A History of Russia, the Soviet Union, and Beyond

A History of
Russia,
the Soviet Union,
and Beyond

Fifth Edition

David MacKenzie
University of North Carolina, Greensboro

Michael W. Curran
The Ohio State University

West/Wadsworth

I(T)P® An International Thomson Publishing Company

Belmont, CA • Albany, NY • Bonn • Boston • Cincinnati • Detroit • Johannesburg •
London • Madrid • Melbourne • Mexico City • New York • Paris • Singapore •
Tokyo • Toronto • Washington

History Editor: Clark Baxter
Senior Developmental Editor: Sharon Adams Poore
Editorial Assistant: Amy Guastello
Print Buyer: Barbara Britton
Marketing Manager: Jay Hu
Production Management: Cecile Joyner / The Cooper Company
Composition: TBH Typecast, Inc.
Copy Editor: Margaret C. Tropp
Art and Photograph Research: Terri Wright
Text and Document Permissions Management: Susan Walters
Interior and Cover Design: Harry Voigt
Cover Art: Kremlin of Tver
Printer: R. R. Donnelley & Sons, Crawfordsville

For more information, contact Wadsworth Publishing Company, 10 Davis Drive, Belmont, CA 94002, or electronically at
http://www.wadsworth.com

International Thomson Publishing Europe
Berkshire House
168-173 High Holborn
London, WC1V 7AA, United Kingdom

International Thomson Editores
Seneca, 53
Colonia Polanco
11560 México D.F. México

Nelson ITP, Australia
102 Dodds Street
South Melbourne
Victoria 3205 Australia

International Thomson Publishing Asia
60 Albert Street
#15-01 Albert Complex
Singapore 189969

Nelson Canada
1120 Birchmount Road
Scarborough, Ontario
Canada M1K 5G4

International Thomson Publishing Japan
Hirakawa-cho Kyowa Building, 3F
2-2-1 Hirakawa-cho, Chiyoda-ku
Tokyo 102 Japan

International Thomson Publishing Southern Africa
Building 18, Constantia Square
138 Sixteenth Road, P.O. Box 2459
Halfway House, 1685 South Africa

 This book is printed on acid-free recycled paper.

Library of Congress Cataloging-in-Publication Data

MacKenzie, David.
        A history of Russia, the Soviet Union, and beyond / David
MacKenzie, Michael W. Curran.—5th ed.
            p.   cm.
        Includes bibliographical references and index.
        ISBN 0-534-54891-1
        1. Russia—History.   2. Soviet Union—History.   I. Curran,
Michael W.   II. Title.
DK40.M17   1998
947—dc21   98-6694

To Bruce, Bryan, and Brendan MacKenzie
To Sara and Elizabeth Curran
And in memory of Peter F. Curran

Preface to the Fifth Edition

THIS VOLUME SEEKS TO PRESENT a clear and objective account and interpretation of the history of the Russians and other eastern Slavs from its beginnings in ancient Rus to the demise of the Soviet Union and after. The length and complexity of this story pose a challenging and difficult task. While emphasizing the history of the Great Russian core of tsarist and Soviet Russia, and now the Russian Federation, we have attempted in this edition to include more fully than before the history and contributions of other east Slavic and non-Slavic peoples. Seeking a reasonable balance among the various periods of Rus, Russian, Soviet, and post-Soviet history, we have sought to give due weight to the often neglected ancient and medieval eras.

The Soviet scheme of historical periodization based on the theory of Marxism-Leninism, accepted without question in the USSR until the Gorbachev era, has been discarded in Russia and most other successor states of the former USSR. Marxist-Leninist teachings that humankind has passed through a series of well-defined socioeconomic states (primitive communism, slavery, feudalism, and capitalism) on a road leading inevitably to the highest stage—communism—have been largely refuted by the events of the past decade. The Marxist tendency to force historical facts and trends into rigid, preconceived patterns is no longer defensible. We, and some of our Russian colleagues, find it inaccurate to designate the history of Rus and Russia from 860 to 1861 as "feudalism," although undeniably the economy and political systems of Kievan Rus and Muscovy did contain feudal elements. Here we accept a scheme of periodization combining geographical and chronological factors—that is, ancient, Kievan, Muscovite, Imperial, Soviet, and post-Soviet eras.

We follow a middle course between the external geographic determinism of the Eurasian school and the organic, inner-oriented approach of S. M. Soloviev, V. O. Kliuchevskii, and Soviet historians. Much of the earlier history of Rus and Russia may be viewed as interaction or conflict between forest and steppe peoples, but the growth of an urban industrial society largely neutralized this factor. Viewing the Russian Empire, as the Eurasians do, as a continuous plain covering much of eastern Europe and northern Asia seems valid, but until the 19th century Siberia's role in Russian development remained minimal. External influences on Russia's evolution—Scandinavian, Byzantine, Asiatic, western European, and recently North American—have been highly significant, but apparently, as the Russian organic school stresses, such influences have neither deflected Russia from its path nor determined its basic internal development. Rus and Russia are neither wholly European nor Asiatic, although they derived important values and institutions from each. Like China, Russia remained essentially a world of its own, absorbing and integrating external elements into a distinctive blend of Orient and Occident.

This book has been conceived out of love for Russia and its diverse peoples. To introduce college and university students to major and continuing controversies among various historical schools —formerly between Soviet and Western historians, and recently among Russian scholars—we have included here a series of Problems that present contrasting views and interpretations of key events. We hope that these Problems will stimulate students to think about major historical issues, to probe further on their own with the aid of the suggested readings, and to reach their own conclusions based on examining the evidence. History, after all, is not primarily memorizing facts and dates, but analyzing and arranging specific data into meaningful patterns.

The authors have sought to present a balanced view of the development and travail of Russia and the Soviet Union. Besides political, military, and diplomatic history—written mostly by Mr. MacKenzie—are chapters on socioeconomic, religious, and cultural developments, composed mostly by Mr. Curran. We have sought to update the fifth edition to include recent cataclysmic changes that produced the collapse of the Soviet Union and to include various interpretations of the Russian past. We have included in this fifth edition more material on women and on non-Russian peoples. Our aim is to write clearly and straightforwardly for both college students and interested lay readers. At the end of each chapter is a list of pertinent suggested readings. Consequently, the Bibliography at the end of the text contains only general and reference works. We welcome any suggestions for further improvement and modification of this ongoing endeavor.

David MacKenzie
Michael W. Curran

Acknowledgments

TO ALL THOSE WHO TAUGHT ME Russian history I owe a profound debt of gratitude; without their inspiration I could not have written this book. To Boris Miller of Stuttgart, Germany, my first teacher in Russian history and the Russian language, who encouraged me to devote myself to lifelong study of the Russian experience, I express heartfelt thanks. At the Russian Institute of Columbia University I had the good fortune to study with Philip E. Mosely, G. T. Robinson, Henry L. Roberts, and John Hazard. Extended visits to the USSR in 1958–59 and 1966 under the auspices of the Inter-University Committee on Travel Grants, and shorter sojourns in 1969, 1974, and 1990, provided me with essential firsthand exposure to Russia and the opportunity to conduct research in Soviet libraries and archives. In Moscow I received advice and encouragement from the eminent Soviet historians S. A. Nikitin and P. A. Zaionchkovskii. During those visits I had the opportunity to travel to many historic cities in European Russia and take photographs, some of which are contained in this book. Contributing their expert advice and suggestions on individual chapters were professors Samuel Baron, David

Griffiths, E. Willis Brooks, and John Keep. They, of course, are not responsible for the errors that this volume may contain. My thanks to my graduate assistant, Bess Smith, for her help in putting together the index for this revised edition. Finally, without the patience and self-sacrifice of my wife, Patricia, neither my trips to the Soviet Union nor the writing of this volume would have been possible.

David MacKenzie

ALTHOUGH IT IS NOT POSSIBLE to acknowledge all of those persons who have contributed to this endeavor, I do wish to recognize some of the most important. I owe a very special debt of gratitude to the two teachers who first introduced me to Russia and Russian history: Michael B. Petrovich of the University of Wisconsin and Werner Philipp of the Free University of Berlin, both now deceased. Their knowledge of Russia and their scholarly enthusiasm have been a source of inspiration over many years. My brief association with the late George C. Soulis, of the

University of California, Berkeley, did much to shape my views of Russian history. Special thanks are due my colleagues at The Ohio State University: Arthur E. Adams, Charles Morley, the late Allan Wildman, and Eve Levin. Their criticisms, encouragement, and constant intellectual stimulation are reflected in this volume. I also wish to express my thanks to the Inter-University Committee on Travel Grants and to the Ministry of Higher and Specialized Education of the USSR, which together provided me with two extended periods of study and research in the USSR, in 1962–1963 and in 1966. The contributions of my two daughters, Sara and Elizabeth, who are just discovering the powerful magnetic qualities of Russian history, are too numerous to recount, as are the contributions of my wife, Ann M. Salimbene; suffice it to say that without their support and encouragement and their understanding patience this work would never have been completed.

Michael W. Curran

F INALLY, WE WISH TO ACKNOWLEDGE the invaluable assistance of Thomas J. Hegarty, University of Tampa; Theresa Lafer, The Pennsylvania State University; Gilbert McArthur, The College of William and Mary; Elaine McClarnand, West Georgia College; Sara W. Tucker, Washburn University of Topeka; Rex A. Wade, George Mason University; A. Benoit Eklof, Indiana University; David M. Griffiths, University of North Carolina, Chapel Hill; Robert Harrison, Southern Oregon State College; Steven Hoch, University of Iowa; Frederick Kellogg, University of Arizona; and Elwood E. Mather, Eastern Montana College, who read through and criticized all or parts of the manuscripts for this or previous editions. Their advice and comments improved the final product considerably, but naturally any mistakes or shortcomings that remain are ours, not theirs.

D.M.
M.C.

A Note on Russian Dates, Names, Measures, and Money

DATING RUSSIAN EVENTS has been complicated by the use in Russia until 1918 of the "Old Style" dates of the Julian calendar, which in the 18th century were 11 days behind those of the Gregorian calendar employed in the West. In the 19th century the lag was 12 days, and in the 20th century it was 13 days. Early in 1918 the Soviet regime adopted the "New Style" Gregorian calendar. Generally we have rendered dates according to the calendar utilized in Russia at the time, except that we have shifted to New Style dates beginning with 1917.

Transliterating Russian names into English presents some peculiar problems. We have adhered largely to the Library of Congress system but have omitted diacritical marks for the sake of simplicity. We have replaced most Russian first names with English equivalents, such as Peter, Nicholas, and Catherine, but we have not used John and Basil instead of Ivan and Vasili.

Russian weights, measures, and distances have been rendered in their English equivalents for the convenience of English-speaking readers. However, Russian rubles have been retained with indications of their dollar value. The ruble, containing 100 kopeks, was worth about 50 cents in 1914. The official value of the Soviet ruble in October 1997 was 5,860 to the dollar. On January 1, 1998, three zeroes were dropped from the value of the Russian ruble; in June 1998 it was 6.1 rubles to the dollar.

Contents

Maps

Illustrations

Figures

Tables

Part One

Early Russia to 1689

THIS SECTION DESCRIBES THE ORIGINS of Rus and of Russia from their settlement by primitive tribal peoples to the accession of Peter the Great. It begins with migrations of nomadic peoples from Asia before the birth of Christ, the struggle between steppe nomads and inhabitants of the forest region, and the formation of Rus. We describe the controversial establishment of the Kievan Rus state in the ninth century, its institutions, and its conversion to Orthodox Christianity in the 10th century. Rus fragments politically in the 12th century preceding the devastating Mongol invasion in 1237–1241. During the subsequent rule of the Golden Horde over semifeudal Russian principalities, Moscow gradually becomes prominent. The region of Great Russia around Moscow is unified after 1450 as Mongol power fragments and weakens. Foundations for autocratic monarchy are laid by Ivan III, Vasili III, and Ivan IV. The extinction of the Muscovite dynasty in 1598 precipitates a "Time of Troubles" involving a political power struggle, conflict between borderlands and the center, and foreign intervention. During the 17th century the new Romanov dynasty, chosen by a national assembly in 1613, consolidates absolutism, reduces independence of the Orthodox church, and fastens serfdom upon the Russian peasantry. Muscovy expands across both Europe and Asia, absorbs part of Ukraine after a long war with Poland, and becomes a vast empire spanning half the globe.

1

Introduction

To place Russian and Soviet history in proper context, one must comprehend the underlying geographic, climatic, and ethnic factors. The peoples of what was until the end of 1991 the Union of Soviet Socialist Republics, often called the Soviet Union, have been shaped by their natural environment and have responded in distinctive ways to its challenges. These responses have made Russia, Ukraine, and the other countries of the former USSR significantly different from the United States or the countries of western Europe.

Geography

The former Soviet Union, of which Russia comprised about three-fourths the area and more than half the population, was a huge country almost three times as large as the United States. Spanning most of eastern Europe and northern Asia, it extended about 6,000 miles east to west across 11 time zones and over 3,000 miles north to south to include about one-sixth of the land area of the globe. By its vastness, resources, and location, the Soviet Union was in a position to dominate the combined landmass of Europe and Asia, called Eurasia.

Most of Russia is a huge plain extending eastward from Poland almost to the Pacific Ocean. Narrowing as one moves across Siberia, it runs out in the plateau and mountainous terrain of eastern Siberia. This expanse is barely interrupted by the low, worn Ural Mountains (maximum height 6,214 feet), which divide Europe from Asia only in part. Between the Urals and the Caspian Sea to the southwest is a gap some 800 miles wide through which successive waves of Asian invaders poured into Europe until the 13th century. Impressive mountain ranges are limited to the frontiers: the Carpathians in the southwest, the Caucasus to the south, and the Pamir, Tien Shan, and Altai mountains on the borders respectively of Afghanistan, India, and China. European Russia, where the main drama of Russian history has been played, is mostly flat and low. The Valdai Hills, a plateau in the northwest where the great European Russian rivers rise, reaches a maximum elevation of only 1,000 feet above sea level.

Flowing slowly through the European Russian plain, the rivers have served throughout history as

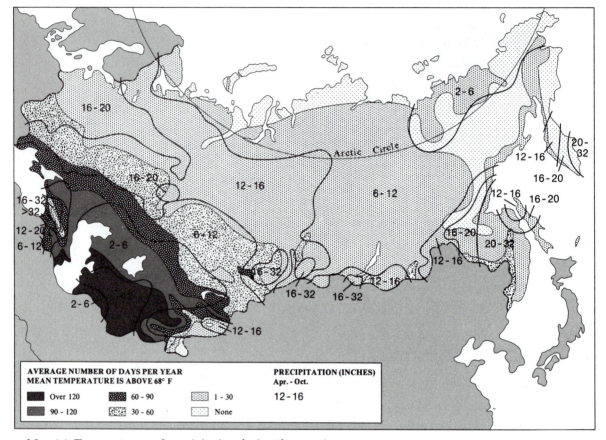

AVERAGE NUMBER OF DAYS PER YEAR
MEAN TEMPERATURE IS ABOVE 68° F

- Over 120
- 90 - 120
- 60 - 90
- 30 - 60
- 1 - 30
- None

PRECIPITATION (INCHES)
Apr. - Oct.

12 - 16

Map 1.1 Temperature and precipitation during the growing season

arteries of communication and commerce. The Northern Dvina and Pechora flow northward into the Arctic basin; most of the others flow southward: the Dniester, Bug, Dnieper, and Don into the Black Sea and the Sea of Azov, and the majestic "mother" Volga, comparable in breadth and importance to the Mississippi, into the Caspian Sea. These rivers and their tributaries form an excellent water communications system, greatly improved in modern times by connecting canals. In Siberia (the region east of the Urals and north of Central Asia) the Ob, Lena, Enisei, and Kolyma rivers, moving northward into the frozen Arctic, are of limited commercial value. Only the Amur, part of the modern boundary with China, moves eastward into the Pacific.

The climate of Russia is continental—that is, marked by extremes of heat and cold. Most of Russia lies in the latitudes of Canada and Alaska. The Gulf Stream, which moderates the climate of the east coast of the United States and the northwest coast of western Europe, affects only the western part of the north Russian coast from Murmansk to Archangel. Extremely cold conditions are more common as one moves eastward (see Map 1.1), but even in European Russia there are no internal mountain barriers to keep icy winds from sweeping down to the Black Sea. Northeast Siberia is one of the world's coldest regions: Temperatures as low as –90°F have been recorded in Verkhoiansk region. However, heat waves occur in European Russia and even Siberia

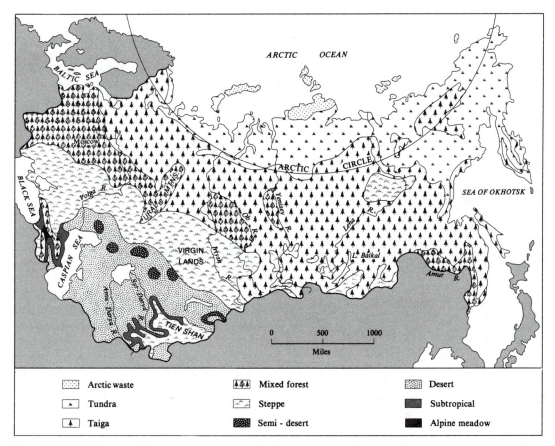

Map 1.2 Vegetation zones

during the summer. In the central Asian deserts temperatures of 120°F are not uncommon. Precipitation in Russia, partly because of the continental climate, is generally moderate or light and often greatest in summer.

There are seven major soil and vegetation zones in the former USSR, stretching generally northeast to southwest (see Map 1.2). About 15 percent of the country in the extreme north is level or undulating treeless plain, called tundra, and 47 percent of it has permanently frozen subsoil. The tundra, a virtually uninhabited wasteland, has many lakes and swamps, with moss and low shrubs the only vegetation. South of it lies the taiga, or coniferous forest in the north and mixed coniferous and deciduous forest farther south.

This vast forest belt, the largest in the world, extends clear across Russia and covers over half its territory. The poor ashy soils, called *podzol,* of the boggy coniferous forest, with their low acid content, are mostly unfit for crops. Agriculture is possible only in cleared portions of the southern forest region. The mixed forest zone to the south, the heart of Muscovite Russia, has richer gray and brown soils. Below this the forest shades into wooded steppe or meadow, mostly with very fertile black soil (*chernozem*), excellent for grains wherever there is sufficient rainfall. Still farther south is mostly treeless prairie like the American Great Plains, extending monotonously for hundreds and hundreds of miles, also a fertile black soil region. East of the Caspian Sea this black soil shades into semidesert, then true desert to the south and east. In the Crimea and along the Caucasian shore of the Black Sea lies a small subtropical region, Russia's Riviera. Early frosts, a short growing season, and barren or frozen soil mean that only about 10 percent of the former Soviet Union is under cultivation, although one-third is potentially arable. In some regions with rich soils, rainfall is often insufficient for crops. Even the black soil region of the southern steppe has a shorter growing season than the American plains.

How has geography affected Russia's history? Until the late 19th century chiefly European Russia should be considered. Siberia remained sparsely populated, its great resources unexploited; Central Asia and the Caucasus were acquired only in the 19th century. European Russia's flat plains fostered colonization and expansion, persistent themes in Russian history for almost 1,000 years. Unworried by waste, Russians cleared forest glades and ploughed up virgin steppelands. In the 19th century a continental colonialism developed as the Russians occupied areas next to their borders.

Geography provided the USSR with natural ocean frontiers on the north and east and with mountain boundaries in the south and southwest. These frontiers were attained after centuries of struggle with Asian invaders and by Russian outward expansion. In the west such natural barriers were lacking. In modern history foreign invasions of Russia have come from the west, and Russian efforts at expansion have focused there. Until the 18th century Russia was largely landlocked, without ready access to warm-water ports or foreign markets. Some historians, such as R. J. Kerner, have interpreted Russian expansion as a drive to secure such ports and unfettered access to the Pacific and to the Baltic, Black, and Mediterranean seas. Vast distances, while contributing to the eventual defeat or absorption of invaders, have complicated the achievement or maintenance of unity and perhaps have promoted highly centralized, authoritarian regimes. The severe climate of the north and Siberia contributed to easy Russian conquest of those regions.

The Peoples

The former Soviet Union, a multinational and multiethnic country, contained almost 180 distinct nationalities and tribes, speaking about 125 languages and dialects, and practicing 40 different religions. Ninety-five groups numbered more than 100,000 people each; 54 had their own national territories. About three-fourths of the Soviet population were eastern Slavs who began as a single people, then separated after the Mongol invasion of 1237–1241 into three major groups: Russians, Ukrainians, and Belorussians.

Russians, or Great Russians, the most numerous people of the former USSR, number about 145 million, or 51 percent of its population (see Map 1.3). They played a dominant historical and political role in both the Russian Empire and the Soviet Union. About five-sixths of ethnic Russians reside in Russia, which occupies almost three-fourths of the former Soviet Union. The remaining 25 million Russians live in other former union republics, mostly in large cities, often holding key political and economic positions.

The almost 45 million Ukrainians, the former USSR's second most numerous national group, are descended directly from the people of Kievan Rus. In the 17th century they were reunited with the Great Russians, initially received autonomy, and then were subjected to direct Russian rule. Presently about 85 percent of Ukrainians live in Ukraine, where they compose about three-fourths of the population. More than 3.5 million Ukrainians reside in Russia.

Belorussians, or "White Russians," number more than 10 million and comprise about 80 percent of the people of Belarus (formerly called Belorussia); some 1.6 million live elsewhere. Belorussia was absorbed into the Russian Empire in the 17th and 18th centuries. Most of the former Soviet Union's approximately one million Poles, the fourth largest Slavic group, entered the USSR involuntarily in 1939 after Soviet annexation of eastern Poland.

The Baltic peoples—some 5.5 million—mostly inhabit the independent countries of Latvia,

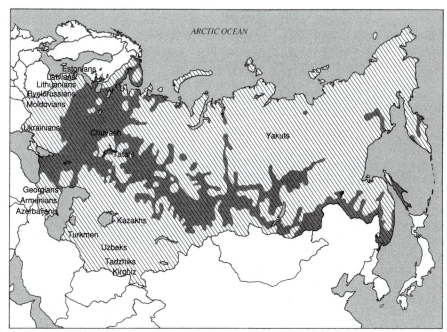

Map 1.3 Chief ethnic groups of the former Soviet Union*

*Predominantly Russian areas are shown in gray.

SOURCE: Joe LeMonnier, *NYT Magazine*, Jan. 28, 1990. Copyright 1990 by The New York Times Company. Reprinted by permission.

Lithuania, and Estonia. After enjoying independence from 1919 to 1940, they were forcibly annexed to the USSR under the Nazi-Soviet Pact of 1939. The three million Lithuanians had a proud heritage of independence as a Grand Duchy, then were linked with Poland until annexed to the Russian Empire in 1795. Latvian and Lithuanian are Baltic Indo-European languages; Estonian is a Uralic tongue closely related to Finnish. All three peoples use the Latin alphabet, are strongly European in outlook, and are mostly Catholic or Lutheran.

The leading peoples of the Caucasus are Armenians, Georgians, and Azerbaijani, and their three countries contain about 15 million people. Many of the 4.4 million Armenians live outside Armenia, within which they represent almost 90 percent of the population. Armenians, like Georgians and Azerbaijani, are heirs of an ancient and proud civilization; their language is Indo-European. Annexed to the Russian Empire in 1828, Armenia enjoyed brief independence from 1918 to 1920, as did Georgia and Azerbaijan, before being forcibly incorporated into the Soviet Union. Neighboring Georgia, with about 5 million people, two-thirds Georgians who are mostly Eastern Orthodox, has an alphabet and language totally different from Russian. Georgia was annexed to Russia in 1801. Unlike their Christian neighbors, most of the Muslim Azerbaijani, who speak a Turkic language, live in former Soviet Azerbaijan; many live in neighboring Iran. The mountainous Caucasus region also contains many smaller groups, some possessing autonomous status.

Muslims, numbering more than 50 million people, are the second largest religious group in the former USSR, after the Eastern Orthodox. In the Volga River basin live smaller Turko-Tatar peoples including the Kazan Tatars, Bashkirs, and Chuvash; the Crimean Tatars are only now returning to their homeland. All are descendants of the Mongol and Turkic warriors who conquered Russia in the 13th century only to be overrun in the subsequent Russian eastward and southward expansion. Further east lies formerly Soviet Central Asia, with some 45 million people comprising five union republics established arbitrarily early in the Soviet era: the Uzbek, Kazakh, Turkmen, Tajik, and Kirghiz republics; they are now independent countries. Their inhabitants are chiefly Muslims with Turkic languages written in Cyrillic, except for the Iranian Tajiks. Between 1730 and 1885 Russian armies conquered Central Asia and renamed it Russian Turkestan. It was absorbed into the Soviet Union by the early 1920s.

Two other significant minorities in the former Soviet Union that lacked union republics of their own have recently emigrated in large numbers. Germans (about 1.5 million), who mostly settled along the Volga River in the 18th century, were scattered during World War II; many have emigrated to Germany. Jews (some 1.8 million) reside chiefly in large cities of European Russia and Ukraine; since 1970 emigration has sharply reduced their numbers.

Russian was the official language of the former Soviet government and army and is spoken natively by about 60 percent of Russia's inhabitants, studied as a second language in all non-Russian schools, and spoken by a majority of other inhabitants of the former USSR. Ukrainian, the second most widespread language of the former USSR, is closely related to Russian, and Belorussian is even closer; all three share a common Cyrillic alphabet. Until 1985 there was a strong trend toward linguistic Russification, which was reversed under Mikhail Gorbachev. Unlike the United States—a melting pot for diverse national and racial elements—the former Soviet Union preserved distinct national territories and languages. There have been disquieting recent trends toward ethnic violence.

Russian Responses to Challenges

Location, climate, and topography have challenged the Russian people severely during a bloody and turbulent history. Historically, Russia was a poor country whose people extracted a precarious living from the soil. Poverty, vulnerability to attack, and poor internal communications combined to produce responses distinguishing Russia significantly from western Europe and the United States. Major Russian responses to severe challenges have included autocracy, collectivism, and mysticism. These concepts may provide keys for unlocking the controversial Russian past.

Autocracy, or statism, conspicuously absent in early Russian history, emerged during the unification of Great Russia after 1450. It persisted until very recently as a centralized monarchical or Communist state with a virtual monopoly of power, except for a few brief "Times of Troubles." During the 16th and 17th centuries autocracy emerged as limitations on the tsar's powers—including an independent hereditary aristocracy, representative institutions such as the assembly of the lands, and an autonomous Eastern Orthodox Church—withered or were subordinated to the state. Though of Byzantine origin, Russian autocracy derived more from the practices of the Mongol Golden Horde than from Byzantine political theory. Russian tsars, such as Peter the Great and Nicholas I, theoretically possessed awesome authority that resembled Oriental despotism more than western European monarchy. However, the Russian autocracy in practice often found it difficult to effect genuine change. Well into the 19th century Russia remained under-governed because the central government could not assert its power effectively throughout a vast empire. Large segments of the population remained removed from direct central control.

After the Mongol era of feudal division, Russia came increasingly under a strong, centralized monarchy. People and property were treated as possessions of the Muscovite state. Growing more powerful over time, the autocracy both mobilized Russia's natural and human resources to resist external invasions and conquered contiguous areas; in the Soviet era it created formidable centralized industrial and military power. Utilizing Byzantine and Mongol political and financial traditions, Russian autocracy used the principle of service to the state to subordinate to its control individuals not protected (as in western Europe) by corporate groups with inherent rights.

Collectivism, unlike the marked individualism of western Europe and the United States, has been another Russian response linked closely with autocracy. Under tsars and commissars, individual enterprise was discouraged and subordination to the state encouraged by all means. Collectivism aided Muscovy, the Russian Empire, and finally Soviet Russia to mobilize resources to combat severe external and internal challenges. Certain collective elements in the Great Russian repartitional commune of the 19th century foreshadowed Soviet collective and state farming. In the century after 1550, autocracy subjected a semifree Russian peasantry to the collective bondage of serfdom, a degrading but vital feature of Russian life until the 1860s.

Finally, the prevalent *mysticism* of the Russian Orthodox tradition and the relative lack of intellectual inquiry within the Eastern Orthodox Church differed greatly from the rationalism and questioning in Western Catholic and Protestant faiths. In Muscovite Russia such matters as the spelling of the name of Jesus and elements of ritual and tradition acquired vast significance for a superstitious populace. The prevalent belief that Russia was the center of the only true faith tended to intensify suspicion of foreigners and their institutions. In a sense Soviet communism, despite a theoretically antithetical ideology, continued this mystical tradition. Until World War II Soviet spokespersons reiterated that the USSR was the only land of socialism and the center of true Marxist faith. Xenophobia—extreme fear of foreigners—persisted and was reinforced deliberately by the Soviet regime.

To be sure, the roles and personalities of rulers —tsarist, Soviet, and Russian—have been important in shaping Russian history and provide a convenient, if not always revealing, method of dividing Russian history into periods. Such major figures as Ivan the Great, Ivan the Terrible, Peter the Great, and Catherine the Great in the tsarist epoch and Lenin and Stalin in the Soviet period stand out above the flood of events. But unless one accepts the "great man/woman" theory of history, viewing an era through the career and character of the ruler exaggerates the importance of personal leadership and oversimplifies complex and continuing trends. Instead, tracing such themes as autocracy and collectivism may prove more effective in giving the reader a comprehension of the evolution of Russia and its people.

Suggested Additional Reading

GEOGRAPHY AND GEOPOLITICS

ADAMS, A. et al. *An Atlas of Russian and Eastern European History* (New York, 1967).

CHEW, A. *An Atlas of Russian History* (New Haven, 1970).

DEWDNEY, J. C. *A Geography of the Soviet Union,* 2d ed. (New York, 1971).

GILBERT, M. *Russian History Atlas* (New York, 1972).

KERNER, R. J. *The Urge to the Sea: The Course of Russian History* (Berkeley, 1942).

LYDOLPH, P. E. *Geography of the USSR,* 3d ed. (New York, 1977).

PARKER, W. H. *An Historical Geography of Russia* (London, 1968).

SUMNER, B. H. "The Frontier," in *A Short History of Russia* (New York, 1949).

TREADGOLD, D. "Russian Expansion in the Light of Turner's Study of the American Frontier." *Agricultural History* 26 (1952): 147–52.

WESSON, R. G. *The Russian Dilemma: A Political and Geopolitical View* (New Brunswick, NJ, 1974).

WIECZYNSKI, J. L. *The Russian Frontier: The Impact of the Borderlands upon the Course of Early Russian History* (Charlottesville, VA, 1976).

PEOPLES AND NATIONALITIES

ALLEN, W. E. D. *A History of the Georgian People* (New York, 1971).

ALLWORTH, EDWARD. *The Modern Uzbeks . . . : A Cultural History* (Stanford, 1990).

BARTOLD, V. V. "Slavs," in *Encyclopedia of Islam,* vol. 4 (Leiden, 1978).

BLUM, D. *Russia, the Land and People of the Soviet Union* (New York, 1980).

DVORNIK, F. *The Slavs in European History and Civilization* (New Brunswick, NJ, 1962).

GOLDHAGEN, E. *Ethnic Minorities in the Soviet Union* (New York, 1968).

GREENBERG, L. S. *The Jews in Russia,* 2 vols. (New Haven, 1944, 1951).

GROUSSET, R. *The Empire of the Steppes: A History of Central Asia,* trans. N. Walford (New Brunswick, NJ, 1970).

HOOSON, D. *The Soviet Union: People and Regions* (London, 1966).

HORAK, S., ED. *Guide to the Study of the Soviet Nationalities* (Littleton, CO, 1982).

HRUSHEVSKYI, M. *A History of the Ukraine* (New Haven, 1941).

KOLARZ, W. *The People of the Soviet Far East* (Camden, CT, 1969).

LANG, D. M. *The Armenians: A People in Exile* (Winchester, MA, 1989).

LANG, D. M. *A Modern History of Georgia* (London, 1962).

OLCOTT, M. *The Kazakhs* (Stanford, 1987).

PIERCE, R. A. *Russian Central Asia, 1867–1917: A Study in Colonial Rule* (Berkeley, 1960).

RAUN, T. *Estonia and the Estonians* (Stanford, 1987).

SENN, A. R. *The Emergence of Modern Lithuania* (New York, 1959).

SMITH, G, ed. *The Nationalities Question in the Soviet Union* (London, 1990).

SUBTELNY, O. *Ukraine: A History,* 2d ed. (Toronto, 1994).

SUNY, R. G. *The Making of the Georgian Nation* (Stanford, 1988).

VAKAR, N. *Belorussia: The Making of a Nation* (Cambridge, MA, 1956).

WHEELER, G. *The Modern History of Soviet Central Asia* (London, 1964).

2

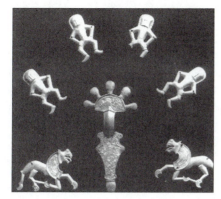

Ancient Rus

The very earliest history of the great Eurasian plain located north of the Black Sea, the region that later comprised the center of the first Rus or Kievan state, is shrouded in mystery because of an almost total lack of historical sources.[1] In recent times, however, archaeology has contributed significantly to our knowledge and understanding of the earliest known inhabitants of this region. That the area was inhabited for many thousands of years before the Christian era and that the region served as the center of a whirlpool for many crosscurrents of cultural influences coming from western Asia, the Black Sea, and the Caucasus Mountains cannot be disputed, but there is no hard evidence to suggest that the region was the aboriginal homeland of Slavic or proto-Slavic peoples. Indeed, very little is known of the origins of the Slavs, and apparently they did

---

[1] We have used the term *Rus* to refer to the territory that would later become Russia. The term *Rus* applies until about 1300, when the process of unification began that would result in the emergence of Great Russia under the aegis of Moscow.

not settle in the Eurasian plain until several centuries after the beginning of the Christian era.

Early Occupants of the Great Eurasian Plain

The great Eurasian plain, the cradle of Russian history, was inhabited by primitive peoples for hundreds of thousands of years before the arrival of the Slavs. Archaeological excavations have unearthed layer upon layer of evidence of human habitation beginning as far back as the Paleolithic Age (the Old Stone Age), dating back more than one million years and extending down to about 8000 B.C. Still clearer evidence of the existence of primitive peoples in the region has been uncovered from the Neolithic era (the New Stone Age), dating back to about 4000 B.C. Finally, beginning at least a thousand years before the Christian era, the Eurasian plain was inundated by wave after wave of migrating peoples moving westward out of Asia and the Middle East. These successive waves of people, each with its own distinctive civilization, left a mark on the region, and the most distant past of this important geographic area has been reconstructed in broad outline by archaeologists rather than by historians.

The first historically recorded people to enter the territory north of the Black Sea coastal region were the Cimmerians, who appeared about 1000 B.C. They were apparently of Thracian stock, and they entered the steppe region as conquerors, imposing their rule on the fragmented primitive peoples already occupying the great plain. Information about the Cimmerians is meager, although archaeological evidence suggests that they were skilled in the use of iron and may have introduced the advantages of iron (as opposed to stone) implements to the indigenous population. The widespread use of iron in the area, however, appears to date from about the seventh century B.C., when the Cimmerians were replaced as the dominant ruling element by the Scythians, whose ethnic origin is a subject of continuing dispute. Some scholars have suggested that they were Iranian; others have argued that they were of Mongol origin; and some Russian scholars have even advanced the view that the Scythians were Slavic or proto-Slavic. As George Vernadsky suggests, all three elements may have existed within the broad Scythian group. Moreover, there was a considerable admixture of Scythian and Cimmerian elements because Scythian culture simply overlaid the older Cimmerian culture and because the survivors of the Cimmerians remained in their former territories as subjects of the Scythians.

At about the same time, the Greeks appeared in the Crimea (a name that may derive from Cimmeria) and spread out along the northern coast of the Black Sea. The Greeks established trading colonies and founded cities in the region. The Greek city Olbia at the mouth of the Bug River was founded in 644 B.C., and the establishment of other centers followed shortly. By entering into trade with the Scythians and other peoples living to the north, these Greek colonies served to link the Eurasian plain with the Hellenistic world of the eastern Mediterranean. Greek sources have provided a wealth of information about the Scythians, although some of the material is not very reliable. Especially valuable is Herodotus's famous *History*, written in the fifth century B.C. Herodotus himself lived for a time in Olbia and collected many kinds of information about the Scythians. Herodotus used the name Scythia to denote not only a geographic area but also in an ethnic sense to apply to all the diverse peoples living within the general territory of the Eurasian plain. The inaccurate use of the term *Scythia* has led to a certain confusion in precisely identifying the Scythians and tracing their origins. The historian Michael Rostovtzeff has suggested an Iranian origin for the Scythians, and it appears that at least the ruling group of the Scythians spoke an Iranian language. The Soviet historian B. D. Grekov claimed that a genetic relationship existed between the Slavs and a portion of the Scythians, the so-called Scythian plowmen. The evidence for this view is tenuous, as it is based on physical similarities of Scythian and early Slavic figures as portrayed in artifacts unearthed by archaeologists. No incontrovertible evidence linking the Scythians with Slavic or proto-Slavic peoples has been turned up to date.

In general, during Scythian times three basic cultural areas may be differentiated within the Eurasian plain: (1) Scythia proper, composed of the lower reaches of the Bug and Dnieper rivers; (2) the Crimean steppe region somewhat to the east; and (3) the Azov steppe region located still farther to the east. All of these territories were occupied by a confederation of related tribes, partly settled agriculturists (the Scythian plowmen referred to by Herodotus) and partly nomads. The dominant group seems to have been a tribe called by Herodotus the Royal Scythians. These various tribes appear to have shared a common language and customs. Another group of tribes of different origin had settled to the west of Scythia proper and were engaged, according to archaeological evidence, in agriculture and animal husbandry. Some Soviet historians have argued that a part of these non-Scythian tribes consisted of proto-Slavic peoples, although no concrete evidence has been produced to support such a view. To the east of Scythia were other groups of people not related to the Scythians but sharing certain common

Map 2.1 Romans and Sarmatians, 200 B.C.–A.D. 200

cultural characteristics with the dominant Scythians. Indeed, there was a degree of cultural homogeneity in the whole region extending from the Caucasus Mountains in the east to the Danube River in the west, and this homogeneity may account for Herodotus's imprecision in identifying the various ethnic groups. The cultural unity of the region was vividly expressed in common weaponry, horse ornaments, and the famous "animal style" in art. The Scythians lived close to nature as herdsmen, hunters, warriors, and agriculturists, and in so doing they acquired a knowledge and understanding of, and respect for, the animal world. Thus animals played an important role in the life and the art of Scythians. The common cultural elements to be found in the whole region

of southern Russia during the Scythian period testify to the existence of extensive trade and cultural contacts among the diverse peoples occupying the Eurasian plain in this early period.

Beginning in the third century B.C. a new group of warrior tribes, the Sarmatians, began to advance into the Eurasian plain, moving out of central Asia (see Map 2.1). The Sarmatians were ethnically Iranian in origin, and by the mid-second century B.C. they had replaced the Scythians as the rulers of south Russia. The Sarmatians were nomadic cattle-breeders who lived in felt huts mounted on wheels to facilitate easy and rapid movement as they followed their wandering herds of cattle and horses. The Sarmatians adopted much of Scythian culture, infusing it with a primitive dynamism of

RIA NOVOSTI/SOVFOTO

Silver human and horse figures from a seventh
century A.D. burial mound; found near village of
Martynovka on the Ros River near Kiev.

their own. The Sarmatians continued the Scythian
practice of maintaining trade with the Greek
colonies on the northern shores of the Black Sea,
and the Sarmatians too were drawn into the eastern Mediterranean cultural sphere. One of the
main groups of Sarmatians, the last to enter the
Eurasian plain, was the Alans, the ruling element
of this confederation of nomadic tribes. One of the
tribes of the Alans was Rukhs-As (the fair-haired
As), and an effort has been made to establish a
link between the terms *Rukhs-As* and *Russian,* the
latter deriving from the former. According to this
now discredited theory, the Rukhs-As emerge as
the ancestors of the modern Russians. Still
another tribe of the Sarmatians was known as the
Roxolani, and Grekov advanced the view that the
term *Rus* derived from this tribal name. Arguing
that the letters *x* and *s* are linguistically inter-
changeable, Grekov theorized that Roxalani
became Rosolani, which in turn was shortened to
Ros and then became Rus. Many such theories of

the origin of the term *Rus* or *Russian* abound, but
none of them can be authoritatively substantiated
at present.

Meanwhile, migration was erupting in another
area, to the north of the Eurasian plain. During the
first century A.D. the Goths began to move out of
Scandinavia, migrating southward into the region
of the lower Vistula River and from there farther
south into the Eurasian plain. As the Goths moved
southward, they conquered and plundered, subduing and absorbing many tribes living in the
Dnieper River basin and dislocating many others.
Mention is made in the historical sources of several such tribes that were overrun by the Goths:
the Venedae, the Sclaveni, and the Antes. Jordanis,
a Goth writing in the sixth century A.D., associated
these tribes with the Slavs; more accurately, he
suggested that the descendants of these tribes
served as the nucleus of the future Slavs. Like their
predecessors, the Goths—a Germanic people
whose way of life was conditioned by the forests
they had traditionally occupied—were a confederation of tribes, but a confederation lacking any real
unified state structure, and so they were able to
impose only a superficial degree of unity on the
diverse peoples then occupying the Eurasian plain.
By the mid-fourth century A.D. the Goths had
become divided into two powerful confederations,
the Ostrogoths (East Goths) and the Visigoths
(West Goths). The Goths in general probably had
not achieved as high a level of culture as either the
Scythians or the Sarmatians, and therefore they
tended to adopt the general culture of the Sarmatians. There is clear evidence of a general cultural
continuity in the Eurasian plain extending from
roughly 500 B.C. to A.D. 500.

The Huns, Avars, and Khazars

During the second half of the fourth century A.D. a
new and terrifying force swept out of Central Asia
into the Eurasian plain and beyond. These were
the fearsome Huns, a powerful and rapidly
expanding people who were prevented from
spilling over into China by the Great Wall, which
had been constructed as a barrier against this

turbulent and aggressive tribe. The Huns, forced to migrate westward, eventually entered the eastern reaches of the Eurasian plain by about A.D. 370. They encountered and crushed the Alans living between the Don River and the Sea of Azov. Many Alans fled westward, pursued by the marauding Huns, who then met the Goths. The momentum of the Huns could not be halted, and what followed is known in historical literature as the Great Migration of Peoples (German: *Völkerwanderung*), in which the advance of the Huns caused tremendous dislocations farther to the west. The Visigoths and Ostrogoths, together with the remainder of the Alans, were forced out of the Eurasian plain by the inexorable advance of the Huns. The Visigoths took refuge in southern Gaul and then moved on into Spain. The Ostrogoths fled first into Thrace and then seized Italy, destroying the Western Roman Empire. A group of the Alans survived the Hunnish attack and moved into the Caucasus Mountains during these vast upheavals, and their descendants survive today under the name Ossetians. Certainly the best-known Ossetian or part-Ossetian of modern times is Joseph Stalin, whose mother was an Ossetian.

The Huns reached their zenith under Attila, who menaced the Eastern Roman or Byzantine Empire in 447, invaded Frankish Gaul in 451, and moved against Italy in 452. The advance of the Huns threatened all of western Europe, but Attila died in 453, and thereafter his far-flung empire rapidly crumbled as a result of jealous rivalries and fratricidal warfare among his less talented successors. Many historians believe that it was during this period of the *Völkerwanderung* that the Slavs began to migrate out of central and eastern Europe in various directions—to the east, to the south, and to the west.

The Huns eventually had to give way to yet another wave of migration into the Eurasian plain, that of the Avars, a mixture of Turkish, Mongolian, and Chinese elements. The Avars conquered the region by the mid-sixth century and amalgamated the remaining Hunnish elements and other surviving groups into a powerful state extending from the Volga River in the east to the Elbe River in the

west. So powerful were the Avars that they were able to pressure the Byzantine Empire into paying tribute in 581, and from Byzantine sources it is clear that Slavic groups participated in these Avar campaigns against the Byzantine Empire. The Slavs were identified as the Sclaveni in Byzantine sources.

Thus Slavic elements, having moved into the Eurasian plain, were now incorporated into the Avar state. The earliest written source of Russian history, *Povest vremennykh let (Tale of Bygone Years)* known as *The Primary Russian Chronicle*, records how the Avars oppressed the Slavic tribes:

> And the Avars [called Obry] made war upon the Slavs and harassed the Dulebians who were Slavs. They [the Avars] did violence to the Dulebian women: when an Avar made a journey he did not cause either a horse or a steer to be harnessed, but gave command instead that three or four or five Dulebian women should be yoked to his cart and be made to draw him. Even thus did they harass the Dulebians.[2]

The Avars held sway in the Eurasian plain until the first quarter of the seventh century and then were decisively defeated by the Byzantines, at which point the Avar state entered upon a period of decay and decline.

Over this welter of diverse peoples, including remnants of the Huns, Avars, Antes, Altaic Turks, and Slavs, there arose in the eighth century a new military power along the northern shores of the Black and Caspian seas—the Khazars, a people of Turkic origin. Although originally nomadic, the Khazars were quickly drawn into commercial relations with the Byzantine Empire and the rising Arab Empire to the east. A lively and lucrative trade developed, with the Khazars serving as middlemen between the Greeks and Arabs and the native tribes living to the north of the Khazar economic sphere. In an effort to maximize trade opportunities, the Khazars extended their control

---

[2] S. H. Cross, "The Russian Primary Chronicle," *Harvard Studies and Notes in Philology and Literature* 12 (1930): 140–41.

David MacKenzie

Old Church in Mtskheta, Georgia, ca. 600 A.D. Christianity came to the Caucasus region long before it was adopted by Kievan Rus.

over numerous Slavic tribes living in the Dnieper River basin. Although many Slavs were compelled to pay tribute, the Khazars maintained a healthy respect for the military prowess of the Slavs. *The Primary Russian Chronicle* relates the account of a Khazar expedition sent out to collect tribute among the Poliane, a Slavic tribe settled along the Dnieper River in the vicinity of the future center of Kiev. "Oh, Kagan [ruler]! This tribute bodes no good. We achieved it with sabres, our single-bladed sword, but their [the Slavs'] weapon is the sword, sharp on both sides. The time will come when they exact tribute from us Khazars, and from other peoples." This was to be a prophetic statement.

For the time being, however, the Khazars maintained at least nominal control over several of the Slavic tribes in the Dnieper River basin and gradually drew them into lucrative trade and commerce. Although the Khazars maintained extensive trade contacts with the Byzantine Empire and provided military assistance to the Byzantines, Greek culture and Greek Christianity made little

headway among the Khazars and the peoples living under their control. To be sure, the Khazars had ample contact with representatives of the three great religions, Christianity, Judaism, and Islam. There is evidence that all three religions actively proselytized among the Khazars, each making moderate progress. Sometime during the late eighth or early ninth century, the Khazar kagan and members of his court were converted to Judaism. No effort was made, however, to make Judaism a state religion. What is important is that the Khazar state, with its extensive commercial contacts, served as a meeting ground or point of confluence for the great civilizations of the period, each of which left some imprint on the Khazars and by extension on those living within the Khazar sphere. The whole area of south Russia was, as a result, a relatively cosmopolitan region. The participation of the Slavs in the trade and commerce of the Khazars provided a bond of unity, but whether this unity expressed itself in any formal state structure is a subject of debate. By the eighth century Slavic tribes had settled permanently in the Dnieper River region and the nucleus of the future Kievan state had been established.

It is evident from the preceding account that numerous groups of peoples moved into and out of the Eurasian plain during the most ancient period of Russia's history. It is also evident that the Slavs were relative latecomers to the region. No definite evidence of their presence in the Eurasian plain is available until about the sixth century. By that time Slavic or proto-Slavic tribes had moved out of central Europe and spread out along the Dnieper River basin. These tribes formed the nucleus of the eastern Slavs, later subdivided into three groups: the Great Russians, the White Russians, and the Little Russians or Ukrainians. Other Slavic tribes moved in other directions—some to the south, into the Balkans, and these formed the nucleus of the southern Slavs. The southern Slavs also became subdivided into various groups: the Serbs, the Croats, the Slovenes, and the Bulgars. Still other Slavic tribes migrated westward, becoming the nucleus of the western Slavs, which later were divided into various ethnic groups: the Poles, the Czechs (or Bohemians), the Slovaks, the Moravians, the Kashubs, and the Wends.

The Primary Russian Chronicle, recording events in the ninth century, refers to 13 eastern Slavic tribes: (1) the Slovenes, located in the north around Novgorod; (2) the Krivichians, located slightly to the south of the Slovenes; (3) the Polochane, in the region of Smolensk; (4) the Viatichians, in the region around the future Moscow; (5) the Severiane, on the eastern bank of the Dnieper River in the region of Chernigov; (6) the Radimichians, on the upper reaches of the Dnieper, to the south of Smolensk; (7) the Derevlians, on the west side of the Dnieper, slightly north of Kiev; (8) the Ulichi, in the region of the Southern Bug River; (9) the Tivertsy, slightly to the west of the Ulichi; (10) the Khorvaty, on the upper reaches of the Dniester River; (11) the Polianians, on the east bank of the Dnieper River, in the region of Kiev; (12) the Dregovichi, on the lower reaches of the Niemen River, to the west of Smolensk; and (13) the Dulebians, located to the west of the Drevliane. Among these widely scattered tribes there was a degree of cultural and linguistic unity, but it is bitterly disputed whether these tribes, or at least some of them, enjoyed in the eighth and early ninth centuries a degree of political unity commensurate with a state structure.

Problem 1

The Formation of Kievan Rus

For more than two centuries scholars have debated how Kievan Rus, the first state on Russian soil, came into being. Did native Slavs or Varangians from Scandinavia create it? When and where did it originate? Which was the crucial factor in its establishment: external Scandinavian influences or the process of internal social and economic change? These questions make up part of the major historical controversies about Rus's beginnings, complicated by the scarcity and the questionable nature of written records from that distant and shadowy epoch.

The historical debate has revolved around the Norman theory, which affirms that the first state in Rus was established in the mid-ninth century by Scandinavian Vikings or Norsemen. The chief Normanists have been Scandinavian and German scholars, although some prerevolutionary Russian historians accepted many of their arguments. Soviet historians, especially after 1935, repudiated the Norman theory completely, and it remained banned in the USSR until recently. They contended that native Slavs had created a state in southern Rus long before the Vikings arrived.

The founders of the Norman theory were the 18th-century German scholars G. Bayer and

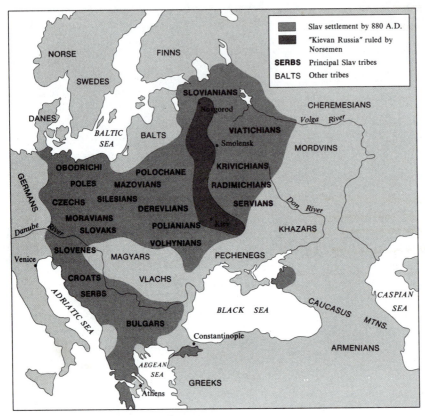

Map 2.2 Slavs and Norsemen by 880

Problem 1 continued

A. Schlözer, working in the infant Russian Academy of Sciences. They relied chiefly upon the account of the formation of Rus in *The Primary Russian Chronicle,* which describes the period from A.D. 852 to 1110, portions of which were probably written in the 12th century by the Kievan monk Nestor. Although the *Chronicle* has come down to us only in later and revised copies, it remains an important, though controversial, source for early Russian history. It states that about 860 the Slavs of the Novgorod region, unable to govern themselves, invited the Scandinavian Vikings, or Varangians, to come and rule over them. The Norman theory, elaborated during the 19th century by V. Thomsen and E. Kunik, was accepted by most contemporary Russian historians.

During the past 50 years scholars working in Soviet Russia, utilizing much new archaeological evidence, especially from burial mounds in northwestern Russia, have subjected the Norman theory to systematic criticism. Rejecting the Normanist emphasis on external Scandinavian influences on Russian development, they stressed the socioeconomic changes that occurred within the eastern Slav tribes and concluded that the first viable Rus political system, or state, emerged from the transition of the eastern Slavs during the sixth to the ninth centuries from primitive communism to feudalism. This process, asserted most Soviet historians, was little affected by Scandinavian incursions, and a state in Rus existed before they arrived. A few Western historians accept many of their arguments. The Soviet challenge forced the Normanists to reexamine their premises and make important concessions, but the Normanists still argue that the Varangians made a substantial contribution to the formation of Kievan Rus. The sections that follow present the main outlines of the controversy over the Norman theory.

The Primary Russian Chronicle

In the year 852 . . . the land of Rus was first named. . . .

859: The Varangians from beyond the sea imposed tribute upon the Chuds, the Slavs, the Merians, the Ves, and the Krivichians. But the Khazars imposed it upon the Polianians, the Severians, and the Viatichians, and collected a squirrel-skin and a beaver-skin from each hearth.

860–862: The tributaries of the Varangians drove them back beyond the sea and, refusing them further tribute, set out to govern themselves. There was no law among them, but tribe rose against tribe. Discord thus ensued among them, and they began to war one against another. They said to themselves, "Let us seek a prince who may rule over us, and judge us according to the law." They accordingly went overseas to the Varangian Russes: these particular Varangians were known as Russes, just as some are called Swedes, and others Normans, Angles and Goths. . . . The Chuds, the Slavs, and the Krivichians then said to the people of Rus: "Our whole land is great and rich, and there is no order in it. Come to rule and reign over us." They thus selected three brothers, with their kinsfolk, who took with them all the Russes and migrated. The oldest, Rurik, located himself in Novgorod; the second, Sineus, in Beloozero; and the third, Truvor, in Izborsk. On account of these Varangians, the district of Novgorod became known as the land of Rus. The present inhabitants of Novgorod are descended from the Varangian race, but aforetime they were Slavs.

After two years Sineus and his brother, Truvor, died, and Rurik assumed the sole authority. He assigned cities to his followers. . . . In these cities there are thus Varangian colonists, but the first settlers were, in Novgorod, Slavs. . . . Rurik had dominion over all these districts. With Rurik there were two men who did not belong to his kin, but were boyars [noblemen]. They obtained permission to go to Tsargrad [Constantinople] with their families. They thus sailed down the Dnieper, and in the course of their journey they saw a small city on a hill. Upon their inquiry as to whose town it was, they were informed that three brothers, Kii, Shchek, and Khoriv, had once built the city, but that since their deaths, their descendants were living there as tributaries of the Khazars. Oskold and Dir remained in this city, and after gathering together many Varangians, they established their dominion over the country of the Polianians at the same time that Rurik was ruling Novgorod.[3]

These excerpts from this semilegendary account suggest that in the mid-ninth century the tribes of Rus, some of them Slavic, were caught between the Varangians of Scandinavia and the Khazar Empire along the Volga River. The Russes, affirms the *Chronicle*, were Scandinavian Vikings who created a state for the tribes of northern Russia. Rus, it continues, was located originally around Novgorod and was ruled by Riurik, founder of the first Rus dynasty; his vassals established Kiev as the capital of Rus. The Rus, it concludes, were descendants of the Varangians and native Slavs.

The Norman Theory

Contemporary Normanists differ somewhat among themselves, but most affirm (1) that the words *Rus* and *Variag* (Varangian) are Scandinavian, (2) that the Rus and the Swedes were identical, and (3) that the latter founded the first Russian state in the Novgorod region. Some Normanists go far beyond this to claim that the Varangians conquered and colonized the east Slav lands, introduced feudal landholding and Christianity into Russia, and created the upper classes of Kievan Rus. Extreme Normanists have

---

[3] Cross, "Russian Primary Chronicle," pp. 144–45.

Problem 1 continued

suggested that the primitive and disorganized eastern Slavs were ushered into civilization and statehood by culturally superior Germanic Varangians.

A scholarly and moderate summary of the Normanist interpretation is that of Stender-Petersen, from which the following excerpts are taken:

> That the Northmen or Normans from mid-Sweden, Östergotland, and Gotland Island played a part in the origin of the Russian state can scarcely any longer be denied seriously. But what this participation consisted of, its extent, and how it occurred must still be considered unresolved questions and over these questions rages the old quarrel between the so-called Normanists and Anti-Normanists. . . . The story of the invitation of the three brothers from across the Baltic, who with the entire Rus people emigrated to the Slav-Finnish frontier regions of northern Russia and settled in . . . Ladoga, Izborsk, and Beloozero, is merely a variant of a passage common to many compositions in various places among the Swedish population in Finland and Estonia. . . . Ture J. Arne . . . after archaeological investigation in Russia, proved that in an archaeological sense Russia was a cultural passageway between the north, especially Sweden, and the East and Byzantium, and that in Russia there was undeniable material evidence of Swedish-Nordic settlements. . . .

> . . . In Soviet sources we get a rather confused and unclear picture of Slav-Russian prehistory, a mosaic of hypotheses that they turn into facts, bald assumptions, and false interpretations whose main purpose is to shatter the Norman theory by any means. . . .

> The Russian state therefore owes its existence not to supposed Viking expeditions by the three legendary brothers who conquered the lands beyond the Baltic Sea and founded a state. . . . We must reckon with the interbreeding of two racial elements. One was the autonomous Slav tribes with their relatively developed agriculture . . ., but the second factor was the Nordic Rus people, originally a Swedish land-grabbing and colonist people who knew how to resist the expansion of the Khazar

kaganate, release itself from dependence on the Swedish king, and so establish its own commercial kaganate around Lake Ladoga. The cooperation between the Slavs of the Dnieper valley and the Normans led to the founding of the Norman-Russian state.[4]

Soviet Anti-Normanism

Recent Soviet historians and a few Western colleagues have sought to refute part or all of the Norman theory. Their critique emphasizes (1) the unreliable nature of *The Primary Russian Chronicle*, (2) that the first state in Rus arose as a result of socioeconomic changes among the eastern Slavs long before the Varangians arrived, and (3) that the Rus were a south Russian tribe living along the Ros River directing a large tribal league that gave its name to the land of Rus. From the sixth to the ninth centuries, claim Soviet historians, occurred a gradual shift of the eastern Slavs from a primitive communal society in which land was held in common to a feudal order in which land became the private property of powerful feudal landowners. By the ninth century feudal states had developed in both eastern and western Europe. Ninth-century Kievan Rus, they affirm, was a fully consolidated feudal state comparable to the Carolingian Empire in the West; the idea that the eastern Slavs lagged behind western Europe in their development is a myth. Archaeological investigation, they conclude, has proved that Kiev and the Kievan state were founded before the Varangians came.

In the detailed *History of the USSR*, the role of the Varangians in the early history of Rus is described as follows:

> The "Norman period" in Russian history has always been exaggerated by bourgeois [Western] scholarship which stretches it out to several centuries, intentionally identifies the Varangian-Normans with the Rus, and attributes to the Varangians the creation of the first Slav state. This

---

[4] Ad. Stender-Petersen, "Der älteste russische Staat," *Historische Zeitschrift* 191 (August–December 1960): 1–17.

has been achieved by selecting tendentious sources, making a tendentious interpretation of disputed passages, and ignoring evidence unfavorable to the "Normanists."

What is the actual role of the Varangians in the history of our fatherland? In the mid-ninth century, when Kievan Rus had already been formed in the mid-Dnieper valley, on the far northern outskirts of the Slav world . . ., there began to appear detachments of Varangians from beyond the Baltic Sea. The Slavs and Chuds drove these detachments away. . . . In 862 or 874 . . . the Varangian konung, Riurik, appeared at Novgorod. From this adventurer, leading a small retinue, has been traced without any real basis the genealogy of all the early Rus princes. . . . The Varangian newcomers did not conquer Rus towns but set up fortified camps nearby. . . . Nowhere did the Varangians control Rus towns. Archaeological findings reveal that the number of Varangian warriors living permanently in Rus was very small.

In 882 one of the Varangian leaders, Oleg, penetrated from Novgorod southward . . . to Kiev where by deception and cleverness he succeeded in killing the Kievan prince, Oskold, and seizing power. With Oleg's name are connected several campaigns for tribute against nearby Slav tribes and the famous campaign of 911 by Rus troops against Tsargrad. Evidently, Oleg did not consider himself master of Rus. It is curious that after the successful campaign to Byzantium he and his Varangian retinue were not in the capital of Rus [Kiev], but far to the north in Ladoga, near their homeland, Sweden. It also seems strange that Oleg, to whom is ascribed wholly undeservedly the creation of the Rus state, disappeared from the Rus horizon without a trace. . . .

The rule of the Varangian, Oleg, in Kiev was an insignificant and brief episode, excessively inflated by a few pro-Varangian chroniclers and subsequent Normanist historians. . . . The Varangians' historical role in Rus was insignificant. Appearing as "discoverers," the newcomers, attracted by the gleam of riches in the already renowned Kievan Rus, plundered northern regions in isolated raids but penetrated only once to the heart of Rus. As to the Varangians' cultural role, there is nothing to be

said. . . . The Varangians had nothing to do with the creation of the [Kievan] state, construction of cities, or establishment of trade routes. They could neither speed up nor significantly retard the historical process in Rus.[5]

A Middle Road

The distinguished early-20th-century historian V. O. Kliuchevskii, whose *Course of Russian History* appeared in the decade before the Bolshevik Revolution, arrived at an interesting compromise between Normanism and its opponents about the origins of the first state in Rus:

> From the beginning of the ninth century and the end of Charlemagne's reign armed bands of pirates from Scandinavia began to roam the coasts of western Europe. . . . About this time along the river routes through our plains began to appear sea rovers from the Baltic who were given the name Varangians. During the tenth and eleventh centuries these Varangians were coming constantly to Rus either to trade or at the invitation of our princes who selected from them their military retinues. But . . . *The Primary Chronicle* records Varangian visits to Rus towns as early as the mid-ninth century. A Kievan legend of the eleventh century exaggerated their numbers, . . . [noting that] these Varangians swarmed into Rus commercial towns in such numbers that they formed a thick layer of their population and submerged the local inhabitants. Thus, according to the *Chronicle*, Novgorodians at first were Slavs and later became Varangians. . . . In the area of Kiev they became especially numerous. According to the *Chronicle*, Kiev was even founded by Varangians. . . . Thus the dim recollection of the *Chronicle* appears to move back the Varangians' arrival in Rus to the first half of the ninth century. . . .
>
> These Baltic Varangians, as well as the Black Sea Rus, according to many signs, were Scandinavians, and not Slavs. . . . These Scandinavian Varangians entered the military-commercial class that arose in the ninth century in the large trading towns of Rus. . . . The Varangians came to us with

---

[5] *Istoriia SSSR s drevneishykh vremen do nashikh dnei*, vol. 1 (Moscow, 1966), pp. 488–91.

Problem 1 continued

different aims and appearance than the Danes brought to the West: there the Dane was a pirate, a coastal brigand; the Varangian was primarily an armed merchant coming to Rus in order to make his way onward to rich Byzantium, there to serve the emperor with profit, to trade, and sometimes to plunder the rich Greeks if the opportunity arose. . . .

The Varangians, settling in the larger commercial towns of Rus, met there a class of armed merchants, socially akin to them and needing them; they were gradually absorbed into it, entering into commercial association with the natives or hiring themselves out for a good price to protect Rus trade routes. . . .

. . . The hazy *Chronicle* account designates the first political units formed in Rus about the mid-ninth century: the city-state, a commercial district administered by a fortified town that served as the commercial center for that region. . . . When the Kievan principality was formed, incorporating the tribes of the eastern Slavs, these formerly independent ancient city-states—Kiev, Chernigov, Smolensk, and others—were absorbed as administrative districts and ready-made subdivisions. . . .

The evolution of this earliest Rus political formation was accompanied elsewhere by the development of a secondary local form: the Varangian principality. In commercial centers where the Varangian immigrants had arrived in especially large numbers, they readily abandoned their role in commercial associations or as hired guards over trade routes and became rulers. . . . The transformation of Varangians from allies into rulers was, under favorable circumstances, achieved rather easily. . . . Thus some fortified towns and their environs under certain circumstances fell into the hands of the overseas immigrants and became

possessions of Varangian konungs. We find a few such Varangian principalities in Rus during the ninth and tenth centuries. . . . The rise of these Varangian principalities explains fully the tale in the *Chronicle* about the beginning of Rus after the invitation of princes from overseas.[6]

Conclusion

The lengthy debate over the origins of Rus persists even as new evidence is uncovered. Soviet scholarship, based largely on intensive archaeological investigation, demolished some of the bolder Normanist claims about the Scandinavian origin of the Kievan state and culture. Soviet historians made a reasonable case for an earlier origin of a Rus state in the vicinity of Kiev. However, they did not succeed in destroying the Norman theory itself, and since 1989 Russian historians have discussed this question far more openly and objectively. Despite efforts to play down Viking presence and influences, Soviet scholars failed to refute abundant evidence on the military and commercial operations of Vikings, or Norsemen, on the soil of Rus. Apparently, most early rulers of Kievan Rus were of Varangian origin. Moderate Normanism, as propounded by Stender-Petersen and H. Paszkiewicz, remains a defensible and provocative interpretation of the history of early Kievan Rus. The continuing controversy surrounding the Norman theory has stimulated intensive investigation of this distant period in several countries, lifting part of the veil that obscured it for so long. As scholars continue their search, many questions remain unresolved. ■

[6] V. O. Kliuchevskii, *Kurs russkoi istorii*, vol. 1 (Moscow, 1937), pp. 126–35.

Suggested Additional Reading

BOOKS

ADLER, M. *The Itinerary of Benjamin of Tudela* (London, 1907).

ARBMAN, H. *The Vikings* (London, 1962).

DUNLOP, D. M. *The History of the Jewish Khazars* (Princeton, 1954).

DVORNIK, F. *The Making of Central and Eastern Europe* (London, 1949).

———. *The Slavs: Their Early History and Civilization* (Boston, 1956).

HARMATTA, J. *Studies in the History of the Sarmatians* (Princeton, 1954).

MILLER, M. *Archeology in the USSR* (London, 1956).

MONGAIT, A. L. *Archeology in the USSR* (London, 1961).

PASZKIEWICZ, H. *The Origins of Russia* (New York, 1954).

———. *The Rise of Moscow's Power,* pp. 13–18 (Boulder, CO, 1983).

———. *Origins of Rus* (Cambridge, MA, 1981).

———. *The Making of the Russian Nation* (London, 1963).

PLETNEVA, S. A., and B. A. RYBAKOV, eds. *Istoriia SSSR* (Moscow, 1966). (Vol. 1 of this Soviet work contains numerous illustrations.)

ROSTOVTZEFF, M. *The Animal Style in South Russia and China* (Princeton, 1929).

———. *Iranians and Greeks in South Russia* (Oxford, 1922).

RYBAKOV, B. *Early Centuries of Russian History* (Moscow, 1965). (A Soviet view.)

SAWYER, P. H. *The Age of the Vikings* (London, 1962).

———. *Kings and Vikings* (New York, 1982).

SHASKOLSKII, I. P. *Normanskaia teoriia v sovremennoi burzhuaznoi nauke* (Moscow, 1965).

STENDER-PETERSEN, A. *Russian Studies* (Copenhagen, 1956).

———. *Varangica* (Aarhus, 1953).

VERNADSKY, G. *Ancient Russia* (New Haven, 1943).

———. *The Origins of Russia* (Oxford, 1959).

WREN, M. *Ancient Russia* (London, 1965).

ARTICLES*

BACKRACH, B. S., and T. NOONAN. "Avars." *MERSH* 2: 180–82.

BRUTZKUS, J. "The Khazar Origin of Ancient Kiev." *SEER* 22 (1944): 108–24.

CHUBATY, N. D. "The Beginnings of Russian History." *UQ* 3 (1946–47): 262ff.

CROSS, S. H. "The Scandinavian Infiltration into Early Russia." *Speculum* 21 (1946): 505–14.

CZEKANOWSKI, J. "The Ancient Home of the Slavs." *SEER* 25 (1946–47): 356–72.

HOWORTH, H. H. "The Avars." *Journal of Royal Asiatic Society,* n.s., 21 (1889): 721–810.

ISSATCHENKO, A. V. "The Varangians in Soviet Archeology Today." *Medieval Scandinavia* 10 (1976): 7–34.

JOHNSON, J. "The Scythian: His Rise and Fall." *JHI* 20 (1959): 250–57.

KAIMYKOV, A. D. "Iranians and Slavs in South Russia." *JAOS* 45 (1925): 68–71.

KIRPICHNIKOV, A. "Connections between Russia and Scandinavia in the Ninth and Tenth Centuries . . ." In *Varangian Problems, S. Sbornik* 64 (1968).

LIKHACHEV, D. "The Legend of the Calling In of the Varangians." In *Varangian Problems, S. Sbornik,* supp. 1 (1970).

NOONAN, T., ed. "Relations between Scandinavia and the Southeastern Baltic/Northwestern Russia." *JB* 13, no. 3 (1982). (Entire issue.)

POLONSKA-WASYLENKO, N. "The Beginnings of the State of Ukraine-Rus." *UQ,* no. 2 (1963): 33–58.

PRITSAK, O. "The Origin of Rus." *Rus. Rev.* (July 1977): 249–73.

RIASANOVSKY, A. V. "The Embassy of 838 Revisited." *JfGO* 10, no. 1 (1962): 1–12.

RIASANOVSKY, N. V. "The Norman Theory of the Origin of the Russian State," in *Readings in Russian History,* vol. 1, ed. S. Harcave, pp. 128–38 (New York, 1962).

WEINRYB, B., comp. "The Khazars: An Annotated Bibliography." *Studies in Bibliography and Booklore* 6 (1963): 11–129.

---

* See the bibliography (p. 705) for a key to journal abbreviations.

3

The Princes of Kievan Rus

During the ninth century, as Varangian and Slav princes formed a federation centering on Kiev and Novgorod in what is now European Russia, the era of Kievan Rus began. Its princes (all belonging to the Riurikid dynasty) and its people soon converted to the Greek Orthodox faith. For more than three centuries Kievan Rus, uniting the eastern Slavs, played a significant though disputed role in medieval civilization. Because Kievan religion and culture came primarily from Constantinople, some scholars consider Kievan Rus an offshoot of Greco-Byzantine civilization. Indeed, the eastern Slavs and many southern Slavs (Serbs and Bulgars) adopted the Cyrillic alphabet, designed in the 860s by two Eastern Orthodox monks from Macedonia. Scandinavian and Byzantine influences interacted and sometimes competed in the country. So important were Kiev's relations with the Byzantine Empire in the political, economic, religious, and cultural realms that some Byzantinists consider Kievan Rus a Byzantine satellite. Soviet historians vehemently and indignantly denied this and affirmed instead the independence, strength, and Slav character of Kievan Rus. Likewise disputed is

whether a cohesive, centralized Kievan state ever existed or whether, on the contrary, Kievan Rus comprised a loose federation, and later confederation, of separate Varangian and Slav principalities. Finally, were the Kievan federation's institutions feudal like those of medieval Europe?

Political History

The history of Kievan Rus may be divided into nearly a century of imperial expansion (878–972); an era of internal consolidation, growth, and prosperity (972–1054); and disintegration after 1054 interrupted by a brief recovery (1093–1132). The prerevolutionary Russian scholar V. O. Kliuchevskii and some Soviet historians consider 1132, when the last effective Kievan prince died, the end of the Kievan era. Many others would date the end of this era from the Mongol invasion a century later. As internal violence increased after 1132 and unity dissolved, Kiev lost its preeminence and Rus divided into several disparate segments and numerous principalities. Nonetheless, a distinctive old Russian political, economic, and cultural order persisted until the Mongol conquest of 1237–1241.

Kievan Rus began its history with a century of bold adventure and far-flung campaigns. Its Varangian and Slav rulers strove to extend their control from the Black Sea to the Baltic, from the Caspian Sea to the Carpathian Mountains. The great attack of the Rus on Constantinople in 860 for booty and concessions constituted part of Viking exploration, conquest, and plundering raids in eastern and western Europe. At first Varangian princes such as Oleg and Igor led these campaigns of Rus; later the eastern Slavs absorbed the Vikings and produced their own princes and heroes. Kievan expansion, seeking mainly trading rights rather than outright conquest, aimed at Constantinople, the Balkans, and Transcaucasia. Repeated assaults by the Rus on Constantinople sought to compel Byzantium to open markets to Rus goods and merchants. To this end Tmutarakan, a small principality in the Azov region, acted for a time as an intermediary between Kievan Rus and Byzantium. Its communications with Kiev were poor, however, and complications with Khazar and Bulgar states along the Volga River frequently distracted the Rus. Unable to fight successfully on two such widely separated fronts, the Kievan princes eventually abandoned their imperial designs.

Not the semilegendary Riurik but Oleg (882?–913), a Varangian prince originally of Novgorod, united Kievan Rus by linking Novgorod with Kiev and fusing his Varangian warriors with the Slav inhabitants. About 878 he moved southward along the Dnieper River and seized Kiev, thus securing a base for further advances. "Oleg set himself up as prince in Kiev, and declared that it should be the mother of Russian cities. Varangians and Slavs accompanied him, and his retainers were called Russes," explains *The Primary Russian Chronicle,* which depicted Oleg as a successful warrior, a shrewd diplomat, and a wise ruler:

> Oleg began to build stockaded towns and imposed tribute on the Slavs, the Krivichians, and the Merians. He commanded that Novgorod should pay the Varangians tribute to the

amount of 300 *grivni* a year for the preservation of peace.[1]

Securing the river route of the Dnieper and its tributaries northward to the Baltic and southward to the Black Sea, in 907 Oleg marched against Constantinople, combining an overland advance across Bulgaria with an assault by some 2,000 ships. After his forces had plundered Constantinople's outskirts, Byzantium granted Oleg a favorable commercial treaty, paid a large indemnity, and admitted Rus merchants to the city. The Russo-Byzantine Treaty of 911 authorized regular and equal trading relations, unthinkable had not Byzantium suffered grave defeats. The Greeks accepted these terms proposed by Oleg:

> The Russes who come hither shall receive as much grain as they require. Whosoever come as merchants shall receive supplies for six months, including bread, wine, meat, fish, and fruit. Baths shall be prepared for them in any volume they require. When the Russes return homeward, they shall receive from your Emperor food, anchors, cordage, and sails, and whatever else is needful for the journey.[2]

Oleg's successor, Prince Igor (913?–945), fought constantly to control east Slav tribes and collect tribute from them. Kiev, noted the Byzantine emperor, Constantine Porphyrogenitus, constituted the central core of Rus; peripheral Slav tribes paid it tribute in furs or money. Each major town of Rus had its prince, belonging to the dynasty of Riurik, but all deferred to the grand prince of Kiev. Igor married Olga (was she a Slav maiden from Pskov, as some claim, or of Scandinavian/Varangian origin?). In 941 Igor's forces attacked Byzantium. Recorded *The Primary Russian Chronicle:*

> The Bulgarians sent word to the Emperor that the Russes were advancing upon Tsargrad [Constantinople] with 10,000 vessels. The Russes set out across the sea, and began to ravage Bithynia. They waged war along the

[1] S. H. Cross, "The Russian Primary Chronicle," *Harvard Studies and Notes in Philology and Literature* 12 (1930): 146–47.

[2] Cross, "Russian Primary Chronicle," p. 150.

Pontus [Black Sea] . . . and laid waste the entire region of Nicomedia, burning everything along the gulf. Of the people they captured, some they butchered, others they set up as targets and shot at, some they seized upon, and . . . drove iron nails through their heads. . . . They burned many monasteries and villages, and took much booty on both sides of the sea.[3]

Eventually, the Byzantines managed to beat off this assault, but in 944 Igor's army, recruited from the Slav tribes and swelled by Pecheneg and Varangian mercenaries, again moved against Byzantium. This time the emperor bought him off with tribute payments, and in 945 he concluded a new and favorable commercial treaty with Rus. The Rus of Igor impressed the Arab chronicler Ibn-Miskawaih as "a mighty nation with vast frames and great courage. They know not defeat, nor does any of them turn his back until he slay or be slain." That same year, while seeking to extort excessive tribute from them, Igor was killed by the Derevlians.

His wife, Olga, the first female ruler of Rus (945–962), avenged her husband's death by luring Derevlian leaders to their deaths:

> When the Derevlians arrived, Olga commanded that a bath should be made ready, and invited them to appear before her after they had bathed. . . . Olga's men closed up the bathhouse behind them, and she gave orders to set it on fire from the doors, so that the Derevlians were all burned to death.

After the army of Olga and her son Sviatoslav had defeated the Derevlians, she imposed heavy tribute and laws upon them before returning to Kiev. To consolidate Kievan power, Olga divided her realm into districts, with a tax collector for each. In 947,

> Olga went to Novgorod, and along the Msta she established trading-posts and collected tribute. . . . Her hunting-grounds, boundary posts, towns, and trading-posts still exist [in 1110] throughout the whole region, while her

sleighs stand in Pskov to this day. . . . After making these dispositions, she returned to her city of Kiev, and dwelt at peace with it.[4]

The Primary Russian Chronicle praised Olga as "the wisest of women," especially because during a visit to Constantinople in 955 she became a Christian. However, her son Sviatoslav and Rus generally remained pagan.

Sviatoslav (962–972), a typical Viking warrior prince despite his Slav name, concentrated on foreign conquests. Some scholars consider him a brilliant general, others a reckless adventurer. Relates the *Chronicle*:

> Stepping light as a leopard, he undertook many campaigns. Upon his expeditions he carried with him neither wagons nor kettles, and boiled no meat, but cut off small strips of horseflesh, game, or beef and ate it after roasting it on the coals. Nor did he have a tent, but he spread out a garment under him, and set his saddle under his head; and all his retinue did likewise.[5]

In campaigns in 964–965 Sviatoslav conquered the Viatichians and Volga Bulgars, who had created a flourishing commercial state, then smashed the Khazars near the mouth of the Volga. Completing east Slavic unification around Kiev, Sviatoslav increased trade with the east. Bribed by the Byzantines, in 967 with a powerful army he aided Byzantium against the Balkan Bulgars, conquered northern Bulgaria, and set up his capital at Pereiaslavets (Little Preslav) on the lower Danube. To objections from Kievans that he was neglecting them, he told his mother and the boyars:

> "I do not care to remain in Kiev, but should prefer to live in Pereyaslavets on the Danube, since that is the center of my realm, where all riches are concentrated: gold, silks, wine . . . , silver and horses from Hungary and Bohemia, and from Rus furs, wax, honey, and slaves."[6]

Kievan Rus under Sviatoslav had commercial and military outposts at both ends of the Black

---

[3] Cross, pp. 157–58.

[4] Cross, pp. 165–66, 168.
[5] Cross, pp. 170–71.
[6] Cross, pp. 172–73.

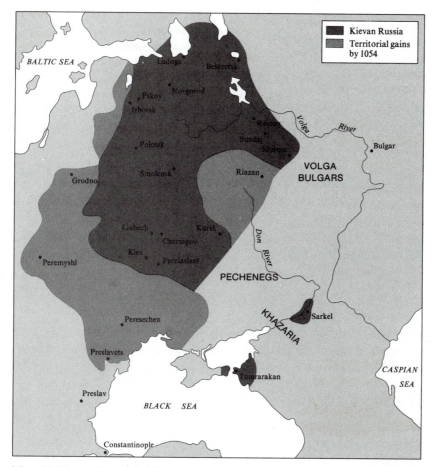

Map 3.1 Kievan Rus, 880–1054

Sea. After Olga's death Sviatoslav left for the Balkans, designating his sons the rulers of Kievan Rus. Had his ambitious Balkan campaigns succeeded, Kievan expansion might have shifted westward, but a Bulgar-Byzantine alliance defeated him and he had to abandon his claims to Bulgaria. On his homeward journey Sviatoslav was ambushed and killed by Pecheneg nomads. Kiev's imperial pretensions in the Balkans ended, but its hold over the Don, Volga, and Azov regions was strengthened.

After an interlude of internal strife Vladimir, Sviatoslav's youngest son and apparently of pure Scandinavian blood, ruled all of Rus (ca. 980–1015) as Vladimir I. A judicious and successful prince, Vladimir reasserted Kiev's authority over the various Slav tribes, expanding Rus to the shores of the Baltic Sea and the eastern frontier deeper into the steppe (see Map 3.1). Early in his reign, related the monkish *Chronicle* writer, Vladimir gave his monumental sexual impulses free rein:

> Now Vladimir was overcome by lust for women. His lawful wife was Rogned. . . . By her he had four sons . . . and two daughters. The Greek woman bore him Sviatopolk; by one Czech he had a son, Vysheslav; by another, Sviatoslav and Mstislav; and by a Bulgarian woman, Boris and Gleb. He had 300

concubines at Vshegorod, 300 at Belgorod, and 200 at Berestovo. . . . He was insatiable in vice. He even seduced married women and violated young girls, for he was a libertine like Solomon. . . . But Vladimir, though at first deluded, eventually found salvation.[7]

The chronicler was alluding in exaggerated fashion to a major event of his reign: the conversion of Vladimir and his people to Orthodox Christianity about 988. This conscious and fateful choice helped set Rus apart from the Latin West and the Moslem East and enhanced Byzantine political and cultural influences. Following his baptism, Vladimir became renowned for practical Christianity and generous hospitality. Making peace with neighboring princes, he defended Kiev's southern and eastern frontiers against nomadic raids. Late in his reign the rebellion of his ablest son, Iaroslav of Novgorod, demonstrated growing rivalry between Kiev and Novgorod, the leading towns of southern and northern Rus.

After Vladimir's death a bloody succession struggle among his sons threatened Kievan Rus's fragile political unity. One son, Sviatopolk, seized Kiev with Pecheneg aid. For murdering his helpless younger brothers, Boris and Gleb (later canonized as the first Russian saints), Sviatopolk was dubbed "the Damned." After losing Pecheneg and Polish support, Sviatopolk was defeated by his brother Iaroslav, who gained control of Kiev in 1019. Then a third brother, Mstislav, defeated Iaroslav, and in 1026 he and Iaroslav partitioned Kievan Rus. Mstislav's death without heirs enabled Iaroslav to reunite Kievan Rus.

Iaroslav the Wise (1036–1054) restored Kiev's leadership and brought Kievan Rus to the peak of its power. He ruled as grand prince from the Black Sea to the Baltic, from the Oka River in the east to the Carpathian Mountains in the west. His defeat of the Pechenegs gave Kiev a generation of respite from nomadic attacks. Europe's royal houses sought marriage alliances with his family. Contemporaries called him *kagan* (khan) or tsar,

as they also called the Byzantine emperor. Under his firm rule Kiev became a magnificent capital and center of learning, rivaling even Constantinople. A learned man, Iaroslav built a large library and may have helped draft Kievan Rus's first written law code, *Russkaia Pravda* (*Russian Justice*). A new citadel was erected in Kiev, and Byzantine masters built fine churches, including the great St. Sofia Cathedral. The first Greek metropolitan of Kiev, appointed in 1039, was subject to the patriarch of Constantinople. But in 1051 Iaroslav, seeking religious autonomy for Rus, convened a bishops' assembly in Kiev that elected a Russian, Ilarion, as metropolitan, though powerful pressure soon forced his resignation. Once this quarrel was settled, Iaroslav's son Vsevolod married a Byzantine princess, recementing Rus-Byzantine relations. Throughout his reign Iaroslav strongly defended all of Kievan Rus's varied interests.

Assigning major towns to his sons to rule, Iaroslav in his *Testament* confirmed their authority over Rus and urged them to live in peace:

> Love one another, since ye are brothers by one father and mother. If ye dwell in amity with one another, God will dwell among you, and will subject your enemies to you, and ye will live at peace. But if ye dwell in envy and dissension, quarreling with one another, then ye will perish yourselves and bring ruin to the land of your ancestors, which they won at the price of great effort.[8]

Iaroslav distributed leading towns to individual sons without dividing the country formally. The prince of Kiev supposedly retained final authority over rulers of other principalities. Henceforth, a town's rank in the *Testament*, a prince's seniority in the dynasty, and war determined succession to the grand princely throne. Theoretically, a hierarchy of thrones existed—Kiev, Chernigov, Pereiaslavl, and so on—but interprincely strife often prevented orderly rotation. Local princes forged strong links with their subjects, and separatism grew.

---

[7] Cross, p. 181.

[8] Cross, p. 231.

Iaroslav's successor, Iziaslav, ruled until 1072, when his brothers forced him to flee. Civil strife persisted under his ineffective successors. To end civil wars, an interprincely conference of Iaroslav's descendants met at Liubech in 1097. The princes, notes the *Chronicle*, told one another:

> Why do we ruin the Russian land by our continued strife against one another? The Cumans [Polovtsy] . . . rejoice that war is waged among us. Let us hereafter be united in spirit and watch over the Russian land, and let each of us guard his own domain.[9]

The Liubech Conference assigned to the princes collectively the keeping of domestic order and the organizing of external defense. Although the seniority principle was retained, each princely line ruled its own territory. Kievan Rus became a loose confederation of independent princes with increasingly tenuous family ties and a vague tradition of national unity.

A severe internal crisis followed the death of Sviatopolk II in 1113. Popular disaffection in Kiev subsided only when Vladimir Monomakh assumed the throne as Vladimir II (1113–1125). Renowned for his writings and numerous successful campaigns against the nomadic Polovtsy, Monomakh restored temporary unity to Kievan Rus and ruled firmly and wisely. Apparently he was a true Christian prince who possessed a practical mind, unusual energy, military ability, and ambition. Soviet historians stressed his patriotism, leadership, and sensible, popular rule. Vladimir's *Testament* depicts his love for his fellow men and his strong sense of responsibility. He urged his sons:

> Forget not what useful knowledge you possess and acquire that with which you are not acquainted. . . . Laziness is the mother of all evil. . . . In the practice of good works, you cannot neglect any item of good conduct.[10]

Following this advice, his eldest son and successor, Mstislav I (1125–1132), exercised authority wisely,

but Mstislav's brother and successor, Iaropolk II (1132–1139), failed to preserve unity, and Kiev's leading role was seriously undermined.

During its final century, Kievan Rus was a loose confederation of virtually sovereign principalities that fought to control Kiev. At times the Riurikid princes united to repel invasions from the steppe, and the Russian Orthodox church supported unity. In 1169 Prince Andrei Bogoliubskii of Suzdal captured and sacked Kiev. He placed a vassal on the Kievan throne but could not reunite Rus. After his death, political fragmentation accelerated. Even before the Mongol invasion, Rus had split into a dozen feuding principalities and several regions: a declining Kiev, the southwest (Galicia and Volhynia), a dynamic northeast (Vladimir-Suzdal), and the republics of Novgorod and Pskov in the northwest (see Map 3.2).

Ruling Rus

Was Kievan Rus wholly or partially "feudal," and what does this term signify? Until recently, Soviet scholars, basing their arguments on Marxism-Leninism, affirmed that feudalism was a class formation common to all medieval Europe. Wrote L. V. Cherepnin:

> The ancient Rus state with its center in Kiev . . . was feudal because it was the organ of the power of feudal landowners dominating over and dependent upon the peasants. And in this respect, there was no difference in principle between Kievan Rus and the medieval states which emerged in the Romano-Germanic countries.[11]

However, the Leningrad scholar I. Ia. Froianov challenged that traditional Soviet view, sanctified by Stalin's *Short Course*, affirming instead that Kievan Rus of the 11th and 12th centuries was prefeudal in social and political structure. Froianov argued that Kievan Rus lacked a system of large-scale service estates or private political authority

---

[9] Cross, p. 279.
[10] Cross, p. 305.

[11] See L. V. Cherepnin excerpt in T. Riha, ed., *Readings in Russian Civilization,* vol. 1, 2d ed. (Chicago, 1969), p. 83.

Map 3.2 The fragmentation of Kievan Rus, 1054–1238

based on landholding.[12] Western scholars tend to view feudalism as a defined political hierarchy of lords and vassals (lesser lords) holding estates (fiefs) in return for service to their overlord. Kievan Rus, asserted the émigré scholar G. Vernadsky, possessed feudal elements such as decentralized princely rule, but its extensive foreign trade did not fit feudal patterns. Even after 1054 a single Riurikid dynasty ruled and all princes were considered equal. Lesser lords could freely shift overlords; the manor was not widespread; and land was bought and sold without restrictions.[13] Western medievalists, stressing vassalage, the fief, and the contract as feudalism's chief features, believe that these never existed fully in Kievan Rus. Such feudal elements as existed in Kievan Rus assumed forms markedly different from those of western Europe.

Was Kievan Rus a "state" in the sense of a unified, centralized country? In the late 19th century N. I. Kostomarov affirmed that old Rus, with a single ruling family of princes, was a federation based on common origin, language, and religion but that each principality retained its peculiarities and separate rule. Soviet historians from the 1930s until 1990 had to emphasize for patriotic reasons the unity and strength of Kievan Rus until 1132. Even after 1139, when principalities developed their own dynasties and foreign policies, they insisted, the concept of the land of Rus persisted. However, to Vernadsky the numerous terms for state in old Rus suggested its heterogeneity—as a number of city-states, some coinciding with ancient Slav tribes, subject in some ways to the grand prince of Kiev.

The Kievan political system, combining princely power with the city-state, contained monarchical, aristocratic, and democratic elements. Even the greatest princes, such as Iaroslav and Vladimir II, were limited rulers, though their model was an absolute Byzantine emperor. Stand-

ing above classes, reflecting popular desires for unity and order, and claiming to be God's representatives on earth, neither Iaroslav nor Vladimir II could achieve absolute authority. Princes ruled their own domains, dispensed justice, led their contingents of warriors, and protected the Orthodox church. By the late 12th century warfare and elections by town assemblies became as important as seniority in the elevation of princes.

Princes ruled with noble councils later known as the *boiarskaia duma,* without whose consent no important decisions were made. The noble council developed out of the princely retinue of warrior chieftains (*druzhina*), whose leading Varangian and Slav members became boyars with estates and commercial interests. Acquiring extensive hereditary lands, boyars grew more independent of the prince than chieftains of his retinue had been. Boyar councils helped make laws, approved treaties, and served as courts of appeal. Their functions were ill defined and differed in various parts of Rus. An inner cabinet (*muzhi perednie*) may have met daily. Important matters were often discussed in plenary council sessions with the prince presiding.

The town meeting (*veche*) had some democratic aspects. Prerevolutionary Russian and many Western historians, affirming the *veche's* popular character and importance, stress that the prince consulted it before reaching important decisions. Most Soviet scholars (but not Froianov) claimed that feudal lords dominated the *veche.* Recently, Froianov claimed that free Kievan farmers ran their own political affairs through the *veche,* which could appoint and remove the prince. This town meeting existed in all Rus principalities, with that of Kiev exercising broader influence. All freemen could participate in *veche* meetings, but only male heads of households voted. Meetings were convened by officials or by ringing the town bell. The wealthy often determined *veche* decisions, but other freemen also participated. Relationships among prince, boyar council, and *veche* varied widely by period and region. Princely authority tended to predominate, except in the northwest,

---

[12] See *Soviet Studies in History,* vol. 24, no. 4, pp. 3–6.
[13] G. Vernadsky, "Feudalism in Russia," in Riha, *Readings,* pp. 69–81.

where aristocratic and democratic bodies gained in power.[14]

Kievan Rus had no central bureaucracy, so each principality was governed by the prince's court. Before 1054 and from 1113 to 1132, the Kievan prince exercised considerable authority over other towns, appointing governors—often sons or other relatives—to rule for him and collect tribute in furs or money for Kiev. After 1054 this Kievan control almost disappeared. Each major town had an elected or appointed chiliarch, or leader of a thousand men, who commanded the town militia and sometimes opposed an unpopular prince.

Armies of individual princes and town militias constituted Kievan Rus's military forces. Princely retinues were relatively small but mobile and well armed. Militia forces of townspeople, usually supplied with horses and weapons by the prince, were mobilized for major campaigns or emergencies. Among the forces confronting steppe nomads, cavalry predominated, sometimes supplemented with peasant infantry. The Kievan warrior wore armor and a helmet, carried a shield, and was armed like western European knights with spear and sword. Bows and arrows were also frequently used. Private princely armies often cooperated to oppose external invasions.

External Relations

Kievan Rus played a significant role in medieval international relations. Until the 12th century its chief commercial and cultural dealings were with the Byzantine Empire, then the leading Christian power. Frequent incursions of steppe nomads greatly influenced Kievan foreign relations, but Rus also dealt with Scandinavia, other Slav lands, and western Europe and traded with the Orient. Rus's international position was favorable in the south, tolerable in the west, but perilous in the southeastern steppe. Its chief external mission, claimed Soviet scholars, was to defend eastern Europe from Asian barbarism. Even after a unified Kievan external policy yielded to rival policies of individual princes, Rus remained important in eastern Europe.

Byzantium remained Kievan Rus's major focus until Constantinople's decline in the 12th century. Some Western historians regard Kiev as a Byzantine satellite, and one tsarist Russian scholar affirmed: "All the laws of the Greco-Roman emperors were binding upon Russia from the moment of their publication in Constantinople."[15] Vehemently denying this, patriotic Soviet scholars claimed equality for Kievan Rus. Tenth-century attacks by Rus on Constantinople forced regular and equal commercial and diplomatic relations upon Byzantium. Rus merchants flocked to Constantinople, and Princess Olga was received with honors befitting an independent sovereign. Dynastic intermarriage made Rus princes feel at home in Constantinople; they visited the city often. Vladimir I married Princess Anna, the emperor's sister; his grandson and two of Iaroslav's grandsons had Greek brides, and a number of prominent Byzantines picked Rus spouses. Rus's adoption of Orthodoxy promoted commercial, political, and cultural ties, as well as some dependence on Byzantium. A fresco depicting Iaroslav the Wise carrying a model of St. Sofia Cathedral of Kiev approaching a figure in imperial robes appears to confirm his vassalage to Byzantium. During the 10th and 11th centuries Byzantine rulers frequently hired Rus military detachments. Kiev and Constantinople were allies at some times; at others Byzantium sought to weaken Rus by allying with Rus's steppe rivals. Byzantine and western European rulers, but not Rus leaders, considered Kiev a satellite of Constantinople, especially in the 11th century. However, Rus never clearly subordinated itself politically to Byzantium.

Nomadic pressure from the east and south periodically imperiled Kievan Rus. Its birth coincided with the peak of the Khazar khanate, a federation of mostly Turkic tribes from the lower Volga and north Caucasus. The Khazars were

---

[14] See Chapter 7 in this text.

[15] V. Ikonnikov, quoted in A. Vasiliev, "Was Old Russia a Vassal State of Byzantium?" *Speculum* 6, no. 3 (1931): 350.

pagan pastoralists whose leaders converted to Judaism. From Itil, their capital on the Volga, they controlled trade in the entire region. Until the Varangians came, states *The Primary Russian Chronicle,* the Slavs paid the Khazars regular tribute, but in the mid-10th century Prince Sviatoslav of Kiev conquered and destroyed their empire.

Sviatoslav's victory exposed Rus to attack from Pechenegs (Patzinaks), a fierce people who migrated into the south Russian (Pontic) steppe and dominated it until about 1040. Arising in Central Asia, then driven westward by the Turks, the Pechenegs lived in felt tents, migrating annually with their herds of horned cattle, horses, and sheep. In the mid-10th century eight Pecheneg tribes formed a military league and invaded Rus. The Byzantine emperor Constantine Porphyrogenitus wrote that Pecheneg lands were divided into eight provinces lying between the Dnieper and Danube rivers, each ruled by a khan. He considered Pechenegs "ravenous" and "covetous," but both Byzantines and the Rus utilized them as mercenary auxiliary troops, periodically bribing them to forestall their fearsome raids. The most intensive Pecheneg-Rus warfare occurred in Vladimir I's reign. To protect his domains Vladimir had many border forts constructed along several Rus rivers. In 992, after a Rus champion had slain the "gigantic and fearsome" Pecheneg champion, Vladimir's troops defeated the Pechenegs on the Trubezh River. In 1036 a large Pecheneg army besieged Kiev until defeated by Prince Iaroslav and Varangian and Novgorod contingents. About the Pechenegs, Russian chronicles said merely that they fought with spears, sabers, and bows and arrows, and drank out of gilded cups made from human skulls. By 1050 most of them had been pushed west of the Dnieper River.

Replacing them were the pagan Polovtsy (Polovtsians), who controlled the Pontic steppes until the Mongol invasion as Rus's most formidable foe. Exploiting chronic civil strife in 12th-century Rus, they even stormed Kiev on occasion, but, incapable of ruling areas of Rus, invariably returned to the steppe. Rus princes conducted their own raids deep into the steppe, taking many Polovtsy women and children as slaves. The Rus-Polovtsy struggle turned into a stalemate.

Did the Polovtsy, as traditional accounts allege, sever Kievan Rus's commercial lifelines to Constantinople? Actually, they wished to exploit Russo-Byzantine trade, not destroy it. Kiev's trade with Byzantium declined only relatively little, and the Volga River trade flourished during the peak of Polovtsy power. As late as 1167, notes a chronicle, Rus's Black Sea trade still operated normally, and even later trade caravans safely traversed the steppe to the Black Sea. The Polovtsy themselves, besides collecting fees from Rus merchants, traded directly with Rus, exchanging their salt, fish, and livestock for finished goods. Rus princes could usually control the Polovtsy, whose threat to Rus has been exaggerated.

By fostering national efforts to repel them, the Polovtsy may have delayed Kievan Rus's disintegration. In 1185, in a famous episode, the Polovtsy defeated Prince Igor of Novgorod-Seversk, took him prisoner, and devastated the Pereiaslavl region. The *Tale of Igor,* the best-known Rus epic, depicts an embryonic national consciousness:

> [Igor], imbued with fighting spirit
> Led his brave troops against the land of the
>   Polovtsians
> For the sake of the Russian land. . . .
> And Igor spoke to his troops:
> "Brothers and soldiers!
> It would be better for us to perish than to
>   surrender." . . .
> "I wish," he said, "to break my spear
> With you, Russian people, at the frontier of the
>   Polovtsian land!
> I want either to die or be able to drink a helmetful
>   of the Don!"[16]

After 1190, Polovtsian pressure against Kievan Rus lessened, then ceased. Successful resistance against the Polovtsy, affirmed Soviet historians,

---

[16] Basil Dmytryshyn, *Medieval Russia: A Source Book, 900–1700,* 3d ed. (Fort Worth, 1991), p. 78. Some Western scholars and the Soviet scholar A. A. Zimin doubt that the *Tale of Igor* was written in the Kievan era.

helped define Rus's national territory and character and protected medieval Europe from possible conquest. Polovtsy continued to participate in civil strife within Rus, but Rus-Polovtsian wars ended. Their treaties were sometimes reinforced by marriage, and some famous Rus princes, such as Andrei Bogoliubskii,[17] were offspring of such unions. Rus and Polovtsy rulers generally respected one another, though Rus chronicles are mostly derogatory about these nomads. In campaigns of 1236–1238 the Mongols, subjugating the Polovtsy, adopted their language and culture. Thousands of Polovtsy fled westward into Hungary.

Kievan Rus also developed significant ties with the Latin West. Military and commercial contacts with Scandinavia persisted into the 11th century, and Rus established relations with the Holy Roman Empire. Princess Olga requested a bishop from Emperor Otto I; later, Vladimir I's marriage to a relative of Otto II reinforced these ties. As a counterbalance to Byzantium, Prince Iaroslav allied with France. The Latin crusaders' sack of Constantinople in 1204 revealed Byzantine decline and the rise of the Latin West. Byzantium's eclipse and Polovtsy incursions shifted much Rus commerce into Western markets, notably through the German town of Regensburg.

The Rus had important dealings with other Slav peoples. About 800 the western boundary of Slav settlement ran from Hamburg on the Elbe southward to Trieste on the Adriatic. Gradually the Germans thrust eastward to the Oder River, and in the early 13th century the Poles invited German Teutonic Knights into East Prussia. Emphasizing Rus–eastern European friendship, Soviet historians stressed their partnership with Czechs, Slovaks, and Poles against the German "drive to the east." In 1017 and 1029, however, Iaroslav cooperated with German princes against the Poles. In the Balkans the Bulgars, a slavicized Asian people, mediated between Rus and Byzantium. They supplied Rus with church books in Slavic translation,

sent priests and translators to Kiev, and fostered Rus-Byzantine commerce. After 1050 Serbian influence on Russian church literature gradually replaced Bulgarian impact, and Rus missionaries were active in Serbia. With western Slavs too there were dynastic intermarriages, despite the schism of 1054 between the Catholic and Orthodox churches.

Rus relations with the Orient were sporadic and limited. In the 10th century Rus's conquest of the north Caucasus opened commercial contacts with Islamic areas to the south and southeast, and numerous Rus merchants visited Baghdad. The Rus also traded with the Volga Bulgars and Khorezm in Central Asia, but Islam inhibited social contacts or intermarriage. After the fall of Tmutarakan in the 11th century, ties with the Orient weakened.

Kievan Rus was usually hospitable to foreigners and to external influences. At first its relationships with Byzantium far overshadowed those with other regions, but its contacts with the Latin West became increasingly significant before the Mongol invasion.

Decline and Fall

Free, productive Kievan civilization succumbed to the invading Mongols for internal and external reasons. Rus's evident political disunity after 1132 resembled that of the Greek city-states before their conquest by Rome. Only the ablest Kievan rulers preserved unity briefly. In its final century Rus's separatism and regionalism prevailed over national unity and cooperation. Fratricidal wars and interprincely disputes reflected the failure of Kievan Rus to create effective central institutions. As the power of boyar councils and town assemblies increased, the princes could no longer control assertive towns.

Geographic factors were also significant. Kiev's leadership had stemmed partly from its location on the great water route "from the Varangians to the Greeks." The relative decline of Kievan-Byzantine trade and Byzantine weakness undermined Kiev's position. Kievan Rus was never secure vis-a-vis the steppe nomads and lacked stable frontiers on the east. Extensive territories

---

[17] See Chapter 5 in this text.

and poor internal communications contributed to Rus disunity.

Kiev's prosperity and strength, affirm some historians, depended on foreign trade. As Byzantium declined commercially, Kiev's trade with it waned. Some Kievan trade passed to the Baltic towns while the economic importance of centers such as Novgorod and Smolensk grew. Kiev's strength was drained further by persistent wars with steppe nomads and by Andrei Bogoliubskii's sack of the city in 1169.

Rising social tensions connected with the growth of feudalism helped tear Kievan Rus apart, argued some Soviet scholars. Antagonism developed among feudal landowners, and peasants gradually lost freedom of movement. In the towns, growing class conflict between the poor and the boyar-merchant ruling element produced serious social revolts.

Finally, external events promoted Kiev's decline and destruction. Rus-Polovtsian wars, exhausting both sides, facilitated the Mongol triumph. Just before the Mongol conquest, however, these conflicts lessened and political conditions in Rus improved, but neither the Rus nor other settled peoples could withstand the tremendous Mongol drive.

Suggested Additional Reading

BOOKS

ARNOTT, P. *The Byzantines and Their World* (New York, 1973).

CONSTANTINUS VII PORPHYROGENITUS. *De administrando imperio*, vol. 1 (Budapest, 1949). Vol. 2, trans. R. Jenkins (London, 1962).

CROSS, S. H. "The Russian Primary Chronicle." *Harvard Studies and Notes in Philology and Literature* 12 (1930): 77ff. (Primary source.)

Galician-Volhynian Chronicle, The, trans. G. A. Perfecky (Munich, 1973).

GREKOV, B. *Kiev Rus* (Moscow, 1959). (Soviet account.)

HURWITZ, E. *Prince Andrej Bogoljubskij* (Florence, 1980).

IBN MISKAWAIH. *The Eclipse of the Abbasid Caliphate*, 7 vols. (Oxford, 1920–21).

KAISER, D. H. Trans. and ed. *The Laws of Rus: Tenth to Fifteenth Centuries* (Salt Lake City, 1992).

MAGOCSI, P. *Galicia: A Historical Survey and Bibliographic Guide* (Toronto, 1983).

POLANSKA-WASYLENKO, N. *Russia and Western Europe, 10th–13th Centuries* (London, 1954).

RYBAKOV, B. *Early Centuries of Russian History* (Moscow, 1965).

———. *Kievan Rus* (Moscow, 1989).

SEIDLER, G. *The Emergence of the Eastern World* (New York, 1968).

TIKHOMIROV, M. N. *The Towns of Ancient Rus* (Moscow, 1959). (Soviet account.)

VERNADSKY, G. *Kievan Russia* (New Haven, 1948).

———. *Medieval Russian Laws* (New York, 1947).

ARTICLES

ANDREYEV, N. "Pagan and Christian Elements in Old Russia." *SR* 21, no. 1 (1962): 16–23.

BOSWELL, A. B. "The Kipchak Turks." *SEER* 6 (1927).

DIMNIK, M. "The Testament of Iaroslav the Wise: A Reexamination," *Can. Slav. Pap.* 29, no. 4 (December 1987): 369–86.

DVORNIK, F. "Byzantine Political Ideas in Kievan Russia." *DOP*, nos. 9–10 (1956): 73–123.

LANTZEFF, G. "Russian Eastward Expansion before the Mongol Invasion." *ASEER* 6 (1947): 1–10.

MASON, R. A. "St. Volodymyr and the Norse Sagas." *Ukrainian Quarterly* 47, no. 2 (Summer 1991): 120–37.

———. "The Mongol Mission and Kievan Rus." *Ukrainian Quarterly* 49, no. 4 (Winter 1993): 385–402.

MILLER, D. "The Kievan Principality in the Century Before the Mongol Invasion. . . ." *Harv. Ukr. Stu.* 10, no. 1/2 (June 1986): 215–40.

NOONAN, T. "Kievan Rus." *MERSH* 16: 130–43.

———. "Pechenegs." *MERSH* 27: 126–33.

———. "Polovtsy." *MERSH* 29: 12–24.

PHILIPP, W. "Russia's Position in Medieval Europe." *Essays in History and Literature*, ed. L. Legters (Leiden, 1972).

RIASANOVSKY, A. V. "Runaway Slavs and 'Swift Danes' . . ." *Speculum* 39, no. 2 (1964): 288–97.

SHULGIN, B. "Kiev: Mother of Russian Towns." *SEER* 19 (1940): 62–82.

STOKES, A. "The Balkan Campaigns of Svyatoslav Igorevich." *SEER* 41 (1962): 466–96.

4

Kievan Rus: Economic Life, Society, Culture, and Religion

By the ninth century the society and culture of the eastern Slavs had undergone considerable development and had achieved relative organization and sophistication. The precise nature of many facets of this society and culture, however, is still subject to debate, owing to incomplete and often contradictory sources.

Economic Life

On the all-important question regarding the nature of Kievan economic life, two historiographic camps may be distinguished. The leading representative of the older view was the eminent Russian historian V. O. Kliuchevskii, who argued that foreign trade constituted the chief determining element in the evolution of the economic life of Kievan Rus, and this view conditioned his evaluation of Kievan social and political life as well. Kliuchevskii's interpretation was challenged by the prominent Soviet authority on Kievan Rus, B. D. Grekov, whose interpretation stemmed from the Marxist view of feudalism, which asserted that agriculture, not foreign trade, was both the chief

occupation of the population and the primary component of the structure of the feudal economy and society. In Kievan Rus, Grekov argued, the crucial social relationships were thus between landowners and unfree peasants. The prevalence of serfdom in Kievan Rus had to be affirmed in order to identify it as a feudal society in Marxist terms. Therefore, Grekov believed agriculture was the key to understanding Kievan society and culture.

Indeed, Kliuchevskii ignored agriculture almost completely, assigning it only a minor role in Kievan life. Grekov, on the other hand, while acknowledging the existence of foreign trade in Kievan Rus, tended to minimize its importance. The essence of Kliuchevskii's view is contained in the following often-cited passage:

> The history of our society would have been substantially different had not our economy been for eight or nine centuries at variance with the nature of our country. In the eleventh century the bulk of the Rus population was concentrated in the black-earth region of the middle Dnieper, and by the mid-fifteenth century it had moved to the Upper Volga

region. It would seem that in the former area agriculture should have been the chief basis of the national economy, and that in the latter foreign trade, forestry, and other industries should have predominated. But external circumstances were such that while the Rus remained in the Dnieper black-earth region they traded in products of the forest and other industries and began vigorously to plow only when they moved to the clayey soil of the Upper Volga.[1]

Grekov countered with an entirely different view: "There is no evidence in our sources to substantiate the basic theses of Kliuchevskii, Rozhkov, and their followers. In Kievan, Novgorodian, and Suzdalian Rus agriculture was the main occupation of the people."[2]

It would appear from a careful reading of the sources that the truth lies somewhere between these two interpretations. The sources, both written and archaeological, provide ample evidence of the existence in Kievan times of a lively and lucrative foreign trade, carried on primarily with the Byzantine Empire, and at the same time there is evidence of extensive local and regional commerce within the Kievan lands. Constantine Porphyrogenitus, ruler of Byzantium from 945 to 959, has left us an invaluable description of the commercial activities of the Slavs in his *De administrando imperio.* He recounted how Russian princes and their agents assembled great trade convoys that sailed down the Dnieper River across the Black Sea to Constantinople, arriving each summer laden with slaves and products of the forest: honey, furs, and wax. According to Porphyrogenitus, the princes and their retinues gathered tribute from the Slavs during the winter; and then with the arrival of spring, huge trees were felled and hollowed out to form boats that transported the collected products down the Dnieper. In Constantinople these prod-

ucts were exchanged for luxury items: silks, wines, fruits, and fine weapons.

However important foreign trade was to the princes and their retinues, the bulk of the population derived a livelihood from agriculture. Archaeological evidence clearly attests that agriculture was the primary occupation of the majority of the population. Excavations have uncovered evidence of the widespread use of the iron plowshare in the south by the eighth century and evidence of the use of a wooden forked plow (*sokha*) in the north. Archaeologists have unearthed evidence of extensive cultivation of wheat, buckwheat, rye, oats, and barley, along with a wide variety of primitive agricultural implements.

In pre-Kievan times various systems of tillage were in use. In the northern forested regions, the slash-and-burn method involved felling trees in the spring, burning them in the autumn, leaving the ashes over the winter, and sowing the cleared land the following spring. The ashes served as fertilizer, and the seeds were broadcast randomly and covered over by means of rakes or tree branches. Such fields were cultivated for anywhere from two to eight growing seasons or until the fertility of the soil was exhausted; then a new plot would be cleared and prepared. The tremendous amount of time and labor involved in this method of farming made extensive cooperation and communal methods essential to success.

In the unforested steppe region to the south, there was no need to clear land, and cultivation was easier. Land was cultivated until its productivity was exhausted, and then new lands would be opened up for cultivation. There was no regular system of crop rotation until Kievan times. Initially, a two-field system prevailed in which a plot of land was cultivated for several years, then left fallow for a number of years, and then replanted. Gradually, as in western Europe, a three-field system was introduced in which crops were systematically rotated and one-third of the land was allowed to remain fallow each year.

The harsh climate and primitive methods of agriculture fostered a need for cooperation and combined effort that resulted in the early

---

[1] V. O. Kliuchevskii, *Boiarskaia duma drevnei Rusi* (Moscow, 1902), p. 13.

[2] B. D. Grekov, *Kievskaia Rus* (Moscow-Leningrad, 1948), p. 35. See the English translation of this work, *Kiev Rus* (Moscow, 1959), p. 70.

emergence of the commune, or *obshchina,* in which land, implements, and livestock were owned in common by groups of people and the obligation to work was shared equally. Two types of communal organization existed in Kievan times: first, family communes made up of blood relatives, or what might be called a patriarchal commune consisting of several related generations; and second, rural or territorial communes made up of unrelated neighbors who banded together to share the burdens of labor and the meager fruits of the earth. Each commune was, to a large extent, self-sufficient, producing all that was needed by the individual members: food, clothing, shelter, and implements. In addition, hunting, fishing, beekeeping, and other forest industries were important supplemental occupations practiced by the rural population.

Social Structure

Having established the importance of trade and commerce for the upper classes—the princes and their retinues—and the importance of agriculture for the bulk of the population, let us now turn to an analysis of the structure of Kievan society. The process of social stratification had begun among the eastern Slavs long before the establishment of the Kievan state. As early as the sixth century, three distinct social categories had emerged: an aristocracy, a class of freemen, and slaves. The social structure became more complex once a formal state framework had been created. The basic judicial sources for the Kievan period are the *Russkaia Pravda (Russian Justice)* of the first half of the 11th century, a collection of laws known as the *Pravda* of Iaroslav's sons of the second half of the 11th century, and the *Russkaia Pravda* (expanded Russian Law) of the 12th century.[3] These law

codes delineate several distinct social categories within Kievan society. The relative social status of individual social groups was reflected in the respective wergeld, or monetary value, placed on an individual's life in cases of unavenged murder.

At the very pinnacle of society in Kievan Rus stood the rapidly proliferating princely family, the House of Riurik. Directly beneath the princely class on the Kievan social ladder were the *muzhi,* or upper-class freemen, who were assigned a wergeld of 80 *grivna.* (There is no general consensus among historians as to the value or precise meaning of this monetary unit; its value must have fluctuated widely during Kievan times.) The *muzhi* made up the *druzhina,* or military retinue, of the princes. Initially, the composition of the *druzhina* was Scandinavian, but by the 11th century Slavic elements freely entered this important social and economic group. These servitors of the prince derived their wealth and social prestige from participation in trade, from war booty, and from grants of land and other rewards and favors bestowed upon them by the prince. The members of the *druzhina* were the closest associates of the prince, serving as his advisers in both military and commercial affairs and acting as his administrative agents in local affairs.

In addition, there was a nonservice aristocracy made up of the descendants of the old Slavic tribal aristocracy and some others who had succeeded in amassing great wealth from lucrative foreign trade or other enterprises. The wergeld for this nonservice aristocracy was fixed at 40 *grivna,* half that of a member of the *druzhina.* Gradually these two aristocracies, the aristocracy of service and the aristocracy of social origin and wealth, merged into the boyar class. The origin of the term *boyar* is obscure, but it was clearly in widespread use by the mid-10th century, and it was used to denote the upper class. As time passed, the House of Riurik increased in size and became divided into groups of senior and lesser princes. The lesser princes often became almost indistinguishable from the boyars. During Kievan times the boyar class was not a closed, corporate class; movement into and out of its ranks was possible. Boyars

---

[3] For an annotated translation of these important documents, see G. Vernadsky, trans., *Medieval Russian Laws* (New York, 1969). It should be emphasized that the use of modern social terminology in this account of the Kievan social structure should not be taken too literally. The terms used in this discussion are modern approximations of the Russian terms that appear in the documents of the time.

maintained the right of departure; that is, they were free to leave the service of one prince and take up service with another prince without jeopardizing their hereditary rights, their privileged social position, or their economic power. They enjoyed, however, no special legal rights and were on an equal footing with other freemen in terms of their right to own land and to participate in trade and commerce.

In a category below the *muzhi* were the *liudi,* or middle-class freemen. The wergeld for *liudi* was fixed by *Russkaia Pravda* at 40 *grivna,* the same as that for a member of the nonservice aristocracy. Sources are vague when it comes to a precise definition of the *liudi.* Many were apparently urban citizens who owned such industrial enterprises as smithies, carpentry shops, and tanneries, whereas others were middle-class merchants involved in local and regional trade as well as foreign trade. Still other *liudi* derived their wealth from property owned outside the city, and finally, some members of this group lived in rural areas as moderately well-to-do landowners. The *liudi* enjoyed no special legal privileges aside from those enjoyed by all freemen.

The lower classes in Kievan society were made up of diverse rural and urban elements. The wergeld for lower-class freemen was fixed at 5 *grivna,* indicating that a substantial gulf separated the upper classes from the lower classes. In the towns and cities the lower classes were known collectively as the *molodshie liudi* (younger men). These were the artisans of various types: tanners, potters, armorers, goldsmiths, glaziers, carpenters, and masons. They were generally employed by the shop owners or merchants, and they were often organized into associations or guilds and lived in designated sections of the city: the potters' section, the carpenters' section, the tanners' section, and so forth.

In the rural areas lower-class people were known collectively as *smerdy* ("stinkers"). This term has been subject to long and still unresolved controversy. Kliuchevskii believed that the *smerdy* were free peasants living on princely land and referred to them as state peasants. Other histori-

ans have advanced the view that two types of *smerdy* existed in Kievan times: village *smerdy* living on communally held land not yet assimilated by the boyar class, and *smerdy* dependent on princes and boyars. The prerevolutionary historian A. E. Presniakov argued that the term *smerdy* was used to denote the entire undifferentiated rural population. Grekov has argued in favor of two types of *smerdy*: the free and the dependent. The free *smerdy,* in his view, were organized into free communes and enjoyed all the rights and privileges of any freemen in Kievan society. The dependent *smerdy* were those living on princely land or boyar land and were required either to perform corvée (labor service) for the landlord or to pay him rent in kind. Dependent *smerdy* were subject to the special jurisdiction of the prince and could not be arrested or prosecuted without the prince's authorization. If a dependent *smerd* died without male heirs, his property reverted to the prince. From the sources, it would appear that the *smerdy* were clearly divided into two groups, the free and the dependent, but it would be a mistake to call dependent *smerdy* serfs, as Soviet accounts often did.

It is difficult to estimate the number of *smerdy* in Kievan Rus, but they clearly constituted the bulk of the rural population, with the free vastly outnumbering the dependent, although the latter probably increased significantly in number during the later Kievan period, when the upper classes turned more and more to landowning as a source of income. Little is known about the way of life, habits, attitudes, and customs of the *smerdy* because the sources invariably concentrate on the upper classes and the urban population.

Two more social categories require mention: the half-free and the slaves. It should be emphasized that serfdom as a legal institution was unknown in Kievan times, but there were social groups whose rights were prescribed by law. These are known in the sources as *zakupy,* whom Vernadsky refers to as the half-free, and a second group known as *cheliad,* or slaves.

As with other aspects of the Kievan social structure, there has been little agreement among historians about a precise definition of the *zakupy.* The *zakup* was not a serf; his relationship with his lord was one of debtor to creditor. The debt incurred was, by agreement, to be repaid by specified labor service rather than money, although money, if available, could be used to pay it off. The debtor was usually a *smerd* who borrowed money for some specific purpose and agreed to repay it with his own labor. The debtor might also be a hired laborer who contracted to receive his wages in advance, thus acquiring a legal debt calling for repayment with interest over a period of time. In this manner, the *smerd* became a *zakup,* or indentured laborer, until his debt was repaid. Soviet historians, especially Grekov, argued that the existence of *zakupy* indicates the growth of feudalism in Kievan times: "The *zakup,* then, is by origin generally a *smerd,* deprived of the means of production and forced by economic circumstances to seek a source of subsistence from the large landowners. This is a symptom of the degradation of the village community under the impact of feudal relationships."[4] This interpretation is tantamount to calling the *zakup* a serf, but clearly his social and economic status was envisaged as being temporary, because once his debt was repaid he immediately became a freeman again with all the rights associated with that category. Still, *zakupy* must have been numerous at certain times because the sources credit them with staging a serious rebellion in Kiev in 1113. Afterward, the legal rights and status of *zakupy* were more clearly defined.

Kievan judicial sources make a clear distinction between the *zakup* and the slave—the *cheliad* or *kholop.* Indeed, the expanded *Russkaia Pravda* provided that if a *zakup* attempted to flee to evade his legal obligation, he *became* a slave. The existence of slavery in Kievan times has been amply documented, and it is clear that slaves were a major element in trade between Kiev and Constantinople. There were two types of slaves: temporary and permanent. The former category was made up of war prisoners, both military and civil-

ian. Usually, with the conclusion of peace such captives were returned on payment of ransom. Otherwise, the captives remained slaves and became part of the war booty. Permanent slavery, according to the expanded *Russkaia Pravda,* resulted from several specific factors. A man became a permanent slave if he sold himself into slavery voluntarily or if he married a female slave without first making an agreement with her lord about his own free status. A person became a slave if he attempted to flee his master in order to evade a legal obligation. From the considerable number of articles on slavery in the expanded *Russkaia Pravda,* it must have been widespread in Kievan Rus.

In summary, the Kievan social structure was complex and stratified, with diverse, clearly delineated social groups. The princely class expanded greatly in Kievan times and occupied the pinnacle of the social structure. Beneath it was the boyar class, which was followed by middle-class freemen, constituting the bulk of the urban population. Lower still were the "younger men" (*molodshie liudi*) in towns and the *smerdy,* or "stinkers," as the bulk of the semiobligated rural population. At the bottom of the social ladder were the half-free and the slaves. Kievan Rus's social structure remained fluid. There were no built-in barriers to social mobility, and movement from one segment of society to another was often determined by chance, opportunity, and skill. Except for the princely class, heredity counted for little in determining one's status.

Urban Life

The land of Rus was known in Scandinavian sources as Gardariki, the land of towns. The Soviet historian M. N. Tikhomirov, the leading authority on old Russian towns, combed the sources and arrived at a figure of 271 towns recorded in Rus in the Kievan era. He admitted that this was a modest estimate.[5] Many towns were founded between

---

[4] Grekov, *Kiev Rus,* p. 275.

[5] M. N. Tikhomirov, *The Towns of Ancient Rus* (Moscow, 1959), p. 43.

Reconstruction of an ancient primitive *gorodishche.*

the 11th and 13th centuries, but the oldest date back to the eighth and ninth centuries and perhaps even earlier. Many early towns developed around the sites of earlier fortified settlements (*gorodishche*), usually located on elevated, easily defended ground situated at strategic points. Kiev, on the hills overlooking the Dnieper River, must have originally been an early *gorodishche. The Primary Russian Chronicle* records that long before the emergence of the Kievan state, three brothers, Kii, Shchek, and Khoriv, "built a town in honor of their eldest brother and named it Kiev. Around the town lay a wood and a great pine forest in which they used to trap wild beasts."[6] Around this small fortified settlement the city of Kiev, "the mother of Russian cities," grew and developed. *The Primary Russian Chronicle* offers two versions of Novgorod's origin. One version ascribes its foundation to the Slavic Slovene tribe; the other attributes its

origin to Riurik and his retinue. The important point is that Novgorod is at least as old as Kiev, if not older. These two urban centers, one at either end of the great waterway, have been extensively excavated by archaeologists, and a great quantity of information has been unearthed that reveals much detail about the nature of life during Kievan times.

The extensive development of urban centers in Kievan Rus, like so many other aspects of Kievan history, has been subject to ongoing controversy. Kliuchevskii, in conformity with his view on the central importance of trade in Kievan society, observed that the earliest towns in Rus were located along the great waterway "from the Varangians to the Greeks" and along the upper Volga River. He noted several exceptions but nevertheless connected the emergence of urban centers with the development of trade and commerce. "These towns emerged as gathering places for Rus trade," Kliuchevskii suggested, "depots where Rus exports were stored and prepared for shipment. Each one of them was a center of some industrial

[6] S. H. Cross, "The Russian Primary Chronicle," *Harvard Studies and Notes in Philology and Literature* 12 (1930): 54.

area and [served as] an intermediary between the latter and the maritime markets. But very quickly events turned these trading centers into political centers and their industrial areas into their dependent regions."[7] The Soviet authority S. V. Iushkov reversed Kliuchevskii's interpretation by arguing that the prince and his retinue settled, with the elders of Slavic tribes, in tribal towns owing to the protection they offered, transforming these places of refuge into political and administrative centers. Later, craftsmen and traders were attracted to these towns and trade and commerce were fostered and developed.[8] Tikhomirov offered still another alternative: "In my opinion, towns arose primarily where agriculture developed, where craftsmen and merchants made their appearance and urban districts took shape around their centers."[9] In this view, developing agriculture and handicrafts in a given region led to the appearance of towns, which in turn led to the development of trade and commerce. Tikhomirov rejected the view that the waterways were vital to the emergence of towns, noting the many urban centers that sprang up at some distance from waterways, but he did not deny that commerce contributed significantly to the growth of towns and helped expand their wealth.

The typical medieval town of Kievan Rus was first of all a walled enclosure, perhaps stemming from the old fortified citadel. Gradually craftsmen and merchants gathered in the immediate vicinity of the citadel, which offered protection in times of danger. These settlements of craftsmen and merchants became known as *posady,* or suburbs. These centers of trade and industry divided, as they grew, into sections, or *kontsy* (sing. *konets*), connected with the practice of a given handicraft or skill (for example, the potters' section, the carpenters' section, and the smiths' section). Central marketplaces gradually emerged in which trade was conducted on a broad scale. Although handi-

crafts and trade dominated the town economy, close contact with surrounding agricultural areas was maintained because the towns needed their products.

The productive capacities of the larger towns were extremely diverse, and many skills became highly developed. A leading Soviet authority, B. A. Rybakov, in seeking to portray Kievan society as the equal of Western societies, identified 64 specific trades in Kievan Rus. Tikhomirov more reliably identified 34 trades, which, although incomplete, suggests the diversity of skills in Kievan times.[10] Archaeological excavations have turned up many examples of these crafts and testify to the high level of craftsmanship in Kievan times.

Most artisans and craftsmen were freemen in business for themselves or were employed by merchants or members of the upper classes, although there were significant numbers of craftsmen who were slaves of princes and boyars. There were also *zakup* craftsmen. The numerous crafts pursued in Kievan times indicate that at least the major towns were highly developed centers of production, engaging in local, regional, and foreign trade. Such major centers as Kiev, Novgorod, Smolensk, Rostov, Suzdal, and Riazan must have been very large, although we do not know their precise populations during Kievan times. Still, their populations must have numbered in the tens of thousands. The populations of other towns rarely exceeded 1,000.

Russian towns in this period were built chiefly of wood. Thus we know little about how these early towns looked because wood is so perishable. One of the greatest ravages of medieval times was fire, and the chronicles record frequent and terrible fires, which wiped out entire towns. Despite its impermanence, wood had obvious advantages because it was plentiful, especially in the northern forest region, and offered better protection from the cold, damp climate than other materials. Wooden structures were easier to heat and provided better insulation than stone or brick build-

---

[7] Kliuchevskii, *Boiarskaia duma drevnei Rusi,* p. 22.

[8] S. V. Iushkov, *Obshchestvenno-politicheskii stroi i pravo Kievskogo gosudarstva* (Moscow, 1949), pp. 257–67.

[9] Tikhomirov, *Towns of Ancient Rus,* p. 60.

[10] Tikhomirov, pp. 91–92.

ings, and wood was easier to work with, being more flexible than stone or brick. Wooden buildings could be constructed quickly with few tools, of which axes were the most important.

In Kievan times, most Russian towns had wooden fortifications, which, in the absence of firearms and heavy siege equipment, offered sufficient protection from external attack. The citadel, or kremlin, of medieval Russian cities was usually constructed on elevated ground, often where two rivers met or on heights overlooking a riverbank. The citadel was surrounded by timber walls much like the stockades around American western forts. The walls were fortified by towers, sometimes constructed on stone foundations for stability and permanence. The number of gates in the wooden stockade depended on the size of the town. Kiev had at least four gates. In major towns one gate was designated the main entrance, and it was often of stone. The remains of the famous Golden Gate of Kiev, modeled after the gates of Constantinople, still exist, and Vladimir's Golden Gate has survived intact. By the 12th century stone walls began to replace the wooden stockades in the major centers.

As towns grew and expanded, the territory of the citadel became too confined to accommodate the entire population, and this led to the establishment of suburbs (*posady*)—new sections built up around the walls of the citadel. These were in turn surrounded by new walls serving as an outer belt of fortifications. As the town developed outside the citadel, recognizable streets emerged and finally whole sections became defined. In larger towns streets were paved with logs. The method of paving streets was uniform in Kievan Rus. Three or four thin wooden poles were laid out longitudinally along the axis of the street. Split half-logs, usually of pine, were notched on the rounded bottom side and laid transversely, side by side, on the thin poles. Thus a stable roadway was constructed, immune to frequent freezing and thawing and accompanying thick mud. Summer and winter sleds were used on these paved streets, the runners moving easily over the flat, uniform surface of the log streets.

Michael Curran

The Golden Gate of Kiev, entrance to the city of Kiev. Built by Iaroslav the Wise, 1019–1054, the Golden Gate was a replica of the Golden Gate of Constantinople. Atop the gate is the Gate Church. Modern reconstruction.

The typical medieval Russian town had several types of buildings: houses, workshops, warehouses, official buildings, and churches. Most buildings were of wood, although stone churches appeared as early as the 11th century in major cities. Most wooden dwellings were of the box-frame type, with logs notched at the end and fitted together much like the log cabins of early America. The living quarters (the *izba*) were square or rectangular, a single large room with a stove in one corner for heating and cooking. The living quarters were often connected to an unheated storeroom or outhouse (*klet*) by a lobby or entryway. Wooden buildings were often decorated with beautiful and elaborate wood carvings on the gables and around the windows, which provided graphic illustrations of folklore and folk symbolism.

Religion and Culture

A major turning point in the history of Kievan Rus and in all of Russian history was the conversion to Christianity, ascribed by tradition to the year 988. Before discussing this momentous event in the development of Russia, we must first briefly sketch the nature of Kievan religion before conversion.

The religion of the early eastern Slavs was a diverse paganism, with no single pantheon of gods accepted by all. Each Slavic tribe worshiped its own group of pagan gods in accordance with its own customs. Nonetheless, there were several common features of Slavic pagan practice. For example, ancestor worship and the worship of nature and of various wood, river, and household spirits were widely practiced among the Slavic tribes. Sacrifices of animals and occasionally of human beings were made to appease and placate these spirits.

Several pagan gods were widely venerated by the ancient Slavs. The earliest written sources make frequent reference to postconversion efforts by the Christian clergy to stamp out pagan practices, especially those of the cult of Rod and Rozhanitsa. These gods represented the concept of fertility, so essential to an agricultural people. The term *rod* means clan or family, and in a broad sense Rod and Rozhanitsa represented the forces of reproduction essential to renew the clan. They may also have represented the forces of fertility inherent in the soil on which the clan's livelihood and prosperity depended. As late as the 13th century, the clergy felt compelled to attack continuing sacrificial rites to these pagan gods.

Vernadsky has suggested that the Russian word for God—*Bog*—may have had an earlier meaning of simply "light"; it is also the root of the Russian word for wealth—*bogatstvo*. The Slavic pagan gods Svarog and Dazhbog, often mentioned in the sources, were associated with the heavens and the sun, respectively, and represented the givers of life, the providers of wealth. Stribog, another fre-

quently mentioned deity, was associated with the air and represented forces controlling the winds. Finally, there was Perun, the god of thunder and lightning, often associated with the Scandinavian god Thor. Deeply rooted in the Slavic mentality, the cult of Perun was later transformed into a cult of the Prophet Elijah, the Christian counterpart to the pagan thunder-god.

In spite of these common features, Slavic paganism did not involve a hierarchical priesthood or the use of elaborate temples. Statues of pagan idols were erected by the early Slavs, and several examples of stone idols have survived, but the diversity of pagan cults and the absence of a formal priesthood meant that organized resistance to the new Christian religion never became unified or consistent, though pagan practices persisted in Russia into modern times.

Christianity was known to the Slavs before 988. Christian influences entered Rus during the early 10th century from a variety of sources: from Byzantium, Scandinavia, and central Europe. We know, for example, from the treaty signed between Prince Igor and the Byzantines in 945 that some members of his military retinue were already Christians. The treaty announced:

> If any inhabitant of the land of Rus, thinks to violate this amity, may such of these transgressors as have adopted the Christian faith incur . . . punishment from Almighty God in the shape of damnation and destruction forevermore. If any of these transgressors be not baptized, may they receive help neither from God nor from Perun.[11]

There was a Christian church in Kiev, the Church of St. Elias, where the baptized Russes swore to observe the conditions of the treaty of 945. We also know that Princess Olga, the wife of Prince Igor, was converted to Christianity and baptized in Constantinople in 955. Yet Christianity did not strike permanent roots at that time, and paganism persisted as the official religion. Nevertheless, these significant early Christian influences

---

[11] Cross, "Russian Primary Chronicle," p. 160.

helped prepare the way for Russia's subsequent conversion.

Paganism was also giving way to more organized religion in many areas bordering on Kievan Rus. By the 980s Kiev was surrounded by peoples who had at least nominally given up paganism in favor of one of the world's great religions. The Khazars (at least the ruling class) had embraced Judaism around 865, and the Volga Bulgars had become Muslim by 920. Christianity was also making rapid progress among Kiev's western neighbors: the Baltic Slavs, the Poles, the Hungarians, the Bulgars, the Danes, and the Norwegians. Kievan Rus, the last great pagan stronghold in the region, found itself increasingly isolated.

About 980 Prince Vladimir, once firmly established on the throne of Kiev, recognized the need to overcome this cultural and religious isolation. A common and unified religion, he realized, would help consolidate his precarious control over eastern Slav lands. Vladimir's extensive foreign contacts offered him various choices of religion. According to *The Primary Russian Chronicle*, Vladimir called together his military retinue and city elders to discuss the religious situation and to investigate the Muslim, Jewish, and Christian faiths.

Vladimir first investigated Islam, being informed by the Volga Bulgars that "they believed in God, and that Mahomet instructed them to practice circumcision, to eat no pork, to drink no wine, and, after death, promised them complete fulfillment of their carnal desires." Vladimir, although impressed by this promise, rejected Islam, saying, "Drinking is the joy of the Russes. We cannot exist without that pleasure." Likewise, he rejected the views of the pope's agents and the Judaism of the Khazars. The chroniclers then recorded the visit of learned Greek scholars from Byzantium, and, as one might have expected, Vladimir was reputedly deeply impressed with their presentation of Orthodoxy.

Vladimir summoned together his boyars and city elders, and said to them, "Behold, the Bulgars came before me urging me to accept their religion. Then came the Germans and praised their own faith; and after them came the Jews. Finally, the Greeks appeared, criticizing all other faiths but commending their own, and they spoke at length, telling the history of the world from its beginning. Their words were artful, and it was wondrous to listen and pleasant to hear them. They preach the existence of another world. Whoever adopts our religion and then dies shall arise and live forever. But whoever embraces another faith, shall be consumed by fire in the next world. What is your opinion on this subject and what do you answer?"[12]

Vladimir was advised to send out his own emissaries to investigate the various faiths at first hand. And it was done. His emissaries reported to Vladimir that they were overwhelmed by Greek Christianity: "Then we went to Greece, and the Greeks led us to the edifices where they worship their God, and we knew not whether we were in heaven or on earth. For on earth there is no such splendor or such beauty, and we are at a loss to describe it." Note that it was the splendor of the church services and the beauty of the churches of Constantinople that so impressed the emissaries, not the spiritual content of Greek Christianity. This preoccupation with external form over internal content was to remain a hallmark of Russian Christianity. After listening to the emissaries, the boyars reminded Vladimir, "If the Greek faith were evil, it would not have been adopted by your grandmother Olga, who was wiser than all other men."[13] Vladimir decided to adopt the Orthodox faith of Byzantium.

The *Chronicle* version is essentially a myth, but it contains a kernel of truth. Vladimir certainly had opportunities to hear the merits of various religions debated in Kiev by Arabs, Jews, Bulgars, and Greeks who visited the city for trade and by Russian travelers. The advantages of accepting Greek Orthodoxy were compelling because of the extensive commercial contacts

---

[12] Cross, pp. 197–98.
[13] Cross, p. 199.

already existing between Kiev and Constantinople. The example of Olga and other Kievan converts to Christianity also influenced him. So his decision appears to have been preordained. What remained was how to arrange the actual conversion.

In this, Vladimir was aided by fortuitous events. The Byzantine emperors, the brothers Basil II and Constantine VIII, threatened by internal and external enemies, desperately needed Kievan military aid. Appealing to Kievan Rus, they offered their sister Anna in marriage to Vladimir in return for his military support. In January 988 Vladimir agreed and promptly dispatched 6,000 troops, with whose help the Byzantine emperors defeated their enemies. Once the immediate threats to the Byzantine Empire had been removed, Basil and Constantine hesitated to send their sister to barbaric Kiev. After all, marriage into the Byzantine imperial family was an honor reserved for the most illustrious ruling families in the Christian world. Vladimir could hardly have been considered worthy of such an honor.

This situation offered Vladimir a great opportunity, for he could now adopt Orthodoxy on his own terms, preventing Kiev from becoming a dependency of Byzantium. Because the Byzantine emperors refused to honor their promise, Vladimir marched against Greek-held territories in the Crimea. In July 988 he captured the Greek city of Kherson, forcing the Byzantines to sue for peace. As a condition of peace Basil and Constantine agreed to send their sister to Kherson, where, after Vladimir's baptism, the wedding took place.

Shortly thereafter, Vladimir returned to Kiev with his new wife and many Greek priests and monks authorized to help him establish Orthodoxy in the Kievan realm. Vladimir "directed that the [pagan] idols should be overthrown, and that some should be cut to pieces and others burned with fire. . . . Thereafter Vladimir sent heralds throughout the whole city to proclaim that if any inhabitant, rich or poor, did not betake himself to the river, he would risk the Prince's displeasure."[14]

By Vladimir's order, Kiev's entire population was baptized in the Dnieper River. Similar orders were sent out to all cities and territories of Kievan Rus.

Thus Kievan Rus entered the ranks of Christian states. This conversion in itself was significant, but even more significant was the fact that Russia's Christianity came from Byzantium. Byzantine influences would shape the development of Russian thought and culture for centuries to come. At the time of Russia's conversion, Christianity was still one, although deep rifts had appeared between the western Latin church and the eastern Greek church. These broadened into an open break in 1054, and after that Kievan Rus nurtured itself on the Byzantine forms and patterns, which became all-pervasive, influencing Russian art, architecture, literature, law, philosophy, and religion.

Byzantine Christianity, while raising Kievan Rus to a new cultural level, introduced into its cultural tradition a degree of rigidity and formalism, which would inhibit future Russian cultural development. Orthodoxy was accepted with the uncritical enthusiasm of the new convert, and Byzantium became the model for Kievan culture as the Russes tried to duplicate the minutest details of the Byzantine Christian tradition. The seductive cultural heritage of the Byzantine Empire remained unquestioned; thus Kievan Rus accepted "the Byzantine achievement . . . without the Byzantine inquisitiveness."[15] The Russes were never able or even inclined to develop or expand on the Byzantine heritage; instead, they tenaciously defended the acquired habits of thought.

Nevertheless, the impact of the conversion cannot be overestimated, even though Soviet historians tended to minimize it. The Soviet scholar Rybakov wrote: "Christianity cannot be counterposed to paganism, since they are but two forms, two variations of the one and the same primitive ideology, differing only in their outward manifestations." Rybakov admitted, however, that the

---

[14] Cross, p. 204.

[15] G. Florovsky, "The Problem of Old Russian Culture," *SR* 21 (March 1962): 14.

church played an important role in consolidating the Kievan state and bringing the culture of Rus closer to the cultural treasures of Byzantium by spreading education and creating enduring literary and artistic traditions. But, in sum, he argued,

> it must be remembered that the Russian people paid dearly for that positive contribution of the church: the poison of religious ideology penetrated (deeper than in pagan times) into all the pores of the people's life, it dulled the class struggle, revived primitive notions in a new form, and for long centuries fastened in the consciousness of the people the ideas of a world beyond, of the divine origin of rulers, and providentialism, i.e., the concept that the fates of people are always governed by God's will.[16]

Later Soviet scholarship took a more balanced and positive view of Christianity in Kievan Rus, recognizing it as a progressive social and cultural development.

At first the conversion was only nominal; pagan practices persisted for many years, especially among the lower classes, to whom the spiritual substance of the new religion was alien. This situation led to a cultural dualism in postconversion Rus, fostered by the existence of a small, highly cultivated, Byzantinized upper class that struggled to assimilate a sophisticated religion and culture while the Slavic masses adhered to the old culture and traditions. At first Christianity overlaid the older culture; then it gradually absorbed and enveloped it.

Almost all aspects of life in Rus felt the impact of the conversion. When a written language was introduced to make Greek Christian beliefs accessible to the Rus, it was Old Church Slavonic, based on the Glagolitic alphabet devised in the ninth century by the apostles of the Slavs, Cyril and Methodius, for Moravian converts to Christianity. The Glagolitic alphabet was developed by their followers into the Cyrillic alphabet (honoring St. Cyril). Church Slavonic, along with Greek and

Latin, became one of Christianity's three great languages. Kievan Rus was flooded with religious tracts and sermons, which along with church service books, all translated into Church Slavonic, formed the backbone of the Russian literary language until the 17th century. In old Rus written literature was almost exclusively religious, and the chronicles too were composed by learned monks and written in religious language. Although painstakingly copied by hand, books must have been produced in considerable numbers, because more than 500 written works from the 11th to the 14th centuries have survived. Because the level of literacy in Rus was extremely low, these written works were accessible only to a few.

The bulk of the population, whose illiteracy prevented direct access to church literature, had their own highly developed oral literary tradition, enough of which has survived to allow us insight into popular folklore. Its basic element was song, in which all life was celebrated from everyday occurrences to great historic events. Especially important were the old sagas (*byliny*), which depicted activities of epic warriors (*bogatyri*), the popular heroes of the Kievan period. The most famous *bogatyri,* members of Prince Vladimir's retinue, were always prepared to defend their prince and native land against all enemies. Each had an individual, fully developed personality and identifiable character traits. Among them was Ilia Muromets, a huge man of peasant stock, a Slavic Paul Bunyan, able to bend nature to his will. Also there was Aliosha Popovich, son of a priest, who accomplished great feats by cunning and cleverness and invariably outsmarted his enemies. Dobrynia Nikitich was a boyar exemplifying loyalty and reliability, a man of action available to perform any task. Finally, there was the humorous and charming Churilo Plenkovich, a true Don Juan, who always had time to charm beautiful women despite terrible danger. Such tales of the exploits of the *bogatyri* were recited by bards and preserved orally from generation to generation. There were also whole cycles of fairy tales replete with magic, mystery, and extraordinary events.

---

[16] B. A. Rybakov, *The Early Centuries of Russian History* (Moscow, 1965), pp. 51, 67.

Such folktales contrasted sharply with the somber, abstract Byzantine religious works.

Perhaps the most remarkable example of the folk genre is *The Tale of Igor,* written in the late 12th century to record the actual struggle of a minor prince and his retinue against the steppe nomads. Skillfully combining Christian and popular pagan traditions, the author produced a highly sophisticated literary work that sounded a call for unity and common action among the princes. The author laments the lack of political unity and cooperation among princes whose selfishness and pursuit of personal glory would doom Kievan Rus.

In art and architecture Byzantine influences were most palpable. The ornate splendor of Byzantine art and architecture, more than an abstract theology, awed the Rus and contributed to their acceptance of Orthodoxy. Church art became the focus of faith for the people of Rus; the great stone churches, icons, frescoes, and mosaics assaulted the senses and lifted people toward heaven, transporting them from the mundane world. These outward manifestations of religion were extremely important in spreading the new beliefs, as Kiev's rulers recognized. Vladimir undertook an extensive building program after his conversion, and his son, Iaroslav the Wise, resolved to give Kiev some of Constantinople's imperial splendor. The climax of Iaroslav's massive building program was the great St. Sofia Cathedral in Kiev. Completed in 1036, it was the most impressive religious structure in Rus and served as the prototype for later stone churches throughout the land. Not only the massive external form of St. Sofia impressed the laity, but also its luxurious internal decorations, frescoes, and mosaics, which are among the finest extant examples of Byzantine art. St. Sofia's interior supplied the basic iconographic models followed in Russia for almost a thousand years.

Smaller in scale but no less impressive was the St. Sofia Cathedral in Novgorod, completed in 1062. It reveals the adaptation of Byzantine forms to northern conditions and tastes. Much external ornamentation typical of the Kiev St. Sofia was eliminated in Novgorod, reflecting the northern desire for uniformity and simplicity. The characteristic Russian onion domes, flared sides, and elongated spires developed early in Novgorod.

Iconography was vital to the Russian religious tradition, and here Byzantine tradition was paramount. Found primarily in the Eastern Orthodox tradition, icons are religiously inspired pictures painted on specially prepared panels of wood. Icons were produced in Russia in great numbers, both for churches and for homes of the faithful. Just as the church was to reflect God's kingdom on earth, so icons served to convey a sense of spirituality and provide an entry into that mystical world lying beyond sense experience. The iconographer, rather than portraying worldly objects and situations, sought to create a link with the boundless eternity of God and to evoke a spiritual reality. Icons were created to foster reverence and aid in worship. They helped instruct an illiterate population by attempting to bring heaven down to earth.

Russian iconographers were especially remarkable for their use of color, and this distinguishes Russian icons from other types. This characteristic reflected the Russians' lively concern with nature. A leading Soviet expert on iconography wrote rather fancifully about a famous Russian icon painter of the late 14th and early 15th century, Andrei Rublev:

> He takes the colors for his palette not from the traditional canons of color, but from the Russian nature around him, the beauty of which he keenly sensed. His magnificent deep blue is suggested by the blue spring sky; his whites recall the birches so dear to a Russian; his green is close to the color of unripe rye; his golden ocher summons up memories of fallen autumn leaves; in his dark green colors there is something of the twilight shadows of the dense pine forests. He translated the colors of Russian nature into the lofty language of art.[17]

Although referring to a later period, this description may be taken as typical of the early Russian regard for the subtleties of color. Indissolubly linked with the ritual and tradition of the Ortho-

---

[17] V. Lazarev, *Andrei Rublev* (Moscow, 1960), p. 19.

dox faith, icons have remained an important element of Russian religious expression.

Administratively, the Russian church was organized like the Byzantine church and was headed by a metropolitan appointed by the patriarch of Constantinople. For the first two centuries all but two of its metropolitans were Greek. Larger towns had bishops, often native Russians, nominated by the princes and confirmed by the metropolitan. At first the clergy were Greek priests and monks, but a native clergy developed rapidly, organized on Byzantine patterns and divided into two general categories: the "black clergy," monks who had taken vows renouncing the earthly world, and the "white clergy," parish priests and deacons whose mission was to minister to the needs of the faithful. Ecclesiastical officials—bishops, abbots, and others—were drawn from the celibate monastic clergy. Parish priests, in contrast to regulations of the Western church, had to be married.

Monasteries were among the most important of church institutions. Many devout Orthodox believed that the Christian ideal could best be achieved in monastic life, and significant numbers chose this ascetic approach. The chief monastery of this era was Kiev's Monastery of the Caves, established in the mid-11th century. Monasteries served to spread Christianity, learning, and the arts. The first Russian libraries were established in monasteries, and it was monks who kept records, composed chronicles, copied books and manuscripts, and engaged in charitable activities, providing care for the sick and the destitute. Monasteries therefore played a key social and cultural role, as well as a vital religious role, in Kievan Rus.

Kievan culture was dominated by the church, and its most lasting achievements—in art and architecture—originated there. Kievan Rus, however, despite some remarkable contributions, was culturally isolated from Latin Christendom and western Europe by the accident of adopting Byzantine Christianity when the two halves of the Christian world were diverging. Although Kievan Rus was the religious offshoot of Byzantium, Russians found Greek civilization largely inaccessible because of the Church Slavonic idiom and the narrow religious preoccupations of the Christian elite. Still, it should be noted that Christianity represented a strong unifying force for Kievan Rus. Cultural influences from a number of sources, including Greek and Latin, began to make inroads in Kiev and other centers. Cultural and spiritual isolation, however, were reinforced by political turmoil and internecine strife, which opened the way to Kiev's external enemies, the Tatars and the Teutonic Knights. In spite of its decline and eventual disappearance, Kievan Rus provided a rich legacy of culture, language, and institutions upon which future generations would build.

Suggested Additional Reading

BOOKS

CROSS, S. H. *The Russian Primary Chronicle* (Cambridge, MA, 1953). (Page references in text are to version in *Harvard Studies and Notes in Philology and Literature* 12 [1930]: 77–320.)

GREKOV, B. D. *Kievan Rus* (Moscow, 1959). (A Soviet interpretation.)

HURWITZ, E., ed. *Studies on Kievan History* (Tempe, AZ, 1980). (A special issue of *Rus. Hist.*, vol. 7, no. 3.)

LENHOFF, G. *The Martyred Princes Boris and Gleb* (Columbus, OH, 1989).

MANN, R. *Lances Sing: A Study of The Igor Tale* (Columbus, OH, 1990).

OBOLENSKY, D. *The Byzantine Commonwealth* (New York, 1971).

Paterik of the Kievan Monastery, trans. M. Heppell (Cambridge, MA, 1989).

PRITSAK, O. *On the Writing of History in Kievan Rus* (Cambridge, MA, 1987).

TIKHOMIROV, M. N. *The Towns of Ancient Russia* (Moscow, 1959).

VERNADSKY, G. *Kievan Russia* (New Haven, 1948).

———. *Medieval Russian Laws* (New York, 1947, 1969).

ZENKOVSKY, S. A., ed. and trans. *Medieval Russia's Epics, Chronicles, and Tales,* rev. ed. (New York, 1974).

———, ed. *The Nikonian Chronicle, Vol. 2: From the Year 1132 to the Year 1240* (Princeton, 1984).

ARTICLES

BIRNBAUM, H. "On Some Evidence of Jewish Life . . . in Medieval Russia." *Viator* 4 (1973): 225–55.

BLUM, J. "The Smerd in Kievan Russia." *ASEER* 12 (1953): 122–30.

BUSHKOVITCH, P. "Towns and Castles in Kievan Rus . . ." *Rus. Hist.* 7, no. 3 (1980): 334–49.

FROIANOV, I. IA. "A New View of the History of Kievan Rus," *Soviet Studies in History* 24, no. 4 (1986): 9ff.

HURWITZ, E. "Kievan Rus and Medieval Myopia." *Rus. Hist.* 5, no. 2 (1978): 176–87 and comments, 187–96.

KAISER, D. H. "Reconsidering Crime and Punishment in Kievan Rus." *Rus. Hist.* 7, no. 3 (1980): 283–93.

———. Review of *Kievskaia Rus* by I. Ia. Froianov (Leningrad, 1974). *Kritika* 12, no. 2 (1976): 70–82.

MACZKO, S. "Boris and Gleb: Saintly Princes or Princely Saints?" *Rus. Hist.* 2, no. 1: 68–80.

NOONAN, T. "The Circulation of Byzantine Coins in Kievan Rus." *Byz. St.* 7, no. 2: 143–81.

———. "Fifty Years of Soviet Scholarship on Kievan History." *Rus. Hist.* 7, no. 3: 334–49.

———. "When and How Dirhams First Reached Russia." *Cahiers du monde* 21, nos. 3–4 (1980): 401–69.

POPPE, A. "The Political Background to the Baptism of Rus . . . " *DOP* 30 (1973): 195–244.

RIASANOVSKY, A. V. "Pseudo-Varangian Origins of the Kievo-Pecherskii Monastery . . ." *Rus. Hist.* 7, no. 3 (1980): 265–82.

RYNDZIUNSKII, P. G., AND A. M. SAKHAROV. "Towns in Russia, Historiography of." *MERSH* 39: 127–36.

VASILIEV, A. A. "Economic Relations Between Byzantium and Old Russia." *JEBH* 4 (1932): 314–34.

ZGUTA, R. "Kievan Coinage." *SEER* 53 (1975): 483–92.

ZORN, J. "New Soviet Work on the Old Russian Peasantry." *Rus. Rev.* 39, no. 3 (1980): 339–47.

5

The Ascendance of the Southwest and the Northeast

The unity of the Kievan state, fragile and tenuous even in the best of times, broke down completely following the death of Grand Prince Iaropolk II in 1139. In the ensuing years the various branches of the House of Riurik vied with one another for supremacy, but none was strong or farsighted enough to exert significantly broad leadership. Occasional interprincely alliances created to oppose the threat of the steppe nomads rapidly gave way to jealous conflicts, and consequently the Kievan state disintegrated into a series of virtually independent principalities, each pursuing its own interests and goals. This period was known in Soviet historiography as "the period of feudal fragmentation" and was viewed as the culmination of a process that had begun in the ninth century with the founding of the Kievan state. This schematic view was perhaps oversimplified, but it is true that separatist tendencies triumphed at least temporarily with the decline of Kiev. Still, it would be an error to ignore persisting elements of unity, fostered in part by the common culture and religion shared by all eastern Slavs and also maintained by vaguely defined familial ties among the various

ruling houses, all tracing their ancestry back to Riurik.

With the decline of trade and commerce centered in the Dnieper region, Kiev ceased to function as the center of a unified state, and the Kievan principality itself descended rapidly to relative insignificance. The decline of Kiev was paralleled, however, by the rise to importance of other regions, most notably the southwestern territories of Volhynia and Galicia and the northeastern territory variously known as Rostov-Suzdal and Vladimir-Suzdal. It is to these two politically important regions that we now turn.

The Southwest

Volhynia and Galicia had formed an integral part of the Kievan state, participating fully in the political, cultural, and religious life of the country. Volhynia, the larger of the two territories, extended westward from Kiev, encompassing the broad fertile plain that stretches from the foothills of the Carpathian Mountains northward into what is present-day Belarus. Galicia, situated along the northern slopes of the Carpathian Mountains, controls the headwaters of the important rivers Pruth and Dniester. Bordering on both Hungary and Poland, Galicia represented the farthest westward expansion of the Kievan state. From earliest times these two territories enjoyed great prosperity resulting both from the fertile soil of the region and from the extensive trade carried on with the West via Hungary and Poland. Both Volhynia and Galicia were relatively secure from the devastating raids of steppe nomads because of their western location. This fact enhanced the region's economic prosperity, and the result was a rapid growth of population and the extensive development of urban centers. From as early as the 11th century the economic prosperity of the southwest, coinciding with the gradual decline of Kiev, was translated into a desire by the Volhynian and Galician princes to act independently of Kiev.

These political ambitions were not to be fully realized until the late 12th century, when Kiev's decline accelerated. The growing political importance of the southwest was converted into virtual independence by one of the most powerful and successful Russian princes of the second half of the 12th century, Iaroslav Osmomysl of Galicia (1153–1187), whose name is thought to mean eight-minded, or exceedingly wise. He succeeded in transforming Galicia into a powerful force in south Russia. His interests were not restricted to the Galician lands; he was concerned with broader issues as well, something clearly attested to by the *Tale of Igor,* which left a memorable and vivid portrait of this remarkable and highly respected prince:

> O Iaroslav Osmomysl of Galicia: You sit high on your gold-forged throne; you have braced the Hungarian [Carpathian] mountains with your iron troops; you have closed the Danube's gates, hurling mighty missiles over the clouds, spreading your courts [laws] to the Danube. Your thunders range over lands; you open Kiev's gates to avenge the Russian land, and the wounds of Igor, turbulent son of Sviatoslav.[1]

---

[1] V. Rzhiga et al., eds., *Slovo o polku Igoreve* (Moscow, 1961), p. 26.

Iaroslav was not merely a local prince but one of the greatest and most powerful princes of the time, one whose power and might were such that he not only guarded the western borders of the Kievan land but could also protect Kiev itself and administer crushing defeats to the steppe nomads, thus avenging Igor's defeat. The wise and enlightened rule of Iaroslav Osmomysl raised immeasurably the power and prestige of Galicia, and the whole of south Russia reflected his glory. Galicia at this time was quite independent of Kiev, forming an important center in its own right.

But without strong rule Galicia was vulnerable to outside interference and harassment. Following Iaroslav's death in 1187, Galicia experienced weak rule, which led to constant intervention by the Hungarian king, who even managed briefly to establish his son on the Galician throne. Only in 1197 were the fortunes of Galicia restored. Strong rule was provided by Galicia's neighbor, Volhynia, in the person of Prince Roman of Volhynia (1197–1205), who united the two territories into a powerful state. For a time Roman even occupied the increasingly insignificant throne of Kiev, from which he mounted several successful campaigns against the steppe nomads, temporarily relieving pressure on Kiev. He was even more successful in opposing the imperialist ambitions of the Hungarians, the Poles, and the Lithuanians, all of whom were intent on controlling southwest Russia. While on campaign against the Poles in 1205, Roman was killed (at the age of 36), leaving two minor sons. As a result of this unfortunate event Volhynia and Galicia entered into a period of internal strife, civil war, and Polish and Hungarian intervention.

The lack of continued strong leadership was one factor that prevented the southwest from assuming the mantle of leadership in the Russian lands. Another deterrent to political stability in the southwest was the intense social conflicts there. The fertile soil of Volhynia and Galicia encouraged the boyar class to carve out great landed estates and bring the local population under increasing control. Furthermore, the success of these ventures also encouraged the boyars to seek to dominate the princely authority and translate their economic power into political power. The result was frequent clashes between boyars and the ruling princes. The boyars were never above appealing to the Poles and the Hungarians for help in achieving their political ambitions. Without strong princely rule capable of curbing the ambitions of the boyar class, political stability was impossible. These tensions broke out into the open after 1205. Roman's son and successor, Daniel, was only four years old when he ascended the throne of Volhynia, and throughout his youth he lived amid bitter and protracted political turmoil that eroded the wealth and power of the territory.

Not until 1221 did Daniel establish himself firmly on the throne of Volhynia and assert his authority, bringing the boyars under his control. It appeared that the fortunes of the southwest were once more on the rise, but in 1223 Daniel was faced with a new and even more potent threat, the Tatars. In this first fateful Rus encounter with a Tatar expeditionary force, the Battle of the Kalka River, he escaped with minor wounds and returned to Volhynia; but the portent for the future was foreboding. Between his first encounter with the Tatars and the full-scale Tatar invasion beginning in 1237, Daniel administered Volhynia wisely, developing trade and commerce, building new cities, and working to restore the unity of Volhynia and Galicia. He accomplished their union in 1238 but had little time to consolidate his power because in 1241 the Tatars swept westward out of Kiev, conquering and pillaging Volhynia and Galicia, thus ending independent existence for these rich territories.

Without the Tatar conquest Volhynia and Galicia might have provided the basis for a resurgence of south Rus and the beginnings of a genuine rapprochement with the West. As it was, however, Volhynia and Galicia declined rapidly after the initial Tatar conquest and during the 14th century were absorbed by their rapacious neighbors; Galicia was incorporated into the Polish state, and Volhynia became part of the expanding Lithuanian state. Both internal conditions and foreign inter-

vention prevented Galicia and Volhynia from inheriting Kiev's political mantle. That honor would be reserved for the northeast—first the territory of Vladimir-Suzdal, later Moscow.

The Northeast

The future of Russia was to be determined not in the southwest but in the northeast, in the plains and forests situated in the region of the Kliazma and Moskva rivers, between the Oka and the Volga. When the eastern Slavs arrived, this northeastern region was occupied by Finnish tribes, which in the ensuing centuries peacefully intermingled with the Slavs. Out of this slow and partial amalgamation emerged the Great Russian nationality. But during the latter part of the ninth century, when the Kievan state was being organized, the northeast was only sparsely settled and certainly did not constitute one of the more important regions of old Rus.

From the 11th century on, however, the history of the northeast becomes extremely complex and important, far more so than that of the southwest. The northeast has occupied the attention of historians to a greater degree because of the subsequent emergence of a new unified Russian state around Moscow, which is located in the forest zone of the northeast. Historians have long debated the rise of the northeast as a prelude to the emergence of Moscow and have tried to ascertain the precise relationship between the northeast and the central Dnieper region of Kiev in an effort to establish the historical continuity, or lack of such, between Kiev and Moscow.

Two basic positions have been taken on this question. The older view, advanced by such historians as S. M. Soloviev and Kliuchevskii, drew a sharp line between Kievan Rus and Muscovite Russia. These historians argued that with the transition of the political center from Kiev to the northeast, to a new geographic region, Russian development moved off in an entirely new direction. They denied any continuity and implied that there was a decisive rupture between the traditions of Kievan Rus and those of northeastern

Rus. Most modern Ukrainian historians agree with Soloviev and Kliuchevskii as to the sharp discontinuity between Kievan and Muscovite history. Other historians, beginning with Presniakov in the early 20th century and continuing with Soviet historians, advanced the view that there was a direct link, a profound historical continuity, extending from Kiev through Vladimir-Suzdal to Moscow. The weight of the evidence seems to support the latter view.

All historians of the northeast agree that during the 12th century there was a massive population shift or migration away from Kiev in the south to the northeast. The northeast was a remote and relatively inhospitable region, less productive agriculturally than the more fertile south. What, then, caused this significant population shift? Precisely the remoteness of the region, which, coupled with the added security afforded by the forest zone, attracted from the south large numbers of settlers who were intent on escaping the constant disruptions and growing insecurity fostered by feuding princes and the ever-present threat of devastating raids by the steppe nomads.

The basic question dividing the two historiographic camps centers on the nature of the Rostov-Suzdal land when this migration was beginning. Kliuchevskii and Soloviev argued that northeastern Rus in the 11th and 12th centuries was a harsh and savage land, quite removed from the traditions of the south. Consequently, a new order of relationships emerged on new and virgin soil. Soloviev cited as evidence for this view the fact that the sources refer to the region as a great and empty land, "where only one town is mentioned as having arisen before the coming of the Varangians—Rostov the Great, from which the whole region received the name the Rostov land."[2] Kliuchevskii, likewise, characterized the Rostov land as more alien to Rus than any of its frontier lands. A new nationality (the Great Russians) and a new political system (the *udel*, or

appanage, system) were, in his opinion, formed under the influence of northeastern geographic and ethnographic conditions, both of which were in sharp contrast to all previous conditions. Kliuchevskii concluded that the consequences of the Russian colonization of the upper Volga were to establish "the earliest and deepest roots of a form of state that will appear in a later period"—that is, the Muscovite period.[3]

Other historians, most notably Presniakov, have argued that the Rostov land was far from being hostile, savage, or primitive. A firmly established way of life built upon complex internal relationships was growing out of the same conditions that prevailed at the time in Kiev, Volhynia, Galicia, and Chernigov. Even before the influx of settlers from the south reached important dimensions in the 12th century, the Rostov land had achieved a high level of culture. Presniakov pointed to the extensive program of building undertaken by the first Suzdal princes. There was a striking increase in the construction of stone churches, and an original and highly sophisticated artistic style had already been elaborated. Such developments, he argued, were possible only in a land with a highly developed urban civilization, a strong tradition of local trades and crafts, and a high overall level of culture. To be sure, the migration contributed much to increasing the material resources of the land and helped transform the Rostov land into the rich and powerful principality of Vladimir-Suzdal, but there was not movement in an entirely new political direction, as had been suggested by Soloviev and Kliuchevskii. Strong ties were maintained all along between the northeast and the south.

In reviewing the history of the northeast, we find that in 1054, at the death of Iaroslav the Wise, the northeast territory passed to one of his younger sons, Vsevolod, as a supplement to the territory of Pereiaslavl. Within less than a century the Rostov land had emerged as an independent principality in the possession of Prince Iuri Dolgo-

---

[2] S. M. Soloviev, *Ob otnosheniiakh Novgoroda k velikim kniaziam* (Moscow, 1846), p. 17.

[3] V. O. Kliuchevskii, *Sochineniia* (Moscow, 1956–59), vol. 1, p. 316.

rukii (Long-Arm) (1149–1157), a younger son of the last great ruler of Kiev, Vladimir II Monomakh. Iuri became one of the most important and powerful princes in Russia, so powerful that he aspired to the supremacy traditionally attached to Kiev's golden throne. For almost a decade (1146–1155) he waged a bitter and tenacious struggle with his nephew Iziaslav for control of Kiev. Only with the death of Iziaslav in 1155 was Iuri finally able to realize his ambition of occupying the throne of Kiev, a position he held for only two years until his own death in 1157.

Iuri Dolgorukii was definitely a prince in the Kievan mold. Encouraged by the growth of the power and prestige of the Rostov land, Iuri, in the best Kievan tradition, sought to gain supremacy over his "brother" princes by establishing himself in Kiev. These aspirations fitted perfectly with Kiev's political traditions. It should be pointed out, however, that Iuri's desire to occupy the throne of Kiev did not imply an abandonment of his northeastern possessions. He merely wished to claim genealogical seniority for the Rostov dynasty. Iuri tried to preserve and strengthen his power in south Russia in order to better pursue his local Suzdal interests. He was motivated in this by a desire to control the territorial center, or what was thought to be the territorial center, of the entire system of interprincely relationships. In other words, his was a policy designed to prevent rival princes from gaining influence that could potentially threaten Suzdal interests, particularly Suzdal's relations with Novgorod, Smolensk, and Chernigov, as well as those with other territories. Only by controlling Kiev could Iuri actively pursue Suzdal interests without fear of external intervention by other princes.

In addition, commercial and cultural interests of great importance also caught Iuri's attention. The commercial and cultural relations between Suzdal and other parts of Russia were extensive and of vital importance if Suzdal was to play a dominant role. A flourishing trade existed between the northeast and the south. Moreover, large quantities of important and valuable prod-

ucts flowed into Suzdal from the west. Iuri was determined to maintain and expand these commercial relations, especially those dependent on the waterway from Novgorod down the Volga, a commercial route that passed through Suzdal. In order to pursue this policy effectively, Iuri had to control Novgorod, or at a minimum ensure Novgorod's cooperation. In an effort to ensure good relations, Iuri tried to place his sons or nephews on the throne of Novgorod. On occasion he was even forced to apply pressure on Novgorod to adopt a pro-Suzdal policy by cutting off its trade routes to the north and the west, thereby crippling Novgorod's economy. It was, in fact, this pressure on Novgorod that brought Iuri into conflict with his nephew Iziaslav, a struggle that eventually centered on control of Kiev. Iuri's success in this struggle in 1155 seriously weakened the hostile forces concentrated in the south, giving him a relatively free hand in the north.

During this same period Iuri embarked on a program designed to strengthen the princely administration in the Rostov land in order to consolidate his position. The result was the consolidation of the territory into a *votchina,* or hereditary holding; that is, Iuri endeavored to make the Rostov land the personal possession of his family. This desire to increase his princely power was reflected in a vigorous building program and extensive colonization. New towns were built and settled by Iuri, and these "younger towns" were considered his private, personal property. To Soloviev this circumstance introduced a new element, one in which "property stood above family relationships, each prince seeing himself as the sole owner of a particular domain, and no longer as a member of a given family, a particular dynasty."[4] Thus emerged the concept of the *udel,* or appanage, a form of property that could be disposed of at will by the owner. Although Soloviev saw this as a sharp break between Kievan political traditions and those of the northeast, there is evidence that the

---

[4] Soloviev, *Ob otnosheniiakh Novgoroda,* pp. 19–20.

same process was occurring in the south, particularly in Volhynia and Galicia.

These efforts to enhance princely power did not go unchallenged. A powerful boyar class in the Rostov land opposed the growth of princely power, which often adversely affected local boyar interests. Adventuresome and costly foreign-policy schemes were particularly resented by the boyars, who felt that the interests of the princely dynasty did not always coincide with their own. The first Rostov princes were frequently challenged by the boyar class. Iuri Dolgorukii moved his capital from Rostov to Suzdal in an effort to get away from the troublesome boyars and avoid open clashes with them. The opposition continued, however, and Andrei Bogoliubskii, Iuri's son and successor, in turn moved from Suzdal to Vladimir for the same reason.

Andrei Bogoliubskii (1157–1174) continued and expanded the policies worked out by his father, concentrating on enhancing his own political power and controlling Novgorod. He too resorted to force to place obedient princes on the throne of Novgorod, sometimes installing his sons, sometimes his nephews. He brought pressure to bear on Novgorod by effectively controlling the vital transport of grain from the Volga region into the city. Andrei also campaigned successfully against the Volga Bulgars to ensure to Suzdal control of the important Volga trade routes. Eventually Andrei was also drawn into a struggle for Kiev as a result of his efforts to control Novgorod. In 1169 Andrei mounted a huge campaign against Kiev, held by Iziaslav's son Mstislav. Andrei captured and sacked Kiev, administering the fatal blow to Kiev's claim to a central position. Andrei seized the grand princely title, but he was even less interested in Kiev itself than his father had been. Having no desire to remain in Kiev, Andrei installed a friendly prince on the throne and established himself in Vladimir, which became a flourishing city and the center of Rus political life. Andrei refused to live in the city of Vladimir and instead built for himself a magnificent palace at nearby Bogoliubovo, from which his surname derives.

Church of the Virgin of the Intercession, at Bogoliubovo on the River Nerl, 1165, a rare example of pre-Tatar architecture that has survived intact.

These moves clearly reflected Andrei's conviction that the fortunes of Rus were tied to the northeast rather than the south.

Andrei's efforts to create a monarchy, to establish the absolute power of the prince, involved him in a conflict with the firmly established boyar class of Vladimir-Suzdal. The tense situation was further aggravated by his ambitious foreign policy, which involved Vladimir-Suzdal in costly wars with the Volga Bulgars, Novgorod, and Kiev. In 1174 the boyars were galvanized into action in the wake of a new and unsuccessful campaign against Kiev, which had been ordered by Andrei, in the words of the chronicler, "out of overweening pride and arrogance." The boyars organized a conspiracy against Andrei, who was assassinated in his palace at Bogoliubovo. This action touched off a bloody rebellion of the local population against the harsh princely administration. Anarchy and strife continued for several years, until Andrei's younger brother Vsevolod managed to bring the situation under control. In 1177 Vsevolod assumed

Michael Curran

Cathedral of the Assumption, Vladimir, 1185–1189.

the title of grand prince and restored princely power to the unchallenged position inaugurated by his brother.

Vsevolod's long reign (1177–1212) marked the zenith of the power of the northeast, a time when Vladimir-Suzdal controlled the thrones of Novgorod and Kiev, reduced many lesser princes to vassal status, and even forced powerful and independent Galicia and Volhynia to reckon with its power. Andrei and Vsevolod tried to justify their authority by appeals to the principle of seniority among the princes. Seniority was now firmly

attached to the principality of Vladimir-Suzdal, but in the hands of Andrei and Vsevolod, it had undergone a significant change. Presniakov argued:

> The earlier Kievan seniority was justified and sustained by the common interests of all elements of Kievan Rus, above all by the task of opposing the steppe nomads. In contrast, the seniority of the Suzdal prince became a force compelling the brotherhood of Rus princes to serve goals and pursue policies that were

either unrelated to or indeed opposed to their own interests.[5]

Thus the Suzdal princes were no longer "the first among equals" but stood significantly higher than any others and could impose their wills on the brotherhood of princes to an unprecedented extent. Still, the Suzdal princes lacked a well-defined set of political priorities. Their interests were dictated by a concern to advance the fortunes of their own territory, Vladimir-Suzdal. The result was bitter hatred, jealousy, and antagonism among the Rus princes. The author of the *Tale of Igor* perhaps expressed the situation best: "O, great Prince Vsevolod! Do you not think of flying here from afar to safeguard the paternal golden throne? For you can splash out the waters of the Volga with your oars, and empty the Don with your helmets!"[6] He implied that Vsevolod should abandon his narrow regional interests, take an interest in the all-Russian problem of invasion by the steppe nomads, and defend the interests of all. His participation in the struggle against the steppe nomads could signify victory for Rus.

In spite of the power and prestige won by the Suzdal princes, the forces of disintegration were at work in the northeast as well, and the region's unity and stability broke down following the death of Vsevolod in 1212. His numerous offspring, who won him the appellation "Big Nest," quarreled bitterly over the inheritance. The principle of patrimonial succession, however, remained intact. This principle, not unique to the northeast, provided that a single princely family was associated with a particular territory and guaranteed the right of all male descendants to share in the inheritance. The rivalry between Vsevolod's two eldest sons, Constantine and Iuri, was finally settled by compromise in 1217, when it was agreed that Constantine would occupy the throne of Vladimir and Iuri the throne of Suzdal, with the former enjoying the title of grand prince. The two elder

brothers then determined the positions to be occupied by the younger brothers. The result was that the Rostov-Suzdal land was divided up into a number of quasi-independent territories, all nominally under the authority of the "senior" prince, the grand prince of Vladimir. Thus the common interests of the whole Rostov-Suzdal land contributed to slow down the disintegration of the land into many separate *votchina* holdings.

Another element contributing to unity was provided by the boyar class. The boyars resented the growth of princely power, but they also generally opposed any change in the ruling dynasty of the region because a new prince would be accompanied by new boyars who could diminish or curtail the influence of the old boyar class. Often such developments led to civil war, which did not serve the boyars' interests. The boyar class, therefore, was intent on supporting the dynastic ambitions of the local princely family as it sought to retain control over the territory.

The principles of unity and consolidation, although somewhat strained after 1212, were maintained, and even after the devastating Mongol invasion they were not lost. They were revived and refined by the principality of Moscow in the 14th century. Nevertheless, the existing political divisions and the rather narrowly defined policies of the Rostov princes made the task of the Tatars easier than it might have been if the senior Russian princes had had a broader political conception or a better understanding of the external threats facing them.

Suggested Additional Reading

There are no satisfactory studies of Volhynia-Galicia or Vladimir-Suzdal in Western languages. Former Soviet scholars are working on an intensive study of the sources for the history of Vladimir-Suzdal. See I. A. Limonov, *Letopisanie Vladimiro-Suzdalskoi Rusi* (Leningrad, 1967).

BOOKS

ALLEN, W. *The Ukraine: A History* (New York, 1940, 1963).

---

[5] A. E. Presniakov, *Obrazovanie velikorusskogo gosudarstva* (Petrograd, 1918), p. 38.
[6] Rzhiga et al., *Slovo,* p. 26.

DOROSHENKO, D. *History of the Ukraine* (Edmonton, 1939).

HRUSHEVSKY, M. *A History of the Ukraine* (New Haven, 1941).

———. *Prince Andrej Bogolijubskij: The Man and the Myth* (Florence, 1980).

PASZKIEWICZ, H. *The Rise of Moscow's Power* (Boulder, CO, 1983).

PRESNIAKOV, A. E. *The Formation of the Great Russian State* (New York, 1971). (Trans. from Russian.)

VORONIN, N. N. *Zodchestvo severo-vostochnoi Rusi XII–XV vekov,* 2 vols. (Moscow, 1961).

ARTICLES

ALLSEN, T. "Mongol Census Taking in Rus, 1245–1275." *HUS* 5, no. 1 (1981): 32–53.

ANDRUSIAK, M. "Kings of Kiev and Galicia." *SEER* 33 (1954): 342–50.

GOLDFRANK, D. "Andrei Bogoliubskii." *MERSH* 1 (1976): 218–21.

HURWITZ, E. "Andrei Bogoliubskii: An Image of the Prince." *Rus. Hist.* 2, no. 1 (1974): 39–52.

———. "Andrei Bogoliubskii: Policies and Ideology." Ph.D. diss., Columbia University, 1972.

WALCK, C. "Settlement Patterns in Rostov-Suzdal Rus, 9th through 13th Centuries." Ph.D. diss., Harvard University, 1980.

6

The Mongols and Russia

Between 1237 and 1241 a nomadic east Asian people, the Mongols,[1] and their Turkic allies conquered most of Rus. Overcoming ill-coordinated resistance by the divided Rus princes, they stormed or occupied most major towns, killed more than 5 percent of the population, and deported thousands into slavery in Asia. The Mongol onslaught shattered Kievan civilization and accelerated the fragmentation of Rus. For more than two centuries Mongol khans from their capitals at Old or New Sarai in the lower Volga region controlled and imposed tribute on the Russian princes. The results of Mongol rule remain debatable, but in any case this last great incursion by Asiatic steppe nomads into eastern Europe had major and long-lasting effects on Russian development.

The 13th-century Mongol invasion of Rus and eastern Europe is somewhat comparable to the fifth-century incursion of Germanic tribes into the Western Roman Empire. Before advancing into Rus, the Mongols had conquered large parts of Asia, causing great destruction and slaughtering all who opposed them. From Rus they moved westward into Poland and Hungary and south-westward into the Balkans, reaching the Adriatic before recoiling into the steppe. Western Europe, whose rulers trembled at the news of their fearsome advance, was spared because of the opportune death of the great khan in Mongolia. The amazing saga of Mongol expansion produced a vast though short-lived empire extending over Eurasian plains and steppe from the Pacific to the Adriatic.

The Mongols, so energetic and successful in war, comprised nomadic clans and tribes, totaling about a million people, that migrated over broad expanses of the Mongolian steppe, north of China, in search of water and pasturage for their flocks. Their religion combined animism, totemism, and shamanism. Before the time of Chingis-khan these primitive sky-worshipers played no significant role in steppe politics and lacked unity and organization. Their property consisted chiefly of

---

[1] The term *Mongol* began to be used during Chingis-khan's lifetime to denote the state, his dynasty, and later the people. It continued to be used in Mongolia and Central Asia, whereas in the western part of the Mongol Empire and in Europe Mongols were called Tatars or Tartars.

extensive pasturelands and herds of sheep, goats, horned cattle, and camels that provided them with food and clothing. Most highly valued in their society was the horse. At age three or four, Mongol children were taught to ride the swift, enduring steppe horses. Steppe life involved constant tension and internecine warfare among clans and tribes.

Chingis-Khan

Temuchin (1167?–1227), later known as Chingis-khan (great ruler or "Prince of the Ocean"), was the son of Esugai, chieftain of a small Mongolian tribe. In his youth, surviving by shrewdness and courage, Temuchin seemed a typical tribal leader engaged in steppe warfare. In a series of bloody victories he defeated his rivals and eventually brought all of the Mongol tribes under his control. In 1206 Mongolia's unification was confirmed and Temuchin's power legitimated by a great council of clan chieftains (*kuriltai*), which named him supreme ruler, or Chingis-khan. Thereafter Chingis considered himself divine, and his slogan became "*One* sole sun in the sky; *one* sole sovereign on earth." He was protected by a personal guard of some 10,000 picked warriors, mostly of aristocratic origin, fighting under his direct orders. For some historians, notes the American scholar Charles Halperin, Chingis was the noble savage whose inspired leadership, flawless judgment, stout character, and military genius catapulted the obscure Mongols to world power. Other historians have viewed him as a bloody gangster whose cruelty galvanized the barbarian Mongols into a holocaust of rapine, death, and destruction.[2] His morality aside, Chingis possessed great military and political ability; he was "a savage of genius," convinced of his divine mission to conquer the world and bring it unity and peace. Declared Chingis: "Man's highest joy is in victory: to conquer one's enemies, to pursue them, to deprive them of their posses-

Temuchin, 1167?–1227, commonly known as Chingis-khan, founder of the great Mongol Empire.

sions, to make their beloved weep, and to embrace their wives and daughters."[3] To the end of his life he remained an illiterate sky-worshiper, but one who appreciated culture. Besides conquest, his principal delights were hunting and gathering numerous concubines.

Chingis's administrative skill and military insight permitted him to greatly outdo previous steppe warlords. With the aid of the *kuriltai*, which contained his chief advisers, Chingis in a few years

---

[2] C. J. Halperin, *Russia and the Golden Horde* (Bloomington, IN, 1985), pp. 21–22.

[3] V. Ia. Vladimirtsov, *Chingis-Khan* (Berlin, 1922), p. 166; quoted in G. Vernadsky, *The Mongols and Russia* (New Haven, 1953), p. 43.

constructed a centralized and absolute monarchy, a coordinated administration, and a strictly disciplined and formidable army. The Mongol state remained basically feudal, with vassals receiving fiefs of herds and accompanying pasture rights. Creating a far-flung empire through conquest, Chingis succeeded in utilizing the Mongols' clan and tribal organization to build an efficient bureaucracy. Thus a single Mongol might be simultaneously a feudal vassal, a clan leader, and an important bureaucrat. This meshing of systems made Chingis's empire cohesive and relatively enduring. His army, also based on the clan-tribal system, comprised detachments of tens, hundreds, thousands, and myriads (ten thousands). Chingis selected the commanders of larger units from among his boyhood friends. The army comprised cavalry capable of great endurance and swift movement. Their chief weapons were bows and arrows shot with great accuracy at a full gallop, techniques practiced from boyhood. Favorite Mongol tactics were surprise and encirclement of their enemies.

Once Chingis had consolidated his regime, he conquered neighboring sedentary civilizations in Asia. To defeat the Chinese Empire, he drafted Muslim and Chinese experts in siege warfare, forging a force that could capture any city. With its numerous siege weapons, innovative tactics, speed, and iron discipline, Chingis's army became an almost invincible machine, capable of coordinated operations on a huge scale. Without the hierarchy of steppe clans and the superiority it gave his mounted bowmen, Chingis could have achieved little, but no one else exploited these advantages comparably. Besides China, Chingis's armies overran Persia and the large central Asian state of Khwarizm.

At the peak of his success and with his armies still advancing, Chingis-khan died in 1227. Unlike the empire of Alexander the Great, which dissolved immediately following Alexander's death, the Mongol Empire continued to expand after Chingis died. His descendants—the Golden Kin—alone could rule the empire and its successor states. Each of his four sons was awarded an appanage (*ulus*) and part of the army. As the new great khan, the great council unanimously elected Ugedei, a capable and energetic ruler who shared his father's concept of universal empire. Juchi, to whom was assigned the western *ulus,* had predeceased his father, so it passed to his son—Chingis's grandson—Batu. The huge cost of Mongol expansion in bloodshed and destruction is undeniable, but the *Pax Mongolica* (Mongolian peace) that ensued prepared the way for the development of commerce and contributed to political and economic growth in many regions. Recruiting conquered peoples as auxiliaries for their armies and administration, the Mongols secured control of caravan routes from China to Persia. The conquest of Eurasia by a people numbering just over one million constituted an amazing triumph of discipline, organization, and leadership.

The Mongol Invasion of Rus

The Mongol invasion of Rus in 1237 was carefully prepared. Fifteen years earlier a Mongol army had defeated an allied force of Rus and Polovtsy at the Battle of the Kalka River, then had retired abruptly into the steppe. This warning went unheeded by the feuding Rus princes; even united, they could scarcely have withstood the Mongol onslaught. At Khan Ugedei's orders, warriors and supplies began to be assembled in 1235. Batu's army, actually commanded in Rus by the redoubtable Subudei, contained a Mongol core of some 50,000 horsemen, but with its Turkic auxiliaries it probably numbered about 120,000 men. Subudei struck initially at the Volga Bulgars, conquering them swiftly, then subdued and enslaved the Polovtsy and Finno-Ugrian tribes. The still uncomprehending Rus princes failed to unite in defense of their land.

The conquest of Rus was achieved by Mongol military tactics developed earlier by Chingis-khan. Large cavalry forces moved in various directions, employing great mobility, sudden attacks, and encirclements. Normally the Mongols enjoyed numerical superiority at the point of attack. With their siege weapons they subdued most resisting towns within a few days. Any resistance provoked devastation and indiscriminate slaughter of the inhabitants. In December 1237 Batu stormed the town of Riazan, then advanced to Moscow, at that time a minor but strategic town of Vladimir-Suzdal, and burned it to the ground. Reigning Grand Prince Iuri sent an army against the Mongols, but it was overwhelmed at Kolomna; he was defeated again and killed in battle in 1238. Vladimir, the chief city of northeast Russia, was swiftly conquered. In 1240 Kiev fell after heroic resistance and was almost wholly devastated; other towns along the southern Dnieper River soon succumbed. Podolia, Volhynia, and Galicia in the southwest were overrun in 1240–1241. Russian chronicles described vividly the destructiveness and vast size of the Tatar forces—"an uncountable multitude, like a swarm of locusts." However, some chronicles tended to exaggerate the Mongol impact on western and northeastern Rus, which emerged with little or limited damage. Their rather literary narratives, notes Paszkiewicz, were mostly by noneyewitnesses, lacking the color and detail found in chronicle accounts of the south and southwest.[4] Thus the Mongols advanced toward Novgorod only to turn back in the face of spring thaws; that city spared itself devastation by prompt submission to Mongol overlordship. Batu's forces scarcely touched the northwest, or Belorussia. In Vladimir, supposedly grievously devastated in 1238, great crowds gathered that very year to mourn the dead, and in the following year Vladimir's Prince Iaroslav won victories over the Lithuanians. Apparently, in the northeast and west life swiftly reverted to near normal after the tragic events of 1238.

After subduing Rus, Tatar (Mongol) armies continued westward into central Europe. They defeated the medieval knightly armies of Poland and Hungary almost simultaneously, in April 1241. That December Batu crossed the frozen Danube into Croatia, ranged widely over the Balkan Penin-

sula, and reached the shores of the Adriatic Sea. So easy were his victories in eastern Europe that Batu apparently intended to move farther westward in search of plunder. Halperin rejects the Soviet claim that, weakened by Rus resistance, the Tatar armies could not continue their European campaign, so that at least indirectly the conquest of Rus had spared western Europe. Actually, Batu's forces had defeated European mounted knights at every encounter. Neither exhaustion nor geography saved Europe, but rather the sudden death of the great khan Ugedei, which precipitated a succession crisis within the Mongol Empire. Learning of Ugedei's death early in 1242, Batu ordered a general withdrawal toward the Volga River. Subsequently, he became too preoccupied with Mongol internal politics and his own domains to resume the advance into Europe.

In Karakorum, the Mongol capital, the great khan's ambitious widow, Teregene Khatun, sought to arrange the succession for Guyuk, her son by Ugedei. Exploiting her powers as regent, she finally prevailed: the *kuriltai* of 1246 named Guyuk, hostile to Batu, as great khan. After Guyuk's death only two years later from drink and debauchery, tension within the Golden Kin subsided. Batu, now the eldest claimant and kingmaker, engineered the *kuriltai*'s election in 1251 of Mongke as great khan. Batu himself was too busy in eastern Europe to aspire to the khanly throne in Karakorum.

The Golden Horde's Suzerainty over Rus

Already in 1242 had emerged the outlines of the khanate of Kipchak, generally known as the Golden Horde, comprising the western territories (*ulus*) of Khan Batu. Its nucleus and the key to its identity were the steppe grasslands north of the Black and Caspian seas (see Map 6.1), which provided excellent pasturage and enabled the Tatars to continue their nomadic life. It also included the upper Volga, the north Caucasus, the Crimea, and much of Central Asia. Remaining a part of the

---

[4] H. Paszkiewicz, *The Rise of Moscow's Power* (Boulder, CO, 1983), pp. 127ff.

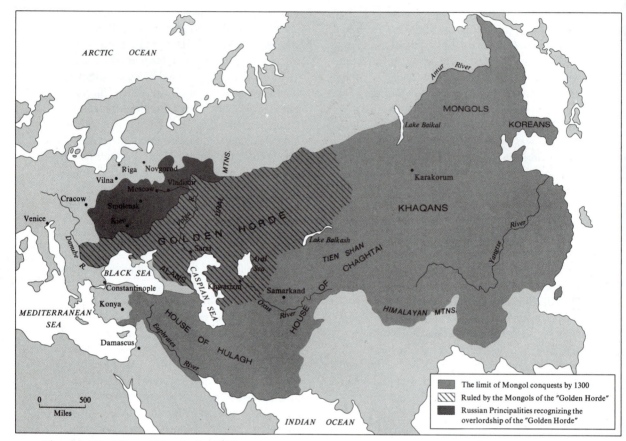

Map 6.1 The Mongol Empire by 1300

Mongol Empire, the Golden Horde promptly achieved broad autonomy under Batu and later virtual independence from the disintegrating empire. Only a small minority of the Golden Horde's population was Mongol. Much more numerous were the Polovtsy and other Turkic tribes; soon the Mongols of the Horde adopted the Turkic language and culture. Batu and his fellow commanders established a strong administration at Old Sarai, founded by Batu between 1242 and 1253 on the east bank of the Akhtiuba River on the lower Volga. Sarai was one of the fortified towns that Batu ordered built on the open steppe. Some Polovtsy settled in these new towns, and Polovtsy played an especially important role at Sarai. William of Rubruck, a Franciscan sent by

Louis IX of France to the Mongols as missionary and envoy, was impressed by the khan's magnificent residence during his visit to Sarai in 1253. From this vast city of tents Batu sought to ensure the obedience and cooperation of the various Rus princes and to collect tribute and army recruits regularly from them.

The Golden Horde rather than Karakorum soon became the true suzerain of Rus. In 1242 Grand Prince Iaroslav I of Vladimir was confirmed in office at Batu's camp, and his son Constantine undertook the long journey to Karakorum in Mongolia to confirm his father's allegiance. Upon Mongke's election as great khan in 1251, all Rus princes had to obtain new patents of authority (*iarlyki*) by traveling to Sarai and prostrating

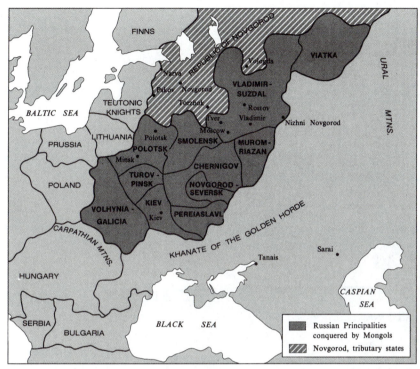

Map 6.2 Mongol conquest, 1237–1300

themselves before the khan. This confirmed the growing decentralization of the Mongol Empire. The Mongols of the Golden Horde, soon coining their own currency, utilized the Mongol census, decimal system of army organization, and postal system (*yam*).

After 1242 the Golden Horde, crushing sporadic resistance, consolidated its hold over nearly all Rus (see Map 6.2). The grave threat to northwest Rus posed by invading Swedes, German crusading knights, and Lithuanians aided Mongol success. This western menace caused Prince Alexander Iaroslavich, the last effective Rus grand prince of the 13th century, to pledge utter loyalty to the Mongol khan and undertake repeated humiliating journeys to his capital at Sarai. Simultaneously, however, he defended Rus valiantly against invasions from the West. In July 1240 a Swedish armada under Karl Birger proceeded up the Neva River from the Gulf of Finland toward

Novgorod and Pskov. As prince of Novgorod, Alexander with his retinue of warriors and the Novgorod militia surprised the Swedes in July 1240 while they were disembarking and forced them to flee in panic. For this exploit he acquired the nickname Nevskii (named after the Neva River). In 1241, aided by the forces of Vladimir, he expelled the German knights from the area of Pskov, Rus's gateway to the west. The following April Alexander Nevskii lured the heavily armed German Teutonic Knights onto the treacherous ice of Lake Chud and through a bold attack destroyed them and delivered Pskov from threatened German conquest. Three years later he defeated the Lithuanians, thus preserving a corner of Rus from direct foreign rule. Soviet historians lauded Nevskii's successful struggle against Germanic invaders while underplaying his unquestioned subservience to the Mongols. Alexander Nevskii became the hero of a classic Soviet film of the

Library of Congress

Icon of Alexander Nevskii, prince of Novgorod.

1930s by Sergei Eisenstein and inspired a cantata by the great Soviet composer Sergei Prokofiev. Nevskii's victories blunted the German drive to the east and prevented western Rus's subjugation by Swedish and German forces.

In the 1250s the Mongols, defeating the rebellious Prince Andrei of Vladimir, gave his throne to Alexander Nevskii. In the west King Daniel of Volhynia, who briefly asserted his independence and defied the Mongols, was forced to flee. Later he too became a loyal vassal of the Horde. In 1262

uprisings organized by town assemblies (*veche*) broke out almost simultaneously in various towns in Suzdalia in northeast Rus but were quickly suppressed. The Rus princes, seeking confirmation of their titles from the khan of the Golden Horde, worked to consolidate their authority within their own appanages. To promote stability, the Horde encouraged this and supported obedient, trustworthy princes, such as those of Rostov, against the town assemblies. In this period the Mongols maintained firm control by superior military strength, periodic raids and punitive expeditions, and Russian awe at their power and administrative efficiency.

The twin aims of the Mongols' administration in Rus were collecting taxes to support both their state apparatus and their military campaigns and securing army recruits to replace their losses. Tatar (Mongol) policies differed in various parts of Rus. In the southwest Tatars displaced Rus princely administration and ruled directly. In most other areas Mongol administration coexisted with that of Rus princes, who were usually allowed to rule their domains as vassals of the Horde and under the vague suzerainty of the great khan of Mongolia. Each prince had to obtain a patent of authority (*iarlyk*) and be installed by an envoy of the Horde, retaining his post during good behavior. However, the khan could revoke this patent at any time. Beginning in 1257, the Mongols conducted a series of censuses in Rus to determine its population and taxpaying capabilities. After the census of 1257 detachments of Mongol and auxiliary troops were assigned to the Rus principalities to assist tax inspectors (*baskaki*), maintain internal order, and ensure obedience. Initially, the Mongols used the grand princely throne in Vladimir as a means to control northeast Rus by granting patents to cooperative princes. However, Vladimir itself, devastated by the Mongol invasion, had been gravely weakened, and many of its inhabitants had fled northward to Rostov. Karl Marx later wrote that the Tatars' traditional policy was to play off the Russian princes against one another and not allow any one of them to become strong.

The Mongol invasion had terrorized the surviving Rus, and their chroniclers considered the Tatars primitive and murderous barbarians, but this is far from the whole story. The Mongols' initial cruel massacres were partly calculated to impose their rule through terror. After the first years, only small Tatar detachments remained in Rus and few Mongols resided there. Adopting Islam in the early 14th century, the Golden Horde simultaneously took over the Persian *diwan* system, the most sophisticated bureaucratic apparatus in the Muslim world. At its peak the Horde,

notes Halperin, was a delicately balanced combination of pastoral nomadism and sedentary bureaucracy.[5] When Tamerlane sacked Sarai in the 1390s, he destroyed the Horde's archives, but this system proved its resiliency after his withdrawal.

The Golden Horde's extensive and sophisticated diplomacy revealed that the Tatars were no longer the barbarian bandits described by the 19th-century Russian historian Sergei Soloviev. The Mongols observed scrupulously the Islamic diplomatic code, including use of the correct paper and script for correspondence. The Horde conducted diplomatic relations with all of eastern Europe, the Middle East, and Central Asia. Thus the traditional view of the Mongol conquest as isolating Rus from Europe and Byzantium appears incorrect. Rus princes visiting Sarai during the 13th and 14th centuries encountered papal envoys, Egyptians, Persians, and merchants from many lands. Most Mongols still lived off their herds, but prosperity was provided by a flourishing international commerce fostered by the *Pax Mongolica,* which made caravan routes secure throughout Eurasia. Silks and spices were conveyed by caravan from the Orient to the Mediterranean and Europe via Sarai and other lower Volga towns. The Horde promoted trade with Egypt, Byzantium, Persia, and Central Asia, as well as with the Hanseatic League via Novgorod.

Mongol administrative control or supervision lasted in most Russian lands for at least a century, and far longer in the northeast. In Galicia it ended in 1349, when that region was annexed to Poland. By 1363 most other western areas of Rus had been absorbed by expanding Lithuania (see Chapter 7). In east Rus the "Tatar yoke" lingered almost another century. However, the Horde suffered political fragmentation very early. In 1280 Nogai, an outstanding Mongol commander, set up his

---

[5] A central council of four top officials (*bekliarbeks*) replaced the *kuriltai,* or Mongol family council; a vizier took charge of the treasury; and a complete replica of the Muslim religious system arose in Sarai. Halperin, *Russia and the Golden Horde,* pp. 26–27.

own Nogai Horde along the Ural River; dual rule prevailed within the Golden Horde until 1299, creating considerable confusion in Rus. Reaching its peak of prosperity early in the 14th century, the Horde divided east Russia among the grand principalities of Vladimir, Moscow, Tver, Riazan, and Nizhnii-Novgorod. Then about 1360 a severe internal crisis developed within the Horde, initially taking the form of a family feud among the sons of Khan Janibeg. This situation encouraged the princes of Rus to play off one Mongol claimant against the other and to assert increasing autonomy. Nevertheless, Rus-Tatar political relationships were slow to change. The grand prince of Vladimir continued to serve the Horde, and Rus princes traveled to Sarai after each new upheaval there to obtain patents of authority. The internal crisis in the Horde, coinciding with the growing strength of Lithuania in the west and of Moscow in the east, gradually undermined the authority of the khan and his hold over the subject peoples. In the mid-15th century the Golden Horde disintegrated; separate khanates were formed in Kasimov (under Moscow's influence), Kazan, Astrakhan, and the Crimea. The remnant of the Golden Horde, known now as the Great Horde, competed with these khanates. This division and internecine strife among the Tatar states prepared the way for Russia's emancipation from tribute payment and Mongol control.

Problem 2

The Mongol Impact

The Mongols undertook to gather and organize Russia as they did their own state in order to introduce into the country law, order, and prosperity. . . . As a result of this policy the Mongols gave the conquered country the basic elements of future Muscovite statehood: autocracy, centralism, and serfdom.[6]

The bloody business begun by Chingiz-khan and continued by his descendants cost the Russians and other peoples of our country dearly. . . . The liberation struggle of peoples against the despotism of Chingiz-khan and his successors was a supreme act of progress.[7]

As these quotations suggest, historians differ greatly in assessing the effects of the Mongol invasion and the "Tatar yoke" upon Rus. Contemporary and later Muscovite chronicles, depicting the invasion as a terrible misfortune for Rus, emphasized the terrible slaughter, disorder, and civil strife. Prerevolutionary Russian historians divided sharply over the effects of Mongol rule. N. M. Karamzin, an early 19th-century nationalist historian, blamed the Tatars for Russian backwardness, but he added that they had "restored autocracy" and strengthened Moscow, which "owed its greatness to the khans."[8] On the other hand, S. M. Soloviev, the leading scholar of the so-called organic school, regarded the Mongols as merely the more powerful successors of the Polovtsy. "We have no reason to assume," he wrote, "any great influence [of the Mongols] on [Russia's] internal administration, as we do not see any traces of it."[9]

Since the Bolshevik Revolution two sharply contrasting views of the Mongol impact have emerged. Soviet historians, repudiating the bal-

---

[6] E. Khara-Davan, *Chingiz-khan kak polkovodets i ego nasledie* (Belgrade, 1925), p. 200.

[7] *Istoriia SSSR* 5 (1962): 119.

[8] N. M. Karamzin, *Istoriia gosudarstva rossiiskogo*, vol. 2, pt. 5 (St. Petersburg, 1842), pp. 215ff.

[9] S. M. Soloviev, *Istoriia Rossii s drevneishikh vremen*, vol. 4 (St. Petersburg, n.d.), p. 179.

anced approach of the 1920s presented by V. V. Bartold, stressed the negative, destructive aspects of the Mongol conquest and argued that Tatar rule delayed the development of a unified Russian culture, economy, and national state. On the other hand, the Eurasian school of Russian émigrés, depicting the Mongol unification of Eurasia as historically progressive, have viewed Russia's unification under Moscow as the direct outgrowth of Mongol rule: "The Russian state was the heir, successor, and continuer of Chingis-khan's historic work."[10] Derived from the Eurasian view is the approach of Professor George Vernadsky, a Russian émigré living in the United States, who assessed Mongol influence by analyzing differences between Kievan and Muscovite Russia. Here is a summary of these three approaches to the nature of the Tatar yoke in Russia.

The Soviet View

The Mongol invasion, Soviet historians agreed, brought terrible physical destruction to Rus towns and villages and dealt severe blows to agriculture, trade, and handicrafts. During the balance of the 13th century repeated Tatar raids devastated new regions and prevented economic recovery. The Rus and other peoples within the territory of the former USSR fought bitterly against the Mongols.

> The heroic defense of their native land and cities by the Russian people was the decisive factor that wrecked the plan of the Tatar-Mongol aggressors to conquer all Europe. The great worldwide significance of the exploit of the Russian people was that it undermined the strength of the Mongol army. The Russian people defended the peoples of western Europe from the approaching avalanche of the Tatar-Mongol hordes and thus secured for them

the possibility of normal economic and social development.[11]

Only Rus's feudal division, claimed another Soviet historian, prevented able Rus princes such as Alexander Nevskii from coordinating massive resistance by peasants and townsmen against the invader. Feudal princes, boyars, and merchants for selfish reasons often collaborated with the enemy. Nonetheless, Rus's vigorous resistance to the Mongols gave it greater autonomy than that of other regions subject to Mongol rule. Instead of administering Rus directly, the Tatars, as Karl Marx noted, "oppressed from a distance."

The invasion and subsequent Mongol yoke, contended Soviet historians, greatly delayed Russia's economic development. Plunder and tribute payments drained silver and other precious metals from the country. The destruction of commercial centers delayed the growth of a money economy. "Russian town handicrafts were completely destroyed. Russia was thrown back by several centuries, and during those centuries when the guild industry of the West shifted to a period of original accumulation, Russian handicraft industry again had to pass through part of that historic path which was traversed before Batu."[12] Likewise, the Mongols undermined Russian agriculture, a basis for towns that might have counterbalanced the influence of feudal lords.

The invasion worsened Russia's international and commercial position, especially toward the West. Weakened by Tatar attacks, the Russian states lost control of the important Dvina River trade route and territory in the West to Lithuania, Sweden, and the Teutonic Knights. Russia's links with Byzantium were mostly cut. Not until the 14th century was there some revival of commerce with Russia's southern and western neighbors. In the Mongol era much of Russian trade shifted

[10] I. R. (Prince Nicholas Trubetskoi), *Nasledie Chingis-khana* (Berlin, 1925), pp. 9, 21.

[11] V. T. Pashuto, *Geroicheskaia borba russkogo naroda za nezavisimost XIII veka* (Moscow, 1956), p. 159.

[12] B. Rybakov, *Remeslo drevnei Rusi* (Moscow, 1948), pp. 780–81.

Problem 2 continued

eastward, although Novgorod remained an important gateway to the West. The net effect of the Tatar yoke on the Russian economy, emphasized most Soviet historians, was overwhelmingly negative. Destroying, looting, and burning, the Mongols gave nothing to the Russian people in return.

Politically, affirmed these historians, the conquest interrupted the gradual consolidation of the Russian lands and deepened feudal divisions. The Mongols shattered the grand princely administration in the northeast and weakened the towns, the supporters of centralization. The centralized Muscovite state of the 15th century emerged, not with the aid of the Tatars, but "contrary to their interests and despite their will." Mongol policy in Russia "was not aimed at creating a unified state out of a divided society, but in every way to hinder consolidation, support mutual dissension of individual political groups and principalities."[13]

The Eurasian View

Emphasizing the necessity to treat the history of the Eurasian landmass as a unit, the émigré Russian scholars of the Eurasian view regard the Mongol invasion as the chief turning point in Russian history. Kievan Rus, they affirm, had merely been "a group of principalities run by Varangian princes" that became historically obsolete. "The political unification of Eurasia was a historic necessity from the beginning, and the people who took this on—the Mongols—were performing a historically progressive and necessary task." What they did for Russia was most significant: "The Mongol yoke summoned the Russian people from a provincial historical existence in small separated tribal and town principalities of the so-called appanage period onto the broad road of statehood." Russia, at first only a province of the Mongol Empire, adopted the

Mongols' concept of the state and later took their place. "The Russian state was the heir, successor, and continuer of Chingis-khan's historic work. . . . The unification of the Russian lands under the power of Moscow was the direct result of the Tatar yoke."

The Mongol impact, assert the Eurasian historians, proved highly beneficial to the Russians. "The Tatars defended Russia from Europe," sparing it from conquest by the West. After the conquest Mongols and the people of Rus coexisted in harmony and peace. From their conquerors the Rus adopted typical Turanian character traits: steadiness, conviction, strength, and religiosity, all of which promoted the development of the Muscovite state. The Mongols assured to Rus secure commercial and cultural relations with the Orient; they enhanced the position of the Orthodox church. In the mid-13th century Alexander Nevskii, prince of Novgorod, faced with a fateful choice, wisely chose the East over the West: "Alexander saw in the Mongols a friendly force in a cultural sense that could assist him to preserve and consolidate Russian cultural identity from the Latin West."

Thus the Eurasian school, largely overlooking the destruction and disruption caused by the Mongol invasion, stressed the Mongols' positive contributions to all aspects of Russian development. It ascribed to them a role similar to that which the Normanists attributed to the Varangians. Both of these schools affirm that external influences outweighed domestic socioeconomic change as a factor in Russia's growth.[14]

Vernadsky's Approach

The problem of the nature of Mongol influence, affirms Vernadsky, a moderate Eurasianist, is many-sided; it involves the immediate impact of the invasion, the direct effects of Mongol rule,

---

[13] A. N. Nasonov, *Mongoly i Rus* (Moscow, 1940), p. 5.

[14] See I. R. (Prince Nicholas Trubetskoi), *Nasledie Chingiskhana;* N. S. Trubetskoi, "O turanskom elemente v Russkoi kulture," *Evraziiskii vremennik* 4 (1925); and Khara-Davan, *Chingiz-khan kak polkovodets i ego nasledie.*

and unintended contributions of the Tatars through delayed action. One can gauge the extent of Mongol influence, he believes, by contrasting the institutions and spirit of Kievan Rus with those of Muscovy—by comparing the pre-Mongol era with the post-Mongol era.

Kievan political life had been free and diversified with monarchical, aristocratic, and democratic elements roughly in balance, but under the Mongols this pattern changed drastically. In place of the Kievan Rus federation, sharp rifts developed between east and west Rus. In the east, the region most exposed to Mongol influences, monarchical power became highly developed. After visiting Muscovy in 1517, Baron von Herberstein affirmed that the grand prince's authority over his subjects surpassed that of any European monarch. Under Mongol rule political life in Rus was curbed and deformed and its traditional balance upset. The Mongols crushed town assemblies because of their defiant independence; landed estates, rather than cities, became the bases of political life. The power of princes grew as checks on their authority crumbled. When the prince of Moscow prevailed over the others, he became the sovereign of east Rus, clothed with awesome power.

Tatar influence on Muscovite administrative and military affairs, asserts Vernadsky, was also profound. "It was on the basis of the Mongol patterns that the grand ducal system of taxation and army organization was developed [in Muscovy] in the late fourteenth to the sixteenth centuries."[15] For more than 50 years the khans of the Golden Horde exercised full and direct power over taxation and conscription in east Rus. When the Rus princes recovered authority over them, they continued the Mongol systems. The Turkic origin of the Russian words for treasury (*kazna*) and treasurer (*kaznachei*) suggest that the Muscovite treasury followed a Mongol pattern. The

division of the Muscovite army into five large units resembled Mongol practice. The Russians adopted the Tatars' tactics of envelopment and their system of universal conscription.

In the social realm, the foundations of the relatively free and mobile Kievan society were chipped away during the Mongol period. Tatar rule helped subordinate the boyars to the ruler and prepared the way for enserfment of the peasantry. When Ivan III announced Rus's emancipation from the Tatar yoke in 1480, the framework of a new service-bound society was virtually complete.

The economic results of the Mongol conquest were mixed. Devastated major cities, especially Kiev, Chernigov, and Suzdal, lost their importance for centuries. Mongol conscription of craftsmen almost exhausted Rus's reservoir of skilled manpower; industry was crippled. In Novgorod the economic depression lasted for 50 years; in east Rus, for a full century. Revival only followed the relaxation of Tatar control. Agriculture, affirms Vernadsky, suffered less and became the leading branch of the Rus economy, especially in the northeast. Mongol regional governors and khans, however, encouraged the development of Rus trade with both east and west.

Mongol rule affected the Orthodox church mostly indirectly but significantly. The devastation and decline of Kiev soon induced the church to shift its center of operations to the northeast. The khans of the Golden Horde issued a series of charters permitting the church to build up its material wealth and influence without fear of state interference or persecution. In many ways it emerged from the Mongol era stronger and richer than before.

The Mongol cultural impact, Vernadsky believes, was considerable. By a process of osmosis Turkish, Persian, and Arabic words entered the Russian language as late as the 17th century.[16] Some of the descendants of Tatars who settled in Rus, such as Karamzin and Peter

---

[15] G. Vernadsky, *The Mongols and Russia* (New Haven, 1953).

[16] For example, *dengi* (money); *tamozhnia* (customs house); *bazar* (bazaar); *balagan* (booth); and *bakaleia* (grocery).

Chaadaev, became outstanding intellectual leaders. Russia adopted the stiff, formal diplomatic ritual of the Orient from the Mongols. In a sense, concludes Vernadsky, Russia itself was a successor state of the Golden Horde.[17]

Conclusion

Today one can no longer deny the important and profound effects of Mongol rule upon Russian development. The contrasting Soviet and

---

[17] Vernadsky, *Mongols and Russia*, pp. 333–90.

Eurasian approaches, while often extreme and one-sided, have deepened our perspective and understanding of this epoch. The linguistic and cultural influences of the Mongol conquest, like the earlier Scandinavian linguistic and cultural influences, seem to have been minor; but the influence of the Mongol conquest on the political and military institutions and concepts of Muscovy, as Vernadsky suggests, was important. The economic effects of the Mongol conquest and rule remain somewhat debatable, but some recent studies suggest that Mongol rule imposed a severe economic burden on Rus, although trade with the Orient brought some benefits. The Mongol impact on Rus was neither wholly positive nor completely negative. ■

Suggested Additional Reading

BOOKS

ALLSEN, T. *Mongol Imperialism: The Policies of the Grand Qar Mongke in China, Russia and the Islamic Lands, 1251–1259* (Berkeley, 1987).

DIMNIK, M. *Mikhail, Prince of Chernigov and Grand Prince of Kiev, 1224–46* (Toronto, 1981).

FEDOROV-DAVYDOV, G. A. *The Culture of the Golden Horde Cities* (Oxford, 1984).

FENNELL, J. *The Crisis of Medieval Russia, 1200–1304* (London, 1983).

HALPERIN, C. J. *Russia and the Golden Horde: The Mongol Impact on Medieval Russian History* (Bloomington, IN, 1985).

———. *The Tatar Yoke* (Columbus, OH, 1986).

HOWORTH, H. H. *History of the Mongols from the Ninth to the Nineteenth Centuries*, 4 vols. (London, 1876–1927).

ISHBOLDIN, B. *Essays on Tatar History* (New Delhi, 1963).

MOSES, L. *The Political Role of Mongol Buddhism* (Bloomington, IN, 1977).

PASZKIEWICZ, H. *The Rise of Moscow's Power* (Boulder, CO, 1983), pp. 127–57.

PRAWDIN, M. *The Mongol Empire: Its Rise and Legacy*, 2d ed. (New York, 1967).

SEIDLER, G. *The Political Doctrine of the Mongols* (Lublin, Poland, 1960).

SILFEN, P. *The Influence of the Mongols on Russia: A Dimensional History* (Hicksville, NY, 1974).

SPULER, B. *Die Goldene Horde* (Wiesbaden, 1965).

———. *The Mongols in History* (New York, 1971).

VERNADSKY, G. *The Mongols and Russia* (New Haven, 1953).

WITTFOGEL, K. *Oriental Despotism* (New Haven, 1957).

YAN, V. *Batu Khan: A Tale of the Thirteenth Century.* (Soviet novel.)

ARTICLES

ALLSEN, T. "Mongol Census-Taking in Rus, 1245–1275." *HUS* 1 (March 1981): 32–53.

CHERNIAVSKY, M. "Khan or Basileus . . ." *JHI* 20 (1959): 459–76.

HALPERIN, C. J. "George Vernadsky, Eurasianism, the Mongols, and Russia." *SR* 41, no. 3 (Fall 1982): 477–93.

———. "Soviet Historiography on Russia and the Mongols." *Rus. Rev.* 41, no. 3 (July 1982): 306–22.

KRADER, L. "Feudalism and the Tatar Polity of the Middle Ages." *Comparative Studies in Society and History* 1 (1958): 76–99.

MAJESKA, G. "Alexander Nevskii." *MERSH* 1: 148–52.

MARTIN, J. "The Lands of Darkness and the Golden Horde: The Fur Trade Under the Mongols, Thirteenth–Fourteenth Century." *Cahiers* 19, no. 4 (1978): 401–22.

NOONAN, T. "Medieval Russia, the Mongols, and the West . . . " *Medieval Studies* 37 (1975): 316–39.

ORCHARD, G. E. "The Eurasian School of Russian Historiography." *Laurentian University Review* 10 (November 1977): 97–106.

RIASANOVSKY, N. V. "The Emergence of Eurasianism." *Cal. SS* 4 (1967): 39–72.

ROUBLEV, M. "The Mongol Tribute," in *The Structure of Russian History,* ed. Michael Cherniavsky (New York, 1970), pp. 29–64.

SAKHAROV, A. "Les Mongoles et la civilisation russe," in *Contributions à l'histoire russe* (Neuchâtel, Switzerland, 1958), pp. 77–97.

SOKOL, E. "Batu Khan." *MERSH* 3: 163–65.

SZCZESNIAK, B. "A Note on the Character of the Tartar Impact upon the Russian State and Church." *SEESt.* 17 (1972): 92–98.

———. "The Scope and Contents of Chingis Khan's Yasa." *HJAS* 3 (1938): 337–60.

VOEGELIN, E. "The Mongol Orders of Submission to European Powers, 1245–1255." *Byzantion* 15 (1940–41): 378–413.

WITTFOGEL, K. "Russia and the East," in *The Development of the Soviet Union,* ed. D. Treadgold (Seattle, 1964), pp. 323–39.

7

Novgorod and Lithuania

During the period of Mongol rule Rus fragmented into several regions that reflected different approaches to the question of political authority. The two leading entities in western Rus were Novgorod and Lithuania—the former a city-state with minimal princely power, the latter a federation of princes and lords. Both contrasted sharply with the increasingly autocratic grand principality of Moscow, especially because of the prominent role played in both by popular assemblies. Soviet scholars viewed the absorption of Novgorod and the Belorussian lands of Lithuania into Muscovy as progressive steps toward the unification of the eastern Slavs under centralized monarchical power. This approach was deplored by some Western scholars who regarded Novgorod and Lithuania as continuing the Kievan Rus traditions of freedom and diversity.

Novgorod

In northwest Rus, at the intersection of several major trade routes, lay the self-governing commercial republic of Novgorod. Known by contemporaries as Lord Novgorod the Great (*Gospodin velikii Novgorod*), it became one of medieval Europe's largest and most important city-states. Novgorod's population at its peak, in the 13th to 15th centuries, was approximately 50,000 to 100,000 people. This made it one of the largest cities in Europe at that time. In Slavic Europe only the city-state of Dubrovnik (Latin: Ragusa), on the Adriatic coast of former Yugoslavia, rivaled Novgorod in prosperity, freedom, and the sophistication and skill of its statecraft. Both Novgorod and Dubrovnik eventually succumbed to superior external forces. Novgorod, maintaining intimate contacts with the West through trade with Baltic German cities of the Hanseatic League, served for several centuries as Russia's chief window on Europe. Until the Muscovite conquest of the 1470s it was never captured or devastated. Escaping direct Mongol invasion by prompt submission and payment of tribute, Novgorod remained autonomous and prosperous until the late 15th century. Controversy persists over the extent and nature of its freedom and as to whether its eventual subjugation to Moscow's rule was a disaster or a blessing for itself and Russia.

Traditional accounts describe Novgorod as a very early military-commercial center of Varangian and Slav princes. Old Rus chronicles agree that the first people to settle the region of Lake Ilmen and Novgorod was the Slovene east Slavic tribe. In 860, states *The Primary Russian Chronicle,* these original inhabitants of Novgorod invited Riurik from Scandinavia to come and rule over them. At first, according to the *Chronicle,* Novgorod enjoyed primacy in Rus, but after Prince Oleg moved southward to Kiev about 880, it was relegated to second place, causing its citizens to resent Kiev's newfound preeminence.

Soviet archaeological excavations and writings altered considerably this older, *Chronicle*-based view. Whereas the *First Chronicle of Novgorod* mentions the town as already existing in 859, the oldest layer unearthed by archaeologists in the city dates from the 920s, and the first streets from 953. Not heavily settled before the mid-10th century, Rus Novgorod was indeed a "new city" (its meaning in Russian), considerably younger than Pskov, its so-called younger brother to the west. Recent excavations in Novgorod have confirmed Artsikhovskii's findings of the mid-1950s that no full-fledged urban community existed in Novgorod's territory in the ninth century.[1] Archaeologists have uncovered 28 layers in Novgorod dating from 953 to 1462. At intervals of seven to 30 years the log streets of the town were relaid. A peculiarly favorable climate preserved these 500 years of wooden Novgorod as well as hundreds of birchbark sheets, some of whose inscriptions have been deciphered. Their number and variety suggest that literacy was much more widespread there than has been hitherto assumed.[2]

Was there an "old town" in or near Novgorod, and if so, where was it located? Based on chroni-

cles and archaeological evidence, argued V. L. Ianin, (English: Yanine) a prestigious Soviet archaeologist, several small settlements probably existed in the Novgorod area during the ninth century. They were apparently located in the earliest boroughs (*kontsy*) of the town: Nerev, Liudin, and Slavno. With the fusion of these small settlements a preurban community probably developed there. Another possible location of the "old town" was in the *Gorodishche,* a mile south of Novgorod.

Geographic position helped determine Novgorod's unusual history and unique role among the Rus states. The city is situated on both sides of the Volkhov River (see Map 7.1), some two miles north of Lake Ilmen. Screened on the east by treacherous bogs and dense forests, it escaped devastation by steppe nomads such as the Pechenegs, Polovtsy, and Mongols. Its location on water routes leading northward to the Baltic Sea, eastward to the Volga River, and southward to Kiev and Byzantium on the famous route "from the Varangians to the Greeks" enhanced its commercial importance during and after the Kievan period. As the logical Rus outlet for trade with the Baltic, it was little affected by Byzantine decline and shifting patterns of trade. Yet Novgorod's position in a food-deficient region made it increasingly vulnerable to pressure from Suzdalia and Muscovy to the northeast and dependent in famine years on grains imported from there or the south.

During the 12th and 13th centuries Novgorod's chief source of wealth was probably its workshops rather than its trade with the outside world. The discovery by Soviet archaeologists of numerous workshops and their products proved that Novgorod was a major center of handicrafts, especially between the 11th and 14th centuries. What ruined the city was not isolation from Byzantium or subjugation to the Golden Horde but conquest and subsequent depredations by Moscow's rulers. Findings in Novgorod excavations reveal that its society resisted innovation. Numerous foreign coins circulated in Novgorod from the 10th century, but no native coins were produced there until the 15th century. In most aspects of life Novgorod in 1450 had advanced little beyond its status in

---

[1] W. W. Thompson, ed., *Novgorod the Great: Excavations of the Medieval City, directed by A. Artsikhovskii and B. A. Kolchin* (New York, 1967).

[2] V. L. Yanine, "The Dig at Novgorod," in *Readings in Russian Civilization,* ed. T. Riha, 2d ed., vol. 1 (Chicago, 1969), pp. 47–59. A birchbark document unearthed recently in Moscow region suggests widespread literacy in northern Russia in medieval times.

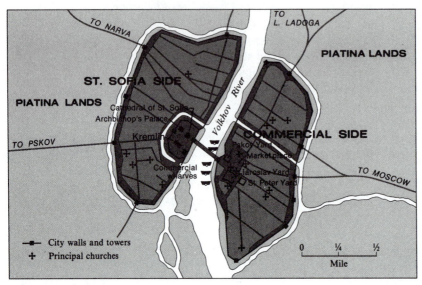

Map 7.1 Novgorod

950, whereas western Europe during those centuries experienced great development and change. This suggests that Rus's backwardness relative to the West, often attributed to the "Tatar yoke," may have resulted partly from lack of innovation.

Whereas Novgorod's early history remains shrouded in legend and controversy, by about 1000 the town had evidently become a major Varangian stronghold. Arriving from Sweden and Baltic islands, the Varangians utilized Novgorod as a principal entry point for their troops and tradesmen. With its sizable Scandinavian garrison Novgorod could serve as a reliable power base both for Vladimir I in his showdown with his brother Iaropolk and for Iaroslav the Wise. During this period Novgorod became a political dependency of the grand prince of Kiev. Watching Novgorod carefully, the Kievan princes normally sent their eldest sons as governors and princes to maintain control of this strategic outpost. But in 1095, after a dispute, Novgorod expelled its prince and invited another to replace him. Seven years later, when the grand prince of Kiev announced his intention to install his son as prince of Novgorod, the latter's emissaries declared: "We were sent to

you, oh Prince, with positive instructions that our city does not want either you or your son. If your son has two heads, then you might send him."[3]

Meanwhile, in 1044, at the instigation of Prince Vladimir, son of Grand Prince Iaroslav of Kiev, Novgorod's first citadel (*Detinets*) was erected. Supported by Kiev, the local prince compelled Novgorod to accept Christianity as a unifying political factor. However, the local citizenry insisted that the principal church, the wooden Cathedral of St. Sofia, built inside the citadel, be subject to Novgorod's bishop and town council (*veche*), not the prince. The latter's residence was removed from the citadel area to the nearby *Gorodishche*. Even then the prince of Novgorod did not involve himself deeply in the town's internal affairs because normally he would expect to succeed to the grand princely throne in Kiev.

In 1136 the Novgorod *veche* asserted the city's sovereign rights by forbidding the prince and his non-Novgorod followers to own estates within its territory. Novgorod became a republic, and Kiev

[3] S. H. Cross, "The Russian Primary Chronicle," *Harvard Studies and Notes in Philology and Literature* 12 (1930): 291.

ceased to interfere in its internal affairs. The power of Novgorod's prince waned, and the boyars were recognized as the predominant element with the right to invite or expel the prince. He had to share judicial power with the lord mayor (*posadnik*). A princely throne was retained inside Novgorod mainly for external reasons. Internally, the prince's authority did not extend much beyond the *Gorodishche;* he served mainly as hired commander of Novgorod's army. Elsewhere in Rus local dynasties established firm roots, but not in Novgorod. The prince lost control over army recruitment to the chiliarch and the town assembly. Even the shrewd Prince Alexander Nevskii (1240–1263) possessed little political authority, and subsequent princes became virtually powerless. Compelled to swear to preserve Novgorod's institutions, the prince could be deposed for violating his contract or infringing on the town's liberties. Elected officials audited his revenues, and the *veche* issued laws without his approval. After 1300, Novgorod shifted its external allegiance to Vladimir, then to Tver or Moscow. Opposing autocracy, Novgorod treated its prince as an outsider with strictly limited and specified powers.

From the 12th century elected officials predominated in Novgorod. Originally dependent on the prince, the lord mayor (*posadnik*) later supervised his rule. Elected by the *veche,* he exercised judicial and administrative authority and dealt increasingly with Novgorod's neighbors and trading partners. He became the spokesman for and was elected from the powerful boyar class. After 1354 his term was limited to one year and the office became a collective boyar oligarchy, first with six members, afterwards swelling to 18, then 24 members. The *posadniks'* short terms allowed most leading boyar families to participate in government. Also important was the chiliarch (*tysiatskii*), who originally commanded 1,000 armed men, 100 raised from each of ten urban "hundreds" (*sotni*). Elected by the town assembly, the chiliarch supposedly represented all free Novgoroders except boyars. Later, the boyars appropriated that office too.

By the 14th century, asserts Ianin, Novgorod was a full-fledged boyar republic. Boyar groups

representing the five boroughs feuded bitterly over key administrative posts. In order to resolve these conflicts and consolidate boyar control, a 50- to 60-member Council of Lords (*sovet gospod*) emerged that acted as the *veche's* executive organ. It has sometimes been called the senate of Novgorod. As the boyars assumed control, poorer free citizens grew frustrated and dissatisfied.

Highly controversial remain the composition and role of the town council (*veche*). The all-Novgorod *veche* was sovereign in theory; many Western accounts depict it as the organ of popular rule. By 1200 the *veche* was inviting or deposing the prince and electing top administrative officials. Initially, all free male citizens theoretically could attend it and could convene a meeting by striking the *veche* bell, the symbol of Novgorod's liberty. Actually, the *veche* was usually summoned by the *posadnik;* normally it met in Iaroslav's court on the commercial side of the city. Decisions were reached by simple oral majority vote. In controversial cases, *veche* meetings could end in street brawls, with the losers sometimes dumped unceremoniously into the frigid Volkhov River. Supposedly, the *veche* dealt with all legislative questions and foreign relations and tried serious crimes, but being large and unwieldy, it met irregularly and lacked regular rules of procedure. Each borough had its local *veche* and elder. Smaller subdivisions (hundreds, streets) also had some self-government. Fifteenth-century documents suggest that the Novgorod *veche* retained considerable vitality to the end.

Whereas George Vernadsky, an émigré historian, considered Novgorod an experiment in participatory democracy, most Soviet scholars depicted it as a boyar republic. The early *veche* contained representative features, concedes Ianin, a Soviet archaelogist, but later the all-Novgorod *veche* was dominated by top boyar families and a few wealthy merchants. Craftsmen, shopkeepers, and petty traders, dependent on the upper classes, lacked real political influence. Controlling the hundreds and all top governmental posts, boyars weakened the veche. Novgorod's conquest, Ianin concludes, merely destroyed a boyar oligarchy.[4]

The Orthodox church was also influential in Novgorod. The 11th-century St. Sofia Cathedral inside the citadel became the city-republic's spiritual center. Symbolically, the town and lands of Novgorod were the patrimony of St. Sofia: "Where St. Sofia is, there too is Novgorod." The archbishop (*vladyka*), directing numerous secular employees and presiding over the Council of Lords, exerted great authority. The archbishop's signature is found on many official documents, and he often acted as spokesman for the city-republic. The church became the single most important landholder in Novgorod. Archbishop Evfimii II (ruled 1429–1458), to avert growing danger from Moscow, sought to assume total control. To prevent this, the boyars supported the monasteries. The archimandrite, heading an extensive monastic community and appointed by the *veche*, offset the archbishop's power. During war or unrest, monastic treasure served Novgorod as a valuable resource.

Novgorod acquired control of vast territories in northern European Russia stretching to the Ural Mountains and the Arctic Ocean. Boyars and merchants organized their colonization, providing resources to outfit expeditions and hew routes through the wilderness. Novgorod's pioneer settlers subdued scattered natives, established forts, and were reinforced by monks. The entire White Sea coast became studded with settlements dependent on Novgorod's boyars or monasteries. These settlements supplied Novgorod with furs, fish, and forest products. In the more southerly regions of the Northern Dvina and Onega rivers the peasant commune prevailed. Novgorod's colonial regions, defended stubbornly and successfully against Muscovite incursions, were divided into five provinces, each subject to a borough and subdivided into districts (*volosti*). Novgorod appointed officials to administer this far-flung

empire and collect tribute, especially furs. The dependencies attempted to escape central administrative control, but except for Pskov, which secured broad autonomy, their revolts were suppressed.

Foreign trade accounted in considerable measure for Novgorod's wealth and prosperity. Since the time of the Varangians it had traded with the Baltic, and from the late 12th century its merchants concluded agreements with traders of Visby on Gotland Island and later with other German merchants of the Hanseatic League. Novgorod sent out merchants to other parts of Rus but rarely maintained them abroad. It lacked a commercial fleet, and its trade was handled largely by German merchants living in a separate settlement, the Peterhof, where they were exempt from arrest and constituted a closed corporation. Novgorod merchants organized trade guilds, the earliest and most powerful of which was the Ivanskoe *sto* (hundred). Novgorod exported furs, wax, and lumber and imported grains, woolens, wine, metals, and sweets. It served as intermediary between other Rus territories and the German world. After 1300 it gradually lost its trade monopoly with the Hanse as German merchants began using the western Dvina route and set up warehouses in Smolensk and Polotsk. After that Novgorod traded increasingly with the rising centers of the northeast, Tver and Moscow. The Novgorod empire retained its commercial prosperity, based partly on its workshops and extensive domains, until the end of its independent existence. In the 15th century it included 18 towns. None of these rivaled Novgorod itself, which attracted agricultural and handicraft products from all parts of its empire. In many ways Novgorod's economy and institutions were comparable to those of the oligarchic commercial republics of Venice and Florence.

Novgorod society, like that of Kiev, remained diversified and relatively mobile. The boyar upper class derived its wealth from trade and ownership of large estates, which provided articles of export, and it controlled credit, moneylending, and the higher political offices. Soviet historians emphasized the "feudal" nature of this class, but it would

---

[4] Ianin's view is summarized in H. Birnbaum, *Lord Novgorod the Great* (Columbus, OH, 1981), pp. 85–88.

seem to have been concerned mainly with commerce rather than manorial landholding. The higher clergy was wealthy and influential, and numerous monasteries possessed large landholdings and enterprises. The clergy remained an open estate: Any citizen of Novgorod could be ordained, and any clergyman might become a layman. Lesser landowners or businessmen not belonging to the ruling aristocracy were known as *zhitye liudi* (well-off people). Merchants were counted as boyars or *zhitye liudi* depending on their wealth and landholdings. Lower-class urban dwellers, known as rye-bread eaters in contrast to the wealthier wheat-bread eaters, included artisans, petty tradesmen, and laborers and were designated collectively as *molodshie liudi* or *chernye liudi.* In rural areas there were free peasants, tenant farmers, and sharecroppers. Slaves (*kholopy*), owned by boyars and wealthy merchants, were more numerous in Novgorod than in Moscow. Although equality before the law was proclaimed by the statutes, it did not exist in actuality. The Novgorod Charter of 1471, like the *Russkaia Pravda* of Kiev, contained a scale of fines for injuring officials that revealed the extent of social inequality. The wealthy dominated the courts, and the poor often suffered injustice. Earlier the *veche* had sometimes defended the legal rights of ordinary citizens.

Soviet accounts stressed the intense class struggle in Novgorod, fueled by the growth of feudal landownership and the exploitation of peasants and the urban lower classes by the boyar-merchant aristocracy. Periodic interruptions of grain imports caused hunger among the city poor and contributed to several urban revolts. In the mid-15th century these social contradictions sharpened, claimed Soviet scholars, undermined Novgorod's unity, and contributed to its fall. The American historian Joel Raba agrees that the boyars, who had formerly fought among themselves, closed ranks, and the *veche* fostered cooperation among the ruling elements. However, Henrik Birnbaum argues that Soviet theories of a Novgorod working class opposing a unified feudal-capitalist urban aristocracy were oversim-

plifications. The boyars, probably not as class-conscious as Soviet scholars suggested, never formed a monolithic power bloc. After assuming full political power about 1400, the boyars fragmented into feuding factions that sought external support.[5]

Externally, Novgorod remained relatively secure from invasion. After repelling Western attacks by Swedes and the Teutonic Knights in the 13th century, it relied upon skillful diplomacy to balance itself between Lithuania and Moscow. Novgorod's political aim continued to be independence. By 1450, however, Moscow and Lithuania had absorbed most of the formerly independent Rus principalities. Early in the 15th century Novgorod had demonstrated its continuing viability by crushing efforts of its dependencies to break away with Moscow's support. Novgorod clearly had less to fear from Lithuania than from Moscow and thus sought friendly ties with lesser princes of the Lithuanian House of Gedymin. During the civil war in Muscovy between Vasili II and Dmitri Shemiaka, Novgorod supported Vasili's boyar opponents. But Novgorod was more dependent economically on Moscow than on Lithuania. Periodic conflicts with the Muscovites, besides costing Novgorod the areas of Torzhok, Vologda, and Volokolamsk, brought suspensions of grain deliveries and Oriental trade. Also, Novgorod had important political links with Moscow: Since about 1300 it had generally selected the Muscovite grand prince as its overlord because he could provide the most protection.

Vasili II's victory in the Muscovite civil war doomed the Novgorod republic. Resentful of Novgorod for supporting his enemies and granting asylum in 1452 to their leader, Dmitri Shemiaka, Vasili acted to restrict its freedom. In 1456 he led a successful military expedition against Novgorod and forced it to sign a humiliating peace. Novgorod preserved its formal independence but had to allow Vasili to collect a special tax (*chernyi bor*)

---

[5] J. Raba, "Novgorod in the Fifteenth Century: A Re-examination," *CSS* 1, no. 3 (Fall 1967): 348–64; and Birnbaum, *Lord Novgorod,* p. 99.

TASS from SOVFOTO

The port of the Novgorod republic at the time of Ivan III.

and Moscow to control its foreign policy. Oblivious of impending disaster, Novgorod's aristocratic factions struggled for power. An influential boyar group headed by the energetic *posadnitsa* (mayor) Marfa Boretskii looked to Lithuania for salvation and arranged for Michael Olelkovich, a lesser Gedymin prince, to become Novgorod's ruler. The Novgorod *veche* in a riotous session approved Boretskii's proposal of a formal alliance with Lithuania against Moscow. Ivan III of Moscow asserted promptly that such a treaty with Catholic Lithuania endangered the Orthodox faith and constituted treason to Rus. With a strenuous propaganda campaign Ivan secured the support of Tver and Novgorod's own dependencies, Pskov and Viatka. When Lithuania failed to send military assistance, Novgorod lay isolated and helpless.

The city-republic's internal disunity, though exaggerated by Soviet historians, contributed to its fall. The boyars, anxious to retain their lands, directed the opposition to Moscow and sought Lithuanian support. On the other hand, the Orthodox clergy feared that Catholic Lithuanians would subvert their church. Archbishop-elect

Feofil refused to send his cavalry against Orthodox Muscovites. Many commoners wavered, confused by the religious issue. To the lower classes good relations with Moscow meant cheap bread and more impartial justice. Consequently, the morale of the large citizen militia was low when it opposed Moscow. Novgorod's troops were untrained and inferior in quality to the smaller Muscovite forces. In 1470 a series of skirmishes culminated in the Battle of Shelon. The Novgorodians were badly beaten and had to accept permanent dependence on Moscow. In 1478, when the boyar party revolted against Muscovite domination, Ivan III sent a massive expedition against the city. Novgorod and its dominions were incorporated into Muscovy, almost doubling the latter's territory, and the *veche* bell was carried off to Moscow. During the 1480s thousands of boyars and merchants were deported and their lands distributed to Muscovite gentry. In 1494 foreign merchants in Novgorod were seized and the Peterhof closed. A window on Europe had been slammed shut.

Pskov, Novgorod's so-called younger brother and its former dependency, suffered a similar fate.

Pskov had developed as early as the eighth century along the Velikaia River trade route, and by the 10th century it was involved in commerce with east and west. Governed in the earlier years by a mayor sent from Novgorod, Pskov after 1260 was ruled at times by Lithuanian princes and came under strong Lithuanian influence. However, the Lithuanian Prince Dovmont, serving in Pskov (1265–1299), led its forces against Lithuania and the Teutonic Knights. In its political and social institutions Pskov resembled Novgorod, but it possessed no colonies. Flourishing from the transit trade with the Baltic, it emancipated itself gradually from direct Novgorodian control. A treaty of 1348 recognized its independence, though Novgorod retained a shadowy suzerainty. When Novgorod proved unable to protect it from the Teutonic Knights, Pskov turned once again to Lithuania. Pskov had a sovereign *veche*, which remained genuinely democratic throughout the 15th century; a prince with limited powers; a council of notables; and two elected mayors. Though suffering from sharp social tensions, Pskov acted consistently as Russia's chief defensive bastion on the west. During Ivan III's reign it recognized Moscow's supremacy, and in 1510 it was formally incorporated into Muscovy.

The conquest by Moscow of the flourishing and vital northwest Russian commercial republics resulted from their internal weaknesses and the simultaneous consolidation of Muscovite absolutism (see Chapter 10). Moscow under Ivan III united eastern Russia's power and resources against city-states that were more advanced culturally and economically but far less cohesive politically. One can surely question Soviet assertions that the fall of these city-states was "progressive" and "historically inevitable." The émigré Russian scholar A. V. Issatchenko asserted that had Novgorod and Pskov been given the opportunity to link themselves with the West, Russia might have overtaken western Europe in the late 16th century.[6] A power-hungry boyar elite may

have doomed the Novgorod republic, but nowhere else in medieval Russia except Pskov did a community approach political self-expression and self-determination as closely as Novgorod. Moscow's destruction and absorption of the commercial republics reduced subsequent chances for Russia to develop representative institutions.

Lithuania

From the 13th century the grand principality of Lithuania, with a large east Slavic and Orthodox population, became an important, powerful, and often independent eastern European state. During the Mongol era Lithuania played a key role in Russian politics; from 1569 to 1795, it constituted part of the Polish-Lithuanian commonwealth.

German sources cite the name Lithuania as early as 1009, and a Lithuanian tribe is mentioned from 1040. Pagan Lithuania emerged during the 11th century as an opponent of the Rus principalities and in the 12th century as a foe of Poland. While neighboring Baltic tribes fell under foreign rule, the coming of the redoubtable Teutonic Knights in Livonia and Prussia (1206–1226) stimulated princes of the Ryngoldas family to undertake Lithuania's unification. As the tribal system in rural areas disintegrated, local organizations of Lithuanian noblemen assumed leadership. Prominent among them was the dynamic Prince Mindaugas who ruled over Novgorod-Litovsk in so-called "Black Russia." After eliminating some of his relatives, he unified most of Lithuania by 1250. Facing enemies on all sides, Mindaugas defeated the Livonian Order while his remaining relatives became rulers of Polotsk and Vitebsk. Thus as its inhabitants sought protection from Mongols and German Teutonic knights, much of Belorussia (White Russia) came under Lithuanian control. Mindaugas, his family, and many other Lithuanians were baptized as Roman Catholics. In 1253, receiving a crown from the pope in Rome, Mindaugas became king of Lithuania. The warlike Lithuanians adopted Russian techniques of training and organization as well as Russian language and culture.

---

[6] A. V. Issatchenko, "Esli by v kontse XV veka . . . ," *Wiener Slavistisches Jahrbuch* 18 (1973): 48–55.

For the next century Mindaugas and his successors, ruling Lithuania, Samogitia, "Black Russia," and portions of Belorussia, resisted growing Germanic pressure from the north and fought the princes of Volhynia and Galicia to the south. Traidenis's rule (1270–1282) completed the unification of Lithuanian tribes into a strong state and saw a major pagan revival that antagonized Orthodox Russians. The able Gediminas (ruled 1316–1341) founded the Grand Principality of Lithuania with a sound administration. Allied with Poland and sometimes with Tver and Riga, Gediminas repelled persistent attacks by the Teutonic Knights. His new dynasty, continuing Lithuanian expansion in the south and east, strengthened ties with Russians through political marriages, extended direct rule over Belorussia, and moved into Volhynia and Galicia. Russian states that were annexed to Lithuania—including Smolensk and eventually Kiev—retained their own language and laws. Under Gediminas Lithuania became a major eastern European power, increasingly Slavic in institutions, language, and culture. Forging friendly relations with the port of Riga, Gediminas channeled Baltic trade through his domains. While most Lithuanians remained pagan, princes who married Russian wives converted to Greek Orthodoxy.

Further Lithuanian southward expansion into Volhynia and Galicia occurred during the dual reign of Algirdas (1345–1377) and Kestutis (1345–1382), two of Gediminas's sons. As the Golden Horde's hold over western Russia loosened, Lithuania reconquered much former Mongol territory (see Map 7.2). By the late 14th century two powerful states had formed in Russia: Lithuania in the west and Moscow in the east. After recapturing Kiev and Podolia from the Mongols, Algirdas in 1363 defeated three Tatar khans at Sinie Vody (Blue Waters) near the mouth of the Bug River and reached the Black Sea. His relations with Moscow grew strained because both were competing for preeminence in Russia. Supporting Moscow's rival, the prince of Tver, Algirdas twice appeared before Moscow but did not assault the Kremlin's new stone walls.

At Algirdas's death, his son, Jogaila, succeeded him as grand prince of Lithuania, feuding with his uncle, Kestutis, until he had Kestutis killed in 1382. Unable to repel the formidable Teutonic Knights unaided, Jogaila married Queen Jadwiga of Poland, also becoming ruler of Poland as King Wladyslaw. In 1385 Jogaila (Polish: Jagiello) signed the Union of Krevo, which signified the virtual incorporation of Lithuania into Poland. He and most Lithuanians abandoned an anachronistic paganism for Catholicism; Lithuanian noble converts obtained all the privileges of the Polish nobility. However, Russian elements opposed restrictions on Orthodoxy, and Lithuanians resented Polish efforts to destroy Lithuania's separate status. In 1392 Jogaila had to recognize the opposition's leader, Vitovt (Lithuanian: Vytautas) as grand prince of Lithuania. After a grand coalition of Lithuania, Russian, and Polish forces defeated the Teutonic Knights decisively at Tannenberg (1410), the Polish-Lithuanian union was modified. Lithuania's incorporation into Poland was reaffirmed, but Lithuanian nobles were allowed to elect the next grand prince subject to Polish approval.

Securing full Lithuanian autonomy, Vitovt (ruled 1392–1430) became the most powerful ruler in eastern Europe. In wars with Moscow he captured Smolensk and, aided by Mongol devastation of Moscow's domains, steadily extended his influence north and east. In 1427 Tver principality recognized Vitovt as its suzerain. At age 80 this mighty warrior finally died after falling from his horse.

A lengthy political crisis followed, but civil strife in Moscow and the Golden Horde prevented them from exploiting it. Lithuanian and Belorussian princes elected Vitovt's cousin Svidrigailo grand prince of Lithuania, but the Poles rejected his claims, proposing instead Vitovt's brother, Sigismund. Conspiracy and strife ended with Sigismund's assassination. In 1442 Lithuanian magnates chose Jogaila's young son, Casimir, as grand prince, and he reunified most Lithuanian lands. In 1445 Poland and Lithuania were

Map 7.2 Lithuanian-Russian state in the 14th century

reunited, largely on Polish terms. Soon thereafter Casimir also became king of Poland and resided in Krakow, but Lithuania remained a separate state. By the Treaty of 1449 Casimir and Vasili II of Moscow pledged mutual nonintervention and assistance to each other against the Mongols, which helped Vasili II consolidate control over eastern Russia (see Chapter 10).

Suggested Additional Reading

NOVGOROD

BARON, S. H. "The Town in Feudal Russia." *SR* 28 (1969): 116–22.

BEAZLEY, R. "The Russian Expansion towards Asia . . . to 1500." *AHR* 13 (1907–8): 731–41.

BIRNBAUM, H. *Lord Novgorod the Great: Essays in the History and Culture of a Medieval City-State* (Columbus, OH, 1981).

———. "Lord Novgorod the Great: Its Place in Medieval Culture." *Viator* 8 (1977): 215–54.

DEJEVSKY, N. J. "Novgorod: the Origins of a Russian Town," in *European Towns . . .* , ed. M. W. Barley (London, 1977), pp. 391–403.

FLORINSKY, M. *Russia: A History and an Interpretation,* vol. 1 (New York, 1953), pp. 110–25.

KLIUCHEVSKY, V. O. *Course of Russian History,* vol. 1 (New York, 1911), pp. 319–69.

LANGER, L. "The Posadnichestvo of Pskov . . . " *SR* 43, no. 1 (1983): 46–62.

———. "V. L. Ianin and the History of Novgorod." *SR* 33 (1974): 114–19.

LEVIN, E. "The Role and Status of Women in Medieval Novgorod." Ph.D. diss., Indiana University, 1983.

———, ed. "Studies of Medieval Novgorod." *SSH* 23, no. 4 (Spring 1985).

———. "Women and Property in Medieval Novgorod: Dependence and Independence." *RH* 10, pt. 2 (1983): 154–64.

MITCHELL, R., and N. FORBES, eds. *The Chronicles of Novgorod (1016–1471)* (London, 1914). Excerpts in *Readings in Russian Civilization,* 2d ed., vol. 1, ed. T. Riha (Chicago, 1969), pp. 20–46.

RABA, J. "Church and Foreign Policy in the Fifteenth-Century Novgorodian State." *CSS* 13, nos. 1–2 (1979): 52–58.

———. "The Fate of the Novgorodian Republic." *SEER* (July 1967): 307–23.

———. "Novgorod in the Fifteenth Century." *CSS* I (Fall 1967): 48–64.

SMITH, R. E. "Some Recent Discoveries in Novgorod." *Past and Present* 3, no. 5 (1954): 1–10.

THOMPSON, W. W., ed. *Novgorod the Great: Excavations of the Medieval City . . .* (New York, 1967).

VERNADSKY, G. "Novgorod," in *Russia at the Dawn of the Modern Age* (New Haven, 1959), pp. 27–66.

YANINE, V. L. "The Dig at Novgorod," in *Readings in Russian Civilization,* 2d ed., vol. 1, ed. T. Riha (Chicago, 1969), pp. 47–59.

LITHUANIA

BACKUS, O. *Motives of West Russian Nobles in Deserting Lithuania for Moscow, 1377–1514* (Lawrence, KS, 1957).

GERUTIS, A., ed. *Lithuania 700 Years,* 2d ed. (New York, 1969).

HALECKI, O. *From Florence to Brest, 1439–1596* (Rome, 1958).

JURGELA, C. R. *History of the Lithuanian Nation* (New York, 1948).

OKINSHEVICH, L. *The Law of the Grand Duchy of Lithuania: Background and Bibliography* (New York, 1953).

ROWELL, S. C. *Lithuania Ascending: A Pagan Empire within East-Central Europe, 1295–1655* (Cambridge, 1996).

SENN, A. *The Emergence of Modern Lithuania* (New York, 1959).

SOBEL, L. "The Grand Principality of Lithuania." *MERSH* 20: 63–68.

VERNADSKY, G. *The Mongols and Russia* (New Haven, 1953).

8

The Rise of Moscow

While the Golden Horde ruled Rus from its steppe capital of Sarai, the obscure Moscow principality on the southern fringe of the grand principality of Vladimir rose to prominence and power. In the 14th century Moscow emerged as Vladimir's successor and the center of both grand princely authority and the Orthodox church. Winning a difficult competition with Tver, another new principality, Moscow became the focus of religious, political, and economic life in northeast Rus. The unexpected victory of Moscow's Prince Dmitri "Donskoi" over Mamai's Mongol army in 1380 shattered the myth of Tatar invincibility and confirmed Moscow's leadership among Rus principalities. How did Moscow achieve such striking successes? Historians cite factors such as excellent geographic position, superior economic resources, astute and long-lived princes, support from the Orthodox church, and a special relationship with the Golden Horde. Did Moscow's rise reflect the artistic pattern woven by the great Russian historian V. O.

Kliuchevskii,[1] the disorderly ebb-and-flow process described in 1918 by A. E. Presniakov,[2] or the internal social and economic growth emphasized by Soviet historians?

The Moscow region has been inhabited for more than 5,000 years. During the 10th and 11th centuries the northern portion was settled apparently by the Krivichians, an east Slavic tribe, and by Slovene refugees from Novgorod. Another east Slavic tribe, the Viatichians, settled the southern part; Moscow's dialect was derived from theirs. The Viatichians, states *The Primary Russian Chronicle,* were of Polish origin and settled along the Oka River. The word *Moscow* (*Moskva*) is traced by some to the Slav word *mosk* (to soak) and the Ugro-Finnish *va* (river); others favor the Ugro-Finnish *mosk* (cow). The basin of the Moskva (Moscow) River, a tributary of the Oka, far from

---

[1] V. O. Kliuchevskii, *Kurs russkoi istorii (Course of Russian History),* vol. 2 (Moscow, 1937), pp. 3–27, originally published 1904–11.

[2] A. E. Presniakov, *The Formation of the Great Russian State* (Chicago, 1970), pp. 45ff. This was originally published in Petrograd in 1918.

SOVFOTO

Moscow in the 12th century, located on the present Kremlin Hill.

being a primeval wilderness in the 11th century, was apparently thickly settled.[3]

Founding and Early Development

The town of Moscow, originally Kuchkovo, seems to have been founded on the lands of an independent-minded boyar, Kuchka. Allegedly, Kuchka refused to pay homage to the visiting Prince Iuri Dolgoruki of Suzdal, who ordered him killed. The town's name may have been changed to Moscow to eliminate memories of the defiant Kuchka. Later, in 1174, his family gained revenge by killing Iuri Dolgoruki's son, Prince Andrei Bogoliubskii.

Russian chronicles first mention Moscow under the year 1147 as a frontier town of the grand principality of Vladimir. That year, now accepted officially as marking the birth of Moscow, Prince Iuri Dolgoruki summoned a distant prince to a meeting with these words: "Come to me, brother, in Moscow." Whether it was then already a town or

merely a princely estate is unknown. In 1156 Iuri reportedly established Moscow as a fortified town. On today's Kremlin Hill he surrounded this settlement with a wooden palisade. Making Moscow a fortress town reflected Iuri Dolgoruki's policy of creating strategic and commercial centers to protect Suzdalia's western border.

Turbulent events in northern Rus provided the background for Moscow's rise. From the late 12th century to the Mongol invasion of 1237, first Suzdal and then Vladimir assumed from Kiev the mantle of all-Russian leadership. During the reign of Andrei Bogoliubskii as grand prince of Vladimir, the Moscow Kremlin was considerably enlarged. Its earthen fortifications were reinforced with rows of logs fastened together with wooden hooks. Moscow and the surrounding villages were burned down during an invasion of Suzdalia in 1177 by Prince Gleb of Riazan, but they were quickly rebuilt. In 1207 Moscow was a concentration point for the army of Grand Prince Vsevolod III ("Big Nest") for a raid on Chernigov principality. Vsevolod installed relatives and obedient princes in Moscow and Novgorod and led resistance to German and Lithuanian incursions from the west. He attacked the Volga Bulgars in the east and vigorously colonized the upper Volga valley.

---

[3] *History of Moscow: An Outline* (Moscow, 1981), p. 13; and H. Paszkiewicz, *The Rise of Moscow's Power* (Boulder, CO, 1983), pp. 175–78.

The chronicles mention Moscow several times after Andrei Bogoliubskii's death in 1174 as a town through which princes passed on journeys and campaigns. Whereas some Soviet scholars asserted that by 1200 Moscow was the capital of a separate principality, the Russian historian Presniakov doubts that an independent Moscow principality existed even in the mid-13th century. However, fierce struggles over its possession suggest Moscow's growing political and economic importance.

Far from the main centers of Suzdalia, young Moscow, developing on the crossroads between the Dnieper and Volga waterways, went to various junior princes of the dynasty of Vsevolod III. Moscow was described by the *Chronicle* as already sizable and densely populated when in 1237 the Mongols burned it and its wooden churches, killed its prince, and departed with much loot. The chronicles provide no more detailed information until 1283, suggesting that Moscow was important mainly as part of Vladimir grand principality. Granted in 1263 to Daniel Aleksandrovich, youngest son of Prince Alexander Nevskii, Moscow thereafter was apparently the capital of a separate principality.

Moscow versus Tver

The Mongol invasion changed conditions in the northeast fundamentally. Suzdalia's trade declined, its colonization eastward halted, and its power waned. As Novgorod and Pskov assumed the chief burden of defending Rus against western invaders, the authority of the Vladimir grand prince declined grievously. Becoming wholly dependent on the Golden Horde, he abandoned his role of leadership and coordination. Some other northern Rus princes now sought to acquire power rather than lands or dynastic seniority. After 1300, "new towns," notably Tver and Moscow, emerged as independent entities contending for the position of declining Vladimir, affirmed Presniakov.

A favorable geographic location and alliance with the Golden Horde promoted Moscow's rise, argued Kliuchevskii. Lying on the Moskva River at the intersection of several major trade routes, Moscow was guarded by dense forests on the east, and to the west more forests and marshes provided considerable protection from external attack. Uprooted by Mongol raids elsewhere, migrants flocked to the Moscow region from the north, west, and south. Settling along the rivers, the newcomers later penetrated their interior tributaries. Even before Moscow became politically important, it attracted titled servitors and princes from many parts of Russia. Its commerce expanded rapidly, providing its princes with customs revenues and helping them outpace their rivals economically.

Moscow, claimed Kliuchevskii, became the ethnographic center of Great Russia. During the 13th and 14th centuries, while Mongols and Lithuanians blocked colonization outside the Volga-Oka region, Moscow's central position and forests protected its growing population from their depredations. Before 1368 Moscow suffered little from Mongol raids, which laid waste to more exposed Riazan, Iaroslavl, and Smolensk. Generally, Kliuchevskii underestimated external factors such as the Mongol invasion and Lithuanian pressure in explaining Moscow's rise. The Moscow princes' position within the House of Riurik, he argued, fostered their untraditional and defiant course. At first they could not aspire to the grand princely throne in Vladimir because of their junior status. They had to provide for their security by bold, untraditional policies. Externally, the Moscow princes were aggressive, the sworn enemies of the grand prince of Vladimir; at home they won a reputation as careful administrators and proprietors.

In the 14th century Moscow gained rapidly in area and power. In 1300 it was an insignificant principality smaller than the present Moscow province. From this central core it expanded in all directions, much as did the French monarchy from the Ile de France around Paris. Just after 1300 the conquest of strategic Mozhaisk on the west and of Kolomna to the south almost tripled Moscow's territory, gave it full control of the Moskva River, and allowed it to exploit its strategic situation at the intersection of trade routes from the east, south, and west. Moscow's southern borders were extended far enough along the Oka River to afford it additional protection against Mongol raids and bring it close to the borders of Riazan principality. Moscow grew by conquest, by settlement of the Volga region, by purchase of territory from other princes, by Mongol military aid, and by treaties with neighboring princes.

Recently the Polish historian Henryk Pasz-kiewicz has disputed Kliuchevskii's arguments. Geographic position, he affirms, did not bring Moscow to the fore. Many other cities, equally well located on convenient river routes, failed to become important politically. The Moskva River basin, with sandy, infertile soil and dense forest interspersed by marshes, could not have attracted many settlers. The soil of Moscow's chief rival, Tver, he adds, was even less fertile. There is nothing in contemporary sources to suggest major migra-tions to Moscow or Tver, or that Moscow was a safe haven from Tatar incursions. After all, Moscow had been easily captured and destroyed by the Mongols in the winter of 1237–1238 while rivers and marshes were frozen. In 1293 Moscow, like other parts of the grand principality of Vladimir, was again devastated by the Tatars. The causes of the rise of Moscow and Tver, Paszkiewicz concludes, should be sought in the external balance of forces and political relations among Vsevolod III's descendants rather than in geographic assets.[4]

In the early 14th century Moscow's most dan-gerous rival was Tver principality. Lying at the confluence of the Volga and Tvertsa rivers about 100 miles northwest of Moscow, Tver had a superb location for trade but was open to attack from all sides. Tver, first mentioned in the chronicles under the year 1209, was apparently settled during the 10th century. At first regarded by Novgorod as an outpost on its border with Suzdalia, Tver for a time was ruled by the princes of Pereiaslavl. After the Mongol conquest its strategic position domi-nating the best route from Suzdalia to Novgorod and its relative security brought it numerous

inhabitants. In 1304, when the contest of Moscow and Tver for supremacy in the northeast began, there was little to choose between them economi-cally or politically; Tver was the stronger militarily. Probably for that reason, the Golden Horde, in order to maintain a balance of power in the east, aided Moscow repeatedly against Tver and against Lithuanian efforts to expand eastward.

Tver and Moscow fought over possession of the grand princely throne in Vladimir and over control of Novgorod. During their contest Prince Mikhail of Tver (1304–1318) sought unwisely to depose Metropolitan Peter, leader of the Orthodox church, who henceforth backed Moscow effectively. In 1317 Mikhail badly defeated a larger Muscovite army at Bortenovo, but the following year the Horde intervened and granted the grand princely title to Prince Iuri Danilovich of Moscow. Mikhail of Tver was condemned and executed in Sarai, capital of the Horde. The Mongols carefully supervised Iuri Danilovich's actions as grand prince. Then, in 1327, Tver revolted against local Mongol merchants and troops, an action that the Tatars may have provoked deliberately. Prince Ivan I of Moscow received support from a powerful Mongol punitive force that captured Tver and sacked it mercilessly. Tver's pretensions to supremacy were shattered; it took the city almost 40 years to recover from this blow. Moscow's success in competition with Tver owed more to initial military weakness than to strength. The Golden Horde and the Orthodox church had proved to be indispensable allies.

Ivan I and His Successors

Ivan I (1328–1340), known as Kalita, or "money-bags," exploited Tver's misfortune to become grand prince of Moscow and Vladimir, as Lithuan-ian pressure on western Russia, especially against Novgorod, helped solidify relations between Moscow and the Horde. In 1328, by shrewd diplo-macy and perhaps bribery, Ivan apparently obtained the khan's patent as grand prince of Vladimir. According to Moscow chronicles, this ushered in a period of peace in northeast Russia; actually, it seems to have been an era of tension

---

[4] Paszkiewicz, *Rise of Moscow's Power,* pp. 199–202.

and instability. Ivan made at least four long trips to Sarai (1332–1339) and followed Mongol instructions carefully. Faced with Lithuanian expansion, the Horde preferred to grant increased authority to the Moscow prince, who now became collector of tribute money from all of the northeastern princes. Simultaneously, Moscow became Russia's chief religious center. After Kiev's fall the metropolitan of the Orthodox church had transferred his headquarters to Vladimir, but on visits to the south he sometimes stayed over in Moscow. A close friendship developed between Ivan I and Metropolitan Peter, who died and was buried in Moscow in 1326. His successor, Theognostus, took up residence in Moscow, became its zealous supporter, and intervened in Novgorod and Pskov on Ivan's behalf. Great material contributions began to flow into Moscow church coffers, and the first stone churches were built in Moscow between 1326 and 1333. After two severe fires Moscow was largely rebuilt; the Kremlin was built of stout oak. The church, centering in Moscow, provided a spiritual basis for unification of Great Russia. Russian 19th-century historians, such as Soloviev and Kliuchevskii, tended to exaggerate Kalita's achievements, hailing him as Moscow's first great statesman and gatherer of the Russian lands. Actually, Moscow's domains increased very little under his rule, and he failed to maintain his authority in Novgorod. Ivan I maintained supremacy over other east Russian princes only by complete subservience to and with the aid of the Golden Horde.

Ivan Kalita's successors consolidated Moscow's strength and sought with varying fortune to maintain its newfound preeminence among north Russian states. In 1340, right after Kalita's death, his son Simeon the Proud (Semen Ivanovich, 1340–1353), Simeon's brothers, and other princes of the grand principality of Vladimir journeyed to Sarai. There Khan Uzbek finally issued a patent (*iarlyk*) to Simeon as grand prince of Moscow and Vladimir. Only a year later the princes had to return to be confirmed in office by the new khan, Chanibek. During his reign Simeon undermined opposition to his rule as grand prince by fomenting discord within the large ruling family of Tver. Although Simeon managed to retain his grand princely title, he remained most insecure because that title was wholly subject to Mongol control. Nonetheless, historians normally credit him with reducing the grand principality's dependence on the Horde. Simeon's brother and successor as grand prince, Ivan II (1353–1359), Paszkiewicz concludes, strengthened Moscow's leading role by conciliating his kinsmen and other Russian princes. In east Russia the Horde remained the only truly independent agent, as did Lithuania in the west. Moscow could merely maneuver within narrow limits. Inspired by a sober realism, Ivan II in his brief reign enhanced Moscow's position.

Dmitri Ivanovich and the Battle of Kulikovo

The reign of Dmitri Ivanovich (1359–1389), later dubbed "Donskoi" (of the Don River) for his victory at Kulikovo in 1380, was an era of crisis with significant results for the history of Russia. As internal divisions grew among the Mongols and within Russia, the old appanage order gradually weakened. When the smoke cleared, a new pattern was taking shape: Moscow's power had increased greatly relative to that of the troubled Horde, which had 22 different rulers between 1357 and 1377. The first of these, Berdibek, murdered 12 brothers in order to seize the throne! Apparently Dmitri Ivanovich, becoming Moscow's ruler at nine, displayed shrewdness and initiative very early. In 1363 his army entered Vladimir (see Map 8.1) and expelled his rival, Dmitri of Suzdal; contemporary chronicles stressed Moscow's military superiority. Dmitri Ivanovich cleverly exploited the Horde's disunity. By the 1360s, as the Horde disintegrated, the power of appointment to the throne of Vladimir was passing inexorably into Russian hands. After the death of Dmitri Ivanovich's younger brother Iuri of Zvenigorod in 1364, Moscow became a compact and prosperous state, able to overawe other principalities militarily and politically. Moscow now repeatedly interfered to determine the rulers of other states such as

Map 8.1 Muscovy, 1340–1389

Rostov and Galich. Lithuanian pressure from the west was also driving east Rus princes together under Dmitri Ivanovich. The Orthodox church under Metropolitan Alexis ably seconded Dmitri's policies, which created bases for eventual Great Russian unity.

During this chaotic period the most powerful Mongol leader was Khan Mamai. From his power base west of the Volga, Mamai in the 1370s allied himself with Tver principality, whose princes continued their fateful rivalry with Moscow. Mamai awarded the *iarlyk* for the throne of Vladimir to Mikhail of Tver, but Vladimir refused to accept

Mikhail as grand prince. In 1375 an alliance of princes in northeastern Rus led by Moscow compelled Tver to accept a humiliating treaty confirming it as Moscow's "younger brother." Khan Mamai's army, seeking to disperse this Moscow-led coalition, met defeat at the Vozha River (1378). With Mamai determined to avenge this setback and punish his disobedient Rus vassals, the stage was set for a showdown between the Horde and Dmitri Ivanovich.

In 1380, refusing Mongol demands for additional tribute, Dmitri Ivanovich mobilized an army of princely and town contingents to defend Rus against Mamai. Acting as grand prince of Vladimir,

Dmitri "sent out envoys to all the princes and military commanders of Rus" to assemble at Kolomna with their forces. Some chronicles claim that Dmitri gathered 200,000 to 400,000 men, but a Soviet account estimated his army at 70,000.[5] The mood in Rus, noted later chronicles, resembled that in Greece before the Battle of Marathon. Few Russians believed that Dmitri could defeat the supposedly invincible Mongols. Princes and towns from many parts of Rus responded, but Novgorod, Tver, and Nizhnii-Novgorod refused to send troops. Seeking to save his own principality, Oleg of Riazan bargained with both sides, then sided with the Mongols. Concluding alliances with Prince Jogaila of Lithuania and with Oleg of Riazan, Khan Mamai swelled his forces with auxiliaries from the Volga, the Caucasus, and the Crimea. Here are excerpts from one chronicle account of the epic Battle of Kulikovo:

> That year Prince Mamai of the Horde, accompanied by other princes and all the Tartar and Polovtsi forces . . . , and supported by Iagailo of Lithuania and Oleg of Riazan, advanced against Grand Prince Dmitri and on September 1 made a camp on the bank of the Oka River. . . . The Grand Prince went to the Church of the Mother of God, where he prayed for a long time; . . . [then] he sent for all the Russian princes, voevodas, and all the people. . . . There never was such a mighty Russian army, for all forces combined numbered some 200,000. . . . Mamai's camp was in a meadow not far from the Don where, with all his forces, he awaited for about three weeks the arrival of Iagailo [Jogaila]. . . .
>
> When Mamai learned of the arrival of the Grand Prince at the Don . . . he said, "Let us move toward the Don before Iagailo arrives there. . . ." At six in the morning the godless Tartars appeared in the field and faced the Christians. There was a great multitude of both; and when these two great forces met they covered an area thirteen versts long. And there was a great massacre and bitter warfare and great noise, such as there never had been in the Russian principalities; and they fought

from six to nine, and blood flowed like a heavy rain and there were many killed on both sides. . . . Shortly thereafter, the godless fled and the Christians pursued them.[6]

As Map 8.2 shows, the Russian army, composed of contingents from most principalities, gathered at Kolomna, south of Moscow. Under the command of Prince Dmitri Ivanovich ("Donskoi") of Moscow, it advanced southward, crossed the Don River, and attacked Mamai's army. The Mongol forces had moved northward to await the arrival of Prince Jogaila's Lithuanians. However, Jogaila failed to arrive. The contingent of Prince Oleg of Riazan originally sided with Mamai but then turned back.

Defeat at Kulikovo shattered the legend of Mongol invincibility. Almost half of the participants on both sides were killed or wounded. Mamai's army disintegrated and fled, and it took the victorious Russian survivors a week to bury their dead. This costly Rus victory resulted from the wise decision of Dmitri "Donskoi" to attack the main Mongol army in the open fields beyond the Don before it could link up with Lithuanian and Riazani forces and invade northeast Russia. Priestly chroniclers dramatized Kulikovo as a crusade against Muslim tyranny; Soviet scholars viewed it as a great national triumph that laid the basis for Russia's subsequent unification and independence. On the surface Kulikovo changed Russo-Tatar relations remarkably little. The army of Dmitri "Donskoi" was too battered to exploit its victory. Northern Rus princes promptly reverted to their habitual disunity, so only two years later Dmitri Ivanovich had to abandon Moscow to the avenging army of Khan Tokhtamysh. Once again Moscow and northern Rus had to submit to Mongol overlordship. However, "gathering the Russian lands" soon resumed, and Dmitri "Donskoi" now proudly called himself "Grand prince of all Russia."

---

[5] *Kulikovskaia bitva* (Moscow, 1980), p. 226.

[6] B. Dmytryshyn, *Medieval Russia: A Source Book, 900–1700* (Hinsdale, IL, 1972), pp. 165–67.

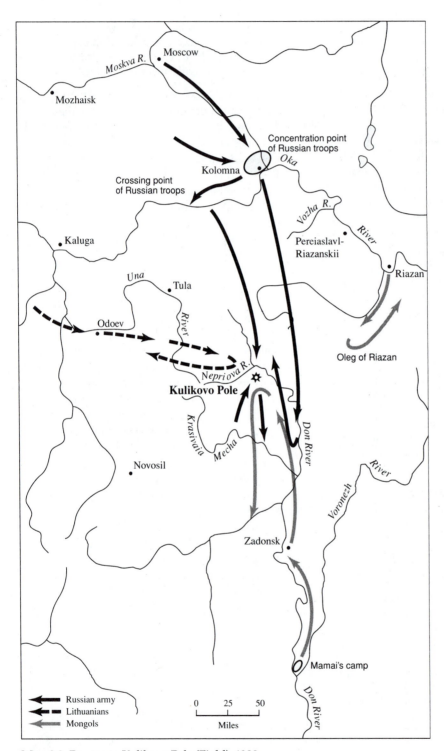

Map 8.2 Routes to Kulikovo Pole (Field), 1380

Russian Historians on Moscow's Rise

Western scholars still tend to accept as accurate much of the imaginative and majestic theory of Moscow's rise advanced by the early 20th-century Russian scholar Kliuchevskii. Politically, Kliuchevskii divided the Russian middle ages into two sharply distinct and contrasting eras. The first was an era of feudal division and disintegration, beginning with Kiev's decline after 1139, when Rus fragmented into hundreds of hereditary princely appanages (*udely*). Then about 1300 began a dramatic reversal, when Moscow's princes started gathering the territories of northern Rus into what became the Muscovite autocratic state. Kliuchevskii summarized:

> During the fourteenth century the north Russian population with the Moscow principality and its prince: . . . (1) came to regard the Moscow grand prince as a model ruler-administrator, creator of civil peace and order, and his principality as the point of departure for a new system of political relationships whose first result was the creation of greater internal peace and external security. (2) They became accustomed to regard the senior Muscovite prince as Russia's national leader in the struggle with external enemies, and Moscow as responsible for the first national victories over pagan Lithuania . . . (3) Finally, northern Russia became accustomed to regard the Moscow prince as the eldest son of the Russian church . . . with whom were bound up the religious and moral interests of the Orthodox Russian people.[7]

In the 1950s the Russian émigré historian Michael T. Florinsky questioned the "logical perfection and consistency" of Kliuchevskii's scheme, arguing that history can seldom be fitted into such nice patterns without major distortion:

> Less romantically minded historians would hesitate to use such a metaphysical concept as that of a new ethnographical formation—in this case Great Russia—"waiting for a leader"

and when the leader was somewhat suddenly discovered, carrying him "to the exalted heights of the sovereign of Great Russia."[8]

Presniakov has written the most comprehensive pre-Soviet Russian account of Moscow's rise.[9] Unlike Kliuchevskii, who treated Muscovite and Kievan Russia as wholly distinct and different chapters in the country's history, Presniakov stressed their close connection and held that Great Russia represented a union between the Novgorod and Suzdalian regions. Whereas Kliuchevskii described successive and sharply contrasting eras of feudal division and unification, Presniakov argued that these processes had existed simultaneously and that the formation of Muscovy was one of ebb and flow. Kliuchevskii emphasized the gathering of lands by Moscow's rulers, but Presniakov depicted the unification of Great Russia as a gradual accumulation of authority and sovereignty by the grand prince of Moscow, achieved by the destruction in fact and the denial in principle of customary law in favor of autocracy.

Early Soviet historians stressed economic factors in Moscow's rise virtually to the exclusion of political ones. Thus M. N. Pokrovskii viewed the 15th-century Muscovite state as "a huge association of feudal landowners" that swallowed its rivals because of Moscow's exceptionally favorable location for trade. The feudal, appanage order was being destroyed by the shift from a natural to a commercial economy and by the creation of a broader market. As early as the 13th century, Moscow had been a populous commercial center with financial resources providing a sound basis for unification. Once the Moscow prince became grand prince of Vladimir, a Novgorod-Moscow alliance became an economic necessity for both parties.[10]

---

[7] Kliuchevskii, *Kurs*, vol. 2, pp. 26–27.

[8] M. T. Florinsky, *Russia: A History and an Interpretation,* vol. 1 (New York, 1953), p. 77.

[9] Presniakov, *Formation.*

[10] M. N. Pokrovskii, "Obrazovanie Moskovskogo gosudarstva," *Russkaia istoriia s drevneishikh vremen,* vol. 1 (Moscow, 1933), pp. 119–57.

After World War II Soviet historians, rejecting Pokrovskii's commercial theory, emphasized instead radical changes in agricultural technology as paving the way for unification around Moscow. The introduction of the three-field system and better plows and better economic conditions attracted landowners, peasants, and artisans to Muscovy. What enriched Moscow was less its location for trade than "the plow, the scythe, and manure on the peasant's fields." Other Soviet scholars, such as V. V. Mavrodin, objected that such an agricultural emphasis denied the significant role of towns and awakening national consciousness. "All progressive elements of the old Russian society [peasants, gentry, merchants, and so on] . . . gravitated toward the grand prince who personified the unity of Russia."[11]

In the post-Stalin era Soviet historians adopted a relatively balanced, multicausal interpretation of Moscow's rise. After 1300, noted *Istoriia SSSR*, when Russia began to recover from the Mongol invasion, agriculture grew, towns revived, and their commercial districts expanded. The existing feudal political division of Russia then hampered its socioeconomic development. External attacks by Mongols, Lithuanians, and Swedes hastened a process of unification that was supported by all progressive classes. Moscow's power, growing under Ivan Kalita, was enhanced by Dmitri's victory at Kulikovo, which helped liquidate feudal division. The growth of productive forces and culture established conditions for the creation of the Great Russian people and language.[12] Later Soviet historians, while emphasizing economic and social factors, also included political aspects of Moscow's rise.

Kliuchevskii's traditional theory clearly requires much revision. The work of Presniakov and such Western scholars as Halperin and Crummey has convincingly shown linkage between the Kievan and Muscovite eras, undermining Kliuchevskii's interpretation of the bloody, chaotic events of appanage Rus. That work has also revealed the vital importance of the Horde's policies in the rise of Moscow. Soviet archaeological findings and intensive study of economic and social factors have deepened our understanding. Nonetheless, Kliuchevskii's classic account remains valuable when revised in the light of recent scholarship.

Suggested Additional Reading

BOOKS

ALMEDINGEN, E. M. *The Land of Muscovy: The History of Early Russia* (New York, 1972).

CRUMMEY, R. *The Formation of Muscovy, 1304–1613* (New York, 1987).

DIMNIK, M. *Mikhail, Prince of Chernigov and Grand Prince of Kiev, 1224–1246* (Toronto, 1981).

FENNELL, J. L. *The Crisis of Medieval Russia, 1200–1304* (London, 1983).

———. *The Emergence of Moscow, 1305–1359* (Berkeley, 1968).

HALPERIN, C. J. *Russia and the Golden Horde* (Bloomington, IN, 1985).

History of Moscow: An Outline (Moscow, 1981).

HOWES, R. C., ed. *The Testaments of the Grand Princes of Moscow* (Ithaca, NY, 1967).

IDE, C., and A. F. IDE. *Women in the Early Middle Ages* (Mesquite, TX, 1981). (Includes women in Russian history.)

KOLLMANN, N. *Kinship and Politics: The Making of the Muscovite Political System, 1345–1547* (Stanford, 1987).

MEYENDORFF, J. *Byzantium and the Rise of Russia: A Study of Byzantino-Russian Relations in the Fourteenth Century* (Cambridge, 1981).

NOWAK, F. *Medieval Slavdom and the Rise of Russia* (New York, 1970). (Reprint.)

PRESNIAKOV, A. E. *The Formation of the Great Russian State* (Chicago, 1970). (Trans. of Petrograd edition of 1918.)

———. *The Tsardom of Muscovy*, ed. and trans. R. F. Price (Gulf Breeze, FL, 1978).

SPULER, B. *The Mongols in History* (New York, 1971).

TIKHOMIROV, M. N. *The Towns of Ancient Rus* (Moscow, 1959).

---

[11] P. P. Smirnov, "Obrazovanie russkogo tsentralizovannogo gosudarstva v XIV–XV vv," *Voprosy istorii,* nos. 2–3 (1946): 89; ibid., no. 4 (1946): 52; and V. V. Mavrodin, *Obrazovanie edinogo russkogo gosudarstva* (Leningrad, 1951), p. 310.

[12] *Istoriia SSSR,* vol. 2 (Moscow, 1966), p. 65.

VERNADSKY, G. *The Mongols and Russia* (New Haven, 1953).

VOYCE, A. *Moscow and the Roots of Russian Culture* (Norman, OK, 1964).

ARTICLES

ANDREYEV, N. "Appanage and Muscovite Russia," in *Introduction to Russian History,* ed. R. Auty and D. Obolensky (Cambridge, 1976), pp. 78–120.

BIRKETT, G. A. "Slavonic Cities, 4: Moscow, 1147–1947." *SEER* 25 (1946): 336–55.

DEWEY, H. "Tales of Moscow's Founding." *CanAmS1St* 6 (1972): 595–605.

———. "The Tver Uprising of 1327 . . . " *JfGO* 15 (1967): 161–79.

HALPERIN, C. J. "The Concept of the Russian Land from the Ninth to the Fourteenth Century." *Rus. Hist.* 2, no. 1 (1974): 29–38.

———. "The Russian Land and the Russian Tsar: The Emergence of Muscovite Ideology, 1380–1408." *FOG* 23:7–103.

KAISER, D. "Church and State in Old Rus." *SR* 36, no. 4 (1977): 658–66.

OSTROWSKI, D. "The Mongol Origins of Muscovite Political Institutions," *SR* 49, no. 4 (1990): 525–42.

PHILIPP, W. "Russia's Position in Medieval Europe," in *Russia: Essays . . . ,* ed. L. Legters (Leiden, 1972), pp. 18–37.

RABA, J. "The Authority of the Muscovite Ruler at the Dawn of the Modern Era." *JfGO* 24, no. 3 (1976): 321–44.

WALCK, C. "Settlement Patterns in Rostov-Suzdal Rus, Ninth through the Thirteenth Century." Ph.D. diss., Harvard University, 1981.

WIECZYNSKI, J. L. "Toward a Frontier Theory of Early Russian History." *Rus. Rev.* 33, no. 3 (1974): 284–95.

9

Society, Culture, and Religion in Appanage Rus

he so-called appanage era—that is, the period of feudal division and political fragmentation of Rus from the mid-12th to the mid-15th centuries—served as a transitional stage in the evolution from Kievan to Muscovite Russia. Social relationships and religious and cultural traditions all developed from the Kievan period without any sharp break or abrupt change in direction. On the other hand, the Mongol invasion and the subsequent Tatar hegemony in Rus caused colossal disruptions and hardships for the Russian people. Life became more difficult and uncertain, but social and economic relations evolved generally along lines well established during the Kievan era.

The Mongol conquest, with its destruction of urban centers, depopulation, and destruction of life and property, altered profoundly the material level of Russian life. The destruction of so many cities was a calamitous blow because they had been centers of handicraft industry, trade, and culture. Long-established patterns of life and production were disrupted or disappeared altogether. The Mongol system of political dependence and reduction of the country's wealth by

imposition of heavy tribute, taxes, and conscription created an inhospitable atmosphere for cultural growth and contributed to economic and cultural stagnation, which made Russia lag significantly behind western Europe.

The Issue of Russian "Feudalism"

An analysis of Russian society and economic life in the appanage era must be preceded by a discussion of feudalism. Efforts to compare Russian institutions of the appanage era with those of feudal western Europe have provoked long and still unresolved historical controversy. Was appanage Russia "feudal"? Largely ignored by 19th-century scholars, this issue was argued sharply between 20th-century Western and Soviet historians of Russia.

Definitions of Feudalism

Feudalism, according to Marxism, is a socioeconomic stage through which every society must pass. Thus Soviet historians until the Gorbachev era had to assert that Russia experienced a feudal stage, broadly designating it as extending from 860 to 1861. Western historians have affirmed, however, that Russia's development differed markedly from western Europe's and point to the lack in Russia of a full-blown feudal order as evidence of that difference.

Both lines of argument have weaknesses. Soviet and Western scholars alike have tried to fit Russian development into abstract historical models. The Soviets' model features "feudal productive relations" in a socioeconomic system in which privileged "feudal lords" dominated peasant masses by monopolizing landownership and other political and judicial rights. Within that broad definition, appanage Rus possessed feudal characteristics.

Many Western historians, by contrast, rejected Soviet claims that Kievan and appanage Rus were feudal. George Vernadsky insisted that a truly feudal regime included a decentralized supreme political authority with a hierarchy of greater and lesser rulers (suzerain, vassals, subvassals) bound by personal contracts. Feudal society, stated Vernadsky, featured a manorial system restricting the peasants' legal status and distinguished between the right to own land and the right to use it. Finally, military service and landholding were linked. These elements, argued Vernadsky, characterized Western feudal societies, and their absence disqualified a society from being classified as feudal. He claimed that suzerain princes had political, economic, and judicial powers and delegated some of them in reciprocal contracts to vassals and subvassals. Thus Kievan and appanage Rus, lacking these features, were not feudal societies.

Soviet historians criticized Vernadsky for creating an "ideal type" of feudalism and measuring Rus society against it to determine whether it was feudal or not. The Soviet historian L.V. Cherepnin argued:

> Feudalism is not an ideally typical construction, not a scheme of development to which the concrete historical paths of separate peoples either correspond or from which they

deviate. Feudalism is a socioeconomic formation that represents a natural stage in its own specific way, and not according to a standard pattern.[1]

Cherepnin suggested that feudalism in Rus was unique and need not have conformed to Western feudalism. There are strong arguments favoring both points of view. Whether appanage Rus was feudal or not depends largely on one's choice of definitions.

Appanage Rus of the 13th to 15th centuries, however, clearly displayed more feudal characteristics than did Kievan Rus. Many features of appanage Rus's economy conformed to traditionally accepted forms of Western feudalism. Appanage Rus was essentially an agrarian society passing through a lengthy political and economic decline. Increasingly, military service was being performed by boyars and other princely servitors. Landholding had become the main source of political power and economic wealth, providing the landowner with extensive control over those living on his land. A manorial system was developing, and along with it a new form of land tenure that contrasted with *votchina,* or patrimonial landholding, was emerging: the *pomestie* system involving the temporary grant of land to a servitor in return for service.

There were important dissimilarities as well. For example, social relations were not determined by contracts of mutual fealty between prince and servitor. Boyars and other princely servitors, not vassals in the strict sense, were free to shift from one prince and take up service with another without jeopardizing their patrimonial rights. No feudal lawbooks or contracts spelling out relationships between lords and their servitors are known to have existed in medieval Rus. No clear-cut standards of rights and obligations governed the mutual relations of prince and servitor. The *votchina* holder was not obliged to perform service for his suzerain, although he often did. Finally, the

---

[1] L. V. Cherepnin et al., *Kritika burzhuaznykh kontsepsii istorii Rossii perioda feodalizma* (Moscow, 1962), p. 84.

peasantry's legal status did not begin to deteriorate seriously until the end of the 15th century.

Clearly, the socioeconomic systems of
appanage Rus and western Europe reveal differences and similarities. To label one feudal and the
other nonfeudal contributes little to explaining
and understanding their differences. Whatever
labels are applied to appanage Rus's socioeconomic structure, one should understand that this
structure was weak when the Mongol invasion
struck, so weak that it could offer little resistance
to the invaders or, subsequently, to the rising
ambitions of the grand princes of Moscow.

Changes in Rus Society

Rus was beset with problems of such vast magnitude in this period that it is surprising that it survived at all. The Mongol invasion, as we have
seen, brought death, destruction, and depopulation of enormous dimensions. Continual Tatar
exactions—heavy annual tribute, escalating tolls,
and many destructive raids by armed detachments
—deepened and prolonged the tragedy. How
much the people of Rus actually paid annually to
the Mongols is unclear from the extant sources,
but in a period of economic depression these large
amounts strained Rus's capacity to pay. Also,
Mongol rule was not the sole burden upon the
Russian people. Lithuanians, Poles, German crusaders, Swedes, and others pressured Rus from
the west, causing further destruction and frequent
warfare, which drained Rus's remaining material
and human resources.

Other calamities afflicted Rus in these years,
including constant princely feuding and competition, epidemics of the Black Death, fires, famine,
and drought. These produced further depopulation, migration, and death. The sources describe at
great length the extent of abandoned land, fallow
fields, and depopulation of towns and whole
regions. All this affected disastrously the level of
Rus productivity, especially in the 13th century.
The number of towns fell by one-half, and
remaining urban centers lost much of their population. Urban handicrafts virtually disappeared as

the Tatars continued to conscript the most talented artisans and craftsmen. The art of stonecut-
ting declined, and most building in stone halted;
glassmaking and enamelwork ceased altogether.
As trade and commerce declined, the populace
retreated into local self-sufficiency, further undermining the economy. Soviet historians quite correctly stressed how seriously these developments
inhibited the rise of an urban merchant class.
These developments also enhanced the importance of landowning as the major source of wealth
and increased the pressure on the rights of free
peasants.

Encouraged by the Tatars in order to fragment
Rus politically, the *votchina* principle of inheritance
spread during the appanage era. Princely families
proliferated, and with each generation territories
were split into smaller parcels so as to provide an
inheritance for each surviving son. Where there
had been one large principality, there emerged
over the years tiny princedoms, often only manorial estates, scarcely able to support a princely family. The inhabitants of these lands became subjects
of the local prince or boyar. As long as the peasantry remained free, the right to leave the land
and reside elsewhere was guaranteed. Uncertain
times, economic insecurity, and Tatar taxation
fostered migration as people sought security and
better economic conditions. This situation brought
growing competition for settlers and agricultural
laborers on the estates of princes, boyars, and the
church. Gradually this competition led to efforts to
curb freedom of movement for the rural population, culminating in 1497 with the restriction of a
peasant's right to leave an estate and take up
residence elsewhere to a two-week period around
St. George's Day (November 26). The process of
peasant enserfment thus began in the appanage
period (see Chapter 14).

As the princely class multiplied, so too did the
boyars, because each prince had a retinue of servitors who themselves became major landowners.
They received immunities and virtually sovereign
powers to govern their estates, administer justice,
collect taxes, and control their subjects without
princely interference. Such immunities granted to

the boyars further undermined peasant rights and freedoms. In addition, landowners appropriated large amounts of hitherto free land to the detriment of the peasantry. As many peasants were transformed from free landowners into renters, their economic status deteriorated markedly.

Role of the Orthodox Church

The landholdings of the church also expanded greatly during the Tatar era. Even in Kievan times, the church had been a landowner on a vast scale, receiving grants of land from the princes and bequests from private individuals seeking God's blessing and the salvation of their souls. During the period of the Tatar yoke the privileged status of the church, enjoying exemption from Tatar taxation and tribute, permitted the monasteries in particular to amass great wealth. Freedom from taxation gave the monasteries great advantages over secular landowners because peasants could live on church property without having to pay Tatar tribute. Monasteries received immunities from princes, who provided them with the same rights and privileges as secular landowners. Monasteries also expanded their holdings by making outright purchases and by colonizing frontier regions where land was simply appropriated to support the monks. By 1500 the church owned an estimated 25 to 30 percent of all cultivated land. Later the church's vested economic interests would create serious political problems for the Muscovite state.

Since its establishment in the 10th century, the Orthodox church had played a major role in Rus life, but never was it more important than in the Mongol era. When the Tatars first appeared, the church had exerted moral leadership by trying to rally Rus princes in a unified resistance to the invaders. When this failed, the church had to accept the Tatar conquest, rationalizing it as God's retribution for Rus's sins.

The church, like all Rus institutions, suffered terribly at first from the conquest. Large numbers of priests and monks, and even the metropolitan, were killed, and many churches and monasteries suffered devastation; but the church's spirit was not broken. Within a short time it revived, and thanks to the Tatar policy of religious toleration, worked out a modus vivendi with the Golden Horde. In return for public prayer for Tatar khans, the church received a guaranteed privileged status by a formal accord in 1266 and concessions even earlier. Besides economic privileges, the Tatars guaranteed the church protection from insults and persecution, and infringement of church rights was punishable by death. The Tatars ensured the church's cultural functions and its economic wealth and power, thus allowing it to become paramount in Rus life.

Some historians have suggested that the accord between the church and the Tatars altered relations between the church and Rus princes by prohibiting the latter from interfering in its affairs. This, however, was not the case. The princes continued to select bishops (subject to Tatar approval) and often encroached on church property as they had done before 1240. In short, despite Tatar mediation, the church remained largely dependent on princely power. The Byzantine tradition of a close church-state relationship was too ingrained to permit any significant alteration of political relations. The church and the princes were mutually dependent, sharing similar interests and long-range goals, and both were dependent on the Tatars. These conditions demanded maximum church-princely cooperation if Rus was to emerge from Mongol domination.

Migrations of the metropolitan see of the Rus church in the appanage era reveal the close identification of religious and secular power. Kiev's political power had been in decline long before its destruction by the Tatars in 1240. The metropolitanate, bound by the inertia of tradition, remained attached to Kiev, although Vladimir-Suzdal had become the chief political center before the Tatars arrived. Nonetheless, there was increasing recognition of the need to relocate the center of church power, especially after the devastating Tatar raid on Kiev in 1299. Kiev's inhabitants, including Metropolitan Maxim, had to flee the city, and in

1300 Maxim, for security and because it was the grand princely center, took up residence in Vladimir. Like his immediate predecessors, Maxim traveled extensively throughout the Rus lands, hoping to keep alive the spirit of national unity in a demoralized country split into many rival principalities, all suffering under the Tatars' heel. In 1303 Maxim died, and in a departure from ancient tradition he was buried in Vladimir, confirming the permanent transfer of religious authority to the northeast.

This action shattered the political aspirations of the southwestern princes, who now had to recognize that they had lost the struggle for all-Rus hegemony to the northeast. To prevent a potential religious dependence on the northeast from becoming a political one as well, the southwestern princes, especially Prince Iuri of Galicia, broke from the jurisdiction of the metropolitan of Kiev (established now in Vladimir) and petitioned the Greek patriarch and the emperor to create a separate southwestern metropolitanate. In 1302 or 1303 the patriarch named the Galician bishop Nifont metropolitan of southwestern Rus.

Soon Nifont died, leaving both Rus metropolitan thrones vacant. The grand prince of Vladimir, Mikhail of Tver, hoped to restore the unity of the Rus metropolitanate and to secure the elevation of another native Rus bishop to the metropolitan throne. Prince Mikhail proposed Abbot Geronti of Kiev, but at the same time Prince Iuri of Galicia supported the candidacy of the Galician bishop, Peter. The Greek patriarch and emperor decided to confirm Peter as metropolitan of Kiev and all Rus in 1308. Although Peter was Iuri of Galicia's candidate, he was appointed to the metropolitan throne of Kiev, now located in Vladimir. The unity of the metropolitanate had been restored, but the new metropolitan was from the southwest.

In 1309 Peter arrived in Vladimir, an unwelcome guest of Prince Mikhail of Tver, whose own candidate had been rejected. Prince Mikhail immediately initiated preceedings to remove Peter, but the trumped-up charges against him were dismissed by an ecclesiastical court and the new metropolitan was confirmed in office. This struggle caused a permanent breach between Metropolitan Peter and Prince Mikhail. Because Mikhail was then involved in a political struggle with the Moscow principality, Peter became Moscow's staunch ally. He endorsed the Moscow princes' political ambitions with the full power and prestige of the Orthodox church. Close relations were established between Peter and Prince Iuri of Moscow, and after 1324 the metropolitan spent much time at the court of Prince Ivan I (Ivan Kalita) of Moscow. They embarked on an extensive building program within the Kremlin walls, and in 1326 the first stone church there was begun, the famous Cathedral of the Assumption. In December 1326 Peter died and, as he had requested, was interred in the still uncompleted cathedral. In retrospect, many historians have concluded that Peter shifted the metropolitan see to Moscow and imparted to Moscow a religious prominence foreshadowing its future political successes as the "gatherer of the Russian lands." Some, such as the church historian N. Zernov, suggested that "the presence in Moscow of the tomb of one so highly revered by all the people, elevated the city to a place of prominence and helped Peter's successor . . . overcome the opposition of other princes to make Moscow his permanent residence."[2] Peter's burial in Moscow may have been important symbolically, but it had little immediate practical significance because Moscow was not then the capital of a grand principality and could not, therefore, aspire to house the metropolitan see of the Orthodox church.

What is significant about Metropolitan Peter is that he established a precedent by lending church support to Moscow in its struggle with Tver, helping create a framework for the Muscovite national mission. After Peter's death Prince Ivan I of Moscow submitted his own candidate for the metropolitan throne, Archimandrite Feodor. The Greeks, however, refused to acknowledge Feodor as a legitimate candidate, claiming that only the grand prince could recommend a candidate.

---

[2] N. Zernov, *The Russians and Their Church* (London, 1964), p. 35.

Church of the Ascension in Kolomenskoe near Moscow (1530–1532).

Finally, the Greeks selected one of their own bishops, Theognostus, in 1328. That same year Prince Ivan I of Moscow secured from the Tatars the right to use the grand princely title, which implied genealogical seniority. When Theognostus arrived in Vladimir to take up his duties as metropolitan, he recognized that power had shifted toward Moscow and promptly moved there. Though Theognostus was of foreign origin, he followed Peter's precedent and firmly supported the process of unification under Moscow's aegis. The metropolitan thus employed the moral authority of the church to support Moscow's political ambitions. The religious authority of Moscow, from Theognostus onward, contributed substantially to its success in uniting Great Russia (see Chapters 8 and 10).

Not only in the political sphere was the church destined to play an important role in Moscow's rise. The church also became a vital, visible symbol of the continuity of Russian history, the embodiment of national unity and strength, remaining the sole national institution to which the Russian people could turn for guidance and inspiration. The spiritual revival fostered by the church during the period of Tatar domination was among its chief contributions. Monasteries played a major role in stimulating the development of Russian civilization. The monastic revival, beginning in the 1330s, left its deepest imprint on the northeast, where the cultural renaissance and the stimulus to colonization were most profoundly expressed.

St. Sergius of Radonezh

St. Sergius of Radonezh (1322–1392) typified the church's role in society. His life and activity constitute one of the brightest chapters in the history of Rus in the bleak Mongol period. Born into a noble family, Sergius at an early age responded to the call of Christ and entered God's service. Determined to lead an ascetic life of isolation and solitude unencumbered by the cares of this world (impossible in an urban Moscow monastery), he took refuge in the impenetrable forest outside. His undeviating devotion to the strictest principles of monastic life—simplicity, contemplation, discipline of the flesh, and hard physical labor—won him a reputation as a true disciple of Christ. People from all walks of life sought him out for guidance, advice, and understanding, hoping to find some of the spiritual tranquillity he so clearly personified. Gradually a few devout and fervent souls decided to remain with Sergius and follow his example. A small brotherhood developed around his isolated retreat, and by 1340 the nucleus of the famous Trinity Monastery had formed. The establishment of a monastery attracted to the remote region settlers who began to carve villages, homesteads, fields, and pastures from the forest, making the monastery the center of a thriving agricultural district.

Sergius's reputation as an ascetic and devoted disciple of Christ spread rapidly in the somber atmosphere of Tatar-dominated Rus. The Trinity Monastery became a place of pilgrimage for the faithful who sought a clearer understanding of themselves and the Christian spirit. All who solicited his advice and guidance, whether princes or peasants, boyars or merchants, were graciously received and counseled. Sergius's message, grounded in Christ's teachings, was disarmingly simple. He preached the need for toleration fortified by love, repentance rooted in humility and self-sacrifice, and kindness and patience born of love and self-effacement. He was always prepared to serve as a mediator of the quarrels that undermined Russian princely cooperation, to promote mutual understanding and national unity.

According to a widely believed legend, Sergius shared credit with Dmitri "Donskoi" and his army for the victory over the Tatars at Kulikovo in 1380. Dmitri appealed to Sergius for advice. Should he negotiate with the Tatars or fight them? Sergius was torn by a crisis of conscience. The devout Christian struggled against the Russian national patriot. Sergius's Christian conscience urged him to advise reconciliation, nonresistance to evil; his national feeling impelled him to grant his blessing to a bloody battle. Initially, he cautioned against confrontation and urged negotiation, but after further prayer and meditation he recognized a great national crusade in the making. God's will made struggle against the infidel Tatars a just and sacred responsibility. Sergius advised Dmitri: "Go forth to do battle against the infidels without fear or hesitation, and you shall triumph." He opened the monastic coffers to support the cause and sent two of his monks with the army. The blessing of so highly venerated a monk endowed the cause with a sense of religious mission and righteousness, which greatly raised the morale of Dmitri's troops. Whether or not this represents an accurate account of Sergius's role in Muscovite affairs, it does present a vivid portrait of the church's key role in the rise of Moscow and in the eventual emancipation of the Russians from the Tatar yoke.

The Russian victory at Kulikovo stimulated a growing sense of national mission in Moscow. St. Sergius of Radonezh contributed profoundly to that growth and to the spiritual revival. Kliuchevskii wrote:

> There are historical names which escape the barriers of time and whose work profoundly influences subsequent generations, because the figure of a personality is transformed into an idea. Such is the case with St. Sergius; in invoking him, the people today still affirm that political strength is well founded only when it is based on moral strength.[3]

Andrei Rublev

The activity of another monk, Andrei Rublev, exemplified another dimension of Russia's spiritual revival. Perhaps the greatest master of Russian iconography, Rublev was one of the few creative geniuses of the age. Under the influence of his remarkable skill, an indigenous tradition of Russian icon painting emerged. Born in the 1370s, Rublev grew up in the atmosphere of religious and national revival stimulated by St. Sergius. As a young man, Rublev may have spent time at the Trinity Monastery and was influenced by the spiritual intensity of Sergius's followers. The earliest example of his work dates from about 1405, when he began decorating the Cathedral of the Annunciation in the Moscow Kremlin. Rublev's teacher, Theophanes the Greek, had been trained in Byzantium and had moved to Moscow shortly after 1400. Theophanes influenced Rublev profoundly, acquainting him with a freer iconographic expression in the use of color and brush strokes. Rublev, responding to the rebirth of national feeling and Theophanes's influence, developed a unique style that influenced Russian painters for generations.

In 1422 Rublev was invited back to the Trinity Monastery to redecorate the Cathedral of the Trinity. At that time he also produced perhaps the most famous Russian icon, the Old Testament

---

[3] V. O. Kliuchevskii, *Ocherki i rechi* (Moscow, n.d.), p. 214.

Old Testament Trinity by Andrei Rublev.

Trinity. This work, inspired by Sergius's memory, was an artistic achievement that testified to his expressive and subtle manner and to his mastery of composition and color. The Old Testament Trinity was considered so perfect in conception and execution that a church council of 1551 declared it the obligatory model for all future icons dealing with that subject. Rublev, with extraordinary vitality, depicted the supreme mystery of

Christian belief—the Trinity—in symbolic yet human form, readily comprehensible to the religious faithful. Striving for simplicity and directness, Rublev reduced his portrayal to the bare essentials. The three angels who appear to Sarah and Abraham in the Old Testament account are portrayed as symbolically representing the Trinitarian nature of God. The serenity and deeply felt religiosity of the three figures are marvelously and subtly expressed. The three figures flow harmoniously together, creating a single impression, yet each remains distinct and unique, the essence of the Trinitarian mystery. The central figure, representing God the Father, stretches his hand over a cup containing the sacrificial lamb as though beckoning the figure to his left, representing Christ, to accept the summons to the supreme sacrifice for the redemption of fallen man. The figure representing Christ is a profoundly moving portrait of resigned acceptance, the Son accepting the Father's will.

Rublev was a master at expressing psychological insight. All his works convey a sense of great dignity and calmness, an impression of eternal verity and tenderness. Using human forms, he penetrated the deepest religious mysteries. Nothing reflected more graphically the successful mission of the church in guiding Rus through the most difficult period of the Tatar yoke than did Rublev's works.

Russian culture, after experiencing a period of decline and stagnation, was powerfully stimulated in the late 14th and early 15th centuries by the religious revival and the growth of national feeling after the Kulikovo victory. The main vehicle of cultural development remained the Orthodox church, which became the focus of the spiritual and secular aspirations of the Russian people.

Suggested Additional Reading

BOOKS

ASCHER, A., et al. *The Kremlin* (New York, 1972).

FAENSEN, H., and V. IVANOV. *Early Russian Architecture* (London, 1975).

FEDOTOV, G. *The Russian Religious Mind: The Middle Ages: The Thirteenth to the Fifteenth Centuries* (Cambridge, MA, 1966).

———. *A Treasury of Russian Spirituality* (New York, 1948).

HAMILTON, G. H. *The Art and Architecture of Russia,* 2d ed. (Baltimore, 1975).

KAISER, D. *The Transformation of Medieval Rus, 1300–1500* (Princeton, 1980).

LAZAREV, V. N. *Russian Icons: From the Twelfth to the Fifteenth Century* (New York, 1962).

MEYENDORFF, J. *Byzantium and the Rise of Russia* (Cambridge, 1981).

ONASCH, K. *Icons* (New York, 1963).

Sergij von Radonez (Munich, 1967). (The life of Sergius of Radonezh.)

VOYCE, A. *The Art and Architecture of Medieval Russia* (Norman, OK, 1964).

ZENKOVSKY, S., ed. *The Nikonian Chronicle, Vol. 4: From the Year 1382 to the Year 1425* (Princeton, 1988).

———. *The Nikonian Chronicle, Vol. 5: 1425–1520* (Princeton, 1989).

ARTICLES

FEDOTOV, G. "Religious Background of Russian Culture." *CH* 12 (1943): 35–51.

HALPERIN, C. J. "A Chingissid Saint of the Russian Orthodox Church . . . " *CanAmSlSt* 9, no. 3 (1975): 324–35.

HELLIE, R. "Muscovy." *MERSH* 23: 214–28.

KLIUCHEVSKII, V. O. "St. Sergius . . . " in *Readings in Russian History,* vol. 1, ed. S. Harcave (New York, 1962), pp. 153–64.

———. "La Trinité d'Andre Roublev." *Gazette des beaux-arts* 54 (1959): 289–300.

LANGER, L. N. "The Black Death in Russia." *Rus. Hist.* 2, no. 1 (1974): 53–67.

———. "The Plague and the Russian Countryside." *CanAmSlSt* 10, no. 3 (1976): 351–78.

MAJESKA, G. "Andrei Rublev." *MERSH* 31: 228–32.

MILLER, D. B. "The Cult of Saint Sergius of Radonezh and Its Political Uses." *SR* 52, no. 4 (Winter 1993): 680–99.

OBOLENSKY, D. "Byzantium, Kiev, and Moscow: A Study in Ecclesiastical Relations." *DOP* 11 (1957): 21–78.

ŠEVČENKO, I. "Intellectual Repercussions of the Council of Florence." *CH* 24 (1955): 291–323.

TIMBERLAKE, C. "Moscow Kremlin." *MERSH* 23: 96–105.

WEICKHARDT, G. G. "The Pre-Petrine Law of Property," *SR* 52, no. 4 (Winter 1993): 663–79.

WIGZELL, F. "Sergii of Radonezh." *MERSH* 34: 77–80.

ZGUTA, R. "The One-Day Votive Church: A Religious Response to the Black Death in Early Russia." *SR* 40, no. 3 (1981): 423–32.

10

The Unification of Great Russia

In the years after Kulikovo the rise of Moscow continued under the successors of Dmitri "Donskoi." It was a process of ebb and flow, with both successes and failures. The reign of Vasili II (1425–1462) proved crucial: Civil war and struggles for the throne were followed by internal consolidation and heightened power for Muscovy and its ruler. Under Ivan III (1462–1505) and his son Vasili III (1505–1533) Great Russia, comprising the northern and eastern parts of European Russia, came under the control of Moscow, whose grand prince gradually acquired extensive authority over his subjects. Great Russian patriotism and a consciousness of the need for unity grew significantly. As the power of Moscow increased, the Golden Horde splintered irrevocably into several feuding khanates. This allowed Muscovite rulers to emancipate Great Russia completely from the Horde's suzerainty. Assisting the emerging and expanding Muscovite state was the Russian Orthodox church, which became virtually independent of supervision from Constantinople. A national army and judicial system weakened the old appanage order. Soviet historians also emphasized the gradual formation of a Great Russian

market. These questions remain: Were Ivan III and Vasili III true autocrats, or were they still limited by the titled aristocracy? Were the unification of Great Russia and the creation of a centralized Muscovite state beneficial or detrimental to the Russian people?

Expansion and the Growth of Grand Princely Power

During Grand Prince Vasili I's bloody, chaotic, and obscure reign (1389–1425), Moscow gyrated feebly between Lithuania and the Golden Horde. Repeated Tatar incursions and internal princely strife caused devastation and disorder. The division of Great Russia among the grand principalities of Moscow, Tver, and Riazan ensured continued Mongol predominance. While permitting Moscow to absorb the principality of Nizhnii-Novgorod and other minor territories along the frontier between Rus and the Tatar domains, the Horde exploited Moscow's continuing rivalry with Tver to keep both dependent. Lithuania under Prince Vitovt expanded eastward almost to Moscow, and only a Mongol victory over the

Lithuanians on the Vorskla River (1399) denied them rule over all of west Russia. Grand Prince Vasili I, hampered by inadequate military strength and inconsistent policies, exerted little influence over Riazan or Novgorod. His position was weakened further by persistent friction with his brothers.

The reign of Vasili II constituted a critical turning point in Muscovite political history. In 1425, at age 10, Vasili became grand prince under a regency headed by the capable Metropolitan Photius and under the protection of the young ruler's grandfather, Prince Vitovt of Lithuania. After these protectors died, Muscovy suffered a severe bout of civil war that threatened to partition it into warring feudal appanages. In this first Muscovite "Time of Troubles" only the loyal support of Vasili's servitors, some boyars, commoners, and finally the clergy ultimately saved him and Muscovy from destruction. In 1433 Iuri Vasilevich, Vasili II's uncle, deposed him and assumed power. The refusal of Vasili's supporters to serve the usurper compelled him to recognize Vasili II temporarily as ruler. However, in 1434 Iuri Vasilevich defeated Vasili, seized Moscow, and installed himself in power. After Iuri's sudden death three months later, his eldest son, Vasili the Cross-Eyed (Kosoi), claimed the throne. Only after a two-year struggle was the pretender defeated and blinded and Vasili II restored to power.

The second phase of this Muscovite dynastic struggle also involved Lithuania and the Tatars. Lithuanian pressure against Novgorod in 1443–1444 induced Vasili II to send his main army against Lithuania. Taking advantage of the situation, Khan Ulug Mehmed, a contender for power in the steppe, invaded Muscovite territory. Vasili hurried to meet him with the forces he could collect in Moscow but was defeated and captured at the Battle of Suzdal (1445).[1] The Golden Horde was now splitting into separate khanates in Kazan, Astrakhan, the Crimea, and Kasimov.

Much to the dismay of Muscovites, it was the founder of the Kazan khanate, Ulug Mehmed, who had captured Vasili II. Traditional accounts attribute Vasili's release to his promise to pay a huge ransom. Edward Keenan, an American scholar, affirms that Vasili's release followed his alliance with the Tatars, who supplied him with auxiliary troops.[2] Soon after returning to Moscow, Vasili II undertook a pilgrimage to nearby Trinity Monastery. Exploiting his absence, Dmitri Shemiaka, a son of Iuri Vasilevich, seized control of Moscow, blinded Vasili and deported him to Uglich, and imprisoned his two young sons. Shemiaka and his followers planned to split Muscovy into independent appanages and destroy grand princely authority. However, their evident selfishness provoked a sharp reaction. The clergy and leading Muscovites induced Shemiaka to release Vasili and his sons. Supported by Tver and his Tatar allies, Vasili captured Moscow, resumed power, and compelled his enemies to make peace.

In the final 15 years of his reign Vasili II, though no great ruler, consolidated his position at home and moved to unify and strengthen Great Russia. Friendship with Lithuania freed Moscow from western threats, and Riazan principality to the southeast became its vassal (see Map 10.1). Shemiaka's appanage was confiscated, and the Moscow metropolitan excommunicated him. His flight to Novgorod gave Vasili a pretext for a campaign against Novgorod in 1456, which prepared its subsequent incorporation into Muscovy (see Chapter 7). Shemiaka's defeat ended Muscovy's civil strife and smashed Great Russia's traditional appanage system irreparably. The emergence of the Moscow-dominated Tatar khanate of Kasimov in 1452 heightened Moscow's prestige in the Muslim world and encouraged many Tatars to enter its service. That same year Moscow ceased paying regular tribute to the disintegrating Horde. Some historians affirm that this date marked Great Russia's de facto independence; others date the removal of the "Tatar yoke" from the abortive

---

[1] G. Alef, "The Battle of Suzdal in 1445 . . . ," in *Rulers and Nobles in Fifteenth Century Muscovy* (London, 1983).

[2] E. Keenan, "Muscovy and Kazan . . . ," *SR* 26 (1967): 554.

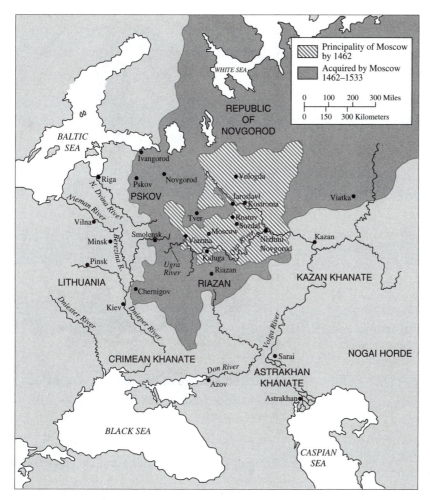

Map 10.1 Rise of Moscow to 1533

Mongol campaign against Moscow in 1480. In any event, Moscow at Vasili II's death was far stronger than before. His gains, prepared by the work of his predecessors and fostered by support from the church, servitor princes, and gentry, constituted a major turning point in Russian political history.

The Russian church became narrowly Muscovite as it achieved independence from crumbling Byzantium. Byzantine leaders, desperately seeking Western aid against the oncoming Turks and yielding to papal pressure, agreed at the Council of Florence (1439) to rejoin the Roman Catholic Church. The violently anti-Catholic Mus-

covites, however, rejected this union and deposed Metropolitan Isidor, their chief delegate to the council. A council of Russian bishops chose Iona, bishop of Riazan, as metropolitan, and he became Vasili's chief adviser. They sought reconciliation with Byzantium, but in 1453 the Turks captured Constantinople and ended the Byzantine Empire. The Russian church became virtually independent, enhancing Moscow's international significance. After Iona the Moscow ruler confirmed metropolitans in office and closer church-state cooperation developed in Muscovy. After 1458, when west Russia formed a separate Uniate church, the Muscovite church asserted its superiority over the Greek church, claiming that it led the Orthodox world and that Moscow's prince was destined to replace the Byzantine emperor. The basis had been laid for the Third Rome theory (that with the apostasy of Rome and the fall of Byzantium, Moscow would replace them) and the later "Greek Project" of Catherine the Great (see Chapter 18).

Ivan III, The Great (1462–1505)

Ivan III, "the Great," like his contemporaries Henry VII of England and Louis XI of France, achieved national unification and centralization and is often called "gatherer of the Russian lands." Aiding his father against Shemiaka and serving as coruler, Ivan was well prepared for power. His father's testament, ensuring Ivan's territorial, fiscal, and political supremacy over four younger brothers, exhorted them to "respect and obey [their] older brother in place of their father." Preferring diplomacy and intrigue to war, Ivan achieved ambitious aims with a minimum of bloodshed. He sought to unite Rus around Moscow and rule it autocratically, and his campaigns, reforms, and marriages occurred as if predestined. Better than other Muscovite rulers, he knew his resources, his goals, and how to attain them. This tall, awe-inspiring, Machiavellian prince—dedicated, hardheaded, and cautious—was feared, not loved.

At his accession Great Russia remained fragmented, and the Kievan tradition of a confederation of equal sovereign princes persisted. Tver to the northwest and the republic of Viatka to the northeast preserved a fragile independence, while Novgorod and Riazan, independent in name, were actually Moscow dependencies. Autonomous Iaroslavl and Rostov, virtually encircled by Muscovite lands, were annexed early in Ivan's reign. Throughout his rule Ivan faced his brothers' claims to compensation and powerful, jealous neighbors: Lithuania and the khanate of Crimea. In handling this complex situation successfully,

Ivan III, "the Great," ruled 1462–1505, "ruler of all Russia" (engraving).

Ivan proved a master tactician and diplomat. His campaigns during the 1460s against Kazan secured Moscow's eastern flank, and during the 1470s he exploited Novgorod's internal dissension, vulnerability, and military weakness to add its broad domains to Muscovy. Novgorod's fall compelled the grand prince of Tver to face Moscow alone. The expulsion of Ivan's envoy and Tver's conclusion of an alliance with Lithuania gave Ivan pretexts to act decisively. In 1485 his army invaded Tver, its boyars defected to him, and its prince fled to Lithuania. Four years later Viatka was similarly incorporated; its populace was largely deported to Moscow and replaced with Muscovites. Except for autonomous Pskov and Riazan, Great Russia had been unified by force.

Ivan III's second marriage was political and controversial. Maria of Tver, his first wife, died in

1467, leaving but one son, Ivan Ivanovich. The papacy, anxious to convert Muscovy to Catholicism and enlist its support against the Turks, arranged Ivan's betrothal to Zoë Paleologus, niece of the last Byzantine emperor. Raised in Rome as a Catholic under papal guardianship, Zoë came to Moscow in 1472 to marry Ivan. Disregarding papal wishes, she became Orthodox and assumed the name Sofia. According to some Russian historians, this "Byzantine marriage" allowed Ivan to claim the vacant Byzantine throne and influenced him to espouse the Third Rome theory and cast off the "Mongol yoke." But recent scholarship minimizes Sofia's direct political influence and affirms that Ivan III had set his basic national policies before she came to Moscow.

In 1480 Khan Akhmad of the Great Horde, allied with Poland-Lithuania, invaded Muscovy in order to reassert Tatar control. On the Ugra River Mongol and Muscovite armies faced each other. Ivan III's eldest son, commanding the Russians, displayed more courage than his father. Some contemporary chroniclers and later historians portrayed Ivan's sudden departure for Moscow as cowardice, though probably he left to reach agreement with his rebellious brothers and ensure united resistance to the Tatars. A chronicle account relates:

> Akhmat arrived at the Ugra with all of his forces, with the intent of crossing the river. When the Tartars came they began to shoot at our [forces] and our [forces] shot at them. Some Tartars advanced against Prince Andrei; others against the Grand Prince. . . . Our forces, using arrows and harquebusses, killed many Tartars; their arrows were falling among our forces but did not hurt anyone. They pushed the Tartars away from the river, though they tried to advance for many days; as they could not cross the river they stopped and waited until it should freeze.[3]

Akhmad's army withdrew without forcing a showdown with the Muscovites, who likewise retired.

Emblem of the Russian state under Ivan III.

Troubles within the Horde and the Polish king's failure to send troops justified this Mongol withdrawal, but Akhmad's retreat ended Moscow's subservience to the Mongol khans.

Great Russia's unification and independence enabled Ivan to inaugurate regular diplomatic relations with foreign powers. In 1486, after he had established ties with the Holy Roman Empire, its envoy, Nikolaus Poppel, hinted that the German emperor might grant Ivan a royal title. Ivan rejected the offer haughtily: "By God's grace we have been sovereigns in our land since the beginning; . . . and as beforehand we did not desire to be appointed by anyone, so now too we do not desire it."[4] Muscovy refused to be anyone's vassal.

In the Baltic region Ivan scored notable successes. In 1492, in order to break the monopoly of Baltic trade held by the German Hanseatic League, he established the port of Ivangorod

---

[3] Quoted in B. Dmytryshyn, *Medieval Russia,* 2d ed. (Hinsdale, IL 1973), p. 192.

[4] Cited in J. L. Fennell, *Ivan the Great of Moscow* (London, 1961), p. 121.

Kremlin of Tver, 15th century, from an icon.

opposite German-controlled Narva, closed Novgorod's foreign settlement, and ended German merchants' special privileges there. As a natural outgrowth of Novgorod's annexation, he sought for Russian merchants the right to trade freely in the Baltic.

Lithuania, whose holdings extended perilously close to Moscow, was Ivan's principal opponent. In undeclared border warfare in the 1480s the Muscovites softened Lithuanian resistance and induced many west Russian princes to shift their allegiance and lands to Moscow. After intensive fighting Viazma province was added to Muscovy by the truce of 1494. Demanding all Lithuanian territory to the Berezina River, Ivan claimed all Kievan Rus lands and entitled himself sovereign of all Russia. Alleged Lithuanian persecution of Orthodox Russians served Ivan as a pretext for further warfare. Ivan allied with the Crimean khan, Mengli-Girei, who wished to plunder Lithuania and Poland. Muscovy and the Crimea had defeated the Great Horde in 1491; a decade later the Crimeans destroyed it completely. The Muscovites defeated the Lithuanians on the Vedrosha River in 1500 but could not capture

Smolensk. In the uneasy truce that followed, Ivan's title and claims to Smolensk remained disputed, but he had achieved a significant expansion westward into Belorussia.

Internal Changes and Conflicts

Within a much enlarged Muscovy, Ivan III consolidated control over disparate and newly annexed territories, built a national administration, and established himself as sovereign rather than first among equal princes. Deporting leading families from annexed regions and replacing them with Muscovite service people and boyars gained him support from an expanding class of loyal gentry servitors and freed him from dependence on older boyar and princely elements. Gradually lesser princes, their appanages absorbed, lost their former independence and became boyars.

In his centralizing policies Ivan overcame strong resistance from appanage princes led by his own brothers, who had at first exercised sovereign authority over considerable territories. As Muscovy expanded, he moved against separatism cautiously but effectively with a minimum of violence, defying tradition by refusing to increase his brothers' appanages. When Iuri of Dmitrov died without heirs, Ivan III seized his appanage and compensated his remaining brothers, Andrei and Boris, minimally. To win their support during Akhmad's invasion of 1480, he made minor concessions; then he took the lands of Novgorod and Tver as they watched helplessly. In a treaty of 1486 his brothers recognized Ivan as sovereign of all Russia, and when Andrei later refused to supply troops, Ivan arrested him and appropriated his domains. Eventually Ivan controlled all of his brothers' territories, effectively undermining separatism and feudal division.

The dynastic crisis of 1497 briefly threatened this newfound unity. Ivan Ivanovich, Ivan III's eldest son, died in 1490 leaving his son, Dmitri, and Ivan III's second son, Vasili, as heirs to the throne. Because in Muscovy an eldest son with a male heir had never predeceased his father, the choice lay with the grand prince. Behind the candidates stood their mothers, Sofia Paleologus and Elena Stepanov. In 1498 Ivan had Dmitri crowned grand prince of all Russia, but four years later Dmitri and his mother were arrested and his title passed to Vasili. Dmitri's defeated faction, some historians claim, represented boyars opposed to centralization.

Muscovite administration developed significantly with territorial expansion. At first Ivan permitted newly annexed territories some autonomy under Moscow-appointed governors (*namestniki*) and district chiefs (*volosteli*). These officials were supported by the "feeding" system (*kormlenie*), in which a portion of local tax revenues provided for their maintenance. Because greedy governors often extorted excessive *kormlenie*, regional charters sometimes specified the amounts and sought to allay local discontent. The White Lake Charter of 1488, furthermore, set rules for apprehending and trying criminals to prevent abuses by local officials. Such regional charters were a first step in unifying Great Russia's administration and legal procedures. Later, to limit the powers of governors, their authority and functions were described

more clearly, and Ivan III appointed agents, usually gentry, to restrict their power.

The first Muscovite national law code, the *Sudebnik* of 1497, required by the transformation of Moscow principality into the extensive Muscovite state, derived largely from *Russkaia Pravda* (see Chapter 3) and charters of Pskov. Boyar courts handled ordinary cases; important ones were heard by a supreme court under the chairman of the Boyar Duma, the supreme legislative and administrative body, and a few cases went to the grand prince for final decision. In the provinces justice was left to officials under the *kormlenie* system. The *Sudebnik*'s prescription of capital punishment for major political crimes, especially armed rebellion, strengthened grand princely authority. Its stipulation that peasants settling accounts with their landlord might move from one estate to another only during St. George's Day in November (see Chapter 14) confirmed the rising influence of service gentry and state secretaries as governing elements.

Muscovy's territorial expansion necessitated a rapid growth of the grand prince's court, which became an unplanned, rather chaotic and inefficient national bureaucracy. Previously, administration had been territorial and decentralized, and as late as 1533 regional princely courts still existed in Novgorod, Tver, Riazan, and Uglich, though their functions were gradually assumed by Moscow-appointed officials. The grand princely court in Moscow had an elaborate hierarchy of officials to handle finances, princely banquets, horses, and weapons. These positions were determined by *mestnichestvo*, a system based on noble birth and posts occupied by relatives, which limited the grand prince's power of appointment. The embryo of the new central administration was the state treasury, whose secretaries (*diaki*) became more specialized, competent, and numerous and assumed the tasks of handling state administration, finance, and foreign affairs. These agencies grew eventually into separate administrative boards (*prikazy*) subject to the Boyar Duma.

A more effective, centralized army developed under Ivan III. Dmitri "Donskoi," lacking a national army, had relied in emergencies on voluntary cooperation by princes and boyars. As the grand princely court expanded under Vasili II, some servitors were assigned to military service, often receiving estates from the government in return. From this practice emerged the service gentry with landholdings (*pomestie*) conditional upon service to the state. Under Ivan III service gentry and boyar children[5] associated with his court constituted the core of Muscovy's cavalry and fostered centralization and grand princely control within the army. The expansion of the gentry militia cavalry, which became the core of the army, reduced Ivan's dependence on the haphazard forces provided by his brothers and boyars. Auxiliary infantry were recruited sporadically from townsmen.

Ivan III urgently needed lands with which to reward his service gentry. In Moscovy the principal categories of land were state (*chernye*), grand princely (*dvortsovye*), church, and patrimonial estates (*votchiny*) of princes and boyars. Most state and grand princely lands were virgin forest or already cultivated by peasants paying state taxes. Ivan could seize lands of individual boyars who defected or resisted his rule, but he dared not challenge the boyar class, which ran his administration. However, in conquered territories such as Novgorod and Tver he was bound by no traditions or restrictions; and by confiscating boyar and church properties there, he obtained by 1500 almost three million acres for distribution to loyal servitors.

Nonetheless, the boyars with large estates still exercised much political influence through the Boyar Duma, the supreme legislative and administrative body, which made important decisions together with the ruler. The grand prince appointed its members and presided when he wished, but *mestnichestvo* tradition required him to select representatives of senior princely and boyar families. Before the Novgorod campaign of 1471

Ivan also consulted the service gentry, but boyar power prevented a repetition of this until Ivan IV's reign. Ivan III limited boyar influence in the Duma by relying more on the *diaki,* usually educated commoners, whom he could appoint and dismiss without consulting the Duma and who were now recognized as Duma members.

Reformers and heretics challenged the conservative leadership of the Orthodox church as Ivan pondered the fate of church lands. In late 14th-century Novgorod the *Strigolniki* (shorn heads) had affirmed that the individual could achieve salvation without the church hierarchy. A century later the Judaizers denied some Christian doctrines and refused to venerate icons or the Virgin Mary. Subscribing to the law of Moses, the Judaizers celebrated the sabbath on Saturday and repudiated church ownership of property. Led by able theologians, they won highly placed converts (Ivan himself sympathized) and seriously threatened the established church. Another threat was posed by the Trans-Volga Elders, led by Nil Maikov (Nil Sorskii) of Sora Hermitage, who denounced church wealth and corruption and espoused an ascetic life in remote monasteries as 13th-century European friars had done. At a church council in 1503 Nil Sorskii with Ivan's support urged monasteries to renounce their landed estates, but Vasili, heir to the throne, backed conservative circles led by Father Joseph.

Joseph Sanin (1439?–1515) had founded Volokolamsk Monastery near Moscow as a bulwark against heresy and reform. Though prosperous, its strict rules stressed ritual, obedience, and submission. The church, argued Joseph, must own property in order to fulfill its functions and attract able clerics. Monks should concentrate on religious matters without having to perform manual labor. Joseph's writings strongly advocated divine-right absolutism. The ruler with authority derived directly from God should be the guardian of his people, supreme judge, and defender of Orthodoxy and should set a Christian example:

> The sun has its task—to shine on the people of this earth; the king has his task too—to take

---

[5] *Deti boyarskie* (boyar children) were military servitors of the grand prince.

care of those under him. You [rulers] received the sceptre of kingship from God, see to it that you satisfy Him who has given it to you. . . . For in body the king is like unto all men, but in power he is like unto God Almighty.[6]

Against an unworthy ruler the subject's only recourse would be passive disobedience. Joseph provided full justification for tsarist absolutism and the subordination of church to state.

Ivan faced a difficult, perplexing choice. On the one hand, the Trans-Volga Elders and the Judaizers backed his desire to seize church land but were political conservatives who supported boyar power. On the other hand, the Josephists espoused Ivan's claims to absolutism but insisted that the church retain its lands and wealth. In 1504 Ivan finally yielded to Vasili, and a church council condemned leading Judaizers to death. Ivan won loyal backing from church conservatives, but the church lost vital, reforming elements.

His last years brought Ivan III disappointment and frustration. His wife and son, whose political views he distrusted, had triumphed; and attempts to control Kazan with Moscow-trained puppet rulers had failed. Worst of all, the Lithuanian war ended indecisively with Smolensk in enemy hands. Although Ivan died unmourned and unloved in October 1505, he fully deserved his title, the Great. Building on sound foundations, he "gathered" the Great Russian lands, undermined separatism, and achieved centralization. He paralyzed the Tatar threat and began reconquering Belorussia and Ukraine from Lithuania. Ivan acquired glory and prestige abroad without ruining Muscovy financially. The price of unity, however, was temporary cultural stagnation and spiritual decline because his suppression of political and religious dissent raised barriers against cultural contacts with the West.

Vasili III (1505–1533)

Ivan III's son Vasili III ably continued most of his policies. The more brilliant reigns of his father and in turn of Vasili's son, Ivan IV, have obscured Vasili's considerable achievements. Though lively and physically active, he displayed a remarkable subtlety. Like his father, Vasili resorted to force only when it was necessary and coerced without cruelty. Baron von Herberstein, who visited his court, asserted with exaggeration: "In the control which he exercises over his people [Vasili] easily surpasses all the rulers of the entire world."[7] Though able to act more authoritatively than Ivan, he was still not a true autocrat. Careful not to offend the boyars as a group, Vasili often consulted with the Boyar Duma, which remained in permanent session. He treated individual boyars disdainfully but neither removed prominent grandees from office nor interfered with their manorial rights. Boyar support remained indispensable to the crown.

Backed by the Josephists, Vasili III continued Ivan's work of centralization. His father's testament granted him 66 towns against 30 for his four brothers combined, and if a brother died intestate, his portion would revert to the crown. Appanage rights were reduced: Vasili's brothers could no longer coin money or deal with foreign powers. Centripetal forces attracted remaining Great Russian lands and princes irresistibly to Moscow. Semi-independent Pskov was annexed in 1510, and Riazan principality was incorporated in 1517. Deportation of their leading families consolidated Moscow's control and allowed Vasili to reward loyal servitors. Muscovite officials were instructed to suppress any opposition.

Joseph Sanin's disciple, Daniel, continued his policies at Volokolamsk and became metropolitan in 1522. Over objections from traditionalists he solemnized Vasili's divorce from a barren first wife and his marriage to Elena Glinskaia. When this marriage produced a male heir, Ivan, Vasili

---

[6] M. Raeff, "An Early Theorist of Absolutism: Joseph of Volokolamsk," in *Readings in Russian History,* vol. 1, ed. T. Harcave (New York, 1962), p. 181.

[7] Cited in G. Vernadsky, *Russia at the Dawn of the Modern Age* (New Haven, 1959), p. 134.

repudiated the conservative religious faction led by the learned Maxim the Greek. Josephism triumphed fully at the church council of 1531, which sentenced the monk Vassian, leader of the Trans-Volga Elders and Daniel's chief opponent, to life imprisonment.

Muscovite expansion helped produce an imperial ideology under Vasili III. Like Ivan III, he used the title Sovereign of All Russia and occasionally tsar—that is, Caesar or emperor. Religious writers elaborated theories to explain his divine authority. According to Spiridon of Tver, Riurik was a descendant of the Roman emperor Augustus; the grand prince of Kiev, Vladimir II, had obtained his crown and regalia from the Byzantine ruler Constantine Monomachus. In 1510 Abbot Filofei of Pskov in a letter to Vasili formulated the famous Third Rome theory: "Two Romes fell down, the third [Moscow] is standing, and there will be no fourth." After Rome's fall, he explained, the center of true Christianity had moved to Constantinople, and after the Byzantine union with Rome of 1439, to Moscow. Filofei did not urge, as some historians assert, Moscow to rule the world but rather emphasized Vasili's duties and responsibilities as Orthodoxy's leading ruler. The sincerely religious Vasili accepted such theories and laid ideological bases for the tsardom of his son, Ivan IV.

Abroad, the defection of Moscow's former ally, the Crimean khanate, complicated Vasili's tasks. Between them began a difficult and protracted struggle. Khan Mohammed Girei's troops reached Moscow's outskirts in 1521 and caused widespread devastation, while the Crimea and Lithuania combated Muscovite influence in Kazan. Trouble with this eastern neighbor induced Moscow to strengthen defenses along the Oka River and settle Cossack frontiersmen in border regions to the south. Vasili also resumed the struggle with Lithuania, and in 1514 the key fortress city of Smolensk was captured and retained. Attempts by Vasili's brothers to use the war to intrigue against him failed. Vasili divided Muscovy between his two sons, but Iuri's death without issue eventually consolidated the entire country under Ivan IV. The unification of Great Russia

under Ivan III and Vasili III and the development of grand princely power and a Muscovite administrative system laid sound bases for the autocracy of Ivan the Terrible.

Suggested Additional Reading

BOOKS

BACKUS, O. *Motives of West Russian Nobles in Deserting Lithuania for Moscow, 1377–1514* (Lawrence, KS, 1957).

———. *Rulers and Nobles in Fifteenth Century Moscovy* (London, 1983). (A collection of articles.)

BARON, S. *Muscovite Russia: Collected Essays* (London, 1980).

BERRY, L. E., and R. O. CRUMMEY, eds. *Rude and Barbarous Kingdom: Russia in the Accounts of Sixteenth Century English Voyagers* (Madison, WI, 1968).

CROSKEY, R. *Muscovite Diplomatic Practice in the Reign of Ivan III* (New York, 1987).

DEWEY, H. ed. and comp. *Muscovite Judicial Texts, 1488–1556* (Ann Arbor, MI, 1968).

GILL, J. *The Council of Florence* (Cambridge, 1959).

GREY, I. *Ivan III and the Unification of Russia* (New York, 1964).

HALECKI, O. *From Florence to Brest, 1439–1596* (New York, 1959).

HELLIE, R., trans. *Readings for Introduction to Russian Civilization: Muscovite Society* (Chicago, 1967).

HERBERSTEIN, S. VON. *Commentaries on Muscovite Affairs*, trans. O. Backus (Lawrence, KS, 1956).

MEDLIN, W. K. *Moscow and East Rome . . .* (Geneva, 1952).

PELENSKI, J. *Russia and Kazan: Conquest and Imperial Ideology, 1438–1560* (The Hague, 1974).

POSSEVINO, A. *The Moscovia*, trans. H. Graham (Pittsburgh, 1977).

PRESNIAKOV, A. E. *The Tsardom of Moscovy*, trans. and ed. R. Price (Gulf Breeze, FL, 1978).

RABA, J. *The Moscow Kremlin: Mirror of the Newborn Muscovite State* (Tel Aviv, 1977).

SOLOVIEV, S. M. *The Age of Vasili III*, trans. and ed. H. Graham (Gulf Breeze, FL, 1976).

———. *The Reign of Ivan III*, trans. and ed. J. Windhausen (Gulf Breeze, FL, 1978).

VERNADSKY, G. *Russia at the Dawn of the Modern Age* (New Haven, 1959).

VON STADEN, H. *The Land and Government of Moscovy . . .* , trans. and ed. T. Esper (Stanford, 1967).

World Congress for Soviet and East European Studies (Harrogate, England, 1990). *New Perspectives on Muscovite History: Selected Papers,* ed. L. Hughes (New York, 1993).

ARTICLES

ALEF, G. "Aristocratic Politics and Royal Policy in Muscovy in the Late Fifteenth and Early Sixteenth Centuries." *FOG* 27: 77–109.

———. "Muscovite History in Recent Soviet Publications." *SR* 20 (1961): 517–22.

DEWEY, H. "The 1497 Sudebnik . . ." *ASEER* 39 (1951): 325–38.

DEWEY, H., and A. KLEIMOLA. "Old Muscovite Amnesties . . ." *Rus. Hist.* 3, no. 1 (1976): 49–60.

EATON, H. "Cadasters and Censuses of Muscovy." *SR* 26 (1967): 54–69.

ESPER, T. "Russia and the Baltic, 1494–1558." *SR* 14 (1955): 458–74.

———. "A Sixteenth Century Anti-Russian Arms Embargo." *JfGO* 15 (1967): 180–96.

———. "Military Self-Sufficiency and Weapons Technology in Muscovite Russia." *SR* 28, no. 2 (1968): 185–208.

FENNELL, J. L. "The Attitude of the Josephians . . ." *SEER* 29 (1950): 486–509.

HALPERIN, C. J. "Kiev and Moscow: An Aspect of Early Muscovite Thought." *Rus. Hist.* 7, no. 3 (1980): 312–21.

———. "Tverian Political Thought in the Fifteenth Century." *Cahiers du monde* 18, no. 3: 267–73.

KAISER, D. H. "Church and State in Old Rus." *SR* 36 (1977): 658–66.

KLEIMOLA, A. "The Changing Face of the Muscovite Aristocracy . . . " *JfGO* 25, no. 4 (1977): 481–93.

MAJESKA, G. "The Moscow Coronation of 1498 Reconsidered." *JfGO* 26, no. 3 (1978): 353–61.

ORCHARD, G. "The Town of Medieval Muscovy." *New Review* 7 (1980): 34–43.

RAEFF, M. "An Early Theorist of Absolutism: Joseph of Volokolamsk." *ASEER* 8 (1949): 79–89.

RYWKIN, M. "Russian Colonial Expansion before Ivan the Dread . . ." *Rus. Rev.* 32, no. 3 (1973): 286–93.

WAUGH, D. "Two Unpublished Muscovite Chronicles." *OSP* 12: 1–31.

YARESH, L. [pseud.]. "The Formation of the Great Russian State," in *Rewriting Russian History,* ed. C. E. Black (New York, 1962), pp. 198–223.

11

Ivan the Terrible (1533–1584)

The lengthy reign of Ivan IV (the Terrible)[1] was crucial to the development of the autocratic, centralized Russian national monarchy. Ivan himself and his epoch still remain rather obscure and controversial because sufficient reliable documentary materials are lacking. Many scholars view Ivan's sporadic cruelty as typifying the crude, self-destructive Asiatic qualities of Muscovy, with its legacy of subjugation to Tatar domination. The reevaluation of Ivan IV's historical role by Soviet scholars beginning in the mid-1930s intensified the debate on whether his reign marked a constructive era of building a strong and progressive state or a period of senseless bloodshed, chaos, and destruction. Few would deny that violence and tyranny often prevailed, but these were also typical of 16th-century Europe. "Bloody Mary" of England, Ivan IV's contemporary, had many Protestants burned at the stake; in France occurred the unprovoked murder of thousands of Huguenots on St. Bartholomew's Day in 1572.

Soviet historians in the Stalin era portrayed Ivan IV's reign as the era when centralized monarchy triumphed over political feudalism represented by the appanage princes. Robert Wipper especially depicted Ivan as a farsighted, progressive statesman who crushed selfish opposition from reactionary princes and boyars. After 1985 Soviet scholars expressed a more balanced view untainted by the need to fit Ivan into a Marxist-Leninist mold. Some, notably D. N. Alshits of St. Petersburg University, view Ivan's tyranny as a precursor of Stalin's totalitarian regime. Did Ivan's autocratic policies, like the Oprichnina, truly smash feudal opposition, or did they undermine the state's economic and political strengths and pave the way for the subsequent "Time of Troubles"?

Minority and Rule with the Chosen Council

Ivan IV's youth was a period of feudal disorder and boyar intrigue that threatened to destroy Muscovy's nascent central institutions. It resembled the anarchy of the Wars of the Roses in

---

[1] The Russian term *groznyi,* used to refer to Ivan IV, is sometimes translated "the dread" or "the awe-inspiring."

England (1450–1485) and of the Fronde (late 1640s) in France, which likewise represented a resurgence of the feudal nobility. In none of these countries was the central bureaucratic apparatus then sufficiently developed or entrenched to govern in an effective and orderly fashion without a strong ruler. When Vasili III died in 1533, his heir, Ivan IV, was only three years old. At first Ivan IV's mother, Elena Glinskaia, directed a regency that resisted the appanage princes and undertook town construction, notably of the Kitai-gorod section of Moscow. But after her death in 1538 powerful boyar families—the Shuiskiis, Belskiis, and Glinskiis—contended for power and wealth. They seized state lands, looted the treasury, and enhanced the power of the Boyar Duma. Unlimited application of the principle of *mestnichestvo,* which stressed noble birth and the position of relatives, undermined the army's effectiveness. As the boyars exiled, executed, and poisoned one another, they, like the French nobility of the Fronde, discredited themselves as a ruling group while support grew among the gentry and merchants for strong central rule.

Ivan IV's character and unhappy childhood inclined him to assert full autocratic power. Information about his youth is fragmentary and disputed, but by the age of nine he had lost both parents and his favorite governess. The boyars, though according him outward respect, scorned and abused him in private. Later Ivan supposedly wrote Prince Andrei Kurbskii:

> What sufferings did I not endure through lack of clothing and from hunger! For in all things my will was not my own. . . . While we [Ivan and his younger brother] were playing childish games in our infancy, Prince Ivan Vasilevich Shuiskii was sitting on a bench, leaning with his elbows on our father's bed with his leg up on a chair. . . . And who can endure such arrogance?[2]

Sudden gyrations between grandeur and neglect, adding to Ivan's emotional instability, stimulated

his intense hatred and suspicion of the old boyar aristocracy. At the age of 13 he first asserted himself by having a chief tormentor, Prince Andrei Shuiskii, executed. Kurbskii relates that young Ivan often hurled pet animals into the palace courtyard and watched their convulsions. With boon companions Ivan engaged in orgies and rode through Moscow trampling people underfoot. According to some sources, Ivan read religious and historical texts avidly, becoming Russia's most literate ruler before Catherine the Great. Edward Keenan cast some doubt on the authorship of many works formerly attributed to Ivan and even questioned his literacy, a view challenged vigorously by Soviet scholars and some Western authorities.[3]

Metropolitan Macarius, a trusted adviser, urged the youthful Ivan to rule as autocrat. Ivan IV's formal coronation in the Kremlin in January 1547 as Muscovy's first tsar enhanced his authority at home and raised his prestige abroad. In February he married Anastasia Zakharina-Koshkina, from an ancient boyar family that supported centralization, but disorders persisted. In June a mysterious fire burned most of Moscow, killing more than 2,700 people. A rebellious mob seized control of Moscow, broke into Ivan's quarters, and left only when convinced that he was not shielding Glinskiis, who were believed to be responsible. Uprisings in Moscow and other towns and peasant revolts revealed grave social tensions and unrest, left young Ivan terrified, and convinced him of the need for reliable support and real power. At the same time, they freed him from the tutelage of the old boyar elite.[4]

Frightened by these events and influenced by Archpriest Silvester, who warned him that God was punishing him for his sins, Ivan entrusted the government to a Chosen Council of leading aristocrats and churchmen. Including Silvester, Macarius, and Alexis Adashev, a courtier of gentry

---

[2] J. L. Fennell, *The Correspondence between Prince A. M. Kurbskey and Tsar Ivan IV* (Cambridge, 1955), p. 75.

[3] E. Keenan, *The Kurbskii-Groznyi Apocrypha* (Cambridge, MA, 1971), pp. 53 ff.

[4] D. N. Alshits, *Nachalo samoderzhaviia v Rossii* (Leningrad, 1988), p. 39.

background, this oligarchy made important decisions and directed the young tsar. Wrote Kurbskii, an advocate of such limited monarchy:

> There gathered around him [Ivan IV] advisers, men of understanding and perfection, . . . and all of these are wholly skilled in military and the land's affairs, . . . and they drew close to him in amity and friendship so that without their advice nothing is planned or undertaken, . . . and at that time those counsellors of his were called the Chosen Council.[5]

To win public support, the government apparently convened an assembly of the land (*zemskii sobor*) composed of members of the clergy, titled aristocracy, and gentry. Ivan S. Peresvetov, a leader of the ordinary west Russian gentry, petitioned Ivan to use men of service like himself to build a reliable army and a centralized monarchy. Greeting Ivan as "a sovereign terrible and wise," Peresvetov denounced boyar limitations on the ruler and proposed royal courts to protect commoners against magnates and governors. For favoring autocracy over feudalism and denouncing slavery, Peresvetov was considered a progressive by many Soviet historians.

Governmental and military reforms heralding oncoming absolutism had begun even under boyar rule. In the Boyar Duma princely families, supplying top political and military figures, were challenged by state secretaries and upper gentry (*dumnye dvoriane*), supporters of central authority. In the provinces the *kormlenie* (tax feeding) system and its officials had become obsolete and corrupt, and frequent rotations of princely provincial governors reduced the judicial and political power of these officials. To prevent princes and boyars from defecting to a foreign suzerain, the grand prince had begun to demand loyalty oaths from them.

The Chosen Council expressed the aspirations of the ordinary gentry, town leaders, and moderate churchmen, many of whom favored a centralized monarchy acting in the public interest. In the army

Ivan Vasilevich, Ivan IV, tsar and grand prince of all Russia, 1530–1584.

mestnichestvo was restricted and sometimes set aside for individual campaigns by the ruler but was not abolished. An official Book of Genealogies (*Rodoslovets*) of noble families was compiled, and the government tried to adjudicate service disputes. Establishment of central command enhanced the effectiveness of gentry forces, and newly formed detachments of royal musketeers (*streltsy*) constituted a regularly paid infantry loyal to the crown. The tsar's control of the army was thus increased without any direct attack on the prerogatives of the feudal lords. Some central administrative departments (*izby*) were reformed on a functional basis, including the Petitions Board, which heard gentry appeals against boyars, and what became the Foreign Office.[6] The grow-

---

[5] J. L. Fennell, ed., *Prince A. M. Kurbsky's History of Ivan IV* (Cambridge, 1965), p. 21.

[6] At first the latter was called the Board of State Secretary I. M. Viskovaty, after the able official who developed it as a separate institution.

ing central secretarial bureaucracy prevailed increasingly over regional courts and officials. An optional *zemskaia* (local self-government) reform gradually replaced governors with local organs having police, judicial, and financial powers and chosen by free peasants and townspeople, not for genuine self-government but to ensure more efficient tax collection. The *Sudebnik* (law code) of 1550, like that of 1497 (see Chapter 10), aimed to improve judicial procedure and protect gentry interests by making governors responsible for their subordinates' misdeeds and by facilitating the alienation of hereditary landholdings. The Chosen Council even sought to assuage the gentry's land hunger, but found little free land and dared not confiscate boyar estates.

In the latter 1550s, indeed until its fall in 1560, the Chosen Council extended these reforms and further curtailed boyar power.[7] The *kormlenie* (tax feeding) system was abolished except in frontier regions, and in the central provinces governors were largely superseded by military men (*voevody*). Freed from their tax collection duties, the gentry became more effective army officers. A law of 1556 regularized and standardized military service, which for noblemen was to last from age 15 to death or incapacitation. It prescribed regular salaries for army service, depending on birth and the size of one's estate. This decree produced a more efficient, loyal army of some 150,000 men, about half of whom were gentry cavalry supplemented with *streltsy* (musketeers), Cossacks, Tatar auxiliaries, and foreign troops. Because army service and the possession of landed estates were made hereditary, the distinction between *votchina* (patrimonial) and *pomestie* (service) lands faded.

In March 1553 Ivan IV's grave illness provoked a brief political crisis that threatened central authority and confirmed his suspicions of princes and boyars. With death seemingly near, Ivan drew up a testament that directed his courtiers to swear allegiance to his infant son, Dmitri. Almost half of the Boyar Duma, however, some perhaps to avoid another chaotic regency, supported his cousin Prince Vladimir Andreevich of Staritsa, the candidate of the appanage princes. Ivan's sudden recovery ended the crisis, but this episode reaffirmed boyar hostility toward Ivan's policies of autocracy and centralization. When Dmitri died, the tsar's newborn son, Ivan Ivanovich, became heir and Prince Staritskii's influence waned.

Compromise prevailed in church reform. To glorify Russian Orthodoxy and outdo the Catholic church, Metropolitan Macarius had church councils canonize 39 saints, more than in the previous 500 years. In 1551 Ivan convened the Hundred Chapters Council (*Stoglav*), named for the 100 questions submitted in Ivan's name, to reform the church and dramatize its independence from foreign control. Reaffirmed was the Byzantine principle of the symphony of church and state: "Mankind has two great gifts from God . . . : the priesthood and the tsardom. The former directs the spiritual needs; the latter governs and takes care of the human things. Both derive from the same origin."[8] The church hierarchy was scolded for holding incomplete services, charging excessive fees, and tolerating corrupt and drunken priests. Though pledging to remedy such abuses, the conclave balked at more drastic reform. Church landholding and tax privileges were restricted (henceforth new land could be acquired only with the tsar's consent), but Ivan's wish to secularize clerical lands was disregarded. Displeased at this half measure, Ivan soon removed from office leading opponents of secularization. In decisions that later became significant, the Hundred Chapters Council approved crossing oneself with two fingers (symbolizing the dual nature of Christ) and the double alleluia (see Chapter 14).

---

[7] A. N. Grobovsky, in *The "Chosen Council" of Ivan IV: A Reinterpretation* (New York, 1969), has argued that the council never existed as an institution but was merely a group of well-intentioned individuals.

[8] Quoted in G. Vernadsky, *A History of Russia.* Vol. 5 *The Tsardom of Muscovy, 1547–1682* (New Haven, 1969), part 1, p. 47.

Generally speaking, the reforms of the Chosen Council consolidated central authority while compromising on key political and social issues. During the 1550s the policies of Ivan IV as ruler and those of the council largely coincided and produced constructive though only partial reforms.

External Affairs

Ivan IV's principal external success—the conquest of Kazan—enhanced his prestige, whereas the subsequent Livonian War in the Baltic left the autocracy gravely weakened. Since the creation of the Kazan khanate in 1445 (see Chapter 10), Moscow had sought to ensure its friendship or vassaldom. Until the 1520s peaceful relations with Kazan, vital to Moscow's eastern trade, were generally preserved and Muscovite campaigns against Kazan aimed to end internal strife there, not to conquer it. Under Vasili III, Kazan, recognizing Moscow's suzerainty, pledged not to select a khan without Russian approval. After 1535, however, frequent raids from Kazan struck Muscovy (see Map 11.1), and numerous Muscovite captives were sold into slavery. In 1551 some sources reported that more than 100,000 Muscovites were held prisoner in Kazan. Muscovite reconnaissance expeditions revealed Kazan's growing military strength. For religious reasons the Orthodox church had long advocated the annexation of Muslim Kazan; for the gentry, Peresvetov stressed the profits and lands to be won. After Safa-Girei's death in 1549 some Kazan magnates backed the Muscovite candidate as khan, but Muscovy's territorial demands encouraged anti-Moscow elements to seize control, to invite Iadigar of Astrakhan to take Kazan's throne, and to prepare for war. Moscow faced a possible Tatar coalition.

In April 1552 Ivan and his advisers decided to attack Kazan. Metropolitan Macarius exhorted the army to fight the infidels who were shedding Christian blood and to free Russian captives. Ivan's large army, besieging the city, shut off its water supply. After breaching the walls with artillery, a major technological innovation, the

Muscovites stormed Kazan, killed many of its defenders, and annexed the khanate. Ivan's troops then moved south to conquer the weaker Astrakhan khanate and opened the entire Volga valley to Russian colonization and the Caspian Sea to Russian trade.

The Volga Tatar region was Muscovy's first major non-Slavic annexation. Neighboring steppe peoples, impressed by Moscow's power, submitted voluntarily to the Russian tsar, successor to the khan of the Golden Horde. Later, as Muscovites moved eastward to the Ural Mountains and beyond, rulers of nomadic west Siberian tribes pledged vague allegiance to Moscow. In 1581 a small private army of Cossacks and steppe fugitives, hired by the wealthy Stroganov merchant family to protect its huge salt and fur empire, moved across the Urals under Ermak Timofeevich, a bold Cossack freebooter. By 1583 his band of Cossacks had conquered the west Siberian domain of Khan Kuchum. Overcoming initial displeasure at this distant involvement, Ivan IV welcomed Ermak's Cossacks as heroes. Eastward expansion under Ivan IV laid the basis for a Eurasian Russian empire (see Chapter 13).

Direct relations between Russia and England were established by accident. In 1553 Richard Chancellor's ship, *Edward Bonaventure,* part of an English expedition seeking an Arctic sea route to China, landed on the shores of the White Sea. For England this amounted to the discovery of Muscovy, which had been virtually unknown to the best-educated Englishmen. Ivan welcomed Chancellor warmly in Moscow and granted the English Muscovy Company a monopoly of duty-free trade with Russia. Carried in English ships, that trade profited both sides: Russia exchanged forest products and furs for English manufactures and luxuries. Anglo-Russian trade stimulated the development of the White Sea port of Archangel, which when Muscovy lost its Baltic ports in the Livonian War, remained its only direct sea link with western Europe. The English tie helped Ivan overcome a blockade by his western neighbors. Livonia and Poland, fearful of Russia's potential strength, were barring technicians and merchants

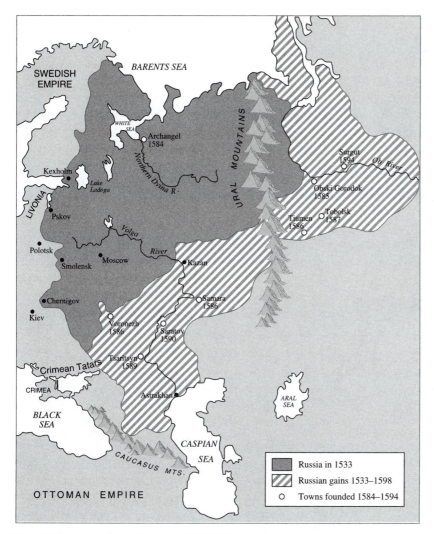

Map 11.1 Expansion of Russia, 1533–1598

from reaching Muscovy. In 1547, when Hans Schlitte, a German adventurer, recruited specialists for Ivan, the Hanseatic League had them arrested.

The Baltic region therefore became for Ivan IV, as later for Peter the Great (see Chapter 15), his chief foreign involvement. In the late 1550s the government debated priorities in foreign policy. Adashev and I. M. Viskovaty, who had been directing foreign relations, favored caution in the West. Believing that the Crimean Tatars were a direct threat to Muscovy, Adashev and Prince

Kurbskii of the Chosen Council urged Ivan to lead the army in person to conquer the Crimea. Ivan and gentry leaders, however, favored attacking Livonia because of its military weakness, the availability of land there, and the importance of the Baltic Sea for Russian commerce. To conquer the Crimea, they argued, would require Polish aid. Soviet historians affirmed that the Livonian War (1558–1582), which would benefit the rising gentry and merchant classes, was progressive, whereas a southward advance, favored by the

Russian merchant of the 16th century.

feudal aristocracy in order to seize new lands, was not. Vernadsky, however, points out that petty gentry and Cossacks then populated the southern borderlands and that Crimean raids into Muscovy affected the entire population. Instead of turning against the Crimea, Ivan became involved in war on two fronts and eventually suffered defeat.

By itself, Livonia, declining and split internally among the Livonian Order, the archbishop of Riga, and autonomous cities, was no match for Muscovy. In 1558 Ivan invaded it, using the pretext of Livonia's alliance with Lithuania. When his troops conquered eastern Estonia and reached Riga's outskirts, Adashev advised peace, provided Ivan could obtain eastern Estonia with the Baltic ports of Narva and Derpt. Ivan reluctantly authorized an armistice, but the Livonian Order used it to secure Lithuania's assistance. In 1560, against

Adashev's advice, Ivan renewed the war in order to conquer all of Livonia. His territorial greed brought Lithuania, Sweden, and Poland together against him and overstrained Muscovy's resources in a war it could not win. Even Robert Wipper, a Soviet historian who praised Ivan highly, admitted that the Livonian War became his obsession and ruined Russia.[9]

The Oprichnina and After

Ivan broke with moderates of the Chosen Council to pursue a risky foreign policy and brutal terror at home. The breach occurred before the death of Anastasia, Ivan IV's beloved first wife, cited by traditional historians as its cause. As military reverses mounted in Livonia, Ivan punished boyar commanders whom he held responsible and promoted ordinary gentry servitors. Contrary to Russian law, Adashev and Silvester were convicted of treason in absentia. The intervention of Metropolitan Macarius prevented their execution, but his death (in December 1563) removed the last restraint upon Ivan's punishment of real or imagined enemies. Repression spread fear and confusion among Muscovite commanders and administrators. Lithuania exploited these fears, promising estates and high positions to Muscovite boyars if they would defect. In 1564, tempted by promised rewards, Prince Kurbskii, a top boyar commander, fled to Lithuania following a major defeat. Other boyar defections followed. The Crimean khan attacked Riazan and carried off numerous captives. Ivan confronted growing opposition to his war policy. Without vindicating Adashev, he could not make peace with Lithuania and fight the Crimean Tatars as the metropolitan and loyal boyars advised. Instead, Ivan established the Oprichnina, or separate royal domain, to crush his opponents and create his personal autocracy.

In December 1564, in a carefully prepared tactical move, Ivan left Moscow with his family, valuables, and many top officials. After prayers at the

---

[9] R. Wipper, *Ivan Grozny* (Moscow, 1947), p. 73.

Trinity Monastery he proceeded to nearby Aleksandrovsk Settlement and dispatched two messages to Moscow. The first, accusing the boyars of treason, announced his abdication as tsar. The second, to the commoners, absolved them of blame and sought their support for a new regime. Receiving a Moscow delegation headed by the metropolitan, Ivan agreed to cancel his "abdication," provided he received a free hand to punish "traitors." In January 1565 he announced the formation of the Oprichnina, or separate domain over which he would exercise full control. Ivan celebrated his return to Moscow by executing some leading boyars.

The Oprichnina produced a territorial division of Muscovy, a new royal court, and a security police (see Problem 3 at the end of this chapter). Centering in Aleksandrovsk Settlement, a temporary second capital, it included scattered portions of Moscow, commercial areas of the northeast, and strategic western frontier towns; eventually it included about half the country. The rest—the *zemshchina*—remained under the regular administration of the Boyar Duma. In Aleksandrovsk Ivan acted as abbot of a "Satan's band" that combined monastic asceticism with violence and debauchery. His *oprichnik* corps, initially 1,000 strong, grew to 6,000 men from all social groups. Massive land transfers that accompanied the Oprichnina dislocated agriculture and army organization. At least 9,000 boyar sons and gentry were evicted from Oprichnina regions.

Forced to choose between making a compromise peace and continuing the Livonian War, in 1566 Ivan sought public support by convening an assembly of the lands, which contained many gentry and merchants. This handpicked assembly approved continuing the war until all Livonia and Riga had been won, but neither it nor Ivan foresaw the war's disastrous outcome.

The church soon felt Ivan's wrath. After Macarius's death he barred top churchmen from his administration. After appointing Philip metropolitan (1566), Ivan discovered Philip's strong opposition to Oprichnina terror when Philip interceded repeatedly for its victims. Having ties with Prince Vladimir Andreevich of Staritsa and Novgorod, alleged proponents of separatism, Philip opposed Ivan's centralizing policies. In 1568, after Philip denounced the Oprichnina openly, he was deposed, exiled to a distant monastery, and finally strangled. The predominance of the state over the church was confirmed.

A reign of terror prevailed during the Oprichnina, as thousands of innocent people from all classes were killed. The mass executions in Moscow in 1570 were unprecedented in their sadism. State Secretary Viskovaty was dismembered publicly as the members of Ivan's entourage each hacked off a part of his body. Ivan himself killed a few people with pike and saber. Other victims had their skin torn off, and for each victim a different painful death was devised. The terror of 1570 also struck at officials of the *zemschchina*, which Ivan wished to subject wholly to his rule.

In the provinces Ivan crushed remnants of separatism and particularism. Receiving anonymous reports of supposed treason in Novgorod, in 1569 he prepared a massive punitive expedition by his private army of *oprichniki* and gave them lists of potentially dangerous people to be killed or arrested. En route, other suspect towns were punished cruelly: In Tver alone some 9,000 people from all social classes were murdered. In Novgorod Ivan confiscated monastic wealth to replenish his treasury, had some 40,000 people killed, and turned Novgorod into a virtual ghost town. Ivan, seeing treason everywhere, eliminated most former advisers, then executed their executioners.

Excesses by debauched *oprichnik* troops, pervasive fear and suspicion, and the splitting of the army into *oprichnik* and *zemshchina* detachments complicated Muscovy's defense. During the Crimean invasion of 1571 Ivan's decision to execute the army's commander-in-chief wrecked morale. The tsar fled to Beloozero, and the army retreated into Moscow while the Crimeans burned its suburbs and carried off some 100,000 captives. The following year Prince M. I. Vorotynskii defeated the Crimean khan decisively, but

Ivan, jealous of his popularity, removed and executed him.

The Livonian War finally turned against Russia. The Union of Lublin (1569), joining the Polish and Lithuanian crowns, created a large and powerful state. In 1572 Stephen Batory, an able military leader, became king and defeated the Russians repeatedly. Militant Polish leaders dreamed of converting Russia to Catholicism. Finally, Ivan appealed to Pope Gregory XIII to mediate. With infidel Turks threatening Europe, he wrote, it was no time for Christians to fight one another. The pope, hoping to bring Muscovy into the fold, dispatched Antonio Possevino, a Jesuit, to settle the Polish-Russian conflict, and by the armistice of 1582 Ivan ceded Polotsk and Livonia to Poland-Lithuania. Meanwhile Sweden, by the armistice of 1583, secured Narva, Ivangorod, and most of the Baltic coastline. Ivan IV's Baltic ambitions lay shattered. An already impoverished Muscovy was further impoverished and had to wait more than a century for an outlet to the western seas.

Ivan's attempts at an alliance with England also failed. Rejecting political ties, Queen Elizabeth I sought more commercial privileges for the English Muscovy Company. Writing Ivan in 1570, she spoke vaguely of an alliance and offered Ivan asylum in case he required it. In 1582 Ivan sought the hand of Mary Hastings, the queen's lady-in-waiting, intimating that he would discard his wife, Maria Nagaia. However, when she bore him a son, the ill-fated Dmitri (see Chapter 12), Ivan's marital and political overtures to England came to naught.

Ivan's final years produced little that was constructive. The Oprichnina, bloody and divisive at home, produced negative effects abroad. In 1572, after executing or disgracing Oprichnina leaders guilty of major crimes, Ivan sought to distance himself from their abuses. Some *oprichniki* lost their privileges, and their organization merged with the *zemshchina*. To deflect public indignation at continuing executions, Ivan proclaimed Simeon Bekbulatovich, a baptized descendant of Chingis-khan, grand prince of all Russia. Assuming the humbler title of prince of Moscow, Ivan pretended to defer to him while sending him secret orders.

Bekbulatovich became his scapegoat for unpopular policies. When the year ended without the catastrophes predicted by soothsayers, Ivan reassumed his titles and named Bekbulatovich grand prince of Tver. One of Ivan's final acts was to kill his heir, Ivan Ivanovich, in a fit of rage. Ivan died in 1584, a disillusioned and broken man.

Ivan's Reign Assessed

Soviet research under Stalin produced favorable assessments of the reign of Ivan IV. He was a Renaissance prince whose methods resembled those of other "terrible" rulers of his time, such as Henry VIII and Cesare Borgia. Ivan's autocracy, one could argue, was essential to defend and expand the realm and dispense justice within it. He had to be cruel and severe in order to curb boyar privilege and deal with disobedient subjects.[10] In the first letter to Prince Kurbskii (or was it instead written by S. F. Shakhovskoi?),[11] Ivan set forth a theory of divine-right monarchy based on the views of Macarius and Joseph of Volokolamsk. God had bestowed his crown, Ivan believed, and he was responsible to God alone. The letter traced autocracy in Russia (incorrectly) to Vladimir I (a limited monarch) and asserted that Ivan belonged to the oldest, most illustrious dynasty in Europe as a direct descendant of the Roman emperor Augustus Caesar. The fall of Byzantium was cited as proof that autocratic rule was necessary in Russia. These views were unoriginal, but the Third Rome thesis combined with assorted biblical texts constituted the most complete Muscovite theory of autocracy. Ivan admonished his sons to learn their trade carefully before becoming tsar:

---

[10] See M. Cherniavsky, "Ivan the Terrible as Renaissance Prince," *SR* 27, no. 2 (1968): 195–211.

[11] Edward Keenan in *The Kurbskii-Groznyi Apocrypha* challenges the authenticity of the entire *Correspondence*, attributes much of it to Shakhovskoi in the 1620s, and questions the authorship of other writings hitherto attributed to Kurbskii and Ivan IV. His conclusions, however, have not been generally accepted.

Muscovite envoys about to be received by the German emperor in 1576. Note that they carry gifts of furs.

You should become familiar with all kinds of affairs: the divine, the priestly, the monastic, the military, and the judicial; with the patterns of life in Moscow and elsewhere; . . . how the administrative institutions function here and in other states. All this you must know yourselves. Then you will not depend on others' advice, you yourselves will give directions to them.[12]

On the other hand, Prince Kurbskii (if it was indeed he) from safe Lithuanian exile advocated limited monarchy and defended ancient boyar rights and the Duma's essential role in government. In letters to Tsar Ivan he justified his defection by the boyars' ancient right to shift suzerains at will. Kurbskii dreamed of a past when boyars were the ruler's equals, not his subjects. Ivan IV, he claimed, had ruled wisely with the Chosen Council. Unfortunately, "such a fine tsar" had later resorted to unnatural personal autocracy to suppress boyar freedom.

Even with recent evidence supplied by Soviet historians, it is difficult to draw up a fair balance sheet for Ivan IV's reign. Negative aspects, stressed by Kliuchevskii and Florinsky, are evident: the vengeful cruelty of Ivan, which snuffed out so many lives, and external failures in the south and west, especially the loss of the Baltic seacoast. It can be claimed that the Oprichnina undermined the state, demoralized the army, and disrupted land relationships, thus contributing powerfully to the coming "Time of Troubles." The great cost of the unsuccessful Livonian War helped fasten serfdom upon the Russian peasantry. Ivan failed to crush the boyars politically, and they remained entrenched in state positions and the Duma. Concludes Vernadsky: "Ivan's policies—both external and domestic—ended in failure."[13]

Soviet historians stressed the brighter side. During Ivan's reign, they noted, political and military centralization triumphed in Muscovy, the antiquated appanage principle was virtually destroyed, and "progressive" gentry and merchant elements rose. The reforms of the 1550s, though compromises, built firm foundations for a powerful monarchy able to protect Russia's security. In foreign affairs Ivan ended the Livonian War without crippling losses, and his eastern conquests began Muscovy's transformation into a Eurasian empire. Chancellor's arrival broke the western blockade, brought in vitally needed technicians, and began mutually profitable Anglo-Russian trade.

[12] Cited in Vernadsky, *Tsardom,* vol. 1, p. 170.

[13] Vernadsky, vol. 1, p. 175.

Farsighted in some ways, nearsighted in others, Ivan and his reign should neither be glorified nor totally condemned. A Soviet apologist for Ivan wrote: "The fate of Ivan IV was the tragedy of a warrior who was beaten by circumstances over which he had no control. He threw all his posses-sions into the scales of fortune, and not only did he lose his newly acquired territories, but the state, which he had only just built up, was shaken to its foundations."[14]

[14] Wipper, *Ivan Grozny,* p. 188.

Problem 3

The Oprichnina

Historians have differed sharply over this major but obscure measure of Ivan IV. Some have ascribed it to Ivan's "change of soul" after the death of Anastasia, his beloved first wife; others, to his quest for security from boyar plots or to a conscious plan to build a centralized autocratic state. The Oprichnina has also been depicted as Russia's first security police, an instrument to destroy the boyar class, and as a weapon of personal terror. A historian's view of the Oprichnina usually reveals his assessment of the entire reign: as constructive and statesmanlike or bloody and despotic. The following selections give divergent interpretations of the Oprichnina's causes, social composition, and significance.

Kliuchevskii's Appraisal

The outstanding prerevolutionary Russian historian V. O. Kliuchevskii asserted that the Oprichnina failed to solve the major political question of the time—conflicts between the ruler and the boyars—and that it was essentially aimless:

> The Oprichnina at first glance . . . represents an institution lacking all political purpose. Actually, while declaring in his message [to Moscow in January 1565] that all boyars were traitors and despoilers of the land, the tsar left its administration in the hands of these same traitors and plunderers. . . . The word *oprichnina* in the sixteenth century was already an antiquated term which the contemporary Muscovite chronicle translated as separate court . . . [and] was borrowed from the ancient appanage language. . . . The Oprichnina of Tsar Ivan was a court economic-administrative institution managing lands set aside to support the tsarist court. . . . [See Table 11.1.] The difference was merely that the Oprichnina with later acquisitions comprised almost half the entire country. . . . But one asks why this restoration or parody of the appanage idea? The tsar indicated an unprecedented task for an institution with such an archaic name: Oprichnina acquired the significance of a political refuge. . . . The idea that he must flee from his boyars gradually took possession of his mind, became an obsession. In his testament written about 1572 the tsar in all seriousness represented himself as an exile, a wanderer. There he writes: "For my numerous sins the wrath of God has been imposed upon me, the boyars have banished me from my property because of their wilfulness. . . ." Thus the Oprichnina was an institution to protect the tsar's personal security. It was given a political goal for which there was no special institution in the existing Muscovite state structure: . . . to wipe out sedition, nesting in Russia primarily among the boyars.
>
> The Oprichnina received the assignment as the highest police in matters of state treason. . . . As a separate police detachment, the Oprichnina obtained a special uniform. The oprichnik had attached to his saddle a dog's head and a broom; these were his insignia of office, and his tasks were to track down, smell out, and sweep away treason and destroy state scoundrels. The oprichnik rode clad in black from head to toe on a black horse with black harness. . . . This was a type of hermit order . . . surrounded with monastic and conspiratorial solemnity. . . .

Table 11.1 Division of Muscovy under the Oprichnina, 1565–1572

Oprichnina	Zemshchina
Territories: Coastal areas, important commercial regions, Stroganov lands in Urals, certain sections and streets in Moscow, central areas where boyar estates located.	*Territories:* All lands not part of the Oprichnina
Capital: Aleksandrovsk Settlement	*Capital:* Moscow
Ruler: Ivan IV, as grand prince of Moscow	*Ruler:* Simeon Bekbulatovich, "ruler of all Russia" (*Gosudar vseia Rusi*)

Oprichnaia Duma
  Oprichnye prikazy
    (Oprichnina bureaus)
□ □ □ ⬚
      ↓
	(Zemskaia) Boyar Duma
	  Zemskie prikazy
	    (regular bureaus)
	⬚ □ □ □
	  ↓

Oprichnina army	*Zemskaia* army
Oprichnina treasury	*Zemskaia* treasury

Problem 3 continued

The boyars could not bring order into the state structure without the ruler's authority, nor could the tsar rule his kingdom in its new boundaries without the boyars' cooperation. . . . Unable to get along or part from one another, they sought to separate, live side by side but not together. The Oprichnina was such an exit from their difficulty. . . . Unable to destroy a governmental system inconvenient for him, he wiped out individuals who were suspicious or hateful to him. In this consisted the political aimlessness of the Oprichnina: . . . it was directed against persons and not an order. . . . It was to a significant degree the fruit of the tsar's excessively fearful imagination. Ivan directed it against the terrible sedition supposedly persisting in boyar circles which threatened to destroy the entire tsarist family. But was the danger really so terrible? The boyars' political strength was undermined, aside from the Oprichnina, by conditions created directly or indirectly by the gathering of Russia around Moscow. . . .

Contemporaries understood that the Oprichnina, removing sedition, introduced anarchy; protecting the sovereign, it shook the bases of the state. Directed against imagined sedition, it prepared the real thing. . . . Colliding with the boyars . . . after

his illness of 1553 and especially after Kurbskii's flight, the tsar exaggerated the danger and became frightened. . . . He began to strike left and right without distinguishing friends from foes. Thus for the direction the tsar gave to the political conflict, his personal character was much to blame.[15]

Two Russian Views

In the introduction to an interesting monograph on the beginnings of the Oprichnina, a leading Russian historian presented this judicious and balanced analysis:

In the historiography of the Russian Middle Ages it is difficult to find a subject that has provoked as many differences and quarrels as the history of the Oprichnina. Some have seen the Oprichnina as the fruit of Tsar Ivan Vasilevich's sick imagination and considered it a historical accident. For others the Oprichnina was a planned, well-thought-out reform, a model of state wisdom, and the expression of objective necessity. Most recently have appeared major monographic studies on the Oprichnina's history, but even now the disputes it has caused are far from over. Generally, there is no

---

[15] V. O. Kliuchevskii, *Kurs russkoi istorii*, vol. 2 (Moscow, 1937, reprint), pp. 188–98.

objection to the fact that the stormy events of the Oprichnina were but a brief episode in Russia's lengthy transition from feudal division to absolutism. In the final analysis the Oprichnina was brought into existence by the conflict between a powerful feudal aristocracy and a rising autocratic monarchy. This conflict of itself, strictly speaking, contains no riddles. The enigma is: under what circumstances could such an ordinary conflict produce the bloody drama of the Oprichnina, unprecedented Oprichnina terror, which quickly outgrew the original narrow bounds of conflict.

Contrary to a very widespread view, the policy of the Oprichnina was never consistent with unified principles unchanged during its entire existence. The Oprichnina's development was marked by many contradictions and shifts. In its first stage Oprichnina policy bears a basically antiprincely direction as is shown by the decree of the Kazan exile and the massive confiscation of princely *votchinas*. The return of the disgraced princes from exile, the calling of the *zemskii sobor* of 1566, and other measures connected with the period of compromise . . . mark the end of the first stage. The chief political event of the Oprichnina's second stage from the political standpoint was the grandiose case of the Staritskii plot, ending with the execution of leaders of the Oprichnina, Boyar Duma, and Novgorod's destruction. The chief victims of Oprichnina mass terror in that period were old Muscovite boyars, church leaders, upper bureaucratic administrators, and in part gentry— the very layers of the ruling class that constituted the monarchy's most solid, traditional support. The Oprichnina's last victims were its own creators and inspirers. In a political sense the Oprichnina ended up by strengthening the power apparatus of the Russian centralized state. In the socioeconomic sphere its main results were the growth of feudal oppression, intensification of tendencies toward serfdom, and also deepening [of] the economic crisis that reached its peak after the Oprichnina in the 1580s.[16]

---

[16] R. G. Skrynnikov, *Nachalo Oprichniny* (Leningrad, 1966), pp. 3–4.

Using the newfound freedoms of *glasnost* (openness), Professor D. N. Alshits of St. Petersburg University argued in a later study, *The Beginning of Autocracy in Russia*, that the Oprichnina constituted Ivan IV's carefully articulated and successful plan both to emancipate himself wholly from restraints imposed by the Chosen Council and to build an unfettered personal autocracy, which became the tsarist regime:

Oprichnina . . . a system of political and economic measures . . . which shook contemporaries and left great though discordant fame over the centuries . . . was the most important act in the life of the terrible tsar. . . . Whoever later "whispered" to the tsar the idea of creating the Oprichnina . . . that idea was first stated by publicists of the government of Adashev-Silvester-Ivan IV [the Chosen Council] . . . stating directly that special military units had to be created to protect the internal security of the state. . . . The appeal to divide the service class into "beloved," "true," and all the rest . . . based on land allotments basically foreshadows the future Oprichnina division of landholdings. . . . The actual government [Chosen Council] carried out a series of practical measures in the spirit of these proposals including the creation of a personal armed guard for the tsar. . . . The advisers and tutors of the tsar—Silvester and Adashev—objectively made a considerable contribution to the basis of future Oprichnina terror. Repeated nine times in "The Tale About Mehmet Saltan" [a work by intimates of Adashev] were appeals to the sovereign to be awesome, to execute and burn offending subjects . . . later turned into fact by Tsar Ivan. . . .

The theory of the autocracy of Ivan the Terrible, to whose formulation and defense he devoted so much of his attention, was permeated with the idea of the Oprichnina. It proposes the division of state servants into those who "serve close by" and those who are not so reliable and "serve farther off." The former "serve close" to the tsar in order to guard him from "criminals," to execute the tsar's will indefatigably and unconditionally and to comprise an apparatus embodying this. . . . The corps of true servants with whose aid he could protect himself and his power from plots of his entourage and of unreliable "counselors" needed to be recruited from the lowborn. The very fact of the elevation of a service person "from the depths to princehood" ["*iz griazi v kniazi*"] must forever bind him to the tsar as a true and devoted servant. . . .

From this it does not follow that Groznyi created his power apparatus solely from the lowborn. In the Oprichnina's highest posts also served titled princes, but . . . the titled in the Oprichnina were intermixed with the lowborn. Such a system reduced the importance of noble birth as such and raised to unparalleled heights . . . people taken from the service masses, sometimes from its lowest elements. The transition to autocracy did not occur immediately. The first step in that direction was the destruction of the actual government's leadership with the expulsion and condemnation of Adashev and Silvester. . . .

The chief catalyst speeding the final transition to autocracy was the Livonian War which required concentrating command in a single center. Under wartime conditions departure from the tsar's service into the service of a ruler in a neighboring country . . . inevitably became military treason. War created a favorable environment for placing blame for failures, defeats and other burdens . . . on military leaders, boyars, gentry, and bureaucrats. Seizing the initiative in making such accusations, the tsar and his faithful servants could direct outbursts of popular rage. . . .

We have spoken of the longstanding factors of the ripening of the Oprichnina . . . the objective factors of the Muscovite state's sociopolitical development, and subjective ones such as the gradual transformation of Tsar Ivan IV into the Oprichnina's creator, Ivan the Terrible, and the lengthy publicistic struggle favoring the creation of autocracy. . . . The final stage . . . [was] a state coup at the top with the purpose of establishing complete and firm authority by the tsar-autocrat. The concrete name of the order created by this coup initially was *Oprichnina*. The more general name it received later . . . in the era of struggle against it was *the tsarist regime*.

The tsar's departure from Moscow on December 3, 1564 is sometimes represented in our historiography as a panicky flight by a man scared to death and unaware whither to direct his steps. R. G. Skrynnikov supposes also that upon his departure from Moscow the tsar had no definite plan. . . . But from the whole context of the chronicle account, it is clear, however, that the tsar wished to create the impression that traitors had forced him to abandon his throne and flee wherever his steps might take him. We recall that Groznyi resorted repeatedly to the threat of abandoning the throne with the aim of political blackmail. . . . Ivan IV, of course, did not for a moment consider renouncing power. . . . Sober political calculation, not hysteria, is revealed in Ivan IV's attempt to "abandon the throne." The struggle of autocracy against the bearers of traditional feudal relationships looked on the surface like an antifeudal struggle and therefore won the support of the broad mass of the population, especially commercial leaders. . . . The tsar never forgot the lessons of [the uprising of] 1547. He knew well how powerful was the force of a popular uprising against . . . the boyars and magnates. . . . Among Muscovites he had the solid reputation of a fighter against the "powerful" and the "plunderers," the reputation of a fighter for truth and justice. . . . Now he could seek "protection" boldly from traitors among the townsmen. . . .

The choice of the moment to deliver the blow—an ultimatum to the Boyar Duma, top churchmen, and service and prikaz rebels—was determined importantly by the increasingly decisive and unconditional support of the Muscovite populace for the tsar in the emerging conflict. . . . Everything was calculated to break the resistance of the old court, to force its leading elements to their knees and compel them to yield on conditions set by the tsar. . . . Opponents of Groznyi hastened to the Aleksandrovsk Settlement to declare their submission. . . . The "sovereign's will" was recognized as the only source of power and rights. Anyone who to a greater or lesser degree expressed disagreement with the tsar's will . . . was subject to punishment including death. This affected primarily "boyars, *voevody*, bureaucrats and churchmen of all ranks. . . ." Thus the "sovereign's will" was recognized as the only source of internal and foreign policy. . . . In the country was established a new regime—tsarist. . . . It was entirely clear that such a "social contract" could not be formed or be consolidated without weapons of compulsion to forge a new autocracy, i.e., without the Oprichnina.[17]

A Western View

George Vernadsky, a prominent American historian of Russian birth, presents a balanced interpretation of Ivan IV's reign. He discusses the origins of the Oprichnina against a background of Lithuanian attacks, boyar defections, and the growing breach between Ivan IV and Muscovy's ruling institution, the Boyar Duma:

> He [Ivan IV] was not only angered; he was frightened. The alternative facing him was either to resign or to enforce his dictatorship by extraordinary measures. . . . The tsar attempted to split the people of Moscow by inciting the commoners against the officials and upper classes. . . . The oprichnina gave the tsar the means to effect his dictatorship and for a time assured his personal safety. . . . In the districts originally taken into the oprichnina, there were few boyar patrimonial estates (*votchiny*). The eviction thus affected mostly the gentry, the *dvoriane*, and the boyars' sons. . . .
>
>   . . . Many an historian expresses the opinion that in spite of all its horrors, the oprichnina performed an important social and political task, . . . shattering the power of the princely and boyar aristocracy in order to clear the way for the rise of the gentry. . . . This policy could have been continued in an orderly way without recourse to such revolutionary measures as the oprichnina. . . . The hasty mobilization of land caused by the oprichnina

and the poor management of landholdings granted to the oprichniki resulted in a general decline of agricultural production. There was under the oprichnina no systematic confiscation of the princely and boyar latifundia. . . .

>   To sum up the historical results of the oprichnina, the havoc it caused added new burdens to Muscovite economics. . . . Hardly less disastrous were the undermining of public morale and the psychological depression of the nation. Perhaps the most tragic result of the oprichnina terror . . . was the destruction of so many gifted personalities. The elite of Russian society had been decimated.[18]

Conclusion

Important differences persist in Russian and Western interpretations of the Oprichnina and of Ivan IV's reign, although since 1985 this divergence has narrowed considerably. Later Soviet and post-Soviet Russian works have abandoned the worshipful praise of Ivan common in the Stalin period, but nonetheless still contend that the Oprichnina and his other major reforms were basically positive and progressive steps necessary to undermine political feudalism and promote absolutism and political centralization. Western historians emphasize somewhat more the Oprichnina's, and Ivan's, senseless violence. The Oprichnina, they argue, was largely counterproductive and contributed to the development of serfdom, the dissolution of the Muscovite state, and the chaos of the "Time of Troubles." This interpretation parallels negative Western reactions to Stalin's collectivization of agriculture in the 1930s and the violence of the Great Purge (see Chapter 34). ■

---

[17] D. N. Alshits, *Nachalo samoderzhaviia v Rossii: Gosudarstvo Ivana Groznogo* (Leningrad, 1988), pp. 102, 105, 109–113, 118–120.

[18] Vernadsky, vol. 5, pt. 1, pp. 107–9, 138–39.

Suggested Additional Reading

BOOKS

ANDERSON, M. S. *Britain's Discovery of Russia, 1553–1815* (London, 1958).

BERRY, L., and R. CRUMMEY, eds. *Rude and Barbarous Kingdom . . .* (Madison, WI, 1958).

BOBRICK, B. *Fearful Majesty: The Life and Reign of Ivan the Terrible* (New York, 1987).

FEDOTOV, G. P. *St. Filip, Metropolitan of Moscow—Encounter with Ivan the Terrible,* trans. and ed. R. Haugh and N. Lupinin (Belmont, MA, 1978).

FENNELL, J. F. *Prince A. M. Kurbsky's History of Ivan IV* (Cambridge, 1965).

———, ed. *The Correspondence between Prince Kurbsky and Tsar Ivan IV of Russia, 1564–1579* (Cambridge, 1955).

GREY, I. *Ivan the Terrible* (London, 1964).

GROBOVSKY, A. *The Chosen Council of Ivan IV: A Reinterpretation* (Brooklyn, 1969).

HELLIE, R. *Enserfment and Military Change in Muscovy* (Chicago, 1971).

KEENAN, E. *The Kurbskii-Groznyi Apocrypha* (Cambridge, MA, 1971).

NORRETRANDERS, B. *The Shaping of Tsardom under Ivan Grozny* (Copenhagen, 1964).

PELENSKY, J. *Russia and Kazan: Conquest and Imperial Ideology (1438–1560)* (The Hague, 1974).

PLATONOV, S. F. *Ivan the Terrible,* ed. and trans. J. L. Wieczynski (Gulf Breeze, FL, 1974).

POUNCY, C., ed. and trans. *The Domostroi: Rules for Russian Households in the Time of Ivan the Terrible* (Ithaca, NY, 1994).

SKRYNNIKOV, R. G. *Ivan the Terrible,* ed. and trans. H. Graham (Gulf Breeze, FL, 1981).

SMITH, R. E. *Peasant Farming in Muscovy* (Cambridge, 1977).

STADEN, H. VON. *The Land and Government of Muscovy* (Stanford, 1967).

TOLSTOY, G., comp. *First Forty Years of Intercourse between England and Russia* (New York, n.d.).

TUMINS, V. *Tsar Ivan's Reply to Jan Rokyta* (The Hague, 1971). (Reprint.)

URBAN, W. *The Livonian Crusade* (Washington, 1981).

WAUGH, D. *The Great Turkes Defiance . . .* (Columbus, OH, 1978).

WILLAN, T. *Early History of the Russia Company, 1553–1603* (Manchester, Eng., 1956).

WIPPER, R. *Ivan Grozny* (Moscow, 1947). (Soviet account.)

YANOV, A. *The Origins of Autocracy: Ivan the Terrible in Russian Historiography,* trans. S. Dunn (Berkeley, 1981).

ARTICLES

BARON, S. "Ivan the Terrible, Giles Fletcher, and the Moscow Merchantry." *SEEJ* 16, no. 4 (1972): 563–85.

BUSHKOVITCH, P. "Taxation, Tax Farming, and Merchants in Sixteenth Century Russia." *SR* 37 (1978): 381–98.

CHERNIAVSKY, M. "Ivan the Terrible as Renaissance Prince." *SR* 27 (1968): 195–211.

DEWEY, H., and A. KLEIMOLA. "Old Muscovite Amnesties: Theory and Practice." *Rus. Hist.* 3, no. 1 (1975): 49–60.

EAVES, R. G., and R. SIMMONS. "Anglo-Russian Relations in the European Diplomatic Setting, 1572–1584." *New Review* 14 (1974): 117–30.

———. "Muscovite Slavery in Comparative Perspective." *Rus. Hist.* 6, no. 2 (1978): 133–209.

EAVES, R. G., and W. WILLIAMS. "Anglo-Russian Relations, 1553–1572." *New Review* 12, no. 3 (1973): 40–51.

HUTTENBACH, H. "The Correspondence between Queen Elizabeth I and Tsar Ivan IV . . ." *FOG* 24 (1978): 101–30.

———, comp. and ed. "Anthony Jenkinson's 1566 and 1567 Missions to Muscovy." *CanAmSlSt* 9, no. 2 (1975): 179–203.

———. "Muscovy and Kazan." *SR* 26 (1967): 548–58.

KLEIMOLA, A. "The Changing Face of the Muscovite Aristocracy." *JfGO* 25, no. 4 (1977): 481–93.

KOLLMAN, J. E. "The Stoglav Council and Parish Priests." *Rus. Hist.* 7, nos. 1–2 (1980): 65–91.

MILLER, D. "The Coronation of Ivan IV of Moscow." *JfGO* 15 (1967): 559–74.

———. "The *Velikie Minei Chetei* and the *Stepennaia Kniga* of Metropolitan Makarii . . ." *FOG* 26, (1979): 263–82.

———. "The Viskovatyi Affair of 1553–54 . . ." *Rus. Hist.* 8, no. 3 (1980): 293–332.

ŠEVČENKO, I. "Muscovy's Conquest of Kazan: Two Views Reconciled." *SR* 26 (1967): 541–47.

———. "On the Authenticity of the Kurbskii-Groznyi Correspondence." *SR* 37 (1978): 107–15.

SZEFTEL, M. "The Epithet *Groznyj* in Historical Perspective," in *The Religious World of Russian Culture,* ed. A. Blane (The Hague, 1975), pp. 101–16.

12

The Time of Troubles

In 1598 the old Muscovite dynasty founded in 1263 died out, beginning a period of disorder and strife known as the Time of Troubles (*Smuta*). Starting as a struggle for the throne, the Troubles deepened into social revolution complicated by foreign intervention. Muscovy was threatened with dissolution and alien rule. Eventually a national movement centering in the Orthodox church expelled the foreign invaders. In 1613 the assembly of the lands elected the Romanov dynasty, resolving the political crisis. Interpretations of the Troubles vary. The traditional approach of the prerevolutionary historian Kliuchevskii emphasized the dynastic issue as their chief cause and concluded that only the election of a "legitimate" ruler ended the turmoil. Soviet historians tended to view the Troubles primarily as an abortive revolution by peasants, slaves, and Cossacks from the borderlands against the boyars, their state, and oncoming serfdom. A secondary Soviet theme was the struggle by lower- and middle-class elements for national liberation. Historians concur that the development of the Russian autocratic state was interrupted. Central authority, lacking legitimacy and power,

was gravely, though temporarily, weakened. Muscovy's social and economic fabric took a generation to recover. What caused the Troubles, why did the Muscovite state virtually dissolve, and which elements led the national resurgence of 1611–1612?

Background and Causes

The causes of the Troubles are complex and extend deep into Muscovite history. The process of unification of the 15th and early 16th centuries, exacting a heavy toll from every social group, left numerous grievances and antagonisms. Ivan IV's extreme policies shattered the traditional order and sowed widespread discontent. His constant wars exhausted Russia's resources while shifts of landowners and peasants during the Oprichnina created near chaos. In 1581 Ivan's senseless act of killing Ivan Ivanovich, his only capable son, presaged the end of the old dynasty. Perceptive contemporary witnesses such as the Englishman Giles Fletcher foresaw a grave crisis should the dynasty die out.

In 1584 every Muscovite class felt insecure and nurtured grievances, which needed only a spark to be expressed violently. Titled magnates had suffered grievously. Expelled from ancestral estates, often in winter, and deprived of political influence and hereditary privileges, they had been harnessed forcibly into state service. During the Oprichnina most of the illustrious families, suffering execution or banishment, had lost much wealth. Growing depopulation of the central provinces threatened many with ruin. The service aristocracy, which had been drawn from virtually every social group except the great lords and under Ivan had become the main bulwark of the army and state, also faced difficult problems. Even some former slaves and priests' sons received *pomestie* (tsar-granted) land. Thus *dvoriane* (gentry) could be army generals with vast estates or humble gentry with plots supporting but a single peasant household. In the south poor *dvoriane* often farmed their own land. Only compulsory army service and the possession of *pomestie* lands bound together this disparate class. Because state lands were inadequate to supply the expanding servitor element, the *pomestie* system was extended aggressively into the Volga valley and the southern borderlands.

The gravest problem confronting the *dvoriane* was a shortage of peasant labor. Rising tax burdens and loss of personal freedom had provoked a massive peasant exodus, often by illegal flight, to the frontiers. In the center many lands and villages were abandoned. By 1585 in the Moscow region only 60 percent of formerly cultivated land was tilled; in the Novgorod area, less than 10 percent. Intensive competition for peasant labor gave wealthier lay and clerical magnates manifold advantages over the lesser gentry. Big lords secured tax exemptions allowing them to offer tenants better economic conditions and more security. Wealthy landlords and especially monasteries exploited their financial advantages unscrupulously and bought the services of tenant farmers from the *dvoriane*. This "exportation" (*vyvoz*) of peasants threatened the service gentry's very existence because without peasant labor its estates became almost worthless.

Noblemen and the state sought to halt peasant departures, which were ruining military servitors and removing taxpayers from the state rolls. The government and private owners acted to bind to the land tenant farmers who had been in residence for a specified number of years. Defined as longtime residents (*starozhiltsy*), they lost their traditional right to depart in the period around St. George's Day. Rising peasant indebtedness further curtailed that right. Customarily a peasant had to settle up with the landowner before leaving, but as taxes mounted, many peasants had to borrow from landlords at exorbitant interest rates. Unable to repay their noble creditors, some peasants became slaves (*kholopy*) or entered into temporary bondage (*kabala*). As the *pomestie* system spread, tenant farmers often became completely dependent on landlords. Often village communities, divided among a number of *dvoriane,* lost rights of self-government. Whereas *dvoriane* obtained state support and protection against magnates, the peasants' only recourses were submission or flight.

Urban dwellers were also affected negatively by the dislocations of Ivan IV's time. State efforts to simplify tax collection by concentrating trade in a few centers impaired urban growth and fostered class rivalries. Wealthy merchants (*gosty*) became government agents responsible for tax gathering; in return they were exempted from taxes and the jurisdiction of regular courts. Because other townspeople assumed their financial burdens, social conflict arose between privileged and non-privileged elements. Urban tradesmen had to compete with tax-exempt commercial settlements (*slobody*) established nearby by boyars and monasteries. Townsmen sought better conditions on the frontiers, thus leaving towns in the center depopulated. Between 1546 and 1582 Novgorod's population shrank from 5,000 to 1,000 households. Only the north escaped grave social and economic problems. Untouched by war, their commerce

RIA-NOVOSTI/SOVFOTO

Boris Godunov—regent 1584–1598, tsar 1598–1605.

stimulated by contacts with England, towns flourished from the northern Volga to the White Sea.

Dynastic Struggle: Fedor I and Boris Godunov (1584–1605)

Ivan IV's death brought to the throne Fedor, his saintly but feeble-minded son. Fedor's brother-in-law, Boris Godunov, descended from a low-ranking boyar family which had long served at the Muscovite court, became the actual ruler. Boris, shrewd and determined, had served in the Oprichnina and married the daughter of a leading *oprichnik.* Through his sister, Irina, wife of Tsar Fedor, he was linked closely with the throne. Early in Fedor's reign Boris Godunov and other boyars associated with the Oprichnina defeated attempts by the princely aristocracy to regain power and reassert their ancient rights. With a minimum of

bloodshed Boris exiled the Shuiskiis, his principal antagonists, and in 1587 became regent (the English styled him aptly: lord protector). Authorized by the Boyar Duma to direct foreign relations, Boris set up his own court, received foreign envoys, and reigned in style. While the incapable Fedor visited monasteries and rang Moscow church bells, Boris won great power and wealth from landed estates and outdistanced his boyar rivals.

As regent, Boris Godunov achieved substantial successes. Contemporaries generally agreed that he had restored order after Ivan's death and that he was unusually able—practical, firm, tactful, and a superb organizer. His government gave generously to the needy, protected the weak, and won gentry support. Boris ended the terror of Ivan IV's time, restored public confidence, and promoted its foreign trade by securing transit rights for Muscovite merchants through Swedish territory. Taxes and service burdens were reduced. In 1589 Boris arranged the creation of a separate Russian patriarchate. Through skillful negotiation and pressure Boris induced Jeremiah II, visiting patriarch of Constantinople, to ordain Boris's supporter Iov (Job) as Russian patriarch. The Russian church ranked last among Orthodox patriarchates, but because the Turks controlled the rest, Muscovy's position was enhanced at home and abroad. Boris acted to restore Muscovite prestige, which had been badly shaken by Ivan IV's defeats. Ably assisted by state secretaries Andrei and Vasili Shchelkalov, he avoided war with Poland and recovered the Baltic territories of Ivangorod and Koporie from Sweden. His excessive caution perhaps prevented further gains. As head of the Kazan Board, Boris fostered Russia's Eurasian empire: Forts erected at Tiumen and Tobolsk consolidated Russian control in western Siberia.

Boris, however, could not solve the crucial internal problems of depopulation, peasant flight, and gentry impoverishment, which had been intensified by Ivan IV's draconian policies; he merely alleviated deep Muscovite social antagonisms temporarily. In the state's interest he backed the *dvoriane* against the magnates, sought to bind the peasantry to the land, and prohibited peasant transfers from small to large estates. The princely aristocracy, seeking revenge, exploited the mysterious death in 1591 of the boy Dmitri, son of Ivan IV and his uncanonical seventh wife, Maria Nagaia. The dubious legality of his parents' marriage weakened Dmitri's claims to the throne. Some historians support the official version of Dmitri's death—that he fell on a knife during an epileptic fit at Uglich. Boris's enemies circulated rumors that his agent Bitiagovskii had murdered the boy to remove an obstacle to Boris's assumption of the throne. This unsubstantiated charge, depicting Boris as a conscience-stricken murderer, was accepted by the 19th-century historian N. M. Karamzin and was incorporated in A. S. Pushkin's play and Musorgskii's great opera *Boris Godunov*. An authoritative Soviet account affirmed that Boris had nothing to do with little Dmitri's death.

Tsar Fedor's death in 1598 without male heirs ended the old Muscovite dynasty. The legitimate hereditary ruler, so important to conservative Muscovites, was no more, and Boris Godunov's best efforts failed to fill the vacuum. Fedor had bequeathed power to his wife, Irina, but she refused the crown. With her consent Patriarch Iov, a Godunov partisan, became regent and convened a *zemskii sobor*, an assembly that, besides clergy and boyars, contained some 300 gentry and 36 merchants. Boris's opponents and many other contemporaries believed that Boris engineered his own election. He probably did not pack the *sobor*, however, and he remained in a monk's cell until it chose him. The other leading contender, Fedor N. Romanov, lacked Boris's advantages of long experience, proven ability as ruler, and broad popular support. Over boyar opposition the *sobor* elected Boris tsar overwhelmingly, and Muscovites expressed warm support by a great procession to the Novodevichii Monastery.

As tsar (1598–1605), Boris Godunov became more isolated and vulnerable. No longer could he control from within the Boyar Duma, which contained his leading opponents. Ruling autocratically, he did not try to develop the *zemskii sobor* as a counterpoise to the Duma. To raise his dynasty's

prestige, he sought to marry his children to foreign royalty. Recognizing Muscovy's need for Western technology, he hired European doctors, engineers, and military men for state service. Conservative churchmen blocked his plans to have German scholars found a university in Moscow, but in 1602 Boris sent 18 youths to study in Europe. To counteract rising dissatisfaction, Boris reverted to a regime of fear. Frontiers were carefully guarded; deportations and confiscations of property were resumed. The severe famine of 1601–3, caused by successive bad harvests, created widespread suffering and unemployment. Boris intensified a public works program and had fortresses, churches, offices, and storehouses built throughout Muscovy. The government distributed grain from its reserves, but general distress and continuing peasant flights promoted brigandage. Late in 1603 Boris had to suppress a major peasant-Cossack revolt led by Khlopko, a Cossack chieftain.

Social Revolt and Foreign Invasion (1605–1610)

Profound social tensions and discontent undermined and finally destroyed the Godunovs. Boris's boyar foes continued to hatch plots while rumors spread that Tsarevich Dmitri had escaped death miraculously in Uglich and that Boris was a usurper. Other accounts labeled him Dmitri's murderer. In 1603 came news that "Dmitri" was in Poland, recognized as the true tsarevich. This Dmitri was probably a native Muscovite prepared for his pretender's role by boyars hostile to Boris. Iuri Mniszech, a Polish magnate of extravagant tastes, viewed him as his opportunity to regain wealth and power and used his daughter as bait. Dmitri became infatuated with Marina, who dreamed of becoming tsaritsa of Muscovy. Early in 1604 Dmitri converted secretly to Catholicism and requested papal protection. He was to marry Marina only when he had become tsar, and he had to promise her father a million zlotys and to make her proprietress of Novgorod and Pskov. Boris declared Dmitri to be Grigori Otrepiev, a fugitive monk from Moscow's Chudov Monastery. Evidently Dmitri's Polish supporters did not believe that he was Ivan IV's son, but he was a convenient tool to subjugate Muscovy and convert it to Catholicism. Dmitri himself apparently believed in his mission.

In the summer of 1604 Dmitri invaded Muscovy with about 2,000 Poles and Ukrainians. Before he reached Kiev, 2,000 Don Cossacks joined him, and soon Russians greatly outnumbered Poles in his army. His strength derived more from the prestige of his name and the social disorder in Muscovy than from the size of his forces. The populace of the southern and western borderlands, the so-called Wild Field, consisting largely of Cossack freebooters, poor gentry, and peasants who had fled from central Muscovy, was volatile, discontented with Moscow, and easily misled. The remnants of the army of the brigand Khlopko had taken refuge there. Some believed Dmitri was authentic, a "fine tsar" who would satisfy their grievances; others joined him to oppose Boris, autocracy, and serfdom. The Pretender and his agents roused this potentially rebellious borderland against the Godunovs. In January 1605, however, Boris's army inflicted a crushing defeat on Dmitri, who barely escaped capture. Retiring to Putivl, he was rescued by some Don Cossacks and soon headed a new army of malcontents.

Moscow's weakness enabled Dmitri to triumph. The sudden death of Boris Godunov in April 1605 removed its only experienced leader. Fedor Godunov, his well-educated 16-year-old son, reigned only six weeks; Fedor's army defected to Dmitri near Kromy. In June Dmitri entered Moscow, Fedor and his mother were brutally murdered, and the Pretender became tsar.

The rule of Dmitri I (1605–1606) was brief and troubled. The anti-Godunov princely aristocracy neither believed in nor supported him. Surrounding himself with Polish favorites and Muscovite adventurers, Dmitri alienated conservative Muscovites by his poorly disguised hostility toward Orthodoxy, his financial exactions from the church, and his disregard for court etiquette. By making lavish gifts and allowing gentry officers to

Cathedral of Our Lady of Smolensk in Novodevichii (New Maiden) Monastery, Moscow.

return to their estates, he won some gentry support, but though intelligent, he proved venal and sensual, haughty and dissolute. The boyars, opposing his efforts to rule independently, exploited rapidly growing popular dissatisfaction with his reign. The wily Prince Vasili Shuiskii, who had confirmed the real Dmitri's death at Uglich and later recognized the Pretender as the legitimate ruler, now told Muscovites that he was an impostor. In the spring of 1606 the elaborate Catholic wedding of Dmitri and Marina, attended by thousands of Poles, further alienated Muscovites and encouraged Shuiskii to instigate a popular uprising. While a mob massacred hundreds of Poles and Lithuanians, boyars invaded the Kremlin and murdered Dmitri. Marina and her father escaped and went into exile.

Moscow boyars then convened a fraudulent *zemskii sobor,* which enthroned Shuiskii as Vasili IV. Shuiskii was of distinguished lineage but modest abilities, and his arbitrary elevation provoked social dissension, then civil war. The entire borderland, which had backed Dmitri, rose against the "boyars' tsar." The dynastic issue slipped into the background as the Troubles became mainly a social revolt. Installing Germogen, the metropolitan of Kazan, as patriarch, Vasili IV secured support from conservative churchmen but alienated the influential Romanovs, whose leader, Filaret, coveted that post. Germogen had the remains of Ivan IV's son Dmitri brought from Uglich to Moscow and canonized him as a saint. Even this action could not destroy a feeling for the Pretender that was rooted deep in popular antipathy to an oppressive regime in Moscow.

The rebellion against Tsar Vasili, which became a great peasant insurrection against serfdom, began in Putivl in the name of Ivan IV's son Dmitri. The ablest and most popular figure in the movement was Ivan Bolotnikov, glorified by Soviet historians as a popular hero and great general. Bolotnikov, a former Don Cossack, had been captured by the Tatars and served for years as a galley slave in Turkey before managing to return to Muscovy. A talented and dynamic leader, he became the commander of a great revolutionary army of peasants, Cossacks, and runaway slaves. Bolotnikov attacked serfdom, the landowning nobility, and the city rich. Inflammatory leaflets urged boyar serfs and city poor to "kill the boyars . . . , merchants and all commercial people" and seize their goods. Bolotnikov considered himself "the great chieftain" serving "the fine tsar, Dmitri Ivanovich" who wished to free the masses. His motley forces defeated Vasili's armies and for three months besieged Moscow. Dissension in Bolotnikov's army between Cossacks who favored freeing the peasants and gentry who opposed it permitted Vasili to drive off the rebels. Throughout 1607 this bitter social struggle raged. Vasili's army finally captured Bolotnikov's base at Tula and seized the rebel leaders. Inadequate organization, social antagonisms within the insurgent ranks, and lack of a clear, positive program doomed this great popular upheaval.

Chain mail of boyar P. I. Shuiskii, *Oruzheinaia Palata,* Armoury Museum, Moscow Kremlin.

Vasili IV's government responded to the challenge with familiar Muscovite police tactics. The borderlands were plundered and devastated; thousands of prisoners were brutally tortured to death, many by slow drowning. Fugitive slaves and serfs were returned forcibly to their lords' control. The right of peasant departure, still sometimes allowed under Boris Godunov, was abrogated completely. The boyar regime took major steps toward establishing serfdom in Russia.

No sooner had Bolotnikov's movement subsided than a second pretender Dmitri challenged Vasili's shaky regime. Polish and Lithuanian lords and adventurers used this vulgar man of unknown origin to attack and plunder Muscovy. King Sigismund of Poland, indignant at the recent massacre of Poles in Moscow, supported them. The Second Pretender proclaimed himself Tsar Dmitri Ivanovich, and by the spring of 1608 a sizable Polish-Lithuanian force had crossed the frontier and was swelled by military servitors, commoners from the Seversk borderland, and survivors from

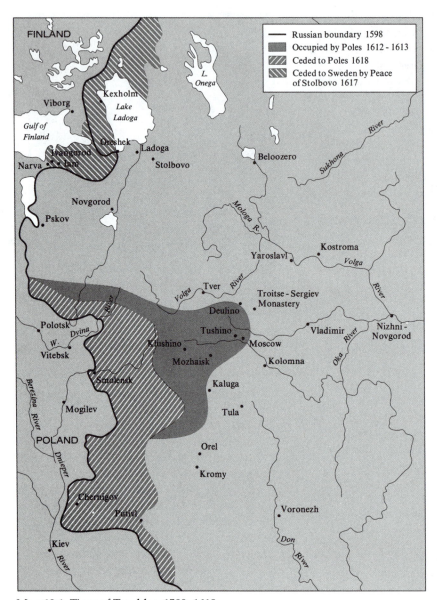

Map 12.1 Time of Troubles, 1598–1618

Bolotnikov's army. The Second Pretender, known to Muscovites as "The Brigand" (*Vor*), met little resistance. Looting as he advanced, he set up headquarters at Tushino, just outside Moscow (see Map 12.1), but could not capture the capital. Iuri Mniszech brought his daughter there, and Marina accepted the reputedly loathsome Brigand as her husband. Two years of civil war ensued. Nobles and rich merchants generally supported Vasili; commoners and some boyars backed the Brigand. A number of illustrious boyars, including Filaret Romanov, defected from Vasili's court to Tushino. Known derisively as "migratory birds," they

Trinity Monastery at Zagorsk, near Moscow (16th century), a chief
center of the Orthodox church and an important Muscovite fortress.

changed sides as the tide of battle shifted. The
Brigand's forces tried to encircle Moscow but were
foiled by a heroic defense of the fortified Trinity
Monastery. The Tushinites next sought to conquer
the north, but its sturdy peasantry and merchants
distrusted the Brigand even more than they did
Tsar Vasili.

Vasili IV, seeking relief and reinforcement,
dispatched his young nephew, Prince M. Skopin-
Shuiskii, to the northwest. By an agreement of
February 1609, Sweden agreed to supply mercenary troops in return for Muscovy's renunciation
of claims to Livonia and Karelia. Skopin's reinforced army defeated the Poles before Moscow
and drove the Brigand south to Kaluga. The
migratory boyars of Tushino, led by Filaret
Romanov, whom the Brigand had named patriarch, negotiated with King Sigismund of Poland,
who was besieging Smolensk. Their agreement of
February 1610 provided that Wladyslaw, the king's
young son, should become Orthodox tsar of Mus-

covy. Before the agreement could be implemented,
the Tushino government dissolved.

Vasili IV's worst troubles seemed over. But
Skopin-Shuiskii died suddenly (some said he was
poisoned), depriving his camp of its ablest figure
and of popular support. In June 1610 the Poles
under Zolkiewski defeated Vasili's poorly led army
at Klushino. Vasili's regime and the old Muscovite
state collapsed. Seven boyars from the Duma
formed a provisional government in Moscow, but
it was not widely obeyed. With Poles and the Brig-
and's Cossacks approaching the city, the Moscow
boyars chose the Poles as the lesser evil. By a
treaty of August 1610, a more conservative version
of the February agreement, Wladyslaw was to
become tsar if he accepted Orthodoxy and ruled
with the Boyar Duma. A 1,200-man "grand
embassy" went to Smolensk to make final
arrangements.

A period of direct Polish rule in Moscow followed. General Zolkiewski occupied the city, consolidated Polish control, and helped defeat the

Brigand. At Smolensk the delegates discovered, however, that King Sigismund coveted the Russian throne himself. Instead of sending his son, he had General Alexander Gosiewski, who replaced the disgusted Zolkiewski, arrest the seven boyars and set up a Polish military dictatorship. When the Muscovite delegates refused to recognize Sigismund as tsar, he had Filaret Romanov and other leaders imprisoned in Poland. At the end of 1610 there was no legal Muscovite government or tsar.

National Revival and the Romanovs' Election (1610–1613)

Polish and Swedish intervention triggered a national movement to liberate the country and restore a legitimate Orthodox Russian tsar. The movement blended religious and national elements in a way that appealed to all Russian social groups. Soviet accounts stress that it was inspired by the patriotism of ordinary townsmen and peasants. The traditional state had disintegrated, but the church as before remained a focus of unity. Late in 1610 Patriarch Germogen, rejecting the Catholic Sigismund, advised Muscovites to accept Wladyslaw as tsar only if he became Orthodox and exhorted other towns to unite against the Poles and Lithuanians. The elderly patriarch, affirm non-Soviet historians, became the spiritual head of a movement to rescue the country from enslavement.

Towns of the still undevastated north and Volga valley responded. After the Brigand's murder (December 1610) his remaining Cossacks became the core of a militia led by Prokopy Liapunov of Riazan, Ivan Zarutskii of Tula, and the boyar Prince Dmitri Trubetskoi, which moved on Moscow. Grave social antagonisms, however, wracked this national militia: The Cossacks aimed to free the serfs while the gentry and merchants sought to restore the old social order. In June 1611 the Cossacks, fearing betrayal to the landlords, murdered Liapunov. The gentry contingents withdrew, and the Cossacks restored their camp at Tushino. A second attempt by middle elements of society to end the Troubles had failed. Meanwhile, King Sigismund had conquered Smolensk and the Swedes had seized Novgorod. Muscovy's complete dissolution seemed near.

Patriotic Russians made new efforts at unity. In August 1611 Patriarch Germogen from his captivity in the Kremlin appealed to Nizhnii-Novgorod, the leading north Volga commercial town, not to submit to Cossacks under the "Baby Brigand," son of Marina and the deceased Brigand. In September Kuzma Minin, an energetic butcher of Nizhnii-Novgorod, exhorted city elders to form a militia financed by voluntary contributions. Minin became the inspirational and financial leader of a movement of Volga towns, which soon involved all of northern and central Russia, led by gentry and merchants against Cossack rule and Polish domination. Prince Dmitri Pozharskii, an experienced commander, assumed control of a sizable militia. Early in 1612 Pozharskii drove the Cossacks from the key Volga city of Iaroslavl, organized his army, and set up a provisional government. Messages went out to other towns to send delegates to a *zemskii sobor*. In August, learning that the Poles were seeking to reinforce and provision their garrison in Moscow, Pozharskii moved toward the city. The Cossack forces in his path disintegrated: Those under Prince Trubetskoi joined Pozharskii; the rest withdrew southward to seek their ideal of land and liberty. The Polish relief force was defeated, and a provisional regime led by Minin, Pozharskii, and Trubetskoi was formed in October. Soviet historians emphasized the significant role of peasant partisan detachments in liberating Muscovy. Pozharskii's army stormed Moscow's inner city, and in October 1612 the starving Polish garrison in the Kremlin capitulated. King Sigismund's attempt to retake the city failed, and Polish dominion in Moscow came to an end.

It remained to prevent new social strife between Cossacks and gentry and to choose a permanent government. Because most of the gentry militia was soon demobilized, Trubetskoi's Cossacks exerted strong pressure upon the *zemskii sobor*, which in January 1613 convened in Moscow to elect a new dynasty. Its membership exceeded 800, estimates Vernadsky, including about 500 provincial delegates. All classes were represented except peasants on private estates, but the assembly was dominated by the gentry and merchant elements that had freed Moscow. One faction of boyars, court officials, and north Russian gentry prepared to back the Swedish prince Charles Philip if he turned Orthodox. Clergy, southern gentry, townspeople, and Cossacks favored a native candidate. The people of Moscow and its vicinity strongly backed Mikhail Romanov, the sickly 16-year-old son of the imprisoned Filaret. Mikhail, the only figure round whom Cossacks and gentry could unite, was acceptable to the older aristocracy and traditionalists because he was weak and because he was related to the old Muscovite dynasty: His great-aunt Anastasia Romanov had been Ivan IV's beloved first wife. After the *sobor* had rejected foreign candidates, support grew for Mikhail. "It was the Cossacks who made your son the sovereign of Muscovy," Filaret learned the following year.[1]

During the interregnum the *zemskii sobor* ruled exhausted, devastated Muscovy as bands of Poles, Swedes, and marauding Cossacks roamed about. While young Mikhail was at the Romanov estate in remote Kostroma, a band of Poles, seeking to abduct him, asked a local peasant, Ivan Susanin, to lead them to the tsar-elect. To save the tsar, Susanin deliberately led them deep into the forest where he and they perished. This episode, the basis for Mikhail Glinka's 19th-century opera *A Life for the Tsar,* revealed the patriotism that had begun to inspire ordinary Russians. Soon afterward, delegates from the *zemskii sobor* arrived to talk with Mikhail Romanov, who at first refused the throne. (The fate of his immediate predecessors was scarcely encouraging.) After the delegates assured him that "the whole land" was demanding him, he yielded, and in July 1613 he was crowned solemnly in the Kremlin as Mikhail I. His coronation inaugurated the Romanovs' 300-year rule and ended the political aspect of the Troubles, but not until 1618 was the fighting ended by treaty with Poland and Sweden.

The Troubles, affirms Florinsky, represented an "abortive social revolution," leaving the structure of Muscovy apparently little changed. But the positions and relationships of the main social groups had altered substantially. The old titled aristocracy, shaken by the Oprichnina, never recovered fully from blows suffered during the years of disorder. The new dynasty would rely more upon state secretaries, military chieftains, and merchants from the middle layers of society, which would provide most of the new bureaucratic aristocracy. The national movement that ended the Troubles drew together and enhanced the influence of the gentry, boyar sons, and merchants. On the other hand, Cossacks, peasants, and slaves, lower social groups that had revolted repeatedly against the center and the traditional order, were defeated and subjugated more firmly to the landlords and the state.

Muscovite autocracy survived the Troubles little altered, but political attitudes had changed. Old traditions had been undermined, and the new concept of "all the land" emerged. In the 16th century, Kliuchevskii notes, Muscovites had considered the ruler as possessor of the land (*votchinnik*) and themselves as tenants subject to his whims; his personal will had been the sole basis for political life. But during the Troubles representative assemblies had elected tsars repeatedly. Although regimes and rulers lacking popular support had been overthrown (Dmitri I and Vasili IV) and from 1610 to 1612 there was no ruler at all, the Muscovite state survived. The *zemskii sobor,* embodying the popular will, evidently constituted an adequate basis for supreme legal authority and could solve fundamental questions such as dynastic change or major foreign war. Hitherto sporadic contacts between Muscovites and foreigners had intensified. Thousands of Poles, Lithuanians, and west Europeans, flocking to Moscow and Tushino, helped convince the Muscovite elite that European

---

[1] S. M. Soloviev, *Istoriia Rossii,* vol. 9 (St. Petersburg, 1894), p. 38; cited in G. Vernadsky, *The Tsardom of Moscow, 1547–1682,* vol. 1 (New Haven, 1969), p. 275.

ways and technology must be mastered. The upper classes began to imitate Western dress, to be influenced by Western culture, and to question long-established institutions and values.

The significance of the Troubles remains debatable. Some historians conclude that they produced little that was new and that the Romanovs restored previous social and political institutions. Soviet accounts emphasized class struggle: that the Bolotnikov movement revealed the tremendous latent force of a discontented peasantry. Muscovy's liberation from foreign domination, they asserted, strengthened national unity although it was many years before the economy recovered from the damage inflicted by foreign interventionists. Some Soviet works made implicit comparisons between foreign intervention during the Troubles and in the Civil War of 1918–1920 (see Chapter 32). Finally, the Troubles can be viewed as a contest between the borderlands (the "Wild Field") and the center. Ultimately the center prevailed: The year 1613 marked the triumph of noble landowners and state power, opening the way for the development during the 17th century of a bureaucratic, autocratic monarchy and serfdom, which were gradually extended to the borderlands. For a generation the Troubles left Muscovy severely weakened economically and with militarily unfavorable and insecure frontiers in the west.

Suggested Additional Reading

BOOKS

BARBOUR, P. *Dmitry Called the Pretender, 1605–6* (Boston, 1966).

BARON, S. H., ed. *The Travels of Olearius in Seventeenth Century Russia* (Stanford, 1967).

BUSHKOVITCH, P. *The Merchants of Moscow, 1580–1650* (London, 1980).

FLETCHER, G. *Of the Russe Commonwealth,* ed. R. Pipes (Cambridge, MA, 1966).

HELLIE, R. *Slavery in Russia, 1450–1725* (Chicago, 1982).

HOWE, S., ed. *The False Dmitri . . . Described by British Eye Witnesses, 1604–1612* (London, 1916).

HUGHES, L. *Russia and the West: The Life of a Seventeenth Century Westernizer, Prince V. V. Golitsyn* (Newtonville, MA, 1984).

MASSA, I. *A Short History . . . of These Present Wars in Moscow . . . to the Year 1610,* trans. and ed. G. E. Orchard (Toronto, 1982).

PERRIE, M. *Pretenders and Popular Monarchism in Early Modern Russia: The False Tsars of the Time of Troubles* (Cambridge, Eng., 1995).

PLATONOV, S. *Boris Godunov,* trans. F. Pyles (Gulf Breeze, FL, 1973).

———. *The Time of Troubles,* trans. J. Alexander (Lawrence, KS, 1970). (The best account in English.)

SKRYNNIKOV, R. G. *Boris Godunov,* trans. and ed. H. Graham (Gulf Breeze, FL, 1982).

———. *The Time of Troubles . . . ,* trans. and ed. H. Graham (Gulf Breeze, FL, 1988).

VERNADSKY, G. *The Tsardom of Moscow,* pt. 1 (New Haven, 1969).

ZOLKIEWSKI, S. *Expedition to Moscow: A Memoir* (London, 1959). (Reprint of a contemporary Polish account.)

ARTICLES

AFANASYEV, G. "Boris Godunov and the First Pretender." *Rus. Rev.* (Liverpool) 2, no. 4 (1913): 31–53.

CRUMMEY, R. "Crown and Boyars under Fedor Ivanovich and Michael Romanov." *CanAmSlSt* 6 (1972): 549–74.

NIKOLAIEFF, A. M. "Boris Godunov and the Ouglich Tragedy." *Rus. Rev.* 20 (1950): 275–85.

ORCHARD, G. "The Frontier Policy of Boris Godunov." *EEHE:* 113–23.

SKRYNNIKOV, R. G., "Boris Godunov's Struggle for the Throne." *CanAmSlSt* 11, no. 3 (1977): 325–53.

VERNADSKY, G. "The Death of the Tsarevich Dmitry . . ." *OSP* 5 (1954): 1–19.

13

The Early Romanovs: Politics and Foreign Affairs

Seventeenth-century Muscovy experienced an agonizing transition from a parochial, religiously oriented society to a secular, partially Westernized, multinational one. Traditional ways were being replaced by disturbing new patterns. Frequent wars and domestic violence imposed onerous burdens on peasants and townsmen. For decades after their formal end in 1613 the Troubles persisted in the form of disorder and brigandage, economic and military weakness. Grievous external challenges promoted the development of autocracy, a bureaucratic state, and a virtual caste system. While ordinary Muscovites were subjected to stricter state controls over religion, residence, and occupation, the elite explored alternatives to traditional policies and institutions. The new Romanov rulers faced monumental tasks, which they could not solve fully, and Russian leaders divided over policy as they faced a western Europe militarily and economically superior and culturally more advanced. Spurning European ways and values, conservatives strove unsuccessfully to preserve self-contained, religious traditions. To protect Russia and bring it out of backwardness, reformers urged the adoption of

Western institutions and the employment of European military and economic experts. Russia survived this difficult and perplexing era and expanded eastward and southward despite its mediocre leadership. Soviet historians emphasized the growth of a unified Russian market as a basis for bureaucratic monarchy, a Russian nation, and a national culture. How did autocracy flourish under often ineffective tsars? Why did representative institutions wither and die? How did Muscovy cope with more advanced neighbors and, despite a blockade, establish closer commercial and political ties with western Europe?

The Rulers and the *Zemskii Sobor*

The early Romanov era presents an apparent paradox of weak tsars with relatives or favorites exercising much actual state authority, yet a steady growth of autocratic power. Contemporaries believed that Mikhail I (1613–1645), who was frail, gentle, and incompetent to govern, had agreed to consult with the Boyar Duma before making decisions. Probably his power was not limited formally, but his government depended at first on leading boyar families, which often treated him scornfully and feathered their nests. In 1619 Filaret Romanov, Mikhail's ambitious and imperious father, returned from Polish captivity. Named patriarch and coruler, he dominated his passive son and directed church and state effectively until his death in 1633. Alexis (1645–1676), Mikhail's son, became tsar at age 16. Humane, religious, and endowed with a keen aesthetic sense, Alexis was more autocratic than Mikhail and achieved greater success at home and abroad. Fedor II (1676–1682), a weakling manipulated by favorites, was succeeded by two young boys—Ivan V, who was mentally deficient, and 10-year-old Peter I, who later became the first masterful Romanov ruler—while Alexis's ambitious daughter, Sofia, acted as regent.

Such weak and ineffective rulers seemed to provide the *zemskii sobor* with opportunities to become a genuine national parliament. Like other eastern European assemblies, it flowered briefly in the 17th century before declining and disappearing. The selection of the Romanovs had ended the political crisis of the Troubles and enhanced the *sobor's* prestige; until Mikhail assumed the throne, it acted as a provisional government. Containing state peasants, provincial merchants, and other elements not included in 16th-century assemblies, the *sobor* met continually until 1615 and functioned regularly until 1622. After Filaret consolidated his power, however, the *sobor* declined and convened irregularly. Its final resurgence came in 1648–1649, when it helped draft the new code (see this chapter under Law). In the early 1650s it met to discuss the annexation of Ukraine, but thereafter there were no more full meetings.

Among the *zemskii sobor's* numerous weaknesses was that it was never a well-defined body with regular composition, representation, or procedure. The infrequent 16th-century *sobory* had comprised government officials and representatives added to the Boyar Duma and the Holy Council of church leaders. In the 17th century, at least in theory, the *zemskii sobor* represented "men of all ranks." The elected representatives were mainly service gentry, merchants, and other

townsmen, though in 1613 state peasants were included. Although government decrees prescribed that men of property and substance be selected, literacy was not required, and in 1648 about half of the deputies were illiterate. Delegates were supposed to represent their constituents by presenting petitions at the *sobor,* and the elected petitioner tended to replace the government agent of earlier *sobory.* At the assemblies with the largest provincial representation, criticism of government measures was loudest.

The *sobor's* competence remained unclear. Unable to initiate legislation or bind the tsar by its decisions, it usually merely confirmed previously made government decisions and provided popular sanction for expensive wars or controversial domestic measures. Except in 1613, when the *sobor* ran the administration and afterward advised the young tsar, its sessions were brief and its delegates conferred little beforehand. The *sobory* of the 1640s, unlike earlier ones, voiced merchant and gentry grievances against the ruling boyars, and the resulting petitions became the basis for many articles of the Law Code of 1649. The Great Sobor of 1648–1649, notes J. H. Keep, tended to divide into an upper house of clergy and boyars and a lower house of elected middle-class representatives. Because the Duma and tsar retained full legislative power, however, Kliuchevskii regards this division as merely a separation of functions. The *sobor's* dual nature—legislative when tsar and Duma were present and consultative otherwise—revealed its institutional immaturity. With its legislative authority based on neither law nor popular will, the *sobor* remained throughout an instrument of the regime. Deputies of various social groups might be questioned separately and their replies compiled into written statements, but there was no regular voting procedure. At times *sobory* criticized government officials and measures, but the regime would then usually dissolve them quickly.

The *zemskii sobor* closely resembled the French Estates General, which also proved ineffective and withered during the 17th century before the strong Bourbon monarchy. At its sessions the *sobor* usually discussed state finances, but unlike the

Reception of a foreign delegation by Tsar Alexis.

English Parliament it never asserted power over taxation. It lacked gentry-merchant cooperation and failed to bargain with the Crown, features that accounted for the House of Commons's unique strength. Like the French Estates General of 1614, the *sobor* was torn by antagonism between greater and lesser lords, and between nobles and townsmen. Influential Russian classes, instead of bargaining with the tsar, became subservient to his authority. Nineteenth-century Slavophiles idealized the *sobor* as a unique representative body that cooperated with the ruler for the common good, but Keep concludes that it basically resembled Western parliaments such as the Estates General and the cortes in Spain.[1]

The *zemskii sobor*, whose peak of influence coincided with an insecure government in a confused country, developed not to limit but to reinforce central authority. Once political centralization was well advanced, it was no longer

needed. The central bureaucracy, consolidated under Alexis, distrusted the representative principle and doubted the *sobor*'s usefulness. Meeting only when the government convened it and possessing inadequate organization and procedure, the *sobor* was helpless and dispensable. Social change undermined its representation: Serfdom removed the peasantry, and gentry and merchants, increasingly dependent on state favor, could no longer voice critical views. The development of autocracy, serfdom, and the caste system doomed representative institutions.

Administration

Centralization became the keynote in central and provincial government, and only a strong tsar was required to establish a true autocracy. The boyars' political decline and the increasing subservience of the church to the state gradually eliminated most restrictions on autocratic power. The *zemskii sobor* elected or confirmed the first Romanovs, but Russia had no clear law of succession or defined

---

[1] J. H. Keep, "The Decline of the Zemsky Sobor," *SEER* 36 (1957): 100–22.

administrative structure. Especially in the late 17th century frequent coups d'état occurred, along with much court intrigue and abuse of power by ambitious favorites, the "accidental men." Muscovite leaders of this time, often lacking self-confidence, looked to the past for solutions. Because the Troubles had destroyed much of the political structure, however, even restoring the old was innovative. Some measures, derived from Muscovite experience, were cautious and lacking in new principles; others traced new paths that led to the reforms of Peter I.

Throughout Europe in the 16th and 17th centuries the size and functions of central governments expanded greatly to handle intensified warfare, new weapons technologies, territorial expansion, and increased taxation. Nowhere was this truer than in the France of Louis XIV (1660–1715). This also largely explains the proliferation of central agencies and officials under the early Romanovs. In Muscovy the authority of these central bureaus (*prikazy*) was never seriously challenged (see Chapter 10). This was because Muscovy possessed a peculiarly unitary and autocratic regime, vast territories, and an increasing variety of peoples yet lacked the medieval Latin administrative traditions of Europe. Meanwhile, a wide gulf opened between Muscovy's privileged "governing elite" and "the governed," which discouraged most people from seeking any redress of grievances.

Bureaus (*prikazy*) in Moscow were created without definite plan, and their jurisdictions were unclear and often overlapping; some were permanent and others temporary. Numbering about 50 under Mikhail Romanov, their annual number at their peak in the late 17th century varied between 60 and 70 (see Figure 13.1). The *prikazy* all possessed a similar hierarchical structure, each consisting of a decision-making board of one to six top officials from Moscow (*moskovskikh chinov liudi*) who were aided by clerks ranging in number from a handful in small, temporary bureaus to several hundred in the largest bureaus. The most important *prikazy* were subdivided into desks

(*stoly*) to facilitate a proper division of labor.[2] Muscovites applied the term *prikazy* indiscriminately to any "government" operation, including the casting of artillery barrels. Temporary *prikazy* first arose during the Oprichnina and continued to be formed until late in the 17th century. This created a cumbersome bureaucratic machine with numerous uncoordinated departments and agencies. Seeking cohesion, the government grouped related departments under one official or merged smaller *prikazy* with larger ones. Late in the 17th century two new agencies were set up: a Bureau of Accounts, which handled state finances, and a Bureau of Secret Affairs, which became the tsar's personal chancellery and supervised other agencies.

Whereas the structure of the *prikazy* remained constant, their personnel expanded and leadership changed hands. In the 16th century bureaus were headed mostly by professional civil servants (*diaki*), but after the Time of Troubles boyars largely replaced them in top posts. This displacement of civil servants by boyars seemingly reflected the superior leadership offered by boyars under the weak early Romanov tsars. Also, civil servants were losing their former good reputation for efficiency and professionalism as they eagerly sought the spoils of the service state: rank, land, and money. Thus during the 17th century *prikazy* were normally headed by a boyar or *okolnichii* (who ranked just below the boyars), assisted by a state secretary (*diak*) and some clerks.[3]

Centralizing tendencies also prevailed in provincial and local government. In each district a governor (*voevoda*) became responsible for finance, law, police, and the army in town and countryside. Unlike the former governors (*namestniki*) (see Chapter 10), *voevody* were supposed to

---

[2] B. Plavsic, "Seventeenth Century Chanceries . . . ," in *Russian Officialdom . . .* , ed. W. Pintner and D. Rowney (Chapel Hill, NC, 1980).

[3] See P. Brown, "Muscovite Government Bureaus," *Rus. Hist.* 10, no. 3 (1983): 268–80; and G. Weickhardt, "Bureaucrats and Boiars in the Muscovite Tsardom," *Rus. Hist.* 10, no. 3 (1983): 331–35.

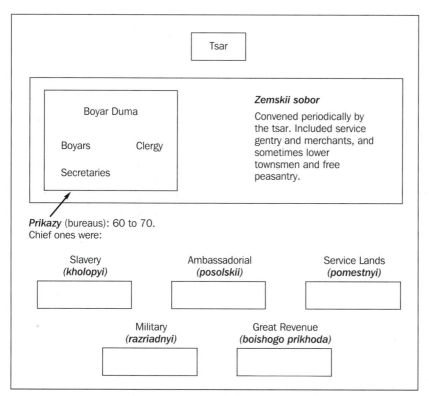

Figure 13.1
Muscovite government in the 17th century

rule for the tsar's benefit. "Feeding" and bribes, though forbidden, persisted nonetheless, and often new governors were descendants of old *namestniki.* Their ill-defined authority encouraged abuse of power and imposed heavy burdens on localities. Provincial representatives to the *zemskii sobor* of 1642 complained: "Your Majesty's governors have reduced the people of all stations to beggary and have stripped them to the bone."[4] Moscow, however, preferred to deal with one appointed governor than with many elected officials.

The *zemstvo* system of local self-government remained vital in the north but withered elsewhere. Elected officials in town offices still

collected taxes for local needs but would seldom disobey the governor to aid their communities. As boards of justice and assessors were disbanded, judicial authority shifted to the governor. Elected mayors executed unpopular policies that the governor and his staff were loath to perform, and *zemstvo* institutions were deprived of initiative but not of onerous responsibility.

Law

Bureaucratic Muscovy urgently needed a new law code. Since 1550 the Boyar Duma and other agencies had issued numerous uncoordinated decrees that made the Code of 1550 obsolete. Tsar Alexis and his boyar advisers provided the initiative: Terrified by the Moscow Revolt of 1648, they convened a Great Sobor to help compose a new

[4] M. T. Florinsky, *Russia: A History and an Interpretation,* vol. 1 (New York, 1953), p. 270.

code from the Acts of the Apostles, the Holy Fathers, decrees of previous tsars, and old charters. Legal sources for the Code of 1649 (*Ulozhenie*) included the *Sudebnik* of 1550, Byzantine codes, and the Lithuanian Statute of 1588. A codification commission of two boyars, a courtier, and two secretaries, urged on by urban revolts, hastily drafted a body of law that often had to cover new situations. The Great Sobor's elected members suggested changes, gave advice, and presented petitions to the Boyar Duma. The result was superficial and inconsistent; its survival until 1833 meant that Russia had to do without a clear or precise collection of laws.

The *Ulozhenie*, Russia's first printed law code, had a preamble, 25 chapters, and 967 articles. The preamble proclaimed that justice would become equal for "men of all ranks," but the *Ulozhenie* subjected most Muscovites to state bondage. Social relationships were defined by establishing a highly stratified class (*soslovie*) system, which prescribed each group's duties and obligations rather rigidly. Almost half of its provisions dealt with the service gentry, whose social and political dominance was confirmed. The *dvoriane* received a virtual monopoly of landed estates farmed by serfs, complete authority over its peasants, and unlimited time to recover escapees. Restrictions were relaxed on *pomestie* estates, which now tended to become hereditary, but all noblemen now had to serve the state. The church retained lands obtained illegally since 1580, but it was forbidden to acquire new ones. Burghers received a monopoly of commerce and industry but were bound to their places of residence. Leading merchants became state wards protected from foreign competition but subservient to detailed government regulations. The *Ulozhenie*, a desperate expedient to protect loyal state servants and the treasury against impoverishment, bound nearly everyone to his class, occupation, and residence.

The Army

War, as R. Hellie notes, was the chief preoccupation of the Muscovite state. Until the mid-17th

century the backbone of the army remained a gentry cavalry designed to combat steppe Tatars. Armed mainly with sabers and bows as late as 1600, it was poorly organized and lacked discipline and staying power. In 1630 *streltsy*, service Cossacks, and small contingents of artillerymen and foreign mercenaries made up the remainder of an army of about 90,000 men. Except for *streltsy*, who had regular regional organizations, this motley army disbanded after each campaign. In 1630 impending war with Poland caused Filaret's government to improve this system by offering huge salaries and large estates to foreign officers and specialists, mainly from Protestant European countries. Colonel Alexander Leslie, a Scot in Russian service, was sent abroad to recruit officers and mercenaries and to buy cannon and muskets. Foreign officers were placed in command of infantry and dragoon regiments, organized and drilled on a European pattern, which threatened the predominance of the gentry cavalry. Between 1630 and 1634 ten such regiments, totaling 17,400 men, were organized—almost half of the army sent to capture Smolensk in 1632. After that campaign failed (primarily because of excessive interference from Moscow) and Filaret died, however, the regiments were disbanded and most of the mercenaries were expelled from Muscovy.

Major reform in military organization and weaponry was forced upon a reluctant regime by the need to combat the more technologically advanced and better-organized armies of Sweden and Poland. In the mid-1640s Tsar Alexis's tutor and favorite, B. I. Morozov, an enthusiastic "Westernizer," revived foreign-style infantry regiments and established in Moscow new military chancelleries that imposed changes to the last detail. The government, insisting that officers possess knowledge, ability, and experience, disregarded *mestnichestvo* (the influence of noble birth and relatives) and traditional boyar privileges. At first most of the top posts went to foreigners, especially in new infantry and dragoon units. During the Thirteen Years War with Poland, as gentry cavalry and *streltsy* revealed their incapacity, the number of infantry armed with new flintlock muskets increased sharply. That war saw the definitive triumph in Muscovy of the "gunpowder revolution," which had swept Europe earlier, and the irreversible decline of the gentry cavalry. By 1681, with 81,000 infantry and only 45,000 cavalry on its rolls, the army had increased greatly in size and was by far the largest force in Europe (more than 200,000 effectives). Even in peacetime the army consumed almost half of the state budget. Most of the threefold increase in cost between 1630 and 1680 went to maintain regiments of foreign type and to pay their officers.

Anxious to make Muscovy self-suffcient in weapons, Mikhail's government modernized the Moscow Cannon Yard, the chief center for artillery manufacture. In 1632 Andrew Vinnius, a Dutch merchant, secured permission to construct and operate a major arms manufacturing plant at Tula, a pioneering effort in the development of Russian industry. By mid-century Russian artillery, now mainly of bronze, was becoming more standardized and accurate. The primitive Russian metallurgical industry, however, still could not fully supply the needs of a rapidly expanding army, and large imports of firearms from European lands were still required.

In the south Moscow created for the first time an effective system of border defenses against Crimean Tatar raids. In 1638 Prince Cherkasskii, governor of Tula, greatly reinforced its defenses. Soon afterward, a French Huguenot engineer designed the Belgorod Line, a formidable fortified network that secured central Muscovy and provided a base for penetration and colonization of the southern steppe. The obsolescent service gentry cavalry was left with little to do.

Such improvements in military organization, discipline, and weaponry prefigured the work of Peter I; though incomplete, they proved highly successful against Poland and the Crimean Tatars. In 1680, however, Muscovy still lacked a regular standing army (in peacetime only *streltsy* and officer cadres remained), and during campaigns "poor" gentry of uncertain skill and morale were still conscripted. Regiments of foreign type were filled by volunteers and by conscription from the peasantry, usually one recruit per 20 households, for infantry and dragoons. The large and costly Muscovite army remained inefficient and over-centralized compared to the Swedish army, and its commanders could not exercise much initiative.

Eastward Expansion

Major expansion to the east and south during the 17th century converted Muscovy into a multinational empire with vast resources. Whereas the conquest of Siberia had to overcome only negligible resistance, the struggle with Poland over Ukraine would strain the country's resources to the utmost and cost heavy casualties.

While the Time of Troubles temporarily reversed Muscovy's advance westward, the Russians surged east to build a huge Eurasian empire (see Map 13.1). Following up Ermak's conquests (see Chapter 11), Muscovites by 1605 controlled the Ob basin, with Tomsk as their outpost facing the Mongol-Kalmyk world. The Troubles failed to slow an advance combining private enterprise and government action. Furs, gold, and adventure lured the Russians onward as their snares and traps, more sophisticated than native ones, depleted the numbers of fur-bearing animals in western Siberia. Hunters and Cossacks, following Siberia's interconnecting river systems, continually sought new territories. Private entrepreneurs, organizing primitive joint-stock companies with all members sharing in the returns, moved along the rivers in small armed bands. Forts built at strategic points subsequently grew into towns, and centralized administration and superior firepower crushed small-scale native revolts against extortion by Russian trappers and adventurers. In 1631 a Cossack force reached Lake Baikal; in 1638 an expedition arrived at the Pacific Ocean; and by 1650 Russia controlled nearly all of Siberia. In eastern Siberia the Russians encountered only scattered tribes: Tungus, Buriats, Mongols, Iakuts, and Paleo-Asiatic tribes engaged mainly in hunting, breeding reindeer, and raising cattle. Together these tribes far outnumbered the invaders, but

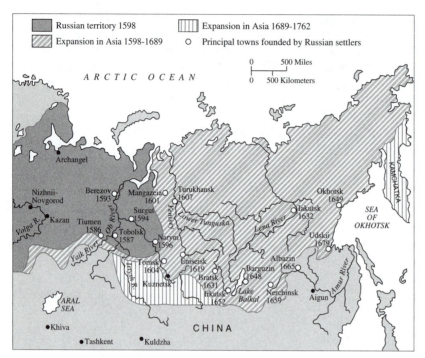

Map 13.1 Russia's eastward expansion, 1598–1762

disunited and lacking firearms, most of them submitted voluntarily to Russian rule.

While losing some western provinces temporarily to Poland and Sweden, Russia was strengthened economically by its eastern acquisitions. In 1613 the Stroganovs, wealthy from Siberian furs, made a large loan to the Moscow treasury. During the 17th century Siberian furs constituted about 10 percent of state revenues. The government fostered mining and agriculture, and by 1645 some 8,000 peasant families had settled in western Siberia. Though criminals and war prisoners were employed in agriculture, the permanent Russian population consisted mostly of peasants seeking free land who eventually produced a grain surplus in western Siberia. Iron mining began in the Tomsk and Kuznetsk areas, and in the 18th century the state established silver and gold mines in the Altai Mountains and east of Lake Baikal.

With a growing financial stake in Siberia, Moscow devoted attention to its administration, which had been handled earlier by the Kazan Board. An independent Siberian Board, set up in 1637 and lasting until 1763, collected tribute systematically and improved communications. *Voevody* (governors) directly responsible to Moscow controlled Siberian towns; the *voevoda* of Tobolsk coordinated their affairs and conducted relations with native peoples.

Russia's southward advance in Siberia caused friction with the new Manchu dynasty of China. Erofei Khabarov's expedition penetrated the Amur valley about 1650, yet few Russian settlers followed. Although Russian merchants and envoys visited China in the 1660s and 1670s, no regular relations resulted. After border clashes in the 1680s Russia and China negotiated the Treaty of Nerchinsk (1689)—(China's first treaty with a European power)—confirming Russia's hold over Siberia but leaving the Amur region to China. For almost two centuries this frontier remained quite stable.

Until the mid-17th century Muscovy remained mostly on the defensive toward Sweden and Poland. By the Peace of Stolbovo (1617) Moscow recovered Novgorod but ceded towns on the Finnish Gulf to Sweden, postponing indefinitely Russia's emergence as a Baltic power. Wladyslaw of Poland failed to capture Moscow, but by the Truce of Deulino (1618) Russia had to renounce strategic Smolensk. This poor beginning reflected Russian weakness in the wake of the Troubles, but it provided a much-needed breathing spell. When the truce expired in 1632, Muscovy attacked Smolensk, but the campaign ended disastrously. Surrounded by the Poles, Moscow's army surrendered and its commander was executed. The "eternal peace" of 1634 confirmed the Truce of Deulino, though Wladyslaw finally renounced claims to the throne of Muscovy.

Annexation of Eastern Ukraine

Developments in Ukraine—meaning the borderland—confronted Muscovy during the 17th century with perplexing and dangerous problems. Ukraine, with Kiev as its political, religious, and cultural center, extended from southern Muscovy to the Black Sea and from the Carpathian Mountains eastward to the Don River. Ukraine was an appropriate name for a country lacking natural frontiers except for the Carpathians. Roughly two-thirds of its territory had remarkably fertile black soil (*chernozem*). Besides Ukrainians, the descendants of the inhabitants of Kievan Rus, the region contained minorities of Poles, Belorussians, Great Russians, and Tatars.

After the decline of Galicia-Volhynia in the 13th century, Ukraine's fate was generally decided in Warsaw, Moscow, or Vienna. While Ukraine declined politically, economically, and culturally in the 14th century, its neighbors—Lithuania, Poland, and Muscovy—were increasing in power. Ancient Kiev, abandoned in 1300 by the Orthodox metropolitan, lost many of its boyars and leading merchants. The Lithuanians, exploiting Ukraine's weakness, seized the small principalities on the left bank of the Dnieper River and in 1362 occupied Kiev, then moved into Podolia. For Ukrainians, Lithuanian rule was preferable to the pitiless rule of the Golden Horde, and Kievan traditions were better preserved in Lithuania than in Muscovy.

Polish expansion had an extensive and lasting impact on Ukrainians, beginning with King Casimir the Great (1310–1370). Casimir's push eastward was hailed as a crusade against heathen Lithuanians and Orthodox Ukrainians. After a Polish-Lithuanian war, the Poles by 1366 occupied all of Galicia and part of Volhynia. This conquest subordinated many Ukrainians to Polish rule, provoking a bitter religious and social conflict lasting several centuries.

First appearing in the 1480s, Slavic Cossacks became the most volatile and warlike element in Ukraine. *Cossacks,* a term probably of Turkic origin, meant free warriors or freebooters; they first fought the Tatars in the steppe. Many Cossacks lacked permanent homes or occupations; others settled along south Russian rivers—the Dnieper, Don, and Volga. Impoverished boyar sons and peasants seeking to escape oncoming serfdom left Muscovy to join their ranks. Thus the bulk of the Cossacks were originally runaway peasants, and most of those living in the Dnieper basin were Ukrainian. The original Cossack country lay south of Moscow, around Tula and Riazan, until Muscovite and Polish colonization forced it further south into Ukraine.

The Ukrainian Cossacks created their own power center. In 1553 on Khortitsa Island in the Dnieper River beyond the cataracts (*Zaporozhe*) they erected the Sich, a fortified camp guarded by wooden ramparts studded with captured cannon. Barring women and children, it served both as a refuge for Cossacks fleeing advancing Polish landlord control and as a means of resisting Crimean Tatar raids into Ukraine. Any male Christian could come to this island fortress to join a Cossack brotherhood that soon numbered about 5,000 men, some 10 percent of whom rotated as its garrison. This "*Zaporozhe* Host" elected its leaders in a noisy council (*rada*) embodying a rough democracy idealized in some Ukrainian accounts. The Sich's economy featured hunting, fishing, and beekeeping, but essentially it was a military trading community whose troops would plunder anyone for "Cossack bread."

Many Ukrainian Cossacks lived in frontier towns obeying only their own elected officers. Seeking to impose control and regular service upon them, the Polish government beginning in 1578 enlisted "registered Cossacks" derived mostly from town residents as a frontier militia. By the early 17th century Ukrainian Cossacks comprised three groups: a wealthier "registered" elite in Polish service, the *Zaporozhe* Host outside the Polish Commonwealth, and the vast majority in the countryside or unregistered in frontier towns. Successful raids into Ottoman territory heightened the Cossacks' self-confidence as the appointed defenders of Christianity.

After 1596, growing Polish pressure and Catholic-Uniate persecution helped unite Orthodox Ukrainians and stimulated revolts against the Polish government and landlords. However, five major Cossack-peasant insurrections in Ukraine between 1593 and 1638 failed for lack of clear aims, leadership, and planning. As clergy and merchants sought Cossack and peasant support, an Orthodox hierarchy was restored in Ukraine in 1620. Four years later Metropolitan Iov of Kiev, failing to secure rights for the Orthodox from the Polish parliament (*seim*), requested Muscovite protection for Ukraine. Because Moscow was then too weak and preoccupied to respond, Iov appealed to the *Zaporozhe* Cossacks to rally to a threatened Orthodoxy. These stateless adventurers, becoming guardians of Orthodoxy and of Russian institutions in Ukraine, sought to expel the Polish lords. As Cossack authority increased along the mid-Dnieper, the Poles constructed Kodak fortress, which threatened the nearby Sich's independence (see Map 13.2). In 1637–1638 the *Zaporozhe* and most of the Cossacks in Polish service revolted unsuccessfully. The Poles virtually ended Sich autonomy, took registered Cossack lands, and forced unregistered Cossacks and Ukrainian peasants to choose between serfdom and rebellion.

The Poles sparked the great Ukrainian revolt of 1648. King Wladyslaw, seeking Cossack support against the Turks, promised to increase the number of registered Cossacks, but the Polish parliament refused to ratify this policy. Bogdan Khmelnitsky, a graduate of a Jesuit college and secretary of the Cossack army, was a delegate to the *seim* who favored expanding the Cossacks' forces and rights. In Khmelnitsky's absence a Polish nobleman seized his estate, killed his youngest son, and abducted his intended bride. Infuriated, Khmelnitsky resolved to lead a Ukrainian revolt against the Poles. Fleeing to the Sich with a few followers in early 1648, the charismatic Khmelnitsky secured the *Zaporozhe* Cossacks' support and was elected as their leader (*hetman*). He built an army of Cossacks and Ukrainian peasants and forged an alliance with the Crimean Tatars. During 1648 his victories stunned the Poles and roused all of Ukraine, but his Cossacks massacred thousands of urban Jews. Entering Kiev in triumph and welcomed into Galicia and Volhynia, Khmelnitsky dreamed of ruling a greater Ukraine from the Don to the Vistula rivers. But his soaring ambitions were checked by growing antagonism between peasants and ordinary Cossacks on one side and the Cossack elite (*starshina*) on the other. The *starshina*, guarding their privileges against the lower classes, restricted the number of registered Cossacks. In 1649 Khmelnitsky made a peace with Poland that restored Cossack self-government and raised the number of registered Cossacks to 60,000; but when hostilities resumed, the Crimeans abandoned him and the Poles defeated him. Forced to accept a treaty that reduced Cossack territory and the number of registered Cossacks, he sought the protection of Moscow as suzerain of Ukraine.

Tsar Alexis and his advisers hesitated, then negotiated cautiously with Khmelnitsky. To accept a protectorate of Ukraine, they knew, would mean war with Poland. Among Ukrainians, ordinary Cossacks and peasants favored Muscovy; the *starshina*, having more in common with the Polish

Map 13.2 Russian expansion in Europe, 1618–1689

szlachta, opposed it. Moscow desired Cossack troops, and its church needed Kiev's scholars and clergy. Nikon's selection as Russian patriarch (see Chapter 14) strengthened the unionist faction in Moscow, and in 1653 a *zemskii sobor* advised Alexis to become protector of Ukraine.

At Pereiaslavl the Cossacks and a Muscovite grand embassy made final arrangements. Khmelnitsky told a Cossack assembly there: "We see that we can no longer live without a tsar." The Pereiaslavl Union placed eastern Ukraine under Moscow's protection and confirmed the autonomy of the Sich, whose elected *hetman* could conduct foreign relations except with Poland and Turkey. Cossacks and Ukrainians swore allegiance to the tsar, but historians still debate whether this meant incorporation, vassaldom, or just military alliance for Ukraine. Seeking to remain independent, Khmelnitsky continued to wheel and deal in typical Cossack fashion with Sweden, Poland, and

Transylvania. The Pereiaslavl Union produced the Thirteen Years War (1654–1667) between Muscovy and Poland. Aided by Cossack forces and Sweden's invasion of Poland, the Russians captured Smolensk and much of Belorussia and Ukraine. Alexis, seeking to unite all eastern Slavs, assumed the grandiose title "Tsar of Great, Little, and White Russia." Then, to Khmelnitsky's dismay, Moscow made a truce with Poland and fought unsuccessfully against Sweden.

Khmelnitsky's death in 1657 plunged Ukraine into chaos and civil war. A brave Cossack with a heroic capacity for vodka, he scarcely deserved subsequent accolades from nationalist Ukrainian historians, although he managed to preserve Ukrainian unity and some balance between the *starshina* and the rank and file. After his death they split irrevocably as his self-appointed successor, Ivan Vygovsky, representing the *starshina*, repudiated the accord with Moscow and reached agreement with Poland and the Crimea. Vygovsky defeated the Muscovites in 1659 only to be unseated by a revolt of ordinary Cossacks. Ukraine divided: The "right bank," west of the Dnieper, under Khmelnitsky's epileptic son, remained Polish; the "left bank" returned to Moscow's control. The Thirteen Years War dragged on at enormous cost to Russia and Poland, producing terrible devastation in Ukraine, until the Turco-Tatar threat induced them to stop fighting.

A farsighted boyar statesman, Afanasi Ordin-Nashchokin, engineered the Andrusovo armistice of 1667 and briefly altered Muscovite foreign policy. He favored peace and alliance with disintegrating Poland to break Sweden's stranglehold over the Baltic. At Andrusovo Russia gained Smolensk and Seversk provinces and eastern Ukraine and occupied Kiev. After more warfare the "eternal peace" of 1686 confirmed these provisions. Because Belorussia reverted to Poland-Lithuania and Ukraine was partitioned, Alexis failed to unite the eastern Slavs. Twenty-five years of bloody war gave Muscovy eastern Ukraine and Kiev, but unable to penetrate the Swedish barrier, it remained blocked from the Baltic and Black seas. Muscovy joined a European coalition of Poland, the Holy Roman Empire, and Venice against the Turks and the Crimean khan, but ill-managed Muscovite campaigns against the Crimea in the 1680s were dismal failures.

Muscovy's strength, prestige, and role in European affairs increased considerably under the early Romanovs. Its foreign relations grew more complex, and Moscow exchanged envoys with all of the important European states. Closer acquaintance with Europe caused imaginative Muscovite statesmen such as Ordin-Nashchokin to question traditional methods and institutions and to use foreign models to overcome persisting Russian backwardness.

Suggested Additional Reading

BOOKS

BASARAB, J. *Pereiaslaval 1654: A Historiographical Study* (Edmonton, Canada, 1982).

BUSHKOVITCH, P. *The Merchants of Moscow, 1580–1650* (Cambridge, England, 1980).

DONNELLY, A. *The Russian Conquest of Bashkiria, 1552–1740* (New Haven, 1968).

FISHER, H. H. *The Russian Fur Trade, 1550–1700* (Berkeley, 1943).

GORDON, L. *Cossack Rebellions: Social Turmoil in Sixteenth Century Ukraine* (Albany, NY, 1983).

HERBERSTEIN, S. VON. *Description of Moscow and Muscovy* (London, 1969). (Reprint).

KERNER, R. J. *The Urge to the Sea . . .* (Berkeley, 1942).

KLYUCHEVSKY, V. O. *A Course in Russian History: The Seventeenth Century,* trans. N. Duddington (Chicago, 1968).

KOTOSHIKHIN, G. K. *O Rossii v tsarstvovanii Alekseia Mikhailovicha,* text and commentary A. E. Pennington (Oxford, 1980).

LANTZEFF, G. *Siberia in the Seventeenth Century* (Berkeley, 1943).

LONGWORTH, P. *Alexis: Tsar of All the Russians* (New York, 1984).

LUPININ, N. *Religious Revolt in the Seventeenth Century . . .* (Princeton, 1984).

MANCALL, M. *Russia and China . . . to 1728* (Cambridge, MA, 1971).

MOUSNIER, R. *Peasant Uprisings in Seventeenth Century France, Russia, and China*, trans. B. Pearce (New York, 1970).

O'BRIEN, C. B. *Muscovy and the Ukraine . . . 1654–1687* (Berkeley, 1963).

PLATONOV, S. *Moscow and the West*, trans. J. Wieczynski (Hattiesburg, MS, 1972).

PORSHNEV, B. F. *Muscovy and Sweden in the Thiry Years War, 1630–1665*, ed. Paul Dukes (Cambridge, 1996).

STEVENS, C. B. *Soldiers on the Steppe: Army Reform and Social Change in Early Modern Russia* (DeKalb, IL, 1995).

SUBTELNY, O. *Ukraine: A History* (Toronto, 1988). (Chapters 7 and 8.)

TREADGOLD, D. *The Great Siberian Migration* (Princeton, 1957).

VERNADSKY, G. *The Tsardom of Moscow, 1547–1682* (New Haven, 1969).

WOOD, ALAN. *The History of Siberia . . .* (London, 1991).

ARTICLES

BARON, S. "The Origins of Seventeenth Century Moscow's *Nemeckaja Sloboda*." *Cal. SS* 5 (1970): 1–17.

———. "Vasilii Shorin: Seventeenth Century Russian Merchant Extraordinary." *CanAmSlSt* 6 (1972): 503–48.

BROWN, P. "Muscovite Government Bureaus." *Rus. Hist.* 10 (1983): 269–330. (Includes complete list of all *prikazy*.)

CHUBATY, N. "Bohdan Khmelnytsky, Ruler of Ukraine." *UQ* 13 (1957): 197–211.

CRUMMEY, R. "Court Groupings and Politics in Russia, 1645–1649." *FOG* 24: 203–21.

———. "Crown and Boiars under Fedor Ivanovich and Michael Romanov." *CanAmSlSt* 6 (1972): 549–74.

———. "Reflections on Mestnichestvo in Seventeenth Century Muscovy." *FOG* 27: 269–81.

DEWEY, H., and K. B. STEVENS. "Muscovites at Play . . ." *CanAmSlSt* 13, nos. 1–2 (1979): 189–203.

DMYTRYSHYN, B. "Russian Expansion to the Pacific, 1580–1700: A Historiographic Review." *SS* 25 (1980): 1–26.

EEKMAN, T. "Muscovy's International Relations in the Late 17th Century: Johan van Keller's Observations." *Cal. SS* 25, no. 1–4 (1991): 179–99.

KEEP, J. "The Decline of the Zemsky Sobor." *SEER* 36 (1957): 100–22.

———. "The Regime of Filaret, 1619–1633." *SEER* 38 (1959–60): 334–60.

KIVELSON, V. "The Devil Stole His Mind: The Tsar and the 1648 Moscow Uprising." *AHR* 98, no. 3 (June 1993): 733–56.

KLEIMOLA, A. "Up through Servitude: The Changing Condition of the Muscovite Elite in the Sixteenth and Seventeenth Centuries." *Rus. Hist.* 6, no. 2 (1978): 210–29.

LOEWENSON, L. "The Moscow Rising of 1648." *SEER* 27 (1948–49): 146–56.

MAZOUR, A. G. "Curtains in the Past." *JMH* 20 (1948): 212–22.

O'BRIEN, C. B. "Muscovite Prikaz Administration of the Seventeenth Century." *FOG* 24 (1978): 223–35.

PHILIP, W. "Russia: The Beginning of Westernization." *New Cambr. Modern History* 5: 571–91.

PLAVSIC, B. "Seventeenth Century Chanceries and Their Staffs," in *Russian Officialdom . . .*, ed. W. Pintner and D. Rowney (Chapel Hill, NC, 1980).

SEVERIN, T. "Conquistadors of Siberia," in *The Oriental Adventure: Explorers of the East* (Boston, 1976), pp. 40–60.

SZEFTEL, M. "The Title of the Muscovite Monarch up to the End of the Seventeenth Century." *CanAmSlSt* 13 (1979): 59–81.

WEICKHARDT, G. "Bureaucrats and Boiars in the Muscovite Tsardom." *Rus. Hist.* 10 (1983): 331–56.

ZGUTA, R. "Witchcraft Trials in Seventeenth Century Russia." *AHR* 82, no. 5 (1977): 1187–1207.

14

The Early Romanovs: Society, Culture, and Religion

The 17th century was an age of momentous social, cultural, and religious change in Muscovite Russia. It was a period of transition in which traditional values and attitudes were challenged and tested by foreign influences, which increased throughout the century, marking a gradual rapprochement between Muscovy and the West. The shock of the Time of Troubles had seriously undermined the state's material well-being and shaken popular confidence in historic traditions and customs. The resulting breakdown of old modes of thought created uncertainty and tension but also a more receptive atmosphere for the spread of foreign influences. Muscovite Russia's confrontation with the West was destined to be neither easy nor peaceful. Spreading foreign influences and growing consciousness of the world beyond the borders of Muscovy affected directly or indirectly almost every facet of Muscovite life.

Foreign Influences

During the Troubles foreigners had entered Russia in unprecedented numbers. Russians had regular and extensive contact with Poles, Swedes, Germans, and many others. Although remaining suspicious of foreigners, Russians were impressed by superior Western technology and captivated by the diverse and spontaneous Western culture. Perceptive Russians realized that if Muscovy was to recover and progress, it would have to learn from more knowledgeable, skilled, and sophisticated Europeans, especially in the vital field of military technology.

Similarly, after the Troubles the impoverished Russian economy allowed foreign capital and entrepreneurs to gain a firm foothold. Along with much-needed capital came many foreign merchants—English, Dutch, and German—who rapidly acquired control of a substantial portion of Russian business activity. The influx of foreigners, both merchants and officers, elicited opposition from native Russians who found it difficult to compete with them. Russian merchants grumbled that English merchants with superior organization, knowledge, and experience were becoming too rich, powerful, and influential, that Russian merchants were losing out in commercial transactions. In a formal petition of 1627 Russian merchants begged the government to prohibit foreigners from engaging in Russian internal trade and to monitor foreigners' activities more closely so as to control widespread bribery, deception, and fraud against their Russian counterparts. Official efforts to regulate foreign merchants had little effect because the foreigners were already firmly entrenched and, more important, because the government and the economy depended on their commercial and industrial skills. Most of the few manufactories of 17th-century Muscovy were established directly by foreigners or with their capital, advice, and skill.

The Russian merchants sought aid from other social groups to combat European influences. The service gentry, dissatisfied with the dominant role of foreign officers in Russian military affairs, resented being commanded by European officers. At the *zemskii sobor* of 1648–1649 merchants and service gentry persuaded the government to recognize the problem of foreign influences.

In 1652 the government, using a plan initiated by Ivan IV in the 1570s, set up a foreign settlement outside Moscow where foreigners were required to reside and do business in isolation from the Russian population. Through this foreign ghetto (*nemetskaia sloboda*) the influence of foreigners on Russian development was more profound than it would have been had they been allowed to operate and live freely in diverse parts of Russia. The foreign ghetto became, noted Kliuchevskii, "a corner of Western Europe sheltering in an eastern suburb of Moscow," a full and tangible example of the diversity of European life. This foreign settlement housed a school; several Protestant churches; practical, well-laid-out European houses and streets; and an aura of bustle and activity. From this "corner" Western culture and customs were transmitted to the Russians.

The spread of foreign influences captivated the imagination of certain enlightened Russians but raised disturbing doubts in the minds of more conservative, traditional segments of society, particularly clergymen, who feared that Protestant and Catholic influences might undermine the purity of the Orthodox faith and popular morality. These fears, coupled with a nagging disquietude about Russian religious traditions, caused complex and explosive religious controversies within the Orthodox church and among the laity, culminating in a great church schism.

Religious Controversies and Heresies

The 17th-century religious problem involved interconnected issues that reflected Russia's changing social, political, and cultural values. On the religious level, controversy developed over proposed changes in church liturgy and ritual. On the political side, a great clash occurred between church and state—between patriarch and tsar—that altered traditional relationships. The religious issue also reflected growing social tensions, as the lower classes in particular protested the growing expansion and secularization of state power and focused their anger and frustration on the question of church reform. The religious controversy reflected a deeper fear that the unique Russian civilization might be destroyed by subtly advancing foreign influences. To many, traditional ways, customs, and attitudes had to be preserved even at the cost of open resistance to the state.

For centuries controversies and heresies, such as those of the *Strigolniki* (shorn heads) and Judaizers in Novgorod (see Chapter 10), had challenged the spiritual authority of the official church. These heresies were apparently stimulated by Western ideas filtering into Western-oriented Novgorod. While combating these movements the church became suspicious and intolerant of deviations from established practice, however minor, and professed a missionary zeal in defending Orthodox purity. The elaboration of the Third Rome theory expressed the messianic mission of the Russian church to maintain Orthodox purity throughout the world. Because, according to the theory, there would be no fourth Rome, Moscow was the last bastion of true Christianity.

In addition, the controversy between the followers of Joseph of Volokolamsk and Nil Sorskii (see Chapter 10) developed awareness of the need to increase the number of religious works available in Church Slavonic translation in Muscovy. To this end the government sought knowledgeable translators abroad. One who responded to this call was Maxim the Greek, a learned monk from Mount Athos in Greece, the center of Orthodox monasticism. Arriving in Moscow in 1518, he was drawn immediately into the religious controversies centering on political and economic questions. Drawing on the spiritual intensity of the monastic traditions of Mount Athos, Maxim joined the ascetic followers of Nil Sorskii and argued for a spiritually revitalized clergy and a church unencumbered by political and economic concerns. While translating from Greek into Church Slavonic, Maxim discovered numerous errors that had crept into Russian church books over the centuries. His findings raised disturbing doubts about the Third Rome's Orthodox purity, doubts that were deepened during the 16th century by visiting Greek prelates who criticized Russian practices for deviating from Byzantine custom. Despite growing awareness of divergence between Russian and Greek practice, even cautious and tentative efforts at reform met with bitter criticism and denunciation. The atmosphere in early 17th-century Muscovy was uneasy, uncertain, and tense, hardly a time to begin difficult and dangerous church reform. Later, new impetus for reform came from an unexpected source: Kiev.

Under the Lublin Union of 1569 the Grand Duchy of Lithuania relinquished to Poland control of the Dnieper River basin, an area populated by peasants and Cossacks who were at least nominally Orthodox but were separated politically and ecclesiastically from Orthodox Muscovy. The patriarch of Constantinople consecrated a metropolitan for this West Russian Orthodox Church to provide the faithful with spiritual guidance and to strengthen the administrative structure of the church. The years after the Lublin Union were difficult ones for the Orthodox population in Pol-

ish territory. In the mid-16th century the religious ferment of the Reformation had penetrated Poland and stimulated a strong Jesuit effort to suppress Protestantism in Poland. The Jesuits, having succeeded with support from the Polish government, pressured the Orthodox under Polish rule to acknowledge papal authority. Their proselytizing activity was so intense that some Orthodox bishops, fearing the destruction of the West Russian Orthodox Church, consented to union with Rome, provided the Eastern ritual and use of Church Slavonic in the services were preserved. These bishops, winning support from the Orthodox metropolitan in Kiev, dispatched a delegation to Rome to negotiate an agreement that split the West Russian Orthodox Church.

Once part of the West Russian Orthodox Church had united with Rome, the Poles increased pressure on the Orthodox remaining under their rule. The Orthodox clergy tried to counter this new offensive but were ill prepared to oppose the incomparably more learned and dynamic Jesuits. Realizing the notorious educational shortcomings of the clergy, the Orthodox metropolitan of Kiev, Peter Mogila, established in 1631 a Kievan Academy "for the teaching of free sciences in the Greek, Slavonic, and Latin languages." Theology, philosophy, natural science, and scriptural criticism together with foreign languages were the main courses taught at this unprecedented educational institution. The Kievan Academy produced a new generation of broadly educated and sophisticated monks, many of whom eventually went to Moscow and the patriarchal printing office, where their scholarly skills and spiritual intensity contributed to growing religious disquietude in the Russian capital. During their studies and activity as translators these scholarly monks noted once again the numerous errors in the Russian service books and ritual. By mid-century the pressure for reform was mounting, but the rapid change and widespread social unrest of this period made it unlikely that any reform movement would succeed. The Russian patriarch Nikon, however, would take up the reform of ritual and church books with great vigor beginning in 1654.

Patriarch Nikon's Church Reforms

The extremely volatile religious issue became further complicated by the introduction of political questions. During Mikhail Romanov's reign the traditional pattern of church-state relations with the secular ruler ascendant had been disrupted. In 1619 Mikhail's father, Filaret, became Russian patriarch. A diarchy was established with patriarch and tsar, father and son, as equals in rank, dignity, and power, marking a significant departure from the traditional Byzantine pattern. This relationship ceased with Filaret's death in 1633, but a precedent had been created that would contribute much to a direct collision between church and state under Tsar Alexis.

To growing religious and political tensions were added deep social frictions, outgrowths of the rigid social structure embodied in the Law Code of 1649 (*Ulozhenie*) and the formalization of serfdom. Reflecting the growing secularization and bureaucratization of life, these frictions contributed to growing restlessness, confusion, hatred, and violence that culminated in local rebellions affecting much of Muscovy. Church reform was the catalyst that ignited this tension into flames of conflict.

In Russian Christianity from its inception, form had been more important than content; ritual had taken precedence over theological content or substance. For most of the Orthodox faithful *how* one performed the ritual and liturgy was far more important than the ideas behind them. Even minor changes in ritual could therefore become matters of life and death, salvation and damnation.

In 1652 Patriarch Joseph died and Tsar Alexis chose as his successor the metropolitan of Novgorod, Nikon, one of the most remarkable religious figures of the 17th century. Born a humble peasant in 1605, amid the turmoil of the Time of Troubles, Nikita Minov was intelligent and ambitious and chose the only upwardly mobile path for one of low social origin—the priesthood. Soon, however, he felt that as a parish priest his talents were being wasted. Persuading his wife to enter a convent, he took monastic vows under the name Nikon.

Nikon was well suited to the rigors of monastic life because he accepted the ascetic views of the Trans-Volga Elders. His spiritual intensity, imposing physical stature (reputedly he was six feet six), and hypnotic personality brought him to his superiors' attention and promoted his rapid rise in the monastic ranks. Named archimandrite of a small monastery in the far north in 1643, he visited Moscow in 1646 and as a visiting prelate was presented to Tsar Alexis. The young, devout tsar succumbed to the spell of Nikon's personality and insisted that he remain in Moscow as archimandrite of Novospasskii Monastery, which housed the Romanov family burial vault. Gradually Alexis became dependent on Nikon's spiritual guidance. In 1648 Alexis appointed Nikon metropolitan of Novgorod, the second highest post in the church hierarchy.

As a member of the devout circle of young clergymen gathering around Alexis, Nikon had acquired a reputation as a reformer. These young clergymen, the Zealots of Piety, including Stefan Vonifatiev (the tsar's confessor), Ivan Neronov, and Simeon Avvakum, sought to revive the Orthodox church spiritually, to enliven dead forms of Orthodox observance, to deepen communication between the clergy and the laity, and to make more tangible the teachings of Christ. Seeking to maintain the national peculiarities of Russian Orthodoxy, these reformers rejected the arguments of Kievan scholars. Russian practice differed from the Greek, they claimed, because Moscow was the Third Rome, the last center of true Orthodox Christianity. Nikon preached this doctrine in Novgorod and became wholly committed to the need for a religious revival.

Recognizing that if reform were to be successful the church needed strong leadership, state support, and internal cohesion, Nikon sought to enhance its power and prestige. He persuaded Alexis to transfer to Moscow the relics of Metropolitan Philip, who had been murdered by order of Ivan IV. Philip was a symbol of the church's moral authority and a folk hero to the people. Nikon was

Nikon (1605–1681), Russian patriarch 1652–1666. State Historical
Museum, Moscow.

prepared to assert church authority, if need be,
even over the state. He imposed rigid ecclesiastical
discipline in the Novgorod region as a pattern for
the entire church.

Nikon's autocratic methods in Novgorod and
his close relationship with Greek prelates worried
his friends among the Zealots of Piety. Nikon was
also urging reform in order to make Russian practices conform to Greek ones. His new views may
have stemmed from ambition and from the desire
to win support from influential Greek prelates.
Alexis, still enchanted by Nikon, ignored the
protests of the Zealots and offered Nikon the
patriarchal throne.

Aware of opposition to his candidacy and of
clerical antagonism toward him, Nikon demurred

until a public demonstration of support was engineered on his behalf. Before agreeing to become patriarch, he insisted upon a free hand to organize and administer the church. He observed:

> Now if you promise to keep the evangelical dogmas, and to observe the canons of the holy apostles and of the holy fathers, and the laws of the pious emperors and tsars; if you allow me to organize the Church, then I shall no longer refuse the supreme archbishopric according to your wish.[1]

He was demanding the total subservience of the tsar and the entire population to his will. Nikon's intention was to make Russian church practices conform with Greek ones. "I am Russian and the son of a Russian," he declared, "but my faith and convictions are Greek."

To implement such a controversial and potentially disruptive reform program required the authority of the earlier diarchy of Mikhail Romanov and Filaret. Alexis, inexperienced and spiritually dependent, granted Nikon many of the powers that Filaret had exercised. Immediately Nikon asserted church independence from secular control and ignored legal provisions of the *Ulozhenie* of 1649 that limited the church's economic and juridical powers. He increased the land holdings of the patriarchate, which had unlimited power over 120,000 peasant households. At first Alexis did not challenge Nikon's inroads on secular power.

Nikon threw himself eagerly into church reform. He ordered changes in the service books and in the spelling of certain key words, ordered that the sign of the cross be made with three fingers instead of two, and instituted other minor changes not involving basic questions of dogma. According to a leading historian of the church Schism, Nikon instituted in Russia "the Greek ambos (pulpit), the Greek episcopal cross, Greek capes and cowls, and Greek plainchant melodies. He welcomed Greek painters and goldsmiths; he began to build monasteries on the Greek model; he had Greek friends whose advice he heeded." The national Russian church was being re-Byzantinized. As the Third Rome bowed to the fallen Second Rome (Constantinople), Nikon's actions were bitterly criticized by defenders of the national Russian religious tradition. His former friend Ivan Neronov admonished him:

> You approve foreigners' laws and accept their doctrines, and yet it was you who used to tell us constantly that the Greeks and Little Russians had lost their faith and their strength and that their ways were evil. Now they are for you saints and masters of religion.[2]

Opposition developed among the clergy and the faithful, who considered Nikon's actions arbitrary and needless.

Challenges to his spiritual authority as patriarch caused Nikon, during Alexis's absence on campaign, to assert strong claims to secular power in order to force through his reforms. Initially supporting Nikon on church reform, Alexis grew apprehensive about his arrogance and appropriation of secular powers. As the patriarch sought omnipotence in both the religious and secular spheres, he threatened the integrity of the secular state. In July 1658 Tsar Alexis, finally asserting his traditional autocratic powers, informed Nikon that the diarchy had ended. This action of Alexis shattered Nikon's ambition to lift the church above the state. Believing that he could negotiate from a position of power, Nikon left Moscow and renounced the patriarchal title, hoping, like Ivan IV, to be invited back on his own terms. Alexis, however, now more independent, refused to request his return. Nikon then claimed that he had not resigned but had merely ceased to be patriarch "in Moscow." From self-imposed exile he asserted openly that ecclesiastical authority was superior to secular authority. For eight years this conflict remained unresolved because Alexis took no action.

---

[1] Quoted in W. K. Medlin, *Moscow and East Rome* (Geneva, Switz., 1952), p. 169.

[2] Quoted in P. N. Miliukov, *Ocherki po istorii russkoi kultury* (Paris, 1931), vol. 2, pt. 1, p. 45.

Nikon's reforms were enforced against growing opposition centering on the Zealots of Piety, Avvakum, and his friends. The Old Ritualists or Old Believers, as they were called, argued that if Moscow were the Third Rome, reform was unnecessary. The Second Rome had fallen into heresy by adhering to the Florentine Union, and its religious inheritance had passed to Moscow. Why, Avvakum asked, should Russian practices conform with those of a church that had rejected pure Orthodoxy? If reforms were necessary, then the Muscovite church had fallen into error and was no longer the true center of Orthodoxy. Because there could be no Fourth Rome, the end of the world must be near and salvation was no longer possible. Acceptance or rejection of the reforms became literally a matter of life and death.

A church council convened in 1666 with Alexis's blessing ended the impasse. Nikon was formally deprived of his title, demoted to simple monk, and banished to a remote northern monastery. The struggle between church and state was settled in favor of the state. The council rejected Nikon's extreme claims of church superiority and endorsed the traditional Byzantine formula of the symphony of church and state. Subsequently the church would fall increasingly under state control.

The Council of 1666, while rejecting Nikon's political claims, accepted and endorsed his reforms, making failure to conform a civil and ecclesiastical offense. This formalized the church Schism because many Russians rejected the reforms, minor as they may appear, and clung tenaciously to the old ways. Few upper-class Russians became Old Believers; the Schism drew its chief support from the peasantry, parish priests (themselves of lower-class origin), and some merchants. Thus the Schism acquired a distinctive social quality. To defend themselves and their principles, Old Believers resorted to flight, passive resistance, and sometimes self-immolation.

The Old Believers remained a disruptive element, often refusing to pay taxes or serve in the army. Continuing to struggle against foreign influences, they came to believe that the sovereign,

Wooden church in the Suzdal principality.

particularly Peter the Great, was Antichrist. Meanwhile the official church fell more and more under state control. The result was a breakdown of the Byzantine cultural tradition as the conservative, inner-directed Muscovite ideology succumbed to external influences. To become a modern European nation, Russia first had to be released from the rigid Byzantine cultural tradition. The greatest legacy of the Schism was to open the way for Peter I's successful program of Westernization and modernization (see Chapter 15).

Because of the Schism and the accompanying bitter sectarian controversy, the Russian church, as James Billington points out, lost its spiritual vitality and moral authority. The Byzantine tradition could not withstand the pressures of rapid social, cultural, and political change. The task of creating a new, more modern, and viable secular culture, begun before Peter, fell to the state. Peter's program of sustained modernization would have been inconceivable without prior weakening of the Byzantine heritage.

Soviet historians explained the Schism mainly by citing the sharpening social contradictions of the 17th century and by emphasizing the rigid social structure and the extension of state power into most aspects of Russian life under provisions of the Law Code of 1649. They concluded that lower-class elements used the issue of church reform to express discontent with an oppressive Muscovite bureaucratic system. The issues of church reform and formalization of serfdom undoubtedly became blurred for many who saw their spiritual and personal freedoms circumscribed by arbitrary government action. The Old Believers, refusing to integrate themselves into the new secularized state, would remain a disruptive dissident group.

The Development of Serfdom

For all classes, particularly the lower classes, life was becoming more difficult and restricted. Service gentry, peasants, and townsmen all found their obligations to the state carefully elaborated in the Law Code of 1649. This code confirmed the completion of the long process of the enserfment of the peasantry. Hardly any other institution of prerevolutionary Russia has been studied as thoroughly and has elicited as much controversy as serfdom. Just how did this institution arise? What made it necessary?

Historians disagree on precisely how serfdom was imposed on the Russian peasantry and especially on the government's role in this enserfment. In the 18th century such historians as V. N. Tatishchev argued that government, by a series of decrees, gradually enserfed the rural population. Other historians argued that the state's role was minor and that serfdom was produced by environmental factors such as long-term residency and the rapid growth of peasant indebtedness. Until recently Soviet historians contended that the Russian peasant had been a serf from the start of the Kievan era.

We have seen that during Kievan times a certain group of peasants, the *zakupy,* had their rights limited, but only temporarily (see Chapter 4). The *zakupy* cannot be considered serfs in the technical sense. Gradually, however, the peasantry's social and economic status deteriorated and the basically free institutions of Kiev yielded to social and economic restrictions. In Kievan times peasants lived in free communes, cooperatively working land owned by the commune. In the Mongol era these communes had to pay tribute, which was collected by the Rus princes acting as the khan's agents. Responsibility for tax collection gave local princes certain administrative and judicial powers over the communes. As a centralized state formed under Moscow, the prince of Moscow made large land grants to noblemen and church officials in return for their support of centralization. More and more land formerly owned by free peasant communes passed into the hands of private individuals or church institutions, thus transforming peasants from free owners of land into renters. These communes had to pay taxes to the prince of Moscow and rent to the landlord, usually a nobleman.

Peasant obligations to landlords consisted of cash payments or payments in kind (*obrok*), labor service (*barshchina*), or a combination of both. Despite the growing weight of these obligations, the individual peasant was free to move about as he wished, not being bound to the land, to the person of the landlord, or even to the peasantry as a class. The individual peasant could leave the countryside altogether and take up residence in town. This very freedom of movement, however, began to work against the long-term interests of the peasant class. Princes and landlords were dependent on peasant labor, which produced much of the revenue vital to upper-class political power and economic well-being. Informal prince-landlord agreements prevented peasants from being lured from one estate to another by more favorable terms.

By about 1500 it was clear that informal agreements were inadequate to curb peasant mobility and compensate for insufficient labor. Ivan III's *Sudebnik* (law code) of 1497 reduced the freedom

Armed Russian peasants, 17th century.

of peasant movement to a brief period each year (the two weeks around St. George's Day, November 26), a major step toward serfdom. The peasant who chose to leave then had to fulfill all of his legal obligations to the landlord and pay a sizable exit fee. Furthermore, dues and services demanded from peasants increased significantly during the 16th century. Peasant indebtedness rose sharply until it became virtually impossible for peasants to leave their landowners, even in the allowable period around St. George's Day.

Another factor detrimental to the peasant was the rapid growth of *pomestie* land tenure in the late 15th and 16th centuries. As the Muscovite state expanded, so too did the need for administrators and army officers. Unable to pay these servitors, the government rewarded them with temporary grants of land (*pomestie*) to be held and exploited during the term of service. Such grants were valuable only if there were peasants available to work the land. The service gentry, whose economic well-being and state service depended on success-

ful management of their estates, clamored for rigid restrictions on peasant mobility. Despite growing economic burdens and legal restrictions, peasants could still be transferred to the estates of wealthy magnates by "exportation" (*vyvoz*), which deprived the service gentry of labor power on their lands. Many peasants also escaped by flight, and many fled during the economic and political chaos of Ivan IV's reign.

Massive peasant flight and "exportation" threatened the entire *pomestie* system and the army. Ivan IV had to restrict further the peasants' right of departure by tying them permanently to the land. In 1570 Ivan began experimenting with a plan to prevent peasant movement. Peasants in designated regions of Novgorod were prohibited from moving for any reason during 1570. A decade later the concept of the "prohibited year" was applied on a national scale, and almost every year thereafter was "prohibited." Occasionally a "free year" would be decreed, but not after 1602. Many town dwellers were also affected by the "prohibited years," which effectively tied them to their communities without the right of movement. Though certain refinements were required, peasants had virtually lost the right to move and serfdom was a fact. Initially, the law decreed a five-year recovery period for a fugitive peasant; he could be tracked down and forcibly returned to the estate within five years of his flight. Later the recovery period was extended to 10, then 15 years, and finally it was abolished altogether, making a fugitive peasant subject to forcible return at any time.

The *Ulozhenie* of 1649 confirmed and codified these measures. All peasants' names were to be included in government registers, which legally attached peasants to the estate where they resided when the registers were compiled. To be sure, the peasant serf was not a slave, and slavery continued to coexist with serfdom. The landowner's power over the peasant's person increased, however, until the distinction between slave and serf virtually disappeared. The serf had no legal means to protect himself against arbitrary actions by his master; his only recourse was flight or violence. The serf owner could make a field serf into a domestic or household serf; eventually the serf could be sold without land, families were separated, and serfs were subjected to corporal punishment and physical abuse.

Thus a large portion of the Russian population was finally enserfed. Peasants made up about 90 percent of the total population, and a majority were directly affected by the *Ulozhenie*'s provisions. Serfdom was imposed from above by government decree to answer the needs of the state and the service class, which constituted the backbone of the Muscovite army, the government's chief support in times of crisis.

Enserfment of the peasantry and growing restrictions on other classes contributed to great social turmoil in 17th-century Muscovy. Around mid-century occurred a series of scattered urban revolts. In 1648 in Moscow the populace rose against the onerous salt tax and rule by unpopular, tyrannical favorites of the tsar. An angry mob besieged Tsar Alexis in the Kremlin until he dismissed his chief favorite, B. I. Morozov, and

Stepan (Stenka) Razin, Cossack leader.

yielded two others to popular vengeance. Subsequent revolts in Pskov and Novgorod expressed similar lower-class grievances against local boyars and Muscovite tyranny. After the government debased the coinage by substituting copper for silver (1656), numerous disorders broke out in 1662, especially in Moscow. The Muscovite autocracy repressed all of these lower-class movements ruthlessly.

The culmination of this general mood of discontent was a massive insurrection in the Don and Volga regions between 1667 and 1671. Like the earlier Bolotnikov rising (see Chapter 12), this was a movement of the turbulent frontier—the "Wild Field"—against the center. It was led by a Don Cossack of outstanding military ability, Stepan (Stenka) Razin. Razin, who came from an established Cossack family near Cherkassk, had served the Cossack host loyally in diplomacy and war before becoming a leader of the downtrodden. The historian N. I. Kostomarov noted that Razin was a man of "enormous will and impulsive activity, . . . now stern and gloomy, now working himself into a fury, now given up to drunken carousing, now ready to suffer any hardship with superhuman endurance."[3]

The upheaval began, as had Bolotnikov's, in frontier urban settlements (*posady*) crowded with drifters, thieves, and laborers, impoverished and resentful of government impositions. Escaped peasants who had taken up residence in Don Cossack settlements resisted Moscow's efforts to recover them for their gentry masters. Initially, Razin's army, destroying local government forces, sought booty along the Volga River and the shores of the Caspian Sea. After seizing Astrakhan in 1669, Razin appealed to the poor to join him in a war against the rich, the boyars, and officialdom to achieve freedom for the common man. As he advanced up the Volga, thousands of peasants flocked to his banners and numerous manor houses were burned. Finally, Razin's motley forces were defeated at Simbirsk by government troops, and he was turned over to the authorities by Cossack elders. He was tortured horribly, quartered, and his body was thrown to the dogs. Again the Muscovite regime wiped out popular revolt brutally, but the indomitable Razin remained a legend, a Robin Hood, to the oppressed lower classes of Russia.

The reign of Tsar Alexis witnessed the rejection of Muscovy's old religious ideology, the Byzantine tradition, and the imposition on society of a straitjacket by the state. These were crucial prerequisites for the full-scale program of modernization and secularization of Peter the Great. The existence of serfdom meant, however, that modernization of the state would create a psychological schism between the upper classes and the mass of the people. Under the impact of Westernization a great cultural cleavage would open up in Russian society that would make understanding and communication between educated society and the masses well-nigh impossible until the latter 19th century. This was the legacy of the momentous social, cultural, and religious developments of the 17th century.

---

[3] Cited in P. Avrich, *Russian Rebels, 1600–1800* (New York, 1972), p. 69.

Suggested Additional Reading

BOOKS

ANDREYEV, N. *Studies in Muscovy* (London, 1970).

AVVAKUM, S. *The Life of the Archpriest Avvakum by Himself* (London, 1924, 1968).

BIRNBAUM, H., and M. S. FLER, eds. *Medieval Russian Culture* (Berkeley, 1984).

BLANE, A., ed. *The Religious World of Russian Culture* (The Hague, 1975).

BLUM, J. *Lord and Peasant in Russia from the 9th to the 19th Century* (Princeton, 1961).

BOLSHAKOFF, S. *Russian Nonconformity . . .* (Philadelphia, 1950).

BUSHKOVITCH, P. *The Merchants of Moscow, 1580–1650* (Cambridge, 1980).

CONYBEARE, F. *Russian Dissenters* (Cambridge, MA, 1921).

CRUMMEY, R. O. *The Old Believers and the World of AntiChrist* (Madison, WI, 1970).

HELLIE, R. *Enserfment and Military Change in Muscovy* (Chicago, 1971).

———, ed. *Readings for Introduction to Russian Civilization: Muscovite Society* (Chicago, 1967).

———, ed. and trans. *The Muscovite Law Code (Ulozhenie) of 1649* (Irvine, CA, 1988).

HUGHES, L. A. J. *Russia and the West: The Life of a Seventeenth Century Westerner, Prince V. V. Golitsyn (1643–1714)* (Newtonville, MA, 1984).

LUPININ, N. B. *Religious Revolt in the Seventeenth Century: The Schism of the Russian Church* (Princeton, 1985).

MEDLIN, W. K. *Moscow and East Rome . . .* (Geneva, 1952).

———. *Renaissance Influences and Religious Reforms in Russia* (Geneva, 1971).

MILIUKOV, P. N. *Outlines of Russian Culture, Vol. 3: Religion and the Church* (New York, 1960).

PALMER, W. *The Patriarch and the Tsar*, 6 vols. (London, 1871–1876).

SZEFTEL, M. *Russian Institutions and Culture up to Peter the Great* (London, 1975). (Reprint.)

WOODCOCK, G., and I. AVAKUMOVIC. *The Doukhobors* (New York, 1968).

ARTICLES

BARON, S. "The Muscovy Company . . . in Russian Foreign Trade." *FOG* 27 (1980): 133–55.

———. "Towns, Trade, and Artisans in Seventeenth Century Russia . . ." *FOG* 27 (1980): 215–32.

CHERNIAVSKY, M. "The Old Believers and the New Religion." *SR* 25 (1966): 1–39.

———. "The Origins of the Noble Official . . . ," in *Russian Officialdom,* ed. W. Pintner (Chapel Hill, NC, 1980), pp. 46–75.

HELLIE, R. "The Church and the Law in Late Muscovy: Chapters 12 and 13 of *Ulozhenie* of 1649." *CanAmSlSt* 25, no. 1–4 (1991): 179–99.

KEEP, J. H. "The Regime of Filaret (1619–1633)." *SEER* 38 (1960): 334–60.

KLEIMOLA, A. "Up Through Servitude: The Changing Condition of the Muscovite Elite in the Sixteenth and Seventeenth Centuries." *Rus. Hist.* 6, no. 2 (1979): 230–42.

LOEWENSON, L. "The Moscow Rising of 1648." *SEER* 27 (1948): 146–56.

MILLER, D. B. "The Viskovaty Affair of 1553–54: Official Art . . . and the Disintegration of Medieval Russian Culture." *Rus. Hist.* 8, no. 3 (1981): 293–332. (With ten illustrations.)

O'BRIEN, C. B. "Agriculture in Russian War Economy in the Later Seventeenth Century." *ASEER* 8 (1949): 167–74.

PELENSKI, J. "State and Society in Muscovite Russia . . ." *FOG* 27 (1980): 156–67.

SPINKA, M. "Nikon and the Subjugation of the Russian Church to the State." *CH* 10 (1941): 347–66.

ZENKOVSKY, S. "The Old Believer Avvakum . . ." *IndSS* 1 (1956): 1–51.

———. "The Russian Church Schism . . ." *Rus. Rev.* 16 (1957): 37–58.

Part Two

Early
Imperial Russia,
1689–1855

THE HISTORY OF IMPERIAL RUSSIA begins with expansion westward and the shift of the capital to St. Petersburg near the Baltic Sea. Peter the Great, a dynamic iconoclast, speeds the Westernization of Russia begun hesitantly by his early Romanov predecessors. The Russian Empire is forged in wars that impose a staggering burden on the impoverished, dependent peasantry. A Westernized elite in Europe-oriented St. Petersburg is set apart increasingly by dress, language, and wealth from the illiterate, impoverished peasant masses. In the late 18th century Catherine II, coming to Russia from a small German state, rules Russia through a privileged nobility and continues Westernization. Catherine's victorious armies partition Poland and wrest the Black Sea's northern shore from the Ottoman Empire. A small noble intelligentsia emerges to question autocracy and serfdom.

Under Alexander I Russia withstands Napoleon's great invasion of 1812, then plays a decisive role in defeating the French emperor. In 1815 imperial Russia reaches its peak of power, prestige, and expansion into Europe. Grievous social problems and economic backwardness are concealed behind an impressive facade of military strength. Only 10 years later the Decembrists begin the organized revolutionary movement; their failure brings to power Nicholas I, whose regime epitomizes fully developed autocracy and police power. Russia's defeat in the Crimean War (1853–1856) reveals its economic underdevelopment, dooms serfdom, and triggers important domestic reforms.

15

Peter the Great: Politics, War, and Diplomacy

The era of Peter the Great (1689–1725) capped a century of increasing autocracy, deepening serfdom, and secularization of Russian life. Centralization, war, and relations with Europe were focal points of Russian domestic and foreign policies, whose basic guidelines had been set in the 17th century. But Peter I's education, interests, and approaches differed radically from those of his predecessors. Unlike them, he exercised fully the absolute powers that they had only begun to build. Under his dynamic leadership, whose significance historians dispute (see Problem 4 at the end of this chapter), Russia acquired a well-organized and powerful army and navy, which enabled it to become a great European power, and developed a more cohesive administration and diplomatic corps. The total subordination of the official church to the state eliminated the last restriction on the ruler's authority. Shifting the capital westward to St. Petersburg symbolized the great changes overtaking Russia under Peter. To support the lengthy war against Sweden, the entire financial and political structure had to be overhauled, not according to a blueprint but by trial and error. The Petrine

reforms combined a lengthy historical development with the dedicated efforts of a uniquely talented and energetic ruler. War requirements triggered many but not all of the changes and often determined their form. Were the reforms so drastic as to make this a revolutionary era? Were they derived from Russian needs or mainly borrowed from more advanced western Europe? Did the Petrine reforms set Russia on a path of greatness and material progress, or did they bring suffering and economic ruin to the Russian people?

Peter's Youth and His Trip to the West

Peter I grew up in a confused, transitional epoch of violence and intrigue resembling in some ways the minority of Ivan IV. Innovative Western ideas and institutions clashed with traditional Muscovite ones. Court factions centering on the two wives of Tsar Alexis contended in the Kremlin's myriad apartments. The first wife was Maria Miloslavskaia, whose children included Fedor, the weakwitted Ivan, and six daughters, of whom Sofia was the eldest (see Figure 15.1). After Maria's death

171

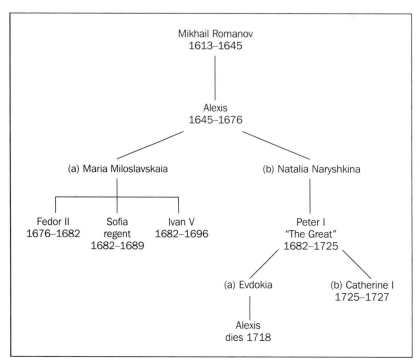

Figure 15.1
The reigns of the early Romanovs

Alexis married Natalia Naryshkina, from an obscure country family, and in 1672 she gave birth to Peter. The Naryshkins displaced the Miloslavskiis temporarily, but for two decades these royal clans waged a bitter struggle for power that made court life turbulent and bloody. Tsar Alexis died when Peter was only four, and Maria Miloslavskaia's weak, ineffective eldest son became tsar as Fedor II (1676–1682). Until he was 10, Peter was brought up in a traditional way in the Kremlin, tutored by Nikita Zotov, a gentle clerk who loved vodka, instructed him none too well in reading and writing, and introduced him to Russian history.

Tsar Fedor's death in April 1682 caused a succession crisis that was complicated by the Naryshkin-Miloslavskii feud. An improvised *zemskii sobor* (assembly) dominated by the patriarch and the Naryshkins proclaimed Peter tsar and his mother regent. Conservative *streltsy* (musketeers)

loyal to the Miloslavskiis reacted with fury. There was no regular law of succession, but according to Muscovite tradition, Ivan, a Miloslavskii, as the elder brother, should have been named tsar. In May, amid rumors that Ivan had been murdered, angry *streltsy,* numbering more than 20,000 in Moscow, revolted; some burst into the Kremlin and in Peter's presence murdered some Naryshkin adherents. After three days of rioting and bloodshed they departed, leaving the Miloslavskii faction in power. Ivan V and Peter I were proclaimed co-tsars, with their elder sister Sofia as regent. Henceforth Peter loathed the Kremlin for its intrigue, court factionalism, and traditionalism.

Between 1682 and 1689 Sofia acted as Russia's first female sovereign in the imperial period. A bulky, unattractive, sensual woman, Sofia was also intelligent, well-educated (most unusual in those times), strong-willed, and insatiably ambitious. Gaining control of the unruly *streltsy,* she had their principal commander, Prince Ivan Khovanskii, apprehended and executed. She ruled with her cultivated, pro-Western, but indecisive lover, Prince V. V. Golitsyn. Their regime announced ambitious plans of reform but soon turned conservative.

After the coup of May 1682, 10-year-old Peter divided his time between the court and living with his mother at nearby Preobrazhenskoe. On ceremonial occasions he and his half-brother Ivan sat together on a dual throne of ivory. Foreign observers remarked that Peter was energetic, strong, and alert; Ivan was apathetic and dull-witted. Peter's formal education was neglected, and while his brothers and sisters learned Latin, Polish, and poetry, he was left largely to his own devices away from court influences. At first he played with toy soldiers; then he began to recruit and drill live ones. Peter filled his play regiments with hundreds of unemployed courtiers and commoners, equipping them from the Kremlin arsenal. Soon he had formed two well-trained battalions of about 300 men each, named Preobrazhenskii and Semenovskii after nearby villages, the nucleus of his subsequent imperial guards. Dressed in full uniform, he would bombard his fake fortress of Pressburg. Some who joined his forces, such as Alexander Menshikov, son of a court equerry, and Prince Mikhail Golitsyn, the future field marshal, became intimate and trusted colleagues. Seeking knowledge of technical and military matters, Peter frequented the German Settlement near Preobrazhenskoe, a separate European town of diplomats, merchants, officers, and artisans, and joined readily in its gay and bawdy life. A Dutchman, Franz Timmermann, taught him rudimentary geometry, the art of fortification, geography, and cabinetmaking. From Brandt, another Dutchman, Peter learned the essentials of ship design and construction. After discovering an abandoned English sailboat, he developed a passion for seafaring. Visits to the White Sea in 1693 and 1694 deepened this interest, and he returned to Moscow determined to create a Russian navy. At the age of 16 Peter was absorbed in three lifelong concerns: soldiers, ships, and European technology. His mother, worried by his unrestrained life at the German Settlement, married him off to Evdokia Lopukhina, a daughter of a conservative nobleman. Soon bored with his dull, conservative spouse, Peter escaped to the German Settlement to drink and carouse.

Princess Sofia sought to achieve full power and remove the growing threat of young Peter. Hoping that victory over the Crimean Tatars would bring glory to her regime, she authorized campaigns under V. V. Golitsyn in 1687 and 1689, but his timidity and poor generalship as well as problems of supply led to failure. In August 1689, aided by a new lover, Fedor Shaklovity, she organized a new *streltsy* conspiracy against the Naryshkins. Warned of the plot, Peter fled to nearby Trinity Monastery, where, joined by his family and personal troops, he appealed to loyal Muscovites and foreign officers to rally to the rightful tsar. Sofia's support crumbled; she was confined in a convent, and Peter's mother ruled as regent until her death in 1694. Most influential at court became Patrick Gordon, a Scottish mercenary and Peter's chief military adviser, and François Lefort, soldier of fortune and boon companion. Lefort introduced Peter to Anna Mons, daughter of a Westphalian merchant, who became his mistress for 10 years.

Peter was a most unconventional man and ruler. Six feet seven inches tall and weighing 240 pounds, he nonetheless retained qualities of a small boy, reveling in noise, buffoonery, and horseplay and combining tenderness and devotion with vicious cruelty. He was curious and a keen observer, and he possessed an excellent memory; obstacles and reverses left him undiscouraged. Like his contemporary Frederick William I of Prussia, he embodied the concept of the ruler as first servant of the state. In every sphere he insisted on "going through the ranks" and doing things himself. He learned many manual skills and a dozen trades, setting an example for the gentry of first-hand knowledge and hard work. Peter hated ceremony, luxury, and artificiality; he disliked subterfuge and expected honesty from his subordinates. Although sincerely religious, he scorned

Library of Congress

Emperor Peter I, 1672–1725.

and even made fun of the hidebound Orthodox clergy. Unlike his predecessors, who generally had remained ensconced in the Kremlin, he wandered restlessly around Russia, open to new ideas and ready to experiment. These qualities helped determine his iconoclastic, innovative policies as tsar.

The Azov campaigns matured Peter as man and ruler. Azov, a Turkish fortress dominating the Sea of Azov, blocked Russian access to the southern seas. The initial campaign of 1695 failed for want of a fleet, able commanders, and skilled engineers. Undismayed, Peter had a fleet built at Voronezh on the Don, severed Turkish communications, and in July 1696 forced Azov to surrender. Entering Moscow to frenzied cheers, Peter became sole tsar and autocrat. The capture of Azov began the struggle with the Turks over the Black Sea, but Peter realized that to win it he required allies.

In 1697 Peter decided to visit western Europe in order to forge an anti-Turkish alliance, study ship construction and European technology, and recruit foreign specialists for Russian service. His experience at the German Settlement had convinced him that Russians must study European techniques, and he had already sent some Russian youths abroad to do so. Hoping that traveling incognito would provide him freedom of movement, he joined the Grand Embassy as simple Peter Mikhailov with about 150 other people. His 14-month journey, unprecedented for a Russian ruler, marked a turning point in his career. In Holland he worked as a laborer in a Zaandam shipyard and spent four weeks in Amsterdam. In England he learned much at the Deptford shipyards and Woolwich arsenal, but he had no use for debates in Parliament or Western constitutional theories. European contemporaries marveled at Peter's outlandish behavior and table manners— he would seize and devour an entire roast!—but they were impressed by his frankness, intelligence, and hunger to learn. Wrote Sophie, electress of Brandenburg: "He is a ruler both very good and very evil at the same time. His character is exactly the character of his country." Wholly convinced now of Europe's technological and economic superiority, Peter recruited more than 750 specialists, mostly Dutch, for Russian service so that they could instruct his countrymen. During his reign Russians streamed westward to study, but Europe's preoccupation with the Spanish succession doomed Peter's hopes for an anti-Turkish coalition.

Learning in Vienna of a new *streltsy* revolt, Peter immediately left for home. The *streltsy*, aiming to restore Sofia, exterminate the boyars, and protect Old Believers, had moved on Moscow, but General Gordon had repelled their uncoordinated attacks. Peter promptly disbanded the disorderly *streltsy* regiments in Moscow, forced Sofia to become a nun, and had several *streltsy* hanged outside her window. He also implicated his wife, Evdokia, divorced her, and forced her to take the veil. Some 800 *streltsy* were executed in Moscow alone, and their corpses left hanging for months. Apparently Peter tortured some of the victims himself, and the numerous executions, revealing his implacable will, convinced Europeans that he was an Oriental despot and Muscovy a backward and barbarous land.

In an effort to Westernize the Russian upper classes, Peter forcibly altered their appearance. Upon his return he shaved off the beards of some of his courtiers. Shaving had been introduced gradually at court, but traditionalists believed that beards symbolized Orthodoxy and were essential for salvation. Patriarch Adrian thundered: "God did not create men beardless, only cats and dogs. . . . The shaving of beards is not only foolishness and a dishonor, it is a mortal sin." Nevertheless, except for clergy and peasants, Russians either had to shave or pay a beard tax (this helped the treasury, since many wealthy Muscovites chose to pay). Peter also disliked the loose-fitting Russian national clothing, with broad sleeves and long coats that hindered movement. For the court and officialdom he prescribed German or Hungarian dress so that Muscovites would not be considered barbarous. This sumptuary rule, however, affected only a tiny minority at court and in towns and marked off the upper class from the peasantry; in their villages peasants still wore beards and national dress. Peter's decrees on Western dress and shaving, while representing a symbolic breach with old Muscovy, aimed also to create new citizens in his own image: energetic, dynamic, and ready to serve him and his new Russia. Conservatives, associating Peter with the "godless" West, strongly opposed these and other reforms.

The opposition gathered around Peter's eldest son, Alexis, and his mother, Evdokia. In childhood Alexis, who rarely saw his father, had learned Latin, French, and German, but he remained passive and pleasure-loving. Evading tasks assigned by his father, he drank heavily. In 1715 his German-born wife, Charlotte, bore a son, Peter, then died. Only weeks later Catherine, Peter I's second wife, also had a son named Peter. As the succession issue further alienated father and son, Alexis renounced his and his son's rights to the throne and fled to Austria. Peter demanded his extradition but promised forgiveness if he returned home promptly. Alexis consented and recognized Peter Petrovich, his father's infant son, as heir. But Alexis, with strong conservative backing, represented an intolerable political threat, and in 1718

Peter accused him of conspiring to destroy St. Petersburg and the fleet and to restore traditional ways. Alexis was interrogated, imprisoned, and apparently murdered in Peter and Paul Fortress, not for overt opposition but as a symbol of resistance to Peter's reforms and tyranny. His death failed to settle the succession: Peter Petrovich soon died, leaving Peter's daughters, Anna and Elizabeth, and Alexis's son, Peter, as possible heirs. In 1722 Peter the Great decreed that he would designate his heir personally. His wife, Catherine, was crowned empress in 1724 but was not designated heir to the throne, and Peter died the next year without naming a successor.

War and Diplomacy

In the almost continuous wars of Peter's reign Muscovite institutions were tested severely, and many were found wanting and discarded. During the grueling conflict with Sweden known as the Great Northern War, Russia became a fully autocratic, military monarchy in which every social group was harnessed into onerous, lifelong state service. Severe early defeats in that war dispersed and discredited traditional military forces and compelled the state to organize a new regular army of conscripts.

Wars were fought to break the bonds of isolation imposed on Russia by geography and hostile neighbors—to acquire seaports and direct commercial and cultural contacts with western Europe. For Peter, as for his great contemporary Louis XIV, war and expansion became the chief aims. Winning access to the seas, however, was a longstanding Muscovite objective. For a century Sweden had dominated the eastern Baltic, periodically blockading Russia, and Gustavus Adolphus had boasted: "Now this enemy [Russia] without our permission cannot sail a single ship into the Baltic Sea."[1] After his western trip Peter concluded that

---

[1] M. A. Alpatov, *Russkaia istoricheskaia mysl i zapadnaia Evropa XII–XVII vv* (Moscow, 1973), p. 314.

with European allies and technology Russia could and must break through to that sea.

During the Grand Embassy he had sounded out leaders of Saxony and Brandenburg who also wished to destroy Sweden's Baltic hegemony. The time seemed ripe because Charles XII, only 16 and reputedly weak and foolish, had just mounted the Swedish throne; his bloated kingdom invited partition. Johan Patkul, a Livonian nobleman whom the Swedes had sentenced to death, organized an anti-Swedish coalition, winning over Denmark and Augustus II of Saxony, who became king of Poland, to his scheme. At Rawa, Peter and Augustus decided to attack Sweden and to allow Russia to regain Ingria and Karelia. Peter pledged to fight after making peace with Turkey, meanwhile assuring the Swedes that Russia desired peace.

Protracted Russian negotiations with the Turks endangered Peter's northern plans. His envoy sought title to the lower Dnieper forts and the Azov region, which Russia had conquered. Peter also demanded regular diplomatic and commercial relations with Turkey, free navigation of the Black Sea, and guarantees to protect Orthodox Christians in the Ottoman Empire. The Turks, however, refused to yield the forts or allow Russian ships in the Black Sea, and Russia had to renounce these claims in order to secure representation in Constantinople. In August 1700 peace was concluded, and the day after the news reached Moscow, Russia declared war on Sweden.

Plunging into a major war before building an effective army, Peter admitted later, was a serious blunder. The motley Russian militia had been recruited hastily and was mostly under foreign officers. The very day Russia entered the war, Denmark made a separate peace with Sweden. Almost 40,000 poorly armed Russians besieged the Baltic port of Narva (see Map 15.1), and Charles XII with 8,000 Swedes rushed to its relief. As a pitched battle loomed between the Swedish professionals and Peter's raw levies, Peter prudently (some say in fright) departed for Moscow. On November 30, 1700, Charles attacked in a blinding snowstorm. Except for the guards regi-

ments, which fought bravely, the Russians fled in panic, abandoning their artillery. The army was shattered and Russia exposed to invasion, but severe weather and illness among his troops dissuaded Charles from a move on Moscow. To Peter's profound relief, he turned westward into Poland to pursue Augustus II, giving Russia a much-needed respite.

In the aftermath of Narva Peter revealed his greatness. The prestige won at Azov was lost, but Peter by incredible efforts raised, trained, and equipped a new and better army. Recruitment and training were regularized, and over the next decade about 200,000 men, mostly peasants and townsmen, were conscripted. Soldiers usually served for life, receiving training at muster points and depots. Initially, peasant soldiers were freed from serfdom, but this policy was abandoned when noble protests grew too loud. Officers, mostly noblemen, likewise served for life. Inscribed in regiments at an early age, most received some education and served several years in the ranks, often in guards regiments, before receiving their commissions. Special schools prepared artillery and engineer cadres. Wartime need at times induced the government to promote able commoners to officer rank. The army's weapons, many produced in Russia, were improved until they equaled European ones. The bayonet was introduced, at first defensively, later in assaults, inaugurating a Russian tradition of cold steel. To replace lost artillery, many church bells in northern Russia were melted down. The new light and heavy artillery became renowned for its accuracy and effectiveness. Peter's tremendous energy, optimism, and organizing skill developed at huge cost a well-equipped, amply supplied standing army. Under pressure of war this regular force, which numbered some 200,000 men by 1725, took shape with strict regulations, based on European models, unified recruitment, and standard uniforms.

Augustus II was kept in the field with subsidies and auxiliary detachments while the Russians conducted a counteroffensive. With Charles tied down in Poland, Russian forces led by Peter him-

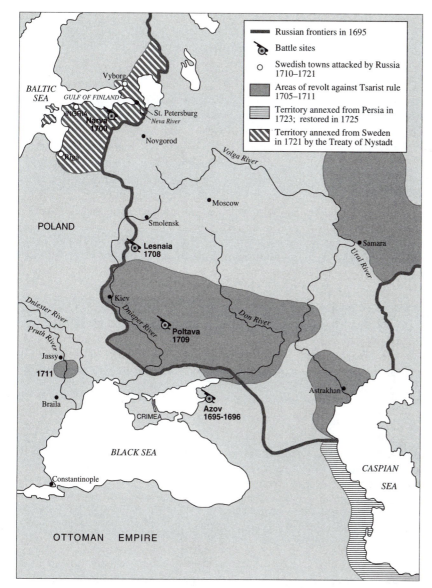

Map 15.1 Russian expansion under Peter the Great, 1695–1725

self or by Menshikov, his intimate friend, seized Ingria from relatively weak Swedish garrisons. In 1703 at the mouth of the Neva River near the Gulf of Finland, Peter founded the city of St. Petersburg. At great expense in lives and resources the future capital was laid out geometrically on swampy, barren land. The next year the capture of Narva

and Derpt climaxed the Ingrian campaign, secured Livonia, and eased direct contacts with the West.

Charles XII, after finally compelling Augustus to make peace, invaded Russia in July 1708 with a veteran army of 46,000 men. Counting on a popular Russian uprising and aid from Hetman Mazepa's dissident Ukrainian Cossacks, Charles planned to advance to Moscow and partition Russia, but finding scorched earth and an elusive, retreating foe, he turned southward into Ukraine to join Mazepa. General Lewenhaupt, with reinforcements and supplies, sought to join him, but Menshikov badly defeated Lewenhaupt at Lesnaia in September and captured his supplies. Peter exulted: "We have never had a similar victory over regular [Swedish] troops, and then with numbers inferior to those of the enemy." Menshikov crushed Mazepa, seized his artillery, and forced Ukraine to submit. Without needed supplies Charles's army suffered severely during the winter. The following spring, as Charles besieged Poltava in Ukraine, Peter's main army came to its relief. In June 1709 some 40,000 Russians fought a decisive battle with the depleted Swedish army of 22,000. The Swedes were dispirited, and Charles, previously wounded, had to be carried on a litter. Peter exhorted his men: "The hour has come in which the destinies of our country will be decided. It is of her that you must think, it is for her that you must fight, . . . and as for Peter, know that he does not cling to his own life provided Russia lives in her glory and prosperity."[2] The Swedish army was mostly destroyed and captured; only Charles, Mazepa, and a few followers escaped into Turkey. The great victory at Poltava ended the Swedish invasion, vindicated Peter's military reforms, and confirmed Russia's rise as a great European power.

The Great Northern War continued because Charles, backed by French diplomacy, persuaded the Turks to declare war on Russia in 1710. Peter overconfidently invaded the Balkans, calling on its Christians to rise against Turkish rule. Only tiny Montenegro responded, and its revolt failed to divert many Turkish troops. Advancing down the Pruth River, Peter's force was surrounded by a huge Turkish army. To save himself and St. Petersburg, Peter was prepared to yield his other northern conquests and even Novgorod and Pskov, but the Turks merely demanded the Azov region. For

two more years Russia faced possible Turkish invasion until Charles overplayed his hand and was expelled from Turkey.

In the north the war dragged on and on. A coalition of Brandenburg, Saxony, Denmark, and Poland gave Russia ineffective support while dynastic marriages involved the country deeply in German politics and roused suspicion among its princes. Anna, daughter of Peter's deceased half brother, married the duke of Courland and later became empress of Russia (see Chapter 17); her sister, Catherine, married the duke of Mecklenburg. Peter's support of German princelings complicated the conflict with Sweden. Russia's allies, he wrote, were "too many gods; what we want, they don't allow; what they advise, cannot be put into practice."[3] But Russian naval and land forces scored many victories. In 1713 all of southern Finland was conquered. A year later Peter's new Baltic fleet, built from scratch during the war, defeated the Swedish galleys at Hangö. Peter's navy, eventually boasting 48 ships of the line, many galleys, and 28,000 seamen, made Russia master of the eastern Baltic and contributed greatly to ultimate victory.[4] The Russians captured the last Swedish fortresses on the southern Baltic shores and raided the Swedish coast, but Charles refused to yield. Even his death in Norway in 1718 did little to hasten peace because British support kept the Swedes fighting.

Finally, in 1721, after a Russian landing near Stockholm, the Swedes yielded. By the Treaty of Nystadt, Russia—though evacuating Finland, paying an indemnity, and pledging not to interfere in Sweden's internal affairs—secured the provinces of Livonia, Estonia, and Ingria; part of Karelia, including Viborg; and Oesel and the Dagoe Islands, a far larger window on the West than Peter had envisioned. The new Baltic provinces were Western, Lutheran, and more

---

[2] Quoted in C. de Grunwald, *Peter the Great* (London, 1956), p. 215.

[3] Quoted in B. Sumner, *Peter the Great and the Emergence of Russia* (London, 1951), p. 85.

[4] A few years after Peter's death, however, only a handful of vessels remained seaworthy. His personal interest was indispensable to the navy.

advanced than Russia proper. They retained separate status and autonomy, and their German nobility continued to rule a Lettish and Estonian populace. Baltic German nobles, entering Russian military and civil service in large numbers, provided able and educated officials, which Russia needed badly.

At the urging of the Senate, which Peter instituted as the supreme organ of the state after abolishing the Boyar Duma in 1711, Peter now accepted the titles of Emperor and the Great. Russia's vast territory and diverse subjects entitled him to the former; his Baltic conquests led prominent contemporaries to accord him the latter. Prussia and Holland immediately recognized his imperial title; other countries followed after bargaining and delay. Russia's international status rose significantly after Poltava, and its voice was heard in all important affairs. "By our deeds in war we have emerged from darkness into the light of the world," noted Peter, "and those whom we did not know in the light now respect us."[5]

Russia showed sporadic interest in the Orient and Central Asia. Peter attempted with little success to increase trade with China. In the northern Pacific Russia annexed Kamchatka Peninsula and the Kurile Islands, and later Captain Vitus Bering, a Dane in Russian service, explored the waters separating Siberia from Alaska, which were named after him. Peter viewed Central Asia as the gateway to India and a potential source of gold. In 1700 he granted the request of the khan of Khiva, faced with rebellion and foreign foes, for Russian citizenship. Later he sought to build a Caspian fleet, and hearing that gold had been discovered along the Amu Darya River, Peter in 1717 sent Prince Bekovich-Cherkasskii with 3,500 men to Khiva. He defeated the Khivans, and then lulled by their peaceful assurances he divided his forces. The Khivans overwhelmed them and killed the Russians or sold them into slavery. A more successful expedition under Captain Bukholts moved up the Irtysh River and in 1716 established a fort

at Omsk, later the capital of western Siberia. Fortified posts at Semipalatinsk and Ust-Kamenogorsk (1718) became bases for subsequent Russian expansion into the Kazakh steppe.

Coveting Persia's Caspian shores, Peter in 1715 sent a cavalry officer, Artemi Volynskii, as envoy to the shah's court. Volynskii concluded a commercial treaty before being expelled. As governor of nearby Astrakhan, he urged Russia to seize Persia's silk provinces along the Caspian. To foster Persia's collapse, Russia aided native rebels. After Dagestani mountaineers nominally subject to the shah attacked some Russian merchants, Peter's army moved in to "restore order" and occupied the Caspian's western shores, including the key port of Baku, in 1722–1723. In Transcaucasia Georgian and Armenian Christians appealed for aid against the Turks, but remembering the Pruth, Peter wisely avoided offending the sultan.

After Poltava Russia played a major diplomatic role in Europe. Insisting on making foreign policy himself, Peter carefully supervised its formulation and engaged periodically in frank personal diplomacy. During a state visit to France in 1717 he proposed an alliance in order to end French machinations in the Ottoman Empire and Sweden. The French would agree merely to a treaty of friendship but recognized Russia as a major diplomatic force.

Peter's ambitious and complex diplomacy forced a reorganization of the Foreign Office along Western lines and a great increase in its personnel. In 1720 the College of Foreign Affairs, personally supervised by Peter, replaced the *Posolskii Prikaz* (Ambassadorial Board). Permanent diplomatic missions were established in leading European capitals, and consuls protected Russian commercial interests. Russian diplomats gradually discarded Oriental etiquette and adopted European methods and dress, but they could decide nothing without consulting Moscow. Peter protected them well: When A. A. Matveev, Peter's ambassador to England, was arrested for debt in 1708, Peter backed him until he was released. An emerging group of skilled diplomats, aided by growing Russian power and a better-organized Foreign Office,

---

[5] Sumner, *Peter the Great,* p. 121.

proved their ability in concluding the Treaty of Nystadt.

Petrine Russia had a mixed record in foreign affairs. Military and diplomatic successes, prepared by Peter's predecessors, altered Russia's relations with Europe fundamentally, but Russian nationalist and some Soviet historians glorified the results unduly. Whether Petrine victories were worth their huge cost and militarization of the Russian state remains debatable. The Great Northern War reduced Sweden to a second-class power and made Russia dominant in the eastern Baltic. Poland was rendered helpless and the way prepared for its subsequent partition, but that scarcely benefited Poland or Russia. Against the Turks nothing was achieved: Peter had underestimated Turkish strength and had counted too much on the Balkan Christians. His marriage alliances with German princes drew Russia into the German quagmire and complicated the succession to the Russian throne. Failing to deflect France from support of Sweden and the Ottoman Empire, Russia began two centuries of alternating cooperation and rivalry with Austria over the Balkans. Peter's war against Persia was unnecessary, and his wars against the Turks ended in failure; but Russia clearly needed the direct links with western Europe secured from Sweden. Peter's conquest of a window on the Baltic and his moving of the capital to St. Petersburg were solid achievements.

Administration

Petrine administrative reforms reflected the general process of state building, which Russia experienced in a manner similar to western Europe. Petrine state reforms, like those of Peter's contemporary, Louis XIV of France, stemmed largely from war requirements. Introduced piecemeal, they were coordinated only late in Peter's reign. They sought to remedy problems produced by the atrophy or near collapse of the cumbersome Muscovite bureaucracy. The new central government, despite its virtual monopoly of political power, failed to exert the controls essential to assure the success of Peter's ambitious schemes, except in

and around major power centers. The new institutions often existed at first only on paper, and some never took proper root.

The early Romanovs, having developed a highly centralized government over which the ruler exercised supreme legislative, executive, and judicial authority, prepared the way for Petrine administration. Seventeenth-century tsars had maintained a lavish court in Moscow costing large sums, sums that Peter later exceeded at Peterhof. The Boyar Duma, no longer based wholly on birth, had become during the 17th century the chief governmental institution—a royal council handling many aspects of national life. It had directed the bureaucracy, drafted legislation, acted as a supreme court, and conducted foreign relations. Under the Duma were 60 to 70 administrative boards (*prikazy*) with overlapping and duplicating jurisdictions. The Duma and the *prikazy*, though centralized and located in Moscow, were disorderly and unstable, and Peter's predecessors entrusted key tasks to favorites, who bypassed this structure. Governors, appointed by and responsible to the *prikazy*, ruled the regional administration and possessed both civil and military authority. As central authority over towns and rural districts grew, self-government withered.

Until 1708 this central administration stumbled along without major structural change. Peter assumed personal charge of foreign and military affairs while the shrunken Boyar Duma implemented his hastily drafted decrees on internal matters. Peter urged the Duma to act independently in his absence but ordered it to keep detailed minutes signed by all members "so that the stupidity of each [member] shall be evident." Meanwhile, new *prikazy* were being created, amalgamated, divided, or renamed. The Admiralty Board administered the new fleet, and the much feared Preobrazhenskii Board ran the secret police, the guards, and recruitment; unlike other *prikazy*, it exercised authority over the entire country. In 1699 the creation of a Board of Accounts (*Ratusha*) to handle state finance heralded coming structural reform. Other *prikazy* had to submit frequent reports to it, and Peter hoped that it could gather enough revenue to support the army. By 1708 the Ratusha collected about two-thirds of state revenues, but because the Treasury and Big Court boards still functioned, financial centralization was incomplete. The Ratusha and the Preobrazhenskii Board revealed the obsolescence and inefficiency of the *prikaz* system.

In order to raise more money locally for the war, the government in 1699 offered towns relief from greedy governors by allowing them to elect mayors if they would pay double taxation to the state. When only a few towns agreed to do this, the authorities dropped double assessment and made elected mayors compulsory. Peter hoped that wealthy merchants would improve the quality of local institutions and raise war revenues, but apathy and a shortage of qualified personnel prevented substantial results. Elected gentry boards, set up in 1702 to assist governors, likewise proved ineffective.

The Ratusha's failure to raise adequate war revenues induced Peter to try decentralization to support the army. In December 1707 Russia was divided into eight huge regions (*gubernii*) under governors whom Peter appointed in 1711. Residing in regional capitals, these governors were expected to be more efficient and accessible than Moscow bureaucrats. Swedish-style provincial boards (*landraty*) of eight to 12 members were created to assist the governors. Later board members assumed charge of new units called *dolia* and were empowered to supervise the governor's work. As *dolia* chiefs, board members were the governor's subordinates; as supervisors, they were theoretically his equals!

Peter experimented with various provincial subdivisions. Beginning in 1711, the *gubernii* were divided into provinces (*provintsii*) and subdivided into districts (*uezdy*). Before these could take root, Peter created *dolia*, each supposedly comprising 5,536 taxable households, to support local army units. Some of the *dolia* coincided with districts; others comprised several districts. This array of political units established for different purposes caused confusion and waste. Petrine provincial legislation revealed neither forethought nor wisdom. Abrupt institutional changes lowered civil service morale and failed to extract maximum revenue.

The creation of the *gubernii* and wartime pressures deepened confusion at the center. Moscow ceased to function as the capital, yet St. Petersburg was still under construction, so government centered wherever Peter happened to be. To fill the void during his absence on the Pruth campaign, Peter replaced the moribund Boyar Duma with a Senate (see Figure 15.2), initially to control the *gubernii*, the courts, government expenditures, and trade. People and institutions were supposed to obey it as they would the tsar. Theoretically, the Senate became, like the Duma before it, the supreme administrative body, the top judicial authority, and a quasi legislature that formulated and interpreted Peter's rough decrees; actually, Senate authority was undermined and often disregarded by Peter's favorites. Originally Peter selected nine senators whose decisions were to be unanimous; but despite their extensive, ill-defined powers, the senators lacked independence and were mostly second-rate men requiring constant supervision.

The structure and procedure of the Senate later grew more complex. An *oberfiskal,* or secret supervisor, was appointed to gather information about unfair court decisions and misappropriations of public funds. Assisted by a growing network of informers (*fiskaly*), he was supposed to indict offenders before the Senate, and for convictions he received half of the fine imposed by the court. In 1715 Peter named an inspector general to enforce Senate decrees, punish negligent senators, and ensure that the Senate performed its duties. Such measures proved inadequate, and Peter had to rebuke and fine senators who brawled, shouted, and rolled on the Senate floor! In 1722 he appointed a procurator general, as "our eye and mandatory in the affairs of state," to head the Senate's secretariat and mediate among the emperor, the Senate, and the Senate's subordinate departments. The procurator was to watch over the Senate, regulate *fiskaly*, preserve order, and report Senate opinions to Peter. Though not a

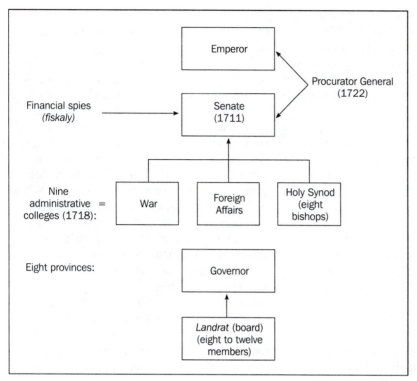

Figure 15.2
Petrine political system, 1721

Senate member and without a vote, he became its de facto president and the mainspring of the administration. Next to the emperor, the procurator became the most powerful man in Russia.

After careful study of foreign models, Peter in 1717 replaced the *prikazy* with administrative colleges, then fashionable in Europe. The German philosopher Leibniz had written Peter: "Their mechanism is like that of watches whose wheels mutually keep each other in movement." Peter believed that the collegial (collective) principle would promote regularity, avoid arbitrary one-man rule, and end corruption in departments of state. Foreign experts organized the colleges and adapted them to Russian conditions. Peter staffed them initially with Swedish war-prisoner volunteers and foreign Slavs and sent young Russians abroad to study their operations. Vice presidents of the new colleges, except foreign affairs, were

foreigners, but only three foreigners per college were permitted, and their presidents were mostly Russian. Not until 1720 did the administrative colleges actually begin to function in foreign affairs, the army, the admiralty, state revenue, commerce, mining and manufactures, state expenditure, justice, and state control. Later new presidents were selected; the procurator general coordinated them with the Senate, and most foreigners were discharged. The administrative colleges soon resembled the former *prikazy* because their boards became tools of the president. They relieved the Senate of many administrative tasks, however, and the judicial college assumed many legal functions. Because the colleges had clear jurisdiction over the entire empire, the central government became more orderly and efficient.

Such changes at the center necessitated further provincial reorganization. In 1718, on the Senate's recommendation Peter adopted local institutions modeled on Swedish ones. The *gubernii,* increased to 11 and later 12, were subdivided into 45, later 50, counties, each under an *oberkommandant* responsible to the governor. The *dolia* were abolished, and the counties, except for military and judicial affairs, became largely self-governing. They were subdivided into districts of about 2,000 households, with local commissars to collect taxes and supervise the police, the economy, education, and even public morals. Regimental districts, set up to raise money for local army units, cut across county boundaries and complicated this neat pattern.

Beginning in 1720, Russian towns adopted institutions like those of the Baltic cities of Reval and Riga. Townspeople were divided by wealth into three guilds, but only first guild members could hold public office. Town councils, headed by a chief magistracy in St. Petersburg, were supposed to collect taxes and run city affairs. They actually did little, and this reform failed to take root. A minority of wealthy merchants, protected by the government, dominated the towns. In 1727 the chief magistracy was abolished and town councils were subordinated to provincial governors. Here foreign models proved inapplicable to Russia's underdeveloped towns.

The Petrine administrative reforms succeeded only in part. A coherent central administration clearly demarcated from local government emerged and lasted with little change for almost a century, but shortcomings were numerous. Judicial, administrative, and executive functions were not clearly separated, and the new agencies were expensive and sometimes superfluous (some colleges were later abolished as unnecessary). Some imported institutions did not work, and trained officials were lacking. The perennial Russian problem of corruption persisted. "We all steal," declared Peter's favorite, Paul Iaguzhinskii. "The sole difference is that some do it on a bigger scale and in a more conspicuous manner than others." Officials were paid inadequately, virtually compelling them to steal, and although Peter crusaded against peculation and encouraged *fiskaly* to uncover abuses, he protected or forgave corrupt favorites. His contempt for regular administrative agencies and his reliance on military men hampered efforts to establish the rule of law. Abysmally low standards of public morality rose little.

The administration, as in the Prussia of Frederick William I, depended greatly on Peter's personal direction and languished in his absence. One of Europe's hardest-working rulers, Peter drafted decrees on every subject and made all important and many minor decisions. He achieved a type of absolutism of which the great "sun king," Louis XIV of France, could only dream. Such personal government deteriorated when Peter was absent and broke down under weak successors; favorites more powerful than the Senate violated the law flagrantly. Guards officers with sweeping powers obtained special missions, especially to punish high-ranking wrongdoers. Peter's numerous administrative spies looking over one another's shoulders confirmed that corruption and malfeasance remained rife. The system functioned well enough to achieve Peter's main objectives but not nearly as efficiently as those of France or Prussia.

Problem 4

Historians and the Petrine Reforms

The reforms of Peter I and their significance have been debated by Russian and foreign scholars ever since his death. Peter the autocrat, like his great contemporary Louis XIV, believed that the state must reform administration and society through reason, but he also believed that in backward Russia barbarous methods would often be required. Like subsequent European enlightened

Problem 4 continued

despots, Peter considered it a duty to uplift and improve his subjects, by force if necessary. His ceaseless activity, inexhaustible energy, and authoritarian methods put a strong personal imprint on the changes that were made. How lasting and beneficial were the Petrine reforms?

Peter's contemporaries mostly considered his reign an era of transformation by the "great reformer." Most 18th-century Russian writers described Peter's work as desirable and far-reaching, considered Europe a valid model, and praised Peter for setting Russia on a progressive course. Prince M. M. Shcherbatov (1733–1790), a leading noble historian and spokesman, believed that Peter had brought Russia forward but at the expense of Russian mores and the titled nobility. Late in the century the liberal noble Alexander Radishchev denounced Petrine despotism but praised Peter for founding St. Petersburg and expanding Russia's territory and power.

Slavophiles and Westernizers

In the early 19th century the Petrine reforms were debated heatedly by Slavophiles and Westernizers (see Chapter 23). For both groups, Peter was a great man—a genius or thundercloud. Glorifying Russian institutions, the Slavophiles condemned Peter for importing Western materialism and subordinating the Orthodox church to the state. While praising Peter's military victories and expansion, N. M. Karamzin deplored his love of foreign customs and his disregard for Russian traditions. Karamzin attributed the deep rift between the upper and lower classes to Petrine reforms of dress. Founding St. Petersburg, with its foul climate and the heavy sacrifice of life that its construction entailed, had been a disastrous blunder. In his memorandum "On the Internal State of Russia" the prominent Slavophile K. Aksakov called Peter I "that greatest of all great men." But the Petrine revolution, "despite all its external brilliance, shows what immense spiritual

evil can be done by the greatest genius as soon as he acts alone, draws away from the people." Peter's predecessors had built soundly, throwing off foreign domination without imitating European models. But then "the state in the person of Peter encroached upon the people, invaded their lives and customs, and forcibly changed their manners and traditions and even their dress." In St. Petersburg Peter had surrounded himself with immigrants who lacked traditional values. "That is how the breach between tsar and people occurred."

The Westernizers lauded Peter for founding the modern, enlightened, secular Russian state. This greatest Russian ruler, wrote Peter Chaadaev, had swept away all Russian traditions: "On one occasion a great man sought to civilize us, and in order to give us a foretaste of enlightenment, he flung us the mantle of civilization; we picked up the mantle, but we did not touch civilization itself." Peter freed Russia from the dead weight of its previous history: He "found only a blank page . . . and wrote on it *Europe* and *Occident*." The radical Westernizer Vissarion G. Belinskii agreed heartily. Peter "opened the door for his people to the light of God and little by little dispersed the darkness of ignorance."

Prerevolutionary Russian Historians

After 1860 Russian historians began denying that Peter's achievements were novel and revolutionary. S. M. Soloviev, the great founder of the "organic school," claimed that reforms had begun before Peter in seven key fields: foreign policy, army reform, administration, taxation, employing foreigners, compulsory service, and education. Only four of Peter's measures were truly innovative: sending Russians abroad, abolishing the patriarchate, creating a navy, and building St. Petersburg. Peter's personality and leadership nonetheless were decisive in modernizing Russia. Sternly teaching civic obligations, Peter invariably explained what he was doing and why. Popular sacrifices under his rule made Russia powerful. "The man who led the people in this feat can justly be called the greatest leader in history." Realizing his duty to civilize Russia, Peter led the way by personal example:

> We must stand astonished before the moral and physical powers of the Reformer. . . . We know of no historical figure whose sphere of activity was as broad as Peter's. . . . He developed entirely on his own, unguided and undeterred by anyone, yet stimulated by a society that was already at a turning point, that wavered between two directions. . . . Peter was endowed with the nature of an ancient Russian epic hero.[6]

The popular Moscow University professor V. O. Kliuchevskii, writing just after 1900, agreed that the early Romanovs had begun reform in most areas and that Peter had become a reformer largely by accident. War had compelled important changes that had aroused all social groups. The Petrine reforms were revolutionary chiefly because of their drastic nature and because of the impression they left on the nerves of Peter's contemporaries. Peter's nature was contradictory: tyranny and cruelty combined with patriotism, dedication to his work, bold plans executed with boundless energy. By despotism and threats Peter sought to inspire independent activity in an enslaved society.

Peter's personal role affected his reforms significantly, wrote P. N. Miliukov, a liberal politician and historian of the early 20th century (see Chapter 27). Performing incredibly varied tasks, Peter had served the state with great dedication and had supplied momentum to a regime working by fits and starts. Though no student of political theory, he was nonetheless strongly influenced by European institutions and ideas. His reforms were derived from western Europe but were profoundly national: "Russia received nothing but the reforms for which she was fitted."

---

[6] S. M. Soloviev, *Istoriia Rossii s drevneishikh vremen*, vol. 18 (St. Petersburg, n.d.), pp. 848–49.

Soviet Historians

Soviet historians after 1917 found little guidance in Marx or Lenin for interpreting the Petrine era. Ascribing to Peter a significant role in implementing change, George Plekhanov, father of Russian Marxism, considered his regime an Asiatic despotism with the autocrat and bureaucracy controlling the means of production and disposing arbitrarily of their subjects' property. "In Europeanizing Russia Peter carried to its extreme logical consequence the population's lack of rights vis-à-vis the state characteristic of Oriental despotism." However, Peter's implementation of the reforms suggested enlightened absolutism. M. N. Pokrovskii, the leading Soviet historian of the 1920s, designated Peter's reign an era of merchant capitalism and criticized the Petrine reforms for creating economic havoc and concentrating power in the bourgeoisie's hands. Peter had been merely a dissolute tool of merchant capitalism. Pokrovskii's *Russian History in Briefest Outline* (1933) discredited Peter in a four-sentence biographical sketch that mainly enumerated his lusts, tortures, and syphilis!

From the mid-1930s, under Stalin's dictatorship, Soviet interpretations of Peter's reign became strongly nationalistic. Repudiating Pokrovskii, who allegedly had disregarded Peter's strengthening of the state and of Russia's position abroad, Stalinist historians rehabilitated both Peter and his reforms; Petrine economic policies were compared with Stalin's Five Year Plans. For Stalinist historians, Peter became a progressive leader whose Russian-inspired reforms had strengthened Russia at home and abroad.

Glorification of Peter persisted to a degree into the Brezhnev era. Academician A. M. Pankratova called Peter "a good organizer and an outstanding statesman" and stressed his positive qualities:

> Peter hated cowardice, falsehood, hypocrisy, and dishonesty. Above all, he hated attachment to old usages which interfered with the country's regeneration. He strove to eliminate all backwardness. . . . Strong-willed, resolute, and persistent, Peter swept aside all obstacles that stood in the way of his

Problem 4 continued

reforms. He was irreconcilable in his fight against backwardness and barbarity.[7]

Here once again we see Peter the hero.

Soviet scholarship under Brezhnev reflected what N. V. Riasanovsky aptly called a bipolar image of Peter and his reforms.[8] Strong nationalism and an element of xenophobia remained, but they were far less pronounced than under Stalin. Extreme praise of Peter, utilized in the Stalin period to build that dictator's image, yielded to a generally sober appraisal of Peter's strengths and weaknesses. Virtual enslavement of an increasingly miserable peasantry and the heavy burden of wars were recognized as negative aspects of Peter's regime. Quotations from Stalin's works and out-of-context citations from other Marxist classics were reduced sharply. Petrine scholarship gained in breadth, sophistication, and quality. Popular rebellions (in Astrakhan and by Kondraty Bulavin; see Chapter 16) against the Petrine reforms remained a popular theme, but the positive image of the Petrine regime created in the 1930s persisted. Military and naval historians still glorified both the victory at Poltava and Peter as founder of the Russian fleet.

In a 1973 volume on Russia during the Petrine reforms, 12 Soviet scholars presented varied essays based on archives and with little ideological intrusion.[9] Editor N. I. Pavlenko wrote:

> Peter's talents were immeasurably broader than Charles XII's. He knew how to hold the sword in a firm hand, but he had mastered the pen with equal success, and he willingly took a chisel and an ax. Diplomacy and military affairs, state building and enlightenment, industry and trade, the way of life

and the mores—this is a far from complete list of the spheres . . . in which Peter intervened authoritatively and upon which he left his mark.[10]

A Recent Russian View

The outstanding St. Petersburg scholar, E. V. Anisimov, in a recent article depicts Peter as the precursor of Bolshevism (notably Stalinism) with his autocratic policies at home and a perilous imperialism abroad. He argues that Peter introduced many negative aspects of the Russian and Soviet political, social, and economic structure.

> We, the people of the late 20th century cannot fully appreciate the explosive effects of the Petrine reforms in Russia. People of the 19th century felt this differently, more sharply, deeply and graphically. The historian, N. P. Pogodin . . . wrote in 1841 about Peter's significance: "In the hands of [Peter] all of our threads were bound in a single knot. Wherever we look, we meet everywhere this colossal figure casting a long shadow over our entire past . . . and who, it seems, we will never lose from view no matter how far we proceed into the future."
>
> . . . Among many habitual symbols of the Petrine era which have become the property of literature and art, one must single out especially a ship under sail with the skipper on the bridge. . . . The ship—and for Peter himself—is the symbol of an organized structure calculated down to the inch, the material embodiment of human thought, of complex movement at the will of a rational man. Even more the ship is the model of the ideal society. . . .
>
> The state is built like a house, affirmed Hobbes.[11] Like a ship, we add. The idea about human, not God-given, nature of the state originated the concept that the state is that ideal instrument for reforming society, of educating the virtuous citizen, ideal institutions with whose aid one can achieve general prosperity. . . . In the years of his reforms in Russia occurred a sharp economic leap. Industrial construction occurred at unprece-

---

[7] A. M. Pankratova, *History of the USSR*, vol. 2 (Moscow, 1966), p. 43.

[8] N. V. Riasanovsky, *The Image of Peter the Great in Russian History and Thought* (New York, 1985), pp. 283ff.

[9] N. I. Pavlenko, ed. *Rossiia v period reform Petra I* (Moscow, 1973).

[10] Pavlenko, p. 101, quoted in Riasanovsky, *The Image*, p. 301.

[11] Thomas Hobbes, English political philosopher (1588–1679), was the author of *Leviathan*, which describes a monster state.

dented tempos. . . . The characteristic feature of this process lay in the leading role of the autocratic state in the economy, its active penetration into all spheres of economic life. . . .

. . . The extreme conditions after the defeat at Narva in 1700 with the loss of artillery provoked the need to rearm and expand the army, determined the character, tempo, and specifics of industrial growth and more broadly Peter's entire economic policy. At its foundation lay the idea of the directing role of the state in the life of society generally and in the economy in particular. . . . The result was disorganization of free entrepreneurship based on market competition. . . . In the first quarter of the 18th century was ruined the wealthiest group of merchants. . . . That was the price paid by Russian entrepreneurs for military victory, but they shared the costs with the rest of the population. . . . Thus active state industrial construction created the economic base essential for a developing nation and simultaneously held back tendencies attracting Russia onto the road of capitalist development on which other European peoples already stood. . . . Was there an alternative to what happened to the economy under Peter, were there other roads and means for her rise? . . .

. . . Gazing intently at Peter's ship of state, we notice that it is above all a warship. Characteristic of Peter's worldview was a relationship to state institutions like to a military unit . . . from the conviction that the army is the most perfect public structure, a model worthy of expanding to the scale of the entire society, tested by the dangerous experience of battle. With the aid of military discipline one can imbue people with a love of order, work, consciousness, and Christian morality. . . .

. . . Of course, service to the country, to Russia, was the most important element of political culture of the Petrine period with its traditions of patriotism. But the basic determining factor was . . . the tradition of identifying authority and the autocrat's person with the state. . . . (In recent history the clearest identification of the person of the ruler with the state, motherland, and people was displayed in the cult of Stalin's person: "Stalin, the will and mind of millions.")

For the political history of Russia subsequently this . . . had the most serious consequences since any action against the bearer of authority, whoever he was—supreme sovereign or petty official—was treated as an action against the state. . . . The most important element of Peter's political doctrine was the idea of paternalism figuratively embodied in the form of a reasonable, farsighted monarch—the father of his country and people. . . . The idea of force as a universal and most effective method of rule was not new. But Peter was probably the first to utilize compulsion with such consistency. . . .

Thus before us is not only a ship but a galley through whose galleries strutted the nobility dressed in military uniform, and to whose thwarts were chained the other classes. . . . Peter transformed a rather amorphous mass of service people "to the fatherland" into a military-bureaucratic corps wholly subordinate to and dependent upon him. . . . What occurred to the social structure of Russia in Peter's time . . . was setting the goal of creating a . . . totalitarian, military-bureaucratic and police state.

. . . Such was the crew of Peter's ship. Now . . . whither was it sailing? What were the goals of the tsar-skipper? The foreign policy conception of Russia during the Northern War underwent basic changes. . . . The Poltava victory allowed Peter to seize the initiative. . . . In the course of dividing Swedish possessions were manifested clearly Russia's pretensions under the influence of brilliant victories on land and sea. . . . The Treaty of Nystadt of 1721 formulated juridically not merely Russia's victory in the Northern War and Russia's acquisitions in the Baltic region but also the birth of a new empire: there was a clear relationship between celebration of the Nystadt treaty and Peter's acceptance of the imperial title. . . . Creation of a military base on the Caspian Sea testified to preparations for a campaign against India. . . . The peculiar "Indian syndrome" which had taken possession of many conquerors . . . did not pass Peter by. . . .

Overall during Peter's reign occurred a serious change in Russia's foreign policy: from deciding vital tasks of national policy it shifted to raising and solving typical imperial problems. The Petrine reforms led to the formation of a military-bureaucratic state with a strongly centralized autocratic authority resting on a serf economy and a powerful army (whose size continued to grow after war

Problem 4 continued

ended). That Peter's ship of state sailed to India flowed naturally from the internal development of the empire. Under Peter were laid the foundations of the imperial policies of Russia of the 18–19th centuries and began to form imperial stereotypes.[12]

_____

[12] E. V. Anisimov, "Petr I: Rozhdenie imperii," *Voprosy istorii*, no. 7 (1989): 3–20 (excerpts).

Conclusion

In both Russia and the West there has been a recent resurgence of interest in this most dynamic, powerful, and controversial tsar. After a generation of Soviet glorification, *glasnost* (openness) has turned a spotlight of criticism onto the giant tsar. How "great" is a ruler whose despotism and wars leave his people destitute and enslaved? What price imperial glory? ■

Suggested Additional Reading

BOOKS

ANDERSON, M. S. *Peter the Great* (London, 1978).

ANISIMOV, E. V. *The Reforms of Peter the Great*, trans. and intro. J. T. Alexander (Armonk, NY, 1993).

BRUCE, P. H. *Memoirs . . .* (New York, 1970). (Reprint.)

CHERNIAVSKY, M. *Tsar and People* (New Haven, 1961).

CRACRAFT, JAMES, ed. *For God and Peter the Great: The Works of Thomas Consett, 1723–1729* (Boulder, CO, 1982).

———. *Peter the Great Transforms Russia*, 3d ed. (Lexington, MA, 1991).

DMYTRYSHYN, B., ed. *Modernization of Russia under Peter I and Catherine II* (New York, 1974).

GRÜNWALD, C. DE. *Peter the Great* (London, 1956).

JACKSON, W. G. *Seven Roads to Moscow* (London, 1957). (On Poltava.)

JONGE, A. DE. *Fire and Water: A Life of Peter the Great* (New York, 1980).

KLYUCHEVSKY, V. O. *Peter the Great* (New York, 1961).

MARSDEN, C. *Palmyra of the North* (London, 1942). (Early St. Petersburg.)

MASSIE, R. *Peter the Great: His Life and World* (New York, 1980).

O'BRIEN, C. B. *Russia under Two Tsars, 1682–1689* (Berkeley, 1952).

PUTNAM, P. B. *Peter, the Revolutionary Tsar* (New York, 1973).

RIASANOVSKY, N. V. *The Image of Peter the Great in Russian History and Thought* (New York, 1985).

SUMNER, B. H. *Peter the Great and the Emergence of Russia* (London, 1951).

———. *Peter the Great and the Ottoman Empire* (Oxford, 1949).

TOLSTOI, A. *Peter the First* (New York, 1959). (Soviet historical novel.)

VOLTAIRE. *Russia under Peter the Great*, trans. F. Jenkins (London, 1983).

ARTICLES

ALEXANDER, J. T. "Petersburg and Moscow in Early Urban Policy." *Journal of Urban Hist.* 8, no. 2 (1982): 145–69.

ALTBAUER, D. "The Diplomats of Peter the Great." *JfGO* 28, no. 1 (1980): 1–16.

ANISIMOV, E. "Birth of an Empire." *SSH* 30, no. 2 (1991): 6–29.

BENSON, S. "The Role of Western Political Thought in Petrine Russia." *CanAmSlSt* 8, no. 2 (1974): 254–73.

BLACK, C. "The Reforms of Peter the Great," in *Rewriting Russian History: Soviet Interpretations of Russia's Past*, C. Black, ed. (New York, 1962), pp. 233–59.

CHERNIAVSKY, M. "The Old Believers and the New Religion." *SR* 25 (1966): 1–39.

HELLIE, R. "The Petrine Army: Continuity, Change, and Impact." *CanAmSlSt* 8, no. 2 (1974): 237–53.

MEEHAN-WATERS, B. "The Russian Aristocracy and the Reforms of Peter the Great." *CanAmSlSt* 8, no. 2 (1974): 288–303.

PERKOWSKI, J. "Peter the Great: A Catalogue of Medals in the Smithsonian Collection." *Numismatist* 95, no. 5 (1982): 1188–1204.

PINTNER, W. M. "The Russian Military (1700–1917): Social and Economic Aspects." *Trends Hist.* 2, no. 2 (1981): 43–52.

WORTMAN, R. "Peter the Great and Court Procedure." *CanAmSlSt* 8, no. 2 (1974): 303–10.

16

Peter the Great:
Social, Economic, and Religious Policies

Peter the Great's reforming activity touched almost every facet of human activity. Social and economic relations were affected by his relentless search for efficiency and productivity. Cultural affairs and church matters were of less immediate practical concern to Peter, but the swift pace of change would not allow these areas to escape attention. Kliuchevskii aptly suggested: "The government's most important and terrible weapon was Peter's pen."[1]

State Service by the Nobility

The military and administrative reforms initiated by Peter could be properly implemented only by an adequately trained and sizable corps of military and civil servants. The chief administrators of the Muscovite state had been members of the capital nobility (*stolichnoe dvorianstvo*), composed of the most prominent and distinguished families, long associated with court service. These old families

---

[1] V. O. Kliuchevskii, *Kurs russkoi istorii* (Moscow, 1937), vol. 4, p. 61.

possessed *votchina* (patrimonial) landholdings on a large scale. In addition, many noble families owning *pomestie* (service) estates around Moscow had been brought to Moscow by earlier tsars to protect the capital. The capital nobility were simply too few and too conservative in spirit to staff the new military and administrative institutions created by Peter's reforming policies.

Peter turned to the provincial nobility living in provincial urban centers and in remote rural areas. Provincial noblemen were notoriously negligent in fulfilling their service obligations. Many sought to hide in dark and distant recesses of remote provinces, so that the central government was often ignorant of their numbers, location, and service obligations. To ascertain these facts, Peter's decree of 1700 ordered all noble landowners to register themselves and all male family members over the age of 10. As soon as their names were registered, noblemen were assigned to specific regiments or civil administrative posts. The number of registered noble families increased dramatically from 3,000 recorded in 1670 to 15,041 in 1700, the extraordinary increase stemming from better recordkeeping. Of the noblemen registered, only about 535 owned more than 100 peasant households, 13 owned between 1,000 and 2,000, and only 5 owned more than 2,000. These figures confirm that noble status encompassed wide divergencies in economic wealth and political power. The 535 families with more than 100 peasant households constituted the noble elite of Russia and would mostly remain such during Peter's reign.

Peter's social program contributed to the gradual amalgamation of the old capital and provincial nobility. This leveling process was indicated by the official adoption of the term *shliakhetstvo* (from the Polish) to designate the entire nobility. On the surface this new name signified a shift away from the paramountcy of family standing in determining state service and toward the elusive quality of suitability for service. The change did not mean, as has so often been suggested, that family status ceased to count. On the contrary, Peter continued to expect the leading families to play prominent roles in state affairs by virtue of their traditional proximity to the centers of state power.

Meritorious service could be expected only from well-educated noblemen, so Peter ordered all nobles between the ages of 10 and 15 taught "mathematics," which to him meant all types of useful information. Though perhaps haphazard, this innovation was a first, halting step toward a totally secular educational system designed to serve state interests. Following his preparatory "education," the young noble was expected at the age of 15 to enter state service at the lowest rank, regardless of his family's social position. Those assigned to military service—by far the majority—were expected to serve two years in the ranks before receiving officers' commissions. One could avoid this demeaning and difficult form of "conditioning" only by being selected to serve in an elite guards regiment, whose members were drawn exclusively from the nobility. Peter used appointment to the guards to foster loyalty, cooperation, and devotion. For the provincial nobility, service in the guards regiments afforded an opportunity to enter the power center around the throne, which for so long had been the capital nobility's exclusive prerogative.

The nobleman was expected to serve the state for life or until incapacitated. His estate was left in the hands of his wife, relatives, or a steward or overseer, and consequently many estates were badly managed and unproductive and the nobility suffered severe economic distress. The success of Peter's new service organization was determined largely by the servitor's economic well-being. To compensate servitors, Peter resorted to the traditional method of land grants, extending both the granting of estates and the ownership of serfs. So that all land would carry service obligations, Peter in 1714 abolished all distinctions between *votchina* and *pomestie* tenure and decreed that henceforth all land was inheritable and carried precise service obligations. Each estate owner now had an incentive to maintain and develop his estate and maximize its productivity; all estate owners were bound to perform specific service to the state in return for the right to exploit their landholdings.

To improve further the nobility's economic status and foster a competitive service atmosphere, Peter decreed new regulations governing inheritance. The aim was to prevent families from so diluting their resources that their continued service became unsatisfactory or impossible. It had long been customary to divide an estate into equal shares for distribution among all remaining heirs. Over centuries this practice had undermined the nobility's economic well-being. Peter proclaimed the law of entail, which provided that land be passed intact from the father to a single designated heir, not necessarily the eldest surviving son. This new law was designed to maintain landholdings as economically viable units capable of supporting the state servitor and to encourage sons not receiving land to carve out for themselves a career in state service, commerce, or industry. These measures, like so many of Peter's plans, were not entirely successful, but they clearly reflected his desire to introduce order, uniformity, and efficiency into the service structure.

The establishment of the Table of Ranks in 1722 capped Peter's efforts to create a dependable and capable class of state servitors. The Table of Ranks recognized three parallel categories of state service: military, civil, and court, each divided into 14 grades. This new hierarchical system formalized the earlier decision that name alone did not assure one of an honorable position in the state. Rank had to be earned, and it was granted only as a reward for meritorious service. Although the Table of Ranks provided that a commoner could acquire hereditary noble status upon achieving the lowest (14th) officer rank or the eighth rank in the civil hierarchy, family status remained significant because Peter continued to expect state leaders to belong to the traditional nobility. Did the Table of Ranks, as many historians contend, have a democratizing influence on the Russian social structure by making noble status accessible to men of talent and ability? In theory, perhaps, and some nonnobles did enter service, but in practice it was generally assumed that an individual was of noble origin before he entered the competitive sphere of the Table of Ranks.

The service structure and the Table of Ranks demanded at least a rudimentary education and began a process that would gradually break down the cultural homogeneity of the Russian people. The upper classes with their Western-oriented education were effectively deprived of traditional Russian culture, and a tremendous chasm opened up in Russian society. The upper and lower classes were separated not only by social position and wealth but also by education and cultural values. In short, the upper classes became increasingly Westernized while the lower classes remained attached to the traditional culture of their ancestors.

The landowners of Russia were then consolidated into a single class of *dvorianstvo* (gentry), which controlled the state apparatus and fostered the spread of Western culture. The nobility's political and economic position was strengthened and consolidated by the establishment of the formal bureaucratic structure of the Table of Ranks.

Increased Burdens of the Peasantry

While the nobility was subjected to regularized, compulsory, and permanent state service, the peasantry bore the major financial burden of transforming Russia into a modern, militarily powerful state. The peasantry endured a rising burden of taxation and provided labor for state and private industry and for the landowning nobility. Under Peter, serfdom, now firmly entrenched, produced the worst forms of exploitation and abuse. The peasantry was affected by Peter's reforms only in the negative sense of suffering greater hardships and heavier burdens.

The tremendous costs of Peter's wars required a reexamination of the tax structure. In old Muscovy state taxes, paid exclusively by peasants and some townspeople, had been assessed according to the number of households. The census of 1678 enumerated some 800,000 taxable households, whereas that ordered by Peter in 1710 listed only 640,000, a disastrous decline in the tax base in the face of growing demands for revenue to pay for the Great Northern War. Many factors explain this decline: inaccurate information, inefficient collection of data, peasant desires to avoid taxes by amalgamating households, the conscription of peasants into the army, and the flight of peasants to outlying areas to escape oppression. The solution to this potentially grave fiscal situation was to substitute a capitation tax, or a tax on individuals, for the former household tax. A decree of 1718 made every nonprivileged male subject to a uniform tax determined by computing the costs of war and administration and dividing that amount by the number of males subject to taxation. The resulting figure was assessed against each male that year. This simple method depended on accurate census information. "Revisions" of the census of 1719 were made several times, until the number of males subject to the capitation or poll tax reached about 5,600,000. This new method represented a new financial burden for the already overburdened peasantry. The amount of tax revenue squeezed from the peasantry increased by a factor of 2½ between 1680 and 1724. Nevertheless, in the first year almost 27 percent of the new tax remained unpaid.

Besides higher state taxes, heavier dues and obligations were imposed on privately owned serfs and state peasants. As the amount of rent in cash or kind (*obrok*) and labor service (*barshchina*) steadily increased during the early 18th century, it became more and more difficult for the serfs to keep body and soul together. The owners of those private serfs who were unable to pay the capitation tax were responsible for paying it, giving them even greater control over the lives of their serfs. The capitation tax had the effect of abolishing the institution of slavery, which had existed side by side with serfdom. Because slaves were not considered persons legally, they paid no taxes, but the new capitation tax had to be paid by *all* male "souls" (*dushi*). Actually, as the landowners' powers increased, serfs became slaves in virtually every way but in name.

Theoretically, the landlord's legal powers over the serfs were almost unlimited, but in reality the situation was quite different. The complexities of rural life, generally archaic agricultural practices, much superstition, and limited labor power sharply limited the landlords' ability to exercise state-granted legal powers. Local custom and conditions often rendered these legal powers impractical and produced compromise. Cooperation and good relations benefited both lord and serf. In theory, the landlord could allot land for peasant use as he wished; more commonly such decisions were made after consulting with village elders rather than disrupting economic relations to everyone's disadvantage. In theory, the landlord could increase or decrease peasant payments in grain, labor, or money for use of the land. In fact, such arbitrary actions were rare so as not to disrupt the delicate balance in rural socioeconomic relations.

A landlord could confiscate a serf's meager personal possessions, but that would not enrich the landlord; it would instead further impoverish and alienate the serf, thus reducing his productivity and value to the lord. The latter could impose corporal punishment even for minor infractions, but this seldom deterred peasants from bad behavior and often rendered them unfit for labor. Serfs resisted landlords' encroachments or arbitrary actions by laziness, feigned ignorance, or negligence. In extreme cases peasants resorted to flight or open rebellion, which imperiled the land-

lords' economic and physical security. The regime pursued fugitives and bloodily suppressed rebellions, but at great cost. Official statistics record over 200,000 cases of flight between 1719 and 1726, which must have cost heavily in expenditures for efforts to recover fugitives and in lost labor.

State peasants were slightly better off than privately owned serfs. The two groups were roughly equal in numbers and had comparable ways of life, and both groups bore crushing burdens of taxation and dues, but state peasants occupied state lands, where their obligations were more precisely defined. State peasants paid the capitation tax and a fixed amount of *obrok* to the state, and they performed some labor service to maintain roads, canals, and bridges. They were legally bound to their villages and could not leave without proper authorization by state officials. Subject to increasing taxation and dues and growing obligations, state peasants also faced the danger of being transformed arbitrarily into private serfs or of being conscripted into government labor gangs to construct new cities, fortifications, and roads or to work as laborers in state-owned mines and industries. During the early 18th century many state peasants were given away by Russian rulers to private individuals or were sold, loaned, or granted outright to owners of private mines and factories as a form of government subsidy. Often these factory serfs were viciously mistreated and exploited, chained to their machines, beaten at whipping posts, poorly housed, and badly fed and clothed. Whole villages of state peasants were haunted by the fear of becoming factory serfs. So terrifying was this prospect that many joined their privately owned brethren in illegal flight.

Escaping serfs fleeing to the south and southeast fed the ranks of the discontented: Cossacks, *streltsy*, army deserters, ethnic minorities, and Old Believers, all of whom awaited an opportunity to revolt. In the fortress city of Astrakhan, government efforts to enforce Petrine reforms of dress and to prohibit beards caused general indignation. In July 1705 soldiers and *streltsy* surprised and destroyed the garrison, killing foreigners (whom

Michael Curran

Stone family dwelling, 17th century.

they associated with the hated reforms), the military governor, and more than 300 noblemen. The insurgents, seizing the property of the rich, formed a rebel government under a merchant, Iakov Nosov. The revolt, supported by Terek Cossacks, soon spread over much of southeast Russia. Peter had to send Field Marshal Sheremetiev with an army to quell the uprising. Insurgents who did not succumb to his troops or to torture by the feared Preobrazhenskii Board were executed in Red Square in 1707.

No sooner had that movement been crushed than a Don Cossack leader appeared to lead the disgruntled against the Petrine regime. Kondraty Bulavin was old enough to recall the revolt of Stenka Razin (see Chapter 14), who, like him, came from a leading Cossack family. In October 1707, with a few followers, he ambushed a government detachment sent into the Don region to round up escaped peasants. Bulavin revived Razin's dream of joining Cossacks of the Don and Dnieper into a united Ukraine to halt Muscovite expansion and encroachments on Cossack freedom. His army of "the insulted and the injured," estimated at 100,000, included Cossacks, peasants,

priests, deserters, barge haulers, and raftsmen. Bulavin fought against serfdom, but his movement, less widespread than Razin's, was chiefly a Cossack rising. In the summer of 1708 he briefly threatened Peter's new and still fragile state structure, which also faced Swedish invasion. Bulavin managed to occupy Cherkassk and become Cossack *ataman* (chieftain) before his undisciplined levies were defeated by a well-trained Muscovite army aided by the Cossack oligarchy. Afterward, some 2,000 Cossacks fled to the Kuban and later across into refuge in Turkey.

Economic Policies

Peter's economic policies were neither new nor innovative. He used the existing economic structure, but with a new urgency stemming from the needs of his new state organization and the need to equip his nascent army and navy. Reduced to simple terms, Peter's economic views were based on a clear recognition of the connection between economic prosperity and national power. Practical considerations combined with the mercantilist doctrine prevalent in Europe provided the "theo-retical framework" for his economic policies. He sought to maximize exports in order to secure a favorable balance of trade, decreed high protective tariffs, sought self-sufficiency, and sought to acquire and preserve hard currency. These were the commonly accepted mercantilist goals of most of contemporary Europe.

Observing the drain on Russia's meager supply of hard currency depleted by expensive imports of military supplies, Peter was determined to make Russia more self-sufficient by encouraging the development of native industry and commerce. The outbreak of the Great Northern War stimu-lated the rapid growth of foundries and armament enterprises organized to supply the army and navy. These industries, initiated by the govern-ment, were rather quickly turned over to private individuals. The government embarked on a pro-gram to survey the country's national resources, the result of which convinced Peter that Russia was superior to other countries in natural resources. He recognized, however, that the state must take the lead in developing them.

Russians were often reluctant to venture into new economic endeavors, forcing the government to encourage private individuals to become involved in economic development. The state offered a variety of fiscal and legal inducements, including monopoly rights, large standing govern-ment orders, outright subsidies, tax exemptions, a free supply of labor (state peasants), and high tariffs for the complete exclusion of foreign com-petition. Even with such generous concessions, the government found it difficult to persuade individ-uals to embark on industrial ventures. Failure or inefficient management of industry brought harsh official reprisals, including heavy fines and even imprisonment. Most of the industrialists came from the merchant class, whose members were often better prepared and more ambitious than noblemen. Because merchants lacked sufficient wealth, the state provided much of the capital for industry. Shortage of capital severely limited Peter's program of industrialization.

Another problem facing the government was an inadequate labor force for new industries. The state used the numerous state peasants at its disposal in both privately and governmentally financed enter-prises. In most cases state peasants were assigned to factories during the winter for such work as construction, building dams, and breaking up coal. The peasants remained in their home villages except while assigned to factories, supporting themselves primarily from agriculture. Private fac-tory owners were permitted to purchase entire villages of serfs who could then be moved to factory sites as permanent factory workers at subsistence wages. Once their ties to the village were broken, they tended to consider themselves workers rather than peasants and were called "possessional peas-ants." Peter also tried to solve a distressing social problem by impressing beggars, prostitutes, crimi-nals, and illegitimate children into the industrial work force. Even fugitive serfs who had found employment in factories were protected against forcible return to their assigned villages. Labor, however, was less of a problem than chronic lack of capital, foreign competition, and the poor quality of products. Still, some 200 large industrial enterprises were established in Russia during Peter's reign (see Map 16.1). In absolute terms success in industrial-ization was modest, but relatively it was enormous, even though some of the enterprises did not long survive Peter. Mining and metallurgy received pow-erful stimuli, as did textiles and armaments—essential industries for a powerful state that was destined to play a prominent international role.

Church Reform

The Orthodox church, weakened during the trau-matic controversies of the 17th century, was deeply affected by Peter's reforming activity. Peter merely completed, however, the subordination of the church to the state begun by his father, Alexis. Following the death of Joachim, patriarch between 1674 and 1690, Peter the Great suffered a setback when his candidate for the patriarchal throne was ignored and Metropolitan Adrian of Kazan was selected. Like his predecessor, Adrian was

Map 16.1 Industry and agriculture, 18th century

extremely suspicious of foreigners and foreign influences in Russia, a fact that did not bode well for the future. Peter's candidate, Markell, metropolitan of Pskov, was, unlike Adrian, open-minded, well read, and well disposed toward foreigners. Markell was hated by the boyars and the clergy, noted one observer, "because of his learning and other good qualities"; Adrian had been chosen because of his "ignorance and simplicity."[2] While Adrian served in undistinguished fashion for the next decade, Peter and his cronies formed the "Most Drunken Council," an insulting

---

[2] R. K. Massie, *Peter the Great*, p. 110.

mockery of the Most Holy Council of church hier-archs. Some historians have tried to connect the drunken parodies of ecclesiastical rites practiced with such delight by Peter and his companions with his bitterness over the defeat of his candidate or with his decision to reform the church. Neither explanation seems to provide an adequate answer because the revelries continued until the end of the reign.

Whatever the explanation, Peter was deter-mined never again to see the church fall into the hands of a person who did not enjoy his full confi-dence. In 1700, when the patriarchal throne fell vacant, Peter refused to sanction the election of a new patriarch. Instead, he turned over the patri-arch's secular duties to the appropriate organs of state administration and referred all ecclesiastical duties to Stefan Iavorskii, metropolitan of Riazan, who served as caretaker of the patriarchate for the next two decades. Peter, certainly, lacked at this point any long-range plan to abolish the patriar-chate as an institution. Indeed, his initial purpose in refusing to allow a new patriarch to be elected was to win time to appropriate for the state some of the revenues of the church and to abolish some of its economic privileges. The time was, after all, one of crisis: The Russians had just been thor-oughly beaten by the Swedes at Narva, and Peter needed revenues and even church bells to melt down to reequip his armies. The absence of a patriarch would facilitate his appropriation of patriarchal and monastic revenues and allow him to have church bells turned into cannon with a minimum of opposition.

Iavorskii remained metropolitan of Riazan, although as temporary head of the church he administered its affairs and was one of Peter's chief advisers on ecclesiastical questions. Iavor-skii's relations with Peter were often stormy and embittered, but the patriarchal "caretaker" never attempted to use the church as a political weapon against Peter. Despite frequent discord, Iavorskii served as head of the church (1700–1721) longer than any previous primate in Muscovite history.

The first indication that Peter was embarking on reforms that would alter the church structure

and administration came in November 1718, when he announced his intention to establish an ecclesiastical college to manage church affairs. This was a logical step, given Peter's familiarity with the organization of the Church of England and other Protestant churches. In an absolute monarchy, he believed, the state was served by three orders—military, civil, and ecclesiastical—over which he, as supreme ruler, had complete authority. Furthermore, revelations about the clergy's role in the conspiracy that led to the death of Alexis, Peter's only son (June 1718), must have convinced him that state control had to be imposed on the clergy. Finally, Peter had just pro-claimed his decision to establish administrative colleges, and an ecclesiastical college would have occurred to him quite naturally.

Peter entrusted the delicate task of drafting the regulations governing the proposed Ecclesiastical College to the bishop of Pskov, Feofan Prokopo-vich, the chief clerical ideologist of the absolute monarchy. Prokopovich's completed draft of the *Ecclesiastical Regulation,* submitted to Peter early in 1720, was promulgated in January 1721 after care-ful scrutiny and revision. The patriarchate had been abolished, noted the *Regulation,* because the administration of the church was "too great a burden for a single man whose power is not hereditary," and seeing no better means to reform the ecclesiastical order, "we hereby establish an Ecclesiastical College."[3] Thus the patriarch was replaced by a consistory of bishops or clerical leaders appointed by the tsar for an indefinite term of office. The *Regulation* suggested 12 as an appropriate and perhaps symbolic number of members for the college, but Peter actually selected only 11 clergymen to serve. The Ecclesias-tical College consisted of a president, two vice presidents, four councillors, and four assessors, each of whom could vote on all issues brought before the college. Iavorskii was appointed presi-dent, Prokopovich became second vice president, and the other appointees were all at least nominal

---

[3] *Ecclesiastical Regulation,* a church charter (described in R. K. Massie, *Peter the Great,* pp. 792–93).

Bishop's palace in Rostov, near Vladimir.

supporters of Peter's regime and among the most enlightened and best-educated clergymen in Russia. Nonetheless, these clerics did not enjoy Peter's complete confidence. In May 1722 he issued a decree providing for the selection of a well-informed and experienced person versed in ecclesiastical affairs, "from among the [army] officers and [to be] made Chief Procurator [of the Holy Synod]." The following month Colonel I. V. Boltin was appointed to that post. The chief procurator was to serve as Peter's "eyes and ears" and act as a watchdog to ensure that the Holy Synod conducted its business properly and with regard for state interests.

Peter's church reform was clearly the most radical of his innovations because it broke most sharply and decisively with the past. The Russian patriarchate was only about a century old, but throughout its brief history it had been a powerful institution that had guarded the autonomy of the church. Precisely this autonomy was incompatible with Peter's conception of absolute monarchy. Prokopovich enunciated this view unequivocally in the *Ecclesiastical Regulation:* "From an adminis-

trative organ embodying the collegial principle there is no reason to fear rebellions and confusions that grow out of the control of the Church by a single individual." No longer could there be two institutions competing for popular loyalty and allegiance; emperor and state could no longer be rivaled by patriarch and church. The autonomy of the church was swallowed up by the state bureaucracy; secular power triumphed over ecclesiastical authority. Declared the oath required of all members of the Holy Synod: "I confess with an oath that the final judge of this ecclesiastical college is the Monarch of all Russia Himself, Our Most Gracious Sovereign."

Suggested Additional Reading

BOOKS

CRACRAFT, J. *The Church Reform of Peter the Great* (Stanford, 1971).

———. *The Petrine Revolution in Architecture* (Chicago, 1989).

KEEP, JOHN L. *Soldiers of the Tsar: Army and Society in Russia, 1462–1874* (Oxford, 1985).

KIRCHNER, W. *Commercial Relations between Russia and Europe, 1400–1800* (Bloomington, IN, 1966).

MULLER, A., trans. and ed. *The Spiritual Regulation . . .* (Seattle, 1972).

RIASANOVSKY, N. V. *The Image of Peter the Great in Russian History and Thought* (New York, 1985).

SEGEL, H. *The Literature of Eighteenth Century Russia . . .*, 2 vols. (New York, 1967).

WITTRAM, R. *Peter I, Czar und Kaiser . . .*, 2 vols. (Göttingen, 1964).

ARTICLES

ALEXANDER, J. "Petersburg and Moscow in Early Urban Policy." *JUH* 8, no. 2 (1982): 145–69.

BISSONNETTE, G. "Did Feofan Prokopovich Really Write *Pravda Voli Monarshei?*" *SR* 40 (1981): 173–93.

———. "Feofan Prokopovich," in *The Eighteenth Century in Russia*, ed. J. Garrard (Oxford, 1973), pp. 75–105.

———. "Peter the Great and the Church as an Educational Institution," in *Essays . . .*, ed. J. Curtiss (Leiden, 1963), pp. 3–19.

CRUMMEY, R. O. "Peter and the Boiar Aristocracy, 1689–1700." *CanAmSlSt* 8, no. 2 (1974): 274–87.

GRAHAM, H. F. "Theophan Prokopovich and the Ecclesiastical Ordinance." *CH* 25 (1956): 127–35.

KAHAN, A. "Continuity in Economic Activity and Policy during the Post-Petrine Period in Russia." *JEH* 25 (1965): 61–85.

———. "The Costs of Westernization in Russia . . ." *SR* 25 (1966): 40–66.

———. "Observations on Petrine Foreign Trade." *CanAmSlSt* 8, no. 2 (1974): 222–36.

LIKHACHEV, D. S. "The Petrine Reforms and the Development of Russian Culture." *CanAmSlSt* 13, nos. 1–2 (1979): 230–34.

MEEHAN-WATERS, B. "The Russian Aristocracy and the Reforms of Peter the Great." *CanAmSlSt* 8, no. 2 (1974): 288–303.

PERKOWSKI, J. L. "Peter the Great: A Catalogue of Medals in the Smithsonian Collection." *Numismatist* 95, no. 5 (1982): 1188–1204.

PINTNER, W. M. "The Russian Military (1700–1917): Social and Economic Aspects." *Trends Hist.* 2 (1981): 43–52.

SERECH, J. "Stefan Yavorsky and the Conflict of Ideologies . . ." *SEER* 30 (1951–52): 40–62.

VON RAUCH, G. "Political Preconditions for East-West Cultural Relations in the Eighteenth Century." *CanAmSlSt* 13, no. 4 (1979): 391–411.

ZERNOV, N. "Peter the Great and the Establishment of the Russian Church." *CQR* 125 (1937–38): 265–93.

ZGUTA, R. "Peter I's 'Most Drunken Synod of Fools and Jesters.'" *JfGO* 21 (1973): 18–28.

17

The Era of Palace Revolutions, 1725–1762

The period between the reigns of Peter and Catherine the Great, though full of complex and important events, has been somewhat neglected by scholars. Nationalist Russian historians called it a "second time of troubles" during which weak rulers dominated by greedy favorites caused disorder at home and impotence abroad. Admirers of Peter I, the architect of reform, Westernization, and Russian power, lamented his successors' indecision and ineffectiveness. But some Russian and Western scholars view this era much more positively. The Russian people, noted Soloviev, no longer oppressed by the state, could deal better with its own problems. With autocracy somewhat relaxed, the nobility adapted better to Western values and succeeded in ending compulsory state service in 1762. As cultural growth continued, bases were laid for intellectual development and greater freedom of expression. The early Soviet historian Pokrovskii affirmed that western European capital dominated Russian internal and foreign policy under Anna Ivanovna; then followed a "new feudalism" and rule by the gentry. Subsequent Soviet accounts, repudiating Pokrovskii's stress on commercial capital, emphasized the heightened contradictions within the ruling feudal landowning class and an intensified mass struggle against it. Should this be called *the* era of palace revolutions because there were similar coups before and afterward? Did Peter I's successors reverse or continue his reforms? Was the political crisis of 1730 a struggle of individuals or feudal factions, or a movement for limited monarchy? Was this an era of rising commercial capitalism or continuing feudalism?

Politics

Coups d'état brought several of the seven rulers between Peter and Catherine to the throne. Peter's decision of 1722 to name his successor arbitrarily and abrogate traditional rules of succession, claimed Kliuchevskii, produced chronic political instability. Peter's failure to name an heir split the Romanov dynasty into an imperial line of his descendants and a royal line from his half brother, Ivan V. Never in Russia or in any other major country did supreme power pass by a line so broken and so exposed to chance, intrigue, and foreign influence. In recurrent succession crises the key role was played by the two (later three) regiments of the Imperial Guard, containing the elite of the Russian nobility and behind which stood titled aristocrats, gentry, and the bureaucracy. Despite these palace coups, most of the period was taken up by the reigns of Anna and Elizabeth, both of whom were unchallenged once they were firmly in power.

In no case could Peter's successors have exercised his tremendous absolute authority. In one sense the years 1725–1730, sometimes designated the "era of collective leadership," resemble the post-Stalin period of 1953–1957 (see Chapter 39). Conservatives and titled aristocrats led by the highly educated prince D. M. Golitsyn and the Dolgorukii family, favoring a traditional succession, backed Alexis's son, Peter, the only surviving male Romanov. Top Petrine bureaucrats such as Prince Menshikov, fearing the loss of their posts, supported Peter I's widow, Catherine, and promised the guards lighter service and more privileges. With backing from the guards, the Senate named the former servant girl autocratic empress. Coarse and ill-educated, Catherine I left most state business to Menshikov and his cronies.

In February 1726 top Russian leaders formed a six-member Supreme Privy Council, all of whose members except Golitsyn were Petrine bureaucrats. The other original members were Menshikov, Fedor Apraksin, Fedor Golovkin, Peter Tolstoi, and Andrew Ostermann. For four years this oligarchy, de facto rulers of Russia, supervised the Senate and the administrative colleges. The problems of this difficult transition period needed an able ruler's full attention; instead, the council members intrigued and played petty politics. Mainly out of apathy they preserved most of Peter's central institutions while discussing futilely how to remedy administrative disorder. Supporting Peter's reforms, Catherine executed his decrees.

The council members, though close collaborators of the Reformer, regarded his work negatively:

> After a discussion of the present condition of the all-Russian state, it appears that almost all

affairs . . . are in bad shape and require immediate rectification.[1]

Attracted by Muscovite administrative practices, the oligarchs condemned the Petrine provincial government for burdening state and people with superfluous officials. They abrogated most of the Petrine regional institutions and restored a single official, the *voevoda*, subject to the provincial governor. Instead of adapting Peter's work to Russian conditions, the Supreme Privy Council rejected innovation, reduced the staffs of the Senate and the colleges, and abolished unpopular procurators and fiscal overseers.

Catherine's death in 1727 brought the boy emperor Peter II (1727–1730) to the throne. Soon thereafter Menshikov was arrested, and the Dolgorukii family with its anti-Petrine policies dominated the Supreme Privy Council, which continued to dissolve Petrine institutions, though they would be restored later. Early in 1728 the court and some central agencies moved to Moscow for the coronation of Peter II, who became a plaything of the Dolgorukiis.

Peter's sudden death (January 1730) without a designated successor sparked a dramatic political crisis. Prince D. M. Golitsyn, the Supreme Privy Council's outstanding leader, persuaded his fellow oligarchs to offer the throne to a widow believed to be docile, Anna of Courland, second daughter of Ivan V. Aiming at limited monarchy, Golitsyn induced the council to adopt "Conditions" obligating the new ruler to act only with the Supreme Privy Council's consent:

1. Not to start war with anyone.
2. Not to conclude peace.
3. Not to burden our loyal subjects with new taxes.
4. Not to promote to high ranks . . . above those of colonel, and not to appoint to high office, and to have the Guard and other regiments under the authority of the Supreme Privy Council.

---

[1] N. P. Pavlov-Silvanskii, "Ocherki po russkoi istorii . . . ," in *Sochineniia*, vol. 2 (St. Petersburg, 1910), pp. 378–79.

RIA-NOVOSTI/SOVFOTO

Empress Anna Ivanovna ruled from 1730 to 1740.

5. Not to deprive [members of] the nobility of life, property, and honor without trial.

6. Not to grant estates and villages.

7. Not to promote either Russians or foreigners to court offices.

8. Not to spend state revenues.[2]

---

[2] M. Raeff, *Plans for Political Reform in Imperial Russia, 1730–1905* (Englewood Cliffs, NJ, 1966), pp. 45–46.

Anna either had to observe these Conditions or lose the crown.

Apparently Golitsyn considered the Conditions a type of bill of rights and an initial step toward a constitutional monarchy dominated by the top aristocracy. "It would be highly expedient to limit the supreme authority by salutary laws," he explained. To top leaders assembled in the Kremlin palace, he declared that Russia had suffered grievously from Peter's despotism and from foreigners imported to operate it, and the council concurred. Three emissaries notified Anna Ivanovna of her selection, explained the Conditions, and secured her signature. The leading Petrine bureaucrats Iaguzhinskii and Prokopovich, however, opposing limited monarchy and council rule, encouraged her secretly to disregard the Conditions and make herself an autocrat.

As opposition to the Conditions and the Council mounted among the assembled gentry, the Council invited them to submit plans for political change. Variously estimated at from seven to 12, most of these proposals were hastily drafted and included specific gentry demands to ease state service and relax training requirements and inheritance laws. The Supreme Privy Council, however, became the chief target of the gentry. Rule by a narrow noble oligarchy, they feared, might take Russia the way of disintegrating aristocratic Poland. Recalling that court cliques had flourished under the early Romanovs, with sovereignty divided among princely families, and that periods without autocracy had produced turmoil and bloodshed, rank-and-file gentry opposed the Conditions strongly. V. N. Tatishchev's complete, well-argued proposal warned that aristocratic rule might bring Russia to ruin. Using Western political theory, notably that of Thomas Hobbes, he urged restoration of the autocracy. Encouraged by overwhelming gentry support for autocracy (and, some claim, popular backing as well) and aided by her powerful favorite, Biron, Anna convened the Senate and the Council of State. In a dramatic scene she tore up the Conditions, proclaimed herself autocratic empress, and ended an abortive attempt at limited monarchy for which tradition and popular support were lacking.

Anna Ivanovna's reign (1730–1740) remains controversial. Nationalist Russian historians have depicted it as a dark page in Russian history, with selfish German favorites exploiting the state, wasting its resources, and betraying national interests. But foreign predominance, notes A. Lipski, a Western historian, was not as great as has been believed. Germans dominated the cabinet, but the Senate remained Russian, and the administrative colleges had no more foreigners than they had under Peter the Great. Furthermore, Germans such as Field Marshal Münnich and Count Ostermann proved able, honest, and loyal to Russia. Under Münnich, president of the War College, "the Russian army was put upon the respectable footing it has since maintained, and a discipline till then unknown was introduced into the troops, thus finishing the work begun by Peter I."[3] Few antinational tendencies are evident in official policies of the 1730s. Anna began her reign with a traditional coronation in the Moscow Kremlin, and in 1732 the court returned to St. Petersburg after four years in Moscow.

Anna, explains a contemporary, "was naturally gentle and compassionate, . . . but she had the fault of weak princes: allowing evil to be done in her name." Nationalists call her rule the Bironovshchina because of the dominant role of Biron (Bühren). This haughty, cruel man established the sinister Secret Chancellery, which arrested many highly placed dignitaries. In his reign of terror many were executed and more than 20,000 were sent to Siberia, often without trial or the empress's knowledge. This practice, in effect, represented a restoration of Peter I's secret police, the Preobrazhenskii Board (see Chapter 15). Executions, favoritism, and abuse of power had existed previously and would recur often. Terror against noblemen was designed partly to silence opponents of autocracy. In 1731 the Supreme Privy Council was abolished and replaced by a Cabinet of Ministers without whose consent nothing important could be done. At first Anna attended it and signed all decrees. When her interest flagged, the cabinet and Biron ruled Russia.

Anna Ivanovna's death (October 1740) brought a baby, Ivan VI, grandson of her sister, Catherine, to the throne, with the unpopular Biron as regent. Only three weeks later Biron was toppled by a palace coup led by Field Marshal Münnich and sent to Siberia. During the regency of Anna,

---

[3] C. H. von Manstein, *Contemporary Memoirs of Russia* (New York, 1968), p. 54.

RIA-NOVOSTI/SOVFOTO

Elizabeth I, empress of Russia from 1741 to 1762.

in court balls and intrigue, Elizabeth neglected government and the populace. Foreign diplomats testified to her inability to reach decisions; documents remained piled on her desk for weeks. Her learning was slight, and she believed that reading was unhealthy! To the joy of nationalists, Münnich and Ostermann were removed and top administrative posts went to native Russians, but Elizabeth promptly named as her heir the German Peter of Holstein (later Peter III), whose mother was Anna, daughter of Peter the Great. Some administrative colleges eliminated under Anna were restored, and the cabinet was abolished. At first Elizabeth presided over a restored Senate, but soon, wearying of personal rule, she turned matters over to her ministers and favorites. Her personal popularity enabled her to abolish the death penalty and release many political prisoners. Elizabeth's chief legacies were more than 15,000 dresses and immense debts (her courtiers followed her dubious example assiduously), but autocracy survived despite the vagaries and inattention of the autocrat.

Society and Economy

Under Peter's successors the *dvorianstvo* (gentry) achieved many cherished objectives and subjected a wretched peasantry to its complete authority. Seeking to satisfy grievances of noblemen in their petitions of 1730, Anna that very year created a third regiment of imperial guards, the Izmailovskii; but she unwisely named as its officers mostly Baltic Germans and Swedes. Biron's rule promoted the nobility's moral unity as the remaining titled noblemen became gentrified. In the relatively peaceful post-Petrine era the state needed fewer noble officers and became more concerned with the economic status of the *dvorianstvo*. Legislation of Anna's reign reinforced the noble's position as landowner and serf owner and eased the burdens of compulsory service, but it failed to satisfy the *dvoriane*, who wished to escape state service altogether. In 1727 many noble officers obtained long leaves without pay to put their

mother of Ivan VI, German favorites contended for power and wealth, aided by foreign ambassadors seeking Russia's international support. This interlude, considered disgraceful by Russian nationalists, ended with another coup on behalf of Elizabeth, the daughter of Peter the Great. Urged on by Lestocq, her doctor, and La Chétardie, the French ambassador, she led the guards in a torchlight procession to the imperial palace and arrested the baby emperor and his ministers. Elizabeth I (1741–1762), beautiful, charming, and popular with the guards, lacked inconvenient moral scruples. Generously rewarding the guards, she promised to deliver Russia from foreign rule. According to Mikhail Lomonosov's panegyric, "Like Moses Elizabeth had come to release Russia from the night of Egyptian servitude; like Noah she had saved Russia from an alien flood."

Elizabeth's return to Petrine policies was only superficial. Like her father, she was impatient, fond of fast travel, and oriented toward Europe, but she was pious, fearful, and indolent. Immersed estates in order. A decree of 1736, reducing compulsory state service to 25 years and allowing one son to remain to manage the estate, created a nonserving *dvoriane* element. Other noblemen, beginning service at the age of 20, could retire at 45 and administer their estates while still vigorous. After the Turkish War (1739) so many noble officers requested retirement that the government restricted the decree's application in order to prevent depletion of the officers corps.

The Cadet Corps, founded by Münnich and beginning to function in 1732, had mollified the gentry because it enabled them to become officers without first serving in the ranks. At first numbering only 200, its student body was soon increased to 360 but still enrolled only some of the prospective officer candidates. Its broad curriculum prepared noblemen for civil as well as military service. In 1732 Russian officer pay was made equivalent to that of foreigners. The state, however, retained tight control over noble education: By a decree of 1737 young nobles had to register for schooling at the age of seven and to take examinations in basic subjects. Those failing the tests could be enrolled as ordinary seamen, which Russian nobles considered a terrible fate.

Noble and state economic interests meshed closely. In 1731 the Senate revoked Peter's unpopular inheritance law of 1714 (see Chapter 16), which the gentry had evaded. Henceforth, immovable property could be divided equally among all heirs, and noblemen again fragmented their estates. *Pomestie* land came under full private ownership, which stimulated the interest of nobles in managing their estates. To encourage noblemen short on capital to revive neglected estates, the government opened a Noble Bank (1754), which loaned up to 10,000 rubles to an individual at low interest rates.

The state also extended the gentry's authority over private serfs. Responsible for the serfs' poll taxes since 1722, noblemen in 1731 became government agents to collect them. No longer could serfs obtain freedom by enlisting in the army, and landowners could order their serfs to marry and could prevent marriages of serfs outside the estate

that cost them labor power. A serf needed his lord's consent to work away from the estate or to purchase land. From 1734 landowners had been supposed to provide food and seed to serfs in hard times, but they rarely did so and the state seldom intervened. The government granted hereditary *dvoriane* a virtual monopoly of estates farmed by serfs by prohibiting other classes from owning such estates, thus separating the hereditary nobility juridically from other social groups.

As the social status of the peasants worsened, their poverty deepened. The Supreme Privy Council considered alleviating the peasant's lot, not because of humanitarian concern but because peasant flight deprived the state of taxpayers and army recruits and the gentry of revenues from rents. Entire villages fled to Poland, to the Don, and to Siberia, and when forcibly returned to an estate, they would often flee again with new companions. The threat of such flights prevented the landowners from raising money rents. The government was also plagued by numerous small-scale peasant uprisings, especially on monastic estates where conditions were particularly bad. Peasant bands, at times numbering thousands, fought pitched battles with government punitive detachments. The state's policy of resorting to military action and brutal punishments instead of seeking to alleviate causes of peasant discontent brought grievous depopulation of many rural areas. Landowners competed feverishly for peasants, who were then forced to pay the taxes of those who had fled. Weaker autocracy in St. Petersburg brought no respite to Russia's impoverished and unfortunate peasantry.

Russian towns continued a slow but steady growth. Especially in the more developed central provinces, there was a peasant influx into urban areas. In 1750, however, the towns still made up only about 3 percent of the total population, and the development of the merchant class, hampered by increasing state favoritism for gentry interests, by no means kept pace with the rapid growth of mercantile elements in western Europe.

The government, though caught between competing merchant and gentry commercial interests, sought with some success to foster Russia's domestic and foreign commerce. Bills of exchange were introduced for merchants in 1729, and a Commercial Bank opened in St. Petersburg in 1754. During the 1740s gentry entrepreneurship began on a significant scale, and in the 1750s the government turned over many state-owned metallurgical works to noblemen. The noblemen, however, proved unable to run them successfully. The gentry did set up flourishing alcohol distilling enterprises, mostly on their estates, as they sought extra income to pay for Western luxuries and travel abroad. As conflict between gentry and merchant entrepreneurs increased, the state granted the nobility a virtual monopoly of alcohol distilling and curtailed the merchants' trading rights. The state, however, stimulated domestic commerce by abolishing internal tolls and charges on the movement of goods (1753), creating virtually free domestic trade. Customs duties on imports made up the lost revenue in a return to Petrine protectionism. Few Russian merchants ventured abroad, and Russia's foreign commerce remained mostly in English hands.

The Anglo-Russian Treaty of 1734 was the era's most significant commercial agreement. England and Russia, though natural trading partners, had been at political odds for years, mainly over Russian naval power in the Baltic Sea. After Peter's death, deterioration of the Russian fleet and Russia's conciliatory approach reduced friction. When normal diplomatic relations were resumed by the two countries in 1731, the Russia Company, a private English concern, actively sought a commercial accord. Throughout the negotiations the English, anxious for markets, raw materials, and naval stores, took the initiative. The Anglo-Russian Treaty helped Russia's balance of payments considerably because Britain normally bought as many Russian goods as any two other countries and paid more cash to Russia than all other European nations combined. The English received most-favored-nation treatment and the right to sell some woolens cheaper than their competitors. Russian consumption of English cloth increased

markedly, and by 1760 average annual English exports to Russia were double the pretreaty level.

This was an era of recurrent budget deficits and incompetent state financial management. The government could not raise poll taxes without swelling the arrears of peasants, increasing their flight, and drawing gentry opposition. In fact, poll tax rates were reduced repeatedly but arrears remained high. To recover revenue lost from direct taxes, Senator P. I. Shuvalov, an enthusiastic amateur financier and project-maker, suggested raising the price of salt and spirits (state monopolies) and devaluating the coinage. Large state sums could not be discovered or accounted for: In 1749 the Senate, seeking back accounts from the College of State Revenue, threatened to lock up its members under guard until they submitted a report! State finances were further burdened by lavish court expenditures and large grants to favorites.

Culture and Westernization

In the considerable cultural gains of the post-Petrine era, the Imperial Court and emerging educational institutions sowed European ideas and values. In Russia court life had greater relative impact than in the West. Most prominent people were received at the Imperial Court, which then alternated between Moscow and St. Petersburg and transmitted its influence to regional centers and noble residences.

Under Anna, prominent, well-educated Germans in her administration (such as Ostermann) and reform-minded Russians (such as Prokopovich) fostered Westernization. The Academy of Sciences (founded 1725), aided by Anna's government, promoted geographic exploration, mapped Russia, and issued the first Russian atlas (1745). Attached to the academy was Russia's first university (opened 1748), whose secondary school educated some future Russian leaders. Under academy auspices was issued the *St. Petersburg News*, the second oldest Russian newspaper, with material drawn from European sources.

Under Elizabeth her favorite, Ivan Shuvalov, promoted educational progress. At his proposal the Senate authorized the opening of Moscow University (1755) with Shuvalov as rector. At first its lectures were mostly in Latin and its students were few, but public debates were held there. Only in the 19th century did it become a distinguished university. Shuvalov's plan to open secondary schools in provincial capitals and primary schools in larger towns was shelved, but two secondary schools opened in Moscow and one in Kazan. Hitherto educational institutions and printing presses had been fully state controlled, but in the 1750s the Academy of Sciences acted as its own censor and the number of printing presses doubled. French cultural influences increased, and prominent Russians corresponded with such philosophes as Voltaire and Diderot. French influences spread beyond court circles as the nobility's educational level rose. Official attitudes toward free expression remained negative, and professors were carefully supervised, but cultural secularization nonetheless caused some erosion of old attitudes and restrictions.

After 1730 a national Russian literature began to develop, fostered by writers who had lived and studied in the West. They adopted prevalent Western classicism but introduced Russian themes and improved the Russian literary language. Prince Antiokh Kantemir, a poet and diplomat, wrote satires that were published posthumously. Russia's first professional men of letters were Vasili Trediakovskii, a prolific translator and writer, and Alexander Sumarokov, a playwright and the director of St. Petersburg's first Russian theater (1756). Mikhail Lomonosov (1711–1765), a peasant's son who became professor of chemistry at the Academy of Sciences, was praised extravagantly by Soviet scholars as a genius and universal man who transformed literature, science, and history. Wrote Alexander Pushkin, the great 19th-century Russian poet:

> Combining unusual strength of will with unusual power of understanding, Lomonosov embraced all branches of knowledge. . . . His-

torian, rhetorician, mechanic, chemist, mineralogist, artist, and poet, he tried everything and penetrated everything.[4]

Less worthy were Lomonosov's odes praising Peter I and his successors and his role in suppressing his rivals' writings. Political and ideological factors, he declared, must prevail over scholarly objectivity. Nonetheless, Lomonosov contributed much to public enlightenment and was Russia's outstanding mid-18th-century intellectual figure.

Sound foundations were laid for the study of Russian history. Especially notable was V. N. Tatishchev's monumental *Russian History,* based on chronicles and other primary materials. At the Academy of Sciences G. F. Müller, a German scholar, who wrote the first thorough study of Siberia, promoted the Norman theory (see Chapter 2), provoking a heated controversy with the patriotic Lomonosov.

In the arts progress was modest. In 1736 an Italian opera company performed at court; under Elizabeth opera performances occurred regularly. An Italian architect, Bartolomeo Rastrelli, designed the magnificent Winter Palace and Smolny Convent, two of St. Petersburg's architectural gems. The National Academy of Arts, also founded by Ivan Shuvalov (1757), stimulated the development of the fine arts.

Foreign Relations

Peter the Great's successors sought sporadically to continue his policies abroad, which had made Russia a great European power. Frequent changes of ruler and political instability, however, encouraged foreign intrigue, bribery of Russian officials, and open interference in Russian affairs. Russian armies scored some major victories, but inept commanders and sudden shifts in state policy prevented significant gains in territory or prestige. Russia's attention focused on the Polish and Turk-

---

[4] Quoted in A. Morozov, *Lomonosov* (Moscow, 1965), pp. 7–8.

ish questions, with weakened Sweden a secondary concern. Nationalist historians such as Kliuchevskii blame German influence in St. Petersburg and unpatriotic diplomacy by German ministers such as Andrew Ostermann for Russia's lack of success abroad. Stalinist historians, however, regarded this as an era of preparation for solving the Polish question and praised Ostermann and A. P. Bestuzhev-Riumin as outstanding diplomats loyal to Russian national interests. Recent Western accounts tend to agree with them.

From 1725 to 1740 Ostermann, a German from Westphalia, formulated and directed Russian foreign policy. Taken into Russian service by Peter the Great and made his private secretary, Ostermann became vice chancellor of the College of Foreign Affairs in 1727. In the crisis of 1730 he feigned illness to avoid compromising himself. Schooled in intrigue, he emerged as Anna Ivanovna's leading diplomat. His contemporary C. H. von Manstein regarded Ostermann as an able minister who knew foreign interests and intentions and was quick of mind, hardworking, "and so incorruptible that he never accepted the least present from any foreign court."

> He had so strange a way of talking that very few persons could ever boast that they had succeeded in comprehending him. Very often foreign ministers, after a conversation of two hours with him, found on leaving his room that they knew nothing more than when they entered. All that he said and all that he wrote could be taken two ways. A master in subtlety and dissimulation, he had perfect command over his passions and could even shed tears when the occasion required.[5]

Ostermann's system was close alliance with Austria and opposition to France, which sought to restrict Russia's influence by supporting Sweden, Poland, and the Ottoman Empire against it. To counter France, Ostermann promoted peace and rapprochement with other European states and England.

In the early 1730s the Polish succession engrossed Ostermann's attention. The wholly dominant Polish aristocracy (*szlachta*) had reduced the elective monarchy to impotence, which encouraged foreign intervention in Polish affairs. The death of the Polish king Augustus II in 1733 provoked a power struggle between Stanislas Leszczynski, sponsored by France and Sweden, and Frederick Augustus, elector of Saxony, backed by Russia and Austria. Regarding Leszczynski's election as a threat to its position in eastern Europe, Russia sent in a powerful army. Leszczynski fled to Danzig but the Russians captured it, and a "confederation" of Polish nobles, obedient to Russia and Austria, elected Augustus III king of Poland. Russia's primacy in Polish affairs was confirmed, and France suffered a major diplomatic defeat.

Anna Ivanovna's ambitious and overconfident advisers led by Field Marshal Münnich provoked war with the Turks. Ill-defined frontiers and periodic raids into Russia by the Crimean Tatars, vassals of the sultan, provided pretexts for conflict. The Turks, opposing growing Russian influence in Poland and recalling the Pruth campaign of 1711 (see Chapter 15), had contempt for the Russian army. The Russian ambassador in Constantinople, however, reported that the Turkish forces were weak and that the Balkan Christians would rise at Russia's signal. Allied with Austria, Russian armies under Münnich gained repeated victories: They invaded the Crimea, captured Azov, Ochakov, and Jassy, and occupied Moldavia. But Russian commanders quarreled, victories went unexploited, and the army's supply system collapsed. Austria made a separate peace, and Russian heroism was largely nullified by inept handling of the peace negotiations with the Porte (the Ottoman government). The Treaty of Belgrade (1739), extravagantly celebrated in St. Petersburg, brought Russia little compensation for 100,000 casualties and millions of expended rubles. Azov was recovered but minus its fortifications. Russian warships and merchant vessels were barred from the Turkish-dominated Black Sea, and the sultan even denied Anna's imperial title.

---

[5] von Manstein, *Contemporary Memoirs,* pp. 334–35.

French mediation in arranging the Treaty of Belgrade improved Franco-Russian relations briefly. Marquis de la Chétardie, the new French ambassador in St. Petersburg, sought to wreck the Austro-Russian alliance and to oust Ostermann. He helped overthrow Ivan VI, enthrone Elizabeth, and remove Ostermann, who died in Siberian exile. A. P. Bestuzhev-Riumin, Ostermann's successor as head of the Foreign Affairs College, had to contend with La Chétardie, Dr. Lestocq, and a pro-Prussian clique around Peter of Holstein, heir to the throne. The French encouraged Sweden to attack Russia, but the Swedes were defeated at Vilmanstrand in Finland. The Treaty of Åbo (1743) reconfirmed the Treaty of Nystadt (see Chapter 15) and added more Finnish territory to Russia.

During the War of the Austrian Succession (1740–1748) Bestuzhev-Riumin resumed Ostermann's pro-Austrian course after overcoming pro-French and pro-Prussian groups. These conflicting court factions, however, helped make Russian policy indecisive and ineffective. La Chétardie, discredited by his intrigues, was expelled, and Bestuzhev-Riumin became chancellor. In 1746 Bestuzhev-Riumin renewed the Austrian alliance and secured an English subsidy for Russian forces protecting England's possessions in Hanover. Russia's role in the War of the Austrian Succession was minor, and it was excluded from the Austro-Prussian settlement of 1748. Bestuzhev-Riumin, having overcome the pro-Prussian faction at court, reached his peak of influence.

In 1756 the Westminster Convention produced an Anglo-Prussian alliance and a fundamental realignment of European powers. In this "Diplomatic Revolution" Russia joined with France and Austria, formerly traditional enemies, to combat growing Prussian power. In St. Petersburg pro-French and pro-British factions strove to win over Empress Elizabeth and bribe her ministers. Chancellor Bestuzhev-Riumin, noted Sir Charles Hanbury-Williams, the British ambassador, remarking that his salary would not allow him to live in his accustomed style, requested a large English pension. To his amazement Hanbury-Williams promised him 12,000 rubles annually for life. Bestuzhev-Riumin was also taking money from other foreign governments without altering his policy. Elizabeth and her ministers decided to join with France and Austria. Three strong-willed women—Elizabeth of Russia, Maria Theresa of Austria, and Madame de Pompadour of France—allied to destroy or weaken Frederick II of Prussia.

During the subsequent Seven Years' War (1756–1763) the 300,000-man Russian army fought bravely, only to be stymied by an incompetent command and St. Petersburg politics. Repeatedly the Russians defeated the great Frederick or fought him to a standstill; they invaded East Prussia, occupied Berlin, and were in a position to dominate central Europe. Contemplating suicide, Frederick was saved by Elizabeth's death (January 1762), which abruptly ended Russia's participation in the war. Peter of Holstein, now Tsar Peter III, reversed Russian policy overnight and threw away Russia's hard-won wartime gains. An admirer of Frederick and the Prussian army, Peter immediately recalled Russian troops, allied with Prussia, and prepared to attack Denmark.

The lavish expenditure of Russian lives and treasure in mid-18th-century wars produced few lasting results. Under Empress Elizabeth Russia continued to play an important role in European power politics and increased its influence in Poland but could not exploit its advantages in manpower and resources. Ostermann's and Bestuzhev-Riumin's pro-Austrian orientation, though hampered by court intrigue and coups d'état, proved sound because Austria was Russia's natural ally against the Ottoman Empire, its most dangerous neighbor.

Conclusion

Denunciations of the era of palace revolutions by Russian nationalist historians appear exaggerated and unduly critical. However, the efforts of Western scholars to rehabilitate the frivolous, inconsequential rulers of this period are not very convincing either. Some of Peter I's policies of domestic reform and expansion abroad continued, and others were reversed, but none was implemented consistently. The short-lived, poorly led governments of these years could not tackle Russia's basic problems of poverty, inefficiency, and corruption. The rulers, often unworthy or uninterested in governing, tended to turn matters over to favorites. Autocracy, threatened in 1730, survived even without capable autocrats largely because the alternatives appeared even worse. The atmosphere of fear, suspicion, and gloom, described by numerous contemporaries, marked little improvement over the Petrine era. Meanwhile, the ascendancy of the nobility and the degradation of the enserfed masses gathered force. More positively, Westernization, education of the elite, and economic and cultural growth continued. There was some respite from Peter I's incessant wars. Should one view this as a period of recovery and relaxation of state pressures or, as nationalist historians affirm, an epoch of humiliation at the hands of greedy foreign favorites? Do the numerous irregular changes of ruler and the repeated coups qualify this as a "second time of troubles"? The answers to these questions depend on one's perspective. However, clearly Russia was directly involved now in the vortex of European diplomacy. The Russian Empire had become a full-fledged European power.

Suggested Additional Reading

BOOKS

CROSS, A. *By the Banks of the Thames: Russians in Eighteenth Century Britain* (Newtonville, MA, 1980).

DANIELS, R. V. *V. N. Tatishchev: Guardian of the Petrine Revolution* (Philadelphia, 1973).

KAPLAN, H. *Russia and the Outbreak of the Seven Years' War* (Berkeley, 1968).

KUDRYAVTSEV, B. B. *The Life and Work of Mikhail V. Lomonosov* (Moscow, 1954).

LEONARD, C. S. *Reform and Regicide: The Reign of Peter III of Russia* (Bloomington, IN, 1993).

MANSTEIN, C. H. VON. *Contemporary Memoirs of Russia . . . 1727–1744* (New York, 1968).

MARHER, G. *Publishing, Printing and the Origins of Intellectual Life in Russia, 1700–1800* (Princeton, 1985).

MEEHAN-WATERS, B. *Autocracy and Aristocracy and the Russian Service Elite of 1730* (New Brunswick, NJ, 1982).

PAPMEHL, K. A. *Freedom of Expression in Eighteenth Century Russia* (The Hague, 1971).

RAEFF, M., ed. *Plans for Political Reform in Imperial Russia, 1730–1905* (Englewood Cliffs, NJ, 1966).

READING, D. K. *The Anglo-Russian Commercial Treaty of 1734* (New Haven, 1938).

ROGGER, H. *National Consciousness in Eighteenth Century Russia* (Cambridge, MA, 1960).

ARTICLES

BELOFF, M. "Russia," in *Readings in Russian History,* vol. 1, ed. S. Harcave (New York, 1962), pp. 265–77.

CRACRAFT, J. "The Succession Crisis of 1730," *CanAmSlSt* 12, no. 1 (1978): 61–84.

DANIELS, R. L. "V. N. Tatishchev and the Succession Crisis of 1730," *SEER* 49 (1971): 550–59.

DASHWOOD, F. "Sir Francis Dashwood's Diary . . . " *SEER* 38 (1959): 194–222.

DUKES, P., and B. MEEHAN-WATERS. "A Neglected Account of the Succession Crisis of 1730 . . ." *CanAmSlSt* 12, no. 1 (1978): 170–83.

DVOICHENKO-MARKOV, D. "Demetrius Kantemir and Russia." *BS* 12, no. 2: 383–99.

HASSELL, J. "Implementation of the Russian Table of Ranks . . ." *SR* 29 (1970): 283–95.

HUNT, N. C. "The Russia Company and the Government, 1730–42." *OSP* 7 (1957): 27–65.

HUNTINGTON, W. C. "Michael Lomonosov and Benjamin Franklin . . ." *RR* 18 (1959): 294–306.

KAHAN, A. "Continuity in Economic Activity and Policy during the Post-Petrine Period in Russia." *JEH* 25 (1965): 61–85.

———. "The Costs of Westernization in Russia . . ." *SR* 25 (1966): 40–66.

KEEP, J. L. "The Secret Chancellery, the Guards, and the Dynastic Crisis of 1740–41." *FOG* 25: 169–93.

LEDONNE, J. P. "The Evolution of the Governor's Office, 1727–64." *CanAmSlSt* 12, no. 1 (1978): 86–115.

LIPSKI, A. "The 'Dark Era' of Anna Ivanovna." *ASEER* 15 (1956): 477–88.

LODGE, R. "Russia, Prussia, and Great Britain, 1742–44." *EHR* 45 (1930): 579–611.

MATLEY, I. "Defense Manufactures of St. Petersburg, 1703–1730." *Geographic Rev.* 71, no. 4 (1981): 411–26.

SCHULZE, L. "The Russification of the St. Petersburg Academy of Sciences and Arts in the Eighteenth Century." *Brit. Jour. for the Hist. of Science* 18, no. 3 (1985): 305–35.

WHITTAKER, C. "The Reforming Tsar: The Rededefinition of Autocratic Duty in 18th Century Russia." *SR* 51, no. 1 (Spring 1992): 77–98.

18

Catherine II Rules and Expands Russia, 1762–1796

In June 1762 a pretty German princess of unusual ability and determination removed her weakling husband from the throne and ruled the Russian Empire as Catherine II. Peter III, her husband, had ruled barely six months but had antagonized many powerful individuals and groups. Nonetheless, in the popular mind he was long credited with liberal policies. The entire period 1762–1796 is often designated the era of Catherine the Great for the remarkable woman who so greatly impressed her contemporaries in Russia and Europe. Some Soviet historians considered her reign an age of enlightened absolutism that aimed to reinforce the nobility's social and political dominance against a rising bourgeoisie. Catherine's rule, they suggested, was a great show from start to finish, revealing effective use of propaganda and publicity by a master craftswoman. Slogans of the European Enlightenment were employed to defend autocracy, serfdom, and expansionism. Most Western scholars, on the other hand, accept Catherine's pretensions as a liberal ruler at first but conclude that the Pugachov Revolt and the French Revolution induced her regime to adopt more rigid and repressive

policies. Was Catherine a true autocrat, or was her regime dominated by favorites and the ruling nobility? How significant were her regime's reforms of provincial government? Did the partitions of Poland with the German powers strengthen or eventually weaken Russia's position in Europe?

Peter III and the Coup of June 1762

After Empress Elizabeth's death in January 1762 Peter of Holstein mounted the throne without opposition as Peter III. At age 13 this grandson of Peter the Great had been summoned to Russia by his aunt, Empress Elizabeth, to become heir to the throne. Despite some efforts to rehabilitate him,[1] Peter was an immature, poorly educated, narrow-minded Holsteiner, scornful of Russian customs and religion. Orphaned in childhood, Peter acted childishly and remained an adolescent mentally

---

[1] M. T. Florinsky, *Russia,* vol. 1 (New York, 1953), pp. 496–99.

211

throughout his life. He worshiped Frederick II of Prussia and Frederick's army but never progressed much beyond playing with soldiers. Although he learned Russian and the Orthodox catechism, Peter remained at heart a German Lutheran. Surrounded by Holsteiners, he sought to build his own little world divorced from things Russian.

During his brief reign some important decrees were issued, attributable more to his advisers' efforts to strengthen their position than to Peter's desire for change. Many political prisoners were freed, and the security police was abolished. Old Believers, allowed to return from exile, were given freedom of worship, and the salt tax was reduced to win lower-class support. Most important, Peter's manifesto of February 18, 1762, freed the nobility from compulsory state service in peacetime and allowed nobles to travel freely abroad and to enter the service of friendly foreign powers.

Other actions, which alienated influential elements, suggest that Peter neither sought personal popularity nor realized the significance of his actions. Church estates were secularized and placed under an Economic College. Wishing to make the church Lutheran, Peter treated Orthodoxy with contempt. He alienated top noblemen by attacking the Senate's powers. Equally foolish was his open admiration for Frederick of Prussia. Wearing Prussian uniforms and decorations, he insisted the guards do likewise. Imposing strict discipline on guards officers, he required them to march in parades. His preference to his Holsteiners for military and civil posts alienated Russian elements vital to his power.

Peter's abrupt reversal of Russian foreign policy hastened his removal. Ending participation in the Seven Years' War against Prussia, he yielded all of Russia's costly gains. The war had been unpopular and many Russians admired Frederick, but Peter's Holstein patriotism, leading him into war against Denmark, triggered his fall. Peter's blatant insults to Russian national feeling and Orthodoxy, and his irregular private life and capricious, irresponsible behavior, compounded his unpopularity. He antagonized leaders and groups as if seeking

deliberately to destroy himself. The public prepared to welcome another ruler.

Catherine, Peter's wife, exploited the growing disaffection to seize power. To her former lover Stanislas Poniatowski she wrote: "Peter III had lost the little wit he had. He ran his head against everything. He wanted to break up the Guards. . . . He wanted to change his religion, marry Elizabeth Vorontsov, and shut me up." The ambitious Catherine catered to Russian Orthodoxy and tradition and dissociated herself from Peter's unpopular policies. When he proposed to lead the guards against Denmark, her opportunity came. After one of their number (P. B. Passek) was arrested, the conspirators moved swiftly.

Early on the morning of June 28 Alexis Orlov, brother of Catherine's lover, Gregory, awakened her at Peterhof Palace: "It is time to get up; all is ready for your proclamation." At the Izmailovskii Regiment's barracks, recalled Catherine, "the soldiers came running out, kissing me, . . . and calling me their deliverer. They began swearing allegiance to me." The other regiments joined her readily. In nearby St. Petersburg the Senate and Synod proclaimed Peter's dethronement, and Catherine was named autocratic empress in Kazan Cathedral. Leading many troops as a colonel of the Preobrazhenskii Regiment, Catherine marched toward Peterhof. Peter sought support at the Kronstadt naval base but was not permitted to land. He returned despondently to Oranienbaum and abdicated meekly. Taken to a nearby estate by Alexis Orlov, he soon died under suspicious circumstances. Catherine's highly colored account reads:

> Fear had given him a diarrhoea which lasted three days; . . . on the fourth he drank excessively. . . . The only things he asked me for were his mistress, his dog, his Negro, and his violin; but for fear of scandal . . . , I only sent him the last three things. . . . The hemorrhoidal colic . . . affected his brain. . . . Despite all the assistance of the doctors, he expired whilst demanding a Lutheran priest. I feared that the officers might have poisoned him, so I had him opened. . . . Inflammation of the bowels and a stroke of apoplexy had carried him off. His

heart was extraordinarily small and quite decayed.[2]

Catherine denied rumors of foul play, but it is generally accepted that Alexis Orlov strangled Peter either on his own initiative or upon Catherine's orders.

Catherine II—Woman and Ruler

Catherine was born as Sophie in 1729 to the ruling family of Anhalt-Zerbst, a small German state on the Baltic. Her education was undistinguished, and her financial and marital prospects were slender. Then in 1744 Empress Elizabeth invited her and her mother to the Russian court. Elizabeth had been engaged to a brother of Sophie's mother, and her elder sister had married the duke of Holstein; so the empress regarded them as part of her family. To stabilize Russia's political future, Elizabeth wanted Grand Duke Peter safely married. En route to Russia, mother and daughter conferred in Berlin with Frederick II, who recruited the mother and charged her to get Elizabeth to ally with Prussia. At the Russian frontier, they were greeted as honored guests of the empress. Rumors spread that Sophie was destined to marry Peter, heir to the throne. Young Sophie, casting her spell over Elizabeth, resolved to remain in Russia, though her mother, soon unmasked as a Prussian spy, was expelled.

Sophie paid court to Peter, who, by her account, was ugly, immature, and boastful. She studied Russian assiduously and won goodwill at the imperial court. Converted to Orthodoxy "without any effort," she was christened Catherine (Ekaterina Alekseevna) and in 1745 married Peter. Her 17-year cohabitation with that perpetual adolescent tested her patience and ambition fully. Catherine described one of Peter's pastimes: In his apartment she saw a large rat hanging from the ceiling. Peter explained that for eating two wax sentries, it had been court-martialed and executed

Catherine II.

and would remain in public view for three days. Soon Paul was born, son of Catherine and probably the courtier Serge Saltykov. Catherine busied herself with amorous adventures, extensive reading, and the study of court politics. She came to the throne as the best-educated, most literate ruler in Russian history. Ambition, vitality, and political shrewdness were her outstanding traits. "I will rule or I shall die," she told the English ambassador in 1757. Frederick II wrote in 1778: "The empress of Russia is very proud, very ambitious, and very vain." Her actions as ruler confirmed the truth of his remarks.

The dubious means by which she achieved power at first helped determine how she ruled. In initial manifestos she posed as a national ruler brought to the throne by public demand and denounced Peter III as a foreigner. "All true sons of Russia have clearly seen the great danger to which the whole Russian Empire has actually been exposed." The foundations of Orthodoxy had been threatened with destruction, and "the

[2] W. Walsh, ed. *Readings in Russian History* (Syracuse, NY, 1959), pp. 186–87.

glory Russia has acquired at the expense of so much blood . . . has been trampled underfoot by the peace lately concluded [with Prussia]." Catherine depicted herself as a defender of Russia's faith and institutions to get the public to forget that she was a German usurper without legitimate claim to the throne and to foster the loyalty of key groups to her regime.

Insecurity induced Catherine to act at first like an official who feared imminent dismissal and to compare herself with a hare being chased in all directions. In state matters she relied principally upon Count Nikita I. Panin, the only experienced statesman among the conspirators, who acted as the de facto chancellor. However, his proposal for a small, permanent Imperial Council to advise the ruler on legislation was blocked by rival court groups and shelved by Catherine. New youthful courtiers like the Orlovs and Princess Dashkova, who rode into power with her, at first treated her as their creature and swarmed around seeking rewards of money, estates, and offices. Catherine was saved from becoming a figurehead by the greed and contention of court factions. At times she heeded the Orlovs' advice and showered favors upon them, but she played them against the Panin group, balancing astutely between these rival elements while building her own power. Early in her reign, to overcome her inadequate knowledge of Russian conditions and the court's isolation from the populace, Catherine undertook excursions to the northeast, the Volga region, and the Baltic provinces, accompanied by a huge suite and the entire diplomatic corps.

For years Catherine's right to the throne was questioned, and abroad many believed that her reign would be brief. She worried about the claims of Ivan VI, imprisoned at Schlüsselberg Fortress since infancy, until in 1764 he was killed by her orders during a rescue attempt by a disgruntled army officer. Even his death failed to dispel the pretenderism produced by Catherine's usurpation and by popular discontent. Three pretenders emerged in 1764 alone and 10 in the next decade, who claimed to be Peter III resurrected, of whom

Emelian Pugachov was the most famous (see Chapter 19). Unlike Catherine, her son Paul possessed a legitimate, hereditary claim to the throne. The Panin faction wished Paul to obtain some power when he came of age in 1772, but Catherine opposed this faction and blocked its efforts. She proclaimed invariably that she was empress by divine plan and popular demand.

Insecurity at home made foreign support and approbation more crucial. In Catherine's correspondence with the philosophes she fostered her reputation as an enlightened monarch. Montesquieu's *Spirit of Laws*, she boasted, stood by her bedside; she urged Diderot to complete the *Encyclopédie* in St. Petersburg. Catherine subsidized the philosophes generously and sought their advice on how to administer Russia. In return, praising her enlightened absolutism, they called her the "Semiramis of the North."

Catherine employed a series of favorites who shared her bed but rarely her power. Ten official favorites in turn occupied quarters next to hers and were loaded with decorations, money, and estates. Gregory Potemkin was by far the most powerful, and only he remained an important statesman after ceasing to be her lover. In old age Catherine chose 22-year-old Platon Zubov. She loved them passionately, especially Gregory Orlov and Potemkin, and she treated her discarded lovers generously, but she alone decided when they must leave the imperial presence. This system enabled her to preserve autocratic power while indulging a sentimental, amorous nature.

The empress, the government's motive force, showed a Germanic devotion to hard, regular labor. Rising regularly at 5:00 A.M., she worked long hours as the true first servant of the state. In 1769 she established the Imperial Council as the chief central political institution. Containing the empire's seven most powerful men, with Catherine presiding, it discussed frankly and secretly vital national issues, especially foreign policy, but it remained purely advisory and in no way limited Catherine's authority. Working closely with her were four or five state secretaries and a few clerks who constituted a type of imperial chancery.

The Legislative Commission

Typical of Catherine's enlightened absolutism were the Legislative Commission and her *Instruction (Nakaz)* to it (see Problem 5 at the end of this chapter). Catherine's travels about Russia in the early 1760s convinced her of the urgent need to replace the antiquated Law Code of 1649 and recast Russian institutions. She set out to become Russia's Justinian and for two years labored over her *Instruction* to the commission, which would provide the government with information about public grievances and desires as a basis for action.

Her manifesto of December 1766 summoned into being a Legislative Commission, reminiscent of the *zemskii sobor* of 1648–1649, to draw up a new law code with the aid of the *Instruction.* The clergy were excluded from the commission as too oppositionist, whereas the nobility (139 deputies) elected one delegate per district. Property-holding townspeople chose 216 delegates; state peasants, 24; single householders, 43; Cossacks, 43; and non-Russians, 51. Deputies from central state institutions (the colleges, Senate, and Synod) brought the total to some 568, too many to compose articles of a law code. The deputies arrived with instructions (*nakazy*) from their constituents somewhat resembling the *cahiers* (instructions) to the French Estates General of 1789. Noble *nakazy* complained about the problems of purchasing and selling estates because of red tape and about competition from merchants; they requested corporate organization for their class. Townsmen countered with demands for a monopoly of commerce, the right to own serfs, and urban self-government. The state peasantry complained of inadequate land.

When the commission convened in July 1767, Metropolitan Dmitri, the church's sole representative, proposed that Catherine be recognized as "the great, wise mother of her country." Using the assembly to legitimate her power, Catherine advertised it to Europe through the philosophes. Once it began discussing a law code and preparing one in 19 committees, official interest in it waned and government deputies rarely attended.

Although 203 sessions of the commission were held, not a single article was drafted. The commission could only discuss and reflect public opinion, not legislate. Confused by Catherine's highly theoretical, vague *Instruction,* the deputies, many of whom were illiterate and unprepared for their work, wrangled among themselves. The old aristocracy urged abolition of the Table of Ranks for admitting people of nonnoble origin, but the service gentry defeated that proposal. Courageous statements by a few deputies urging limitations on serfdom alarmed the government. A noble deputy, Gregory Korobin, advocated breaking the lord's unlimited power over his serfs, giving serfs property rights, and limiting their obligations by law.

Although Catherine used the commission to strengthen her autocracy, she refused to let it limit her power. The philosophe Diderot hoped that it would become permanent, but after the Russo-Turkish War began in 1768, Catherine prorogued the commission, though some of its committees worked until 1774. Their proposals for reforming provincial and urban government were used in subsequent imperial legislation. Diderot commented sadly: "The Russian empress is doubtless a despot."

Administrative Changes

At her accession, Catherine recalled later, the government was near collapse and unable to perform its functions. State credit was poor, the deficit was large, and governmental institutions lay in disorder, run by incompetent and corrupt officials. The Senate, supposed to supervise the administration, could handle little business and was, in Catherine's words, "apathetic and deaf." Catherine ignored proposals to transform the Senate into an elected legislature of 600 to 800 members. Instead, in 1763 it was divided into six specialized departments and its staff considerably enlarged. Though the Senate's political importance declined further, it could handle much more business promptly and efficiently. Rather than consult directly with the Senate, Catherine enhanced the powers of the procurator general, a post held for

many years by the industrious and loyal Prince
A. A. Viazemskii. By 1768 Catherine could already
point to major achievements in central administration: considerable surplus revenues, former
debts paid, and state credit restored. The state's
capacity to govern improved dramatically. During
the 1780s several administrative colleges, superfluous because of provincial reform, were closed.
In the chief colleges—the army, the admiralty, and
foreign affairs—one-man administration had by
then largely replaced former collective decision
making. Finally, the Table of Ranks was reorganized, the number of officials increased considerably, and their salaries raised. Corruption,
although not eliminated, was reduced to more
tolerable levels.

In local government the empress could act as
an enlightened despot without imperiling autocracy. In the 1760s the salaries of most provincial
officials were raised, and their jurisdiction was
clarified. Appointed procurators supervised all
levels of provincial administration, and governors
were encouraged to exercise real authority and
initiative. Such bureaucratic absolutism failed to
prevent the Pugachov Revolt of 1773–1774 (see
Chapter 19), but the revolt brought the state and
nobility into closer harmony and cooperation and
revealed the incapacity of the old local administration. Afterward, concern for internal security stimulated Catherine to carry out far-reaching reform,
a move that was also prompted by the vastness
of the old provinces, territorial and population
increases, and the nobility's expressed desire to
participate in local government. Using materials
from the Legislative Commission and private
petitions to the Senate, Catherine drafted most of
the Fundamental Law of 1775. She boasted to
Voltaire: "This is the fruit of five months' work
carried out by me alone."

The Fundamental Law became the basis of
Catherine's domestic policy for the rest of her
reign, and its institutions lasted until 1861. By now
she was a complete and experienced autocrat
served by able and loyal officials, and the reforms
owed much to the advice of Jakob Sievers, the able
and industrious governor of Novgorod. Provincial

administration was rationalized and simplified.
The former *gubernii* and *provintsii* were replaced
with 41 new *gubernii.* By the end of Catherine's
reign territorial expansion had increased this
number to 50, a number that changed little to the
end of the empire. Each *guberniia,* with 300,000 to
400,000 male "souls," was divided into districts
(*uezdy*) with 20,000 to 30,000 "souls." The top
regional official was the viceroy (*namestnik*), who
administered two to four *gubernii* along the frontiers with semiregal authority. The Tula governor-
generalship was inaugurated with an elaborate
ceremony in a great hall in which the new viceroy
addressed the assembled nobility from the steps of
a throne beneath the empress's portrait. A governor (*gubernator*) headed each *guberniia,* and the
gubernii received a uniform administrative structure. As Montesquieu had advised, administrative,
judicial, and financial functions (but not powers)
were carefully separated. State decrees were transmitted to the *gubernii* through a provincial board
over which the governor presided. A subsidiary
board supervised tax collection, expenditures, and
economic affairs, and a Board of Public Charity ran
schools and hospitals. A police official (*kapitan-
ispravnik*), elected by the nobility, administered
each *uezd.* Except for Moscow and St. Petersburg,
which had the status of provinces, towns were run
by lower-ranking state-appointed officials.

The provincial court system reflected mainly
noble desires and Montesquieu's principles. Criminal and civil courts were established in each
guberniia capital while at the district and local
levels separate courts for nobility, townspeople,
and peasantry perpetuated old estate distinctions.
Catherine introduced English-style courts to reconcile complainants and plaintiffs and to free
those arrested without due cause, but these courts
decided only minor cases.

In 1785 Catherine's Charter to the Towns (and
Charter to the Nobility) (see Chapter 19) completed the recasting of regional administration.
The growth of commercial and monetary relationships in towns and urban petitions preceded
changes in town government. The urban population was divided into six categories based on

property, education, and wealth, including all urban property holders of whatever estate, and commercial and industrial elements were divided into guilds by wealth. A complex system of town self-government emerged that guaranteed control to men of wealth. A town assembly (*duma*) would select a six-member board to run urban services. These elective institutions were supervised by the provincial governor.

In frontier regions and newly incorporated territories Catherine pursued vigorous centralization and Russification. Favoring a single system of imperial administration, she disregarded national differences and destroyed remnants of autonomy. In 1764 she confided to Prince Viazemskii that perhaps Ukrainian and Baltic rights could not be abolished immediately, but "to call them foreign and treat them as such would be more than a mistake; it would be, indeed, plain stupidity."[3]

The full weight of this repressive policy struck Ukraine, where the autonomous tradition of the Cossacks still threatened Russian control. In 1768 Russian troops crushed an uprising by ordinary Cossacks against the elite (*starshina*), and seven years later the Sich itself was suddenly attacked and destroyed. *Starshina* aristocrats cooperating with Russia were rewarded with officer rank and estates. Some rank-and-file Cossacks, rather than submit, fled to the Ottoman Empire. Volga, Ural, and Don Cossacks also lost their freedom, and the Russian army absorbed their regiments. In 1781 the last remnants of Ukrainian autonomy were snuffed out: The left-bank Ukraine became a governor-generalship of three provinces ruled by Russians. The Baltic provinces' special status also ended: After a census had been conducted, the poll tax was introduced, and in 1783 the region became a governor-generalship.

Prince Potemkin, Catherine's powerful favorite and empire builder, ruled newly acquired areas in south Russia and the north Caucasus effectively. With his military background, administrative skill, and physical attractiveness to Catherine, he rose

rapidly until he headed the War College and all administration in "New Russia." In the 1780s with unremitting energy he settled colonists and built towns, notably Sevastopol, a naval base in the Crimea, and Ekaterinoslav on the Dnieper. Potemkin's work in the south strengthened Russia economically and enhanced its power in the Black Sea. In 1784 he was given large state funds to organize a triumphal visit of Catherine and Joseph II of Austria to "New Russia." From St. Petersburg to Kiev, stations were built and supplied with horses taken from the populace, triumphal arches constructed, and villages erected. Foreign observers, perhaps jealous of these successes, asserted that Potemkin's villages were made of cardboard, originating the expression "Potemkin village," but his achievements in bringing order and prosperity to a vast region were undeniable. He died theatrically in 1791 on an Oriental rug in the midst of the steppe and was buried in the city of Cherson on the Dnieper.

External Affairs

Catherine II has been called "the Great" partly for her diplomatic and military victories. At home she faced peasant revolts, pretenders, and noble opposition; abroad she could exhibit her diplomatic flair and satisfy her ambition. During her reign Russia's territory, prestige, and international importance increased markedly, though at heavy cost. The results of her diplomacy remain debatable, especially the alliance with Prussia and the partitions of Poland. A friendly and allied Poland, if feasible, might have proved preferable to one divided with the German powers.

At Catherine's accession, Russia's chief external concerns were Poland and the Ottoman Empire. Immediate Russian objectives were to advance southward to the Black Sea, to cultivate the rich grainlands of southern Ukraine, and to develop foreign trade, but all of this was impossible while the Crimean Tatars, Turkish vassals, controlled the northern Black Sea coast. Russia's goals in Poland were, for national and religious reasons, to annex largely Orthodox Belorussia and western Ukraine

---

[3] Florinsky, *Russia,* vol. 1, p. 555.

and to gain security from a potential western invasion. The international situation seemed favorable: Prussia had been weakened in the Seven Years' War (1756–1763); Austria had suffered heavy losses; Sweden was no longer a major threat; and the Ottoman Empire had begun to decline. Only Russia emerged from the Seven Years' War with unimpaired resources.

Catherine, like Peter I, directed Russian foreign policy personally. She told Potemkin: "I wish to rule for myself and let Europe know it!" Schooled in intrigue since childhood, she soon mastered contemporary diplomatic techniques. Russia's greatness, she realized, would exalt her own and lessen her dependence on the nobility. By hard work, knowledge of Europe, patience, and courage, she surmounted all external crises with great aplomb. To restore Russia's prestige, shaken by Peter III's policies, she broke his alliance with Prussia and announced: "Time will show everyone that we won't follow anyone's tail." Toward Europe, Catherine's tone was confident, though she realized that Russia needed five years of peace to restore its finances and guarantee domestic order.

For almost 20 years her chief assistant in foreign affairs was Nikita I. Panin, senior member of the Foreign Affairs College and architect of the Northern System. Catherine supported this capable nobleman until his pro-Prussian policy became outdated. His Northern System aimed to align satisfied powers (Russia and Prussia) against attempts at revenge by disgruntled Austria and to remove hostile French influence from Russia's borders. The nucleus of the system was the Russo-Prussian Alliance of 1764, which sought to preserve the status quo in Poland and Sweden, thus guaranteeing their impotence. Panin also secured an alliance with Denmark, and Great Britain in 1766 signed a commercial treaty. Until 1768, though opposed by some influential Russians, the Northern System appeared to achieve its aims.

Events in neighboring Poland had inclined Catherine to adopt Panin's concept. Then in turmoil, Poland remained one of Europe's largest countries, with about 280,000 square miles and more than 11 million people. However, an elective kingship and domination by a few powerful magnate families had gravely undermined royal power and resources. When King Augustus III died in 1763, Russia and Prussia backed Stanislas Poniatowski, Catherine's former lover and member of the pro-Russian faction, as his successor. As to the unimpressive Poniatowski, Catherine confided that "he had less right [to the throne] than the others and thus should be all the more grateful to Russia." Refusing to marry him, Catherine urged Poniatowski to wed a Catholic Pole before the Diet convened. The other major candidate, the elector of Saxony, was supported by Austria, France, and most Poles. To ensure a "free" election, Russia bribed members of the Diet and surrounded its chamber with troops. Poniatowski's election in September 1764 gave Panin his first success over the Catholic powers.

In their controversial alliance of 1764 Russia and Prussia agreed to maintain Polish institutions unaltered and to seek equal rights for Orthodox and Protestant minorities. The alliance, claimed a Soviet account,[4] allowed Russia to dominate Poland, play a major European role at slight cost, and restrain the sultan. Kliuchevskii, however, viewed it as a blunder because exhausted Prussia needed Russia, not vice versa. Earlier Catherine had called Prussia Russia's worst enemy; so now she had to change her tune.[5]

At first Catherine used the Prussian alliance to consolidate Russia's position in Poland. Supported by patriotic elements, Poniatowski planned major constitutional reforms. However, Russia and Prussia insisted that Poland retain its archaic elective monarchy and the liberum veto,[6] under which a single opposition vote could defeat any measure introduced into the Diet. Catherine supported the claims of Polish Orthodox dissidents, especially

---

[4] V. P. Potemkin, ed., *Istoriia diplomatii*, vol. 1 (Moscow, 1941), p. 287.

[5] V. O. Kliuchevskii, *Kurs russkoi istorii*, vol. 5 (Moscow, 1937), p. 37.

[6] A free veto held by all members of the Diet that could block legislation or election of a king.

numerous in Lithuania and eastern Poland, to equal religious, civil, and political rights with the Catholic majority. To win Catherine's support, their spokesman in Russia, Bishop Koniski, declared that the dissidents were her loyal subjects. She exploited their cause to gain increased leverage in Poland. When the Diet of 1766 refused to accord the dissidents political equality, Catherine ringed Warsaw with Russian troops until it gave in. A Russo-Polish treaty of February 1768 placed Poland's constitution under Russia's protection "for all time to come." Freedom of worship was proclaimed, and dissidents were accorded full civil and political rights. In March 1768 conservative Polish patriots formed the "Confederation of Bar" in Ukraine against the Russian-dominated regime in Warsaw and sought Austrian and French backing. As Poniatowski's weak rule threatened to collapse, the Polish Senate requested Russian "protection." A four-year struggle ensued before the Russian army could crush the confederacy and bring Poland under complete Russian domination.

The Polish issue now became linked with the Turkish problem. To prevent Russia from absorbing Poland, Austria and France bribed Turkish officials, who used an accidental Russian border crossing as a pretext to declare war on Russia. Though Russia was unprepared, Catherine was confident of victory. Her forces, superior in training, equipment, and command, invaded the Danubian Principalities (Moldavia and Wallachia) and largely freed them from Turkish rule. Using Balkan Christians against the Turks, Catherine urged them to revolt. A Russian fleet, advised by British officers, defeated the Turks at Chesme and Scio, but the Balkan Christian risings failed. The Russians captured Azov and Taganrog and occupied the Crimea, revealing their rising power. Soon both sides wanted peace. Russian finances were strained, and plague raged in Moscow. Austria sought to halt the war in order to prevent Ottoman dismemberment, and Frederick II of Prussia urged Poland's partition, threatening to cancel his alliance with Russia otherwise. Catherine agreed reluctantly to a partition to avoid conflict with the German powers. Over Poniatowski's

objections the three eastern powers each occupied part of Poland (see Map 18.1). Russia acquired eastern Belorussia and part of Latvia while Prussia and Austria took mainly lands inhabited by Poles. Russian gains may have been justified on national grounds, but they undermined Polish independence.

When the Russo-Turkish War resumed, Austria withdrew support from the Porte, but France urged the Turks to continue fighting. Though Russia's efforts were complicated by the Pugachov Revolt, during 1773–1774 General P. A. Rumiantsev and the brilliant new general, A. S. Suvorov, won repeated victories, crossed the Danube River and the Balkan Mountains, and forced the Turks to yield.

The Treaty of Kuchuk-Kainarji (July 1774) ceded Azov, Enikale, and Kerch Straits to Russia, secured Russia's access to the Black Sea, and enabled it to build a fleet there and send merchant ships into the Mediterranean. The Crimea secured political "independence" from the Porte. Russia expanded westward to the Bug River and acquired part of the northern Caucasus. Freed finally from Tatar threats, Russia could now develop its agriculture and trade in southern Ukraine. For a Turkish indemnity Catherine evacuated the Danubian Principalities, but they remained a de facto Russian protectorate. The sultan recognized a vague Russian right to protect rights of Orthodox Christians in Constantinople, providing a pretext for subsequent Russian intervention in the Balkans. Confirming Russian emergence as a Black Sea power, Kuchuk-Kainarji was an important turning point in its relations with a declining Porte, although Catherine had not expelled the Turks from Europe.

Russia soon exploited its advantage by incorporating the Crimea. Crimean "independence" provoked fierce Russo-Turkish competition. In 1775 Devlet-Girei, a Turkish tool, seized the Crimean throne, and the Porte again appointed its judges and customs officials. The next fall Russian troops backed the pro-Russian pretender, Shagin-Girei, and named him khan. In 1783 Catherine, citing

Map 18.1 Expansion and partitions of Poland, 1772–1795

alleged Turkish violations of Kuchuk-Kainarji, annexed the Crimea, which enhanced Russia's security in the south, gave it Black Sea ports, and strengthened its position in the Caucasus.

By the late 1770s Russia was drifting away from Prussia toward Austria. Catherine mediated the German powers' conflict over the Bavarian succession and as a guarantor of their peace became a protector of the moribund Holy Roman Empire. In 1780 Catherine and Joseph II, the new Austrian emperor, discussed an alliance against the Porte and their spheres of interest. Catherine offered Austria northern Italy and even Rome; not to be outdone, Joseph suggested that Russia might occupy Constantinople. The Austro-Russian alliance of 1781, which confirmed the status quo in Poland, stipulated that if the Turks violated Kuchuk-Kainarji or attacked Russia, Austria would join Russia in war. The pro-Prussian Panin and his

followers were ousted, and Russian foreign policy under Potemkin and A. A. Bezborodko grew more aggressive.

The Austrian alliance promoted Potemkin's and Catherine's grandiose "Greek Project" to chase the Turks from Europe, partition the Balkans, and, as Catherine put it, restore "the ancient Greek monarchy on the ruins of . . . barbaric rule." This neo-Byzantine empire was to be ruled by Catherine's grandson, appropriately named Constantine, but the Russian and Greek crowns were not to be combined. To Joseph II Catherine suggested creating a buffer state of Dacia, formed from Bessarabia, Moldavia, and Wallachia. Austria concurred with the Greek Project, and Britain viewed it as a way to foment a Russo-Turkish war. The British had been alienated by Catherine's Declaration of Armed Neutrality of 1780, which was directed at Britain. The declaration supported neutral coun-

SOVFOTO

General A. S. Suvorov, 1730–1800, the ever-victorious general.

tries' efforts to protect their merchant shipping and revealed Catherine's ambition to play a leading international role.

A Russo-Turkish war broke out in 1787 after Catherine and Joseph had inspected Russia's new domains in the south: Ukraine and the Crimea. Accusing Russia of violating Kuchuk-Kainarji, the Turks demanded the return of the Crimea, then suddenly attacked southern Russia. General Suvorov, however, repelled the Turks, and Austria joined Russia. Then Sweden, egged on by France, attacked Russia (June 1788), forcing Catherine to fight on two widely separated fronts. The Swedish war ended in stalemate, and the Treaty of Verela of 1790 restored the prewar boundaries.

Although Austria made a separate peace, Russia eventually defeated the Porte. The great Suvorov won major victories at Fokshany, Rymnik, and Ismail as other Russian forces captured Akkerman and founded the port city of Odessa.

The Black Sea fleet under Admiral F. F. Ushakov defeated the Turks repeatedly. Reaching the Danube, a Russian army opened the way into the Balkans with its bayonets. Britain sought vainly to organize a European coalition against Russia and even planned a naval demonstration in the Baltic. Finally, the sultan yielded, and by the Treaty of Jassy (1791) he renounced all claims to the Crimea and Georgia. Russia obtained Ochakov and advanced its southern frontier to the Dniester River. Catherine hailed Jassy as a great triumph, though it fell far short of her aims and compensated Russian sacrifices poorly, but she never abandoned the Greek Project. A secret Austro-Russian agreement of 1795 planned to dismember the Ottoman Empire, and only Catherine's death blocked a Russian effort to seize Constantinople. Russian victories encouraged the Balkan Christians to seek to throw off the Turkish yoke.

During the Turkish war Polish patriots, with Prussian backing, secured major reforms at the Four Years Diet (1787–1791) and got Russian troops withdrawn. By the May Constitution of 1791 the liberum veto and the right of confederation were abolished and Poland briefly became a hereditary monarchy. Austria and Prussia approved, but Catherine called this constitution "revolutionary." She helped organize a confederation to "restore ancient Polish liberties," which appealed to Russia for aid. When 100,000 Russian troops invaded Poland, Poniatowski revoked the May Constitution, and its supporters fled abroad. In 1793 Russia and Prussia, in a second partition, sliced up more than half of Poland. Russia obtained the rest of Belorussia and western Ukraine, and the remainder of Poland became a Russian protectorate. British and French protests were ineffective, and a mortal blow was struck at Polish statehood.

Within Poland, national feeling boiled over: In 1794 the bourgeoisie, intelligentsia, city poor, and even some serfs rallied behind Thaddeus Kosciuszko in a desperate anti-Russian movement. To win mass support, Kosciuszko proclaimed the serfs free, but the nobility blocked this. The insurgents massacred Russian garrisons in Warsaw and Vilna, defeated Prussian and Russian units in the field, and forced the Prussians to withdraw. Suvorov, however, led a massive Russian invasion, defeated Kosciuszko at Maciejowice, and captured him.

Early in the uprising Bezborodko, Catherine's chief adviser, delimited the shares of the eastern powers for a final partition. Russia reached agreement with Austria and then imposed its terms on Prussia. In this third partition of 1795 Russia obtained Lithuania, Courland, and parts of Podolia and Volhynia. Soviet historians claimed that these former Kievan lands were Russia's by historic right and that incorporation benefited their people. Actually, Russia, Prussia, and Austria shared the responsibility for Poland's destruction fairly equally.

The French Revolution preoccupied Catherine in her last years. At first, expecting the Bourbons to crush the revolt, she underestimated its scope. After the French royal family was arrested in 1791, she became the first European sovereign to recognize a French regime in exile. After considering joining in the Austro-Prussian military intervention of 1792 against France, Catherine commented: "I'll break my neck in order to involve the Vienna and Berlin courts. . . . I want to entangle them in the affair in order to have free hands. . . . I have many unfinished enterprises."[7] Only Catherine's death prevented a Russian expeditionary force from joining Great Britain and Austria in fighting the French Directory.

Catherine's foreign policy has been variously interpreted. Traditional nationalist historians hail Russia's westward expansion, and some Soviet scholars, without praising Catherine or condoning tsarist methods, applaud the results. Acquiring the Crimea and southern Ukraine, they note, fostered the development of Russia's resources. Solving the Polish question was "historically progressive"

because it united the eastern Slavs and rejoined Ukrainian and Belorussian lands with the motherland. Catherine's foreign policy, though promoting noble interests, often corresponded to the incorporated peoples' interests.[8] On the other hand, Florinsky deplored the expense in lives and treasure to conquer territory inhabited partly by Tatars, Poles, and Lithuanians, who detested Russian rule. Two major blunders, argued Kliuchevskii, denied Catherine greater success abroad: Ending the traditional alliance with Austria and adopting the Northern System embroiled Russia with Austria and France, whose support Russia needed against the Porte. The Russo-Prussian Alliance, he argued, prevented a separate solution of the Polish and Turkish issues, reduced Russian gains against the Porte, and forced Russian acceptance of Frederick's plan of Polish partition. Instead of annexing only those areas where Orthodox eastern Slavs predominated, Catherine antagonized the Slav Poles with squalid partitions. These benefited mainly the German states because Russia in the 19th century would thrice have to fight Polish nationalism. In the south, Catherine, dreaming of driving the Turks from Europe, sought prematurely to rouse the Balkan Christians to revolt. The partitions of Poland and the Greek Project created fears in Europe that an insatiable Russia menaced its political independence. The coquette, argued Kliuchevskii, fell victim to the clever Prussian soldier, Frederick.[9]

Despite such persuasive arguments, it is undeniable that Russia under Catherine II achieved a major expansion of territory and population in the west and south. Firmly established on the Black and Baltic seas and controlling much of Poland, Russia could develop more freely its commercial, political, and cultural links with Europe. Some of Catherine's victories later rang hollow, but in her time few denied her great ability and achievements in foreign affairs.

---

[7] A. V. Khrapovitskii, *Dnevnik* (Moscow, 1901), p. 226.

---

[8] *Istoriia SSSR*, vol. 3 (Moscow, 1967), pp. 550–51.
[9] Kliuchevskii, *Kurs russkoi istorii*, vol. 5, pp. 44–46.

Problem 5

Was Catherine II
an Enlightened Despot?

The generation before the French Revolution of
1789 is often called the Age of Enlightened
Absolutism. Many Europeans looked to philosopher monarchs who by knowledge, virtue, and
example could uplift their people politically,
economically, and morally. Previously there had
been few such sovereigns, but during the latter
18th century a sizable group of them ruled simultaneously: Frederick II ("the Great") of Prussia,
Joseph II of Austria, Catherine II of Russia, and
Charles III of Spain, to name the most prominent.
Some historians view enlightened absolutism, or
despotism, as a method of rule that utilized the
philosophy of the Enlightenment to make government more efficient and took a positive interest in
the welfare and rights of all its citizens. Others
consider it merely absolutism that employed the
distinctive tone of the times while using the
forms and pursuing the goals of earlier autocrats.
Unlike their immediate predecessors (Frederick
William I in Prussia, Maria Theresa in Austria,
and Peter the Great in Russia), who had established centralized autocracies concerned with
public welfare, reduced noble privilege, and
created a common state citizenship, the enlightened despots shared a common devotion to
Enlightenment culture, sought to apply rational
knowledge to government, and professed certain
ideals admired in their era. Imbued with the
concept of natural law and the program of the
French philosophes, they attempted to govern by
new progressive principles. The enlightened
despots were driven by a strong desire to know
and experience life on this earth and to assert
their mastery in politics and diplomacy. All of
them dedicated long hours to state business, but
rather than reveling in administrative detail for
its own sake (like Philip II of Spain), they
believed that supervision of these details by a

rational ruler was necessary in order to execute
sound and consistent policies. To a greater or
lesser extent the enlightened despots aimed to
improve peasant well-being (at least on Crown
lands), develop trade and industry, eliminate
economic restrictions, rule in a just and orderly
way under law, and abrogate cruel and unusual
punishments. Frederick II summed up one of
their ideals: "I am the first servant of the state."
Elsewhere he explained: "The prince is to the
nation he governs what the head is to the man—
it is his duty to see, think, and act for the whole
community."[10] The enlightened despots shared
this attitude of benevolent patriarchal
absolutism.

Did Catherine II live up to the principles of
enlightened absolutism and to the ideals of the
philosophes whom she so admired, or did she
merely pay them lip service? Was she a hypo-
crite, as her critics claimed, or did she truly
believe in and seek to implement her professed
intentions? One should remember that Catherine,
especially at first, was much less secure on the
throne than were her contemporaries in Prussia
and Austria. As a German-born widow who had
usurped the throne and was widely believed to
have conspired in her husband's mysterious
death, she had to placate the powerful with various concessions. Following are pertinent sections
of the *Instruction* (*Nakaz*), her major political
work, and analyses of her actions.

Nakaz (1766)

More than three-fourths of the 22 chapters and
655 articles of "The Instructions to the Commis-
sioners for Composing a New Code of Laws,"
which constituted the most complete statement of
Catherine's theories of government and society,

---

[10] Quoted in R. P. Stearns, *Pageant of Europe* (New York, 1961),
p. 290.

were borrowed verbatim from Montesquieu, the German cameralists, Beccaria, Quesnay, and the French Encyclopedists. The *Nakaz* stressed typical Enlightenment concepts of natural law, freedom, and humanitarianism. When Catherine submitted it to her advisers, they insisted on deleting the boldest sections, especially those on serfdom. Soviet and some Western historians have affirmed that the *Nakaz* was circulated only abroad for propaganda purposes and was forbidden at home; actually, it went through eight editions in Catherine's lifetime and was sold publicly in Russia but was banned in France and in Russia later under her son, Paul I. Some of the articles of the *Nakaz* follow:

1. The Christian Law teaches us to do mutual Good to one another as much as possibly we can.
3. . . . Every individual citizen in particular must wish to see himself protected by Laws which . . . should defend him from all attempts of others that are repugnant to this fundamental rule.
6. Russia is a European State.
9. The sovereign is absolute, for there is no other authority but that which centers in his single person that can act with a vigor proportionate to the extent of such a vast dominion.
12. . . . It is better to be subject to the Laws under one Master than to be subservient to many.
13. What is the true end of Monarchy? Not to deprive people of their natural Liberty; but to correct their Actions in order to attain the *Supreme Good.*
15. The Intention and the End of Monarchy is the Glory of the Citizens, of the State, and of the Sovereign.
33. The Laws ought to be so framed as to secure the Safety of every Citizen as much as possible.
34. The Equality of the Citizens is . . . that they should all be subject to the same Laws.
35. This Equality requires Institutions . . . to prevent the rich from oppressing those who are not so wealthy as themselves.
38. *Liberty is the Right of doing whatsoever the Laws allow.*
96. . . . All Punishments, by which the human Body might be maimed, ought to be abolished.
123. The Usage of Torture is contrary to all the Dictates of Nature and Reason; even Mankind itself cries out against it. . . .
194. *The Innocent ought not to be tortured;* and in the Eye of Law, every Person is innocent whose crime is not yet *Proved.*
313. Agriculture is the first and principal Labour which ought to be encouraged in the People; the next is the Manufacturing of our own produce.[11]

Catherine as Ruler

The liberal prerevolutionary Russian historian Alexander Kizevetter presented an interpretation of Catherine's political methods and successes that emphasizes her personal role. Responsible for putting the new system of state and social relationships in final legal form, Catherine and her team harvested the field which their predecessors had "plowed, sown, and cultivated." Failure would have nullified many previous political efforts. Catherine's brilliant successes and the resplendent halo around her name resulted from the fact that the fundamental task of her era corresponded to key traits in her personality. "By nature she was not a plower or a sower."

The resourceful empress overcame numerous and complex obstacles, primarily with flexibility and hard work. "In her statesmanship she followed people and circumstances rather than led them." Probing the sources of Catherine's triumphs, Kizevetter argued that she possessed an extraordinary personality that featured an unusual combination of passionate desires and

---

[11] *Documents of Catherine the Great* (Cambridge, 1934), pp. 215ff.

Problem 5 continued

great self-control in choosing means to achieve these desires. "Catherine never lost this ability to play on people's heartstrings" and she did so constantly. Often the empress made those close to her feel her authority, but she could reveal apparent trustfulness and a disarming sense of humor with her interlocutor or "suddenly flash a ray of royal favor upon him." Catherine was an expert at self-promotion and exploiting others for her own benefit. Notably during her initial months in power she reiterated in numerous documents the fiction that she had assumed power from Peter III with her subjects' unanimous support.

Catherine's lofty reputation in Europe was vital to building her authority and success at home. Of vital importance to her was her celebrity as a freedom-loving, enlightened, and liberal ruler, an image she worked hard to spread throughout Europe. Many of her official statements were directed much more to European than to Russian opinion. She readily secured foreign writers to glorify her rule. Outstanding intellectual leaders, headed by the great Voltaire, allowed her to exploit their talents while they sang the praises of the "northern Minerva."

"Her correspondence," noted Kizevetter, "served not only to camouflage her moods but also to touch up facts she did not want revealed as they really were." Thus, during a severe Russian famine, Catherine described to Voltaire how happy and prosperous were Russian peasants, knowing that he would spread the word through Europe. For Catherine appearances took precedence over reality. After years of self-delusion, she grew convinced that only good could come from her and her efforts, "that everybody around her and under her wing was bound to prosper and bloom with happiness."[12]

---

[12] Marc Raeff, ed. *Catherine the Great: A Profile* (New York, 1972), pp. 4–17.

A Soviet View of Russian Enlightened Despotism

A Soviet work, *History of the USSR*, gives this highly critical view of Catherine's role, emphasizing its socioeconomic foundations:

The policy of "enlightened absolutism" was a general European manifestation. . . . To revolutionary-democratic reforms the theoreticians of "enlightened absolutism" opposed a peaceful means of eliminating obsolete feudal institutions. Such a path of development, retaining the key positions in society for the nobility, suited the monarchs. As a result was formed an "alliance of philosophers and kings." Monarchs invited into their service ideologists of "enlightenment," were in correspondence with them, called them their teachers, and themselves worked on the composition of political tracts. State decrees spoke of "the general good," "national benefit," of the concern of the state for the needs of "all loyal subjects." These words never conflicted as sharply with actuality as during the rule of "enlightened rulers." During the reign of Catherine II the slogans of the Enlightenment were utilized for the defense of serfdom and to forestall the approaching economic decline of the nobility. By old methods alone the working people of the country could not be held in obedience. . . .

Step by step the government satisfied the aspirations of the "noble" class, created conditions to adapt the *votchina* economy to commercial relationships. In many instances the expectations of the nobility, especially elements of it that, renouncing aristocratic snobbery, engaged in trade and industrial enterprise, coincided with the hopes of merchants and industrialists. If, however, the interests of these two classes came into conflict, absolutism satisfied the demands of the nobility at the expense of the merchants and industrialists. . . .

In the "enlightened age" of Catherine II trade in peasants reached broad proportions. Serfs, like slaves, were sold at markets, exchanged for horses and dogs, and lost at cards. . . . To a question of Denis Diderot about the relationship between masters and serfs in Russia the Empress gave the following cynical reply: "No definite conditions exist between master and serf, but each master, possessing common sense, seeks to treat his cow carefully, not exhaust her and not demand from her too much milk." Naturally, all "masters" sought to ensure that this "milk" should constantly increase. . . .

. . . The convening of the Legislative Commission and all its activity bore a demonstrative, sham character, clearly illustrating the aspirations of "enlightened absolutism," without changing anything in the social or political structure but achieving "quiet and calm" in the country. . . . By creating this representative organ, Catherine intended to strengthen her position on the throne. . . . [The *Instruction*] prepared minds for the transition from feudalism to bourgeois society. . . . The Legislative Commission fulfilled . . . the task of strengthening absolutism in the interests of the nobility.[13]

Catherine the Republican Empress

An American scholar, David Griffiths, has provided a balanced, judicious reinterpretation of Catherine's reign, disagreeing with many traditional views of Western and Soviet scholars:

The conventional Soviet analysis is unconvincing from the point of view of personality theory, since it assumes that the empress passed her entire adult life in a state of tension between her liberal utterances and her conservative policies. Politically, it explains nothing: a "liberal" image abroad would hardly help secure her hold on the throne. And such a reputation within Russia could only serve to undermine her position: for the literate elements in society—the nobility and the merchantry—would react with suspicion to alien political tenets. Both analyses, Western and Soviet, suffer from a more fundamental shortcoming: the use Soviet as well as non-Soviet historians make of terms such as republican, liberal, and conservative displays a lack of historical perspective. . . . The terms liberal and conservative were not, and could not be, applied by contemporaries to Catherine II . . . [who], on the other hand, was referred to, and referred to herself, as a republican; but the connotation was far from

that envisioned by those who would equate republicanism with liberalism. Only with the advent of the French Revolution did these three labels acquire the specific modern designations with which we associate them today. Hence the utilization of post-revolutionary terminology to describe pre-revolutionary political activity is inappropriate. . . .

In much of the governmental sphere Catherine II did little more than follow in the footsteps of Peter I. Her obligation to . . . Peter I was freely acknowledged . . . by her inability to abide any criticism of him; her policies, too, are of a piece with Peter's handiwork. The stress on rationalization, categorization, and ordering was common to both rulers. In one very prominent respect, however, Catherine II modified (so she believed) Petrine practice. She deemed despotism a necessary feature of rule earlier in the century. . . . Many Western commentators, Montesquieu among them, thought despotism endemic to Russia. But Catherine disagreed: the very success of Peter's reforms was proof of Russia's common destiny with the rest of Europe; with the reforms of the Petrine era behind it, she maintained Russia was ready for government by the rule of law. . . . Equal application, and equal observance, of the law, rather than separation of powers or constitutional limitations on the sovereign, was the solution she insisted to be best adapted to Russian tradition and circumstances. . . .

Social ordering via constituted bodies is frequently condemned as a form of class rule by modern scholars, who imply that Catherine II violated her own public pronouncements—consciously, as Soviet scholars assert—by granting a disproportionate share of the privileges to the nobility while further oppressing the peasantry. This interpretation fails to make the necessary distinction between estates in feudal societies and classes in capitalist societies. . . . To sustain this misinterpretation Soviet and non-Soviet scholars alike have distorted the content and hence the intent of Catherine's legislative activity. . . .

The 1785 Charter to the Nobility will serve as a first case in point. A close examination of the Charter, commonly misrepresented as a major concession to the nobility, reveals that it consolidated existing privileges rather than bestowing new privileges and that their enjoyment was still contingent upon successful performance of service obligations.

---

[13] *Istoriia SSSR*, (Moscow, 1967), vol. 3, pp. 428, 433, 435, 445–47.

Problem 5 continued

. . . It should now be apparent that Catherine II was hardly an early version of a modern public relations expert, conducting her own lavish campaigns to improve her image at home and abroad by deluding public opinion. The gap between her words and actions was no greater than that of any other ruler of the time, and where it existed it often signified nothing more than the limitations inherent in eighteenth century absolutism. Close examination of her reign reveals a clear correlation between the tenets of Montesquieu's *De l'esprit des lois*, the principles professed in the *Nakaz*, the equally advanced practices recorded in the Complete Collection of Russian Laws, and their evaluation by enlightened contemporaries. Her policies, in sum, were very much in harmony with the ideas of the age.[14]

Catherine II may have been empress of the nobility, but by building an orderly bureaucratic monarchy she subordinated them gently but effectively to the state. Though brought to power by the guards, she soon escaped their tutelage and selected her statesmen for their ability and their loyalty to the Crown. Her seeming concessions to the nobility were a means to achieve full autocratic power and personal rule. Catherine built support for herself with bonds of self-interest, not terror. Her model was Le Mercier's "legal despotism," not Montesquieu's separation of powers. Her governmental reforms—making the nobility her administrative agents—gave them the shadow of authority but gave the substance to the Crown. The self-government she granted dramatically to nobles and towns proved largely conditional. Her greatness, notes Leo Gershoy,[15] lay in flouting the logic she so admired in the philosophes and in uniting contradictions through patience, courage, and realistic flexibility. Like Peter I, she made royal absolutism a cement of state. Securing the old regime by essential concessions, she reconsolidated its central and local institutions, enhanced absolutism, and made Russia safe for aristocracy and unlimited monarchy for another century. ∎

[14] D. Griffiths, "Catherine II: The Republican Empress," *JfGO* 21 (1973): 324, 327–28, 343–44.

[15] L. Gershoy, *From Despotism to Revolution* (New York, 1944), pp. 106–26.

Suggested Additional Reading

BOOKS

ANDERSON, M. S. *The Eastern Question, 1774–1923* (London, 1966).

CATHERINE II. *Documents of Catherine the Great . . .* (Cambridge, 1934).

———. *The Memoirs of Catherine the Great* (New York, 1957).

CROSS, A. "By the Banks of the Thames"; Russians in Eighteenth Century Britain (Newtonville, MA, 1980).

DASHKOVA, E. *The Memoirs of Princess Dashkov* (London, 1958).

DE MADARIAGA, I. *Britain, Russia and the Armed Neutrality of 1780* (New Haven, 1962).

———. *Russia in the Age of Catherine the Great* (New Haven, 1981). (Comprehensive.)

DUKES, P. *Russia under Catherine the Great,* 2 vols. (Newtonville, MA, 1977).

———, ed. and trans. *Catherine the Great's Instruction (Nakaz)* (Newtonville, MA, 1977).

FISHER, A. *The Russian Annexation of the Crimea . . .* (Cambridge, 1970).

FOUST, C. *Muscovite and Mandarin: Russia's Trade with China . . . 1727–1805* (Chapel Hill, NC, 1969).

GLEASON, W. *Moral Idealists, Bureaucracy, and Catherine the Great* (New Brunswick, NJ, 1981).

GRIFFITHS, D., and G. MUNRO, eds. and trans. *Catherine II's Charters of 1785 to the Nobility and the Towns* (Bakersfield, CA, 1991).

JONES, R. E. *Provincial Development in Russia: Catherine II and Jacob Sievers* (New Brunswick, NJ, 1984).

KAPLAN, H. *The First Partition of Poland* (New York, 1962).

KLIER, J. D. *Russia Gathers Her Jews . . .* (Dekalb, IL, 1966).

LEDONNE, J. P. *Ruling Russia: Politics and Administration . . . 1762–1796* (Princeton, 1984).

LONGWORTH, P. *The Art of Victory: The Life of . . . Suvorov* (London, 1965).

MAKAROVA, R. *Russians on the Pacific, 1743–1799,* trans. and ed. R. Pierce and A. Donnelly (Kingston, Ontario, 1975).

OLDENBOURG, Z. *Catherine the Great* (New York, 1965).

RANSEL, D. L. *The Politics of Catherinian Russia* (New Haven, 1975).

SOLOVIEV, S. M. *The Rule of Catherine the Great: War, Diplomacy and Domestic Affairs, 1772–1774,* ed. and trans. G. E. Munro (Gulf Breeze, FL, 1991).

TOWNSEND, C. *The Memoirs of Princess Natalja B. Dolgorukaja* (Columbus, OH, 1977).

TROYAT, H. *Catherine the Great* (New York, 1980).

ARTICLES

ANDERSON, M. "Great Britain and the Russo-Turkish War of 1768–74." *EHR* 79 (1964): 39–58.

BARTLETT, R. P. "Foreign Settlement in Russia under Catherine II." *New Zealand Slavonic Journal,* n.s. 1: 1–22.

DAVISON, R. "'Russian Skill and Turkish Imbecility': The Treaty of Kuchuk-Kainardji Reconsidered." *SR* 35, no. 3 (1956): 463–83.

GIVENS, R. D. "Eighteenth Century Nobiliary Career Patterns . . .," in *Russian Officialdom . . . ,* ed. W. Pintner (Chapel Hill, NC, 1980), pp. 106–29.

GRIFFITHS, D. "Catherine II: The Republican Empress." *JfGO* 21 (1973): 323–44.

———. "Nikita Panin, Russian Diplomacy, and the American Revolution." *SR* 28 (1969): 1–24.

HALECKI, O. "Why Was Poland Partitioned?" *SR* 22 (1963): 432–41.

JONES, R. E. "Catherine II and the Provincial Reforms of 1775 . . . " *CSS* 4 (1970): 497–512.

KAMENSKII, A. "Catherine the Great." *SSH* 30, no. 2 (1991): 30–65.

LEDONNE, J. "Appointments to the Russian Senate, 1762–1796." *Cahiers du monde* 16, no. 1 (1975): 27–56.

LENTIN, A. "Beccaria, Shcherbatov, and the Question of Capital Punishment in Eighteenth Century Russia." *CSP* 24, no. 2 (1979): 128–37.

———. "The Pugachev Revolt," in *Rural Protest . . . ,* ed. H. Landsberger (New York, 1974), pp. 194–256.

LORD, R. H. "The Third Partition of Poland." *SEER* 3 (1924): 481–98.

MARCUM, J. "Catherine II and the French Revolution: A Reappraisal." *CSP* 16, no. 2 (1971): 187–201.

MEEHAN-WATERS, B. "Social and Career Characteristics of the Administrative Elite, 1689–1761," in *Russian Officialdom . . . ,* eds. W. Pintner and D. Rowney (Chapel Hill, NC, 1980), pp. 76–105.

MENNING, B. W. "G. A. Potemkin and A. I. Chernyshev: Two Dimensions of Reform and the Military Frontier in Imperial Russia." *PCRE* 1: 237–50.

RAEFF, M. "The Domestic Policies of Peter III . . ." *AHR* 75 (1970): 1289–1310.

RASMUSSEN, K. "Catherine II and the Image of Peter I." *SR* 37 (1978): 51–69.

THADEN, E. "Estland, Livland, and the Ukraine: Reflections on Eighteenth Century Autonomy." *JBS* 12, no. 4: 311–17.

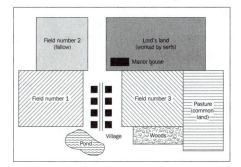

19

Catherine II:
Economic, Social, and Cultural Policies

In the late 18th century Russia experienced economic and intellectual growth, but its social relations deteriorated. The slow growth of commerce and money relationships prepared future industrialization, but agriculture, still weighted down by serfdom, remained backward and unproductive. While the upper and middle nobility reached their zenith of economic influence and dominated regional administration, the peasantry plumbed new depths of poverty and degradation. An intelligentsia began to emerge and criticized abuses hesitantly. Soviet historians emphasized the development of capitalist forms despite the predominance of feudal-serf relationships, and they dramatized the scope of the Pugachov Revolt, which they call "the Peasant War." How much economic growth occurred under Catherine? Was serfdom already declining economically? Did the regime ameliorate or worsen peasant conditions? What were the causes and significance of the Pugachov Revolt? What relationship existed between Catherine's government and the intellectuals?

The Economy

Under Catherine the serf-based economy reached its apogee. Russia remained basically an agrarian country low in productivity—though not notably backward by contemporary European standards—in which methods and systems of cultivation changed little. In the central region the three-field system prevailed. In the Black Soil region, which was becoming Russia's breadbasket, the long fallow system developed: The land was cultivated continuously for a number of years and then left fallow, sometimes for a decade or more, before being recultivated. New lands north of the Black Sea and in the Crimea, Don, and north Caucasus added significantly to Russian grain production, and in the south some plantation-type estates arose. Changes in landownership and rents presaged serfdom's decline as merchants and wealthy peasants, especially in the north, challenged noble predominance in landholding. In non–Black Soil areas, rising commercial activity accelerated a shift to money *obrok* (annual rent); in Black Soil regions *barshchina* (labor service) prevailed. Nomadic peoples from the Volga to the Pacific, spurred by

Russian settlers and state legislation, were shifting to settled agriculture. By 1800, Russians far outnumbered native peoples in Siberia.

Some Soviet and Western accounts challenge the older view that negative state policies slowed Russia's economic development after Peter I. To be sure, state policy became less vigorous, but it fostered industry through supervision, subsidies, and tax exemptions. The regime permitted more economic freedom, abolished some state monopolies, lowered tariffs, and stimulated private industries. Between 1725 and 1800, claims W. Blackwell,[1] the economy grew considerably as foundations were laid for the metallurgical and textile industries and peasant handicrafts expanded. However, industry represented only a small segment of the national economy with few employees.

Imprecise statistics make the evaluation of industrial progress difficult. Soviet historians affirmed that in the late 18th century the number of factories doubled to about 1,200. However, "factory" (*fabrika*) was a vague term; the great increase in industrial concerns included tiny shops with only a few employees. Most industry was conducted in these or in peasant cottages, and estimates of industrial workers in 1800 vary from less than 200,000 (Blackwell) to 500,000. Large-scale enterprise grew slowly, but by 1800 Russia had hundreds of factories and mines, thousands of small plants and shops, and was a leading iron producer. Industrial goods lacked wide markets in Russia; the state and the nobility purchased most military and luxury products. Light industry, notably that producing linen and silk, showed marked gains. Russia underwent superficial military industrialization while remaining, like all countries of the 18th century except England, basically agrarian.

Noble entrepreneurs, seeking additional revenues, engaged in liquor distilling, the manufacture of woolens, and metallurgy. Distilling, a noble monopoly, required little technology and had a ready market, abundant raw materials, and serf

labor. In the Urals the state, to foster private enterprise and rid itself of responsibility, granted factories and serf workers to noblemen, generals, and bureaucrats, but many noble enterprises soon failed or changed hands.

The labor force was changing in character. Hired workers (often still serfs on *obrok*) were widely used in the light industry of the towns and rural areas of non–Black Soil areas. Recruited from Russian, Chuvash, and Mordovian villages, they were paid substantial wages initially, but industrial wages generally were so low that many workers were hopelessly indebted to factory owners. Metallurgical plants, especially in the Urals, employed mainly serf labor. Incentives to introduce machinery were lacking, and inventions were little used or forgotten: A steam engine constructed by I. Polzunov at an Altai factory remained idle. Late 18th-century Russian industry, despite significant growth, retained primitive methods and crude output.

Though Russia's domestic and foreign trade expanded considerably, aided by population increases, imperial expansion, improved internal security, and official encouragement, the early Soviet view (Pokrovskii) that this was an era of commercial capitalism is much exaggerated. For a time Catherine continued efforts to liberalize domestic trade and provide merchants with easier credit. Responding to requests in the Legislative Commission for greater economic freedom, in 1775 she eliminated most monopolies and allowed anyone to operate an industrial enterprise, but noble landlords, not merchants, benefited most. Russia under Catherine, noted a foreign observer, had fewer restrictions on domestic trade than most European countries, and relatively liberal tariff policies stimulated Russian foreign trade. In 1782 the tariff rates increased somewhat over those of 1766 (from 20 to 30 percent of value), but they still afforded Russian industry only modest protection. Only in the 1790s, for political and fiscal reasons, did the state adopt protectionist measures and prohibit trade with revolutionary France.

Exports reflected Russia's largely agrarian economy. After the mid-1780s exports of iron, the chief industrial product, declined because of high tariffs

---

[1] W. Blackwell, *The Beginnings of Russian Industrialization, 1800–1860* (Princeton, 1968), pp. 27–28.

and the technological backwardness of the iron industry. Other leading exports were hemp, flax, linen cloth, timber, hides, and furs. Grain shipments were encouraged, but major growth in the grain trade came later. Leading Russian imports were luxury articles for noblemen and well-to-do merchants and woolen cloth for uniforms. Russia's foreign trade almost trebled in value from 1775 to 1795, but the quantitative increase was much less because of the ruble's depreciation. In 1794 the Commerce Department admitted that the balance of trade, depicted officially as favorable, may have been adverse.

Russia's best customer was Great Britain, notably for naval supplies, and most of the Russian exports were carried by English ships. England remained a coveted trading partner because it bought much more than it sold to Russia, and political frictions failed to disrupt the relationship. The Anglo-Russian commercial agreement of 1734 (see Chapter 17), highly favorable to England, was reaffirmed by a convention of 1766 and renewed in 1793. Russian commercial accords with Denmark, Portugal, and France reduced somewhat British preeminence in the Russian market.

By 1800 St. Petersburg handled more than 60 percent of Russian maritime commerce, and other Baltic ports (Riga, Narva, and Tallinn) handled most of the rest. What remained went chiefly through White Sea ports; southern seaports (Taganrog, Kherson, Odessa, and Sevastopol) had just begun to develop. The Treaty of Kuchuk-Kainarji allowed Russian merchantmen to use the Turkish Straits, but Russian ships were few and the Turks rarely permitted the passage of other foreign merchant vessels; Black Sea commerce remained mostly in Turkish hands. Through Astrakhan, Russia supplied European products and its own industrial goods to Asia and traded European goods to Asians at trade fairs in Orenburg, Semipalatinsk, and Petropavlovsk. Economically backward compared to the leading European states, to Asian neighbors Russia was an advanced country.

Catherine's financial policies were only a partial success. A sharp increase in national wealth (state revenues swelled from 17 million rubles in 1762 to 78 million in 1796) must be viewed against depreciation of the ruble and a fourfold increase in expenditures. Income came mostly from the poll tax (33 percent), spirits (25 percent), salt (7–10 percent), customs levies (10 percent), and conquered territories, but embezzlement by tax collectors probably exceeded the amount reaching the treasury. Even in peacetime the army took more than one-third of the budget. Lavish state expenditures, inept financial administration, and frequent wars induced the treasury in 1768 to issue paper banknotes (assignats); by 1796 they had depreciated about one-third. Extensive foreign borrowing weakened the ruble's value abroad. By 1796 state indebtedness totaled 215 million rubles and annual interest payments almost 6 million rubles. Under Catherine taxes rose some two and one-half times, including inflation, with the heaviest burden falling on the unfortunate peasantry.

What the state of the economy was under Catherine remains in dispute. N. D. Chechulin asserted that economic advances in the 18th century were negligible,[2] but industrial and commercial expansion belies this negative verdict. Developing money relationships, noted a Soviet source with apparent justice,[3] preparing the way for capitalist development and the decline of serfdom, forced changes in the landlord economy. Russia was progressing economically, though not as rapidly as advanced western European countries.

The Society

The Russian Empire, like most other regions of Europe, experienced rapid population growth in the 18th century. The population grew, according to official statistics, from about 14 million in 1724 to 36 million in 1796 (including about 7 million Poles incorporated during the partitions of Poland).[4] Table 19.1 provides data on Russia's population growth.

---

[2] N. D. Chechulin, *Ocherki po istorii russkikh finansov v tsarstvovanii Ekateriny II* (St. Petersburg, 1906).
[3] *Istoriia SSSR*, vol. 3 (Moscow, 1967), pp. 395ff.
[4] Ia. E. Vodarskii, *Naselenie Rossii za 400 let* (Moscow, 1973), p. 56.

Table 19.1
Population of the Russian Empire,
1724–1858

Revision (census)	Date	Estimated population (millions)
1	1724	14
2	1734–1735	16
3	1762–1764	19
4	1782–1783	28
5	1796	36
6	1811	41
7	1817	45
8	1835	60
9	1851	68
10	1858	74

SOURCE: Jerome Blum, *Lord and Peasant in Russia* ... (Princeton, 1961), p. 278.

Catherine's reign has often been called the golden age of the Russian nobility. The *dvorianstvo* scored notable progress, notably in wealth and cultural development. Nonetheless, the autocracy in its ceaseless state-building efforts redefined the nobility's role in society in conformity to state interests and restricted the growth of noble power and influence. Noble unity and esprit de corps should not be exaggerated. Within noble ranks persisted vast differences in status and political interests. As a minister of Nicholas I noted later, the nobility was an estate extending "all the way from the steps of the throne almost to the peasantry."[5] Books of nobility, held by the government until 1785, then by noble provincial corporations, described gradations important to its members. Old noble families (for example, Dolgorukii, Golitsyn) still claimed superiority; next came titled nobles (barons, counts). These top categories compared to the French nobility of the sword. Some noblemen had acquired their status since 1700 from civil or military service or through patent, like French nobles of the robe. Ennoble-

ment through state service prevented the *dvorianstvo* from becoming a closed caste, and service rank (*chin*) largely determined a noble's power and prestige. The upper nobility flaunted elegant manners, Parisian French, and Western dress and attended special schools. Shallow imitation of European customs made some noblemen virtual foreigners, conspicuous by their laziness, their vanity, and their contempt for Russian ways. Nonetheless, after 1725 the *dvorianstvo* had a sense of corporate unity and sought to confirm their rights. From the state they won important concessions culminating in emancipation from compulsory state service (1762). Noblemen wanted these privileges confirmed in writing, and at the Legislative Commission they requested a major role in local government.

Catherine, sympathetic to their aspirations, declared in French shortly after her accession: "*Je suis aristocrate* [I am an aristocrat]." Without noble support she could neither remain in power nor govern her empire. Thus the early Soviet view of Pokrovskii that Catherine's policies were probourgeois does not stand up. J. Blum's study shows that most of her legislation favored noble interests.[6] Later Catherine became less dependent on the nobility by granting its main desires while restoring Crown control over its activities.

The Charter to the Nobility (1785), marking the *dvorianstvo* ascendancy, aimed to regularize noble affairs. Noble status, defined as good birth or superior rank gained through state service and previously acquired privileges, was expressly reaffirmed. In each province noblemen organized as a corporate group; a noble assembly met triennially to elect officials in the province and its districts. All noblemen could attend, but only property holders over the age of 25 who had risen in state service could vote and hold office. Noble desires for a political role were satisfied while the state retained control over the noble assemblies, which lacked real power of initiative or the ability to block government measures. The *dvorianstvo* received

---

[5] M. T. Florinsky, *Russia,* vol. 2 (New York, 1953), p. 802, note.

[6] J. Blum, *Lord and Peasant in Russia* ... (Princeton, 1961), p. 352, note.

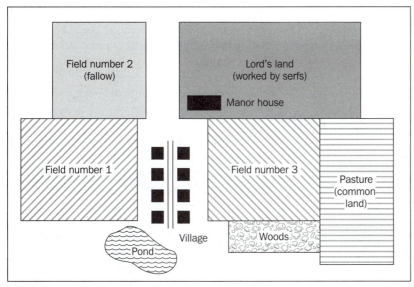

Figure 19.1
A large noble estate, 18th century

The sketch depicts a private noble estate under serfdom. Note the division between the lord's land, undivided and worked by serf labor under *barshchina*, and the three fields, one always lying fallow to recover its fertility. In repartitional communes the other two fields were divided into strips of various widths and periodically reassigned. The amount of land assigned to each peasant household depended on the number of males in the household. A few strips were set aside to provide for the indigent. Small plots around peasant huts were often sown to vegetables. Pasture and pond were used by the entire peasant community. In hereditary communes the field strips were not repartitioned but were owned by the households. *Dvorovye* (house serfs) received no land and worked in and around the manor house.

apparent self-government while the state retained the substance of power. Nonetheless, the Charter promoted the rule of law because at least one group had defined rights and some freedom.

A noble's economic and social status depended on the number of his serfs, not the amount of his land. At first Catherine gave away lands with state peasants, mostly to about 100 families. (Historians have often suggested that this occurred throughout her reign. Actually, Catherine largely abandoned this practice soon after seizing power.) Top noblemen owned far more serfs than plantation owners did slaves in the United States. A few great magnates with tens of thousands imitated the standards of the imperial court. Count P. B.

Sheremetiev, the richest, owned 2,500,000 acres and 185,000 serfs. He had palaces in Moscow and St. Petersburg and a lavish country estate at Kuskovo known as "little Versailles." Well-to-do nobles possessed 500 serfs or more, but in 1777 only 16 percent owned more than 100 serfs and almost one-third had fewer than 10 apiece. These pauper nobles, unless they entered state service, often lived with their serfs under a single humble roof and ate with them at a common table. Insistence on subdividing their estates among all heirs and high living produced pauperization. The government curbed their luxurious tastes by forbidding expensive carriages and clothing, but nobles still incurred huge debts.

Under Catherine serfdom reached its maximum extent and development. In 1796 the peasantry— private serfs and state peasants—comprised more than 90 percent of the population. As the taxes of the peasantry increased, its personal and economic status deteriorated. Secularization of church lands brought some one million privately owned serfs under state administration, undoubtedly improving their lot. At her accession, Catherine announced that "natural law" commanded her to promote the well-being of all her people, and she considered applying Enlightenment concepts of law and justice to the peasantry, but noble opposition helped dissuade her. In the Baltic provinces she suggested restrictions on serfdom, but they were not widely applied. Later she limited serfdom's scope somewhat by prohibiting the enserfment of orphans, war prisoners, illegitimate children, and other free people, or reenserfment, but such measures affected relatively few. Serfs were still forbidden to petition the Crown for redress of their grievances, and by abandoning the serfs to their lords' untender mercies, Catherine deepened the evils of serfdom. Her agents were merely to "curb excesses, dissipation, extravagance, tyranny, and cruelty" by the lords, but rarely were such matters investigated. Serfdom spread to Ukraine and Belorussia. After 1765, when the administration of court and imperial peasants was combined with that of state peasants, two major categories remained: private serfs (53.2 percent) and state peasants (45 percent).

The peasant's position depended on his work and obligations. In the north and center, where most state lands were located, the system of *obrok* was common; it was vital to peasant survival in the north, with its relatively short growing season. Under this system, taxes or dues were payable in kind (for example, grain) or in money, or both, for use of the land and on a peasant's outside earnings; however, in many cases peasants had to make payments in kind or cash *and* perform labor service (*barshchina*). In Tver province in 1783 peasants derived less than half their cash income (only about one-quarter of their total income) from agriculture; the rest came from handicrafts and labor in state or private enterprises. A major price

revolution occurred between 1725 and 1800. Grain prices increased more than 5 times while total dues paid by state peasants rose only 3.6 times. The burden of dues increased, but generally at a slower rate than prices. Nonetheless, in the forest region where most peasants still lived, dues per acre were roughly double those of the early 20th century.[7]

In southern Black Soil areas, forced labor service (*barshchina*) prevailed, unlimited by law until 1797. Traditionally, a *barshchina* peasant worked three days per week for the landowner, three days for himself, and rested on Sunday, but lords often required four or five days *barshchina* per week and continuous labor while their harvests were gathered. *Barshchina* peasants were generally more dependent on the lord than those under *obrok.* In the late 18th century, noted V. I. Semevskii, 44 percent of the Great Russian peasants were under *obrok,* 56 percent under *barshchina.* Usually, *barshchina* provided lords with a better return than *obrok.*

On sizable estates numerous courtyard people (*dvorovye*) worked in the lord's household performing specialized functions as clerks, scribes, or craftsmen of various types. Generally landless, they were indistinguishable from slaves except for paying state taxes and being subject to conscription. As noble ostentation grew, hundreds of them were employed, especially to impress visitors. Lords could punish them brutally with little fear of state action.

Russian landlords were miniature monarchs and viceroys of the state to ensure serf obedience and labor. "Except for imposing the death penalty," declared Catherine, "the landlord can do anything that enters his head on his estate." The lord's whim determined serf obligations; the lord's legal responsibilities were minimal and rarely enforced. After 1765, lords could deport serfs to forced labor in Siberia or send them into the army

---

[7] G. T. Robinson, *Rural Russia under the Old Regime* (New York, 1932), pp. 27–28. On grain prices in Russia, see B. N. Mironov, *Khlebnye tseny v Rossii za dva stoletiia (18–19 vv.)* (Leningrad, 1985), pp. 173, 186.

as recruits. Included in the estate's inventory from 1792, serfs could be sold individually or in families, with or without land; they were commonly exchanged for dogs and horses and gambled away at cards. Lords could beat serfs almost to death (even deaths were seldom investigated) but were dissuaded from killing them by moral and economic considerations. Masters could decide serf marriages—permission to marry outside the estate usually involved a large fee—and sometimes insisted upon the first night with the new peasant bride.

How could one escape serfdom? A serf soldier who served his time or became a war prisoner was emancipated when released. A few lords voluntarily freed their serfs, and some wealthy serfs purchased their freedom. By 1796 there was a sizable group of freedmen who had to join the army or another estate within a year or revert to serfdom. For most serfs the only way out was flight to areas without landlords. As state authority tightened over frontier areas, this escape became ever more difficult. Serfs who migrated to Siberia became state peasants because Siberia had neither landlords nor serfdom.

Urban growth remained slow, and so Russia's bourgeoisie lacked the size and influence of the bourgeoisie in western Europe. Even after a fourfold increase under Catherine, townsmen constituted only about 4 percent of the population (see Table 19.2). Catherine apparently wished to build up an urban middle class as a counterpoise to the nobility, but she had only modest success. A sparse urban population distinguished Russia socially from western Europe.

The clergy declined greatly under Catherine as secularization of its lands increased church dependence on the state. The government reduced the number of clergy by closing many monasteries, and Catherine made the church wholly subservient to the state. The Holy Synod punished Arseni Matseevich, archbishop of Rostov, her chief clerical critic and an opponent of secularization, as an example to others by reducing him to a simple monk and imprisoning him for life in a remote monastery. Catherine, however, granted toleration to Old Believers and revoked their double taxa-

Table 19.2
Russia's urban growth, 1724–1851

Date	Urban population	Percentage of total population
1724	328,000	3.0
1782	802,000	3.1
1796	1,301,000	4.1
1812	1,653,000	4.4
1835	3,025,000	5.8
1851	3,482,000	7.8

SOURCE: Jerome Blum, *Lord and Peasant in Russia* ... (Princeton, 1961), p. 281.

tion. To attract colonists and foster her liberal image, she allowed Protestants and Catholics freedom of worship. Her secular emphasis and tolerance accorded fully with the Age of Reason.

The Pugachov Revolt, 1773–1774

During the early 1770s a great Cossack, tribal, and peasant revolt raged from the Urals to the Volga region, threatening to engulf the landlords and Catherine's regime. Called the Peasant War by Soviet historians, the Pugachov Revolt was the greatest rural upheaval of Russian history down to 1905. "The entire populace was for Pugachov," wrote the poet Alexander Pushkin. "Only the nobility openly supported the government." After 1930 Soviet historians glorified and often exaggerated what they considered the last spontaneous peasant rebellion against feudalism. They rejected the thesis of Semevskii, a 19th-century Populist historian, that the Ural Cossacks directed the revolt, as they rejected early Soviet assertions that it was a worker-peasant revolution. Western scholars stress the revolt's traditional elements: the demand for legitimate rule and Old Believer rights. A Soviet-era American historian called it a "frontier jacquerie."[8]

---

[8] J. Alexander, "Recent Soviet Historiography on the Pugachov Revolt," *CSS* 4 (1970): 617.

The revolt's causes were many and deep-rooted. The spread of serfdom to Ukraine and the Don region and heavier taxation produced much peasant discontent. Forced serf laborers in Ural mines and factories worked under frightful conditions. Bashkirs and other national minorities were alienated by Russian seizure of much of their land, and the state had been depriving Cossacks of autonomy and forcing onerous service upon them. Among the Volga and trans-Volga peasantry were many Old Believers who opposed church and state. The mysterious death of an emperor who had permitted Old Believers to return to Russia and a foreign woman's usurpation of power gave Peter III undeserved popularity. Rumors spread that he had intended to emancipate the serfs, and, believing deeply in the tsar's benevolence, many peasants concluded that their "fine tsar" still lived. Support for pretenderism was the means of expressing their grievances.

Shaky state control over southeastern Russia facilitated revolt. Orenburg was the center of a huge, remote province where Tatars outnumbered Russians and the latter were mainly Cossacks and factory serfs hostile to the regime. Government troops were few and dispersed among many forts. Insurrection now, as earlier (see Chapters 12 and 14), began among Ural Cossacks whose autonomy had been whittled away and who were being conscripted to fight the Turks. Early in 1772 brutal actions by a government commission investigating Cossack complaints provoked open revolt. Its stern repression and the indemnity imposed on the Ural region created an explosive situation.

Early in 1773 a Don Cossack, Emelian Pugachov, came to the Urals and fanned tinder into flame. Born in the same settlement as Stenka Razin, he had participated in the first Turkish War, then refused to return to the army and wandered around the southeastern frontier. He realized how deep popular dissatisfaction was and resolved to exploit it. Like Razin, he was a bold, determined leader with military experience. Proclaiming himself "Peter III," he appeared on the Ural River as the "fine tsar" of peasant dreams. Led by the clergy, the inhabitants of Iletskii Gorodok greeted

Emelian Ivanovich Pugachov, leader of the peasants' revolt of 1773–1774.

him with bread and salt as "Emperor Peter Fedorovich," a scene repeated in towns and villages throughout the Ural region. Peasants, Ural workers, lower townsmen, and non-Russians joined his Cossacks. Pugachov's forces captured many Ural forts, seized their artillery, and besieged Orenburg. Most of his followers merely wished to capture Orenburg and seize some property, but Pugachov believed that if Orenburg fell, the road to St. Petersburg would lie open and Catherine's regime would fall. General A. I. Bibikov's forces defeated him, however, and lifted the siege.

With his remaining followers Pugachov moved westward to the Volga region, where thousands of peasants flocked to his banner. As his undisciplined levies captured Saratov and most of Kazan, panic gripped noblemen and some government leaders. Pugachov's manifesto of late July 1774 pledged to free the peasantry from serfdom, recruitment, and the poll tax:

We order by this our personal ukase: whosoever were hitherto gentry in their estates and domains, these opponents of our rule and perturbators of the empire and despoilers of the peasant shall be caught, punished, and hanged, and treated just as they . . . have treated you peasants.[9]

The insurgents killed some 3,000 landowners and local officials, mostly that summer. But untrained peasants were no match for government regulars. After a catastrophic defeat near Tsaritsyn (now Volgograd), Pugachov fled into the steppe, where some followers betrayed him to the authorities. Chained hand and foot, Pugachov was taken to Moscow in an iron cage. There he was interrogated, executed, and his body burned. His chief followers and thousands of peasants were also executed.

The Pugachov Revolt had far-reaching significance. By revealing a chasm of popular disaffection, it drew the nobility and the state together, tightening further the bonds of serfdom. Curiously, the revolt demonstrated the strength of the ideals of legitimate monarchy and the Old Belief among the peasantry; in a sense it was a revolution fought for reactionary goals. Whereas Semevskii and many Western scholars conclude that the revolt failed and discouraged mass peasant upheaval for more than a century, Soviet accounts asserted that it shook the feudal system, heightened peasant class consciousness, and inspired abolitionists such as Alexander N. Radishchev. The revolt apparently induced Catherine to reform provincial and local government, and by crushing Pugachov and restoring order, her regime revealed its effectiveness and power.

Education and Culture

Peter I's military-educational institutions had languished after his death, but Catherine II developed education for the elite considerably. After Peter, so anxious were noblemen to avoid service

at sea that the Naval Academy's complement went unfilled. Moscow University, founded in 1755 to train specialists for the state, began with 100 students but had only 82 in 1782, and its professors often did not deliver their lectures or gave them in French or Latin. The Cadet Corps, established in 1731 for gentry sons, however, flourished. Private boarding schools, stressing French, dancing, and other subjects desired by the nobility, had more success than state schools, and noble families employed many well-qualified and often radical French tutors.

Catherine's educational policy reflected her personal enlightenment, though less was achieved than she had hoped. Her first educational adviser was Ivan Betskoi, inspired by Locke, Rousseau, and the Encyclopedists, who urged Catherine to raise a breed of superior Russians in special state boarding schools. As director of the Cadet Corps, Betskoi stressed general education over military subjects and abolished corporal punishment. Women's education was begun: In 1764 Smolny Convent in St. Petersburg became a school for noble girls and flourished under court patronage and direction, and in 1765 a school for nonprivileged girls (except serfs) opened. Originally Catherine intended that boys' and girls' schools have identical curricula, but she later abandoned this advanced concept. Announced a government commission: "The intent and goal of the rearing of girls consist most of all in making good homemakers, faithful wives, and caring mothers."

When lack of teachers and public interest wrecked Catherine's dream of creating new men and women, she adopted the narrower goal of giving some Russians a general education. She employed Janković de Mirjevo, a Serbian graduate of Vienna University recommended by Joseph II, to set up Russia's first general-education schools. A statute of 1786 authorized a network of elementary, intermediate, and high schools of Austrian type, and high schools opened in 26 provincial capitals. The intermediate schools were dropped, but elementary schools open to children of all estates were set up in many different centers. Most of the pupils were sons of merchants, artisans, and

[9] Quoted in J. Alexander, *Autocratic Politics . . . 1773–1775* (Bloomington, IN, 1969), p. 151.

minor officials. Many were enrolled forcibly, and some existing schools had to be closed to secure sufficient attendance at new institutions. A central teachers college supplied instructors, and de Mirjevo translated many Austrian texts for their use. In 1796, despite faltering official and public support, more than 22,000 students were enrolled in the new public schools, a substantial achievement for its time. Despite Catherine's encouragement, only some 7 percent were females, mostly from St. Petersburg province. Catherine's reign marked a turning point in the development of Russian education.

In culture it was an era of laying foundations and absorbing lessons from the West. The modern Russian language, spurred by Petrine reforms of the alphabet, developed gradually. Foreign words and expressions, incorporated at first at random, were later included more systematically. The resulting literary language, richer and more flexible than Church Slavonic, was equally removed from popular speech and from old Church Slavonic but resembled the colloquial language of the broader literate public emerging from new state schools. Michael Lomonosov contributed the first true Russian grammar (1755), and leading writers compiled a complete dictionary (1789–1794).

In literature there were clashing styles, imitation of foreign authors, secularization, and sentimentalism, and abundant foreign works were available to noblemen schooled in French. Miliukov notes that two cultural strata developed and grew apart: the educated elite and the merely literate. The former adopted every new Western literary trend, whereas the broader public with its simpler tastes helped vivify the elite's artificial style. Foundations were laid for a creative national Russian literature.

Catherine's reign revealed signs of independent Russian literary achievement. The leaders— G. R. Derzhavin, Denis Fonvizin, and Nicholas Karamzin—built upon such earlier pioneers as Antiokh Kantemir. Lomonosov, Russia's universal man, was noted in literature chiefly for his odes. Alexander Sumarokov composed tragedies and comedies and directed the first permanent Russian theater. Toward the end of the century, public

demand for love literature finally provoked a response: The ode gradually yielded to tragedy, tragedy to high comedy, and finally to emotional light comedy. Sumarokov's classical tragedies, inspired by Jean Racine, were succeeded by the plays of Iakov Kniazhnin, which were devoted more to adventure and emotion. Fonvizin, noted for his plays *The Adolescent* and *Brigadir,* satirized Frenchified noblemen and portrayed realistically the behavior of the provincial gentry. Karamzin, author of the first nationalistic Russian history, catered to ordinary tastes with his sentimental *Poor Liza.* In architecture and painting native achievement was likewise considerable, although many leading architects and artists were foreigners. Catherine and wealthy noblemen erected luxurious palaces in the prevalent neoclassical style, and imposing public buildings were erected in "Russian imperial" style. Outstanding Russian architects included V. I. Bazhenev, known for a plan to reconstruct the Moscow Kremlin; M. F. Kazakov, designer of Moscow University and the Kremlin's Administration Building; and I. E. Starov, builder of Alexander Nevskii Cathedral and the lavish Tauride Palace of Prince Potemkin in St. Petersburg. The works of these architects and writers, though based on foreign models, created a sound basis for the more brilliant achievements of the 19th century.

The Russian Enlightenment

Westernization and the increased leisure of noblemen contributed to a significant development of Russian thought. A Populist historian, Ivanov-Razumnik, called the small group of educated noblemen deeply interested in ideas that emerged under Catherine "the intelligentsia." It was, he affirmed, a hereditary group outside estate or class seeking the physical, mental, social, and personal emancipation of the individual. Intelligent noblemen such as Nicholas Novikov and A. Radishchev reflected the ideals and beliefs of the Enlightenment.

That European movement, extending from about 1715 to 1790, centered in Paris, but many western and some eastern European areas contributed to it. The Enlightenment was based on foundations laid by the 17th-century "scientific revolution," which drastically altered views of the cosmos and humans' place in it and culminated in Sir Isaac Newton's laws of motion. Generally, Enlightenment thought was characterized by (1) skepticism about traditional ideas and authorities, (2) rejection of revealed religion as the basis of authority in favor of a profoundly secular emphasis, (3) confidence in the power of science and reason and optimism about human capabilities and potential perfectibility, and (4) a relentless search for the truth. The Enlightenment profited from the spread of French values and language across the continent. Its values and ideas were expounded and spread by the philosophes, including Montesquieu, Voltaire, and Rousseau. Most of them were men of letters and publicists, not professional philosophers. Many of them were bourgeois, but some were noblemen. A few were atheists, but most were deists who believed devoutly in natural law. The philosophes favored political, social, or economic reforms to place humans in harmony with nature. While rejecting or questioning older institutions or practices such as divine-right monarchy, serfdom, autocracy, and torture, they disagreed sharply as to how reform should proceed. These European philosophes inspired their educated Russian contemporaries, including Catherine II. Emphasizing the originality of Russian thought, Soviet historians argued that a multiclass intelligentsia had begun earlier around Lomonosov. Some Western scholars, considering the figures of Catherine's reign to be isolated individuals, believe that the Russian intelligentsia began with the Decembrists in the 1820s.

Prince M. M. Shcherbatov was the old aristocracy's leading ideologist and writer. He defended serfdom as necessary and desirable: Most serfs, he pontificated, were "satisfied with their lords who cared for them like children." In *Journey to the Land of Ophir* (1787) he described an ideal state where most people were slaves dependent on a nobility with a monopoly of land. The monarch, supervised constantly by a powerful elite, could do

nothing without his council of lords. In *Petition of the City of Moscow on Being Relegated to Oblivion* (1787) he recalled Moscow's ancient glory and called shifting the capital to St. Petersburg unnatural. Shcherbatov prefigured the Slavophiles' subsequent depiction of St. Petersburg as an alien, harmful element in Russian life. *On the Deterioration of Russian Morals* indicted the autocratic system and denounced Catherine's court for luxury, corruption, and arbitrariness. In his sophisticated defense of aristocracy Shcherbatov used fully the terminology and works of the philosophes.

Between 1750 and 1770, affirmed a Soviet work,[10] there developed a multiclass intelligentsia fostered by new institutions of higher education such as the Academic University (1748), Moscow University, and the Academy of Arts (1758). These *raznochintsy*[11] criticized the prevalent noble ideology in a rationalist manner, and Lomonosov's followers especially advocated a middle-class ideology based on reason and natural law. Lomonosov, who embodied the supposed diversity and originality of Russian scholarship, believed that history should glorify the fatherland and its people, not princes, and that Russia must overcome its backwardness and its dependence on the West. American scholars, however, note that most *raznochintsy* identified by Soviet scholars were actually noblemen.

Many members of the educated upper classes found Freemasonry the principal outlet for their growing frustration and their deepening sense of alienation. Introduced into Russia as early as the 1730s, it became a significant movement only under Catherine II. A Christian movement existing outside the formally established churches, Masonry provided the Russian nobleman with an opportunity to serve his fellowman through educational and philanthropic activities and created a framework for the development of profound religious feelings and aspirations no longer offered by the Orthodox church. In secret or semisecret

---

[10] M. M. Shtrange, *Demokraticheskaia intelligentsiia Rossii v XVIII veke* (Moscow, 1965).

[11] Literally "men of various ranks"—that is, different social groups.

lodges the Russian nobleman identified with the higher calling of Christian service in an atmosphere of brotherhood and common purpose.

Nicholas Novikov (1744–1818)—Freemason, journalist, and philanthropist—was the key figure in developing Russian humanitarian liberalism. Viewing individual moral development as the basis for happiness and material progress, Novikov popularized the Enlightenment, brought culture to remote areas, and instructed a generation of Russian noblemen. He saw Freemasonry as a potential counterbalance to the rationalism, hedonism, and frivolous atmosphere of St. Petersburg. Disillusioned with the casual social dilettantism of Masons in the capital, Novikov organized his own more serious lodge. In Moscow after 1779 he and his followers organized an independent program of educational and philanthropic activities to alleviate human misery—aid to the sick, starving, and homeless—and spread Enlightenment through lending libraries, publishing houses, and translation programs. These activities helped reestablish Moscow as a thriving intellectual center.

Novikov favored free expression but not transformation of the political or economic order. He wished to "be useful to men of good sense"—to inculcate virtue, well-being, happiness, and self-knowledge. "Let us endeavor above all to love man" and "attack vice, wickedness, and inhumanity," he wrote in *On Man's High Estate* (1787). His journals, to which many progressives contributed, propagated liberal, humane social thought. In *The Drone* he satirized reactionary noblemen. Squire Nedum (Thoughtless) submits a plan to the government: "No creatures are to exist in the whole world except members of the gentry; the common people should be wholly exterminated." Later, in *The Painter,* Novikov described the excesses of serfdom and how it demoralized lords and peasants. His indirect satiric critique of abuses was most effective, and in the 1780s he developed the largest private publishing enterprise in Russia.

In 1786 Novikov fell into disfavor when Catherine discovered that his press was publishing books illegally. Six years later he was arrested for espousing Masonic views viewed by the empress

Library of Congress

Alexander N. Radishchev, 1749–1802.

as subversive because of their foreign origin. He fell victim to Catherine's intense fear of the French Revolution.

Alexander N. Radishchev (1749–1802) attacked serfdom and autocracy directly. The son of a well-to-do landowner of Saratov province, he attended the Corps de Pages in St. Petersburg, then studied for five years at Leipzig University in Saxony. As protocolist for the Russian Senate after 1771, Radishchev read many documents relating to the peasantry; in the office of an army division he studied the Pugachov Revolt. In 1780 he joined the customs service in St. Petersburg, and in 1790 he became its director.

Radishchev's conventional bureaucratic career shielded daring literary activity. As Russia's first "repentant nobleman," he could not reconcile his progressive ideas with tyranny and exploitation in

Russia. To him autocracy was "the state of affairs most repugnant to human nature." The ruler should be "the first citizen of the national society." In 1789 he submitted unsigned *A Journey from St. Petersburg to Moscow* to the censors, who approved it for publication with some deletions. Radishchev's serfs ran it off on his private press, excisions and all! Catherine read it with rising fury, finding intolerable his rejection of autocracy and serfdom and his personal attacks on Potemkin: He was "a rebel worse than Pugachov." In *A Journey* the traveler learns of the horrible nature of serfdom en route to Moscow: It is "a hundred-headed monster" repugnant to human nature, natural law, and the social contract, which must be gradually but completely abolished. (Later Russian abolitionists could add little.) Landowners in the name of reason, morality, and self-interest should end voluntarily a system economically and morally disastrous for all. The alternative was a mass revolution, which Radishchev seemed to welcome: "Oh, would that the slaves burdened with heavy shackles should rise in their despair and with the irons that deprive them of freedom crush our heads!" Actually, he sought to persuade the lords and the state to forestall revolution with timely reform.

Radishchev and Novikov were Russian philosophers whose ideas were largely of foreign origin. Rousseau's *Social Contract* influenced Radishchev deeply, and the American Revolution inspired his "Ode to Liberty" (1783), which demanded freedom and an end to censorship. Soviet historians, stressing his debt to Lomonosov's materialist philosophy and the Pugachov Revolt, portrayed him as a pioneer of the Russian revolutionary tradition who prepared people to accept revolution as the sole means to a better order. Western and prerevolutionary Russian scholars generally view Radishchev as a liberal reformer and *A Journey* as the first program for political democracy and equality in Russia. His purpose, they argue, was to persuade the old regime to change before it was too late.

The French Revolution illuminated Radishchev's message with falling fortresses and burn-ing manor houses. Finding the book "quite flagrantly insurrectionary," Catherine had Radishchev imprisoned in Peter and Paul Fortress, where he was interrogated by the torturer of Pugachov. He was condemned to death, but Catherine commuted his sentence to 10 years of exile in Siberia. She ordered *A Journey* seized and burned, but some copies escaped, circulating from hand to hand in Moscow and St. Petersburg.

At first the French Revolution had found widespread approval in Russia, but later the nobility and the regime became alarmed by its violence. With the execution of Louis XVI, Catherine retreated into open reaction and sought to isolate Russia from revolutionary thought. Belated repression, however, could not undo Russia's participation in the Enlightenment. The ideas of Radishchev, spreading among the educated public, prepared the way a generation later for the Decembrist movement.

Suggested Additional Reading

BOOKS

ALEXANDER, J. T. *Autocratic Politics in a National Crisis: The Imperial Government and Pugachov's Revolt, 1773–1775* (Bloomington, IN, 1969).

———. *Catherine the Great* (New York, 1989).

———. *Emperor of the Cossacks: Pugachov and the Frontier Jacquerie of 1773–1775* (Lawrence, KS, 1973).

BATALDEN, S. *Catherine II's Greek Prelate: Eugenios Vulgaris in Russia, 1771–1806* (Boulder, CO, 1982).

BLANCHARD, J. *Russia's "Age of Silver" . . .* (New York, 1989).

BROWN, W. E. *A History of Eighteenth-Century Russian Literature* (Ann Arbor, MI, 1980).

GARRARD, J. G., ed. *The Eighteenth Century in Russia* (Oxford, 1973).

GLEASON, W. J. *Moral Idealists, Bureaucracy, and Catherine the Great* (New Brunswick, NJ, 1981).

GRIFFITHS, D. M., ed. "The Russian Enlightenment (II)." *CanAmSlSt* 16, nos. 3–4 (1982).

HITTLE, J. M. *The Service City: State and Townsmen in Russia, 1600–1800* (Cambridge, MA, 1979).

JONES, G. *Nikolay Novikov: Enlightener of Russia* (Cambridge, 1984).

JONES, R. E. *The Emancipation of the Russian Nobility, 1762–1785* (Princeton, 1973).

LANG, D. *The First Russian Radical: Alexander Radishchev, 1749–1802* (London, 1959).

———. *Russia in the Age of Catherine the Great* (New Haven, 1981).

———. *A Russian Philosophe: Alexander Radishchev* (The Hague, 1964).

MADARIAGA, I. *Catherine the Great: A Short History* (New Haven and London, 1990).

MARKER, G. *Publishing, Printing, and the Origins of Intellectual Life in Russia, 1700–1800* (Princeton, 1985).

RADISHCHEV, A. N. *A Journey from St. Petersburg to Moscow,* trans. L. Wiener, ed. R. Thaler (Cambridge, MA, 1958).

RAEFF, M. *The Origins of the Russian Intelligentsia: The Eighteenth Century Nobility* (New York, 1966).

———, ed. *Catherine the Great: A Profile* (New York, 1972).

ROGGER, H. *National Consciousness in Eighteenth Century Russia* (Cambridge, MA, 1960).

ROZMAN, G. *Urban Networks in Russia, 1750–1800* (Princeton, 1976).

SHCHERBATOV, M. M. *On the Corruption of Morals in Russia,* ed. A. Lentin (New York, 1969).

ARTICLES

BECKER, C. "Raznochintsy: The Development of the Word and the Concept." *ASEER* 8 (1959): 63–74.

BLACK, J. L. "Catherine II's Imperial Society for the Education of Noble Girls . . . " *Slav. Eur. Educ. Rev.* 2: 1–11.

BROWN, J. H. "The Free Economic Society and the Nobility, 1765–96." *CanAmSlSt* 14, no. 3 (1980): 427–35.

KAHAN, A. "The Costs of Westernization in Russia: The Gentry and the Economy in the Eighteenth Century." *SR* 25 (1966): 40–66.

———. "Some Western Sources of Radishchev's Political Thought." *Revue des Études Slaves* 25 (1949): 73–86.

LONGWORTH, P. "Peasant Leadership and the Pugachov Revolt." *Journal of Peasant Studies* 2 (1975): 183–205.

MCARTHUR, G. H. "Freemasonry and Enlightenment in Russia: The Views of N. I. Novikov." *CanAmSlSt* 14, no. 3 (1980): 361–75.

MCCONNELL, A. "The Origin of the Russian Intelligentsia." *SEEJ* 8 (1964): 1–16.

NASH, C. "Educating New Mothers: Women and the Enlightenment in Russia." *HOEQ* 21, no. 3 (1981): 301–16.

PETROVICH, M. "Catherine II and a False Peter III in Montenegro." *ASEER* 14 (1955): 169–94.

RAEFF, M. "Pugachov's Revolt," in *Preconditions of Revolution in Early Modern Europe,* ed. R. Forster and J. Green (Baltimore, 1970), pp. 161–202.

———. "State and Nobility in the Ideology of M. M. Shcherbatov." *ASEER* 19 (1960): 363–79.

RANSEL, D. "Ivan Betskoi and the Institutionalization of Enlightenment in Russia." *CanAmSlSt* 14, no. 3 (1980): 327–38.

SUMNER, B. H. "New Material on the Revolt of Pugachov." *SEER* 7 (1928–29): 113–27, 338–48.

20

Bureaucratic Monarchy:
Paul and Alexander I, 1796–1825

Between 1796 and 1855 the Russian imperial regime grew more centralized and bureaucratic, partially recovering its authority over the landed nobility. The trend during the earlier era of Palace Revolutions (1725–1762) toward enhanced noble influence and independence from state control was reversed. Early 19th-century Russian monarchs began imposing limitations on the noble landowners' hitherto virtually unlimited powers to control their serfs and to restrict serfdom itself. However, they shied away from any decision to emancipate the serfs. In their reassertion of central authority they won growing support from bureaucrats, many of whom now derived their income and influence primarily from state service, not from landed estates and serf rents.

Paul and his son Alexander I, both believers in enlightened absolutism, ruled Russia between 1796 and 1825. In peaceful periods between the Napoleonic Wars, they sought by different means to strengthen and centralize the administration. The collegial principle, predominant theoretically since Peter I, was discarded for monocratic ministries organized on military, hierarchical princi-

ples. Holding jealously to their autocratic powers, both sovereigns believed that in Russia a powerful ruler was the only proper instrument of progress and popular well-being. After heroic sacrifices in the struggle with Napoleon, many Russians hoped for political and social reform from the enlightened Alexander, only to be rudely disillusioned by his reactionary and repressive policies. A few Russians turned unsuccessfully to revolutionary conspiracy to achieve the changes of which they dreamed.

Paul I

The brief reign of Paul I (1796–1801) remains controversial and disputed. According to traditional accounts, it was a failure at home and abroad because it lacked a consistent program and because Paul I was psychotic. Some recent historians, questioning this thesis, provide a more sympathetic picture and credit Paul with constructive domestic policies and considerable achievements despite his undeniable arbitrariness and volatility. They deny that Paul was mentally unbalanced.

Tsar Paul I, 1745–1801, son of Catherine the Great.

Paul's personal life as heir had a profound impact on his conduct of affairs as emperor. He was afflicted with mental problems stemming from events in early life. Born in 1754, he was uncertain whether his father was Peter III (Catherine's husband) or one of her lovers. Empress Elizabeth soon removed Paul from his mother, Catherine, and placed him in the hands of nurses whose inept care weakened his health. His mother had little time for Paul and less interest in him. At

six he began his formal education under his chief tutor, the watchful Nikita Panin, Catherine's close adviser. When Paul was only eight, his supposed father, Peter III, was deposed and murdered. Whatever Paul's feelings toward him, this violent death contributed to psychological stress, which was soon reflected in erratic behavior. Paul became quick-tempered, impulsive, inconsistent, and generally high-strung. A tutor described his young student's behavior: "Paul has an intelligent mind in which there is a kind of machine that hangs by a mere thread; if the thread breaks, the machine begins to spin, and then farewell to reason and intelligence."[1]

Court gossips persuaded Paul that his mother would share power with him when he reached maturity. Catherine II, of course, had no such intention, and when Paul turned 18, she refuted such rumors. Paul felt wrongfully deprived of his inherent right to rule, whereas Catherine was wary, regarding Paul more than ever as a potential threat to her rule. Deepening mutual suspicion and mistrust produced mutual alienation. Paul developed a morbid hatred of his mother and all that she stood for.

To keep Paul isolated from state affairs, Catherine tried to divert him by arranging his marriage to Princess Wilhelmina of Darmstadt in 1773. Paul refused to be diverted: He was heir to the throne, and his views on important questions merited consideration. He submitted a detailed proposal for reorganization of the army, which Catherine ignored completely, thus throwing him into a frenzy of anger and bitterness.

Soon after his first wife died in 1776, Paul married Princess Sophie of Württemberg. The births of his first two sons—Alexander in 1777 and Constantine in 1779—further alienated Paul from his mother. Because Catherine considered bypassing her son in favor of one of her grandsons, she immediately removed them from their parents' care in order to supervise their upbringing and education.

In 1782 Paul retired despondently to his estate at Gatchina outside St. Petersburg to begin a long, frustrating wait for his mother's death. Lacking contact with the St. Petersburg court, he retreated into his own little military world. Paul gathered a small personal army, organized, equipped, and drilled in the Prussian style that he so admired. Military exercises became an outlet for his pent-up emotions. Woe to the man who had a button out

of place or an unpolished weapon! For 14 years Paul awaited power, vowing to destroy everything his mother had done. Catherine's hatred for her son festered to such an extent that she decided to make her grandson Alexander her successor, but she died unexpectedly in 1796 before she could formalize this decision.

Once he had assumed power, Paul issued a series of decrees designed to subvert everything his mother had done. He filled the capital with his Gatchina "army" and exiled hundreds who had served Catherine. Paul also emptied the prisons, releasing such victims of Catherine as Radishchev and Novikov. Where Catherine had tried decentralization, Paul fostered centralization. Dismissals, transfers, and appointments proceeded at a dizzying pace. Wallowing in the pomp and circumstance of power, Paul insisted that high and low grovel before him in recognition of his august authority. The army was reorganized and re-equipped on the Prussian model, dressed in Prussian-style uniforms, and subjected to draconian discipline. Paul established a watch parade (*Wachtparade*) on the Prussian model to instruct soldiers and their officers. In a cocked hat, huge jackboots, and frock coat, holding a stick in his hands, the emperor would yell out "One, two, three!" even in subzero cold. The watch parade became a semiofficial institution at which Paul would issue decrees, receive reports, and set audiences. No one dared set foot on the parade ground without money in his pocket and a change of clothes in his knapsack because the emperor might order any unit not "up to snuff" directly to Siberia! The discipline, orderliness, and conventions of the parade ground had always been Paul's overriding concern and remained so during his imperial rule.

Pursuing his avowed aim of reversing his mother's policies, Paul sought to curb the nobility and subordinate it more completely to the state. Catherine had cultivated noble support by granting concessions culminating in the Charter to the Nobility. Unconcerned with noble privileges, Paul rescinded most of the Charter's provisions. His attitude toward noblemen was summed up by a

[1] P. Miliukov et al., *History of Russia,* 3 vols. (New York, 1968), vol. 2, p. 140.

comment he made to the Swedish ambassador: "Only he is great in Russia to whom I am speaking, and only as long as I speak [to him]."[2] Paul was acutely aware that during the 18th century the nobility had acquired great political power based on its ability to influence the succession to the throne by staging palace coups. Peter the Great's vague law of succession of 1722, allowing each sovereign to select his or her own successor, accounted for successful noble intervention on several occasions. Anxious to limit this power and determined to prevent future legitimate rulers from being deprived of the right to exercise power, Paul issued a new law of succession the day of his coronation in April 1797. Henceforth succession would follow the principle of primogeniture: descent in the direct male line. Paul abolished the provincial noble corporations stemming from Catherine's efforts to decentralize the administration and instead appointed bureaucrats to perform their duties. To regulate relations between noble landowners and their serfs, he issued a decree forbidding landowners to force serfs to work their lands on Sundays and holidays and suggested a maximum of three days a week of *barshchina* as in the best interests of lords and serfs. These measures, directed primarily against the nobility, did not represent a well-conceived plan of social reform but rather a desire to annul some privileges that Catherine had granted nobles in return for their support of her usurpation of power. Paul restored the right of individual peasants to petition the crown, prohibited the sale of serfs without land in Ukraine, and ordered some measures to improve the well-being of state and court peasants. He extended serfdom, however, by transferring in his short reign more than half a million state and crown peasants to the control of private landowners.

Paul favored enlightened absolutism and held a high view of the sovereign's role as the guardian of his subjects and the promoter of their well-being. He sought to establish a more rational, centralized, and efficient bureaucratic system. Restoring some government departments abolished by Catherine, his regime laid the bases of the ministerial reform implemented by his son. Lacking experience and often poorly advised, however, Paul pursued no definite plan, and his legislation lacked guiding principles.

Toward the end of his reign a deepening mood of uncertainty and fear paralyzed the emerging bureaucratic structure, cowed the nobility, and weakened the economy. The populace from top to bottom lived in increasing fear of an arbitrary, capricious emperor, fond of dismissing a general in disgrace one day and recalling him with praise and honor the next. A police straitjacket tightened upon Russian society, arbitrary arrests multiplied, and insecurity rose among the elite. Decrees prohibited everything smacking of revolutionary France, which Paul feared as much as Catherine had. Many feared that the empire could not long survive under Paul's high-handed and inconsistent rule. The familiar idea of a palace coup won support among high officials and army officers, who explored cautiously the idea of removing Paul and elevating his son Alexander to the throne. Among the leaders of the conspiracy was Nikita Panin (nephew of Paul's tutor), who had been Paul's foreign minister; Count Peter von der Pahlen, military governor of St. Petersburg; and the Zubov brothers.

For a long time Alexander refused to countenance any action against his father, but months of artful persuasion and Paul's arbitrariness won Alexander over to the conspiracy on the condition that Paul's life be spared. Pahlen pledged that no harm would befall Paul, though he knew full well that such a promise could not be kept. There is no concrete evidence to suggest that Alexander knew in advance of plans to murder Paul or accepted this as the price of gaining power. Alexander's grudging approval of a coup stemmed from Paul's dangerous foreign policy (see Chapter 21) and from Paul's resolve to exclude all of his sons from the succession in violation of his own decree. Alexander thus participated in the final prepara-

---

[2] V. Kliuchevskii, *Kurs russkoi istorii*, vol. 5 (Moscow, 1937), p. 220.

tions and selected the date: March 23, 1801. To his dismay, the conspirators beat and strangled Paul, which brought Alexander to the brink of collapse. Guilt and remorse never left him. Meanwhile there was general rejoicing that Paul's nightmarish reign had ended.

Paul's reign revealed the potential dangers and weaknesses of autocracy. Absolute power wielded irresponsibly and inconsistently endangered the entire state. Noblemen now realized that autocratic power could destroy privileges as well as grant them. Paul's efforts to outlaw some of the worst abuses of serfdom and to introduce legislative controls over it had only slight impact but dramatized the pressing need to alleviate the crushing weight of peasant obligations. Alexander I had to grapple with autocracy and serfdom, twin pillars of the Old Russian system, but he proved no more successful than his predecessors in finding solutions in their inherent contradiction: the need to modernize while maintaining intact traditional social and political forms.

Political Policies of Alexander I

Alexander I (1801–1825) mounted the Russian throne at the age of 23, confused, grief-stricken, and guilt-ridden. His entire life had been plagued with contradictions: Caught between a grandmother who supervised his education and a father who feared him as a rival, Alexander tried to love these strong-willed and antagonistic people. He was thrust back and forth between the sophisticated St. Petersburg court life of Catherine and Paul's crude and vulgar barracks life at Gatchina. The moral laxity, self-indulgence, and hypocrisy at court appalled him no less than the brutality and pettiness of Gatchina. In trying to please both grandmother and father, Alexander led a chameleonlike existence, constantly shifting moods to please one or the other. It proved even more difficult to reconcile Russian reality with his liberal education in the humanitarian principles of the Enlightenment under his Swiss tutor, F. C. La Harpe. Harsh military training under Paul's trusted

lieutenant, Count A. A. Arakcheev, contrasted wholly with La Harpe's progressive views. To characterize Alexander as weak, docile, vacillating, and contradictory, however, is superficial. On the contrary, once he became emperor, Alexander proved single-minded, imperious, stubborn, and domineering.

A staggering array of problems faced the new ruler. Paul's rule had left the country morally and physically exhausted, the economy in disarray, corruption and inefficiency endemic, and foreign policy confused and contradictory. Inexperienced and with few trusted friends, Alexander was temporarily at the mercy of the conspirators. They were eager to stabilize the new regime, and Alexander cooperated. His first acts aimed to restore confidence in government and promote economic recovery. A general amnesty freed some 12,000 people sentenced without trial under Paul. To stimulate the economy, all restrictions on imports and exports were lifted. Educational institutions were given support after having languished for years without funds. The Charter to the Nobility was officially reaffirmed. Once again nobles could travel abroad, take service with friendly powers, use private printing presses, elect their officials, and form provincial assemblies. Nobles were guaranteed freedom from corporal punishment and the poll tax and from having to billet troops. These measures aimed to restore noble confidence and foster security and stability.

Alexander soon recalled several youthful friends who had been sent abroad by his distrustful father. Returning to Russia, Prince Adam Czartoryski, Nicholas Novosiltsev, and Count Victor Kochubei, together with Count Paul Stroganov, constituted the Unofficial Committee, an informal group that met with Alexander over coffee to discuss general policy. These young Anglophile aristocrats (except Novosiltsev) favored abolition of serfdom and advocated enlightened absolutism, but neither they nor Alexander were democrats or desired a constitutional regime in the British sense. They and Alexander aimed to establish the rule of law in place of Paul's arbitrary despotism and to institute orderly, efficient government with separation of functions, not powers. All of them, including Alexander, wished to transform Russia into a more modern country, but gradually and without radical change. Alexandrine "constitutionalism," therefore, operated within narrow confines and did not include any limitations on the emperor's autocratic powers.

Alexander has often been portrayed as a liberal whose reform plans were frustrated by Russia's backwardness and entrenched upper-class privileges and vested interests. Allen McConnell, however, has argued persuasively that the liberals were the conspirators who lifted Alexander into power. The Zubovs and Pahlen in particular planned to transform the empire's basic political structure by granting genuine legislative powers to the Senate, powers traditionally exercised by the sovereign alone. Such a program, if implemented, would have imposed crucial limitations on the ruler and altered the state structure. Alexander, however, never sanctioned such drastic change and opposed vigorously and successfully all efforts to limit his authority. Once he felt secure, was assured of a loyal army, and was surrounded by his youthful friends, he moved against the conspirators, who posed a threat to his power. They were removed or exiled by the end of 1801. Once he was rid of the conspirators, the tone of Alexander's administration changed. Liberal-sounding initial measures were abruptly halted, and plans to reform the Senate, revise the law code, and issue a promised Charter of the Russian People were shelved. Now in full control, Alexander resolved to preserve full traditional monarchical authority. This decision may have been a crucial turning point in Russian political development—a turning away from constitutional or representative government.

Alexander drew closer to his young friends and discussed state affairs with them in secret. They all agreed that serfdom was inequitable and odious, but they failed to suggest serious measures to reform or abolish it. To be sure, members of the professional and merchant classes were given the right to purchase estates with serfs (formerly only nobles could) on the ground that they would be more humane serf owners, and public advertisement of serfs for sale without land was prohibited. Alexander, however, continued to turn over state lands and peasants to private individuals, though not as rapidly as Paul had done.

Only the Free Agriculturalists' Law of 1803, permitting landowners to free their peasants individually or in groups, was intended to benefit private serfs. This decree, however, did not confront the fundamental issues of serfdom and affected very few serfs. Perhaps recalling the fate of his father and grandfather (Peter III), Alexander would not risk measures that would have provoked intense noble hostility.

Alexander's most important and lasting administrative reform was the creation in September 1802 of government ministries. The Petrine administrative colleges, some of which had atrophied, were replaced by eight ministries: foreign affairs, war, navy, finance, interior, justice, commerce, and education. In theory the ministers were accountable to the Senate, which was to be a mediator between the sovereign and the administration. In practice the ministries completed the creation of a bureaucratic, centralized system administered by powerful officials directly responsible to the emperor. The new ministers were not to form a cabinet and consulted little among themselves on broad issues of policy. Each minister, heading a centralized department organized on military lines, reported directly to and received orders directly from Alexander. Confirming that Alexander did not conceive of the Committee of Ministers as a cabinet was his appointment of liberals, conservatives, and even reactionaries as ministers, men who could not possibly act collectively with unanimity. Members of the Unofficial Committee were all appointed to positions within the ministries: Czartoryski became deputy minister of foreign affairs; Novosiltsev, deputy minister of justice; Stroganov, deputy minister of the interior; and Kochubei, minister of the interior. Admiral N. S. Mordvinov, the navy minister, shared the political views of the Unofficial Committee, whereas G. R. Derzhavin, the minister of justice, was a confirmed reactionary.

The Committee of Ministers, however, did meet with Alexander to discuss important policy issues. The group, with its conflicting political views, remained largely a sounding board, with the tsar deciding all matters personally. Once Alexander became embroiled in conflict with Napoleon, the Committee of Ministers was empowered to decide all but the most important questions by majority vote. Absorbed in foreign policy, Alexander late in 1803 even ceased to meet with the Unofficial Committee. As relations between the tsar and his young friends grew strained, they began resigning their government positions to go into the army, education, or private life.

Education was a bright spot in an otherwise uninspired domestic policy. The shortage of adequately trained personnel, Alexander realized, hampered the proper functioning of bureaucratic monarchy because the educational system could not supply enough educated men to run the country. Creation of the Ministry of Education in 1802 showed that Alexander was determined to remedy this deficiency. This ministry supervised all educational institutions, including libraries, museums, printing presses, and censorship. Early in 1803 a new school statute divided the empire into educational districts, each of which was to have a university. A curator was to be the district's chief educational authority, responsible directly to the minister of education. Previously the only functioning university had been in Moscow (founded in 1755). Existing universities in Vilna (largely Polish) and Derpt (German) were revived, and new ones were founded in Kharkov and Kazan. St. Petersburg University was founded in 1819, bringing the total to six. Each university was to train teachers, disseminate knowledge, and supervise preparatory schools in its district. The educational system was open in theory to all classes, to anyone with the academic qualifications. Such egalitarianism offended the nobility, which wished to have education restricted to the privileged.

Clearly, the few serfs or nonnobles who possessed the necessary interest or qualifications scarcely threatened the upper classes. Nevertheless, a stated goal of the new system was to uncover and develop talent and skills useful to the state. Educational advances were perhaps modest in absolute terms, but relatively, progress was significant. Those officials with even a rudimentary education, however, remained few, and educational deficiencies continued to hamper bureaucratic efficiency.

Involvement in the coalition wars against Napoleon (1805–1807) distracted Alexander's interest from even modest domestic changes. Only after the Tilsit Treaty (1807) did he again consider projects for internal reform. His unpopular alliance with France, however, made the atmosphere at home less favorable for reform than it had been in 1801–1804.

Speranskii's Reform Program

The spearhead for reform came from a remarkable nonnoble bureaucrat, Mikhail Speranskii, son of an Orthodox priest. Born in a small village of Vladimir province in 1772, Speranskii had been educated at the local seminary; then, owing to his unusual ability and interest, he was sent to the Alexander Nevskii seminary in St. Petersburg to continue his education. Within two years his progress at what was then the best ecclesiastical school in Russia was such that he was appointed to the faculty. By 1795 he was already among the best-educated men in Russia, thoroughly familiar with advanced concepts of law, philosophy, politics, mathematics, and rhetoric as well as theology. Though assured of a brilliant academic career, he entered government service in 1797. A born bureaucrat, he possessed the ability to make even the most complex materials simple and understandable. His extraordinary stylistic brilliance made his memorandums and reports models of elegance, grace, and precision. Within three months he had risen to the eighth civil rank, which conferred hereditary nobility; by 1798 he

RIA-NOVOSTI/SOVFOTO

Mikhail M. Speranskii, 1772–1839, statesman and reformer of Imperial Russia.

occupied the sixth rank, equivalent to the rank of colonel in the army.

Count Kochubei, upon becoming interior minister in 1802, requested Speranskii's transfer to his ministry. As head of its Second Department, Speranskii handled police functions and internal welfare and drafted important measures such as the Free Agriculturalists' Law. In 1807 he attracted Alexander's personal attention when he began, in Count Kochubei's absence, to brief the tsar regularly on the ministry's activities. Impressed with Speranskii's ability to prepare succinct reports and to administer the ministry's complex affairs, Alexander relied on him increasingly for advice. When Alexander met Napoleon at Erfurt in 1808, Speranskii was there as a civilian observer. In a famous remark Speranskii told Alexander: "They [the French] have better institutions, we have better men." Soon Speranskii became deputy minister of justice, headed a commission to codify Russian laws, and was commissioned by

Alexander to draw up a plan to improve Russia's institutions.

By 1809 Speranskii had prepared a comprehensive plan for a largely new governmental system that would transform Russia from an autocracy based on the sovereign's absolute whim into a "true monarchy" based on the rule of law. The emperor would retain sovereign power and remain the source of all authority, but there would be separation of functions among three branches of government (see Figure 20.1). These functions would be coordinated by a Council of State containing the emperor's closest advisers. The executive branch would comprise the eight reformed ministries. An entirely new legislative branch would include elected assemblies (*dumy*) and executive boards (*pravleniia*) culminating in an indirectly elected State Duma. That body would meet annually, as long as its agenda required, to consider only those questions that the ministers submitted to it. This Duma, reminiscent of Muscovy's *zemskii sobor,* would lack all legislative initiative. Freed from bureaucratic control, the judicial branch would consist of courts at each of the four levels. The Senate, containing civil and criminal departments, would serve as a supreme court and review the decisions of lower courts.

The entire political system would be based on three social groups, which would no longer be rigid castes. Only the nobility, by virtue of education and real property, would possess full civil and political rights. The middle class (merchants, townspeople, free peasants) would enjoy basic civil rights, and its members would be able to vote if they owned real property. The third estate (peasants, workers), lacking political rights, could enter the middle class by acquiring property. This scheme reflects the stake-in-society concept of John Locke and the American Federalists and might well have provided a sound basis for political and social progress.

Historians differ as to whether Speranskii's plan advocated a *Rechtsstaat,* a state based on the rule of law, or was a genuine attempt to establish a

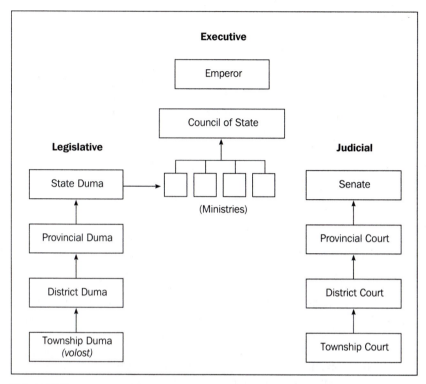

Figure 20.1
Speranskii's plan of 1809

limited, constitutional monarchy of Western type.[3] Alexander, however, found totally unacceptable any proposal limiting his authority, and so the only section of Speranskii's plan to be implemented was the one providing for the creation of a Council of State (1810) (see Figure 20.2). This body functioned as a sounding board for new legislation to the end of the empire. Speranskii was appointed secretary of state responsible for the Council of State's operation.

Speranskii's power was second only to that of the emperor himself. Concentration of such power in the hands of a single person, especially a social

upstart, naturally produced enmity and jealousy. Speranskii's foes among the nobility multiplied as his responsibilities and Alexander's dependence on him grew. Intent on improving the efficiency of the bureaucracy, Speranskii introduced compulsory examinations as the only entrée into state service and for promotion to the higher ranks. Speranskii's efforts to resolve the financial crisis by proposing a progressive tax on noble property infuriated the aristocracy. Speranskii had enemies even within the tsar's own family: A conservative circle formed around Catherine Pavlovna, Alexander's favorite sister. A leading figure associated with this circle was N. M. Karamzin, author of a spirited and patriotic defense of Russia's past traditions, *A Memoir on Ancient and Modern Russia*, which defended unlimited autocracy and stressed the role and status of the nobility. Karamzin's analysis of Russia's past and present, a classic

---

[3] M. Raeff, *Michael Speransky* . . . (The Hague, 1957), contains a full description of the plan. D. G. Christian's articles argue in favor of the view that the plan called for constitutional monarchy.

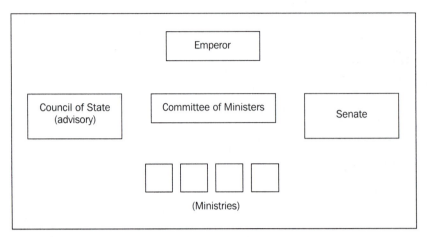

Figure 20.2
Administrative system under Alexander I, 1810

expression of Russian conservative thought, articulated the views of the privileged class.

Speranskii's most vocal enemies, not content with attacking his political views, resorted to slander and innuendo to undermine his position and accused him of being a French agent, negotiating secretly with Napoleon and trying to subvert Russia by introducing French legal and administrative practices. Alexander evidently recognized these accusations to be ridiculous, but faced with rising anti-French feeling, he could ill afford to keep Speranskii in office. In March 1812 Alexander capitulated reluctantly to "public opinion" and dismissed Speranskii, ending the reform era prematurely. There had been little concrete accomplishment as preparations for the confrontation with Napoleon shunted reform into the background, nor would the reforms be revived after the war.

The Arakcheevshchina

The last decade of Alexander's reign has customarily been viewed as one of unmitigated reaction associated with the sinister figure of Count A. A. Arakcheev. Indeed, the period is often called the Arakcheevshchina, or the rule of Arakcheev. Accu-

rate assessment of these years requires proper perspective, taking into account the atmosphere prevailing in Russia and the personalities of Alexander and his associates.

Russia's decisive contribution to Napoleon's defeat gave it unprecedented prestige abroad. Alexander "the Blessed," "the Savior of Europe," personified this new glory and renown. Victory, of course, had been achieved by the sacrifice and courage of the Russian people, among whom, in all social ranks, arose a mood anticipating major internal changes. Peasants yearned for reward in the form of emancipation and a lessening of their burdens. Educated society hoped for freer institutions and more cultural freedom. To satisfy such high expectations would have required radical reforms, which Alexander considered impractical and dangerous.

The traumatic events of the Napoleonic Wars had altered Alexander's political outlook. He was influenced deeply by the religious mysticism of Baroness von Krüdener, who had revealed that he was God's chosen instrument for the redemption of mankind. Alexander had been introduced by Prince A. N. Golitsyn to Bible study in 1812. Golitsyn then founded the Russian Bible Society with close ties to Protestant and Catholic circles.

Alexander did not renounce his hopes of reform, but he became more fearful of revolution. Insisting upon constitutions for defeated France and the restored Kingdom of Poland, he continued to consider reform for Russia. Speranskii, recalled from exile and appointed governor general of Siberia, hoped that a reformed bureaucracy and thorough reorganization of the legal code would gradually change the empire into a semiconstitutional monarchy. The emperor enthusiastically approved Novosiltsev's draft constitution but then failed to proclaim it. Disturbing events in Europe contributed to growing malaise in Russia. Student associations, secret societies, assassinations, and minor revolts in Europe worried Alexander and made him unwilling to permit the people any voice in the process of government.

While he toyed with constitutional ideas, Alexander depended heavily on Count Arakcheev, who occupied a position similar to that held by Speranskii earlier. Arrogant, cruel, power-hungry, and vindictive, Arakcheev, though doggedly loyal, represented the dark side of the political forces of Alexander's last decade; he is associated with the military colonies, which he administered. Their precise origin is unknown, but there were many precedents in Russia, Austria, and Prussia. Arakcheev had organized his own estates along quasimilitary lines, and Alexander may have derived the concept of military colonies from them. The tsar aimed to improve the military and reduce the costs of a huge standing army. He voiced humanitarian concern for his troops, who had to serve 25 years, separated from their families. The military colonies were designed to remedy all of these problems. Army recruits with their families were to be settled on state lands, combining military training and exercises with agricultural pursuits.

Begun on an experimental basis before the Napoleonic invasion, colonies became widespread afterward. Initially they were an experiment in social reform designed to improve living conditions and the socioeconomic status of recruits. Colonists were to be granted inviolability of property and sufficient land to till free of charge. Freed from all state taxes and forced labor service, each

was to be given a horse and living quarters, and the infirm were to be cared for. This experiment might have served as a model for future emancipation, except that reality did not conform to theory. A chief aim of military colonies was to reduce the costs of a huge standing army, equal to those of Austria and Prussia combined. The provisions just outlined would have bankrupted an already overburdened treasury. Under Arakcheev's administration, the reality included merciless exploitation, misery, mismanagement, and open resistance. Alexander denounced the military colonists for being ungrateful for the opportunities provided by the state. "There will be military colonies whatever the cost, even if one has to line the road from Petersburg to Chudovo with corpses," he thundered when informed of open unrest in the colonies. He expanded these infamous institutions to include almost a third of the million-man Russian army.

The military colonies were unpopular with their inmates, who suffered draconian discipline and frequent corporal punishment. The colonies combined some of the worst features of serfdom and army barracks and were bitterly denounced by liberals as barbaric. As violent protests by military colonists increased, even conservative elements expressed fear that uprisings in the colonies might touch off a general insurrection. The notorious military colonies revealed again Alexander's callousness toward a peasantry that had served him so well in war.

The Decembrist Revolt

Alexander's fear of the lower classes promoted distrust of all social groups, notably the youthful noblemen who had served as junior officers in the Russian advance across Europe. As many of them abandoned military careers and entered universities, Alexander took alarm at the rapid spread of "Jacobinism," of liberal and radical ideas that were perhaps tolerable when discussed secretly by top government leaders but were potentially explosive when debated publicly. There was also a growth of obscurantist, reactionary views tinged with religious mysticism. Alexander selected as minister of education Prince A. N. Golitsyn, director of the Russian Bible Society and procurator of the Holy Synod. Education and religion thus became inextricably connected. As head of the Bible Society, Golitsyn was tolerant toward Protestant and Catholic churches and toward religious sectarians, but as minister of education he espoused reactionary and intolerant views and unleashed a host of obscurantist bureaucrats upon the educational system. He aimed to root out all liberal and controversial influences from the schools and universities. Universities were purged of professors who disagreed with Golitsyn's bureaucrats or who had been dismissed for "teaching in a spirit contrary to Christianity and subversive of the social order." Such men as Mikhail Magnitskii and Dmitri Runich—curators, respectively, of the Kazan and St. Petersburg school districts—sought to transform educational institutions into docile purveyors of official rhetoric and conservatism. Magnitskii recommended that Kazan University, as a dangerous and unnecessary institution, be closed completely. Alexander would not go that far, but he encouraged increasing vigilance and control. The universities were emasculated, and the cause of learning suffered severe blows.

With the peasantry ground down by serfdom and military colonies, what opposition there was developed within the aristocracy. In the tradition of Radishchev, educated noble army officers recognized the glaring contradictions and shocking injustices of the Russian system. These young men, upon returning home, were struck by the enormous gulf separating European social and political life from Russia's. These officers, mostly veterans of the Russian army of occupation in France, had absorbed liberal and radical ideas there and had experienced the freer atmosphere of western Europe. These experiences equipped them with a heightened social consciousness and greater interest in public affairs. They were acutely conscious of contradictions in Alexandrine policies: Alexander the Blessed abroad but Alexander the Despot at home; constitutions and civil liberties for foreign countries, and even for Poland and Finland within the Russian Empire, but serfdom and military colonies for Russia. The most powerful country in Europe, Russia was shamefully backward in domestic affairs. European events also stimulated Russian thought as revolts in Spain, Naples, and Piedmont in 1820–1821 reflected popular opposition to reactionary postwar governments.

In such circumstances idealistic, liberal-minded young Russian aristocrats naturally sought to act in defense of freedom and justice. In Russia public debate of fundamental issues was impossible, and this situation promoted the formation in 1816 of the first secret society, the Union of Salvation. Founded by elite guards officers, all members of prominent and distinguished noble families, the Union of Salvation, like similar secret societies springing up in western Europe, resembled a Masonic lodge, with a constitution and degrees of initiation. Prominent among its small membership were Nikita Muraviev, Prince Sergei Trubetskoi, and Paul Pestel, young men who hoped to revivify Russia by abolishing serfdom and military colonies and introducing a constitutional regime. They disagreed, however, on how to achieve these broad aims. In 1818 this informal group was reorganized as the Union of Welfare, with an elaborate apparatus but a vague political creed ranging from mild reformism to radical revolution. Members were urged to spread enlightenment through philanthropic activity similar to that of Masonic lodges. The Union of Welfare attracted some 200 members, mostly from the guards regiments and chiefly veterans of the Napoleonic Wars. By 1820 the government knew of its existence, and faced with official threats, the Union decided to disband. A few members maintained a smaller supersecret society with headquarters in St. Petersburg. Colonel Pestel, who had been transferred to the south, organized a second secret group.

Three major groups of what were subsequently called Decembrists emerged after 1820: a Northern Society in St. Petersburg, a Southern Society in the south, and the Society of United Slavs on the southwestern frontier. These groups were separated by distance and differing political views. The Northern Society, representing the upper gentry, tended to be more moderate, whereas the more radical Southern Society sought to enlist the support of ordinary soldiers scorned by their northern brethren. The Society of United Slavs was largely composed of poor gentry and was the only Decembrist element to favor a mass revolution; soon it merged with the Southern Society.

Nikita Muraviev, leader of the Northern Society, produced a constitution for Russia that incorporated the moderate views of his wealthy gentry colleagues. Its preamble summarized his political philosophy:

> The experience of all nations and of all times has proved that autocratic government is equally fatal to rulers and society; that it is not in accordance with the rules of our sacred religion or with the principles of common sense; it is not permissible to let the basis of government be the despotism of one person; it is impossible to agree that all rights shall be on one side and all duties on the other.[4]

Muraviev demanded the abolition of serfdom and military colonies and the prohibition of all social distinctions. His constitution guaranteed freedom of speech, religion, and assembly, and landowners were assured of the right to own their estates. Following the U. S. Constitution, Muraviev envisaged a Russia divided into thirteen states and two provinces. A bicameral National Assembly consisting of a Supreme Duma and a Chamber of Representatives would exercise legislative power, but the franchise and officeholding would be restricted to men of wealth and property. Each state and province was to have both state and local assemblies. Executive power would be entrusted to a hereditary emperor with powers similar to those of the American president. Muraviev envisioned a liberal constitutional monarchy run by the nobility.

Pestel and the Southern Society rejected Muraviev's constitution as "legalized aristocracy."

This son of the governor-general of Siberia and the first dedicated Russian revolutionary composed *Russkaia Pravda* (Russian Justice) to guide a provisional government after the revolution had overthrown tsarism. All existing social institutions would be abolished: serfdom, military colonies, and aristocratic privileges and titles. All men were to be considered equal. Pestel advocated a centralized government, a single culture, and a single language, which clearly was to be Russian. Except for the Poles, who would become independent, national and religious minorities must abandon their institutions and faiths in a Russia "one and indivisible," in contrast to the federalism implicit in Muraviev's constitution. Pestel would concentrate legislative authority in a unicameral National Assembly with broad powers and elected by universal male suffrage. Executive power was to be held by a five-member State Council elected by the National Assembly (like the French Directory of 1795–1799). To implement this political program, Pestel envisioned the need for an authoritarian provisional government for a decade or so. Then it would yield its powers to a centralized republic that would exert absolute control over its citizens' behavior and thoughts through the clergy and police. Like the radical and puritanical French Jacobins of the 1790s, Pestel would bar card playing and all dissipation. Private property was to be "sacred and inviolable," but half of the land, much of it confiscated from the large serf owners, would be state-owned and distributed to those who wished to work it in accordance with need. Pestel's vision fused in strange combination Great Russian nationalism, Jacobin republicanism, dictatorship, and elements of socialism.

Most members of the Northern Society were horrified at Pestel's political and social program, especially at the violent minority seizure of power that Pestel advocated. Persuasion and peaceful change were the principles upon which Muraviev wished to act. Still, vague discussions were held between the two groups, and there was tacit agreement that some action would be taken in 1826. Early in 1825 Muraviev and Trubetskoi were temporarily replaced as leaders of the Northern

---

[4] Marc Raeff, *The Decembrist Movement* (Englewood Cliffs, NJ, 1966), p. 103.

Society by Kondraty Ryleev, a radical poet sympathetic with Pestel's views. While in Kiev, Trubetskoi agreed with Pestel to establish closer ties between the two societies, and that fall he began to arrange a closer alliance with the southerners. Soon events interrupted all theoretical planning. On November 19, 1825, Alexander I died unexpectedly in Taganrog on the Sea of Azov.

Alexander and his wife were childless, and normally the throne would have passed to Constantine, his younger brother. Unknown to virtually everyone, Constantine had renounced all rights to the throne in 1820 after divorcing his first wife to marry a Polish countess. Continuing to reside in Poland, he took little interest in Russian court affairs. In 1823 Alexander had formally designated his youngest brother, Nicholas, as heir apparent. A sealed copy of a manifesto to that effect was kept in Moscow; other copies were deposited in state institutions with instructions to open them in the event of Alexander's death. Though vaguely aware of all this, Nicholas was uncertain of his status, and so he immediately swore allegiance to Constantine and ordered that this oath be administered throughout the empire. When Constantine failed to accept or renounce the throne and remained in Warsaw, the resulting confusion and uncertainty afforded the conspirators opportunity to act. They had agreed that Alexander's death by natural causes or assassination would trigger an attempt to overthrow the government. Nicholas learned of a possible conspiracy in St. Petersburg and the south and resolved to have himself proclaimed emperor on December 14, 1825, and then to have the oath of allegiance administered to the troops. The Northern Society's leaders agreed to stage a revolt on December 14. Trubetskoi, selected as "dictator," had just three days to prepare an uprising.

The conspirators made no definite plans and few preparations, anticipating that their troops would follow orders at the appointed time. Many clearly recognized the hopelessness of their cause. "We are destined to die!" Ryleev announced melodramatically. December 14 was a comedy of errors. Ryleev was ill, and "Dictator" Trubetskoi

failed to appear. Only about 3,000 troops on Senate Square in St. Petersburg refused the oath of allegiance to Nicholas, and even they did not understand why. The conspirators made no attempt to enlist support from a sympathetic crowd of commoners, which had gathered on the edge of the square. When the government failed to disperse the rebel troops peacefully, Nicholas ordered his men to fire. In the volley of canister shot that followed, many rebels and even more innocent bystanders were killed or wounded. The rebels fled, and the abortive revolt came to an ignominious end. The Southern Society, out of touch with events in the capital, acted somewhat later but with similar lack of success. Pestel had been arrested even before December 14, and the two companies of the Chernigov Regiment that rebelled under the Muraviev-Apostol brothers were soon subdued. Nicholas set up a commission of inquiry to investigate the entire Decembrist affair. It interrogated more than 600 people, of whom 121 were brought to trial before a special tribunal of five judges (one was Speranskii). Five leaders were sentenced to death; 31 were exiled to Siberia for life; and the remaining 85 were exiled for shorter periods.

The Decembrist Revolt is often considered the last of the palace coups common in the 18th century, but the revolt on Senate Square aimed at a fundamental alteration of the system of government, not the mere replacement of one ruler by another. In this sense the Decembrist Revolt began a genuine revolutionary movement led by the intelligentsia that would culminate in the Revolution of 1917. The Decembrist Revolt was unique as the only time until 1917 that revolutionary ferment would center in the ranks of army officers. For the balance of the century the army would support the autocracy. The revolt became a powerful myth inspiring generations of Russian radicals, who saw the Decembrists as heroic defenders of the rights of man. Soviet historians have hailed these noble revolutionaries as the first Russians to build a revolutionary organization and prepare armed action against tsarism. The revolt failed because it lacked preparation and adequate leadership, but also because it was premature. Only a tiny minority of the population had any comprehension of the ideas that motivated the Decembrists to act. Like their successors, the Decembrists, isolated from the populace, did not represent and could not articulate popular needs except in the vaguest way.

The Alexandrine era closed, as it had opened, on a note of violence. The promise of fundamental reform enunciated in 1801 was blocked by Alexander's stubborn insistence on maintaining his full autocratic powers. Speranskii's approach, which might have prepared the way for a constitutional monarchy based on law, was not given a chance. Serfdom and autocracy remained as the apparently unshakable core of the Russian imperial system.

Suggested Additional Reading

BOOKS

ALMEDINGEN, E. M. *The Emperor Alexander I* (London, 1964).

CZARTORYSKI, A. *Memoirs and Correspondence with Alexander I*, ed. A. Gielgud, 2 vols. (Hattiesburg, MS, 1968). (Reprint.)

DZIEWANOWSKI, M. K. *Alexander I: Russia's Mysterious Tsar* (New York, 1990).

JENKINS, M. *Arakcheev: Grand Vizir of the Russian Empire* (New York, 1969).

MAZOUR, A. G. *The First Russian Revolution 1825: The Decembrist Movement* (Stanford, 1937).

———. *Women in Exile: Wives of the Decembrists* (Tallahassee, 1975).

MCCONNELL, A. *Tsar Alexander I: Paternalistic Reformer* (New York, 1970).

MCGREW, R. *Paul I of Russia, 1754–1801* (New York, 1992).

MIKHAILOVICH, N. *Scenes of Court Life* (London, n.d.).

PALMER, A. *Alexander I: Tsar of War and Peace* (London, 1974).

PIPES, RICHARD. *Karamzin's Memoir on Ancient and Modern Russia . . .* (Cambridge, MA, 1959).

RAEFF, MARC. *The Decembrist Movement* (Englewood Cliffs, NJ, 1966).

———. *Michael Speransky, Statesman of Imperial Russia . . .* (The Hague, 1957).

———. *Siberia and the Reforms of 1822* (Seattle, 1956).

RAGSDALE, HUGH, ed. *Paul I: A Reassessment of His Life and Reign* (Pittsburgh, 1979).

———. *Tsar Paul and the Question of Madness . . .* (New York, 1988).

STRAKHOVSKY, L. *Alexander I of Russia* (New York, 1947).

ARTICLES

LANG, D. "Radishchev and the Legislative Commission of Alexander I." *ASEER* 6 (1947): 11–24.

LOEWENSON, L. "The Death of Paul I . . ." *SEER* 29 (1950): 212–32.

MCCONNELL, A. "Alexander I." *MERSH* 1: 126–32.

———. "Alexander I's Hundred Days." *SR* 28 (1969): 373–93.

MCGREW, R. "A Political Portrait of Paul I . . ." *JfGO* 18 (1970): 503–29.

NARKIEWICZ, O. "Alexander I and the Senate Reform." *SEER* 48 (1969): 115–36.

RAGSDALE, H. "Paul I." *MERSH* 27: 64–73.

———, ed. "The Reign of Paul I." *CanAmSlSt* 7, no. 1 (1973): (entire issue).

VERNADSKY, G. "Reforms under Alexander I . . ." *RoP* 9 (1947): 47–64.

21

War and Diplomacy, 1796–1825

Russia played a vital role in European power politics during the French Revolution and the Napoleonic era. Under Paul I it joined European efforts to block French expansion and began a successful Mediterranean policy. Under Alexander I Russia fought Napoleon in central Europe (1805–1807), repelled Napoleon's invasion of 1812, and headed the European resurgence that overthrew him in 1814. Victory over Napoleon brought Russia to its peak of power in the tsarist period and gave it predominance in eastern Europe. Personal shortcomings prevented Alexander from exploiting Russian victories fully, and afterward, in upholding the Vienna Settlement, he followed in Austria's wake. What were Russia's aims in Europe? Why the alternating cooperation and conflict with Napoleon? Which factors defeated the French invasion of Russia? How did Russia's great victory over Napoleon affect its foreign policy afterward?

Paul I

Paul hated and feared revolutionary France even more than his mother did and sought by every

means to bar Jacobin principles from Russia. At first he refused to join an anti-French coalition, partly because his advisers feared foreign war would worsen Russia's financial and administrative problems, and he negotiated with the French Directory to restore the relations that Catherine had suspended. Assuming an increasing role in foreign policy, Paul sought to consolidate his empire, remain neutral in the Anglo-French struggle, and avoid binding commitments abroad.

A French challenge to Russian interests in the eastern Mediterranean and central Europe upset his cautious approach. In 1798 Napoleon launched a program of conquest: He seized Malta, the Ionian Islands, and Egypt and invaded Syria. The deeply religious Paul had long been interested in the Maltese Order of the Knights of St. John, and his first foreign agreement (January 1797) was with the order's grand master after the French had confiscated its assets in France. That November he was named a protector of Malta, and French seizure of the island in June 1798 triggered Russian intervention in the Mediterranean. Imbued with a mystic aim to revive chivalry in Russia and Europe, Paul wished to lead a crusade against the "infidel" French Revolution. He viewed the order as the vanguard of counterrevolution and strove to build an international movement to support traditional churches and monarchies.

The Second Coalition against France, headed by Russia and Great Britain, also included Austria, the Ottoman Empire, and Naples. The unprecedented Russo-Turkish alliance, provoked by the French threat, was the basis for anti-French action in the eastern Mediterranean. After Napoleon's invasion of Egypt caused the Porte to declare war on France and seek Russian aid, a Russo-Turkish expedition under Vice Admiral F. F. Ushakov liberated the Ionian Islands. While the war lasted, Russia sent its warships freely through the Turkish Straits and used Ionian bases to exert strong influence in the eastern Mediterranean. Simultaneously, Russia established important political ties with the Balkan Christians (Paul decorated and subsidized the prince of Montenegro). On land Austro-Russian forces fought the French in Italy as General Suvorov scored repeated victories, but growing suspicion soon estranged the allies. In the war's most dramatic (but futile) episode Suvorov's army struggled heroically through the Swiss Alps, but Austria's withdrawal from Switzerland induced Paul to recall Suvorov, and the Second Coalition dissolved without real result.

In 1800 Paul's policy shifted as Anglo-Russian tension grew over the enhanced Russian role in the Mediterranean. After the British captured Malta from the French, Russia seized British property and sailors and suspended commercial and diplomatic relations. A Russo-Swedish alliance (October 1799) became the cornerstone of a second League of Armed Neutrality to protect neutral seaborne trade against British seizures. Great Britain and Russia drifted toward war while Paul undertook rapprochement with Napoleon's Consulate, which, he believed, was no revolutionary threat. Responding to Napoleon's peace overtures, Paul supported him against Great Britain and proposed a Franco-Russian expedition against British India as part of plans for southward expansion. Napoleon, approving the Indian venture, delayed sending troops, but in February 1801 Paul

ordered 22,000 Cossacks through the central Asian deserts toward India. His murder, preventing full implementation of this fantastic scheme, averted war with Great Britain.

Paul's foreign policy seemingly lacked coherence or overall planning. Except in the Mediterranean, where Russian power was increased temporarily, little was accomplished. Paul's hatred of revolution drew him initially into an anti-French coalition similar to the Holy Alliance of his son Alexander, but whim, not national interest, predominated in his foreign policy.

Alexander I: Orientation and Initial Policies, 1801–1804

Alexander and his chief advisers, defending monarchical and aristocratic values, were profoundly oriented to Europe and sought to preserve a balance of power. At times they sought to promote peace abroad in order to concentrate on domestic reform; at other times they involved Russia deeply in European power struggles. Alexander himself made the chief policy decisions and often conferred with foreign ambassadors and heads of state. Viewing foreign relations theoretically, he stressed neither pragmatic security nor commercial interests. He considered war a justifiable extension of diplomacy but entered into it reluctantly, mostly for defensive reasons. "If I make use of arms . . . ," he stated in 1801, "it will be only to repulse an unjust aggression." "What need have I to increase my empire?" he asked Chateaubriand in 1823. "Providence has not put 800,000 soldiers at my orders to satisfy my ambition but to protect religion and justice and to preserve those principles of order on which human society rests."[1]

At first Alexander, anxious to pursue domestic reform, sought general European peace. To avert war with Great Britain, he recalled the Cossacks sent to India and freed British property in Russia.

---

[1] Quoted in P. Grimsted, *The Foreign Ministers of Alexander I* (Berkeley, 1969), pp. 44–45.

Lord Nelson's destruction of the Danish fleet (April 1801) damaged the Russian-led League of Armed Neutrality; but only two months later an Anglo-Russian convention was signed and normal relations were restored. In October Alexander and Napoleon reached an agreement to respect Ionian independence and Neapolitan neutrality, and the tsar promoted Anglo-French talks culminating in the Peace of Amiens. To achieve rapprochement with England, Alexander then sacrificed the League of Armed Neutrality. Russia also resumed good relations with Austria while continuing to protect the small German states. Acting Foreign Minister Victor Kochubei's "passive system" of nonintervention appeared to be successful.

Alexander, preferring a weak Porte under Russian protection to partition of the Ottoman Empire, continued the Russo-Turkish alliance, which guaranteed Russia's position in the eastern Mediterranean. Rejecting suggestions for a partition, he declared that Russia favored Ottoman integrity. Meanwhile, Russia's Black Sea commerce, protected by its fleet, rose from 5.5 percent of its total seaborne trade in 1802 to 12.9 percent in 1805.

Anti-French feeling soon developed at the Russian court, however, fostered by Alexander I's Anglophile "young friends." As Napoleon's ambitions unfolded and relations with Great Britain improved, Russian ties with France deteriorated. Viewing himself as the champion of liberty, Alexander came to identify Napoleon with despotism, especially after the abduction and execution of the Duke d'Enghien, a member of the Bourbon family, from neutral Baden in March 1804. Napoleon's insulting response to Russian protests over this incident led to the severing of diplomatic relations, and Russia moved into the waiting arms of England.

Coalition Wars, 1805–1807

Great Britain resumed war with Napoleon in 1803 and eagerly sought continental allies. When Russia and Austria responded favorably, a Third Coalition formed against France, organized chiefly by Prince Adam Czartoryski, assistant Russian foreign minister and Alexander's intimate friend. Czartoryski, a Polish aristocrat, aimed at maximum Russian involvement abroad in order to reconstruct Europe and resurrect Poland under Russia's wing. N. Novosiltsev, bearing Czartoryski's instructions, went to England on a secret mission (November 1804) to arrange an alliance against Napoleon. His instructions advocated an Anglo-Russian league to restrict France to its natural frontiers while assuring the French that their national interests would be secured, and outlined ambitious Russian territorial goals: all of Poland, Moldavia, Malta, Constantinople, and the Turkish Straits. If the Ottoman Empire collapsed, Great Britain and Russia were to confer on its partition. Prime Minister William Pitt raised objections over Malta and the Straits, then consented to an Anglo-Russian alliance to liberate non-French regions from Napoleonic rule. In return for British subsidies, Russia would supply most of the land forces. Some Russian leaders opposed this alliance, but Alexander finally ratified it. Austria and Russia had agreed earlier that in a war with France, Austria would raise 235,000 men and Russia 115,000. Sweden and Naples also joined the Third Coalition.

The campaign of 1805 brought disaster to the allies. Napoleon, marching eastward, forced an Austrian army at Ulm to surrender. General M. I. Kutuzov's Russian army joined the main Austrian force in Bohemia, but poor Austrian generalship and Alexander's impatience for military glory wrecked the prospects of the allies. Kutuzov's sound advice to await reinforcements was rejected, and at Austerlitz (December 1805) Napoleon won a decisive victory. Kutuzov extracted the bulk of his army, but Austria made peace and Prussia became pro-French, while the Third Coalition expired ingloriously.

Napoleon next expanded in the Balkans, inducing Austria to cede Dalmatia, Istria, and Kotor (Cattaro) to his Kingdom of Italy. Admiral D. N. Seniavin, commanding Russia's Mediterranean fleet, resolved to deny the French use of Kotor, ator and flocked to his banners. That winter the Russians and French fought two bloody, indecisive battles in East Prussia. Finally, Napoleon won a hard-earned victory at Friedland (June 1807). Alexander, distracted by wars against the Porte and Persia and dissatisfied with British subsidies, decided on peace. He was influenced by court pressures and Russia's financial and military exhaustion.

M. I. Kutuzov (1745–1813), commander in chief 1812–1813.

Tilsit and the Franco-Russian Alliance, 1807–1812

In June 1807 Napoleon and Alexander met alone on a raft in the Niemen River, which separated the French and Russian forces. Reportedly the tsar declared that he hated the English as much as Napoleon did. "If so," Napoleon supposedly declared, "then peace is concluded," and at Tilsit Alexander and Napoleon concluded peace and a secret alliance against Great Britain. Alexander made his own decisions and was not duped by Napoleon as some contemporaries believed. For Alexander survival of his empire was paramount: Russia needed peace and friendship with France, he believed, in order to recover its strength. In the Tilsit bargaining Alexander proved a more stubborn, calculating negotiator than Napoleon had anticipated.

The Tilsit accords created a rough division of Europe into French and Russian spheres of interest, and Russia became Napoleon's junior partner in his efforts to force Great Britain to submit. Prussia lost all of its territory east of the Elbe, and from its Polish lands Napoleon erected the Duchy of Warsaw, a French satellite state. Russia received the Polish district of Belostok but yielded its Mediterranean foothold to France and recognized Napoleon's brothers as kings of Naples and Westphalia. Admiral Seniavin's fleet, losing its bases and blocked from the Black Sea, surrendered to the British. Alexander pledged secretly to mediate between France and England and to declare war on Great Britain if he failed; in return, Napoleon would try to mediate a Russo-Turkish settlement, or failing that, would "make common cause" with

persuaded the Austrians to yield it to him, and allied Russia with Montenegro. Dominating the Adriatic, Seniavin blockaded the French in Dubrovnik and tightened Russian ties with the Balkan Slavs. Napoleon's agents, bribing the sultan with promises of territorial gain, however, persuaded the Turks to fight Russia. After the sultan's arbitrary removal of the rulers of the Danubian Principalities provoked Russia to occupy them, the Porte declared war on Russia (October 1806) and closed the Straits. Alexander then authorized his Balkan commanders to cooperate with Serbian insurgents under Karadjordje and secure Serbia's autonomy from the Turks.

Late in 1806 a Fourth Coalition formed against France as Prussia replaced fallen Austria. King Frederick William III, angered by arbitrary French actions in west Germany and swayed by Alexander, demanded a French withdrawal to the Rhine. Napoleon responded with a lightning stroke, destroying the main Prussian forces at Jena and capturing Berlin before the slow-moving Russians arrived. The Poles greeted Napoleon as their liber-

Russia. A secret alliance treaty committed France and Russia to fight side by side with all of their resources in any European conflict.

The French alliance proved so unpopular in Russia that some called Alexander "Napoleon's henchman," and there was even talk of a palace coup; but Alexander persisted in his dealings with Napoleon. As foreign minister, he appointed N. P. Rumiantsev, a wealthy serf owner who favored ties with France. Although Tilsit allowed France to dominate most of the continent, establish a French base on Russia's borders, and win Polish support, it nonetheless gave Russia an urgently needed breathing spell, preserved shrunken Prussia's independence, and enabled Russia to acquire Finland. For Russia, the worst consequences of Tilsit were conflict with Great Britain and membership in the French Continental System, which Napoleon had proclaimed in 1806 in order to bar British goods from Europe.

A breach with Great Britain followed. After the British destroyed the Danish fleet to prevent its use against them, Russia broke relations with Great Britain and declared war on it. Early in 1808 Napoleon proposed to Alexander a joint campaign against British India and possible partition of the Ottoman Empire, promising Russia the Danubian Principalities and northern Bulgaria; France would take Albania and much of Greece. France and Russia, however, clashed over Constantinople and the Straits (Rumiantsev insisted on these), negotiations broke down, and the expedition against India was abandoned.

One consequence of Tilsit was a Russo-Swedish war. Because King Gustav IV of Sweden, allied with Great Britain, remained stubbornly anti-French, Napoleon encouraged Alexander to seize the Swedish province of Finland, and Rumiantsev persuaded him to make this move in order to assuage Russian patriotic opinion and protect St. Petersburg. Within six months the Swedes were driven from Finland and ceded it to Russia (1809), though guerrilla warfare revealed Finnish hostility to Russia. To calm this resistance, Alexander pledged to respect Finnish laws, religion, and

institutions; Finland became a grand duchy within the Russian Empire.

At the Erfurt meeting of Napoleon and Alexander (1808), Napoleon tried to tighten his alliance with Alexander by recognizing Russia's claims to Finland and the Danubian Principalities, but Alexander refused to join France in a war against Austria. In fury Napoleon threw down his hat and stamped on it, but to no avail. Talleyrand, the French foreign minister, foreseeing Napoleon's ultimate fall, secretly urged the tsar to resist his demands. When Austria rose in 1809, Russian troops on the Galician frontier moved in only to prevent the Poles from uniting Galicia with the Duchy of Warsaw. Napoleon finally defeated Austria, but he deeply resented Russia's inaction, and he was angered further by the refusal of Alexander's sister to marry him.

The Franco-Russian alliance broke down for many reasons. Like Adolf Hitler after him (see Chapter 38), Napoleon aimed to control all Europe. His bloated ambitions and arrogance conflicted with vital Russian interests in the Balkans, the Straits, and Poland, and his arbitrary annexation of Oldenburg, a north German state ruled by a relative of the tsar, confirmed the divergence of Napoleon and Alexander. Their economic differences also increased because Russia had joined the Continental System most reluctantly and its participation remained halfhearted. Anglo-Russian trade dwindled, but Alexander did not enforce measures against British contraband. Russian merchants and landowners, hurt by a Continental System that prohibited normal trade with England, complained vehemently. Alexander's decree of December 1810 imposed heavy customs duties on French imports, and he refused to close Russian ports to neutral vessels. Franco-Russian economic interests proved incompatible, and trade with Great Britain remained vital to Russia. Talleyrand kept exhorting Alexander to form a coalition against Napoleon: "You must save Europe." In 1811–1812, though Rumiantsev espoused loyal cooperation with France, both sides prepared for conflict.

Napoleon Invades Russia, 1812

The War of 1812 (Soviet historians call it the "first fatherland war") decided Franco-Russian competition for European supremacy. Western scholars often attribute Napoleon's defeat in Russia to distance, bad roads, and climate, whereas Soviet historians emphasize General Kutuzov's brilliant strategy and generalship and the heroism and patriotism of the Russian people. All of these factors, as well as Russia's size and manpower reserves and Alexander I's courage and persistence, contributed to victory in a campaign described graphically in Leo Tolstoy's immortal novel *War and Peace* (see Chapter 29).

Napoleon hoped by conquering Russia to deny all continental markets to Great Britain and encompass its defeat. "In five years I shall be ruler of the world; there remains only Russia, but I shall crush her," he declared in 1811. Europe's fate rested upon Russia's ability to resist a French invasion. By pressure and force, Napoleon had built a formidable European coalition based on military alliances with weakened Austria and Prussia. (Privately their rulers assured Alexander that their participation would be only nominal.) Most Poles, believing that French victory would restore their independence, supported Napoleon. On the eve of the invasion Russia managed to erase potential threats on the north and the south. Welcoming a Russian pledge to help it recover Norway, Sweden secretly allied with Russia; and the Turks, whom Napoleon had hoped would tie up Russian forces and even invade Ukraine, were defeated repeatedly by General Kutuzov. Russian willingness to return most of the Danubian Principalities and Turkish losses outweighed French pressure. The Treaty of Bucharest (May 1812), giving Russia Bessarabia and part of the Caucasian Black Sea coast, released sizable Russian forces and contributed to victory over the French. Once the war began, Russia allied with Great Britain and Spain, Napoleon's other enemies.

On June 24, 1812, without a declaration of war, Napoleon's Grand Army of some 400,000 men (almost 600,000 with later reinforcements) invaded Russia. It included about 250,000 French, many Poles (who fought willingly), and Germans, Italians, and Spaniards (mostly recruited forcibly). Facing them were some 200,000 Russians in three armies: one under the supreme commander, Barclay de Tolly; a second under Prince P. I. Bagration; and reserves under General Alexander Tormasov. The Russians, though heavily outnumbered, were roughly equal to the Grand Army in armament and superior in morale. Initial numerical inferiority compelled them to retreat into the interior, avoiding a decisive battle and destroying foodstuffs and supplies.

Napoleon's precise objectives in Russia remained obscure, though he evidently wished to engage and destroy the Russian army near the frontier and restore Russia to obedient partnership. Soviet historians argued that Napoleon (like Hitler later) aimed to exclude Russia from the Baltic and Black seas, take away its western lands, and thrust it into Asia. Moving through friendly Lithuania and eastern Poland, Napoleon reached Vilna on June 28. He decided against emancipating the Russian serfs, explaining that rousing such savages against the nobility would make orderly government impossible. The possible effects of such a proclamation are hard to gauge. In mid-August, when Napoleon reached Smolensk on the road to Moscow, there was heavy fighting but no decisive battle, and the Russian armies linked up and withdrew eastward. Personal friction among Russian commanders and public outcry at their retreat induced Alexander to remove Barclay and name the aged but popular Field Marshal Kutuzov commander in chief.

Plunging eastward, Napoleon met Kutuzov's forces at Borodino, about 75 miles west of Moscow (see Map 21.1), where on September 7 was fought the greatest battle of the campaign and Napoleon's career. The French captured key positions, but Napoleon withheld his guard, which might have destroyed the battered Russian army. Withdrawing to Fili near Moscow, Kutuzov consulted his generals at a council of war, then decided to abandon Moscow. This unpopular but wise move brought Alexander I's prestige to its

Map 21.1 Napoleonic Wars and Russia

nadir. He turned over the army to Kutuzov and the government to his ministers, but his unwavering determination to resist and his refusal to negotiate while the French remained on Russian soil contributed significantly to ultimate victory.

Napoleon entered Moscow on September 14, expecting supplies and Russian peace offers, but as the French occupied the largely deserted city, fires broke out and, fanned by a strong wind, destroyed most of it. Napoleon had to flee the Kremlin in haste. The fires probably broke out spontaneously as French soldiers looted the city. To Napoleon's dismay, Alexander and Kutuzov refused to parley, while at Tarutino, southwest of Moscow, lay Kutuzov's army guarding armament and supply centers and the unconquered south. Kutuzov was being steadily reinforced while French strength dwindled and numerous partisans and mobile Cossack units raided their communications. Napoleon's position in Moscow became untenable.

On October 19 Napoleon abandoned Moscow, intending to retreat southward, but Kutuzov's army barred the way; and after a bitter battle at Maloiaroslavets, the French retreated westward toward Smolensk, harried by the Russians. Poor Russian coordination, the hesitancy of the Russian generals, and Napoleon's ability permitted his escape across the Berezina River. Then the cold completed the Grand Army's destruction, and fewer than 30,000 ragged, half-frozen troops recrossed the Niemen. The Russian campaign undermined Napoleon's strength, but his escape prolonged his rule for two years and required a costly war to liberate Europe.

Liberation of Europe and the Vienna Settlement, 1813–1815

Russian leaders split over whether merely to expel the invader or to free Europe. Kutuzov favored a nationalist policy of concentrating on Russia's affairs because, as far as he was concerned, "that accursed island [England] could sink out of sight." The sentiments of Rumiantsev and Count Arakcheev were similar, but Alexander, encouraged by the British ambassador and Baron vom Stein, a liberal German statesman, resolved to deliver Europe from Napoleonic tyranny. His decision launched Russia on expensive wars abroad as his sense of mission blended with the desire to wreak vengeance on Napoleon and to liberate Paris. Neglecting urgently needed reform at home, Alexander turned his face toward Europe.

Russia's victory over the Grand Army and awakening patriotism in Germany triggered a national rising there against French rule. As Russian troops moved into Prussia, the king and people greeted them enthusiastically. Supported by

Russia, Prussia declared war on France and led a German war of liberation. As Prussian and Russian forces fought Napoleon, Austria temporized. Emperor Francis did not wish to fight Napoleon, his new son-in-law, and Foreign Minister Metternich opposed a liberal, national German war of liberation. During a summer truce Metternich tried in vain to arrange a compromise peace, then reluctantly brought Austria into the anti-French coalition. This decision turned the scale, and at Leipzig (October 1813) an allied force, almost half of which was Russian, defeated Napoleon decisively and threw him into France.

Determined to crush Napoleon, Alexander led his forces into France, and the Allies (Great Britain, Russia, Prussia, and Austria) pledged in the Treaty of Chaumont (March 1814) to fight until final victory. On March 30 Alexander and his Prussian junior partner, Frederick William III, entered Paris. Talleyrand, having already abandoned Napoleon, persuaded Alexander to demand Napoleon's abdication and the Bourbons' return as French constitutional monarchs. Alexander, enjoying paramountcy in Europe, failed to exploit or retain it, and in a state visit to Great Britain alienated the court with tactless support of the Whig opposition. Inconsistency, idleness, and deepening mysticism cost him diplomatic leadership, which was seized instead by Metternich and the clever Talleyrand.

Alexander's determination to restore a Polish kingdom under his rule alienated western European governments and public opinion and almost broke up the Congress of Vienna, which convened in the Austrian capital to work out a European settlement. At its first session, the Polish-Saxon question was hotly debated. Sympathetic in a sense with Polish national aspirations, Alexander treated kindly the Poles who had fought for the French and with Czartoryski drew up plans for a constitutional Poland, including the former Duchy of Warsaw, Prussian Poland, and Austrian Galicia. Prussia and Austria were to be compensated, the former with Saxony, but Metternich strongly opposed strengthening Russia and Prussia so much. Lord Castlereagh of Great Britain, fearing

Russian domination of Europe, seconded Austrian objections, and Talleyrand exploited this opening to secure full French participation at the congress by backing Russia's opponents. The Polish-Saxon issue provoked a secret Austro-British-French alliance in January 1815 against the claims of Russia and Prussia, and war threatened until a compromise was negotiated. Prussia kept some of its Polish lands, Austria retained Galicia, Cracow became a free city, and Russia obtained the rest of Poland as a constitutional kingdom.

Napoleon's escape from Elba temporarily reunited the powers. The British and Prussians defeated Napoleon at Waterloo in June 1815 without Russian participation, but Russian troops entered Paris and joined in a subsequent Allied occupation of France (1815–1818). The Congress of Vienna confirmed Russia's claims to Finland and Bessarabia and its status as the greatest European land power.

The Concert of Europe

Russia played a major though quieter role in European affairs during Alexander I's final decade. Anxious to preserve the great power alliance and the balance of power, Alexander sought good relations with the east European monarchies (Austria and Prussia) and with more liberal France. In his idealistic, mystical quest for European peace and harmony, he composed in 1815 a Holy Alliance based on Christian principles for signature by his fellow monarchs in order to ensure peace and mutual aid. Signed eventually by most of the European rulers, it lacked practical significance but symbolized the unity of the conservative European monarchies.

More substantial was the Concert of Europe (1815) to bring together periodically leaders of the great powers to preserve peace and the Vienna Settlement. Once the unifying menace of French expansion disappeared, however, rifts deepened, especially between Russia and Great Britain. At the Aix-la-Chapelle Congress (1818), Castlereagh of Great Britain rejected a Russian proposal for

regular, intimate great power cooperation, and it was decided to evacuate Allied troops from France and grant it equality in European affairs. At subsequent congresses at Troppau, Laibach, and Verona (1820–1822), the powers discussed what to do about revolutions against legitimate rulers. Convinced that revolutionary conspiracy threatened all European regimes, Alexander proposed common action against it. At Verona he declared: "My sword is at the service of France," but the French showed no desire to use it. He offered Russian troops to crush revolts in Italy and Spain, but Austria demurred. Great Britain refused to sanction intervention in the domestic affairs of continental states and blocked the eastern monarchies' efforts to restore Latin America to Spanish control. Verona was the final congress, but the eastern powers still collaborated closely to uphold the Vienna Settlement.

Continuing to control foreign policy closely, Alexander between 1815 and 1822 pursued a flexible course of cooperation with France and Austria. In the foreign office he maintained both I. A. Capodistrias, a liberal Greek aristocrat, and Karl Nesselrode, a convervative Austrophile. Capodistrias, favoring constitutionalism and moderate reform, espoused Greek independence; Nesselrode, self-effacing and obedient, established close ties with Metternich.

The abortive Greek Revolt of 1820–1821 severely tested Alexander's balancing act between constitutionalism and status quo conservatism. The Greek question, preoccupying European diplomacy in the 1820s, revealed Russia's acute dilemma over the Eastern Question—involving the future of the Ottoman Empire and the Turkish Straits—and threatened to involve it in war with the Porte. Dominating commercial and intellectual life in the Ottoman Empire, the Greeks in 1814 at their colony in the Russian port of Odessa founded *Philike Hetairia* (Society of Friends) to liberate Greece from Turkish rule. Early in 1821 Alexander Ypsilanti, a Greek officer in the Russian army, left Russia illegally and invaded Turkish-held Moldavia, sparking revolts in Greece and appeals for Russian support. Capodistrias, some army officers, and expansionists in St. Petersburg advocated war against the Porte. Alexander I remained passive, torn between sympathy for Orthodox Christians and opposition to revolts against legitimate rulers. Ottoman collapse, he realized, might destroy the Concert of Europe and provoke intolerable great power rivalries. In 1822 Capodistrias's approach was repudiated: The tsar, fearing revolution, turned toward Austria and sent a secret mission to Vienna to reach agreement about Greece with Count Metternich.

Russia's relations with the United States improved after a severe crisis in the early 1820s. Russians had moved south from Alaska and in 1812 had founded Fort Ross north of San Francisco Bay; between 1815 and 1817 there were indirect Russian efforts to influence or control Hawaii. Alexander's desire to restore Spanish rule in Latin America provoked Anglo-U.S. opposition, expressed in the U.S. Monroe Doctrine of December 1823. Alexander, an admirer of the U.S. Constitution who had corresponded with President Jefferson, decided to negotiate rather than provoke complications with the United States. A treaty of April 1824 restricted Russian claims in Alaska to the region north of 54°40', and Russia both pledged to respect freedom of navigation and fishing in North American coastal waters and renounced intervention in Latin America. By abandoning further expansion in North America, Alexander facilitated subsequent friendly Russo-U.S. relations.

During his final years Alexander largely withdrew from governmental affairs and left ordinary diplomacy to Nesselrode. This withdrawal signified a partial surrender to Metternich, although Alexander never wholly abandoned his constitutional aspirations. He continued to oppose Metternich indirectly by sending abroad liberal envoys, such as Pozzo di Borgo, and by maintaining direct contacts with French leaders. Metternich, by siding with the Porte, blocked Alexander's efforts at a compromise solution of the Greek problem.

The Alexandrine epoch coincided with the peak of Russian power and influence in Europe.

Russian prestige was high after the defeat of Napoleon's invasion and the liberation of Europe, partly because of Alexander's able diplomacy and his continuing commitment to European affairs.

Suggested Additional Reading

BOOKS

ATKIN, M. *Russia and Iran, 1780–1828* (Minneapolis, 1980).

AUSTIN, P. B. *1812: The Great Retreat* (London, 1996).

———. *1812: The March on Moscow* (London, 1993).

———. *1812: Napoleon in Moscow* (London, 1995).

BARRATT, G. *Russia in Pacific Waters, 1715–1825* (Vancouver, 1981).

BASHKINA, N., et al., eds. *The United States and Russia: The Beginning of Relations, 1765–1815* (Washington, 1980).

BOLKHOVITINOV, N. N. *The Beginnings of Russo-American Relations, 1775–1815,* trans. E. Levine (Cambridge, MA, 1976).

CAULAINCOURT, A. *With Napoleon in Russia,* ed. J. Hanoteau (Westport, CT, 1977). (Reprint.)

GRIMSTED, P. *The Foreign Ministers of Alexander I* (Berkeley, 1969).

JOSSELSON, M., and D. JOSSELSON. *The Commander: A Life of Barclay de Tolly* (Oxford, 1980).

KUKIEL, M. *Czartoryski and European Unity, 1770–1861* (Princeton, 1960).

MINISTERSTVO INOSTRANNYKH DEL SSSR. *Vneshniaia Politika Rossii XIX i nachala XX veka, Seriia Pervaia, 1801–1815* (Moscow, 1960). (A wealth of diplomatic documents, some in French, on the period.)

PARKINSON, R. *The Fox of the North: The Life of Kutuzov* (New York, 1976).

PIERCE, R. *Russia's Hawaiian Adventure, 1815–1817* (Kingston, Ontario, 1976).

PIVKA, O. VON. *Armies of 1812: Vol. 1, The French Army . . .* (New York, 1977).

PURYEAR, V. *Napoleon and the Dardanelles* (Berkeley, 1951).

———. *Détente in the Napoleonic Era: Bonaparte and the Russians* (Lawrence, KS, 1980).

RAGSDALE, H., ed. *Imperial Russian Foreign Policy* (Cambridge and New York, 1993).

SAUL, N. *Russia and the Mediterranean, 1797–1807* (Chicago, 1970).

TARLE, E. *Napoleon's Invasion of Russia, 1812* (New York, 1942). (Soviet view.)

TOLSTOY, L. *War and Peace.* (Outstanding historical novel of Russia and the Napoleonic Wars.)

ARTICLES

ANDERSON, M. S. "British Public Opinion and the Russian Campaign of 1812." *SEER* 34 (1956): 408–25.

ATKIN, M. "The Pragmatic Diplomacy of Paul I: Russia's Relationships with Asia, 1796–1801." *SR* (1979): 60–74.

CHANDLER, D. "The Russian Army at War, 1807 and 1812." *Hist. Today* 20 (1970): 867–74.

GRIMSTED, P. "Czartoryski's System for Russian Foreign Policy, 1803: A Memorandum." *Cal. SS* 5 (1970): 19–91.

JEWSBURY, G. "Comte de Langeron and His Role in Russia's Wars against the Porte and French, 1805–1814." *PCRE* 1: 222–30.

KEEP, J. L. "The Russian Army's Response to the French Revolution." *JfGO* 18, no. 4 (1970): 500–523.

MCNALLY, R. T. "The Origins of Russophobia in France, 1812–1830." *ASEER* 17 (1958): 173–89.

MORLEY, C. "Czartoryski's Attempts at a New Foreign Policy under Alexander I." *ASEER* 12 (1953): 475–85.

PERKINS, D. "Russia and the Spanish Colonies, 1817–1818." *AHR* 28 (1923): 656–72.

QUESTED, R. "Further Light on the Expansion of Russia in East Asia, 1792–1860." *JAS* 29 (1969–70): 327–45.

RAGSDALE, H. "A Continental System in 1801 . . ." *JMH* 42 (1970): 70–89.

SCHERER, S. "Alexander I, the Prussian Royal Couple, and European Politics, 1801–1807." *Michigan Academy* 13 (1980): 37–44.

22

Social, Economic, and Cultural Development 1796–1855

Imperial Russia reached a lofty plateau in its development in the era after the defeat of Napoleon. Internationally, Russia was unchallenged by rivals as the dominant military power, epitomizing stability and legitimacy, the unyielding bastion against unorthodox and revolutionary ideas. The empire enjoyed tremendous prestige and exercised great power and influence in Europe. Though beset with sporadic outbursts of peasant discontent and rumblings from disgruntled officers and intellectuals, the autocracy controlled internal developments firmly and blocked all organized opposition. The empire's external power, however, concealed grave social and economic problems. Among the perceptive there was a nagging uneasiness, a vague disquietude about the future. With the empire's rapid growth came new and perplexing problems.

The period from Paul's accession to Nicholas I's death in 1855 brought a very rapid growth of population, from 37.2 million to 59.2 million, excluding Finland, Russian Poland, and the Caucasus (they brought the total to 72.7 mil-

lion).[1] The peasantry numbered 32.6 million "souls" in 1795, or 90 percent of the population; by 1857 it had increased to 48.4 million, still almost 84 percent. This mass of humanity was divided almost equally between privately owned serfs and state peasants. Whereas in 1719 private serfs had accounted for 71 percent of the total population and state peasants for only 19 percent, by 1857 the landowners' serfs constituted only 51 percent of the peasant class and 46 percent of the population, revealing a significant change in the composition of the peasantry. In the mid-19th century Russia remained an overwhelmingly peasant, agrarian country.

The Nobility

The nobility, increasing in absolute numbers, decreased as a percentage of the population. By the fifth revision (census) of 1795, male nobles numbered 363,000 (2.2 percent of the population);

---

[1] Ia. Vodarskii, *Naselenie Rossii za 400 let* (Moscow, 1973), p. 54.

269

the 10th revision of 1858 recorded 464,000 (1.5 percent).[2] Only about 700 families could trace their noble status back before 1600. Noble status, either inherited or earned through state service, entitled the holder to own populated estates—that is, to own peasant serfs. Noblemen enjoyed not only high social status but real economic, civic, and judicial privileges. As we have seen (see Chapter 19), however, there were many impoverished noble families, chiefly because of the traditional and ancient practice of dividing property equally among the male heirs, a practice that produced the fragmentation of estates into smaller and smaller parcels with each generation. Impoverishment and the general economic climate of the early 19th century forced many serf owners to borrow extensively to maintain their living standards and social status and to keep themselves afloat financially. Serf owners borrowed by mortgaging their serfs to banks or private individuals. By 1859 fully two-thirds of the male serf population was mortgaged. Indebtedness was not confined to small, marginal proprietors. Even great magnates found it increasingly difficult to live within their incomes and were forced to borrow on a grand scale. Count Sheremetiev, Russia's largest landowner, was reputedly six million rubles in debt by 1859. Contributing to this indebtedness were extravagant living patterns, inflation, and low returns from inefficiently run estates.

Despite its economic difficulties, the nobility remained *the* privileged social class, with many exclusive rights and privileges. Their income, however inadequate, came chiefly from landed estates rather than government salaries, commercial ventures, or investments. Many commoners aspired to become gentlemen-landowners because a noble title, and hence the right to own serfs, could be earned by talent and hard work. Thus the noble class increased steadily in size despite efforts to prevent this. Between 1795 and 1858 the nobility increased by more than 100,000 males. As long as the government needed more civil servants, there

was no reason to abolish the Table of Ranks, which, providing a way to acquire nobility, served as a powerful device to attract the ablest individuals into state service. Nicholas I sympathized with noble demands to restrict access to the nobility and issued a decree in 1845 to tighten up the provisions governing the Table of Ranks. Henceforth the rank of major in the army (eighth rank) would confer hereditary nobility, whereas titular councillor (ninth rank) in state service would bestow only personal nobility, a status that could not be transmitted to heirs. Achievement of rank five (actual state councillor) conferred hereditary noble status. These provisions made the acquisition of nobility through state service more difficult but failed to satisfy noble demands for the creation of a closed class.

In 1832 the government allayed some of the frustration of those who had acquired wealth or distinction but not nobility by creating the title "honored citizen" to recognize special achievement in business, science, and the arts. The title could be either personal or hereditary, and it granted the holder many privileges, including exemption from the capitation tax, recruitment, and corporal punishment. Still, the title was conferred sparingly, and it failed to satisfy those intent on the social distinction of noble status.

Urban Centers

The Russian urban population grew faster in this period than any other demographic category. Numbering 1.6 million in 1795, or roughly 4 percent of the population, it had risen by 1858 to 5.4 million, or more than 9 percent.[3] Much of the urban population lived in the two capitals. In 1800 Moscow had about 300,000 inhabitants and St. Petersburg slightly fewer; by 1864 St. Petersburg had grown to 586,000 while Moscow had increased to only 378,000. St. Petersburg was clearly the empire's economic, cultural, and

---

[2] *Istoriia SSSR*, no. 4 (Moscow, 1971), p. 164.

[3] P. G. Ryndziunskii, *Gorodskoe grazhdanstvo doreformennoi Rossii* (Moscow, 1958), p. 334.

administrative center. Whereas in 1811 few other towns had more than 25,000 people, by 1864 rapid urban growth had produced 12 towns with populations of more than 50,000.[4] Clearly, 19th-century Russia was urbanizing rapidly, largely because of a growing internal market and expanding foreign trade and manufacturing.

Russian towns contained a populace very diverse in wealth and social status. In the capitals lived the wealthiest noblemen, who could maintain splendid town mansions besides their country estates. Many moderately wealthy noblemen had residences in Moscow and in a descending scale in other provincial centers. There was a relatively small well-to-do merchantry (*kupechestvo*), divided into three guilds by wealth and social status. Beneath the merchants were artisans and skilled workers, organized into corporations (*tsekhi*) with their own rules and regulations. A large miscellaneous group of petty bourgeoisie (*meshchanstvo*) remained a rather vague and imprecise social category. Then there were government bureaucrats and a small group of intellectuals. Together these nonnoble urban residents were the Russian counterpart of the Western middle classes, or bourgeoisie. Yet there were profound differences between the urban middle class in Russia and in western Europe. The Russian middle class did not stand for individualism, free enterprise, and political democracy, as did the middle classes in the West. The autocracy maintained as tight a control over townsmen as it did over the rural elements.

The intelligentsia was in the process of formation in this period and would become the chief advocate in Russia of free institutions and political liberties. Urban groups—merchants, bureaucrats, artisans, and intellectuals—did not constitute a Russian equivalent of the western European bourgeoisie, as has been stated. They were not socially homogeneous and thus could not wield the influence or pressure that the European bourgeoisie exercised so successfully.

As urban centers developed, they presented a vivid kaleidoscope of the extremes of Russian life. The incredible display of ostentatious wealth by the upper classes, with their opulent pleasure palaces and town houses, contrasted with shocking and degrading poverty. The empire's wealth was poured into building up St. Petersburg, which the rulers resolved to make the most imposing and beautiful city in Europe. Yet alongside stately mansions, impressive official buildings, and resplendent imperial residences stood the distressing slums, hovels, doss houses, and wretched taverns of the lower classes, portrayed graphically in Fedor Dostoevsky's famous novels *Crime and Punishment, The Idiot,* and *Poor Folk.*

Industrial Development

Russia's industrial development and technological progress stagnated compared to more advanced western Europe. By 1860 Russian industry lagged even further behind the West than in 1800. The government during this era pursued conservative, unimaginative economic policies featuring protective tariffs, fiscal restraint (to prevent excessive debt and inflation), and financial support for noblemen. The government favored industrial expansion officially but in practice did little to promote it, partly because of fears of a host of social problems associated with rapid growth of the factory system, partly because of distaste for speculative Western capitalism.

Typifying the conservative state economic policies of this era was the finance minister (1823–1844) Count E. F. Kankrin. A German who had come to Russia as a youth, he served in the quartermaster corps before being appointed finance minister through Arakcheev's influence. Kankrin never developed a consistent economic philosophy, but he considered himself a "practical" man able to make adjustments. He was primarily a mercantilist and a consistent opponent of free trade. Socially, he favored the status quo and aristocratic predominance. Kankrin's credit policies

---

[4] The 12 towns were Odessa, Kishinev, Saratov, Riga, Vilna, Kiev, Nikolaev, Kazan, Tbilisi, Tula, Berdichev, and Kharkov. W. H. Parker, *An Historical Geography of Russia* (Chicago, 1969), p. 262. Also see Chapter 17 in this text.

were clearly anti-industrial: He refused to provide direct state loans to industry that could readily have been provided through state banks. Instead, he had state banks loan large sums to an indigent nobility who squandered much of the money on luxuries. Kankrin abhorred the idea of an unbalanced budget or private banking; he opposed Admiral N. S. Mordvinov's enlightened projects for private provincial banks. A high tariff policy protected domestic industries, but its main purpose was revenue, not industrial growth. As to railroads, Kankrin saw no benefit in them whatsoever. They separated men from nature, he complained, broke down class barriers (which he wanted to preserve), and increased the restlessness of the younger generation. He seems to have envisioned hordes of disorderly youths tearing around the country in railroad cars! Railroads, concluded Kankrin, were a needless luxury, and anyway they would never carry freight! Kankrin's rigid balance-the-budget conservatism reflected the bureaucrats' approach toward the economy under Nicholas I. The state, as the American historian Walter Pintner points out, was unwilling to foster economic development until forced to do so by painful defeat in the Crimean War.

Despite the sluggish Russian economy of the early 19th century, there were notable achievements in certain areas. According to official statistics, the number of industrial enterprises rose from about 2,400 in 1804 to 15,400 by 1860. These figures are conservative estimates because some types of manufacturing firms were not counted and because many small operations may have been concealed by owners to evade taxes. Fewer than 10 percent of manufacturing enterprises employed more than 100 workers. Workers in industry, according to official figures, increased from a paltry 95,200 in 1804 to 210,600 in 1825 and to 565,000 in 1860, including both hired free laborers and serf workers, mostly state peasants. A surprising number of serfs became successful industrialists. Serfs of the Sheremetiev family were pioneers of the Russian cotton industry, which developed in the village of Ivanovo, owned by the Sheremetievs.

Soviet historians, challenging the official industrial employment figures, argued that they are disproportionately low and substituted higher ones: 225,000 industrial workers in 1804 (only 27 percent free hired laborers) increasing to 862,000 in 1860 (56 percent free). Many industrial workers were seasonal laborers working in factories during the off-season and returning to the village at the peak agricultural periods, spring and autumn. Whichever figures are accepted, clearly only a tiny minority of the population engaged in regular factory work in 1860.

The leading branches of industry in the early 19th century were woolen, linen, and cotton textiles; leather processing; and the sugar beet industry. Woolen textile manufacturing, largely for the army, with only 29,000 workers in 1804, employed more than 120,000 people by 1860. The work was carried on largely in primitive estate factories, though enterprising Old Believer merchants in Moscow were beginning to create a basis for a modern woolen industry by midcentury. Cotton textiles grew even faster, from 8,000 employees in 1804 to 152,000 workers by 1860. At first Russia depended on imported English cotton cloth, which was printed and sold domestically. During the Napoleonic Wars the flow of English cotton imports was temporarily interrupted, forcing the Russians to develop their own manufacture of cotton cloth. After 1842 the latest spinning machinery was imported from England by thrifty serf craftsmen and Old Believer merchants. A thriving cotton textile industry was established to meet a large internal demand for cotton cloth and to supply markets in the Middle East and China.[5]

The oil and coal industries, so essential to modern industrial societies, remained largely undeveloped in Russia during this period. Iron and steel production lagged, and it was soon evident that Russian iron products, turned out mostly by unfree labor, could not compete in price or quality with English ones manufactured in mechanized mills. The backwardness of such key industries

---

[5] P. A. Khromov, *Ekonomicheskoe razvitie Rossii v XIX–XX vekakh* (Moscow, 1967), p. 31.

helps account for the relative stagnation of the Russian economy.

Modest railroad construction, despite Kankrin, began in the 1830s. A short line connecting St. Petersburg with the imperial summer residence at Tsarskoe Selo opened in 1837, more as a curiosity for Nicholas I and his family than as an experiment in a new form of transportation. Several prominent Russians realized the railway's revolutionary potential and promoted its construction. In 1839 F. Bulgarin, a leading publicist, wrote:

> Are the complaints justified that the industrial spirit of our age has stifled the poetry of life? We do not think so! It seems to us that from the creation of the world there has not been an idea more poetic and majestic than the project for a railroad from Petersburg to Moscow and from there . . . to Odessa.[6]

Work began in 1842 to link the two capitals by rail. The project was completed in 1852 with the help of an American engineer, G. W. Whistler, who convinced the Russians to use a wider gauge than that in Europe, at a time when railroad gauges were not standardized anywhere. By 1855 about 660 miles of track had been built, only a tiny beginning, and there was no railroad to Odessa. The Russians, however, were committed to a 5-foot gauge, whereas most of continental Europe adopted a 4-foot 8 1/2-inch gauge.[7]

After victory over Napoleon, Russia took on a modest but significant role in international economic affairs. By 1850 the volume of Russian foreign trade exceeded Austria's, though it was only 18 percent of Great Britain's. Russia exported largely raw materials and foodstuffs, and it imported manufactured goods and luxuries. As early as 1822, Russia adopted a high protective tariff, mainly to raise revenue and discourage excessive imports. In spite of a generally backward economy, Russia maintained a favorable balance of trade throughout most of Nicholas's reign, largely by means of grain exports. The Crimean War had a depressing effect on the Russian economy and especially on foreign trade, which dwindled to almost nothing during the war.

The early 19th-century Russian economy was characterized by backwardness owing to the persistence of an agrarian economy based on serfdom. Still, there were important signs of industrial activity and accumulation of private capital, particularly among Old Believers and Jews and some enterprising serfs. These social outcasts were often persecuted and restricted, forcing them to pool their resources and engage in economic activities scorned by the upper class. Old Believers formed the core of the Russian textile industry, whereas Jews dominated banking, retail trade, and vodka distribution. Serfs were encouraged to engage in commercial ventures by masters seeking additional revenue. The most enterprising serfs accumulated capital and built factories and shops, some of which became the nuclei of future large enterprises, such as the Ivanovo textile industry. The government, however, remained cautious, failing to recognize the significant social and economic changes that were occurring. The dynamic changes in western Europe became fully evident only with Russia's defeat in the Crimean War, which eventually forced a change in official thinking and policies.

Literature

The political conservatism and obscurantism so widespread in Russia early in the 19th century did not preclude a tremendous outburst of cultural creativity. Russian literature and music showed unprecedented vigor and originality after a long apprenticeship in the schools of western Europe.

A necessary prerequisite for an original literature was a modern literary language, whose development owes much to Russia's greatest 18th-century scholar and scientist, Mikhail Lomonosov, often called the "father of Russian literature" for his linguistic reforms. Lomonosov

---

[6] Quoted in T. Koepnick, *The Journalistic Careers of F. V. Bulgarin and N. I. Grech,* Ph.D. diss., Ohio State University, 1976.

[7] See R. M. Haywood, "The Question of a Standard Gauge for Russian Railroads, 1836–1860," *SR* 28, no. 1 (1969): 72–80.

helped shape the Russian language for poetic expression by developing a suitable system of versification and poetic structure. His textbooks of rhetoric and grammar set standards for the modern Russian literary language. His poetry, in a ponderous classical style, demonstrated his theories of versification and became the model for subsequent 18th-century Russian poetry. As a nationalist, Lomonosov believed that the Russian language was superior to all others as a vehicle of expression. He distinguished three linguistic levels —high, middle, and low—each characterized by many Old Church Slavonic elements.

The greatest Russian 18th-century poet, Gabriel R. Derzhavin (1743–1816), further elaborated Lomonosov's theories and language. An innovator within the narrow bounds of classicism, Derzhavin was set apart from his predecessors and contemporaries by his imaginative power, which presaged the romantic movement.

Nicholas Karamzin's literary work[8] helped turn Russian literature away from classical models and toward the romantic movement. His *Letters of a Russian Traveler* (1791) introduced a delightfully casual, colloquial style and a genteel, cosmopolitan sensibility to the reading public. His name is associated with the school of sentimentalism, and his short novel *Poor Liza* (1792) won him instant fame as a writer. Karamzin's efforts to use the cultivated conversational Russian of his day, infused with French phrases and influences, was challenged by Admiral A. Shishkov (1753–1841), who passionately defended the purity of the Russian language and attacked Karamzin's cosmopolitan language. Refusing to become involved in polemics, Karamzin abandoned literature in favor of history. From 1803 until his death in 1826 he was the official court historiographer, and his monumental *History of the Russian State*, while ignoring the Russian people, provided dramatic portraits of Russian rulers and eulogized absolute monarchy. The *History* was widely read and inspired generations of Russian artists—notably

Alexander S. Pushkin, 1799–1837.

Alexander Pushkin, who drew heavily on its materials.

The poet V. A. Zhukovskii (1783–1852) and a few colleagues formed the Arzamas Society, which advanced Karamzin's literary reforms and attacked the conservative Shishkovites with epigrams, puns, and insulting witticisms. Seeking to translate Karamzin's literary reforms into poetry, Zhukovskii in his works helped to create a new language of poetry based on that of Karamzin and well suited to the literary romanticism of the period. Zhukovskii portrayed masterfully the inner spiritual world and intimate thoughts and feelings. His poetry gained unprecedented popularity and began a Russian cult of poetry that continues to this day.

As a poet, Zhukovskii was completely overshadowed by the towering figure of his friend Alexander S. Pushkin (1799–1837). Indeed, one cannot discuss modern Russian literature without dealing with Pushkin, Russia's great national poet. Declared the prominent literary critic, Vissarion G. Belinskii (1811–1848): "To write about Pushkin means to write about the whole of Russian literature; for just as previous Russian writers explain

---

[8] For Karamzin's political views, see Chapter 20.

Pushkin, so Pushkin explains the writers who followed him." Pushkin has always been ranked by Russians with the greatest literary figures of all time, such as Shakespeare and Goethe. Virtually all leading Russian writers of the 19th and 20th centuries have paid homage to Pushkin's artistic genius and have acknowledged their debt to him. Pushkin's genius was manifested in his ability to speak on behalf of all Russians, not just the elite. He embodied the Russian people and articulated the latent creativity of the Russian spirit.

Born in 1799 into an old but undistinguished noble family, Pushkin was descended on his mother's side from Peter the Great's black favorite from Abyssinia, Abraham Hannibal. Pushkin was extremely proud of both his noble origin and his African ancestry. Though, like so many Russian noblemen, he grew up in an atmosphere of French culture, books, and tutors, he developed early and lasting ties with the Russia of the common people from his beloved nursemaid, Irina, who told him traditional Russian folktales, which he later included in some of his greatest creations.

Even Pushkin's schoolboy verse bore the mark of genius, and by the time he had completed his formal schooling in 1817, he was an established poet openly associated with Zhukovskii and the Arzamas Society. His first major work, *Ruslan and Liudmila* (1820), based on a fairy tale heard from his nurse, was brilliant in language and poetic artistry. His reputation rested equally upon radical and irreverent poems known only in manuscript copies because of censorship. These poems attacked evils of Russian society, particularly serfdom and hypocrisy, and induced the authorities to exile the young poet to the south of Russia. He lived in the Caucasus and the Crimea and settled in Odessa on the Black Sea. These "exotic" places were reflected in such vibrant poems as *The Prisoner of the Caucasus* and *The Fountain of Bakchisarai.*

Pushkin returned to the family estate at Mikhailovskoe in Pskov province in 1824, and in its solitude and isolation produced one masterpiece after another: the great historical drama *Boris Godunov,* recalling Shakespeare and inspired by Karamzin; and the beginning of perhaps his greatest work, *Eugene Onegin.* In that novel in verse Pushkin portrays the classic "superfluous man," an insipid misfit who suffers from boredom. Eugene inspires the love of the passionate Tatiana, then rejects her love in favor of aimless wandering. Tatiana enters into an arranged marriage with a "fat general." Eugene gradually realizes the value of what he had so casually spurned and returns to declare his love for Tatiana, but she refuses his advances and remains loyal to her husband. Apparently a romantic tale of unrequited love, *Eugene Onegin* in fact indicts shallow and selfish Byronic romanticism. Tatiana, the archetype of the great Russian literary heroine, is passionate yet sensible, honest, loyal, and long-suffering.

A shorter, more intense Pushkin masterpiece is *The Bronze Horseman* (1833), a paean to Peter the Great and his monumental city on the Neva River. It is named from the French sculptor Falconet's majestic equestrian statue of Peter, commissioned by Catherine the Great. Pushkin contrasts the power of nature and Peter's vision with the suffering and tragedy of the helpless government clerk, Eugene, pursued by rampaging floodwaters that sweep away his fiancée and her family and by the statue of the bronze horseman that comes to life in his anguished mind. Eugene is a literary archetype, a model of the downtrodden, defenseless common man buffeted by forces beyond his control and comprehension, adrift in the murky waters of destiny.

Drawing upon similar sources is *The Queen of Spades,* a fine Pushkin short story. Set in St. Petersburg, it records with mounting psychological tension the adventures of a callous army officer who terrorizes an old lady to death in an effort to obtain her secret of winning at cards. The old woman's spirit appears and reveals to the greedy youth a false version of the secret, causing him to lose a fortune. His life and reputation destroyed by avarice, he goes mad. Realistic portrayals of character set against exotic backgrounds and situations won Pushkin enormous popularity.

At the zenith of his creative powers Pushkin was killed in a senseless duel in 1837. It was as though he foresaw his tragic end when he described in *Eugene Onegin* the duel between Onegin and the poet Lenskii. After Lenskii has been shot and killed, Pushkin writes:

> His hand upon his breast lays lightly,
> And drops. His clouded eyes betray
> Not pain, but death. Thus, sparkling whitely
> Where the quick sunbeams on it play,
> A snowball down the hill goes tumbling
> And sinks from sight, soon to be crumbling.
> Onegin frozen with despair,
> Runs to the poor youth lying there,
> And looks and calls him. . . . But no power
> Avails to rouse him: he is gone.
> The poet in the very dawn
> Of life has perished like a flower
> That by a sudden storm was drenched;
> Alas! the altar-fire is quenched.[9]

Russian educated society was outraged by Pushkin's pointless death. How could such a thing be allowed to happen? None dwelt on that question more intensely than the young army officer Mikhail Lermontov (1814–1841), who castigated society for permitting such a senseless waste of genius. Pushkin had been the victim of a system that rewarded mediocrity and ignored talent and artistic brilliance:

> You whose eager flock surrounds the throne,
> You, the slayers of genius and freedom,
> You hide in the shadow of the law;
> But justice and truth, for you, are dead letters![10]

Lermontov's poem *On the Death of Pushkin* circulated widely in manuscript because censorship prevented critical views from appearing in print. His forceful writing won over the educated and gave him recognition.

Descendant of a Scottish soldier of fortune, Lermontov was exiled repeatedly to remote areas because of his restless, romantic spirit and unconventional behavior. Officialdom judged his great-

Library of Congress

Nicholas Gogol, 1809–1852.

est poem, *The Demon,* unfit for publication because of its "blasphemous" theme: love between a demon and a mortal. Unpublished in Lermontov's lifetime, it inspired later generations.

In Caucasian exile Lermontov completed his greatest prose work, *A Hero of Our Time* (1840), which analyzed contemporary Russian society vividly in an easygoing, natural style. It contributed much to an emerging literary realism and naturalism in Russia. The novel's hero, the proud and passionate Pechorin, inspired real and fictional imitators. Lermontov, who had condemned Russian society for Pushkin's death, died at age 27 in a duel over an absurd point of honor. Lermontov wrote relatively little but ranks among the giants of Russian literature.

Nicholas Gogol (1809–1852), a master of the romantic realism that became a hallmark of Russian literature, was born to a lesser gentry family in Ukraine. His literary career began in 1831 with *Evenings on a Farm near Dikanka* (1831), a collec-

---

[9] Quoted in *The Poems, Prose, and Plays of Alexander Pushkin,* ed. A. Yarmolinsky, trans. B. Deutsch (New York, 1936), p. 240.

[10] Quoted in H. Troyat, *Pushkin* (New York, 1970), p. 605.

tion of stories based on Ukrainian folktales, legends, and daily life; it was a microcosm of his later great works. In later collections of stories, *Mirgorod* (1835) and *Arabesques* (1835), Gogol continued using folk and historical tales. Other stories, including "Nevskii Prospekt," chronicled the lives of lower-middle-class people of St. Petersburg. The most famous of these St. Petersburg tales is "The Overcoat" (1842). Poor, lamentable Akaki Akakievich, a petty clerk, makes incredible sacrifices to buy a new overcoat so as to transform himself from a worm into a real human being. Alas, the coat is stolen, and Akaki perishes in a futile effort to recover it. His spirit haunts those who refused to help him find it.

Among Gogol's masterpieces is the comedy *The Inspector General* (1836), inspired by A. S. Griboedov's famous play *The Misfortune of Being Clever* (1823), the first great Russian social comedy. *The Inspector General* humorously satirizes provincial Russian life and the self-satisfied inferiority (Russians called it *poshlost*) of townspeople. The play centers on a case of mistaken identity as the rascal Khlestakov is taken for a powerful government inspector traveling incognito to audit the local administration. The townspeople overwhelm him with hospitality; the ladies flatter him, the gentlemen compliment and try to deceive him. The boorish Khlestakov survives because the townspeople are even stupider than he. He robs them blind, then leaves an insulting letter making fun of their gullibility before disappearing. The play received a mixed response. Nicholas I liked it, but upper-class society accused Gogol of undermining the established order. Others saw the play as an accurate portrayal of Russian provincial life. Gogol had held a mirror up to Russian society, and some disliked what they saw. The critic Belinskii called Gogol "a great comic painter of real life."

Whereas *The Inspector General* focused on one provincial town, Gogol's epic novel *Dead Souls* (1842) ranged all over Russia. The hero, Chichikov, is a middle-aged scoundrel who travels about buying up the names of dead serfs before they can be removed from official registers in order to use

the serfs as collateral for a huge bank loan. Gogol again focuses on the greed, stupidity, and corruption of much of Russian society. "God, what a sad country our Russia is!" exclaimed Pushkin after reading a draft of *Dead Souls*. It is a comic epic with sidesplitting humor as well as black humor and mordant satire. Gogol was the true founder and leading practitioner of Russian romantic realism and occupies a pivotal place in literary history.

Music

The more limited Russian achievements in music, painting, and architecture were little known abroad. Imitative in the 18th century, early 19th-century Russian music is chiefly identified with Mikhail Glinka (1804–1857), a composer of genius. He founded the national school of Russian music that developed so brilliantly thereafter.

Glinka's operas drew upon the peculiar musicality of his friend Pushkin's writings. Most great 19th-century Russian composers derived their opera librettos from his creations.[11] Despite the lack of a Russian musical conservatory, Glinka received excellent private tutoring in St. Petersburg where he met Zhukovskii, Pushkin, and other leading writers. Because a musical career was considered unworthy of an aristocrat, Glinka's family tried to dissuade him from it. Eventually he persuaded them to let him visit Italy, where he studied for several years. Returning to Russia in 1834 a convert to Italian opera, Glinka decided to compose a truly Russian opera in subject matter and music. Accepting Zhukovskii's suggestion of the story of the peasant hero, Ivan Susanin (see Chapter 12), Glinka completed his opera *Ivan Susanin* in 1836. After Nicholas I praised it highly, he renamed it *A Life for the Tsar*. Glinka drew heavily on Russian folk music to depict Ivan's heroic plan to save Mikhail Romanov from capture

---

[11] Notably Glinka's *Ruslan and Liudmila*; Dargomyzhskii's *Rusalka* and *The Stone Guest*; Musorgskii's *Boris Godunov*; Tchaikovskii's *Eugene Onegin, Mazeppa*, and *The Queen of Spades*; Rimskii-Korsakov's *Tsar Saltan* and *The Golden Cockerel*; and Rachmaninov's *Aleko* and *The Covetous Knight*.

Mikhail Glinka, 1804–1857.

Painting and Architecture

Early 19th-century Russian painting and architecture produced no towering figures such as Pushkin, Gogol, or Glinka. Nonetheless, significant progress was made toward independence, originality, and national artistic expression, influenced by developments in literature.

The upsurge in national feeling and his desire to foster imperial prestige induced Alexander I to make St. Petersburg a beautiful and splendid city, a capital befitting the most powerful state in the world. Revealing his cosmopolitanism in his preference for European neoclassicism, he selected as architects a Russian, Vasili Stasov (1769–1848); an Italian, Carlo Rossi; and a Frenchman, Auguste Montferrand—all strongly influenced by the prevalent Greek classicism. Their styles resembled those found in any European capital of the time or in the eastern United States. These architects' works completed the classical configuration of St. Petersburg. In Winter Palace Square, Rossi erected the semicircular and grandiose General Staff building. He also built the Mikhailovskii Palace (now the Russian Museum), Alexandrinskii (now Pushkin) Theater, and Theatrical Square just off Nevskii Prospect. Stasov, though trained in western Europe, adapted traditional Russian architectural styles to neoclassicism. He renovated the Winter Palace, Peterhof, and the great palace at Tsarskoe Selo and designed its famous Lyceum, where many prominent Russian noblemen, including Pushkin, would study. Several large Orthodox churches testify to Stasov's skill at synthesizing classical and Byzantine styles. In Winter Palace Square, Montferrand added a towering granite monolith, erected in 1829, to commemorate the Russian victory over Napoleon. His most impressive work is St. Isaac's Cathedral, a very un-Russian church but an architectural treasure house in exterior design and interior decoration. These architects completed the carefully planned development of official St. Petersburg.

Early 19th-century Russian painting, like architecture, followed European styles rather unimaginatively, adopting an academic style that utilized

by the Poles in 1613. Susanin dies but saves the Romanov dynasty and Russia. *A Life for the Tsar,* a great popular success, won for Glinka adulation from educated society. In the USSR the title reverted to *Ivan Susanin* and the libretto was revised to stress Susanin's devotion to country and people, not just the tsar.

Audiences and critics judged Glinka's second opera, *Ruslan and Liudmila,* based on Pushkin's fairy tale, a failure. Glinka was dismayed, knowing that musically it was superior to his previous work. Glinka's music had a vitality and richness unprecedented in Russia. *Ruslan and Liudmila* is a more Russian opera than *Ivan Susanin,* which is essentially an Italian opera with a veneer of Russian folk music. Misunderstood at the time, *Ruslan and Liudmila,* a great pioneering work of Russian national music, was Glinka's masterpiece. Glinka was to Russian music, noted a leading Soviet scholar, what Pushkin was to Russian literature. A musical genius, he set the stage for a musical outpouring later in the century.

classical and Old Testament themes and stressed draftsmanship rather than conceptualization. The Russian Academy of Arts, founded in the 18th century, resembled the European art academies. The academic painter Karl Briullov (1799–1852), the most famous artist of the age, was called "the Russian Raphael" for his gigantic painting *The Last Day of Pompeii,* but posterity has not sustained this judgment. Briullov himself realized that his paintings, devoid of bold conceptualization and originality, resembled those of many other academic painters.

The fate of Alexander Ivanov (1806–1858) resembled Briullov's. The gifted son of a leading Petersburg academic painter, Ivanov received the best art education available in Russia, then settled in Rome to create masterpieces in the style of the Renaissance masters. Stimulated by the "success" of Briullov's *The Last Day of Pompeii,* Ivanov resolved to create a work surpassing all previous religious painting. He labored over his magnum opus, *The Appearance of Christ to the People,* for more than 25 years, but when it was finally exhibited in St. Petersburg in 1855, it was an artistic failure, as even he realized.

Early 19th-century Russian culture was characterized by a new independence and national consciousness that stimulated a great creative outburst, first in literature, then in music and the fine arts. For all of its originality and creativity, this half century was merely a prelude, a portent of the superb accomplishments to come in the arts during the second half of the century.

Suggested Additional Reading

ECONOMY AND SOCIETY

BLACKWELL, W. *The Beginnings of Russian Industrialization, 1800–1860* (Princeton, 1968).

BUSHNELL, J. "Did Serf Owners Control Serf Marriage? Orlov Serfs and Their Neighbors, 1773–1861," *SR* 52, no. 3 (Fall 1993): 419–45.

CRISP, O. "The State Peasants under Nicholas I." *SEER* 37 (1959): 387–412.

FREEZE, G.L. *The Parish Clergy in Nineteenth Century Russia* (Princeton, 1983).

LOWE, H-D. *The Tsars and the Jews: Reform, Reaction and Anti-Semitism in Imperial Russia, 1772–1917* (New York, 1993).

MIRONOV, B. "Bureaucratic or Self-Government: The Early 19th Century Russian City," *SR* 52, no. 2 (Summer 1993): 233–55.

MOON, D. *Russian Peasants and Tsarist Legislation on the Eve of Reform: The Interaction of the Peasantry and Official Russia* (New York, 1992).

PINTNER, W. *Russian Economic Policy under Nicholas I* (Ithaca, N Y, 1967).

PIPES, R., trans. and ed. *Karamzin's Memoir on Ancient and Modern Russia* (Cambridge, MA, 1959).

SUNDERLAND, W. "Russian Peasants on the Move: State Peasant Resettlement in Imperial Russia, 1805–1830," *Rus. Rev.* 52, no. 4 (October 1993): 472–85.

CULTURE

(Virtually all of the literary works referred to are available in English translation.)

ASAFIEV, B. *Russian Music from the Beginning of the Nineteenth Century,* trans. A. Swan (Ann Arbor, MI, 1953).

BLACK, J. *Nicholas Karamzin and Russian Society* (Toronto, 1975).

BREYER, L. *Dostoevsky: The Author as Psychoanalyst* (New York, 1989).

COTTEAU, J. *Dostoevsky and the Process of Literary Criticism* (New York, 1989).

CROSS, A. G. *Anglo-Russica: Aspects of Cultural Relations between Great Britain and Russia in the 18th and Early 19th Centuries: Selected Essays* (New York, 1993).

———. *N. M. Karamzin: A Study of His Literary Career* (Carbondale, IL, 1971).

DANIELS, G., ed. *A Lermontov Reader* (New York, 1965).

DRIVER, S. *Pushkin: Literature and Social Ideas* (New York, 1989).

FANGER, D. *The Creation of Nikolai Gogol* (Cambridge, MA, 1979).

FLYNN, J. *The University Reform of Alexander I* (Washington, 1988).

GARRARD, J. *Mikhail Lermontov* (Boston, 1982).

LAVRIN, J. *Lermontov* (New York, 1959).

LEONARD, R. *A History of Russian Music* (New York, 1968).

MAGARSHACK, D. *Pushkin: A Biography* (New York, 1967).

MAGUIRE, R. A. *Exploring Gogol* (Stanford, 1994).

———, ed. *Gogol from the Twentieth Century* (Princeton, 1974).

ORLOVA, A. *Glinka's Life in Music . . .* , trans. R. Hoops (Ann Arbor, MI, 1988).

SIMMONS, E. *Pushkin* (Cambridge, MA, 1937). (Still the best biography.)

TROYAT, H. *Divided Soul: The Life of Gogol,* trans. N. Amphoux (New York, 1975).

VICKERY, W. *Alexander Pushkin* (New York, 1970).

YARMOLINSKY, A., ed. *The Poems, Prose, and Plays of Alexander Pushkin* (New York, 1964).

23

The "Iron Tsar"

The Marquis de Custine, a French aristocratic visitor, wrote in *Russia in 1839*:

> The more I see of Russia the more I agree with the Emperor when he forbids Russians to travel and makes access to his own country difficult for foreigners. The political system of Russia would not resist twenty years of free communication with western Europe.[1]

Ruling Russia from 1825 to 1855 was Nicholas I, called the "Iron Tsar" for his tightfisted militarism. This final epoch of autocracy combined with serfdom was comparable in its absolutism and personal monarchy to the reign of Peter the Great. Many Soviet accounts depicted Nicholas I as a rigid status quo conservative, but Western and some tsarist Russian historians point out that he carried through, mostly early in his reign, some cautious but constructive reforms. Nicholas's personal autocracy notwithstanding, Russian society displayed a remarkable moral and intellectual ripening. This circumstance helps explain the

apparent paradox that an era of rigorous censorship and repression could also be one of great intellectual and literary vitality and achievement. Was Nicholas a reactionary or a reform conservative? Did his regime prepare the way for subsequent reform or render it more difficult? How did his militarism affect Russian government and society? Why, despite his devotion to the army and the resources he lavished upon it, was Russia defeated in the Crimean War, and what did that defeat signify?

The Ruler and His Ideology

Nicholas I epitomized his autocratic, militaristic regime. He ascended the throne at the age of 29, competently educated though not prepared as specifically as his elder brothers to rule. General M. I. Lamsdorf, his chief tutor, was a narrow, strict disciplinarian who had developed Nicholas's sense of military duty to an extreme degree. Though intelligent, Nicholas was narrow-minded and unimaginative, and during his visits to Europe as grand duke he preferred authoritarian, militaristic Prussia. Whereas Alexander I had observed

---

[1] Astolphe de Custine, *Lettres de Russie* (Paris, 1946), p. 139.

John Massey Stewart

Tsar Nicholas I, 1796–1855.

Stated the French observer Custine: "The Emperor of Russia is a military commander and each one of his days is a day of battle." Only God was his superior, Nicholas believed; all others owed him unquestioning loyalty and obedience. Such divine-right absolutism was virtually dead in western Europe.

After removing his brother's worst advisers—Arakcheev, Runich, and Magnitskii—Nicholas selected some capable and some incompetent subordinates. The conservative but cultured Count S. S. Uvarov as minister of education and the able reformers Counts P. D. Kiselev and Speranskii were counterbalanced by such a poor diplomat and general as Prince A. S. Menshikov.

The official creed was Autocracy, Orthodoxy, and Nationalism—the famous triad proclaimed in Uvarov's circular of 1833 and reiterated constantly for the next 20 years. Orthodoxy, believed Nicholas and his followers, represented the true faith of all right-minded citizens. Assisted by state, family, and school, the church was to inculcate the Christian virtues of obedience, humility, and morality, and Russians should learn only what was proper to their station in life. The non-Orthodox were liable to persecution. Of autocracy, the empire's basic law declared: "The tsar of all the Russias is an autocratic and unlimited monarch. God Himself commands us to obey the tsar's supreme authority, not from fear alone, but as a point of conscience." Anyone blaspheming or insulting the emperor could be decapitated. Russian autocracy combined Western divine-right theory with the awesome authority of the Mongol khans. Russia, many asserted, required autocracy, and its whole history justified it. "The Russian people," wrote Mikhail Pogodin in 1826, "is marvelous, but only in potential. In actuality it is low, horrid and beastly"—and must be led firmly. Nationalism, the least defined of the three doctrines, portrayed Russia as a youthful, pure, and separate entity with a unique past and a brilliant future. Russian customs and language, it was suggested, were superior to those of the decadent West. Under Nicholas were anticipated the subsequent concepts of Russification and Pan-Slavism.

Russia theoretically from above, Nicholas scrutinized it from below as if it were a piece of machinery in need of repair. As a third brother, he had never been given much official responsibility. Profiting from free discussions with those waiting to see his brother, he came to power with a few simple, realistic political ideas.

Nicholas looked so impressive that the French ambassador, struck by his bearing, called him an educated Peter the Great. Nicholas kept Peter's bust on his desk and claimed to emulate him as a ruler, but his severe appearance, unlike Peter's, concealed fear and deepening pessimism as he sought to make Russia an impregnable fortress. Orderly, precise, and duty-bound, his chief delights since childhood had been army reviews, formal parades, and the minutiae of military life.

Meanwhile, national consciousness was emerging gradually among non-Russian peoples of the empire. Of the greatest potential significance was Ukraine, containing the empire's second most populous nationality. Being formed during the early 19th century was a Ukrainian intelligentsia that researched Cossack traditions, collected a rich peasant folklore, and developed Ukrainian as a separate Slavic language. The initial center was Kharkov University (founded 1805), but with the opening of St. Vladimir's University (1835), Kiev assumed Ukrainian cultural leadership. While perfecting the Ukrainian language, these intellectuals asserted that Ukrainians shared a glorious past. Thus *Istoriia Rusov* (*History of the Rus*) (1846) glorified and romanticized the Cossack past, especially Bogdan Khmelnitsky, and viewed Ukrainians as a separate people deserving of self-government. Ukraine, it argued, not Russia, was the lineal descendant of Kievan Rus. Taras Shevchenko, Ukraine's greatest poet, in his initial collection of poems, *Kobzar* (*The Bard*) (1840), fervently opposed tsarist Russian autocracy, praised Cossack leaders who had opposed Russian rule, and advocated Ukrainian self-determination. In this work Ukrainian as a literary language first achieved true excellence. The Brotherhood of Saints Cyril and Methodius (1847), the first modern Ukrainian ideological organization, advocated a Slavic federation led by Ukraine with Kiev as its capital. Uncovering the nonpolitical Brotherhood, Nicholas I's tyrannical regime arrested its leaders. Shevchenko, considered its ringleader, was sentenced to 10 years' forced labor in Siberia.[2]

Administration

Nicholas sought to strengthen, improve, and repair the existing administrative system bureaucratically, without public participation. He examined personally the complaints and proposals of the Decembrists, and rejecting reactionary advice to repeal Alexander I's administrative reforms, he encouraged moderates to suggest some changes. A secret committee of leading officials was set up in 1826 to study papers left from Alexander's reign. After three years' work it proposed modest improvements in the administrative and social structure, leaving autocracy and serfdom intact. Legislative, judicial, and executive organs in national and provincial government were to be clearly separated. The State Council would advise the emperor on legislation; the Senate, yielding administrative tasks, would become a supreme court. The Revolutions of 1830 interrupted the committee's work, and few of its recommendations were implemented, but Nicholas did consider them.

Impatient with regular official channels, Nicholas from 1826 built up a private bureaucracy of several sections—His Majesty's Own Imperial Chancery—that bypassed ordinary administrative organs and enhanced the tsar's personal power. The Second Section, dominated by Count Speranskii, undertook to codify Russian law. All decrees and acts since the *Ulozhenie* were collected, ordered chronologically, and published as *The Complete Collection of Laws of the Russian Empire* (1833). Speranskii also codified military law and the laws of the western borderlands. Codification, perhaps Speranskii's greatest achievement, marked a significant and essential step toward the rule of law, a basis for the improvement of justice, and spurred development of the Russian legal profession.

The Chancery's Third Section, the most notorious to many Russians, symbolized Nicholas's entire regime. Count A. K. Benkendorf had warned Alexander I about secret societies and proposed a special elite political police recruited from moral men of breeding that would be "feared and respected." The Third Section was established under Benkendorf in 1826 to coordinate the regular and political police, gather information, and conduct surveillance of heretical religious groups, subversive or suspect people, and all foreigners.

[2] Orest Subtelny, *Ukraine: A History* (Toronto, 1988), pp. 227, 236–37.

It administered political prisons, handled censorship, and arrested and exiled subversives. Benkendorf was an unusual police chief: kindly, humane, and so forgetful that it was said he sometimes forgot his own name! The Third Section, with agents scattered over the empire, watched state institutions and submitted reports on the public mood. Nicholas hoped that it would also promote efficiency and reduce red tape. The gendarmes' blue uniforms appeared wherever domestic trouble existed or was suspected. The Third Section was independent and powerful but uncovered very little subversion.

Aiming at efficient government, Nicholas tried to reduce personnel and paperwork. His personal inspections of St. Petersburg offices caused panic among their bureaucrats. Trusted officials were sent to the provinces to conduct rigorous inspections (see Nicholas Gogol's humorous literary version in *The Inspector General*), and one report of a tax official ran to 15,000 pages. Forty carts, hired to bring the report from Moscow to St. Petersburg, disappeared en route without trace! Efforts to create an efficient, European bureaucracy failed despite the tsar's best efforts, largely because poorly educated officials could not apply complex laws that they often misunderstood. Poorly paid provincial officials stole or took bribes to support their families. Because lower officials evaded responsibility, trivial matters came to ministers or to the emperor for decision. At the top were some able, patriotic men, but in the provinces, where bureaucracy proliferated, the wheels of state often turned largely by corruption.

The Army

Nicholas I's military despotism rested on the pillars of bureaucracy, church, police, and army. To Nicholas the last was the most important, and he lavished great attention and resources on it. His system must therefore be judged partly on the army's effectiveness and showing in war. As supreme commander, Nicholas sought to improve its efficiency, but he always suspected intelligent,

educated officers, fearing a repetition of the Decembrist Revolt. Instead, he relied largely on the 18th-century traditions of General Suvorov: "The bullet is a fool, the bayonet is a hero." Technology, strategy, and tactics were neglected.

Field Marshal F. I. Paskevich, Russia's top military man from 1827 to 1855 and greatly admired by Nicholas, epitomized the shortcomings in the army command. A harsh disciplinarian, he guarded a swollen reputation won in easy victories over Persia, the Porte, and the Poles. Despite sporadic objections by Nicholas, he emphasized formal regulations, parade ground routine, and precise marching over realistic combat training:

> Uniformity and organization reached the point where a whole infantry division of four regiments of twelve battalions (not less than 9,000 men) formed in columns, performed all the movements, marching in step . . . , and keeping the ideal alignment in rank and depth. The manual of arms by whole regiments struck one by its "purity." . . . [Here], according to the views of the times, lay the guarantee of success in war.[3]

Promotions were based solely on seniority while the most innovative military minds and the most daring commanders were unused or forced into premature retirement. A conservative, anti-intellectual military establishment was epitomized by the motto of General N. O. Sukhozanet, fussy commander of the General Staff Academy: "Without knowledge victory is possible, without discipline never." Brutal, unreasoning discipline reduced the academy's low enrollment to a trickle and deprived Russia of the able staff officers it needed so badly during the Crimean War.

The Russian army, the largest in Europe, numbered 859,000 in the peacetime year of 1850, but many troops were tied down in garrison duty and internal security (some 145,000 in 1853). Thus Russia's field army was not much larger than the French or the Austrian. The stifling restrictions of serfdom made an effective reserve system impos-

---

[3] Quoted in J. S. Curtiss, *The Russian Army under Nicholas I, 1825–1855* (Durham, NC, 1965), p. 119.

sible, and the huge standing army and an unwieldy, overcentralized military bureaucracy overburdened taxpayers and unbalanced the budget. Even trivial decisions often had to be made by the minister of war. Enlisted men, mostly serfs, served 25 years and were punished brutally by their noble officers. In 1827 Nicholas ordered two Jewish escapees whipped 12 times through a column of 1,000 men. "God be thanked," commented the tsar. "There has been no death penalty with us and I shall not introduce it."[4]

The army command, overconfident and self-satisfied after victories over weaker opponents (Poles and Turks), turned its back on technical innovation. Its successes had been achieved by discipline, numbers, and the stoic courage of the Russian soldier. Infantrymen were supplied with antiquated muskets and given virtually no target practice. Marching on the parade ground could not prepare men for battle. The cavalry, except for the Cossacks, was clumsy and loaded down with heavy, useless equipment. Its horses were pampered and overfed and lacked endurance. Only the artillery and engineers, containing some of the ablest officers, remained innovative and abreast of their western colleagues. While western European armies adopted modern weapons and had trained reserves, Nicholas's army—his pride and joy—reflected Russia's backward economy and the worst features of autocracy and serfdom. Tested severely for the first time in the Crimean War, it was found wanting.

The Intelligentsia

Intellectually, Nicholas's reign was a strange combination of stifling censorship and highly creative literature and thought. The full weight of censorship, however, hit literature and the press with severity only from 1848 to 1855, and even then it lacked the thoroughness of Soviet censorship. Particularly from 1838 to 1848 a wide variety of

---

[4] Curtiss, *The Russian Army*, p. 49.

material was published with the aid of relatively liberal censors.

The suppression of the Decembrist Revolt temporarily blighted the bright promise of the St. Petersburg intelligentsia, that tiny minority of educated people who were vitally concerned with ideas. Executions or exile of Decembrist leaders frightened other intellectuals; the first decade of Nicholas's reign was marked largely by intellectual emptiness, fear, and somnolence. Nonetheless, some remarkable writers—Pushkin, Zhukovskii, Gogol, and Lermontov—lived and worked in St. Petersburg and wrote some of their finest works. In these years some Russian intellectuals renounced the French Enlightenment for Germanic theories such as Schelling's, and especially Hegel's dialectical idealism came into vogue. Schelling's writings stimulated both the doctrine of official nationalism and later idealistic theories of purposeful evolution. In St. Petersburg, however, the bureaucracy and the police were too omnipresent for a free development of ideas, and the government sponsored or watched over the leading press organs.

Moscow was freer, its university more distinguished, and a sizable group of leisured, cultured noblemen resided there. In the 1830s Moscow University became the center of Russian intellectual life and inspiration. Groups of professors and students earnestly discussed moral and philosophical problems, and many published their views in the *Moscow Telegraph* (1825–1834). Of the three major groups, two were associated directly with the university. One, headed by Alexander Herzen (see Chapter 27) and N. P. Ogarev, espoused the views of early western socialists until it was denounced to the police in 1834. A second, the so-called Stankevich Circle (from a leader, N. V. Stankevich), included Professor T. N. Granovskii, whose lectures on general history aroused widespread interest for their liberal viewpoint. The circle's leading Hegelian, until he emigrated in 1840, was Mikhail Bakunin, later a founder of anarchism, and it also included Vissarion Belinskii, the first professional Russian man of letters not from the gentry (see Problem 6 at the end of this chapter). A third group, later called the Slavophiles, contained A. S. Khomiakov and the Kireevskii and Aksakov brothers, all land-owners knowledgeable about agriculture and the peasantry.

A few Russians were turning to a socialism derived from the French utopians and centered on a peasantry whose discontent was rising. Wrote Count Benkendorf, head of the Third Section: "Every year the idea of freedom spreads and grows stronger among the peasants owned by the nobles. In 1834 there have been many examples of peasant insubordination to their masters . . . purely from the idea of obtaining the right to freedom."[5] Responding to peasant yearnings for land and liberty, members of the intelligentsia laid the foundations of populism. Alexander Herzen, the leading early Russian socialist, combined ele-ments of Slavophilism and Westernism (see Prob-lem 6) and suggested agrarian socialism as the solution to Russia's problems. In his memoirs Herzen described how the Decembrists' sacrifice had inspired him: "The stories of the revolt and the trial . . . shook me deeply. A new world opened for me and became the center of my spiritual life. . . . The execution of Pestel and his comrades woke me forever from my youthful dreams."[6] He and his young friend N. P. Ogarev vowed to dedicate their lives to the struggle that the Decembrists had begun, and they adopted many of the ideas of Charles Fourier and other European socialists. Sharing the Westernizers' passion for science and the belief that Russia must be Europeanized, Herzen called Hegel's philosophy of development "the algebra of revolution," but he rejected West-ern industrialism, urbanism, and materialism. While denouncing the Slavophiles' Orthodoxy and nationalism as "fresh oil for anointing the tsar, new chains laid upon thought," he shared

their veneration of Russian institutions and their faith in the peasantry. Unlike them, he viewed the commune, purged of feudal elements, as the basis for Russia's socialist regeneration.

The Petrashevskii Circle of the late 1840s reflected the narrow, abstract, and utopian nature of nascent Russian socialism. This small group, mostly lesser gentry in government service, dis-cussed socialist ideas and built paper utopias but made no concrete plans to implement them. M. V. Petrashevskii was an idealistic, eccentric dreamer and minor foreign office official who adopted Fourier's ideas wholeheartedly. His pamphlets urged emancipation of the serfs and setting up phalansteries combining private property and collective ownership. The Russian commune minus its feudal aspects, he believed, equaled Fourier's phalanstery. Within this circle, N. A. Speshnev's small communist faction advocated a tightly organized, centralized organization to direct a peasant revolt that would be followed by dictatorship and large-scale collective agriculture. Petrashevskii summarized his difference with Speshnev: "Fourierism leads gradually and natu-rally to what communism wishes to impose immediately and forcibly."

The Revolutions of 1848 alarmed Nicholas I as the French Revolution of 1789 had frightened Catherine II. To quarantine Russia from revolu-tionary contagion, his Buturlin Committee policed the press so carefully that little could be published. Even Count Uvarov, the regime's official spokes-man, was removed as minister of education for defending the universities against reactionaries who wanted to close them down! In April 1849 the police uncovered the Petrashevskii Circle. Though it was harmless, the authorities sentenced many Petrashevtsy to death, including the young writer Fedor Dostoevsky. Moments before execu-tion, their sentences were commuted. In 1850 universities were forbidden to teach philosophy and European constitutional law. As Orthodoxy, autocracy, and nationalism were enforced rigidly by a militaristic regime, gloom and despair settled over the Russian intelligentsia.

---

[5] Quoted in F. Venturi, *Roots of Revolution* (New York, 1960), p. 65.
[6] Venturi, *Roots of Revolution*, p. 2. See *The Memoirs of Alexander Herzen*, 6 vols. (New York, 1924–28), 1: 61.

Foreign Affairs

Until the Crimean War, Russia, believed to be the strongest European land power, with its Austrian and Prussian allies, upheld Metternich's system of conservative absolutism. Nicholas stood ready to use his powerful army to repress foreign revolutions, but his foreign policy, though aggressive in tone, aimed to preserve the status quo, not extend Russian boundaries. To avoid general European conflict, Nicholas kept lines of communication open with the Western powers. Even strong suspicion of his allegedly expansionist policy in Great Britain did not prevent practical cooperation at times. Among his specific goals were to regulate Russia's relationship with Poland and to consolidate Russia's favorable position in the Balkans. Like his predecessor, Nicholas maintained personal control over foreign policy. Foreign Minister Count Nesselrode, inherited from his brother Alexander I, remained an obedient mouthpiece. Later a breakdown in communications between Nicholas and Count Nesselrode helped involve Russia in the Crimean War. In foreign affairs Nicholas was direct, blunt, stubborn, and often rigid.

The Polish Revolt (1830–1831) brought Russia closer to the other eastern powers but alienated it from France. Nicholas had upheld reluctantly his obligations as constitutional king of Poland until the French Revolution of 1830 encouraged Polish nationalists and radicals to overthrow the Warsaw government. The Poles received only sympathy from the West, and Nicholas's commander, General Paskevich, captured Warsaw (September 1831); but Polish resistance helped prevent Russian intervention in western Europe, and Nicholas had to accept a neutral Belgium and the July Monarchy in France. As thousands of Poles fled into exile in France, Nicholas's Organic Statute (1832) divided Poland into provinces and incorporated it directly into the empire.

In the Caucasus, Russian expansion continued as Paskevich defeated Persia (1826–1828). The Treaty of Turkmanchai gave Russia most of Persian Armenia with Erivan and moved the frontier to the Araxes River. The Caucasian lowlands had been won fairly easily, but Russia's control of the mountain regions remained insecure. In the late 1820s there developed in Daghestan a strong Muslim resistance movement known in Russia as Muridism. Its leader, Kazi Mullah, proclaimed a holy war on Russia. Religious and national hatred of Russians combined with resentment at their occupation of mountain lands. After Kazi Mullah's death (1834), Shamil, a brilliant commander of the Muslim resistance force, led the mountaineers in guerrilla warfare and for two decades inflicted humiliating defeats on Nicholas's troops. Shamil's movement, encouraged by the British in order to contain Russia, prevented firm Russian control of the Caucasus.

In Central Asia by 1850 small Russian forces, sometimes without official initiative, had established firm control over the broad Kazakh steppe and its nomadic population. Major revolts by Isatai Taimanov (1836–1838) against local Kazakh rulers and by Kenesary Kasimov (1837–1847) against the Russians were quelled. Russian forces, occupying Fort Perovskii on the Syr River and Fort Vernoe (the future Alma-Ata) farther east, brought the ill-defined frontier close to rich oases ruled by the semifeudal khanates of Khiva, Kokand, and Bukhara. In the Far East, N. N. Muravev (Amurskii), governor-general of eastern Siberia (1847–1861), advanced into the Amur region, claimed but not settled or firmly controlled by decaying Manchu China. Captain G. I. Nevelskoi, authorized to explore the Amur River, raised the Russian flag at the river's mouth. Nicholas I, dismissing Nesselrode's cautious objections, declared: "Where once the Russian flag has flown, it must not be lowered again." Muravev founded Khabarovsk on the Amur (1854) and penetrated Sakhalin Island offshore, and the delighted emperor made him a count. Simultaneously, Admiral E. V. Putiatin entered Nagasaki, Japan, weeks after Commodore Perry of the United States reached Tokyo, opening Japan to external influences. The Russo-Japanese treaty of 1855 provided for extraterritorial rights, trade, diplomatic relations, and joint administration of Sakhalin Island.

The Eastern Question remained a chief focus of Russian foreign policy during the 19th century. Should Russia act politically or militarily to protect Orthodox and Slav Balkan Christians against the Muslim Turks, or instead defend a legitimate monarch—the sultan—against a rising tide of national revolts in the Balkans? Nicholas I generally considered relations with the sultan more important than wooing rebellious Balkan Christians. "The advantages of maintaining the Ottoman Empire in Europe," he affirmed, "exceed the inconveniences that it presents." A weak, pliant Ottoman Empire under Russian tutelage still seemed preferable to a partition that might provoke a European war. At times Nicholas dealt with the sultan alone; at others he supported the Christians. But usually he sought to cooperate in the Balkans with the European powers. He and Nesselrode, fearing that the Ottoman "sick man" might die, believed that plans must be made just in case.

In the late 1820s Russian influence in the Ottoman Empire increased greatly, alarming Great Britain, which worried about its far-flung imperial interests. Anglo-Russian imperial rivalry over predominance in Ottoman affairs would persist throughout the 19th century, threatening repeatedly to provoke war between them. However, in 1826 Russia, backed by France and Great Britain, secured domestic autonomy for the Greeks. Russia and Turkey concluded the Akkerman Convention, which confirmed autonomy for Serbia and the Danubian Principalities under the sultan and provided free passage through the Turkish Straits for Russian merchant ships. But when a Turkish fleet was destroyed at Navarino Bay (1827), the sultan repudiated Akkerman and declared war on Russia. At first Russian armies made little headway in the Balkans, but in the Caucasus Paskevich conquered some of the southern Black Sea coast and captured the powerful Kars fortress. In 1829 Field Marshal I. Dibich's forces took Adrianople and threatened Constantinople while Paskevich

conquered Erzurum in Anatolia. In the ensuing Treaty of Adrianople (1829), the sultan had to reaffirm Akkerman, make the Danubian Principalities a Russian protectorate, and cede to Russia the southern Danube delta and more Black Sea coastline. Merchant ships of all countries at peace with the Porte (Ottoman Empire) could now use the Straits. In 1830 the powers arranged the independence of Greece, and the Porte became dependent on Russia.

Ottoman subservience to Russia increased still further after Mehemet Ali, pasha of Egypt, revolted in 1832, invaded Syria, and defeated a Turkish army. In desperation the sultan turned to Russia, which prevented Mehemet from taking Constantinople and helped the powers arrange peace. The Treaty of Unkiar-Skelessi (July 1833) provided that Russia would aid the Porte militarily upon request and that the Turks would close the Dardanelles to foreign warships. By this treaty with the Ottoman Empire, Russia safeguarded its vulnerable Black Sea coast and claimed the right to intervene at will in Turkish affairs. Unkiar-Skelessi marked a high point of Russian power in the Straits question. At Münchengrätz (September 1833) the Austrian emperor and the Prussian crown prince met with Nicholas and accepted Unkiar-Skelessi. Austria and Russia agreed to preserve the Ottoman Empire and prevent Mehemet from taking any of European Turkey.

Russia could not keep the Porte in subjugation for long. The British ambassador, Lord Ponsonby, counterbalancing Russian influence in Constantinople, helped the Sultan regain freedom of maneuver. While Nicholas remained moderate and defensive, Ponsonby and a journalist, David Urquhart, whipped up anti-Russian feeling in Great Britain. When Mehemet Ali revolted again and another Near Eastern crisis erupted (1839–1840), the powers restricted him to Egypt, and Unkiar-Skelessi lapsed. The powers signed a Straits Convention (1841) with the Porte, which barred foreign warships from the Straits while the sultan was at peace. Russia remained secure unless the Porte was a belligerent. This compromise merely delayed a confrontation between Russia and the Western powers.

Early in 1848 the French July Monarchy and Metternich's regime fell as revolution engulfed Paris, Vienna, Berlin, and Budapest. Nicholas feared that it might spread to Russian Poland and wished to restore the July Monarchy by force, but the outbreaks in central Europe prevented him from doing so. Instead, he guarded Russia's position in Turkish affairs and supported the Austrian Habsburgs. When radicals took power in Wallachia, Russian troops occupied neighboring Moldavia and aided the Turks in suppressing the rebels. Nicholas grew convinced that the Hungarian Revolution, led by Lajos Kossuth's liberal nationalists, was part of an anti-Russian conspiracy. He wrote Paskevich: "At the head of the rebellion . . . are our eternal enemies, the Poles." In May 1849, responding to a request by the young Austrian emperor, Franz Josef, Paskevich crushed the Hungarian Revolution. Russia restored Austrian leadership in German affairs, blocked Prussian action, and upheld the Vienna Settlement. These successes made Nicholas I very overconfident.

The Crimean War, 1853–1856

The Crimean conflict—the diplomatic and military climax to Nicholas's reign—revealed the disastrous failure of his policy. Clashing Russian and Franco-British interests in the Ottoman Empire, inept diplomacy, and miscalculations on both sides led to war. A trivial "quarrel of monks" sparked a costly, useless war between Russia and Turkey, backed by several European powers. Roman Catholic and Orthodox priests argued over rights at the Holy Places in Jerusalem, and their respective claims were backed by France and Russia.

In February 1853 Nicholas sent Prince A. S. Menshikov on a diplomatic mission to Constantinople to reassert Russian prestige against France. Menshikov secured the resignation of the Turkish foreign minister and reached agreement on the Holy Places, but the Turks, supported by Stratford de Redcliffe, the British ambassador, rejected his haughty demands for a secret Russo-Turkish alliance and denied Russia's rights to "protect" the Porte's Orthodox Christians. Some Soviet accounts suggested that Redcliffe provoked war deliberately. In May Menshikov left Constantinople angrily, severing Russo-Turkish relations; in July Nicholas ordered Russian troops into the Danubian Principalities.

Menshikov's demands drew Great Britain and France together behind the Turks. To Nicholas's dismay, they and the German powers protested Russia's occupation of the Principalities. The Porte blocked the Vienna Note, a European attempt at compromise, and London rejected a revised version of the note. A Franco-British fleet sailed through the Dardanelles, and the Porte declared war on Russia (October 1853). Emotional British reactions to Admiral N. S. Nakhimov's destruction of the Turkish fleet at Sinop ended chances to localize the conflict. Though the Turks had been the aggressors, London denounced the Russian action as a "massacre." When Nicholas ignored a Western ultimatum to evacuate the Principalities, France, Great Britain, and later Sardinia joined the Turks in the war.

The causes of the Crimean War remain debatable, but evidently neither the allies nor Russia planned aggression or desired war. London believed that Russian intervention in the Ottoman Empire would lead to Russian control and threaten vital British interests; Napoleon III of France needed success abroad to prop up his regime at home. Hostility toward and suspicion of Russia, especially in Great Britain, contributed to the war. Western leaders believed that they had to stop Russia and restore Europe's balance of power. For his part, Nicholas overrated Russia's strength and sought by bluster to reassert undefined Russian rights to "protect" the Christians. He apparently did not intend to seize Constantinople or partition the Ottoman Empire, but only to consolidate Russian influence there.

During the war Russia's strategic position was unfavorable. Nicholas had planned to invade the Balkans with the aid or friendly neutrality of the

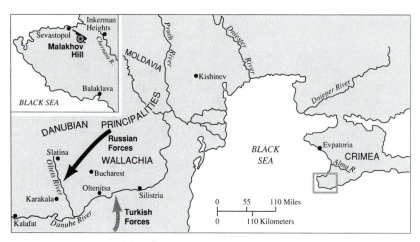

Map 23.1 Russia and the Crimean War, 1853–1856

German powers. Instead, they allied with one another (April 1854); Austria mobilized against Russia and agreed with the Turks to a joint occupation of the Danubian Principalities. Austria's "monstrous ingratitude" (for Russian aid in 1849) rendered Russia's position there exposed, and Nicholas's efforts to rouse the Balkan Christians failed. Field Marshal Paskevich, the commander in chief, considered the Austrian threat awkward and kept many troops in Poland. Other Russian forces fought the Turks in the Caucasus and watched Shamil, and still others protected St. Petersburg against possible invasion. Such a dispersal of troops and cautious Russian commanders prevented proper use of Russia's huge army.

In the campaigns of 1854–1855 the Russians won in the Caucasus but lost on the Danube and in the Crimea (see Map 23.1). After making probing attacks along the Danube and suffering minor setbacks, Russian forces withdrew behind the Pruth, and Austria occupied the Principalities. Then a Franco-British expeditionary force of 60,000 men landed in the western Crimea (September 1854). After Prince Menshikov's smaller Russian force, marching northward to meet it, suffered defeat at the Alma River, only hasty fortification of Sevastopol on the landward side and Allied slowness saved the chief Russian naval base from immediate capture. Menshikov, reinforced

from the Danubian front, tried to throw the Allies off Inkerman Heights near Sevastopol into the sea, but he failed to use his numerical superiority. Poor coordination and ignorance of the terrain (a detailed map of the region reached Menshikov *after* the battle!) contributed to a major Russian defeat. In the ensuing siege of Sevastopol, the defenders fought heroically, but superior allied firepower pulverized their positions while both armies suffered severely from disease and cold. Early in 1855 Nicholas, knowing that his huge military machine could not even protect Russian soil, died of pneumonia and was succeeded by his son, Alexander II. In September the Allies captured key Malakhov Hill and compelled the Russians to evacuate Sevastopol, but the Russian capture of Kars in the Caucasus somewhat offset the Crimean defeats.

Throughout the war the diplomats tried to arrange a compromise settlement. In August 1854 France, Great Britain, and Austria agreed upon Four Points as a basis for peace: All powers, not just Russia, should regulate the status of Serbia and the Principalities; all states were to navigate the Danube freely; the Straits Convention of 1841 was to be revised; and Russia was to renounce claims to exclusive protection of Orthodox Christians. In December 1855 Austria threatened to enter the war unless Russia accepted the Four

Points and two additions. Realizing that Russia could not fight Austria too, Alexander II agreed to a peace conference in Paris and accepted the Four Points. Russia ceded southern Bessarabia to Moldavia and consented reluctantly to "neutralize" the Black Sea by dismantling its fleet and naval bases there.

The Crimean defeat and the Paris treaty, though galling, did not threaten Russia's great-power status, but Russia had lost the predominance on land that it had enjoyed since 1814. Ottoman disintegration was arrested, and Russian prestige in the Balkans was reduced. Russia's

defeat and Austria's support of the Western powers destroyed the unity of the three eastern monarchies. Timid and incompetent leadership, inferior weapons, and inadequate communications had caused Russia's defeat. The complete lack of railroads south of Moscow had complicated the supply problems of the Crimean army. The war revealed Russia's technological and economic backwardness compared to the Western powers and the need for drastic internal reform. The new ruler, Alexander II, and his advisers learned these harsh lessons and were determined to restore Russian power and influence.

Problem 6

Whither Russia? Slavophiles versus Westernizers

After publication in Russia (1836) of Peter Chaadaev's first *Philosophical Letter* (Herzen called it "a pistol shot in the dead of night"), a great debate erupted within the intelligentsia over Russia's past history and future role. Two major schools of thought emerged—generally known as Slavophiles and Westernizers—which criticized the regime of Nicholas and were suspected by it. Sir Isaiah Berlin, an English historian, believed that Chaadaev's *Letter* began "a marvelous decade" of effort by a small intelligentsia, in attitude half-Russian and half-foreign, cut off from the populace and standing between an oppressive regime and a sea of wretched but disorganized peasants.[7] Few ideas presented in this debate were original: Russian intellectuals seized eagerly upon European ideas, often considering them the ultimate truth. Russian thinkers of the 1840s compare in outlook and in the raising of major issues to the French

philosophes of the late 18th century. Below are summarized Chaadaev's *Letter* and some views of the Slavophiles and Westernizers from their principal spokesmen.

Chaadaev: First Philosophical Letter

Peter Ia. Chaadaev (1793–1856) fought in the Napoleonic Wars and then became associated with the Decembrists and was a close friend of the great liberal poet Alexander Pushkin. Resigning from the army in 1821 to immerse himself in the works of religious writers, in 1823 he went abroad, where he was deeply influenced by Catholicism and French conservative thought. Between 1828 and 1831 he wrote eight philosophical letters in French, of which the first and most spectacular was published in Russia by N. I. Nadezhdin's *Telescope* in 1836. Chaadaev's views were strongly pro-European and pro-Catholic; he was profoundly pessimistic and negative about Russia's past:

> It is one of the most deplorable traits of our peculiar civilization that we are still discovering truths which other peoples, even some much less advanced than we, have taken for granted. The reason

---

[7] I. Berlin, "A Marvellous Decade, 1838–48," *Encounter* 4 (June 1955): 27–39.

is that we have never marched with the other peoples. We do not belong to any of the great families of the human race; we are neither of the West nor of the East, and we have not the traditions of either.

Chaadaev viewed Russia's history as essentially worthless:

> A brutal barbarism to begin with, followed by an age of gross superstition, then by a ferocious and humiliating foreign domination, the spirit of which has passed into the national state—that is the sad history of our youth. . . . We live in a narrow present, without a past and without a future, in the midst of a dead calm.

That was bad enough, but the following passage infuriated the authorities and nationalists who had glorified Russian traditions and institutions:

> We are alone in the world, we have given nothing to the world, we have taught it nothing. We have not added a single idea to the sum total of human ideas; we have not contributed to the progress of the human spirit, and what we have borrowed of this progress we have distorted.

Neither Peter I nor Alexander I, though exposing Russia to European civilization, had been able to civilize it:

> There is something in our blood that resists all real progress. In a word we have lived, and we live now, merely in order to furnish some great lesson to a remote posterity. . . . We are a blank in the intellectual order.

Chaadaev attributed this cultural vacuum to the fact that "we went to wretched Byzantium," whereas Europe had been schooled by Catholicism. He held out only the vague hope that in the future Russia might save European civilization.[8]

The government responded by closing down the *Telescope* and exiling its editor. Concluding

[8] From *Russian Intellectual History: An Anthology,* edited by Marc Raeff, copyright © 1966 by Harcourt Brace Jovanovich, Inc. and reprinted by permission of Humanities Press International, Inc., Atlantic Highlands, NJ. Pp. 162ff.

that Chaadaev must be mad, it placed him under a physician's care, a practice revived in the 1960s under Brezhnev. In his *Apology of a Madman* (1837), Chaadaev protested that he was a patriotic Russian but that love of truth must precede love of country. Admitting that he had been too pessimistic about Russia's history, he held out the vague hope that Russia might have some positive future mission. Utilizing Europe's experience and avoiding its mistakes, including capitalism, Russia should be guided by "the voice of enlightened reason and conscious will."

Chaadaev's writings helped spark the development of the Slavophiles and the Westernizers, groups that objected for different reasons to Russia's existing social and political system. Repelled by bureaucratic absolutism, serfdom, the atmosphere of fear, and the suppression of thought, they demanded civil liberties and reform. However, this tiny, emerging Russian intelligentsia split sharply over its view of humanity, the Russian past, the nature of the status quo, and where Russia should be headed. The terms *Slavophile* and *Westernizer*, deliberately vague and chosen to deceive the censor, suggested two fundamentally different types of civilization: traditional Russo-Byzantine versus modern, rational, and European. After the Revolution of 1848 the publications of both groups were suppressed by Nicholas I's regime.

The Slavophiles

The leading Slavophiles—A. S. Khomiakov and the Kireevskii and Aksakov brothers—were romantic nationalists who idealized Russian Orthodoxy and the institutions of old Muscovy, notably the *zemskii sobor* and the peasant commune, which they believed exemplified the distinct, superior qualities of the Russian people: unity, obedience, and harmony with the tsar. Replying to Chaadaev, Khomiakov agreed that some Russians lacked history and traditions, but only the Westernized and rootless minority that had lost contact with the people (*narod*) and sought salvation in Europe. Rejecting a Westernization that they associated with the Petrine reforms, the Slavophiles denounced the bureaucracy for alienating the tsar from his people. The Slavophiles opposed constitutional government as alien and divisive, but their more liberal members (Iu. Samarin, V. Cherkasskii) were later leaders in emancipating the serfs. For them, salvation lay in a conservative utopia, in a return to the people, their ancestral religion, and traditional community life. Wrote K. S. Aksakov in a memorandum submitted to Alexander II in 1855:

> The Russian people is not a people concerned with government. . . . It has no aspiration now toward self-government, no desire for political rights . . . [or] power. [This had been proven at the dawn of Russian history] when the Russians of their own free will invited foreigners to rule over them—the Varangians. . . . [In 1612 the people] chose a tsar and having wholly entrusted their fate to him, they peaceably laid down their arms and returned to their separate homes. . . . The spirit of the people is the guarantee of tranquility in Russia and security for the government. . . . For Russia to fulfill her destiny, she must follow her own ideas and requirements, and not theories which are alien to her. . . . The Russian people *has no concern for government* . . . , has no desire to limit in any way the power of the authorities . . . , is apolitical and consequently does not contain so much as an embryo of revolution or a trace of desire for a constitutional order.

What, then, do the Russian people desire?

> To retain their internal communal life, their way of life. . . . The essential qualities of the Russian people are good, its beliefs are holy, its way is righteous. . . . The Russian people, having renounced the political realm and given unlimited powers to the government, reserved for themselves *life*—their moral and communal freedom, the high purpose of which is to achieve a Christian society.

Aksakov, while advocating absolute monarchy and noting the ancient and traditional division in Russia between "tsar's business" and "people's business," also glorified the old Muscovite *zemskii sobor:*

> The power of the state must be absolute . . . it must be a monarchy. . . . In recognizing the absolute power of the monarch, [the Russian] retains complete independence of spirit, conscience, and thought. . . . It is one of the state's duties to protect freedom of public opinion. [The *zemskii sobor*] consisted of representatives of all the social classes. . . . Their only purpose was to elicit expression of *opinion.* . . . The people of Russia gathered at these assemblies at the summons of the tsar and not out of a vainglorious desire to orate, as they do in Parliament, or to seek power. . . . Our [Muscovite] tsars gave full rein to public opinion among the peasantry . . . by asking them to elect judges . . . and by giving full latitude to peasant meetings to decide all matters pertaining to their own administration.

On the other hand, Aksakov argued that the West had "abandoned the spiritual path," had been "lured by vanity into striving for power," and was thus on the verge of collapse. Consequently, Russian rulers had been wrong to adopt "false" Western principles, as during the reign of Peter I:

> We must now speak of a period when the government—not the people—violated the principles of Russia's civil order and swerved Russia from her course. . . . The revolution wrought by Peter, despite all its outward brilliance, shows what immense spiritual evil can be done by the greatest genius as soon as he acts alone, draws away from the people, and regards them as an architect does bricks. Under Peter began that evil which is still the evil of our day. . . . Contempt for Russia and for the Russian people soon became an attribute of every educated Russian intent upon aping Western Europe. That is how the breach between the Tsar and the people occurred.

Turning to the present condition of Russia, Aksakov described what should be done to remedy its shortcomings:

> Russia's present condition is one of internal dissension glossed over by unscrupulous lies. . . . The general corruption and the weakening of moral principles in society have reached vast proportions. Bribery and organized robbery by officials are terrifying. . . . The main root of the evil is our repressive system of government—repression of

Problem 6 continued

freedom of opinion and of moral freedom. . . . A man is not even expected to think right, he is expected not to think at all. . . . The specific remedy for the ills of modern Russia is . . . to revert to the essential principles which are consonant with her spirit. . . . Let there be reserved for the government unlimited freedom to *rule*, which is its prerogative, and for the people full freedom of social and spiritual life under the government's protection. Let the government *have the right to action* and consequently the power of law; let the *people have the right of opinion* and consequently freedom of speech.[9]

The Westernizers

Chaadaev and the Slavophiles stimulated the Westernizers to develop a philosophy of history and refute their conservative approach to Russian problems. Repudiating the Slavophiles' stress on collectivism and determinism, the Westernizers were ardent individualists and voluntarists. Wrote T. N. Granovskii, a liberal history professor at Moscow University: "The goal of history is the moral, enlightened individual, emancipated from fatalistic determining factors and a society founded on postulates."[10] Westernizers tended to neglect the masses and to conclude that history is the product of enlightened, autonomous, and critical minds. Much less unified in ideology than the Slavophiles, the Westernizers were positivists with deep faith in science and technology. They believed that Russian development should follow western Europe's, not pursue its own path. Most of them were atheists or deists who repudiated Orthodoxy and all established churches. Contrary to Slavophile claims, the Westernizers were patriotic Russians who wished not to substitute Western institutions for Russian ones but to lift Russia to Europe's

Vissarion G. Belinskii, 1811–1848, literary critic and leading Westernizer.

level of educating and modernizing society. Besides freedom of speech and press, many espoused constitutional government. Some, such as Professors Granovskii and K. D. Kavelin, were liberal moderates; others, such as Vissarion Belinskii, were democrats or radicals. The Westernizers proclaimed Peter I their mentor and admired his rational, secular reforms; they deplored his cruelty and rejected the autocracy he epitomized.

Vissarion Belinskii (1811–1848) became the Westernizers' most militant spokesman. A radical and an atheist, he was much quoted and admired by Soviet historians. At first an ardent Hegelian and a social conservative, Belinskii became the leading Russian advocate of freedom, democracy, and humanitarianism. Expelled from Moscow University for attacking serfdom, he developed into the most brilliant, incisive literary critic of

---

[9] Raeff, *Russian Intellectual History*, pp. 231ff.

[10] T. N. Granovskii, *Sochineniia* (Moscow, 1900), p. 445, quoted in A. Walicki, *The Slavophile Controversy* (Oxford, 1975), p. 425.

Problem 6 continued

his age. In his best-known political work, *Letter to Gogol* (1847), written in Austria, Belinskii castigated the famous conservative writer for his *Selected Passages from Correspondence with Friends*, a defense of Nicholas I's regime:

> One cannot remain silent when, under the cloak of religion and the protection of the knout [whip], falsehood and immorality are being preached as truth and virtue. . . . You know Russia well only as an artist and not as a thinking man.

Like Voltaire, to whom he compared himself implicitly, Belinskii denounced the Orthodox church as a corporate entity:

> Russia sees her salvation not in mysticism, not in asceticism, not in pietism, but in the achievement of civilization, enlightenment, and humanitarianism. What she needs is neither sermons (of which she has heard enough!) nor prayers (she has mumbled enough of those!), but an awakening in her people of the sense of human dignity . . . ; she needs rights and laws conforming not to Church doctrine but to common sense and justice. . . . Instead, she offers the dreadful spectacle of a country in which men trade in men . . . ; a country, finally, which not only affords no guarantees for personal safety, honor, and property but which cannot even maintain internal order and has nothing to show but vast corporations of officeholding thieves and robbers.

In this work, which circulated widely inside Russia, Belinskii attacked boldly the official doctrines of Nicholas's regime:

> [The Orthodox church] has ever been the support of the knout and the toady of despotism. [It had nothing in common with Christ], the first to teach men

the ideals of liberty, equality, and fraternity. . . . Our clergy is held in general contempt by Russian society and the Russian people. . . . Take a closer look and you will see that the Russian people are deeply atheistic by nature. They still have many superstitions, but not a trace of religious feeling. [The public] holds the Russian writers to be its only leaders, its only defenders and saviours from the black night of Autocracy, Orthodoxy and Nationalism.

Finally, Belinskii sought to point the way forward toward the achievement of a new and freer Russia:

> The most topical, the most vital national questions in Russia today are the abolition of serfdom, the repeal of corporal punishment, and the introduction, as far as possible, of the strictest possible application of at least those laws which are already on the books.[11]

Conclusion

While the Slavophiles and Westernizers struggled to define a future role for Russia, the Crimean War revealed the traditional system of autocracy, serfdom, and Orthodoxy to be hollow and incapable of solving Russia's domestic problems or of maintaining its power abroad. Nicholas's critics, notably Belinskii, pointed the way toward the reform of Russian institutions, especially the abolition of serfdom. In the midst of the war a new tsar, Alexander II, mounted the throne. Although conservative and traditional in some ways, he was realistic enough to attempt major reforms in order to save the imperial regime. ■

---

[11] Raeff, pp. 253–58.

Suggested Additional Reading

BOOKS

BARKER, A. J. *The War against Russia, 1854–1856* (New York, 1971).

BAUMGART, W. *The Peace of Paris, 1856,* trans. A. Saab (Santa Barbara, CA, 1981).

BELINSKII, V. G. *Selected Philosophical Works* (Moscow, 1956).

BLACK, J. L. *Nicholas Karamzin and Russian Society in the Nineteenth Century* (Toronto, 1975).

CARR, E. H. *The Romantic Exiles . . .* (Cambridge, 1981). (Reprint.)

CHRISTOFF, P. *An Introduction to Nineteenth Century Slavophilism: Khomjakov* (The Hague, 1961).

CURTISS, J. S. *The Russian Army under Nicholas I, 1825–1855* (Durham, NC, 1965).

———. *Russia's Crimean War* (Durham, NC, 1979).

CUSTINE, A. DE. *Journey for Our Time: Russia—1839,* ed. and trans. P. P. Kohler (London, 1980). (Reprint.)

EVANS, J. L. *The Petrashevsky Circle, 1846–1848* (The Hague, 1974).

GAMMER, M. *Muslim Resistance to the Tsar: Shamil and the Conquest of Chechnia and Daghestan* (Portland, OR, 1994).

HERZEN, A. *My Past and Thoughts,* 6 vols. (London, 1924–1927).

INGLE, H. *Nesselrode and the Russian Rapprochement with Britain, 1836–1844* (Berkeley, 1976).

LENSEN, G. *Russia's Japan Expedition of 1852–1855* (Westport, CT, 1982). (Reprint.)

LINCOLN, W. B. *In the Vanguard of Reform: Russia's Enlightened Bureaucrats, 1825–1861* (De Kalb, IL, 1982).

———. *Nicholas I* (Bloomington, IN, 1978).

MACKENZIE, D. *Ilija Garašanin: Balkan Bismarck* (Boulder, CO, 1985). (Especially Chap. 8, "Confrontation with Russia, 1850–1853," pp. 113–40.)

MALIA, M. *Alexander Herzen and the Birth of Russian Socialism* (Cambridge, MA, 1961).

MONAS, S. *The Third Section* (Cambridge, MA, 1961).

MOSELY, P. E. *Russian Diplomacy and . . . the Eastern Question in 1838 and 1839* (Cambridge, MA, 1934).

ORLOVSKY, D. *The Limits of Reform: The Ministry of Internal Affairs . . . 1802–81* (Cambridge, MA, 1981).

PRESNIAKOV, A. E. *Emperor Nicholas I of Russia . . .* (Gulf Breeze, FL, 1974).

PURYEAR, V. *England, Russia, and the Straits Question, 1844–56* (Berkeley, 1931).

RIASANOVSKY, N. V. *Nicholas I and Official Nationality . . .* (Berkeley, 1959).

———. *A Parting of Ways: Government and the Educated Public in Russia, 1801–1855* (Oxford, 1976).

RIEBER, A. J. *Merchants and Entrepreneurs in Imperial Russia* (Chapel Hill, NC, 1982).

SAAB, A. P. *The Origins of the Crimean Alliance* (Charlottesville, VA, 1977).

SEATON, A. *The Crimean War: A Russian Chronicle* (New York, 1977).

SQUIRE, P. S. *The Third Department . . .* (Cambridge, 1968).

WALICKI, A. *A History of Russian Thought from the Enlightenment to Marxism* (Stanford, 1979).

———. *The Slavophile Controversy* (Oxford, 1975).

ARTICLES

BALMUTH, D. "The Origins of . . . Censorship Terror." *ASEER* 19 (1960): 497–520.

BERLIN, I. "Russia and 1848." *SEER* 26 (1947): 341–60.

BOLSOVER, G. H. "Nicholas I and the Partition of Turkey." *SEER* 27 (1948): 115–45.

BROOKS, E. W. "Nicholas I as Reformer: Russian Attempts to Conquer the Caucasus, 1825–1855," in *Nation and Ideology . . . ,* ed. Ivo Banac (Boulder, CO, 1981), pp. 227–63.

HAYWOOD, R. "The Development of Steamboats on the Volga River . . . 1817–65," in *Research in Economic History,* ed. P. Uselding (Greenwich, CT, 1981), pp. 127–92.

HORVATH, E. "Russia and the Hungarian Revolution, 1848–49." *SEER* 12 (1933): 628–45.

KAPLAN, F. "Russian Fourierism of the 1840's . . ." *ASEER* 17 (1958): 161–72.

LEWAK, A. "The Ministers of Nicholas I . . ." *Rus. Rev.* 34, no. 3 (1975): 308–23.

———. "The Polish Rising of 1830." *SEER* 9 (1930): 350–60.

———. "Russia on the Eve of Reform: A *Chinovnik's* View." *SEER* 59, no. 2 (1981): 264–71.

MCNALLY, R. "The Origins of Russophobia in France, 1812–30." *ASEER* 17 (1958): 173–89.

PINTNER, W. "Civil Officialdom and the Nobility in the 1850's," in *Russian Officialdom . . .* (Chapel Hill, NC, 1980), pp. 227–49.

———. "The Social Characteristics of the Early Nineteenth Century Russian Bureaucracy." *SR* 29 (1970): 429–43.

PIPES, R. "The Russian Military Colonies, 1810–31." *JMH* 22 (1960): 205–19.

ROWNEY, D. K. "Structure, Class, and Career: The Problem of Bureaucracy, and Society in Russia, 1801–1917." *Social Science Hist.* 6, no. 6 (1982): 87–110.

SMOKE, R. "The Crimean War," in *War: Controlling Escalation,* ed. R. Smoke (Cambridge, MA, 1977), pp. 147–94.

Part Three

Modern Russia,
1855 to the Present

DURING THE PAST 140 TURBULENT YEARS Russia has undergone pervasive political, social, economic, and cultural changes under the last tsars and several Soviet and post-Soviet leaders: Lenin, Stalin, Khrushchev, Brezhnev, Gorbachev, and Yeltsin. Assuming power during and after the Crimean War, Alexander II's regime instituted the "Great Reforms" (especially the emancipation of the serfs), which created a liberalized tsarist system. Under Alexander III conservative monarchy was restored, but the large-scale railroad construction and state-sponsored industrialization of Finance Minister Sergei Iu. Witte fostered rapid economic change. Russia absorbed Central Asia and expanded in the Far East. Its defeat by Japan triggered the Revolution of 1905. Under pressure, Nicholas II inaugurated semiconstitutional monarchy. During this Duma monarchy public education was extended, and Count Peter A. Stolypin began to replace communal agriculture with private farming. Reform and reaction under the last tsars were followed by the calamity of World War I, bringing military defeat, financial breakdown, and governmental paralysis. In the 1917 revolutions tsarism yielded to democracy, and democracy to Soviet communism. Authoritarianism, absent during 1917, was gradually restored by Lenin and perfected by the dictator Stalin. Through forced collectivization Stalin transformed agriculture. The Five Year Plans and universal education made the Soviet Union a powerful modern state. Millions of lives were snuffed out in Stalin's Great Purge. After the terrible travail of World War II, wherein the USSR and the United States emerged as the superpowers, Stalin established a bloc of eastern European satellite states. In the post-Stalin era the USSR at first raised living standards and relaxed political terror but still poured resources into heavy industry and military strength. In an authoritarian and stagnating Soviet system the Communist Party retained preeminent power until its position was undermined in the Gorbachev era. Then in 1991 the USSR disintegrated into 15 sovereign states linked loosely in a Commonwealth of Independent States.

24

Political Reform and Minorities, 1855–1904

The death of Nicholas I and the Crimean defeat ended the old regime of undiluted autocracy and serfdom in Russia. The year 1856, with its remarkable openness, debate, and demands for reform, is comparable to the recent Gorbachev period in the USSR. Alexander II, the new emperor, pursued from the start more pragmatic and enlightened policies than his father. The Great Reforms (1855–1874) of his reign, compared by some to the far-reaching changes in the USSR under Gorbachev, released forces of change that gradually transformed patriarchal Russia as it adjusted to rising industrial capitalism. The reforms, though partial and incomplete, were opposed by entrenched conservative interests, which sought, sometimes successfully, to reverse or impede change. This opposition made the half century after the Crimean War an era of ebb and flow, of conflict between modernizing and traditional elements.

The Great Reforms remain controversial. Did Alexander's government seek to create a modern, progressive Russia, or merely to avert revolution and save the nobility by halfhearted concessions? Did the reforms place Russia on the path, earlier traversed by western Europe, toward parliamentary government and social reform, or were they, as many Soviet historians claimed, mere palliatives, altered later by the rigidly conservative regime of Alexander III?

Alexander II and the Emancipation

The emperor, retaining full autocratic powers, remained the prime mover in the Russian political system. In the midst of the Crimean War Alexander II, well prepared and well intentioned, assumed power at the age of 37. His father and tutors had stimulated his sense of duty and his concern for the military; the poet Zhukovskii had reinforced his romantic, humanitarian impulses. Though no scholar, Alexander was well versed in foreign languages, and Count Speranskii had coached him in Russian law and politics. He was the first tsar to have visited Siberia (1837) and traveled extensively in Russia and Europe. Alexander married a German from Hesse-Darmstadt, christened Maria Alexandrovna in Russia, and Prussia remained his favorite European country.

Library of Congress

Alexander II, tsar 1855–1881.

Nicholas I had entrusted him with important state duties and had allowed him to run the government during his absences. Alexander's character was a curious mixture of strengths and weaknesses. Tending to shy away from obstacles, he had combated irresolution and weak will since childhood, but he could be very stubborn. He was irritable and emotional, but he possessed sound common sense and sincere patriotism, and he wanted to do what was right. Generally, Alexander chose able advisers and supported them loyally even against strong opposition.

Designated the "tsar-liberator" by some, Alexander II played a vital, probably decisive part in the emancipation of the serfs. He acted more from conservative than from liberal motives and sought as Russia's "leading nobleman" to protect legitimate interests of the nobility. Shaking off indecisiveness and weak will, he directed the difficult campaign at every step. War Minister Dmitri A. Miliutin wrote:

The tsar showed at this time such unshakable firmness in the great state undertaking he had personally conceived that he could ignore the murmurings and grumblings of the clear opponents of innovation. In this sense the soft and humanitarian Emperor Alexander II displayed greater decisiveness and a truer sense of his own power than his father who was noted for his iron will.[1]

Alexander was not the frightened man depicted by Soviet accounts. Letters to his trusted friend Prince A. I. Bariatinskii emphasized that in an emancipation designed to take Russia along the path of progress, the ruler must seize the initiative: "Autocracy created serfdom and it is up to autocracy to abolish it." In 1856 he warned the Moscow nobility: "It is better to begin to abolish serfdom from above than to wait until it begins to abolish itself from below. I ask you, gentlemen, to think over how all this can be carried out." This speech jolted the nobility out of its apathy but failed to win substantial support for emancipation among noblemen.

Initially, the press was permitted to discuss the emancipation issue, but the emperor, to protect his autocratic powers, had the Emancipation prepared bureaucratically. He appointed a secret committee to examine the problem, most of whose members were conservative noblemen, though liberals such as S. S. Lanskoi and N. A. Miliutin dominated the Ministry of Interior, which prepared the specific statutes. The tsar prodded the reluctant Main Committee and ordered the provincial nobility to create committees to draw up emancipation procedures. Rejecting the landless emancipation favored by conservative gentry, Alexander in 1858 visited key provinces and stressed the need for a landowning peasantry. Soviet accounts attributed his initiatives largely to a rising tide of peasant disorders. Alexander Herzen's émigré newspaper, *The Bell*, rejoiced: "Thou hast triumphed, O Galilean!" When editor-

---

[1] Quoted in A. J. Rieber, ed., *The Politics of Autocracy: Letters of Alexander II to Prince A.I. Bariatinskii, 1857–1864* (Paris, 1966), p. 21.

ial commissions (set up to decide how much land should go to the peasants and on what terms) delayed, Alexander appointed his liberal brother, Grand Duke Constantine, to head them. The Emancipation Act, after a brief discussion in the State Council, was signed by Alexander on February 19, 1861, the sixth anniversary of his accession. To prevent peasant disturbances, the authorities announced the Emancipation the Sunday before Lent, and it was proclaimed to the peasants in church and in their villages. The peasants' initial joyous reaction at liberation soon yielded to dismay or anger when they realized that they would not receive free and clear all of the lands they had worked previously.

The Emancipation Act of 1861, relating only to private serfs, granted them immediate personal freedom. The statute was so lengthy, complex, and often so vague that it is no wonder the peasants failed to understand it. The reform was to proceed in three phases: a brief transition, a phase of "temporary obligation," and a redemption period. For the first two years former serfs were expected to perform traditional services for the landowners while reaching agreements with them on lands, boundaries, and obligations. Such "inventories" were to be drawn up by mutual agreement or with the aid of peace mediators (*mirovye posredniki*) appointed by the Crown from the gentry. If the peasants and lords failed to draw up an inventory, the mediator was to do so.

Numerous peasant disturbances developed because the peasants were reluctant to accept onerous or unfair terms; some charters had to be completed without peasant approval. Many peasants expected that "real freedom" would follow this two-year interlude, and when such rumors proved false, some refused regular-sized land allotments, accepting free-of-charge dwarf plots ("beggars' allotments") instead. About one-fourth of the maximum norm, these proved insufficient to support a peasant family. Most possessors of "beggars' allotments" became tenant farmers. In areas where land was abundant and rents low, some peasants preferred beggars' allotments, which freed them from redemption payments and

allowed them to rent land at relatively low cost. Other peasants, once the inventories had been completed, became "temporarily obligated": They paid their usual *obrok* or performed *barshchina* while the lords retained ownership of the land. For the first nine years after 1861 all former serfs, except those taking beggar allotments, had to accept a standard-sized allotment. Household serfs, though personally free, usually received no land and often had to work for the landlord. "Temporary obligation" lasted until both parties agreed on a procedure to redeem the land. Finally, the government set 1883 as the date by which all peasants must begin redeeming their land. After deducting noble debts, the state advanced to the landowners about three-fourths of the amount due them in interest-bearing securities. The peasants were to repay the government over a period of 49 years and to pay the remaining quarter directly to the lords.

Land allotments varied in size by region— Black Soil, non–Black Soil, and steppe. Maximum and minimum norms were set for each province, but the lord was guaranteed at least one-third of his estate. In Great and New Russia the land was generally transferred to the repartitional commune; in Ukraine, where the hereditary commune prevailed, allotments became the hereditary possession of individual households. In the western provinces under the land reform of 1864, because the landlords were largely Polish, the mostly Belorussian, Ukrainian, or Lithuanian peasantry received all land previously worked at below its market price. In the west and infertile north and east, allotments usually equaled or exceeded preemancipation standards. In the fertile Black Soil region, however, they were smaller, and reductions ("cutoffs") on behalf of the nobility exceeded 25 percent. In the Black Soil zone the land was somewhat overvalued, and in the north greatly overvalued, to compensate nobles for the loss of labor power or peasant side earnings.

Other categories of peasants obtained better terms. In 1863 the imperial peasants (826,000 registered males in 1858) received allotments about equal to the maximum accorded private peasants in their region and were to begin redemption payments within two years. The next year emancipated state peasants were ascribed to work in metallurgical factories. A law of November 1866 assigned to state peasants—mostly in northern and eastern Russia and Siberia—all of the lands previously worked in return for higher *obrok* payments; in 1886 redemption payments replaced *obrok*. Because "cutoffs" were rare and state peasants had worked more land than private serfs, the state peasants were considerably better off. For all peasants the household and commune, regarded by the state as guarantors of order and stability, were reinforced, receiving most of the nobility's former judicial and police powers.

The significance of the emancipation settlement is still debated. Most liberal Western historians consider it a major step in modernizing Russia that only an autocratic government could have carried out. For Soviet scholars, the Emancipation was a "bourgeois reform" extracted from a reluctant government by peasant pressure. The former serf owners who executed it, however, imposed many feudal survivals, galling restrictions, and excessive payments on the peasantry. The emancipation settlement, claims a Soviet general history,[2] created conditions that fueled subsequent revolutionary peasant explosions. Thus some historians emphasize the progress achieved, others the remaining restrictions and problems. The Emancipation did produce a single class of free villagers who were, however, still clearly demarcated socially and administratively from other groups and governed by their own regulations and standards. Emancipation did not and could not solve Russia's longstanding agrarian problem of low productivity.

Other Social and Political Reforms

The end of serfdom encouraged, and in some cases required, other significant changes. Most of these changes were drafted or suggested during the late 1850s; after 1861 their enactment and implementation met with increasing opposition from conservative noblemen in and outside the government. During the 1860s contending factions within the bureaucracy and Alexander's indecision caused shifts, delays, and confusion in government policies. Such disputes, claims a Soviet account,[3] were over what concessions had to be made to preserve autocracy against the threat of revolution. On the one hand, magnates with vast estates, such as Count P. A. Shuvalov, favored only minimal concessions to improve existing laws and institutions coupled with repression of radicals and liberals. More liberal officials of the new generation, especially the Miliutin brothers and Count P. A. Valuev, favored new basic institutions, and some even proposed a constitutional regime. Alexander's vacillation between these groups helps account for alternating liberalism and repression. Generally, the government adopted a middle course of limited reforms designed to make a constitution unnecessary.

Censorship and Education

Even before the Crimean War ended, the government permitted a revival of Russian intellectual life, which had been stifled by the post-1848 repression. Under a liberalized censorship, Russian-language periodicals, some quite radical in approach, increased from 25 to almost 200 between 1855 and 1862. After 1858 the government limited the press in its discussion of controversial policies, especially in foreign affairs, but the press law of 1865, which largely abolished prior censorship by officials of the Ministry of Education for books and journals, generally confirmed the liberal trend. For newspapers, a new system of punitive censorship, involving warnings and suspensions, marked an advance over the old system of prior censorship. Though the authorities still often seized or suspended radical publications, for

---

[2] *Istoriia SSSR* (Moscow, 1968) vol. 5, pp. 7–9.

[3] *Ibid.*

most of Alexander II's reign the press enjoyed greater freedom than it did before his reign or immediately after it. Whereas Nicholas I had sought to permit only publications beneficial to the state, Alexander generally permitted whatever did not endanger it.

Higher education experienced heartening progress. When the Crimean War ended, restrictions on university admissions were lifted, courses in philosophy, European government, and international law were reinstituted, and enrollments increased some 50 percent in four years. Foreign scholarly works were freely imported, and Russian students again traveled and studied abroad. In May 1861, however, strict temporary rules caused serious student disorders at Russian universities, and Admiral E. V. Putiatin, the new minister of education, urged that the universities be closed. But in December Alexander dismissed Putiatin and appointed an outstanding liberal, A. V. Golovnin, to his post. The charter of June 1863 gave the universities considerable autonomy and academic freedom. Faculty councils controlled university affairs and elected rectors, and the universities entered a period of growth and creative activity.

For the first time the government sought to educate the Russian masses. In the early 1860s an unofficial public effort established some 500 literacy clinics for adults. In July 1864 the Ministry of Education issued the Public School Statute, the first major proposal in Russia for a national system of primary schools. District school boards were created, including representatives of the ministry, the Holy Synod, and other agencies. The new zemstva assemblies (see this chapter, under "Local Self-Government") also made encouraging progress; by 1880 they supported, at least in part, most of the 23,000 elementary schools in European Russia. Under their auspices some village schools were opened in the latter part of Alexander's reign. City councils (dumy) did similar work in larger towns.

The Ministry of Education's limited resources were devoted mainly to secondary education based on German and French models. Golovnin's statute of 1864 stated the liberal all-class principle, a vital innovation of this epoch: "The gymnasia and progymnasia are for the education of children of all conditions without social or religious distinction." Classical and modern curricula were considered equally valid, though only graduates of the classical gymnasia had sure access to the universities. Debate continued over the relative merits of classical and practical-scientific studies. Golovnin's liberal approach yielded in 1866 to the rigid discipline of Count Dmitri Tolstoi, minister of education until 1880. Tolstoi, a fervent advocate of classicism, by the law of June 1871 imposed the "Greco-Roman bondage" under which the gymnasia stressed Greek and Latin to the detriment of Russian language and history. His purpose was to discipline the students, steer them away from revolution, and make access to universities difficult for nonprivileged elements. Nonetheless, both gymnasia and Realschulen (practical schools emphasizing science and modern languages) expanded in numbers and improved in quality. A law of 1870 provided for the opening of women's gymnasia, largely locally supported. Women's universities (women were not admitted to the existing ones) were opened in the provincial capitals Kiev and Kazan beginning in 1869.

Local Self-Government

The highly significant zemstvo reform of January 1864 marked a shift from the appointed local officials of Nicholas I to a measure of self-government. The old system of bureaucratic tutelage led A. M. Unkovskii of Tver province to complain in 1859 that without official permission people "dare not repair a miserable bridge or hire a schoolteacher." That same year Alexander instructed a special commission to propose a new system of local government. After the Emancipation ended their direct power over the peasantry, noblemen agitated for a larger role in local affairs. Some liberal gentry urged a national representative assembly like the old zemskii sobor. In February 1862 the Tver nobility, renouncing special tax and class privileges, petitioned the tsar to convene an assembly elected by the entire land. Alexander responded angrily by having the Tver leaders imprisoned. Noble assemblies, warned the Ministry of Interior, must submit no petitions going beyond local needs. The central government opposed a national assembly or constitution.

Instead, in January 1864 the tsar approved the *zemstvo* system, which provided for the election of district and provincial assemblies by landowners, peasantry, and townspeople. Introduced in some provinces in 1865, *zemstva* were gradually extended by 1914 to 43 of the 50 provinces of European Russia. Each class group was to elect representatives (*volost* elders selected peasant deputies) to a district assembly primarily on the basis of landownership and property value, a weighted franchise that ensured the predominance of landowners. In 1867 at the district level nobles held 42 percent, peasants 38 percent, and townsmen about 20 percent of the seats. District *zemstva* elected delegates to provincial assemblies, where the gentry, because of their dominance at the district level, occupied almost three-fourths of the seats. At each level the assembly chose an administrative board to execute its decisions. Despite gentry predominance, the *zemstva* reflected the all-class principle, as for the first time the various classes participated together in local government in an elected assembly.

The sphere of *zemstvo* activity was carefully limited by law to local tasks that the central government lacked the personnel or the desire to perform. Supervised by police and crown officials, they were to fill the gap between the *mir* (peasant commune) and provincial governors. The *zemstva* were to build roads and bridges, construct and operate village schools, establish public hospitals and clinics, and improve agricultural techniques. Local taxes on landed property and commercial wealth were to finance their activities. Though the taxing power of the *zemstva* was severely restricted, their revenues grew steadily and they employed more and more professional people: agronomists, teachers, and doctors. Despite a jealous bureaucracy, they improved conditions in rural Russia considerably and were far superior to anything that had existed previously. Serving as schools of self-government, the *zemstva* gradually undermined the principle of autocracy and agitated for national representation. Some Soviet historians, however, quoting Lenin, regarded them as a halfhearted gesture by the autocracy: "The *zemstva* were doomed from the very start to play the part of the fifth wheel on the coach of Russian state administration, a wheel tolerated by the bureaucracy only so long as its own powers were not at stake."[4] This statement reflects Lenin's contempt for liberalism but fails to do the *zemstva* justice.

The municipal law of 1870, based on Russian and European practice, represented progress toward urban self-government. The eight largest cities, accorded the status of provinces, were placed under commandants, whereas other cities were treated as equivalent to districts and subordinated to provincial governors. Important towns were to elect city councils (*gorodskie dumy*) under a system resembling the Prussian, reserving most influence to the merchant elite, which paid the most taxes. Though provincial governors sharply restricted their competence and tax revenues, the city *dumy* accomplished much in providing elementary education, building hospitals, paving and lighting streets, and creating other city services, especially in the two capitals. The city council elected an executive body consisting of a mayor (*golova*) and several members, which was closely regulated by the Ministry of Interior or the provincial governor. Although most city dwellers were excluded from public office and deprived of real influence, the law of 1870 still represented progress toward self-government.

Judicial Reform

Nowhere was reform more urgently needed than in the court system. Under Nicholas I legal procedure had been antiquated, cumbersome, and cor-

---

[4] V. I. Lenin, *Sobranie sochineniia,* 5th ed. (Moscow, 1960), vol. 5, p. 35.

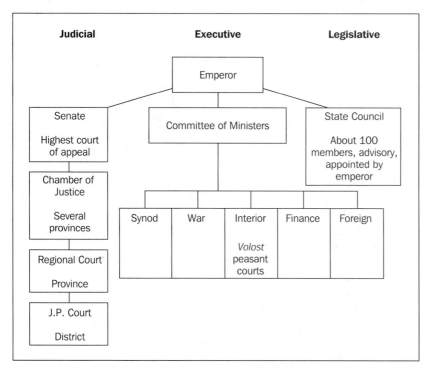

Figure 24.1
Russian Imperial Government, 1855–1905

rupt. Frequently judges had been untrained and open to bribery; the accused often languished in jail for years before their cases were tried. Alexander II declared in 1856, "May justice and mercy reign in our courts!" but not until 1862 did he decide to establish a new system of justice. The law of November 1864 introduced enlightened European judicial practices and in each province not subject to administrative control set up a system of regular courts with judges who would serve for life. Justice of the peace courts (see Figure 24.1) were established in the countryside and the towns to try lesser cases and became highly popular for their simple, swift, and impartial procedures. In the regular courts, public jury trials were introduced for more important cases, and a brilliant Russian bar developed. This new judicial system took firm root, but it required decades to extend the new courts from the capitals to more remote parts of European Russia and the borderlands.

Many cases fell outside or were removed from the jurisdiction of the new courts. After 1872, crimes against the state were tried, often secretly, by special courts under the Ministry of Interior, and the minister of interior could banish suspicious or politically dangerous people to remote parts of the empire without trial. Three additional court systems continued to function outside the regular one. *Volost* courts, originally set up for state peasants by Count Kiselev, were extended to former serfs as a part of emancipation legislation. Using oral customary law and staffed by often illiterate peasant judges, they tried minor civil and criminal cases involving peasants under the Ministry of Interior. Thus peasant contacts with the modern judicial system were minimal (except for the justice of the peace courts), which helped perpetuate the peasants' separate status. Ecclesiastical courts under the Holy Synod handled all cases involving the clergy, church property, and divorce. Finally, the War Ministry maintained courts for military personnel and areas under martial law. Despite these severe limitations, the judicial reforms of 1864 were strikingly successful and promoted the rise of an able legal profession. The principle of equality before the law helped undermine the old estate system.

Military Reform

Under an able war minister, Dmitri A. Miliutin (1861–1881), described as "the most daring and radical spirit among the reformers," the Russian army was transformed and modernized. Miliutin's long tenure of office, his energy, and the tsar's support enabled him to carry through comprehensive changes despite powerful opposition. Earlier he had fought against Shamil in the Caucasus and served 15 years as a leading professor at the Military Academy. During travels to western Europe he had pointed out the numerous shortcomings of Nicholas I's army. As chief of staff to Field Marshal A. I. Bariatinskii (1856–1860), he had reorganized the military command in the Caucasus and contributed greatly to that region's pacification. Appointed war minister at Bariatinskii's urging, Miliutin acted to create a more efficient, less expensive army and to ensure Russia's security. First he reduced the term of service to 15 years and abolished most corporal punishment. In 1864, 15 regional military districts replaced the overcentralized system of Nicholas and strengthened local authority. Miliutin also reorganized the central army command and greatly reduced its personnel and paperwork. A liberal reform of military justice was effected along the lines of the judicial reform of 1864. Military gymnasia, providing a broader education and open to all classes, replaced the exclusive cadet corps for training officers, and primary schools were set up to provide literate recruits.

During the late 1860s growing noble reaction imperiled military and other changes. In April 1866 D. V. Karakozov, a nihilist student, attempted unsuccessfully to assassinate Alexander II, frightening him and increasing the influence of conservative noblemen and officials. Count P. A. Shuvalov, chief of gendarmes and spokesman for former serf owners, dominated the government for the next seven years. Prussia's decisive victory over France (1870–1871), which dramatized the issue of Russia's national security, however, enabled Miliutin to secure approval for universal military training. He had advocated this reform since the early 1860s, but only in 1874 did he finally overcome vehement opposition from Shuvalov and Bariatinskii, the chief defenders of traditional gentry privileges. The law of January 1874 proclaimed that "the defense of the fatherland forms the sacred duty of *every* Russian citizen." At the age of 20 all able-bodied males, with a few exceptions, were subject to a maximum of six years' active service and some years in the reserves. The term of service depended on one's education (a university graduate had to serve only six months). The tsar, despite his sympathy with the conservatives, supported Miliutin because of the importance of universal training for national security. Universal military service enabled Russia to establish trained reserves, and the Russian army, thanks to Miliutin's dedicated work, became a more effective fighting force with high morale. As subsequent wars would reveal, however, serious shortcomings remained.

Significance of the Great Reforms

The Great Reforms, despite their limitations and inconsistencies, changed Russia fundamentally. The all-class principle reduced the privileges and predominance of the nobility and increased the rights of other groups. The regime sought to integrate the freed serfs into Russian society, but peasants remained inferior and were subject to many discriminatory practices. A liberalized censorship and educational progress stimulated the rise of public opinion and increased literacy. The concepts of greater equality before the law, universal liability to military service, and local self-government all weakened autocracy. The reforms thus created a basis for more rapid social, economic, and even political evolution. Soviet historians viewed the reforms as marking Russia's transition from feudalism to capitalism and its adaptation to bourgeois values and a capitalist economy. They stressed correctly that because the regime protected and favored noble interests, many aspects of serfdom and feudal inequality survived. Many of the most liberal changes were later halted or reversed, which revealed the continuing power of conservative interests. Older attitudes and institutions, though shaken, persisted side by side with the new in continual friction and conflict, and the shallowness of political change left the Great Reforms incomplete.

Legally, Alexander remained an unlimited autocrat, and to preserve absolute power he blocked the creation of a national parliament or constitution. He controlled the executive branch by simultaneously keeping in office liberal and conservative ministers, whom he appointed and dismissed and who were responsible to him alone. He presided over the Committee of Ministers (see Figure 24.1), a loose, uncoordinated body whose members rarely consulted one another on their policies and took pride in keeping their colleagues ignorant of their activities. The appointed State Council of 75 to 100 top civil and military officials debated prospective laws, but neither its decisions nor its advice was binding, and the emperor and his ministers initiated all legislation. The effective operation of the central administration depended largely on the emperor, so chaos threatened if he failed to provide adequate leadership.

Treatment of Minorities before 1905

Alexander II's attitude toward national and religious minorities remained generally liberal and moderate, but in Poland an armed rebellion caused him to resort to Russification and repression, which heralded official policies after 1881. During the liberal years after 1855 some Polish émigrés returned home, and a reform-minded

Agricultural Society was created with branches throughout Russian Poland. Though Alexander warned the Poles not to expect political changes, Polish radicals agitated for broad autonomy or independence and opposed the moderate approach of Alexander Wielopolski, appointed head of a Polish commission on religion and education. Wielopolski wished to introduce needed reforms, make Russian rule more tolerable, and cooperate with Russian liberals such as Grand Duke Constantine. Late in 1861, as student and worker demonstrations broke out in Warsaw, Wielopolski's policies were repudiated, and radical defiance of his decree on conscription in January 1863 touched off armed rebellion.

The Polish insurrection against Russia lasted more than a year and doomed the hopes of the moderates. Polish lords supported the Warsaw radicals while the enserfed peasantry remained largely passive. The rebels, hopelessly outnumbered and incompetently led, found few sympathizers in Russia and obtained only moral support abroad from France and England. Alexander's government crushed them, then implemented a drastic land reform in 1864, which undermined the nationalistic landowners. Count M. M. Muraviev, known subsequently as "the hangman of Vilna," successfully "pacified" Poland. The property of the Polish Catholic church was mostly confiscated, the clergy put on the state payroll, and the church subordinated to the Russian Ministry of Interior. In 1875 Russian Poland was divided into 10 provinces. Russian regulations on secondary education were extended there in 1872, and at Warsaw University Russian was the required language of instruction. Repression in Poland helped discredit Russian Pan-Slavism (see Chapter 26), but Alexander had little choice: The romantic Polish nobility had prepared its own ruin.

In Finland Alexandrine liberalism proved more successful. A reform program stimulated trade, developed communications, and spread education. The Russian governor-general, Count F. F. Berg, backed Finnish liberals who favored a railway into the interior to aid the timber industry and agriculture. In 1863 the Finnish Diet, convened for the first time since 1809, approved plans to modernize the economy and promote public education. Meeting regularly thereafter, the Diet steadily extended Finnish autonomy. Alexander II observed the Finnish constitution scrupulously because the Finns sensibly restricted themselves to measures he would tolerate.

The status of Russian Jews improved considerably under Alexander II. Some categories, notably merchants, doctors, and intellectuals, were permitted to reside outside the Pale of Jewish Settlement urban areas in western Russia designated for Jewish residence by Catherine II's regime. Jewish military recruitment was placed on the same basis as that for other citizens. As restrictions relaxed, Jews tended to assimilate with the Russian population. Anti-Semitism, however, remained strong in the lower bureaucracy and among the public.

Ukrainian national activities revived after Nicholas I's death. Ukrainophile veterans, including the poet Shevchenko (released from exile in 1856), historian Mykola Kostomarov, and some younger men, formed a *hromada* (society) in St. Petersburg to improve the lives of Ukrainian peasants. In 1861 they finally won permission to publish *Osnova*, the first Ukrainian-language periodical in the Russian Empire, which stimulated national consciousness among the intelligentsia. Meanwhile, a Kiev student society set up a network of Sunday schools for illiterate peasants. But in July 1863 St. Petersburg cracked down by prohibiting all Ukrainian publications except literary works. Pontificated Interior Minister P. A. Valuev, the Ukrainian language "has never existed, does not exist, and shall never exist." In the early 1870s Ukrainophiles resumed cautious activity. A Kievan branch of the Imperial Geographical Society, formed in 1873, studied Ukrainian folklore and poetry; the Shevchenko Literary Society, created in Lwow, later became an unofficial Ukrainian academy of arts and sciences. Mykhailo Drahomaniv, a youthful democratic member of the Kiev *hromada*, boldly advocated reorganizing the Russian Empire into a loose confederation of autonomous regions,

asserting that Ukrainians had lost much under Russian rule.

Russian repression cut short these promising trends. Drahomaniv, rather than abandon his radical views, went into exile and periodically issued *Hromada*, the first Ukrainian political journal. Worried by a rising Ukrainian national consciousness, St. Petersburg authorities recommended a total prohibition on importing and publishing Ukrainian books, on using Ukrainian on stage, or on teaching in the language. Concurring, Alexander II in May 1876 issued the Ems Decree, which crippled Ukrainophile activities and closed Kiev's branch of the Geographical Society.[5] Crushed in Russia, Ukrainian national activities flourished in freer Austrian Galicia, which emerged as a nucleus for a Ukrainian nation. Despite this repression, Alexander II generally pursued more tolerant policies toward the empire's minorities than did his successors.

Following the theories of K. P. Pobedonostsev, Alexander III's onetime tutor and later minister, the regime from 1881 to 1905 pursued active discrimination against the empire's national and religious minorities. Favoring Russians and Orthodox everywhere, it sought to turn these minority elements into Russian Christians. Russification, fostered by a central bureaucracy intolerant of diverse traditions, languages, and faiths, was supported for security reasons by the Orthodox clergy and the military. It represented a conscious attempt in the form of Great Russian domination to achieve Uvarov's vague concept of nationalism (see Chapter 23), and it paralleled the policies of some other European countries in the age of neo-imperialism. Among those who suffered most were the Baltic Germans, the Finns, and the Armenians, who had shown unswerving loyalty to the imperial regime.

Russification was introduced to Finland and intensified in the western borderlands. Finland, which had enjoyed the broadest autonomy of any region of the empire, began in 1890 to experience

---

[5] Orest Subtelny, *Ukraine: A History* (Toronto, 1988), pp. 279–86.

gradual Russian encroachment. The independent Finnish postal service was abolished (1890), and the Russian language was later introduced forcibly into certain Finnish institutions. In 1899, in violation of the Finnish constitution, St. Petersburg proclaimed that imperial laws would take precedence over Finnish laws. Under the narrow-minded Governor-General N. I. Bobrikov (1898–1904), the separate Finnish army was abolished and the Finnish Senate had to speak Russian. Such high-handed measures provoked growing Finnish passive resistance and antagonism toward Russia.

In Russian Poland remnants of autonomy were eliminated. In 1885 the Polish Bank became the Warsaw Office of the Russian State Bank; after 1885 all subjects in Polish schools, except the Polish language, were to be taught in Russian. Repression of Ukrainian nationalism intensified, but nationalist, democratic, and socialist movements, stimulated by literature from freer Ukrainian areas under Austrian rule, continued a slow growth. Mykhaylo Hrushevsky, a Russian-born Ukrainian scholar made professor of Ukrainian history at Lwow University in Austrian Poland in 1894, continued Drahomaniv's tradition. In the Baltic provinces the regime launched a campaign against Lutheranism and separate German

schools. The German University of Dorpat was closed, then reopened as the Russian Iurev University. The police and court systems in the Baltic provinces were Russified, embittering many loyal public servants.

The anti-Semitic Alexander III and Nicholas II enacted stringent laws against Jews. Pobedonostsev declared: "One-third will die out, one-third will become assimilated with the Orthodox population, and one-third will emigrate." Pogroms—unofficial mob violence against Jews and their shops—grew more frequent and were often condoned by the authorities. The "Temporary Rules" of 1882, enforced until 1905, forbade Jews to live outside towns or large villages and forced them into business and certain professions. In 1887 the Ministry of Education established Jewish quotas for secondary schools and universities: 10 percent in the Pale of Settlement, 3 percent in the capitals, and 5 percent elsewhere. Jews were virtually prohibited from becoming lawyers and lost the right to vote in *zemstvo* elections while still having to pay *zemstvo* taxes! Many Jews responded by emigrating, especially to the United States, and some entered the revolutionary movement. Bigoted decrees undermined the loyalty of minorities, especially in the western borderlands, and helped stimulate revolutions in 1905 and 1917.

Problem 7

Why Did Alexander II Free the Serfs?

Emancipation of the Russian private serfs in 1861 and of the court and state peasants in 1863 and 1866, respectively, constitutes the most significant and controversial act of Alexander II's reign. Some scholars consider it the greatest reform by a European government in the 19th century. It affected roughly 85 percent of Russia's population and began to transform its peasant masses from virtual slaves bound to the land into

free citizens and property holders. Some historians still describe the struggle over emancipation as one between "liberals" and "planters," though it is difficult to find avowed liberals or planters involved in the legislative process. During the working out of the reform legislation the reformers held secondary and tenuous positions, whereas their detractors held high offices. Most of the nobility revealed its opposition and resentment toward emancipation but demonstrated less cohesion and political capacity than one might expect from an elite class. Because senior

Problem 7 continued

bureaucrats involved in the reform lacked requisite skills, lower officials and outsiders were able to play key roles in drawing up the reform legislation. Writes Daniel Field:

> The manifest inadequacy of the government's nebulous and moderate program of 1857, coupled with a formal, public commitment to a reform of serfdom, impelled the regime to adopt a far more venturesome program in 1858 and enact it with substantial modifications in 1861.[6]

Why did Alexander II take this fateful step, which his predecessors (including his strong-willed father, Nicholas I, who had denounced serfdom as immoral) had refused to do? Is there a single explanation of the decision to emancipate? The official tsarist view depicted emancipation as a personal and generous decision by the new sovereign. Prerevolutionary liberal historians, on the other hand, stressed the role of an aroused public opinion directed by abolitionist writers (reform was "in the air"), which exerted decisive pressure on the government.

The Official Tsarist View

Tatishchev's official biography of Alexander II presents the Emancipation as the personal decision of an emperor convinced that serfdom was a great social evil and that the Crimean defeat had made a reorganization of the state administration imperative. Tatishchev emphasizes Alexander's concern that the nobility agree to and cooperate with his efforts at reform:

> The Crimean War revealed the unsatisfactory condition of many branches of state administration whose improvement Alexander II considered his immediate task. The young sovereign considered serfdom a great social evil whose elimination his predecessors had already repeatedly thought about and about which all the best Russian minds had long dreamed. From the first day of his reign

Alexander Nikolaevich [Alexander II] firmly resolved to implement the noble intentions of Empress Catherine II and Emperors Alexander I and Nicholas I, to achieve what they had backed away from because of the difficulties associated with implementing an act affecting and changing all aspects of the state and social order of Russia. He planned to undertake it only with the consent and the active participation of the nobility, not doubting its readiness to waive its rights to own souls [serfs] and to make this sacrifice voluntarily for the benefit and dignity of the country. This was the meaning of his first address to the nobility of Petersburg immediately after he mounted the throne, when, receiving their delegation, he expressed the hope that "the nobility will be in the full sense of the word a truly noble class, in the forefront of all that is good."

. . . Meanwhile from the first days of the reign vague rumors about the desire of the new sovereign to emancipate the peasants from serfdom began to spread in society both among the landowners and among the peasants, causing among both groups agitation so strong that Emperor Alexander considered it essential, at the first opportunity, to explain to the nobles the true meaning of his intentions. Soon after the conclusion of the Treaty of Paris on March 30, 1856, the emperor utilized a brief stay in Moscow in order, while receiving representatives of the nobility of Moscow province, to address them as follows: "I have learned, gentlemen, that among you have spread rumors of my intention to destroy serfdom. In refuting various unfounded reports on such an important matter, I consider it essential to declare to all of you that I do not intend to do this now. But, of course, you yourselves understand that the existing order of owning souls cannot remain unchanged. It is better to begin to destroy serfdom from above than to await the time when it begins to destroy itself from below. I ask you, gentlemen, to consider how all this can be carried out. Pass on my words to the nobility for their consideration."

In the tsar's speech to the Moscow nobility was clearly stated both the sovereign's personal view of serfdom and the wish for the nobility to take upon itself the initiative in the matter of its destruction. The emperor considered it a necessary condition for success that nowhere would the legal order be violated and that prior to the issuance of the new

---

[6] D. Field, *The End of Serfdom* (Cambridge, MA, 1976), pp. 3–5.

legislation, private serfs not express impatience and remain wholly obedient to their masters.[7]

Soviet Views

Until the 1960s Soviet historians, quoting extensively from the works of Marx, Lenin, and Stalin, placed overwhelming emphasis on peasant discontent as a cause of emancipation. They asserted that emancipation had been enacted reluctantly by a fearful tsarist regime vulnerable during a "revolutionary situation" of 1859–1861.[8]

P. A. Zaionchkovskii Later Soviet scholarship shifted to a multicausational explanation of the abolition of serfdom. Here is an outstanding example from the pen of one of the pioneers, Zaionchkovskii, taken from the introduction to *The Abolition of Serfdom in Russia*:

> The abolition of serfdom in Russia was a precondition ensuring the consolidation of capitalism. The reason that induced the government to undertake this reform was the crisis of the feudal-serf system. The existence of serfdom dictated the economic and political backwardness of Russia. As long as serfdom was retained, the development of industry and the rise of agriculture were impossible. The crisis of the feudal-serf system provoked the sharpening of class contradictions, finding expression in the growth of antifeudal ideology and the rise of the peasant movement, especially during the 1850s. Therefore, the question of serfdom and its liquidation was the central problem of social and ideological struggle in the first half of the nineteenth century.
>
> The Crimean War, revealing with utmost clarity all the backwardness of the serf-holding state, compelled the government of Alexander II to

undertake reform. The fear of peasant uprising played a major role. However, under existing circumstances, the abolition of serfdom by revolutionary means was impossible. The peasant movement represented a spontaneous struggle unilluminated by any political consciousness. There were no other forces capable of fighting against autocracy. The bourgeoisie, economically dependent on tsarism, although favoring the liquidation of serfdom, lacked the decisiveness with which the Third Estate in France had entered the struggle against the feudal regime [in 1789]. The Russian bourgeoisie was incapable of revolutionary struggle against the autocracy. . . . Revolutionary democrats, reflecting the aspirations of the peasantry, were very few and did not represent any real force. As a result the revolutionary situation . . . could not develop into a revolution.[9]

L. G. Zakharova In a recent article Professor Zakharova of Moscow State University, basing her findings chiefly on Soviet archives without reference to the "classics of Marxism-Leninism," emphasizes the positive roles in the emancipation process of public opinion, Alexander II, and liberal bureaucrats. Reflecting the "new thinking" of the Gorbachev era, her multicausational approach resembles that of Western interpretations.

> The removal of serfdom in Russia in 1861 and the resultant reforms . . . was the greatest event or "turning point" in Russian history. . . . On the eve of reform, the year, 1856, was the thaw, or: why the serf monarchy undertook the removal of serfdom . . . Prince D. A. Obolenskii, serving in the Navy Ministry . . . left in his diary characteristic entries. October 16, 1856: "In general there is a force upon which I am beginning to lay great hopes. . . . People are beginning to breathe freely; that in itself is a powerful prescription for recovery." . . .
>
> The first powerful blow to the Nicholaevian system was delivered from outside. Defeat in the Crimean War (1853–1856) revealed the true condition of serf Russia. It not only emerged from the war defeated but in international isolation. The

[7] S. S. Tatishchev, *Imperator Aleksandr II . . .* , 2 vols. (St. Petersburg, 1903), vol. 1, pp. 300–303.

[8] M. V. Nechkina, "Reforma 1861 goda kak pobochnyi produkt revoliutsionnoi borby," in *Revoliutsionnaia situatsiia v Rossii v 1859–1861 gg.* (Moscow, 1962), pp. 7, 9, 10. On Marxism, see Chapter 27; on Lenin's ideology, see Chapter 27.

[9] P. A. Zaionchkovskii, *Otmena krepostnogo prava v Rossii*, 3d ed. (Moscow, 1968), pp. 3–4.

Problem 7 continued

reactionary Holy Alliance of Russia, Prussia and Austria, created after the Napoleonic Wars, had fallen apart. The foreign policy of Nicholas I had turned out bankrupt. Concern about the prestige of the country in European public opinion . . . was revealed by the first steps of the government of Alexander II, even before the peasant question was raised. . . .

Dissatisfaction gripped every layer of society inspiring a flood of accusatory handwritten statements and plans of reform, "an underground literature." It seemed as if all thinking Russia had taken up the pen. . . . Returning at this time from exile M. E. Saltykov-Shchedrin [a leading satirical writer], coming to Moscow, then to St. Petersburg . . . , was amazed by the freedom with which everyone talked everywhere about everything. . . . *Glasnost* (openness) arose spontaneously from below. The government followed in the wake of events, renouncing extraordinary censorship prohibitions, but then utilized *glasnost* as a weapon. . . . In Russia, "like mushrooms after a rain," as [Leo] Tolstoy expressed it, were issued publications embodying the thaw. . . . *Glasnost* . . . carried a charge of optimism and bright hopes, inducing the government and society to act, and drove away fear which had permeated the Nicholaevian system. The emancipation of the moral forces of society preceded the reforms and were their precondition.

A powerful economic stimulus operated also. The realization that free labor was more advantageous than serf, that serfdom, as the government had known earlier, was hampering the development of agriculture and commercial production of grain, incited the removal of serfdom. . . . Already in January 1857 was revealed to the ruling circles and to Alexander II the true and extremely grave and threatening financial situation. . . . A well-known economist L. V. Tengoborskii in a memorandum in the tsar's name concluded: "It is essential to take immediately the most decisive measures to curtail expenditures . . . ; otherwise state bankruptcy is inevitable." The threatening financial crisis stimulated the leadership to seek reforms and especially aroused Alexander II. . . . "The former system has outlived its age," was the verdict of one of its ideologists, M. P. Pogodin. . . .

Alexander II . . . already as heir to the throne had participated in state affairs, in the work of secret committees on the peasant question. He was neither a liberal nor a fanatical reactionary. Prior to ascending the throne he lacked a program of his own. . . . But coming to the throne during the crisis of the old system and the awakening of public opinion which demanded reform, he was able to realize this and began seeking new solutions and new men. . . . In the Interior Ministry the activity of liberal bureaucrats was manifested especially. . . . From this ministry came the leader of the liberal bureaucracy, N. A. Miliutin, who in 1856 . . . was already prepared to solve the basic issue: the peasant question. . . . His memorandum served as a model for the reform of 1861. It was important that in the apparatus of authority were new people with their own program. They united and were prepared under favorable circumstances to take the matter of reforms into their hands. Among the nobility were also some adherents of liberal reforms although they comprised a clear minority. . . .

The role of peasant movements in the preparation of ending serfdom has ever since the 1930s generally been exaggerated by Soviet sources, but while overcoming that exaggeration, one need not go to the other extreme. . . . Although there was no direct threat of an insurrection, memories of the Pugachov Revolt . . . increased fears of the leadership.[10]

Western Views

During the post–World War II era European and American scholars have debated whether economic, political, military, or personal factors were decisive in Alexander II's decision to free the Russian serfs.

Alexander Gerschenkron A leading American economist of Russian origin, Alexander Gerschenkron, emphasizes economic considerations.

The question of whether, on the eve of the reform, the system of serfdom was disintegrating for economic reasons or whether its vitality and viability were still essentially unimpaired has been the

---

[10] L. G. Zakharova, "Samoderzhavie, biurokratiia i reformy 60-kh godov XIX v. v Rossii," *Voprosy istorii*, no. 10 (1989): 3–8.

subject of much controversy. But even those who, like the present writer, tend toward the latter view must admit that the development of the non-agrarian sectors of the economy was virtually premised upon the abolition of serfdom.

To say this, however, does not at all imply that promotion of economic development was a para-mount objective of the emancipation. . . . The authors of the Russian reform either considered industrialization undesirable or, at best, were indif-ferent to it. The actual procedures chosen reflected these attitudes. In many ways they were bound to hamper rather than facilitate economic growth. . . . Over wide parts of the country (and particularly in the black-earth belt) the peasants received a good deal less land than had been customarily assigned to them prior to the reform. Second, there was the question of the magnitude of the quitrents (*obrok*) to be paid by the peasants as compensation for land allotments. . . . It might be argued that the two features of the Russian reform just mentioned should have provided a favorable climate for subse-quent industrialization; the inadequacy of the peasants' landholdings in conjunction with the considerable financial obligations imposed upon the peasants' households could have been expected to favor the flight from the country and thus to provide a large reservoir of labor supply to the nascent industry. Such might have been the conse-quences indeed, if the reform and the later legisla-tive measures had not erected considerable barriers to land flight by strengthening the *obshchina,* the village commune, wherever it existed.[11]

W. Bruce Lincoln An American historian, W. Bruce Lincoln, argues that Alexander II initi-ated reform for a complex set of reasons that included restoring the nation's power status and role in European affairs.

Defeat in the Crimean War immediately challenged Russia's single claim to membership in the commu-

nity of great powers. As the quality of armaments technology began to counterbalance the number of armed forces in determining a nation's power, Russians began to debate how to prevent any fur-ther erosion of their nation's international standing. No one doubted that Russia must move decisively into the industrial age, for a nation without heavy industry and railroads could not hope to be counted among the great powers of the West. At the same time, the young Alexander II and his advisers knew that Russia no longer could afford to support an army of more than a million men in peacetime. European nations had begun to experiment with small standing armies that could be supplemented by a large system of ready reserves in time of war. Yet, as General Dmitrii Miliutin stated flatly in a memorandum in March 1856, no nation that drew its soldiers from a servile population dared to return them to bondage after training them in the use of arms.

Dangerously weakened finances, a local admin-istration that had failed to connect her people with their government, a pre-modern system of law in which semiliterate judges still presided over cata-strophically backlogged law courts, the problems of developing modern industrial and transportation networks in a society that had not yet entered the industrial age, and an army in which a term of military service was akin to a sentence of penal servitude all had to be considered in plotting Rus-sia's course after the Crimean War. Across all of these, serfdom continued to cast its retrograde shadow, for modern armies and modern industry required a free citizenry and a mobile labor force.

Serfdom's was not the only dark shadow that lay upon the Russian political and social landscape when the Crimean War ended in 1856. Although the army could not be modernized and industry could not be developed so long as serfdom remained, emancipation posed other problems whose resolution seemed fully as complex as serf-dom itself. Emancipation would free Russia's nobil-ity of its responsibilities for collecting taxes, assembling recruits, and administering justice to more than 20 million peasants. At one liberating stroke of the tsar's pen, these responsibilities would shift to the shoulders of the government, yet there were no current institutions that could integrate so many new citizens into the fabric of Russia's

[11] A. Gerschenkron, "Problems and Patterns . . . ," in *The Transformation of Russian Society,* ed. C. E. Black (Cambridge, MA, 1960), pp. 42–43. Reprinted by permission.

Problem 7 continued

national life. Nor could the nearly bankrupt imperial treasury finance an emancipation.

Not only did the Crimean defeat challenge Russia's claim to great power status but it called into question the principles that had directed her national life and government since the time of Peter the Great. To develop Russia's traditional institutions along the lines followed by Nicholas I and his predecessors—to bring them to the level of perfection implied by Uvarov's slogan "Orthodoxy, Autocracy, and Nationality" and proclaimed as truth by defenders of Official Nationality—meant, in fact, to weaken Russia, not to strengthen her ability to confront the disconcerting challenges of the Crimean defeat. "Orthodoxy, Autocracy, and Nationality" articulated a political outlook that no longer had a place in Europe's experience, just as it described a social order that could not hope to survive among modern nations that had entered the industrial age. Even though Peter the Great had used them to win membership in the European great power community for Russia, such principles now could only carry Russia further away from the West.[12]

---

[12] W. Bruce Lincoln, *The Great Reforms* . . . (DeKalb, IL, 1990), pp. 37–39. Copyright ©1990 Northern Illinois University Press. Used by permission of the publisher.

Conclusion

Both Russian and Western scholars have been moving toward multicausational explanations of the decision to emancipate. Undoubtedly, both the regime and the nobility feared growing peasant discontent, but that fear increased most *after* the decision to emancipate had been reached. There may have been a "crisis of the servile economy," but the serf owners do not appear to have realized it at the time, and they feared economic ruin and peasant upheaval if the serfs were emancipated. Nor is there much evidence in primary sources that the Crimean defeat convinced contemporary Russian leaders that serfdom must be abolished. And whereas Alexander's personal role in deciding on emancipation was crucial, one should not view him as a benevolent liberal. He came to power in 1855 as a profoundly conservative and traditionally minded man who was linked powerfully with the past. Thus the decision to free the serfs involved a variety of complex, interacting factors and considerations. ■

Suggested Additional Reading

BOOKS

AMBLER, E. *Russian Journalism and Politics, 1861–1881: The Career of A. S. Suvorin* (Detroit, 1972).

BALMUTH, D. *Censorship in Russia, 1865–1905* (Washington, 1979).

EMMONS, T. *The Emancipation of the Russian Serfs* (New York, 1970).

———. *The Russian Landed Gentry and the . . . Emancipation* (Cambridge, 1968).

ENGEL, B. A. *Between the Fields and the City: Women, Work, and Family in Russia, 1861–1914* (Cambridge, 1995).

FIELD, D. *The End of Serfdom . . .* (Cambridge, MA, 1976).

FROHLICH, K. *The Emergence of Russian Constitutionalism, 1900–1904* (The Hague, 1981).

GREENBURG, L. *The Jews in Russia,* 2 vols. (New Haven, CT, 1951).

HABERER, E. E. *Jews and Revolution in Nineteenth Century Russia* (Cambridge, 1995).

HOCH, S. *Serfdom and Social Control in Russia: Petrovskoe, a Village in Tambov Province* (Chicago, 1986).

KLIER, J. D. *Imperial Russia's Jewish Question, 1855–1881* (Cambridge, 1995).

LINCOLN, W. B. *The Great Reforms: Autocracy, Bureaucracy, and the Politics of Change in Imperial Russia* (Dekalb, IL, 1990).

LONG, J. *From Privileged to Dispossessed: The Volga Germans, 1860–1917* (Lincoln, NE, 1988).

MOSSE, W. E. *Alexander II and the Modernization of Russia* (New York, 1958).

ORLOVSKY, D. *The Limits of Reform: The Ministry of Internal Affairs . . .* (Cambridge, MA, 1981).

PINTNER, W. M., and D. K. ROWNEY, eds. *Russian Officialdom . . .* (Chapel Hill, NC, 1980).

PRYMAK, T. M. *Mykhailo Hrushevsky: The Politics of National Culture* (Toronto, 1987).

RIEBER, A. J., ed. *The Politics of Autocracy . . .* (Paris, 1966).

ROGGER, H. *Russia in the Age of Modernization and Revolution, 1881–1917* (New York, 1983).

THADEN, E. *Conservative Nationalism in Nineteenth Century Russia* (Seattle, 1964).

———. *Russification in the Baltic Provinces and Finland, 1855–1914* (Princeton, 1981).

VAKAR, N. *Belorussia . . .* (Cambridge, MA, 1956).

WEISSMAN, N. *Reform in Tsarist Russia: The State Bureaucracy and Local Government, 1900–1914* (New Brunswick, NJ, 1981).

WHELAN, H. *Alexander III and the State Council . . .* (New Brunswick, NJ, 1981).

ZAIONCHKOVSKII, P. A. *The Abolition of Serfdom in Russia,* trans. and ed. S. Wobst (Gulf Breeze, FL, 1978).

———. *The Russian Autocracy Under Alexander III,* trans. D. D. Jones (Gulf Breeze, FL, 1976).

ARTICLES

ARONSON, I. M. "The Attitude of Russian Officials in the 1880's toward Jewish Assimilation and Emigration." *SR* 34, no. 1 (1975): 1–18.

BENFORD, B. L. "Tsarist Nationalist Policy and the Baltic Germans . . ." *CanRStNat* 2, no. 2 (1975): 317–33.

EMMONS, T. "Russia's Banquet Campaign." *Cal.SS* 10 (1975): 45–86.

KOPRINCE, R. "The Russian Conscription Law of 1874." *Heritage Review* 11, no. 3 (1981): 3–12.

MOSSE, W. E. "Russian Bureaucracy: . . . the Imperial State Council, 1897–1915." *SR* 39, no. 4 (1980): 616–32.

PEARSON, T. "The Origins of Alexander III's Land Captains: A Reinterpretation." *SR* 40, no. 3 (1981): 384–403.

PEREIRA, N. G. "Alexander II and the Decision to Emancipate the Russian Serfs, 1855–61." *CSP* 22, no. 1 (1980): 99–115.

RIEBER, A. J. "Alexander II: A Revisionist View." *JMH* 43, no. 1 (1971): 42–58.

VIOLETTE, A. "The Grand Duke Konstantin Nikolaevich and the Reform of Naval Administration, 1855–70." *SEER* 52 (1974): 584–601.

WORTMAN, R. "Judicial Personnel and the Court Reform of 1864." *CSS* 3, no. 2 (1969): 224–34.

25

Social and Economic Development, 1855–1904

After 1861 Russia underwent major socioeconomic change as state policies unquestionably promoted the process of modernization triggered by the Emancipation. For centuries Russian regimes had repeatedly mobilized national resources to protect the country's independence and promote its prestige. Now, in the half century between the Emancipation and World War I, the government employed its financial resources to construct and operate railroads and to establish heavy industries and purchase their products. As towns grew and railroads and factories were built at an increased rate, Russia began to overcome the backwardness imposed by a severe climate, poor soil, lack of communications, and isolation from Europe. After three decades of slow, preparatory growth, economic development intensified in the 1890s and again between 1906 and 1914.

Profound social changes accompanied this economic surge. As the nobility and clergy declined, there emerged a dynamic, professional middle class, a small industrial bourgeoisie, a better-off peasant element, and an industrial proletariat. The old, rigid social system weakened despite state aid to traditional privileged classes designed to help them cling to their positions and status. Nonetheless, the "two Russias" described by Alexander Herzen persisted:

> On the one hand, there was governmental, imperial, aristocratic Russia, rich in money, armed not only with bayonets but with all the bureaucratic and police techniques taken from Germany; on the other, there was the Russia of the dark people, poor, agricultural, communal, democratic, helpless, taken by surprise, conquered, as it were, without battle.[1]

The extent and type of capitalist development in Russia and how much this development affected the peasantry are still debated by historians. Many Western scholars emphasize the persistence of traditional communal agriculture and handicrafts (*kustar*). Soviet historians, following Lenin's *Development of Capitalism in Russia* (first published in 1898, published in its final form in 1906), stressed peasant differentiation, the growth

---

[1] Quoted in C. E. Black, ed., *The Transformation of Russian Society* (Cambridge, MA, 1960), p. 590.

of the industrial proletariat, and the triumph of capitalism and the bourgeoisie. How did the emancipation settlement affect the economic and social position of the peasantry and nobility? What problems did Russia face in industrializing? How did these problems compare with the problems of other industrializing countries, and how did the state attempt to solve them? Was there an agrarian crisis in Russia at the end of the 19th century? What effects did state policy have on the various social groups?

The Peasant World

As late as 1930 Russia remained a predominantly agrarian country whose people resided chiefly in the countryside, where the peasant's life was controlled almost wholly by the village commune (*mir*). Adapted to local conditions and traditions, communes varied widely. Most comprised small villages of four to 80 households (20 to 500 people) engaged primarily in agriculture. Defining a peasant's entire existence from birth to death, the commune determined land allotments, use of communal resources, dues and taxes, division of property, and permission for external employment. The commune provided for orphans, the indigent, and the aged, and maintained schools and clinics. Supervising religious rites, it also handled fire fighting and flood control, and protected villages from disease. It was in charge of measures relating to births, deaths, marriages, family feuds, and contacts with the external world and its authorities.

As an economic institution the commune determined land allotments and their distribution to individual households. It also coordinated agricultural decisions; allocated and collected taxes; coordinated construction and maintenance of roads, bridges, and communal buildings; and managed its business affairs. Serving as the peasants' legal and administrative agency, it provided police protection and administered justice. The *mir* took responsibility for rural schools, religious observances, and other community activities. In short, the commune provided for the peasants' needs and defended their interests within and outside. It was a democratic but highly structured entity within which the individual was subject to the collective as expressed by a village assembly (*skhod*) composed of male heads of households. Normally, *skhod* decisions, which were binding on the commune, were unanimous, with the minority yielding to the majority. "At every step the collective 'we' took precedence over the individual 'I.'"[2]

The peasant commune fostered a homogeneous, cohesive rural society based on common interests and values. Designed to balance income and needs, not produce a profit, the *mir* by its periodic redistribution of land prevented individual households from accumulating wealth or from advancing at others' expense. The commune sought to insulate households from increasing poverty with a safety net of mutual assistance, with better-off peasants helping the less fortunate and providing for widows and orphans. A household's taxes and dues to the state were based on ability to pay as determined by amount of land, number of livestock, and income. Although the most prosperous and impoverished peasants often found *mir* rules stifling, the vast majority welcomed the security they provided. "Who is greater than the commune?" they asked. "The commune is . . . greater than man."[3]

The Great Reforms intensified differentiation in Russian society and accelerated bourgeois tendencies affecting the peasant commune. Peasants gradually became involved in commercial activities of an expanding national market. More ambitious peasants produced for external markets, utilized credit, and engaged in cooperative activities. Such economic trends, plus rising literacy rates and growing influence of urban cultural values, fostered individualism among a minority of better-off peasants. On the other hand, an indication of

[2] B. Mironov, "The Russian Peasant Commune . . . ," in *The World of the Russian Peasant* . . . , B. Eklof and S. Frank, eds. (Bloomington, IN, 1990), p. 18.
[3] Quoted in Mironov, "The Peasant Commune," p. 23.

declining rural living standards was a decline in vodka consumption in the 1870s in excess of 11 percent, although most peasants considered vodka a necessity. Furthermore, a rising number of peasants were rejected for military service for physical reasons. As living standards for most peasants deteriorated after 1861, their dependence on the omnipresent commune increased.

The spread of primary education in the late-19th-century Russian countryside was a positive but often ignored development. The number of primary schools increased from just over 8,000 in 1856 to more than 87,000 in 1896.[4] By 1914 some formal education was available to most peasants. Peasants themselves spearheaded this expansion, recognizing the value of literacy under difficult economic conditions. Only after 1891 did the state assume a leading role, exploiting education to inculcate patriotism and respect for Orthodoxy. Peasants often viewed such state involvement as interference with their commune, causing many to remove their children from school. Most children who attended school did so only for about two years and then dropped out. Nonetheless, literacy rates rose significantly in the late 19th century, and peasants exerted constant pressure on the state to achieve universal education. By 1914 more than half the children of the Empire were enrolled in various schools.

Despite the spread of rural literacy, peasants retained many traditional superstitions; their popular religion blended old beliefs and superstitions with Orthodox Christianity. Taking their religion seriously, peasants believed strongly in Christ, the Virgin Mary, and the sacraments. They attended church on prescribed holidays, fasted, and mortified the flesh while understanding little about church dogma. From church ritual and icons they acquired a highly visual understanding of religion. The people, noted a 19th-century clergyman, "have not the slightest conception of the faith, the true path to salvation, or the basic tenets of

Orthodoxy."[5] Every peasant hut displayed a favorite icon to protect the family and ensure its well-being. Peasants believed that saints guided their daily lives.

The peasant hut (*izba*), not the church, served as the focus of life. The local priest (*pop*) was not usually a community leader. A peasant himself, usually illiterate and totally dependent economically on the commune, he often fell victim to demon vodka. The priest performed such necessary functions as baptisms, marriages, and burials for fees, often paid in vodka. Penury forced some priests to labor in the fields. Complained one bishop: "Many priests, to alleviate their poverty, devote all their time and energy to agricultural toil," preventing them from providing religious instruction to their parishioners.[6] Local priests, often viewed as buffoons or drunks, were believed by peasants to be no match for evil forces lurking everywhere. The world of the devil and evil spirits influenced the peasant imagination powerfully. These forces had to be appeased, peasants believed, to ward off illnesses, crop failures, and famines.

The peasant world lay within the commune, a complex world drawing heavily upon ancient cultural traditions and beliefs that reflected a continuing struggle with nature and mysterious forces. Dealing with this world as best they could, peasants expressed their resignation and optimism in a popular religion based on a belief in salvation and an afterlife and focusing on nature's unpredictable forces.

Agriculture

The Emancipation hastened the development of a money economy and capitalist relationships, but it failed to solve the problems of the peasantry and nobility. Still poor and discontented, peasants

---

[4] Ben Eklof, "Peasants and Schools," in Eklof and Frank, *World of the Russian Peasant,* p. 116.

[5] Quoted in Gregory Freeze, *The Parish Clergy in Nineteenth Century Russia* . . . (Princeton, 1983), p. xxiv.
[6] Freeze, *Parish Clergy,* p. 61.

Chloe Obolensky, *The Russian Empire, 1855–1914* (New York, 1979), p. 166.

An *izba* (peasant hut) in the mid-Volga region, about 1870.

were unsure whether the Emancipation had benefited them economically. Increasing by almost one million people per year, the rural population rose from roughly 50 million in 1861 to 79 million in 1897. Especially in the fertile, overpopulated Black Soil provinces there was growing pressure on the land, and land prices rose rapidly. Noble "cutoffs" at the Emancipation had made peasant allotments in European Russia in 1877 smaller than those of peasants under serfdom. Between 1877 and 1905 the average allotment per household declined by about one-third. Peasant tax burdens remained heavy, with redemption charges and *zemstvo* dues added to their former obligations, although the state did seek to reduce them by abolishing the poll tax (1886), lowering redemption debts, and granting partial moratoriums. Even in the Black Soil region most peasants could not meet their taxes from their allotments alone. Their tax debts rose until in 1900 they exceeded a peasant's average annual tax assessment for 1896–1900. Peasant woes, claims the American scholar G. T. Robinson, were compounded by heavy state reliance on indirect taxes.[7] However, rising indirect tax receipts and increased peasant consumption of sugar, tea, and other items indicate that their economic position was improving.[8]

The peasant's problem was less insufficient land than lack of sufficient incentives to use new techniques to increase productivity. Allotments of Russian peasants, averaging 35 acres per household in 1877, were almost four times as large as the average French farm. To be sure, allotments in the Black Soil region were smaller, ranging down to 16 acres per household in Poltava province. Yields per acre were also far lower than in western Europe or even the United States. Russian peasants had little reason to fertilize the land thoroughly, plow deeply, or diversify and rotate their crops. Under a system of periodic repartition and low grain prices there was little incentive to

---

[7] G. T. Robinson, *Rural Russia under the Old Regime* (New York, 1949), p. 96.

[8] J. Y. Simms, "The Crisis in Russian Agriculture . . . ," *SR* 36, no. 3 (1977): 377–97.

A general view of the village Kurejka, Turukhansk district, Krasnoyarsk territory, where J. Stalin was exiled by the tsarist government in 1913–1917.

improve the land and much reason to exploit it ruthlessly.

Rather than adopting new techniques, Russian peasants found less satisfactory solutions. Communes and individual households bought or rented additional land. By 1900 they rented some 52.7 million acres, mostly in small plots. Aided by the Peasant Bank, created in 1883, peasants between 1897 and 1903 purchased almost 15 million acres.[9] But their land hunger drove up prices so high that fewer could afford to buy subsequently. From rented lands, despite feverish exploitation, they barely received a subsistence wage. This "hunger renting" and an increasing shortage of work animals revealed the peasant's plight. In 1900, workhorses averaged only about one per household.

Many peasants left their villages temporarily or permanently. During the industrial spurt of the 1890s many sought seasonal employment, especially in the central provinces. Village authorities usually allowed this practice if the peasants

returned in the spring to plow the fields and pay their share of taxes. In the Black Soil provinces a more common solution was migration—at first to New Russia, the north Caucasus, and the Trans-Volga, later to Turkestan and Siberia. During the 1870s and 1880s many peasants departed illegally; later the state fostered the settlement of Russia's vast Asian domains. From 1894 to 1903 emigration to Asia reached a peak of some 115,000 annually, many of the emigrants taking the new Trans-Siberian Railroad. But the natural population increase in the rural areas of European Russia was almost 14 times the net loss from emigration. In the forest provinces peasants relied heavily on traditional handicrafts to eke out their incomes during the off-season. These crafts were carried on independently in peasant huts by primitive cooperatives, or they were organized by outside entrepreneurs. Handicrafts that had to compete with factory industry disappeared or declined, but in 1900 handicrafts still employed more people than factory industry.

How far had peasant differentiation and capitalist development proceeded in the Russian village? In *The Development of Capitalism in Russia,*

---

[9] Robinson, *Rural Russia,* p. 101.

Lenin asserted that about 17 percent of the peasantry had become *kulaki* ("rural bourgeois") and 11 percent "rural proletarians" lacking arable land or livestock. Communal agriculture, he claimed, was disintegrating. Lenin pointed to a marked difference between regions of the north and center following the "Prussian pattern," in which landowners remained dominant and feudal survivals were strong, and the borderlands, where the "American pattern" of an independent farmer class was accelerating capitalist development. Disputing Lenin's findings were the Populists, who affirmed that the *mir* (peasant commune) remained unshaken and that the Russian peasantry was still fundamentally equal in land and wealth. G. T. Robinson, who takes a middle position in this controversy, notes how few Russian farmers—only 150,000 in 1906—had fully consolidated holdings like those in the United States. The collective traditions of the *mir* still predominated; in 1905 about three-fourths of the peasant allotments in European Russia were still of the repartitional type.

The nobility, despite official favoritism, was declining economically. The Emancipation statutes, though drawn to favor the landowners, brought ruin or decline to most. Technological backwardness, slowness to adjust to new conditions, and lack of initiative were more to blame than shortage of capital. Many lords, unable to compete with the more efficient western European producers, sold out. On private nonallotment land in European Russia, half of it noble, the average yield of spring wheat in 1899–1903 was only one-third that of lands in Germany. In the south some large plantations operated by hired labor persisted, but noble landownership declined in every province and decade from the Emancipation to 1905—from some 197 million acres in 1877 to 140 million in 1905. At first townsmen were the chief buyers of noble lands; later peasant purchases gained much more rapidly.

Russian agriculture, noble and peasant alike, was stimulated in the post-Emancipation years by rising grain prices, by the peasants' need for cash to pay taxes and dues, and by railway construction, which made it easier to market grain. The area under cultivation rose significantly, and Russian grain exports surged dramatically during the 1860s and 1870s; the level of grain exports was the main reason for Russia's persistently favorable balance of trade. Toward the end of the century, however, higher foreign tariffs and falling international grain prices slowed the increase in grain exports. By 1905 Miliukov could refer to a Russian agrarian crisis.[10]

Industry and Finance until 1891

The Crimean defeat ushered in a new chapter in Russian economic history marked by the development of a capitalist economy. Soviet historians, regarding the entire period of 1861–1917 as Russia's capitalist phase, asserted that between 1861 and 1890 the country was transformed swiftly into a capitalist country. Western scholars, on the other hand, tend to regard those decades as an era of slow growth preparatory to rapid development after 1890. Did Russia pursue a new path and set a pattern for the modernization of backward countries, or was its development basically a process of Westernization—that is, of following techniques worked out earlier in western Europe?

Whatever the model, the Russian state played a more prominent role in fostering economic development than did most European governments. Alexander II's regime, realizing the disastrous consequences of economic backwardness, eliminated hampering restrictions by lowering tariffs and encouraging an influx of foreign products and capital. The government recognized the need for railroads, and it was their construction, not emancipation, that proved crucial in Russia's economic growth. The strategic advantages of railroads were recognized first, and their economic benefits only later. Finance Minister Mikhail Reutern (1861–1878) wrote Alexander II: "Without railways and mechanical industries Russia cannot be considered secure in her boundaries. Her influence in

[10] P. Miliukov, *Russia and Its Crisis* (Chicago, 1905).

Europe will fall to a level inconsistent with her international power and her historic significance."[11] Because the impoverished treasury could not afford to build railroads, private companies were encouraged and foreign loans sought. In 1865 the government, deciding that Russia needed an extensive railway network, provided subsidies and guarantees to numerous small private firms to construct lines that the state considered essential. There ensued an orgy of construction and speculation comparable to the railway boom that occurred at the same time in the United States. Many of these private firms, poorly financed and inefficient, went bankrupt in the depression of 1873–1876, and many others borrowed heavily from the state. In the 1880s the government reversed its policy, constructed the major lines itself, bought up many private railways, and created an expanding state-owned system. By 1890, major economic regions were interconnected and linked with the principal ports. The railway network grew from only 600 miles in 1857 to 11,730 miles in 1876 and more than 22,000 miles in 1895. However, even the roughly 40,000 miles of railroads that Russia boasted in 1914 were clearly inadequate for a country of its size, and branch lines were few.

Meanwhile the Finance Ministry, seeking to overcome Russia's poverty, faced complex and interrelated problems: stabilizing the currency, balancing the budget, financing railway construction, achieving a favorable trade balance, and attracting foreign investment in industry. Finance Minister Reutern took office with a treasury impoverished by war, a badly unbalanced budget, and a ruble whose value had been undermined. The grave banking crisis of 1858 endangered reform and induced the government to place the chief financial costs of emancipation and redemption of the land on the peasantry.[12] A new State Bank was established, with branches throughout Russia. The creation in 1862 of a unified state budget enabled the Finance Ministry to coordinate the government's economic activities and develop a degree of state planning. Reutern discovered that heavy foreign imports, low tariff rates, and rising state expenditures on railways were producing large budget deficits. To conceal Russia's poverty, he set up an extraordinary budget, financed by foreign loans, for new arms and railroad construction. To attract foreign loans, Reutern tried but failed to make the ruble convertible into a given amount of gold. To increase revenues, he developed indirect taxation and raised the poll tax rates. The balance of trade and payments, however, remained negative, evidence that Russia was living beyond its means. The Russo-Turkish War of 1877–1878 wrecked Reutern's efforts and plunged the country deeply into debt.

Finance Minister N. K. Bunge (1881–1886) tried a different approach. A modest rise in tariff rates restricted imports, produced additional revenue, and helped protect Russian industry. Seeking long-term economic improvement, Bunge abolished most of the direct taxes on the peasantry, including the poll tax, and set up land banks to assist peasants and nobles with credit. Unable to balance the budget, Bunge resorted to more foreign loans, until interest on them consumed more than one-third of the budget.

Coming to the Finance Ministry from industry, I. A. Vyshnegradskii (1887–1892) reversed Bunge's policies. He balanced the budget and built up a surplus by reducing expenditures and increasing state revenues. This policy required taxing the peasantry heavily and forcing grain exports to the limit to pay for imports from abroad. "We must export though we undereat," declared Vyshnegradskii prophetically. A drastic tariff imposing levies averaging one-third the value of imports was enacted in 1891; it remained the cornerstone of Russian state economic policy until 1917. Providing almost one-fourth of state revenues, it improved the balance of payments and increased Russia's bullion reserves. When the harvest of 1891 failed, however, the overburdened peasantry

---

[11] T. Von Laue, *Sergei Witte and the Industrialization of Russia* (New York, 1963), p. 9.

[12] Steven Hoch, "The Banking Crisis, Peasant Reform and Economic Development in Russia, 1857–1861," *AHR* 96, no. 3 (June 1991): 795ff.

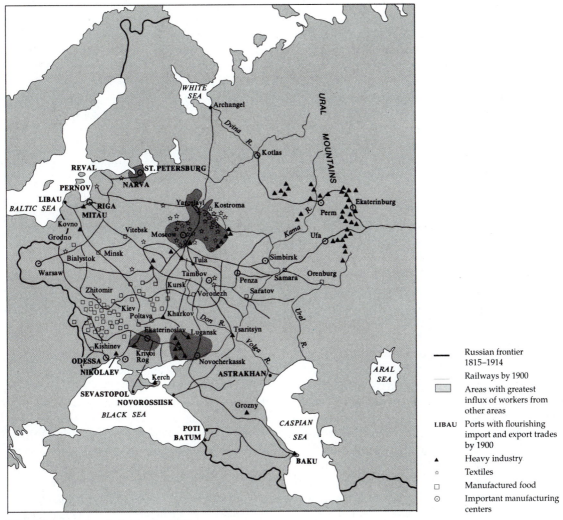

WHITE SEA
Archangel
Dvina R.
Kotlas
URAL MOUNTAINS
REVAL
ST. PETERSBURG
PERNOV
NARVA
LIBAU
BALTIC SEA
RIGA
MITAU
Yaroslavl   Kostroma
Ekaterinburg
Perm
Kovno
Vitebsk
Moscow
Kama R.
Ufa
Grodno
Minsk
Bialystok
Tula
Simbirsk
Warsaw
Tambov
Orenburg
Zhitomir
Kursk
Penza
Samara
Voronezh
Saratov
Kiev
Poltava
Kharkov
Don R.
Tsaritsyn
Ekaterinoslav
Lugansk
Volga R.
Kishinev
Krivoi Rog
Ural R.
ODESSA
Novocherkassk
NIKOLAEV
ARAL SEA
Kerch
ASTRAKHAN
SEVASTOPOL
NOVOROSSIISK
Grozny
BLACK SEA
CASPIAN SEA
POTI
BATUM
BAKU

	Russian frontier 1815–1914
	Railways by 1900
	Areas with greatest influx of workers from other areas
LIBAU	Ports with flourishing import and export trades by 1900
▲	Heavy industry
○	Textiles
□	Manufactured food
⊙	Important manufacturing centers

Map 25.1 Russian industry by 1900

had no reserves. The government admitted, "Our peasant economy has come to a full collapse and ruin," and disastrous famine forced Vyshnegradskii from office. By 1892 the Finance Ministry, despite a variety of approaches, had found no formula to overcome Russia's poverty.

Until 1890 industrial development proceeded at a modest pace. At first the emancipation settlement did little to assist it and in fact contributed to the industrial slump of the early 1860s, especially in the Ural industries (see Map 25.1), which had

employed mostly serf labor. Industrial growth was hampered by low peasant purchasing power, a shortage of domestic capital and skilled labor, and an inadequate transportation system. Also, the *mir* blocked permanent peasant migration to the cities. The relaxation of restrictions on the importation of foreign capital and goods and the judicial and administrative reforms of the 1860s, however, created a more favorable climate for business activity. The government gradually lost its fear of industrialization and by the 1890s, in order to strengthen Russia's position in world affairs, accepted it as a central goal.

Before 1890, although small-commodity production and handicrafts predominated, strong bases were laid for large-scale industry, especially in textiles and food processing. Among domestic manufactures, only the textile industry had an assured home market. The per capita consumption of cotton goods roughly doubled between 1860 and 1880. Sugar refining expanded markedly, and, despite greater domestic consumption, Russia began to export sugar. Metallurgy, however, developed slowly, and Russia's share in world production of cast iron fell during the first post-Emancipation decades. During the 1880s the Donets Basin became an important iron and steel region. Most of its factories were owned by foreign capitalists, who received favorable prices, especially for iron rails, from the government. The English capitalist John Hughes established a large factory at Iuzovka (now Donetsk) in the heart of this region. The southern iron and steel plants were more modern and productive than those of the Urals. Also in the 1870s the oil industry began to grow rapidly at Baku in the Transcaucasus.

Private capitalism now flourished in Russia. Between 1861 and 1873, 357 joint-stock companies with a combined capital of more than a billion rubles were formed, a vast increase over pre-Emancipation days. The Russian government strongly encouraged private companies and credit facilities. Native entrepreneurs, however, were too few, their time horizons too restricted, and their methods too antiquated for rapid industrial and commercial development. In the 1880s industrial growth remained sluggish as the impoverished villages checked demand.

Finance and Industry: The Spurt of the 1890s

The achievements of the preparatory era permitted major financial gains and fostered the industrial boom of the 1890s. Both were largely attributable to Sergei Iu. Witte, minister of finance

(1892–1903), perhaps the ablest minister of the late tsarist period. Of German background, Witte graduated from the new Odessa University and made a brilliant career in private business before entering state service as a railway expert. Self-confident and dynamic, he moved easily among bureaucrats and business leaders. After being appointed finance minister, he reformed the Finance Ministry into an efficient general staff for economic development. In his first budget report Witte affirmed that the government was responsible for the whole economy and should develop its resources and "kindle a healthy spirit of enterprise." Firmly backed by Alexander III, he developed the boldest and most ambitious economic program since that of Peter the Great.

The Witte system was based on considerations of power politics. "International competition does not wait," he warned. Unless Russia developed its industries swiftly, foreign concerns would take root: "Our economic backwardness may lead to political and cultural backwardness as well."[13] Thus Witte's work was filled with a sense of urgency and the belief that Russia's industrialization was a race against time. His plan was to stimulate private enterprise and exploit Russian resources through a vast state-sponsored program of railway construction, which would trigger the expansion of heavy industry, especially metallurgy and fuels. Developing these industries would spark light industry; eventually agriculture would perk up as growing industrial cities demanded more foodstuffs. General prosperity would raise tax yields and recompense the government for its heavy initial capital outlays.

Witte's program, with its concentration on heavy industry and its substitution of the state for timid and inadequate private capital, in many ways presaged Stalin's more ruthless Five Year Plans (see Chapter 35). An experiment in state capitalism, it suggested a way by which a backward country could overtake the industrial front-

---

[13] Von Laue, Th. *Sergei Witte and the Industrialization of Russia*, pp. 34–35.

runners. Finance Minister Witte channeled about two-thirds of the government's revenues into economic development, thus fueling Russia's first major industrial boom. His most ambitious project was the Trans-Siberian Railroad, which was pushed through on schedule on an economy budget. As other parts of his planned development of Siberia he promoted peasant colonization and new shipping routes, and he envisioned the Trans-Siberian line as the means to penetrate and dominate Asian markets. Russia's European rail network was double-tracked, and lines were built to major ports. Everywhere construction was carried on at a feverish pace: From 1898 through 1901 more than 1,900 miles of railway line were constructed annually. That construction stimulated a boom in the iron and steel industry of the Donets Basin, whose large and modern plants used the latest German and American technology. The Witte upsurge seized hold of all industry, but especially heavy industry. The average industrial growth rate in the 1890s was approximately 8 percent annually, the highest of any major European country. During that decade pig iron output trebled, oil production rose two and one-half times, and coal output doubled.

Witte's financing of the industrial upsurge was masterful. Heavy indirect taxation, falling largely on peasants and lower-class townsmen, met most of the government's ordinary expenses, and a state liquor monopoly with stores throughout Russia increased government revenues considerably. The high tariff of 1891 produced large sums for the treasury. For extraordinary expenditures, especially railroad construction, Witte relied chiefly upon foreign loans, primarily French. He was favored by an abundance of foreign money seeking investment and by the Franco-Russian Alliance of 1893, which induced the French government to foster private investment in Russia. In order to balance his overall budget, Witte had to continue borrowing abroad, but he maintained a high credit rating there by prompt payment of dividends in gold. To preserve a favorable trade balance, he forced agricultural exports and curtailed imports, and, above

all, he sought a stable currency convertible to gold. After stabilizing the paper ruble, he increased the state gold reserves, and in 1897 he finally put Russia on the gold standard. This action enhanced Russia's international prestige, created a stable currency, and encouraged foreign investment.

In the late 1890s, however, the Witte system showed signs of strain and came under increasing public attack. Ultranationalist publications blamed it for Russia's supposed agricultural decline and for growing foreign economic influence. Witte's vast authority and his advocacy of ever-wider reforms (notably abolition of the *mir*) in order to promote industry aroused the opposition of conservative and Slavophile officials, especially Pobedonostsev. They and Nicholas II opposed Witte's efforts to streamline the autocracy and adapt it to 20th-century needs. Despite his strenuous public relations campaigns and his optimistic statistical predictions, his program of industrialization through sacrifice became ever more unpopular. The traditional view of Soviet and Western scholars that Witte's policies contributed to an agrarian crisis at the end of the 19th century by exhausting the capacity to pay off the lower classes has been challenged. James Simms, an American historian, cites rising peasant consumption and increasing state tax receipts as evidence to the contrary, and Olga Crisp notes that the cotton industry, whose products were purchased by the peasantry, was little affected by the economic slump of 1900–1903.[14] In any case, Witte had proved that rapid economic growth in a backward country was possible if the state mobilized its resources. His system laid a sound basis for subsequent Russian industrial development.

Social Change

Russia's social structure changed fundamentally after 1861. The old categories of the class (*soslovie*)

---

[14] Simms, "Crisis in Russian Agriculture," pp. 377ff; and O. Crisp, *Studies in the Russian Economy before 1914* (New York, 1976), p. 32.

system persisted in official usage, but traditional privilege was undermined by new elements that did not fit the old patterns: a professional middle class, a capitalist peasant element, and an industrial working class. Industrialization, urbanization, and the legislation of the Great Reforms promoted social mobility. The Emancipation deprived hereditary noblemen of their chief privilege—the right to own serfs—and the new courts largely disregarded estate, title, and wealth. Universal military service, abolition of the poll tax, and participation in the *zemstva* lessened peasant isolation from society, while increasing sales of noble lands to merchants and peasants reduced the nobility's economic power and social prestige.

After 1880, however, the development of new social groupings was hampered by a conservative government anxious to preserve the traditional order. Separate land banks for peasants and noblemen gave the latter preferential treatment, and some schools were reserved for noble children. The *zemstva* and city *dumy,* in which social groups mingled, were severely restricted in power and function. New groups, such as industrial workers and kulaks, failed to break fully with tradition or to form economic organizations to promote their interests.

The census of 1897, more informative about social groups than previous ones, nonetheless retained the old categories. Hereditary noblemen (including top civil and military officials and some professional men) with their dependents numbered 1,220,169 people. Many of them embodied the attitudes of the novelist Ivan Goncharov's Oblomov—a superfluous, guilt-ridden landowner trained only for leisure who spent most of his day in a bathrobe trying to get up. Most of the 630,119 "personal noblemen" listed were government servants. Ecclesiastics of all faiths numbered 342,927, more than two-thirds of them Orthodox and about 9 percent Catholic. In the Orthodox hierarchy the small but privileged "black" (monastic) clergy, often of noble origin, held the top positions. The "white" (parish) clergy were not far above the peasantry in social and economic

status. Townspeople were divided into three categories according to tax payments. The two top groups, "distinguished citizens" (342,927) and "merchants" (281,179), dominated urban economic and political affairs and included many professional people. Other city dwellers— *meshchane* (13,386,392)—included artisans, petty tradesmen, and most of the urban workers. The bulk of Russia's population still consisted of peasants (96,896,648), including industrial workers who still belonged legally to the commune. Cossacks (2,928,842), mostly independent farmers, were listed separately.

Soviet accounts, asserting that the peasant had renounced his patriarchal heritage to become a full-fledged proletarian, claimed that the working class was far larger than the official tsarist statistics suggested. The number of industrial workers employed in manufacturing, mining, and transportation in European Russia, noted Lenin, grew from 706,000 in 1865 to 2,208,000 in the years 1900–1903. He listed the following breakdown of mass groups under the 1897 census: well-off smallholders, 23.1 million; poor smallholders, 35.8 million; proletarians, 22 million; and semiproletarians, 63.7 million. About 1900, affirmed Lenin, 44 percent of the peasant families in Moscow province and 56 percent of those in Vladimir province labored not in agriculture but in industry, trade, or services, but the official tsarist statistics, to conceal the proletariat's growth, still listed them as peasants.[15]

Recent Western studies, on the other hand, portray the tsarist Russian industrial workers as half peasant. The Emancipation, leaving some four million peasants landless or with dwarf allotments, created a sizable labor reservoir. Migrating to nearby industrial centers, peasants mastered industrial skills more slowly than did new workers in the West, thus delaying the development in Russia of a modern industrial working class. Even in 1900, 90 percent of the Russian urban workers

---

[15] V. I. Lenin, *Sobranie sochinenii,* 5th ed. (Moscow, 1960), vol. 3, p. 505.

David MacKenzie

Nineteenth-century wooden dwelling in Riazan.

were legally classified as peasants, still belonged to communes, sent home part of their earnings to families or relatives, and returned there periodically. Low industrial wages and miserable living conditions also delayed the formation of a hereditary proletariat. As the 1897 census noted, some 60 percent of Russian workers lived alone, many in filthy employer-owned barracks. The unskilled usually had to leave their families in the village; normally only skilled and semiskilled workers could afford to maintain regular family life. Conditions improved gradually, and an industrial proletariat did develop, but even in 1917, J. Gliksman emphasizes, it remained half peasant and represented but a small fraction of the population.[16] States R. Johnson: "The typical worker had one foot in the village and one in the factory but showed little inclination to commit himself irrevo-

cably to either alternative."[17] Because of the capital-intensive nature of Russia's industrialization, the working class was small and more inclined to radicalism than in the West.

Lenin, claims H. Seton-Watson,[18] also exaggerated the extent of differentiation among the peasantry before 1905. Kulaks neither constituted a social class nor were regarded as such by other villagers. Instead, peasants, mainly conscious of their difference from nobles and townspeople, retained a strong sense of solidarity. Rural class conflict, if it existed, pitted peasant against nobleman, not kulak against poor peasant. On the eve of the 1905 Revolution, Russia was undergoing

---

[16] J. Gliksman, "The Russian Urban Worker . . . ," in *The Transformation of Russian Society,* ed. C. Black (Cambridge, MA, 1960), pp. 312–17.

[17] R. Johnson, *Peasant and Proletarian . . .* (New Brunswick, NJ, 1979), p. 50. Of Moscow's population of 1,170,000 (1902), 73 percent were migrants, mostly from nearby provinces, and 67 percent were legally peasants. Migrants constituted 93 percent of the factory work force in Moscow. Johnson, p. 31.

[18] H. Seton-Watson, *The Russian Empire, 1801–1917* (Oxford, 1967), pp. 545–46.

profound social change, but new groupings based on economic interest had not yet replaced the old categories. The process was furthest advanced among professional men, least among peasants.

During the post-Emancipation era, the state acted, albeit reluctantly, to protect industrial workers and regulate factory conditions. In 1859 the governor-general of St. Petersburg, supported by progressive manufacturers, favored installing safety devices, improving sanitary conditions in the factories, and forbidding child labor under the age of 12. On the other hand, Moscow industrialists, like the British classical liberals, favored freedom of contract and unrestricted child labor. These attitudes reflected varying local conditions: St. Petersburg recruited labor from distant provinces and had to pay higher wages, whereas in Moscow abundant cheap labor was available from nearby rural districts. Thus St. Petersburg entrepreneurs put more emphasis on skill, labor productivity, and machinery. Finance Minister Bunge's regulatory legislation of 1882 reflected the views of the St. Petersburg group: It forbade the labor of children under the age of 12 and restricted the hours of those under 15. There were too few inspectors to enforce this legislation strictly, but their reports on deplorable factory conditions brought increased governmental intervention. A 14-hour day was the norm, and many workers were paid in kind under a type of industrial serfdom. In 1885, after worker disorders, legislation prohibited night work for women and for boys under the age of 17 and required that wages be paid in money. The law of 1897 set a maximum of 11.5 hours for all workers and 10 hours for night work, but many manufacturers still evaded the regulations, and workers opposed them. Before the 1905 Revolution few Russian workers were unionized, and workers lacked the right to strike or bargain collectively.

Religion

After 1855 the administration of the Orthodox church remained stagnant while the need for

St. Petersburg's Church of the Savior's Blood, built on the site of Alexander II's assassination in 1881.

reform became increasingly evident. The emperor was "the supreme defender and preserver of the dogmas of the ruling faith," but he rarely intervened directly in matters of dogma. The Holy Synod, which included the three metropolitans, the exarch of Georgia, and eight or nine bishops appointed by the tsar, handled matters of dogma and the discipline of the clergy and administered church property and parochial schools. The dominant official in the church was the overprocurator, a layman who since 1824 had enjoyed the status of a minister of state. He acted as the intermediary between the tsar and the Holy Synod, was the only church official with direct access to the ruler, and really ran the church's affairs. Pobedonostsev held this key post from 1880 to 1905. In 1914 the Orthodox church had 64 dioceses and more than 50,000 priests. Lay officials, headed by the secretary of the consistory, a miniature overprocurator, ran diocesan affairs.

The Orthodox church closely resembled the bureaucratic autocracy it served. Even minor matters required decisions by high lay officials, so that it often took many months to get the repair of church buildings authorized. Parishioners had no part in selecting their priests or in disbursing church funds. The priests lived among the villagers, but their seminary education and their frequent collection of high fees for their services led to divergence in outlook. Priests were expected by the police to aid the authorities by reporting anything suspicious learned in confession. The moral tone of the monastic clergy was deplorable. In 1906 a Kazan church publication reported that the environs of Russian monasteries were populated largely by the offspring of their monks!

The state church was privileged and wealthy. By law a Russian was automatically considered Orthodox from birth unless he was inscribed officially as a member of another faith. The children of mixed marriages were supposed to be brought up as Orthodox. The salaries of bishops averaged 20 times those of industrial workers, and although sworn to poverty, the bishops received additional revenue from monasteries and diocesan homes. Only the Orthodox could conduct missionary work freely and maintain church-related schools. Despite these manifold advantages, by 1900 the Orthodox church, corrupt and worldly, was clearly decaying. Its influence with the Russian people was fading. Most of the intellectuals had left it, although in the early 20th century such conservative intellectuals as Peter Struve, N. Berdiaev, and Sergei Bulgakov led a back-to-the-church movement. Factory workers tended to be much less devout than the peasantry they had come from. Serious dissension developed between parish priests and the pampered church hierarchy; yet before 1905 attempts at church reform failed utterly. Russian Orthodoxy, unlike Western Protestant and Catholic churches, was bound to a rigid autocracy and failed lamentably to adapt to a new age.

Other religious groups suffered discrimination and persecution, especially after 1881. Dissenters were forbidden to construct new churches, ring church bells to announce services, or hold open religious processions. But all except extreme sectarians could practice their faith, engage in trade and industry, and hold minor offices. Some sectarian groups, especially the Stundists (similar to Baptists) and Dukhobors, were severely persecuted, and the latter were virtually compelled to

emigrate. Official figures issued in 1901 that purposely underestimated the number of dissenters listed only 1,028,437 Old Believers, 176,199 Sectarians, and 969,102 "others," whereas official data published in 1859 had listed 9,300,000 Old Believers. J. S. Curtiss estimates that in 1900 the Old Believers (17,500,000) and Sectarians (1,500,000) constituted more than 15 percent of the population of the Russian Empire, leaving out Poland and Finland.[19] Catholics and Jews were persecuted less for their religion than for national and economic reasons. The regime made no concerted effort to undermine Islam in the Caucasus, the Volga valley, and Central Asia, where it was widely practiced. Religious discrimination, however, doubtless contributed much to rising minority dissatisfaction with the imperial regime.

Suggested Additional Reading

BOOKS

ANDERSON, B. *Internal Migration during Modernization in Late Nineteenth Century Russia* (Princeton, 1980).

ARONSON, MICHAEL. *Troubled Waters: The Origins of the 1881 Anti-Jewish Pogroms in Russia* (Pittsburgh, 1991).

BERNSTEIN, L. *Sonia's Daughters: Prostitutes and Their Regulation in Imperial Russia* (Berkeley, 1995).

BLACK, C. E., ed. *The Transformation of Russian Society: Aspects of Social Change since 1861* (Cambridge, MA, 1960).

BLACKWELL, W. *The Industrialization of Russia,* 2d ed. (Arlington Heights, IL, 1982).

BUNGE, N. K. *The Years 1881–1894 in Russia . . .* (Philadelphia, 1981).

CHRISTIAN, D. *Living Water: Vodka and Russian Society . . .* (New York, 1990).

CRISP, O. *Studies in the Russian Economy before 1914* (New York, 1976).

CURTISS, J. S. *Church and State in Russia . . . 1900–1917* (New York, 1940).

EKLOF, B., and S. FRANK. *The World of the Russian Peasant . . .* (Boston, 1990).

---

[19] J. S. Curtiss, *Church and State in Russia, 1900–1917* (New York, 1940), pp. 137–39.

FITZLYON, K., and T. BROWNING, comps. *Before the Revolution: A View of Russia under the Last Tsar* (Woodstock, NY, 1979).

FRIEDEN, N. *Russian Physicians in an Era of Reform and Revolution, 1856–1905* (Princeton, 1981).

GLICKMAN, R. I. *Russian Factory Women . . . 1880–1914* (Berkeley, 1984).

HOGAN, H. *Forging Revolution: Metal Workers, Manufacturers and the State in St. Petersburg, 1890–1914* (Bloomington, IN, 1993).

JOHNSON, R. *Peasant and Proletarian . . .* (New Brunswick, NJ, 1979).

LENIN, V. I. *The Development of Capitalism in Russia* (Moscow, 1956).

MACEY, D. *Government and Peasant in Russia, 1861–1906 . . .* (Dekalb, IL, 1987).

MANNING, R. T. *The Crisis of the Old Order in Russia: Gentry and Government* (Princeton, 1982).

MAYNARD, J. *The Russian Peasant and Other Studies* (New York, 1962).

MCCAFFRAY, S. P. *The Politics of Industrialization in Tsarist Russia: The Association of Southern Coal and Steel Producers, 1874–1914* (DeKalb, IL, 1996).

MCKAY, J. P. *Pioneers for Profit: Foreign Entrepreneurship and Russian Industrialization, 1885–1913* (Chicago, 1970).

OWEN, T. C. *Capitalism and Politics in Russia: Moscow Merchants, 1855–1905* (Cambridge, 1981).

RANSEL, D. *Mothers of Misery: Child Abandonment in Russia* (Princeton, 1988).

RIEBER, A. J. *Merchants and Entrepreneurs in Imperial Russia* (Chapel Hill, NC, 1982).

ROBBINS, R., JR. *Famine in Russia, 1891–92 . . .* (New York, 1975).

ROBINSON, G. T. *Rural Russia under the Old Regime* (New York, 1949).

ROGGER, H. *Russia in the Age of Modernization and Revolution, 1881–1917* (New York, 1983).

SEMYONOVA TIAN-SHANSKAIA, O. *Village Life in Late Tsarist Russia*, ed. D. Ransel (Bloomington, IN, 1993).

STITES, R. *The Women's Liberation Movement in Russia . . .* (Princeton, 1978).

TUGAN-BARANOVSKY, M. I. *The Russian Factory in the Nineteenth Century* (Homewood, IL, 1970).

VON LAUE, T. *Sergei Witte and the Industrialization of Russia* (New York, 1963).

VUCINICH, W. S., ed. *The Peasant in Nineteenth Century Russia* (Stanford, 1968).

WCISLO, F. W. *Reforming Rural Russia: . . . 1855–1914* (Princeton, 1989).

WESTWOOD, J. N. *A History of Russian Railways* (London, 1964).

WOROBEC, C. D. *Peasant Russia . . . in the Post-Emancipation Period* (Princeton, 1991).

ZELNIK, R. E. *Labor and Society in Tsarist Russia: The Factory Workers of St. Petersburg, 1855–1870* (Stanford, 1971).

———. *A Radical Worker in Tsarist Russia: The Autobiography of S. I. Kanatchchikov* (Stanford, 1986).

ARTICLES

ABBOT, W. "Crime, Police, and Society in St. Petersburg, 1866–1878." *Historian* 40, no. 1 (1977): 70–84.

———. "Moscow in 1897 as a Preindustrial City." *Amer. Sociological Review* 39, no. 4 (1974): 542–50.

BROWER, D. "Labor Violence in Russia in the Late Nineteenth Century." *SR* 41, no. 3 (1982): 417–31 and following comments.

EKLOF, B. "Peasant Sloth Reconsidered . . ." *Jour. of Social Hist.* 14, no. 3 (1981): 355–85.

ENGEL, B. "Russian Peasant Views of City Life, 1861–1914," *SR* 52, no. 3 (Fall 1993): 446–59.

FREEZE, G. "P. A. Valuyev and the Politics of Church Reform, 1861–62." *SEER* 56, no. 1 (1978): 68–87.

GIFFIN, F. "The First Russian Labor Code: The Law of June 3, 1886." *Rus. Hist.* 2, no. 2 (1975): 83–100.

GOLDSMITH, R. W. "Economic Growth of Tsarist Russia, 1860–1913," in *Economic Development and Cultural Change* (Chicago, 1961), vol. 9, pt. 2, pp. 441–75.

HAMBURG, G. M. "The Russian Nobility on the Eve of the 1905 Revolution." *Rus. Rev.* 38, no. 3 (1978): 323–38.

PORTAL, R. "The Industrialization of Russia," in *Cambridge Economic History* (Cambridge, 1966), vol. 6, pt. 2, pp. 801–72.

REICHMAN, H. "The Rostov General Strike of 1902." *Rus. Hist.* 9, no. 1 (1982): 67–85.

SIMMS, J. Y. "The Crisis in Russian Agriculture at the End of the Nineteenth Century." *SR* 36, no. 3 (1977): 377–97.

STITES, R. "The Women's Liberation Issue in Nineteenth Century Russia," in *Women in Eastern Europe and the Soviet Union*, ed. Tova Yedlin (New York, 1980), pp. 20–30.

VON LAUE, T. H. "Russian Peasants in the Factory, 1892–1903." *JEH* 21 (1961): 61–80.

———. "Tsarist Labor Policy, 1895–1903." *JMH* 34 (1972): 135–45.

26

Diplomacy and Empire, 1855–1905

The Crimean defeat shook tsarism, damaged its prestige, and forced Alexander II and his advisers to consider new external policies. Revealing the old army's inadequacy, the war exposed Russia to nationalist agitation in the western borderlands and to British incursions along its vulnerable southern frontiers. Russia could not maneuver freely until it restored its Black Sea defenses and cleaned up matters left from Nicholas's reign: unrest in Poland, resistance in the Caucasus, and unstable boundaries in Central Asia. Absorbed in domestic change, especially army reform, Russia could not fight a major war and needed to break up the Crimean coalition. Alexander's closest advisers agreed that the Crimean defeat must be avenged and the prewar frontiers regained but disagreed over how these goals were to be achieved. Generally, the Foreign and Finance ministries advocated caution and traditional diplomacy, while the War Ministry, the Asiatic Department, and army commanders urged expansion along the southern frontiers to restore Russian prestige by force. Russia's viceroy in the Caucasus, Prince A. I. Bariatinskii, advocated that region's speedy pacification and its use as a base

to conquer Central Asia and threaten Great Britain in India. He viewed Russia's mission as bringing European civilization and Christianity to Asia, but he failed to convert Alexander II to reckless expansion there. The emperor believed that the empire's European and Balkan frontiers were more vital, and the Eastern Question, he noted, "interests us more than all that happens in the rest of Europe." Alexander would not adopt unreservedly Foreign Minister A. M. Gorchakov's preference for working with the European powers in the Balkans, yet his hatred of revolutionary movements led him to oppose a Pan-Slav crusade there. Lacking any overall plan, the emperor was pushed this way and that by conflicting advice. Like previous Russian rulers, he could not separate the Polish and Turkish issues or overcome Austrian opposition to Russian predominance in the Balkans.

During the half century after 1855 Russia pacified the Caucasus, conquered Central Asia, and advanced in the Far East. Except between 1894 and 1904, when Russia was preoccupied with its expansion in the Far East, official Russian diplomacy focused on Europe and the Balkans and in general

aimed to preserve a balance of power and to cooperate with other powers to maintain peace. At key
junctures (1878 and 1885), Russian leaders, to prevent war with major powers, made concessions that
distressed the advocates of a unilateral, forward
foreign policy. In 1904, however, the adventurists
temporarily dominated the leadership itself, with
disastrous results—that is, the Russo-Japanese War.
How much influence did military and Pan-Slav
elements exert on policy decisions? How did the
Foreign Ministry's role change during this era? Why
did Russia expand in Central Asia (see Problem 8 at
the end of this chapter) and the Far East and
become involved in war with Japan in 1904?

Relations with Europe until 1875

In the first post–Crimean War years, antagonism
toward Austria and Great Britain drew Russia
closer to France. Though Napoleon III refused to
cancel the humiliating Black Sea clauses of the
Paris Treaty, France and Russia cooperated against
Austria to promote Rumanian independence and
the nationalist course of Prince Mihailo Obrenović
of Serbia; and Russia's benevolent neutrality and
French support of Sardinia against Austria in 1859
contributed to Italian unification. The Polish revolt
of 1863 (see Chapter 24) ended this Franco-
Russian entente and produced Russo-Prussian
cooperation against the rebels. This change
enabled Gorchakov to defy Western demands for
Polish amnesty and autonomy and to emerge as
the triumphant spokesman of a resurgent Russia.
The subsequent Russo-Prussian entente was
cemented by Alexander II's respect for his uncle,
King William I of Prussia.

   During the 1860s Otto von Bismarck, the Prussian statesman, exploited Russia's dislike for the
Paris Treaty and its domestic preoccupation to unify
Germany by force. Originally considering Bismarck
his pupil, the vain Gorchakov later had to recognize
the Prussian statesman as his master. During the
Austro-Sardinian War of 1859, Russia tied down
Austrian troops that might have fought France,
thus gaining revenge for similar Austrian action

during the Crimean War. Prussia's defeat of France
in 1871, aided by Russia's benevolent neutrality,
enabled Gorchakov, with Bismarck's support, to
denounce the Black Sea clauses; the London Conference of 1871 reluctantly recognized this high-
handed action. Now Russia could rebuild its Black
Sea fleet and its Crimean bases. Gorchakov thus
achieved the peak of his career, but the price was
high: a powerful German Empire that upset the
European balance and stretched ominously along
Russia's exposed western frontiers.

   Chancellor Bismarck sought to preserve his
new Germany by keeping defeated France isolated. The emperors of Germany, Austria-Hungary, and Russia met and in 1873 formed the
Dreikaiserbund (Three Emperors' League), a loose
and fragile entente based on similar conservative
ideologies and institutions and a determination to
keep Poland partitioned.

Pan-Slavism and the Eastern Question until 1878

The Great Reforms made Russia more attractive to
Habsburg and Ottoman Slavs, and Gorchakov's
opposition to the Paris Treaty brought official Russian policy closer to nationalist and Pan-Slav
desires. In the Balkans in the post-Crimean era
Russia sought to rebuild its prestige, regain influence over Orthodox Slavs, and obtain free access to
the Turkish Straits. During the 1860s Gorchakov
aimed to strengthen the Serbia of Mihailo Obrenović and encourage Serbian leadership of Balkan
Christians against the Turks. Around Serbia formed
a Balkan League, including Greece and Montenegro, which was supplied with arms by the Russian
War Ministry. Prince Mihailo, however, tempted by
Austrian territorial offers, backed away from conflict, and his murder (May 1868) shattered the
league and Russia's hopes of Balkan hegemony.

   Bellicose Russian Pan-Slavs exerted increasing
influence as official Russia shifted to support the
Balkan status quo and embrace the German powers. Pan-Slavism had first developed among western Slavs, notably the Czechs, as a movement to
unite Slav peoples culturally and free them from

alien rule. Russian Pan-Slavism, the offspring of Slavophilism and resurgent nationalism, renounced a cultural humanitarian emphasis for militant national imperialism. Regarding Russia as the superior "big brother" for "younger" Slav brethren of the west and south, its spokesmen often excluded Poles and other non-Orthodox Slavs from their proposed Slav federations. A small group of Russian noblemen, army officers, and writers, including Fedor Dostoevsky, expounded Pan-Slav doctrines that stimulated sympathy among educated Russians for Slavs under foreign rule. N. Ia. Danilevskii's lengthy *Russia and Europe* (1872), the "Bible" of Pan-Slavism, predicted Slav triumph in an "inevitable conflict" with Europe and the formation of an all-Slav federation centering in Constantinople. R. A. Fadeev, a retired major general, proclaimed in 1869: "Russia's chief enemy . . . is the German race"; Russia must "extend her preeminence to the Adriatic or withdraw again beyond the Dnieper." Its historic mission was to lead Orthodox Slavs in war against the Germans until "the Russian reigning house covers the liberated soil of Eastern Europe with its branches under the supremacy of the tsar of Russia."[1] In western Europe Fadeev's pamphlet, translated into English in 1876, raised the specter of Russian imperial rule of Slav satellite states all over eastern Europe.

Until 1875 only small, uninfluential groups in Russia advocated Pan-Slav doctrines, but during the Balkan Crisis of 1875–1878, using the Slav committees of Moscow and St. Petersburg, Pan-Slavs achieved temporary dominance. Earlier the Moscow Committee had merely educated a few foreign Slavs in Russia and aided Orthodox churches abroad. In 1867 it had sponsored a Slav Congress in Moscow, but Russian claims of primacy for Orthodoxy and the Russian language had alienated many western Slav guests. During the Balkan crisis the Pan-Slavs exploited official indecisiveness and a divided Foreign Ministry to

achieve unusual influence. Within the ministry the Diplomatic Chancellery, staffed largely by diplomats of foreign origin with European connections and high social positions, handled relations with the powers and favored cooperation with Europe. The Asiatic Department, responsible for Asia, the Balkans, and the Near East, contained many Russian nationalists and people of Balkan background. In the Balkans its work was coordinated by the embassy in Constantinople, run between 1864 and 1877 by Count N. P. Ignatiev, a Pan-Slav and former director of the Asiatic Department, who favored a unilateral Russian solution of the Eastern Question.

In July 1875 Orthodox Serbs in the Turkish provinces of Hercegovina and Bosnia revolted and were supported, at first unofficially, by Serbia, Montenegro, and Russian Slav committees (see Map 26.1). Alexander II and Gorchakov, seeking a compromise European solution, proclaimed Russia's nonintervention, but Ambassador Ignatiev encouraged Balkan Slavs to aid the insurgents and the Serbian states in their fight against Turkey. Pan-Slav activists in Russia, backed by the heir and court ladies, organized public medical and financial aid for the embattled Slavs. Coordinating this aid program, the Slav committees sent the Pan-Slav general M. G. Cherniaev to direct Serbia's armies and recruited several thousand Russian volunteers to serve under him. To the Russian public and many Slavs abroad, Cherniaev symbolized unselfish Russian aid for the cause of Slav liberation, though he and his officers actually sought to transform Serbia into a Russian satellite. The Turks finally defeated his forces, and to prevent Serbia's destruction, Russia issued an ultimatum to the Turks in October 1876, which halted their advance.

Pan-Slav agitation and Alexander II's sense of honor drew Russia into the costly Russo-Turkish War of 1877–1878. Eventually the Russian army, after embarrassing setbacks at the Turkish fortress of Plevna, reached the outskirts of Constantinople. Shelving Gorchakov's program of cooperation with Europe, the tsar allowed Ignatiev to impose on the Turks the Treaty of San Stefano (March

---

[1] R. A. Fadeev, *Opinion on the Eastern Question* (London, 1876).

Map 26.1 Russia and the Balkans, 1876–1885

1878), which envisioned a Big Bulgaria under Russian military occupation. This action provoked near panic in England, which feared Russian seizure of Constantinople and the Straits. England and Austria threatened war unless Russia submitted its treaty to the powers for approval. Alexander II, reluctant to fight a European coalition, agreed to the Congress of Berlin, directed by Chancellor Bismarck of Germany, which accorded Russia only its minimum aims: southern Bessarabia and Kars and Batum in the Caucasus. Big Bulgaria was reduced and split up, and Austria-Hungary occupied Bosnia and Hercegovina. Serbia, rebuffed by Russia, turned to Austria-Hungary. The Berlin Treaty recognized the independence of Serbia, Montenegro, and Rumania and Bulgaria's autonomy, but it preserved the Ottoman Empire and let Austria-Hungary dominate the western Balkans. Russian Pan-Slavs and nationalists were furious; they and most government leaders agreed that Russia had been cheated and humiliated at Berlin.

The Caucasus and Central Asia

Under Alexander II Russia finally pacified the Caucasus. After Field Marshal Bariatinskii and his chief of staff, D. A. Miliutin (see Chapter 24), had reorganized the Caucasus command, systematic operations by able commanders and assurances to Muslim tribesmen that they could retain their faith and customs brought speedy success. In 1859 Shamil, leader of the mountaineers, was forced to surrender, and by 1864, after many Circassians sought refuge in Turkey, the west Caucasus tribes had also been subdued. The Caucasus now provided Russia with secure natural boundaries in the south and bases for expansion in Asia.

Central Asia, lying east of the Caspian Sea and south of Siberia (see Map 26.2), became the next arena of Russian imperial expansion. At slight cost Russia annexed a region more than twice the size of France with vast potential wealth. For reasons resembling those motivating European overseas

To Astrakhan   To Orenburg   To Omsk

Turgai

CASPIAN
SEA

KAZAKH STEPPE

Raim

Aral
Sea

HUNGRY STEPPE

Balkhash

Perovsk   Suzak

TURKESTAN

Krasnovodsk

KHIVA   Kyzyl-Kum
Desert

Turkestan   Pishpek   Kulja
Arys R.   Vernoe
Chimkent   Aulie - Ata   Issyk - Kul

TRANSCASPIA

Central Asian

Khiva

Kara-Kum
Desert
Geok-Tepe

Djizak   Tashkent

Bukhara

R. R.

Ashkhabad   Merv   BUKHARA   CHINA

Samarkand   Kokand

PERSIA
(IRAN)

AFGHANISTAN

INDIA

Map 26.2 Central Asia, 1850–1914

imperialism, Russia moved deep into Muslim Asia. No serious geographic or military obstacles hindered Russia from filling the Central Asian power vacuum. This policy was favored by the War Ministry, frontier governors and generals, and nationalist diplomats, whereas the Foreign Ministry, fearful of British reactions, opposed major advances, and the Finance Ministry pleaded poverty. Having to make the final decisions, the emperor backed cautious advances, though frontier generals at times took action independently of the War Ministry, committing the government to unwanted conflicts and territory. The imperial family, tempted by glory and prestige, sanctioned most of these conquests and rewarded those reponsible for them.

Between 1864 and 1885 small Russian forces seized most of Turkestan in Central Asia from the weak, poorly organized Muslim khanates of Kokand, Khiva, and Bukhara. In 1864, after Colonel Cherniaev and Colonel N. A. Verevkin closed the remaining gap in Russia's steppe

defense lines, Cherniaev seized Chimkent fortress on the edge of the oasis region. Foreign Minister Gorchakov pledged publicly that Russia would halt there, but Cherniaev disregarded instructions and captured Tashkent (June 1865), Central Asia's chief commercial center. Though removed for insubordination, Cherniaev had committed Russia to absorb the Muslim oases. In 1867 the emperor appointed General K. P. Kaufman governor-general of Turkestan. He built an administration from scratch, won native respect, and began developing Turkestan's resources. In 1873 Khiva became a Russian protectorate, and three years later Kokand khanate became Fergana province, later the empire's chief cotton-growing region. In 1881 General M. D. Skobelev conquered fierce Turkoman tribesmen to the southwest.

Under Alexander III Russia expanded until it reached British-controlled areas. The occupation of Merv oasis (1884) caused fears ("Mervousness") in London for India's security. In 1885 Russia's advance to the Afghan border almost provoked war with Great Britain, but the two countries agreed to a compromise frontier and ended their acute rivalry in Central Asia. An agreement in 1895 gave Russia natural frontiers in the mountainous Pamir region. The Central Asian Railroad (begun in 1881) and the Orenburg-Tashkent line (completed in 1905) linked firmly with central Russia strategic Turkestan, which produced increasing amounts of cotton and silk for Russian industries.

After 1880 Anglo-Russian rivalry grew over weak and corrupt Persia. Military and civilian agents steadily extended Russian influence, and the Cossack Brigade of Persia (founded in 1879), led by Russian officers, served as a spearhead against the British. London considered Persia an outpost in its Indian defense system; Russian leaders saw it as ripe for the plucking. "The entire northern part of Persia," declared Count Witte, "was intended, as if by nature, to turn in the future . . . into a country under our complete protectorate." In Persia the British lost much ground to Russia in competition for trade and influence.

Europe and the Balkans, 1881–1905

Under Alexander III, Russia remained at peace. The emperor rarely interfered directly in foreign affairs, and when he did, as in Bulgaria, disaster resulted. Foreign policy was directed by Foreign Minister N. K. Girs, a highly trained, prudent, and experienced Swedish Protestant. He restrained nationalists and militarists, kept Russia out of war, and induced the emperor to accept most of his views. Girs favored close relations with Germany but finally, albeit reluctantly, had to prepare the way for an alliance with France.

A second Dreikaiserbund was formed soon after Alexander III's accession. Germany in 1879 had allied with Austria-Hungary. Fearing diplomatic isolation and loathing republican France, Russian leaders swallowed their hurt pride and found Bismarck happy to admit them to "the German club." The three partners pledged neutrality if one of them were fighting a fourth power.

The Dreikaiserbund guaranteed closure of the Turkish Straits to foreign warships and enhanced Russia's security, but it cost Russia freedom of action in the Balkans. Though accepting this policy of Girs, Alexander agreed with the Pan-Slavs that Constantinople must eventually be Russian. Russian nationalists denounced the Dreikaiserbund as treason to Russia's national mission and predicted a Russo-German war. Bonds linking the three eastern monarchies remained fragile, but the Pan-Slavs could not oust Girs or undermine his policy.

In the Balkans after 1878 Serbia became an Austrian satellite and Bulgaria a Russian one, but each great power alienated the leaders of its protégé. Commercial and political treaties bound Serbia to Austria, but King Milan's Austrophilism caused rising public sympathy for Russia in Serbia. In Bulgaria, liberated by Russia in 1877, conflicting policies by Russian ministries and the tactlessness of Russian officers who dominated the army and administration stimulated national feeling.

In September 1885 a crisis erupted when Bulgarian nationalists seized control in Eastern Rumelia and proclaimed its union with Bulgaria under Prince Alexander of Battenberg. Refusing to recognize an act that he had not initiated, Alexander III ordered home all Russian officers. To secure territorial compensation, Serbia attacked Bulgaria but met with decisive defeat. Austria intervened to prevent disaster to its Serbian protégé and restored peace without territorial changes. The tsar then had the Bulgarian prince abducted to Russia and forced him to abdicate, while Baron A. V. Kaulbars, a Russian general, assumed control of Bulgaria. When the defiant Bulgarians chose Ferdinand of Coburg as their ruler, the tsar recalled his officers and broke relations. Great Britain and Austria, reversing their position of 1878, protested Russian bullying and supported Bulgarian unification. Russia lost its Bulgarian bastion temporarily, and its Balkan position was weakened. Austro-Russian tension, revealed anew by the Bulgarian crisis, destroyed the Dreikaiserbund. Russian nationalists, led by M. N. Katkov, fanned anti-German feeling, but Bismarck and Girs managed to preserve Russo-German diplomatic cooperation. Though their Reinsurance Treaty of 1887 did not square fully with the Austro-German alliance, it provided Russia and Germany with a measure of security. Russia, however, was already increasing its financial links with France, foreshadowing their subsequent alliance.

Russo-German relations deteriorated rapidly after Bismarck's forced retirement in 1890. When Emperor William II of Germany refused to renew the Reinsurance Treaty, the way lay open for reconciliation between autocratic Russia and republican France on the bases of power and national interest. France needed a continental ally against Germany; Alexander III wished to restrict German power. French loans to Russia and French fear that Great Britain might join the Triple Alliance pushed France and Russia together. In 1891, during the French fleet's official visit to Kronstadt, the tsar stood bareheaded while "La Marseillaise," anthem of revolution, was played. Common fear of Germany proved more potent than ideological hostility. France and Russia pledged in 1893 to aid each other with all their forces if either were attacked by Germany. As their defensive military alliance opposed the Triple Alliance of Germany, Austria, and Italy, two formidable power blocs split Europe, although room for diplomatic maneuver remained.

After the Bulgarian crisis a generally pacific Russian policy in the Balkans produced an accommodation with Austria-Hungary. With Russia absorbed in the Far East and Austria-Hungary weakened by domestic problems, they agreed in 1897 that neither power would annex Balkan territory unless the Turks collapsed in Europe. In that event, Austria could annex Bosnia, Hercegovina, and Novi Pazar, occupied since 1878; other Turkish possessions would be divided so as to prevent predominance by a single Balkan state. The Straits would remain closed to foreign warships. Temporarily the rivals placed the Balkans "on ice," and even the bitter rivalry of Serbia, Bulgaria, and Greece over Macedonia and a major uprising there failed to disrupt an accord that the

Austrian and Russian rulers reaffirmed at Mürzsteg in 1903.

Russia in the Far East until 1914

In the half century after the Crimean War Russia conquered the Maritime Province, penetrated north China, and encroached upon Japanese interests in Korea. In aims and methods, Russia's Far Eastern expansion resembled that of other European powers. At the expense of decaying Manchu China, Russia sought railroad concessions, commercial privileges, warm-water ports, and spheres of interest.

N. N. Muraviev (Amurskii), governor-general of Eastern Siberia (1847–1861), exploited China's weakness and absorption in war against Great Britain and France to seize the Amur and Ussuri regions. Hitherto China had refused to recognize Russian control of the Amur basin, but Muraviev forced the local Chinese commander to confirm in the Treaty of Aigun (May 1858) Russia's claims to the Amur's left bank from the Aigun River to the sea and to place the Ussuri region under joint Sino-Russian administration. In June Admiral E.V. Putiatin exploited the Western powers' defeat of China to conclude the Treaty of Tientsin, which granted Russia trading rights obtained earlier by Great Britain, France, and the United States. As Western forces prepared to attack Peking, Muraviev advanced southward and in July 1860 founded the port of Vladivostok (Ruler of the East) near the Korean frontier (see Map 26.3). In December Count Ignatiev negotiated with China the Treaty of Peking, which confirmed the previous treaties and gave Russia territory between the Ussuri River and the Pacific. In the 1960s China would complain that Russia had seized the Maritime Province illegally.

In the 1860s St. Petersburg liquidated its Alaskan venture. The fur trade there was dwindling, and the inefficient Russia-America Company was deeply in debt to the government. During the U.S. Civil War, Russia and the Union government shared hostility to England. Viewing Alaska as an economic burden and as indefensible against

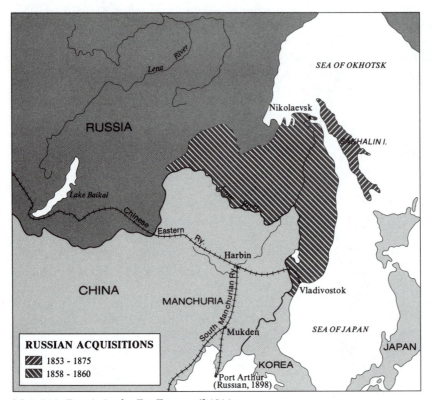

Map 26.3 Russia in the Far East until 1914

British Canada, Russian leaders decided to sell it to the United States. They hoped that this action would create a balance of power in North America and increase Anglo-American rivalry. Since 1854 the Russian and American governments had discussed the sale of Alaska informally. In March 1867 Baron E. Stoeckl, the Russian ambassador, and Secretary of State William Seward signed a treaty transferring Alaska to the United States for $7,200,000. Stoeckl used $200,000 to bribe American senators to ratify the treaty! Considering Alaska's present economic and strategic importance, in ratifying "Seward's Folly" the United States had unwittingly struck a rare bargain.

Russia's position in the Far East remained vulnerable. Siberia's settlement lagged, and Russian port facilities, naval bases, and overland communications were inadequate. To be sure, by the Treaty of St. Petersburg (1875) Russia had obtained from Japan the large offshore island of Sakhalin, valuable for oil and fisheries. Japan, however, modernizing rapidly, displayed increasing interest in the Asian mainland.

A group of Russian scholars, journalists, and military men known as *Vostochniki* (Easterners), like the Pan-Slavs for the Balkans, advocated further imperial expansion in Asia. With its essentially non-European culture and values, they argued, Russia was destined to develop or incorporate much of Asia and to protect Europe from the "yellow peril." Mongolia and Sinkiang longed to join Russia, affirmed the explorer M. N. Przhevalskii: "Those poor Asiatics look to the advance of Russian power with the firm conviction that its advent is synonymous with the beginning of a . . . life of greater security for themselves." V. P.

Vasiliev, a leading Sinologist, predicted in 1893 that Russia would liberate Oriental peoples "oppressed by the tyranny of internecine strife and impotency." Prince E. E. Ukhtomskii, journalist and student of Oriental philosophy who influenced Nicholas II deeply, believed that once opened by modern communications, Siberia would become Russia's Eldorado: "For Russia there is no other course than to become . . . a great power uniting the West with the East, or ingloriously and imperceptibly to tread the downward path." Count Witte (see Chapter 25) translated some of these vague imperial dreams into reality. Earlier Muraviev had suggested a transcontinental railroad, but Witte persuaded the government to start building the Trans-Siberian Railroad in 1891. Witte envisioned it as replacing the Suez Canal as the bearer of Russian and European goods to Oriental markets, and his memorandum of 1892 outlined a broad program of Russian economic expansion in the Far East.

The Sino-Japanese War of 1894, revealing China's weakness, stimulated European imperial powers to press forward. In 1895 Witte, to prevent Japan from securing a foothold on the Asian mainland, obtained Franco-German diplomatic support. Posing as guardians of China's "territorial integrity," France, Germany, and Russia insisted that Japan return to China the Liaotung Peninsula containing Port Arthur, a strategic warm-water port. Urging peaceful Russian economic penetration of north China, Witte favored a passive, friendly China as Russia's ally against Japan. By the Li-Lobanov agreement of 1896, negotiated by Witte with China's foreign minister, China authorized a private Russian-controlled corporation to build and operate a Chinese Eastern Railroad across northern Manchuria, shortening the route to Vladivostok by more than 300 miles. In 1898 Nicholas II, over Witte's objections and urged on by War Minister A. N. Kuropatkin, ordered Port Arthur occupied and forced China to grant Russia a 36-year lease of the Liaotung Peninsula—the very region that Russia had compelled Japan to renounce in 1895! Constructing the South

Manchurian Railroad from Port Arthur northward to Harbin, where it joined the Chinese Eastern, the Russians dominated all of Manchuria economically. In 1900 the Chinese Boxer Rebellion erupted against foreign imperialism. After the Boxers attacked Russian railways in China, Kuropatkin's troops occupied Manchuria, and Kuropatkin told Witte that it would become a Russian protectorate like Bukhara.[2]

The Russian government was seriously divided over Far Eastern policy. As the Foreign Ministry lost control of the situation, Russia embarked upon an ill-considered, aggressive course. Foreign Minister V. N. Lamsdorf and Finance Minister Witte still favored peaceful economic penetration of China while avoiding conflict with Japan, but an adventurist clique of former guards officers (A. M. Bezobrazov and V. M. Vonliarliarskii) and titled aristocrats (Grand Duke Alexander Mikhailovich and Count I. I. Vorontsov-Dashkov) converted Nicholas II to reckless expansion. Late in 1897 Bezobrazov obtained a timber concession on the Yalu River on the Manchurian-Korean border, a first move toward Russian annexation of Korea, a region that Japan considered its rightful sphere. Naval leaders seeking Korean bases supported Bezobrazov's group. In May 1903 Bezobrazov became secretary of state for Far Eastern affairs, and Admiral E. I. Alekseev became imperial viceroy over the entire region east of Lake Baikal, responsible for relations with China, Korea, and Japan. Witte had warned the Foreign Ministry in vain that misunderstandings with Japan must be removed because "an armed clash with Japan in the near future would be a great disaster for us."

Japan sought accommodation with Russia. In 1901 the Ito mission visited St. Petersburg but failed to achieve agreement, partly because of Bezobrazov's growing influence with Nicholas II. Japan offered to guarantee Manchuria as a Russian sphere if Russia would respect Japanese predominance in Korea. Russian moderates, such as

---

[2] S. Iu. Witte, *The Memoirs of Count Witte* (Garden City, NY, 1921), vol. 1, p. 10.

Witte, favored a settlement of this kind, but Bezo-brazov's group was supported by naval and military elements. Interior Minister V. K. Pleve declared that bayonets, not diplomats, had made Russia and that "in order to restrain revolution, we need a little victorious war." Nicholas II, blissfully confident, wrote William II of Germany: "There will be no war because I do not wish it." He and the extremists, grossly underrating Japan, disregarded clear warning of its impending action.

Problem 8

Why Did Russia Expand in Central Asia?

Between 1850 and 1895, Russians, moving south from the previously conquered Kazakh steppe, occupied the Syr and Amu river valley oases and advanced to the borders of Afghanistan and India. This expansion created Russian Central Asia, a large imperial domain that in 1914 covered 655,427 square miles and contained millions of Turkic Muslims with a culture wholly different from Russia's. Why should already vast tsarist Russia, absorbed by domestic problems and with an impoverished treasury, move to the Himalaya and Hindu Kush mountains? Tsarist accounts, often remarkably frank, stressed considerations of power, trade, and Russia's civilizing mission. Following are statements by conquerors of the Turkestan region, a contemporary justification by Foreign Minister Gorchakov, and a retrospective view by an official tsarist source of 1914. Soviet historians, understandably, emphasized economic motives: the growing appetites of industrial and commercial elements for raw materials and markets and demands by these elements that the government protect their trade caravans and representatives in Central Asia. Soviet authors stressed the supposed threat of British imperialism to which Russia responded by occupying Turkestan. Later Soviet accounts also included military, political, and prestige motives. Finally, a Cold War–era Western article summarizes and assesses various factors in the Russian expansion.

Tsarist Views: The Conquerors

General M. G. Cherniaev, a leading and reckless frontier general who conquered much of Turkestan (1863–1866), played a semi-independent role in central Asian expansion. Here are a few of his declarations:

> This point [Aulie-Ata] is important to us both commercially and militarily because it lies at the intersection of routes from Kokand and Tashkent. With the capture of Aulie-Ata we have acquired the entire Trans-Chu region.[3]

> In view of the fact that Kokand's concentrations grow daily, that our [native] population is losing confidence in us, . . . I decided, in order to cover Aulie-Ata and the nearby nomads, . . . to advance toward Chimkent.[4]

> Chimkent is scarcely known to Europeans even by map and its conquest cannot cause much noise, and having some 5,000 natives with me, we can dress ourselves in the clothing of the defenders of an exploited people.[5]

> Everyone feels that it would be calmer for us in Chimkent if [Tashkent] were either independent or belonged to us, but in Petersburg, of course, they know better.[6]

> I could not remain indifferent to the [Bukharan] emir's machinations and was compelled without

---

[3] To his parents, June 29, 1864; Cherniaev Archive, Amsterdam.

[4] To Diugamel, July 6, 1864, *Turkestanskii krai*, comp. A. G. Serebrennikov (Tashkent, 1908–1915), 17: 213–14.

[5] To Poltoratskii, August 20, 1864, *Turk. krai* 18: 113–16.

[6] To Poltoratskii, January 22, 1865, *Turk. krai* 18: 33.

awaiting arrival of reinforcements on the line to advance now along the road to Tashkent.[7]

To withdraw from [Tashkent] would give the emir [of Bukhara] vast prestige in Central Asia and strengthen him with all the sinews of war concentrated in Tashkent. Consequently, I resolved to seize the city by open force. . . . Please call the attention of the emperor to this handful of tireless, intrepid warriors, who have established the prestige of the Russian name in Central Asia commensurate with the dignity of the Empire and the power of the Russian people.[8]

N. A. Kryzhanovskii, governor-general of Orenburg and Cherniaev's immediate superior, sounded the theme of "the white man's burden":

It seems to me that it is time to stop catering to the languages and customs of our weak neighbors [the khanates]. We can compel them to conform somewhat to our customs and impose our language on them. In Central Asia we alone must be the masters so that with time through us civilization can penetrate there and improve the lives of those unfortunate offspring of the human race.[9]

General K. P. Kaufman, who was appointed in July 1867 as the first governor-general of Russian Turkestan and who completed its conquest, spoke of insecurity and disorder there upon his arrival:

All this indicates *the necessity* to strike at Bukhara and induce it by force of arms to make peace, and then by a single stroke subdue unconditionally the lands occupied by us so far, remove any thought or possibility of subordination to other than the Russian state. (Alexander II commented: "I find this very sensible.")[10]

War Minister Miliutin, the superior of the above-mentioned conquerors, noted in 1862 Turkestan's significance as a threat to British India:

In case of a European war we should especially value the occupation of [Kokand khanate] bringing us closer to the northern regions of India. . . . Ruling in Kokand, we can constantly threaten England's East Indian possessions. This is especially important since only there can we be dangerous to this enemy of ours.[11]

Official Memorandums (1864)

After Russian troops seized the towns of Chimkent and Turkestan on the fringes of Tashkent oasis, Foreign Minister Gorchakov submitted a memorandum to Alexander II that was soon sent to European powers to reassure them about Russian expansion. The memorandum sought to explain and justify Russian conquests:

The relationship of Russia to Central Asia . . . reveals that, despite our constant wish not to expand our territory with conquests, we, under the influence of the insistent demands of our commerce and some kind of mysterious but irresistible attraction to the Orient, have constantly advanced into the depths of the steppe. . . . The intentions of our government toward this area have undergone continual and fundamental changes. . . . Motivated by a sincere desire not to be drawn into making new acquisitions, we have had to obey willy-nilly the attraction of inexorable necessity. . . . [Russia's] natural and legitimate desire is not to imitate Europe, not to expand her already vast territories, but to retain all her resources for internal development, but a strictly peaceful policy is impossible for a powerful and civilized state bordering upon half-wild tribes. These tribes must either themselves rise because of internal revolt to the same level of civilization or be devoured by a powerful neighbor.[12]

[7] To Kryzhanovskii, May 2, 1865, *Turk. krai* 19: 146–47.

[8] To Kryzhanovskii, July 7, 1865, *Turk. krai* 19: 244–54.

[9] To Stremoukhov, September 3, 1865, *Turk. krai* 20: 47–48.

[10] *Voenno-istoricheskii sbornik* 2 (1916): 159–60.

[11] A. L. Popov, "Iz istorii zavoevanii Srednei Azii," *Istoricheskie zapiski* 9 (1940): 211.

[12] Gorchakov to Alexander II, October 31, 1864, *Turk. krai* 18: 165–67.

Problem 8 continued

Gorchakov stated his opposition to an advance beyond Chimkent because this would create longer Russian frontiers and involve the expense and responsibility of administering millions of central Asian Muslims.

A memorandum written slightly later by the foreign and war ministers suggested that chance had played a major part in Russian expansion:

> Until recently all of our acquisitions in that region [Central Asia] have been made not on the basis of a definite system, not to achieve a specific goal, but under the influence of temporary circumstances and personal, sometimes one-sided views of local commanders. In view of the vast area of the Kirgiz steppe occupied gradually by us . . . , one involuntarily reaches the conclusion that in Russia's advance to the southeast there is a definite law not yielding to human considerations, and that occupying the middle and lower parts of the Syr-Daria, we inevitably, sooner or later, will also occupy its upper reaches, that is, the entire Kokand khanate. Truly, Russian possessions in Central Asia would then achieve natural limits: the Tien Shan Range . . . and the sands of Kyzyl-Kum. . . . At the present time the further extension of our holdings in Central Asia would not accord either with the views of the government or the interests of the country.[13]

Asiatic Russia (*Aziatskaia Rossiia*)

In 1914 an official tsarist publication titled *Asiatic Russia* summarized and evaluated Russian expansion in Central Asia a generation after its completion. It emphasized Muslim hatred and agitation against Russia; attacks on Russian settlers, merchants, and diplomats by savage tribes; and the need for defensible frontiers. Nowhere did it suggest that either the Russian government or frontier commanders had been aggressive or greedy.

The Muslim world with every generation became more hostile to Russia. The khans of Khiva, Bukhara, and Kokand . . . constantly spurred on the Kazakhs to hostile action. . . . The khans . . . with Oriental cunning shifted the responsibility for keeping the people quiet onto the Russians and Russia. . . . Only by subduing [the khanates] could the Kazakh country become Russian not only in name but in fact. . . . Pacification of the Steppe was only possible by terrorizing or subduing those khanates who adopted a bold attitude toward Russia. . . . From this followed the conclusion that it was necessary to deliver a decisive blow against the khanates, and by the 1850s the Russian government had adopted this course.

. . . It only remained to join the fortified town of Vernoe with a cordon to Fort Perovsk for the Kazakh territory to be cut off from external influences hostile to Russia. . . . By 1864 our troops . . . captured the towns of Turkestan, Chimkent, and others. The line was now closed up. . . . The Steppe had been crossed and the Russians were now established in a very rich and fruitful region. . . .

But our occupation of the new line did not bring peace to the Central Asian steppes. The khanates . . . , in their half-brigandish existence, did not appreciate the significance of the events which had taken place nor did they have a proper understanding of the power of Russia. . . . The Asiatic nomads . . . had no desire to reconcile themselves to the new situation and to see around them Russian garrison towns. Incited from without, they plundered our merchants, attacked small detachments, and detained not only our traders, but our ambassadors, and incited the native population of the towns captured by us to start a . . . holy war against the infidels.[14]

Soviet Views

For two decades after the Bolshevik Revolution, Soviet historians, led by Pokrovskii, denounced what they called the brutal tsarist imperial conquest of Central Asia, attributing it mainly to

---

[13] Gorchakov and Miliutin to Alexander II, November 20, 1864, *Turk. krai* 18: 196–98.

[14] *Aziatskaia Russiia*, from G. Wheeler, *The Modern History of Soviet Central Asia* (London, 1964), pp. 235–44.

Problem 8 continued

typical bourgeois greed for markets, land, and raw materials; they discounted British threats as justifying that conquest. After 1937, however, the party line shifted, and Central Asia's incorporation into the Russian empire was considered a "lesser evil" than having its peoples ruled by the British or remaining under reactionary Muslim khanates. Soviet historians until Gorbachev stressed the British danger and economic motives for tsarist expansion. Wrote S. S. Dmitriev:

> At this time [the 1850s] Russia's ancient economic ties with Central Asia increased sharply. Commercial relations between Orenburg, Nizhnii-Novgorod, and Irbit on the one side, and Khiva, Bukhara, and Tashkent on the other, became regular. . . . Russian government policy contributed to this development. . . .
>
> . . . Central Asia was essential to tsarist Russia not only as a source of raw materials, especially as a cotton base for Russian cotton textile manufactures, but as an important market for the sale of goods produced by Russian industry. The Russian bourgeoisie sought new sources of raw materials, new markets for its industrial products. The narrow domestic market [of Russia] could not satisfy the demands of an industry developing rapidly in the postreform period. . . . No less than the bourgeoisie, Russian noble landowners were also interested in acquiring Central Asia. The acquisition of new colonies permitted capitalism to develop in breadth relatively easily and thus delayed the inevitable basic destruction of survivals of serfdom in the country's landowning structure. . . .
>
> . . . Central Asia interested Russian tsarism also as a new region of colonization for the "excess" population of Russia, as a new source of money for the treasury, and as a convenient military base to halt England's expansionist policy directed at the interior of Asia. New conquests in Central Asia also opened to an important and influential group of military and civilian Russian nobles and bourgeois easy possibilities for feudal-military plunder of the new colony. . . . The English bourgeoisie [from 1830] sought thirstily to seize more and more new colonies as markets for

the goods of its capitalist industry and to obtain valuable raw materials.[15]

N. A. Khalfin, a Soviet specialist on Central Asia, affirmed:

> Rapid industrial development made the question of expanding markets particularly acute. Russian entrepreneurs submitted to the Finance and Foreign ministries various petitions, requests, and memoranda that solicited the increase of opportunities to sell their products, especially about "creating in Central Asia favorable conditions for the activity of Russian merchants. . . ." The tsarist government responded sympathetically. . . . Through expansion abroad it counted on weakening class contradictions within the country, which were becoming extremely sharp. . . . By an active and successful foreign policy it sought to distract the attention of the popular masses from severe internal problems. . . . Advances in Central Asia, where the opponent was weak, gave promise with small expenditures of securing for Russian entrepreneurs profitable markets and sources of raw materials, for military men a chance to distinguish themselves, for the service gentry administrative posts, for landowners reserves of land for resettlement, etc. . . .
>
> In the early 1860s the most important branch of Russian industry—textiles—developed an urgent need for cotton. . . . However, the U.S. Civil War . . . reduced the imports of cotton into Russia, 1861–65. . . . The interruption in the receipt of American cotton compelled the [Russian] government, merchants, and industrialists . . . to view differently the question of turning the Central Asian khanates into sources of raw materials. Though during the cotton famine, the prices of Central Asian cotton in Russia jumped upward sharply, its importation increased significantly. . . . The difficulty of obtaining this vital raw material for the Russian textile industry caused sharp concern in commercial-industrial circles and among all those connected with eastern policies. . . . Central Asia, regarded hitherto by Russian merchants and industrialists primarily as a profitable market, now acquired the significance of an important

---

[15] S. S. Dmitriev, "Sredniaia Aziia i Kazakhstan v 1860–1880-kh godakh: Zavoevanie Srednei Azii," in M. V. Nechkina, ed., *Istoriia SSSR* (Moscow, 1949), pp. 578–81.

source of industrial raw materials. Russian newspapers and journals were filled with articles and comments about turning Central Asia into the cotton farm of the Russian empire.[16]

A Western View

Firuz Kazemzadeh, a leading American scholar, assessed the validity of these tsarist and Soviet explanations for expansion:

> Many attempts have been made to uncover the motives behind Russia's expansion in Central Asia and the Middle East. . . . Soviet writers have stressed the economic forces which supposedly made it inevitable. . . . Indeed, Russian trade with the khanates of Turkestan had been growing rapidly ever since the middle of the eighteenth century . . . ; however, the volume of this trade was relatively small and there is very little evidence that the Russian bourgeoisie had sufficient influence on the government to induce it to undertake large-scale conquests in the interests of a rather insignificant industry. Moreover, the alleged interests of the bourgeoisie fail to explain the origins of Russia's eastward expansion, a process which had begun long before the post-reform period. . . . In the case of Central Asia Russian expansion cannot be explained exclusively in economic terms. The same objections apply to the assertion that the conquest of Central Asia was in the interests of the serf-owning gentry who hoped that the acquisition of new territories would somehow postpone . . . "the liquidation of the survivals of serfdom. . . ."
>
> . . . Up to 1917 the British habitually referred to a "military party" at St. Petersburg . . . that was supposed to have pushed the tsars, often against their better judgment and will into dangerous Asiatic adventures. Prince A. M. Gorchakov and his successor, N. K. Giers, found it convenient to blame the military for Russia's every embarrassing

action, for every unfulfilled obligation, every broken promise. However, in fact, the military were tightly controlled from St. Petersburg, all their moves being decided on at the highest governmental level. . . .

> The large-scale advance of 1864 was undertaken on the initiative of [War Minister] Miliutin and his generals and carried out in spite of the objections of Gorchakov and the diplomats. . . . The pressure exercised by the military was perhaps the decisive factor in Russia's conquest of Turkestan and Transcaspia. The generals, frustrated by the Crimean fiasco, were impatient and angry. More than any other group in the Empire they were imbued with a nationalist-imperialist ideology of the Panslavist type . . . and clamored for expansion. It meant everything to them: quick promotion, decorations, fabulous loot, unlimited opportunities for enrichment through dishonest management of army funds, excitement and adventure.[17]

Conclusion

Neither tsarist nor Soviet explanations of Central Asian expansion are wholly convincing, though each contains part of the truth. The advances, though initiated by government decision, greatly exceeded official intentions and plans. The security arguments of tsarist officials and generals seem partly justified and partly spurious, but Russian leaders believed that Russia would be strengthened if India were put under threat. Gorchakov's arguments about the need to protect Russian trade, chance, and a great power's tendency to expand to natural limits likewise appear sincere. Soviet historians, correctly noting Russia's growing economic interests in Central Asia, have exaggerated their importance, the influence of mercantile interests, and ostensible British threats. Tsarist Russia expanded into Central Asia for many reasons, but especially to win prestige and glory for its army and regime. ■

---

[16] N. A. Khalfin, *Prisoedinenie Srednei Azii k Rossii* (Moscow, 1965), pp. 137–45.

[17] F. Kazemzadeh, "Russia and the Middle East," in *Russian Foreign Policy*, ed. Ivo Lederer (New Haven, 1962), pp. 493–97.

Suggested Additional Reading

BOOKS

BECKER, S. *Russia's Protectorates in Central Asia . . .* (Cambridge, MA, 1968).

CURZON, G. *Russia in Central Asia in 1889* (New York, 1967). (Reprint.)

ENCAUSSE, H. C. *Islam and the Russian Empire: Reform and Revolution in Central Asia* (Berkeley, 1988).

FULLER, W. C. *Civil-Military Conflict in Imperial Russia, 1881–1914* (Princeton, 1985).

JELAVICH, C. *Tsarist Russia and Balkan Nationalism . . .* (Berkeley, 1958).

KALMYKOV, A. D. *Memoirs of a Russian Diplomat . . . 1893–1917* (New Haven, 1971).

KAZEMZADEH, F. *Russia and Britain in Persia, 1864–1914* (New Haven, 1968).

LENSEN, G. *Balance of Intrigue: International Rivalry in Korea and Manchuria, 1884–1899* (Tallahassee, FL, 1982).

MACKENZIE, D. *Imperial Dreams, Harsh Realities: Tsarist Russian Foreign Policy, 1815–1917* (Fort Worth, 1994).

———. *The Lion of Tashkent . . .* (Athens, GA, 1974).

———. *The Serbs and Russian Pan-Slavism, 1875–1878* (Ithaca, NY, 1967).

MALOZEMOFF, A. *Russian Far Eastern Policy, 1881–1904* (Berkeley, 1958).

MILLER, D. H. *The Alaska Treaty* (Kingston, Ontario, 1981).

MORGAN, G. *Anglo-Russian Rivalry in Central Asia, 1810–1895* (London, 1981).

OKAMOTO, S. *The Japanese Oligarchy and the Russo-Japanese War* (New York, 1970).

PETROVICH, M. *The Emergence of Russian Panslavism, 1856–1870* (New York, 1956).

PIERCE, R. *Russian Central Asia, 1867–1917 . . .* (Berkeley, 1960).

RAGSDALE, H., ed. *Imperial Russian Foreign Policy* (Cambridge and New York, 1993).

ROMANOV, B. *Russia in Manchuria, 1892–1906* (Ann Arbor, MI, 1952).

ROSEN, R. R. *Forty Years of Diplomacy,* 2 vols. (New York, 1922).

RYWKIN, M., ed. *Russian Colonial Expansion to 1917* (London, 1988).

STARR, RICHARD, ed. *Russia's American Colony* (Durham, NC, 1987).

SUMNER, B. H. *Russia and the Balkans, 1870–1880* (Oxford, 1937).

———. *Tsardom and Imperialism in the Far East and Middle East, 1880–1914* (London, 1940).

TAYLOR, A. J. *The Struggle for the Mastery of Europe, 1848–1918* (Oxford, 1954).

WALDER, D. *The Short Victorious War: The Russo-Japanese Conflict* (New York, 1974).

WARNER, D., and P. WARNER. *The Tide at Sunrise: A History of the Russo-Japanese War* (New York, 1974).

WITTE, S. I. *The Memoirs of Count Witte* (Garden City, NY, 1921).

ARTICLES

BAYLEN, J. O. "The Tsar and the British Press: Alexander III and the Pall Mall Gazette, 1888." *EEQ* 15, no. 4 (1981): 425–39.

ESTHUS, R. "Nicholas II and the Russo-Japanese War." *Rus. Rev.* 40, no. 4 (1981): 396–411.

HAMILTON, C. I. "Anglo-French Seapower and the Declaration of Paris." *Int. Hist. Rev.* 4, no. 2 (1982): 166–90.

LONG, J. "Franco-Russian Relations during the Russo-Japanese War." *SEER* 52 (1982): 213–33.

MACKENZIE, D. "Expansion in Central Asia: St. Petersburg vs. the Turkestan Generals, 1863–1866." *CSS* 3, no. 2 (1969): 286–311.

———. "Kaufman of Turkestan . . . , 1867–1881." *SR* 26, no. 2 (1967): 265–85.

———. "Russian Views of the Eastern Crisis, 1875–1878." *EEQ* 13, no. 1 (1979): 1–24.

———. "Turkestan's Significance to Russia, 1850–1917." *Rus. Rev.* 33, no. 2 (1974): 167–88.

MORRILL, D. L. "Nicholas II and the Call for the First Hague Conference." *JMH* 46, no. 2 (1974): 296–313.

WILLIAMS, B. "Approaches to the Second Afghan War . . ." *Int. Hist. Rev.* 2, no. 2 (1980): 216–38.

27

Opposition to Tsarism, 1855–1905

It would be a mistake to assume that the Russian people have always remained docile and obedient under a repressive regime. Although modern Russian history has witnessed political autocracy, serfdom, and repression, it has also seen massive peasant revolts, two great revolutions in 1905 and 1917, and successful popular resistance to an attempted conservative coup in 1991. Whenever autocratic government weakened or controls were relaxed, popular upheavals erupted, virtually unmatched in violence and destructiveness (except in 1991).

A vibrant new intellectual climate marked the first decade of Alexander II's reign, as numerous liberal and radical newspapers and periodicals appeared. "Everyone is talking, everyone is studying, including people who never before read anything in their lives," wrote the historian K. D. Kavelin. Contacts with Europe, severed by Nicholas I, were renewed; hopes for drastic change soared. In London in 1857 Herzen and Ogarev began publishing the fortnightly newspaper *Kolokol* (*The Bell*), which called upon the living to bury the dead past, oppose prejudice and

oppression, and work for a bright Russian future. *Kolokol* attacked evils of the old system and at first hailed government plans for emancipation. With a remarkable 2,500 subscribers, it was read in Russia by intellectuals, bureaucrats, and the tsar himself.

In the post-Crimean epoch, a diversified liberal and radical opposition developed against the autocracy. Liberals, aiming to reform and improve the system peacefully, competed with revolutionaries who sought to overthrow it. The liberals found it difficult to pursue their work without a parliament and in the face of governmental repression. Determined radicals, often using despotic methods and organizations, answered police repression with terrorism, secrecy, and ruthlessness. Before 1890 they looked mostly to the peasantry as their army of revolution; afterward Marxism grew rapidly, and its adherents wooed a rising urban working class. Soviet historians devoted most of their attention to Marxist Social Democrats and claimed that only a workers' party could have taken Russia to socialism. Recent Western scholars, often rejecting this thesis, have turned more to agrarian socialists and liberals. Why did Russian liberalism remain relatively weak? Why did radical movements develop so many splits? Was a Marxist triumph in Russia inevitable, as Soviet accounts suggested? Did the autocracy help determine the opposition's aims and means?

Liberalism and Radicalism, 1855–1870

The relaxation of censorship, increased contacts with Europe, and government overtures stimulated liberal gentry to advocate reform. The Nazimov Rescript (November 1857), which made public the tsar's intention to free the serfs, urged the Lithuanian gentry to draw up proposals on land reform; similar rescripts went to all of the Russian provinces. In Tver province the liberal gentry leaders A. M. Unkovskii and A. A. Golovachev composed a memorandum that criticized the bureaucracy and the official reform proposals and advocated full and immediate emancipation and an equal role for gentry committees in working it out. The Tver gentry committee's majority project (1858), incorporating most of this memorandum, urged landowners to favor emancipation with land, the abolition of *barshchina* and patrimonial rights, and an all-class, elected local administration. The minority proposal from the Kaluga Province committee also urged reform of army recruitment and the courts, accountability of bureaucrats to the courts, and public primary schooling. Strongly influenced by liberal European thought and Russian university lectures, such liberal views won considerable support among the middle gentry in the provinces.

Liberal gentry ideology evolved further in the provincial gentry assemblies of 1859–1860. The Tver assembly protested government violations of noble rights and affirmed a major public role for the gentry. When the authorities exiled Unkovskii for this, he wrote Alexander II:

> I never thought that the problem of peasant emancipation could be decided by the gentry or its representatives, but I have always been convinced that for the success of this transfor-

mation the conscious sincere cooperation of the gentry is necessary.[1]

These gentry assemblies, transforming lifeless corporate bodies into vehicles to express independent interests and crystallize public opinion, were unprecedented in Russia. Summoned to discuss national issues in elected bodies for the first time, the provincial gentry discussed economic, political, and legal reform. As official reform plans matured, however, the regime gradually restricted public initiative, and in November 1859 it forbade the gentry assemblies to debate the peasant question. Nonetheless, they continued to voice strong opposition to the extension of bureaucratic control and demanded full local self-government in return for the imminent loss of seignorial rights. The most vocal assemblies, those of Tver, Iaroslavl, Riazan, and Vladimir, advocated immediate obligatory redemption of land by the peasantry, drastic judicial reform, and all-class elective local self-government.

After the Emancipation, gentry assemblies pressed for political and administrative change and criticized the emancipation statutes. The Tver provincial gentry assembly resolved (February 1862):

> Gentry are deeply convinced that the government is not capable of realizing [further reforms]. The free institutions to which these reforms lead can come only from the people. . . . The gentry . . . indicate that the path onto which [the government] must venture for the salvation of itself and of society . . . is the gathering of representatives from the entire people without distinction as to class.

To dramatize gentry demands for local self-government, the Tver assembly went on to renounce its class privileges:

> The gentry, by virtue of class advantages, have so far escaped fulfillment of the most important public obligations. Sovereign, we consider it a grievous fault to live and enjoy the benefits

---

[1] Quoted in T. Emmons, *The Russian Landed Gentry* (Cambridge, 1968), p. 281.

of the public order at the expense of other classes. . . . We most loyally request Your Majesty to be allowed to take upon ourselves a part of state taxes and obligations.[2]

However, instead of meeting with the Tver leaders or heeding their recommendations, Alexander II ordered their arrest.

During 1861–1862 Russian publicists abroad, such as A. Koshelev and Herzen, fostered a semi-constitutional gentry movement for a consultative assembly, or *zemskii sobor*. Underground leaflets such as *Velikoruss* (June–October 1861), advocating a constitution, responsible ministers, jury trials, and freedom of religion and the press, declared: "The educated classes must take the handling of affairs from the incapable government into their own hands." The regime blocked gentry constitutionalism and punished its leaders while conceding to gentry wishes by facilitating the redemption of land and outlining liberal *zemstvo* and judicial reforms (see Chapter 24). This took the steam out of the gentry opposition, and a Moscow petition (1865) for a national consultative assembly was gentry constitutionalism's last gasp.

After 1865 gentry liberalism centered in the new *zemstva*. Leaders such as I. I. Petrunkevich of Chernigov aimed to convert them into "a school of self-government and by this means prepare the way for a constitutional state order." They aimed to expand *zemstvo* activities to the maximum and to take from the autocracy most of the control over rural affairs. In Chernigov Petrunkevich's program to aid the peasantry included free primary education, better material conditions, and justice under law.[3] Such liberals as Petrunkevich sought a society in which the individual would be central and self-governing, private property would be guaranteed, and law would be supreme. *Zemstvo* liberals strove to persuade the regime to accept their "small deeds" in raising popular cultural and material well-being, hoping that it

Nikolai G. Chernyshevskii (1828–1889), leading radical of the 1860s and author of *What Is to Be Done?*

would eventually grant a national *zemstvo* or even a constitution.

Meanwhile young intellectuals, led by N. G. Chernyshevskii and N. A. Dobroliubov, determined to remake the world through reason, turned enthusiastically to radicalism. Some of them were priests' sons who were estranged from existing values and institutions and convinced that partial reforms were useless. These radicals gathered around a journal, *The Contemporary*. Soviet scholars regarded Chernyshevskii, a leading contributor, as the chief precursor of Bolshevism and praised his materialism and his scorn for liberalism. Chernyshevskii dreamed of changing history's course by building a perpetual motion machine to abolish poverty. He and Dobroliubov stressed the intellectual's duty to awaken, educate, and lead the toiling masses. Viewing the *mir* (peasant commune) as the basis for decentralized

---

[2] Emmons, *Russian Landed Gentry,* pp. 341–43.
[3] C. Timberlake, "Ivan Il'ich Petrunkevich . . . ," in *Essays on Russian Liberalism* (Columbia, MO, 1972), p. 18ff.

agrarian socialism, Chernyshevskii affirmed that Russia, unlike Europe, could avoid capitalism and move directly to socialism. In *What Is to Be Done?*, composed in prison (1863), he described a socialist utopia achieved by relentless, practical revolutionaries who would "impose their character on the pattern of events and hurry their course." Now few, they would multiply rapidly, and "in a few years . . . people will call unto them for rescue, and what they say will be performed by all." Chernyshevskii's "toiler's theory" asserted that labor was entitled to all that it produced, but he derived his socialism more from Fourier than from Marx. Twenty years in Siberian exile made him a revolutionary martyr.

Dmitri Pisarev (1840–1868) reflected the uncompromising radicalism of the intelligentsia "sons" of the 1860s who attacked the values and beliefs of the "fathers" of the 1840s. "Here is the ultimatum of our camp: what can be smashed should be smashed; what will stand the blow is good; . . . at any rate hit out left and right."[4] This thrilled rebellious adolescents fighting the establishment. The writer Ivan Turgenev dubbed their ideology nihilism, and Bazarov, the hero of his novel *Fathers and Sons*, was Pisarev thinly disguised. A convinced Westernizer, Pisarev believed that an educated elite with modern science and European technology would uplift the masses and destroy autocracy.

During the early 1860s small groups of intelligentsia discussed ways to spread propaganda and achieve revolution. N. Shelgunov's dramatic leaflet *To the Younger Generation* (1861) urged the educated youth to reject Western parliamentary models and rely upon the *mir*. "We trust in our own fresh forces. We believe that we are called upon . . . to utter our [own] words and not follow in the wake of Europe." Another leaflet, *Young Russia* (1862), by Peter Zaichnevskii, a Moscow University student, proposed a republic and local assemblies based on the peasant commune: "Russia is entering the revolutionary period of its existence. The interests of the masses are irreconcilable with those of the imperial party, landowners, officials, and tsar. Their plundering of the people can only be stopped by a bloody, implacable revolution." The police speedily dissolved such radical groups.

In the mid-1860s, a small group of Moscow intelligentsia led by Nicholas Ishutin, a follower of Chernyshevskii, plotted direct, violent action. A secret band of terrorists known as Hell was to destroy autocracy. In April 1866 a student, Dmitri V. Karakozov, Ishutin's cousin, shot at the tsar. He missed (and apologized to Alexander II before being executed!), and the Ishutin circle was broken up.

In the ensuing reaction Russian exiles developed conspiratorial ideas. In 1869 Sergei Nechaev, a Moscow University student in Geneva, Switzerland, and the romantic revolutionary Mikhail Bakunin composed *Catechism of a Revolutionary*, which stressed that revolutionaries must be professional, dedicated, and disciplined:

> The revolutionary is a doomed man. He has no interests, no affairs, no feelings, no attachments of his own. . . . Everything in him is wholly absorbed by one sole, exclusive interest . . . revolution. He must train himself to stand torture and be ready to die. . . . The laws, the conventions, the moral code of civilized society have no meaning for him. . . . To him whatever promotes the triumph of the revolution is moral, whatever hinders it is criminal.[5]

Later Lenin, praising the *Catechism* highly, patterned his Bolshevik party upon it. Nechaev returned briefly to Russia in 1870 and set up a small organization, "The People's Reckoning" (*Narodnaia Rasprava*), which murdered a member for planning to betray it to the authorities.[6]

Revolutionary Populism

In the 1870s a broader movement of revolutionary intelligentsia heeded Herzen's appeal: "Go to the

---

[4] Aurahm Yarmolinsky, *A Century of Russian Radicalism*, p. 120.

[5] A. Yarmolinsky, *Road to Revolution* (London, 1957), p. 156.
[6] Fedor Dostoevsky based his novel *The Possessed* on this incident and the character Peter Verkovenskii on Nechaev.

SOVFOTO

Alexander I. Herzen (1812–1870), founder of
Russian socialism and publisher of *The Bell*
(*Kolokol*), 1858–1867.

people." Populism (*narodnichestvo*) combined
idealistic faith in the peasantry with determination
to overthrow the old social and political order by
force. Lacking central organization or a cohesive
ideology, populism advocated a peasant socialism
derived largely from Herzen. The Populists
regarded European large-scale factory industry as
degrading and dehumanizing, denied that an
industrial revolution must precede socioeconomic
progress, and believed that only farmers led the
good, natural life. Using intelligence and free will,
Russians could avoid European errors. Like
Rousseau, the Populists believed that bad institutions had corrupted men and that the state had
fostered inequality, injustice, and oppression.
Popular revolution, not parliaments, would produce a decentralized socialist order. The Populists
idealized the people (*narod*), especially the peas-

antry, as a mystical, irresistible, and virtuous force
whose traditional institutions—the *mir* and the
primitive producers' cooperative (*artel*), with their
collective landholding and quasi self-government
—would become socialist once the old order was
destroyed. Convinced that peasants in the *mir*
were practicing rudimentary socialism, the Populists disregarded clear signs of its disintegration
before an advancing money economy. They
emphasized ethical and humanitarian values and
faith in collective institutions, but they disagreed
about revolutionary organization, the intelligentsia's relationship to the people, and how and
when to achieve revolution. In the early 1870s the
émigrés Bakunin and P. L. Lavrov had small fol-
lowings of socialist youth; later Peter N. Tkachev's
views tended to prevail.

Mikhail Bakunin, a founder of anarchism with
long experience in tsarist prisons, urged an immediate, spontaneous mass uprising (*bunt*) by the
peasantry. Regarding much of the intelligentsia
as a privileged elite that despised the people,
Bakunin appealed, not to reason or science, but to
emotion, feeling, and mass instincts: "The Russian
peasantry are socialists by instinct and revolutionaries by nature. . . . We must not act as schoolmas-
ters for the people; we must lead them to revolt."
The existing state must be totally destroyed, and a
free federation of peasant communes should
replace it. A romantic apostle of freedom, Bakunin
opposed "the authoritarian communism of Marx
and the entire German school." He helped inspire
the "going to the people" movement of 1874, and
his influence grew during the 1870s, but no true
Bakuninist organization was ever established in
Russia. When the anticipated popular uprising
failed to break out, Bakunin's following dwindled.[7]

P. L. Lavrov's more moderate, cautious
approach grew popular. Lavrov, a mathematics
professor, achieved prominence with his legally
published *Historical Letters* (1870). For their education, intellectuals owed a debt to the people, and
they should repay it by preparing the people for

---

[7] F. Venturi, *Roots of Revolution* (New York, 1960), pp. 429–36.

revolution: A "critically thinking" elite should propagandize and agitate among the people. Abroad, in his journal, *Forward!,* Lavrov developed a complete Populist program. He borrowed Marx's tenets of the increasing misery of the masses and the worldwide socialist revolution but was uncertain whether revolution in Russia would precede or follow full capitalist development. He emphasized careful preparation of a peasant revolution by the intelligentsia (Bakuninists derisively dubbed his followers "the preparationists"). Dedicated intellectual revolutionaries were to explain socialism to the masses and recruit members from their ranks. (Lavrov worked it all out mathematically!) Local uprisings, directed by a revolutionary organization, would fuse in a nationwide revolution. Afterward a strong central government would be needed temporarily, but Lavrov repudiated dictatorship.

Peter N. Tkachev, the heir of nihilism and Ishutin, led a small Jacobin faction that rejected Lavrov's patient approach. Tkachev's views, expressed in the émigré newspaper *The Tocsin,* combined populism, Marxism, and Blanquism. Like Bakunin, Tkachev urged immediate action, but he believed that the masses must be led by a centralized, elite organization of revolutionaries, a disciplined party able to impose its will. His writing was filled with urgency: Unless revolution came soon, capitalism would destroy the *mir.* "This is why we cannot wait. This is why we insist that a revolution in Russia is indispensable . . . at the present time." A temporary dictatorship would follow armed overthrow of the old order, but it would wither away once the people had been educated in socialism. Tkachev appealed desperately for immediate revolution until he finally went insane. Later Lenin described his plan for seizing power as majestic.

Populism's practical achievements were few. Its main early organization, the Chaikovskii Circle (Lavrovist), was broken up by arrests. In 1873–1874, after a famine in the Volga region, more than 3,000 young urban intellectuals "went to the people" to spread socialist ideas and prepare revolution, but the peasants responded to this unorga-

nized, naive "children's crusade" by turning over many of the ragged agitators to the police; the rest returned home disillusioned. The failure of the "going to the people" episode discredited Lavrovism and dissipated some of the naive idealism of Russian Populists. In 1876 a broader Populist organization, the second Land and Liberty (the first was founded in 1861), demanded all land for the peasants and conducted the first mass revolutionary demonstration in Russia, at Kazan Cathedral in St. Petersburg. The police arrested its leaders, and two big trials were held. In 1879 Land and Liberty split, mainly over the issue of terrorism. Moderates founded their own organization and newspaper, *Black Repartition,* which repudiated terrorism and violence, but soon its leaders (George Plekhanov, Lev Deutsch, and Vera Zasulich) fled abroad. An extremist, preterrorist element created *Narodnaia Volia* (the People's Will), based on ideas of Nechaev and Tkachev. Its secret Executive Committee plotted to assassinate the tsar and other high officials in order to disorganize the regime and trigger popular revolution. In March 1881 the People's Will murdered Alexander II, but within two years the police had destroyed it and broken the revolutionary movement.

Before the 1860s few women played roles in revolutionary activity. Under Alexander II, female radicalism at first involved only acts of individual defiance and participation in radical circles. Revolutionary proclamations of the 1860s, often distributed by women, mostly failed to mention women's rights, except for Zaichnevskii's pamphlet, *Young Russia* (1862), which demanded complete women's emancipation, civil and political equality, and abolition of marriage and the family. Becoming the Bible for Russian feminists and revolutionaries, Chernyshevskii's novel *What Is to Be Done?* described the emancipation of Vera Pavlovna, the model of the new socialist woman, from family control and her escape from an arranged marriage. Love and sexual fulfillment, she concludes, are less important for women than economic independence. Only about 65 of some 2,000 Russian revolutionaries in the 1860s were women, but they were involved in radical circles such as Ishutin's and in the Dressmaking Shop of the Ivanova sisters in Chernyshevskii's novel, in which educated women and lower-class seamstresses lived, worked, and read radical authors together.

That women composed about one-eighth of revolutionary Populists in the 1870s, most of them well educated, reflected the growing women's movement. As revolutionaries, women could aspire to equality and rise to top leadership posts, proving themselves capable of things undreamed of by traditional society. About one-third of the Executive Committee of the People's Will were female, and they were subsequently incarcerated in the worst prisons alongside male terrorists. A prominent leader of the People's Will was Vera Figner (1852–1942), an aristocratic woman who studied medicine and worked among the peasantry as a Populist follower of Bakunin. In 1876 she joined Mark Natanson and others in Land and Liberty to organize a massive peasant uprising. Concluding that only violent revolution could overturn tsarism, she joined the Executive Committee and held the People's Will together for two years after Alexander II's assassination. Betrayed to the police, she served 22 years of solitary confinement in a fortress and then was exiled, finally returning to Soviet Russia after 1917. Another prominent revolutionary was Sofia Perovskaia (1853–1881), daughter of the St. Petersburg governor-general. Revolutionaries admired her for her simplicity, love of common people, stoicism, coolness, and courage. During the "going to the people" movement, she agitated among St. Petersburg workers and was prominent in the Chaikovskii Circle. As a leader of the Executive Committee, Perovskaia prepared Alexander II's assassination, placed the bomb throwers, and gave the signal. Apprehended with her lover, terrorist Andrei Zheliabov, she confessed freely and was the first female Russian political prisoner to be hanged (1881).

Women played a vital and growing role in the Russian revolutionary movement, both in its Populist phase and later in the Marxist movement.

Setting an example of dedication to violent struggle, they created precedents for the numerous women who participated in the revolutions of 1905 and 1917. Wrote Lenin in 1918: "From the experience of all liberation movements, it can be noted that the success of revolution can be measured by the extent of the involvement of women in it."[8]

The Development of Marxism

By 1881 the more naive, idealistic elements of the intelligentsia had been eliminated or discredited. The Populist movement, after the failure of "going to the people" and faced with police persecution following the tsar's assassination, was in disarray. Urban-bred revolutionaries, still idealizing the peasantry, had not bridged the gulf in education, attitudes, and lifestyles that separated them from the rural masses. Economic conditions were changing rapidly, and an industrial working class with more revolutionary potential was emerging. Alexander III's stifling autocracy, allied with rising business interests, heightened the revolutionaries' despair and isolation. Radical youths of the 1880s, dismayed by Populist defeats and illusions, searched for a new, comprehensive theory to explain disturbing new economic facts. Some found their answer in Marxism, which began to attract intellectuals and link them with the industrial working class.

Karl Marx (1818–1883), whose forebears included Jewish rabbis, and Friedrich Engels (1820–1895), son of a wealthy German manufacturer, derived their cohesive theory of "scientific socialism" from many sources, ingeniously weaving ideas of others into a system to explain the "laws of history." Their complex and sometimes contradictory theory reflected European ideas of progress and the perfectibility of humanity. Marx, the philosopher, and Engels, the publicist, combined in a unique intellectual partnership. Marx owed much to the system of dialectical idealism of

---

[8] V. I. Lenin, *Polnoe Sobranie Sochinenii,* 5th ed. (Moscow, 1960), vol. 36, p. 186.

Karl Marx (1818–1883), founder of "scientific socialism."

SOVFOTO

the outstanding German philosopher G. W. F. Hegel, accepting his method of reasoning (dialectic) and his belief that the conflict of opposites and the resulting synthesis produce progress, unfolding in stages and culminating in perfection. However, Marx rejected Hegel's belief that ideas create reality and responded negatively to his conservative political and social views. Marx adopted Ludwig Feuerbach's atheism and materialism: How people earn their daily bread determines their actions and outlook ("Man is what he eats"). Antagonistic social classes (for example, bourgeoisie versus proletariat), affirmed Marx, contend over the means of production (land, factories, and tools). Economic elements (means of production and worker-owner relationships), he argued, make up the substructure of society and basically determine its superstructure (government, law, religion, ideas). A person's economic and social status largely determines what he or she does, writes,

and thinks. Nonetheless, Marx retained a strong belief in human dignity and the goal of freedom.

Applying their philosophy to history (historical materialism), Marx and Engels shared Hegel's view of human evolution by inexorable laws through a series of stages toward freedom. Each successive historical stage—primitive communism, slavery, feudalism, capitalism, and socialism—reflects a more mature form of production. Passage from one stage to the next results inevitably from conflict between a class (for example, the bourgeoisie) controlling the means of production and the one it exploits (for example, the proletariat). As one mode of production yields to a more advanced one and the exploited class achieves greater freedom, a new stage develops, usually by revolution.

Capitalism, explained Marx, is that historical stage in western Europe during which the bourgeoisie (especially factory owners) exploits the proletariat. At first, with its numerous small, competing firms, capitalism is revolutionary and dynamic, the most productive system yet devised. However, workers, the creators of value, receive back in wages only a fraction of the value their labor creates; capitalists pocket the rest ("surplus value") as profit. As weaker firms succumb, competitive capitalism will evolve into its opposite—monopoly. The industrial work force will absorb much of the peasantry and the lesser bourgeoisie, until the proletariat becomes the vast majority of the population. As overproduction and unemployment grow, so too will worker dissatisfaction and class consciousness. Fully developed capitalism will produce mountains of goods that miserably paid workers cannot afford to buy.

Revolutions, Marx predicted, would occur first in advanced capitalist countries. They would be led by communists—class-conscious workers and intellectuals—defined as "the most advanced and resolute section of the working-class parties of every country . . . which pushes forward all others." In 1848 Marx believed that such revolutions would generally be violent because the ruling capitalists and feudal lords would not yield their wealth and power voluntarily, but that they would be democratic because the vast oppressed majority would dispossess a tiny minority of exploiters. In 1872 Marx declared that there were countries, such as the United States, England, and perhaps Holland, where the workers might achieve their goals peacefully. These differing views on the necessity of revolution would be reflected later in a split between European democratic socialists and Russian Bolsheviks.

Following the demise of capitalism, a transitional era of unspecified length—the dictatorship of the proletariat (which Marx never defined precisely)—would prevail. Workers the world over would unite to cast off their chains and establish socialism everywhere. A workers' state would run the government and the economy, distribute goods fairly to the people, and educate them in socialist values. Coercing only former exploiters, it would be more democratic than "bourgeois democracy" because it would represent the workers, the vast majority. Once it had achieved its purposes, the workers' state, or at least its coercive aspects, would wither away. Private property, class struggle, and exploitation would disappear, yielding to a perfect socialist order of abundance and freedom called *communism.* Marx described this system in 1875:

> After the subordination of the individual to the division of labor, and therewith also the antithesis between mental and physical labor has vanished . . . ; after the productive forces have also increased with the all-round development of the individual, and all the springs of cooperative wealth flow more abundantly— only then can the narrow horizon of bourgeois right be crossed in its entirety and society inscribe on its banner: From each according to his ability, to each according to his needs![9]

Here, in describing the future socialist society, Marx becomes a pure Utopian. His predictions were predicated on the transformation of human nature, which, as events in socialist countries would confirm, was totally unrealistic.

Did Marxian theory, conceived for western Europe, with its more liberal, humanitarian traditions, apply to backward, autocratic Russia? Marx learned Russian, read Chernyshevskii, and corresponded with Russian socialists, but his and Engels's views on Russia were uncertain and inconsistent. Thus Marx suggested in 1877 that Russia might escape capitalism and move directly from feudalism to socialism *if* capitalist elements within the *mir* were eliminated and *if* proletarian revolutions occurred soon in western Europe. In 1881, anxious to see tsarism overthrown, Marx replied to Vera Zasulich, a leading Russian Populist and later Marxist, that his research on the *mir* had "convinced him that this community is the mainspring of Russia's social regeneration," provided it could "eliminate the deleterious influences which assail it from every quarter."[10] After Marx's death, however, Engels wrote sadly that these conditions had not been fulfilled, so that Russia was doomed to undergo capitalism after all. On Russia, Marx and Engels seemed to be of two minds.

In the 1870s Marxist ideas began to circulate in Russia. The abstruse and technical *Das Kapital* (1867, 1885, 1894) was published openly, as were other nonpolitical Marxist works. In 1875 the first significant workers' organization in Russia, the South Russian Workers Alliance, was founded in Odessa, but soon its leaders were arrested. Three years later the Northern Alliance of Russian Workers, with more than 200 active members, arose in St. Petersburg, but until the mid-1880s Russia had few Marxists and no Marxist movement.

George Plekhanov (1856–1918), though of noble origin, "reared a whole generation of Russian Marxists," Lenin said. Earlier Plekhanov had sought to create a scientific populism, but even then he had stressed the industrial workers' revolutionary potential. In 1879 he became editor of *Black Repartition,* the moderate Populist newspaper, but discouraged by its failure and the poor

---

[9] Quoted in R. Tucker, *The Marx-Engels Reader,* 2d ed. (New York, 1978), p. 531. For more on Marxism, see R. N. Carew-Hunt, *The Theory and Practice of Communism* (New York, 1958) and *Marxism: Past and Present* (New York, 1954).

[10] Tucker, *Marx-Engels Reader,* p. 675.

results of agitation among the peasantry, in 1880 he fled into Swiss exile. Believing that in Russia the commune was being undermined and industry was developing, Plekhanov in Geneva converted to Marxism. He was attracted by its orderliness and by Marx's claim to have discovered the laws of historical development. In Switzerland he, Paul Akselrod, and Vera Zasulich set up an independent Marxist group, the Liberation of Labor (1883), which for the next two decades acted as an embryo Russian Social Democratic party. Its members translated Marxist works and sent pamphlets into Russia, but at first Russians remained apathetic. In *Our Differences* (1885) Plekhanov denounced the People's Will for urging terrorism and minority insurrection. Industry was growing in Russia: "We must recognize that in this sphere the present as much as the [near] future belongs to capitalism in our country." Plekhanov affirmed that Russia, like western Europe, must pass through capitalism to reach socialism; only the proletariat, sparked by the intelligentsia, could organize a true socialist revolution. He balanced between voluntarist and determinist aspects of Marxism: The proletariat needed knowledge and organization, but the laws of history would surely bring defeat to the bourgeoisie. "The Social Democrats," he exulted, "are swimming along the current of history."

The Russian intelligentsia viewed Marxism and populism as separate, competing movements. In 1885 D. Blagoev, a Bulgarian student, established the first Marxist study group in Russia; soon these groups became popular among university students and workers. The famine of 1891, revealing peasant helplessness, stimulated Marxism's growth as younger intellectuals such as V. I. Ulianov, later known as Lenin, rejected populism and turned to the workers. In St. Petersburg a Central Workers Circle linked worker groups and Marxist intellectuals, and in 1893 Ulianov joined one of them, beginning an illustrious revolutionary career. Marxist literature then mostly stressed determinism, affirming incorrectly that capitalist development was undermining the *mir* and proving populism wrong. Arkadi Kremer's pamphlet *On*

Agitation (1894), however, warned that Marxists must not just study and theorize but must learn workers' grievances and exploit them. His associate Julius Martov met Ulianov and merged his Vilna group with those in St. Petersburg. In 1895 major strikes in the textile industry revealed the workers' revolutionary energy and dispelled naive faith in Marxist study circles, but many Marxist leaders, including Ulianov and Martov, were arrested and exiled to Siberia.

Some Russian Marxists, influenced by European currents, turned away from revolution. Eduard Bernstein, a German Social Democrat, was attacking some of Marx's main premises, claiming that socialism could be reached by gradual, nonviolent, democratic means. In Russia Peter Struve and Sergei Bulgakov argued that capitalism would evolve gradually into socialism. The movement of Economism developed, stressing "spontaneous" development and peaceful agitation to encourage workers to demand economic benefits from employers. Many Russian workers seemed more interested in shorter hours and higher pay than in revolution. Meanwhile, an attempt by Russian Marxist "politicals," who advocated active struggle against the regime, to form a national Social Democratic party failed when the leaders of their secret Minsk Congress of 1898 were arrested.

The youthful Lenin (Ulianov) helped reinvigorate Russian Marxism and turn it back toward revolution. He too was of noble background (his Soviet biographers glossed this over) because his father as school inspector in Simbirsk earned hereditary nobility. Vladimir Ilich was raised in a conservative, disciplined, religious household. In 1887 his elder brother, Alexander, whom Vladimir greatly admired, was executed for trying to assassinate Alexander III. Vladimir Ilich was greatly influenced by his brother's death and by his favorite author, Chernyshevskii. Chernyshevskii's *What Is to Be Done?* convinced him that "strong personalities" would impose their pattern on history. Expelled from Kazan University after a student demonstration, Ulianov later passed the bar examination in St. Petersburg and practiced law briefly in Samara. Though he admired the

Library of Congress

Vladimir Ilich Lenin (1870–1924).

dedication of the Narodovoltsy (People's Will), he became a Marxist (1892). He attacked the Populists, affirming in *Who Are the Friends of the People?* (1894) that Russia was well advanced along the path to capitalist development. In his major work written in Siberian exile, *The Development of Capitalism in Russia* (1899), he argued that differentiation of the peasantry into a rural proletariat and bourgeoisie proved that the commune was disintegrating irrevocably.

After his exile Lenin and Plekhanov became Orthodox Marxism's chief spokesmen against revisionism. Restating Plekhanov, Lenin affirmed that revolution was absolutely essential in Russia and urged Social Democrats to lead an organized, class-conscious working class. Attacking the view of the Economists, a faction of Russian Marxism, that workers could develop cohesion spontaneously while improving their economic status, he argued that by itself the working class could develop only trade unionism. Marxists must provide conscious leadership, not trail behind the

masses. In 1900 Lenin and Martov joined older émigrés of the Liberation of Labor (Plekhanov, Akselrod, and Zasulich) to found the newspaper *Iskra* (*The Spark*) in Stuttgart, Germany, to combat revisionism and consolidate Marxist ideology and organization. In its first issue Lenin, using his pseudonym for the first time, stressed the need for active political work:

> The task of Social Democracy is to instill social democratic ideas and political consciousness into the mass of the proletariat and to organize a revolutionary party unbreakably tied to the spontaneous labor movement. . . . We must train people who will dedicate to the revolution not a free evening but the whole of their lives.

In *What Is to Be Done?* (1902), a sizable pamphlet containing his main ideas on party organization, Lenin stressed the need for a small, centralized body of professional revolutionaries from the intelligentsia to serve as the vanguard of the working class in its struggle to achieve socialism. "Give us an organization of revolutionists, and we will overturn the whole of Russia."

Iskra's leaders moved to reorganize the Russian Social Democratic party. In July 1903 a Second Congress (the abortive Minsk meeting of 1898 was designated the first) convened in Brussels, Belgium. Because *Iskra* controlled 33 of the 43 delegates, its program was mostly approved. After the Belgian authorities compelled the congress to move to London, a struggle between Lenin and Martov over party membership and organization developed within the *Iskra* group. Arguing for an elite party, Lenin insisted that membership be limited to active participants in a party organization. Martov advocated a broad, mass party: "The more widely the title of party member is extended, the better." That, Lenin objected, would inundate the party with opportunists. Plekhanov, the party's elder statesman, sided with Lenin, but at first Martov's more democratic formula prevailed, 28 to 22. After the congress rejected the Jewish Bund's demand for autonomy, however, the Bundists walked out; they were soon joined by the defeated Economists. These walkouts, engineered by Lenin, who worked frantically to secure victory, gave his "hard" faction a majority of two over Martov's "softs." Lenin promptly dubbed his group Bolsheviks (majority men) and obtained a psychological edge over Martov's faction, which meekly accepted the name Mensheviks (minority men). Lenin sought to exploit his slim majority to impose his views on membership and organization and make the party a centralized organization of professional revolutionaries. Instead, the Second Congress split the Social Democrats (SDs) irreconcilably. Soon after the congress the Mensheviks took over *Iskra* and won a majority on the central committee as well. Less disciplined and united than the Bolsheviks, the Mensheviks believed that the first revolution in Russia must be bourgeois and must establish a democratic republic. The Mensheviks' differences with the Bolsheviks, at first over seemingly minor matters of party organization, steadily widened. The Mensheviks favored a broad, democratic, and genuine workers' party, not a narrow conspiratorial elite mainly of intellectuals. In 1905 Paul Akselrod, a leading Menshevik, urged Russian workers to form their own trade unions and party under worker leadership, to draft their own program rather than accept dictation from professional intellectual revolutionaries like Lenin. As Bolsheviks and Mensheviks feuded and his former *Iskra* colleagues accused Lenin of employing dictatorial methods and creating a state of siege in the SD party, young Leon Trotskii (Lev Bronstein), a brilliant polemicist and orator, stood between the factions and sought to mediate their differences.

From Populism to the Socialist Revolutionaries (SRs)

Populism recovered slowly from the destruction of the People's Will. Populist ideologists of the 1880s and early 1890s denounced capitalism and argued desperately that it must never come to Russia. However, younger Populists calling themselves Socialist Revolutionaries (SRs) agitated among new factory workers of peasant origin. In the capitals the Marxists outdid them, but in provincial centers the SRs won much support. Some Populist exiles returned, including Catherine Breshko-Breshkovskaia, who won converts around the country and became known as "the grandmother of the revolution."

In the late 1890s three centers of SR activity emerged. In 1896 the Union of Socialist Revolutionaries was founded in Saratov and won followers in the Moscow and Volga regions. Declared its Lavrist program, *Our Tasks* (1898): "Propaganda, agitation and organization . . . , such are the tasks of preparatory work at present." The program emphasized winning political freedom, and deferred revolution to an indefinite future. A southern element from Voronezh and Ukraine advocated a constitution, agitation among the peasantry, strikes by agricultural workers, and boycotts against landlords. A third group, formed in Minsk by Breshko-Breshkovskaia and A. Gershuni, a young Jewish scientist, featured terror as its chief weapon against autocracy. In 1898 the police frustrated an attempt to establish an SR party in Russia, but in 1900 an underground organization and newspaper, *Revolutionary Russia*, were set up in Kharkov. Two years later elements from the various SR groups met in Berlin to establish the Socialist Revolutionary party.

Its chief ideologist was Victor Chernov (1876–1952), an SR organizer in Tambov province, who accepted some Marxist doctrines and recognized capitalist development in Russia. Urging the SRs to agitate in factories and include workers in "the people," Chernov admitted that the proletariat would lead the revolution against capitalism but affirmed that the peasantry would be "the fundamental army." In the new society, socialized enterprise in the towns would complement reorganized socialist communes. Chernov, like the Populists but unlike the Marxists, stressed free will, passion, and creativity, but he stood ready to collaborate with Marxists and urban workers to overturn capitalism.

Unlike the Social Democrats, the dynamic, rapidly growing SR party never had a large or well-disciplined formal membership. Forming many local groups around various leaders, the SRs propagandized vigorously among peasants and factory workers. Unlike their Populist forebears, the SRs enjoyed considerable support from workers and white-collar people in provincial towns, though they remained peasant-oriented. The SRs never produced a truly outstanding leader, and they lacked the organizational cohesion to link their massive peasant following with a town-bred intellectual leadership. Within the party, but actually independent of it, was the small, highly disciplined Combat Detachment, led by the terrorists A. Gershuni and Evno Azev. Between 1902 and 1905 it assassinated two interior ministers, the Moscow governor-general, and other officials. Thus the tsarist police considered the SRs more dangerous than the more academic, theoretical SDs.

Liberalism Organizes

Nineteenth-century Russian liberalism, despite considerable achievements through the *zemstva*, never attained cohesion, but on the eve of the 1905 Revolution, reinforced with former revolutionaries, it broadened into a vigorous, effective national movement seeking a national *zemstvo* union, constitutional reform, and civil liberties.

Until 1898 the *zemstva* remained the main arena of the liberals, and gradualism remained their chief approach. *Zemstvo* leaders, anxious to promote public welfare, felt keenly the lack of a national organization, but their activities continued to expand despite official restrictions. By 1900 the *zemstva* employed more than 70,000 agronomists, doctors, and teachers. This professional personnel, known as the "Third Element," helped democratize the *zemstva* until both their gentry and professional members supported constitutional reform and civil rights. The Slavophile liberals' chief spokesman, the conscientious D. N. Shipov (1851–1920), chairman of the Moscow provincial *zemstvo* board, favored the joint administration of Russia by tsar and people through a national consultative assembly and hoped that the

tsar would heed his appeals. Petrunkevich, active in the Chernigov and Tver provincial *zemstva* since 1868, led the *zemstvo* constitutionalists. The Slavophile liberals still awaited governmental concessions, and Shipov, despite official rebuffs, sought to extend the *zemstva* to additional provinces and create a national *zemstvo* union. The regime's refusal to permit that, its repressive actions of 1899–1900, and the Slavophile liberals' submissiveness strengthened the constitutionalists.

Defectors from revolutionary socialism reinforced liberalism among the professional intelligentsia. During the 1890s the Legal Populists, led by N. K. Mikhailovskii, stressing ethical principles and the individual, abandoned revolutionary views to cooperate with the liberals. The Legal Marxists, headed by N. Berdiaev and Peter Struve, likewise rejected revolution. Struve, author of the Marxist manifesto of 1898 at Minsk, broke with the SDs to advocate liberal gradualism. The Economists S. Prokopovich and his wife, E. D. Kuskova, like the English Webbs, advocated "pure trade unionism" to satisfy the workers' economic needs. Kuskova's *Credo* (1899), depicting orthodox Marxists as narrow sectarians, urged Economists to support the liberals.

At the turn of the 20th century the Russian liberals acquired a press and a more cohesive political program. The liberal gentry set up *Beseda*, a private discussion group that included Slavophiles and constitutionalists. After 1896 *zemstvo* liberals of all shadings met irregularly to agitate for a national *zemstvo* union, and in May 1902 the first congress of *zemstvo* officials, 52 leaders from 25 provinces, met without official authorization at Shipov's home. This semilegal action set a pattern for the liberals in 1905. The founding in Stuttgart in 1902 of the periodical *Osvobozhdenie* (*Liberation*), edited by Struve and financed by a Moscow landowner, established a militant liberal press organ. Adopting a radical constitutionalist line, it became almost as influential as Herzen's *Bell*. In 1903 the Union of Liberation was formed in Switzerland. Designed to unite the entire non-Marxist intelligentsia, its membership comprised many outstanding theorists and activists. In January 1904 its leaders met in private apartments in St. Petersburg and pledged to work to abolish autocracy, establish constitutional monarchy, and achieve universal, secret, and direct suffrage in equal constituencies—the "four-tailed" suffrage—for a national parliament. The Union's national council met regularly until the 1905 Revolution.

Before 1905 the opposition movements were developing greater cohesion and clearer programs. The liberals, led by such pro-Western intellectuals as P. N. Miliukov, were supported by much of the growing professional middle class and some of the provincial *zemstvo* gentry. The socialists generally agreed on the need to overthrow the tsarist autocracy and establish a less rigidly centralized popular government. They differed sharply, however, over timing and means, over how their movement or party should be organized, and over which elements should constitute and lead it. The SRs, with an urban intellectual leadership and a mainly peasant rank and file, opposed a Marxist workers' party, the SDs, which was split among the Bolsheviks, the Mensheviks, and smaller factions.

Reactionary Tsarism, 1881–1904

The assassination of Alexander II by a terrorist from the People's Will organization brought his son, Alexander III (ruled 1881–1894) to the Russian throne, inaugurating 25 years of reaction and political stagnation. Would the autocracy survive this sudden murder or provoke, as the revolutionaries hoped, confusion and a popular revolution? The new ruler, a powerful, unimaginative man of 36, although honest and straightforward, was conservative, nationalistic, and religious. After the death in 1865 of his elder brother, Nicholas, Alexander's previously limited education was broadened. He was instructed by the eminent historian S. M. Soloviev, but especially by a private tutor, the prominent jurist K. P. Pobedonostsev.

On the day of his death, Alexander II's ministers had been scheduled to meet with him to discuss the proposals of Interior Minister M. T. Loris-Melikov for a consultative assembly and how they were to be implemented. However, from

his accession, Alexander III relied primarily upon Pobedonostsev, procurator of the Holy Synod, who turned him away from the liberal principles of his father's last will. Pobedonostsev predicted disaster for Russia if even Loris-Melikov's very limited constitutional proposals were realized. Pobedonostsev's victory brought the removal or resignation of remaining liberal ministers, headed by War Minister D. A. Miliutin. As tutor to both Alexander III and his son, Nicholas II, Pobedonostsev and his ideology largely determined their outlook and policies.

Pobedonostsev elaborated the most complete, consistent theory of autocracy and status quo conservatism that Russia had known. As the "gray eminence" of moribund tsarism, he contributed much to the "dogma of autocracy," which helped block essential political change and provoked radical opposition. Basing his views on Uvarov's triad of Orthodoxy, Autocracy, and Nationalism (see Chapter 23), Pobedonostsev argued that men and women were by nature unequal, weak, and vicious. Russians, he believed, required strong leadership and a firm hand. A onetime Slavophile who emphasized the differences between Russia and the West, he felt that Western institutions were not limbs that could be grafted onto the Russian tree. Favoring the concentration of political power in the autocrat and in the central administration, he opposed local self-government, counting instead on traditional romantic bonds between tsar and people. To him constitutional government was anathema: "I hear everywhere the trite, accursed word 'constitution.' A Russian revolution . . . is preferable to a constitution. The former could be suppressed and order restored . . . ; the latter is poison to the entire organism."[11] Although a distinguished jurist, Pobedonostsev rejected the rule of law and civil liberties as restrictions on autocracy. Orthodoxy, he declared, was the only true faith, and only one religion should be tolerated in Russia. Rigid censorship by the Holy Synod must shield Russians

---

[11] Robert F. Byrnes, *Pobedonostsev. His Life and Thought* (Bloomington, IN, 1968), p. 155.

from Western liberal and radical ideas while the Orthodox church imbued them with correct ideas. Unity was indispensable—one tsar, one faith, one language—so national and religious minorities must be converted, assimilated, or expelled by ruthless Russification. Pobedonostsev's program was mainly negative: to preserve paternalistic noble and bureaucratic authority and a rigid status quo. To a remarkable extent he persuaded Alexander III and Nicholas II to adopt principles and policies that intensified revolutionary opposition to the autocracy.

For the first year of Alexander III's reign, the Slavophile Count N. P. Ignatiev, following a distinguished diplomatic career (he had negotiated the treaties of Beijing and San Stefano), was minister of the interior and the leading governmental figure. Although conservative, Ignatiev and his fellow Slavophiles opposed Pobedonostsev's full-blown authoritarianism. Instead, they proposed reviving the zemskii sobor (Assembly of the Lands) of old Muscovy as an institution. On the occasion of the tsar's coronation scheduled for May 1883, Ignatiev proposed that some 3,000 deputies be elected from traditional Russian classes—nobles, merchants, clergy, and some 1,000 peasants—to demonstrate the Russian people's unity and loyalty to the monarchy. However, Pobedonostsev opposed that idea as representing a form of constitutionalism by allowing elected deputies to discuss matters of state. Ignatiev was forced to resign in May 1882 by Pobedonostsev, his former sponsor.

The ensuing reactionary regime, centering in Pobedonostsev and Count Dmitrii A. Tolstoi as minister of education, emasculated the Great Reforms with bureaucratic counterreforms. The land captain law of 1889 abolished the justice of the peace courts except in Moscow and Odessa and transferred their functions to judges appointed by the Interior Minister. Land captains, usually hereditary noblemen, were to supervise peasant affairs and exercise administrative and judicial powers; they could rescind decisions of village assemblies and volost courts. They were to keep the peasantry under official control and

noble tutelage. In 1890 peasant representation in zemstvo assemblies was reduced, and the Interior Minister's authority over the zemstva was tightened. A law of June 1892 greatly reduced city electorates, so that in St. Petersburg only 7,152 persons could vote. Without actually abolishing local self-government, the central authorities aimed to curtail it and stifle local initiative. Nonetheless, zemstva and city councils continued to achieve much. They employed many youthful experts and professional people, who continued to press for political change.

Under Alexander III external peace and internal passivity hid a widening gap between the claims of autocracy and its performance. After the tsar's Moscow coronation the remnants of the People's Will were easily crushed, and full authority was given to Count Tolstoi. Alexander himself, intellectually limited and cautious, opposed any experimentation with traditional government. Often he simply issued orders without any previous consultation or discussion.

Regime leaders under Alexander III, notably Pobedonostsev and Dmitrii Tolstoi, were imbued with a type of historical pessimism, fearing loss of mastery over a world moving too fast for them. They sought by all means to postpone the disintegration of the old order. The poverty and emptiness of the official ideology stemmed partly from its lack of a real social basis. In this period tsarism sought to appear to be a government of the entire Russian people, standing above class and party, only to be left without solid support anywhere. The prevalent calm in public life failed to halt an erosion of the regime's moral and political authority that continued right to the 1905 Revolution and after. Russia had entered a crisis of authority with declining respect for established rules and for those who enforced them.[12]

Alexander III's sudden death by stroke in 1894 brought Nicholas II (ruled 1894–1917) to the throne amid hopes for liberal change. Though

---

[12] Hans Rogger, *Russia in the Age of Modernization and Revolution, 1881–1917* (London and New York, 1983), pp. 11–13.

more intelligent than his father, Nicholas appeared irresolute and was strongly influenced by reactionaries. As heir he had made a trip around the world, which gave him an abiding enthusiasm for Asia and Russia's "Asian mission." Shortly before his accession, he married Alexandra of Hesse ("Alix"), a deeply conservative and religious woman who dominated him and reinforced his piety and belief in autocracy. Nicholas remained devoted to his wife and family while becoming increasingly isolated from Russian reality. His chief interests, noted in his carefully kept diary, were trivial: hunting, yachting, tennis, and military reviews.

The accession of the youthful and personable Nicholas II encouraged liberals to expect relaxation of restrictions on the press and on political activity. However, in January 1895 at a reception for delegates of *zemstvo*, town, and noble assemblies, Nicholas dashed these hopes abruptly. He warned them to abandon "senseless dreams" about an increased role for *zemstva*. "I, devoting all my strength to the welfare of the people, will uphold the principle of autocracy as firmly and unflinchingly as my late unforgettable father."[13] Though he appeared weak and indecisive in contrast with his formidable father, Nicholas II actually revealed much firmness and obstinacy. When it was a question of protecting his power prerogatives or defending his prejudices, Nicholas could be as determined as his father. Even more poorly prepared than Alexander to bear the burdens of imperial rule, Nicholas had little knowledge of the world, men, or politics to assist him with the difficult decisions that only the tsar could make. His training proved adequate only for the ceremonial functions of a constitutional monarch. Dominated by Pobedonostsev and reactionary Prince V. P. Meshcherskii, Nicholas believed firmly that constitutions and parliaments were evil.

During the first decade of Nicholas's rule, the prestige of an autocrat who refused to listen to the knowledgeable was gravely damaged. Prior to 1905 Nicholas remained a conscientious and industrious ruler, spending many hours reading and annotating state papers, but most of the matters he dealt with were trivial, minor affairs that his subordinates should have handled. The result was a gradual near paralysis of initiative at the center. Soon in the salons of St. Petersburg spread the witticism: Russia does not need a constitution to limit the monarchy because it already has a very limited monarch. At first Nicholas displayed reasonable judgment in state affairs, retaining Count Witte and other capable men in office, but he treated his imperial ministers like servants. Even the independent-minded Witte in his presence often behaved like a subaltern, bowing and scraping obsequiously. By the turn of the century Nicholas was tending to heed and be influenced by irresponsible adventurers ready to lead the country to disaster. The initial decade of his reign was outwardly quiet and uneventful, while beneath the surface an opposition movement matured, based upon rising discontent and dismay with a paternalistic autocratic system.

Suggested Additional Reading

ASCHER, A. *Pavel Axelrod and the Development of Menshevism* (Cambridge, MA, 1972).

AVRICH, P. *Anarchist Portraits* (Princeton, 1988).

BALABANOFF, A. *My Life as a Rebel* (New York, 1938).

BARON, S. H. *Plekanov: The Father of Russian Marxism* (Stanford, 1963).

BERGMAN, J. *Vera Zasulich: A Biography* (Stanford, 1983).

BILLINGTON, J. *Mikhailovsky and Russian Populism* (New York, 1958).

BYRNES, R. F. *Pobedonostsev: His Life and Thought* (Bloomington, IN, 1969).

CARR, E. H. *Mikhail Bakunin* (New York, 1961).

CHERNYSHEVSKY, N. G. *What Is to Be Done?* (New York, 1961). (Novel.)

DAN, F. *The Origins of Bolshevism* (New York, 1970). (Translation.)

EMMONS, T. *The Russian Landed Gentry* (Cambridge, 1968).

---

[13] Hugh Seton-Watson, *The Russian Empire* (Oxford, 1967), p. 549.

ENGEL, B. A. *Mothers and Daughters: Women of the Intelligentsia of Nineteenth Century Russia* (Cambridge, 1983).

ENGEL, B. A., and C. ROSENTHAL, eds. *Five Sisters: Women against the Tsar* (Boston, 1987).

FIGNER, V. *Memoirs of a Revolutionist* (New York, 1927).

FISCHER, G. *Russian Liberalism* (Cambridge, MA, 1958).

GETZLER, J. *Martov* (New York, 1967).

GLEASON, A. *Young Russia: The Genesis of Russian Radicalism in the 1860s* (New York, 1980).

HAIMSON, L. *The Russian Marxists . . .* (Cambridge, MA, 1955).

HERZEN, A. I. *My Past and Thoughts,* 6 vols. (New York, 1924–1928). (Also reprints.)

JUDGE, E. H. *Plehve: Repression and Reform in Imperial Russia, 1902–1904* (Syracuse, NY, 1983).

KEEP, J. L. *The Rise of Social Democracy in Russia* (Oxford, 1963).

KROPOTKIN, P. *Memoirs of a Revolutionist* (New York, 1927). (Also reprints.)

LAMPERT, E. *Sons against Fathers . . .* (London, 1965).

LAVROV, P. L. *Historical Letters,* ed. J. Scanlan (Berkeley, 1967).

NAIMARK, N. *Terrorists and Social Democrats: The Russian Revolutionary Movement under Alexander III* (Cambridge, MA, 1983).

PAPERNO, IRINA. *Chernyshevsky and the Age of Realism* (Stanford, 1988).

PIPES, R., ed. *The Russian Intelligentsia* (New York, 1961).

POMPER, P. *The Russian Revolutionary Intelligentsia,* 2d ed. (Arlington Heights, IL, 1993).

———. *Sergei Nechaev* (New Brunswick, NJ, 1979).

PORTER, C. *Women in Revolutionary Russia* (Cambridge, 1987).

RANDALL, F. N. *N. G. Chernyshevskii* (New York, 1967).

SCHAPIRO, L. *Rationalism and Nationalism in Nineteenth Century Russian Thought* (New Haven, 1967).

SENN, A. E. *The Russian Revolutionary Movement of the 19th Century as Contemporary History* (Washington, 1993).

THADEN, E. C. *Conservative Nationalism in Nineteenth Century Russia* (Seattle, 1964).

TIMBERLAKE, C., ed. *Essays on Russian Liberalism* (Columbia, MO, 1972).

TREADGOLD, D. *Lenin and His Rivals, 1898–1906* (New York, 1955).

TURGENEV, I. *Fathers and Sons* (New York, Modern Library). (Novel.)

VENTURI, F. *Roots of Revolution . . .* (New York, 1960).

WILDMAN, A. K. *The Making of a Workers' Revolution* (Chicago, 1967).

WOLFE, B. *Three Who Made a Revolution* (New York, 1964).

WOOD, A. *The Origins of the Russian Revolution, 1861–1917,* 2d ed. (London and New York, 1993).

WORTMAN, R. *The Crisis of Russian Populism* (London, 1967).

YARMOLINSKY, A. *Road to Revolution* (London, 1957).

ZIMMERMAN, J. *Mid-Passage: Alexander Herzen and European Revolution, 1847–1852.* (Pittsburgh, 1989).

28

War, Revolution, and Reform, 1904–1914

The turbulent decade 1904–1914, ushered in by the disastrous Russo-Japanese War, witnessed a crucial race in Russia between reforms and revolution and alternating periods of radicalism and reaction. The major revolution that erupted in 1905 in the midst of the war with Japan brought masses of workers and peasants, under intelligentsia leadership, for the first time into a broad, popular movement against the autocracy. Although the revolution proved a partial failure and was succeeded by political reaction, the tsarist system was nonetheless altered significantly. A semiconstitutional monarchy with a national parliament sought, albeit hesitantly, to tackle Russia's perplexing problems. Important agrarian reform was undertaken, and industrialization continued. While the armed forces were being reorganized and modernized in the aftermath of defeat, a weakened Russia sought to recover prestige abroad while avoiding conflict. By 1914 a measure of success seemed to have crowned these efforts. Partially industrialized Russia, though plagued by social turmoil, was advancing economically and maturing politically. Why did the Revolution of 1905 fail to overthrow tsarism? How genuine was

the constitutional monarchy that succeeded unlimited autocracy? Was Russia in 1914 truly moving toward parliamentary government, prosperity, and social harmony, or was it headed toward a massive social revolution?

The Russo-Japanese War, 1904–1905

A humiliating military defeat by Japan fostered revolution in European Russia that compelled the tsarist regime to make major concessions to the peoples of the Russian Empire. As in the Crimean War, Russia blundered poorly prepared into a needless war that could benefit it little. Allied with Great Britain since 1902 and enjoying American sympathy, Japan held the stronger diplomatic position because the Franco-Russian alliance did not apply to the Far East. Russia's population, army, and fleet were far larger than Japan's, and its resources were much greater, but the war was fought more than 6,000 miles from Russia's industrial and population centers, and at the outset Japan was stronger locally on land and sea. Russian leaders were negligent and overconfident;

Admiral Alekseev, the commander-in-chief, was incompetent and at odds with the army commander, General Kuropatkin. The uncompleted Trans-Siberian Railroad could transport only two divisions of reinforcements per month. From the start the war was highly unpopular in Russia, whose soldiers failed to comprehend why they were fighting on Chinese soil. Each defeat in the Far East heightened in European Russia the agitation and demonstrations that became the 1905 Revolution.

The war began in January 1904 with sudden Japanese attacks on the scattered Russian Far Eastern fleet. Japanese land forces in Korea defeated weak Russian units on the Yalu River and moved into southern Manchuria. Port Arthur, the main Russian naval base, was besieged. Its Russian garrison fought heroically to repel several Japanese assaults, only to have its commander surrender needlessly to the enemy in December 1904. In Manchuria superior Japanese forces defeated General Kuropatkin repeatedly. After the great Battle of Mukden early in 1905, Kuropatkin abandoned that city and retired northward. By then Japanese resources were nearly exhausted, and Russian reinforcements kept arriving, but Russian morale was low from repeated setbacks and a rising tide of revolution in European Russia. In February 1905 Japan asked the American president, Theodore Roosevelt, to mediate the conflict.

Then Russia suffered a final, devastating blow. Late in 1904 the Baltic Fleet was sent around the world to wrest control of the seas from Japan. While crossing the Dogger Bank in the North Sea, Russian ships accidentally sank some English fishing boats, almost triggering war with Great Britain. When Admiral Z. P. Rozhdestvenskii's obsolescent Russian battleships engaged Admiral Togo's main Japanese fleet in Tsushima Strait in May 1905, most of them were destroyed or captured. After this defeat the tsar, facing revolution at home, agreed to seek peace.

At the peace conference in Portsmouth, New Hampshire, in August 1905, Count Witte, summoned from retirement to lead the Russian delegation, rejected Japanese demands for a money

indemnity and for all of Sakhalin Island. Witte managed to win American public sympathy, but the Treaty of Portsmouth ceded Liaotung Peninsula, including Port Arthur, and southern Manchuria to Japan. Russia recognized Japanese preeminence in Korea while Japan permitted Russia to hold northern Manchuria and the Chinese Eastern Railroad.

The Russo-Japanese War, costing each side some 450,000 casualties, proved futile but significant for Russia. Japan had halted Russia's imperialist drive in the Far East and weakened its position there, but with retention of northern Manchuria and the Maritime Province including Vladivostok, Russia remained an important Pacific power. Russia's defeat weakened the Franco-Russian alliance and encouraged Germany to pursue an aggressive policy in Europe; and by ending British fears of Russian imperialism, it fostered their subsequent rapprochement. This first major Asian victory over a European power began to undermine European imperialism in the Orient. Defeat by Japan discredited tsarism at home and helped force it to grant important political and economic concessions to the Russian people.

The 1905 Revolution

Historians differ widely over the meaning of the 1905 Revolution. Most Western scholars regard it, like the European revolutions of 1848, as a liberal-democratic movement in which workers and peasants acted largely spontaneously. Early Soviet accounts, such as Pokrovskii's, agreed, but Stalinist historians dramatized and glorified Bolshevik leadership of the proletariat in a "bourgeois-democratic revolution." Most scholars affirm that 1905 was the dress rehearsal for the greater 1917 revolutions because similar parties and mass elements participated, though with less cohesion and militancy in the first case.

Revolution occurred in 1905 because industrial workers, intellectuals, peasants, and ethnic minorities found their repressive, unresponsive government unbearable. Supporting the govern-

Bloody Sunday. The demonstrators led by Father Gapon are
attacked by the tsar's cavalry in St. Petersburg.

ment were a large and cohesive bureaucracy, a
vast police network, the nobility, the church, and
the army, but until Witte was returned to office
(October 1905), the regime used these still powerful elements ineptly. The depression of 1900–1903
and bad harvests had brought hard times to Russia; and an increasingly articulate opposition
sought political freedom, civil liberties, and social
reform.

The assassination (July 1904) of Interior Minister V. K. Pleve removed the only dynamic government figure. Replacing him with the mild Prince
Peter Sviatopolk-Mirskii, Nicholas II made minor
concessions to the public. In Paris in October
1904, the Liberation movement and socialists
agreed to agitate for the replacement of autocracy
with a democratic regime based on universal suffrage, and by December most educated Russians
were criticizing the regime. In many cities, political
banquets were held similar to those before the
Paris revolution of 1848.

The revolution began on "Bloody Sunday"
(January 9, 1905). With police cooperation, the
priest Father George Gapon had organized St.
Petersburg factory workers to deflect them from

revolutionary ideas. When news came of Port
Arthur's fall, a strike of locomotive workers spread
through the giant Putilov plant and several other
St. Petersburg factories. Gapon urged the workers
to petition the tsar to end the war, convene a constituent assembly, grant civil rights, and establish
an eight-hour workday, all also goals of the Liberationists. On January 9, a snowy Sunday morning,
Gapon led one of several columns of workers from
various parts of the city toward the Winter Palace.
The marchers—men, women, and children—bore
icons, sang hymns, and clearly intended no violence. When they disregarded orders to halt, the
tsar's uncle, Grand Duke Vladimir Aleksandrovich,
ordered troops to fire on the crowd, and hundreds
of the unarmed workers were slaughtered.

Bloody Sunday united the Russian people
against the autocracy and undermined its faith in
the tsar. During January, half a million workers
struck, and assemblies of nobles and *zemstva*
issued sharp protests. As students and professional people joined the workers, St. Petersburg
became the center of nationwide agitation. Except
for Socialist Revolutionary terrorists, however,

Heller model 1:400 constructed by Bruce MacKenzie

The battleship *Potemkin,* named after Catherine II's influential favorite and launched in 1900, was the last Russian predreadnought ship to be built. Constructed in Nikolaev shipyard, it combined French and German designs. The *Potemkin* weighed 13,000 tons and was 378 feet long. The mutineers who took over the ship in June 1905 later surrendered to Romanian authorities.

there was relatively little violence. At their congress in March, the Liberationists demanded a constituent assembly, universal suffrage (including women), separation of church and state, autonomy for national minorities, transfer of state and crown lands to the peasants, an eight-hour workday, and the right to strike. Revolutionary socialists, mostly in exile, squabbling over tactics, played little part in this movement.

In May and June, the opposition organized, the strike movement expanded, and a naval mutiny erupted. Fourteen unions of professional people established the Union of Unions to coordinate their campaign for a constituent assembly. P. N. Miliukov, head of the Union of Liberation, was elected its president, giving liberals in 1905 a unity that socialists and conservatives lacked. Although Bolsheviks and many Socialist Revolutionaries favored armed insurrection, other socialists cooperated with the Union. At the textile center of Ivanovo-Voznesensk, virtually the entire work force struck, some 70,000 workers. Their strike

committee, calling itself a *soviet* (council), took on governmental functions such as price regulation. On June 14, the crew of the new battleship *Potemkin* mutinied under a red flag and forced the government to deactivate the Black Sea Fleet.

Some minority nationalities of the Empire— notably in Russian Poland, the Baltic provinces, Finland, and the Caucasus—took uncoordinated but sometimes violent action during 1905, aiming chiefly to win autonomy within the Russian Empire. At the same time Ukrainian nationalism emerged for the first time as a considerable force, combining intelligentsia and peasantry. In August 1905 Muslims organized politically at Nizhnii-Novgorod, demanding elimination of all legal discrimination against their faith.

Nicholas II's response to all this was to announce the Bulygin Duma (named after the new Minister of Interior, A. G. Bulygin), a consultative assembly to be elected by a limited suffrage favoring rural elements. It would be able to speak but not act, and autocracy would be preserved. This temporarily split the opposition three ways: *Zemstvo* moderates favored participating in such elections, the Union of Unions urged a boycott and agitation for a constituent assembly, and revolutionaries advocated an armed uprising.

The spreading mass unrest forced greater governmental concessions. Peasant disorders grew in many regions. Radical demands by the Peasant Union, formed in July, revealed that contrary to official expectations, the peasantry had joined the opposition. The workers forced the government's hand: History's first general strike began spontaneously September 19 with a walkout by Moscow printers, which then was joined by bakers and factory workers. Spreading to St. Petersburg, it halted railroad, telegraph, and telephone service completely. In all Russia, only one newspaper, a conservative Kiev daily, was published, and in mid-October mobs controlled the streets of leading cities. The workers' strike committee in St. Petersburg became a soviet and selected a 22-man executive committee under Leon Trotskii and a Menshevik, G. Khrustalev-Nosar.

Powerless to halt the strike, the regime fell into panic and virtual paralysis. Count Witte advised either a military dictatorship or a constitution. Unable to find a dictator and faced with general revolt in town and countryside, the tsar yielded. His October Manifesto (October 17) promised a constitution, civil liberties, and a national parliament (Duma) elected by a broad suffrage without whose consent no bill was to become law. It also legalized most strikes and ended peasant redemption payments. Two days later, Nicholas revived the Council of Ministers, creating a unified executive branch, and named Witte premier. Nicholas was in despair because he had broken his pledge to maintain autocracy unaltered.

The tsar replaced reactionary ministers, but liberal leaders refused to join the government, and socialists and most liberals spurned the Manifesto. The two months after it was issued were the most disorderly of 1905. In those "days of freedom," the St. Petersburg Soviet, coordinating a growing soviet movement, decreed the end of censorship, newspapers ignored censorship restrictions, and

the public began exercising rights that the Manifesto had promised. In October and November rural violence reached its peak, and national minorities agitated for autonomy or independence. Naval mutinies broke out at Kronstadt, Vladivostok, and Sevastopol, and in November postal and telegraph workers struck, touching off new railroad strikes. Government troops suppressed peasant revolts and arrested the St. Petersburg Soviet's leaders, but the Soviet, supported by the Peasant Union and the socialists, proclaimed economic war against the regime and called for another general strike. In December the Moscow Soviet led a weeklong armed workers' rebellion, but it was suppressed after bitter street fighting reminiscent of the Paris "June Days" of 1848, and thousands of Moscow workers were shot or deported. The regime had now recovered its nerve, and after the Moscow Soviet called off its faltering general strike, the revolution gradually subsided. Opposition newspapers were closed, and the "days of freedom" ended.

Tsarism survived 1905 for reasons not present in the fatal crisis of 1917. Quick and honorable conclusion of the Russo-Japanese war in August localized disaffection in the armed forces, mutinies were suppressed, and most peasant soldiers remained loyal. The timely political and economic concessions of the October Manifesto satisfied most moderates, isolated radical elements, and divided advocates of social change from advocates of political change. Many top revolutionaries were in exile. Mass groups were uncoordinated and lacked good leadership, and their protest movements peaked at different times. The bureaucracy and police backed the regime solidly. Finally, at a crucial time Witte secured a large loan from France, which was anxious to prop up its ally, Russia, so it would not have to face Germany alone. Nonetheless, the 1905 Revolution aroused the Russian people politically and gave them a taste of freedom. The government restored order but not the awe it had formerly inspired in the masses. Tsarism had a last chance but under altered conditions.

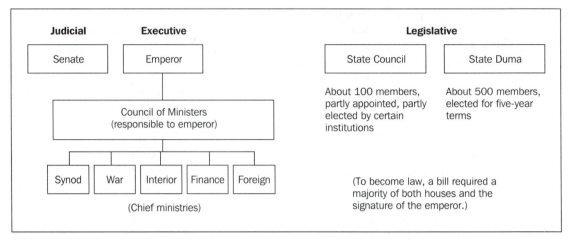

Figure 28.1
Russian Imperial Government (1906–1917)

Creation of the Duma Monarchy, 1905–1906

The most dangerous time for a bad government, noted the 19th-century French writer Alexis de Tocqueville, is when it begins to change for the better. Bloody Sunday had shattered the myth of the tsar as a benevolent, omniscient father. A new principle of political authority was needed, but as the revolution ebbed, Nicholas II salvaged most of his autocratic powers, fired Witte, and blocked creation of a true parliamentary regime. Further trouble portended between "society" and the government as the Manifesto's promises were hedged with restrictions, infuriating the leftist liberals and making them into defiant obstructionists.

Decrees and acts of the next six months laid foundations for a regime satisfying neither side. To the liberals' dismay, an imperial manifesto of February 1906 created a bicameral legislature. (See Figure 28.1.) The hitherto wholly appointive State Council was reorganized as a conservative upper chamber, half of it appointed by the emperor, half of it elected by various social bodies (*zemstva*, municipal dumas, the nobility, and universities, for example). Though most males over the age of 25 could vote for deputies to the lower house, the State Duma, the electorate was divided into the

traditional classes: landowners, peasants, and townspeople. A weighted, indirect franchise favored landowners and peasants and excluded many workers. It represented the belated realization of Speranskii's scheme of 1809 (see Chapter 20), not the "four-tailed" suffrage of liberal demands. The government expected the Duma to be a conservative assembly.

The Duma's powers were very limited. Russia's constitution, the Fundamental Laws of April 1906, described the emperor now as "autocrat" instead of "unlimited autocrat." He retained power to declare war and appoint and dismiss ministers of state, who were responsible to him alone. Duma members could question ministers, but the latter did not have to give satisfactory replies, and the crown retained all powers not specifically given to the legislature. To become law, a measure had to pass both houses, and the emperor retained absolute veto power. Article 87 of the Fundamental Laws further restricted Duma authority by authorizing ministers to govern by decree during Duma recesses, provided the Duma approved such decrees subsequently. The Duma's ability to obstruct the executive was slight because the emperor determined the duration of its sessions and could prorogue it at will if he set a date for

Table 28.1 Russian political parties and programs, 1905–1917

Party	Program
RSDLP (Social Democrats), 1898. Splits 1903 into: 1. Bolsheviks 2. Mensheviks	Marxist (overthrow of tsarism; establishment of a workers' state) 1. Stress violent revolution 2. Orthodox Marxists; move toward nonviolent, parliamentary socialism
SRs (Socialist Revolutionaries), 1900	Peasant socialism (violent overthrow of tsarism; establishment of federal state; confiscation of estates without compensation)
KD (Constitutional Democrats), 1905	Liberal-democratic (constitutional monarchy or a republic; all civil rights; ministerial responsibility; land reform)
Trudoviks (Labor faction), 1906	Radical groups favor drastic land reform; national autonomy for minority peoples; civil liberties
Octobrists, 1905	Conservatives (program of "October Manifesto"; limited monarchy; mild reform; rule of law)
United Nobility, 1906	Faction or pressure group to promote noble interests; mainly conservative
Union of the Russian People, 1905	Extreme conservatives ("orthodoxy, autocracy, and nationalism"; racist)

new elections. The Duma could neither overturn the ministry nor revise the Fundamental Laws, and its control of the purse was severely restricted. (It had no control over court expenses and little over the army or state debt.) Could any legislature operate effectively under such limitations?

Amidst continuing revolutionary disturbances, the electoral campaign for the First Duma began in December 1905. Excitement and expectancy gripped Russia, as for the first time political parties (see Table 28.1), though still not legal, contended in national elections. The SRs, deciding at their first open congress in Finland to boycott the elections and promote violent revolution, demanded socialization of the land, its issuance to peasants on the basis of need, and a federal system with full national self-determination for non-Russians. At their Fourth Congress in Stockholm (spring 1906), the SDs restored surface unity, but serious Bolshevik-Menshevik differences persisted. Initially, most SDs favored boycotting the elections, but then the

Mensheviks decided to participate. Arguing that Bolsheviks could use the Duma to denounce tsarism, Lenin shocked his colleagues by voting with the Mensheviks. As revolutionary parties scarcely competed in the elections, peasants voted mostly for the Trudovik (Labor) group, largely SR in ideology but peaceful in tactics. Among the nonrevolutionary parties, the most radical was the Constitutional Democrats (Kadets, KD), ably led by Miliukov and Struve from the Union of Liberation and Petrunkevich from the *zemstva*. Abandoning temporarily their call for a constituent assembly, the Kadets campaigned for full parliamentary rights for the Duma, alienation of large estates with compensation, and more rights for labor. The Octobrist party, led by Alexander I. Guchkov and representing moderate *zemstvo* leaders, business, and liberal bureaucrats, accepted the October Manifesto. Aiming to strengthen constitutional monarchy and civil liberties, it opposed real land reform and national self-determination. The extreme right, especially the ultranationalist Union of the Russian People, denounced the Duma and the Jews and demanded restoration of unlimited autocracy.

The election revealed Russia's radical mood and dismayed the government. The Kadets (180 seats) with their allies organized and dominated the First Duma, and the peasant Trudoviks had about 100 deputies. There were 18 Menshevik Social Democrats, 17 Octobrists, 15 extreme Rightists, and about 100 deputies from national and religious minorities.

In the Winter Palace's elegant St. George's room, the tsar opened the First Duma on May 10, 1906. He, his court, and ministers, magnificent and bejeweled, occupied one side of the hall. Opposite sat the staid State Council, and behind them crowded the 500 Duma delegates: bearded peasants, Mensheviks in worker blouses, and minority groups in national costume. The contrast between the elite and popular representatives resembled that at the French Estates-General of 1789. In a brief, colorless "Address from the Throne" Nicholas II, like Louis XVI, gave the legislature no directives.

Organizing the Duma, the Kadets elected one of their own, Sergei Muromtsev, as speaker. Their reply to the tsar's "Address" demanded fully democratic suffrage, abolition of the State Council as an upper house, ministerial responsibility to the Duma, and amnesty for all political prisoners, but Nicholas and his ministers refused such exorbitant demands. Obsessed by European precedents and blind to Russian realities, Miliukov spurned compromise. I. L. Goremykin, the faded and servile bureaucrat who had replaced Witte as premier, responded for the tsar that the Duma's requests were all "inadmissible." The Duma promptly declared no confidence in the government, which simply ignored it. Because the Kadets failed to use existing Duma powers, vital issues such as land reform, minority rights, and education were neglected. Secret Duma discussions with the tsar on a Kadet or coalition ministry proved fruitless. The Kadets' doctrinaire approach and Nicholas's

suspicion doomed the First Duma and ultimately the constitutional experiment. When the Duma appealed directly to the public on the land question, Nicholas dissolved it without ordering new elections.

The Kadets responded with illegal defiance. When troops closed the Duma, some 180 delegates, mostly Kadets and Trudoviks, went to Vyborg, Finland, where Muromtsev proclaimed it reconvened. Miliukov drew up the Vyborg Manifesto, which urged Russians not to pay taxes or supply army recruits until the Duma met again, but there was little public response, and the Manifesto's signers were tried, jailed briefly, and disfranchised. Losing many talented leaders, the Kadets never fully recovered their political leadership.

Originally dedicated to promoting the broad, liberal development of Russia into a parliamentary democracy, the Kadets gradually became a narrower party of the professional middle class confined largely to towns and increasingly suspicious of the masses. After 1906 the Kadets began to hedge on their democratic aims, tending to prefer constitutional monarchy. To many workers and peasants the Kadets were "bourgeois," a party favoring gradual change while preserving upper-class privilege and social order.

After the Duma's dissolution Peter A. Stolypin, since July 1906 premier and minister of interior, made frequent use of Article 87, which allowed the executive to rule by decree. This last statesman of imperial Russia dominated the political scene for the next five years. Stolypin, a well-to-do landowner, had been a provincial marshal of nobility who in 1905, as governor of Saratov province, had ruthlessly repressed peasant disorders. He was an impressive orator, thoroughly convinced of his rectitude, who favored bold measures and strong-arm tactics. A Russian nationalist, Stolypin viewed repression as the prelude to reform by an enlightened autocracy. Proclaiming a state of emergency, he instituted field courts-martial against SR terrorists, who were killing hundreds of police, priests, and officials. By the spring of 1907, the trials had effectively broken the revolutionary movement.

To the government's chagrin, the short-lived Second Duma (February–June 1907) was more extreme and less constructive than the first. Both SDs and SRs participated in the elections, but Stolypin declared leftist parties illegal and forbade their campaign literature. Almost half those elected were socialists, but they failed to form a bloc and disdained collaboration with the Kadets, who had lost ground. The Duma debated Stolypin's agrarian reforms (see this chapter, under "Economic and Social Development") heatedly, then refused to approve them. Violent SD attacks on the army infuriated the tsar who, urged on by the Union of Russian People, dissolved the Duma. The first constitutional phase ended in complete deadlock between the Duma and the executive.

Political Development, 1907–1914

Stolypin's decree of June 1907, dubbed a coup d'état, altered the original electoral laws arbitrarily to produce a Duma "Russian in spirit." Declared Stolypin: "We don't want professors, but men with roots in the country, local gentry, and the like." Blatantly violating the Fundamental Laws, his measure ensured that subsequent elections would be far from democratic. The government reduced peasant representation drastically, guaranteeing that noblemen would choose almost half the electors. Non-Russians lost most of their seats. Only about 2.5 percent of the population voted for the Third Duma, in which the Octobrists emerged as the largest party, the extreme Right was greatly strengthened, and the Kadets were further weakened. On the left, Trudoviks and Social Democrats each had 14 deputies. This "Masters' Duma" proved so satisfactory to the government that it was allowed to serve out its full five-year term. Though the State Council blocked many progressive laws, the Duma nonetheless approved Stolypin's agrarian reforms, promoted universal education, extended local self-government and religious freedom, and expanded its control of the budget. Even the Third Duma marked an advance over the Pobedonostsev era: All political points of

view were represented, political parties operated openly, and newspapers debated public issues. Whenever possible, the Duma protected and broadened civil liberties by drawing public attention to government abuses.

Outwardly, the Fourth Duma (1912–1917), more than half noblemen, seemed still more conservative. The strengthening of right and left at the expense of the political center revealed dangerous political polarization, but even many conservative deputies defended the Duma and observed parliamentary forms. The Duma's tragedy, noted Thomas Riha, was that "too few were learning too slowly" in a political oasis far from the masses. The government often treated it as a mere department, and the emperor, until dissuaded by his ministers, considered making the Duma merely advisory.

Non-Russian elements were strongly represented in the First Duma of 1906. There were 51 Polish deputies united in a Polish Circle, about 40 Ukrainian nationalists, and 30 Muslims, most of whom cooperated with the Kadets. Under this pressure the imperial government restored the Finnish Diet as a single chamber of 200 members elected for a three-year term by a system of proportional representation and virtual universal suffrage of both sexes. Finland thus became the first country in eastern Europe to grant the vote to women.

From this atmosphere of reluctant concessions to the nationalities by a beleaguered imperial regime in 1905, their situation deteriorated sharply during the years 1907–1914. They faced a conservative imperial government and hostility by most of the Russian people. Polish schools reverted to their pre-1905 Russified condition, and the Ukrainian nationalist movement was subjected to vigorous repression. Baltic Germans were favored by the Russian regime, whereas other Baltic peoples (Estonians, Latvians, and Lithuanians) were suppressed. A law of the Russian Duma in 1910 reduced the Finnish Diet to the status of a provincial assembly before dissolving it altogether; Finland was then governed dictatorially by decree as an occupied and hostile country. Simultaneously, persecution of the Jews was intensified. The policies of the Russian imperial government generally alienated most national minorities completely, preparing the way for their common revolt against Russian rule in 1917–1918.

Until late in 1911 Stolypin ran the executive branch capably, if high-handedly. He used Article 87 to bypass the legislature whenever it obstructed his measures. At first he enjoyed Nicholas II's confidence and support; later he offended the imperial family. In September 1911 Stolypin was assassinated in the Kiev opera house by a double agent who received a ticket from the chief of police! Succeeding him as premier was Finance Minister V. N. Kokovtsov, who was able and moderate but lacked his predecessor's independence and dynamism. In late 1913 the emperor removed him under pressure from the empress and Grigori Rasputin, whose influence Kokovtsov had opposed consistently. The aged and incompetent Goremykin replaced him.

The revolutionary movement, though plagued by police infiltration, recovered somewhat after 1912 from its eclipse under Stolypin. The SRs were appalled by the exposure of Evno Azev, head of their Combat Detachment, as a police agent. Arrests and double agents also weakened the SDs. According to Trotskii, Bolshevik membership had shrunk in 1910 to 10,000. Early in 1914 Roman Malinovskii, Bolshevik leader in the Duma, was exposed as a police spy. Abroad, Lenin maintained his own organization and blocked efforts to reunite the party. In 1912 he convened a conference in Prague and set up a separate Bolshevik party. Later that year the so-called August Bloc under Martov and Trotskii held a separate Menshevik conference, and in 1913 separate Menshevik and Bolshevik factions were formed in the Duma. The Bolsheviks retained their revolutionary fervor, whereas the Mensheviks tried to create a legal, trade union–oriented labor movement run by the workers themselves.

How were the Bolsheviks faring in 1914? Some Western accounts, emphasizing their demoralization, cite declining circulation of *Pravda* (their party newspaper); Lenin's isolation in SD ranks; a small, weak party in Russia; and loss of popularity among Russian workers. Only the outbreak of World War I, claims British scholar Leonard Schapiro, prevented the Bolsheviks' demise. A Soviet source, however, asserted that by July 1914 the Bolsheviks had the support of four-fifths of Russian workers and were leading a militant strike movement in St. Petersburg. Leopold Haimson, an American historian, agrees that Bolsheviks were outdoing Mensheviks in the capitals because their revolutionary program and tactics appealed to many new workers. Bolshevik success, if success it was, reflected worker militancy more than skillful, perceptive leadership.

Economic and Social Development

Important economic and social change occurred between 1906 and 1914. Industrial growth was lifting Russia out of backwardness, and the Stolypin agrarian reforms were creating a basis for a new class of independent farmers. Social inequality was lessening as workers and peasants obtained higher incomes, greater mobility, and more rights.

Stolypin agreed with the socialists that a communal peasantry was potentially revolutionary. His government's aim, therefore, was to abolish the *mir* (peasant commune), free the peasant from it, and foster individual farming. Stolypin explained to the Duma in 1908: "The government has put its wager not on the drunken and the weak but on the sober and the strong—on the sturdy individual proprietor." In November 1906, after the First Duma, he decreed that in communes without a general repartition since 1882, a householder could claim ownership of all plow land worked in 1906. In case of a repartition, he could demand land held before 1882 plus land received in a repartition, provided he paid the commune the original redemption price. This policy encouraged peasants to shift from repartitional to hereditary tenure. The law of June 1910 dissolved all communes with no general repartition since 1861. After one peasant in such a commune applied for an ownership deed, all land in it became private. In repartitional and hereditary communes the head of the household received ownership of the land, a policy that encouraged or even forced younger males to go to the city. Stolypin's ultimate objective was consolidation of scattered strips into Western-style farms.

How successful were these land reforms? Stolypin stressed the need for 20 years of peace to implement them, but they were halted in 1915. Though the government appointed many survey-ors and exerted great pressure, results were incon-clusive. In some areas, such as the northwest, there was noteworthy progress, but in others there was little change. Concludes a recent work: "Nowhere did peasants share the government's enthusiasm for the *khutora* (a private farm)."[1] By 1915 more than half of Russian peasant house-holds had hereditary ownership of their allotments, but less than 10 percent were fully consolidated individual farms.[2] Agricultural tech-niques and output improved considerably on such farms, but village collectivism, though weakened, remained prevalent. Many communes, supposed to be dissolved by the law of 1910, never were. After a big initial push, state enforcement lagged. Thus in 1917 most Russian peasant households still lived in the traditional *mir.*

Who benefited from the reforms? According to Soviet accounts, only a minority of wealthy peas-ants. Stolypin sought to end strip farming and carry through an agricultural revolution, reply recent Western accounts. Viewing the process as a race against time, Lenin feared that Stolypin's reforms would transform the dissatisfied peas-antry, upon which he counted for the future, into a class of loyal, conservative peasant proprietors.

The government encouraged colonization of Siberia to absorb dispossessed younger peasants and to increase farm output. About half of Siber-ian wheat was exported abroad or to other parts of Russia. Siberia, however, lacking a local nobility, promoted rugged individualism and a bourgeois ethos that distressed conservatives. After a visit in 1910, Stolypin called Siberia "an enormous, rudely democratic country which will soon throttle Euro-pean Russia." The government also promoted peasant land purchases through the Peasant Bank. In 1914 European peasantry owned more than four times as much land as the nobility (460 to 108 million acres). The vast state and imperial hold-ings (390 million acres) were mostly unsuited to agriculture. By 1917 most Russian crop land was already in peasant hands.

After 1905 significant industrial progress occurred, though the government did not promote it with Witte's single-minded determination. The economy now was more mature and the official role less marked. The Finance Ministry, despite creation of a separate Ministry of Trade and Indus-try, still controlled the keys to industrial develop-ment but used them more cautiously. Finance Minister V. Kokovtsov (1906–1913), stressing bal-anced growth, sought to maintain the gold stan-dard and a high tariff to uphold Russia's foreign credit and to balance the budget. Thanks to a spurt in new railroad building, the growth rate almost equaled that of the Witte period. Excellent har-vests, large exports, and wider prosperity en-hanced Russia's overall economic performance, although in 1914 it still had the lowest per capita wealth of the major powers, and its industry trailed that of England, Germany, the United States, and France.[3] Industrial progress now, instead of impoverishing the population, was combined with agricultural growth and modest prosperity.

---

[1] Judith Pallott and Denis Shaw, *Landscape and Settlement in Romanov Russia, 1613–1917* (London, 1990), p. 186.

[2] In 1915, of the roughly 14 million peasant allotments, some 5 million remained under repartitional tenure. About 1.3 million were subject to automatic dissolution but had not actually been dissolved, and 1.7 million had been affected to some degree. About 4.3 million holdings had fully hereditary title in scattered strips, and more than 1.3 million had been partially or completely consolidated into farms. Geroid T. Robinson, *Rural Russia* (New York, 1949), pp. 215–16.

[3] In total volume of industrial production in 1913, France exceeded Russia 2.5 times, England 4.6, Germany 6, and the United States 14.3. P. Liashchenko, *History of the Russian National Economy* (New York, 1949), p. 674.

Russia had overcome its backwardness, claimed Kokovtsov, and only the Bolshevik Revolution interrupted its "swift and powerful development."

Geographical distribution of Russian industry changed little, but consolidation and foreign ownership increased. In 1912 the central industrial region produced more than one-third of all manufactures, followed by Ukraine, the northwest, and the Urals. In manufacturing, the largest labor force was in metalworking and textiles. Soviet accounts stressed that foreign interests initiated most industrial combinations in this "era of imperialism." In 1902 French capitalists fostered creation in southern Russia of Prodameta, a metallurgical cartel; by 1910 its member firms produced about three-fourths of the empire's iron products and almost half its rails. The Duma, however, prevented it from becoming a full-fledged trust, a circumstance that revealed big industry's limited influence in imperial Russia. Other combinations formed in sugar (1887) and oil (1904). Foreign influence and investment in Russian industry were considerable, but Soviet claims that Russia had become a semicolonial appendage of Western capitalism were exaggerated. A tsarist source estimated foreign investment in Russia in 1916 at 2.243 billion rubles, more than half of it in mining, metallurgy, and metalworking, with the French holding almost one-third of the total, followed by the British, Germans, and Belgians.

Railroad construction remained the key to Russian industrial booms. The 6,600 miles of line built between 1902 and 1911 triggered an annual industrial growth rate of almost 9 percent between 1909 and 1913 and overall economic growth of about 6 percent annually between 1906 and 1914. Private railroad lines were more efficient, but the state owned about two-thirds of the network, and rising revenues from its lines enabled the government to pay interest on railroad loans and still have a surplus. Nonetheless, in 1914 Russia's external debt (5.4 billion rubles) was one of the world's largest.

Russia's foreign trade increased considerably in volume, but its direction and structure changed little. In 1913 exports were worth more than 1.5 billion rubles and imports 1.374 billion. Russia still exported mostly agricultural goods (grain 44 percent, and livestock and forest products 22 percent). Industrial exports (10 percent) went mostly to backward Asian lands. Germany bought about 30 percent of Russian exports and supplied 47 percent of its imports; Great Britain stood second with 17.5 percent and 13 percent, respectively.

The empire's population rose by almost one-third between 1897 and 1913, to more than 165 million (excluding Finland). Mainly responsible were a birthrate much higher than in western Europe and a declining death rate. The east had the highest growth rates, but three-fourths of the population resided in European Russia. Despite industrialization and urban growth, cities in 1913 contained only 16 percent of the population.

Russian society in 1914, undergoing transition and with numerous inequities and frictions, remained dominated by a nobility that guarded its privileges jealously against the bourgeoisie. Impoverished lesser gentry were selling their lands rapidly, but large landowners retained much wealth and strengthened their influence at court. After 1906 a pressure group, the Council of the United Nobility, protected their interests. Within the Orthodox church, the elite black (monastic) clergy remained in control and blocked needed reform. In an expanding bourgeoisie, Moscow entrepreneurs led the commercial and industrial elements; St. Petersburg remained the financial center. Outside the capitals, the bourgeoisie was often cautious and stodgy and engaged mainly in local trade and industry. Within the Russian middle class, liberal professions exceeded industrial and commercial elements in numbers and influence.

Among the peasantry, slow differentiation was speeded somewhat by the Stolypin reforms, but the mass of middle peasantry was still growing numerically. There were tensions in the village between an upper crust of kulaks and proletarians and semiproletarian elements, but the basic rural rivalry pitted peasant against noble. Peasant isolation was diminishing, and with freedom of movement gained after 1906, many younger peasants migrated to the cities. Peasant inferiority and poverty were lessening but remained potential dangers to the regime.

Far from suffering increasing misery, as Marx had predicted, Russian industrial workers after 1905 found their status and economic position improving. Sharply reduced summertime departures for the village revealed growth of a largely hereditary proletariat. By 1914 more than three million workers labored in mines and factories, about one-half in enterprises with more than 1,000 employees. Such large factories enhanced worker consciousness and solidarity and facilitated agitation by socialists and union organizers. Real wages rose considerably but still lagged far behind those in Europe because of a plentiful labor supply and low labor productivity. Increasingly unionized skilled and semiskilled workers were now usually paid enough to maintain a normal family life. Working conditions were also improving. After 1912 the 10-hour day prevailed; accident and sickness compensation, partly paid by employers, was instituted; and factory inspection increased. Theoretically legalized in 1905, strikes remained virtually prohibited, and unions were barred from organizing public meetings. Strikes were few in 1907–1910, but an industrial revival and a massacre of workers in the British-owned Lena goldfields (April 1912) sparked a resurgence: Some 700,000 workers struck in 1912; 900,000 in 1913; and about 1.5 million in the first half of 1914. St. Petersburg metalworkers—the most literate, highest paid workers—were also the most militant.

Wage levels and living conditions, bad enough for working men, remained far worse for women, who generally received only about two-thirds the pay of males. Many working women remained below a normal subsistence level, as conditions in small sweatshops were appalling and unregulated. Nonetheless, the poorly educated working women in tsarist Russia were mostly docile and obedient and proved difficult to organize in unions or politically. Women's education and literacy lagged far behind that of men: In 1903–1905 only 13.7 percent of Russian women were literate, compared with 32.6 percent of men.

No genuine Russian women's movement emerged until the 1905 Revolution, which brought women consciousness and organization but few tangible benefits. Two separate movements developed: a feminist women's suffrage organization and a socialist movement sharply opposed to it in methods and goals. Early in 1905 the feminist All-Russian Union for Women's Equality was formed, seeking "freedom and equality before the law without regard to sex." Centering in St. Petersburg, it developed branches all across Russia. In April in the capital it convened the first political meeting for women in Russian history, drawing about 1,000 people and laying a basis for the Union's first congress in Moscow in May. The Union demanded an immediate constituent assembly elected without distinctions of sex, nationality, or religion; equality of the sexes under law; protection of women workers; and equal educational opportunity for women at every level. In July it joined the Union of Unions.

During and after 1905 the feminist movement focused on the issue of women's suffrage, which was denied by the October Manifesto but supported increasingly by liberal and radical political parties. However, in 1908, under pressure of political reaction, the women's union collapsed as antagonism escalated between feminists and socialists. In 1910 feminist activity revived around the weekly *Women's Cause.* The largest feminist organization in Russia had fewer than 1,000 members by 1917, minuscule compared to those in the West. Most feminists came from the middle class and were led chiefly by nongentry university graduates. Confronting powerful foes on left and right, Russian feminism failed to persuade the Duma to give women the vote.

Also emerging from the 1905 Revolution was a small women's socialist movement, which encountered hostility or indifference from male workers and most Social Democratic leaders. Its outstanding leader was Alexandra Kollontai, born in 1872, an energetic nonconformist who began as a Populist before becoming a Marxist follower of Plekhanov. The 1905 Revolution turned Kollontai into a dedicated revolutionary who wrote and

Women's demonstration, 1905.

distributed socialist literature, raised money, and marched with workers. "Women and their fate have occupied my whole life," she recalled later. Finding support in the Union of Textile Workers, mostly women, she gave Marxist lectures and organized public meetings that emphasized the themes of exploitation and social liberation. After spending the years of reaction abroad, Kollontai returned to lead a revival of the women's socialist movement (1912–1914), remaining its chief link with the European International Socialist Women's Movement. In March 1913 Kollontai promoted the first celebration of International Women's Day in Russia.

Foreign Affairs, 1906–1914

Defeat in the war with Japan, the 1905 Revolution, and indebtedness restricted Russia's freedom of action abroad, and dreams of an expanded Asian empire lay shattered. Settling outstanding dis-

putes in the Far and Near East, Russia concentrated again on Europe and the Balkans in an effort to regain lost prestige. The Foreign Ministry's task was to prevent exploitation of Russia's military weakness by other powers. Until 1914, it averted disaster by repeated diplomatic retreats under German pressure.

In the Far East, relations between Russia and Japan were transformed as Russian leaders learned from their defeat. Both powers were anxious to protect their mainland interests and moved toward partnership. The United States's Open Door policy, an apparent screen for economic penetration of Manchuria, fostered a series of Russo-Japanese agreements. In 1910 Russia recognized Japan's special interests in Korea and south Manchuria in return for Japan's pledge to respect Russian domination of northern Manchuria and Outer Mongolia. Russia encouraged Mongolia to escape Chinese control; in 1912 it proclaimed its "independence" and became a de facto Russian protectorate. On the eve of World War I, Russia's position in the Far East was secure.

Powerful imperial Germany absorbed much of Russia's attention. In 1904–1905 William II, to undermine the Franco-Russian alliance, offered the tsar the defensive Björkö Treaty. Although the naive tsar signed it, Foreign Minister Lamsdorf and Count Witte persuaded him to ignore it and stick to Russia's alliance with France. When Germany sought to humiliate France in Morocco (1905–1906), Russia backed France loyally at the Algeciras Conference in return for a large French loan. The French alliance remained the cornerstone of Russian foreign policy until the end of the empire, and growing German military and naval strength fostered rapprochement between Russia and England. German leaders believed that Anglo-Russian imperial rivalries were insoluble, but Japan's defeat of Russia caused London to abandon fears of Russian expansionism. The friendship of Russia and England with France encouraged the British Liberal cabinet, realizing that it could not defend Persia, to seek agreement with Russia. Foreign Secretary Lord Grey wrote: "An entente between Russia, France, and ourselves would be absolutely secure. If it is necessary to check Germany, it could then be done."[4]

Serious obstacles had to be overcome on the Russian side. Foreign Minister Alexander Izvolskii (1906–1910), who reasserted his ministry's role (sometimes rashly), had to neutralize pro-German feeling at court and overcome the old Turkestan military men who coveted all of Persia. The Anglo-Russian Convention of August 1907 left Afghanistan and Tibet in the British sphere; unfortunate Persia was partitioned into a British sphere in the southeast and a huge Russian zone in the north, separated by a neutral area. Anglo-Russian rivalry in Persia continued but became tolerable and peaceful. By 1914 Russia dominated most of it, but England accepted this as the price of containing Germany.

---

[4] Memorandum of February 20, 1906, quoted in A. J. P. Taylor, *The Struggle for Mastery in Europe 1848–1918* (Oxford, 1954), pp. 441–42.

Izvolskii hoped that Great Britain would now assist him in revising the Straits Convention to let Russian warships pass through the Bosphorus, but he was disappointed. His interest in the Straits coincided with Austria's more dynamic Balkan policies. Conrad von Hötzendorf, Austrian chief of staff, wished to crush Serbia by preventive war, whereas Alois von Aehrenthal, the foreign minister, aimed to annex Bosnia and Hercegovina, which Austria had occupied since 1878. (See Map 28.1.) At Buchlau (September 1908), Aehrenthal and Izvolskii agreed that Russia would support their annexation by Austria in return for Austrian backing to revise the Straits Convention. Austria annexed Bosnia and Hercegovina, but Izvolskii could not win the other power's consent on the Straits question. Angered by Austria's absorption of two Serbian-speaking provinces, Serbia demanded territorial compensation, but because Germany backed Austria, Russia dared not support Serbia's claims. Russia and Serbia had to back down before the German powers. The Bosnian crisis discredited Izvolskii and gave warning of a general war over the Balkans.

Succeeding Izvolskii as foreign minister was S. D. Sazonov (1910–1916), a conscientious diplomat who lacked firm control over his subordinates. As Pan-Slav tendencies revived, Russian consuls N. G. Hartvig in Belgrade and A. Nekliudov in Sofia advocated a forward policy. In 1912, with their warm encouragement, a Balkan League of Serbia, Bulgaria, Montenegro, and Greece was formed. In October, disregarding official Russian and Austrian warnings, the League attacked Turkey and conquered Macedonia. Austria, however, blocked Serbia's aspiration to Adriatic ports, and Russia yielded again to German threats. In a second Balkan war of 1913, Bulgaria, seeking control of Macedonia, attacked the Serbs and Greeks, but they, aided by Romania and Turkey, defeated Bulgaria and seized Bulgarian Macedonia. This victory smashed the Balkan League, turned embittered Bulgaria toward the Central Powers (Germany, Austria-Hungary, and Italy), and damaged Russian prestige. Serbian nationalism intensified further as the Austrian

Map 28.1 Russia and the Balkans, 1912–1914

military awaited an opportunity to crush Serbia completely.

In the Balkans before 1914, Russian and Austrian imperialism clashed and Russo-German tension was sometimes severe, but war between Russia and the Central Powers was far from inevitable. Russo-German friction over the Berlin to Bagdad Railway and over German attempts to dominate the Straits was settled peacefully. The Romanovs remained pro-German, supported by the Duma Right, which sought to buttress autocracy against Western liberal parliamentarism.

Suggested Additional Reading

ASCHER, A. *The Revolution of 1905: Vol. I. Russia in Disarray* (Stanford, 1988).

BOCK, M. *Reminiscences of My Father, Peter A. Stolypin* (Metuchen, NJ, 1970).

CHARQUES, R. *The Twilight of Imperial Russia* (London, 1958, 1974).

EDELMAN, R. *Gentry Politics on the Eve of the Russian Revolution: The Nationalist Party, 1907–1917* (New Brunswick, NJ, 1980).

———. *Proletarian Peasants: The Revolution of 1905 in Russia's Southwest* (Ithaca, NY, 1987).

EDMONDSON, L. H. *Feminism in Russia, 1900–1917* (Stanford, 1984).

GATRELL, P. *Government, Industry and Rearmament in Russia, 1900–1914* (Cambridge, 1994).

GEIFMAN, A. *Thou Shalt Kill: Revolutionary Terrorism in Russia, 1894–1917* (Princeton, 1993).

HAIMSON, L. "The Problem of Social Stability in Urban Russia, 1905–1917," *Slavic Review* 23 (1964): 619–42; and 24 (1965): 1–22. Comments by Mendel and von Laue in 24 (1965): 23–46.

HARCAVE, S. *The Russian Revolution of 1905* (London, 1970).

———, trans. and ed. *The Memoirs of Count Witte* (New York, 1990).

HEALY, A. E. *The Russian Autocracy in Crisis: 1905–1907* (Hamden, CT, 1976).

HENNESSY, R. *The Agrarian Question in Russia, 1905–1917. The Inception of the Stolypin Reform* (Giessen, Germany, 1977).

HOSKING, GEOFFREY. *The Russian Constitutional Experiment . . . 1907–1914* (New York, 1973).

IZVOLSKY, A. P. *Recollections of a Foreign Minister* (New York, 1921).

KOKOVTSOV, V. N. *Out of My Past* (Stanford, 1935).

LEIKIN, E., trans. and ed. *The Beilis Transcripts: The Anti-Semitic Trial That Shook the World* (Northvale, NJ, 1993).

LINCOLN, W. B. *In War's Dark Shadow: The Russians Before the Great War* (New York, 1983).

MAKLAKOV, V. A. *The First State Duma* (Bloomington, IN, 1964).

MANNING, R. T. *The Crisis of the Old Order in Russia* (Princeton, 1983).

MCCAULEY, M., and P. WALDRON, eds. *Octobrists to Bolsheviks . . . Documents . . .* (Baltimore, 1984).

MCNEAL, R., ed. *Russia in Transition, 1905–1914* (New York, 1970).

MEHLINGER, H. D., and J. M. THOMPSON. *Count Witte and the Tsarist Government in the 1905 Revolution* (Bloomington, IN, 1972).

MILIUKOV, PAUL. *Political Memoirs, 1905–1917,* ed. A. Mendel (Ann Arbor, MI, 1967).

MILLER, M. S. *Economic Development of Russia, 1905–1914,* 2d ed. (London, 1967).

OBERLANDER, E., et al. *Russia Enters the Twentieth Century . . .* (New York, 1971).

POSPIELOVSKY, D. *Russian Police Socialism: Experiment or Provocation?* (London, 1971).

RAWSON, D. C. *Russian Rightists and the Revolution of 1905* (Cambridge, 1995).

REICHMAN, HENRY. *Railwaymen and Revolution: Russia, 1905* (Berkeley, 1987).

RICE, C. *Russian Workers and the Socialist-Revolutionary Party Through the Revolution of 1905–07* (New York, 1988).

RIHA, T. *A Russian European: Paul Miliukov . . .* (Notre Dame, 1968).

ROBSON, R. A. *Old Believers in Modern Russia* (DeKalb, IL, 1996).

SABLINSKY, W. *The Road to Bloody Sunday* (Princeton, 1976).

SCHLEIFMAN, N. *Undercover Agents in the Russian Revolutionary Movement: The SR Party, 1902–1914* (New York, 1988).

SEREGNY, S. J. *Russian Teachers and Peasant Revolution . . .* (Bloomington, IN, 1989).

STAVROU, T. G., ed. *Russia Under the Last Tsar* (Minneapolis, 1969).

SURH, G. D. *1905 in St. Petersburg: Land, Society and Revolution* (Stanford, 1990).

SZEFTEL, M. *The Russian Constitution of April 23, 1906* (Brussels, 1976).

THADEN, E. *Russia and the Balkan Alliance of 1912* (University Park, PA, 1965).

TROTSKY, L. D. *1905,* trans. A. Bostock (New York, 1972).

VERNER, A. M. *The Crisis of Russian Autocracy: Nicholas II and the 1905 Revolution* (Princeton, 1990).

WEINBERG, R. *The Revolution of 1905 in Odessa: Blood on the Steps* (Bloomington, IN, 1993).

WILLIAMS, R. C. *The Other Bolsheviks: Lenin and His Critics, 1904–1914* (Bloomington, IN, 1986).

ZENKOVSKY, A. V. *Stolypin: Russia's Last Great Reformer,* trans. M. Patoski (Princeton, 1986).

29

Cultural Developments, 1855–1917

The late 19th century witnessed a spectacular flowering of Russian culture. Nicholas I's death removed an oppressive weight from Russian life and ushered in a relatively liberal era that, combined with a powerful national upsurge, produced remarkable cultural creativity. Individuals in literature, art, music, and architecture began to experiment with new modes of expression. Frank discussion of the plight of the peasantry and emancipation focused attention on this long-neglected segment of society. The daily lives of commoners and the drama and pathos of peasant life captured the imagination of Russian artists.

Literature

Russian literature entered a Golden Age associated primarily with Turgenev, Dostoevsky, and Tolstoy, all among the world's greatest novelists. This triumvirate, building upon the legacy of Pushkin, Lermontov, and Gogol, became the most consummate practitioners of literary realism. Under their tutelage, Russian literature achieved great international acclaim.

Turgenev (1818–1883)

Ivan Turgenev, a nobleman well educated by private tutors, studied at Russian and German universities and became an ardent Westerner. Through his works this most Western of Russia's major writers taught Europeans to appreciate Russian literature. His short stories about peasant life, based on personal observation, appeared in *The Contemporary,* a leading journal of literature and criticism and were later published as *A Sportsman's Sketches* (1852), winning him recognition as a leading author. The stories denounced serfdom while portraying the serf as compassionate and dignified. Publication that same year of his laudatory obituary of Nicholas Gogol, who had satirized official corruption and social injustice, brought brief imprisonment and banishment. In 1853, pardoned and having returned to the capital with an enhanced reputation, Turgenev became literary Russia's chief spokesman.

Turgenev embodied the new spirit pervading Russian life. In his first novels, *Rudin* (1856) and *Nest of Gentlefolk* (1859), he depicted the well-intentioned but unrealistic idealism of the older generation. In the novel *On the Eve* (1860), he

Library of Congress

Ivan Turgenev (1818–1883).

described aspirations of the new generation, tried to reveal life as it really was, and faced the toughest issues of the day. In these novels the critics found beauty, truth, simplicity, and sensitivity, hailing his descriptive powers, portrayal of character, and insight.

Fathers and Sons (1862), Turgenev's most famous novel, described the generational conflict between men of the 1860s—Arkadi and the nihilist Bazarov—and men of the 1840s—Arkadi's father and uncle. Conservative critics condemned Turgenev for apparently approving radicalism by depicting Bazarov too positively. The left criticized Bazarov as a caricature of the younger generation's aspirations. Except for Dmitri Pisarev (on whom Bazarov was based), who praised the novel, most radical critics claimed Turgenev had exhausted his talent. The general rejection of *Fathers and Sons* crushed Turgenev's ego. Settling in western

Europe, he visited Russia rarely. His novel *Smoke* (1867), revealing his disillusionment with Russia, stressed the arrogance and deceitfulness of Russian aristocrats and émigrés.

Turgenev's last novel, *Virgin Soil*, which analyzed the "going to the people" movement of the 1870s, revealed that as his fame in Europe grew, he had lost touch with Russian life. With his international reputation, Turgenev was more at ease among Europe's literary elite than among Russians. Unreconciled with his beloved Russia, he died in a village near Paris.

Dostoevsky (1821–1881)

If Turgenev was the stylistic master of realism, Fedor Dostoevsky strove to be "a realist in a higher sense," plumbing the depths of humanity's soul and laying bare conflicts within human nature. His metaphysical realism dealt with the meaning and purpose of life. For him ideas had a tangible, palpable quality. Seeking to overcome divisions in Russian life, he discovered that only by surmounting the division between humans and God could Russian life be restored to wholeness. Dostoevsky wrote:

> I am a child of the age, a child of unbelief and skepticism. I have been so far, and shall be I know to the grave. . . . If anyone proved to me that Christ was not the truth, and it really was a fact that the truth was not in Christ, I would rather be with Christ than with the truth.[1]

Throughout his life he sought to know and understand Christ. Believing deeply in Russia and its people, he tried similarly to believe in God. A character in *The Possessed* blurts out: "I believe in Russia. I believe in Orthodoxy. . . . I believe that Christ will come again in Russia." This was Dostoevsky's own conviction, proclaimed in his writings.

The son of a well-to-do but miserly doctor, Dostoevsky was an engineering student in St. Petersburg when he learned of his father's murder

---

[1] Quoted in E. H. Carr, *Dostoevsky* (New York, 1931), pp. 281–82.

Library of Congress

Fedor Dostoevsky (1821–1881).

by peasants. With his inheritance he soon resigned his army commission to devote himself to literature.

"We have all sprung from Gogol's 'Overcoat,'"[2] Dostoevsky once remarked. Indeed, his first novel, *Poor Folk* (1845), is related to "The Overcoat." An exchange of letters between a young girl and an aging government clerk exposes the pathos and constant struggle of the downtrodden for human dignity. The novel revealed Dostoevsky's intense concern with psychological torment, self-sacrifice, and alienation—key themes of his later great novels. At 23 he was already recognized as a leading Russian author, but the cool response to his second novel, *The Double* (1846), gravely wounded

his vanity. He attended the radical Petrashevskii Circle partly from boredom and curiosity. But Nicholas I's regime equated nonconformity with treason, and Dostoevsky was arrested in April 1849. Convicted of crimes against the state, Dostoevsky was sentenced to death, but at the execution site his sentence was commuted to eight years of Siberian exile. Being snatched from the jaws of death stimulated his deep interest in human psychology and torments of the mind.

Dostoevsky recorded his prison sojourn vividly in *Notes from the House of the Dead* (1861), a work that resembles Alexander Solzhenitsyn's *Gulag Archipelago* (see Chapter 43). His imprisonment, a turning point in his life, caused an intellectual reorientation affecting his entire outlook. He discovered two sources of inspiration for his later views: the New Testament and "the people" of Russia.

Allowed to return to St. Petersburg in 1859, Dostoevsky and his brother, Mikhail, entered journalism as partners, but suppression by the authorities and financial failure resulted in disaster. In 1864 the deaths of his wife and beloved brother plunged him into grief; his debts brought him close to bankruptcy. In that disastrous year Dostoevsky ventured into philosophy in *Notes from Underground*. Releasing his despair, he sought to answer Chernyshevskii's utopian novel, *What Is to Be Done?* (see Chapter 27). Chernyshevskii believed people were inherently good and rational; Dostoevsky argued that people could use their free will to choose between good and evil, and he presented people as irrational and contradictory. A man's ability to choose, claimed Dostoevsky, was the root of his freedom. He developed these ideas further in his major novels.

The great novels *Crime and Punishment* (1866), *The Idiot* (1869), *The Possessed* (1871–1872), and his profound final work, *The Brothers Karamazov* (1879–1880), constitute a related cycle dealing with contemporary Russian issues, reflecting stages in Dostoevsky's elaboration of Christianity, and portraying the "underground man." *Crime and Punishment* reveals the tragic failure of Raskolnikov, a poor student, to assert his individuality

---

[2] A famous short story written by Gogol in 1842.

"without God" by senselessly murdering a pawn-broker and her sister. Raskolnikov succeeds only in denying his humanity and Christian spirit. In *The Idiot* Dostoevsky portrays saintly idiocy—a long revered Russian trait—in Christlike Prince Myshkin, an impotent epileptic, long confined in mental institutions. Returning to society, he becomes enmeshed in the lives of "ordinary" people who find him amusing and wholly gullible. Exploiting his kind generosity, they turn him into a real madman. By his actions Myshkin fosters Christian compassion and, like Christ, is ridiculed and abused.

The Possessed depicts socialism's alleged destructiveness. A ruthless nihilist, Peter Verk-hovenskii, persuades followers to murder a fellow conspirator for planning to squeal to the police. Reacting to the "Nechaev Affair," a contemporary event (see Chapter 27), Dostoevsky was convinced that socialism was morally bankrupt. In *The Possessed* he depicts the alienation resulting from rejecting Christianity. The theater of the struggle between good and evil is all Russia which, Dostoevsky feared, socialism threatened with destruction. A powerful indictment of the revolutionary movement, the novel provoked criticism from radicals and conservatives. Undaunted, he continued his quest for personal spiritual peace and salvation for Russia.

In his greatest novel, *The Brothers Karamazov,* Dostoevsky tried to resolve issues that had long tormented him. Old Feodor Karamazov is murdered by one of his four sons, provoking a great theological debate between Ivan Karamazov and his younger brother Alyosha over the existence of God. The debate culminates in the famous "Legend of the Grand Inquisitor," portraying in parable form the human conflict between material well-being and belief in God. Christ reappears in Spain during the Inquisition and is recognized by the Grand Inquisitor, who threatens to burn him at the stake because Christ asks people to grant Him allegiance freely without coercion. Freedom of choice, warns the Grand Inquisitor, threatens the happiness of people who beg for authoritarianism in order to be free of the responsibility of freedom.

Count Leo Tolstoy (1828–1910) in his study.

Like the Grand Inquisitor, socialist revolutionaries offered people material well-being at the cost of their freedom, contended Dostoevsky. Society was doomed unless it embodied Christ's ideal; the Russian people possessed a Christlike harmony that could redeem humanity. Russia's and humanity's salvation were to be found in spiritual rebirth by voluntary acceptance of Christ's spirit.

Tolstoy (1828–1910)

From a prosperous noble family south of Moscow, Leo Tolstoy was tutored at home, attended Kazan University, then left it to open a school for peasant children on his estate. Joining the army in 1851, he served in the Caucasus, beginning his literary career there with a widely acclaimed autobiographical trilogy, *Childhood, Boyhood,* and *Youth* (1852–1857). In *Sevastopol Stories* he recorded his impressions of Sevastopol's siege in the Crimean War. After the war Tolstoy resigned from the army and traveled in Europe. Returning to his estate in 1862, he married and devoted himself to writing and his family.

His great novels, *War and Peace* and *Anna Karenina,* stem from this tranquil period. *War and Peace* (1869), a vast literary canvas of the Napoleonic era, probes lives of people from all social groups. Vast panoramas, great battles, agonizing retreats, and Napoleon's historic encounter with General Kutuzov serve as backdrop for Tolstoy's historical and moral philosophy. The novel's heroine and Tolstoy's ideal woman is Natasha Rostova, whose experiences mirror mighty historical forces. Ordinary people move history, not vaunted leaders like Napoleon, he believed. Tolstoy viewed Napoleon as a mere puppet, manipulated by forces beyond his control. To Tolstoy history had an inner logic that worked itself out through people as agents, not creators. Despite numerous characters and varied human experiences, *War and Peace* is a remarkably unified masterpiece perfectly integrating Tolstoy's philosophy with his artistry.

In *Anna Karenina,* an outstanding social novel (1877), Tolstoy discusses family issues, emancipation, the role of women, and the nobility's economic decline. The focus is the triangle of Anna, her husband, and her lover, Count Vronskii. Contrasting with Anna and Vronskii's tempestuous affair is her friend Kitty's marriage to the idealistic landowner, Levin. Anna and Vronskii struggle against social conventions that deny them happiness. Bitterness and guilt corrupt their relationship until Anna, to find peace, commits suicide and Vronskii's life is ruined.

Tolstoy's later works lack the intensity and depth of these masterworks. In the late 1870s he underwent a religious conversion dramatically recounted in *A Confession* (1882). Rejecting conventional Orthodoxy for a rationalistic Christianity based on nonresistance to evil, he urged rejection of all coercive institutions: church, state, and private property. His critique of contemporary society brought his public excommunication in 1901. Tolstoy's denunciation of the nobles' greed and his repudiation of private property caused conflict with them while the state viewed him as a dangerous revolutionary. His unconventional views on marriage and the family expressed in *The Kreutzer Sonata* (1889) and *The Devil,* published posthumously, provoked bitter family dissension. At 82, signing over his property to his estranged wife, Tolstoy set out on a pilgrimage and died a few days later at a house in Riazan province. Justifi-

ably, he is known as the last "true giant of the reformist aristocratic intelligentsia." He searched restlessly for answers to the meaning of life and history.

Chekhov (1860–1904)

Anton Chekhov was the last great figure of 19th-century Russian literature. Born in Taganrog on the Sea of Azov, son of a greengrocer and grandson of a serf, he grew up in poor health amidst provincial boredom, middle-class piety, and straitened finances. When his family moved to Moscow, Anton remained in Taganrog, supporting himself by tutoring and running errands. He was a carefree youth with an extraordinary sense of humor, evident in his later stories. His literary career began in 1880 with stories hastily written for pulp magazines under a pseudonym. Besides paying for medical school, his writings gave him the reputation of a prolific but mediocre writer. When one story was noticed by the literary elite upon its publication in 1885, Chekhov was invited to St. Petersburg and met Alexis Suvorin, editor of *New Times,* a prominent daily. Impressed with Chekhov's ability, Suvorin urged him to make writing his career. Much flattered, Chekhov continued writing short stories whose quality improved as their quantity decreased. In 1888 the Academy of Sciences gave him the prestigious Pushkin Prize. Amidst this growing success came warnings of tuberculosis, which would end his life prematurely. Foreseeing death, Chekhov wrote between 1889 and 1897 many fine stories reflecting personal restlessness and a belief that Russia required sweeping changes. Recurrent themes are human vanity, weaknesses, and melancholia. His characters often yearn for a richer, more beautiful future.

Always fascinated by the theater, Chekhov in 1895 wrote a serious play, *The Sea Gull,* but its first performance flopped because the director and actors misunderstood it. Two years later it was presented by a new theatrical company formed by K.S. Stanislavskii and V.I. Nemirovich-Danchenko: the famous Moscow Art Theater. Its directors

Anton Chekhov (1860–1904).

(Stanislavskii and Nemirovich-Danchenko) and actors understood its subtleties, and *The Sea Gull* became a sensation. In close association with Stanislavskii's theater, Chekhov from 1899 to 1903 wrote the immortal plays *Uncle Vania, The Three Sisters,* and *The Cherry Orchard.* Lacking clear plots or dramatic climaxes, they are studies in human psychology. Understatement, lack of suspense, little action—Chekhov's literary characteristics—succeed brilliantly on stage. Chekhov wrote with great enthusiasm for life and unfaltering optimism about the future. He lived in a Russia entering a century of momentous change.

Chekhov died in the summer of 1904 while taking a health cure in Germany, leaving a rich legacy of plays, stories, letters, and essays that deeply influenced writers in Russia and abroad. He brought the Golden Age to a close, though Russian literature continued to be creative and original. The last tsarist decades witnessed another outburst of creative energy, called the Silver Age. The transitional figure was Maxim Gorkii (1869–1936), whose literary credo evolved from classical realism through neoromanticism to socialist realism.

Gorkii (1868–1936)

From a lower-middle-class family, Maxim Gorkii (born A. M. Peshkov) saw his modest social status deteriorate rapidly after his father's premature death. On the streets at a tender age, he was educated by surviving in hostile Nizhnii-Novgorod. Gorkii wandered ceaselessly through southern Russia, learning much from those he met and gaining insight into life's problems. (The pseudonym Gorkii means "bitter," and for him it was a constant reminder of his miserable childhood as a street urchin.) He gained sympathy for the downtrodden. Gorkii's first published work was *Makar Chudra* (1892), a tale of love, passion, and violence among gypsies. His realistic early works reflect preference for broad social themes and reveal his humanitarianism. Portraying vividly a little-known world, Gorkii's stories were well received. His collected stories, issued in two popular volumes in 1898, made his reputation as a forceful writer. In 1902 he was elected an honorary member of the Academy of Sciences; when the government annulled this award on political grounds, Gorkii's popularity soared. On close terms with revolutionaries, he often supported the Bolsheviks after 1903.

In 1902 Stanislavskii's Moscow Art Theater staged with limited success his drama *The Lower Depths,* an unconventional play set in a decaying boardinghouse filled with drunks, prostitutes, and thieves. Translated, it soon became a hit in western Europe. In this call for freedom, Gorkii defended the dignity of people ground down by tsarism. The authorities banned it in the provinces and branded Gorkii a dangerous radical.

Gorkii's tendentious novels were less successful artistically. One, *Mother* (1907), was written on an ill-fated visit to the United States. Participating in the 1905 Revolution, Gorkii had been arrested and

Library of Congress (Alice Boughton)

Maxim Gorkii (1868–1936).

then released, provided he left Russia. Disillusioned with the United States, he bitterly criticized American society in *The City of the Yellow Devil* (1907), a collection of stories about New York. He finally settled in Italy, where his villa on the Isle of Capri became a haven for political exiles and an artists' and writers' colony. In his absence his reputation in Russia dwindled, but the great autobiographical work, *Childhood* (1913), and *Among Strangers* (1915) restored it. During the Romanovs' tercentenary in 1913, he returned to Russia, wrote for the Bolshevik press, and edited a Marxist journal, *Annals.* Gorkii rejoiced at tsarism's collapse but was unenthusiastic about the Bolshevik coup in November. Quarreling frequently with Lenin, Gorkii eventually made peace with him and continued writing in the Soviet era.

Decadence and Symbolism

Other writers criticized Gorkii for continued commitment to a literary realism they considered outmoded. Many grew preoccupied with form and beauty. A general European romantic revival influenced these new trends in Russia, where it was called the Decadent movement and later Symbolism. Such writers stressed aesthetics and "art for art's sake." Mysticism, individualism, sensualism, and demonism were its hallmarks. Language became vague and obscure to create symbolic images and sounds; poetry revived. Younger Symbolists included the great Alexander Blok, Andrei Beli, and Nicholas Gumilev. These poets formed a closely knit group that contributed to the same journals and created poetry of technical perfection, pure tonal harmony, and sheer beauty. Little affected at first by World War I and Russia's social crisis, most welcomed the March but not the November Revolution. Afterward some sought exile abroad; others remained in Russia hoping to influence the new regime. Taking their toll on Russian culture, war and revolution pointed in uncharted directions.

Music, painting, and architecture paralleled, though belatedly, developments in literature. Painting and music responded favorably after the Crimean War and were influenced by realistic aesthetics. Architecture was less affected until the turn of the 20th century.

Music

The Russian Music Society, founded in 1859, fostered musical activity, promoted conservatory training, and encouraged public music appreciation. Anton Rubinstein, a leading pianist and composer, and his younger brother, Nicholas, established branches in Moscow and some 30 provincial centers. Conservatories were founded in leading Russian cities to provide musical education. The Society organized several symphony orchestras and smaller performing ensembles and sponsored concerts all over Russia. Conservative in musical taste and theory, the Society followed the Rubinsteins, who viewed German schools of composition as models to emulate.

The Five

Despite the Society's remarkable popular success and rising interest in music, its conservative credo was challenged. A small group of composers—the famous "Five" or "Mighty Handful"—sought to initiate a revolution in Russian music and direct it along new paths. These men seemed an unlikely revolutionary group. Its leader and organizer was Mily Balakirev, its only trained musician, an excellent pianist and conductor, but only a mediocre composer. Cesar Cui, trained as an engineer, later became a general of army engineers. Modest Musorgskii was a Guards officer and later an official in the Transport Ministry. Alexander Borodin, trained as a medical doctor, eventually became a chemistry professor. Nicholas Rimskii-Korsakov became a naval officer and later a music professor at the St. Petersburg Conservatory. From diverse backgrounds and with differing professional interests, they did not always agree but shared common musical ideals and attitudes.

The Five, as successors of Glinka, aimed to create a Russian national school of music based on native folk and church music. Rejecting strict Western rules of technical form, they preferred a freer, more flexible style associated with folk music. They abhorred imitation of foreign models and scorned Italian opera as devoid of content and dramatic effect. Bitter polemics erupted between Rubinstein's conservatives and Balakirev's musical nationalists, which publicized and popularized music. In 1862, to counter Rubinstein's Music Society, the Five organized the Free School of Music to promote their musical theories and perform their works. Their great champion and defender of the nationalist musical trend was the distinguished art and music critic Vasili V. Stasov (1824–1906), whose caustic polemics and enthusiastic reviews won for the Five a large and loyal following.

Balakirev and Borodin were the creators of the Russian symphony and contributed much to symphonic theory. Musorgskii, Rimskii-Korsakov, and Borodin were geniuses of Russian opera, and their works remain in the repertoire throughout the world. Borodin worked 18 years on his great opera, *Prince Igor,* first performed in 1890 with great success. Based on the disputed 12th-century epic *The Tale of the Host of Igor* (see Chapter 4), it is a heroic national saga.

Library of Congress

Modest Musorgskii (1839–1881), portrait by Ilia Repin.

Modest Musorgskii is renowned for his monumental music drama, the opera *Boris Godunov,* one of Russia's greatest works of art. The composer studied carefully the history and language of the 16th century and was influenced by old Russian church music. The opera's hero was not Tsar Boris but the suffering Russian people, epitomized by a simpleton. Adapting Pushkin's play, Musorgskii wrote much of the libretto and stated: "My music must reproduce the people's language even in the most insignificant nuances."[3] *Boris Godunov,* in its original stark, tense version with no female lead, was rejected as insufficiently operatic by St. Petersburg's Marynskii Theater. Completely revising the score, Musorgskii added a "Polish" third act with Marina as prima donna and a revolutionary scene. The new version was performed successfully until 1882, when it was withdrawn under

[3] V. Seroff, *Modeste Moussorgsky* (New York, 1968), p. 90.

pressure from Alexander III's regime, which disliked its revolutionary implications. Rimskii-Korsakov, Musorgskii's friend, completely reorchestrated *Boris Godunov,* and his polished version scored triumphs in Europe and the United States. Musorgskii also composed most of *Khovanshchina,* a second folk opera based on the Moscow *streltsy* (musketeers') revolt of 1682. Completed and revised by Rimskii-Korsakov, it has remained a favorite in Russia. *Pictures at an Exhibition,* a piano suite also composed by Musorgskii, is best known in Maurice Ravel's orchestral version. Rimskii-Korsakov's operas, little known outside Russia, include *Sadko,* an old folktale of Novgorod, and *The Golden Cockerel,* also based on a fairy tale.

Tchaikovsky (1840–1893)

Among the first students at the St. Petersburg Conservatory, opened in 1862, was Peter I. Tchaikovsky, destined to become the best-known Russian composer. Like many of his contemporaries, Tchaikovsky was trained not for a musical career but for the civil service, serving briefly in the Ministry of Justice. After studying music privately, he enrolled in the Conservatory. He was such an excellent student that he was invited to join the faculty of the new Moscow Conservatory in 1866, and he worked and taught there for 12 years. His association with the Rubinsteins, and with Moscow, fostered enmity with the Five in St. Petersburg, which obscured how much they shared and how close they were in musical tastes and attitudes. Some critics describe Tchaikovsky's music as cosmopolitan and Western while calling that of the Five nationalist and Russian, but this dichotomy ignores their common origins and national feelings.

Tchaikovsky composed some of his finest music in Moscow. Despite recurring mental crises, he completed four symphonies; several operas, including *Eugene Onegin* (adapted from Pushkin); concertos; and his greatest ballet, *Swan Lake.* Then a period of acute depression and nervous tension prevented his composing so intensely and creatively. In 1889 another creative burst began with

his second major ballet, *The Sleeping Beauty,* soon followed by a third, *The Nutcracker,* one of his most popular compositions. Then he composed his Sixth Symphony ("Pathetique"), often considered his masterpiece. First performed in St. Petersburg in 1893 under the composer's direction, it was soon acclaimed as one of the greatest of Russian musical works.

Tchaikovsky acquired an international reputation even in his lifetime. In his last years he traveled extensively, conducting his music all over the world, and was specially honored at the opening of Carnegie Hall in New York City in 1891. Nationalists criticized his music as too Western and imitative of foreign models, but Igor Stravinsky, his worthy successor, stressed repeatedly its uniquely Russian qualities.

By 1900 Russian music had achieved great maturity, international recognition, and general respect. A group of brilliant teachers took up the cause in Russian conservatories, molding a new generation of composers that carried on the traditions of the Five and Tchaikovsky. Among the most talented were Sergei Rakhmaninov, a great pianist whose romantic compositions won plaudits worldwide, and Alexander Glazunov, composer and teacher. A pair of innovative Russian composers, Alexander Scriabin and Igor Stravinsky, like the Symbolists in poetry, opened up entirely new vistas. Alexander Scriabin (1871–1915), enrolled in the Moscow Conservatory at age 16, revealed prodigious ability as pianist and composer. He dabbled in mysticism, devoured Decadent poetry, and wrote poetry himself. Influenced by the Symbolists, Scriabin rejected the musical realism of the Five and Tchaikovsky's academicism to chart a new musical course. Inspired by romanticism, the occult, and the Decadents, Scriabin concluded that art must transform life, overcoming pain, ugliness, and evil and realizing the Kingdom of God on earth. He viewed the artist as a new messiah to redeem humankind and infuse life with new creative energy. His *Poem of Ecstasy* had eerie, haunting qualities, music he characterized as mystico-religious, the basis for a new harmonic system.

Scriabin's compositions, notably his piano music, influenced Stravinsky, Sergei Prokoviev, and Dmitri Shostakovich, the Russian giants of the 20th century, and have experienced a revival in the West.

Stravinsky (1882–1971)

Igor Stravinsky represents the first tide of musical influence flowing *from* Russia *into* Europe. Unlike most of his contemporaries, Stravinsky was self-taught, until he was tutored by Rimskii-Korsakov. His early career was closely associated with the famous Russian impresario, Serge Diagilev (1872–1929), who was impressed by his early works. Preparing the program for the first season of the revolutionary Ballet Russe de Monte Carlo in Paris, Diagilev asked Stravinsky to orchestrate two Chopin pieces for the ballet. Thus began a revolutionary and highly productive association— Diagilev, the organizer and man of ideas; Stravin-sky, the innovator whose scores would revolution-ize music; Mikhail Fokine, the choreographer whose ballets would become modern classics; Leon Bakst, a brilliant set and costume designer; and Vaslav Nijinsky, a great ballet dancer. Together in 1910 they created a stunning and opulent pro-duction of *The Firebird,* based on an old Russian folktale. The result was a great international tri-umph. In 1911 the same company staged *Petrushka,* a ballet teeming with new ideas and musical forms.

Stravinsky's radical orchestral style and boldly innovative music shocked many listeners. In 1913 Diagilev staged Stravinsky's revolutionary ballet, *The Rite of Spring,* whose brutal realism, violence, and extraordinary vitality created a public scandal. In these early works, Stravinsky was a musical descendant of Musorgskii's realism and national-ism, utilizing the rich tradition of Russian folk music. Before World War I he lived in France and Switzerland and adopted a neoclassical style reflected especially in the ballet *Pulcinella* (1919), based on themes by Pergolesi. Although he became a French citizen in 1934, Stravinsky was attracted increasingly to the United States. One of

Igor Stravinsky (1882–1971).

Library of Congress

the first major foreign composers to use jazz in his works, he moved to the United States at the out-break of World War II. He revisited Russia, triumphantly, only in his final years. The creativity of Russian music in the twilight of the tsarist monarchy, epitomized by Stravinsky, parallels the flowering of Russian literature in its Golden Age.

Painting

Russian painting developed rapidly during the late 19th century, finally emancipating itself from neo-classicism, long imposed by the Academy of Arts. Younger artists challenged old artistic conventions and strove to develop realism and nationalism. In 1863 the entire graduating class of the Academy defied its rigid policies after "The Festival of the Gods in Valhalla" was decreed as compulsory subject matter for a competition to determine who would be selected to continue their studies in Italy. Refusing to participate, the students demanded the right to select their own subjects freely. When the authorities demurred, 14 students resigned from the Academy to form their own artistic cooperative (*artel*), soon becoming the Society of Traveling Art Exhibitions; it dominated Russian art into the 1890s. The Society's young nationalist artists rejected the Academy's cosmopolitan and neoclassical approach. Annual exhibitions were organized in St. Petersburg and then toured throughout Russia. Exhibitions of the so-called Itinerants (artists of the Society) acquainted audiences with recent works by Russia's best artists. The critic Vasili V. Stasov staunchly defended the Itinerants, who promoted artistic realism based on portrayals and interpretations of real Russian life. Emphasizing content over form and composition, they were by no means indifferent to color and design. Often protesting against injustice, inequality, and exploitation, they realized that in order to make serious social statements their art had to display sound form, too. They considered themselves artists first, not mere propagandists.

The moving forces behind the Society of Traveling Art Exhibitions were Ivan Kramskoi and Vasili Perov, who were organizers and entrepreneurs as well as skillful artists. Kramskoi was a fine painter whose portraits of prominent leaders reveal great psychological insight and understanding. Perov, of humble origin, depicted lower-class life and problems. His searching criticism of the hypocrisy and moral turpitude among Orthodox clergy brought him into conflict with the authorities.

The most famous and successful 19th-century Russian artist was Ilia Repin (1844–1930). Though of humble origin, he studied at the Academy of Arts and won a prestigious traveling fellowship to study in Italy. *The Volga Boatmen* (1870–1873), designed as a group portrait of the human beasts of burden who hauled heavy barges up the Volga River, won him a reputation throughout Europe. This painting revealed a brutal exploitation widespread in Russia. Repin knew each of the people depicted in the painting and recorded their tragic lives in his memoirs. Another devastating social critique was his *Religious Procession in Kursk Province* (1880–1883), suggesting the clergy's arro-

Library of Congress

Ilia Repin (1844–1930), self-portrait.

gance and aloofness, police brutality, and quiet suffering of the peasantry. In the 1880s, turning to history, Repin in *Tsar Ivan and the Body of His Son* (1881–1885) showed Ivan IV moments after he had clubbed his eldest son to death, suggesting the corrupting influence of unlimited autocracy. Repin won greater recognition for Russian art, but after the Bolshevik Revolution he retired to his country house in Finland and refused to return to Soviet Russia.

Beginning in the 1890s, the Russian art world too revolted against the canons of realism and nationalism. Younger artists such as Mikhail Vrubel (1856–1911) broke with the Itinerants' realism. His abbreviated and tragic career contributed much to turning Russian art away from traditional approaches. After studying philosophy, he enrolled in the Academy of Arts and became a successful designer and mural painter skilled at church decoration. In an artwork every element was important to him: form, line, color, design, and subject matter. Vrubel advocated "art for art's sake"—art created for aesthetic purposes—an idea the realists considered outrageous. Suffering from serious mental stress, Vrubel was obsessed by demons, particularly after illustrating Lermontov's story "The Demon." Vrubel produced a powerful, brooding devil, but still unsatisfied, he finally produced a huge figure with contorted features and an expression of terrible despair that mirrored his own accelerating breakdown. He placed this figure against a background of dark swirling colors reminiscent of European Impressionism. Then he went insane and was confined in an asylum until his death. In his short career Vrubel helped shake Russian art loose from crystallized forms of realism and influenced poets and composers.

The foundations of a new direction in Russian art were firmly established in 1898 by the group Mir Iskusstva (World of Art), named after the journal it published (1898–1904). This group of young, cosmopolitan aristocrats was led by Serge Diagilev, Alexander Benois, Leon Bakst, and Dmitri Filosofov. Diagilev, the moving force and impresario, began with successful exhibitions of advanced Russian and European art. The journal attracted talented, avant-garde artists, essayists, and poets who wrote daring articles on various topics. The journal advocated "art for art's sake" and publicized new artistic trends. The success of *Mir Iskusstva* encouraged similar publications, such as *Byloe* (Past Years) and *The Golden Fleece,* which informed their readers of new European trends and attempted to integrate Russian and European art. Movements such as Symbolism, Futurism, and Cubism all found supporters and practitioners in Russia. The best-known Russian artists of this period included young Marc Chagall, Vasily Kandinskii, and K. Malevich, who helped shape the development of modern art.

Architecture

Russian architecture lacked the originality and striving for national forms of expression revealed in literature, music, and painting; it was dominated largely by foreign architects and styles. But about 1900 some Russian architects sought con-

sciously to create a new national style based on Russian medieval structures. The Slavic Revival, a rebirth of interest in Russia's past, affected all aspects of Russian culture. Iconography was rediscovered as a developed art form, and its carefully prescribed principles influenced and inspired many architects. The Slavic Revival caused architects to turn to traditional Russian wooden structures for inspiration and to translate them into innovative stone and brick structures. Slavic Revival architecture, found all over Russia, centered in Moscow, as epitomized by the Historical Museum. A leader in this movement was A. V. Shchusev (1873–1949), who designed several Orthodox churches in traditional Novgorod and Pskov style and built Moscow's Kazan Railroad Station in the style of 17th-century Muscovy.

Thus Russian culture between the Crimean War and World War I revealed to the world tremendous vitality and originality in most fields. For the first time Russian culture, notably in Stravinsky's music, began to influence international standards rather than responding to or imitating Western trends. On the eve of World War I, Russian culture was extraordinarily dynamic and diverse, exciting and energetic. War and revolution dampened but failed to destroy the creative impulses of the Russian intelligentsia.

Suggested Additional Reading

ANDREW, J. *Women in Russian Literature* (New York, 1988).

ASAFIEV, B. *Russian Music from the Beginning of the Nineteenth Century,* trans. A. Swan (Ann Arbor, MI, 1953).

BERLIN, I. *The Hedgehog and the Fox: An Essay on Tolstoy's View of History* (New York, 1953).

BOUSOVA, E., and G. STERNIN. *Russian Art Nouveau* (New York, 1988).

COSTLOW, J. T. *Worlds Within Worlds: The Novels of Ivan Turgenev* (Princeton, 1989).

EIKHENBAUM, B. M. *The Young Tolstoy,* trans. G. Kern (Ann Arbor, MI, 1972).

EMERSON, C. *Boris Godunov: Transpositions of a Russian Theme* (Bloomington, IN, 1987).

———. *Modest Musorgsky and Boris Gudonov* (Cambridge, 1994).

FANGER, D. L. *Dostoevsky and Romantic Realism* (Cambridge, MA, 1965).

FAUCHEREAU, S. *Moscow, 1900–1930* (New York, 1988).

FRANK, J. *Dostoevsky,* 3 vols. (Princeton, NJ, 1980–1987).

GRAY, C. *The Great Experiment: Russian Art 1863–1922* (London, 1962).

GRIERSON, R., ed. *Gates of Mystery: The Art of Holy Russia* (Fort Worth, 1993).

GROSSMAN, L. *Dostoevsky: A Biography,* trans. M. Mackler (New York, 1975).

GUSTAFSON, R. F. *Leo Tolstoy: Resident and Stranger* (Princeton, 1986).

HELDT, B. *Terrible Perfection: Women and Russian Literature* (Bloomington, IN, 1987).

HINGLEY, R. *Chekhov: A New Biography* (New York, 1976).

HOISINGTON, S. *A Plot of Her Own: The Female Protagonist in Russian Literature* (Evanston, IL, 1995).

LAYTON, S. *Russian Literature and Empire: Conquest of the Caucasus from Pushkin to Tolstoy* (New York, 1994).

LEONARD, R. *A History of Russian Music* (New York, 1968).

MAUDE, A. *The Life of Tolstoy,* 2 vols. (Oxford, 1987).

NEUBERGER, J. *Hooliganism: Crime, Culture and Power in St. Petersburg, 1900–1914* (Berkeley, 1993).

OBOLENSKY, C. *The Russian Empire: A Portrait in Photographs* (New York, 1979).

PYMAN, A. *A History of Russian Symbolism* (New York, 1994).

RABINOWITZ, S., ed. *The Noise of Change: Russian Literature and the Critics (1891–1917)* (Ann Arbor, MI, 1986).

SALMOND, W. *Arts and Crafts in Late Imperial Russia* (Cambridge, 1996).

SEELEY, F. F. *Turgenev: A Reading of His Fiction* (New York, 1991).

SIMMONS, E. J. *Chekhov: A Biography* (Boston, 1962).

THOMPSON, D. O. *The Brothers Karamazov and the Poetics of Memory* (New York, 1991).

TROYAT, H. *Tolstoy* (Garden City, NY, 1967).

VALKENIER, E. *Ilyia Repin* (New York, 1990).

———. *Russian Realist Art: The State and Society: The Peredvizniki and Their Tradition* (Ann Arbor, MI, 1977).

YARMOLINSKY, A. *Turgenev. The Man, His Art and His Age* (New York, 1959).

30

War and Revolution, 1914–1917

In August 1914 imperial Russia, its armed forces still being reorganized, refused to yield to Austro-German pressure and entered World War I. Initially, the war produced unity, patriotic resolve, and predictions of quick victory. As it dragged on, it revealed Russia's bureaucratic ineptitude, disunity in the army and government, and financial disarray. Military defeats and the regime's incompetence undermined morale among soldiers and civilians alike. In March 1917, in the midst of this great conflict, the tsarist regime was overthrown by a popular revolution. What caused the sudden collapse of the Romanov regime, which had ruled Russia for more than 300 years? Was it economic backwardness, social conflicts, bureaucratic bungling, or incompetent military leadership—or a combination of these—that accounted for Russia's defeat in World War I? This chapter probes the complex relationship between the war and the coming of revolution in March 1917.

Russia Enters World War I

On June 28, 1914, a Bosnian student linked with the Serbian national movement assassinated

Archduke Francis Ferdinand, heir to the Austrian throne, in Sarajevo, Bosnia, sparking war among the European powers, Japan, and later the United States. The assassination alone did not cause the war. World War I resulted from increasingly rigid alliance systems that divided Europe between the Triple Alliance (Germany, Austria-Hungary, and Italy) and the Triple Entente (Great Britain, France, and Russia) and involved the prestige of all powers; from a precipitous growth of armaments and militarism; from intense nationalism, especially in Serbia and France, expressed in hatred of their national enemies, Austria and Germany; and from imperial rivalries. In this tense, intolerant atmosphere, diplomats could not reach reasonable compromises.

Russian leaders, at first not unduly alarmed by the Sarajevo murder, went on vacation. The Russian public and press, although mostly anti-Austrian and pro-Serbian, were not violently so. In mid-July the Russian government even sent the quartermaster-general on a routine mission to the Caucasus. By July 20, Russian leaders had returned to St. Petersburg to greet President Poincaré of France, who spent three days there on a previously arranged state visit. French and Russian chiefs reaffirmed their solemn obligation under the Franco-Russian Alliance.

No sooner had Poincaré departed than Austria-Hungary issued an ultimatum to Serbia that was so framed as to be unacceptable. Russian Foreign Minister S. D. Sazonov exclaimed, "That means European war!" but he urged Serbia to make a conciliatory reply, appeal to the powers, and not resist Austria militarily. He requested Austria to give the Serbs more time to answer, but Russia, assured of French support, resolved not to back down.

The mobilization of Russia's army became a vital factor in the last days before war broke out. On July 24 the Council of Ministers empowered War Minister V. A. Sukhomlinov to mobilize only districts facing Austria. Sazonov saw this as mainly a diplomatic move to back Serbia. Sukhomlinov and Chief of Staff N. N. Ianushkevich agreed to this partial mobilization, though subordinates objected that there were no plans for it and that to improvise them might disrupt full mobilization later. On July 25 the tsar and his ministers, learning that Serbia's reply had not satisfied Austria, agreed to support Serbia at any cost. Austria mobilized and, on July 28, declared war on Serbia, and Sazonov announced that Russia would carry out partial mobilization.

Meanwhile, Russian staff officers had convinced their chiefs, and finally Nicholas II and Sazonov, that partial mobilization was impractical. On July 29, with the Austrians bombarding Belgrade, the Russian chief of staff issued the decree of Nicholas II, authorizing full mobilization. Nicholas, receiving the Kaiser's telegram warning of the consequences, rescinded this order, but on July 30 Sazonov and the military chiefs persuaded him to authorize general mobilization. Germany demanded that Russia demobilize; when it refused, Germany declared war on Russia, then on France. After Germany violated Belgian neutrality, England joined France and Russia on August 4. The Central Powers (Germany and Austria-Hungary) now faced a coalition of Serbia, Russia, France, and England.

Russia's responsibility for World War I remains debatable. German and Western revisionist historians argue that its general mobilization doomed German and British efforts to head off conflict. But the tsar and Sazonov, who opposed war, concluded that partial mobilization would disorganize the Russian army. Another retreat in the Balkans, they believed, might destroy Russia's credibility as a great power. Also, Austria was the first to mobilize, declare war, and begin hostilities against Serbia, an ally of Russia. Like all great European powers in 1914, Russia bore some responsibility, but its leaders went to war reluctantly after failing to find a peaceful solution. Soviet historians, following Lenin, considered World War I a clash of rival imperialist powers, with Germany and Austria-Hungary bearing primary responsibility.

War Aims and Wartime Diplomacy

Russia entered the war without clear aims except to protect itself and Serbia. At first no specific territorial claims were made against Germany, and Sazonov merely denounced German militarism and pledged to restore a "free" Poland. In September 1914 he told the French and British ambassadors that Russia advocated reorganizing Austria-Hungary into a triple monarchy, ceding Bosnia, Hercegovina, and Dalmatia to Serbia and restoring Alsace-Lorraine to France. As an afterthought he requested free passage for Russian warships through the Turkish Straits. Grand Duke Nicholas, Russia's commander in chief, urged the peoples of Austria-Hungary to overthrow Habsburg rule and achieve independence, but other Russian leaders did not pursue this nationalist tack. Like other members of the Entente, Russian leaders expected victory to provide them with a program of war aims.

Early defeats and Turkish entry into the war ended official Russian reticence. After Germany persuaded the Ottoman Empire to join the Central Powers (November 1, 1914), the tsar favored expelling it from Europe and solving "the historic task bequeathed to us by our forefathers on the shores of the Black Sea." Nationalists and liberals in the Duma and press took up the refrain. Only securing Constantinople, Professor Trubetskoi of Moscow University declared, would guarantee Russia's independence. P. N. Miliukov, leader of the Kadets and the liberal opposition in the Duma, echoing the general nationalist euphoria, demanded that Russia seize the Straits and Constantinople, and to do so became the principal Russian war aim.

The Entente powers pledged, in September 1914, not to conclude a separate peace and to consult on peace terms, but they disagreed over war plans and aims. As a basis for a future peace they concluded secret treaties and agreements. In December 1914 Grand Duke Nicholas, lacking forces to capture or garrison the Straits, urged Sazonov to obtain them by diplomacy. London, to keep Russia fighting, responded warmly. "As to Constantinople, it is clear that it must be yours," the English king told the Russian ambassador.[1] In 1915 the British undertook a Dardanelles campaign to force open the Straits and develop a supply line to Russia; its failure helped doom Russia instead to eventual defeat. In March 1915 Sazonov insisted that if the Entente won, the Straits and environs go to Russia; England, then France, agreed. The tsar told the French ambassador, Maurice Paléologue: "Take the left bank of the Rhine, take Mainz; go further if you like."[2] Later, secret inter-Allied agreements arranged a partition of the Ottoman Empire. Russia would obtain the Straits, eastern Anatolia, and part of the southern coast of the Black Sea. The former Crimean powers promised this, knowing that without Russia they would lose the war. Thus the Russian government and liberals were committed to an imperialistic peace, which aroused no popular enthusiasm at home.

The Army and the Fronts

Russia began World War I with unity, optimism, and loyalty to the Crown, a situation unlike the public apathy prevalent at the beginning of the Japanese war. Domestic quarrels and differences seemed forgotten, and the strike movement, so threatening in July, ended abruptly. Virtually the entire Duma pledged to support the war effort, except for a few socialists who refused to vote war appropriations. The enthusiasm was largely defensive; the Russian people believed that the war was being fought to defend Russia and Serbia. In the cities this spontaneous patriotism became anti-German: The name of St. Petersburg was changed to Petrograd, and there were anti-German riots. The villages, however, remained ominously silent.

At first the generals and nationalist press proclaimed that the Russian "steamroller" would move to Berlin and end the war in a few weeks. In the West, this myth of Russian invincibility was widely believed. Actually, the army, its leadership split between "patricians" and "praetorians" (aristocratic and professional elements), reflected the deep rifts in Russian government and society. Though contemporaries claimed that the army had been unprepared, the military *was* prepared for a replay of the Russo-Japanese War. As the German General Staff realized, the Russian army had recovered completely from that defeat and possessed more infantry and mobile guns in the east than the Germans did. What hampered the Russian army in 1914 was divided command, incompetent leadership, and failure to mobilize industry. Grand Duke Nicholas, the impressive-looking six-foot-six commander in chief appointed at the last moment, lacked real authority and knew neither his subordinates nor military plans. In General A. A. Polivanov's words, he "appeared entirely unequipped for the task and . . . spent much time crying because he did not know how to approach his new duties."[3] His military bearing made him popular with the men, who mistook his severity for competence. In August 1915 Nicholas II, who knew even less, replaced him, continuing a disastrous Romanov

---

[1] Quoted in Maurice Paléologue, *An Ambassador's Memoirs* (London, 1923), vol. 1, p. 297.

[2] Paléologue, *Ambassador's Memoirs,* vol. 1, p. 297.

[3] Quoted in M. T. Florinsky, *Russia: A History and an Interpretation* (New York, 1953), vol. 2, p. 1320.

tradition of placing members of the imperial family in top military posts. War Minister Sukhomlinov, who had put through needed reforms before the war, succumbed to intrigues by his political and military foes.[4] High army commands, despite Sukhomlinov, were filled largely by seniority, not proven ability. Abler company-grade officers, killed in large numbers in the first months, could not be replaced, producing a grievous officer shortage.

General conscription swelled a peacetime force of 1.35 million men to almost 6.5 million, with no comparable increase in trained officers. During the war, more than 15 million men were called up— some 37 percent of all Allied soldiers—but only a fraction could be equipped; they were poorly led and early in the war were inadequately supplied. The rank and file were mostly illiterate peasants ignorant of why they fought. Red tape and lack of a unified command or agreed war plan produced much confusion. Shortages of shells and rifles soon developed, mainly from lack of planning and failure to mobilize industry. The autocracy was unprepared for the overwhelming complexity of total war, which necessitated mobilizing the entire population to support it, but other belligerents also proved ill-prepared.

Within the army command, prewar controversies between those favoring an offensive against weaker Austria-Hungary and others advocating an invasion of Germany remained unresolved. The army was split among competing fronts, strategies, and generals jealous of one another; men and resources were wasted. Appeals for help from the hard-pressed French and British in the west persuaded the Russian high command to dispatch two armies under Generals P. K. Rennenkampf

and A. V. Samsonov (personal enemies) into East Prussia. Inadequate maps, inaccurate intelligence, and poor coordination between the armies and their commanders produced defeat. The Germans rushed in reinforcements from France, and General von Hindenburg trapped Samsonov's army at Tannenberg. Some 300,000 men were lost, Samsonov apparently shot himself, and Russian morale was seriously damaged. Revealing German tactical superiority and ending Russian dreams of a march to Berlin, Tannenberg proved "that armies will lose battles if they are led badly enough."[5] However, a Russian offensive against the smaller, poorly armed, and unreliable Austro-Hungarian army led to occupation of Galicia and heavy Austrian losses and ended hopes by the Central Powers for quick victory in the east.

Unlike the positional trench warfare in France, a war of maneuver persisted on the eastern front. In April 1915 the Germans, reinforcing their armies, scored a breakthrough in Russian Poland. A devastating four-hour artillery bombardment smashed Russian trenches and scared their ill-trained defenders from their posts. Galicia was reconquered, and the Russians retreated hastily, abandoning Poland and part of the Baltic provinces. An unwise Russian scorched-earth policy produced swarms of refugees who poured into Russian cities and demoralized the population. Severe shortages of war matériel and even food plagued the Russian forces. Their artillery had few shells while German guns fired ceaselessly; many Russian soldiers even lacked rifles. Losses and desertions soared, officers lost faith in their men, and morale plummeted. Rumors spread: "Britain will fight to the last drop of Russian blood." Commented one Russian soldier: "We throw away our rifles and give up because things are dreadful in our army, and so are the officers."[6] Only swampy terrain, overextended German supply lines, and the heroism of the Russian soldier prevented utter collapse. During 1915, while the western front had a long breath-

---

[4] Sukhomlinov, notes Norman Stone in his revisionist treatment of Russia in World War I, was hated by Duma liberals for his autocratic methods and by old guard, aristocratic military elements for his reforms. Accused of corruption, he was imprisoned by the tsarist and Provisional governments, though the charges were never proven. Norman Stone, *The Eastern Front* (New York, 1975), pp. 24–32.

[5] Stone, *Eastern Front*, p. 59.
[6] Stone, p. 170.

ing spell, Russia bore the main pressure of the Central Powers.

In the winter of 1915–1916 began a surprising recovery. Though few of the promised war supplies came from Russia's allies, Russian industry in a great effort produced more than 11 million shells during 1915, proving its capacity to support a modern war. Unofficial efforts by *zemstva,* Duma deputies, and other public-spirited groups left the army far better equipped and supplied. By mid-1916, the Russian army enjoyed a considerable superiority in both men and matériel over the Central Powers. The new war minister, A. A. Polivanov, and Chief of Staff M. Alekseev were abler than their predecessors. General A. A. Brusilov's sudden but carefully prepared attack in Galicia (May 1916) shattered Austrian lines and forced the Germans to send reinforcements (see Map 30.1). This action revealed Russia's renewed ability to fight and induced Romania to join the Allies. In the Caucasus, Russian forces prevailed against poorly organized Turkish armies, capturing Erzurum and Trebizond in 1916 and penetrating deep into Anatolia.

Thus the Russian army, despite poor command and organization, played a vital part in World War I. It tied down much of the Central Powers' strength and repeatedly saved the western front from disaster. However, the cost to Russia was staggering: more than 3 million soldiers killed and wounded and 2.7 million captured and missing. Though they coped well with Austrians and Turks, Russian forces were usually defeated by the Germans. These defeats, speeding deterioration of relations between Russian officers and their men, demoralized the army and contributed greatly to the downfall of the tsar's regime.

The Home Front

Modern war, the supreme test of a nation's soundness, reveals both strengths and hidden weaknesses. Few had foreseen before 1914 that in an age of industrialization and technology war would require a total mobilization of a nation's resources.

Russia proved most inadequately prepared to face such a total conflict. On the one hand, World War I triggered rapid growth of Russian machine-tool and chemical industries and swelled the industrial proletariat. On the other hand, it ruthlessly exposed Russia's inadequate transportation system, fumbling government, and chaotic finances. It revealed the tsar's incompetence and isolation, heightening the problems of a disintegrating regime and a disgruntled public. The terrible weaknesses on the home front, more than military shortcomings, produced defeat and revolution. Interior Minister Peter Durnovo's memorandum to Nicholas II in February 1914 proved prophetic:

> A war involving all of Europe would be a mortal danger for Russia and Germany regardless of which was the victor. In the event of defeat . . . social revolution in its most extreme form would be inevitable in our country.[7]

The Economy

Agriculture suffered less than industry from the ill-considered mobilization of Russian manpower. Because of rural overpopulation and prewar wastage of labor, peasant farms were able to operate almost normally, despite the loss of most male laborers. In some unoccupied provinces, acreage under cereal crops actually increased as women, children, and old men took up the slack. Large estates, which had produced most of the surplus for home and foreign markets, were harder hit because they could not obtain hired laborers, machinery, or spare parts. Despite increased demand, the total Russian grain and potato harvest and meat production fell by about one-third during the war. At first peasant soldiers ate better in the army than they had at home, but by 1917 the front was receiving less than half the grain it required. As commanders searched for food, their soldiers grew hungry and dissatisfied.

Even in 1917 Russia possessed enough food for both civilians and soldiers. The virtual cessation of

---

[7] Quoted in M. Heller and A. Nekrich, *Utopia in Power . . . ,* trans. P. Carlos (New York, 1986).

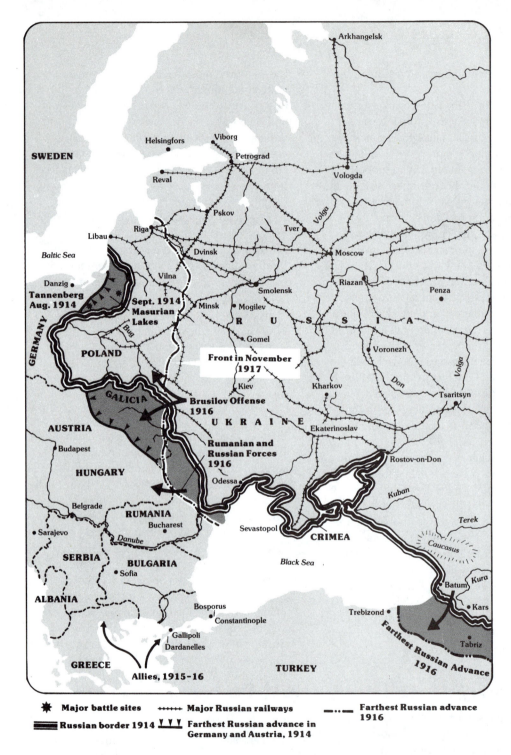

SWEDEN

Arkhangelsk

Helsingfors

Viborg

Petrograd

Reval

Vologda

Volga

Pskov

Riga

Tver

Libau

Dvinsk

Moscow

Baltic Sea

Vilna

Riazan

Danzig

Tannenberg Aug. 1914

Sept. 1914 Masurian Lakes

Minsk

Smolensk

Mogilev

Penza

GERMANY

Bug

POLAND

Gomel

R U S S I A

Voronezh

Volga

Front in November 1917

GALICIA

Kiev

Brusilov Offense 1916

U K R A I N E

Kharkov

Don

Tsaritsyn

AUSTRIA

Budapest

Ekaterinoslav

Rumanian and Russian Forces 1916

HUNGARY

Rostov-on-Don

Odessa

Kuban

Belgrade

RUMANIA

Terek

Sarajevo

Bucharest

Sevastopol

CRIMEA

Caucasus

Danube

SERBIA

BULGARIA

Black Sea

Kura

Sofia

ALBANIA

Batum

Kars

Bosporus

Constantinople

Trebizond

Farthest Russian Advance 1916

Gallipoli
Dardanelles

Tabriz

GREECE

Allies, 1915–16

TURKEY

✸ **Major battle sites**   +++++ **Major Russian railways**   —··— **Farthest Russian advance 1916**

▬ **Russian border 1914** ⋎⋎⋎ **Farthest Russian advance in Germany and Austria, 1914**

Map 30.1 Russia in World War I, 1914–1918

SOURCE: Adapted from *A History of Russia,* Fifth Edition, by Nicholas V. Riasanovsky. Copyright © 1963, 1977, 1984, 1993 by Oxford University Press, Inc. Used by permission.

Hungry Petrograd in World War I.

food exports and diminished use of grain to manufacture vodka roughly balanced production declines. Government policy contributed to shortages: Artificially low state prices for grain deprived farmers of production incentives while prices of manufactured goods they desired rose rapidly. Peasants, therefore, consumed more grain and brewed their own alcohol while speculators hoarded grain and awaited higher prices. Because shipping foodstuffs to the cities was complicated by a worsening transportation crisis, by 1917 the cities in the northern consuming provinces were hungry while in Ukraine and Siberia food was relatively abundant.

Transportation, the economy's weakest link, was nearing breakdown by 1917. The railroad system, which had barely met ordinary peacetime needs, had a low carrying capacity and inferior connections with seaports. (Only a narrow-gauge line went to Archangel, and not until 1916 was a railroad built to the new port of Murmansk.) Wartime needs virtually monopolized a railway system further overburdened by the retreat in Poland and massive evacuation of civilians. Railroad cars and spare parts, formerly obtained largely in western Europe, became critically short. The government spent 1.5 billion rubles to improve the network and build additional lines; it ordered American railway equipment, but it did not arrive until late in 1917. On the eve of the March Revolution, a crisis in railroad transport worsened the problems of industry and food supply.

Because at first the government had no deferment system, industry was crippled by mobilization of irreplaceable skilled labor. Much of the labor force came to be composed of women, children, and war prisoners. Initially, many factory owners pursued "business as usual," and some curtailed production because of mobilization, disruption of foreign business connections, and expected decreases in domestic demand. Unprecedented need for munitions and war supplies placed an intolerable burden on industry, which could not get essential raw materials and fuel. (More shells were used in a month than in a year of the Russo-Japanese War.) The loss in 1915 of Russian Poland, the Empire's most industrialized region, reduced production by about one-fifth. To be sure, certain branches of industry, spurred by war demand, grew rapidly: Metalworking trebled in 1916, and chemicals expanded 250 percent. Rifle production in August 1916 was 11 times that of 1914 but was still insufficient.

Red tape and lack of government planning further complicated industry's problems. The official hands-off policy lasted until appalling munitions shortages spurred public action. During 1915 industrialists, Duma members, *zemstva,* and municipalities formed military-industrial committees, which improved the supply picture greatly. But government action was too little and too late. By 1917 industrial production was falling sharply in a growing economic crisis. Yet Soviet accounts exaggerated the wartime growth of monopolies and trusts to support their claims that in Russia finance capitalism was maturing, thus preparing the way for socialism.

The war badly disrupted Russian foreign trade. In the first year exports fell to about 15 percent of the prewar level and later recovered to only 30 percent. Imports, dropping sharply at first in 1916, were double the prewar value in 1917—mainly war supplies and equipment sent by the Allies through Siberian ports. Instead of the 47 million ruble export surplus of 1913, the wartime Russian trade deficit totaled some 2.5 billion rubles. Incompetent government wartime financing damaged the Russian economy. At the outset Russia seemed in better financial shape than in the Russo-Japanese War, but the Treasury expended as much in a month of World War I as in a year of the war against Japan. A drastic fall in customs and railway receipts cut Treasury revenues, and an incredible blunder robbed it of the liquor tax. The finance minister ordered state liquor stores closed during mobilization and introduced legislation to raise liquor prices to combat drunkenness. A decree of August 1914 kept liquor stores closed throughout the war. Such pioneering in prohibition cost the Treasury about 700 million rubles annually—about 25 percent of its total revenue. Peasants brewed their own liquor, and illicit vodka sales brought huge profits to dealers but nothing to the Treasury. New wartime taxes barely covered this loss, and state revenues fell far short of war expenditures. Income and war profits taxes were low and introduced too late. Huge domestic and foreign loans and massive use of the printing press financed the war. Foreign nations, chiefly Great Britain, loaned Russia some 8 billion rubles, accelerating a sharp decline in the ruble's exchange value, which produced rampant inflation, loss of confidence in the currency, and a rapid rise in living costs. Russia grew ever more dependent financially upon its allies.

The serious economic strain of the war helped bring on revolution and made it more profound. The basic economic framework, especially of peasant agriculture, remained sound, but food supplies in the swollen cities of Petrograd and Moscow became increasingly inadequate as the overstrained railway system deteriorated. With paper rubles losing their value, there was little incentive for peasants to ship their grain to the cities. Although the masses' purchasing power rose, people found little to buy. Russian resources were wasted and misused by incompetent officials.

The Government

During the war the tsarist regime revealed its inability to govern the country and disintegrated rapidly. Nicholas II, retaining his faith in autocracy, Orthodoxy, and nationality, failed to supply leadership; he believed that constitutional government was evil and that the public could not be allowed to help run Russia. Though interfering little with the Duma, he largely ignored it and absorbed himself in family affairs and problems. Ever more dominated by Empress Alexandra, he and his family were estranged from the public and the bureaucracy. "The characteristic feature of the imperial family," noted a trusted minister, "is their inaccessibility to the outside world, and their atmosphere of mysticism." Empress Alexandra, who hated the Duma and liberal ministers with a passion, was largely responsible for this isolation, and as Rasputin's hold over her grew, she interfered more and more in state affairs. The most influential of several "men of God" to influence the superstitious empress, Rasputin had been introduced at court in November 1905. She found this semiliterate, debauched (his motto was "Redemption through sin"!), but dynamic Siberian peasant indispensable to preserving her hemophiliac son, Alexis (born 1904), and the dynasty. Rasputin managed through hypnotism to stop the tsarevich's bleeding, and to the imperial couple he embodied the Russian people.

When Nicholas II took command of the army in September 1915, control over the government passed to the empress and Rasputin. Believing that she could save Russia from revolution, Alexandra relied completely on Rasputin, who lacked clear political aims; she was surrounded with unscrupulous, greedy adventurers. When the more competent, liberal ministers, appointed under public pressure early in 1915, protested Nicholas's decision to become army chief, the empress, to preserve autocracy, removed them from office. A nonentity, Boris Stürmer, was named premier. "A country cannot be lost whose sovereign is guided by a man of God," Alexandra wrote Nicholas. "Won't you come to the assistance of your hubby now that he is absent . . . ?" Nicholas queried. "You ought to be my eyes and ears there in the capital. . . . It rests with you to keep peace and harmony among the ministers."[8]

---

[8] Bernard Pares, *The Letters of the Tsar to the Tsaritsa, 1914–1917* (London, 1929) and *Letters of the Tsaritsa to the Tsar, 1914–1916* (London, 1923).

The final disgraceful year of Romanov rule was marked by "ministerial leapfrog" as the empress and Rasputin shifted ministers with bewildering speed. The last premier, Prince N. D. Golitsyn, begged to be relieved of his tasks, which he did not know how to perform. Late in 1916 Rasputin's behavior became intolerable even to loyal monarchists. An ultraconservative Duma delegate, V. M. Purishkevich, and two grand dukes invited Rasputin to a banquet, fed him cake laced with cyanide, shot him, and finally drowned him in a canal. This was a terrible blow to the empress, but she and A. D. Protopopov continued to rule and hold seances to recall Rasputin from the dead. On the eve of the March Revolution, the government was inactive, divided, and in an advanced state of decay.

Meanwhile, the Duma had risen to unprecedented national leadership. After the war began, the Duma set up a provisional committee to aid the wounded and war sufferers and to coordinate its war work. At first, the Duma supported the government unconditionally, but early in 1915 it agitated with *zemstvo* and municipal representatives for a responsible ministry. That summer, about two-thirds of the Duma, excluding the extreme left and right, formed a Progressive Bloc led by Kadets and Octobrists, which advocated a government capable of winning public confidence, political amnesty, religious freedom, and freedom for trade unions. Though most of the ministers accepted this program, Premier Goremykin stubbornly rejected it as an illegal attempt to limit the autocrat's power. During 1916 the Duma's relations with the executive branch deteriorated sharply when deputies led by Miliukov accused the government and the tsarina of conspiring with the Germans. Censorship deleted the sharpest Duma attacks, but its debates were widely publicized and it was winning a public following. The fatal weakness that prevented the Duma from representing and leading the Russian people in 1917 was an electoral process of indirect and weighted voting that favored the landed nobility. Thus the majority of Russians were still not politically represented.

The Revolutionary Movement

The government's ineffectiveness and inability to win liberal support provided revolutionaries with a rare opportunity. In 1915, after the defeat in Galicia, strikes grew more numerous and continued to mount until the March Revolution, but the socialist parties in Russia remained too disorganized and fragmented to prepare a revolution. Their leaders mostly remained in exile in Siberia or Europe, out of touch with Russia. Initially, the SDs in the Duma denounced the war as the product of aggressive capitalism and urged the proletariat to oppose it. The Bolshevik deputies, more aggressively antiwar than the Mensheviks, were soon arrested, tried, and exiled to Siberia. Social Democrats abroad were divided by the war. Plekhanov, splitting with Lenin and the majority, urged Russian workers to fight against Prussian imperialism and with the Western democracies to final victory. Lenin, in his *Theses on War* (1914), written in Switzerland, denounced World War I as imperialist and exhorted Russian workers to help defeat tsarism, to turn the conflict into a civil war, and to prepare revolution. Lenin accused the Second International and its leader, Karl Kautsky, of betraying the proletariat by voting for a fratricidal war. At international socialist conferences at Zimmerwald (1915) and Kienthal (1916), the minority Leninist left urged a civil war of workers against all capitalist governments, but most European socialists supported their governments in World War I.

The Bolsheviks' Russian rivals were likewise divided. The Menshevik organizational committee in Switzerland, including Martov, Akselrod, and A. S. Martynov, denounced the war and advocated eventual revolution but sought to restore unity to international socialism. Rather than favor Russia's defeat, they exhorted workers to exert pressure on all governments to conclude a democratic peace without annexations and indemnities. In Russia, an important Menshevik group around the publication *Our Dawn (Nasha Zaria)* advocated noncooperation with the regime without hampering the war effort; later it favored defense of Russia

against invasion. The SRs, still dispirited, were split among a right actively supporting the war effort, Chernov's pacifist center, and a sizable left internationalist wing favoring defeat of tsarism. In Russia and abroad, socialists divided into three main groupings: patriots, centrists (defensists and pacifists), and defeatists advocating revolution.

Bolshevik organizations in Russia were tougher and more resilient than their rivals. The British scholar Leonard Schapiro claims that Bolshevik wartime activity was intermittent and ineffective, but Soviet accounts asserted that the Bolsheviks led the workers' struggle against the war from the start, steadily expanded their organization, and followed Lenin's instructions. Although the police "liquidated" the Petrograd Committee 30 times and arrested more than 600 Bolsheviks, the party nonetheless expanded its membership and activities. By late 1916 the Bolsheviks, numbering perhaps 10,000, were led by A. G. Shliapnikov (Lenin's man), V. M. Molotov, and P. A. Zalutskii. Though Soviet historians exaggerated Bolshevik strength and leadership of the workers, the party represented a considerable force ready, unlike Mensheviks and SRs, to exploit a revolutionary situation.

The March Revolution

In five days—March 8–12, 1917 (February 23–27 Old Style)[9]—a mass movement in Petrograd overturned the tsarist government. The eyewitness accounts of N. N. Sukhanov, a moderate socialist, and French ambassador Maurice Paléologue stress that it was spontaneous and not led by a party or organization. Western historians and early Soviet accounts, such as Trotskii's *History of the Russian Revolution*, accept this view, whereas Stalinist historians overstate Bolshevik leadership of the masses.

---

[9] New Style dates, like those used in western Europe, will be used from this point onward instead of Old Style dates of the Julian calendar, which by the 20th century were 13 days behind the New Style dates.

In previous months the Petrograd strike movement had steadily gathered momentum. A strike by some workers at the Putilov factory, Russia's largest, became general, and on March 7 the management locked out the workers. Though the government and tsar had received numerous warnings of impending revolution (from foreign ambassadors and Duma president M. V. Rodzianko), they made no concessions. Nicholas II, confident that nothing unusual was afoot, left his palace at Tsarskoe Selo near Petrograd on March 7 for military headquarters at Mogilev. The authorities had a detailed plan for suppressing an uprising: First the 3,500 police were to be used, then Cossacks with whips, and finally troops from the 150,000-man garrison. The plan, though later implemented, proved ineffective.

Revolution began in Petrograd on March 8, International Women's Day. In the large factories of Vyborg district, women in bread lines and strikers began spontaneous demonstrations, which spread to the Petersburg side. (See Chapter 31, Map 31.1.) Women textile workers, the most downtrodden segment of the Petrograd proletariat, supplied the impetus. In the streets appeared placards with slogans: "Down with the war!" "Give us bread!" and "Down with autocracy!" That day, notes Sukhanov, "the movement in the streets became clearly defined, going beyond the limits of the usual factory meetings. . . . The city was filled with rumors and a feeling of 'disorders.'" Fearing conflict with the authorities while the party was weak, the Bolsheviks, who controlled Vyborg Borough Committee, relegated revolution to the indefinite future, not realizing that one was in progress. In March, noted Trotskii, the higher the revolutionary leaders, the further they lagged behind the masses. Next day (March 9), continued Sukhanov, "the movement swept over Petersburg like a great flood. Nevskii Prospect [the main shopping street] and many squares in the center were crowded with workers." Mounted police were sent to disperse the demonstrations, then Cossacks were ordered out. They charged the crowds halfheartedly and often chatted amicably with the workers.

By March 10 "the entire civil population felt itself to be in one camp united against the enemy —the police and the military." Proclamations of the garrison commander, General S. S. Khabalov, threatening stern punishment for demonstrators, were torn down, police were disarmed or vanished from their posts, and factories and streetcars halted operation. Khabalov sent in troops, but the crowds, avoiding clashes with them, sought to win them over.

Early on Sunday, March 11, workers advanced from outlying districts toward Petrograd's center. Stopped at the bridges, they poured across the solidly frozen Neva River, dodging bullets. At the tsar's orders, Khabalov sent thousands of infantry into the streets. On Nevskii Prospect, soldiers fired on crowds, killing many and terrorizing the rest; that afternoon the Vyborg Borough Committee considered calling off the strike. The critical moment of the revolution had come. In the evening, after police fired on a crowd, soldiers of the passing Pavlovskii Regiment mutinied, fired on the police, then returned to barracks, resolved not to fire again at strikers, and appealed to their comrades to join them. This was the military's first revolutionary act of 1917.

On the fifth day (March 12) workers streamed into the factories and in open meetings resolved to continue the struggle. Armed insurrection grew irresistibly from events while the Bolshevik headquarters staff looked on despondently, leaving the districts and barracks to their own devices. Soldiers mutinied in growing numbers and joined crowds of workers.

New centers of authority sprang up before old ones had disappeared. The government had ordered the Duma prorogued, but on March 12 some members elected a Provisional Committee under the Duma president, Rodzianko, representing all groups except the right, "to restore order in the capital and establish contact with public organizations and institutions." Reflecting views of the Progressive Bloc, the Committee sought to save the dynasty with a responsible ministry. Simultaneously, the Petrograd Soviet was reborn while mutinous troops freed worker and socialist leaders from the city's prisons. Proceeding with the troops to the Tauride Palace and aided by the trade union leaders, they created the Provisional Executive Committee of the Soviet of Workers' Deputies. At the Petrograd Soviet's first meeting that evening some 250 delegates were present, but new ones kept entering the noisy, chaotic session. No political party proposed a definite plan or took decisive leadership. When soldier deputies asked to join, the organization became the Soviet of Workers' and Soldiers' Deputies. Henceforth, this spontaneous fusion of popular elements led the revolution.

The tsarist government and dynasty came to a swift, unlamented end. By March 14 the entire garrison of Petrograd had defected, and the tsarist ministers were arrested. The Duma's Provisional

Committee selected a Provisional Government from liberal members of the Progressive Bloc, the "government having public confidence," which the bourgeoisie had long sought. Learning of the deteriorating situation in Petrograd, Nicholas II decided to rejoin his family at Tsarskoe Selo, but railroad workers halted his train and forced him to return to Pskov, headquarters of the northern front. Behind events as usual, he agreed now to a responsible ministry, but his commanders unanimously advised abdication. On March 15 delegates Guchkov and V. V. Shulgin, sent to Pskov by the Provisional Committee, secured Nicholas's abdication in favor of his brother, Grand Duke Mikhail. Rumors of Mikhail's impending rule caused such indignation among the workers that he wisely renounced his claims, and on March 15, 1917, Romanov rule ended in Russia.

Problem 9

Did World War I Cause the Collapse of Tsarism?

What is the relationship between the defeat of a regime in war and its overthrow? What is the connection between war and revolution? Did Germany's defeat of the Russian imperial army cause or trigger the collapse of tsarism in March 1917? Without war, was it likely that the regime could have survived in liberalized form, turning perhaps into something resembling the British constitutional monarchy? Or, conversely, did the war delay tsarist collapse by generating a final outburst of Russian patriotism? Was the regime's disintegration so far advanced in 1914 that it would soon have collapsed in any case? Were social and political tensions rising or declining in Russia in 1914? Finally, could either the tsarist regime, without war, or a liberal successor have confronted 20th-century problems successfully?

The Soviet Position

An official Soviet account, written during the rule of N. S. Khrushchev, emphasizes the approaching collapse of tsarist Russia and the revolutionary upsurge just before World War I, as well as the growing strength and cohesion of the Bolsheviks in leading the discontented masses:

> The cost of living was rising, and the position of the worker was deteriorating. An official industrial survey revealed that while annual wages averaged 246 rubles, annual profit per worker averaged 252 rubles. . . . Incredible poverty reigned in the countryside. Stolypin's agrarian policy had, as its direct result, the mass impoverishment of the peasants and enrichment of the kulak [better-off peasants] bloodsucker. . . . The Russian countryside presented a picture of omnipotent feudal landlords, bigger and richer kulak farms, the impoverishment of a vast mass of middle peasants, and a substantially increased mass of landless peasants. . . . The situation left no doubt whatever that the Stolypin policy had collapsed.

Tsar Nicholas and family, the tsar seated second from left.

Problem 9 continued

Its collapse brought out more saliently than ever the profound contradictions throughout Russia's social and political system. It demonstrated anew that the tsarist government was incapable of solving the country's basic social and economic problems. . . . Poverty, oppression, lack of human rights, humiliating indignities imposed on the people—all this, Lenin emphasized, was in crying contradiction to the state of the country's productive forces and to the degree of political understanding and demands of the masses. . . . Only a new revolution could save Russia. . . .

The Bolsheviks' prediction that a new revolutionary upsurge was inevitable proved to be true. Everywhere there was growing discontent and indignation among the people. The workers saw in the Bolshevik revolutionary slogans a clear-cut expression of their own aspirations. . . . Of all the political parties then active in Russia, only the Bolsheviks had a platform that fully accorded with the interests of the working class and the people generally. . . .

The workers' movement continued to grow in scope and strength. There were over one million strikers in 1912, and 1,272,000 in 1913. Economic struggles were intertwined with political ones and culminated in mass revolutionary strikes. The working class went over to the offensive against the capitalists and the tsarist monarchy. . . . In 1910–1914, according to patently minimized figures, there were over 13,000 peasant outbreaks, in which many manor houses and kulak farmsteads were destroyed. . . . The unrest spread to the tsarist army. . . . Mutiny was brewing in the Baltic and Black Sea fleets. A new revolution was maturing in Russia.

Together with the rise of the working-class movement, the party of the working class, the Bolshevik Party, grew and gained in strength. . . . Amidst the difficulties created by their illegal status, the Bolsheviks *reestablished a mass party*, firmly led and guided by its Central Committee. . . . Everywhere—in mass strikes, street demonstrations, factory gate meetings—the Bolsheviks emphasized that revolution was the only way out, and put forward slogans expressing the people's longings: a democratic republic, an eight-hour working day, confiscation of the landed estates in favor of the peasants.

Meanwhile the waves of the working-class movement rose higher and higher. In the first half of

Problem 9 continued

1914 about 1,500,000 workers were involved in strikes. . . . On July 3 the police opened fire on a workers' meeting at the Putilov Works in St. Petersburg. A wave of indignation swept over the country. The St. Petersburg Bolshevik committee called for immediate strike action. . . . Demonstrations began in protest against the actions of the tsarist authorities and the war, which everyone felt was about to break out. The strike wave spread to Moscow; barricades were thrown up in St. Petersburg, Baku, and Lodz.

Russia was faced with a revolutionary crisis. The landlords and capitalists were accusing each other of inability to put out the flames of revolution. . . . The tsarist government adopted "emergency" measures, the capital was turned into a veritable military camp. . . . The advance of the revolution was interrupted by the outbreak of the world war.[10]

The Pessimists' View

Leopold Haimson, writing in *Slavic Review* in 1965, presents an interesting analysis of conditions in Russia on the eve of World War I, in some ways refuting and in others supporting the preceding Soviet assertions:

> The four-day interval between the last gasps of the Petersburg strike and the outbreak of war may not altogether dispose of the thesis of Soviet historians that only the war prevented the strike movement of July, 1914, from turning into a decisive attack against the autocracy. . . . Yet surely much of the conviction of this argument pales in the light of the two glaring sources of political weakness that the strike revealed from its very inception . . . the failure of the clashes in St. Petersburg to set off anything like the all-national political strike, which even the Bolshevik leaders had considered . . . a necessary condition for the armed assault against the autocracy . . . [and] the inability of the Petersburg workers to mobilize, in time, active support among other groups in society. . . . No demonstrations, no public meetings, no collective petitions—

no expressions of solidarity even barely comparable to those that Bloody Sunday had evoked were now aroused. . . . Thus, . . . the most important source of the political impotence revealed by the Petersburg strike was precisely the one that made for its "monstrous" revolutionary explosiveness: the sense of isolation, of psychological distance, that separated the Petersburg workers from educated, privileged society.

. . . The crude representations to be found in recent Soviet writings of the "revolutionary situation" already at hand in July, 1914, can hardly be sustained. Yet when one views the political and social tensions evident in Russian society in 1914 in a wider framework and in broader perspective, any flat-footed statement of the case for stabilization appears at least equally shaky. . . .

By July, 1914, along with a polarization between workers and educated, privileged society . . . , a second process of polarization—this one between the vast bulk of privileged society and the tsarist regime—appeared almost equally advanced. Unfolding largely detached from the rising wave of the labor movement, this second process could not affect its character and temper but was calculated to add a probably decisive weight to the pressure against the dikes of existing authority. By 1914, this second polarization had progressed to the point where even the most moderate spokesmen of liberal opinion were stating publicly, in the Duma and in the press, that an impasse had been reached between the state power and public opinion, which some argued could be resolved only by a revolution of the left or of the right. . . .

Indeed, by the beginning of 1914 any hope of avoiding a revolutionary crisis appeared to be evaporating even among the more moderate representatives of liberal opinion. Under the impact of the blind suicidal course pursued by the government and its handful of supporters, the Octobrist Party had split at the seams. . . .

Indeed, many signs of economic and social progress could be found in the Russian provinces of the year 1914—the introduction of new crops, new techniques and forms of organization in agriculture, and the industrialization of the countryside; growing literacy among the lower strata and invigorated cultural life among the upper strata of provincial society. But no more than in the major cities were these signs of progress and changes in

[10] *History of the Communist Party of the Soviet Union* (Moscow, 1960), pp. 163–64, 169–70, 173, 175–76, 182–83.

Problem 9 continued

the localities to be viewed as evidence of the achievement or indeed the promise of greater social stability. . . ."Official" and "unofficial" Russia had now turned into two worlds completely sealed off one from the other.[11]

The Optimists' View

Leonard Schapiro, a British historian, stresses the weakness and disorganization of the Bolsheviks on the eve of World War I, providing a sharp contrast to Soviet accounts:

> The Bolsheviks, or those of them who supported Lenin, could now [1914] no longer persist in their policy of maintaining the split [with the Mensheviks] at all costs. . . . There was also more unity now on the non-Bolshevik side than ever before. . . . If Lenin were isolated in his intransigence, there was every chance that many of his "conciliator" followers, who had rejoined him in 1912, would break away again. The Bolshevik organization was, moreover, in a poor state in 1914, as compared with 1912. The underground committees were disrupted. There were no funds, and the circulation of *Pravda* had fallen drastically under the impact of the split in the Duma "fraction."
>
> Intensive propaganda for unity now began inside Russia. The Mensheviks and organizations supporting them drew up an appeal to the Russian workers, blaming the Bolsheviks for the split, and urging support for the efforts of the International to reunite the whole party. But it was too late. War broke out . . . and before long, the Russian social democrats were rent asunder by new and even less reconcilable dissensions.[12]

Alexander Gerschenkron, an American economic historian, argues that Russia was following the path that western Europe had taken earlier and suggests that without war it would have avoided revolution:

Russia before the First World War was still a relatively backward country by any quantitative criterion. . . . Nevertheless . . . Russia seemed to duplicate what had happened in Germany in the last decades of the 19th century [in industrial development]. One might surmise that in the absence of the war Russia would have continued on the road of progressive westernization. . . . The likelihood that the transformation in agriculture would have gone on at an accelerated speed is very great. . . .

As one compares the situation in the years before 1914 with that of the [18]90s, striking differences are obvious. In the earlier period, the very process of industrialization with its powerful confiscatory pressures upon the peasantry kept adding . . . to the feeling of resentment and discontent until the outbreak of large-scale disorders became almost inevitable. The industrial prosperity of the following period [1906–1914] had no comparable effects, however. Modest as the improvements in the situation of peasants were, they were undeniable and widely diffused. Those improvements followed rather than preceded a revolution, and accordingly tended to contribute to a relaxation of tension. . . .

Similarly, the economic position of labor was clearly improving. . . . There is little doubt that the Russian labor movement of those years was slowly turning toward revision and trade-unionist lines. As was true in the West, the struggles for general and equal franchise to the Duma and for a cabinet responsible to the Duma, which probably would have occurred sooner or later, may well have further accentuated this development. . . .

. . . It seems plausible to say that Russia on the eve of the war was well on the way toward a westernization or, perhaps more precisely, a Germanization of its industrial growth.[13]

An English View

In a recent study of the Russian Revolution and how it affected the Russian people, the English scholar Christopher Read writes:

---

[11] Leopold Haimson, "The Problem of Social Stability in Urban Russia, 1905–1917: II," *SR* 24, no. 1 (March 1965): 1–3, 8–10.

[12] Leonard Schapiro, *The Communist Party of the Soviet Union* (New York, 1959), pp. 139–140.

[13] "Patterns of Economic Development," in C. Black, *The Transformation of Russian Society* (Cambridge, MA, 1960), pp. 57–61.

Problem 9 continued

We need to look at the immediate causes of the collapse of tsarism, the particular conjuncture that brought about the emergence of the Provisional Government and the abdication of Nicholas II. There can be no doubt that, in the short term, it was Russia's disastrous performance in the First World War that brought about the final destruction of tsarism.

The initial impact of the war was favourable to the regime. Internal conflicts were put to one side as the whole country took up the national cause of fighting the enemy. Militarily, too, the tsarist army scored some limited successes that may even have been decisive in preventing a rapid German victory (in France). . . . The moment of success was brief. The new German reinforcements soon pushed the Russians back and even started to advance into Russian Poland.

Worse quickly followed. The 1915 campaigning season was a series of unmitigated catastrophes from which the autocracy never recovered. The Russian army was soon in headlong retreat as the Central Powers marched forward into the Carpathians and through Poland. . . . Warsaw was evacuated in early and mid-August. . . . Reinforcements going to the front were met by a constant stream of civilian refugees and bedraggled, broken units heading into the interior to regroup.

. . . From 1915 on, the regime was caught in a trap. It could only save itself by undermining its erstwhile closest supporters and abandoning all it held dear. Essentially, this was only an acute form of the problem it had faced since the mid-19th century, but in the turmoil of total war the old tactics of evading the real issues and diverting or repressing opposition were even more ineffective than usual.

The final scene of the autocracy's long-drawn-out demise was played out within the limits of the situation that emerged in the high summer of 1915. The crisis of August 1915 brought all the conflicting pressures into focus. The military commanders thought the only solution was that they should have more power. The civilian government were afraid that, given the military's incompetence, such a development would hasten disaster. . . . The more competent members of the administration were horrified by the continuing encroachment of the military on their preserve. As the front fell back, the army chiefs demanded that more and more of the rear territory should be put under military rule. The government was determined to resist this process, not only because of its natural inclination to preserve its own power, but also because of the total incompetence of some of the army commanders when it came to politics and the administration of civilians.

. . . Thus, by 1916 the basic elements of tsarism's final crisis were in place. . . . Had the autocracy been prepared to make a major gesture of reconciliation with the Duma a new start might still have been possible, but nothing illustrates the entrenched obtuseness of Nicholas II and those around him better than the events of the last months of the dynasty.[14]

Conclusion

Neither "optimists" nor "pessimists" have proved their case fully, yet both present valid arguments. Unquestionably, there was serious social tension and a major worker upsurge early in 1914, yet to call this a "revolutionary situation" appears to be as misleading as to claim that one existed in 1861. The workers remained largely isolated from the rest of Russian society; their movement was confined mainly to the larger cities. To be sure, the alienation of educated society from a narrow-minded regime was evident and growing, as was fragmentation of the political parties (notably Kadets and Octobrists). On the other hand, Russia for the first time was experiencing self-sustaining industrial and agricultural growth, as well as an unparalleled degree of prosperity. ■

---

[14] Christopher Read, *From Tsar to Soviets: The Russian People and Their Revolution* (New York and Oxford, 1996), pp. 35–38.

Suggested Additional Reading

BERNSTEIN, H. *The Willy-Nicky Correspondence, 1914–17* (New York, 1918).

BRUSSILOV, A. A. *A Soldier's Notebook, 1914–18* (Westport, CT, 1971).

BUCHANAN, G. W. *My Mission to Russia,* 2 vols. (New York and London, 1923).

BURDZHALOV, E. *Russia's Second Revolution: The February 1917 Uprising in Petrograd,* trans. and ed. Don Raleigh (Bloomington, IN, 1987).

DE JONG, A. *The Life and Times of Grigorii Rasputin* (New York, 1982).

EDELMAN, R. *Gentry Politics on the Eve of the Russian Revolution* (New Brunswick, NJ, 1980).

FRANCIS, S. R. *Russia from the American Embassy* (New York, 1971).

GEYER, D. *The Russian Revolution: Historical Problems and Perspectives* (New York, 1987).

GOLOVIN, N. N. *The Russian Army in the World War* (New Haven, CT, 1931).

GRAYSON, B. L. *Russian-American Relations in World War I* (New York, 1979).

GRONSKY, P. P., and N. I. ASTROV. *The War and the Russian Government* (New Haven, CT, 1929).

HASEGAWA, T. *The February Revolution: Petrograd 1917* (Seattle, 1981).

KATKOV, G. *Russia 1917: The February Revolution* (New York, 1967).

KNOX, A. *With the Russian Army: 1914–1917* (New York, 1921).

LIH, L. *Bread and Authority in Russia, 1914–1921* (Berkeley, 1990).

MANDEL, D. *The Petrograd Workers and the Fall of the Old Regime* (New York, 1984).

MASSIE, R. *Nicholas and Alexandra* (New York, 1967).

MCKEAN, R. *St. Petersburg Between Revolutions . . . June 1907–February 1917* (New Haven, CT, 1990).

MICHELSON, A. M., et al. *Russian Finance During the War* (New Haven, CT, 1928).

ODINETS, D. M., and P. J. NOVGORODTSEV. *Russian Schools and Universities in the World War* (New Haven, CT, 1929).

PALÉOLOGUE, M., *An Ambassador's Memoirs,* 3 vols. (New York, 1972).

PARES, B. *The Fall of the Russian Monarchy . . .* (New York, 1939; reprint, New York, 1961).

———, ed. *The Letters of the Tsar to the Tsaritsa, 1914–1917* (London, 1929).

———. *The Letters of the Tsaritsa to the Tsar . . .* (London, 1923).

PAVLOVSKY, G. *Agricultural Russia on the Eve of Revolution* (London, 1930).

PEARSON, R. *The Russian Moderates and the Crisis of Tsarism, 1914–1917* (New York, 1977).

POLNER, T. I., et al. *Russian Local Government During the War and the Union of Zemstvos* (New Haven, CT, 1930).

PORTER, C. *Women in Revolutionary Russia* (New York, 1988).

PURISHKEVICH, V. M. *The Murder of Rasputin,* ed. M. Shaw (Ann Arbor, MI, 1985).

READ, C. *From Tsar to Soviets: The Russian People and Their Revolution* (New York and Oxford, 1996).

RODZIANKO, M. V. *The Reign of Rasputin* (London, 1927).

RUTHERFORD, W. *The Russian Army in World War I* (London, 1975).

SENN, A. E. *The Russian Revolution in Switzerland* (Madison, WI, 1971).

SIEGELBAUM, L. H. *The Politics of Industrial Mobilization in Russia, 1914–1917* (New York, 1983).

SMITH, C. J. *The Russian Struggle for Power, 1914–17* (New York, 1956).

SOLZHENITSYN, A. *August 1914* (New York, 1972). (Historical novel.)

STONE, N. *The Eastern Front* (New York, 1975).

THURSTON, R. *Liberal City, Conservative State: Moscow and Russia's Urban Crisis, 1906–1914* (New York, 1987).

WILDMAN, A. K. *The End of the Russian Imperial Army . . .* (Princeton, 1979).

ZAGORSKY, S. O. *State Control of Industry in Russia During the War* (New Haven, CT, 1928).

31

From March to November 1917

The politically freest, most exciting year in Russian history was 1917, and it has generated more controversy than any other. Bolshevik victory in November brought to power an intransigent, antiliberal element. Ever since 1917, Soviet and Western historians have debated why the Bolsheviks won and what it signified for humankind. The Soviet view presented Bolshevik victory as the inevitable result of historical development. The Bolsheviks, it noted, assumed power for the proletariat under Lenin, their revered leader. A few Western historians, such as E. H. Carr, agree that the Bolsheviks were bound to triumph because of their clear purpose and determination. Some Western accounts, especially Robert Daniels's *Red October,* stress spontaneity and the role of chance in 1917. Others cite conspiracy as the decisive factor, but most Western histories reject an explanation of the outcome on the basis of a single factor.

How do the Revolutions of March and November 1917 compare with one another? Were the events and outcome in 1917 predetermined? Did the Provisional Government's liberal democratic experiment founder because of Russia's weak

constitutional tradition, because it failed to keep its promises, or because it kept Russia in World War I? What produced Bolshevik victory: Lenin's and Trotskii's leadership, superior organization, an attractive program, mass action, or a combination of these elements? Did the Bolsheviks win because of their strengths or their opponents' weaknesses and blunders?

The "Dual Power"

In March 1917, a "Dual Power," to use Trotskii's phrase, succeeded tsarism. Dual power, he noted, does not necessarily imply equal division of authority or a formal equilibrium, and it arises from class conflict in a revolutionary period when hostile classes rely upon incompatible ruling institutions—one outlived, the other developing. The Provisional Government, argued Trotskii, represented a Russian bourgeoisie too weak to govern long; the Petrograd Soviet was a proletarian organ, which surrendered power initially to the bourgeoisie. Both convened, at first, in the Tauride Palace, where they competed for loyalty and popular support.

The Provisional Government represented landed and industrial wealth, privilege, and educated society. Its premier and interior minister, Prince G. E. Lvov, a distinguished aristocrat and wealthy landowner, had been a prominent *zemstvo* leader and member of the right wing of the Kadet party. "I believe in the great heart of the Russian people filled with love for their fellow men. I believe in this fountain of truth, verity, and freedom," declared this idealistic Slavophile liberal. "An illustrious but notoriously empty spot," commented Trotskii.[1] Lvov's government, despite good intentions, was poorly equipped to maintain order or to govern Russia. Its dominant figure and real brains was Foreign Minister Paul Miliukov, the erudite but unrealistic history professor who had led the Kadet party since 1905. War Minister Alexander I. Guchkov, a big Moscow industrialist, strove to preserve army discipline and create reliable military support for the regime. Finance Minister M. I. Tereshchenko owned property worth some 80 million rubles, spoke excellent French, and was a ballet connoisseur. Only A. F. Kerenskii, Minister of Justice and leader of the leftist Labor Group, represented even vaguely those who had unseated the tsar. A young lawyer of rare oratorical power and febrile energy, he believed fully in the revolution and his own destiny, but Kerenskii, noted Trotskii, "merely hung around the revolution." The Petrograd Soviet had barred its members from the Government, but Kerenskii, a vice-chairman of the Soviet, after a dramatic speech, secured permission to enter the cabinet.

This liberal Provisional Government was to exercise authority only until a democratically elected constituent assembly could establish a permanent regime. "Its orders," noted War Minister Guchkov, are "executed only insofar as this is permitted by the Soviet . . . which holds in its hand the most important elements of actual power such as troops, railroads, the postal and telegraph service." The Provisional Government pledged to

A. F. Kerenskii (1881–1970).

prepare national elections with all possible speed, and the constituent assembly became an article of faith—the holy grail of Russian democracy—for moderates and revolutionaries, including Bolsheviks. Meanwhile the Government took what steps it could toward democracy by granting full freedom of speech, press, assembly, and religion, and equality to all citizens. An amnesty released political prisoners and allowed exiles to return. Provincial governors were abolished, and local governmental officials were to be elected. Unprecedented freedom and euphoria prevailed in Russia. All restrictive legislation imposed on national and religious minorities under tsarism was abolished, and the administration of the borderlands was placed mostly in local hands.

The Petrograd Soviet, hastily formed and ill-defined in membership, powers, and procedure,

---

[1] M. T. Florinsky, *Russia: A History and an Interpretation* (New York, 1953), vol. 2, p. 1384.

promptly took charge in the capital and coordinated other soviets that sprang up throughout
Russia. On March 15 it had 1,300 members; a
week later soldier delegates swelled the number
to more than 3,000. Even when reduced to its
former size, it was too large and noisy to do much
real business. A small Executive Committee,
chaired by the Menshevik N. S. Chkheidze, was
chosen to reach and implement important decisions. Moderate socialists dominated it and the
Soviet, with Bolsheviks in opposition. At first,
party affiliations were unimportant in the Soviet.

The drama of Russia in 1917 was captured
wonderfully by this eyewitness, the radical American journalist John Reed:

> Lectures, debates, speeches—in theatres,
> circuses, schoolhouses, clubs, Soviet meeting-
> rooms, Union headquarters, barracks. . . .
> Meetings in the trenches at the front, in village
> squares, factories. . . . What a marvelous sight
> to see the Putilov factory pour out its 40,000 to
> listen to Social Democrats, Socialist Revolu-
> tionaries, Anarchists, anybody, whatever they
> had to say, as long as they would talk! For
> months in Petrograd, and all over Russia, every
> street-corner was a public tribune.[2]

The Soviet approved the Government's initial
program and measures, but their relations soon
grew strained over control of the army and foreign
policy. On March 14 the Soviet's army section
issued Order No. 1, which authorized all army
units to elect soldier committees and send representatives to the Soviet. Enlisted men were to
obey their officers and the Government only if
their orders did not conflict with the Soviet. This
Order, confirmed most reluctantly by War Minister
Guchkov, prevented the Government from controlling the army and further undermined army
discipline. Meanwhile, Foreign Minister Miliukov
insisted that the March Revolution had not
changed Russian foreign policy: Russia would
fulfill its commitments to the Allies and fight for

"lasting peace through victory." Allied governments and the United States, which had entered
the war in April, quickly recognized the Provisional Government and supplied it generously
with war credits. Russia, insisted Miliukov, must
obtain Constantinople and the Straits and "merge
the Ukrainian provinces of Austria-Hungary with
Russia." This expansionist program based on
secret inter-Allied treaties provoked a Soviet
appeal, on March 27, to European peoples to overthrow their imperialist governments and achieve a
just and democratic peace "without annexations
and indemnities." Meanwhile, until peace came,
the Russian Revolution must defend itself. Within
the Government, Miliukov and Guchkov contended with ministers who repudiated an imperialist peace, though for the time being an
atmosphere of democratic unity muted these
differences.

The Bolsheviks Gain Leaders and a Program

Moderates controlled the Government and Soviet,
but the Bolsheviks grew into a formidable opposition. Late in March, L. B. Kamenev and Joseph
Stalin (I. V. Djugashvili) returned to Petrograd
from Siberian exile. Briefly turning the Bolsheviks
to the right, they pledged to support the Provisional Government in a defensive struggle against
Germany. (Later Stalin blamed Kamenev for this
rightist orientation, claiming that he had always
opposed the Provisional Government and the
war.) Though described by N. N. Sukhanov in
1917 as "a grey blur," Stalin was an able organizer
and contributed from behind the scenes to Bolshevik victory, but neither he nor Kamenev supplied dynamic leadership.

Lenin's return to Russia in mid-April proved
vital to Bolshevik success. In Switzerland, directing
a small group of socialist émigrés, he had feared
that he would not live to see the revolution.
Though taken unaware by the March Revolution,
he grasped its significance immediately and
telegraphed his party comrades: "Our tactic:
absolute lack of confidence, no support to the new

---

[2] John Reed, *Ten Days That Shook the World* (New York,
1987), p. 11.

Government."[3] His "Letters from Afar" to *Pravda,* the Bolshevik newspaper, envisioned an armed seizure of power by the proletariat fused with an armed populace. To arrange his return home, Lenin negotiated through Swiss socialists with the German government, which readily consented to send home socialists dedicated to overthrowing a pro-Allied government and ending Russia's participation in the war. Temporary identity of interests and even Lenin's receipt of "German gold," though, does not prove his opponents' assertion that he was a German agent. Lenin was prepared to accept help from whatever source (only the Germans provided it) without compromising his principles or altering his goals. He and other Russian socialist exiles passed through Germany on a sealed train.

At Petrograd's Finland Station on April 16, the Bolsheviks gave Lenin a triumphal welcome, although he had been in neither the Soviet nor the Duma. The Soviet's chairman, Chkheidze, greeted him: "We think that the principal task of the revolutionary democracy is now the defense of the revolution from any encroachment, either from within or without . . . , the closing of democratic ranks. We hope that you will pursue these goals together with us." Lenin, disregarding Chkheidze, turned to the entire Soviet delegation:

> Dear Comrades, Soldiers, Sailors and Workers! I am happy to greet in your persons the victorious Russian revolution, and greet you as the vanguard of the worldwide proletarian army. . . . The piratical imperialist war is the beginning of civil war throughout Europe. . . . The worldwide socialist revolution has already dawned. . . . Germany is seething. . . . Any day now the whole of European capitalism may crash. The Russian revolution accomplished by you has prepared the way and opened a new epoch. Long live the worldwide socialist revolution.[4]

Lenin's exhortation caused dismay and incredulity among most Bolshevik leaders, who were moving toward accommodation with the Provisional Government.

The following day—April 17—Lenin presented a series of proposals, known as his "April Theses," to the Petrograd Bolshevik Committee. "The basic question," explained Lenin, "is our attitude toward the war." Because the new Provisional Government favored continuing in World War I, he condemned it as "imperialistic through and through." There must be "no support for the Provisional Government; exposure of the utter falsity of all its promises." He added, "Not the slightest concession must be made to 'revolutionary defensism'! . . . since the war on Russia's part remains a predatory imperialist war. . . . Russians must transform this 'imperialist war' into a civil war against capitalism." According to Lenin, Russia was moving from the first, bourgeois, stage of the revolution to its second stage, "which is to place power in the hands of the proletariat and the poorest strata of the peasantry." The Bolsheviks must tell the masses that the Soviet of Workers' Deputies was "the only possible form of revolutionary government."[5] Spurning Western parliamentary democracy, Lenin advocated a republic of soviets of worker and peasant deputies. The police, army, and bureaucracy were to be abolished. Private lands must be confiscated and all land in Russia nationalized. All banks should be merged into one general national bank under the Soviet. Bolsheviks should seize the initiative to form a revolutionary international. However, the Petrograd Committee rejected Lenin's "April Theses" 13 to 2, *Pravda* dubbed them "unacceptable," and Plekhanov, the father of Russian Marxism, declared: "A man who talks such nonsense is not dangerous." Lenin argued, cajoled, and persuaded until three weeks later an all-Russian Bolshevik conference approved his program by a wide margin. The

[3] V. I. Lenin, *Collected Works,* vol. 23, pp. 297ff.
[4] N. Sukhanov, *The Russian Revolution* (New York, 1962), vol. 1, pp. 272–73.

[5] V. I. Lenin in "The Tasks of the Proletariat in the Present Revolution," *Pravda,* April 17, 1917, reprinted in *The Lenin Anthology* (New York, 1975), pp. 295–301.

Bolsheviks took over the initial Soviet program: bread, land, and peace.

In May, Leon Trotskii returned from exile in New York and, in July, joined the Bolsheviks with his followers. Lenin had adopted (or stolen) Trotskii's idea of permanent revolution: Instead of awaiting full development of capitalism, Russia could move directly to socialism by revolution. When Trotskii, the most effective orator of the Revolution, joined Lenin, its ablest strategist and organizer, the Bolsheviks gained a great advantage in leadership.

The Revolution Moves Left (May–July)

As Lenin won control of the Bolsheviks, a severe crisis shook the Provisional Government. It was touched off by Foreign Minister Miliukov's May 1st Note, which rejected a separate peace and pledged that Russia would fight to the end to secure "sanctions and guarantees." The profoundly patriotic Kadet party, led by Miliukov, wished almost unanimously to fight to final victory. This stance alienated the Kadets from war-weary soldiers and workers. The Soviet viewed Miliukov's Note as a thin disguise for an imperialist peace, notably seizure of the Turkish Straits, which he had advocated repeatedly. Massive, spontaneous demonstrations of workers and soldiers erupted in Petrograd and Moscow with the slogans "Down with Miliukov!" and "Down with the Provisional Government!" The demonstrators could have overturned the Government, but when the latter disavowed the Note, the Soviet prohibited further demonstrations. Nonetheless, Miliukov, disliked for his cool arrogance, and Guchkov, the conservative war minister, were forced to resign.

Since the Soviet's Executive Committee now permitted member parties to join the Provisional Government, the cabinet was reorganized as a coalition of nine nonsocialist (mainly Kadet) and six socialist ministers. Its dominant figure was Alexander Kerenskii, a right-wing SR, as war and

navy minister. Victor Chernov, the SRs' chief ideologist, became minister of agriculture. Supported by most peasants and many soldiers, the SRs retained, by far, the largest popular following, but they were starting to disintegrate. During 1917 they achieved none of their social program, especially drastic land reform. Their mass support became dissatisfied with the leadership. By entering the Government, moderate socialists became vulnerable to Bolshevik criticism of their inaction, mistakes, and continuation of the war. The extremist Bolsheviks, like the Jacobins (radicals in the French Revolution), profited from the moderates' passivity and incompetence as rulers and war leaders.

The coalition ministry's policies differed little from its predecessor's. Caught between Allied insistence upon a total military effort and Soviet pressure for a democratic peace, the Government issued vague statements to mask internal divisions. War Minister Kerenskii, Foreign Minister Tereshchenko, and Premier Lvov advocated an active war role. Responding to French pleas to tie down German troops in the east, Kerenskii prepared a great offensive in Galicia, hoping thereby to revive army morale, provide the regime with reliable troops, and secure Allied financial and political support. A patriot and a democrat, he believed that a free Russia was linked indissolubly with the Allied cause. Conservatives of the Kadet party expected an offensive to restore order in Russia and perhaps bring military victory. Kerenskii toured the front to whip up patriotic enthusiasm. Special volunteer "shock battalions" were recruited to lead the way. Kerenskii's oratory was applauded warmly, but it had few lasting effects on the war-weary Russian troops.

In June 1917 moderate socialists seemed securely in control of the Government and the Soviet. When the first all-Russian Congress of Soviets opened on June 16, the Bolsheviks and their allies had only 137 out of 1,000 delegates. The Menshevik Tseretelli told the delegates that the Government was safe; no party in Russia would say "Give us power!" To his surprise, Lenin shouted "Yes, there is one!" and attacked the bourgeoisie, demanding that the war be ended and capitalist aid repudiated. The moderate majority disregarded Lenin, but in the factories Bolshevik strength and worker radicalism were rising. On June 23 the Bolsheviks, pressed by workers and soldiers, agreed to lead a demonstration against the Government, but the next day the Congress of Soviets called it off. A week later, however, a demonstration organized by the Congress to display revolutionary unity was dominated by such Bolshevik slogans as "End the war!" The Bolsheviks, not the Soviet, now clearly led the Petrograd workers.

On July 1 Kerenskii's much heralded offensive began in Galicia with a great artillery barrage. After initial gains against the Austrians, it was halted after 12 days, and on July 19 German and Austrian forces counterattacked and easily broke through Russian lines. Demoralized Russian troops threw down their weapons and fled. Their panicky retreat ended only after all Galicia had been lost and enemy attacks ceased. On July 25 the Government restored the death penalty for desertion, but this action failed to revive the army's will to fight.

As the Russian offensive faltered, disorders broke out in Petrograd (July 16–18) following the resignation from the Provisional Government of four Kadet ministers who opposed the cabinet's decision to grant demands for autonomy by the Ukrainian Rada (Assembly). Troops of the garrison, sailors from the Kronstadt naval base, and factory workers clashed with Government supporters. The Bolshevik-dominated First Machine Gun Regiment, after refusing to leave for the front, began the demonstrations. Some 500,000 soldiers and workers marched on the Tauride Palace to force the Soviet to assume power. Radical Bolsheviks from the Military Organization and Petersburg Committee supported this movement, but more cautious Central Committee leaders considered it premature. The Bolshevik party finally decided, reluctantly, to lead the demonstration. The Soviet's Executive Committee, though frightened, refused to take power or implement

Bolshevik demands. Without clear purpose, the demonstrators, after roughing up some ministers, gradually dispersed, and the July Days petered out. Later Stalin explained the curious Bolshevik tactics: "We could have seized power [in Petrograd] . . . , but against us would have risen the fronts, the provinces, the soviets. Without support in the provinces, our government would have been without hands and feet." Lenin, too, believed that national support for the Bolsheviks was still inadequate. Their unwillingness to lead damaged the Bolsheviks temporarily among militant soldiers and workers.

Kornilov and the Rightward Shift (July–September)

As the July Days ended, the Provisional Government and Petrograd Soviet regained control. Guard regiments in Petrograd, hearing that Lenin was a German agent, rallied to the Government, and a reaction set in against the Bolsheviks as newspapers published documents accusing their leaders of treason. The Government disarmed the First Machine Gun Regiment and occupied Bolshevik headquarters. The next day, troops searched *Pravda*'s editorial office, wrecked its press, and closed down Bolshevik newspapers. The Bolshevik Military Organization wished to resist, but the workers were cowed. Realizing that the party had suffered a severe setback, Lenin convinced the Central Committee of the need to retreat. He considered standing trial to refute the Government charges, but fearing that he might be murdered in prison, Lenin took refuge in Finland. Trotskii and some other Bolshevik leaders were arrested.

Kerenskii, reshuffling the coalition cabinet on July 25, replaced Prince Lvov as premier. Mensheviks and SRs held most ministerial posts, but the moderate Government failed to implement the measures that the impatient masses demanded. Kerenskii, the democrat, began his rule with half-hearted repression. Insurgent troops and civilians mostly retained their arms, and though the central

Bolshevik apparatus was shaken, Bolshevik support in Petrograd's factories continued to grow. By mid-August the Bolshevik party numbered about 200,000 members, compared with 80,000 in April, and had outstripped the Mensheviks, whose support declined partly because of the inactivity of the Provisional Government.

Early in August Kerenskii again reshuffled his cabinet and moved into the Winter Palace, seat of the tsars. To build support for his shaky regime before the elections to the Constituent Assembly, he convened the Moscow State Conference drawn from Russia's elite: members of the four Dumas, the soviets, the professions, and army leaders. The Bolsheviks boycotted the Conference (August 26–28) and sought to embarrass it with a general strike in Moscow. Instead of strengthening Kerenskii's government, the Conference exposed the chasm between conservatives and moderate socialists.

As the Moscow State Conference met, General Lavr Kornilov emerged as leader of the conservatives. The son of a Siberian Cossack with a reputation for bravery and rigid discipline, he had been appointed commander in chief of the army by Kerenskii on July 31. Though Kornilov lacked political acumen (General Alekseev described him as "a man with the heart of a lion and the brains of a sheep"), he headed a movement of bourgeoisie, landowners, and the military organized by Rodzianko and Miliukov. About August 20 he ordered his Cossacks and Caucasian Wild Division to take up positions within striking distance of Moscow and Petrograd. After talking with Kerenskii, Kornilov told his chief of staff: "It is time to hang the German supporters and spies with Lenin at their head and to disperse the Soviet . . . once and for all." When Kornilov entered the chamber of the Moscow State Conference, the Right cheered wildly; the Left applauded Kerenskii with equal warmth. The Conference convinced Kornilov that Kerenskii was too weak to restore order in Russia. Supported by conservative Duma leaders, financiers, and the Allied powers, Kornilov pushed plans to march on Petrograd

and crush the revolution. Learning of the conspiracy, Kerenskii secured authorization from socialist members of his cabinet to take emergency measures, but the Kadet ministers resigned. Kerenskii's dismissal of Kornilov as commander in chief, on September 9, forced the general's hand.

The threat of a military coup united Petrograd socialists, who mobilized workers and soldiers to defend the revolution. While Kerenskii postured equivocally, hoping that Kornilov would crush the Bolsheviks and leave him in command, the Soviet's Executive Committee set up a "Committee for Struggle against Counterrevolution" to coordinate resistance. Bolshevik leaders were released and directed the Committee's work, and arms were gathered everywhere to equip the Red Guard, a workers' militia. Kronstadt sailors, pouring in to defend Petrograd, swiftly rounded up Kornilovites. The Executive Committee instructed army committees and railroad and telegraph workers to obstruct Kornilov's advance; his small forces were enveloped and never reached Petrograd. His troop trains were delayed or derailed while Bolshevik agitators turned his soldiers against their officers. The Wild Division, won over by a Moslem delegation, elected a committee that apologized to the Petrograd Soviet for participating in a counterrevolutionary plot. Kornilov and his supporters were arrested, and the only serious Rightist attempt in 1917 to seize power fizzled out ingloriously.

The Rising Tide (September–November)

After Kornilov's defeat, the Bolsheviks rode a wave of mass discontent that finally overwhelmed the weak Provisional Government. In the Kornilov affair, the party had displayed leadership and control of the workers, who were becoming increasingly radical. On September 13 the Petrograd Soviet approved a Bolshevik resolution for the first time; five days later this action was repeated in Moscow. On September 22, when the Petrograd Soviet again voted Bolshevik, the moderate Executive Committee, interpreting this as a vote of no confidence, resigned, and soon thereafter Trotskii was elected chairman. Control of the principal soviets gave the Bolshevik party a strategic base as important as radical Paris was for the French Jacobins in 1792.

Kerenskii's moderate regime might still have survived had it acted swiftly to begin land reform, end the war, and convene the Constituent Assembly, but it did none of these. Alexander Verkhovskii, the new war minister, urged Russia and the Allies to conclude a just peace and carry out immediate social reforms, but the Provisional Government, ignoring his suggestions, soon removed him. Instead, Kerenskii made more cabinet changes and proclaimed Russia a republic. On September 27 he convened a 1,200-man Democratic Conference in Petrograd, drawn from soviets, trade unions, *zemstva*, and cooperatives. Representing mostly the Russian educated classes, whose influence and popular support were dwindling, this Conference voted to establish the Council of the Republic, or Preparliament, dominated by moderate socialists but including nonsocialists and some Bolsheviks. At the Council's first meeting, on October 20, Trotskii denounced it and the Bolsheviks walked out; the other deputies took no action.

Extreme elements were growing at the expense of the moderates. Between July and October, while the Bolshevik vote in Moscow city elections rose from 11 to 51 percent, and the Kadets (now the conservatives) from 17 to 26 percent, the moderate SRs dropped from 58 to 14 percent. Chernov, the only SR leader of real stature, was a theoretician, not a practical politician. Its other leaders (Kerenskii and Savinkov) grew more conservative while the militant rank and file drew closer to the Bolsheviks. As the SRs neared an open split, the Mensheviks were losing worker support to the Bolsheviks. The radical masses were rejecting moderate leaders and parties and moving the revolution to the left.

The breakdown of the army, which had been developing since March, contributed greatly to extremism. Kornilov's fiasco hastened the collapse of discipline among the exhausted troops; the men regarded officers as enemies of the revolution. For months thousands of peasant soldiers had been deserting their units and filtering back to their villages, ragged, hungry, and disgruntled. Soldier soviets in most army units swung toward the Bolsheviks, who accelerated the trend with leaflets and agitation. National groups demanding independence also helped dissolve the army, until by November few reliable units remained.

The peasantry moved spontaneously during 1917 to seize and divide up landowners' estates, though at first they had waited and listened to Government promises. In May the first National Peasant Congress in Petrograd, wholly SR-dominated, outlined a program: All property in land was to be abolished, even for smallholders, and land was to belong to the entire people. Anyone might use land if he tilled it himself; hired labor was to be prohibited. Final solution of the land question was to be left to the Constituent Assembly. By midsummer, angered by official grain requisitioning, shortages of manufactured goods, and postponement of land reform, the peasants began to act. Violent land seizures and murders of landowners grew in number week by week, reaching a peak in October and November. The Bolsheviks did not lead the peasants, but exploited their discontent. The Government, helpless to protect landlord property, reluctantly recognized local peasant committees and soviets, which controlled much of the countryside. By November most peasants backed leftist SRs who were cooperating with the Bolsheviks.

The workers grew more discontented as they were squeezed by galloping inflation, dwindling food supplies, and shrinking real wages. Food riots and long lines of hungry workers became common in the cities. Disorder mounted in factories as strikes intensified and industrial sabotage and murders of hated foremen by workers increased. The owners, lacking essential raw materials and fuel, shut down many factories, but the workers believed that such closures were meant to prevent strikes for higher wages. The Government could neither mediate between workers and employers nor coerce the workers. By November the rapidly growing trade union movement had more than 2 million members. Moderate socialists retained influence in central trade union conferences, but by June more radical local factory committees were endorsing Bolshevik proposals for worker control of the factories, and by November factory committees and district soviets in Petrograd were firmly Bolshevik. The largely spontaneous and militant worker movement converged with the Bolshevik drive for political power and supplied the mass base for the Bolshevik Revolution. By November peasants were seizing the land and workers the factories, soldiers were deserting and making peace, and soviets were taking power. All this coincided with the Bolshevik short-term program.

With increasing urgency national minorities—almost half the population of the Russian Empire—demanded autonomy or independence. In March 1917 the Provisional Government, while promising the Poles independence and making concessions to the Finns, refused to recognize Ukraine as a separate administrative entity. Ukrainian moderates established a Central Council (Rada) in Kiev that favored autonomy, but Ukrainian radicals soon dominated the Rada and pushed it toward independence. In June the Rada demanded that Petrograd recognize Ukrainian territorial and administrative autonomy and permit separate Ukrainian army units. Though sympathetic, the Provisional Government avoided specific promises and admonished: "Wait until the Constituent Assembly." By July the Rada was virtually an independent government, but the Ukrainian national movement remained fragmented. Ukrainian quarrels with Petrograd over the extent of autonomy merely weakened liberal and moderate socialist elements in Russia. Native nationalist movements also developed rapidly in the Baltic provinces, soon to become independent as Latvia, Lithuania, and Estonia. In Central Asia the Russians had crushed a Kazakh revolt in 1916, but during 1917 Kazakh congresses in Orenburg

demanded a "Greater Kirghizia." Almost everywhere the Provisional Government's control over the borderlands was slight, moderate socialists leading the Petrograd government temporized, and the Bolsheviks exploited the resulting confusion.

Kornilov's defeat signaled a sharp upturn in Bolshevik popularity. To Lenin, still hiding in Finland, the achievement of Bolshevik majorities in leading soviets proved that it was time to strike. The soviets could become the foundation for a revolutionary regime. "They represent a new *type* of state apparatus which is incomparably higher, incomparably more democratic," he wrote. Crucial for Lenin were majorities in the chief soviets, not victories in parliamentary elections. The Bolsheviks were now strong in the capitals, Volga cities, the Urals, Donets Basin, and Ukrainian industrial centers, while their allies, the Left SRs, had widespread support among peasants and soldiers. No longer could an isolated Red Petrograd be crushed by the rest of Russia.

Lenin and Trotskii, certain that it was time to seize power, had to convince the Central Committee in Petrograd. Lenin's slogan was "Insurrection now!" With majorities in the Petrograd and Moscow soviets, he wrote the Central Committee in late September, "The Bolsheviks can and must take power into their own hands."[6] To await the Constituent Assembly, warned Lenin, would merely enable Kerenskii to surrender Petrograd to the Germans. "The main thing is to place on the order of the day *the armed uprising in Petrograd and Moscow. . . . We will win* absolutely *and* unquestionably."[7] Insurrectionary detachments should be formed and placed in position immediately. Shocked by Lenin's urgent messages, the Central Committee burned one of his letters and disregarded the other.

Early in October Lenin moved to Vyborg, closer to the capital. Bolshevik leaders in Petrograd were calling for the Second Congress of Soviets, set for

---

[6] Lenin, *Collected Works,* vol. 26, pp. 19–21.
[7] Lenin, *Collected Works,* vol. 26, pp. 83–84.

Red Guards on a street in Petrograd.

early November, to assume power peacefully. In the pamphlet *Will the Bolsheviks Retain State Power?* Lenin insisted that the masses would support a purely Bolshevik government. Nothing except indecision could prevent the Bolsheviks from seizing and keeping power until the world socialist revolution triumphed. As the Central Committee stalled, Lenin wrote in *The Crisis Has Matured* (October 12): "We are on the threshold of a world proletarian revolution" that the Bolsheviks must lead. If the Central Committee showed misguided faith in the Congress of Soviets or Constituent Assembly, its members would be "miserable traitors to the proletarian cause." When this, too, was disregarded, Lenin threatened to resign and campaign in the lower ranks of the party.

On October 20 Lenin came to Petrograd in disguise to convert the Central Committee to armed insurrection. He and 11 Committee members argued through the night of October 23–24 in the apartment of the unsuspecting Sukhanov. They approved a Political Bureau (subsequently Politburo) of seven: Lenin, Zinoviev, Kamenev, Trotskii, Stalin, Sokolnikov, and Bubnov. After long debate, the idea of armed uprising was approved in principle, though Zinoviev and Kamenev, arguing that armed insurrection would be contrary to Marx's teachings, remained opposed and kept the party leadership in turmoil until the November Revolution. Trotskii urged that the insurrection be coordinated with the imminent Second Congress of Soviets, thus giving it a measure of legitimacy, and he stuck to this position despite Lenin's demand for immediate action. Without Lenin's and Trotskii's leadership, it seems unlikely that the Bolsheviks would have taken power.

The November Revolution

Unlike the spontaneous overthrow of tsarism, the November Revolution was an armed seizure of power by one party under cover of the Second Congress of Soviets. Had the Bolsheviks not acted in November, Trotskii concludes, their opportunity would have passed.

Preparations for an armed showdown were haphazard on both sides. Trotskii, chairman of the Petrograd Soviet and its Military Revolutionary Committee (MRC), directed the insurrection and

UPI/Corbis-Bettmann

Leon Trotskii (1879–1940).

was the most active Bolshevik leader at large in Petrograd. The MRC and the Bolshevik Military Organization won over or neutralized the 150,000-man Petrograd garrison. Composed mostly of overage, sick, or green troops, the garrison leaned politically toward the SRs, but was loyal to the Soviet and to whoever kept it away from the front. The MRC sent revolutionary commissars to all its regiments, ousted Government commissars, and won control. When the garrison recognized MRC and Soviet authority on November 5, the Government was virtually powerless, but the uprising was "postponed" until the meeting of the Second Congress of Soviets on November 7.

The Provisional Government remained outwardly confident. Colonel G. P. Polkovnikov, commander of the Petrograd Military District, announced he was ready for trouble. Premier Kerenskii hoped the Bolsheviks would act so that the Government could crush them. The Govern-

ment had a thorough defense plan that anticipated most Bolshevik moves and concentrated on holding the city center and Neva bridges (see Map 31.1). Kerenskii had some 1,000 military cadets, officers, and Cossacks—sufficient, he believed, to paralyze Bolshevik centers if used boldly.

As both sides waited, Government strength ebbed. On November 5 Trotskii and Lashevich literally harangued the garrison at Peter and Paul Fortress into surrendering and procured weapons there for 20,000 Red Guards. Next morning the Government sent military cadets to close down Bolshevik newspapers and moved to the Winter Palace the Women's Battalion of Death, recruited by Kerenskii in June to shame Russian males into fighting. Accusing Lenin of treason and ordering MRC leaders arrested, Kerenskii sought plenary powers from the Preparliament to crush the Bolsheviks.

Government moves and Lenin's exhortations prodded the MRC into counteraction. "The situation is impossibly critical. . . . A delay in the uprising is equivalent to death," Lenin told the Central Committee. Early on November 7 Red Guards and sailors occupied railroad stations, the State Bank, and the central telephone exchange without resistance. Kerenskii lacked troops that would defend his regime and left Petrograd to locate loyal units outside. The capture of the Winter Palace that evening was anticlimactic and virtually bloodless. About 10 P.M., when the Women's Battalion tried a sortie, the besiegers rounded it up, raped a few, and dispersed the rest. The ministers surrendered meekly to invading Red Guards and were placed under house arrest. In this "assault," unduly glorified in Soviet accounts, only six attackers and no defenders were killed. The Provisional Government had fallen almost without resistance.

Bolshevik Petrograd withstood Kerenskii's counterattack combined with an internal revolt. At Pskov, Kerenskii had persuaded General N. N. Krasnov to move on Petrograd with about 700 Cossacks, and on November 12 they occupied Tsarskoe Selo, just to the south. The previous day, however, an uprising in Petrograd by military

1. Winter Palace
2. Palace Square and Alexander Column
3. General Staff
4. Admiralty
5. Ministry of War
6. Marinsky Palace
7. Pavlov Barracks
8. Bolshevik Military Organization
9. Bolshevik Secretariat, Fall 1917
10. Bolshevik Printing Plant
11. Telephone Exhange
12. State Bank
13. Central Post Office
14. Central Telegraph Office
15. Kexholm Barracks
16. Baltic Crew Barracks
17. Menshikov Palace (First Congress of Soviets)
18. Location of Aurora, Oct. 25
19. Ksheshinskaya Mansion
20. Sukhanov's Apartment (Bolshevik Central Committee, Oct. 10)
21. Bolshevik Editorial Office
22. Mikhailovsky Artillery School
23. Site of Sixth Party Congress
24. Vyborg District Bolshevik Headquarters
25. Fofanova's Apartment (Lenin's Hideout)
26. Arsenal
27. Peter–Paul Fortress
28. Finland Station
29. University
30. Tauride Palace
31. Smolny Institute
32. Putilov Factory

Map 31.1 Petrograd, 1917

cadets organized by moderate socialists had been crushed. Red Guards and sailors repelled Krasnov's feeble attack on Petrograd, and his force, neutralized by Red propaganda, melted away.

Kerenskii escaped in disguise and eventually reached England.

In most of Russia the Bolsheviks established control in a few weeks. In Moscow there were several days of severe fighting before the Red

Guards[8] overcame military cadets and stormed the Kremlin on November 15, but there was no active defense of the Provisional Government elsewhere. Georgian Mensheviks set up a nationalist regime, and in Kiev the Ukrainian Rada took over, but these actions did not then threaten Bolshevik rule. The Bolsheviks generally favored nationalist movements against the old Russian Empire.

Screened by the Second Congress of Soviets, the Bolsheviks created a new regime even before the Government yielded. Lenin emerged from hiding the afternoon of November 7 to tell the Petrograd Soviet: "The oppressed masses themselves will form a government. The old state appa-

---

[8] The Red Guards numbered about 20,000 in Petrograd and between 70,000 and 100,000 in all Russia. D. N. Collins, "A Note on the Numerical Strength of the Russian Red Guard in October 1917," *Soviet Studies* 24, no. 2 (October 1972): 270–80.

ratus will be destroyed root and branch. Now begins a new era in the history of Russia."[9] That evening the Second Congress of Soviets convened with Bolsheviks predominating (390 out of 650 delegates). After verbal fireworks, the moderate socialists denounced the Bolshevik coup as illegal, walked out, and went into opposition. The remainder (Bolsheviks and Left SRs) set up an all-Bolshevik regime: Lenin became president of the Council of People's Commissars, Trotskii foreign commissar, and Stalin commissar of nationalities. Lenin read his Decree on Peace, which urged immediate peace without annexations and indemnities, the end of secret diplomacy, and publication of all secret treaties. To win peasant support, he issued the Decree on Land, which confiscated state and church lands without compensation. Lenin was acting swiftly to implement his promises.

---

[9] Lenin *Collected Works*, vol. 26, pp. 247–48.

Problem 10

Why Did the Bolsheviks Win?

The seizure of power by the Bolshevik Party of Lenin and Trotskii in November 1917 (October by the Old Style calendar), was a crucial turning point in Russia's political history, and one of the most momentous events in modern world history. This and the subsequent bitter civil war placed Russia squarely on a path leading toward Stalin's totalitarianism and the epic transformations of agriculture and industry in the 1930s. The Russian Revolutions of 1917, unlike the French, American, or Chinese conquest of power, occurred in wartime amid military defeat, economic collapse, and governmental disintegration. How did the Bolshevik party—with scarcely 250,000 members and apparently weaker than its socialist rivals, the Mensheviks and SRs— achieve power in a vast peasant country whose

people had just discarded the 300-year authoritarian regime of the Romanovs and made Russia briefly into "the freest country in the world"? Was this Bolshevik takeover, condemned by many contemporary Russian socialists as Blanquism, or insurrection for its own sake, consistent with Marxism? In the 1840s Marx had predicted that socialism would inevitably replace capitalism through a violent revolution, but initially in fully developed capitalist countries. Was Bolshevik victory the inevitable outcome of Russia's historical and economic development, or an accidental by-product of Russia's defeat and breakdown in 1917?

The Soviet View

Soviet and many Western scholars have ascribed Bolshevik success primarily to the Bolsheviks' strengths. Official Soviet accounts, holding to the orthodox Marxist view, emphasized that the November Revolution was the inevitable outcome of Russian historical development, but also ascribed great importance to the decisive role of the Bolshevik party and Lenin's individual qualities of leadership. Declared *The History of the USSR* in 1967:

> The October armed insurrection in Petrograd was the first victorious proletarian uprising. The insurrection triumphed because the Bolshevik Party was armed with the Leninist theory of socialist revolution and utilized the experience of past uprisings of the workers. The Party, guided by the teachings of Marxism, treated insurrection as an art, insured its organization and decisiveness. The Central Committee of the party correctly utilized revolutionary forces . . . V. I. Lenin worked out the plan of insurrection and conscientiously executed it. . . .
>
> The success of the October insurrection was the result of the vast organizational activity of the Bolshevik Party and its Central Committee. The Bolsheviks were at the head of the insurgents. By their bravery and courage, their unexampled devotion to the revolution, they raised the masses to this heroic feat. The soul and brain of the insurrection was the great Lenin. Wherever he was in the hours of insurrection . . . , he was in the center of events. . . . The October armed uprising in Petrograd . . . showed what heroic deeds the people can accomplish when led by the Marxist-Leninist party.[10]

The 27th Party Congress in 1986 adopted a revised "Program of the Communist Party of the Soviet Union," which reiterated these themes, attributing Bolshevik victory to the well-organized, revolutionary Russian working class led by the Bolsheviks under Lenin. The March Revolution, argued that document, had failed to deliver the Russian masses "from social and political yokes" or from the burden of the "imperialist war," and it had not resolved social contra-

dictions. "Thus a socialist revolution became an undeniable demand."

> The working class of Russia was distinguished by great revolutionary qualities and organization. At its head stood the Bolshevik Party, hardened in political struggles and possessing an advanced revolutionary theory. V. I. Lenin armed it with a clear plan of struggle after formulating theses on the possibility of the victory of a proletarian revolution under conditions of imperialism originally in one of a few separate countries.
>
> At the summons of the Bolshevik Party and under its leadership the working class undertook a decisive struggle against the power of capital. The party united in one powerful stream the proletarian struggle for socialism, peasant struggle for the land, the national-liberation struggle of the oppressed peoples of Russia, into a general [*obshchenarodnoe*] movement against the imperialist war and for peace, and directed it with the overthrow of the bourgeois order.[11]

Western Views

Many Western accounts also consider the Bolshevik victory as the inevitable outcome of the momentum of an invincible party, or the product of clever, even diabolical, plotting by Lenin. On the surface, in November 1917 the Bolsheviks possessed many strengths: a highly centralized, disciplined organization, leadership, and mass support. Although indecisive, unsure, and weak back in March, the party allegedly had become a potent instrument under Lenin and Trotskii, who combined organizational skill, intellectual and oratorical power, and ruthless purpose to exploit opportunities that arose late in 1917. The Bolsheviks' mass following—the industrial workers of Petrograd and Moscow—was militant, impatient, and readily mobilized, living mostly in well-defined workers' quarters. Lenin's short-term program, outlined in his "April Theses," of bread, land, peace, and all power to the soviets

---

[10] *Istoriia SSSR s drevneishikh vremen do nashikh dnei* (Moscow, 1967), vol. 7, pp. 145–46.

[11] *Programma Kommunisticheskoi Partii Sovetskogo Soiuza* (Moscow, 1986), pp. 6–7.

coincided largely with the workers' aspirations at that moment.

However, one can also view the reasons for Bolshevik success in more negative terms: the product of fortunate accidents, circumstances, and divisions, weaknesses, and mistakes of their opponents. The Bolsheviks' chief socialist rivals —the SRs and Mensheviks—were badly split internally. Indeed the SRs by November were becoming two parties: a right wing favoring peaceful methods and moving toward democratic socialism, and a radical, terrorist Left that would ally with the Bolsheviks. Both of these rivals lacked cohesion and discipline, failed to put forward practical programs, and proved unable to mobilize mass support. The thesis of Professor Crane Brinton about the weaknesses of moderates in periods of revolution seems pertinent: "The moderates in control of the formal machinery of government are confronted by . . . radical and determined opponents. . . . This stage [dual sovereignty] ends with the triumph of the extremists." Continues Brinton:

> Little by little the moderates find themselves losing the credit they had gained as opponents of the old regime, and taking on more and more of the discredit [as] . . . heir to the old regime. Forced on the defensive, they make mistake after mistake.[12]

Thus the Right SRs, Mensheviks, and Kadets were all moderate parties caught between an intransigent leftist opposition (Bolsheviks) and a weak and incompetent Provisional Government, which they had joined and whose blunders and foot-dragging exacerbated their internal weaknesses. The Provisional Government's ineffectiveness provided the Bolsheviks with the opportunity to take power. Establishing in March 1917 broad personal and political freedom in Russia, that government failed to implement

promptly its most important pledge: to hold elections for a Constituent Assembly. Had that Assembly been convened in late summer or early fall 1917, as was wholly feasible, Bolshevik opportunities might have disappeared with the creation of a legitimate and permanent Russian government. Instead, Premier Kerenskii resorted to legalistic devices, harangues, and exhortations and kept Russia locked in a disastrous and unpopular war. Given the deepening mood of popular extremism in the fall of 1917, his democratic regime was virtually foredoomed to failure.

In sharp contrast to the Soviet thesis that the Bolsheviks succeeded because of their correct theory, careful plans, and decisive action with mass support, the American scholar Robert Daniels argues that the Soviets fostered a myth with little basis in reality and that the Bolshevik Revolution succeeded because of an incredible series of accidents and miscalculations by its opponents.

> One thing that both victors and vanquished were agreed on . . . was the myth that the insurrection was timed and executed according to a deliberate Bolshevik plan. . . . The stark truth about the Bolshevik Revolution is that it succeeded against incredible odds in defiance of any rational calculation that could have been made in the fall of 1917. . . . While the Bolsheviks were an undeniable force in Petrograd and Moscow, they had against them the overwhelming majority of the peasants, the army in the field, and the trained personnel without which no government could function. . . . Lenin's revolution . . . was a wild gamble with little chance that the Bolsheviks' ill-prepared followers could prevail against all the military force that the government seemed to have, and even less chance that they could keep power even if they managed to seize it temporarily. To Lenin, however, it was a gamble that entailed little risk, because he sensed that in no other way and at no other time would he have any chance at all of coming to power.

Nor was the subsequent exaltation of Lenin's leadership really accurate.

There is some truth in the contentions, both Soviet and non-Soviet, that Lenin's leadership was deci-

---

[12] Crane Brinton, *The Anatomy of Revolution*, rev. ed. (New York, 1965), p. 137. In his classic study, Brinton compares the English, American, French, and Russian revolutions.

Problem 10 continued

sive. By psychological pressure on his Bolshevik lieutenants and his manipulation of the fear of counterrevolution, he set the stage for the one-party seizure of power. But . . . in the crucial days before October 24 [November 6], Lenin was not making his leadership effective. The party, unable to face up directly to his brow-beating, was tacitly violating his instructions and waiting for a multi-party and semi-constitutional revolution by the Congress of Soviets. Lenin had failed to seize the moment, failed to nail down the base for his personal dictatorship—until the government struck on the morning of the 24th of October. Kerenskii's ill-conceived countermove was the decisive accident.[13]

An American View

Professor Richard Pipes, a conservative American scholar, in a recent full-length treatment of the Russian Revolution, stresses errors of the moderates and conservatives, as well as the leadership qualities of Lenin and Trotskii, as fostering Bolshevik victory in 1917. Pipes ascribes great importance to the "Kornilov Affair" as undermining the authority of Kerenskii's Provisional Government:

> The clash fatally compromised his [Kerenskii's] relations with conservative and liberal circles without solidifying his socialist base. The main beneficiaries of the Kornilov Affair were the Bolsheviks: after August 27 the SR and Menshevik following on which Kerensky depended melted away. The Provisional Government now ceased to function even in that limited sense in which it may be said to have done so until then. In September and October, Russia drifted rudderless. The stage was set for a counterrevolution from the left. Thus when Kerensky later wrote that "it was only the 27th of August that made [the Bolshevik coup of] the 27th of October [November 7 New Style] possible," he was correct, but not in the sense in which he intended.

During August 1917, continues Pipes, the Bolsheviks "were reasserting themselves as a political force."

> They benefited from the political polarization which occurred during the summer when the liberals and conservatives gravitated toward Kornilov, and the radicals shifted toward the extreme left. Workers, soldiers, and sailors, disgusted with the vacillations of the Mensheviks and SRs, abandoned them in droves in favor of the only alternative, the Bolsheviks.
>
> The Kornilov Affair raised Bolshevik fortunes to unprecedented heights. To neutralize Kornilov's phantom putsch . . . , Kerensky asked for help from the Ispolkom. . . . But since the Bolshevik Military Organization was the only force which the Ispolkom could invoke, this action had the effect of placing the Bolsheviks in charge of the Soviet's military contingent. . . . A no less important consequence of the Kornilov Affair was a break between Kerensky and the military. . . . The officer corps . . . despised Kerensky for his treatment of their commander [Kornilov], the arrest of many prominent generals, and his pandering to the left. When, in late October, Kerensky would call on the military to help save his government from the Bolsheviks, his pleas would fall on deaf ears. . . . It was only a question of time before Kerensky would be overthrown by someone able to provide firm leadership. Such a person had to come from the left. . . .
>
> The growing disenchantment with the soviets and the absenteeism of their socialist rivals enabled the Bolsheviks to gain in them an influence out of proportion to their national following. . . . As their role in the soviets grew, they reverted to the old slogan: "All Power to the Soviets." . . . In the more favorable political environment created by the Kornilov Affair and their successes in the soviets, the Bolsheviks revived the question of a coup d'état. . . . The Kornilov incident convinced him (Lenin) that the chances of a successful coup were better than ever and perhaps unrepeatable.[14]

Despite such revisionist Western views, in the USSR the concept of a carefully conceived Marxist revolution with wide popular support was

---

[13] Robert Daniels, excerpted from *Red October: The Bolshevik Revolution of 1917.* Copyright © 1967 Robert V. Daniels. Reprinted with the permission of Charles Scribner's Sons.

[14] Richard Pipes, *The Russian Revolution* (New York, 1990), pp. 464–67, 471–72.

Problem 10 continued

cultivated assiduously and on the whole success-fully. This was accompanied by the rather incon-gruous assertion that the success of the

revolution depended heavily on the individual leadership and driving energy of its guiding genius, Lenin. This evident contradiction reflects the persistent dichotomy in Marxism between determinism (inexorable laws) and voluntarism (dynamic leadership). ■

Suggested Additional Reading

ABRAHAM, R. *Alexander Kerensky* (New York, 1987).

ADAMS, A., ed. *The Russian Revolution and Bolshevik Victory* (Boston, 1972).

AVRICH, P. *The Russian Anarchists* (Princeton, 1967).

BOLL, N. M. *The Petrograd Armed Workers Movement in the February Revolution (February–July 1917)* (Washington, 1979).

BRINTON, C. *The Anatomy of Revolution* (New York, 1965).

BROWDER, R., and A. KERENSKY, eds. *The Russian Provisional Government, 1917*, 3 vols. (Stanford, 1961).

BROWER, D. R., ed. *The Russian Revolution: Disorder or New Order?* (Arlington Heights, IL, 1986).

BUNYAN, J., and H. H. FISHER, eds. *The Bolshevik Revolution, 1917–1918: Documents and Materials* (Stanford, 1934).

CARR, E. H. *The October Revolution: Before and After* (New York, 1971).

CHAMBERLIN, W. H. *The Russian Revolution, 1917–1921*, 2 vols. (New York, 1935).

CHERNOV, V. *The Great Russian Revolution* (New Haven, CT, 1936).

CLARK, K. *Petersburg, Crucible of Revolution* (Cambridge, MA, 1995).

DANIELS, R. *Red October: The Bolshevik Revolution of 1917* (New York, 1967).

———. *The Russian Revolution* (Englewood Cliffs, NJ, 1972).

DUNE, E. *Notes of a Red Guard,* ed. and trans. D. Koenker and S. Smith (Urbana, IL, 1993).

ELWOOD, R. C., ed. *Reconsiderations on the Russian Revolution* (Cambridge, MA, 1976).

FERRO, M. *October 1917: A Social History of the Russian Revolution,* trans. N. Stone (Boston, 1980).

———. *The Russian Revolution of February 1917 . . . ,* trans. J. Richards (Englewood Cliffs, NJ, 1972).

FRANKEL, E., et al. *Revolution in Russia: Reassessments of 1917* (Cambridge and New York, 1992).

GALILI, Z. *The Menshevik Leaders in the Russian Revolution* (Princeton, 1989).

GILL, G. J. *Peasants and Government in the Russian Revolution* (New York, 1979).

HARTLEY, L. *The Russian Revolution* (New York, 1980).

HEALD, E. *Witness to Revolution: Letters from Russia, 1916–1919,* ed. James Gidney (Kent, OH, 1972).

HILL, C. *Lenin and the Russian Revolution* (New York, 1978).

HORSBRUGH-PORTER, A., ed. *Memories of Revolution: Russian Women Remember* (New York, 1993).

KAISER, D. H., ed. *The Workers' Revolution in Russia, 1917: The View from Below* (Cambridge, 1987).

KATKOV, G. *The Kornilov Affair . . .* (London, 1980).

KERENSKII, A. F. *The Catastrophe . . .* (New York, 1927).

———. *The Crucifixion of Liberty* (New York, 1934).

———. *Russia and History's Turning Point* (London, 1965).

KOENKER, D. *Moscow Workers and the 1917 Revolution* (Princeton, 1981).

KOENKER, D., and W. G. ROSENBERG. *Strikes and Revolution in Russia, 1917* (Princeton, 1990).

LOCKHART, R. H. B. *The Two Revolutions: An Eyewitness Study of Russia, 1917* (London, 1957).

MAWDSLEY, E. *The Russian Revolution and the Baltic Fleet* (London, 1978).

MELGUNOV, S. P. *The Bolshevik Seizure of Power* (Santa Barbara, CA, 1972).

MILIUKOV, P. N. *The Russian Revolution: Vol. I. The Revolution Divided: Spring 1917,* trans. T. and R. Stites (Gulf Breeze, FL, 1978).

MOHRENSCHILDT, D. VON, ed. *The Russian Revolution of 1917: Contemporary Accounts* (New York, 1971).

PALÉOLOGUE, M. *An Ambassador's Memoirs,* 3 vols. (New York, 1972).

PETHYBRIDGE, R. *The Spread of the Russian Revolution: Essays on 1917* (London, 1972).

——, ed. *Witnesses to the Russian Revolution* (London, 1964).

PIPES, R. *The Russian Revolution* (New York, 1990).

——, ed. *Revolutionary Russia: A Symposium* (New York, 1969).

RABINOWITCH, A. *The Bolsheviks Come to Power* (New York, 1976).

——. *Prelude to Revolution: . . . the July Uprising* (Bloomington, IN, 1969).

RADKEY, O. H. *The Agrarian Foes of Bolshevism: . . . Russian Socialist Revolutionaries . . .* (New York, 1958).

READ, C. *From Tsar to Soviets: The Russian People and Their Revolution* (New York and Oxford, 1996).

REED, J. *Ten Days That Shook the World* (New York, 1919, and reprints).

ROSENBERG, W. *Liberals in the Russian Revolution: The Constitutional Democratic Party, 1917–1921* (Princeton, 1974).

SAUL, N. E. *Sailors in Revolt: The Russian Baltic Fleet in 1917* (Lawrence, KS, 1978).

SCHAPIRO, L. *The Russian Revolution of 1917: The Origins of Modern Communism* (New York, 1984).

SERGE, V. *Year One of the Russian Revolution* (New York, 1972).

SLUSSER, R. *Stalin in October: The Man Who Missed the Revolution* (Baltimore, 1987).

SOBOLEV, P. N., ed. *The Great October Socialist Revolution,* trans. D. Skvirskii (Moscow, 1977).

SUKHANOV, N. N. *The Russian Revolution of 1917,* 2 vols., ed. J. Carmichael (New York, 1962).

SUNY, R. G. *The Baku Commune 1917–1918 . . .* (Princeton, 1972).

SUNY, R. G., and A. ADAMS, eds. *The Russian Revolution and Bolshevik Victory: Problems in European Civilization,* 3d ed. (Lexington, MA, 1990). (Includes and discusses various viewpoints.)

THOMPSON, J. M. *Revolutionary Russia, 1917* (New York, 1981).

TROTSKY, L. *The History of the Russian Revolution,* 3 vols. (New York, 1932).

WADE, R. *The Russian Search for Peace: February–October 1917* (Stanford, 1969).

WILDMAN, A. *The End of the Russian Imperial Army . . .* (Princeton, 1980).

WILLIAMS, A. R. *Through the Russian Revolution* (New York, 1978).

32

Civil War and Communism, 1917–1921

After the November Revolution it took the Bolsheviks, governing a divided, war-torn country, a decade to achieve full military and political control and begin to build a new autocracy. After making peace with the Central Powers with the Treaty of Brest-Litovsk, they defeated their domestic counterrevolutionary opponents in a bitter civil war (1918–1921) complicated by foreign intervention. They moved simultaneously to destroy the old state, political parties, society, and economic order and erect new socialist ones. By 1927 they had succeeded in their destructive mission, but had taken only initial and tentative steps in socialist construction. One can divide this first decade of Bolshevism in power into the hectic initial months, a period of extremism and revolutionary fervor (1918–1921), and one of recovery, compromise, and power struggle (1921–1927). In 1918–1919 it seemed dubious that the Soviet regime could retain power in semibackward Russia without revolutions abroad. Provided they succeeded, could the Bolsheviks build socialism in isolated Soviet Russia? Why and how did they win the Civil War? Why did the Allies intervene, and how did this affect the outcome? Was "War Communism" an unplanned response to the war crisis or a conscious effort to build socialism?

First Steps, 1917–1918

After the Bolshevik coup in Petrograd, many Russian and foreign leaders believed that Bolshevik rule would be but a brief interlude and that Lenin could not implement his program of bread, land, and peace. Predicting that 240,000 Bolsheviks, running Russia for the poor, could "draw the working people . . . into the daily work of state administration," Lenin counted on imminent European revolutions to preserve his infant regime; otherwise, its prospects appeared dim. Bolshevik leaders recalled the Paris Commune of 1871, in which radical Paris was crushed by conservative France, and their initial measures seemed designed to make a good case for posterity in case world capitalism overwhelmed them.

Bolshevik power spread swiftly from Petrograd over central Russia, but it met strong opposition in borderlands and villages, from other socialist parties, and even from some Bolsheviks. Lenin, however, acted decisively to crush other socialist parties, dissident Bolsheviks, and workers' groups in Russia proper. Mensheviks and Right SRs were demanding a regime of all socialist parties without Lenin and Trotskii, who had led the "un-Marxian" November coup. Right Bolsheviks under Gregory Zinoviev and Lev Kamenev temporarily left the Central Committee and proclaimed: "Long live the government of Soviet parties!" Retorting that the Congress of Soviets had approved his all-Bolshevik regime, Lenin called the Rightists deserters and until they submitted, threatened to expel them from the party. Bringing a few Left SRs into his government, Lenin hailed it as the dictatorship of the proletariat (Bolsheviks) and poor peasantry (Left SRs). This action completed the split of the SRs.

The Constituent Assembly represented a severe political challenge because during 1917 the Bolsheviks had pledged to convene it. Even after November *Pravda* proclaimed: "Comrades, by shedding your blood, you have assured the convocation of the Constituent Assembly." Lenin knew his Bolshevik party could not win a majority, but he found it too risky to cancel the scheduled and promised elections. Held only three weeks after the Bolshevik coup, the elections to the Constituent Assembly were the only fundamentally free elections contested by organized and divergent political parties under universal suffrage ever held in Russia until 1991, when Boris Yeltsin was elected Russian president. Despite continuing political turmoil, more than 40 million votes were cast using secret, direct, and equal suffrage. Despite some intimidation and restrictions imposed on the Kadets and the Right, the elections were remarkably fair and orderly. The SRs obtained about 58 percent of the vote, the Bolsheviks 25, other socialists 4, and the Kadets and the Right 13 percent. Soviet accounts stress that major cities returned Bolshevik majorities and that many SR votes were cast for pro-Bolshevik Left SRs. Nonetheless, non-Bolshevik parties had won the elections.

Lenin swiftly neutralized, then dissolved the Constituent Assembly. In December the Kadets were banned as counterrevolutionary, and their leaders and many right-wing socialists were arrested. The Constituent Assembly, warned Lenin, must accept the Soviet regime and its measures or be dissolved. When the Assembly convened in Petrograd January 18, 1918, it was surrounded by sharpshooters, and armed Red[1] soldiers and sailors packed its galleries. After Bolshevik resolutions were defeated and Chernov, a moderate SR, was elected president, the Bolsheviks walked out. Early next day, on Bolshevik orders, a sailor told Chernov to suspend the session because "the guards are tired." Red troops then closed down the Assembly and dispersed street demonstrations in its behalf. Moderate socialists during the Civil War tried to use the Assembly as a rallying point, only to find that most peasants knew nothing about it. The Constituent Assembly's dissolution marked the demise of parliamentary democracy in Russia.

Old political agencies, principles, and parties were crushed ruthlessly. Decrees abolished the Senate, *zemstva*, and other organs of local self-government. Even before counterrevolutionary threats materialized, the sinister Cheka (Extraordinary Commission), an incipient Soviet secret police, began Red terror under the dedicated Polish revolutionary Felix Dzerzhinsky. The imperial family, transported to Ekaterinburg (Sverdlovsk) in the Urals, was murdered at Lenin's orders in a cellar in July 1918.[2] The Left SRs, who left the cabinet after Brest-Litovsk and sought to overthrow the regime, were expelled from the soviets and proscribed. At the December 1920 Congress of Soviets, individual Mensheviks and SRs appeared legally for the last time.

At first Lenin sought to achieve his short-term economic program without antagonizing mass

---

[1] The Bolsheviks were known as the Reds; their nonsocialist opponents, from monarchists to Kadets (KD), were known as the Whites.

[2] Unsubstantiated reports abound that the tsar's daughter Anastasia—or even the entire family—escaped execution and went abroad. The remains of nine bodies were discovered in 1991; subsequent DNA testing proved that Anastasia did not survive the massacre. See Robert K. Massie, *The Romanovs: The Last Chapter* (New York, 1995).

Michael Curran

Bolshevik Headquarters, Smolny Institute in Petrograd, where the
Revolution was first declared won.

elements. The peasantry were allowed to seize
landowners' estates and divide them up into small
holdings. Worker committees were authorized to
take over factories. "Workers' control"
undermined private capitalism, dislocated production, and fed economic chaos. All banks, railroads,
foreign trade, and a few factories were nationalized, but a mixed economy functioned for the time
being. The Supreme Council of National Economy
(*Vesenkha*) was created to coordinate economic
affairs and supervise regional economic councils
(*sovnarkhozy*), which ran local activities. These
initial efforts at economic planning proved rather
ineffective.

The Bolsheviks acted promptly to destroy the
traditional patriarchal family, army, and church
associated with the tsarist regime and clear the
way for a new socialist society. Early in 1918 they
adopted the Western calendar. Marriage and
divorce were removed from church control, and
only civil marriage was recognized. One spouse
could cancel a marriage before a civil board with-

out citing reasons, then notify the absent partner
of the "divorce" by postcard. Incest, bigamy, and
adultery were no longer prosecuted. In the army,
ranks and saluting were abolished, and officers
were to be elected. A major campaign against the
Orthodox church began because Lenin considered
religion as part of the Marxist superstructure that
must reflect economic conditions. Declared Lenin,
"God is before all a complex of ideas produced by
the stupefying oppression of man"; he predicted a
struggle between religion and the socialist state
until the former disappeared. Orthodoxy's link
with tsarism, the Bolsheviks believed, made it
counterrevolutionary and an obstacle to building
socialism. Lenin warned, however, that attacking
religious "superstitions" directly might alienate
the masses from the Soviet state. Instead, a multifaceted campaign began to pen the church in a
corner until it withered and died. A decree of
February 1918 separated church and state and
deprived churches of property and rights of ownership. The church hierarchy was destroyed and its

lands, buildings, utensils, and vestments nationalized. Believers had to apply to a local soviet to secure a place of worship and religious articles, and parish churches could operate only with irregular donations of believers. Twenty years of intensive Soviet persecution of all religions had begun.

Lenin had promised peace, and the Russian army had disintegrated to the point where it could no longer fight. When the Allies failed to respond to his Decree on Peace, Lenin urged a separate peace, but only German advances on Petrograd, in February 1918, overcame Central Committee opposition to such a peace. Lenin considered the Treaty of Brest-Litovsk (Soviet Russia's separate peace with the Central Powers), despite its severity, essential for his regime's survival. The Baltic provinces and the entire Ukraine were surrendered to German occupation. As he predicted, it provided a breathing space, allowed demobilization of the army, and perhaps saved the Soviet regime.

Civil War, 1918–1920

The Russian Civil War between the Bolsheviks (Reds) and their political opponents (Whites) did as much to create the USSR as the Revolutions of 1917, argues one American scholar.[3] Bolshevik objectives in November 1917 were unclear, but the merciless civil strife between Reds and Whites laid the foundations of the autocratic Soviet system. The Bolshevik party was hardened and militarized, systematic terror began, extreme economic policies were adopted, and implacable hostility developed toward the West. The Civil War, though not wholly responsible for these developments, made Bolshevik policies much more draconian.

After moving to Moscow early in 1918, Lenin's regime came under intense military and political pressure. As White forces approached, Lenin set up a ruthless emergency government, which sought to mobilize central Russia's total resources.

"The republic is an armed camp," Nicholas Bukharin declared. "One must rule with iron when one cannot rule with law." Relatively democratic norms of party life in 1917 yielded to dictatorship, and local popular bodies were suppressed. Lenin made major political and economic decisions and reconciled jealous subordinates. Wisely, he let Trotskii handle military affairs, confirmed his decisions, and defended the able war commissar against intrigues by Stalin and others. Jakob Sverdlov ran the party organization until his death in 1919; Stalin then assumed that role. The Eighth Party Congress in 1919 created the first operating Politburo with five full members (Lenin, Trotskii, Stalin, Kamenev, and N. M. Krestinskii) and three candidates (Bukharin, Zinoviev, and M. Kalinin), constituting Bolshevism's general staff.

In January 1918 Lenin, proclaiming the Third Congress of Soviets the supreme power in Russia, had it draft a constitution. At the Congress some delegates advocated genuine separation of powers and autonomy for local soviets, but the successful Stalin-Sverdlov draft instead outlined a highly centralized political system that concentrated all power in top government and party bodies. The Constitution of 1918, disfranchising former "exploiters" (capitalists, priests, and nobles) and depriving them of civil rights, supposedly guaranteed all democratic freedoms to the working class. Urban workers received weighted votes to counteract the peasantry's huge numerical superiority. Between congresses of soviets, a 200-member Central Executive Committee was to exercise supreme power and appoint the executive, the Council of People's Commissars. A hierarchy of national, regional, provincial, district, and local soviets was to govern Soviet Russia. The Constitution, however, omitted mention of the Bolshevik party, possessor of all real political power!

As the Soviet regime consolidated political control over central Russia, long repressed national aspirations for independence disintegrated the former tsarist empire until Russia was reduced virtually to the boundaries of 1600. The Civil War, like the Time of Troubles (see Chapter

---

[3] Peter Kenez, *Civil War in South Russia: The First Year of the Volunteer Army* (Berkeley, 1971).

12), brought political conflict, social turmoil, foreign intervention, and ultimate national Russian resurgence and reunification. Soviet accounts stressed heroic Russian resistance in both instances to foreign aggression. The southern frontier—the "Wild Field"—again became a refuge for rebels against a shaky regime in Moscow, and western borderlands broke away to secure independence. Anti-Communist Finns defeated Bolshevik-supported Red Finns to create an independent Finland, and the Baltic states of Latvia, Lithuania, and Estonia, assisted by German occupiers, declared independence and retained it until 1940. In Ukraine a moderate General Secretariat signed a treaty with the Germans who occupied that region and set up a puppet regime under "Hetman" Skoropadski, opposed by Bolsheviks and many Ukrainian nationalists. In Byelorussia an anti-Communist group, the Hromada, declared independence, but the national movement there was less developed and lacked a broad popular following. In the Caucasus a Transcaucasian Federative Republic existed briefly in 1918 before yielding to separate regimes in Georgia, Armenia, and Azerbaijan under British protection. In Central Asia Tashkent was an isolated Bolshevik fortress in a sea of disunited Moslems. The SRs created regimes in western Siberia and at Samara on the Volga, while Cossack areas of the Urals and the North Caucasus formed a Southeastern Union. Russia had almost dissolved.

To undermine the tsarist empire and the Provisional Government, the Bolsheviks had used the slogan of national self-determination. However, as early as 1903 most Russian Social Democrats, preferring, like Marx, large, centralized states, had rejected federalism. Viewing nationalism as a capitalist by-product that would disappear under socialism, the Bolsheviks underestimated its power and attractiveness, though Lenin exploited national movements to bring his party into power. He advocated political self-determination in 1917 for every nation in the Russian Empire, but aimed to reunite them subsequently with a Russian socialist state. Grigorii Piatakov, a Bolshevik leader in Ukraine, expressed the party's view bluntly:

On the whole we must not support the Ukrainians, because their movement is not convenient for the proletariat. Russia cannot exist without the Ukrainian sugar industry, and the same can be said in regard to coal (Donbass), cereals (the black earth belt), etc.[4]

Realizing that without the resources of the western borderlands Soviet Russia would not be a major power, Lenin strove to reconcile advocacy of national self-determination with Soviet Russian unity. At his instruction Joseph Stalin formulated a Bolshevik doctrine of "proletarian self-determination" limited to "toilers," denying it to the bourgeoisie and intelligentsia. National independence would be recognized only "upon the demand of the working population"—meaning, in fact, local Bolsheviks subject to control by Moscow.

Civil War and Allied Intervention, 1918–1920

Opposition to Lenin's government began in November 1917 but at first was disorganized and ineffective. Many Russians believed that the Soviet regime would soon collapse, and an ideological gulf divided conservative military elements from moderates and socialists. In August 1918 Fania Kaplan, a terrorist, attempted to kill Lenin and wounded him severely. In the Don region General M. V. Alekseev, former imperial chief of staff, began organizing anti-Bolshevik elements soon after November into the Volunteer Army, which became the finest White fighting force. Before the Bolsheviks seized Russian military headquarters at Mogilev, some leading tsarist generals (Kornilov, A. I. Denikin, and others) escaped and joined Alekseev. The anti-Bolshevik White movement included socially and ideologically disparate elements lacking in unity and coordination. Former tsarist officers exercised military and often political leadership and played a disproportionate role. Though some were of humble origin, their educa-

---

[4] Quoted in R. Pipes, *The Formation of the Soviet Union* (Cambridge, MA, 1954), p. 68.

Library of Congress

V. I. Lenin and sister in Moscow, 1920.

tion and status separated them from a largely illiterate peasantry. White soldiers were mostly Cossacks, set apart from ordinary peasants by independent landholdings and proud traditions. Officers and Cossacks had little in common ideologically with Kadet and SR intellectuals except antipathy for Bolshevism.

Facing this motley opposition was a Red Army, created in January 1918. At first an undisciplined volunteer force, by late 1918—after Trotskii had become war commissar—it became a regular army with conscription and severe discipline imposed by former imperial officers. Trotskii defended this risky and controversial policy as "building socialism with the bricks of capitalism." To get Red soldiers to obey their officers, officers' families were often held hostage to ensure the officers' loyalty. Trotskii raised uncertain Red Army morale by appearing in his famous armored train at critical points. In August 1918, at Sviiazhsk near Kazan, he rallied dispirited Red troops and helped turn the tide against the SRs. Soviet historians gave him little credit for this brilliant feat of inspiration and organization, which saved the regime.

Full-scale civil war and Allied intervention followed an uprising in May 1918 of the Czechoslovak Brigade in Russia. The Czechs had joined

the imperial Russian army during World War I and, surviving its collapse, remained perhaps the best organized military force in Russia. Wishing to go to the western front to fight for an independent Czechoslovakia, the Czechs quarreled with Soviet authorities. Then they seized the Trans-Siberian Railroad, cleared the Reds from most of Siberia, and aided their White opponents. The Allies, claim Soviet accounts, employed the Czechs to activate all enemies of Red power and intervened militarily to overthrow the Soviet regime. Western accounts claim that Allied intervention was designed to restore a Russian front against Germany. President Wilson allowed United States participation in the Allied expeditions to north Russian ports in the summer of 1918 only after the Allied command insisted it was the sole way to win World War I.[5] Such individual Allied leaders as Winston Churchill and Marshal Foch, however, did aim to destroy Bolshevism through intervention. The Soviet-Western controversy over its nature and purpose still rages.

The Civil War, fought initially with small Russian forces of uncertain morale, grew in scope and bitterness. Villages and entire regions changed hands repeatedly in a fratricidal conflict in which both sides committed numerous atrocities. At first the main threat to the Soviet regime came from the east. In August 1918, SR troops, encouraged by the Czechs' revolt, captured Kazan and the tsarist gold reserve and formed SR regimes in Samara and in Omsk in western Siberia. After the Red Army regained Kazan, the SRs in Omsk were ousted by Admiral A. Kolchak, who won Czech and later Allied support for his conservative Siberian regime. Early in 1919, pledging to reconvene the Constituent Assembly, Kolchak moved westward toward Archangel and Murmansk, controlled by the Allies and the White Russian army of General Evgenii Miller. By late summer, however, the Red Army had forced him back across the Urals (see Map 32.1). White and Allied armies hemmed

---

[5] George Kennan, *Russia and the West Under Lenin and Stalin* (Boston, 1960), p. 64.

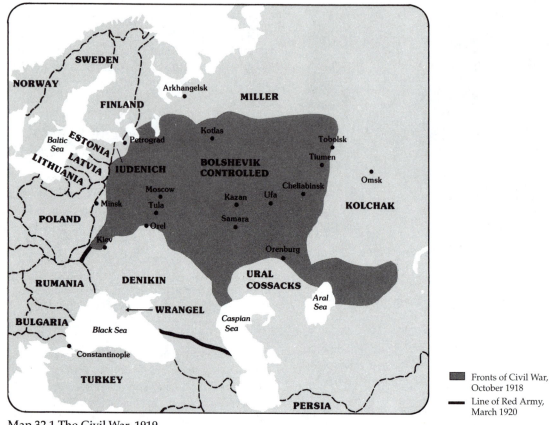

Map 32.1 The Civil War, 1919

SOURCE: Treadgold, Donald W., *Twentieth Century Russia*. Fourth Edition, © 1976, 1972, 1959, by Rand McNally College Publishing Company, Chicago. Map, page 114.

in the Bolsheviks on every side. In the west General Iudenich, commanding a British-equipped White army in Estonia, advanced close to Petrograd in October 1919, but Trotskii rallied its defenders and Iudenich's army dissolved. The chief military threat came from the south. Early in the fall of 1919 General Denikin, commanding Don Cossacks and the elite Volunteer Army equipped with British tanks, reached Orel, 250 miles south of Moscow. Then numerically superior Red forces counterattacked and drove him back, and in March 1920 the British evacuated the remnants of his army from Novorossiisk.

The Bolsheviks gradually reasserted military and political control over the tsarist borderlands, except for Poland, Finland, and the Baltic states. In the west, they dissolved the Byelorussian *Rada* and incorporated Byelorussia. After the Central Powers withdrew from Ukraine at the end of 1918, the Ukrainian nationalist Directory ousted their puppet, Hetman Skoropadski. Conservative and liberal nationalist elements competed with the Red Army for control of Ukraine, which experienced anarchy and turmoil. Early in 1919 the Red Army removed the Directory, but much of Ukraine was conquered by Denikin's Whites. In 1920 Red forces restored the rule of Ukrainian communists, now wholly subservient to Moscow, virtually ending the abortive Ukrainian struggle for independence. Though the Allied powers recognized de facto independence of the three Caucasian republics early in 1920, Moscow's rapprochement with Turk-

Michael Curran

The monument to the Legendary Machine Gun Cart at Kakhovka,
site of an important battle of the Civil War fought in Ukraine.
Horse-drawn machine gun carts of this type were instrumental in
the Bolsheviks' victory in the Civil War.

ish nationalists paved the way for Soviet incorporation of the Transcaucasus. That spring the Red Army occupied Azerbaijan; in December unfortunate Armenia succumbed; and in March 1921 Red forces conquered Menshevik-controlled Georgia against strong resistance. In Central Asia the Bolsheviks conquered the khanates of Khiva and Bukhara and set up several artificial client national states. Bands of mounted Basmachi guerrillas resisted Red rule in Turkestan until the mid-1920s. With most of the former Russian Empire reunited forcibly with its Great Russian core, the way was prepared for creation of the Soviet Union.

By then the Allies, except for the Japanese in Vladivostok, had departed and White resistance had weakened, but a Soviet-Polish war prolonged Russia's agony. To reconstitute a Greater Poland, the forces of Marshal Joseph Pilsudski invaded western Ukraine and captured Kiev in May 1920. A Soviet counteroffensive carried General M. N. Tukhachevskii's Red Army to Warsaw's outskirts, and Lenin sought to communize Poland. The Poles, however, with some French support, rallied, drove out the Red Army, and forced Soviet Russia

to accept an armistice and later the unfavorable Treaty of Riga (March 1921). Soviet preoccupation with Poland enabled Baron Peter Wrangel, Denikin's successor and the ablest White general, to consolidate control of the Crimea. Wrangel employed capable Kadet leaders to carry through land reform, won peasant support, and occupied considerable areas to the north. After the Soviet-Polish armistice in October 1920, the Red Army smashed Wrangel's resistance and forced the evacuation of some 150,000 Whites to Constantinople.

The Whites lacked coordination and were plagued by personal rivalries among their leaders. They denounced Bolshevism, but affirmed nothing. Denikin and Kolchak were moderates who lacked effective political or economic programs. Their slogan—"A united and indivisible Russia"—alienated national minorities and played into Bolshevik hands. White generals made military blunders, but their political mistakes and disunity proved decisive. Allied intervention was of dubious value: Foreign arms and supplies aided the Whites, but were insufficient to ensure victory and let the Reds pose as defenders of Mother Russia.

Bolshevik propaganda portrayed White generals (wrongly) as reactionary tools of Western imperialism and (more correctly) as aiming to restore the landlords. Conversely, the Reds possessed able leadership, a disciplined party, clever propaganda, and a flexible policy of national self-determination. The Red Army had central positions, better discipline, and numerical superiority. Retaining worker support in the central industrial region and controlling its railways, the Bolsheviks won the Civil War as they had won power in 1917, with superior leadership, unity, and purpose.

Russian women, theoretically granted full civil, legal, and electoral equality in January 1918 by the new Bolshevik regime, played significant roles, some quite novel, during the Civil War. Their participation in medical services and combat was far broader than in World War I. In the Civil War, Russian women fought on every front and with every weapon; the female machine-gunner made frequent appearances in early Soviet literature. From October 1919 women's activities were coordinated by Zhenotdel, the Women's Department of the Party's Central Committee, and by 1920 women were being conscripted for noncombatant service and held important positions in the Red Army's political departments. Inessa Armand, a close friend of Lenin, was Zhenotdel's first director. She, along with Alexandra Kollontai and Nadezhda Krupskaia, Lenin's wife, were leaders of women's rights in early Soviet Russia. An estimated 74,000 women participated in the Russian Civil War, suffering casualties of about 1,800.

"War Communism": An Economic Disaster

During the Civil War the government adopted War Communism, an emergency program of nationalization, grain requisitioning, and labor mobilization. With the Whites holding the richest food-producing regions, in Lenin's words, "Hunger and unemployment are knocking at the doors of an ever greater number of workers . . . ,

Nadezhda K. Krupskaia (1869–1939), Lenin's wife, women's activist, who unsuccessfully opposed Stalin's drive for power.

there is no bread." In May 1918 he launched a "crusade for bread," and in June all large-scale industry was nationalized and labor conscripted. This development marked the true beginning of War Communism. State administration of industry by the Supreme Council of National Economy (*Vesenkha*) and its numerous boards proved to be inefficient. Almost one-fourth of Petrograd's adult population became officials, perhaps outnumbering actual factory workers. According to Maurice Dobb, an English economist, representatives of some 50 boards surrounded a dead mare in the streets of Petrograd and disputed responsibility for disposing of its carcass! In a speech in Moscow in 1922, Lenin admitted:

> Carried away by a wave of enthusiasm . . . , we thought that by direct orders of the proletarian state, we could organize state production and distribution of products communistically in a land of petty peasants. Life showed us our mistake.

By 1920 industrial production—a victim of inefficiency and civil war—had fallen to one-fifth of the 1913 level.

In the countryside, as the Bolsheviks denounced "rich" peasants (kulaks), Sverdlov warned that the Soviet regime would survive "only if we can split the village into two irreconcilably hostile camps, if we succeed in rousing the village poor against the village bourgeoisie." Red Army detachments aided "committees of the poor" (*kombedy*) to seize "surplus" grain—everything above a bare minimum for subsistence—from kulaks and middle peasants. Compulsory grain deliveries, though later regularized, amounted to virtual confiscation because peasants were paid in almost worthless paper currency. When farmers hid their grain, sold it on the black market, or brewed vodka, the government responded with forcible seizures. Lacking incentives, the peasantry reduced sowings, and agricultural output under War Communism fell to about one-half of what it had been. Government attempts to organize collective farms and cooperatives failed because few peasants would enter them voluntarily, and only fear that the Whites would restore landlordism kept some peasants loyal to the Bolshevik regime.

With most state expenditures financed by the printing of money as needed, the ruble was undermined and paper currency became almost worthless. Worker rations were free, and wages were paid mostly in kind. As doctrinaire Bolsheviks rejoiced at an increasingly moneyless economy, production plummeted. With the government unable to obtain enough food for the cities, illegal bagmen brought foodstuffs to city dwellers in return for consumer goods. A black market thrived.

Once the Civil War ended, the population found War Communism unbearable. In the winter of 1920–1921, in the Don and Volga regions, Ukraine and north Caucasus peasant uprisings broke out. Soviet sources blame SR-led kulaks, but most middle peasants joined the revolts as the worker-peasant alliance, the cornerstone of Soviet power, tottered. Grain requisition detachments were attacked everywhere, and in February 1921 the Cheka reported 118 separate peasant uprisings. In Tambov province Alexander Antonov, a former SR, led almost 50,000 insurgent peasants demanding "Down with Communists and Jews!" and "Down with requisitioning!" From all over Russia peasant petitions demanded a fixed tax on agricultural produce instead of grain seizures. In the towns the situation was equally dismal: Industry and transport lay idle, workers starved, and city life was falling apart. Despite the Reds' military victory, Soviet Russia seemed about to collapse.

The Kronstadt Revolt of 1921

In March 1921 a major revolt by sailors of the Kronstadt naval base on Kotlin Island near Petrograd confirmed Lenin's decision to yield to peasant demands to scrap War Communism. Ironically, Red sailors, the most revolutionary, pro-Bolshevik element during 1917, led an insurrection against the Bolshevik regime only four years later. As in March 1917, hunger was again a factor. A one-third reduction in the bread ration triggered worker strikes and demonstrations in Petrograd in February. These encouraged the crews of two warships of the disaffected Baltic Fleet to draw up a list of demands. Their Petropavlovsk Resolution condemned War Communism and demanded elections to the soviets by secret ballot, the abolition of grain requisitioning and state farms, and full freedom for peasants on their land. Advocating anarcho-syndicalism, the sailors sought land, liberty, and a federation of autonomous communes. The Resolution appealed to the Soviet regime to live up to its Constitution of 1918 and grant rights and freedoms that Lenin had proposed during 1917. A Provisional Revolutionary Committee led by S. M. Petrichenko, a sailor of Ukrainian peasant background, seized control of Kronstadt, whose Communist party virtually dissolved. During their two-week regime the Kronstadt rebels recaptured briefly the enthusiastic idealism and freedom of the March Revolution.

Fearing for their power, the Bolshevik authorities, realizing the Kronstadt uprising might ignite a massive rebellion in Russia, sought from the start to discredit it as a White émigré plot manipulated from abroad. They depicted the Kronstadt sailors of 1921—whom Trotskii in 1917 had called "the pride and glory of the Russian Revolution"— as demoralized, drunken roughnecks. Actually, the revolt was native and spontaneous. Declared Petrichenko, "Our revolt was an elemental movement to get rid of Bolshevik oppression . . . [so] the will of the people will manifest itself." Spurning conciliation or concessions that might have averted bloodshed, Bolshevik leaders headed by Trotskii demanded that the "counterrevolutionary mutineers" immediately lay down their arms. When the rebels rejected his ultimatum, the Red Army launched an infantry assault across the ice from Petrograd, only to be repulsed. In the final attack of March 16, some 50,000 Red troops finally conquered defiant Kronstadt. The bloody suppression of the revolt revealed the Bolshevik regime as a repressive tyranny relying on naked force. Kronstadt, admitted Lenin, "lit up reality better than anything else." Revealing the need for new economic policies and a relaxation of state pressure, the revolt marked the end of the Russian revolutionary movement.[6]

Suggested Additional Reading

ADAMS, A. *The Second Ukrainian Campaign of the Bolsheviks* (New Haven, CT, 1963).

AVRICH, P. *Kronstadt 1921* (Princeton, 1970).

BASIL, J. D. *The Mensheviks in the Revolution of 1917* (Columbus, OH, 1984).

BRADLEY, J. F. *Civil War in Russia, 1917–1920* (New York, 1975).

BRINKLEY, G. *The Volunteer Army and the Allied Intervention in South Russia, 1917–1921* (Notre Dame, IN, 1966).

BROVKIN, V. N. *The Mensheviks After October . . .* (Ithaca, NY, 1988).

———, ed. and trans. *Dear Comrades: Menshevik Reports on the Bolshevik Revolution and Civil War* (Stanford, 1991).

BUNYAN, J., and H. H. FISHER, eds. *Intervention, Civil War and Communism in Russia, April–December 1918: Documents and Materials* (Baltimore, 1936).

BURBANK, J. *Intelligentsia and Revolution: Russian Views of Bolshevism, 1917–1922* (Oxford, 1989).

D'ENCAUSSE, H. C. *The Great Challenge: Nationalities and the Bolshevik State, 1917–1930* (New York, 1992).

DENIKIN, A. *The Russian Turmoil* (London, 1922).

FIGES, O. *Peasant Russia, Civil War, and the Volga Countryside in Revolution, 1917–1921* (New York, 1989).

FISCHER, L. *The Life of Lenin* (New York, 1964).

FOOTMAN, D. *Civil War in Russia* (New York, 1962).

GELDERN, J. VON. *Bolshevik Festivals, 1917–1920* (Berkeley, 1993).

GETZLER, I. *Kronstadt, 1917–1921: The Fate of a Soviet Democracy* (Cambridge, 1983).

KAZEMZADEH, F. *The Struggle for Transcaucasia, 1917–1921* (New York, 1951).

KENEZ, P. *Civil War in South Russia: The First Year of the Volunteer Army* (Berkeley, 1971).

KENNAN, G. F. *Soviet-American Relations, 1917–1920,* 2 vols. (New York, 1967).

KINGSTON-MANN, E. *Lenin and the Problem of Marxist Peasant Revolution* (Oxford, 1983).

LEHOVICH, D. *White Against Red: The Life of General Denikin* (New York, 1974).

LINCOLN, W. B. *Red Victory: A History of the Russian Civil War* (New York, 1989).

LUCKETT, R. *The White Generals . . .* (London, 1987).

MORLEY, J. W. *The Japanese Thrust into Siberia, 1918–1920* (New York, 1957).

NOVE, A. *An Economic History of the USSR, 1917–1991* (London and New York, 1992).

RADKEY, O. *The Election to the Russian Constituent Assembly of 1917* (Cambridge, MA, 1950).

———. *The Unknown Civil War in Russia* (Stanford, 1976).

RESHETAR, J. S., Jr. *The Ukrainian Revolution, 1917–1920* (Princeton, 1952).

SERVICE, R. *Lenin: A Political Life: Vol. 3. The Iron Ring* (Bloomington, IN, 1995).

SHOLOKHOV, M. *The Quiet Don* (New York, 1966). (Historical novel of the Civil War.)

SWAIN, G. *The Origins of the Russian Civil War* (London and New York, 1996).

ULLMAN, R. H. *Intervention and the War: Anglo-Soviet Relations, 1917–1920,* 2 vols. (Princeton, 1961, 1968).

---

[6] Paul Avrich, *Kronstadt 1921* (Princeton, 1970).

UNTERBERGER, B. *America's Siberian Expedition, 1918–1920* (Durham, NC, 1956).

VERNECK, E. *The Testimony of Kolchak and Other Siberian Material* (Stanford, 1935).

VOLKOGONOV, D. A. *Lenin: A New Biography,* trans. and ed. Harold Shukman (New York, 1994).

WHITE, J. A. *The Siberian Intervention* (Princeton, 1950).

WRANGEL, P. N. *The Memoirs of General Wrangel* (London, 1929).

33

The New Economic Policy and Power Struggle, 1921–1927

In March 1921, in the face of a rising tide of peasant uprisings and the Kronstadt Revolt, the 10th Congress of the Soviet Communist Party under Lenin's leadership scrapped the disastrous economic policies of War Communism. In their place were instituted the basic elements of a New Economic Policy (NEP), described by Lenin as a step backward toward capitalism in order to prepare the way for a subsequent surge forward toward the promised land of socialism. NEP promoted the recovery of the Soviet economy devastated by seven years of war and doctrinaire Bolshevik economic experimentation. NEP also relaxed somewhat the economic and political pressures exerted by the state and allowed more scope to individual enterprise and creativity. Did NEP represent a genuine retreat toward capitalism or the initial stage of socialist construction? Did it signify Lenin's abandonment of the more extreme features of the Bolshevik dictatorship in favor of moderate policies and the slower advance toward socialism advocated by N. I. Bukharin?

Lenin suffered his first cerebral stroke in May 1922, which triggered a major struggle over the succession among the principal Soviet leaders. Stalin and Trotskii soon became the chief contenders for power, but neither was given Lenin's full blessing. How did Stalin, a "grey blur" in 1917, eventually defeat his rivals and achieve absolute power in the Soviet Union? Did Stalin's triumph signify a logical continuation of Leninist rule and principles or a dastardly betrayal of the ideology of Marxism-Leninism?

Economic and Political Controls of NEP

Lenin had written that tactical retreats would sometimes be necessary. To save the regime, the peasantry had to be wooed and the worker-peasant alliance restored. Toward this end, Lenin, overcoming objections to "compromise with capitalism," persuaded the 10th Party Congress to end grain requisitioning and approve a fixed tax in kind per acre. Initially, the New Economic Policy was a limited move to stimulate peasant production for the urban market, but by late 1921 private buying and selling had swept the country. Private

Red Army passing in review before Trotskii (first from left, marked with an X) in Red Square, ca. 1918.

ownership was restored in consumer sectors, while the state retained control over the "commanding heights"—large industry, transport, and foreign trade.

Postponing socialist agriculture indefinitely, NEP stimulated small private farming. Class war in the village was abandoned, and richer peasants were allowed to prosper. Once they had paid their tax in kind, farmers were free to dispose of their surplus and were guaranteed secure tenure. Within limits, they could lease additional land and hire labor. With these stimuli, agriculture recovered rapidly until threatened by the "scissors crisis" of 1922–1923. Marketing their grain in order to buy consumer goods, farmers found that industrial prices, kept up by inefficient state trusts, were

three times higher relative to agricultural prices than before World War I. Farmers again curtailed their marketings of grain and purchases of manufactures. When this reaction threatened economic recovery by reducing urban food supplies and causing consumer goods to pile up, the government forced state industry to lower prices and to prune excess staff. These measures overcame the worst effects of the scissors.

Scrapping War Communism also fostered industrial recovery. Denationalization began in May 1921, and soon about 4,000 small firms controlled three-fourths of retail and 20 percent of wholesale trade. Inefficient state enterprises were forced to close, and free contracts among remaining state firms gradually replaced centralized allocation of raw materials and equipment. State-owned big industry employed more than 80 percent of all workers, but handicrafts and small firms with up to 20 employees were private. Real wages recovered roughly to prewar levels, but unemployment became an increasing problem. By 1923 the USSR possessed the first modern mixed economy, with both state and private sectors. A degree of economic planning was achieved by Gosplan (State Planning Commission).

In 1924–1925 the mixed NEP economy, overcoming currency difficulties and the price scissors, reached its peak. As state-controlled big industry coexisted with individual and family enterprises, production in industry and agriculture neared prewar levels. In 1927 about 25 million farms, held through communal arrangements, composed 98.3 percent of all agricultural units, while state and collective farms included only a tiny minority of peasants and land. Some 350,000 peasant communes with their village assemblies, not local soviets, dominated rural life. More than 90 percent of the peasantry belonged to *mirs* and had reverted to traditional strip farming and periodic land redistribution. Millions of households still used wooden plows, and half the 1928 grain harvest was reaped by scythe or sickle! Whereas Soviet sources divide the peasantry neatly into kulaks, middle peasants, and poor peasants, actually each group shaded into the next. Middle peasants, poor by European standards, often lacked horses. Redefined to suit political convenience, kulaks were estimated at 5 to 7 percent of the total, yet only 1 percent of households employed more than one laborer. Nonetheless, the resurgence of the kulaks suggested peasant differentiation and capitalist revival. Individual farmers sought to consolidate their land and increase production for the market, but success meant being labeled "kulak exploiters." In 1925 the sown area was about that of 1913, but the grain harvest was some 10 percent smaller. Whereas Stalin claimed that only half as much grain was marketed in 1927 as in 1913, recent studies report that marketings in 1927 almost equaled the 1909–1913 average. Urban demand for grain was rising while

peasants, discouraged by low prices, ate better and sold less. Grain exports, which reached 12 million tons in 1913, were only 300,000 tons in 1927–1928.

Party moderates, led by Bukharin, advocated continuing NEP indefinitely in order to reach socialism. Peasant prosperity, they argued, would stimulate rural demand for industrial goods and increase marketable agricultural surpluses. In 1925 Bukharin declared, "Peasants, enrich yourselves!" but soon had to repudiate that slogan. The party's goal, he stated, was "pulling the lower strata up to a high level," because "poor peasant socialism is wretched socialism." Lower industrial prices would spur peasant demand and achieve socialism without coercion "at a snail's pace."

Serious economic problems still faced Russia in 1927. A primitive peasant agriculture barely surpassed prewar levels of productivity. An overpopulated countryside inundated towns with unskilled workers, threatening Bolshevik industrial goals and urban-rural market relationships. As industrial growth leveled off, the economy, unable to draw from capital accumulated under tsarism, faced hard decisions on how to generate more investment and savings. Grain marketings were insufficient to support industrial progress, yet short of coercion, the only ways to increase them were to provide cheaper consumer goods or to raise farm prices significantly.

The experience and results of NEP were debated and reassessed in the USSR under Gorbachev after 1985. At the 27th Party Congress of February 1986, Gorbachev himself advocated "something like a Leninist food tax (*prodnalog*) in the new conditions of today" to stimulate lagging agricultural production. The numerous Soviet articles in 1987–1989 that referred to NEP were overwhelmingly favorable and often exaggerated its beneficial economic results. Soviet specialists attributed NEP's successes primarily to the economic freedom it gave the peasant. Some stressed the efficiency of individual peasants producing for the marketplace, whereas others, apparently with official approval, argued that voluntary peasant cooperatives were needed for any long-term solution of agrarian problems. Many Soviet intellectuals praised the NEP years as an era of political, legal, and cultural freedom.[1]

How much did Soviet women benefit from this increased freedom? Proclaiming a women's emancipation and equality that they failed to implement fully in practice, the Bolsheviks had created Zhenotdel, directed after Inessa Armand's death by Alexandra Kollontai (1920–1921). She emphasized the liberation of "women of the East," notably Muslim women of Central Asia, from their traditional subservience. Opposing the increasing centralism and bureaucracy overtaking the Bolshevik party, Kollontai advocated creative efforts by the workers themselves; in 1921 she drafted and distributed the program for the Workers' Opposition faction, advocating syndicalism. Lenin and his colleagues, denouncing the Workers' Opposition as a threat to party unity and discipline, removed Kollontai from Zhenotdel and packed her off to Norway on a minor diplomatic mission. Her political career was over, but later she became the first Soviet ambassador to Sweden. Lenin's regime, while providing educational and economic equality for women, granted them little political power. Before November 1917 only three women had served in the party leadership; few thereafter even reached the Central Committee, and no woman served on the Politburo until Ekaterina Furtseva achieved full membership, 1957–1961. Observed Kollontai correctly in 1922: "The Soviet state is run by men." Soviet women enjoyed broad civil rights but little political power.

Under NEP, though a degree of freedom persisted, political controls were tightened. Remaining Menshevik and SR leaders were exiled, and late in 1921 a party purge excluded about one-fourth of the Bolshevik membership. Within the party, factions were banned and political dissent became more dangerous. Punitive powers of the expanding central party apparatus over the members increased, and decision making by top leaders grew more arbitrary. Party decrees, however, failed to end debate or factions during NEP, even though the defeated might be expelled or lose their posts.

The Constitution of 1918 had proclaimed federalism, but relations among Soviet republics remained undefined until December 1922, when a unified, centralized Union of Soviet Socialist Republics replaced the several independent republics. Within the huge Russian Republic (RSFSR) were 17 autonomous republics and regions for national minorities, all ruled from Moscow. Other republics, such as Ukraine and Byelorussia, had to accept the RSFSR's constitution verbatim. Because the soviets were subordinate to party direction and other Communist parties were Russian led, the Russian party's Central Committee exercised full de facto power everywhere. The RSFSR government became the highest state authority in all areas occupied by the Red Army. Soviet histories under Gorbachev, minimizing national resistance to integration in Soviet Russia, attributed the USSR's formation partly to "imperialist" pressure and foreign plots to overthrow Soviet power. Actually, it resulted mainly from the Red Army's subjugation of tsarist borderlands, such as Transcaucasia. When Red troops entered Vladivostok in 1922, following Japanese withdrawal, the Far Eastern Republic dissolved instantly and merged with the RSFSR. The nominally independent republics of Khiva and Bukhara in Central Asia were abolished in 1924 and their territory distributed arbitrarily among five new Soviet republics: Uzbek, Turkmen, Tajik, Kazakh, and Kirghiz.

The new USSR was an apparent compromise between Bolshevik desires for centralization and autonomist aims of nationalists and federalists in the borderlands. The Bolsheviks viewed the USSR as a stage in the advance toward an ultimate worldwide Soviet state. Within it, national minorities often enjoyed less autonomy than under tsarism. Gone were their political parties and separate religious and cultural institutions, though they received linguistic autonomy, distinct national territories, and political representation—a fake federalism, concealing complete Russian and

---

[1] R. W. Davies, ed., *Soviet History in the Gorbachev Revolution* (Bloomington, IN, 1989), pp. 28*ff.*

Bolshevik predominance that failed to win the support of the nationalities.

Once Lenin achieved power, his doctrines changed considerably. Before the November coup he had declared in *State and Revolution:*

> To destroy officialdom immediately, everywhere, completely—this cannot be thought of. . . . But to *break up* at once the old bureaucratic machine and to start immediately the construction of a new one which will enable us gradually to reduce all officialdom to naught, this is *no* Utopia, it is the experience of the [Paris] Commune, the . . . direct and urgent task of the revolutionary proletariat.[2]

Capitalism had so simplified governmental functions, Lenin believed, that ordinary workers could perform such "registration, filing and checking." He had conceived of a "state apparatus of about 10, if not 20 million" class-conscious workers as part-time civil servants. (How poorly he understood the problems of running an industrial society!) Once in power, the flexible Lenin discarded former views that proved inapplicable. The transition to socialism, he admitted in 1918, would require bourgeois experts, and in 1920 he conceded sadly: "We have to administer [the proletarian state] with the help of people belonging to the class we have overthrown" and pay them well. In his final years Lenin, in his writings, grew cautious and reformist. Criticizing War Communism's "furious assaults," he described "exaggerated revolutionism" as dangerous in domestic policy and advocated "conquering peacefully" by careful economic construction.[3] The contrast between his militant views in 1917–1920 and the reformist, evolutionary emphasis of 1921–1923 makes one wonder which was the "real" Lenin.

Nonetheless, Lenin bequeathed an elitist doctrine and party as one foundation of a new autocracy (others were provided by tsarism, the Civil

War, and War Communism). His central doctrine —the dictatorship of the proletariat—he had defined as "power won and maintained by the proletariat against the bourgeoisie, power unrestricted by any laws."[4] Having designed a theoretically centralized party able to strike ruthlessly and outlawing factions within it (which failed to end factionalism), he hoped that "democratic centralism" would encourage free intraparty debate, then unanimous action. Discussion was to be free until a decision was reached, then all party members were expected to execute it loyally. Although Lenin prevailed within the party not by force or because of any position he held, but by persuasion, charisma, and moral stature, nevertheless he left to Stalin certain tools which Stalin used to build his brutal dictatorship: a centralized party, predominant central organs, subservient soviets, and police terror. It was Lenin who authorized creation of a secret police and who banned factionalism within the party. By applying these elements ruthlessly and vindictively, Stalin altered the Soviet system fundamentally.

The Struggle over Succession

In May 1922 Lenin suffered his first stroke. Through his writings, pragmatic leadership, and ability to handle people, he had dominated Bolshevism since its inception, and his semiretirement sparked a struggle for succession within the party. Lenin named no successor, and his "Testament," or "Letter to the Congress" of December 1922, found fault with all the leading contenders. Increasingly dismayed by Stalin's Great Russian chauvinism and brutal domination of the party apparatus, Lenin wrote, "Comrade Stalin, having become *gensek* [General Secretary] has concentrated boundless power in his hands, and I am not sure that he will always manage to use this power with sufficient caution." He had a second stroke in December 1922. In January 1923 he added, "Stalin

---

[2] Lenin, *Polnoe Sobranie Sochineniia,* 5th ed. (Moscow, 1962), vol. 33, pp. 48–49.

[3] "The Immediate Tasks of the Soviet Government, April 1918," in R. Tucker, ed., *The Lenin Anthology* (New York, 1975), pp. 441–44.

[4] Ibid., p. 464.

John Massey Stewart

Joseph Stalin: Tsarist police photograph.

is too rude. . . . I propose to the comrades that they devise a way of shifting Stalin from this position." Apparently, only a third stroke in March 1923 prevented Lenin from removing Stalin. Concern for the party and their own positions induced other contenders at first to form a collective leadership and present a united front. Behind the scenes the struggle for succession went through several phases until Stalin triumphed. These issues were debated fiercely: Where was the Revolution heading? Would NEP lead to capitalism or socialism? How should Russia be industrialized? Factions, though illegal, were too ingrained in party traditions to be easily eradicated, though politics grew ever more dangerous and secretive. By Lenin's death in 1924, four major groups had formed: a Stalin faction, the Trotskii Left, Bukharin's moderates, and a Zinoviev-Kamenev group based in Leningrad.

Joseph Stalin, the eventual winner, was born in 1879 as Iosif Vissarionovich Djugashvili of semiliterate Georgian parents descended from serfs. As a boy, Soso was devoted to his mother and rebelled against a drunken father and all authority. An excellent student who expected to excel in everything, he idealized Koba, a fearless 19th-century Caucasian mountain chieftain, and adopted his view of vindictive triumph as a worthy goal in life. He resented the strict discipline at the Tiflis Orthodox seminary and was expelled as a socialist in 1899. Between 1902 and 1917 he was arrested and exiled repeatedly for underground revolutionary activity. He became a Bolshevik soon after the faction's formation; as Lenin's admiring disciple, he modeled himself after his hero and adopted the name Stalin partly because it resembled Lenin. Stalin adopted a Great Russian outlook and dedicated his life to revolution. His *Marxism and the National Question* (1913) established him as a major leader and a mature Marxist. In 1917, as a party organizer and close colleague of Lenin, he belonged to the Bolshevik general staff. The SR memoirist, N. Sukhanov, recalled Stalin then as "a grey blur, looming up now and then dimly, and not leaving any trace." During the Civil War he gained military experience and political influence but was intensely jealous of Trotskii, who overshadowed him. The traditional Western view of Stalin as a nonintellectual "organization man," building the party state, however, actually fitted Sverdlov better. Stalin handled crises well, but he was too impatient, hot tempered, and uncooperative to be a gifted organizer or administrator. In 1923 he confided to Kamenev: "The greatest

Stalin's birthplace, surrounded by the Stalin museum, in Gori, Georgia.

delight is to mark one's enemy, prepare everything, avenge oneself thoroughly, and then go to sleep."

Aiming to control the Bolshevik movement, Stalin achieved his commanding position through the politics of power and influence and by cultivating a political following built up over the years. In exile, using Machiavelli's *The Prince* as a primer, he studied the strategy and tactics of politics. He had an intuitive eye for men's strengths and weaknesses and how to exploit them. After Sverdlov's death in 1919, Stalin acquired key posts in the Orgburo (concerned with organizational matters), Politburo, and Secretariat; election as general secretary consolidated his organizational position. Stalin dominated the party apparatus that Sverdlov had built, forged his personal machine, and obtained a controlling voice on party bodies that selected and placed personnel.

Stalin exploited cleverly the cult of Lenin, which developed during the leader's final illness. Lenin had prohibited public adulation of himself and detested ceremony, but after his death his teachings—Leninism—became sacred doctrine. Official decrees ordered monuments to Lenin erected all over the USSR, renamed Petrograd as Leningrad, and authorized a huge edition of his writings. Stalin urged that Lenin's body be embalmed and placed on public display in a tomb on Red Square, although his widow, Trotskii, and Bukharin all protested that this was un-Marxian. As Lenin's devoted disciple, Stalin gathered the reins of power and won public acclaim.

Before achieving full power, Stalin survived some tense moments. In May 1924 a Central Committee plenum heard Lenin's "Testament," which urged Stalin's removal as general secretary. But Zinoviev and Kamenev, who had formed a triumvirate with Stalin in 1922, supported him out of fear of Trotskii (see Table 33.1). Stalin used the triumvirate to undermine Trotskii, whose inept tactics and arrogance antagonized many party members, and who spurned overtures from Kamenev and Zinoviev when Stalin's rise might still have been prevented. Only after his rivals had voted him into all positions of power did Stalin begin an open struggle with them. His repetitious,

Table 33.1
Participants in the Soviet Power Struggle, 1922–1929

1922–1925	Triumvirate: Stalin-Zinoviev-Kamenev
1925–1928	Stalin-Bukharin versus Trotskii-Kamenev-Zinoviev
1929–1953	Stalin in power

catechistic style won support from younger, semi-educated Bolsheviks, who sought a single authoritative chief to lead their party forward.

In 1925 the triumvirate broke up: Zinoviev and Kamenev drifted belatedly toward Trotskii, while Stalin joined Bukharin's moderates. At the 14th Congress, Kamenev, too late, challenged Stalin's credentials as the new party chief, but Stalin's machine defeated him and broke up Zinoviev's Leningrad organization. Because Stalin still lacked enough prestige to seize sole power, his alliance with Bukharin proved most advantageous. As chief theorist and spokesman for NEP, Bukharin shielded Stalin from accusations that he was usurping Lenin's place and compensated for his lack of ideological clout. Through 1927 Stalin supported NEP, Bukharin's gradualist economics, and his ideological warfare against Trotskii.

During the growing debate over socialist construction, Stalin developed his major theory: socialism in one country. He had declared at a Bolshevik conference in April 1917, "The possibility is not excluded that Russia will . . . blaze the trail to socialism." In 1925 Bukharin affirmed that the USSR could build its own socialism gradually but added, "Final practical victory of socialism in our country is not possible without the help of other countries and of world revolution." Posing as a moderate and Lenin's true interpreter, Stalin restated the Leninist view in *Foundations of Leninism* (1924):

> To overthrow the bourgeoisie the efforts of one country are sufficient; for the final victory of socialism, for the organization of socialist production the efforts of one country, particularly of a peasant country like Russia, are insuf-

ficient; for that the efforts of the proletariats of several advanced countries are required.[5]

To prove that Trotskii and his theory of world revolution were anti-Leninist, however, Stalin later that year suddenly asserted that Russia alone could organize a completely socialist economy with advanced industry and high living standards. He developed the nationalistic view that Russia alone might blaze the trail of socialist construction. Soviet Russia, the pioneer of proletarian revolution, could construct a fully socialist society by its own exertions with or without revolutions abroad. To ensure that the old order would not be restored, however, the proletariat must win power in "at least several other countries." Carefully selecting his quotations, Stalin insisted that this was Lenin's theory, too. Stalin's program of Russian self-sufficiency in building socialism proved highly effective, especially among new, young party members and a burgeoning Soviet officialdom, composed largely of semieducated worker and peasant elements. These greedy and often incompetent officials welcomed Stalin's nationalism and growing "personality cult." The new bureaucracy, manipulated by Stalin, replaced the proletariat as the bearer of socialism.[6] The doctrine of socialism in one country made Stalin an authoritative ideological leader who could shrug off his opponents' belated criticisms.

In 1926–1927 Stalin defeated and silenced the Left with support from the Bukharinists. Trotskii and Zinoviev were removed from the Politburo and the latter ousted as Comintern chief. Trotskii's denunciations of the Stalin-dominated Politburo as "Thermidorean," his critique of its blunders in foreign policy, and his street demonstration of November 1927 hastened his expulsion from the party and exile. As Zinoviev and Kamenev recanted their views to save their party membership, only the Bukharinists stood between Stalin and complete power.

---

[5] Quoted in R. Tucker, *Stalin as Revolutionary, 1879–1929* (New York, 1973), p. 371.
[6] See Moshe Lewin, "The Social Background of Stalinism," in R. Tucker, ed., *Stalinism* (New York, 1977), pp. 111*ff.*

Soviet Russia under NEP was a one-party dictatorship modified by social pluralism—an economic compromise between socialism and capitalism. Though the state sector predominated in industry and was growing, the private sector remained vital and dominant in agriculture. Most Soviet citizens, especially peasants, worked and lived far from party or state control, which did not extend far outside the urban centers. NEP was an era of rival theories, contention, and exciting experiments. Tolerance of political, economic, and social diversity marked it as a period of liberal Communism, recovery, and civil peace. As Stalin built his party autocracy, however, these compromises could not long endure.

Problem 11

From Lenin to Stalin: Continuity or Betrayal?

Who, if anyone, was responsible for putting Soviet Russia on a course leading to renewed autocracy, repression, and massive purges? Was this the work of Lenin or Stalin, or was it inherent in Bolshevism or in the previous development of Russian history? Were there fundamental differences in approach, policy, and personality between Lenin and Stalin? Was Stalin's regime the logical culmination of Leninism, or did his one-man rule and personality cult represent a breach with and repudiation of Bolshevik ideals and practice? Did Stalin's dictatorship constitute an aberration, a temporary interruption of a Bolshevik tradition of "collective leadership," as N. S. Khrushchev would later intimate?

Until 1960 most Western scholars stressed elements of continuity between early Bolshevism and the Stalin era. This theory of the "straight line" was later reinforced by Alexander Solzhenitsyn's *Gulag Archipelago*, which traced the roots of mass terror and the system of forced labor camps to the first days of Lenin's regime. Western scholars tended to view Stalin's "great transformation" of 1929–1933 as perfecting an inherent, inevitable totalitarianism.

Recently some Western historians, using newly accessible Soviet materials, have challenged this continuity thesis. These revisionists argue that Stalinism differed fundamentally from earlier Bolshevism—that Stalin's policies were so violent and extreme that they changed the very nature of the Soviet state and Bolshevik party. By emphasizing statism, Great Russian nationalism, and anti-Semitism and by encouraging his own deification, Stalin repudiated the beliefs of Lenin and his "Old Bolshevik" colleagues, such as Trotskii, Zinoviev, and Bukharin. To view Stalinism as merely the outgrowth of the militant Lenin of *What Is to Be Done?* (1902), argues Stephen Cohen, is a grievous oversimplification. Instead, Bolshevism evolved over the years from an unruly, loosely organized group of independent-minded revolutionaries into the centralized, bureaucratic organization of the 1920s; under Stalin the Communist Party was terrorized and its influence sharply reduced. In actuality, the Bolshevik party had never been quite the disciplined vanguard of professionals advocated in *What Is to Be Done?* Even official party historians complained repeatedly that its history was one of "factional struggle." Despite the ban on factions engineered by Lenin in 1921, the party remained oligarchical or, as Bukharin put it, "a negotiated federation between groups, groupings, factions, and tendencies." Thus, Cohen concludes, the party's "organizational principles" did not produce Stalinist dictatorship and conformity.[7]

---

[7] S. Cohen, "Bolshevism and Stalinism," in R. Tucker, ed., *Stalinism: Essays in Historical Interpretation* (New York, 1977), pp. 19–29. See also Tucker, *The Soviet Political Mind* (New York, 1963).

Indicative of the widely disparate views on the relationship between the regimes of Lenin (1917–1923) and Stalin (1928–1953) are the following excerpts: two from official Soviet publications, one by a Soviet dissident scholar, one from a recent Russian biography of Stalin, two from statements by Soviet émigrés, and two from Western accounts.

Official Soviet Interpretations

History of the Communist Party of the Soviet Union (Bolsheviks): Short Course (New York, 1939) is the official party history prepared ostensibly by the Central Committee following the Great Purge (discussed in Chapter 34). It was edited and perhaps partly written by Joseph Stalin and reflects the "classical" Stalinist interpretation of the purges. The "dregs of humanity" referred to in the text included the leading "Old Bolsheviks," the closest colleagues of Lenin—the original leaders of Soviet Russia, the Bolshevik party, and the Third International (Comintern)!

In 1937, new facts came to light regarding the fiendish crimes of the Bukharin-Trotsky gang. The trial[s] . . . all showed that the Bukharinites and Trotskyists had long ago joined to form a common band of enemies of the people, operating as the "Bloc of Rights and Trotskyites." The trials showed that these dregs of humanity, in conjunction with the enemies of the people, Trotsky, Zinoviev, and Kamenev, had been in conspiracy against Lenin, the Party, and the Soviet state ever since the early days of the October Socialist Revolution. The insidious attempts to thwart the Peace of Brest-Litovsk at the beginning of 1918, . . . the deliberate aggravation of differences in the party in 1921 . . . , the attempts to overthrow the Party leadership during Lenin's illness and after his death, . . . the vile assassination of Kirov . . . —all these and similar villainies over a period of 20 years were committed, it transpired, with the participation or under the direction of Trotsky, Zinoviev, Kamenev,

Bukharin, Rykov and their henchmen, at the behest of espionage services of bourgeois states.

. . . These Whiteguard pygmies, whose strength was no more than that of a gnat, apparently flattered themselves that they were the masters of the country, and imagined that it was really in their power to sell or give away the Ukraine, Byelorussia, and the Maritime Region. . . . These contemptible lackeys of the fascists forgot that the Soviet people had only to move a finger, and not a trace of them would be left. The Soviet court sentenced the Bukharin-Trotsky fiends to be shot. . . . The Soviet people approved the annihilation of the Bukharin-Trotsky gang and passed on to the next business.[8]

History of the Communist Party of the Soviet Union (Moscow, 1960), issued during the modified one-man rule of N. S. Khrushchev, reflects denunciation of Stalin's crimes after 1934 balanced by praise for his economic achievements, as expressed by the 20th Party Congress of 1956. Note that no attempt is made here to rehabilitate "Old Bolshevik" leaders such as Trotskii, Zinoviev, and Bukharin.

The victory of socialism created favorable conditions for the extension of Party and Soviet democracy. But in spite of that, there were direct violations of Party and Soviet democracy resulting from what was later defined by the Party as the cult of Stalin's personality. Stalin began to develop into a law certain restrictions in inner-Party and Soviet democracy that were unavoidable in conditions of bitter struggle against the class enemy and his agents. He began to violate the standards of Party life worked out by Lenin, the principle of collective leadership, deciding many important questions on his own. In Stalin's actions a discrepancy arose between word and deed, between theory and practice. . . . Starting from correct Marxist premises, he warned against impermissible exaggerations of the role of the individual in history, but in practice he encouraged the cult of his own personality.

Stalin rightly stressed the necessity of strengthening the Soviet State in every possible way, of keeping a watchful eye . . . on the machinations of the hostile capitalist encirclement; . . . to be on

---

[8] *History of the Communist Party of the Soviet Union (Bolsheviks): Short Course* (New York, 1939), pp. 346–48.

guard against . . . the routed opposition groups of the Trotskyists, Zinovievites. . . . On the other hand, in 1937, when Socialism was already victorious in the U.S.S.R., Stalin advanced the erroneous thesis that the class struggle in the country would intensify as the Soviet State grew stronger. . . . In practice it served as a justification for mass repressions against the Party's ideological enemies who had already been routed politically. Many honest Communists and non-Party people, not guilty of any offense, also became victims of these repressions. During this period the political adventurer and scoundrel, Beria,[9] who did not stop short at any atrocity to achieve his criminal aims, worked his way into responsible positions in the State, and, taking advantage of Stalin's personal shortcomings, slandered and exterminated many honest people, devoted to the Party and the people. In the same period a despicable role was played by Yezhov. . . . Many workers, both Communists and non-Party people, who were utterly devoted to the cause of the Party, were slandered with his assistance and perished. Yezhov and Beria were duly punished for their crimes.[10] . . . Although the mistakes resulting from the cult of Stalin's personality retarded the development of Soviet society, they could not check it, and still less could they change the Socialist nature of the Soviet system.[11]

A Dissident Marxist Historian

Roy Medvedev is a Russian Marxist scholar who became absorbed in study of the Stalin era after Khrushchev's revelations at the 20th and 22nd Party Congresses. However, by the time he had completed his book *Let History Judge: The Ori-*

gins and Consequences of Stalinism in 1968, the Brezhnev regime was moving toward a partial rehabilitation of Stalin and it had to be published in the United States. Medvedev was subsequently expelled from the party but remains a Marxist living in Russia. This book represented an "insider's" view of the Stalin phenomenon. Medvedev accepted Khrushchev's view that Stalinist terror and the personality cult were temporary departures from an essentially sound Soviet system, but he was much more vigorous in denouncing that terror.

To many people in the Soviet Union the mass repression of 1937–38 was an incomprehensible calamity that suddenly broke upon the country and seemed to have no end. Explanations abounded, some of them representing a search for the truth, but more attempting to escape the cruel truth, to find some formula that would preserve faith in the Party and Stalin. . . . One widespread story was that Stalin did not know about the terror, that all those crimes were committed behind his back. Of course it was ridiculous to suppose that Stalin, master of everyone and everything, did not know about the arrest and shooting of members of the Politburo and the Central Committee, . . . about the arrest of the military high command and the Comintern leaders. . . . But that is a peculiarity of the mind blinded by faith in a higher being. This naive conviction of Stalin's ignorance was reflected in the word, *yezhovshchina,* "the Yezhov thing," the popular name for the tragedy of the thirties . . . , a new version of the common people's faith in a good tsar surrounded by lying and wicked ministers. But it must be acknowledged that this story had some basis in Stalin's behavior. Secretive and self-contained, Stalin avoided the public eye; . . . he acted through unseen channels. He tried to direct events from behind the scenes, making basic decisions by himself or with a few aides . . . preferring to put the spotlight on other perpetrators of these crimes, thereby retaining his own freedom of movement.

Some confusion about the nature of Stalin's power must be cleared away. By the end of the twenties and the early thirties he was already called a dictator, a one-man ruler . . . , but the unlimited dictatorship that he established after

---

[9] After the Great Purge had reached its climax in 1937 under N. I. Yezhov, Stalin had him executed and made Lavrenti Beria head of the security police (NKVD).

[10] Yezhov was executed, apparently at Stalin's orders, in 1938. Beria was purged in June 1953 after apparently attempting to overthrow the government and was executed either before or after his "trial."

[11] *History of the Communist Party of the Soviet Union* (Moscow, 1960), pp. 512–13.

Problem 11 continued

1936–38 was without historical precedent. For the last fifteen years of his bloody career Stalin wielded such power as no Russian tsar ever possessed. . . . In the years of the cult, Stalin held not only all political power; he was master of the economy, the military, foreign policy; even in literature, the arts, and science he was the supreme arbiter. . . .

It was an historical accident that Stalin, the embodiment of all the worst elements in the Russian revolutionary movement, came to power after Lenin, the embodiment of all that was best. . . . The Party must not only condemn Stalin's crimes; it must also eliminate the conditions that facilitated them. . . . Stalin never relied on force alone. Throughout the period of his one-man rule he was popular. The longer this tyrant ruled the USSR, coldbloodedly destroying millions of people, the greater seems to have been the dedication to him, even the love, of the majority of people. . . .

One condition that made it easy for Stalin to bend the Party to his will was the hugely inflated cult of his personality. . . . The deification of Stalin justified in advance everything he did. . . . All the achievements and virtues of socialism were embodied in him. . . . Not conscious faith, but blind faith in Stalin was required. Like every cult, this one tended to transform the Communist Party into an ecclesiastical organization with a sharp distinction between ordinary people and leader-priests headed by their infallible pope. The gulf between the people and Stalin was not only deepened but idealized. The business of state in the Kremlin became as remote and incomprehensible for the unconsecrated as the affairs of the gods on Olympus. . . . Just as believers attribute everything good to God and everything bad to the devil, so everything good was attributed to Stalin and everything bad to evil forces that Stalin himself was fighting. "Long live Stalin!" some officials shouted as they were taken to be shot.[12]

---

[12] Roy A. Medvedev, *Let History Judge: The Origins and Consequences of Stalinism* (New York, 1968), pp. 289–90, 355, 362–63.

A Contemporary Russian Historian

D. A. Volkogonov, a prominent military historian, wrote *Triumph and Tragedy,* the first complete biography of Stalin published in the USSR. "I want to show that the triumph of one person can turn into a tragedy for the whole people," Volkogonov explained. As director of the Institute of Military History, Volkogonov used many reminiscences and documents from the hitherto secret archives of the Defense Ministry, stressing how Stalin's psychotic personality resulted in tragedies for the Soviet people. "I am profoundly convinced that the socialist development of society could have avoided those dark stains . . . if a deficit of popular authority had not developed after the death of Lenin." But none of the other available leaders, Volkogonov concluded, would have been preferable to Stalin:

> If Trotskii had been in charge of the Party, even more burdensome experiences would have awaited it, involving loss of our socialist achievements—all the more because Trotskii did not have a scientific and clear programme for the construction of socialism in the USSR. Bukharin had such a programme . . . , but in spite of his great attractiveness as a person . . . and his humanity Bukharin for a long time did not understand the necessity of a sharp leap by the country in the growth of its economic power.[13]

Soviet Émigrés

Born in Brussels, Belgium, in 1890 of Russian émigré parents, Victor Serge (Viktor L. Kibalchich) became a radical socialist and after the Russian Revolution returned to Soviet Russia. He joined the Bolshevik party and became prominent in the Comintern, barely escaping to the West before the Great Purge. Like his "Old Bolshevik" contemporaries, Serge greatly

---

[13] D. A. Volkogonov, "Fenomen Stalina," *Literaturnaia gazeta,* December 9, 1987; *Trud,* June 19, 1988; and *Pravda,* June 20, 1988. These excerpts are from Volkogonov's book, translated as *Stalin: Triumph and Tragedy,* trans. Harold Shukman (New York, 1991).

Problem 11 continued

admired and idealized Lenin, but was profoundly disillusioned by Stalinist tyranny.

> Everything has changed. The aims: from international social revolution to socialism in one country. The political system: from the workers' democracy of the soviets, the goal of the revolution, to the dictatorship of the general secretariat, the functionaries, and the GPU [secret police]. The party: from the organization, free in its life and thought and freely submitting to discipline, of revolutionary Marxists to the hierarchy of bureaus, to the passive obedience of careerists. The Third International: from a mighty organization of propaganda and struggle to the opportunist servility of Central Committees appointed for the purpose of approving everything, without shame or nausea. . . . The leaders: the greatest militants of October are in exile or prison. . . . The condition of the workers: the equalitarianism of Soviet society is transformed to permit the formation of a privileged minority, more and more privileged in comparison with the disinherited masses who are deprived of all rights. Morality: from the austere, sometimes implacable honesty of heroic Bolshevism, we gradually advance to unspeakable deviousness and deceit. Everything has changed, everything is changing, but it will require the perspective of time before we can precisely understand the realities.[14]

In his massive, three-volume work, *The Gulag Archipelago, 1918–1956,* Alexander Solzhenitsyn, a great contemporary Russian writer forcibly exiled from the USSR in 1974, describes the labor camp system in the USSR and its history, based on personal experience and the testimony of 227 witnesses. Begun in 1958, *Gulag* was first published abroad in 1973. Arbitrary arrest and detention, argues Solzhenitsyn, originated with Lenin in 1918 and was merely extended and intensified under Stalin. He sees repression as an inalienable part of an evil Soviet totalitarianism.

---

[14] Victor Serge, *From Lenin to Stalin* (New York, 1973), pp. 57–58.

Note how Solzhenitsyn's interpretation of Lenin differs from that of Roy Medvedev, who considers him a true Marxist, invariably adhering to norms of socialist legality.

> When people today decry the *abuses of the cult* [of Stalin's personality], they keep getting hung up on those years which are stuck in our throats, '37 and '38. And memory begins to make it seem as though arrests were never made *before* or *after*, but only in those two years. . . . The *wave* of 1937 and 1938 was neither the only one nor even the main one, but only one, perhaps, of the three biggest waves which strained the murky, stinking pipes of our prison sewers to bursting. *Before* it came the wave of 1929 and 1930 . . . which drove a mere 15 million peasants, maybe even more, out into the taiga and the tundra. . . . And *after* it was the wave of 1944 to 1946 . . . when they dumped whole *nations* down the sewer pipes, not to mention millions and millions of others who . . . had been prisoners of war, or carried off to Germany and subsequently repatriated. . . .
>
> It is well known that any *organ* withers away if it is not used. Therefore, if we know that the Soviet Security organs or *Organs* (and they christened themselves with this vile word), praised and exalted above all living things, have not died off even to the extent of one single tentacle, but instead, have grown new ones and strengthened their muscles—it is easy to deduce that they have had *constant* exercise. . . .
>
> But even before there was any Civil War, it could be seen that Russia . . . was obviously not suited for any sort of socialism whatsoever. . . . One of the first blows of the dictatorship was directed against the Cadets—the members of the *Constitutional Democratic Party.* At the end of November 1917 . . . the Cadet Party was outlawed and arrests of its members began. . . . One of the first circulars of the NKVD [initially the Cheka, renamed NKVD in 1934], in December 1917, stated: "In view of sabotage by officials . . . use maximum initiative in localities, *not excluding* confiscations, compulsion, and arrests." . . . V. I. Lenin proclaimed the common, united purpose [in January 1918] of "purging the Russian land of all kinds of harmful insects." And under the term *insects* he included not only all class enemies but also "workers malingering at

Problem 11 continued

their work. . . ." It would have been impossible to carry out this hygienic purging . . . if they had had to follow outdated legal processes and normal judicial procedures. And so an entirely new form was adopted: *extrajudicial reprisal,* and this thankless job was self-sacrificingly assumed by the Cheka . . . , the only punitive organ in human history which combined in one set of hands investigation, arrest, interrogation, prosecution, trial and execution of the *verdict.*[15]

Western Views

An American specialist in Russian affairs, George F. Kennan served in the U.S. Foreign Service from 1926 to 1953, including a stint as ambassador in Moscow. Following his retirement he became a professor at the Institute for Advanced Studies in Princeton, New Jersey, where he wrote *Soviet-American Relations, 1917–1920. Russia and the West Under Lenin and Stalin,* from which the following passage is excerpted, was based on lectures delivered at Oxford and Harvard universities, 1957–1960. After World War II Kennan won renown as the author of the "containment theory" that advocated preventing Soviet expansion by means of non-Communist alliances and bases.

> It remains only to mention the contrast between Stalin, as a statesman and [Lenin]. . . . The differences are not easy ones to identify, for in many instances they were only ones of degree and of motive. Lenin, too, was a master of internal Party intrigue. He, too, was capable of ruthless cruelty. He, too, could be unpitying in the elimination of people who seriously disagreed with him. . . . No less than Stalin, Lenin adopted an attitude of implacable hostility toward the Western world.
>
> But behind all this there were very significant differences. Lenin was a man with no sense of inferiority. Well-born, well-educated, endowed with

a mind of formidable power and brilliance, he was devoid of the angularities of the social parvenu, and he felt himself a match for any man intellectually. He was spared that whole great burden of personal insecurity which rested so heavily on Stalin. He never had to doubt his hold on the respect and admiration of his colleagues. He could rule them through the love they bore him, whereas Stalin was obliged to rule them through their fears. This enabled Lenin to run the movement squarely on the basis of what he conceived to be its needs, without bothering about his own. And since the intellectual inventory of the Party was largely of his own creation, he was relieved of that ignominious need which Stalin constantly experienced for buttressing his political views by references to someone else's gospel. Having fashioned Leninism to his own heart's desire out of the raw materials of Marx's legacy, Lenin had no fear of adapting it and adjusting it as the situation required. For this reason his mind remained open throughout his life—open, at least, to argument and suggestions from those who shared his belief in the basic justification of the second Russian Revolution of 1917. These people could come to him and talk to him, and could find their thoughts not only accepted in the spirit they were offered but responded to by a critical intelligence second to none in the history of the socialist movement. They did not have to feel, as they later did under Stalin, that deep, dangerous, ulterior meanings might be read into anything they said, and that an innocent suggestion might prove their personal undoing.

> This had, of course, a profound effect on the human climate that prevailed throughout the Soviet regime in Lenin's time. Endowed with this temperament, Lenin was able to communicate to his associates an atmosphere of militant optimism, of good cheer and steadfastness and comradely loyalty, which made him the object of their deepest admiration and affection and permitted them to apply their entire energy to the work at hand. . . . While Lenin's ultimate authority remained unquestioned, it was possible to spread initiative and responsibility much further than was ever the case in the heyday of Stalin's power. This explains why Soviet diplomacy was so much more variegated and colorful in Lenin's time than in the subsequent Stalin era. In the change from Lenin to Stalin, the

---

[15] Alexander Solzhenitsyn, *The Gulag Archipelago, 1918–1956* (New York, 1973), vol. 1, pp. 24–25.

Problem 11 continued

foreign policy of a movement became the foreign policy of a single man.[16]

Stephen Cohen, professor of politics at Princeton University, has specialized in the Soviet period and written an outstanding biography of Nikolai Bukharin, a leading theoretician and close colleague of Lenin.

While the internal party battles of 1923–9 constituted prolonged attempts to reconstruct the power and authority previously exercised by Lenin, the idea that there could be a successor—a "Lenin of today"—was impermissible. Lenin's authority within the leadership and in the party generally had been unique. Among other things, it had derived from the fact that he was the party's creator and moving spirit, from his political judgment which had been proved correct so often and against so much opposition, and from the force of his personality, which united and persuaded his fractious colleagues. In no way did it derive from an official post. As Sokolnikov pointed out: "Lenin was neither chairman of the Politburo nor general secretary; but nonetheless, Comrade Lenin . . . had the decisive political word in the party." It was . . . a kind of charismatic authority, inseparable from Lenin as a person and independent of constitutional or institutional procedures.

Some of his heirs intuitively understood this and commented on it in different ways. "Lenin was a dictator in the best sense of the word," said Bukharin in 1924. Five years later, describing Lenin as the singular "leader, organizer, captain, and stern iron authority," and contrasting his pre-eminence with Stalin's brute machine power,

Bukharin tried to explain further. "But he was for us all *Ilich*, a close, beloved, person, a wonderful comrade and friend, the bond with whom was indissoluble. He was not only 'Comrade Lenin,' but something immeasurably more."[17]

Conclusion

A wide divergence of views persists among scholars about the relationship between Lenin's rule and that of Stalin. Among Communists, Lenin remains a generally respected, even revered figure, but viewpoints about Stalin range from hero worship by Russian and Georgian neo-Stalinists, to the relatively balanced verdicts of the Khrushchev years, to bitter denunciation by Roy Medvedev and most writers and historians under Gorbachev. Many Soviet citizens, notably workers, appeared to believe that Stalin's positive contributions to the USSR outweighed his monstrous crimes. Those crimes were downplayed under Brezhnev when the emphasis once again was placed on Stalin's achievements as collectivizer, industrializer, and war-time leader. Even under Gorbachev many military memoirs continued to praise Stalin's leadership during World War II. Solzhenitsyn's view, on the other hand, repudiates Soviet totalitarianism in toto, Lenin included, in favor of Russian nationalism and neo-Orthodoxy. Whether Stalin's regime represented a continuation of Lenin's principles and rules or their antithesis remains debated. Among those Russian citizens who harbor feelings of nostalgia for the past, Stalin's strength, authority, and achievements contrast sharply with the pain and suffering of post-Communist Russia. ■

[16] George F. Kennan, *Russia and the West Under Lenin and Stalin* (Boston, 1960), pp. 256–58.

[17] Stephen Cohen, *Bukharin and the Bolshevik Revolution* (New York, 1971), pp. 223–24.

Suggested Additional Reading

BALL, A. M. *Russia's Last Capitalists: The NEPMEN 1921–1929* (Berkeley, 1987).

CARR, E. H. *A History of Soviet Russia,* 10 vols. (New York, 1951–1972).

CHASE, W. *Workers, Society, and the Soviet State: Labor and Life in Moscow, 1918–1929* (Champaign, IL, 1990).

COHEN, S. *Bukharin: A Political Biography* (New York, 1974).

D'AGOSTINO, A. *Soviet Succession Struggles . . . from Lenin to Gorbachev* (Winchester, MA, 1987).

DANIELS, R. *The Conscience of the Revolution: Communist Opposition in Soviet Russia* (Cambridge, MA, 1960).

DESAI, M., ed. *Lenin's Economic Writings* (Atlantic Highlands, NJ, 1989).

DEUTSCHER, I. *The Prophet Unarmed: Trotsky, 1921–1929* (Oxford, 1951).

FISHER, H. *The Famine in Soviet Russia, 1919–1923 . . .* (Stanford, 1927).

JAKOBSON, M. *Origins of the GULAG: The Soviet Prison Camp System, 1917–1934* (Lexington, KY, 1993).

KOLLONTAI, A. *The Workers' Opposition in Russia* (Chicago, 1921).

KRUPSKAIA, N. *Memories of Lenin* (London, 1942).

LEWIN, M. *Lenin's Last Struggle* (New York, 1968).

MEYER, A. *Leninism* (Cambridge, MA, 1957).

PAGE, S. *Lenin and World Revolution* (New York, 1959).

PIPES, R. *The Formation of the Soviet Union* (Cambridge, MA, 1954).

READ, C. *Culture and Power in Revolutionary Russia . . .* (New York, 1990).

REIMAN, M. *The Birth of Stalinism: The USSR on the Eve of the "Second Revolution,"* trans. G. Saunders (Bloomington, IN, 1987).

SERGE, V. *From Lenin to Stalin* (New York, 1973).

SIEGELBAUM, L. *Soviet State and Society Between Revolutions, 1918–1929* (Cambridge, 1992).

TARBUCK, K. *Bukharin's Theory of Equilibrium* (Winchester, MA, 1989).

TROTSKY, L. *The Revolution Betrayed* (Garden City, NY, 1937).

TUCKER, R. *Political Culture and Leadership in Soviet Russia from Lenin to Gorbachev* (New York, 1987).

———. *Stalin as Revolutionary, 1879–1929* (New York, 1973).

———, ed. *Stalinism: Essays in Historical Interpretation* (New York, 1977).

ULAM, A. *The Bolsheviks* (New York, 1965).

VOLKOGONOV, D. *Lenin: A New Biography,* trans. H. Shukman (New York, 1994).

———. *Stalin: Triumph and Tragedy,* trans. H. Shukman (New York, 1991).

VON LAUE, T. *Why Lenin? Why Stalin?* 2d ed. (Philadelphia, 1971).

ZALESKI, E. *Planning for Economic Growth in the Soviet Union, 1918–1932* (Chapel Hill, NC, 1971).

34

The Politics of Stalinism, 1928–1941

By 1928 Stalin had ousted Trotskii and the Left opposition and taken major steps away from Lenin's collective leadership and freer intraparty debate. Moving toward personal rule, Stalin acted to secure predominant power over party and state by crushing the Right opposition and purging other colleagues of Lenin who retained influential positions. He manipulated the Lenin cult and created the monstrous myth of his own omniscience. To secure awesome power, the Stalin regime crushed passive opposition from the peasantry and secured control over the countryside by forcibly collectivizing agriculture. With the rapid industrialization of the Five Year Plans, it won support from a growing working class. (These economic policies will be discussed in Chapter 35.) A seemingly monolithic state swallowed society as most Soviet citizens became state employees, subject to increasing party supervision and controls. After all significant opposition had seemingly been overcome, Stalin launched the Great Purge of 1936–1938, which eliminated the Old Bolsheviks and left his minions apparently triumphant over a purged party, army, and state, and over a supine and frightened populace.

Recently, however, the monolithic, apparently unified nature of the Stalin regime depicted in most Western and dissident Soviet accounts has been sharply disputed. Recent specialized studies, notes J. Arch Getty, have revealed that policymaking in the early Stalin years was often uncertain and tentative. Like Hitler, Stalin employed an indirect, sometimes erratic "formula of rule" in the 1930s. Differences of opinion persisted within the party, and Soviet administration was chaotic, irregular, and confused. Getty concludes: "Although the Soviet government was certainly dictatorial, . . . it was not totalitarian."[1]

In the Stalinist political system, theory and practice were often totally at odds. The federal system and Constitution of 1936 gave national minorities and the Soviet people the appearance of self-government and civil rights; actually power, although inefficient, resided primarily in a self-perpetuating party leadership in Moscow. Did Stalin's aims and methods derive from Ivan the Terrible? Was he a loyal Marxist and true heir of Lenin, or an Oriental

---

[1] J. Arch Getty, *Origins of the Great Purges* (Cambridge, 1985), p. 198.

Joseph Stalin (1879–1953).

despot paying mere lip service to Marxism-Leninism? Did he truly initiate all decisions, as was claimed officially, and did contending factions remain concealed within the party? How did Stalin's political system actually function? And why was the Great Purge undertaken?

Intraparty Struggles and Crises, 1929–1934

A growing personality cult aided Stalin's drive to dominate the party and rule the USSR. Launched cautiously at the 14th Congress in 1925, it developed notably after Stalin's 50th birthday (December 21, 1929), celebrated as a great historic event. In contrast with Lenin's modest, unassuming pose, the Stalin cult by the mid-1930s took on grandiose, even ludicrous forms. At a rally during the Purges in 1937, N. S. Khrushchev, Stalin's eventual successor, declared slavishly:

These miserable nonentities wanted to destroy the unity of the party and the Soviet state. They raised their treacherous hands against Comrade Stalin . . . , our hope; Stalin, our desire; Stalin, the light of advanced and progressive humanity; Stalin, our will; Stalin, our victory.[2]

Within the party, the area of dissent narrowed, then disappeared. As Stalin crushed the Left in 1926–1927, it became clear that he would exclude factions or individuals who opposed his personal authority. But though Trotskii and the rest were stripped of influential positions, they still underestimated Stalin. Trotskii's expulsion from the USSR in 1929 brought predictions that power would pass to a triumvirate of Bukharin, Alexis Rykov, and M. P. Tomskii, who appeared (mistakenly) to dominate the Politburo selected after the 15th Congress.

Once the Left had been broken, Stalin adopted a moderate stance, and split with the Right led by Bukharin. The Stalin-Bukharin struggle developed behind the scenes during a growing economic crisis: Better-off peasants (kulaks), taxed heavily by the regime, withheld their grain from the market. Whereas Bukharin favored further concessions to the peasantry, including raising state grain prices, Stalin began urging strong action against the kulaks and officials who sympathized with them. Denouncing the still unnamed opposition for blocking industrialization, Stalin used his control of the Secretariat and Orgburo to remove Bukharin's supporters from key party and government posts. Belatedly contacting Kamenev from the broken Left, Bukharin warned "*He* [Stalin] will strangle us." He added:

Stalin . . . is an unprincipled intriguer who subordinates everything to the preservation of his power. He changes his theories according to whom he needs to get rid of at any given moment. . . . He maneuvers in such a way as to make us stand as the schismatics.[3]

[2] Quoted in E. Crankshaw, *Khrushchev's Russia* (Harmondsworth, England, 1959), p. 53.
[3] Quoted in I. Deutscher, *Stalin* (London, 1949), p. 314.

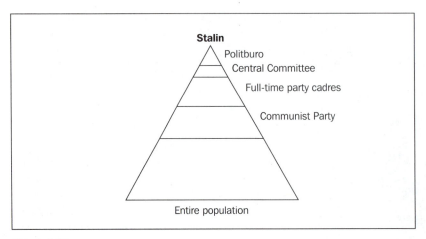

Figure 34.1
Politics of Stalinism

By early 1929 Stalin attacked the Right openly and told a Politburo meeting, "Comrades, sad though it may be, we must face facts: a factional group has been established within our party composed of Bukharin, Tomskii, and Rykov" that was blocking industrialization and collectivization. Though the Right controlled the Moscow party organization, Stalin won majority support in the Politburo, bypassed the Moscow leaders, and broke their resistance. In April 1929 the Central Committee condemned the Right and removed its leaders from their posts; in November they surrendered, recanted their views, and bought themselves a few years of grace. (See Figure 34.1.)

Open political opposition in the party ended, but during 1932–1933 Stalin faced a grave economic and political crisis. Forced collectivization had brought on famine and hunger in the cities and provoked widespread nationalist opposition, especially among Ukrainian peasants. As Stalin's popularity fell to its nadir, Trotskii's *Bulletin of the Opposition* declared abroad: "In view of the incapacity of the present leadership to get out of the economic and political deadlock, the conviction about the need to change the leadership of the party is growing." Trotskii reminded his readers of Lenin's "Testament," which had urged Stalin's removal as general secretary. In November 1932,

after Nadezhda Allilueva, Stalin's second wife, spoke out about famine and discontent, the overwrought Stalin silenced her roughly, and she apparently committed suicide. Victor Serge notes that Stalin submitted his resignation, but none of the Politburo's obedient Stalinist members dared accept it. Finally V. M. Molotov said, "Stop it, stop it. You have got the party's confidence," and the matter was dropped.

Stalin surmounted this personal danger and the economic and political crisis in the country. Opposition remained unfocused, confused, and leaderless. In 1932 Stalin had Kamenev and Zinoviev expelled from the party and exiled to Siberia, but after more abject recantations, they were allowed to return. After similar admissions of guilt, other Old Bolsheviks received responsible posts. They might have tried to kill Stalin, but who would rule in his place? Even Trotskii declared, "We are concerned not with the expulsion of individuals but the change of the system." Stalin temporarily adopted a moderate, conciliatory course. His speech of January 1934 called for consolidating earlier gains and inaugurated a brief period of relative liberalism. Within the Politburo the youthful and popular Leningrad party chief, S. M. Kirov, backed by Voroshilov and Kalinin, supported concessions to the peasantry and an end to terror;

hard-liners such as Molotov and Kaganovich opposed them. During 1934 Stalin apparently wavered indecisively between these groups.

The Great Purge

This interlude ended with Kirov's murder in December 1934. The supposed assassin, Nikolaev, and his accomplices were promptly apprehended, tried secretly, and shot. They were described officially as Trotskyites working for the clandestine, foreign-directed United Center, which had allegedly plotted to kill Stalin and other top leaders. Zinoviev and Kamenev, supposedly implicated in the plot, were sentenced to penal servitude.

Ominous changes proceeded in the political police. Early in 1934 the secret police (GPU), which had gained a sinister reputation, was dissolved. Its tasks were assumed by the People's Commissariat of Internal Affairs (NKVD), which combined control over political, regular, and criminal police. Henrikh Iagoda, its first chief, perhaps fearing that Kirov's liberal line threatened his power, may have engineered the assassination at Stalin's order. NKVD employees were highly paid and obtained the best apartments and other privileges. This "state within a state" maintained a huge network of informers, kept dossiers on millions of persons, and spied on all party agencies. Special sections watched the NKVD's own regular personnel, whose members were expected to show loyalty first to the NKVD and only secondarily to the party. Special NKVD courts, exempt from control by government or judicial agencies, were set up to conduct secret trials.

While surface calm prevailed, Andrei Zhdanov, Kirov's successor as Leningrad party chief, conducted a ruthless purge there, deporting tens of thousands of persons to Siberia, and the NKVD prepared the greatest mass purge in history. In May 1935 a Special Security Commission was created to investigate all party members, "liquidate enemies of the people," and encourage citizens to denounce suspected counterrevolutionaries and slackers. Its members included Stalin,

N. I. Yezhov (later head of the NKVD), Zhdanov, and Andrei Vyshinskii, subsequently chief prosecutor at the public trials. That spring 40 members of Stalin's personal bodyguard were tried secretly for conspiracy, and "terrorists" were hunted in every party and Komsomol (Young Communist League) agency. As the rapidly growing NKVD justified its existence by uncovering conspiracies everywhere, Stalin ordered careful surveillance even of Politburo members.

A reign of terror was unleashed, dwarfing that of the French Revolution. Perhaps that precedent had previously deterred Stalin, who once remarked, "You chop off one head today, another one tomorrow. . . . What in the end will be left of the party?" Unlike the French case, terror in Russia reached its murderous peak two decades after the Revolution. The French terror claimed about 40,000 victims; Stalin's from 1935 to 1938 killed hundreds of thousands and sent millions into exile.[4] Stalin, not the NKVD, initiated the Great Purge and approved executions of prominent figures. A Stalinist account explained:

> The Trotsky-Bukharin fiends, in obedience to the wishes of their masters—the espionage services of foreign states—had set out to destroy the party and the Soviet state, to undermine the defensive power of the country, to assist foreign military intervention . . . [and] to bring about the dismemberment of the USSR . . . , to destroy the gains of the workers and collective farmers, and to restore capitalist slavery in the USSR.[5]

The party had to become an impregnable fortress to safeguard the country and the gains of socialism from foreign and domestic enemies. Stalin added: "As long as capitalist encirclement exists, there will be wreckers, spies, diversionists, and murderers in our country, sent behind our lines by

---

[4] In 1989 demographer Paul Robeson, Jr., estimated that the USSR during the Stalin era had about 29.3 million "excess deaths" from terror and famine.

[5] *Short History of the Communist Party* (New York, 1939), p. 347.

the agents of foreign states." The Soviet public found this distorted view credible.

Three great public trials of party leaders accused of treason were held in Moscow. At the Trial of the Sixteen (August 1936), Prosecutor Vyshinskii accused Kamenev, Zinoviev, and others of conspiring to overthrow the regime and to remove Stalin and other Politburo leaders. After confessing and incriminating the Right opposition, the defendants were convicted and shot. When this severe treatment of Lenin's old colleagues provoked opposition in the Central Committee, Stalin removed Iagoda and appointed as NKVD chief Yezhov, under whom the purge reached its bloody climax. Each group of defendants incriminated the next in a chain reaction of denunciations. At the Trial of the Seventeen (January 1937), featuring Piatakov, Muralov, and Radek (all Old Bolshevik leaders), the accused confessed to treasonable dealings with Germany and Japan. The greatest public spectacle of them all, the Trial of the Twenty-One (March 1938) included Bukharin, Rykov, and Iagoda. Foreign espionage agencies, claimed the prosecutor, had set up a "bloc of Rightists and Trotskyists" on Soviet soil to bring a bourgeois-capitalist regime to power and detach non-Russian regions from the USSR. Allegedly Bukharin had been a traitor since 1918. Vyshinskii concluded his prosecution with the invariable appeal, "Shoot the mad dogs!" and the leading defendants would be executed.

Why did the accused, many of them prominent, courageous revolutionaries, publicly admit crimes they could not have committed, when their confessions constituted the only legal basis for conviction? Most had recanted several times already, each time admitting greater guilt, and hoped to save their lives, positions, and families. Some believed that the party, to which they had dedicated their lives, must be right. The defendants, mostly middle-aged, were broken down by lengthy NKVD interrogations and sleeplessness, or were hypnotized by the terror. Doubtless they hoped to save something from blasted careers by bowing to Stalin's tyranny.

Those who were tried and executed, or died by other means, included all surviving members of Lenin's Politburo except Stalin and Trotskii, the defendant in chief tried in absentia. A former premier, two former chiefs of the Comintern, the trade union head, and two chiefs of the political police were executed. Survivors must have wondered how the great Lenin could have surrounded himself with so many traitors and scoundrels. In 1914, to be sure, Roman Malinovskii, Lenin's close colleague, had been exposed as a police agent. The legacy of police infiltration of revolutionary organizations under tsarism provided some basis for believing the revelations of the 1930s.

The Great Purge decimated the leadership corps of the Soviet armed forces. The military chiefs, especially Marshal Tukhachevskii, who had made the Red Army an effective fighting force, apparently had been highly critical of the early trials. In May 1937 he and other prominent generals were arrested, accused of treasonable collaboration with Germany and Japan, and shot. None of them resisted or attempted a military coup. Purged later were most members of the Supreme War Council, three of five marshals, 14 of 16 army generals, and all full admirals. About half the entire officer corps was shot or imprisoned, a terrible insult to Red Army patriotism and a grave weakening of the armed forces. (After Stalin's death, all leading military figures who were purged were rehabilitated, many posthumously, and declared innocent of all charges brought against them.)

In addition to Old Bolsheviks, many Stalinist party leaders were eliminated. Purged were 70 percent of the Central Committee members and candidates chosen in 1934. At the 18th Party Congress in 1939, only 35 of 1,827 rank-and-file delegates from the previous congress were present! From the party and army the purge reached downward into the general populace as friends and relatives of those purged were arrested. Thousands of ordinary citizens were denounced orally or by poison-pen letters, often out of jealousy and meanness, of crimes they had not and could not have committed. For two years (1937–1938), most of a helpless population lived in abject terror of sudden arrest and deportation. Special targets for arbitrary arrest included former members of other political parties and former White soldiers, priests, intellectuals (especially writers), Jews and other national minorities in Russian towns, and professionals who had been abroad. Many ordinary workers and peasants were also denounced and forced to confess to imaginary crimes against the state. Stalin even issued orders to arrest a percentage of the population. His bloodthirstiness grew as members of all social groups were rounded up.

Why this terrible bloodbath? wondered the survivors. Some victims were scapegoats for economic failures of the early 1930s. Stalin's chief motive, suggests the British scholar Isaac Deutscher, was to destroy those who might lead an alternate regime or criticize his policies. This strategy required killing or exiling party and military men trained by purged leaders, then rebuilding the chief levers of Soviet power: the party, the army, and the security forces. The general public may have been involved deliberately to create the climate of fear essential to Stalin's total control. The need for millions of forced laborers in the Arctic and Siberia supplied a reason for mass deportation of workers and peasants. Perhaps Stalin became utterly mad, making pointless the search for rational explanations. Certainly casualties were too great to be justified by ordinary political or social aims. Robert Conquest's estimate of about 8 million purge victims in camps by 1938, plus another million in prisons, seems reasonable. During the 1930s a huge NKVD empire of forced labor camps and prisons, begun in the White Sea area under Lenin and described graphically in Alexander Solzhenitsyn's *Gulag Archipelago,* mushroomed in European Russia and Siberia. Major projects included constructing the White Sea and Moscow-Volga canals, double-tracking the Trans-Siberian Railway, and gold mining in the frigid Kolyma region. Usually fed below the subsistence level and working under extremely arduous conditions, the inmates died off rapidly only to be replaced by new millions.

In December 1938, with the arrest of master purger Yezhov, blamed for excesses ordered by Stalin, the purge's intensive phase ended. By then half the urban population of the USSR was on police lists, and 5 percent had actually been arrested.[6] Large-scale terror remained endemic to the Soviet system until Stalin's death. The epilogue to the Great Purge was the brutal murder of Trotskii in Mexico (August 1940) by an NKVD agent, the son of a Spanish Communist. Besides terrorizing the USSR, the purge opened up numerous vacancies in civil and military posts, filled by obedient but often inexperienced men who ensured Stalin's omnipotence. The Politburo lost most of its power and became Stalin's rubber stamp, while his private Secretariat became a modern Oprichnina. Otherwise the purge altered the Soviet political system remarkably little.

The Great Purge necessitated the rewriting of Communist Party history. Directed by Zhdanov and Stalin's secretaries, historians prepared the *History of the All-Union Communist Party (Bolshevik): Short Course* (1938). Apparently Stalin corrected the manuscript and wrote the section on philosophy. Portraying Stalin as Lenin's only true disciple, the *History* claimed that other Old Bolsheviks had conspired against Lenin and the party since 1917. Thus the all-powerful dictator had altered history to serve his present purposes. After 1938 Stalin worked intensively to foster patriotism, restore unity, and rebuild the army leadership and the armed forces as the Nazi threat to the USSR grew.

Government and Party Organization

The Stalin regime combined systematic terror and massive use of force with a democratically phrased

---

[6] See R. Conquest, *The Great Terror* (New York, 1968).

constitution, apparent federalism, and representative institutions. Operating ostensibly through a hierarchy of soviets, the political system was run actually by the party leadership and NKVD. Often theory and practice were wholly at odds, and in many ways Stalinism marked a return to tsarist autocracy. Stalin himself, no longer the apparently patient, humble, and accessible party functionary of the early 1920s, retreated into the Kremlin's recesses or to his country villa at nearby Kuntsevo. Rarely appearing in public, he clothed himself in mystery, and many in the younger generation regarded him and his oracular pronouncements with awe and reverence. Once his rivals had been eliminated, he grew more dictatorial and, after 1938, became an all-powerful father figure. His Politburo contained bureaucrats and party officials, not active revolutionaries or creative ideologists as in Lenin's time. Men such as Molotov, Kaganovich, and Kuibyshev, though able administrators, were narrow and ignorant of foreign lands. In the Politburo, Stalin listened impatiently to their arguments, then often decided an issue with a sarcastic remark or vulgar joke. All important matters were decided there, under the dictator's jealous eye.

The legal basis of this Soviet political system was the Constitution of 1936. Constitutions under Marxism were supposed to reflect existing socioeconomic conditions and had to be altered as these conditions changed. Earlier Soviet constitutions (1918 and 1924), with a franchise heavily weighted to favor urban elements and excluding "exploiters," represented the proletarian dictatorship's first phase. In November 1936 Stalin explained to the Eighth Congress of Soviets that because rapid industrialization and collectivization had eliminated landlords, capitalists, and kulaks, "There are no longer any antagonistic classes in [Soviet] society . . . [which] consists of two friendly classes, workers and peasants." Restrictions and inequalities in voting could be abolished, and a democratic suffrage instituted. The Stalin Constitution, he claimed, would be "the only thoroughly democratic constitution in the world." It was designed to win approval abroad.

The promises of the Stalin Constitution (finally superseded by a new one in 1977) often meant little in practice. "The USSR," it proclaimed, "is a federal state formed on the basis of a voluntary union of equal Soviet socialist republics." Most republics, however, had been conquered or incorporated forcibly, and the predominance of the Russian Republic, with about half the population and three-fourths the area of the Union, negated equality. Theoretically, a republic, as formerly, could secede, but to advocate secession was a crime and a "bourgeois nationalist deviation." Only the working class, through its vanguard, the Soviet Communist Party, could approve secession or create and abolish republics. In 1936 Transcaucasia split into Azerbaijan, Armenia, and Georgia, which were admitted as separate republics; then the Kazakh and Kirghiz republics in Central Asia were added. A Karelo-Finnish Republic was created partly out of territory taken from Finland in 1940, but it was abolished equally arbitrarily in 1956. The Moldavian Republic was established also in 1940, mostly from territory acquired by treaty with Hitler, and the formerly independent Baltic countries of Estonia, Latvia, and Lithuania were occupied and became Soviet republics. An amendment of 1944 permitted republics to establish relations with foreign countries (none ever did so), and Ukraine and Byelorussia obtained separate United Nations representation in 1945. Smaller national groups (more than 100 in the Russian Republic alone) obtained autonomous republics and national areas, plus legislative representation.

Soviet federalism provided an illusion of autonomy and self-government, but the central government, retaining full power, repressed any group or individuals who advocated genuine autonomy or independence, especially in Ukraine, populous and agriculturally valuable. Each nationality received its own territory, language, press, and schools, but the Russian-dominated all-Union Communist Party supervised and controlled them. This federal system, in Stalin's words "national in form, socialist in content," though preferable to tsarism's open Russification and assimilation, perpetuated Russian rule over most areas of the old empire. National feeling persisted nonetheless among many minority peoples of the USSR.

Under the Stalin Constitution a bicameral Supreme Soviet became the national legislature, supposedly the highest organ of state authority. The Council of the Union was directly elected from equal election districts, one deputy per 300,000 population. The Council of Nationalities represented the various administrative units: 25 deputies from each union republic, 11 from autonomous republics, and so on. Delegates, elected for four-year terms by universal suffrage, received good pay during brief sessions but, unlike members of the U.S. Congress, retained their regular jobs and had no offices or staffs. A Presidium, elected by both houses, could issue decrees when the Soviet was not meeting, and its chairman was titular president of the USSR. Bills became law when passed by both houses. Under Stalin, however, the Supreme Soviet never recorded a negative vote. It was a decorative, rubber-stamp body without real discussion or power of decision. Below it lay a network of soviets on republic, regional, provincial, district, and village or city levels—more than 60,000 soviets in all—with some 1,500,000 deputies elected for two-year terms. Sovereign in theory, soviets were controlled in fact at every level by their party members and parallel party organizations. Elections were uncontested with only one candidate, selected by the party, in each election district.

The Constitution entrusted executive and administrative authority to the Council of People's Commissars (called the Council of Ministers after 1946). Some ministries operated only on the all-union level, others there and in the republics, and still others in the republics only. Theoretically, but not in practice, these ministries were responsible to the soviets. Coordinating the administrative and economic system, the Council of People's Commissars possessed more power than the Con-

stitution suggested. The Supreme Court of the USSR headed a judicial system including supreme courts in the republics, regional courts, and people's courts. Lower courts were elected and higher ones chosen by the corresponding soviet. Judges, supposedly independent, were subject to party policies, and many important cases were tried in secret by the NKVD.

Article 125 of the Constitution promised Soviet citizens freedom of speech, conscience, press, assembly, and demonstrations "in conformity with the interests of the working people and in order to strengthen the socialist system." Citizens were guaranteed the right to work, education, rest, and maintenance in sickness and old age. Article 127 pledged freedom from arrest except by court decision. In fact, the Soviet people never enjoyed most of these rights. As the new constitution was printed, the NKVD was conducting mass arrests and deportations without trial. The state assigned workers to jobs arbitrarily and prohibited strikes and independent trade unions. Constitutional rights could be used only to support the regime, not to criticize it.

The Stalin Constitution, unlike its predecessors, at least suggested in Article 126 the true role of the Communist Party:

> The most active and politically conscious citizens in the ranks of the working class, working peasants, and working intelligentsia voluntarily unite in the Communist Party of the Soviet Union, which is the vanguard of the working people in their struggle to build communist society and is *the leading core of all organizations of the working people, both public and state.* [Italics added for emphasis.][7]

Still organized on Leninist principles, the party remained an elite force of about 4 percent of the population in which intellectuals and bureaucrats outnumbered ordinary workers. Operating supposedly by democratic centralism, it exercised decisive authority over domestic and foreign affairs. Under Stalin all power passed to higher

[7] *Constitution (Fundamental Law) of the Union of Soviet Socialist Republics* (Moscow, 1957), p. 103.

party organs co-opted by the leaders, not elected democratically as the party rules stipulated. The rank and file could merely criticize minor short-comings and lost all influence over the self-perpetuating leadership. The party became Stalin's monolithic, disciplined, and increasingly bureaucratic instrument. Intraparty debate avoided major issues and was limited to *how* to implement decisions, with no discussion of alternative policies or leaders.

The all-union congress, a periodic gathering of leaders from the entire USSR, theoretically exercised supreme authority within the party. Once factions were banned (1921) and the Right was defeated (1929), however, congresses lost power to initiate policies. Important decisions were made in advance by the Politburo and approved unanimously by the congress, which merely ratified policies of the leadership pro forma. In Lenin's time, the Central Committee, supposedly elected by the congress to direct party work between congresses, was an important decision-making body; under Stalin it grew in size (to 125 full members and 125 candidates in 1952) but declined in power. It comprised mostly regional party secretaries and ministers from the all-union and republic governments.

The Central Committee, stated the party rules, elected three subcommittees—the Politburo, Orgburo, and Secretariat; in fact, they determined the Committee's membership and policies. With about a dozen full members and a few candidates, the Politburo ostensibly "directs the work of the Central Committee between plenary sessions." It always included the most powerful party and state officials and decided the chief domestic and foreign policy issues; after 1920 it was the main power center in the USSR. Its meetings were secret and its debates presumably free. Stalin purged the Politburo, refilled it with his own men, and made it an instrument of his personal power. During the 1930s it experienced great insecurity and high turnover; after that its members enjoyed much stability of tenure. The Orgburo, Stalin's original power base, directed the party's organizational work until its merger with the Politburo in

1952. The Secretariat directed the party's permanent apparatus. Stalin, as general secretary with four assistants, managed its professional staff and controlled all party personnel and appointments.

With five levels the party, like the soviets, was directed centrally by its all-union organs (see Figure 34.2). Thus the Ukrainian party, run generally by Great Russians, was controlled from Moscow, which decided its policies and personnel. Lower party officials were often sacrificed as scapegoats for unpopular or mistaken national policies. Some regional party secretaries became miniature Stalins, dictating to frightened subordinates. At the bottom of the party hierarchy stood some 350,000 primary organizations, or cells, composed of at least three members, in villages, collective farms, factories, offices, and military units. Acting like nerves of the human body, they permeated and controlled all organizations and agencies.

Party membership was open, in theory, to all persons over 21 years of age (over 18 for Komsomol members). Applicants filled out a detailed questionnaire, submitted recommendations from three members in good standing to a primary party organization, and served at least a year's candidacy. Applications had to be approved by the primary organizations and ratified by the district party unit. Rank-and-file members performed party work besides their regular jobs. They had to pay dues, work actively in agitation and propaganda among their fellows, explain Marxian theory and the party line, and set examples of leadership and clean living. Their rewards included power and influence because the party was the only road to political success, plus material benefits. Disobedient or undisciplined members were reprimanded, censured, or in graver cases, expelled. Periodic purges were designed to cleanse the party of opportunists, slackers, and the disloyal. Under Stalin, Communists occupied the key positions in most walks of life; factory managers, collective farm chairmen, school superintendents, and army officers were generally party members. Within the party, urban elements predominated over rural ones and Great Russians over national minorities.

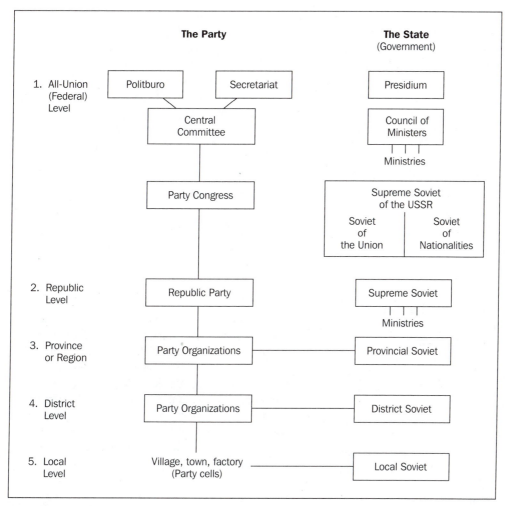

Figure 34.2
Soviet power centers under Stalin

Both the Communist Party of the Soviet Union and the Soviet government were organized on five levels, from the all-union hierarchy at the top to the local bodies at the bottom. At each level, the party organization controlled the corresponding governmental (soviet) bodies. Of the 15 Soviet socialist republics, the Russian Republic was by far the largest. Among the others were Ukraine, Byelorussia, Georgia, and Armenia. Each republic possessed its own supreme soviet and ministries. Autonomous republics (for smaller nationalities) also had their own supreme soviets and councils of ministers. The Communist Party of each republic was subordinated to the All-Union party organs.

The highly centralized Stalinist political system was based on interlocking presidia of the party and the state. The main decisions, made by Stalin personally and approved by the Politburo, were transmitted by lower party organs, soviets, trade unions, and media of mass communication to the people. The party manipulated the soviets skillfully to maintain links with the population and provide a semblance of legitimate rule. The main weaknesses were lack of local initiative and the absence of any legal means to transmit power from one leader or group of leaders to another. This intensified intrigue, suspicion, and power struggles behind the scenes at the top.

Stalinism

Stalin had risen in the party as an organizer and administrator, not an ideologist. Marx had been a theorist, not an active revolutionary; in Lenin, the two aspects were in rare balance. At first Stalin marched carefully in Lenin's footsteps (his chief theoretical work was *Problems of Leninism*), but once in power he altered and gravely distorted the doctrines of Marx and Lenin. Stalin's major doctrinal innovation—socialism in one country—developed accidentally and pragmatically during his struggle with Trotskii (see Chapter 33). Trotskii's apparently contrasting theory of "permanent revolution" stressed using the Comintern (Communist International, organization of Communist parties) to foment revolutions abroad; Stalin emphasized building socialism in Russia first. They differed somewhat over means and tactics, but shared the goal of an eventual global triumph of communism. But could socialism be *completely* built in a single country? Stalin claimed in 1936 that it had already been *essentially* constructed in Russia, although final victory must await worldwide revolution. Stalin's national emphasis won him continuing support from industrial workers, the intelligentsia, and military men, as well as from a party anxious to believe that Russians could build socialism themselves. Socialism in one country provided the ideological basis and social

support for forced collectivization and the Five Year Plans.

Since Stalin claimed that socialism had triumphed in the USSR and that class enemies had been broken, why was proletarian dictatorship not withering away, as Marx had predicted? Stalin had already answered this question in rather cynical fashion at the 16th Party Congress in 1930:

> We are in favor of the state dying out, and at the same time we stand for the strengthening of the dictatorship of the proletariat, which represents the most powerful and mighty authority of all forms of state which have existed up to the present day. The highest possible development of the power of the state with the object of preparing the conditions of the dying out of the state? Is this contradictory? Yes, it is contradictory. But this contradiction is a living thing and completely reflects Marxist dialectics.[8]

Apparently Stalin derived this view from Lenin's statement that state machinery must be perfected in the lower phase of socialism before withering. To justify strengthening the proletarian state, Stalin argued that hostile capitalist powers, surrounding the USSR, threatened armed intervention. Until "capitalist encirclement" was replaced by socialist encirclement of capitalism, the proletarian state must remain strong and alert, eliminate "bourgeois survivals," and hasten the transition to the final goal—communism.

Stalin was reacting instinctively against a Marxian internationalism that had already been undermined by the apparent failure of world revolution. For Stalin the interests of the Soviet fatherland clearly preceded those of the international proletariat and foreign Communist parties. Thus in the years before World War II, Soviet nationalism and patriotism were developed partly as an affirmation of what the working class had built in the USSR and partly to counter separatism in the borderlands. The regime fostered pride in Soviet industrial and technological achievements, with considerable success among workers and the younger generation. The shift away from interna-

---

[8] *Problems of Leninism* (Moscow, 1933), vol. 2, p. 402.

tionalism was reflected in repudiation of the works of the Marxist historian M. N. Pokrovskii, who had condemned Russian tsars and imperialism unreservedly. From the mid-1930s there occurred a selective rehabilitation and even praise of such rulers as Peter the Great and Ivan the Terrible for unifying and strengthening Russia. Tsarist generals such as Suvorov and Kutuzov, and certain admirals in the Crimean War, were glorified for defending their country heroically. New Soviet patriotism contained elements of traditional Great Russian nationalism, which Stalin had adopted. Through Soviet nationalism—one positive aspect of socialism in one country—Stalin sought to overcome and replace narrower national loyalties within the USSR.

The Stalinist political system established patterns of authority, many of which—unlike Stalin's cult of personality—persisted until the end of the USSR in 1991. With maximum use of force and terror, Stalin crushed all political opposition, as Ivan the Terrible had sought but failed to do. Stalin created perhaps the most powerful centralized state in history, with a developed industry and a vast bureaucracy. In so doing, he perverted Marxist ideology almost beyond recognition by accumulating personal power analogous to that of Oriental despotism. The Communist Party, though supreme over obedient soviets, was itself eventually transformed into a bureaucracy of frightened automatons by the Great Purge. Stalin's successors would repudiate mass terror and the cult of individual dictatorship, but not a centralized regime.

Suggested Additional Reading

ADAMS, A. *Stalin and His Times* (New York, 1972).

BAUER, R., A. INKELES, and C. KLUCKHOHN. *How the Soviet System Works* (Cambridge, MA, 1956).

BERMAN, H. J. *Justice in the USSR* (New York, 1963).

CARMICHAEL, J. *Stalin's Masterpiece: The Show Trials and Purges of the Thirties* (New York, 1976).

CARR, E. H. *The Bolshevik Revolution: Socialism in One Country, 1924–1926,* 3 vols. (London, 1958–1964).

CONQUEST, R. *The Great Terror* (New York, 1968).

———. *Inside Stalin's Secret Police: NKVD Politics, 1936–1939* (Stanford, 1985).

———. *Stalin and the Kirov Murder* (Oxford and New York, 1990).

DANIELS, R., ed. *The Stalin Revolution* (Lexington, MA, 1990).

DAY, R. B. *Leon Trotsky and the Politics of Economic Isolation* (New York, 1973).

DE JONG, A. *Stalin and the Shaping of the Soviet Union* (New York, 1986).

DEUTSCHER, I. *Stalin: A Political Biography,* 2d ed. (New York, 1967).

DJILAS, M. *The New Class* (New York, 1957).

ERICKSON, J. *The Soviet High Command . . . 1918–1941* (New York, 1962).

FAINSOD, M. *How Russia Is Ruled,* 2d ed. (Cambridge, MA, 1963).

———. *Smolensk Under Soviet Rule* (Cambridge, MA, 1958).

FRIEDRICH, C. J., and Z. K. BRZEZINSKI. *Totalitarian Dictatorship and Autocracy,* 2d ed. (New York, 1966).

GETTY, J. A. *Origins of the Great Purges . . . 1933–1938* (Cambridge, 1985).

GLUCKSTEIN, D. *The Tragedy of Bukharin* (London, 1994).

HAZARD, J. N. *The Soviet System of Government,* 5th ed. (Chicago, 1980).

HOCHSCHILD, A. *The Unquiet Ghost: Russians Remember Stalin* (New York and London, 1994).

HYDE, A. M. *Stalin, the History of a Dictator* (New York, 1982).

KATKOV, G. *The Trial of Bukharin* (New York, 1969).

KOESTLER, A. *Darkness at Noon* (New York, 1951). (Novel relating to the Great Purge.)

LEVYTSKY, B., comp. *The Stalinist Terror in the Thirties: Documentation from the Soviet Press* (Stanford, 1974).

LEWIS, J. *Stalin: A Time for Judgment* (New York, 1990).

MARPLES, D. R. *Stalinism in Ukraine in the 1940s* (New York, 1992).

MARRIN, A. *Stalin* (New York, 1988).

MEDVEDEV, R. A. *Let History Judge: The Origins and Consequences of Stalinism* (New York, 1971, 1973).

NOVE, A. *Stalinism and After,* 3d ed. (London, 1989).

———, ed. *The Stalin Phenomenon* (New York, 1993).

ORWELL, G. *1984* (New York, 1949). (Novel on totalitarianism.)

RESIS, A., ed. *Molotov Remembers: Inside Kremlin Politics* (Chicago, 1993).

SCHAPIRO, L. *The Communist Party of the Soviet Union,* rev. ed. (New York, 1970).

SERGE, V. *Memoirs of a Revolutionary, 1901–1941* (New York, 1963).

SOLZHENITSYN, A. *The Gulag Archipelago, 1918–1956,* 3 vols. (New York, 1974–1975).

———. *One Day in the Life of Ivan Denisovich* (New York, 1963). (Novel about labor camps under Stalin.)

THORNILEY, D. *The Rise and Fall of the Rural Communist Party, 1927–39* (New York, 1988).

TROTSKY, L. D. *The Revolution Betrayed* (Garden City, NY, 1937).

———. *Stalin: An Appraisal of the Man and His Influence* (New York, 1941).

———. *Trotsky's Notebooks, 1933–1935,* trans. and ed. P. Pomper (New York, 1986).

TUCKER, R. *Stalin in Power: The Revolution from Above, 1928–1941* (New York, 1990).

———, ed. *Stalinism: Essays in Historical Interpretation* (New York, 1977).

TUMARKIN, N. *Lenin Lives! The Lenin Cult in Soviet Russia.* (Cambridge, MA, 1983).

ULAM, A. *Stalin: The Man and His Era* (New York, 1973).

URBAN, G. R., ed. *Stalinism: Its Impact on Russia and the World* (New York, 1982).

VOLKOGONOV, D. *Stalin: Triumph and Tragedy,* trans. and ed. H. Shukman (New York, 1991).

VYSHINSKY, A. *The Law of the Soviet State* (New York, 1948).

35

The Great Transformation

Once the economy had recovered to prewar levels and Stalin had consolidated his power, he launched the "Second Socialist Offensive" of rapid industrialization and forced collectivization of agriculture. This policy followed a bitter debate within the party over how to modernize the Soviet economy. In the decade after 1928, the USSR became a major industrial country, collectivized its agriculture, and acquired the basic economic and social forms that characterize it today. The price paid for these advances by the Soviet people, however, was very high. Did Stalin's "revolution from above" reflect Marxist-Leninist principles or betray the ideals of 1917? Were rapid industrialization and forced collectivization necessary and worth their terrible cost, or was Bukharin's alternative of gradual evolution toward socialism preferable? Should Stalin be called "the great" for overcoming Russia's backwardness and weakness? If so, then 1929 marks a greater turning point in Russian history than 1917. After continuing to smash or remodel traditional social pillars—family, school, and church—why did Stalin retreat toward tsarist patterns in the later 1930s and make concessions to the church?

The Great Industrialization Debate, 1924–1928

During the mid-1920s, leading Soviet politicians and economists debated Russia's economic future. They agreed on goals of socialism and industrialization, but disagreed on how they could best be achieved. The success of the New Economic Policy (NEP) meant that survival was not at issue, but in a largely hostile world the USSR, unlike tsarist Russia, had to rely on its own resources to industrialize.

The party Left, led by Trotskii but with Evgeni Preobrazhenskii as chief economic spokesman, advocated rapid industrial growth at home while promoting revolutions abroad. The key to industrialization and socialism, Preobrazhenskii argued, was "primitive socialist accumulation": Lacking colonies to exploit, the USSR must obtain necessary investment capital by keeping farm prices low and taxing private farmers heavily. NEP, he believed, could restore the economy, but it could not produce the vast capital required for industrialization and the development of transportation and housing. Central state planning would permit immediate major investment in heavy industry.

The Left accused the Stalin-Bukharin leadership of favoring kulaks, "surrendering" to NEP men, and isolating the USSR. It stressed the intimate connection between developing Soviet socialism and ending "our socialist isolation." Opposing forcible expropriation of kulaks, Trotskii believed that revolutions in advanced countries would promote Soviet industrialization.

Bukharin, chief official spokesman and later leader of the Right, urged the continuation of NEP until the USSR gradually "grew into" socialism. Leftist "superindustrializers and adventurers" would alienate better-off peasants, undermine the worker-peasant alliance, and threaten the regime. Taxing peasants heavily would price industrial goods beyond their reach and induce them to market less grain. Instead, industrial prices should be cut and peasants encouraged to produce and save freely. Agricultural surplus would provide investment capital, expand the internal market, and stimulate industrial production. Citing Lenin's last writings, Bukharin advocated gradual "agrarian cooperative socialism." He overestimated peasant economic power and considered the peasant-worker alliance inviolable. Unless Soviet industrialization were more humane than under capitalism, he warned, it might not produce socialism. "We do not want to drive the middle peasant into communism with an iron broom." Bukharin spoke of "moving ahead slowly . . . dragging behind us the cumbersome peasant cart," and of creeping "at a snail's pace."

All leading Bolsheviks viewed industrialization as a vital goal and realized that it must rely mainly on internal resources. Agreeing that investment capital must be shifted from agriculture into industry, they differed over how much to take and how to take it. Bukharin emphasized development of the internal market, imposition of progressive income taxes, and voluntary savings. Such methods, retorted the Left, would produce too little capital because peasants would consume most of the surplus. Bolsheviks agreed that central planning was needed, but what did this involve? The Left advocated a single, state-imposed plan stressing rapid growth of heavy industry. Bukharin

called that "a remnant of War Communist illusions" that disregarded market forces of supply and demand; instead, he would stress consumer industry.

The factions also argued about capitalist elements in the countryside. Official figures of 1925 stated that poor peasants composed 45, middle peasants 51, and kulaks 4 percent of the peasantry. Asserting that more than 7 percent were kulaks, who were exploiting and dominating the village, the Left argued that continuing NEP would restore capitalism. Peasant differentiation had increased, replied Bukharin, but kulaks were still less than 4 percent, and state control of large-scale industry prevented any serious capitalist danger. Class conflict in the countryside, he predicted, would subside as the economy approached socialism.

As the debate continued, these differences lessened. Bukharin began to admit the need for rapid growth; Preobrazhenskii warned of its considerable risks. The chief beneficiary of this apparent synthesis was Stalin. Supporting Bukharin during the debate, he expelled the Left and stole its plank of rapid industrialization. To break peasant resistance, he combined it later with forced collectivization and demanded industrial goals far higher than those of the Left.

Bukharin's gradualist solution was doomed as the private sector lost its ability to compete with the state sector. Taxing heavily the profits of private producers, imposing surcharges for transportation and exorbitant levies on kulaks, the state squeezed private producers severely. By cutting industrial prices despite severe shortages of industrial goods, the state undermined the basis of NEP, which was based upon a free market and incentives. To the party, the stagnation of the restored Russian economy by 1926 was intolerable because without rapid growth the party's élan and morale would deteriorate.

Some later Soviet accounts claimed that the demise of the NEP was natural and inevitable. Unlike capitalist countries, the USSR could not exploit colonies, conduct aggressive wars, or obtain foreign credits. To achieve socialism the state had to industrialize quickly by concentrating resources in its hands and tapping all sources of internal capital, especially agriculture. Accepting most of Preobrazhenskii's theory of primitive socialist accumulation, some Soviet historians concluded that the populace, especially the peasantry, had to make major sacrifices in order to achieve industrialization. Recent Western studies, however, conclude that NEP agriculture could have satisfied immediate urban needs; they question the necessity and value of collectivization, either to solve the grain problem or to increase capital formation.[1]

Forced Collectivization

Stalin's adoption in 1929 of a policy of forced collectivization of agriculture provoked a grim struggle between the regime and the peasantry. One factor in his decision was an apparent grain crisis in 1927–1928. Farm output had reached prewar levels, but grain marketings remained somewhat lower (though higher than Stalin claimed), largely because of government price policies. Better-off peasants, awaiting higher prices, withheld their grain, and the state could not obtain enough to feed the cities or finance new industrial projects. Peasants, roughly 80 percent of the Soviet population, operated about 25 million small private farms; collective and state farms were few and unimportant.[2] Most peasants still carried on traditional strip farming and remained suspicious of the Soviet regime. Kulaks tended to be literate, enterprising, and hardworking, envied by other peasants for their relative prosperity but respected for their industry. Employing a hired worker or two and perhaps renting out small machines to poorer neighbors, kulaks performed most of their own labor and

scarcely qualified as capitalists or semicapitalists, as Soviet historians described them.

Marx and Lenin—and even Stalin before 1928—had never suggested *forced* collectivization. Marx intimated that large industrial farms would evolve gradually. Lenin considered collective, mechanized agriculture essential to socialism but warned that amalgamating millions of small farmers "in any rapid way" would be "absolutely absurd." Collective farming must develop "with extreme caution and only very gradually, by the force of example without any coercion of the middle peasant."[3] Following this advice closely, Stalin told the 15th Party Congress in 1927:

> What is the way out? The way out is to turn the small and scattered peasant farms into large united farms based on cultivation of the land in common, go over to collective cultivation of the land on the basis of a new higher technique. The way out is to unite the small and dwarf peasant farms *gradually but surely, not by pressure but by example and persuasion,* into large farms based on common, cooperative collective cultivation of the land. . . . There is no other way out.[4] [Italics added for emphasis.]

Perhaps from ignorance or misinformation, Stalin disregarded Lenin's warnings and his own statements. Touring the Urals and Siberia in January 1928, he arbitrarily closed free markets, denounced hesitant officials, and had grain seized from the peasants. His "Urals-Siberian method" marked a return to War Communism's forced requisitioning. Faced with strong Rightist protests, Stalin retreated temporarily, but during 1928–1929 this brutal method was used repeatedly in scattered areas. Bukharin objected to it as "military-feudal exploitation" of the peasantry and referred to Stalin as Chingis-khan. Until he had destroyed the Right, Stalin refrained from a general assault on private agriculture, and the First Five Year Plan, approved in 1929, proposed that state and collective farms provide only 15 percent of agricultural

---

[1] J. Karcz, "From Stalin to Brezhnev . . . ," in J. Millar, ed., *The Soviet Rural Community* (Urbana, IL, 1971), pp. 36ff. See also R. W. Davies, *Soviet History in the Gorbachev Revolution* (Bloomington, IN, 1989), especially pp. 40–46.
[2] In 1928 individual farmers tilled 97.3 percent of the sown area, collectives 1.2 percent (of which 0.7 percent were of the loose *toz* type), and state farms 1.5 percent.

[3] Lenin, *Collected Works* (New York, 1927–1942), vol. 30, p. 196.
[4] Stalin, *Works* (Moscow, 1953–1955), vol. 10, p. 196.

output. The predominance of private farming seemed assured indefinitely.

Late in 1929, after crushing the Right, Stalin moved abruptly to break peasant resistance and secure resources required for industrialization. Voluntary collectivization had clearly failed, and most Soviet economists doubted that the First Plan could be implemented. Recalled N. Valentinov, a Menshevik: "The financial base of the First Five Year Plan was extremely precarious *until Stalin solidified it by levying tribute on the peasants in primitive accumulation by the methods of Tamerlane*."[5] Stalin may have viewed collectivization also as a means to win support from younger party leaders opposed to kulaks, NEP men, and the free market. Privately, he advocated "industrializing the country with the help of *internal* accumulation," à la Preobrazhenskii. Once the peasantry had been split and rural opposition smashed, Stalin believed that rural proletarians would spearhead collectivization under state direction. The grain shortage induced the Politburo to support Stalin's sudden decision for immediate, massive collectivization.

A great turn was underway, Stalin asserted in November. The Central Committee affirmed obediently that poor and middle peasants were moving "spontaneously" into collectives. In secret, Stalin and his colleagues had ordered local officials to try out massive collectivization in selected areas. When results seemed positive (the number of collective farmers had allegedly doubled between June and October), Stalin ordered general collectivization, led by some 25,000 urban party activists. Entire villages had to deliver their grain to the state at low prices. Kulaks were deliberately overassessed for grain deliveries, then expropriated for failure to obey. The party had not discussed how to implement collectivization, and so initial measures were sudden, confused, and ill prepared. Many officials interpreted them to mean incorporating all peasants in *kolkhozy* (collective farms). Stalin and Molotov pressed for speed,

overruled all objections, and rejected proposals for private peasant plots and ownership of small tools and livestock. Local officials took Stalin at his word.

The initial collectivization drive provoked massive peasant resistance and terrible suffering. Isaac Deutscher notes that rebellious villages, surrounded by Red Army detachments, were bombarded and forced to surrender. So much for voluntary, spontaneous collectivization! Within seven weeks about half the peasantry had been herded into collectives, but bringing in as little as possible, the peasants slaughtered more than half the horses, about 45 percent of the large cattle, and almost two-thirds of the sheep and goats in Russia. In December 1929 Stalin authorized liquidation of the kulaks:

> Now we are able to carry on a determined offensive against the kulaks, eliminate them as a class. . . . Now dekulakization is being carried out by the masses of poor and middle peasants themselves. . . . Should kulaks be permitted to join collective farms? Of course not, for they are sworn enemies of the collective farm movement.[6]

Poor neighbors often stole kulaks' clothing and drank up their vodka, but Stalin prohibited their dividing kulak land because he thought if they did so they would be reluctant to enter collectives. By a decree of February 1930, "actively hostile" kulaks were to be sent to forced labor camps; "economically potent" ones were to be relocated and their property confiscated. The "least noxious" kulaks were admitted to collectives. A party history claimed that only 240,757 kulak families were deported, but eventually deportation overtook nearly all so-called kulaks, up to 5 million persons counting family members. Few ever returned, thousands of families were broken up, and millions of peasants were embittered. Soviet sources claim that such excesses reflected peasant hatred of kulaks, but there is little evidence to

---

[5] Ruthless Central Asian conqueror of the early 15th century.

[6] Quoted in *Istoriia KPSS* (Moscow, 1959), p. 441.

Table 35.1 Agricultural output during collectivization

Category	1928	1929	1930	1931	1933	1935
Grain (million tons)	73.7	71.7	83.5	69.5	68.4	75.0
Cattle (million)	70.5	67.1	52.5	47.9	38.4	49.3
Pigs (million)	26.0	20.4	13.6	14.4	12.1	22.6
Sheep and goats (million)	146.7	147.0	108.0	77.7	50.2	61.1

SOURCE: Adapted from A. Nove, *The Soviet Economy*, 2d ed. (New York, 1967), p. 186.

support this claim. In March 1930, with the spring sowing threatened by lack of seed grain, Stalin in an article "Dizzy with Success" called a temporary halt and blamed overly zealous local officials for excesses he had authorized. Interpreting this retrenchment as a repudiation of compulsory collectivization, the majority of peasants hastily left the *kolkhozy*.

After a brief pause, peasants were lured into collectives by persuasion and discriminatory taxation. By 1937 nearly all land and peasants were in *kolkhozy*; remaining individual peasants worked inferior land and paid exorbitant taxes. But *kolkhoz* peasants were demoralized: Crops lay unharvested, tractors were few, and farm animals died of neglect. Large grain exports to western Europe in 1930–1931 exhausted reserves, and city requirements increased. In 1932, amid widespread stealing and concealment of grain, collectivization hung by a thread and was maintained by force. In Ukraine and north Caucasus, the state seized nearly all the grain, causing a terrible famine, which the Soviet press failed to report. (Table 35.1 reveals the impact of collectivization.) Between 1928 and 1933, forced collectivization cost the Soviet Union roughly 27 percent of its livestock and contributed to the death of some 5 million persons, mostly peasants, in the famine of 1932–1934, notes J. Karcz. Damage to agriculture during this period was so severe that it could contribute little to the initial Five Year Plans. Collectivization was supposed to ensure more agricultural products for towns and industry, but though state grain procurements increased dramatically from 1928 to 1931, procurement of other products, notably meat and industrial products, declined sharply.

At first collective farm organization and management were confused. The city activists sent to supervise collectivization and manage the farms misunderstood the peasantry and made many blunders. Peasant rights in *kolkhozy* were few and vague, and pay was low. The regime initially favored state farms (*sovkhozy*) as being fully socialist, but their inefficiency and costliness provoked second thoughts, and after 1935 they received less emphasis.

The Model Statute of 1935 described the *kolkhoz* as supposedly a voluntary cooperative whose members pooled their means of production, ran their own affairs, and elected their officials in a general meeting. Actually local party organizations nominated farm chairmen and issued orders to farms, while state procurement agencies and Machine Tractor Stations (MTS) assured party control. The state-controlled MTS received all available machines and tractors and rented them to *kolkhozy*. Only after fixed requirements were met (taxes, insurance, capital fund, administration, and production costs) were *kolkhoz* members paid from what remained according to their work. Wages varied sharply according to skill and the farm's success, but as late as 1937, 15,000 *kolkhozy* paid their members nothing at all. The statute recognized the peasant's right to a private plot of up to one acre per household and some livestock. This grant created the chief private sector in the economy. After 1937 *kolkhozy* produced mainly grain and industrial crops (cotton, sugar beets, flax); private peasant plots provided most meat, milk, eggs, potatoes, fruits, and many vegetables. Peasants sold these products after paying taxes. Low state prices, however, discouraged agricultural output. Industrial prices in 1937 were far higher than in 1928–1929, a recurrence of the price "scissors" against the peasant. On *kolkhozy* there was much coercion and unhappiness, but as the output of private plots increased, living conditions gradually improved.

During the last prewar years arbitrary state decisions, ignoring local conditions, caused agriculture to stagnate or decline. In 1939 the party reduced the allowable size of private plots and transferred millions of acres to collective control. Stricter discipline and compulsory minimums of labor days were instituted for collective farmers, and fodder shortages brought a decline in already low *kolkhoz* livestock production. Crop yields and private livestock ownership declined substantially, but state procurements for urban consumption and for exports rose. Providing few incentives, collective farming remained very unpopular with Soviet peasants. Even by Soviet official figures, agricultural output increased very little during the 1930s. To achieve rapid industrialization and socialism, Stalin had uselessly sacrificed Russia's best, most enterprising farmers. Less compulsory methods, such as those of NEP, might well have proved less costly and more effective.

Industry: The Five Year Plans

One rationale for collectivization was to ensure food supplies adequate to support the rapid industrialization of the First Five Year Plan, which aimed immediately to provide a powerful heavy industry and only later an abundant life. The plan's psychological purpose was to induce workers and young people to make sacrifices, by holding before them a vision of the promised land of socialism in their own lifetimes. The state would benefit because the economy would become fully socialist, production and labor would be wholly state controlled, and security against capitalist powers would be strengthened. Stalin stated in February 1931: "We are 50 to 100 years behind the advanced countries. We must cover this distance in 10 years. Either we do this or they will crush

us." Ten years and four months later, Hitler invaded the USSR!

The First Five Year Plan did not inaugurate Soviet economic planning. Gosplan (State Planning Commission) had operated under NEP, and there had been annual control figures (see Chapter 33). As private market forces declined, central economic control increased. The goods famine of 1926–1927 promoted state distribution of key commodities, especially metals, and regulation of production. Soviet economists had long discussed a Five Year Plan, but serious work on one began only in 1927.

Realistic early drafts of the First Plan in 1928 yielded to optimistic (and fantastic) variants in 1929. In 1927 Gosplan's mostly nonparty professional staff outlined a plan for relatively balanced growth, with industry to expand 80 percent in five years; it recognized probable obstacles. Party pressure, however, soon forced estimates upward, and resulting variants represented overly optimistic predictions made largely for psychological purposes. The version of S. G. Strumilin, a leading party planner, allowed for possible crop failures, little foreign trade or credits, and potentially heavier defense spending, but it set goals far exceeding those of the Left, which Stalin had denounced as superindustrialist. Stalin boasted in 1929:

> We are going full steam ahead toward socialism through industrialization, leaving behind the age-long "Russian" backwardness. We are becoming a land of metals . . . , automobiles . . . , tractors, and when we have put the USSR on an automobile and the muzhik on a tractor, let the noble capitalists . . . attempt to catch up. We shall see then which countries can be labeled backward and which advanced.[7]

Because 1928 was a successful year, goals were boosted higher. In April 1929 the 16th Congress approved an optimal draft of the plan, which assumed that no misfortunes would occur. Gross industrial output was to increase 235.9 percent

---

[7] Quoted in Maurice Dobb, *Soviet Economic Development Since 1917* (New York, 1948), p. 245.

and labor productivity 110 percent; production costs were to fall 35 percent and prices 24 percent. To fulfill such goals would require a miracle (in which Stalin presumably did not believe!). In December 1929 a congress of "shock brigades" urged the plan's fulfillment in four years; soon this became official policy. Constantly sounding notes of urgency, Stalin forced the tempo and brought former party oppositionists into line. Riding a wave of overoptimism, party leaders chanted: "There is no fortress that the Bolsheviks cannot storm." Perhaps Stalin knowingly adopted impossible targets largely for political reasons. Those urging caution were denounced as "bourgeois" wreckers working for foreign powers.

During the First Plan some wholly unanticipated obstacles appeared. The Great Depression in the United States and Europe made Soviet growth look more impressive, but it dislocated world trade and made imported foreign machinery more expensive relative to Soviet grain exports. Defense expenditures, instead of declining, were increased in response to Japanese expansion in East Asia. Ignorance and inexperience of workers and managers caused destruction or poor use of expensive foreign equipment, blamed on deliberate wrecking and sabotage. Resources were used inefficiently: Industrial plants often lacked equipment or skilled workers. The inexorable drive for quantity brought a deplorable decline in quality as strains and shortages multiplied.

The First Plan had mixed results. Vast projects were undertaken, but many remained unfinished. Some, such as the Volga–White Sea Canal, were built by forced labor; others reflected genuine enthusiasm and self-sacrifice. At Magnitogorsk in the Urals, previously only a village, a great metallurgical center arose as workers and technicians labored under primitive conditions to build a bright socialist future. As industrial output rose sharply, the regime announced late in 1932 that the plan had been basically fulfilled in four years and three months; in fact, goals were surpassed only in machinery and metalworking, partly by

statistical manipulation.[8] Nonetheless, the new powerful engineering industry reduced Soviet dependence on foreign machinery. Fuel output rose considerably, but iron and steel fell far short because necessary plants took longer to complete than anticipated. Supposed increases in consumer production concealed sharp declines in handicrafts. To the party, the First Plan was a success (though goals for steel were fulfilled only in 1940, for electric power in 1951, and for oil in 1955) because industrial expansion and defense output could now be sustained from domestic resources. Lifting itself by its own bootstraps, the USSR was vindicating Stalin's idea of socialism in one country. Consumer production, agriculture, and temporarily military strength, however, were sacrificed to a rapid growth of heavy industry. (See Map 35.1.)

Labor was mobilized and lost much freedom. Once the state controlled all industry, Stalin declared trade union opposition anti-Marxist: How could the proletariat strike against its own dictatorship? Early in 1929 Tomskii and other trade union leaders were removed and replaced by Stalinists. Henceforth trade unions were to help build socialist industry by raising labor productivity and discipline. Unions exhorted workers to raise production and organize "shock brigades." Factory directors took control of wages, food supplies, housing, and other worker necessities. Russian workers, losing the right to strike or protest against their employer, reverted to their status of 75 years earlier, and Stalin's attitude toward labor resembled that of early Russian capitalists. By 1932 unemployment disappeared in towns and a seven-hour day was introduced, but real wages fell sharply. As millions of untrained peasants, escaping collectivization, sought industrial jobs, labor discipline deteriorated. Machinery was ruined, and workers hunted for better conditions. (In 1930, the

---

[8] Overfulfillment in machinery resulted chiefly from assigning high prices in 1926–1927 rubles to many new machines, thus increasing the "value" of total output. See A. Nove, *The Soviet Economy* (New York, 1967), p. 192.

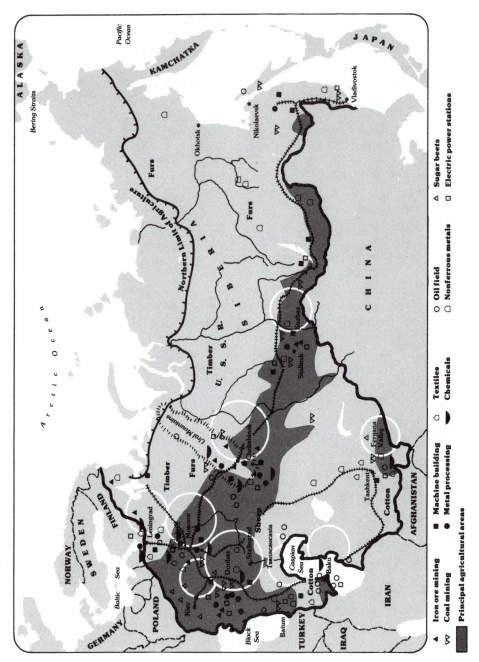

Map 35.1 Industry and agriculture to 1939

SOURCE: Adapted from *A History of Russia, Second Edition* by Nicholas V.
Riasanovsky. Copyright 1969 by Oxford University Press, Inc. Used by permission.

average worker in the coal industry shifted jobs three times!) Cities grew rapidly, housing construction lagged, and urban services were grievously overtaxed.

Burgeoning industrial employment and rising incomes without a comparable rise in consumer goods or services spurred inflation. Seeking to achieve impossible goals, managers hired more and more labor, sending wage bills skyrocketing. Rationed goods remained cheap, leaving people much money but little to buy. By 1929 a wide gap opened between official and private prices. To absorb excess purchasing power, the government in 1930 instituted the turnover tax in place of many excise levies. Generally imposed at the wholesale level, it amounted to the difference between the cost of production and the retail selling price. In 1934, for instance, the retail price of rye was 84 rubles per centner (100 kilograms), of which 66 rubles was turnover tax. Its burden fell mainly on the peasantry because the state paid them so little for their grain; in this way, agriculture indirectly financed the Five Year Plan.

A Soviet account in the Brezhnev period, claiming that the situation at home and abroad required rapid industrialization, barely mentioned Stalin's crucial role in launching it. The First Plan, it continued, erected the foundations of a socialist economy and turned the USSR into an industrial-agrarian state as enthusiastic shock workers completed the plan ahead of schedule. The workers themselves, resolving to complete the plan in four years, were supported by the party and the plan's success represented a great victory for socialism. While admitting serious shortcomings, these Soviet historians asserted that the party quickly remedied the difficulties.[9]

By 1932 the Soviet economy was badly overstrained; 1933 brought shortages and privation. The Second Five Year Plan, redrafted during its first year, was adopted in February 1934 by the 17th Congress. More realistic than the First Plan, its execution was aided by more experienced plan-

ners and managers. Unlike its predecessor, final goals were lower than preliminary ones. Heavy industrial targets were mostly met, and machinery and electric power output rose dramatically. Labor productivity surpassed expectations, and technical sophistication improved as the First Plan's investments bore fruit. The Second Plan stressed consolidation, mastering techniques, and improving living standards. Initially a greater increase was planned for consumer goods than for heavy industry, but then came a shift toward heavy industry and defense. Consumer goals were underfulfilled, and per capita consumption fell below the 1928 level. Completed metallurgical works in Magnitogorsk, Kuznetsk, and Zaporozhye further reduced Soviet dependence on foreign capital goods, relieved the strain on the balance of payments, and permitted repayment of earlier debts. By 1937 the basic tools of industry and defense were being made in the USSR. Growth followed an uneven pattern: After a bad year, 1933, came three very good ones in industry and construction, and then relative stagnation began in 1937 (between 1937 and 1939 steel production actually declined). Table 35.2 shows some results of the two plans.

During the Second Plan labor productivity rose substantially and industrial employment fell below estimates as training programs gradually created a more skilled labor force. Pay differentials widened, rationing was gradually abolished, and more consumer goods were made available. After 1934 high prices of necessities stimulated harder work under the prevailing piecework system. Labor productivity was improved by Stakhanovism, a by-product of "socialist competition." In September 1935 Alexis Stakhanov, a Donets coal miner, by hard work and intelligent use of unskilled helpers, produced 14 times his norm. Fostered by the party, Stakhanovism spread to other industries, and low labor norms were raised. Harsh penalties for absenteeism and labor turnover reduced these problems and improved labor discipline. However, the Great Purge, Soviet historians later admitted, swept away managers, technicians, statisticians, and even foremen. The shaken survivors often

---

[9] *Istoriia SSSR* (Moscow, 1967), vol. 8, pp. 475–83.

Table 35.2 First and Second Plan results

Category	1927–1928	1932 (target)	1932–1933 (actual)	1937 (target)	1937 (actual)
National income in 1926–1927 rubles (billions)	24.5	49.7	45.5	100.2	96.3
Gross industrial output (billions of rubles)	18.3	43.2	43.3	92.7	95.5
Producer goods	6.0	18.1	23.1	45.5	55.2
Consumer goods	12.3	25.1	20.2	47.1	40.3
Gross agricultural production (billions of 1926–1927 rubles)	13.1	25.8	16.6	—	—
Electricity (100 million Kwhs.)	5.05	22.0	13.4	38.0	36.2
Hard coal (millions of tons)	35.4	75.0	64.3	152.5	128.0
Oil (millions of tons)	11.7	22.0	21.4	46.8	28.5
Steel (millions of tons)	5.9	19.0	12.1	17.0	17.7
Machinery (millions of 1926–1927 rubles)	1,822.0	4,688.0	7,362.0	—	—

SOURCE: Adapted from T. Nove, *The Soviet Economy*, 2d ed. (New York, 1967), pp. 191, 225.

rejected responsibility. This reaction, and the growing shift of resources into arms production, created an industrial slowdown after 1937.

The diversion of resources into defense plagued the Third Five Year Plan (1938–1941), which the Nazi invasion interrupted. Industrial output increased an average of less than 2 percent annually, compared with 10 percent under the first two plans. Progress remained uneven, with much growth in production of machinery, but little in steel and oil. New western frontier territories such as the Baltic states considerably increased productive capacity. Labor was severely restricted in mobility and choice of occupation, the work week rose to 48 hours, and workers required permission from their enterprise to change jobs. A million high school students were conscripted for combined vocational training and industrial work.

In summary, rapid industrialization (1928–1941) brought increases in heavy industrial production unprecedented in history for a period of that length, as shown in Table 35.3. The USSR became a leading industrial power, but living standards, real wages, and housing conditions declined. Dire predictions made during the industrialization debate came true: Bukharin foresaw the human sacrifices and inflation, and Preobrazhenskii's concept of primitive socialist accumulation was implemented by methods that appalled him. (He was executed for protesting the excesses of collectivization.)

Shifts in Social Policies

A continued assault on social institutions associated with the old regime accompanied the Second Socialist Offensive. After 1933 or 1934 policy shifted to consolidation of Soviet institutions that often resembled their tsarist models, and emphasis on discipline and social stability was renewed to overcome unfavorable effects of the preceding offensive. Social policies of 1934–1941 represented "a great retreat,"[10] or Soviet Thermidor, except that they coincided with the bloody terror of the purges.

---

[10] See Nicholas Timasheff, *The Great Retreat* (New York, 1946).

Table 35.3
Selected statistical indicators, 1928–1940
(1928 = 100)

Category	1940 Output (in percent of 1928)
Industrial production	263
Industrial materials	343
Ferrous metals	433
Electric power	964
Chemicals	819
Machinery	486
Consumer goods	181
Agricultural production	105
Crops	123
Animal products	88
Individual consumption (per capita)	93
Real wages	54
Capital stock	286
Urban housing space (per capita)	78

SOURCE: Stanley H. Cohen, *Economic Development in the Soviet Union* (Lexington, MA, 1970), p. 39.

Efforts to undermine the traditional family in order to strengthen the socialist state continued during the First Five Year Plan. Husbands and wives were often assigned to different cities, yet any available job had to be accepted. When a teacher complained of being separated from her husband, the Labor Board advised her to find a husband at her new job. In Stalingrad, "socialist suburbs" featuring single rooms were built, but only bachelors would live in them. Such policies did weaken family ties, but the by-products were grim. Free divorce and abortion caused a serious decline in birthrates, which threatened the supply of labor and army recruits. Moscow medical institutions in 1934 recorded only 57,000 live births and 154,000 abortions. Early in 1935 divorces numbered more than 38 per 100 marriages. Communities were confronted with spiraling juvenile delinquency and hooliganism. Children were beating up their schoolteachers!

In 1934–1935 the regime—largely for economic reasons—shifted course abruptly. "The family," it was now stated officially, "is an especially important phase of social relations in socialist society" and must be strengthened. Marriage is "the most serious affair in life" and should be regarded as a lifelong union; men who changed their wives like shirts were threatened with prosecution for rape. In 1939 the journal of the Commissariat of Justice proclaimed:

> The State cannot exist without the family. Marriage is a positive value for the Socialist State only if the partners see in it a lifelong union. So-called free love is a bourgeois invention and has nothing in common with the principles of conduct of a Soviet citizen.[11]

Marriage was now dignified with well-staged ceremonies in comfortable registration centers. Soon wedding rings were being sold again, and non-Communists frequently reinforced the civil ceremony with a church wedding. Strict regulations, replacing the quickie divorce of earlier days, greatly curtailed divorces and raised fees sharply. Divorce became more difficult and expensive to obtain in the USSR than in many of the United States, and unregistered marriage, instituted in 1926, was abolished. After June 1936 abortion was permitted only if the mother's life was endangered or to prevent transmission of serious illness. Parental authority was reinforced, and young people were urged to respect and obey parents and elders. Motherhood was glorified (Stalin made a pilgrimage to Tiflis to show how much he loved his old mother), and mothers of large families were compensated. After destroying the old extensive patriarchal family, the authorities reinforced the new Soviet nuclear family.

Joseph Stalin, the self-styled "man of steel," emphasized women's economic and personal dependence, reflecting the attitude of male superiority prevalent in the Caucasus and Central Asia. To Stalin women epitomized ignorance and conservatism, threatening social progress: "The woman worker . . . can help the common cause if

---

[11] Quoted in Timasheff, *The Great Retreat*, p. 198.

she is politically conscious and politically educated. But she can ruin the common cause if she is
downtrodden and backward." Under Stalin's rule
there was strong emphasis on women's duties and
responsibilities at home and at work, while less
and less was heard of their former oppression. In
the Stalin era the role of women was transformed
primarily by industrialization, collectivization, and
urbanization. Their massive influx into the Soviet
work force after 1929 coincided with greatly
expanded educational opportunities, growth of
child-care institutions, and protective legislation
for all workers, but not equal pay. However, unlike
early Bolshevik libertarian concern with female
emancipation, the Soviet aim was no longer to
enhance women's independence but to improvise
a response to urgent needs created by rapid
urbanization and burgeoning female employment.
Development of social services, such as child-care
centers, because of the low priority assigned to
them by the Stalin regime, failed conspicuously to
keep pace with demands.

Experimentalism in education yielded during
the First Plan to a structured, disciplined school
program. Not Leninist theory, but industry's insistent demands for trained specialists triggered the
shift. Applicants to higher educational institutions
were found to be woefully deficient in reading
skills and parroted vague generalizations. In 1929
A. Lunacharskii, chief exponent of experimentalism, was removed, and a shift to serious study
began under the slogan "Mastery of knowledge."
In 1931–1932 came partial curricular reforms:
Teaching of Marxism was reduced, history revived,
and "progressive education" was largely abandoned. Book learning, academic degrees, systematic textbooks, and traditional grading practices
were reemphasized. Examinations were reinstituted after a 15-year lapse. Noisy, undisciplined
classrooms disrupted by hooligans yielded to
quiet, disciplined ones as the authority of teachers
and professors was restored. Decrees from above
specified every detail of instruction and school
administration as a new Soviet school emerged,
patterned after the conservative tsarist school of

the 1880s. Curricula resembled tsarist and European ones, and pupils were dressed in uniforms
like those of the 1880s. For pragmatic reasons, a
retreat to traditional models began earlier in education than in other fields. The authoritarian
school reflected the Stalinist autocracy.

Soviet religious policies fluctuated. During the
First Plan there was a widespread campaign to
close churches. In 1930 the Soviet press reported
the burning of icons and religious books by the
carload, and restrictions, disfranchisement, and
discriminatory taxation plagued the clergy. The
atheist League of Militant Godless, featuring the
young and growing to almost 6 million members,
induced many collective farms to declare themselves "godless." Then between 1933 and 1936,
partly to allay peasant discontent, came some
relaxation of persecution. The Stalin Constitution
of 1936 restored the franchise to clergymen and
gave them full civil rights. The Purge of 1937–1938
brought another wave of persecution, but few
priests were executed. After 1938 a more tolerant
religious policy developed to win popular support
and counter the rising threat of Nazi Germany.
Christianity was now declared to have played a
progressive, patriotic role in Russian history. Violence against churches and believers was forbidden, and the closing of churches and political trials
of clergymen were halted. The regime adopted a
subtler approach of emphasizing that scientific
advances had made religion outmoded. Soviet
leaders, recognizing the persistence of religious
belief, sought to use it to consolidate their power.
The Soviet census of 1937 revealed that more than
half the adult population still classified themselves
as believers. (The census takers were sent to
Siberia!) Meanwhile, the Orthodox church recognized the regime and wished to cooperate with it
to achieve greater social discipline, a strong family,
and restriction of sexual activity. Twenty years of
official persecution had greatly weakened the
church as an organization and reduced markedly
the numbers of the faithful, but had strengthened
their faith. Marxism-Leninism had proved an
inadequate substitute for religion.

During the 1930s the Stalin regime, abandoning experimentalism and radical policies, retreated toward tradition and national and authoritarian tsarist patterns. There emerged an increasingly disciplined, status-conscious society headed by a new elite of party bureaucrats, economic managers, engineers, and army officers, which differed sharply in attitudes and habits from the revolutionary generation.

Problem 12

Forced Collectivization: Why and How?

The transformation of Russian agriculture under Stalin from 25 million individual farms into several hundred thousand collective and state farms was one of the 20th century's most dramatic and important events. It involved a massive conflict between the Soviet regime and the peasantry, the destruction of many of the best Soviet farmers and much of the livestock, and produced a terrible famine in 1933. Soviet collectivized agriculture, plagued by low productivity, lack of incentives for farmers, and incompetent organization, sought without conspicuous success to satisfy domestic needs. Was forced collectivization necessary or wise? Why was it undertaken? Who was responsible for the accompanying mass suffering? Here these issues are explored from various viewpoints, including Stalin's contemporary speeches, a Soviet account from 1967, and the work of a Soviet historian published in the West.

Stalin's View

Stalin and his Politburo colleagues claimed in 1929 that it was necessary to collectivize agriculture to achieve economic progress and socialism. They affirmed that the decision to collectivize was imposed upon them by kulak treachery and the insistent demands of an expanding industry. Poor and middle peasants, Stalin claimed, were entering collective farms voluntarily and en masse. Declared Stalin as forced collectivization began:

The characteristic feature of the present collective farm movement is that not only are the collective farms being joined by individual groups of poor peasants . . . but . . . by the mass of middle peasants as well. This means that the collective farm movement has been transformed from a movement of individual groups and sections of the laboring peasants into a movement of millions and millions of the main mass of the peasantry. . . . The collective farm movement . . . has assumed the character of a mighty and growing *antikulak* avalanche . . . paving the way for extensive socialist construction in the countryside [speech of December 27, 1929].

At the beginning of forced collectivization Stalin, summarizing the party's problems and achievements in agriculture, stressed the rapid development of a new socialist agriculture against desperate resistance from "retrograde" elements:

The party's third achievement during the past year . . . [is] the *radical change* in the development of our agriculture from small, backward *individual* farming to large-scale advanced *collective* agriculture, to joint cultivation of the land . . . , based on modern techniques and finally to giant state farms, equipped with hundreds of tractors and harvester combines.

. . . In a whole number of areas we have succeeded in *turning* the main mass of the peasantry away from the old, *capitalist* path . . . to the new *socialist* path of development, which ousts the rich and the capitalists and reequips the middle and poor peasants . . . with modern implements . . . so as to enable them to climb out of poverty and enslavement to the kulaks onto the high road of cooperative, collective cultivation of the land. . . . We have succeeded in bringing about this *radical change* deep down in the peasantry itself and in

Problem 12 continued

securing the following of the broad masses of the poor and middle peasants in spite of incredible difficulties, in spite of the desperate resistance of retrograde forces of every kind, from kulaks and priests to philistines and Right Opportunists.

. . . Such an impetuous speed of development is *unequaled* even by our socialized large-scale industry. . . . All the objections raised by "science" against the possibility and expediency of organizing large grain factories of 40,000 to 50,000 hectares each have collapsed. . . .

What is the new feature of the present collective-farm movement? . . . The peasants are joining the collective farms not in separate groups, as formerly, but as whole villages, *volosts*, districts, and even *okrugs*. And what does that mean? It means that *the middle peasant is joining the collective farm* [November 1929].

Only a month later, however, Stalin hinted that forcible means were having to be employed after all:

It is necessary . . . *to implant* in the village large socialist farms, collective and state farms, as bases of socialism which, with the socialist city in the vanguard, can drag along the masses of peasants.

In March 1930, at his colleagues' insistence, Stalin temporarily halted forced collectivization. His article "Dizzy with Success" blamed local party workers and extremists for errors and perversions of official policy:

People not infrequently become intoxicated by such successes, . . . overrate their own strength. The successes of our collective-farm policy are due . . . to the fact that it rests on the *voluntary character* of the collective-farm movement and *on taking into account the diversity of conditions* in various regions of the USSR. Collective farms must not be established by force. That would be foolish and reactionary. The collective-farm movement must rest on the active support of the main mass of the peasantry. . . . In a number of the northern regions of the consuming zone . . . , attempts are not infrequently made to *replace* preparatory work for the organization

of collective farms by bureaucratic decreeing . . . , the organization of collective farms on paper.

. . . Who benefits from these distortions, . . . these unworthy threats against the peasants? Nobody, except our enemies! In a number of areas of the USSR . . . attempts are being made . . . to leap straight away into the agricultural commune. . . . They are already "socializing" dwelling houses, small livestock, and poultry. . . .

How could there have arisen in our midst such blockhead excesses in "socialization," such ludicrous attempts to overleap oneself? . . . They could have arisen only in the atmosphere of our "easy" and "unexpected" successes on the front of collective farm development . . . as a result of the blockheaded belief of a section of our Party: "We can achieve anything!" [March 2, 1930].

In his report to the 17th Congress in January 1934, Stalin hailed the results of rapid collectivization in the USSR:

From a country of small individual agriculture it has become a country of collective, large-scale mechanized agriculture. . . . Progress in the main branches of agriculture proceeded many times more slowly than in industry, but nevertheless more rapidly than in the period when individual farming predominated. . . . Our Soviet peasantry has completely and irrevocably taken its stand under the Red banner of socialism. . . . Our Soviet peasantry has quit the shores of capitalism for good and is going forward in alliance with the working class to socialism.[12]

The Official Position, 1967

The *History of the USSR* (Moscow, 1967), issued early in the Brezhnev era, while defending the necessity and correctness of collectivization and stressing the voluntary entry of many peasants into *kolkhozy*, admitted the widespread use of force and "administrative methods" (secret police). It credited the party (not Stalin) with successfully implementing collectivization, but criticized the

---

[12] J. Stalin, *Works* (Moscow, 1955), vol. 12, pp. 131–38, 147, 155, 198–206; vol. 13, pp. 243–61.

extremism of some party leaders. Stalin was reprimanded mildly, and his role in deciding upon and
implementing collectivization was deemphasized.

Under conditions of worsening international relations, increasing economic difficulties, and the
growth of class struggle within the USSR, the Communist Party had to achieve simultaneously industrialization and the socialist reconstruction of
agriculture. Life demanded a colossal application of
energy by party and Soviet people and sacrifices. . . .

In the course of fulfilling the First Five Year
Plan, the Communist Party came out decisively for
speeding the tempo of constructing socialism.
Collectivization was part of that construction. The
decision that it was necessary to reduce the period
of implementing it ripened gradually. . . . In the
spring of 1929 were heard the words "full collectivization" for the first time as a practical task. . . .
In the second half of 1929 the village seethed as in
the days of the revolution [of 1917]. At meetings of
the poor peasants, at general village assemblies
only one question was raised: organizing *kolkhozy.*
From July through September 1929 were attracted
into *kolkhozy* as many peasants as during the whole
12 years of Soviet power. And during the last three
months of 1929 the numerical growth of *kolkhozy*
was twice as fast again. This was, as the party
emphasized, "an unprecedented tempo of collectivization, *exceeding the most optimistic
projections.*" . . .

The choice of the moment for a transition to massive collectivization was determined by various
reasons. Among them the most important was the
spurt in the country's economy. Socialist construction
was advancing at an accelerating pace. The industrial population was growing considerably faster than
had been assumed. The demand for commercial
grain and raw materials rose sharply. The inability of
small peasant production to supply a growing industry with food . . . became unbearable. It became clear
that the economy of the country could not be based
on two different social foundations: big socialist
industry and small individual peasant farming. . . .

One of the new methods of struggle of the kulaks
against the policy of the Soviet state in 1928–29

was so-called kulak self-liquidation. The kulaks
themselves reduced their sowings, sold their stock
and tools. "Kulak self-liquidation" thus began
before the state shifted to a policy of consistent
liquidations of the kulaks as a class. . . .

Along with the achievements in socialist reconstruction of the village, inadequacies were revealed. . . . Such a leap was to a significant degree
caused by serious extremes, by the broad use of
administrative measures. . . . In a majority of cases
local leaders themselves forced by every means the
process of collectivization. . . . Leaders of one
region issued at the beginning of 1930 the following slogans: "Collectivize the entire population at
any cost! Dekulakize no less than seven percent of
all peasant farms! Achieve all this by February 15
[1930] without delaying a moment!" . . . Administrative methods, violation of the voluntary principle
in *kolkhoz* construction, contradicting the Leninist
cooperative plan caused sharp dissatisfaction
among the peasantry. . . . All that represented a
serious danger for the country, for the alliance of
the working class with the peasantry. In the struggle against these extremes rose all the healthy
forces of the party. The Central Committee was
inundated by letters of local Communists, workers,
and peasants. . . . Numerous signals of the dissatisfaction of the peasantry with administrative methods of *kolkhoz* construction caused serious concern
in the Central Committee. Thus the party and
government in February and March 1930 took a
series of emergency measures to correct the situation in the countryside. . . . On March 2, 1930, was
published the article of I. V. Stalin, "Dizzy with
Success" . . . against leftist extremes. . . . Many
people noted, to be sure, that it had come too l..
when extremes had taken on a massive character.
. . . One must note that in describing the causes of
the extremes, I. V. Stalin was one-sided and not
self-critical. He placed the entire blame for mistakes and extremes on local cadres, accused them
of dizziness and demanded harsh measures against
them. This caused a certain confusion among party
workers, which hampered the task of eliminating
excesses.[13]

---

[13] *Istoriia SSSR* (Moscow, 1967), vol. 8, pp. 443, 541–43,
553–57.

Problem 12 continued

A Dissident Marxist Historian

Roy Medvedev, a Marxist historian, in *Let History Judge* (New York, 1973), published in the USSR under Gorbachev about 1990, castigates forced collectivization and Stalin's role in it. Unlike the previous selection, which ascribed "mistakes" mainly to a few "leftists," Medvedev points directly at Stalin and the Politburo and suggests that forced collectivization was unwise and unnecessary. He ascribes Stalin's decision to pursue forced collectivization and elimination of the kulaks mainly to economic conditions for which Stalin and his colleagues were responsible.

> The economic miscalculations of Stalin, Bukharin, and Rykov and the kulaks' sabotage of grain procurement brought the USSR at the end of 1927 to the verge of a grain crisis. . . . Mistakes . . . in the previous years did not leave much room for political and economic maneuvering, [but] there were still some possibilities for the use of economic rather than administrative measures, that is for the methods of NEP rather than War Communism.

Medvedev attributed the traumatic implementation of collectivization to Stalin's incompetent and disastrous leadership:

> His inclination toward administrative fiat, toward coercion, instead of convincing, his oversimplified and mechanistic approach to complex political problems, his crude pragmatism and inability to foresee the consequences of alternative actions, his vicious nature and unparalleled ambition—all these qualities of Stalin seriously complicated the solution of problems that were overwhelming to begin with.
>
> . . . Stalin could not appraise correctly the situation taking shape in the countryside. At the first signs of progress [of collectivization] he embarked on a characteristically adventurous course. Apparently, he wanted to compensate for years of failures and miscalculations in agricultural policy and to astonish the world with a picture of great success in the socialist transformation of agriculture. So at the end of 1929, he sharply turned the bulky ship of agriculture without checking for reefs and shoals. Stalin, Molotov, Kaganovich, and several other leaders pushed for excessively high rates of collectivization, driving the local organizations in every possible way, ignoring . . . difficulties. . . .
>
> Although at the beginning of the 30s, grain production decreased, bread was in short supply, and millions of peasants were starving, Stalin insisted on exporting great quantities of grain. . . . Moreover, Soviet grain was sold for next to nothing. . . . The most galling aspect of the sacrifices that the people suffered—the peasants most of all—is that they were unnecessary. . . . The scale of capital investment in industry, which Stalin forced in the early 1930s, was too much for the economy to bear.

Stalin was likewise responsible, claims Medvedev, for the extreme tempo and excessive socialization of the initial collectivization drive. The Central Committee's draft decree had suggested a slower pace:

> At his [Stalin's] insistence the draft was stripped of rules indicating what portion of livestock and farm implements should be collectivized. In the final version the period of collectivization was reduced in the North Caucasus and Mid-Volga to one to two years and rules were omitted concerning socialization of the instruments of production. . . . The peasants' right to keep small livestock, implements, and poultry was omitted. Also deleted were guidelines for liquidating the kulaks. . . . Material and financial resources needed to organize hundreds of collective farms had not been set aside. . . . Most of the local party, soviet, and economic organs . . . were not prepared for total collectivization in such a short time. In order to carry out the orders that came from above . . . , almost all party and Soviet organs were forced to put administrative pressure on the peasants and also on the lower officials. . . . Such methods absolutely contradicted the basic principles of Marxism-Leninism.[14]

Soviet Views under Gorbachev

Under the Gorbachev regime, Soviet writings about Stalin's policy of forced collectivization exhibited much continuity with critiques from the Khrushchev period. However, there was far more

---

[14] Roy Medvedev, *Let History Judge* (New York, 1973), pp. 69*ff.*

Problem 12 continued

outright condemnation of forced collectivization as a whole as well as of Khrushchev's agricultural policies. Thus academician V. A. Tikhonov claimed that the kulaks had virtually disappeared during the Civil War period (1918–1920), so that those "dekulakized" by Stalin from 1929 to 1933 were peasants who produced somewhat more than the average—that is, the ablest and thriftiest Soviet farmers; Tikhonov described forced collectivization as an unmitigated disaster. Sociologist V. Shumkin stated bluntly:

> Stalin decided to eliminate NEP prematurely, using purely administrative measures and direct compulsion; this led, speaking mildly, to pitiable results. Agricultural production was disrupted; in a number of districts of the country famine began. In towns measures against artisans and small producers in practice destroyed a whole sphere of services. The lives of tens of millions of people . . . were filled with incredible deprivations and difficulties, often at the limit of purely biological existence.

And the economist V. Seliunin castigated Stalin's "Year of the Great Break" (1929) instituting forced collectivization as the "year of the breaking of the backbone of the people."[15]

A Western View

Recent Russian critiques of forced collectivization tend to confirm the findings of an outstanding Western study by Moshe Lewin,[16] who generally endorsed Medvedev's conclusions. Lewin affirms that Stalin, in asserting that the middle peasant was entering the *kolkhoz* voluntarily, was arguing from false premises:

> There were no grounds for suggesting that there had been a change of attitude among the mass of the peasantry with regard to the *kolkhozes*. The supposed change was a product of Stalin's peculiar form of reasoning which consisted of taking the wish for the deed. It followed that the peasants were being won over because this spring *there would be* 60,000 tractors in the fields, and in a year's time there would be over a hundred thousand.

As to the results of forced collectivization, Lewin concludes:

> The rash undertaking of the winter 1929–30 cost the country very dearly. . . . Indeed, it is true to say that to this day Soviet agriculture has still not fully recovered from the damaging effects of that winter.

The cost of collectivization was enormous: "Seldom was any government to wreak such havoc in its own country."[17] Economically, forced collectivization was counterproductive even in the short run, concludes James Millar; in the long run it had no economic rationale at all.[18] It is revealing that forced collectivization à la Stalin was not tried elsewhere in eastern Europe. Instead, wealthier farmers were squeezed out, as Lenin had suggested, by economic measures and their managerial talents used in the collective farms. ∎

[15] R. W. Davies, *Soviet History in the Gorbachev Revolution* (Bloomington, IN, 1989), pp. 49–50. The three Soviet articles cited by Davies—by Tikhonov, Shumkin, and Seliunin—were all published in 1987 or 1988.

[16] Moshe Lewin, *Russian Peasants and Soviet Power: A Study of Collectivization* (New York, 1975).

[17] Lewin, *Russian Peasants and Soviet Power*, pp. 457, 515.

[18] James Millar, "Mass Collectivization . . . ," *Slavic Review*, December 1974, p. 766.

Suggested Additional Reading

BELOV, F. *A History of a Soviet Collective Farm* (New York, 1955).

BERGSON, A. *The Real National Income of Soviet Russia Since 1928* (Cambridge, MA, 1961).

BERLINER, J. S. *Factory and Manager in the USSR* (Cambridge, MA, 1957).

BLACKWELL, W. *The Industrialization of Russia . . .* (New York, 1982).

BROWN, E. *The Soviet Trade Unions and Labor Relations* (Cambridge, MA, 1966).

CARR, E. H. *Foundations of a Planned Economy, 1926–1929* (New York, 1972).

CONQUEST, R. *The Harvest of Sorrow: Soviet Collectivization and the Terror-Famine* (New York, 1986).

CURTISS, J. S. *The Russian Church and the Soviet State* (Boston, 1953).

DANIELS, R. V., ed. *The Stalin Revolution* (Lexington, MA, 1972).

DAVIES, R. W. *The Industrialization of Soviet Russia: Vol. 3: The Soviet Economy in Turmoil 1929–1930* (Cambridge, MA, 1989).

———. *The Soviet Collective Farm, 1929–1930* (Cambridge, MA, 1980).

——— et al. *The Economic Transformation of the Soviet Union, 1913–1945* (Cambridge, 1993).

DEUTSCHER, I. *The Prophet Outcast: Trotsky, 1929–1940* (Oxford, 1963).

DUNMORE, T. *The Stalinist Command Economy* (New York, 1980).

EDMONDSON, L., ed. *Women and Society in Russia and the Soviet Union* (Cambridge, 1992).

ERLICH, A. *The Soviet Industrialization Debate . . .* (Cambridge, MA, 1960).

FARNSWORTH, B., and L. VIOLA, eds. *Russian Peasant Women* (Oxford, 1992).

FITZPATRICK, S. *Stalin's Peasants: Resistance and Survival in the Russian Village After Collectivization* (New York, 1994).

GERSCHENKRON, A. *Economic Backwardness in Historical Perspective* (Cambridge, MA, 1962).

GOLDMAN, W. *Women, the State and Revolution: Soviet Family Policy and Social Life, 1917–1936* (Cambridge, 1993).

HODGEMAN, D. R. *Soviet Industrial Production, 1928–1951* (Cambridge, MA, 1954).

HOFFMAN, D. L. *Peasant Metropolis: Social Identities in Moscow, 1929–1941* (Ithaca, NY, 1994).

HOLZMAN, F. D. *Soviet Taxation* (Cambridge, MA, 1955).

HUNTER, H., and J. SZYMER. *Faulty Foundations: Soviet Economic Policies, 1928–1940* (Princeton, 1992).

JASNY, N. *Soviet Industrialization, 1928–1952* (Chicago, 1961).

KRAVCHENKO, V. *I Chose Freedom* (New York, 1946).

LAIRD, R. D., ed. *Soviet Agriculture and Peasant Affairs* (Lawrence, KS, 1963).

LEWIN, M. *Russian Peasants and Soviet Power . . .* (New York, 1975).

MALE, D. J. *Russian Peasant Organization Before Collectivization . . .* (Cambridge, 1971).

MORRIS, M. W. *Stalin's Famine and Roosevelt's Recognition of Russia* (Lanham, MD, 1994).

NOVE, A. *Was Stalin Really Necessary?* (London, 1964).

POSADSKAYA, A. *Women in Russia: A New Era in Russian Feminism,* ed. and trans. K. Clark (New York, 1994).

PREOBRAZHENSKY, E. A. *The Crisis of Soviet Industrialization,* ed. D. Filtzer (White Plains, NY, 1979).

ROSENBERG, W. G., and L. H. SIEGELBAUM, eds. *Social Dimensions of Soviet Industrialization* (Bloomington, IN, 1993).

SHOLOKHOV, M. *Virgin Soil Upturned* (New York, 1959). (Novel.)

SMITH, K., ed. *Soviet Industrialization and Soviet Maturity: Economy and Society* (London, 1986).

STALIN, J. *Problems of Leninism* (Moscow, 1940).

SWIANIEWICZ, S. *Forced Labor and Economic Development . . .* (London, 1965).

TIMASHEFF, N. *The Great Retreat* (New York, 1946).

VIOLA, L. *The Best Sons of the Fatherland: Workers in the Vanguard of Soviet Collectivization* (New York, 1989).

WHEATCROFT, S. G., and R. W. DAVIES, eds. *Materials for a Balance of the Soviet National Economy, 1928–1930* (Cambridge, 1985).

ZALESKI, E. *Stalinist Planning for Economic Growth,* trans. and ed. M. C. MacAndrew and J. Moore (Chapel Hill, NC, 1979).

36

Soviet Culture under Lenin and Stalin, 1917–1953

From the very outset of the Soviet regime, culture became the handmaiden of politics and could not be viewed in isolation from it. However, profound differences in cultural policy developed in the era of Lenin and Stalin. Under so-called War Communism (1917–1921) there was no real official policy on cultural affairs because Bolshevik leaders were beset on all sides by foreign and domestic enemies and were therefore too preoccupied to formulate one. Many outstanding Russian writers, artists, and musicians sought refuge abroad, and some remained there. During the New Economic Policy (1921–1928) liberal and permissive policies toward the arts generally prevailed. Experimentation and debate were largely accepted as essential for a healthy cultural life, and some émigré intellectuals returned to Soviet Russia. Then, in 1929, Stalin's "revolution from above" altered irrevocably the nature of Soviet society and restructured the country. Cultural and scientific life could not escape the momentous transformations fostered by forced collectivization and rapid industrialization and urbanization. As Stalin loomed ever larger in all spheres of life, the freewheeling culture of NEP, with its lively debates and numer-

ous controversies, ended abruptly. No longer could one remain neutral or aloof; independent views were no longer tolerated. Party-mindedness (*partiinost*) became paramount. Following considerable relaxation of party pressures and controls during World War II, the screws of conformity tightened once again over Soviet cultural life in Stalin's final years.

Initial Policies

The November Revolution caused no abrupt break with established cultural patterns and traditions. Indeed, during the first years of the Soviet regime Russian culture underwent little apparent change. Having seized power, the Bolsheviks strove desperately to retain it, leaving them little time or energy to devote to the arts. They realized that they could not introduce pervasive cultural controls with their limited trained personnel. But the disruptions of revolution and civil war meant that little of enduring cultural value was produced. Scarce paper was quickly consumed to print Bolshevik propaganda leaflets and revolutionary tracts. Artists who managed to continue working found little demand for their works, and basic materials were in short supply and poor in quality; musicians faced similar problems. Concert halls were often filled with raucous political debates and revolutionary agitation. Deaths from hunger, disease, war, and execution had severely thinned the ranks of the intelligentsia. Emigration was an escape from what seemed to many to be the onset of the apocalypse. Many prominent artists chose to live in foreign exile rather than face an uncertain life in Soviet Russia. Émigrés included such leading artists as Maxim Gorkii, Alexis Tolstoy (a distant relative of Leo Tolstoy), Igor Stravinskii, Sergei Prokofiev, and Marc Chagall. Some returned later to the Soviet Union; others resided abroad permanently.

The chaotic uncertainty of the early years of Soviet rule constituted only one obstacle to elaborating a coherent cultural policy. From an ideological or theoretical vantage point there was equal confusion and uncertainty. In Marxism, culture was part of the superstructure. Only changes in the substructure (methods of production) would bring changes in the arts. A new socialist culture would emerge only gradually after a new economic order and a genuine proletarian society had taken shape.

Lenin outlined this moderate view of culture as a basis for a Soviet policy toward the arts:

> Art belongs to the people. It must have its deepest roots in the broad masses of the workers. It must be understood and loved by them. It must be rooted in, and grow with their feelings, thoughts, and desires. It must arouse and develop the artist in them. Are we to give cake and sugar to a minority while the mass of workers and peasants still eat black bread? So that art may come to the people, and people to art, we must first of all raise the general level of education and culture.[1]

This was neither very new nor even particularly Marxist, but it echoed what V. V. Stasov had

espoused in the 19th century in defending the art of the Itinerants and the music of The Five. Art had to be rooted in the life of the people, be clear and understandable, and serve a useful purpose: to educate the people. This became the essence of the Soviet concept of art.

Lunacharskii: The Politics of Culture

Anatol Lunacharskii (1875–1933) was responsible for making Lenin's views on culture and art a reality. The son of a successful tsarist civil servant, Lunacharskii studied philosophy and literature and developed sophisticated, cosmopolitan tastes. Joining the Bolshevik party in 1904, he described himself as "an intellectual among Bolsheviks, and a Bolshevik among the intelligentsia." As the party's leading cultural authority, Lunacharskii was the natural choice to be the first People's Commissar of Education. From 1917 to 1929 he guided the Soviet regime's efforts to improve education and develop a socialist culture. He proved a skillful, imaginative administrator, exercising considerable authority flexibly and tolerantly. He sought to initiate and oversee a program of basic education to teach the illiterate masses— 60 to 70 percent of the population—to read and write. He aimed to secure the allegiance of the artistic intelligentsia and emphasize their social obligations to the state. He had to persuade party leaders of the importance of the arts in order to conduct an effective cultural program. Recognizing the need for a delicate balance between conservative social elements, on the one hand, and fanatical enthusiasm for new directions and radical demands for a complete break with the past, on the other, he worked frantically to prevent wanton destruction of churches and sculptures associated with the old regime by those aiming to obliterate "bourgeois culture." Seeking to preserve the best of Russia's heritage, Lunacharskii refused to be limited by it.

Lunacharskii strove to restrain enthusiasm by proletarian supporters of the new regime and to persuade anti-Communists to shift to neutrality or

---

[1] Quoted in Sheila Fitzpatrick, *The Commissariat of Enlightenment* (New York, 1971), p. 24.

Library of Congress

Anatol Lunacharskii (1875–1933).

support the Soviet order. He preferred persuasion and patience to pressure and coercion. His was a reasonable voice in an era of impatience and intolerance. His actions were generally sensible and humane in an inhumane, irrational age. As commissar of education he encouraged give-and-take, in clear contrast to the rigid authoritarianism of the Stalin era. The 1920s represented a type of "Golden Era" of Soviet culture, an age of experimentation and innovation.

The "ideological reorientation" implied by the revolution soon affected social life and schools. Radicals predicted that the traditional family would wither away and urged a sharp breach with bourgeois social patterns. In education the curriculum was transformed to stress practical learning, promote economic specialization and material production, and develop socially responsible individuals. Schools were to be nondiscriminatory, free, and compulsory until age 17. Schooling and work experience were to be integrated; ideological loyalty and Soviet patriotism were incorporated

into the curriculum. Schools were to become political and economic instruments to overcome Russia's backwardness. Lunacharskii's commissariat made significant educational progress despite shortages of buildings, teachers, and books. By 1926 literacy had risen to about 51 percent of those over age nine.

Soviet Culture in the Making: *Proletkult* and Other Vanguard Groups

To implement a wide-ranging educational program, Lunacharskii had to recruit "bourgeois specialists" needed to train future "socialist specialists." Wishing to alienate no one, Lunacharskii helped finance numerous literary, artistic, and educational groups that retained much freedom and autonomy. Among the groups his commissariat sponsored was the Association of Proletarian Cultural and Education Organizations (*Proletkult*). Founded in 1917 (before November) by A. A. Bogdanov as an outlet for working-class cultural activity and to promote a broad educational program, Proletkult created workers' cultural clubs, toilers' universities, and palaces of culture. In August 1918 Proletkult sponsored a conference of proletarian writers that urged setting up an All-Russian Union of Writers of "working-class origin and viewpoint." That first effort failed, but the idea was not forgotten. However, Proletkult's aggressiveness caused friction with Lunacharskii's commissariat. Their competition finally induced Lenin to intervene. In 1920 he ordered Proletkult merged with the commissariat; he would not allow Proletkult to undermine Lunacharskii's more traditional approach.

In opposition to Proletkult's aim to reorient culture radically, there emerged a group of writers that Trotskii dubbed the Fellow Travelers. These "bourgeois specialists" were mostly established prerevolutionary writers who remained in Soviet Russia. They analyzed problems of adjustment in a new and alien world and wrote of the Revolution, the Civil War, and their effects on individuals. Less interested in cosmic historical forces than the proletarian writers, they wrote about romantic love, violence, and passion. In 1921 some Fellow Travelers formed a loosely organized fraternity known as the Serapion Brotherhood (from a hermitlike character of the early-19th-century German Romantic writer E. T. A. Hoffman). Lacking clear aesthetic doctrines, the Brotherhood sought to preserve artistic freedom. "Most of all," wrote one, "we were afraid of losing our independence." By 1924, however, the Brotherhood's unity began to crumble.

Another literary group of this period was associated with *Pereval* (The Mountain Pass), the first important Soviet "thick" journal—that is, one with serious intellectual content, with essays on politics, economics, literature, and the arts. The *Pereval* group consisted largely of young writers dedicated to the Revolution; more than half were party members. Regarding emerging Soviet society as transitional, they criticized as well as praised it. Favoring artistic freedom, they advocated literary "sincerity" and artistic "realism" and stressed each writer's unique personality as critical in developing talent. Their humanistic outlook was uncomplicated by ideology. Individualism and humanism brought *Pereval* into conflict with militant proletarian writers, who accused it of a lack of revolutionary enthusiasm. Lunacharskii monitored such disputes to prevent them from becoming disruptive.

Larger, more influential organizations of proletarian writers grew from the Proletkult movement.[2] They claimed to be the only true literary spokespersons for the working class. In their journal, *On Literary Guard,* they attacked the Fellow Travelers and *Pereval* writers aggressively. In 1925 these proletarian groups convened the first All-Union Conference of Proletarian Writers as a forum to attack "bourgeois" writers for opposing the revolution and espousing bourgeois

values such as individualism. Their accusations against the Fellow Travelers were mostly groundless, but there was open debate, not intimidation. The Fellow Travelers vigorously defended their literary freedom and intellectual integrity.

These intense debates provoked the party to issue a formal statement on culture, "The Policy of the Party in the Field of Artistic Literature." It revealed that many leading Bolsheviks were sophisticated culturally and understood that artistic creativity could not be dictated. The party accepted a variety of literary trends reflecting the diversity of NEP. Remaining aloof from partisan debate, the party advocated fair competition among the groups, guaranteeing that cultural ferment would persist and that proletarian writers would not devour the Fellow Travelers.

Painting and music of the 1920s revealed similar patterns of struggle between "left" and "right" factions. The Soviet musical world was split by intense debates between warring factions. The Association for Contemporary Music (ASM) maintained close ties with western European musical circles, thus assuring Soviet composers contact with advanced and progressive Western ideas. ASM in turn acquainted the West with the best music of Soviet composers. Such Western contacts proved especially stimulating to young composers like Dmitri Shostakovich (1906–1975). Members of ASM rejected completely the idea that music was a political tool.

Opposing the ASM were proletarian musicians, many of whom had participated in the short-lived Proletkult, which collapsed in 1920. The Russian Association of Proletarian Musicians (RAPM), founded in 1923, sought to embody proletarian ideology in music. Its members rejected most past composers and adopted a negative attitude toward the classical heritage. Scorning ASM's more traditional composers, they announced a life-and-death struggle with "decadent formalism" of "bourgeois" composers. Seeking to mediate, Lunacharskii cautioned the proletarian musicians not to forcibly "revolutionize" Russian music. Uneasy coexistence prevailed in music until the end of the 1920s.

---

[2] The Moscow Association of Proletarian Writers (MAPP) was founded in 1923; the Russian Association of Proletarian Writers (RAPP) and the All-Union Combined Association of Proletarian Writers (VOAPP) were founded in 1928.

Literature

Two Poets of the Revolution

Uncertainty and ambiguity pervaded Russian literature of the early Soviet period. This was reflected clearly in the last works of the brilliant Symbolist poet Alexander Blok (1880–1921). Well established in 1917, Blok welcomed the Revolution as the painful birth of a new world order, yet its violence frightened him. He stood precariously over a widening gulf between old and new, uncertain where to leap. Two famous poems written in 1918 amid revolution and civil war revealed his—and the intelligentsia's—ambiguous reactions. *The Scythians* celebrated the Revolution as an elemental expression of the Russian national spirit: "Yea, we are Scythians, / Yea, Asians, a slant-eyed, greedy brood." Russia, proclaimed Blok, had long shielded a haughty and ungrateful Europe from the Mongol hordes. Now, to collect that debt, it beckoned to Europe to join it in promoting peace and cooperation for the welfare of humanity: "Come unto us from the black ways of war, / Come to our peaceful arms and rest. / Comrades, before it is too late, / Sheathe the old sword; may brotherhood be blest." If Europe spurned this call to peace, a Scythian and Asiatic horde would descend and destroy corrupt, dying Western civilization.

Even more somber and controversial was Blok's foreboding poem *The Twelve,* which elicited enormous interest and impassioned debate. Did Blok intend *The Twelve* to affirm the Revolution, or to predict destruction of a refined and ancient culture? Was it a hymn of praise or a deceitful blasphemy? The "twelve" are Red Army soldiers tramping through Petrograd in a blizzard, intent on murder and pillage against the bourgeois enemy. The poem begins forebodingly: "Black night, / White snow, / The wind, the wind! / It all but lays you low, / The wind, the wind, / Across God's world it blows!" The Revolution, like the wind, sweeps all before it. After recording the soldiers' bloody acts, the poem ends cryptically: "Forward as a haughty host they tread. / A starved mongrel shambles in the rear. / Bearing high the

Alexander Blok (1880–1921).

banner, bloody red, / . . . With mist-white roses garlanded! / Jesus Christ is marching at their head."[3] Thus 12 terrorists become the 12 apostles, vanguard of a new era, following Christ and leading humanity into a new millennium, justifying a destructive revolution. Is that what Blok meant?

These were Blok's last two poems. His final diary entries, written as he was dying in 1921, confirm his despair and personal incompatibility with the Soviet era: "At this moment, I have neither soul nor body. . . . Vile rotten Mother Russia has devoured me . . . as a sow gobbles one of its suckling pigs."[4] Trying to leap to the new, he had slid into the abyss.

Another major poet devoured by Mother Russia and the Revolution was Vladimir Mayakovskii

---

[3] A. Yarmolinsky, ed., *An Anthology of Russian Verse, 1812–1960,* trans. Babette Deutsch (New York, 1962), pp. 109, 120.

[4] Quoted in Marc Slonim, *Modern Russian Literature* (New York, 1953), p. 206.

(1893–1930). No other writer identified so closely with the Revolution received such adulation. A prominent Futurist poet before 1917, Mayakovskii hailed the November Revolution, joined the Bolshevik party, and confidently set out to create a new "proletarian art" appealing to the masses. A "cultural radical" who rejected all bourgeois art as obsolete, he argued, "The White Guard is turned over to a firing squad: Why not Pushkin?" Art now must celebrate the Revolution, the proletariat, the machine—all modern life. Futurists regarded themselves as the vanguard of proletarian culture, and Mayakovskii was out in front. To achieve these grandiose aims, he and his friends organized LEF (Left Front in Art), whose members proclaimed art that was utilitarian to the state. "Art for art's sake" repelled him. To engage in idle dilettantism during historic change was to betray art. Commenting on current issues, he even put his poetry to work selling products in the service of the people and the Revolution.

Typical of his approach was the poem *150,000,000* (the 1919 population of Soviet Russia), published in 1920: "Its rhythms—bullets, / its rhymes—fires from building to building, / 150,000,000 speak with my lips . . . / Who can tell the name / of the earth's creator—surely a genius? / And so / of this / my / poem / no one is the author."[5] It depicts the struggle between good and evil, socialism and capitalism, Moscow and Chicago, and 150 million Russians and the rest of the world. This blatantly propagandist work was a failure. Lenin chastised Mayakovskii for printing *150,000,000* in 5,000 copies; 1,500 "for libraries and cranks" would have been enough, he claimed.

Among Mayakovskii's most popular works were two plays, *The Bedbug* (1929) and *The Bathhouse* (1930), revealing his growing disillusionment with a Soviet regime that to him was increasingly remote from the heroic dreams of the Revolution. In *The Bedbug* a worker, Prisypkin, becomes a self-important bureaucrat indulging his

bourgeois tastes and values. A fire set by his drunken guests disrupts his wedding day. Everyone except Prisypkin and one bedbug are incinerated. Fifty years later, Prisypkin and the bedbug are found perfectly preserved in a block of ice. Prisypkin recovers fully after thawing out, but his miraculous resurrection is a mixed blessing for the purified future Communist society he now enters. His bourgeois habits—drinking, smoking, and swearing—and especially the "ancient disease" of love all prove contagious and potentially disruptive. Thus the authorities display him and the bedbug in a cage as curiosities. Prisypkin symbolized everything Mayakovskii hated in himself and in Soviet citizens of the late 1920s. Revolutionary fervor and self-sacrifice had begun to fade, replaced by "bourgeois" values: self-satisfaction, complacency, and pursuit of the material. Soviet society, he feared, was fostering a generation of Prisypkins.

The Bathhouse more directly indicted Soviet life, notably the Stalinist bureaucracy, which radiated vulgarity characteristic of Stalinism at its worst, with its anti-intellectualism, crudeness, and sterility. Mayakovskii was continuing a literary tradition, dating back at least to Gogol, in which literature was used to expose bureaucratic humbug, abuse of power, and corruption. Dreams given substance by the Revolution had begun to dissipate, Mayakovskii felt, like bubbles in the air. The spontaneity and freedom of NEP were yielding to a soulless bureaucratic state supported by a vast police apparatus resembling that of tsarism. His efforts to publicize and ridicule shortcomings of Soviet society were attacked viciously by petty, narrow-minded bureaucrats who felt the sting of his critiques. Their attacks only convinced him that his assessment was accurate.

Harassed by enemies, adrift in a society that spurned his high standards, beset with personal problems, and suffering from boredom and isolation, Mayakovskii shot himself in April 1930. His suicide note avoided self-pity: "Don't blame anyone for my death, and please don't gossip about it." His tragic death shocked the entire intelligentsia. He had been *the* poet of the Revolution,

---

[5] Quoted in Edward J. Brown, *Russian Literature Since the Revolution* (New York, 1969), p. 54.

spokesman of the working class, and the advocate of socially useful literature, yet his suicide seemed to many a slap in the face of the Revolution. But even in death he served it. His legacy as a poet and a symbol has been enormous, and his genius unchallenged.

Two Novelists of Dissent

Mayakovskii's prose counterpart was Evgenii Zamiatin (1884–1937), author of the influential anti-utopian novel *We*. Joining the Bolshevik party as a youth, he soon found the atmosphere sectarian and petty and left it before the Revolution. Zamiatin began publishing stories in 1911 and was well known by 1914. During World War I he spent much time in England supervising ship construction for the Russian navy. After the Revolution he found it difficult to fit into Soviet society, finally finding employment only with the help of his friend, Maxim Gorkii, as a lecturer on literature. Zamiatin became the spiritual godfather of the Serapion Brotherhood but not a formal member. *We* (1920), circulated but not published in the USSR until 1989, appeared in English translation in 1924, the first of many Soviet writings to enjoy great success in the West.

In *We* Zamiatin reveals a frightening vision of the society he saw emerging in the Soviet Union. He foresaw both a degeneration of communism and the destruction of freedom and individuality by the monolithic state. *We* satirizes a future utopian city where science provides every convenience (including a glass cover to protect it from the elements), but its people have been reduced to ciphers. "Wise authorities" control every facet of human activity—work, thought, leisure, and sex. Transparent living quarters and constantly monitored activity eliminate privacy. Every thought and utterance is recorded; every deviation from the norm is ruthlessly suppressed. The novel's hero is D-503, a rebel against sterile conformity who dares to engage in free thought, to love, and to show interest in nature; he is a more sophisticated Prisypkin. D-503 eventually is "reprogrammed"

(destroyed) and his "irrationality" ended by the "wise authorities."

Zamiatin's novel warned of future dangers to freedom and individuality stemming from the regime's manipulation of science, thus anticipating Aldous Huxley's *Brave New World* and George Orwell's *1984*. *We*, of course, could not then be published in the Soviet Union. Zamiatin's other writings, too, alienated the Soviet authorities, who in 1929 launched a vicious campaign of vilification (a familiar practice later) against him. Prevented from publishing, he was forced to resign his teaching position and was ostracized by all. Finally, in 1931, Gorkii personally delivered Zamiatin's letter of appeal to Stalin:

> For me as a writer to be deprived of the opportunity to write is a sentence of death. Matters have reached a point where I am unable to exercise my profession because creative writing is unthinkable if one is obliged to work in an atmosphere of systematic persecution that grows worse every year.[6]

Owing to Gorkii's intercession, Zamiatin and his wife were allowed to leave the USSR in 1932.

Zamiatin's contemporary, Boris Pilniak (pen name of Boris Vogau, 1894–1937), was an influential and popular Fellow Traveler with great impact on Soviet literature of the 1920s. His first and most important work, a novel, *The Naked Year* (1922), was a series of vignettes of the Revolution that recount the cruelty and hatreds it unleashed and portray with compelling pathos the suffering and optimism of this age. Pilniak sympathized not with the Bolsheviks but with all those seeking freedom, whether anarchists, SRs, or disillusioned Bolsheviks. He shared Zamiatin's concern about the dangers to human freedom and individuality from efforts to organize all life by a preconceived plan. Pilniak's "The Tale of the Unextinguished Moon" resembled closely the actual death of Red Army commander in chief Mikhail Frunze. A Red Army Civil War hero falls ill; the party orders him

---

[6] Quoted by Michael Glenny in his introduction to E. Zamiatin's *We* (New York, 1972), p. 12.

to undergo surgery, which he knows instinctively will kill him. The party leader—"Number One"—insists that the hero be repaired so as to remain useful, like a piece of machinery. Pilniak castigates this callous attitude, and in his story the Red Army commander dies on the operating table as if cut down on the battlefield. This story provoked a storm of criticism, and Pilniak and the editors of the journal in which it appeared had to denounce it publicly as "a gross error."

Pilniak was thus already suspect when his short novel *Mahogany* appeared in Germany in 1929. Pilniak had sent it there for publication simultaneously with the Soviet edition to gain international copyright protection because the USSR then did not subscribe to the International Copyright Convention. The novel was issued in the USSR in 1930 only after complete rewriting, under the title *The Volga Falls to the Caspian Sea*. It describes construction of a dam and a hydroelectric plant that will destroy a historic town. The theme is the struggle between history and technological progress; Pilniak clearly sympathizes with history. His heroes are not construction workers but mahogany collectors who cherish true craftsmanship and preserve the old in the face of the advance of the new.

The Cinema

"The cinema is for us the most important of all the arts," declared Lenin. As a means of mass communication in an era of mass culture, the cinema is unsurpassed. Sophisticated messages can be filmed, duplicated, distributed, and projected on screens for millions of people, with little technical equipment and personnel. Thus conditions were right to develop Soviet cinema. Most prerevolutionary Russian film directors, actors, and technical personnel left Russia after the Revolution. Thus, unlike literature, music, and painting, the Soviet cinema had no "bourgeois specialists" to worry about and was free to develop on its own. The first Soviet film directors were young enthusiasts whose spontaneity, ingenuity, and artistry deeply influenced Soviet filmmaking.

Two important early Soviet directors were Lev Kuleshov, who directed his first film at age 17, and Dziga Vertov, who filmed the Civil War at age 20. Vertov's Civil War documentaries helped shape future Soviet films. He developed the "camera-eye" (*kino-glaz*) concept, which records what is occurring live. The director gives meaning to the raw experience recorded by the camera by cutting and arranging—editing—the film. Thus the film becomes an instrument that interprets and educates. Later Vertov perfected his techniques, recording scenes from Soviet life, editing them, and arranging them into virtual filmed newspapers, calling them "film truth" (*kino-pravda*) after the newspaper *Pravda*.

Lev Kuleshov applied Vertov's techniques to feature films, utilizing Vertov's documentary realism to stimulate the viewer's imagination and anticipation and making film both an intellectual and a visual experience. He used his simple equipment creatively and intelligently. He combined documentary footage with pure fiction to create an artistic montage, and he paved the way for Sergei Eisenstein, the greatest Soviet film director.

Trained as an architect, Eisenstein (1898–1948) worked as a poster artist during the Civil War. As a set designer he joined the Proletkult theater, where he was influenced by the director, V. E. Meierhold. Later, after staging his own theatrical productions, he moved exclusively to cinema in 1924. He combined Meierhold's theatrical techniques—stressing the visual, caricature, and contrast—with Kuleshov's documentary montage to develop his own imaginative style. Eisenstein's first film, *Strike* (1924), which began as a documentary, became a powerful portrait of the inequities of capitalist Russia. Eisenstein's use of visual symbolism enhanced the film's psychological impact. He jolted audiences with powerful scenes and shocked them with startling visual effects, creating a "film-fist" (*kino-kulak*) to pummel the viewer. *The Battleship Potemkin* (1926), Eisenstein's greatest cinematic triumph, depicted the mutiny of the crew of the *Potemkin* in Odessa in the 1905 Revolution. The hero is the battleship, which sustains the crew's revolutionary enthusiasm. The film indicted tsarist callousness, represented by the mechanical march down the steps of Odessa harbor by a phalanx of tsarist troops and by the repulsive image of maggot-infested meat fed to the battleship crew by inhumane officers. *The Battleship Potemkin* demonstrated how significant a political instrument the cinema could be. Still, in the 1920s Eisenstein's films were not great popular successes. Audiences preferred lighter foreign imports, and party censors suspected Eisenstein's unorthodox methods. By the late 1920s he began having trouble with the authorities.

Vsevolod Pudovkin, another major Soviet director of the 1920s, was less original than Eisenstein but more popular with audiences. Relying on professional actors and a clear story line, which gave his works smoothness and continuity, Pudovkin drew his subject matter from works of fiction. He involved the viewer in development of individual characters rather than in great historic events. His often sentimental and unsophisticated films were very influential in a developing Soviet cinema. His most critically acclaimed film was *Mother* (1926).

By the late 1920s party authorities, becoming more interested in the cinema, moved to control it as they did other arts. The party supported Vertov's "film-eye" documentary techniques, harnessed to the industrialization drive of the 1930s. Some imaginative directors and prominent film actors emigrated in protest.

Education

From the inception of the Bolshevik regime, the party placed high priority on eliminating illiteracy, which was especially widespread in rural areas but also affected many urban workers. As early as 1919 a campaign was inaugurated to eradicate illiteracy: The *likbez* (liquidation of illiteracy) aimed at expanding the educational system, emphasizing practical education and hands-on experience. In 1921 so-called *rabfaki* (workers' schools) were established in factories to offer instruction in basic reading, writing, and arithmetic. Evening classes

were held in factories; their success may be measured by the millions who learned the rudiments of literacy in their crash courses.

The effort to create a "workers' culture" resulted from a desire to develop a new cultural and educational level worthy of the new era. However, the result was often a lowering of the overall cultural level, as many intellectuals, officials, and white-collar workers sought to identify completely with the new "leading class" and began to dress and speak like workers, carefully disguising their more refined tastes and attitudes.

Despite the assault on illiteracy and creation of a new workers' culture, the party did not neglect higher education. Intent on training a new generation of scientists with the proper political and intellectual outlook, the party established a Communist Academy rivaling the old Imperial Academy of Sciences and staffed largely by members of the old guard. A number of Communist universities were also established. A limited coexistence between these institutions prevailed until the late 1920s. In general, Bolshevik attitudes prevailed in the social sciences (economics, history, politics), whereas prerevolutionary views predominated in the natural sciences and humanities.

Education at all levels had two fundamental purposes: (1) to train a new generation in socialist thinking and counteract lingering bourgeois influences and (2) to establish a solid foundation for a new socialist culture expressed in all the arts and sciences. A correct socialist world outlook among the students was emphasized. If that could be established early and then continuously reinforced, the subjects studied would assume an appropriate "socialist character" no matter what they were—literature, chemistry, economics, or astronomy. Intensive efforts were made to open up educational opportunities for the former lower classes, notably workers.

Science

As the 1920s progressed—a period of relative freedom and peaceful coexistence between the

Marxist and non-Marxist camps—tensions grew and a showdown was clearly inevitable, the outcome of which was never really in doubt. Scientists experienced a growing intolerance at the hands of the party on issues of central scientific and philosophical importance, such as Freudian psychology, Einstein's theory of relativity, quantum mechanics, and modern genetic theory. Intellectual debates over interpretation of these theories, crucial to the development of 20th-century science, acquired political overtones. Serious scientists found it increasingly difficult to reconcile dialectical materialism, as interpreted by the party, with basic principles of quantum mechanics or Einstein's relativity theory. Many scientists chose to retreat from public debate about scientific theory and pursue their own research unobtrusively. Thus many gifted scientists shunned controversial theoretical work, which was viewed as politically dangerous if one ended up on the losing side of a theoretical debate.

Nowhere were these dangers more apparent than in genetics. The controversies that plagued Soviet genetics for more than a generation were typical of those affecting many aspects of Soviet intellectual life. Traditional geneticists agreed that a gene reproduces itself essentially unchanged from generation to generation, with very infrequent instances of mutation. Soviet scientists tended to reject that view as not squaring with Marxism's dialectical materialism. Some Soviet geneticists now suggested that evolution involved a series of adaptations to environmental conditions capable of transmission to subsequent generations—that is, the inheritance of acquired characteristics. Such a view was consistent with the Soviet view that the USSR had created an entirely new and superior social environment from which triumphant Soviet men and women would emerge. The debate between traditionalists and Soviet Lamarckians moved back and forth during the 1920s. (Lamarck, a pre-Darwinian philosopher, had formulated the idea that acquired characteristics could be transmitted to successive generations.) Only with the emergence under Stalin of a young pseudoagronomist, Trofim D.

Lysenko, would the genetics debate take on real and dire political dimensions. During the New Economic Policy politics did not impinge seriously on scientific work, but the specter of dialectical materialism hung malevolently over an infant Soviet science like the sword of Damocles. The agony of Soviet genetics would begin with the emergent Stalinist dictatorship of the 1930s.

Toward the end of the 1920s, tension and unease developed in scientific circles and in all realms of Soviet culture, as the party manifested impatience at the slow pace of development. In 1928 a mere 6 percent of all scientific workers were members of the Communist Union of Scientific Workers (*Varnitso*). Among scientists the party was winning few adherents, and the Academy of Sciences remained impervious to party influence. The frightening possibility arose that the party might be excluded from the country's intellectual life. Advocacy of peaceful coexistence between party and nonparty scientists was deleted abruptly from official pronouncements as the party began with increasing regularity to assert its authority in scientific matters. With the consolidation of Stalin's position and the rise of the cult of personality, Stalin began to intervene in scientific debates. Soon his arbitrary view became official and exclusive in all branches of learning.

Stalinist Culture, 1929–1953

Tightened controls on Soviet intellectual life began soon after Stalin's consolidation of power with an attack on the Academy of Sciences, which had sought to remain aloof from political involvement. Using a method typical of his drive for power, Stalin insisted that Academy membership be expanded and proceeded to nominate carefully selected candidates. By 1929 older academicians had been mostly replaced by aggressive party-minded members who transformed the Academy into a tool of Stalinist cultural policy. After a pliable majority had been seated, some distinguished older members were arrested beginning in 1930, including Sergei Platonov and Evgenii Tarle, highly respected nonparty historians. This campaign brought the prestigious Academy into line in support of the Five Year Plan. Those who resisted or evaded the party's demands paid dearly for it in the Great Purge of 1936–1938.

The party now intervened in such fields as linguistics. Nicholas Marr, a distinguished linguist, had applied Marxist theory to linguistics. Language, Marr argued, was an aspect of social life that reflected productive relations. As part of the superstructure, language would reflect fundamental changes in the socioeconomic base. A new socialist language would emerge as socialist productive relations developed, he predicted. Marr discerned an embryonic socialist language in Russian and non-Russian languages of the USSR. After Marr's death in 1934, Stalin distorted his views to claim that Russian was socialism's international language to which non-Russian languages must yield. This became a theoretical basis for a new Russification of Soviet national minorities.

A flagrant example of party interference in Soviet intellectual life was in genetics. Collectivization enabled unscrupulous individuals to win party support for preposterous theories. Lysenko argued that classical genetics, disregarding dialectical change, had misinterpreted the genetic process. Lysenko claimed that hereditary characteristics resulted from an organism's dialectical interaction with its environment. He argued that altering the environment would change organisms' natural properties; these changes could then be transmitted to succeeding generations. This amazing theory was supplemented by the belief that organisms could somehow select which acquired characteristics could be passed on. This belief coincided with and reinforced the conviction that the November Revolution had begun a new era in which a new, superior Soviet individual would emerge. Change the environment and change humankind! With conditions ripe for a new genetic theory, Lysenko became Stalin's scientific hero.

With such support, Lysenko asserted first that he could turn winter wheat into spring wheat merely by treating the seeds, then that he could transform one species into another (for example,

wheat into rye). His experiments, though never duplicated outside his laboratory, were officially hailed as epitomizing socialist science. Lysenko convinced few scientists, but the omnipotent Stalin accepted his assertions fully. Thus Lysenko acquired enormous power, destroyed his enemies, and made his views into "scientific law." Even Nicholas Vavilov, the USSR's most distinguished geneticist, who was elected president of the International Congress of Genetics in 1939, succumbed to Lysenko's intrigues, perishing in prison after valiant efforts to maintain his scholarly integrity. Lysenko's impact on Soviet biology and agriculture was disastrous. His harebrained schemes inflicted untold damage on crops and livestock, but he was so formidable that agronomists falsified tests of his theories, fearing they might be "planted" for opposing them. Promoted by Stalinist terror, Lysenkoism destroyed most Soviet genetics research for a generation.

Scientists, like artists, were expected to serve the party and Stalin unequivocally. The spirit of inquiry, long characteristic of Russian and Soviet science, died, and many branches of science suffered irreparable harm. Science, art, and literature all became the party's humble servants. Many talented people retreated into abstract, theoretical studies, hoping to avoid the risks of applied science that might endanger their positions and even their lives. Writers composed for their desk drawers; scientists left their laboratories for their private offices. Zhores Medvedev, distinguished scientist and chronicler of the Lysenko affair, described the general atmosphere:

> An unprecedented number of discussions took place in 1935–37 in all fields of science, the arts and literature. As a rule, because of the historical conditions, they were all harsh. Differences of opinion, approach, method, and evaluation of goals are completely natural occurrences in science. Truth is born from argument. But in the environment of the massive repressions of the thirties, the spy hunts and centralized inflaming of passions, and under the conditions of a feverish search after the "enemies of the people" in all spheres of human activity, any scientific discussion tended to become a

struggle with political undertones. Nearly every discussion ended tragically for the side represented by the more noble, intellectual, honest, and calm men, who based their arguments on scientific facts.[7]

Only the strength and courage of many men and women dedicated to the pursuit of truth allowed Soviet science and culture to survive at all in this hostile environment.

The political ambiguity of many works of the Fellow Travelers in literature and the lack of conformity in other cultural fields could no longer be tolerated in Stalinist Russia. By 1929 Stalin's personal dictatorship began to impinge directly on the lives of Soviet citizens as industrialization and collectivization moved forward. Stalinist controls were now extended over every aspect of culture. One sign of the shift away from the tolerance of NEP days was Lunacharskii's removal as commissar of education early in 1929. Shortly after came the first signs of tightening party control over literature.

Partiinost in Literature

The Stalinist technique of extending party controls to literature, repeatedly used and continually refined, was to settle on scapegoats and thus terrorize an entire group into obedience. Scapegoats in literature were Pilniak, heading the All-Russian Union of Writers, and Zamiatin, leading the Leningrad Union of Writers. The attack on them and, by implication, on all Fellow Travelers, signaled a sharp change in literary policy. The prosecution totally bungled charges brought against Pilniak and Zamiatin of arranging publication of their works abroad to avoid Soviet censorship. Both writers presented solid evidence that they had not authorized such foreign publications. Their embarrassed accusers then asserted that these works (and those of other Fellow Travelers)

were "anti-Soviet"—defined as any hostile or neutral position. Either one favored socialist construction in the USSR, or one became an "enemy of the people." The message was clear: Fellow Travelers must cease writing unless they wrote politically "correct" literature.

Zamiatin, Pilniak, and their supporters were removed as leaders of the All-Russian Union of Writers, more than half of whose members were purged; it became the All-Russian Union of Soviet Writers, stressing "Soviet." NEP tolerance ended, yielding to an era of "party-oriented" literature. Fellow Travelers now had to prove their "solidarity" with the proletariat, serve the party, and help construct socialism. The Russian Association of Proletarian Writers (RAPP) now dominated the literary scene. Pilniak recanted, but Zamiatin stood his ground and later appealed successfully to Stalin. RAPP, led by Leopold Averbakh and Alexander Fadeev, strongly pressured the Fellow Travelers and attacked "neobourgeois elements" in literature.

RAPP proved ineffective in controlling literature because its members rejected the party view that writings could be produced by directive. Trumpeted a 1930 *Pravda* editorial: "Literature, the cinema, and the arts were levers in the proletariat's hands which must be used to show the masses positive models of initiative and heroic labor." This "positive" emphasis proved too simple and one-sided even for the sincere proletarian writers Averbakh and Fadeev. To them literature had to depict life honestly, both the negative and the positive. Despite their enthusiastic pro-regime stance, proletarian writers of RAPP were out of step with party authorities, who wanted literature and art to portray the heroic struggle to achieve socialism only positively and optimistically and viewed culture as a party weapon to propagandize and mobilize the masses. RAPP writers were still too wedded to "objective art" and individualism, so RAPP was dissolved in 1932. Diverse literary groups were abolished, and henceforth all writers had to belong to a monolithic Union of Soviet Writers, which was wholly party-dominated.

---

[7] Zhores Medvedev, *The Rise and Fall of T. D. Lysenko,* trans. I. M. Lerner (New York, 1971), pp. 5–6.

A New Aesthetic: Socialist Realism

More than two years passed before the full impact of the 1932 decisions was felt. Much opposition to party control of literature had to be overcome before the authorities could convene an open writers' congress to formalize the situation. The First All-Union Congress of Soviet Writers met in August 1934. Of the 590 Soviet delegates, more than 60 percent were party members; many prestigious foreign guests were also present. At the congress Andrei Zhdanov (1896–1948) emerged as the party's new authority on cultural affairs and presented the main address, which outlined Soviet literature's future form and content:

> Our Soviet literature is not afraid of being called tendentious, because it *is* tendentious. In the age of the class struggle a non-class, non-tendentious, apolitical literature does not and cannot exist. In our country the outstanding heroes of literary works are the active builders of a new life. . . . Our literature is permeated with enthusiasm and heroism. It is optimistic, but not from any biological instinct. It is optimistic because it is the literature of the class which is rising, the proletariat, the most advanced and most prospering class.[8]

This was the genesis of "socialist realism," the aesthetic that until the mid-1980s dominated every facet of Soviet culture. Zhdanov defined it as the portrayal of "real" life in all its revolutionary development, the aim of which was to promote the masses' ideological reeducation in socialism. Endorsement of the new doctrine by Gorkii, who presided over the congress and lent his enormous prestige to the new policy, made the doctrine respectable. Delegate after delegate rose mechanically to reiterate Zhdanov's remarks and to endorse "socialist realism." So carefully orchestrated was the congress that even the most prominent writers dared not protest openly against literature's complete identification with party goals. How far would Stalin go to ensure confor-

mity to his "literary" views? In 1934, to be a practicing writer one had to join the Writers' Union and accept its statutes embodying Zhdanov's concepts. Compare this with the tolerant attitude of the 1925 party resolution on literature!

The enormous significance of the First Congress and of "socialist realism" was not recognized immediately. Literary contacts with Western writers increased, and many translations of "progressive" Western authors appeared in the USSR, including works by Hemingway, Dreiser, and Dos Passos. Despite the imposition of narrow-minded socialist realism and the terror of the Great Purge, some decent literature was still being produced as authors skirted ingeniously around socialist realism's dogmas. An example was Iuri Krymov's *Tanker Derbent* (1938), which focused on the personal problems of men engaged in intense competition in the oil shipping business on the Caspian Sea.

Nazism's triumph in Germany and gathering war clouds in the 1930s stimulated Russian nationalism. In 1934 a new orientation in historical writing was decreed. M. N. Pokrovskii (1868–1932), a friend of Lunacharskii, had promoted a Marxist orientation among Soviet professional historians and had virtually eliminated national history from school curricula. History was reduced to vague sociological categories involving class struggle. National heroes were deleted from history texts, and a generation of Soviet schoolchildren grew up largely ignorant of their past. In 1934 Pokrovskii and his followers were denounced as anti-Marxists who had denied Russian history's progressive development. National history and a cult of national heroes were revived. Many authors sounded patriotic themes in their plays and novels. Many works dealt with wars by the Russian people against foreigners. The leading historical novel of the period was Alexis Tolstoy's unfinished three-volume *Peter I* (1929–1944), which became a great popular success considered comparable to Leo Tolstoy's *War and Peace.* Based on extensive research, *Peter I* depicted the "Great Transformer" of Russia very positively.

---

[8] A. Zhdanov et al., *Problems of Soviet Literature* (New York, n.d.), p. 21.

Appearing simultaneously was Mikhail Sholokhov's four-volume *The Quiet Don* (1928–1940), which masterfully portrays the lives of peasants and Cossacks during World War I, the Revolution, and the Civil War. Sholokhov focused on the moral and psychological problems of individuals struggling to understand events that were engulfing them. Soviet critics claimed that *The Quiet Don* embodied concepts of socialist realism, but it resembles very little the precepts of Zhdanov and the hack writers of the 1930s. Conceived on a scale comparable to *War and Peace, The Quiet Don* traces life in a quiet Cossack village before World War I. As war's outbreak disrupts the village, Sholokhov measures its impact on individuals and families. The second volume probes the difficulties of war, growing discontent, and the Revolution's impact on villagers' lives. The last two volumes record the bitter fighting of the Civil War. The novel touched a responsive chord in Soviet readers, who discovered in it more substance, originality, and power than in all the proletarian writers' Five Year Plan novels. The first parts of the novel were so moving that many grew skeptical about its authorship. Some claimed Sholokhov had obtained the manuscript of a White Army officer killed during the Civil War and passed it off as his own work. Such charges were denied officially, but rumors persisted (repeated later by Solzhenitsyn) that Sholokhov did not write *The Quiet Don*. Without concrete evidence to the contrary, we must assume that Sholokhov was the author and that his study of human resiliency and fortitude represented a rare bright spot in Soviet literature of the Stalin era.

Literary Victims of Stalinism

The Great Purges (1936–1938) constituted a frightening, sterile period in Soviet history when virtually no one felt safe. The purge cut deeply into intelligentsia ranks. (In the 1970s Solzhenitsyn claimed that more than 600 writers disappeared.) Many established writers were publicly branded "enemies of the people" and disappeared without trace until hastily "rehabilitated" after

Stalin's death. The literary intelligentsia was ordered to devour itself, and the Soviet cultural world was terrorized. Those terrible years revealed awesome contrasts—heroism, cowardice, hypocrisy, and shrewd maneuvering. Some hastily denounced friends as traitors, spies, and Trotskyites. Others tried to remain unnoticed or waited in meek resignation. The result was devastation of Soviet culture. The untalented and unscrupulous emerged as Soviet spokespersons. The list of great talents lost in the purge reads like a Who's Who of Soviet literature.

Prominent among the distinguished literary victims of Stalinism was Osip Mandelshtam (1892–1938), a highly educated Jewish poet and one of the 20th century's most talented writers. His elaborate poetry was replete with magnificent archaisms revealing strong Greek Orthodox influence. In 1933 his work was criticized for not reflecting Soviet life and for "distorting reality." Unusual outspokenness doomed Mandelshtam. Recalled the writer V. Kataev, "He was a real opponent of Stalin. . . . [In 1936 or 1937] he was shouting against Stalin; what a terrible man Stalin was." For writing an acid poem about the dictator, he was arrested during the Great Purge and died in a labor camp.[9]

The Nazi invasion of June 1941 offered a respite from the terror and the inanities of socialist realism. The struggle for national survival against the Germans required unity and cooperation, possible only in a more tolerant, flexible atmosphere. Culture was enlisted in the war effort; party controls, including censorship, were relaxed; and writers and artists were freer to express their talents. Many writers became war correspondents, went to the front, and reported about personal heroism, great battles, and partisan warfare. Some of this writing was sheer propaganda to bolster morale; some was first-rate eyewitness reporting; a few pieces qualified as literature. Ilia Ehrenburg (1891–1967) wrote a memorable two-volume collection, *War* (1941–1942), an extremely moving

---

[9] Under the aegis of *glasnost* Mandelshtam was "rehabilitated," and his poetry is again in fashion.

portrait of a nation resisting the Nazi onslaught. The sieges of Leningrad and Stalingrad (especially K. Simonov's *Days and Nights* about Stalingrad) and cases of personal sacrifice and heroism provided material for hundreds of literary works that inspired and informed the people. This literary outpouring reflected greater party tolerance and flexibility early in the war, reminiscent of NEP. Writers and artists who contributed to the war effort were allowed greater latitude than at any time since the 1920s.

As victory approached, the war-weary Soviet people anticipated being allowed to pursue their interests without interference. Terrible sacrifices had brought triumph and unprecedented prestige to the USSR. Was it not time to loosen the heavy-handed Communist dictatorship and create better lives for all? During the war hints of change were evident everywhere. Strident party ideology was toned down during wartime cooperation with the Western democracies. The Soviet people expected this more open atmosphere to continue, only to be disillusioned cruelly by an abrupt return to prewar harshness.

As early as 1943, when the Red Army began a sustained counteroffensive, the party deplored erosion of ideological orthodoxy. Renewed party ideological vigilance was shown in an attack in late 1943 on the popular satirist Mikhail Zoshchenko (1895–1958), whose humorous collection of autobiographical sketches, *Before Sunrise,* was being successfully serialized in a Soviet journal. Party publications denounced them as unpatriotic "vulgar philistinism" (a favorite term of opprobrium in the postwar era). The series was halted abruptly. Several other prominent writers were criticized for disregarding party guidelines, which reminded them that there were limits to the party's tolerance. Cultural controls remained, but many hoped for liberal changes in postwar party policies toward culture. Some delegates to the first postwar Soviet writers' conference (May 1945) openly opposed renewed party interference in cultural matters.

The party quickly made it clear that such "harmful attitudes" and wartime lapses of disci-

Anna Akhmatova (1888–1966).

Library of Congress

pline would no longer be tolerated. On August 14, 1946, a Central Committee resolution condemned two prominent Leningrad journals, *The Star* and *Leningrad,* for publishing ideologically harmful apolitical works, kowtowing to bourgeois culture, and disparaging Soviet values. This party resolution contained in germ the *Zhdanovshchina,* or era of Andrei Zhdanov's ideological dominance. *Leningrad* was closed down, and a party bureaucrat who became editor of *The Star* obediently banished from its pages "debased" works of Zoshchenko, the poet Anna Akhmatova (1888–1966), and others holding their "antiparty" views. The party again chose scapegoats to initiate a new crackdown, focusing on Leningrad's journals and authors. The party—actually Stalin—feared the city's traditional Western orientation and peculiar sense of independence after heroically surviving a three-year wartime siege. Nor was the choice of Zoshchenko and Akhmatova accidental. Influenced by prerevolutionary models, both had won recognition before 1917 and neither had praised the Soviet regime.

Elaborating on the Central Committee resolution at a meeting of Leningrad writers, Zhdanov bitterly denounced Zoshchenko's story "The Adventures of a Monkey" (1945), which had appeared in *The Star*. Zhdanov saw something sinister in this apparently harmless satire about a monkey who escapes from a zoo:

> If you will read that story carefully and think it over, you will see that Zoshchenko casts the monkey in the role of supreme judge of our social order, and has him read a kind of moral lesson to the Soviet people. The monkey is presented as a kind of rational principle having the right to evaluate the conduct of human beings. The picture of Soviet life is deliberately and vilely distorted, and caricatured so that Zoshchenko can put into the mouth of his monkey the vile, poisonous anti-Soviet sentiment to the effect that life is better in the zoo than at liberty, and that one breathes more easily in a cage than among Soviet people. Is it possible to sink to a lower political and moral level? And how could the Leningraders endure to publish in their journals such filth and nonsense?[10]

Zoshchenko's work, concluded Zhdanov, was "a vile obscenity." Unless he changed his ways, he could not remain a Soviet writer.

Zhdanov devoted even greater vituperation to Akhmatova, a most distinguished Russian poet. Her poetry's main themes were love and religion, which required her to remain mostly silent in the 1930s. She resumed publishing her lyric poems during and after the war in Leningrad journals. Declared Zhdanov brutally:

> [Her] subject matter is throughout individualist. The range of her poetry is pathetically limited. It is the poetry of a half-crazy gentlelady, who tosses back and forth between the bedroom and the chapel. . . . Half-nun and half-harlot, or rather both nun and harlot, her harlotry is mingled with prayer.[11]

This was no idle criticism, but rather a lethal vendetta.

These official denunciations were quickly translated into action. Both writers were expelled summarily from the All-Russian Union of Writers. Zoshchenko, a broken man, lived in poverty and loneliness until his death in 1958. Akhmatova, too, was forced to remain silent, living isolated and poor, sustained only by her great moral courage until she could publish again after Stalin's death.

Anticosmopolitanism and the Arts

The campaign against nonconformity, not limited to literature, also engulfed cinema and the arts. Numerous films and artistic works were pilloried as insufficiently ideological or too Western. To ensure clarity about the party's new policies, the Central Committee began issuing a weekly, *Culture and Life*. Its first issue announced:

> All forms and means of ideological and cultural activity of the party and the state— whether the press, propaganda and agitation, science, literature, art, the cinema, radio, museums, or any cultural and educational establishment—must be placed in the service of the Communist education of the masses.

Culture and Life castigated the "degenerate bourgeois culture of the West" and its followers in the USSR. A grave accusation against nonconformists was "cosmopolitanism," defined as servility to Western bourgeois culture. Part of this campaign was to glorify everything Soviet and emphasize Stalin's universal genius. *Culture and Life*, Zhdanov's speeches, and the growing Stalin cult spelled out in narrow limits what cultural workers must do. The results were disastrous. Soviet culture was reduced to a parody of itself. With everything in Soviet life idealized, the Soviet people were touted as the world's most advanced and progressive people with the most creative, original culture. The harsh facts of life in the postwar USSR were ignored. Any attempt to describe Soviet life realistically was branded a slander.

---

[10] Quoted in Brown, *Russian Literature*, pp. 226–27.
[11] Quoted in Brown, p. 227.

The anticosmopolitan campaign peaked after Zhdanov's mysterious death in 1948, but its roots lay in the immediate postwar period and were first elaborated in Zhdanov's 1946 speeches. "Cosmopolitan" became a synonym for unpatriotic and anti-Soviet. Everything in the West was condemned, and imitating Western models was considered toadyism, or servility before Western bourgeois culture. Any deviation from approved party policies could be labeled cosmopolitanism, the equivalent of treason. Writers ceased to write, wrote for the desk drawer, or produced party-approved drivel and then had to face themselves.

Music

The only branch of cultural activity to survive the deadly party directives was music, perhaps because the USSR boasted some of the world's most talented and famous composers: Prokofiev, Shostakovich, Aram Khachaturian, and N. Ia. Miaskovskii. Idolized by party and public alike as exemplars of Soviet creativity, they were awarded year after year every honor and prize the Soviet Union could bestow. There was also a group of remarkable performers: the violinist Oistrakh, the pianist Sviatoslav Rikhter, and the cellist Mstislav Rostropovich.

Direct and oppressive political intervention by the party began in 1936 against Shostakovich's opera, *Lady Macbeth of Mtsensk,* based on Nicholas Leskov's novella of 1865. An innovative and controversial work, Shostakovich's opera enjoyed a triumphal premiere in Leningrad in January 1934. During the next two years *Lady Macbeth* achieved unparalleled success for a new Soviet work, with more than 170 performances in Moscow and Leningrad. Soviet critics, while criticizing the opera's more lurid aspects, hailed it as reflecting "the general success of socialist construction, of the correct policy of the party." Such an opera, they gushed, "could have been written only by a Soviet composer brought up in the best traditions of Soviet culture." The youthful Shostakovich had "torn off the masks and exposed the false and

lying methods of the composers of bourgeois society." So poorly were the implications of socialist realism then understood, noted a Western critic, that *Lady Macbeth* was then accepted as its epitome.[12]

All went well for *Lady* and its composer until Stalin saw the opera. Having just heard and praised a patriotic piece for its realism and positive hero, Stalin, whose musical tastes were very conservative, found *Lady Macbeth* repulsive, raucous, and obscene. An unsigned and therefore authoritative article in *Pravda* on January 28, 1936, titled "Confusion Instead of Music," denounced the work as formalist and vulgar, a repudiation of operatic form:

> The listener is flabbergasted from the first moment of the opera by an intentionally ungainly, muddled flood of sounds. Snatches of melody, embryos of musical phrases, drown, escape and drown once more in crashing, gnashing, and screeching. Following this "music" is difficult, remembering it is impossible.[13]

A week later another *Pravda* article denounced Shostakovich's ballet on Soviet themes, *A Limpid Stream,* destroying his career as a ballet composer. With the Great Purge underway, the composer's friends climbed swiftly aboard the bandwagon of criticism. This was a clear warning to composers and other creative artists to conform to the dictates of socialist realism as interpreted by the party and by Stalin personally.

Then the storm subsided, allowing the chastened Shostakovich and other composers to resume writing, but they were more careful to avoid experimental forms of musical expression. During World War II Shostakovich and Prokofiev in particular were once more in vogue, rewarded generously for compositions such as the former's Symphony no. 7 (1942), the *Leningrad* Symphony, and the latter's opera *War and Peace,* based on

[12] Boris Schwarz, *Music and Musical Life in Soviet Russia* (Bloomington, IN, 1983) pp. 119*ff.*

[13] D. MacKenzie, "D. D. Shostakovich," in *MERSH* 35 (1983), pp. 33–34.

patriotic themes. Until the beginning of 1948 the Soviet musical world enjoyed a degree of artistic freedom and creative independence out of reach of the literary and artistic intelligentsia. Suddenly, in January 1948, Zhdanov announced that this adulation had been a terrible mistake, that these "great" composers were anti-Soviet hacks, unworthy to use the title "Soviet composer." How did this abrupt about-face occur?

A curious silence descended over the Soviet musical world beginning in December 1947, when some long-awaited premiere performances went practically unnoticed in the press and a number of secondary musical figures simply disappeared without mention. Then, in January 1948, Zhdanov presided over a turbulent meeting of composers and musicians. On February 10th the party Central Committee issued a resolution on music comparable to that on literature of 1946. This resolution on music viciously attacked long-honored and respected artists. The resolution announced:

> The state of affairs is particularly bad in the case of symphonic and operatic music. The Central Committee has here in mind those composers who persistently adhere to the formalist and anti-people school—a school which has found its fullest expression in the works of composers like Comrades Shostakovich, Prokofiev, Khachaturian, Shebalin, Popov, Miaskovskii, and others. Their works are marked by formalist perversions, anti-democratic tendencies which are alien to the Soviet people and their artistic tastes.[14]

The composers were further accused of creating music incomprehensible to the masses. "Disregarding the great social role of music, [these composers] are content to cater to the degenerate tastes of a handful of estheticizing individualists." The intent of the resolution was to drag serious music down to the level of "pop music."

> The divorce between some Soviet composers and the people is so serious that these com-

posers have been indulging in the rotten "theory" that the people are not sufficiently "grown up" to appreciate their music. They think it is no use worrying if people won't listen to their complicated orchestral works, for in a few hundred years they will. This is a thoroughly individualist and anti-people theory, and it has encouraged some of our composers to retire into their own shells.[15]

Thus music was not serving as a vehicle to reeducate the masses in the spirit of socialism! Give the people what they want, Zhdanov told the composers—simple ditties they could sing and hum while they merrily filled, or overfilled, their production quotas.

The impact of the decree on Soviet music was as disastrous as that of the 1946 decree on literature. Khachaturian and Prokofiev adapted themselves as best they could to the new party demands. Shostakovich publicly repented for past "errors," then went right on composing as he always had, making an occasional obeisance to the party authorities. Miaskovskii, already an elderly man whose career stretched back into prerevolutionary times, was destroyed by the resolution and died embittered and defeated in 1951. Prokofiev's work deteriorated in his last years, a change for which the resolution on music of 1948 was at least in part responsible.

These decrees on music and literature must be viewed as part of a general anti-intellectual policy designed to drag culture down to the level of the masses rather than lift the masses up to the level of a sophisticated, creative culture. The Zhdanov-shchina represented the triumph of the Stalinist bureaucratic mentality, which enjoyed kicking around those with genuine talent and ability. Zhdanov died in August 1948, but unfortunately his policies did not die with him. One of the supreme ironies of the postwar era was the renaming of the famous University of Leningrad (in 1991 renamed St. Petersburg University) to honor this man who had done so much to poison

---

[14] N. Slominsky, *Music since 1900*, 4th ed. (New York, 1971), pp. 684–88.

[15] Quoted in A. Werth, *Russia: The Postwar Years* (New York, 1971), pp. 356, 358.

the intellectual climate of the Soviet Union. It took the death of Stalin to unleash winds of change and usher in a more tolerant and creative atmosphere.

Suggested Additional Reading

LENINIST CULTURE, 1917–1929

ALEXANDROVNA, V. (pseud.). *A History of Soviet Literature,* trans. M. Ginsburg (Garden City, NY, 1963).

BARNES, A. *Boris Pasternak . . . ,* vol. 1 (New York, 1989).

BAROOSHIAN, V. D. *Russian Cubo-Futurism, 1910–1930* (The Hague, 1974).

BEREDAY, G. F., et al., eds. *The Changing Soviet School* (Boston, 1960).

BLOK, A. *The Twelve,* ed. A. Pyman (Durham, England, 1989).

BROWN, E. J. *Major Soviet Writers: Essays in Criticism* (London, 1973).

———. *Russian Literature Since the Revolution* (Cambridge, MA, 1982).

CHAPPLE, R. L. *Soviet Satire of the Twenties* (Gainesville, FL, 1980).

COMPTON, S. *Russian Avant-Garde Books, 1917–34* (Cambridge, MA, 1993).

ENTEEN, G. M. *The Soviet Scholar-Bureaucrat: M. N. Pokrovskii and the Society of Marxist Historians* (University Park, PA, 1978).

ERMOLAEV, H. *Soviet Literary Theories, 1917–1934* (New York, 1963, 1977).

FAUCHEREAU, S. *Moscow, 1900–1930* (New York, 1988).

FITZPATRICK, S. *The Commissariat of Enlightenment . . . 1917–1921* (Cambridge, 1970).

———. *The Cultural Front: Power and Culture in Revolutionary Russia* (Ithaca, NY, 1993).

GELDERN, J. VON. *Bolshevik Festivals, 1917–1920* (Berkeley, 1993).

GORKII, M. *On Literature* (Seattle, 1973).

GUERMAN, M. *Art of the October Revolution* (New York, 1979).

HINGLEY, R. *Nightingale Fever: Russian Poets in Revolution* (New York, 1981).

JANECEK, G. *The Look of Russian Literary Avant-Garde Visual Experiments, 1900–1930* (Princeton, 1984).

JOSEPHSON, P. R. *Physics and Politics in Revolutionary Russia.* (Berkeley, 1991).

KENEZ, P. *Cinema and Soviety Society, 1917–1953* (Cambridge, 1992).

KOPP, A. *Soviet Architecture and City Planning, 1917–1953* (New York, 1970).

LEACH, R. *Vsevolod Meyerhold* (Cambridge, 1989).

MAGUIRE, R. A. *Red Virgin Soil: Soviet Literature in the 1920s* (Princeton, 1968).

MOLLY, L. *Culture in the Future: The Proletkult Movement . . .* (Berkeley, 1990).

POGGOLI, R. *The Poets of Russia, 1890–1930* (Cambridge, MA, 1930).

ROMAN, G. H., and V. H. MARQUARDT. *The Avant-Garde Frontier: Russia Meets the West, 1910–1930* (Gainesville, FL, 1995).

RUSSIAN MUSEUM. *Soviet Art: 1920s–1930s* (Leningrad, 1988).

SIEGELBAUM, L. H. *Soviet State and Society Between Revolutions* (New York, 1992).

STANISLAVSKY, C. *My Life in Art,* trans. J. J. Robbins (London, 1967).

STRUVE, G. *Russian Literature Under Lenin and Stalin* (Norman, OK, 1971).

TROTSKY, L. *Literature and Revolution* (Ann Arbor, MI, 1960).

TSIVIAN, Y. *Early Cinema and Its Cultural Reception,* trans. A. Bodger (New York, 1994).

YOUNGBLOOD, D. J. *Movies for the Masses: Popular Cinema and Soviet Society in the 1920s* (New York, 1992).

STALINIST CULTURE, 1929–1953

AKHMATOVA, A. *The Complete Poems,* 2 vols., trans. J. Hemschemey (Somerville, MA, 1990).

BOFFA, G. *The Stalin Phenomenon,* trans. Nicholas Fersen (Ithaca, NY, 1992).

BORDWELL, D. *The Cinema of Eisenstein* (Cambridge, MA, 1993).

BOWLT, J. E., ed. and trans. *Russian Art of the Avant-Garde . . . , 1902–1934* (New York, 1976).

BOWRA, C. M. *Poetry and Politics, 1900–1960* (Cambridge, 1966).

BROWN, E. J. *The Proletarian Episode in Russian Literature, 1928–1932* (New York, 1953, 1971).

DUNHAM, V. *In Stalin's Time: Middle-Class Values in Soviet Fiction* (New York, 1976).

EHRLICH, V. *Modernism and Revolution: Russian Literature in Transition* (Cambridge, MA, 1994).

ERMOLAEV, H. *Mikhail Sholokhov and His Art* (Princeton, 1982).

FITZPATRICK, S. *Education and Social Mobility in the Soviet Union, 1921–1934* (New York, 1979).

FITZPATRICK, S., A. RABINOWITCH, and R. STITES, eds. *Russia in the Era of NEP: Explorations in Soviet Society and Culture* (Bloomington, IN, 1991).

GARRARD, J., and C. GARRARD. *Inside the Soviet Writers' Union* (New York, 1990).

GLEASON, A., et al., eds. *Bolshevik Culture: Experiment and Order in the Russian Revolution* (Bloomington, IN, 1985).

GRAHAM, L. *Science and Philosophy in the Soviet Union* (New York, 1970).

GÜNTHER, H., ed. *The Culture of the Stalin Period* (New York, 1990).

HAYWARD, M. *Writers in Russia: 1917–1978,* ed. Patricia Blake (San Diego, 1983).

HAYWARD, M., and L. LABEDZ, eds. *Literature and Revolution in Soviet Russia, 1917–1962* (New York, 1963).

HOLMGREN, B. *Women's Works in Stalin's Time: On Lidia Chukovskaia and Nadezhda Mandelstam* (Bloomington, IN, 1993).

JORAVSKY, D. *The Lysenko Affair* (Cambridge, MA, 1970).

KENEZ, P. *Cinema and Soviet Society, 1917–1953* (New York, 1992).

KREBS, S. D. *Soviet Composers and the Development of Soviet Music* (New York, 1970).

MARSH, R. *Images of Dictatorship: Portraits of Stalin in Literature* (London, 1989).

MATHEWSON, R. W. *The Positive Hero in Russian Literature* (Stanford, 1978).

MCDONALD, I. *The New Shostakovich* (Boston, 1990).

MEDVEDEV, Z. A. *The Rise and Fall of T. D. Lysenko,* trans. I. M. Lerner (Garden City, NY, 1971).

MILLER, F. J. *Folklore for Stalin: Russian Folklore and Pseudo-folklore of the Stalin Era* (Armonk, NY, 1990).

ROBIN, R. *Socialist Realism: The Impossible Aesthetic,* trans. Catherine Porter (Stanford, 1992).

ROSENBERG, W. G., ed. *Bolshevik Visions: First Phase of the Cultural Revolution in Soviet Russia,* 2 vols. (Ann Arbor, MI, 1989).

RUBENSTEIN, J. *Tangled Loyalties: The Life and Times of Ilya Ehrenburg* (New York, 1996).

SCHWARZ, B. *Music and Musical Life in Soviet Russia, 1917–1981* (Bloomington, IN, 1983).

SCHWEITZER, V. *Tsvetaeva.* trans. R. Chandler and H. T. Willetts (New York, 1992).

SICHER, E. *Jews in Russian Literature After the October Revolution* (Cambridge, 1995).

SLONIM, M. *Soviet Russian Literature . . . , 1917–1967* (New York, 1967).

STEWART, B. H. *Mikhail Sholokhov: A Critical Introduction* (Ann Arbor, MI, 1967).

STITES, R. *Russian Popular Culture: Entertainment and Society Since 1900* (New York, 1995).

———, ed. *Culture and Entertainment in Wartime Russia* (Bloomington, IN, 1995).

STRUVE, G. *Russian Literature Under Lenin and Stalin, 1917–1953* (Norman, OK, 1971).

TARKHANOV, A., and S. KAVTARADZE. *Architecture of the Stalin Era,* trans. by R. Whitby, J. Whitby, and J. Paver (New York, 1992).

TAYLOR, R., and I. CHRISTIE, eds. *Inside the Film Factory: New Approaches to Russian and Soviet Cinema* (New York, 1991).

TAYLOR, R., and D. SPRING, eds. *Stalinism and Soviet Cinema.* (New York, 1993).

VARSHAVSKY, S., and B. REST. *The Ordeal of the Hermitage: The Siege of Leningrad, 1941–1944* (Leningrad and New York, 1985).

WALSH, S. *The Music of Stravinsky* (New York, 1988).

YARMOLINSKY, A., ed. *A Treasury of Russian Verse* (New York, 1949).

37

Soviet Foreign Relations to 1941

After the Bolshevik Revolution, Soviet foreign policy comprised an intricate combination of national and ideological elements. Some Western historians, stressing the elements of continuity between tsarist Russian and Soviet policies, have argued that geography and historical experience determine a country's basic interests, regardless of political regime. Emphasizing such persistent aims as the desire for security, urge for access to the sea, manifest destiny in Asia, and leadership of the Slav peoples, they contend that Soviet policy was pragmatic and power oriented. Other foreign scholars (notably Western ex-Communists), at least until the 1960s, considered Marxism-Leninism paramount and a blueprint for world domination. Soviet leaders, they argued, sought by every means to create a world Communist system run from Moscow and regarded relations with the capitalist world as a protracted conflict that would last until one side triumphed. Believing that all Soviet moves aimed to promote world revolution, this group concluded it was fruitless, even harmful, for the West to make agreements with the USSR. A middle view interpreted Soviet foreign policy as combining tradi-

tional and ideological elements: Revolutionary beliefs and ideology predominated at first, then pragmatic nationalism increased as Soviet leaders gradually reverted to more conservative policies based on power, geography, and history.

An important ideological foundation for Soviet foreign policy was provided by Lenin's pamphlet *Imperialism, the Highest Stage of Capitalism* (1916), which long remained established doctrine in Soviet Russia. Written in Swiss exile in the midst of World War I, it updated and globalized Marxism despite being singularly unoriginal. (It was based chiefly on works of two European socialists, J. A. Hobson and Rudolf Hilferding.) The pamphlet revealed Lenin's thinking about the capitalist world, positing an inevitable and protracted conflict between it and Soviet socialism. Lenin defined imperialism as finance or monopoly capitalism, controlled by bankers, that had developed from the earlier industrial capitalism of Marx's time:

> Imperialism is capitalism in that stage of development in which the domination of monopoly and finance capital has taken shape; in which the export of capital has acquired

pronounced importance; in which the division of the world by international trusts has begun, and in which the partition of all the territory of the earth by the greatest capitalist countries has been completed.

A relentless search for raw materials, markets, and investment opportunities had provoked quarrels among leading capitalist countries, ending in World War I. That war, Lenin predicted, would bring capitalism crashing down, breaking first like a chain at its weakest link, perhaps in Russia. Eventually imperialism would succumb to its internal contradictions—among imperialist powers and power blocs, and between individual imperialist countries and their rebellious overseas colonies. The final outcome, gloated Lenin, could only be worldwide socialist revolution and the demise of capitalism.

What were the major aims of Soviet foreign policy until 1941? At first Lenin and Trotskii strove to foment revolution abroad because they believed that otherwise world capitalism would crush Soviet Russia. War-weary Europe, especially Germany, seemed ripe for revolution, and Comintern leaders long remained confident that one would occur. A second, apparently conflicting aim soon emerged and became paramount: to preserve the Soviet regime and power base, if need be at the expense of foreign Communists. Moscow, therefore, sought to divide capitalist powers, prevent anti-Soviet coalitions, and woo colonial peoples. As long as their military weakness persisted, Soviet leaders aimed to avoid war with major capitalist powers.

To achieve these goals Soviet leaders forged a variety of instruments. The Comintern and Soviet party coordinated the Communist parties that developed in most foreign countries. Because until 1945 the USSR was the only Communist power, most foreign Communists looked to Moscow for inspiration and direction. Especially under Stalin, Communist parties abroad became subservient to Soviet policy. Each had a legal organization, which propagated Soviet views in democratic countries, was represented in legislatures, led labor unions,

and criticized anti-Soviet cabinets. Illegal underground bodies, operating if the open ones were suppressed, conducted subversion and sabotage. Soviet commercial missions and skillful radio and newspaper propaganda supplemented the work of these parties.

The Soviet regime instituted a new diplomacy. As commissar of foreign affairs, Trotskii believed initially that diplomacy would soon disappear because world revolution was supposedly imminent. He declared confidently: "We'll issue a few decrees, then shut up shop." At Brest-Litovsk he had repudiated the norms and even the dress of old, secret European diplomacy, but once the revolutionary wave subsided, Soviet diplomacy became important and its diplomats donned traditional formal dress. Moscow, however, scorned permanent accommodation with other nations, and Soviet diplomacy prepared the way for future expansion by lulling capitalist countries into false security, winning temporary concessions, and splitting the capitalist camp. Whereas under Lenin diplomacy remained innovative and flexible, Stalin bound his diplomats with rigid, detailed instructions.

The Soviets before 1941 made little use of force —the ultimate sanction in foreign policy— because of military weakness. During the Polish-Soviet War of 1919–1920, they attempted unsuccessfully to spread revolution on Red Army bayonets, but only in 1939–1940 was force used effectively against weaker Finland and the Baltic states.

In matters of foreign policy, Lenin's voice proved decisive. In the first months of the regime, policies were debated freely in the Central Committee and Politburo, and sometimes he was outvoted. Then the Politburo, under Lenin's direction, became the chief policymaking body in foreign affairs, and its decisions were transmitted to the People's Commissariat of Foreign Affairs (Narkomindel) for implementation. Lenin formulated foreign policy and built up the Soviet diplomatic service; the foreign commissar had no more independence than a tsarist foreign minister. Noted

Foreign Commissar Georgi Chicherin right after Lenin's death:

> In the first years of the existence of our republic, I spoke with him by telephone several times a day, often at length, and had frequent, personal interviews with him. Often I discussed with him all the details of current diplomatic affairs of any importance. Instantly grasping the substance of each issue . . . , Vladimir Ilich [Lenin] always provided in his conversations the most brilliant analysis of our diplomatic situation and his counsels . . . were models of diplomatic art and flexibility.[1]

The autocratic tsarist tradition in foreign affairs was restored fully by Stalin. Let us now examine Soviet policies chronologically. Each of the five periods between 1917 and 1941 reflected a different approach toward the antagonist—the capitalist world.

First Revolutionary Era, 1917–1921

For the new Soviet government, a first priority was to redeem Bolshevik pledges to take Russia out of World War I. That war, which Lenin had long proclaimed to be an imperialist struggle, had undermined both the tsarist regime and its successor, the Provisional Government. Lenin's "Decree on Peace," approved on November 7, 1917, by the Second All-Russian Congress of Soviets, had been foreshadowed by his fourth "Letter from Afar" in March, in which he had stated that the Petrograd Soviet should repudiate treaties concluded by previous Russian governments. The Decree on Peace proposed to all warring peoples and their governments "to begin immediately negotiations for a just and lasting peace . . . without annexations . . . and indemnities." It continued: "The [Soviet] government abolishes secret diplomacy and . . . expresses the firm intention to carry on all negotiations absolutely openly before all the people and immediately begins to publish

in full the secret treaties concluded or confirmed by [previous Russian governments]."[2] Following this declaration was President Wilson's "Fourteen Points" (January 1918), which resembled it closely in phraseology. Lenin urged all belligerents to conclude an immediate armistice, during which their representatives could negotiate a permanent and nonimperialistic peace settlement. One purpose of his Decree was to provoke general peace negotiations so that a weak Soviet Russia need not face the Central Powers alone. Bolshevik leaders may have believed also that the appeal would touch off revolutions throughout Europe.

The allied powers ignored Lenin's appeal and his Soviet regime, but the German imperial government responded eagerly to his call for an armistice. Disregarding Lenin's demagogic appeal to German workers, the Berlin government and high command saw great potential strategic and psychological advantages from concluding a separate peace with Soviet Russia. By liquidating the eastern front, Germany could shift millions of troops westward and perhaps deliver a knockout blow in France to Allied armies before American troops could arrive in great force.

Leon Trotskii, after firing diplomats of the Provisional Government, had taken charge of the new People's Commissariat of Foreign Affairs (Narkomindel). Believing world revolution to be imminent, and traditional European secret diplomacy outmoded, Trotskii directed the new agency haphazardly with inexperienced personnel until replaced in March 1918 by Georgi Chicherin, who restored order and improved efficiency.

Peace negotiations between Soviet Russia and the Central Powers dragged on with interruptions from late December 1917 until March 1918 at Brest-Litovsk, German headquarters for the eastern front. The Soviet delegation, soon headed by Trotskii himself, proposed a peace without annexations and delivered inflammatory revolutionary appeals over the heads of the German delegates to the war-weary peoples of Europe. General Max

---

[1] *Izvestiia,* January 30, 1924, p. 2.

[2] A. Rubinstein, *The Foreign Policy of the Soviet Union* (New York, 1972), pp. 51–52.

von Hoffman of Germany, however, aiming to erect satellite states in western Russia, insisted that all German-occupied areas be separated from Russia. To obtain Ukrainian resources, the Germans reached agreement with the anti-Bolshevik Rada (February 9th) and detached all of Ukraine from Russia. These stiff German territorial demands caused Trotskii to suspend negotiations in January and return to Petrograd.

The Bolshevik Central Committee now held its first great debate over foreign policy. Left Bolsheviks and Left SRs urged a revolutionary war to promote the triumph of world revolution. Lenin argued that preservation of revolution in Russia must take precedence over the uncertain prospects of world revolution and over the interests of the international proletariat. He demanded an immediate end to the war: "For the success of socialism in Russia, . . . not less than several months will be necessary . . . to vanquish the bourgeoisie in our own country." The Central Committee approved Trotskii's compromise formula of "no war, no peace"; that is, Russia would neither fight nor sign a treaty with Imperial Germany.

The Germans responded with a swift offensive toward Petrograd. As they advanced, the alarmed Bolshevik leaders, including Lenin, favored seeking aid from the Allies. Despite efforts in this direction by unofficial Allied agents in Russia, Allied governments ignored these overtures. With the Germans approaching Petrograd, Lenin finally convinced the majority of the Central Committee to accept new, harsher German peace terms.

In the summer of 1918 the Allies intervened militarily in Russia's civil war (see Chapter 32). According to Soviet historians, they sought to overthrow Bolshevism, set up spheres of interest, and exploit Russia's resources. Claimed *Pravda* in September 1957:

> The organizer and inspirer of armed struggle against the Soviet Republic was international imperialism . . . [which] saw in the victory of the socialist revolution a threat to its own parasitical existence, to its profits and capital.

To throttle the young Soviet republic, the imperialists, led by the leading circles of England, the USA, and France, organized military campaigns against our country.

But George Kennan, a leading American diplomat, asserted that the Allies had aimed to restore an eastern front, win the war, and keep their supplies out of German hands. British and French military leaders pushed for intervention, but President Wilson sent token U.S. forces most reluctantly. Allied troops did little fighting in Russia, but the Allies equipped and supplied Russian White forces long after World War I ended. Proponents (Churchill) argued that Allied intervention prolonged White resistance and stalled world revolution; recent opponents (Kennan) claim that it helped alienate Soviet Russia from the West. Allied intervention produced international stalemate because neither Soviet Russia nor the West could destroy the other; this situation suggested that outside powers cannot decide a civil war in a major country.

Allied hostility fed the extreme Soviet policies of those years. As German revolutionary socialists (Spartacists) fought for power in Berlin, Lenin, in January 1919, invited leftist European socialists to the First Comintern Congress. Of 35 delegates who attended, only 5 came from abroad, and even they did not truly represent their parties. Russian-dominated from the start, the Comintern, or Third International, gave Lenin a nucleus for a world Communist movement, though it was too feeble then to organize revolutions abroad. During the Second Comintern Congress of August 1920, as the Red Army advanced in Poland, delegates from 41 countries waxed optimistic over prospects for world revolution, until Soviet defeat before Warsaw dashed their hopes. Twenty-one conditions for admission, which sought to impose the Russian party's tight discipline, were approved, but for some years the Comintern remained a loose collection of parties with factions and heated debates. By 1924, when it became a disciplined tool of Soviet policy, revolutionary opportunities abroad had dwindled.

The Allies excluded war-torn Soviet Russia from the Paris Peace Conference of 1919. Soviet-Western ideological and military antagonisms were at their peak, and in the West people were searching for Communists under every bed. Before the Conference, Prime Minister David Lloyd George of Great Britain wrote:

> Personally, I would have dealt with the Soviets as the de facto government of Russia. So would President Wilson. But we both agreed that we could not carry to that extent our colleagues at the Congress nor the public opinion of our countries which was frightened by Bolshevik violence and feared its spread.[3]

Preoccupied with Germany, the Allies neglected Soviet Russia and its relationship with Europe. (See Map 37.1.) This rebuff fed Bolshevik hostility to the peace settlement and the League of Nations, which the Soviets regarded as a potential capitalist coalition against them, and drew the two outcasts—Weimar Germany and Soviet Russia—together.

In 1919 halfhearted private Allied overtures to Soviet Russia failed, but during 1920 relations began to improve. Once the Allies withdrew from Russia and the White armies were defeated, the Bolsheviks sought Western aid to restore Russia's wrecked economy. Lloyd George, favoring recognition of Soviet Russia and restoration of normal economic ties, helped end the Allied blockade. "We have failed to restore Russia to sanity by force. I believe we can save her by trade," he told Parliament. The Polish-Soviet War delayed normal relations, but by early 1921 Red Army defeats in Poland and Western desires to win Russian markets laid a basis for accommodation.

Accommodation, 1921–1927

Lenin warned Moscow leftists late in 1920 that an era of coexistence with capitalism was dawning.

European capitalist economies were reviving, and even the intransigent Trotskii admitted, "History has given the bourgeoisie a fairly long breathing spell. . . . The revolution is not so obedient, so tame that it can be led on a leash as we imagined."[4] The Polish conflict, ended by the Treaty of Riga (March 1921), left Soviet Russia weakened. Ukraine proper became a Soviet republic, but Poland acquired parts of Belorussia and western Ukraine. After seven years of strife, Russia's economy faced collapse. Lenin, confronting peasant uprisings and the Kronstadt revolt, launched the New Economic Policy at home and a conciliatory policy toward the West.

To strengthen itself for subsequent conflict, Soviet Russia now sought diplomatic recognition, trade, and credits from the West. Recognition would provide some security against attack and aid Soviet efforts to divide capitalist countries and win trade concessions. The West reacted favorably because European industries needed export markets and their governments, never truly committed to overthrowing the Soviet regime, longed for normal relations. Obstacles to settlement included Comintern propaganda in the West and its colonies and, in particular, Russian debts. Western claims, totaling about 14 billion rubles (roughly 7 billion dollars), included pre–World War I tsarist debts, wartime borrowing, and compensation for nationalized European property; the Soviets made huge counterclaims for damage done by Allied intervention. The West agreed that wartime debts and Allied damage to Russia nearly canceled each other out, but the French especially sought repayment of the prewar debt, most of which they held, and reimbursement for confiscated property. When Russia demurred, debt negotiations broke down; but the Soviets, making token concessions on propaganda, obtained some short-term credits, trade agreements, and diplomatic recognition from all major powers except the United States. Even this refusal of recognition did not prevent

---

[3] Quoted in George Kennan, *Russia and the West Under Lenin and Stalin* (Boston, 1960), p. 124.

[4] Quoted in Kennan, *Russia and the West,* p. 179.

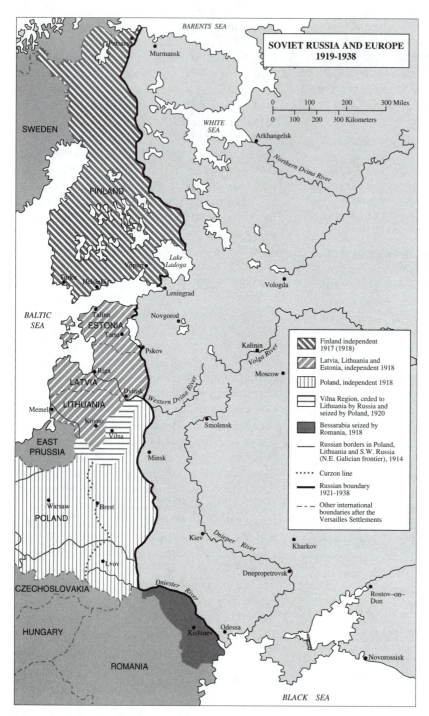

Map 37.1 Soviet Russia and Europe, 1919–1938

extensive U.S. technological assistance and some Soviet-American trade during the 1920s.

The shift to accommodation enhanced the role of Soviet diplomacy directed by an able professional, Georgi Chicherin (foreign commissar, 1918–1930). An ex-Menshevik of noble birth who had once worked for the tsarist foreign ministry, Chicherin was an idealistic socialist, dedicated, scholarly, and hardworking. However, with his dubious past (from a Bolshevik standpoint), he never achieved high rank or influence in the Soviet Communist Party. Abroad, he had to contend with the Comintern, Profintern (international trade union organization), secret police, and foreign trade and tourist agencies. Furthermore, the Narkomindel lacked even the degree of authority enjoyed by the tsarist foreign office. After 1919 formulation and decision making in both foreign and domestic affairs were concentrated in the Politburo of the Russian Communist Party, rather than the Party Congress or Central Committee. During Lenin's illnesses of 1922–1923, the Politburo decided foreign policy issues collectively, then transmitted its decisions to Chicherin for implementation. However, when healthy, Lenin formulated basic theoretical and practical concepts of foreign policy himself and devoted much attention to organizing the new Soviet diplomatic service. His fertile political imagination and tactical skill made him preeminent in determining the general outlines of early Soviet foreign policy. With Lenin acting basically as his own foreign minister, Chicherin's position resembled that of Foreign Minister Gorchakov in the 1860s—executing policies already determined by the head of state. The Politburo frequently bypassed the Narkomindel, the rival Comintern did not keep it informed, and the government, affirming that the Comintern was an independent agency, disclaimed responsibility for its moves. Nonetheless, Chicherin achieved real gains by persistent diplomacy.

The Genoa Conference (April 1922) marked his, and Soviet Russia's, diplomatic debut. In western Europe, Genoa was conceived as an international effort to restore Europe's depressed economy by drawing in both of its pariahs—

Weimar Germany and Soviet Russia. At the opening session of the Conference, Chicherin declared:

> While maintaining . . . their communist principles . . . , the Russian delegation recognize that in the present period of history, which permits the parallel existence of the old social order and of the new [socialist] order now being born, economic collaboration between the states representing these two systems of property is imperatively necessary for the general economic reconstruction.[5]

To the West, Chicherin held out alluring prospects of extensive trade with Soviet Russia and lucrative investment in nascent Siberian industries, coupling this with a proposal for general disarmament. However, his main objective remained to separate Weimar Germany from the victor powers and reach a diplomatic accord with it.

Chicherin achieved this objective brilliantly at Rapallo, Italy. Exploiting Western coolness and snubs toward the Germans at Genoa, he induced Weimar delegates to meet with him at nearby Rapallo. To the consternation of the British and French, Germany and Soviet Russia promptly concluded the Treaty of Rapallo involving mutual diplomatic recognition, cancellation of debts and claims, and agreements to expand and normalize trade. Although Western liberals viewed Rapallo as a sinister Soviet-German conspiracy, the Germans regarded it as inaugurating for them an independent foreign policy and escape from the consequences of defeat in World War I. The Soviets considered Rapallo a model agreement with a bourgeois state, leaving them full freedom of action. They interpreted it as splitting European capitalism and enabling them to reach useful accords with the weaker segment. Rapallo, Moscow concluded, scotched dangers of European economic action against Soviet Russia and brought it out of diplomatic and economic isolation. Simultaneously, clandestine military cooperation was taking shape: The Germans were constructing arms factories in Soviet Russia and

---

[5] Jane Degras, ed., *Soviet Documents on Foreign Policy* (New York, 1951–1953, 1983), vol. 1, p. 298.

trying out new weapons, including tanks, prohibited to them by the Treaty of Versailles. (The Soviets had a share of the weapon production.) During the severe crisis that confronted Weimar Germany during 1923, policy differences surfaced between Narkomindel and the Comintern. While Chicherin supported the Weimar government and Soviet Russia shipped grain to Germany, the Comintern backed efforts by the German Communist Party to overthrow it. The Comintern suffered a grave reversal as evidence mounted that prospects for a Communist revolution in Germany were all but dead. Continuing rivalry between Narkomindel and Comintern, however, reflected merely differing tactics, not a conflict of basic aims.

Chicherin's policy of normalizing relations with the rest of Europe, though generally successful, also suffered setbacks. During Anglo-Soviet negotiations for trade and credits erupted the "Zinoviev Letter" (October 1924), whose authenticity remains disputed. Supposedly containing instructions from the Comintern president to British Communists to subvert the armed forces, the letter caused a furor, provoking a "Red scare" in Great Britain, contributing to the downfall of the Labor government, and severely straining Anglo-Soviet relations. Another diplomatic reverse followed: The Locarno Agreements of 1925 between Germany and the former Allied powers excluded the USSR completely and achieved a brief era of apparent European unity and harmony. Despite such reverses, Chicherin's diplomacy, by ending Soviet isolation and reaching accord with Weimar Germany, enhanced Soviet security and contributed to its economic recovery. Only a year after Locarno the Soviet-German Treaty of Berlin (April 1926), reaffirming the provisions of Rapallo, stipulated neutrality if either country were attacked by a third power.

However, Soviet hostility toward the League of Nations persisted. From its inception the League had been viewed in Moscow as a concealed capitalist coalition against Soviet Russia. Soviet hostility resulted partly from the latter's exclusion from the Paris Peace Conference of 1919 and partly because the League was dominated in the inter-

war period by leading capitalist powers, Great Britain and France. Furthermore, international stability and prosperity, fostered by the League, would reduce Communist prospects for world revolution. A Soviet press statement on the League of Nations declared in November 1925:

> We regard the League of Nations . . . not as a friendly association of peoples working for the general good, but as a masked league of the so-called Great Powers, who have appropriated to themselves the right of disposing of the fate of weaker nations. . . . Certain Powers are counting on using Germany to assist in carrying out . . . their hostile designs against the USSR. . . . The League is a cover for the preparation of military action for the suppression of small and weak nationalities.[6]

Not until 1934 would the Soviets alter their hostility toward the League.

Asia had remained secondary in Soviet policy. Lenin recognized the revolutionary potential of colonial peoples in undermining Western imperialism, but Soviet Russia was too weak to exploit it. Soviet Russia promptly repudiated tsarist imperial privileges and spheres of interest, most of which it could not retain anyway. To weaken Franco-British influence in the Near East and enhance Soviet security, Lenin supported such nationalists as Kemal Pasha of Turkey. The Soviets appealed to colonial peoples, notably at the Comintern-sponsored Baku Congress of September 1920. Zinoviev told delegates from 37 nationalities: "The Communist International turns today to the peoples of the East and says to them: 'Brothers, we summon you to a Holy War first of all against British Imperialism.'"[7] This was purely a propaganda campaign, but later many Asian revolutionaries were trained in the USSR, with profound consequences for the West.

Justifiably, Soviet leaders regarded China as the key to Asia. They promptly condemned European imperialism there and renounced most special

---

[6] Degras, *Soviet Documents*, vol. 2, pp. 65–66.
[7] Quoted in Louis Fischer, *The Soviets in World Affairs, 1917–1929* (Princeton, 1951), vol. 1, p. 283.

Russian privileges, though in 1921 the Red Army entered Outer Mongolia, ostensibly pursuing White generals, and established a Communist puppet government. Mongolia served until 1991 as a buffer and Russian base on China's frontier. During the early 1920s Moscow maintained formal relations with the weak Beijing government while Soviet agents, led by Mikhail Borodin, penetrated the Canton regime. Its leader, Sun Yat-sen, who had led the Chinese Revolution of 1912, aimed to expel foreign imperialism and to achieve national unity and social reform. With Borodin's aid, he built the Kuomintang (Nationalist Party) on the model of the Soviet Communist Party. Sun's death in 1925 left a vacuum in Canton soon filled by Chiang Kai-shek, a young Moscow-trained nationalist officer. The Stalin-Trotskii struggle affected Soviet policy: Convinced that China was entering her bourgeois-democratic revolution, Stalin favored proletarian participation in a national bloc including peasants and bourgeoisie and urged the Communists to enter the Kuomintang. Trotskii, however, advocated an armed Communist uprising and a direct transition to socialism in China. Stalin's policy prevailed, but during his northward expedition in 1926, Chiang slaughtered Communists in Shanghai, expelled Soviet advisers, and soon ruled much of China. Stalin's policies there, based on inadequate knowledge of the situation, had plainly failed.

Neoisolationism, 1928–1933

Stalin's ascendancy brought a return to autocracy in Soviet domestic and foreign policies and produced a docile and subservient Comintern. Removing potential and actual rivals from positions of power and influence at home and launching forced collectivization and massive industrialization, Stalin abroad raised as a smokescreen the danger of imminent attacks on the USSR by powerful capitalist states. Envious and distrustful of cosmopolitan, intellectual Old Bolsheviks such as Zinoviev and Bukharin, he acted to undermine their influence and sever ties with European

socialism. In these years occurred a marked growth of deliberate isolation from European affairs.

In his report to the 15th Party Congress (December 1927), Stalin intimated that a major shift in Soviet foreign policy was imminent and raised the specter of renewed capitalist assaults against the USSR:

> Whereas a year or two ago it was possible and necessary to speak of . . . "peaceful coexistence" between the USSR and the capitalist countries, today . . . *the period of "peaceful coexistence" is receding into the past,* giving place to a period of imperialist assaults and preparation for intervention against the USSR.[8]

Soon afterward Stalin accused France, which he considered the dominant European power, of making preparations to attack the Soviet Union, which he surely did not believe and for which there was not a shred of evidence. The Sixth Comintern Congress of September 1928, an obedient Stalinist body, proclaimed the USSR to be the sole bastion of world revolution and stressed that all Communist parties owed exclusive allegiance to Moscow; their local interests must be subordinated to preserving the USSR.

While accusing Western capitalist nations of plotting war, Stalin emphasized that Soviet foreign policy sought consistently to preserve peace. At the 16th Congress of June 1930 he affirmed:

> As a result of this policy of negotiating trade and non-aggression pacts . . . we have succeeded in maintaining peace . . . in spite of a number of provocative acts . . . of the warmongers. We will continue to pursue this policy of peace with all our might. . . . We do not want a single foot of foreign territory, but we will not surrender a single inch of our territory to anyone.[9]

Indeed, despite Stalin's intransigent and frequently alarmist tone, Soviet foreign policy in

---

[8] Joseph Stalin, *Works* (Moscow, 1955), vol. 10, pp. 282*ff.*
[9] Stalin, *Works,* vol. 12, pp. 268–69.

these years remained cautious and pacific, avoiding confrontations with capitalist powers. Stalin appears to have counted on the preservation of world peace during the First Five Year Plan and continued to sound this theme until 1939.

The Great Depression (1929–1933) convinced Moscow of the correctness of its policy line against Western democratic socialists. Predicting the imminent demise of world capitalism, Soviet leaders concluded that this would leave Social Democrats as the only important remaining barrier throughout the world to the conquest of power by the working class led by the Communists. Declared Politburo member V. M. Molotov: "Social fascism with its 'left' wing is the last resource of the bourgeoisie among the workers."

Stalin's theory of "social fascism," which claimed that Western socialists had adopted fascist policies, helped undermine democracy in Weimar Germany and bring Adolf Hitler to power. Stalin detested the democratic, pro-Western policies of the German Social Democrats (SPD), but he also distrusted the large and volatile German Communist Party (KPD) and doubted he could control it if it achieved power. Thus, Stalin, playing Communists against Social Democrats, ordered the KPD to collaborate with the Nazis against a Weimar Republic undermined by the Depression. Believing that the capitalists were already in power in Germany and that the Nazis were likewise bourgeois, Stalin concluded that Hitler in power, rather than launch a revolution against capitalism, would crush moderate socialism and cause Germany's defection from the Western camp and its dependence on the USSR. To desperate pleas by German Social Democrats for Communist aid against the Nazis, the reply of the Soviet embassy was: The road to a Soviet Germany lies through Hitler. Thus Stalin bears considerable responsibility for the triumph of Nazism in Germany, which later would prove so costly to the USSR. Even after Hitler assumed power (January 1933), Stalin persisted in regarding France as the chief Soviet foe, apparently out of ignorance about German conditions and excessive faith in Leninism.

In the Far East, Stalin pursued a cautious, defensive course. In 1928 he severed relations with Chiang's nationalist regime, and the next year, after local authorities seized the Chinese Eastern Railway, the Red Army restored it to Soviet control. Once Japan seized Manchuria in 1931 and turned it into the puppet state of Manchukuo, Stalin became gravely concerned about Japanese militarism. Reinforcing the Red Army in the Far East, he sought agreement with Japan, even offering to sell it the Chinese Eastern Railway. He restored relations with Chiang, tried to prevent Sino-Japanese cooperation against the USSR, and sought rapprochement with the United States.

Meanwhile the USSR was advocating peace and disarmament for Europe. Maxim Litvinov, Chicherin's longtime assistant who succeeded him as foreign commissar in 1930, proposed total disarmament at the Geneva Disarmament Conference of 1932 but found little response. In January 1933 Hitler assumed power in Germany and influenced Stalin to alter his foreign policy. Deep in the Depression, the West no longer threatened the USSR, but the chief beneficiaries were not Communism but aggressive German Nazism and Japanese militarism.

Collective Security, 1934–1937

Worried by the rising Nazi threat, Stalin gradually abandoned isolationism and opposition to the Versailles system to seek reconciliation with the West. During 1932 the Soviets had normalized relations with such neighbors as Finland, Estonia, and Poland, then with France. In 1934 Soviet diplomacy tried to erect an east European alliance to protect its western borders, but Poland demurred. Meanwhile, diplomatic relations were established with the United States. Soviet leaders, admiring American enterprise and efficiency, had long desired recognition from the United States, but conservative Republican presidents, Communist propaganda, and unpaid Russian debts had blocked it. Invited to Washington by President Franklin Roosevelt, Litvinov provided assurances on propaganda and legal protection for Americans

SOVFOTO

Maxim M. Litvinov (1876–1951) as Soviet ambassador to the United States (1941–1943) in his Washington, D.C., office with Lenin looking over his shoulder. As commissar of foreign affairs (1930–1939), Litvinov was associated with a policy of collective security against Hitler.

in the USSR. In November 1933 the United States recognized the USSR, and William Bullitt, who had led an unofficial mission to Russia in 1919, became the first American ambassador there. Receiving him warmly and ignoring strong American isolationism, Stalin mistakenly expected the United States to block Japanese penetration of China.

By 1934, after the Polish-German pact, Stalin realized that Nazism represented a real danger to the USSR. Though holding out an olive branch to Hitler, he noted that "revanchist and imperialist sentiments in Germany" were growing. Hitler's nonaggression pact with Poland roused Soviet fears that he might encourage the Poles to seize Ukraine. Growing concern over Germany accelerated a Soviet shift toward the Western democracies.

In September 1934 the USSR finally joined the League of Nations and abandoned its hostility to the Paris peace settlement. Litvinov, a Jew, an anti-Nazi, and a pro-Westerner, became a convincing spokesman for Soviet cooperation with the West. He used the League of Nations to proclaim a Soviet policy of peace, disarmament, and collective security against aggression. Contrary to assumptions in the West, Litvinov never made policy but merely executed Stalin's orders. His sincere belief in the new line won the confidence of Western liberals and socialists, but the League's failure to halt Italy in Ethiopia in 1935 revealed once again its weakness as a peacekeeping instrument.

Stalin also sought security through mutual defense pacts. In May 1935 France and the USSR, driven together again by fear of Germany, concluded a mutual assistance pact, but it lacked the military teeth of the old Franco-Russian alliance; politically divided France took almost a year to ratify even a watered-down version. The USSR pledged to aid Czechoslovakia militarily against a German attack if the French did so first, as Stalin insured cautiously against being drawn into war with Germany while the West watched.

The Comintern obediently adopted a new Popular Front policy. Its Seventh (and last) Congress of July–August 1935 announced that all "progressive forces" (workers, peasants, petty bourgeoisie, and intelligentsia) should cooperate against fascism, the most dangerous form of capitalist imperialism. Communists were instructed to work with socialists and liberals while retaining their identity within the Popular Front.

Failures of collective security in 1936 caused growing Soviet disillusionment. In March Nazi troops marched into the Rhineland in clear violation of the Versailles and Locarno treaties, using French ratification of the pact with the USSR as justification. Disregarding feeble French and British protests, the Germans refortified the Rhineland. This action shattered the collective security approach and, by weakening the French position, undermined the Franco-Soviet pact, shifting the balance of power to Germany. Stalin realized that he could not count on the West to resist Nazi aggression, which was now likely to turn eastward. Soon Stalin began the Great Purge, eliminating rivals in case he later had to deal with Hitler. The West's apathy toward the Spanish Civil War, beginning in July, reinforced Stalin's suspicions. While Germany and Italy supported General Francisco Franco's fascist revolt against the Spanish Republic, the West proclaimed nonintervention. The USSR, explaining that it was aiding the Popular Front against fascism, provided important military aid to the Republic, saved Madrid from early capture, and greatly prolonged the conflict. Stalin may have hoped to draw the West into the war or thought that lengthy fascist involvement in Spain would delay a move against the USSR. However, during 1937 he withdrew most military aid from Spain and purged Russian Communists associated with it as Trotskyites. Soviet efforts to cooperate with the West against Hitler before World War II virtually ended.

The Nazi-Soviet Pact, 1939–1941

The formation of the Axis (Germany and Italy) in October 1936 and its conclusion of the Anti-Comintern Pact with Japan in November apparently deepened antagonism between communism and fascism, but Stalin was already abandoning collective security. For him 1937 was a year of watchful waiting abroad and relentless purging at home. Litvinov covered his retreat by continuing to advocate collective resistance to fascism.

Nazi gains during 1938 demolished the remnants of collective security and alienated the USSR from the appeasement-minded West. Hitler's annexation of Austria drew only ineffectual Western protests, and Stalin doubtless concluded that the West would not fight Hitler to save eastern Europe. Litvinov warned repeatedly that time was running out if the West wanted Soviet cooperation against fascism. Collective security's last gasp was the May Crisis between Germany and Czechoslovakia: The Czechs mobilized, the West and the USSR pledged aid if Czechoslovakia were attacked, and Hitler backed down. But at the Munich Conference in October, with the USSR excluded, France and Great Britain surrendered

the Czech Sudetenland to Hitler and made Czechoslovakia indefensible. Western appeasement and Stalin's purge of the Red Army, which weakened the USSR, had destroyed collective security.

Tension with Japan stimulated Stalin's desire to settle with Hitler. He had tried to appease Japan by selling it the Chinese Eastern Railway in 1935. The outbreak of the Sino-Japanese War in 1937 temporarily relaxed pressure on the USSR. Stalin signed a friendship treaty with China and supplied Chiang with arms and credits. When the Japanese army probed the Soviet border in major attacks at Changkufeng (July 1938) and Nomonhan (May 1939), it was repulsed with heavy losses, apparently convincing Tokyo that expansion into Siberia would be too costly.

By 1938 Stalin had eliminated all opposition and could dictate to the Politburo. "Stalin thought that now he could decide all things alone and that all he needed were statisticians," recalled N. S. Khrushchev. "He treated all others in such a way that they could only listen to and praise him."[10] In May 1939 V. M. Molotov, Stalin's loyal secretary, replaced Litvinov as foreign commissar, suggesting that Stalin was preparing a major move in foreign policy. Molotov imposed rigid conformity upon the hitherto flexible and cosmopolitan Narkomindel, as Stalin sought to reverse the Brest-Litovsk Treaty of 1918 and obtain a recognized sphere of influence in eastern Europe.

During early 1939 the West and the Nazis vied for Soviet support. In March Hitler's occupation of the rest of Czechoslovakia finally ended Western appeasement. France and Great Britain belatedly guaranteed the integrity of Poland and Romania but failed to convince Stalin that they would really fight Hitler. In a speech to the 18th Party Congress in March Stalin, accusing the West of trying to provoke a Soviet-German conflict, warned that the USSR would not be drawn into a war "to pull somebody else's chestnuts out of the fire." In August the West finally sent military missions to

---

[10] *Khrushchev Remembers* (Boston, 1970), pp. 297, 299.

UPI/Corbis-Bettmann

Foreign Commissar Viacheslav M. Molotov (1890–1986) signing Nazi-Soviet Pact in August 1939. He served as foreign commissar and foreign minister 1939–1949 and 1953–1957. Standing left to right: German Foreign Minister Joachim von Ribbentrop, Stalin, and V. Pavlov.

Russia, but it had moved too slowly and indecisively. Hitler, having decided to attack Poland, had already begun intensive negotiations with the USSR.

On August 23, 1939, the Nazi-Soviet Pact, concluded in Moscow between former ideological archenemies, shocked the world. (See Problem 13 at the end of this chapter.) That fateful agreement included a public nonaggression pact pledging absolute neutrality if either partner were attacked by a third power. Securing Hitler's eastern flank, the pact encouraged him to invade Poland on September 1. A secret territorial protocol partitioned Poland, with the USSR to receive roughly the eastern third. Latvia, Estonia, Finland, and Bessarabia were assigned to the Soviet sphere, and Lithuania was added to it later. (See Map 37.2.) Reflecting the worst traditions of the old secret diplomacy, the two dictators' cynical bargain resembled the alliance of 1807 between Napoleon

and Alexander I. Once again Russia, bribed with temporary peace and eastern European territory, gave a Western tyrant a free hand to deal with Europe and England. Stalin apparently interpreted the pact as a diplomatic masterstroke, securing the USSR from invasion, giving it a buffer zone, splitting the capitalist world, and encouraging its parts to fight, all of which might enable Russia to become the arbiter of Europe.

If so, Stalin's hopes were soon shattered. He was appalled at the awesome Nazi blitzkrieg that rolled over Poland, the Low Countries, and France; he watched helplessly as the Soviet Union, having agreed to supply Germany with raw materials, became economically dependent on Germany. At Hitler's insistence the Soviet-controlled Comintern abandoned its hostility to Nazism. Seeking compensation, Stalin occupied the Baltic states militarily, deported many of its citizens to Siberia, then engineered a sham plebiscite that, Moscow claimed, overwhelmingly (more than 99 percent) approved their annexation to the USSR. The Soviets also demanded Finnish territory near Leningrad in exchange for part of Soviet Karelia. When the Finns refused, the Red Army attacked but met heroic resistance, suffered huge casualties, and displayed embarrassing weakness in the aftermath of the military purge. This unprovoked Soviet aggression, which the Soviets justified as an essential defensive measure, brought sharp Western condemnation and expulsion from the League of Nations, and almost provoked war with the West. Once Finnish defenses had been broken, Stalin hastily concluded peace, taking much of the Karelian Isthmus and many of the Finnish bases. Later in 1940 he seized Bessarabia and northern Bukovina from Romania to protect vulnerable Ukraine.

Despite their large and mutually profitable trade, friction increased between Germany and the USSR. As early as July 1940 Hitler apparently decided to invade Russia, and Soviet stubbornness during the Molotov-Ribbentrop talks in November merely confirmed his decision. The German foreign minister tried in vain to turn Soviet aspirations southward to the Persian Gulf against Great

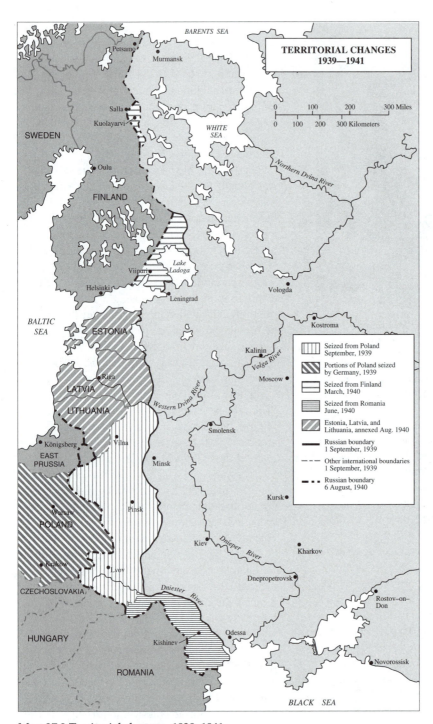

Map 37.2 Territorial changes, 1939–1941

Britain. Abandoning any pretense of Marxist internationalism, Molotov stated Soviet demands in pragmatic, power-political terms. The Soviet Union, he declared, would accept Ribbentrop's proposals on politicoeconomic cooperation only on the following terms:

1. Provided that the German troops are immediately withdrawn from Finland, which under the compact of 1939, belongs to the Soviet Union's sphere of influence. . . .

2. Provided that within the next few months the security of the Soviet Union in the [Turkish] Straits is assured by the conclusion of a mutual assistance pact between the Soviet Union and Bulgaria, which geographically is situated inside [its] security zone . . . and by the establishment of a base for land and naval forces of the USSR within range of the Bosphorus and Dardanelles by means of a long-term lease.

3. Provided that the area south of Batum and Baku in the general direction of the Persian Gulf is recognized as the center of the aspirations of the Soviet Union.

4. Provided that Japan [renounces] her rights to concessions for coal and oil in northern Sakhalin.[11]

Molotov's statement marked an evident return to traditional 19th-century tsarist objectives, secret diplomacy, and even language—"spheres of influence," military bases, and long-term leases. Nazi-Soviet friction over Finland and the Turkish Straits resembled that between tsarist Russia and Napoleonic France preceding the French invasion of Russia in 1812.

---

[11] R. J. Sontag and J. Beddie, eds., *Nazi-Soviet Relations, 1939–1941* (Washington, 1948), pp. 258–59.

Problem 13

The Nazi-Soviet Pact: Then and Now

Prevalent historical opinion remains that the conclusion of the Nazi-Soviet Pact on August 23, 1939, gave Hitler the green light to invade Poland just eight days later, thus touching off World War II. Still disputed, however, is whether Stalin, the realistic statesman, had a genuine alternative in 1939 to an accord with Hitler. Could the Red Army, shattered by the terrible purge of its officer corps in 1937–1938, have resisted a Nazi invasion then? Would Hitler indeed have invaded the Soviet Union had Stalin aligned the USSR with the Western powers, Great Britain and France? Would Hitler have attacked Poland, already backed by the Western powers, without guaranteed neutrality from the Soviet

Union? Was there a realistic chance for a military alliance between the xenophobic Stalin and the Western powers in 1939, given the abject surrender by France and Great Britain to the Axis powers in September 1938 at the Munich Conference, which had excluded the USSR? How much responsibility for the outbreak of World War II actually rests on the shoulders of Stalin's USSR?

Another series of questions relates to Stalin's motives and objectives, which have recently been scrutinized by Russian historians and commentators. This debate centers around the secret additional protocol of August 23 on territorial divisions in eastern Europe and the subsequent protocol of September 28, 1939, under which the USSR secured Lithuania while surrendering Warsaw and portions of central Poland to Germany. Can Stalin's actions be defended on the grounds of security—a defensive move to create a buffer zone to protect the USSR against a possible subsequent Nazi attack? Or was Stalin's objective primarily expansionist—an aggressive move to secure control of the Baltic states and eastern Poland while agreeing with Hitler to destroy an independent Slav Poland? Probably it represented a combination of the two aims. Some Soviet commentators condemned the pact and protocols as violations of Leninist principles in foreign affairs. Leaders in the Baltic republics have argued that their incorporation into the USSR in 1939–1940 took place forcibly against the background of secret agreements that were illegal both under international law and in light of Leninist principles. If their incorporation was indeed involuntary, were the Baltic republics not therefore justified in demanding secession from the USSR?

Some basis for answering these questions can be provided by examining the relevant documents from 1939: the Soviet-German Nonaggression Pact, the secret territorial protocol of August 23, and the additional secret protocol of September 28. Foreign Minister Molotov provided the official Soviet explanation of reasons for the Nazi-Soviet Pact. Half a century later, in 1989, the debate over the pact intensified, and excerpts from that Soviet debate, both Russian and Baltic, have also been included.

The Treaty of August 23, 1939

ARTICLE 1: Both High Contracting Parties obligate themselves to desist from any act of violence, any aggressive action, and any attack on each other, either individually or jointly with other powers.

ARTICLE 2: Should one of the High Contracting Parties become the object of belligerent action by a third power, the other High Contracting Party shall in no manner lend its support to this third power. . . .

ARTICLE 4: Neither of the two High Contracting Parties shall participate in any grouping of powers

whatsoever that is directly or indirectly aimed at the other party.

Disputes between the two nations were to be settled through "friendly exchange of opinion" or through arbitration (Article 5). The treaty was to run for 10 years; if neither party denounced it a year before its scheduled expiration, the treaty would be extended automatically for five more years.

ARTICLE 7: The present treaty shall be ratified within the shortest possible time. . . . The agreement shall enter into force as soon as it is signed.

For the government of the German Reich	With the full power of the Soviet government
J. von Ribbentrop	V. M. Molotov[12]

The Secret Additional Protocol of August 23, 1939

The undersigned plenipotentiaries of each of the two parties discussed in strictly confidential conversation the question of the boundary of their respective spheres of influence in eastern Europe. These conversations led to the following conclusions:

1. In the event of a territorial and political rearrangement in the areas belonging to the Baltic States (Finland, Estonia, Latvia, Lithuania), the northern boundary of Lithuania shall represent the boundary of the spheres of Germany and the USSR. In this connection the interest of Lithuania in the Vilna area is recognized by each party.

2. In the event of a territorial and political arrangement of the areas belonging to the Polish state the spheres of influence of Germany and the USSR shall be bounded approximately by the line of the rivers Narew, Vistula and San. The question of whether the interests of both parties make desirable the maintenance of an independent Polish state and how such a state should be bounded can only be definitely determined in the course of further political developments. . . .

---

[12] Sontag and Beddie, *Nazi-Soviet Relations*, pp. 76–77.

4. This protocol shall be treated by both parties as strictly secret.

    v. Ribbentrop   V. Molotov[13]

The Secret Supplementary Protocol of September 28, 1939

When German armies marched into Poland on September 1, 1939, the Soviet Union remained neutral according to the terms of the Nonaggression Pact. On September 17 Soviet armies invaded eastern Poland and occupied the region assigned to it by the Secret Additional Protocol. At Soviet request, on September 28 in Moscow von Ribbentrop and Molotov signed a Secret Supplementary Protocol. This document amended the Secret Protocol of August 23 under Article 1

> to the effect that the territory of the Lithuanian state falls to the sphere of influence of the USSR, while, on the other hand, the province of Lublin and parts of the province of Warsaw fall to the sphere of influence of Germany. As soon as the Government of the USSR shall take special measures on Lithuanian territory to protect its interests, the present German-Lithuanian border . . . shall be rectified in such a way that the Lithuanian territory situated to the southwest of the line marked on the attached map should fall to Germany.[14]

This protocol confirmed that Nazi Germany had assigned all the Baltic states to the Soviet sphere.

The Official Soviet Explanation: 1939

On August 31, 1939, Foreign Minister Molotov provided this interpretation of the preceding Nazi-Soviet agreements in a speech to the Supreme Soviet of the USSR. Emphasizing the tense international situation that then prevailed in Europe and Asia, Molotov declared:

> In view of this state of affairs, the conclusion of a nonaggression pact between the USSR and Germany is of tremendous positive value, eliminating the danger of war between Germany and the Soviet Union. In order more fully to define the significance of this pact, I must first dwell on the negotiations which have taken place in recent months in Moscow with representatives of Great Britain and France . . . for conclusion of a pact of mutual assistance against aggression in Europe. . . . The initial proposals of the British Government were, as you know, entirely unacceptable . . . ; they ignored the principle of reciprocity and equality of obligations. . . . These negotiations encountered insuperable obstacles. . . . Poland, which was to be jointly guaranteed by Great Britain, France and the USSR, rejected military assistance on the part of the Soviet Union. . . . After this it became clear to us that the Anglo-French-Soviet negotiations were doomed to failure. . . . The British and French military missions came to Moscow without any definite powers and without the right to conclude any military convention. . . .
>
> The decision to conclude a nonaggression pact between the USSR and Germany was adopted after military negotiations with France and Britain had reached an impasse. . . . It is our duty to think of the interests of the Soviet people, the interests of the USSR. . . . In our foreign policy towards non-Soviet countries, we have always been guided by Lenin's well-known principle of peaceful coexistence of the Soviet state and capitalist countries. . . . The Non-Aggression Pact . . . marks a turning point in the history of Europe, and not only of Europe. Only yesterday, the German fascists were pursuing a foreign policy hostile to us. . . . Today, however, the situation has changed and we are enemies no longer. The art of politics in the sphere of foreign relations . . . is to reduce the number of enemies and to make the enemies of yesterday good neighbors. . . . The two largest states of Europe have agreed to put an end to the enmity between them, to eliminate the menace of war and live in peace with the other. . . . Is it really difficult to understand that the USSR is pursuing and will continue to pursue its own independent policy,

---

[13] Sontag and Beddie, p. 78.

[14] Sontag and Beddie, p. 107.

Problem 13 continued

based on the interests of the peoples of the USSR and only their interests?[15]

Thus Molotov justified the agreements with Germany on the basis of Soviet national interests and the "insuperable obstacles" to an accord with the Western powers. He made no allusion whatsoever to the establishment of Soviet-German spheres of interest.

Soviet Views of the Agreements: 1989

A. N. Iakovlev, a member of the Soviet Politburo, in a *Pravda* interview published on August 18, 1989, declared that "serious researchers" agreed that when Stalin authorized Ribbentrop's visit to Moscow on August 22, 1939, the Soviet Union no longer had any choice of partners. Unable to prevent war by itself and having failed to enlist England and France as allies, "the only thing left for it to do was to think about how to avoid falling into the maelstrom of war for which the USSR was even less prepared in 1939 than in 1941." As to the Secret Additional Protocol of September 28, 1939, Iakovlev stated:

> From a political standpoint . . . , it represented a deviation from Leninist norms of Soviet foreign policy and from Lenin's break with secret diplomacy. . . . [The protocol] conflicted with the sovereignty and independence of a whole series of countries [including the Baltic states] . . . and with the treaties which the USSR had previously concluded with those countries, with our commitments to respect their sovereignty, territorial integrity and inviolability. In my opinion, Stalin took an unjustified risk in giving his blessing to Molotov's signature to the "territorial-political rearrangement" of Poland. . . . The venture could have ended with the USSR's being drawn into the war rather than being

given a breathing spell. . . . This way of acting by the Soviet leaders then in no way reflected the will of the Soviet people and was not in tune with their mood. I think we will be acting responsibly . . . by unequivocally condemning the prewar Soviet leadership's departure from Leninist principles of foreign policy.

Asked to compare the Nonaggression Pact of August 23, 1939, with the Secret Supplementary Protocol of September 28, Iakovlev found them to be qualitatively different:

> The first was a treaty made in peacetime; the second was concluded with a country [Nazi Germany] which had committed an overt act of aggression. The first was basically in keeping with the international practices of the time; the second essentially cast doubt on the USSR's status as a neutral—if it did not undermine that status—and pushed our country toward unprincipled cooperation with Nazi Germany. There was no direct need at all for the September 28 treaty. . . . For opportunistic motives, however, in late September Stalin made a move that entailed major political and moral costs in order, as he supposed, to fix Hitler firmly in a position of mutual understanding—not with the USSR, but with Stalin himself.[16]

On August 23, 1989—the 50th anniversary of the Nonaggression Pact—an interview with F. N. Kovalev, director of the Foreign Ministry's Diplomatic Historical Administration, appeared in the Soviet newspaper *Izvestiia*. Discussing the forced incorporation of the Baltic republics of Latvia, Lithuania, and Estonia into the USSR, Kovalev said:

> When the agreements were signed in August 1939, what was primarily intended was to establish a definite boundary to German fascist expansion. And only that. It was certainly not intended, say, that the Baltic republics would eventually be incorporated into the USSR. The purport of Moscow's instructions to our representatives in the Baltic republics . . . was that Soviet garrisons stationed in the Baltic republics on the basis of treaties . . . concluded with them in late September and Octo-

---

[15] V. M. Molotov, "The Meaning of the Soviet-German Non-Aggression Pact," Speech to the Supreme Soviet, August 31, 1939. In Alvin Rubinstein, *The Foreign Policy of the Soviet Union* (New York, 1960), pp. 145–51.

[16] Interview with A. N. Iakovlev, *Pravda*, August 18, 1989.

Problem 13 continued

ber 1939 should in no way interfere in those countries' internal affairs. There could be no question of any Sovietization of the three Baltic republics . . . but the presence of Soviet garrisons created an atmosphere in which leftist forces and democratic circles in the three republics began to step up efforts which ultimately led to the events that occurred in 1940 [incorporation]. From my viewpoint . . . , the Baltic republics then faced a very clear alternative; either side with Hitler or the USSR.[17]

On August 28, 1989, *Izvestiia* reported from the Lithuanian capital of Vilnius that the presidium of the Lithuanian Supreme Soviet had examined the conclusions reached by its commission studying the Soviet-German treaties of 1939. The

---

[17] Interview with F. N. Kovalev, *Izvestiia*, August 23, 1989.

assertion that Lithuania's incorporation into the Soviet Union in 1940 had been illegal, affirmed that Moscow newspaper, "is leading the republic of Lithuania into a political impasse and will be of little help during the transition to economic independence."[18]

Conclusion

Soviet and Russian views on the Nazi-Soviet agreements of 1939 have changed significantly over the years. Under Gorbachev the Nonaggression Pact of August 23 was disavowed as mistaken and "anti-Leninist," as were Soviet-German accords over spheres of influence. The Soviet incorporation of the Baltic states in 1940, facilitated by the Nazi-Soviet Pact, was finally reversed in 1991 when Latvia, Lithuania, and Estonia became independent countries, and Russian troops were later withdrawn. ∎

---

[18] "Search for the Road Together," *Izvestiia*, August 28, 1989.

Suggested Additional Reading

ANGRESS, W. T. *Stillborn Revolution: The Communist Bid for Power in Germany, 1921–1923* (Princeton, 1963).

BELOFF, M. *The Foreign Policy of Soviet Russia, 1929–1941,* 2 vols. (London, 1947–1949).

BORKENAU, F. *World Communism: A History of the Communist International* (Ann Arbor, MI, 1962).

BRANDT, C. *Stalin's Failure in China, 1924–1927* (Cambridge, MA, 1958).

BROWDER, R. P. *The Origins of Soviet-American Diplomacy* (Princeton, 1953).

BUDUROWYCZ, B. *Polish-Soviet Relations, 1932–1933* (New York, 1963).

CARR, E. H. *German-Soviet Relations Between the Two World Wars, 1919–1929* (Baltimore, 1951).

———. *Twilight of the Comintern, 1930–1935* (New York, 1983).

CRAIG, G., and FELIX G., eds. *The Diplomats, 1919–1939* (Princeton, 1953). (See chapters on Chicherin and Litvinov.)

CROWE, D. M. *The Baltic States and the Great Powers: Foreign Relations, 1938–1940* (Boulder, CO, 1993).

DANIELS, R. *Russia: The Roots of Confrontation* (Cambridge, MA, and London, 1985).

DEGRAS, J. *Calendar of Soviet Documents on Foreign Policy, 1917–1941* (New York, 1948).

———, ed. *The Communist International, 1919–1943* (New York, 1956).

———, ed. *Soviet Documents on Foreign Policy, 1917–1941,* 3 vols. (New York, 1951–1953, 1983).

DMYTRYSHYN, B., and F. COX. *The Soviet Union and the Middle East: A Documentary Record of Afghanistan, Iran and Turkey, 1917–1985* (Princeton, 1985).

EUDIN, X., and H. FISHER, eds. *Soviet Russia and the West, 1920–1927* (Stanford, 1957).

———, and R. NORTH, eds. *Soviet Russia and the East, 1920–1927* (Stanford, 1957).

———, and R. SLUSSER, eds. *Soviet Foreign Policy, 1928–1934,* 2 vols. (University Park, PA, 1966–1967).

FILENE, P. G. *Americans and the Soviet Experiment, 1917–1933* (Cambridge, MA, 1967).

FISCHER, L. *Russia's Road from War to Peace . . .* (New York, 1969).

———. *The Soviets in World Affairs . . . 1917–1929,* 2d ed. (New York, 1960).

FREUND, G. *Unholy Alliance: Russo-German Relations from the Treaty of Brest-Litovsk to the Treaty of Berlin* (New York, 1957).

GARRISON, M., and A. GLEASON, eds. *Shared Destiny: Fifty Years of Soviet-American Relations* (Boston, 1985).

GOLDBERG, H. J., ed. *Documents of Soviet-American Relations: Vol. I. Intervention, Famine Relief, International Affairs, 1917–1933.* (Gulf Breeze, FL, 1993).

GROMYKO, A. A., and B. N. PONOMAREV. *Soviet Foreign Policy 1917–1980,* 2 vols. (Moscow, 1981).

HASLAM, J. *Soviet Foreign Policy, 1930–1933: The Impact of the Depression* (New York, 1983).

HILGER, G., and A. G. MEYER. *The Incompatible Allies: A Memoir History of German-Soviet Relations 1918–1941* (New York, 1953).

HULSE, J. W. *The Forming of the Communist International* (Stanford, 1964).

KENNAN, G. F. *Russia and the West Under Lenin and Stalin* (Boston, 1960).

KOCHAN, L. *Russia and the Weimar Republic* (Cambridge, 1978).

MACKENZIE, D. *From Messianism to Collapse: Soviet Foreign Policy, 1917–1991* (Fort Worth, TX, 1994).

MCKENZIE, K. E. *Comintern and the World Revolution, 1928–1943 . . .* (New York, 1964).

MCLANE, C. B. *Soviet Policy and the Chinese Communists, 1931–1946* (New York, 1958).

MOSELY, P. E. *The Kremlin and World Politics* (New York, 1961).

NELSON, D. N., and ROGER ANDERSON, eds. *Soviet-American Relations: Understanding Differences, Avoiding Conflicts* (Wilmington, DE, 1987).

ROBERTS, G. *The Unholy Alliance: Stalin's Pact with Hitler* (Bloomington, IN, 1989).

RUBINSTEIN, A. Z., ed. *The Foreign Policy of the Soviet Union* (New York, 1972).

SONTAG, R. J., and J. BEDDIE, eds. *Nazi-Soviet Relations* (Washington, 1948).

SUVOROV, V. *Icebreaker: Who Started the Second World War?* (London, 1990).

SWORD, K., ed. *The Soviet Takeover of the Polish Eastern Provinces, 1939–1941* (New York, 1991).

TROTTER, W. *The Russo-Finnish Winter War of 1939–1940* (Chapel Hill, NC, 1990).

ULAM, A. *Expansion and Coexistence . . . 1917–1973,* 2d ed. (New York, 1974).

ULDRICKS, T. J. *Diplomacy and Ideology: The Origins of Soviet Foreign Relations, 1917–1930* (London, 1980).

WEINBERG, G. *Germany and the Soviet Union, 1939–1941* (New York, 1972).

WHITE, S. *The Origins of Detente: The Genoa Conference and Soviet-Western Relations, 1921–1922* (London and New York, 1985).

ZENKOVSKY, S. A. *Pan-Turkism and Islam in Russia* (Cambridge, MA, 1960).

38

War and Reconstruction, 1941–1953

Between 1941 and 1945, the USSR fought the greatest war in Russian history. Despite poor military preparation and massive popular hostility to the Stalin regime, Soviet Russia eventually defeated the Nazi invasion, and the Red Army advanced triumphantly into central Europe. The USSR was joined by Britain and the United States, but Soviet relations with the West were complicated by suspicion and differences over strategy and war aims. The Soviet role in World War II and Stalin as wartime leader remain controversial: Was Soviet Russia caught by surprise in 1941 and, if so, why? Why did the Red Army suffer terrible early defeats, then recover and defeat Germany? How important was Allied aid in the Soviet victory, and how great were the respective Soviet and Western roles in defeating Germany and Japan?

When the war ended, Stalin reimposed tight controls over a Soviet people yearning for liberalization and relaxation. Reindoctrinating or imprisoning millions exposed to Western influences during the war, he again isolated the USSR and blamed the West for domestic hardships. Heavy industry was stressed again at the consumer's

expense, but reconstruction was rapid, and the USSR soon produced atomic and hydrogen weapons. Soviet Russia achieved dominance over eastern Europe, except for Yugoslavia, which escaped Stalin's grasp in 1948. Soviet expansion and Western resistance produced the Cold War between the two superpowers, and in Asia Communist China emerged as a huge Soviet ally. How did postwar Stalinism compare with the prewar regime? How and why did the Soviet Union win control of eastern Europe? Was Stalin mainly responsible for the Cold War?

Invasion

At dawn on June 22, 1941, more than 3 million German and auxiliary troops from Nazi-controlled Europe crossed the Soviet frontier on a 2,000-mile front. Their unprovoked attack inaugurated what the Soviets called "the great fatherland war," the greatest land conflict in world history, and a struggle that tested the Soviet regime and people to the limit. Despite accurate warnings from Soviet spies (such as Richard Sorge in Tokyo) and foreign intelligence of impending German attack, the Nazis achieved complete tactical surprise. At first, uncertain whether it was invasion or a provocation, Moscow ordered Soviet troops to remain passive. Apparently Stalin believed that Hitler would not attack if the USSR fulfilled its commitments under the Nazi-Soviet Pact. Finally, at noon on June 22, eight hours after the Nazis attacked, Deputy Premier Molotov informed the Soviet people of the German assault. Stalin, in a state of shock, remained in seclusion for several days at his dacha outside Moscow. When Ambassador Schulenburg delivered the German declaration of war, Foreign Minister Molotov queried: "Do you believe that we deserved this?"

Hitler's aim in Operation Barbarossa was to crush the "barbarian" USSR by crippling the Red Army in encirclements near the frontier, then to advance to the Archangel-Astrakhan line. Moscow, Leningrad, and most of European Russia would be occupied, and Russian remnants expelled into Asia. Nazi Germany would obtain sufficient oil, grain, and manpower to dominate Europe and defeat England. Hitler and his commanders were confident that these objectives could be achieved before winter.

At first Nazi victories exceeded even Hitler's expectations. Soviet frontier forces were overwhelmed and hundreds of planes destroyed on the ground as Soviet soldiers and civilians were stunned by the suddenness and power of the German onslaught. In four weeks General Heinz Guderian's tank forces pierced to Smolensk, only 225 miles from Moscow, while the northern armies sliced through the Baltic states toward Leningrad. Hundreds of thousands of demoralized Soviet troops surrendered; border populations in eastern Poland, the Baltic states, and Ukraine welcomed the Germans with bread and salt as liberators from Stalinist tyranny.

Overconfidence and fanaticism caused Hitler and his associates to overlook or fumble golden military and political opportunities. On July 19 Hitler rejected Guderian's plea for an immediate strike against Moscow, ordering him instead against Kiev. That operation netted more than 600,000 Soviet prisoners, but produced fatal delay

in assaulting Moscow, the key to Soviet power, which was very vulnerable in the fall of 1941. By October the Germans had occupied most of Ukraine and surrounded Leningrad, but Red Army resistance was stiffening. Guderian was now unleashed, and by early December reached Moscow's outskirts, but an early winter, lack of warm clothing and tracked vehicles, and major Siberian reinforcements stalled his advance. The year 1941 ended with a Soviet counteroffensive that drove the Nazis back from Moscow, opened a relief route into Leningrad, and recaptured Rostov in the south. (See Map 38.1.) Hitler's attempt to achieve quick victory in Russia had failed.

The Germans wasted unique chances to overturn Stalin's regime. Nazi agencies in Russia pursued conflicting policies. Many German army leaders and foreign officials sought Russian popular support, but Nazi party and SS elements treated the people as subhumans, exterminating or exploiting even those ready to cooperate with Germany. Alfred Rosenberg's Ministry for the East favored autonomous German-controlled satellite states in non-Russian borderlands, but Goering's economic agencies grabbed their resources for Germany. No single course was implemented consistently, but German eastern policy (*Ostpolitik*) was brutal and inefficient. The Nazis aimed to colonize choice areas with Germans and exploit Soviet resources, but they achieved remarkably little. Occupying some 400,000 square miles of Soviet territory with 65 million people and rich grain areas, the Germans obtained only a fraction of what they secured from France or from Nazi-Soviet trade agreements. Incompetent and corrupt German officials, who flooded the USSR like carpetbaggers, contributed to this economic failure as they disregarded popular aspirations for religious freedom, self-government, and decollectivization. Himmler's extermination detachments liquidated not just Bolsheviks but also thousands of innocent men, women, and children.

Why the initial Soviet collapse followed by recovery? Stalinists blamed setbacks on the Nazi surprise attack and credited recovery to a loyal populace that rallied to the motherland. Later

NORWAY

SWEDEN

FINLAND

Helsinki

DENMARK

BALTIC
SEA

ESTONIA

Riga LATVIA

LITH.

Danzig

EAST
PRUSSIA

Vilna

Berlin

Torgau

Minsk

Bialystok

Warsaw

POLAND

Brest-Litovsk

CZECHOSLOVAKIA

Vienna

AUSTRIA

Budapest

HUNGARY

Lvov

ROMANIA

Belgrade

YUGOSLAVIA

Bucharest

ITALY

Sofia   BULGARIA

ALBANIA

GREECE

Istanbul

Athens   Izmir

CRETE

Leningrad
Tikhvin

Archangel

N. Dvina

Kotlas

Vologda

Kirov

Kalinin

Gorkii

Kazan

Volga

Moznaisk

Moscow

Smolensk   Tula

WHITE
RUSSIA   Orel

Kuibyshev

Kursk

Farthest
German
Advance
1941—1942

Kiev

Kharkov

Voronezh

UKRAINE

Dneprtr

Don

Stalingrad

Dnepropetrovsk

Rostov-on-Don

Astrakhan

Kerch   Kuban

Sevastopol   Yalta

Novorossiisk

Mozdok

Terek

BLACK SEA

CAUCASUS

Batum   Tiflis

Erivan

Ankara

Erivan

TURKEY   IRAN

SYRIA   IRAQ

Axis and occupied areas
June 22, 1941

1938 boundaries

Russian boundary, 1941

Front lines in Russia

—·—·— 1941   •••••• 1942

—···— 1943   ▪▪▪▪▪▪ 1944

Russian and allied
drives 1941—1945

Map 38.1 USSR in World War II

Source: Adapted from *A History of Russia*, Second Edition by Nicholas V. Riasanovsky.
Copyright © 1969 by Oxford University Press, Inc. Used by permission.

Khrushchev blamed early defeats mainly on Stalin's deafness to warnings of attack and inefficiency in using the breathing spell of the Nazi-Soviet Pact. In the West many attributed Soviet collapse to a revolt of the borderlands and Soviet recovery mainly to Nazi brutality. The American political scientist George Fischer suggested that Stalin's initial paralysis of will had left an army and population used to dictation without instructions; once he reasserted leadership, the Soviet people again obeyed the regime.

By the end of 1941 the Soviet leadership had regained widespread public support. After two weeks of silence and seclusion (some reports claim he suffered a near nervous breakdown), Stalin appealed to the Soviet people by radio for national resistance to an invader seeking to turn them into "the slaves of German princes and barons" and to restore the tsar and the landlords. A scorched earth policy must deny the Germans factories, food, and matériel. Stalin's call for guerrilla warfare behind German lines was reinforced by skillful patriotic propaganda. Soon forests in the German rear were infested with partisans who tied down many German troops and disrupted communications. A State Committee for Defense, headed by Stalin and including Molotov, Voroshilov, Beria, and Malenkov, became a war cabinet. As de facto commander in chief, Stalin concentrated military and political leadership in his own hands. In that capacity he made many arbitrary and harmful military decisions, often interfering in tactical matters, about which he knew little. Stalin's mistakes apparently contributed to major Red Army defeats, especially in the initial Nazi advance in 1941, but his decision to remain in threatened Moscow in October 1941 halted panic provoked by the movement of diplomats and government offices to Kuibyshev on the Volga. If Stalin is partially to blame for early Soviet defeats, he deserves some credit for the Red Army's outstanding victories during 1944–1945.[1] His wartime leadership remains controversial.

---

[1] A. Seaton, *Stalin as Military Commander* (New York, 1976), p. 271.

The Grand Alliance—Britain, the USSR, the United States, and later France—formed against the Nazis and their allies in 1941 sent significant aid to the USSR. The day after the invasion Prime Minister Churchill of England offered the USSR friendship and military aid, while refusing to recant his earlier attacks on Bolshevism. After President Roosevelt's adviser Harry Hopkins went to Moscow in July, the United States began Lend-Lease assistance to Russia, which totaled some 15 million tons of supplies worth more than $11 billion. Anglo-American aid contributed to the Soviet repulse of German attacks in 1942 and proved indispensable in subsequent Soviet counteroffensives. Japan's attack on Pearl Harbor in December 1941 brought the United States into the European war as well.

The 1942 Campaign: The Turning Point

In 1941 German losses were so heavy that in 1942 Hitler's offensive had to be more limited. The Nazis still retained the potential to reach the Archangel-Astrakhan line and knock out the USSR, but Hitler removed most of his high command and interfered frequently in military decisions, with disastrous results. Instead of trying to envelop and capture Moscow, he sought economic and psychological objectives: seizing the Caucasus oil fields and Stalingrad on the Volga.

In June the Germans broke through the Don front, but Soviet resistance at Voronezh prevented an advance to the mid-Volga. Nazi armies rolled east, then southward into the Caucasus, but were halted short of the main oil fields. Stalingrad became the focus and symbol of the entire Soviet-German war. In bitter street fighting during August and September, Stalingrad was virtually reduced to rubble. Despite brave Soviet resistance, General von Paulus's Sixth Army captured most of the city, but his army was bled white in frontal assaults instead of crossing the Volga and encircling the city. Heroic Soviet defense, Siberian reinforcements, and U.S. equipment turned the tide. In November a massive Soviet counteroffensive broke through Romanian and Italian lines on the exposed northern German flank and cut off the entire Sixth Army. After relief efforts failed, von Paulus and the hungry remnants of his army surrendered. Here was the psychological and perhaps military turning point of the Soviet-German war. After Stalingrad the Nazis were mostly on the defensive, and ultimate Allied victory in World War II became a matter of time and blood.

In 1942 the Nazis again neglected a major political weapon. In July Lieutenant General Andrei Vlasov, an able Soviet commander, surrendered with his men and agreed to help Germany achieve a free, non-Bolshevik Russia. He denounced the Soviet regime, collective farms, and Stalin's mass murders. Some on the German General Staff wished to use him and several million Soviet war prisoners against Stalin. Named head of a Russian National Committee, Vlasov sought to form an army of liberation (ROA), but Hitler blocked its use until German defeat was inevitable. The Germans employed more than a million Soviet volunteers as cooks, drivers, and orderlies, but not in combat.

To counter an appalling desertion rate, Stalin appealed to Russian traditions and completed a reconciliation with the Orthodox Church. Soviet soldiers were told to serve the fatherland without socialist obligations. The army restored ranks, saluting, insignia, and officer privileges reminiscent of tsarist times, and the regime's tone became strongly nationalist. At the 25th anniversary of the Bolshevik Revolution (November 1942), Soviet leaders, instead of calling for world revolution, stressed Slav solidarity. To convince the West that the USSR had abandoned world revolution, Stalin abolished the Comintern in 1943 and rewarded the loyal Orthodox hierarchy by restoring the patriarchate under state supervision. A church synod unanimously elected Metropolitan Sergei patriarch in September 1943; Sergei then proclaimed Stalin "the divinely anointed." These moves promoted unity and countered German efforts to foment disloyalty, but did not signify changes in Stalin's domestic or foreign aims.

Inter-Allied relations remained good in 1942, primarily because the USSR badly needed Lend-Lease supplies. Even then, friction developed over a second front and over Poland. Throughout 1942 Stalin pressed for a cross-Channel invasion; he was only partially mollified by the Allied invasion of North Africa in November. Stalin sought Western recognition of the USSR's June 1941 frontiers, but England and the United States, though making concessions, refused to sanction Soviet annexation of eastern Poland and the Baltic states.

Soviet Offensives and Allied Victory, 1943–1945

After Stalingrad, with brief exceptions, Soviet armies were on the offensive everywhere and bore the heaviest military burden until victory was achieved. After the defeat of a German offensive at Kursk in July 1943, producing the greatest tank battle in history, the Red Army attacked, jabbing ceaselessly at various points. U.S. tanks, trucks, and planes ensured the success of the Soviet drive westward by making the Red Army highly mobile. The Red Army's numerical superiority grew steadily. By the summer of 1944 the Germans were outnumbered about three to one, and the Soviets commanded the skies and used their artillery effectively. Named chief of the Soviet General Staff in 1941, Marshal Georgii Zhukov led the defense of Moscow later that year and also directed the great Soviet counteroffensive of 1943–1945. His U.S. counterpart was General Dwight Eisenhower. The Germans could merely delay the Soviet advance and hope to exploit Allied divergences.

Once the Allies were advancing everywhere, their relations cooled. Both the Soviets and the West feared that the other might make a separate peace, though there is little evidence that either planned to do so. As Soviet armies advanced, Stalin's attitude hardened as he sought to dominate eastern Europe and Germany. The Western allies, still sensitive in 1943 over the absence of a true second front, proved vulnerable to Stalin's diplomacy. Hitherto Soviet war aims had been defensive: to preserve Soviet frontiers, the Communist system, and Stalin's total control. Now Stalin sought also Carpatho-Ukraine from Czechoslovakia to forestall Ukrainian disaffection. The USSR joined in the formation of the United Nations in 1942 and approved its high-sounding declarations, but Stalin never accepted Western democratic aims. He refused to alter his views or make major concessions to his partners. Stalin realized that the surest way to achieve his aims was to advance westward as far as possible, then secure what he wanted from the West. Stalin and Molotov, notes George Kennan, played their cards skillfully and carefully while the Western allies, holding a stronger hand, remained confused, divided, and unrealistic and let the Soviets score large gains.

Poland was the stickiest issue in inter-Allied relations. Early in 1943 the Germans discovered the corpses of thousands of Polish officers in the Katyn Forest near Smolensk. The Soviets accused the Nazis of the murders, but evidence was strong that Soviet security forces had killed the Poles in 1940.[2] Assertions of Soviet responsibility by the Polish government in exile in London induced Stalin to sever relations with them. At Teheran in November 1943 Churchill proposed the Curzon Line of 1920 as Poland's eastern frontier, with Poland to be compensated in the west at German expense. Stalin promptly agreed and suggested the Oder-Neisse Line as the western boundary. Poland's drastic shift westward would make it dependent on Soviet favor. Churchill finally persuaded the London Poles to accept this bargain; but when their new leader, Stanislas Mikolajczyk, went to Moscow in July, the USSR had already recognized the Communist-dominated Lublin Committee political group in Poland and turned over to it liberated Polish territory. Because the Western allies took no firm stand, Mikolajczyk was powerless. In August 1944, with the Red Army in Praga, across the Vistula River from Warsaw, Poles aligned with the London exiles rose against the

Nazis: General Bor's men fought heroically, but the Soviet army did not aid them. Once the Germans had destroyed this core of potential opposition to a Soviet-dominated Poland, the Red Army drove the Nazis from Warsaw.

The second-front issue caused serious inter-Allied friction until the Normandy invasion of June 1944. At the Moscow foreign ministers' conference (October 1943), the Soviets sought a definite Western pledge to invade France by the next spring. At the Teheran Conference in November, Churchill's idea of invading the Balkans, partly to prevent Soviet control there, was blocked by Stalin, whose support of Overlord, the American plan to invade France, ensured its adoption. The Normandy invasion relieved Soviet fears of a Nazi-Western separate peace and speeded the end of the war. Later Soviet historians claimed that Normandy was invaded to prevent a Soviet sweep to the Atlantic but contributed little to Germany's defeat.

As Soviet forces advanced through Poland and the Balkans, Churchill sought to delimit postwar spheres of influence, a proposal Roosevelt repudiated as immoral. In October 1944 Churchill proposed a numerical formula for influence in eastern Europe: 90-percent Soviet influence in Romania and Bulgaria and similar British control in Greece; Yugoslavia and Hungary would be split 50–50. Such formulas, however, meant little: The USSR could gain total control in its sphere by military occupation.

In February 1945, with Allied armies at the border of or inside Germany, the Big Three met at Yalta in the Crimea to outline a postwar settlement. Because the Red Army controlled most of Poland, only united and determined Western action might have salvaged some Polish independence. The West (especially Roosevelt), however, wished to continue cooperation with the USSR after the war. In regard to Polish frontiers, Stalin insisted on the Curzon Line, overcoming half-hearted Western efforts to obtain Lvov and the Galician oil fields for Poland. In the west, Poland was to administer the region to the Oder-Neisse Line until the peace conference, and more than 7

---

[2] In 1990 the Soviet Union admitted responsibility for the Katyn Forest Massacre.

Churchill, Roosevelt, and Stalin at Yalta, February 1945.

million German residents were expelled. Stalin insisted that the West repudiate the London Poles and recognize the Soviet-controlled Lublin Committee as the core of a new Polish government; the West proposed a wholly new regime formed from all political parties. Finally the Allies agreed to broaden the Soviet-dominated Polish provisional government and hold "free and unfettered elections" as soon as possible, but Stalin secured his basic aim: a Soviet-dominated Poland. Germany was to be de-Nazified, demilitarized, and occupied, and France was to receive an occupation zone from the Western share. The USSR would receive half of a suggested total of $20 billion in German reparations. The Allies also agreed on voting in the United Nations and, by secret protocols, to Soviet entry into the Far Eastern war. Soviet gains at Yalta resulted from a strong military position, shrewd bargaining, and Western uncertainty.

After Yalta, Allied armies advanced swiftly. The Red Army overran Hungary, much of Austria, and crossed the Oder River. The Americans surged across the Rhine, and as Nazi resistance collapsed, the British urged them to occupy Berlin. General Eisenhower, however, halted at the Elbe River, then turned south to destroy the reputed German fortress in Bavaria. On April 17 Marshal Zhukov began his final offensive against Berlin, and on the 25th Soviet and American forces joined on the Elbe. While the Red Army was storming Berlin, Hitler committed suicide, and on May 8, 1945, his successors surrendered unconditionally.

The USSR and the Far Eastern War

The United States had long sought Soviet participation in the war against Japan, but until victory in Europe was in sight, Stalin avoided the issue. Japanese neutrality in the German-Soviet war had permitted him to bring in Siberian troops to stop the Germans at Moscow and Stalingrad. Late in 1943 Stalin hinted to the United States that the

USSR would enter the Pacific conflict soon after Germany's defeat. At Teheran Roosevelt assured Stalin that Russia could recover territories lost in the Russo-Japanese War. U.S. military chiefs estimated before Yalta that without Soviet participation it would take the United States 18 months and cost up to a million casualties to subdue Japan after Germany's surrender. Consequently, to ensure Soviet entry into the war against Japan, at Yalta Roosevelt accepted Stalin's demands for territory and spheres of interest in China and agreed to secure Chiang Kai-shek's consent to them.

On August 8, 1945, two days after the American atomic attack on Hiroshima, the USSR declared war on Japan. Justifying his action, Stalin cited somewhat lamely the "treacherous Japanese attack" in 1904 and the "blemish on the tradition of our country" left by Russia's defeat. "For 40 years we, the men of the older generation, have waited for this day." Stalin omitted to mention that in 1904 Russian Social Democrats had encouraged the Japanese to beat Russia quickly and later had celebrated Russia's defeat! Large Soviet forces overwhelmed the Japanese in Manchuria, continuing operations even after Japan's surrender on August 14. Soviet accounts claimed that the Red Army's invasion of Manchuria, not the atomic bomb, caused Japan's surrender and brought the subsequent victory to the Chinese Communists. For one week's participation in the fighting, the USSR was rewarded generously: It recovered southern Sakhalin, Port Arthur, Dairen, and the Manchurian railways, secured all the Kuril Islands, and occupied North Korea. General MacArthur, however, rejected Soviet demands for an occupation zone in Japan.

The USSR's balance sheet in World War II revealed some gains in territory and population at enormous human and material cost. About 265,000 square miles of territory with some 23.5 million people were annexed forcibly to the Soviet Union of 1939: the Baltic states, eastern Poland, Bessarabia, northern Bukovina, eastern Karelia, Carpatho-Ukraine, northern East Prussia, and the Kuril Islands. Estimates of Soviet war deaths range

from 20 to 27 million, about half civilians.[3] By contrast, German casualties were about one-third as great; U.S. losses of 295,000 were 72 times less! The Soviets suffered about 38 percent of all fatalities caused by World War II, partly because the massive conflict was fought over their territory for three and one-half years, during which the invading Nazis sought deliberately to annihilate Jews and enslave other nationalities. The criminal negligence of its political and military leaders increased Soviet losses. At Stalin's orders Soviet commanders often sought to win battles at any cost, sending many soldiers to needless slaughter. Mass civilian starvation, notably in besieged Leningrad, and Stalin's deportation of more than a million people from the Crimea and Caucasus led to additional deaths.[4] The Nazi invaders caused colossal material damage: They destroyed 1,710 towns and working settlements and more than 70,000 villages, leaving 25 million Soviet citizens homeless; they wrecked some 32,000 industrial plants and tore up more than 40,000 miles of railway.[5] At war's end, western European Russia was devastated. The country emerged from the conflict depleted in manpower and its economy a shambles. Is it any wonder that the Soviet people long retained a pervasive fear of war?

Postwar Stalinism

Domestic Affairs

As World War II ended, the exhausted Soviet people hoped for liberal change, freedom, and well-being. Instead Stalin restored total control,

---

[3] According to N. S. Khrushchev in 1961, Soviet deaths equaled 10 million soldiers and 10 million civilians. Soviet figures from 1973 (*Istoriia SSSR*, Moscow, 1973, vol. 10, p. 390) for the European republics listed as "killed and tortured to death" 6,844,551 civilians and 3,932,256 war prisoners. Western historians have come up with a total of 21.3 million—13.6 million soldiers and 7.7 million civilians killed, or 11 percent of the Soviet population in 1941.

[4] Mikhail Heller and Alexander Nekrich, *Utopia in Power: The History of the Soviet Union from 1917 to the Present* (New York, 1982), pp. 443–44.

[5] *Istoriia SSSR* (Moscow, 1973), vol. 10, p. 390.

resumed rapid industrialization, and isolated the USSR from the West. After the brief euphoria of victory celebrations, Stalin reimposed terror and party dominance, concealing rather successfully from the West signs of mass discontent revealed early in the war.

At war's end, some 5 million Soviet citizens were outside Soviet borders. At Yalta the Allies agreed to help one another bring home those of their citizens living abroad. About 3 million Soviet war prisoners, forced laborers, and defectors resided in areas under Western control, mostly Germany, and about 2 million in Soviet-occupied regions. Until 1947 Western authorities cooperated by urging or forcing (as with General Vlasov) Soviet citizens to return home. In displaced persons camps, U.S. troops forced many to leave with Soviet officials. Western leaders believed naively that with the war over, all but traitors and criminals would happily return home. About half a million "nonreturnables" stayed in the West by claiming they were Baltic or Polish nationals or by melting into the populace of disorganized Germany. The formerly pro-Soviet American journalist Louis Fischer noted that when Soviet Russians had a choice, they "voted against the Bolshevik dictatorship with their feet." Others committed suicide or redefected on the way to the USSR. Between 1945 and 1948 some 20,000 Soviet soldiers and officers defected from occupation forces, though until 1947 they were usually turned over to the Soviets for execution by their units. By 1948 Western cooperation ceased, but so did most opportunities to defect.

Returning Soviet soldiers and civilians, having seen Europe at first hand, confronted Stalin with a massive "debriefing" problem comparable with that of the tsarist regime after the Napoleonic Wars. Both governments solved it by repression and cutting ties with Europe, not with needed reforms. Isolation was essential for Stalin because Soviet living standards had fallen sharply while Russia's productive capacity had grown. His regime could not admit failure to produce abundance. Refusing economic dependence upon the West, Stalin found an alternative in quarantining his people. Thus Stalin exiled many returning POWs to Siberia and other distant regions.

Even before the war ended, a campaign began against the supposedly decaying "bourgeois" West. Closed party meetings learned: "The war on fascism ends, the war on capitalism begins" anew. Stalin's victory toast to the Russian people began the glorification of everything Russian while minimizing or ignoring debts to the West. In a February 1946 speech, Stalin reaffirmed that while capitalism survived, war was inevitable; he revived the bogey of capitalist encirclement to justify internal repression and economic sacrifice. In 1946 began the Zhdanovshchina—an ideological campaign associated with Andrei Zhdanov, Leningrad party chief, who emerged during the war as heir apparent to Stalin. (See Chapter 36.) Zhdanov, who had proclaimed socialist realism *the* acceptable art form in 1934, urged a struggle against foreign influences in Soviet life that amounted to ideological war with the West in order to demonstrate socialism's cultural superiority. "Our role . . . is to attack bourgeois culture, which is in a state of miasma and corruption." Soviet intellectuals were denounced for subservience to Western influence or using Western themes or sources. The economist Eugene Varga was castigated for doubting there would be a postwar depression in the United States. Zhdanov's campaign, demanding absolute conformity to party dictates, stifled Soviet intellectual development.

Stalin's assertions of Russian achievement reached absurd extremes. Russian or Soviet scientists were credited with almost every major scientific discovery of modern times. The desire to prove Russian self-reliance reflected a persistent Russian inferiority complex toward the West. In 1950 Stalin, attacking the late N. Marr's linguistic theories, suggested that in the socialist future a single superior language, presumably Russian, would prevail. As in the 1930s, T. D. Lysenko, an obscure plant breeder, was encouraged to denounce Western genetic theories and Soviet scientists who accepted them. (See Chapter 36.) Stalin combined xenophobic Russian nationalism and anti-Semitism: Jews were "homeless bourgeois cosmopolitans." Connected with Israel's emergence as a state and the desire of Soviet Jews to emigrate there, this campaign featured ugly anti-Semitic cartoons and severe persecution, though certain prominent Jews such as Lazar Kaganovich and the writer Ilia Ehrenburg were spared to "prove" that the regime was not anti-Semitic.

Soviet economic problems in 1945 were staggering. About one-fourth of the nation's capital resources had been destroyed, including some two-thirds in Nazi-occupied regions. Industrial and agricultural outputs were far below prewar levels; railroads were damaged or disrupted. United Nations relief and British and Swedish credits aided reconstruction, as did reparations from Germany and former Axis satellites such as Finland. Newly sovietized eastern Europe had to supply minerals, foodstuffs, and machinery, and German war prisoners helped rebuild devastated cities. Without major U.S. credits, which Stalin had hoped for, however, the reconstruction burden fell largely on the Soviet people. The Fourth Five Year Plan, stressing heavy industry and mineral production, aimed at complete rebuilding and at exceeding prewar levels in industry and agriculture. Prewar "storming" and rigid labor discipline were revived; slave labor controlled by the NKVD was used extensively. Heavy investment in construction sought to overcome a catastrophic urban housing shortage. In heavy industry the plan was largely fulfilled, although spectacular industrial growth rates partly reflected restoration of existing capacity in western Russia. More than half the 2,500 industrial plants shifted eastward during the war remained there, heightening the importance of new Siberian industrial areas. Consumer production and agriculture, however, lagged seriously, and during Stalin's lifetime Soviet living standards remained among the lowest in Europe.

With drought and severe shortages of livestock plaguing agricultural recovery, food rationing continued until December 1947. Wartime peasant encroachments on collective farms were ended, and Khrushchev, who was a close colleague of

Stalin and who was placed in charge of the Ukraine, vigorously recollectivized the western Ukraine. By 1950 the 250,000 prewar collectives had been amalgamated into about 125,000, but Khrushchev's ambitious scheme to build agricultural cities (*agrogoroda*) with peasants living in massive housing projects foundered on peasant opposition and lack of funds. In 1948 in the eastern Ukraine Stalin inaugurated a giant afforestation program, called modestly his "plan to transform nature," to stop drought and sandstorms, but it achieved little. Stalin continued to neglect agriculture as, ensconced in the Kremlin, he apparently believed stories of agricultural prosperity related by fearful subordinates. Meanwhile collective farmers remained miserably poor and lacked incentives to produce.

Nonetheless, Stalin's draconian policies brought major heavy industrial growth and some agricultural recovery. By 1953 the USSR, the world's second greatest industrial power, was moving toward Stalin's seemingly fantastic 1960 goals of 60 million tons of steel, 500 million metric tons of coal, and 60 million metric tons of oil.

Foreign Affairs

In the first postwar years the USSR greatly expanded its influence in Europe and Asia. Stalin, despite a U.S. atomic monopoly until 1949, built a bloc of satellite states in eastern Europe and promoted Communist victories in China, North Korea, and North Vietnam. His blustering tone and actions, however, then caused the West to rearm and ended opportunities for advances. Soviet expansion clashed with U.S. containment to produce the Cold War.

Between 1945 and 1948 the Soviet Union established complete control over eastern Europe. According to Soviet accounts, Communist states there emerged from native revolutions against exploitative landlords and capitalists. To construct a security shield against a German resurgence or possible Western action, Stalin ensured control in eastern European countries by "progressive elements"—that is, pro-Soviet regimes. Stalin wished to use these countries' resources to rebuild the Soviet economy and their territory to influence events in central Europe.

Soviet methods of achieving control varied, but the general pattern was similar, except in Yugoslavia where Marshal Tito won power independently. Red Army occupation was the first step, except in Czechoslovakia and Yugoslavia. National Communist parties, decimated during the war, were rebuilt and staffed mainly with Soviet-trained leaders subservient to Moscow. Usually the Soviets secured key levers of power for Communists—the army, police, and information media. Then coalition governments were formed from all "democratic, antifascist" parties. With NKVD aid, political opposition was intimidated, disorganized, and fragmented. Conservative parties, accused (often falsely) of collaborating with the Nazis, were banned while socialist parties were split, then merged forcibly with the Communists. Resulting socialist unity parties allowed Communists to control the working-class movement. Elections were often delayed until the Communists and their allies were assured of victory.

Poland, whose control was vital for Soviet domination of eastern Europe and influence in Germany, reflects these techniques clearly. Despite Yalta guarantees, Poland succumbed to Soviet domination after mild Western protests. During the war the Nazis and Soviets had decimated its intelligentsia and officer class. Then the Red Army occupied Poland, and the Communist-dominated Lublin Committee formed the nucleus of a coalition government. Mikolajczyk and three other London Poles were included, but they were powerless against the Communists, who controlled the chief ministries and forced the socialists into a coalition. Mikolajczyk, very popular with peasants, democrats, and conservatives, probably would have won a free election, but the police intimidated members of his Peasant party. In the manipulated elections of 1947 the leftist bloc won, and Mikolajczyk escaped into exile.

In Czechoslovakia the script was different but the results similar. It was the only eastern European country with an advanced industry and strong democratic traditions. A genuine democrat, Eduard Beneš, returned as president. At first the Communists (and the USSR) were popular, won 38 percent of the vote in the 1946 elections, and took over several key ministries. Under Beneš Czechoslovakia was friendly toward the USSR and sought to be a bridge between East and West, but Stalin could not tolerate a democracy on his borders. In February 1948, when democratic elements tried to force the Communist interior minister to resign, the Communists, supported by armed workers and a Red Army demonstration on the frontier, seized power and forced Beneš to resign. Klement Gottwald established a Communist regime subservient to Moscow.

Soviet expansion in eastern Europe and tension over Germany helped produce the Cold War. In March 1945 Stalin and Roosevelt exchanged heated notes over Poland; the Potsdam Conference in July revealed widening Soviet-Western differences. President Truman (who succeeded to the presidency after Roosevelt's death) and Foreign Minister Ernest Bevin of Britain (who replaced Churchill during the conference) criticized Soviet policies in eastern Europe that violated the Yalta accords. Rapid deterioration of Soviet-Western relations stemmed partly from suspicion left after Western intervention in Russia in 1918–1919 and partly from deepened differences between Soviet and Western ideologies and political systems after Stalin renewed autocracy in Russia. With the common enemy defeated, there was little to hold the USSR and the Western powers together. Stalin's xenophobia and paranoia were contributory: He considered the cessation of Lend-Lease in May 1945 and refusal of postwar American credits unfriendly acts, which they do not seem to have been. In a speech in February 1946, Stalin blamed the West for World War II and was pessimistic about prospects of future Soviet-Western friendship. Churchill's "Iron Curtain" speech at Fulton, Missouri, on March 5, 1946, cited by Western revisionist historians as having launched the Cold War, came a month later. Churchill described prophetically the Soviet domination of eastern Europe:

From Stettin on the Baltic to Trieste on the Adriatic an iron curtain has descended across the Continent. All these famous cities and the populations around them lie in the Soviet sphere and are subject, in one form or another, not only to Soviet influence, but to a very high and increasing degree of control from Moscow.[6]

The Iranian crisis was the first skirmish in the Cold War. During World War II Allied troops had occupied Iran to guard supply routes to the USSR, but they were supposed to withdraw afterward. Soviet troops, however, remained in Iran, ostensibly to protect the Baku oil fields, while in the north the Soviets, barring Iranian troops, fostered a Communist-led movement for autonomy. Accusing the USSR of interfering in its domestic affairs, Iran appealed to the United Nations, where it received strong support from the United States and Britain. In April 1946 the Soviets, after signing an agreement with Iran for joint exploitation of its oil resources, reluctantly pledged to withdraw. Once the Red Army had left, Iran suppressed the northern separatists, and its parliament rejected the Soviet-Iranian treaty.

In the eastern Mediterranean, Soviet pressure and British weakness produced another crisis. Demanding the return of Kars and Ardahan (Russian from 1878 to 1918) and bases in the Turkish Straits, Stalin massed Soviet troops on Turkey's borders and conducted a war of nerves, but Turkey refused concessions. In neighboring Greece, the Soviets, Yugoslavia, and Bulgaria supported a Communist-led guerilla movement against the conservative British-backed government. Because Roosevelt had hinted at Yalta that U.S. forces would withdraw from Europe within two years, Stalin hoped to dominate the region once Britain pulled out of Greece. To his surprise, President Truman in March 1947 pledged economic and military support to Greece and Turkey, describing the issue as a struggle between democracy and Communism. Reversing traditional U.S. iso-

lationism, this "Truman Doctrine" began a permanent U.S. commitment to Europe. The USSR denounced it as subversive of the United Nations and a "smokescreen for expansion."

In June 1947 the U.S.-sponsored Marshall Plan for European recovery confronted Stalin with a difficult decision because all European states were invited to participate. Molotov attended preliminary meetings, and Poland and Czechoslovakia showed deep interest, until Stalin abruptly recalled Molotov, forbade east European participation, and denounced the Marshall Plan as concealed American imperialism. Doing so was a serious blunder: Soviet acceptance probably would have doomed the plan in the U.S. Congress, thus enhancing Soviet prospects of dominating western Europe. Instead Stalin set up the Council of Mutual Economic Assistance (Comecon) as an eastern European equivalent. But until 1953 Comecon served largely as a device to extract resources from the satellites for the USSR.

George Kennan, a leading U.S. expert on the USSR, in July advocated long-term containment of the Soviet Union by strengthening neighboring countries until Soviet leaders abandoned designs of world domination. "For no mystical Messianic movement—and particularly not that of the Kremlin—can face frustration indefinitely, without eventually adjusting itself in one way or another to the logic of that state of affairs."[7] Kennan urged the West to adopt a patient policy of strength and await changes in Soviet conduct.

Creation of the Soviet-dominated Cominform (Communist Information Bureau) in Belgrade in September 1947, ostensibly to coordinate the Communist parties of France, Italy, and eastern Europe, deepened ideological rifts with the West. At its founding congress Zhdanov, confirming the end of Soviet-Western cooperation, described the division of international political forces into two major camps: imperialist (Western) and democratic (Soviet). Zhdanov, stating that coexistence between them was possible, warned that the

---

[6] *New York Times*, March 6, 1946, p. 4.

[7] "The Sources of Soviet Conduct," *Foreign Affairs* (July 1947), pp. 581–82.

United States had aggressive designs and was building military bases around the Soviet Union.

Soon the breach widened further. The Czech coup of February 1948 ended any Western illusions about Soviet policy in eastern Europe. Early that year the British and U.S. zones in Germany merged and a currency reform was implemented. Stalin responded in June by cutting off rail and road traffic to Berlin—despite a 1945 four-power agreement that guaranteed access—in order to expel the West from that city. Some U.S. generals, such as Lucius Clay, favored forcing the blockade, but instead the United States flew in necessary supplies until Stalin lifted the siege in May 1949. Separate German regimes were soon formed: the Federal Republic in the west and the German Democratic Republic, a Soviet satellite, in the east. Alarmed and united by the Berlin crisis, the countries of western Europe and North America formed the North Atlantic Treaty Organization, a collective security system to counter huge Soviet conventional forces with European and American armies and atomic weapons.

In June 1948 Stalin's expulsion of the Yugoslav Communist Party from the Cominform opened a breach in eastern European communism. Previously Tito had been a loyal Stalinist, but for Stalin his independent policies and tight control over his party and state proved intolerable. The Soviets accused the Yugoslavs of slandering the Red Army and the USSR and deviating from Marxism-Leninism. Behind the verbiage lay more fundamental conflicts: Tito, already dominant in Albania, aspired to lead a Balkan federation that would break Soviet domination. Stalin overrated Soviet power ("I will shake my little finger and there will be no more Tito. He will fall."), tried to remove Tito, and ordered his satellites to blockade Yugoslavia. But the Yugoslavs rallied behind Tito, who turned to the West for support, and danger of general war probably restrained Stalin from invading Yugoslavia. Tito developed a national communism that diverged markedly from that of the USSR in ideology, economy, and politics.

Stalin promptly purged other potential eastern European Titos. In Poland Wladyslaw Gomulka was removed in 1949 as the party's general secretary; in other satellites there were show trials and forced confessions resembling the Soviet purges of 1937. Soviet control was ensured by an elaborate network that included Soviet troops, diplomats, secret police agents, and "joint companies" under Soviet control. Bilateral treaties enabled the USSR to exploit the satellites economically while Stalin's towering figure dominated a monolithic eastern European bloc.

In October 1949 the Chinese Communist victory over the Nationalists created a huge Eurasian Communist bloc of more than 1 billion people. Moscow, while aiding the Communists secretly, maintained formal ties with Chiang Kai-shek to the end. Mao Tse-tung, like Tito, had controlled a party and territory before achieving power, and China was too vast to become a satellite. In February 1950, after two months of tough bargaining in Moscow, Stalin and Mao concluded a mutual defense treaty against Japan and the United States. The USSR retained its privileges, treaty ports, and control of Outer Mongolia in return for modest amounts of economic aid, but a united Communist China would clearly be harder to control than a weak Nationalist China.

In his last years Stalin continued a forward policy while carefully avoiding war. Soviet support for national liberation movements tied down large British and French forces in Malaya and Indochina. In June 1950, after Secretary of State Dean Acheson hinted that the United States would not defend South Korea, Stalin encouraged the Soviet-equipped North Koreans to invade it, but a prompt military response by the United States and other United Nations members prevented a Communist victory. Subsequent Chinese intervention in Korea, probably arranged by Stalin, produced a stalemate but enhanced China's independence of Moscow. The United States in 1951 concluded a separate peace with Japan, which emerged as its partner in the Pacific. Stalin's miscalculations in Asia revealed the limitations of Soviet power and the fact that opportunities for expansion had vanished.

The 19th Party Congress and Stalin's Death

In October 1952 Stalin convened the 19th Congress, the first party congress in 13 years. It approved the Fifth Five Year Plan, which featured the development of power resources, irrigation, and atomic weapons. The party now numbered more than 6 million members, but its top organs had become self-perpetuating and it had lost its proletarian character. Stalin instructed Khrushchev, former party boss of Ukraine, to revise party statutes and carry through reform. Top party bodies were recast: A larger Presidium replaced the Politburo, and the Orgburo and Secretariat were merged. Georgii Malenkov had been Stalin's heir apparent since Zhdanov's sudden and mysterious death in 1948. Malenkov's 50th birthday in January 1952 was celebrated with much fanfare, and he delivered the chief report at the Congress. But his position was under challenge, and before Stalin's death there was much jockeying for position within the party hierarchy.

Stalin had drawn the party line for the Congress in *Economic Problems of Socialism in the USSR*. Often considered his political testament, it discussed the transition from socialism to communism in the USSR without setting a timetable and emphasized the deepening crisis of capitalism. Stalin predicted that wars among capitalist states had become more likely than an anti-Soviet coalition. Stressing this theme at the Congress, Malenkov hinted that Soviet expansion would end temporarily while the USSR overtook the United States in military technology.

In January 1953 *Pravda* claimed that nine Kremlin doctors, six of them Jews, had hastened the deaths of high Soviet officials, including Zhdanov. This "Doctors' Plot," part of Stalin's crude anti-Semitic campaign, may have been engineered partly by Alexander Poskrebyshev, sinister head of Stalin's personal secretariat. Seemingly it was one event in a power struggle between the nationalist former adherents of Zhdanov and the more internationally oriented faction of Malenkov and Beria, the secret police chief. The atmosphere of suspicion and fear in Moscow suggested strongly that Stalin was planning a new purge. On March 4, however, Stalin, who long had suffered from heart trouble and high blood pressure, had a massive stroke and died the next day. The Malenkov-Beria group, facing demotion or destruction at his hands, may have speeded his demise, ending a quarter century of personal dictatorship and bloody brutality unmatched in world history. But unlike Hitler, who left only ruins, Stalin bequeathed to his successors a powerful industrial state that owed much to his determination and satanic energy. Because Stalin failed to designate a successor, and the Soviet system provided no legal means to select one, a ruthless power struggle was inevitable.

Suggested Additional Reading

ANDREYEV, C. *Vlasov and the Russian Liberation Movement* . . . (Cambridge, 1987).

ARMSTRONG, J. A. *Soviet Partisans in World War II* (Madison, WI, 1964).

ARONSEN, L., and M. KITCHEN. *The Origins of the Cold War in Comparative Perspective . . . 1941–48* (New York, 1988).

BACON, E. *The Gulag at War: Stalin's Forced Labour System in the Light of the Archives* (New York, 1994).

BIALER, S. *Stalin and His Generals* . . . (New York, 1969).

BRZEZINSKI, Z. *The Soviet Bloc: Unity and Conflict*, 2d ed. (Cambridge, MA, 1961).

BUHITE, R. D. *Soviet-American Relations in Asia 1945–1954* (Norman, OK, 1981).

CARRELL, P. *Scorched Earth: The Russian-German War, 1943–44* (Boston, 1970).

CHUIKOV, V. I. *The Battle for Stalingrad* (New York, 1964).

CLARK, A. *Barbarossa: The Russian-German Conflict, 1941–1945* (New York, 1965).

CLEMENS, D. S. *Yalta* (New York, 1970).

CONQUEST, R. *The Nation Killers: Soviet Deportation of Nationalities* (New York, 1970).

COOPER, M. *The Nazi War Against Soviet Partisans, 1941–1944* (New York, 1979).

COUNTS, G. S. *The Country of the Blind: The Soviet System of Mind Control* (Westport, CT, 1959).

CRAIG, W. *Enemy at the Gates: . . . Stalingrad* (New York, 1973).

DALLIN, A. *German Rule in Russia, 1941–45* (New York, 1957, 1980).

DOUGLAS, R. *From War to Cold War 1942–48* (New York, 1981).

DMYTRYSHYN, B. *Moscow and the Ukraine, 1918–1953* (New York, 1956).

DUNN, W. S., JR. *The Soviet Economy and the Red Army, 1930–1945* (Westport, CT, 1995).

ERICKSON, J. *The Road to Berlin: Continuing the History of Stalin's War with Germany* (Boulder, CO, 1983).

FEIS, H. *Churchill–Roosevelt–Stalin* (Princeton, 1957).

FISCHER, G. *Soviet Opposition to Stalin* (Cambridge, MA, 1952).

FUGATE, B. *Operation Barbarossa* (Novato, CA, 1984).

HAHN, W. G. *Postwar Soviet Politics . . . 1946–53* (Ithaca, NY, 1982).

HARBUTT, F. *The Iron Curtain: Churchill, America, and the Origins of the Cold War* (New York and Oxford, 1986).

HARRISON, M. *Accounting for War: Soviet Production, Employment, and the Defence Burden, 1940–1945* (Cambridge, 1996).

HERRING, G. *Aid to Russia, 1941–46 . . .* (New York, 1973).

HOLLOWAY, D. *Stalin and the Bomb: The Soviet Union and Atomic Energy, 1939–1956* (New Haven, CT, 1994).

KORIAKOV, M. *I'll Never Go Back: A Red Army Officer Talks,* trans. N. Wreden (New York, 1948).

KUZNETSOV, A. *Babi Yar,* trans. D. Floyd (New York, 1970).

LIDDELL-HART, B. H. *The Red Army . . .* (Gloucester, MA, 1956).

LUCAS, J. S. *War on the Eastern Front 1941–45* (New York, 1982).

LYONS, G., ed. *The Russian Version of the Second World War* (New York, 1983).

MASTNY, V. *Russia's Road to the Cold War . . .* (New York, 1979).

MCCAGG, W. O. *Stalin Embattled, 1943–1948* (Detroit, 1978).

NEKRICH, A. M. *The Punished Peoples . . . ,* trans. G. Saunders (New York, 1978).

PATERSON, T. G., and R. J. MCMAHON, eds. *The Origins of the Cold War* (Lexington, MA, 1991).

PETROV, V., comp. *June 22, 1941* (Columbia, SC, 1968).

REDLICH, S. *War, Holocaust and Stalinism* (Toronto, 1995).

REINHARDT, K. *The Turning Point: The Failure of Hitler's Strategy in the Winter of 1941–42,* trans. Karl B. Keenan (Oxford and New York, 1992).

RZHESHEVSKY, O. *War and Diplomacy: The Making of a Grand Alliance* (Toronto, 1996).

SALISBURY, H. *The 900 Days: The Siege of Leningrad* (New York, 1969).

SEATON, A. *Stalin as Military Commander* (New York, 1976).

SHULMAN, M. *Stalin's Foreign Policy Reappraised* (Cambridge, MA, 1963).

SIMONOV, K. *Days and Nights* (New York, 1945). (Novel on Stalingrad.)

SNELL, J., ed. *The Meaning of Yalta* (Baton Rouge, 1956).

STEENBERG, S. *Vlasov* (New York, 1970).

TARRANT, V. E. *Stalingrad: Anatomy of an Agony* (New York, 1992).

VITUKHIN, I., ed. *Soviet Generals Recall World War II* (New York, 1981).

WERTH, A. *Russia at War, 1941–45* (New York, 1964, 1984).

WOHLFORTH, W. C. *The Elusive Balance: Power and Perceptions during the Cold War* (Ithaca, NY, 1993).

ZAWODNY, J. K. *Death in the Forest: . . . the Katyn Forest Massacre* (Notre Dame, 1980).

———. *Nothing But Honour: The Story of the Warsaw Uprising, 1944* (Stanford, 1978).

ZHUKOV, G. E. *Marshal Zhukov's Greatest Battles* (New York, 1969).

ZINNER, P. *Communist Strategy and Tactics in Czechoslovakia, 1918–1948* (New York, 1963).

39

The Khrushchev Era, 1953–1964

Stalin's death in March 1953 touched off a power struggle involving the major forces in the Soviet system: the party, the state, the army, and the police. As Stalin's successors tried new methods of rule and sought public support, controls over the USSR and eastern Europe were relaxed considerably. Nikita S. Khrushchev (1894–1971), the eventual winner, lacked Stalin's absolute authority and wooed the public by denouncing Stalin's crimes, improving living standards, and barnstorming around the country. Khrushchev retained the chief features of the Soviet system, but he instituted important changes. Abroad, revolts in Poland and Hungary loosened Soviet control over the satellites. Between the USSR and Communist China ideological and political conflict erupted, which produced a Communist world with several power centers and varying approaches. How and why did Khrushchev win the power struggle in the USSR? How great was his authority afterward? Why did he institute de-Stalinization, and what were its effects? How fundamental were the differences between Khrushchev's Russia and Stalin's? How did the Soviet position in world affairs change

under Khrushchev? How was he viewed by his successors?

Politics: Repudiating Stalinism

After Stalin's death, the principle of collective leadership revived and individual dictatorship was repudiated. As Stalin was placed in the Lenin-Stalin Mausoleum, his chief pallbearers—Georgii Malenkov, Lavrenti Beria, and V. M. Molotov—appealed to the populace for unity and to avoid "confusion and panic." Briefly Malenkov held the two chief power positions of premier and first party secretary, but within two weeks he resigned as first secretary, and in September Khrushchev assumed that post. Marshal Zhukov, the World War II hero, became deputy defense minister as genuine collective rule and surface harmony prevailed.

In April 1953 *Pravda* announced that the "Doctors' Plot" had been a hoax. There was a shake-up in the secret police, and its chief, Beria, suddenly posed as a defender of "socialist legality" and urged liberal revisions of the criminal code. In June his security forces apparently tried a coup, but

SOVFOTO

Stalin's coffin being carried out of the House of Trade Unions in March 1953. Right to left: L. Beria, G. Malenkov, Vassily Stalin (J. Stalin's son), V. Molotov, Marshal Bulganin, L. Kaganovich, and N. Shvernik.

party, state, and army leaders combined against him. Beria was arrested and may have been shot in the Kremlin by Marshal Zhukov. In December his "execution" was announced, and he became an "unperson." Subscribers to the *Great Soviet Encyclopedia* were instructed to remove his biography and paste in an enclosed article on the Bering Sea! The secret police came under closer party control.

For the rest of 1953 the Soviet press featured a jovial-looking Malenkov as the principal leader, who stressed consumer goods production and

pledged that Soviet living standards would soon rise markedly. *Izvestiia,* the government newspaper, pushed this proconsumer line until December 1954, but *Pravda,* the party organ controlled by Khrushchev, denounced it as "a belching of the Right deviation . . . , views which Rykov, Bukharin, and their ilk once preached." (And they had been executed!) In February 1955 Malenkov resigned as premier, citing "inexperience" and accepting blame for agricultural failures. Marshal N. A. Bulganin, a political general and Khrushchev appointee, replaced him as premier.

Khrushchev, like Stalin, consolidated his power behind the scenes. A genuine man of the people, he epitomized the revolutionary principle: careers open to talent. Khrushchev was born in Kalinovka, a village in Kursk province near the Ukrainian border; his ancestors were serfs, his father a peasant, then a coal miner, and his own childhood full of hardships. His image while Soviet leader reflected his peasant heritage. Attending the parish school, Khrushchev was the first member of his family to become literate. He joined the Bolshevik party in 1918, worked by day and attended school at night, fought in the Civil War, and revealed leadership and strong ambition. In 1929, still rough and uncouth, he was sent to the Moscow Industrial Academy to complete his education. By sheer ability and drive he came to lead its party organization. Three years later he became a member of the Central Committee and in 1935 headed the key Moscow party organization and guided it through the Great Purge. Invaluable to Stalin, he kept making speeches while others fell silent. In 1938 he was assigned to Ukraine, completed ruthless purges there, and the next year entered the Politburo as a full member. During and after World War II he served as boss of Ukraine. Throughout his career Khrushchev displayed toughness, resourcefulness, practicality, and a frank independence uncharacteristic of Stalin's henchmen. In 1950, surviving the failure of his untimely agricultural cities scheme, he stormed again into the inner circle of power.

After Malenkov's fall, Khrushchev was the most powerful member of the collective, sharing power with Premier Bulganin and Defense Minister Zhukov. During 1955–1956, he and Bulganin traveled to eastern Europe and Asia and undermined the power position of Foreign Minister Molotov. Meanwhile Khrushchev was replacing his rivals' supporters in the Secretariat with his own men.

Khrushchev dominated the 20th Party Congress of February 1956. In a dramatic secret speech, he denounced the crimes of the Stalin era and began building up his own image as Lenin's loyal follower as steps toward full power. (See Problem 14 at the end of this chapter.) He overcame strong conservative opposition to the proposed speech by threatening to denounce Stalin publicly. In the speech, he accused Stalin of fostering a personality cult, claiming infallibility, and liquidating thousands of honest Communists and military leaders out of paranoidal suspicion. Stalin, he claimed, had gravely weakened the Red Army by executing its top leaders, and his inaction in June 1941 had brought the USSR to the brink of defeat. Khrushchev's speech established him as a reform leader campaigning for basic political changes and won him wide support from younger provincial party leaders. He sought to break the hold that Stalin retained over the party even from the grave, absolve himself of responsibility for Stalin's crimes, and dissociate himself from the dictator's closest lieutenants, Molotov and Malenkov. Khrushchev depicted Stalinism as an aberration and urged a return to Leninism and collective leadership. Molotov's resignation as foreign minister in June 1956 confirmed the power of Khrushchev's forces.

Opposition to Khrushchev was weakened, not broken. The upheavals in Poland and Hungary in late 1956 (discussed later in this chapter) temporarily lowered his prestige. By creating regional economic councils (*sovnarkhozy*), Khrushchev aimed to break the technocrats' hold over the central economic ministries, but this action stimulated his opponents to desperate countermeasures. In June 1957, while Khrushchev and Bulganin visited Finland, his rivals united, secured a Presidium majority, and voted him out of office. Returning hastily, Khrushchev proved his mastery over the party apparatus. He weaned waverers (Voroshilov, Bulganin, Saburov, and Pervukhin) from his chief opponents (Malenkov, Molotov, Kaganovich, and Shepilov) and insisted that the Central Committee vote on his removal. With Marshal Zhukov's support, Khrushchev's provincial supporters were flown to Moscow. The Central Committee then reversed the Presidium's action and expelled his chief rivals, henceforth dubbed the "antiparty group." Through maneuver and compromise, Khrushchev had won a decisive though limited victory.

Khrushchev moved swiftly to consolidate his power. Marshal Zhukov, accused of building a personality cult in the Red Army, was removed from the Presidium and as defense minister and replaced by Marshal Rodion Malinovskii. In March 1958 Bulganin resigned and Khrushchev became premier, confirming his predominant role in party and state. He became an undisputed and very popular leader, with enthusiastic support from the Soviet people who enjoyed his informality, his appearances around the country, and his well-publicized trips abroad. However, even during his six years of personal rule, Khrushchev never possessed Stalin's authority. He could not dictate to the Presidium, and he needed almost four years to remove his opponents from their posts. The "antiparty" leaders were exiled but not imprisoned, and even then Khrushchev's reform program was opposed strongly by a conservative group led by Mikhail Suslov.

Nikita Khrushchev represented something new and exciting for the Soviet public: an ordinary-looking Russian, open and garrulous, who had a real flair for public relations. Unlike Stalin, a suspicious paranoid ensconced within the Kremlin, Khrushchev plunged boldly into crowds and expressed his opinions flamboyantly. He was a risk taker and innovator who promised to improve living conditions for average people. He contrasted with Stalin in character and approach as dramatically as Gorbachev would later differ from his elderly predecessors. However, city intellectuals scorned Khrushchev for his ungrammatical Russian and boorish, often reckless behavior.

Once in power, Khrushchev reduced the apparatus of terror and rebuilt the party as his chosen instrument of power. Malenkov had released some political prisoners, but Khrushchev released millions, especially in 1956. Victims of Stalin's terror were rehabilitated, often posthumously, notably Marshal Tukhachevskii and other Red Army leaders purged by Stalin. Police influence declined, and

Nikita Khrushchev (1894–1971).

a more relaxed and hopeful political climate developed. Khrushchev sought popularity by mixing with the people, traveling around the USSR, and delivering homey speeches to workers and peasants. Unlike Stalin, the Kremlin recluse, Khrushchev remained informal, jovial, and talkative, bringing new and able people from industry to revive the party, which Stalin had demoralized by terror. Promoting his youthful provincial supporters, he increased party authority over the technocrats. Like Lenin, Khrushchev stressed persuasion, not coercion, and party congresses, rare under Stalin, now met regularly.

In January 1959 Khrushchev convened a special 21st Congress to approve a Seven Year Plan to begin building communism. Khrushchev launched a miniature personality cult, which described him as "Lenin's comrade-in-arms" and architect of the transition to communism. Urging preparation of a new party program, he stressed that the state's coercive aspects were "withering away" and that some administrative and police functions could be transferred to "public" organizations such as the Komsomol. Opponents, however, objected to any premature dissolution of the state, and after the congress Khrushchev's erratic behavior and policy shifts revealed his continuing problems with the opposition.

The 22nd Congress of October 1961 convened mainly to adopt a new party program, which proclaimed: "The present generation of Soviet people shall live under communism." But at the congress Khrushchev renewed his anti-Stalin campaign and depicted Stalin's atrocities publicly in greater depth and detail. He accused Stalin of authorizing Kirov's assassination in 1934, which led to the Great Purge, and linked Molotov and Voroshilov with him in that affair. "Antiparty" elements, he claimed, had executed Stalin's repressive policies, whereas his own regime had broken cleanly with the past. In response to demands of some delegates, Stalin's body was removed from the mausoleum and reburied in the Kremlin wall. Moderates in the Presidium (Aleksei Kosygin, Mikhail Suslov, and Anastas Mikoian), however, blocked Khrushchev's efforts to expel "antiparty" leaders from the party. Then the Cuban missile crisis shattered his prestige, and only at the Central Committee's June 1963 plenum, which named Leonid Brezhnev and Nicholas Podgorny (his allies in the Presidium) as party secretaries, did Khrushchev seem to recover his authority. The "antiparty" leaders were expelled from the party but not tried. Khrushchev's 70th birthday in April 1964 was appropriately celebrated by the Soviet press, but he was not portrayed as absolute or indispensable. His struggle with the opposition remained inconclusive and his victory incomplete. Khrushchev's personal rule lasted only six years, 1958–1964.

After 1953 the relaxation of some totalitarian controls enhanced the Soviet regime's legitimacy for most of the population. With the overpowering authoritarian image of Stalin gone and brutal police repression ended, a political reform movement developed among younger intellectuals and those released from Stalin's camps. This movement aimed at democratization, civil liberties, and preventing a reversion to Stalinism. Marxist-Leninist ideology became less effective and credible. The critical reaction of youthful dissidents ("sons") to the values of Stalinist "fathers" was reflected in the reactions of Vladimir Osipov, later editor of the underground journal *Veche,* to Khrushchev's secret speech:

> Overthrown was the man who had personified the existing system and ideology to such an extent that the very words "the Soviet power" and "Stalin" seemed to have been synonymous. We all, the future rebels, at the dawn of our youth, had been fanatical Stalinists [and] had believed with a truly religious fervor. . . . Khrushchev's speech and the 20th Congress destroyed our faith, having extracted from it its very core . . . . , Joseph Stalin.[1]

The ensuing Hungarian Revolution profoundly affected Soviet university students. In Leningrad alone, some 2,000 were disciplined or expelled for condemning Soviet armed intervention in Hungary. They formed a number of political and literary groups that produced self-published (*samizdat*) underground journals.

Toward the non-Russian nationalities of the USSR Khrushchev pursued generally conciliatory policies while pushing efforts at linguistic and cultural Russification. Some of the peoples Stalin had deported during World War II were allowed to return home, but the Crimean Tatars and Volga Germans remained conspicuous exceptions. Finally, in 1964, Khrushchev rehabilitated the Volga Germans by decree in an effort to improve relations with West Germany, but he did not restore their autonomous republic. Crimean Tatar petitions to the government to permit their return to their ancestral homeland were pointedly ignored.

---

[1] Quoted in H. Morton and R. Tökes, *Soviet Politics and Society in the 1970s* (New York, 1974), p. 10.

Economy: Focus on Agriculture

After 1953, despite some major policy changes, the Soviet economy retained the chief strengths and weaknesses of the Stalin period and was run by men trained under Stalin. It remained a centrally planned economy in which heavy industry and defense were emphasized, though the consumer sector now received more resources. Under Malenkov the collective leadership, to win public support, pledged that for the first time since 1928 consumer industry would grow faster than heavy industry. In April 1953 food prices were considerably reduced, but since key items such as meat were in short supply, the result was long lines and shortages. Compulsory bond purchases were reduced and the worker's take-home pay increased, but not the supply of available goods.

Khrushchev emphasized agriculture and began with a frank statement on its sad condition. Soviet collective farming in 1953 was unproductive and unworthy of a great power: Half the population barely fed the other half. Soviet livestock herds, noted Khrushchev, were smaller than in 1928 or even 1916. Heavy taxes on private peasant plots discouraged production of desperately needed meat, milk, and vegetables. These shortcomings must be overcome in two to three years, warned Khrushchev, always in a hurry. During the next five years many steps were taken to foster agricultural growth. State prices for farmers' compulsory deliveries and over-quota shipments were raised sharply, especially for grains. In 1954 the average price paid for all agricultural products was more than double the 1952 level; in 1956 it was two and one-half times higher. The state assumed most collective farm transportation costs, wrote off their old debts, and reduced taxes on private plots and limitations on private livestock holdings. Tractor and fertilizer production were expanded. Greater incentives to farmers and increased state investment in agriculture stimulated a 50-percent rise in output between 1953 and 1958.

Khrushchev's most controversial gamble was plowing up millions of acres of semiarid soil in the virgin lands of northern Kazakhstan. Reviving a plan of 1940 that had never been implemented, he sought to solve the grain shortage by greatly increasing the cultivated area of the USSR. By the end of 1956, 88.6 million additional acres had been placed under cultivation, an area equal to the total cultivated land of Canada. Hundreds of new state farms were created, some 300,000 persons permanently relocated in Kazakhstan, and additional hundreds of thousands helped bring in the harvest. Leonid I. Brezhnev, then second party secretary of Kazakhstan, directed this campaign. In 1955 drought brought a poor crop and threatened Khrushchev's position, but an excellent harvest in 1956 apparently vindicated his risky experiment: Kazakhstan alone provided 16 million tons of grain.

The Sixth Five Year Plan, approved in 1956 by the 20th Congress, set ambitious goals for agriculture, including a grain output of 180 million tons. In 1957 began a hectic campaign to overtake the United States in per capita production of meat, milk, and butter. Khrushchev toured the country, made many speeches, and dismissed numerous officials. He pushed the development of state farms at the expense of collectives (*kolkhozy*) and amalgamated the latter into larger units. (*Kolkhozy* decreased from 125,000 in 1950 to 69,100 in 1958.) In 1958 Machine Tractor Stations were abolished and *kolkhozy* were forced to purchase their machines.

Industrial growth in the 1950s continued to be rapid despite management problems. The Fifth Plan's goals were mostly fulfilled, and the Sixth Plan prescribed creation of a third major metallurgical base in Kazakhstan and western Siberia. Industrial management, however, became entangled with Khrushchev's drive for political supremacy. In February 1957 Khrushchev's scheme to scrap central industrial ministries in Moscow and replace them with regional economic councils (*sovnarkhozy*), eventually 107 in number, under Gosplan was approved. Causing a massive exodus of ministry personnel to the provinces, it made regional party secretaries virtual economic dictators. Khrushchev achieved his political aim of weakening the ministerial hierarchy but not the

economic goal of greater industrial efficiency. The
sovnarkhozy were supposed to overcome supply
problems, avoid duplication, and improve regional
planning, but they catered to selfish local interests,
and individual enterprises often received no clear
directives or got conflicting orders from various
agencies. In the partial recentralization of 1963,
sovnarkhozy were reduced in number and 17 larger
economic planning regions were created.
Khrushchev's insistence in 1962 on splitting party
organizations into industrial and agricultural
hierarchies caused much confusion and uncertainty, especially because *sovnarkhozy* rarely corresponded with the new party units. By 1963
industrial and agricultural management were
chaotic.

Meanwhile, in 1959, the Sixth Five Year Plan
had been scrapped in midcourse in favor of
Khrushchev's grandiose Seven Year Plan "to construct the bases of communism."[2] It featured
heavy investment in the chemical industry, non-
solid fuels, and development of Asiatic Russia. In
1961 Khrushchev raised some of the plan's goals,
including steel output. During its first years industrial progress remained impressive, but thereafter
declining growth rates in industry and agriculture
made a mockery of Khrushchev's 1961 party program, which foresaw the attainment by 1980 of
industrial output and living standards far exceeding those of capitalist countries. In 1963 the Seven
Year Plan was abandoned as impossible of
achievement, a tacit admission that the party
program likewise was unrealizable.

Agricultural stagnation and lagging labor productivity slowed overall Soviet economic growth
after 1958. Agricultural output, supposed to rise 70
percent during the Seven Year Plan, increased only
14 percent (crops only 7 percent). Bad weather

was a factor, especially in 1963, but other reasons
were more important. Suddenly dissolving most
Machine Tractor Stations and compelling the
collective farms to purchase their machinery virtually bankrupted poorer farms. Dispersed among
kolkhozy, the machines could not be properly
maintained or repaired. Because *kolkhozy* lacked
the capital to purchase new machinery, the agricultural equipment industry was brought to the
verge of ruin. This poorly thought out and irresponsibly executed reform had a depressing effect
on collective farm production.

Equally harmful was Khrushchev's optimistic
but ill-conceived campaign, announced in May
1957, to overtake the United States in production
of meat, milk, and butter within three to four
years. This campaign provoked what the Med-
vedevs call "the Riazan fiasco." Responding to
Khrushchev's appeal, A. N. Larionov, ambitious
party secretary of Riazan province, pledged to
more than double meat deliveries to the state in
1959. This goal was achieved by slaughtering beef
and milk cows and buying animals and meat from
other provinces; Larionov became a Hero of
Socialist Labor. However, by 1960 Riazan's agriculture was ruined, its herds decimated, and its
kolkhozy in debt. With Riazan unable to deliver
even half its normal quota of meat and grain, the
"heroic" Larionov shot himself. National production of meat fell sharply, and Khrushchev's boast
to overtake America in meat production became
a bad joke.[3] Thus Khrushchev's personal campaigns, interference, and hasty reorganizations did
considerable harm. He did not create the nation's
agricultural problems, but his policies often made
them worse. In March 1962 he told the Central
Committee:

> Communism cannot be conceived of as a table
> with empty places at which sit highly con-
> scious and fully equal people. . . . It is necessary
> to double and triple the output of major farm
> products in a short period. . . . The develop-

---

[2] Khrushchev's Plan called for an increase of 62 to 65 percent in national income (58 percent was achieved); 80
percent in gross industrial output (84 percent achieved);
grain, 164 to 180 million tons (121 million achieved); and
meat, 6.13 million tons (5.25 million achieved). See Alec
Nove, *An Economic History of the USSR, 1917–1991* (New
York, 1992), p. 363.

[3] Roy Medvedev and Zhores Medvedev, *Khrushchev: The
Years in Power,* trans. A. Durkin (New York, 1978), pp.
80–100.

ment of agriculture is an integral part of the creation of the material and technical bases of communism.

Instead Soviet grain production in 1963 fell 27 million tons below the high point reached in 1958, and millions of tons had to be imported from the United States and Canada. Poor economic performance after 1958 made Khrushchev increasingly vulnerable politically.

Beginning in 1958 the Soviet wage system was reformed with a trend away from the piece rates that had been prevalent under Stalin. New minimum wages in town and country gave the lowest paid workers substantial increases. To cut pay differentials, some higher salaries (for example, those of professors) were reduced. The workweek was gradually shortened, maternity leaves were lengthened, and industrial pensions and disability benefits were much improved. The currency reform of 1961 exchanged 1 new ruble for 10 old ones; the rate of 4 rubles to the dollar was altered arbitrarily to 0.90 rubles per dollar. As direct taxes were further reduced, the turnover tax remained the chief source of state revenue.

In foreign trade, important changes occurred under Khrushchev. The USSR abandoned Stalin's policy of exploiting the European satellites economically, scrapped the joint companies that had done so, and paid fairer prices for eastern European goods. In 1954 the multilateral Council for Mutual Economic Assistance (Comecon) was revived, though most Soviet trade with eastern Europe remained bilateral. The USSR moved into the foreign aid field and, in 1953 China received a long-term Soviet credit of 520 million rubles. (The Soviets had removed equipment worth more than three times that much from Manchuria in 1945!) After Khrushchev visited India in 1955, a major program of foreign economic aid to that country began, partly to compete with the United States in the Third World. The Soviets supplied goods on credit, especially to India and Egypt, for later repayment in goods. Soviet imports and exports increased sharply. Using 1955 as the base year (100), imports in 1950 had been 54.6 and

exports 56.7. By 1958 they were 148.4 and 130, respectively.[4]

Living standards of most Soviet citizens improved considerably under Khrushchev, but this rise whetted their appetites for more. Beginning in 1956, housing construction spurted and private home building received more state support. Even millions of new apartments, mostly in massive, ugly blocks derisively dubbed "Khrushchev slums," could not satisfy demand. Between 1953 and 1964 the Soviet population rose from 188 to 228 million, mostly in cities. Just before his fall, Khrushchev declared that the chief task of the near future was "a further rise in the living standard of the people. . . . Now when we have a mighty [heavy] industry, the party is setting the task of the more rapid development of the branches that produce consumer goods." Performance did not match these promises.

Foreign Affairs: Crises in the Communist Bloc Countries

Soviet foreign policy quickly discarded its rigid Stalinist mold to adopt flexible, varied tactics. Malenkov began the shift and Khrushchev, stressing peaceful coexistence with the West from February 1956, continued and extended this new approach. It had to overcome a conservative hardline opposition, led first by Molotov and later apparently by Suslov, which favored a more aggressive anti-Western course. Stalin's successors found it increasingly difficult to maintain leadership of the Communist bloc and world Communist movement in the face of Chinese and Yugoslav challenges.

After Stalin's death, the collective leadership promoted détente with the West and China, as Premier Malenkov warned that nuclear war might destroy all humankind, not just capitalism. In July 1953 an armistice ended the Korean War, and at

---

[4] A. Nove, *An Economic History of the USSR* (London, 1969), p. 352.

the Geneva Conference of 1954 the USSR supported settlement of the Indochina conflict, although no settlement was forthcoming. The tone and manners of Soviet diplomacy began to mellow. Unable to coerce China, Soviet leaders courted it, promising technical aid, loans, and experts to assist Chinese industrialization, and agreed to end special privileges, abolish joint companies, and return Port Arthur to China.

Soviet leaders wished to prevent West Germany from rearming and entering NATO, but they refused to sacrifice their East German satellite. Early in 1954 a four-power conference called to reach a general German settlement ended in stalemate. After West Germany joined NATO, the Soviets in May 1955 set up the Warsaw Pact, a defensive alliance of the satellites and the USSR, with the latter commanding all the military forces, thus legalizing the presence of Soviet troops in eastern Europe.

Foreign trips by top Soviet leaders, beginning in 1955, fostered a new image of Soviet foreign policy. Khrushchev made a pilgrimage to Belgrade, blamed the Soviet-Yugoslav breach of 1948 on Beria, and over Molotov's strong objections achieved reconciliation with Marshal Tito. The expanding Soviet foreign aid program and the wooing of such neutral countries as India signified the replacement of Zhdanov's two-camp thesis (socialism versus capitalism) with a more flexible three-camp concept to include neutral countries. In May 1955 the USSR signed an Austrian peace treaty, which ended four-power occupation and made Austria a neutral country. (See Map 39.1.) Apparently Moscow hoped that West Germany would leave NATO in order to achieve German reunification on a similar basis. This policy culminated in the Geneva Summit Conference (July 1955) between President Eisenhower and a smiling Khrushchev and Bulganin. The amiable "Geneva spirit" produced no substantive agreements, but reduced Cold War tensions and enhanced Khrushchev's prestige abroad.

A crisis confronted the USSR in eastern Europe in 1956. Without Stalin's awesome image, the unpopular satellite regimes proved vulnerable to public agitation for change. As Soviet controls relaxed and a degree of diversity appeared, a workers' uprising in East Germany (June 1953) had to be crushed by Soviet tanks. Khrushchev's secret speech further undermined the satellite regimes. In June 1956 riots in the Polish industrial city of Poznan swelled into a national movement of liberalization and brought the hasty restoration of Wladyslaw Gomulka, purged by Stalin, as first secretary of the Polish Communist Party. When top Soviet leaders stormed into Warsaw on October 19, the new Polish leadership presented a united front. In a compromise solution, Poland won domestic autonomy while remaining in the Warsaw Pact and pledging loyalty to the USSR in foreign affairs. Such "domesticism" became a model for other eastern European countries. Preserving Soviet domination of the region, it freed the USSR from detailed supervision of domestic affairs in the satellites.

Meanwhile in Hungary a broad popular movement led by students and intellectuals demanded drastic political reforms. Premier Imre Nagy failed to halt Stalinist Hungary's rapid disintegration. After a revolt in Budapest (October 23), Nagy announced that Hungary would leave the Warsaw Pact, become a neutral country, and restore a multiparty system. Much of the Hungarian army joined the insurgents, who appealed to the West for aid. Janos Kadar, hastily named the new first secretary of the Hungarian Communist Party, "invited" in Soviet troops, which soon crushed the rebels as thousands of Hungarians fled into exile. The Soviet response in Hungary showed that the USSR would act militarily within its sphere of interest whenever Communist rule was threatened, demonstrating anew that Communist control in eastern Europe was based not on consent but on Soviet bayonets and the unreliability of satellite armies.

Toward the West, Khrushchev combined "peaceful coexistence" with bluster and threats. To him coexistence meant avoiding war and preventing nuclear rearmament of West Germany. The USSR sponsored the Rapacki Plan (October 1957), named after the Polish foreign minister, for a

Russian occupied zones in Austria (evacuated in 1955) and Germany

British, French, and American occupied zones

The "Iron Curtain" in 1948

Former German and Czechoslovak territory annexed by Russia in 1945

Principal areas of anti-Soviet protest and revolt 1953–1968 crushed by Soviet military intervention (East Germany, Hungary, Czechoslovakia) and by strong political pressure (Poland)

Map 39.1 USSR and Eastern Europe, 1945–1989

SOURCE: Adapted with permission of Macmillan Publishing Co., Inc. from *Russian History Atlas* by Martin Gilbert. Cartography by Martin Gilbert. Copyright © by Martin Gilbert.

nuclear-free zone in central Europe. Khrushchev's caution in 1958 during crises over Taiwan and Lebanon involving the United States distressed hard-liners in Moscow and Beijing. The growing Chinese challenge helped provoke Khrushchev to deliver an ultimatum to the West over Berlin in November 1958, hoping to force Western powers out of that city. When his ultimatum instead stimulated Western unity and determination, Khrushchev backed down. His erratic policies toward the West reflected his weakness at home and vulnerability to conservative critics.

At a meeting in November 1957 to celebrate the 40th anniversary of the Bolshevik Revolution, the 12 ruling Communist parties issued the Moscow Declaration, which stressed the unity of the socialist camp headed by the USSR. The Yugoslavs, affirming that every country should determine its own road to socialism, refused to sign and accused the USSR of bureaucracy and departures from true Marxism-Leninism; Moscow retorted that Tito was a revisionist kowtowing to U.S. imperialism. Although the second Soviet-Yugoslav dispute (1958–1961) avoided an open breach, Yugoslav independence and the potential threat of national communism to Soviet leadership were reaffirmed.

After 1957 Soviet foreign policy was influenced strongly by the triangular Soviet-U.S.-Chinese relationship. Khrushchev was caught between his desire for détente with the West and the maintenance of Soviet leadership of the Communist Bloc against more militant China. Seeking to score points against "American imperialism" in the Middle East, he backed Arab states against pro-Western Israel and Turkey and rattled his rockets. The growing Soviet commitment to the Arabs proved expensive, especially the construction for Egypt of the Aswan Dam, which the United States had refused to finance.

Renewed Soviet overtures to the United States ended in failure. After his Berlin ultimatum had failed to budge the West, Khrushchev at the 21st Congress (January 1959) made warm references to the United States, and in September he became the first Russian ruler to visit the United States. This trip was a personal triumph for Khrushchev and cemented his relationship with a flexible President Eisenhower; they agreed to hold a summit conference in Moscow in 1960. When a U.S. U-2 reconnaissance plane spying over Soviet territory was shot down and its pilot captured, Eisenhower took responsibility for the flight but refused to apologize officially. An angry Khrushchev then sabotaged the summit and withdrew his invitation to Eisenhower to visit the USSR.

More serious was a growing rift between the USSR and China, which now became public and disrupted Bloc unity. Between 1957 and 1960, though their relations seemed harmonious, mounting Soviet criticism of China's industrial "Great Leap Forward" suggested that China might reach communism before the USSR. Khrushchev's party program of 1961 was in direct response to this Chinese challenge. The Chinese also condemned Soviet détente with the West. In 1960 began thinly concealed mutual vilification: The Chinese attacked Yugoslav "revisionism," and the Soviets denounced the Stalinist Albanian regime, which sought Chinese support, as "dogmatic," but clearly they were striking at each other. Sino-Soviet tension was only partly ideological. Mao was now the senior leader of world communism, and in intra-Bloc disputes the Chinese adopted an orthodox, Stalinist line, which was supported by some of the Soviet "antiparty group." Militance in promoting revolution and national liberation won the Chinese widespread support in Asia and Africa. A unified Communist China challenged the Soviet position in Asia and posed a potential threat to underpopulated Siberia. Noting niggardly Soviet economic aid to them, the Chinese complained that Khrushchev was more generous to nonaligned India and Egypt. Asserting that tsarist Russia in the 1850s had acquired the Maritime Province unfairly, Chinese maps showed portions of the Soviet Far East as Chinese territory. Khrushchev withdrew some Soviet technicians from China and sought to dissuade the Chinese from developing nuclear weapons, but in 1959 Beijing decided to manufacture its own. In April 1960 *Red Flag,* a Beijing journal, denouncing Khrushchev's policy of coexistence with capitalism, affirmed that nuclear war would destroy imperialism but not the socialist camp. At the Romanian Party Congress in June, Khrushchev, quarreling violently with the Chinese delegates, castigated their leaders as nationalists, adventurers, and "madmen" seeking to unleash nuclear war.

Attempts to resolve the Sino-Soviet dispute failed. In the summer of 1960 a world Communist

Congress in Moscow, representing 81 parties, sought to restore unity. Khrushchev, however, clashed with the Chinese over power-political issues. Soon afterward Albania, smallest and most backward of European Communist states, defied Khrushchev openly, praised Stalin, relied upon Chinese support, and boycotted the Soviet 22nd Congress. Chou En-lai, after defending Albania at the congress, left suddenly and was greeted vociferously in Beijing. Romania also began to assert independence of the USSR, especially in economic matters, and established good relations with China. In 1963 Romania proclaimed virtual neutrality in the Sino-Soviet dispute and even voted occasionally against the Soviet Union in the United Nations. The Sino-Soviet quarrel promoted polycentrism in the Communist world and disintegration of the Bloc.

After President John Kennedy's inauguration in 1961, Khrushchev sought concessions from the youthful American leader as compensation for his troubles in the Bloc. Cuba and Berlin were the key issues. In January 1959 Fidel Castro, heading a radical insurgent movement, took power in Cuba with Communist support and soon aligned himself with the Soviet Union. In April 1961 Cuban exiles supported by the United States sought unsuccessfully to overthrow the Castro regime in the inept Bay of Pigs invasion, whose failure revived Khrushchev's self-assurance. Meeting Kennedy in Vienna that June, Khrushchev threatened to sign a separate peace with East Germany unless an overall German settlement was reached soon. The ensuing Berlin crisis, however, revealed Kennedy's coolness and determination. To halt a westward surge of refugees, the East German regime built the Berlin Wall, which stood until late 1989. Finally Khrushchev removed his time limit on a German settlement and advocated nuclear-free zones in Europe and the Far East.

In the fall of 1962 the Cuban missile crisis threatened to provoke nuclear war between the USSR and the United States. Khrushchev had been seeking to conclude a German peace treaty and prevent China and West Germany from acquiring nuclear weapons. His decision to install medium-range missiles in Cuba was apparently a gamble to solve mounting domestic and foreign problems with one bold stroke: Once his missiles were installed, he might bargain with the West over Berlin and nuclear-free zones. U.S. aircraft detected the Soviet installations, however, and President Kennedy ordered a sea blockade of Cuba (October 22). Khrushchev had the choice of withdrawing the missiles or fighting a United States far superior in long-range missiles and local naval power. Khrushchev prudently chose withdrawal, only to be taunted by the Chinese for "adventurism" in placing the missiles in Cuba and cowardice in removing them!

Peaceful resolution of the missile crisis improved Soviet-American relations. In 1963 the United States, the USSR, and Britain agreed to ban the testing of nuclear weapons in the atmosphere. A "hot line" was set up between Washington and Moscow to reduce the danger of accidental nuclear war. Khrushchev's freedom of maneuver was sharply restricted by the Sino-Soviet quarrel. During 1963–1964 he tried but failed to round up support for a world Communist conference to expel the Chinese and reassert Soviet hegemony over world communism.

Khrushchev's Fall

In October 1964 Khrushchev was suddenly removed from power. The official statement of October 16 in *Pravda* declared:

> The plenum of the Central Committee satisfied the request of N. S. Khrushchev to relieve him of the duties of first secretary of the Central Committee, member of the Presidium of the Central Committee and chairman of the Council of Ministers of the USSR in connection with advanced age and poor health.

Actually his health was good, and many statesmen older than he were directing their countries' destinies. Subsequently his successors accused Khrushchev of "harebrained schemes," recklessness at home and abroad, fostering a new personality cult, undignified behavior, and dangerous experimentation. His prestige had suffered severely from the Cuban crisis, and between 1960 and 1963 he had almost been toppled on several occasions, but in 1964 his power still far exceeded that of other Presidium members. Apparently a powerful coalition of interest groups organized against him. While Khrushchev was on vacation in the Crimea, after he had refused to depart gracefully, the Presidium voted him out of office and disregarded his demand to submit the issue to the Central Committee. Having antagonized the military leaders by reducing the size of the ground forces, Khrushchev this time lacked the army support to reverse the verdict. Overnight Khrushchev became emeritus—an unperson rarely mentioned and relegated to obscurity but granted a fine apartment and limousine. The transfer of power, smooth and orderly, to Brezhnev and Kosygin marked a peaceful evolution of the Soviet political system away from Stalinist terror. The Presidium had become a society of relative equals, whose collective weight exceeded that of an individual leader.

A combination of foreign and domestic failures caused Khrushchev's unexpected downfall. His Presidium colleagues blamed him for the Cuban fiasco and setbacks in Berlin. The intensifying conflict with China had split the world Communist movement and encouraged Albania and Romania to assert full or partial independence. The Soviet position in eastern Europe, and with it Soviet security, were imperiled. At home the Soviet economy was stumbling. Industrial growth rates were falling, agriculture had stagnated, and Khrushchev's boasts of soon overtaking the United States sounded hollow. His decision in 1962 to split the party into industrial and agricultural segments had created confusion and antagonized party traditionalists and technocrats. Reduction of Soviet ground forces and efforts to promote détente with the West had alienated influential military men. Khrushchev's hasty reforms and mistakes welded together a potent conservative coalition. However, his basic policies —de-Stalinization, reducing terror, aiding agriculture and the consumer, and increasing contacts with the West—were apparently sound. Khrushchev had led the Soviet Union through the difficult post-Stalin transition, ensured the party's predominance, and maintained the Soviet Empire without resort to mass terror.

Problem 14

De-Stalinization: Stalin's Role in the Purges and in World War II

Was Joseph Stalin a "great revolutionary despot" (Deutscher) or a monster worse than Caligula, as his successor, Khrushchev, suggested in 1956? Did Stalin exemplify Soviet communism or represent an aberration from it because of his "cult of personality" after 1934? Why was the Great Purge launched, and what were its results? Did Stalin or his generals deserve blame for Soviet defeats early in World War II or the credit for eventual victory? Should Stalin be praised for his wartime leadership, or should he have been shot for failing to prepare or lead the country adequately? These and similar issues were debated inside and outside the Soviet Union after Khrushchev's "secret speech" in February 1956 at the 20th Party Congress lifted part of the veil that had shrouded Stalin's actions.

Stalinist Defense

The following sources glorify Stalin's leadership, contending that he was a genius and that what he did was necessary and correct. The first is an excerpt from the *History of the All-Union Com-*

munist Party (Bolshevik): Short Course, published originally in 1938. Approved by Stalin and sometimes attributed at least partly to him personally, this official party history seeks to explain and justify the Great Purge, then underway.

The successes of socialism in our country gladdened . . . all honorable citizens of the USSR . . . , but infuriated more and more the . . . yesmen of the defeated classes—the miserable remnants of the Bukharinites and Trotskyites. These gentlemen . . . sought revenge upon the party and people for their failures. . . . On December 1, 1934 in Leningrad at Smolny, S. M. Kirov was mostly foully murdered with a shot from a revolver. The murderer, arrested at the scene of the crime, turned out to be a member of an underground counterrevolutionary group which was organized from members of the anti-Soviet Zinovievite group in Leningrad. . . . This group set itself the aim of murdering the leaders of the [Soviet] Communist Party. . . . From the depositions of the participants . . . it became evident that they were connected with representatives of foreign capitalist states and received money from them. The participants in this organization who were uncovered were sentenced by the Military Tribunal of the Supreme Court of the USSR to the extreme punishment—shooting.

Soon thereafter the existence of an underground counterrevolutionary "Moscow center" was established. Investigation and trial clarified the vile role of Zinoviev, Kamenev, Evdokimov, and other leaders of this organization in arousing among their followers terrorist inclinations and to prepare the murder of members of the Central Committee and the Soviet government. . . . Already then in 1935 it became clear that the Zinovievite group was a hidden White Guardist organization which fully deserved to be dealt with like the White Guardists. . . .

The chief inspirer and organizer of this whole band of murderers and spies was the Judas, Trotskii. Aiding Trotskii and executing his counterrevolutionary instructions were Zinoviev, Kamenev, and their Trotskyist yesmen. They prepared the defeat of the USSR in case of an attack on it by the imperialists, they became defeatists toward the worker-peasant state, they became the despicable servants and agents of the German and Japanese fascists.[5]

The following excerpts from a speech by Khrushchev in 1939 show him as a loyal follower of Stalin, praising the dictator and his work slavishly; they are included in a volume of similar speeches dedicated to Stalin.

Today, on the 60th anniversary of Comrade Stalin's birth, all eyes will be turned on our great leader of nations, on our dear friend and father. Working people all over the world will write and speak words of love and gratitude about him. Their enemies will foam at the mouth with rage when . . . speaking on this theme. The working men of the world see in Comrade Stalin their leader, their liberator from the yoke of capitalism. . . . The imperialists of all countries know full well that every word uttered by Comrade Stalin is backed by a people of 183,000,000 strong, that every idea advanced by Comrade Stalin is endorsed by the great and mighty multinational Soviet people. . . .

The biography of Comrade Stalin is the glorious epic of our Bolshevik party. . . . Lenin together with Stalin created the great Bolshevik party. . . . In Comrade Stalin the working class and all toilers possess the greatest man of the present era, a theoretician, leader, and organizer of the struggle and victory of the working class. . . . All nations of the Soviet Union see in Stalin their friend, their father, their leader. . . . Stalin is the father of his people by virtue of the love he bears them. Stalin is the leader of nations for the wisdom with which he guides their struggle. . . . The army and the navy are the creation of our great Stalin, who increases their might with every day.[6]

Khrushchev's Critique

In his "secret speech" of February 24–25, 1956, Khrushchev detailed Stalin's crimes and blunders while concealing that as Stalin's loyal follower he had participated in them. Khrushchev did not condemn Stalin unconditionally because

[5] *Istoriia VKP(b), Kratkii kurs* (Moscow, 1946), pp. 309–12.

[6] Quoted in Marin Pundeff, ed., *History in the U.S.S.R.* (San Francisco, 1967), pp. 135–39.

Problem 14 continued

that would have meant repudiating industrialization, collectivization, and social benefits. While affirming Stalin's contributions in the Revolution and Civil War and in building socialism until 1934, Khrushchev focused on an aberration: the cult of the individual leader and its destructive results. World War II generals led by Marshal Zhukov had pressed Khrushchev to rehabilitate purged military leaders and the Red Army's reputation, partly by discrediting Stalin's wartime leadership. Engaged in a bitter power struggle, Khrushchev may have believed he could undermine conservative opponents such as Molotov by destroying the image of Stalin as an all-wise, all-powerful leader. He glorified Lenin as embodying socialist modesty, comradely behavior, and socialist legality and posed as his true follower. Declared Khrushchev:

> At present we are concerned . . . with how the cult of the person of Stalin gradually grew . . . , the source of a whole series of exceedingly grave perversions of party principles, party democracy, of revolutionary legality. . . . The great harm caused by the violation of collective direction of the party and . . . accumulation of immense and limitless power in the hands of one person, the party Central Committee considers it absolutely necessary to make the material pertaining to this matter available to the 20th Congress.

Marx and Lenin, Khrushchev reminded the delegates, had denounced any cult of an individual leader. Lenin had invariably displayed great modesty while emphasizing the role of the people and party in making history. Instead of dictating to his colleagues, "Lenin never imposed by force his views upon his co-workers. He tried to convince; he patiently explained his opinions to others." Lenin had realized Stalin's grave character defects, but premature death had prevented him from removing Stalin from office. After Stalin assumed power:

> Grave abuse of power by Stalin caused untold harm to our party. . . . Stalin . . . absolutely did not toler-

ate collegiality in leadership and work, and practiced brutal violence. . . . Stalin acted . . . by imposing his concepts and demanding absolute submission to his opinion. Whoever opposed this concept . . . , was doomed to removal from the leading collective and to subsequent moral and physical annihilation. . . . Stalin originated the concept "enemy of the people" . . . which made possible the use of the most cruel repression, violating all norms of revolutionary legality against anyone who in any way disagreed with Stalin.

During the Great Purge, continued Khrushchev:

> Stalin . . . used extreme methods and mass repressions at a time when the Revolution was already victorious, . . . when the exploiting classes were already liquidated, . . . when our party was politically consolidated. . . . Stalin showed in a whole series of cases his intolerance, his brutality and his abuse of power. . . . He often chose the path of repression and physical annihilation, not only against actual enemies, but also against individuals who had committed no crimes against the party and the Soviet government.

Generally the only proof of guilt was a "confession" exorted by force and torture. Such incongruous methods, noted Khrushchev, were employed when the Revolution had already triumphed, the exploiters had been wiped out, and socialism had been firmly established. "In the situation of socialist victory there was no basis for mass terror in the country." This terror had been blamed on N. I. Yezhov, chief of the security police, but clearly Stalin had made the decisions and issued the arrest orders.

Khrushchev, seeking to discredit Stalin's role as the chief Soviet leader in World War II, accused Stalin of failing to prepare the USSR for war, of disregarding numerous clear warnings of impending German attack, and of gross incompetence and negligence in directing military operations. Moreover, after victory Stalin denied the crucial role of his generals and people in achieving victory, taking all the credit for himself. Khrushchev noted the improbable role that many Soviet war novels and films attributed to Stalin. Supposedly harkening to Stalin's "genius," the

Red Army had retreated deliberately, then coun-terattacked and smashed the Nazi invaders. Such works ascribed the glorious victory achieved by the heroic Soviet people solely to Stalin's brilliant strategy. Stalin blamed early severe Soviet defeats on the German surprise attack, though Hitler had announced his intent to destroy com-munism back in 1933. In the months before the attack, numerous warnings came from the West, Soviet diplomats, and military men that a Nazi invasion was imminent, but Stalin disregarded them. "Despite these particularly grave warnings, the necessary steps were not taken to prepare the country properly for defense and to prevent it from being caught unaware," said Khrushchev.

Khrushchev was equally critical of Stalin's performance as wartime commander in chief. When the Nazis invaded, Soviet troops had orders not to return fire because Stalin just could not believe that war had really begun. In border areas much of the Soviet air force and artillery were lost needlessly, and the Germans broke through. Believing that the end was near, Stalin declared in panic, "All that Lenin created we have lost forever." For a long time Stalin neither directed operations nor exercised real leadership. He was ignorant of the true situation at the front, which he never visited except for one brief look at a stabilized sector, yet his constant interfer-ence with military operations caused huge man-power losses. Exclaimed Khrushchev derisively, "Stalin planned operations on a globe . . . and traced the front line on it!" As a result, early in 1942 the Germans surrounded large Red Army units in the Kharkov area, and hundreds of thou-sands of soldiers were lost. Yet Stalin believed that he was always right and never made mis-takes. "This is Stalin's military genius; this is what it cost us," declared Khrushchev.

Right after Soviet victory, Stalin began unfairly to denigrate the contributions to victory of many top Red Army commanders. "Stalin excluded every possibility that services rendered at the front should be credited to anyone but himself." All Soviet victories, Stalin claimed, had been due solely to his courage and genius. In the postwar Soviet film *The Fall of Berlin* (1949), only Stalin issued orders; there was no mention of the military commanders, the Politburo, or the government. "Stalin acts for everybody . . . in order to surround Stalin with glory, contrary to the facts and to historical truth."[7]

Post-Khrushchev Debate on Stalin

On February 16, 1966, at the Institute of Marx-ism-Leninism in Moscow, a discussion was held on a book by Soviet historian A. M. Nekrich, *June 22, 1941*, which used the "secret speech" to blame Stalin for Soviet unpreparedness. This debate reflected a major issue disputed in the USSR throughout the more open Khrushchev era. It related not only to Stalin's alleged mistakes and crimes, but also to the role of Khrushchev in implementing de-Stalinization. The debate was wide open by Soviet standards then, though most participants and the audience believed that Nekrich had not gone far enough in criticizing Stalin. In the extracts that follow, note the critical attitude of Professor G. A. Deborin of the Insti-tute of Marxism-Leninism in Moscow toward the fallen Khrushchev and his partial defense of Stalin.

Deborin Nekrich adopts an erroneous position; he explains everything by the obstinate stupidity of Stalin himself. That is a superficial analysis. . . . Stalin was not the only person involved. . . . It is unnecessary to refer to Khrushchev's declarations which are not objective. . . . Insofar as [Stalin] received false information, Stalin reached false conclusions. He placed too much hope in the Ger-man-Soviet pact, . . . but Stalin's estimate of Ger-man intentions was endorsed by all those around him. So Stalin cannot be considered solely respon-sible for his mistakes.

---

[7] N. S. Khrushchev, "The Crimes of the Stalin Era," *The New Leader*, 1956.

Problem 14 continued

Anfilov (General Staff) And now let us come to the beginning of the war. If all our forces had been completely ready for action, which was entirely Stalin's responsibility, we should not have begun the war with such disasters! And in general the war would not have been so long, so bloody, and so exhausting. . . . Stalin remains the chief culprit.

Dashichev (General Staff) [Nekrich] should have gone deeper. . . . It was [Stalin] who made the situation in which the country then found itself [in 1941]. Stalin's greatest crime was to have eliminated the best cadres of our army and our party. All our leaders understood the international situation, but not one of them was courageous enough to fight to get the necessary measures taken for the defense of the country. . . . The driver of the bus is responsible for every accident that happens through his fault. Stalin assumed the responsibility for every accident that happens through his fault. Stalin assumed the responsibility of sole driver. His guilt is immense.

Slezkin (Institute of History of the Academy of Sciences) I was at the front and took part, at the age of 19, in the June 1941 fighting. There can be no hesitation in saying that Stalin's behavior was criminal. There was a vicious circle of personality cult, provocation and repression. Everyone tried to please his superior by supplying only the information that might gratify him. . . . All this was the cause of immeasurable damage to the country and everyone is guilty in his own way. . . . And the responsibility is heavier in proportion to one's place in the hierarchy. . . . Stalin is the chief culprit.

Peter Yakir (Institute of History of the Academy of Sciences) Some of the speakers . . . have referred to "Comrade Stalin." . . . Stalin was nobody's comrade and above all, not ours. Stalin impeded the development of our armaments by eliminating many eminent technicians, and among them the creators of our artillery. . . . In the concentration camps there were millions of able-bodied men, specialists in every department of the country's economic and military life. And the task of guarding them absorbed considerable forces.

Snegov [who had been imprisoned in one of Stalin's labor camps] Nekrich's book is honest and useful. If a unit is disorganized on the eve of combat, . . . then that unit suffers a defeat. The head of such a unit is generally shot by order of the high command. . . . Stalin was both the supreme commander, and the head of the unit and that unit, in a state of disorganization, was our whole country. Stalin ought to have been shot. Instead of which, people are now trying to whitewash him. . . . How can one be a Communist and speak smoothly about Stalin who betrayed . . . Communists, who eliminated nearly all the delegates of the Eighteenth Congress . . . , and who betrayed the Spanish Republic, Poland, and all Communists in all countries?

Deborin It has not been my task to defend or justify Stalin. What is needed is to examine the personality cult more deeply in all its aspects. . . . It is strange that Snegov should hold the same view [as West German Professor Jacobson]. Comrade Snegov, you ought to tell us which camp you belong to!

Snegov The Kolyma [concentration] camp.

Nekrich It is Stalin who bears the chief responsibility for the heavy defeat and all the tragedy of the first part of the war. All the same, nobody ought to provide his superiors with inexact information because it will give them pleasure. Stalinism began because of us, the small people. Stalin wanted to trick Hitler; but instead of that he got himself into a maze which led to disaster. He knew better than anyone about elimination of the leading cadres and the weaknesses of the army.[8]

Gorbachev's Position

President M. S. Gorbachev continued and in some ways deepened the critique of Stalin that General Secretary Khrushchev began in 1956. Public pressure virtually compelled Gorbachev to

---

[8] Selected excerpts reprinted from *June 22, 1941: Soviet Historians and the German Invasion* by Vladimir Petrov, pp. 250–61, by permission of The University of South Carolina Press. Copyright © 1968 by The University of South Carolina Press in cooperation with the Institute for Sino-Soviet Studies, The George Washington University, Washington, D.C.

address the Stalin issue in his speech of November 2, 1987, but he failed to face it squarely.

> To remain faithful to historical truth we have to see both Stalin's indisputable contribution to the struggle for socialism, to the defense of its gains, as well as the gross political mistakes and the abuses committed by him and his circle, for which our people paid a heavy price and which had grave consequences for society. Sometimes it is said that Stalin did not know about many incidents of lawlessness. The documents at our disposal show that this is not so. The guilt of Stalin and his immediate entourage before the party and the people for wholesale repressive measures and acts of lawlessness is enormous and unforgivable. This is a lesson for all generations.[9]

In his speech of November 25, 1989, Gorbachev returned to this theme, arguing that Stalin's unfortunate legacy—a centralist bureaucratic system—had to be replaced if the USSR was to progress.

> Why did Stalin succeed in imposing on the Party and on all of society his program and his methods? . . . Stalin played cleverly upon the revolutionary impatience of the masses, on the utopian and egalitarian tendencies of any mass movement, on the vanguard's aspiration for the quickest possible achievement of the desired goal. . . . The idea of socialism became equated more and more with an authoritarian command and bureaucratic administrative system.
>
>   . . . An ever greater rift [opened] between the theory of Marxism and reality, between the humane ideals and practice. A bureaucratic, extremely centralized economic and political system acted by its own laws. And theory had . . . to create the illusion of the "correctness" of these actions. . . . In the name of the achievement of "the great idea" of socialism were justified the most inhumane means. . . . The 20th Congress, rejecting and condemning the dark sides of the Stalin regime and its ex-

tremes, generally left unchanged the bureaucratic system itself. It managed to survive, aided by a new illusion that it was enough to eliminate the extremes of the Stalinist regime—and the liberated energy of socialism in the near future could bring our society to the higher phase of communism. Stalinist distortions led to the loss of the main content of the Marxist and Leninist concept of socialism: an understanding of the individual as the goal, not the means.[10]

Two Western Evaluations

The U.S. scholar Severyn Bialer, in his introduction to Soviet wartime memoirs, seeks to strike a balance between exaggerated praise of Stalin and Khrushchev's one-sided and partisan denunciation. Up to 1953, he points out, Soviet war history had glorified Stalin as an infallible and omnipotent genius. Soon after Stalin's death "war history came to serve the cult of the party," whose infallibility replaced Stalin's. Khrushchev's attack in 1956 had aimed to use Stalin's crimes as a lever to achieve power:

> The singlemindedness with which Khrushchev concentrated on his goal . . . led him to seek not comprehension, not rectification, but destruction of Stalin's role as war leader. . . . Soviet war memoirs testify to Stalin's complete control over the political, industrial, and military aspects of the Soviet war effort. . . . The Soviet dictator personally made every wartime decision of any importance. He alone seems to have possessed the power to impose his will on both civilian and military associates alike. . . .
>
>   . . . It appeared to [Western observers] that Stalin had an extraordinary grasp of war goals and major long-range plans for conducting the war and a talent for adjusting the conduct of military operations to political realities. . . . On the second level, that of tactical and technical expertise, Western observers were struck by Stalin's mastery of detail. . . . Their descriptions are corroborated in the memoirs of Soviet commanders and industrial managers. . . .
>
>   The task of military leadership is located to an overwhelming extent, however . . . in the area of

---

[9] M. Gorbachev, *October and Perestroika: The Revolution Continues, 1917–1987* (Moscow, 1987), p. 21.

[10] *Pravda*, November 26, 1989, pp. 1–3.

operational leadership which involves planning and control of large-scale military operations—battles and campaigns. In this middle area . . . , Stalin made no real contribution. . . . Stalin's crucial contribution to victory . . . [derived] from his ability to organize and administer the mobilization of manpower and material resources. . . . Stalin . . . regarded his role as that of arbiter and ultimate judge of his generals' strategic plans and operational designs. His major asset as a military leader was the ability to select talented commanders and to permit them to plan operations, while reserving for himself the ultimate power of decision. . . .

Thus what was crucial to Soviet survival and eventual victory was Stalin's ability to mobilize Soviet manpower and economic resources over a sustained period, his ability to assure the political stability of his armed forces and the population at large despite disastrous initial defeats, and his ability to recognize and reward superior military talent at all levels under his command. . . . It was in just the area of Russia's greatest need that Stalin showed his greatest strength. . . . He was above all an administrator better suited to directing the gigantic military and civilian bureaucracy than to initiating and formulating military plans.[11]

The historian Robert Conquest, who has written authoritatively on the Stalin terror, provides this largely negative evaluation of Stalin in a recent book:

The long-term effects of the life which ended in Kuntsevo on that night in March [1953] . . . were dreadful and enduring. . . . Meanwhile, the politico-economic system Stalin had created remained in being. It was only in the late 1980s that the Soviet leadership saw that the Stalin-style "command economy" had ruined the country. . . . [In the late 1980s] there came a campaign of continuous, wholesale and devastating revelation of the truth about Stalinism and about Stalin personally— including . . . the digging up of mass graves. . . .

Stalin was in almost every way an outsider. He had no natural allegiance to his family, his home, his nation, his schoolmates. He was neither a Georgian nor a Russian. He was neither a worker nor an intellectual. . . . His marital life was an empty front. His social life was an imperfectly maintained pretense, which eventually degenerated into forced jollity with coarse and terrified toadies. . . . As so often with Stalin, we seem to find normal human faculties either lacking or withered to vestigial form. One of his outstanding characteristics was, in many respects, a profound mediocrity melded with a superhuman willpower. It is as though he had a very ordinary brain, but with some lobes extravagantly overdeveloped. . . . It is clear that a profound feeling of insecurity was thickly woven into his personality. This manifested itself in the continuous falsification of his part in events. . . .

The question of whether Stalin was, or became, insane is now being publicly argued. . . . That he was psychologically abnormal is clear enough. . . . Above all, he was by nature cruel. . . . For Stalin's personal inclination to terror and death, it is indeed hardly necessary to do more than look at the record. . . . Impersonally ordering and signing scores of thousands of death sentences, as often as not of men who had supported him in all his earlier acts of tyranny. . . . And he inflicted not only death, but also torture, giving personal instructions on the beating of innocent prisoners. Despots who revelled in killing and torture are to be found in various periods of history, and among them Stalin occupies a very high place. But . . . he ruled not only by terror but also by falsification. . . . The image of a tiger came to the minds of many: not merely the quintessential beast of prey, the most dangerous killer in the jungle, but also one that lies in wait for its victim with no more than an occasional sign of impatience.[12] ■

---

[11] *Stalin and His Generals: Soviet Military Memoirs of World War II*, ed. Severyn Bialer (New York, 1969), pp. 34–44.

[12] Robert Conquest, *Stalin: Breaker of Nations* (New York, 1991) pp. 314–19.

Suggested Additional Reading

BOFFA, G. *Inside the Khrushchev Era* (New York, 1963).

BRESLAUER, G. W. *Khrushchev and Brezhnev as Leaders* (London, 1982).

BURLACHUK, F. F. *Khrushchev and the First Russian Spring: The Era of Khrushchev Through the Eyes of His Advisor* (New York, 1991).

CHOTINER, B. A. *Khrushchev's Party Reform* (Westport, CT, 1984).

COHEN, S., ed. *The Soviet Union Since Stalin* (Bloomington, IN, 1980).

CRANKSHAW, E. *Khrushchev: A Career* (New York, 1966).

CRUMMEY, R. O., ed. *Reform in Russia and the USSR: Past and Prospects* (Urbana, IL, 1989).

DALLIN, A., ed. *The Khrushchev and Brezhnev Years* (New York, 1992).

DINERSTEIN, H. S. *The Making of a Missile Crisis: October 1962* (Baltimore, 1976).

FEIFER, G. *Justice in Moscow* (New York, 1964).

FILTZER, D. *Soviet Workers and De-Stalinization: The Case of the Modern System of Soviet Production Relations, 1953–1964* (New York, 1992).

FRANKLAND, M. *Khrushchev* (New York, 1967).

GITTINGS, J. *Survey of the Sino-Soviet Dispute, 1963–1967* (New York, 1968).

GRIFFITH, W. E. *Albania and the Sino-Soviet Rift* (Cambridge, MA, 1963).

HILSMAN, R. *The Cuban Missile Crisis: The Struggle over Policy* (Westport, CT, 1996).

HYLAND, W., and R. SHRYOCK. *The Fall of Khrushchev* (New York, 1969).

KHRUSHCHEV, N. S. *Khrushchev Remembers* (Boston, 1971).

———. *Khrushchev Remembers: The Last Testament* (Boston, 1974).

LEE, W., and R. STAAR. *Soviet Military Policy Since World War II* (Stanford, 1986).

LINDEN, C. A. *Khrushchev and the Soviet Leadership, 1957–1964* (London, 1967).

MCCAULEY, M., ed. *Khrushchev and Khrushchevism* (Bloomington, IN, 1987).

MEDVEDEV, R., and Z. MEDVEDEV. *Khrushchev: The Years in Power* (New York, 1978).

NOGEE, J. L. and R. DONALDSON. *Soviet Foreign Policy Since World War II*, 4th ed. (New York, 1992).

PISTRAK, L. *The Grand Tactician: Khrushchev's Rise to Power* (New York, 1961).

PLOSS, S. *Conflict and Decision-Making Process in Soviet Russia: A Case Study of Agricultural Policy, 1953–1963* (Princeton, 1965).

RICHTER, J. G. *Khrushchev's Double Bind: International Pressures and Domestic Coalition Politics* (Baltimore, 1994).

ROTHBERG, A. *The Heirs of Stalin: Dissidence and the Soviet Regime, 1953–1970* (Ithaca, NY, 1972).

ROTHSCHILD, J. *Return to Diversity: A Political History of East Central Europe Since World War II*, 2d ed. (New York and Oxford, 1993).

RUSH, M. *Political Succession in the USSR*, 2d ed. (New York, 1965).

SMOLANSKY, O. *The Soviet Union and the Arab East Under Khrushchev* (Lewisburg, PA, 1974).

STOKES, G., ed. *From Stalinism to Pluralism: A Documentary History of Eastern Europe Since 1945* (New York and Oxford, 1991).

SYROP, K. *Spring in October: The Polish Revolution of 1956* (New York, 1958).

TATU, M. *Power in the Kremlin: From Khrushchev to Kosygin* (New York, 1969).

TOMPSON, W. J. *Khrushchev: A Political Life* (New York, 1995).

ULAM, A. *New Face of Soviet Totalitarianism* (New York, 1965).

WOLFE, B. *Khrushchev and Stalin's Ghost* (New York, 1957). (On the secret speech.)

ZAGORIA, D. *The Sino-Soviet Conflict, 1955–1961* (Princeton, 1962).

———. *Vietnam Triangle: Moscow, Peking, Hanoi* (New York, 1967).

ZINNER, P. *Revolution in Hungary* (Cambridge, MA, 1961).

ZUBOK, V., and C. PLESHAKOV. *Inside the Kremlin's Cold War: From Stalin to Khrushchev* (Cambridge, MA, 1996).

40

The Brezhnev Era, 1964–1982

A fter the Politburo removed Khrushchev from power abruptly in October 1964, a collective leadership assumed control, led by Leonid I. Brezhnev (1906–1982) and Alexei N. Kosygin (1904–1980), both engineers. Following a concealed power struggle with Kosygin and other rivals, Brezhnev gradually accumulated power and by 1971 had established modified one-man rule over the USSR. Despite declining health and vigor after 1975, he dominated the Soviet scene until early 1982. The new leaders, repudiating Khrushchev's risky economic and political experiments at home and his flamboyant foreign policy, acted cautiously, stressing efficiency, order, and stability. Abandoning Khrushchev's de-Stalinization campaign, they returned partially to Stalinism. The new oligarchs tightened controls over intellectuals and dissidents and at first combined industrial and agricultural growth with an impressive military buildup. Abroad, the USSR tightened its control of eastern Europe after invading Czechoslovakia in 1968 while pursuing détente and arms control agreements with the West. China confronted it with ideological and geopolitical challenges that threatened to provoke a Sino-Soviet war. Was the

Brezhnev period an "era of stagnation," as M. S. Gorbachev later characterized it, or did it pursue reform? Were genuine stability and consensus achieved, or did resurgent minority peoples, especially Muslims, begin to undermine an apparently solid Soviet Empire? Why did economic growth slow dramatically after 1970? What were the implications of Soviet invasions of Czechoslovakia in 1968 and Afghanistan in 1979 and severe tensions with a liberalizing Poland in 1980–1981?

Politics: Brezhnev's Rise

After Khrushnev's sudden ouster, an oligarchy in the Presidium (renamed the Politburo in 1966) and Secretariat of the party's Central Committee, headed by Brezhnev, Kosygin, N. V. Podgorny, and Mikhail Suslov, assumed power. Right after Khrushchev's removal, *Pravda* castigated his methods rather than his specific policies:

> The Leninist Party is an enemy of subjectivism and drift in communist construction. Wild schemes, half-baked conclusions and hasty decisions and actions divorced from reality; bragging and bluster; attraction to rule by fiat;

unwillingness to take into account what science and practical experience have already worked out—these are alien to the Party. The construction of Communism is a living, creative undertaking. It does not tolerate armchair methods, one-man decisions, or disregard for the practical experience of the masses.[1]

Subsequently Khrushchev was not criticized by name and under Brezhnev was hardly ever mentioned by the press, almost as if he had never ruled the USSR. Consigned to the oblivion of retirement, he was supplied with an apartment and limousine and retained his country dacha. Khrushchev appeared in public only at election times to cast his ballot. As a pensioner, he wrote two volumes of fascinating memoirs and died of heart disease in 1971.[2]

The new leaders, at first insecure, were absorbed in a protracted power struggle that raged beneath a placid surface from the day of Khrushchev's removal. A veil of anonymity, sobriety, and secrecy enveloped them as they jockeyed for position. Group and individual photographs were avoided so as not to reveal the leaders' order of prominence. In the Presidium, which soon reasserted primacy over the Secretariat, former Khrushchev supporters at first retained their posts. Some Western observers did not expect this collective leadership to last, but it proved surprisingly durable and effective. Powerful interest groups competed behind the scenes: the party apparatus, high state administrators, "steeleaters" (heavy industry), and less influential army and police elements. None of these lobbies could dictate to or ignore the interests of the others; clashes among them generally ended in compromise. Whereas the successors of Lenin and Stalin soon had achieved complete or modified one-man rule, this time the top posts of secretary general (Brezhnev) and premier (Kosygin, later N. A. Tikhonov) remained in different hands.

The coup of October 1964 was apparently planned by Mikhail Suslov, chief party ideologist, and executed by opponents of Khrushchev who considered Brezhnev the most acceptable moderate replacement. At the outset Brezhnev's position was highly vulnerable and insecure because he could count on only one sure ally in the Presidium: Andrei Kirilenko. The other members of the Presidium included independent senior figures (Suslov, Kosygin), rivals for his post as first secretary (Podgornyi), Khrushchev protégés, and party elders Shvernik and Mikoian. Brezhnev's status grew even more precarious when Aleksandr Shelepin and Peter Shelest, the Ukrainian party chairman, became full members of the Presidium. The new party first secretary began by wooing elements alienated by Khrushchev's reforms: the party, industrial managers, bureaucrats, and the military. Promptly rescinding Khrushchev's most unpopular policies, the new regime ended his short-lived division of the party and insistence on rotating its leaders. Brezhnev sought to replace conflict and suspicion among powerful interest groups with cooperation and consensus, summed up in the slogan "Trust in cadres." In official life a more relaxed atmosphere prevailed as disagreements were limited to ascertaining the best means to achieve agreed goals. The frenetic administrative reorganizations of the Khrushchev era virtually ceased.

Confounding the skeptics, Brezhnev emerged as a clever and adroit politician and a master of compromise. Within 18 months, after achieving working control of the Secretariat, he had begun to emerge from a pack of contenders as first among equals. A Presidium consensus enabled him to replace followers of Khrushchev with his own adherents. Brezhnev in December 1965 had Podgornyi "promoted" to titular president of the Supreme Soviet. That July Konstantin Chernenko, a faithful personal associate, was named to a key post in the Central Committee. The following April Presidium member Kirilenko, a senior supporter, was appointed to the Secretariat, where he acted as Brezhnev's watchdog for personnel matters. A leading rival, A. Shelepin, who had boasted

---

[1] *Pravda*, October 17, 1964, quoted in J. Dornberg, *Brezhnev: The Masks of Power* (New York, 1974), p. 184.
[2] *Khrushchev Remembers* (Boston, 1971); and *Khrushchev Remembers: The Last Testament* (New York, 1974).

outside the Kremlin that Brezhnev soon would be replaced by "a man with a little more dynamism and authority," was undermined; he and Podgornyi lost their seats in the Secretariat.[3] The 23rd Party Congress (March–April 1966), naming Brezhnev secretary general of the party, confirmed his superior power. A Western diplomat admitted having underestimated Brezhnev's acumen: "We just didn't give him enough credit. . . . Everybody wrote him off as a party hack, as a colorless *apparatchik,* as a compromise candidate."

Leonid Brezhnev had risen from lowly origins by hard, persistent work, mainly in the party apparatus. Born in 1906 in Ukraine of Russian worker parents, he was graduated from a classical gymnasium and later obtained a degree as a metallurgical engineer. From 1938 on, his career was linked closely with Khrushchev's. Serving as a political commissar in World War II, Brezhnev became a major general, and once in power his military career was inflated beyond measure. Leaving the military service in 1946, Brezhnev, as a chosen member of Khrushchev's entourage, became party chief in Zaporozhe and a member of the Ukrainian Politburo. In the early 1950s he served as party chief in Moldavia, then in Kazakhstan. Under Khrushchev he became a secretary of the Central Committee and a member of the Politburo. Kicked upstairs in 1960 as titular president of the USSR, he returned from that political graveyard to true power. After Kozlov's stroke in April 1963 (a stroke of fortune for Brezhnev!), he was restored to the Secretariat and became Khrushchev's heir apparent. In the brutal world of Soviet politics, Brezhnev succeeded through patronage, manipulation, and maneuver. He built a strong political machine—the so-called Dnieper Mafia—of officials from his home region. Brezhnev won the reputation of being efficient, quiet, sensible, and of keeping a low profile—a man of experience and moderation.

Soviet leaders under Brezhnev operated as an exclusive, self-renewing elite, or *nomenklatura,* living in a very private world. The roughly 25 members of the Politburo (Presidium until 1966) and Secretariat, stressing stability and order, had defined rules of conduct that none could disregard with impunity. They acted purposefully to prevent Politburo disputes' being aired in the much larger Central Committee by manipulating its semiannual plenums. If agreement could not be achieved, the plenum would be delayed. Politburo members who violated these procedures would be punished, often by losing their posts. If a non-Politburo member criticized the leaders' policies at a plenum, he would normally be dismissed. The oligarchs jealously guarded special decision-making powers that separated them from lower party bodies, which merely executed Politburo decisions. Even junior members of the Secretariat or candidate members of the Politburo belonged to this privileged elite. Under Brezhnev, four or five top men were included: the premier, titular president, and the top three party secretaries. The Secretariat, normally chaired by Brezhnev, managed the party machine and appointed candidates to all senior posts. Moscow-based Politburo members possessed advantages over party leaders of Leningrad, Ukraine, or Kazakhstan, who normally could not attend weekly Politburo meetings.[4]

Powerful Politburo members representing major interest groups blocked Brezhnev's initial efforts at supremacy. However, between 1966 and 1971 Brezhnev removed or isolated leading rivals and accumulated power without dictating to the Politburo. His authority spread outward from the party base to include foreign policy, state affairs, and agriculture. In 1967 he ousted his main rivals from the Secretariat, and the 24th Party Congress in 1971 confirmed his personal ascendancy as he enlarged the Politburo to include his cronies. Brezhnev's summit diplomacy with Western leaders reaffirmed his authority. During 1973 leading representatives of important interest groups entered the Politburo: Marshal Andrei Grechko (defense minister), Iuri Andropov (KGB chief),

[3] Harry Gelman, *The Brezhnev Politburo* (Ithaca, NY, 1984), pp. 74–79.

[4] Gelman, *The Brezhnev Politburo,* pp. 51–58.

and Andrei Gromyko (foreign minister). In May 1975 Alexander Shelepin, his only remaining major rival, was removed from the Politburo; and the July 1975 Helsinki Security Conference vindicated his policy of détente. Changes announced by the 25th Party Congress of 1976 confirmed Brezhnev's supremacy. By then 10 of 16 full Politburo members were his appointees, and his rivals had been weakened and isolated. In 1977, asserting that the USSR had entered the phase of "developed socialism," Brezhnev assumed the title President of the Soviet Union. Despite repeated bouts of illness beginning in 1975, which sharply reduced his capacity to work, Brezhnev remained in command, repeatedly removing younger men who might aspire to replace him. In October 1980 Premier Kosygin retired and died two months later. He was replaced as premier by Nikolai A. Tikhonov, an elderly Brezhnev crony. Careful not to groom a dynamic successor, Brezhnev placed his stamp firmly on an entire era of Soviet history and retained preeminent authority until 1982, his final year of life. His legacy was stability, orderly procedure, and stagnation.

Under Brezhnev the role of the party was further enhanced, and tenure at all levels became more secure. After 1964 there were some abrupt removals from the Politburo, but few changes in the Central Committee or lower. In 1977 only 2 percent of party members failed to retain membership. Party congresses after 1971 were to convene every five years to coincide with Five Year Plans. Losing some of its power, the Central Committee was expanded to 241 full members and 155 nonvoting candidates, 90 percent of whom were reelected in 1976. The party continued to grow, reaching 17.4 million members in 1983. Now almost 10 percent of the adult population, it was losing its Leninist vanguard character; its apparatus of full-time paid workers exceeded 250,000. Meanwhile the educational level and technical expertise of party members had risen sharply. About 25 percent of them were women, but few held important positions and none were in top party agencies. Under "developed socialism" the party was to initiate major reforms, coordinate a complex socioeconomic system, and push forward a cautious bureaucracy. The theme of party control over the ministries was emphasized. Party spirit (*partiinost*), declared Brezhnev, must be combined with expertise.

Western scholars wondered whether the Brezhnev regime represented a stable oligarchy or a modified one-man rule. Was it reverting to Stalinist autocracy or permitting freer debate? Concealing its rivalries from the public, the Brezhnev leadership projected an image of harmony and unity. One Western scholar, Zbigniew Brzezinski, called the Brezhnev regime a "government of clerks" that, seeking to preserve its power and privileges, had repudiated social change. With a decaying ideology, its leaders presided over a petrifying political order. However, Robert Daniels stressed institutional pluralism in which the chief agencies—party, state, army, and police—shared power. Brezhnev adopted no major policies that would endanger the influence of any of them. Stalin's "permanent purge" of top officials had yielded to a remarkably stable leadership. With wider-ranging debate in the Soviet press, important decisions were reached after extensive discussion and compromise. The party became a "political broker," reconciling and mediating differences among several bureaucracies.

Khrushchev's removal by a large Politburo majority served as a deterrent to a potential dictator. Totalitarian discipline, pointed out French Sovietologist Michel Tatu, could be reimposed only by a massive purge, which party leaders scrupulously avoided. In some ways Brezhnev had fewer prerogatives than democratic chief executives. Lacking sole decision-making authority, he could have policies imposed on him by a Politburo majority that could dismiss or retire him at any time. He required his colleagues' consent to alter the composition of the Politburo or Secretariat.

After a brief, relatively liberal interlude, the Brezhnev regime cracked down on political dissent, with enforcement by the KGB under the able direction of Iurii V. Andropov, Brezhnev's eventual successor. De-Stalinization ended abruptly. Beginning in 1965, memoirs by leading Soviet generals

Table 40.1 Ethnic groups as a percentage of total population

Ethnic groups	1897	1926	1959	1970	1989
Russians	44.4	47.5	54.6	53.4	50.8
Ukrainians	19.4	21.4	17.8	16.9	15.4
Byelorussians	4.5	3.6	3.8	3.7	3.5
Tatars	1.9	1.7	2.4	2.5	—
Turko-Moslems	12.1	10.1	10.3	12.9	15.4
Jews	3.5	2.4	1.1	0.9	0.7
Europeans (Georgians, Armenians, Latvians, Estonians)	3.9	3.6	3.8	3.8	3.8
Lithuanians	1.3	1.2	1.1	1.1	1.1
Finns	2.3	2.2	1.5	1.4	1.4
Moldavians (Romanians)	1.0	1.2	1.1	1.2	1.2

of World War II praised Stalin's wartime leadership, which Khrushchev had castigated. Stalin and the party, went the new line, fully aware of the Nazi danger in 1941, had taken essential precautions, then guided the heroic Soviet people to victory. A prominent neo-Stalinist intimate of Brezhnev, S. Trapeznikov, described the Stalin era in *Pravda* in October 1965 as "one of the most brilliant in the history of the party and the Soviet state." Brezhnev agreed with powerful party conservatives that discussion of Stalin's crimes and forced labor camps must cease. Official treatment of Stalin grew increasingly positive, with only perfunctory criticism of his cult of personality. In an abortive attempt to rehabilitate Stalin completely, Devi Sturua, ideological secretary of the Georgian Communist Party, declared in October 1966:

> I am a Stalinist because the name of Stalin is linked with the victories of our people in the years of collectivization and industrialization. I am a Stalinist because the name of Stalin is linked with the victories of our people in the Great Patriotic War [World War II]. I am a Stalinist because the name of Stalin is linked with the victories of our people in the postwar reconstruction of our economy.[5]

A closed nationwide "seminar" of party ideological officials applauded.

Nationalism and Dissent

During the Brezhnev era, nationalism revived in various parts of the USSR. "Of all the problems facing Moscow the most urgent and the most stubborn is the one raised by the national minorities," wrote Hélène d'Encausse prophetically.[6] Brezhnev's official goal of a "fusion of the nations" was resisted by non-Slavic elements seeking genuine Soviet federalism and autonomy. Efforts at Great Russian linguistic and educational assimilation, effective with smaller ethnic groups, failed in the Caucasus, Lithuania, and Central Asia, where religion (Catholicism or Islam) reinforced a local sense of historic and national identity. The Soviet regime provided few mosques for its large Muslim minority, but many worshiped unofficially. Muslim leaders, affirmed d'Encausse, were making communism a by-product of Islam. (For statistics on the relative size of ethnic groups, see Table 40.1.)

The Brezhnev regime persecuted "bourgeois nationalism," especially in the Ukraine. In April 1966 two Ukrainian literary critics were accused of smuggling "nationalist" verses to the West.

[5] Stephen F. Cohen, ed., *An End to Silence* (New York, 1982), p. 158.

[6] Hélène Carrère d'Encausse, *Decline of an Empire: The Soviet Socialist Republics in Revolt* (New York, 1979), pp. 231, 274.

Map 40.1 The Soviet political units in 1970

V. Chornovil, who reported their trial to the world and denounced KGB tactics, was sentenced to forced labor. That fall Articles 190/1 and 190/3, making it a crime to spread "slanderous inventions about the Soviet state and social system" or to "disturb public order," were added to the Soviet criminal code and were used frequently against nationalists and other dissidents. In 1972 Peter Shelest, the Ukraine's political boss, was removed partly for glorifying Ukrainian history and culture and seeking to re-Ukrainize its political apparatus. The Brezhnev regime reacted harshly to efforts by national minorities to assert their rights or to complaints of Russian domination. (See Map 40.1.) While declining as a percentage of the total Soviet population, Great Russians remained dom-

inant and privileged, holding with other Slavic elements most top political positions. In the socioeconomic realm, most non-Russians lost ground relative to Great Russians. Industrial development and urbanization centered in Slavic republics with a low rate of population increase and growing labor shortages. In contrast, Turkic-Muslim areas suffered from economic under-development, growing labor surpluses, and rapid population increases. In Muslim urban centers non-Muslims, only 21 percent of the total Muslim-area population in 1970, frequently took the best jobs. A 44-percent increase in the Turkic-Muslim population from 1959 to 1970 created powerful demographic pressures in Central Asia, with a large rural population surplus and intensified pressures on agriculture.[7]

Frequently the Brezhnev regime imprisoned dissidents in psychiatric hospitals. In 1966 the writer Valeri Tarsis, in exile in England, published *Ward Seven*, which described compulsory treatment in a Moscow psychiatric hospital. "I believe in God and I cannot live in a country where one cannot be an honest man," wrote Tarsis. The USSR "is not a democratic country; this is fascism."[8] The Politburo declared Tarsis insane and a traitor and deprived him of Soviet citizenship! In 1967 former major general Peter Grigorenko, campaigning for the right of Crimean Tatars to return home from exile, was arrested, committed to a hospital for the criminally insane, and beaten by the KGB. Explained another dissident, Vladimir Bukovskii:

> The inmates are prisoners, people who committed actions considered crimes from the point of view of the authorities . . . but not . . . of the law. And in order to isolate them and punish them somehow, these people are declared insane and kept in the ward of the psychiatric hospital.[9]

Andrei Amalrik, a young historian, compared dissident trials under Brezhnev with medieval heresy trials. "Recognizing their ideological hopelessness, they [the leaders] cling in fear to criminal codes, to prison camps, and psychiatric hospitals."[10] Losing his job, Amalrik was convicted of "parasitism" and served 16 months in Siberia at hard labor.

Many scientists and intellectuals joined the dissident Human Rights Movement. Its leading statement was the *Sakharov Memorandum*, published abroad in 1968 by the outstanding scientist Andrei Sakharov. His protest reflected growing support by Soviet scientists for civil liberties and democratization. Citing the deadly danger to humankind of nuclear war, overpopulation, bureaucracy, and environmental pollution, Sakharov urged Soviet-American cooperation to save civilization. The Soviet and American systems, borrowing from each other, were converging toward democratic socialism, he argued. Castigating Stalinism and its vestiges, Sakharov urged democratic freedoms for the USSR and denounced collectivization as an "almost serflike enslavement of the peasantry." He demanded rehabilitation of all Stalin's victims: "Only the most meticulous analysis of the [Stalinist] past and its consequences will now enable us to wash off the blood and dirt that befouled our banner."[11] In May 1970 Sakharov warned Brezhnev that unless secrecy was removed from science, culture, and technology, the USSR would soon become a second-rate provincial country.

Despite a severe crackdown by the Brezhnev regime, Soviet dissent during the 1970s expanded as one component of an emerging "contrasystem" with a flourishing illegal "second economy" and a major system of underground religious belief and *samizdat* publications.[12] Under Brezhnev, Soviet dissent acquired a history, heroes, and martyrs. According to Amnesty International, more than 400 Soviet dissidents were imprisoned or restricted in their movements after 1975, notably before important events such as the Moscow Olympics of 1980. A steadily growing volume of dissident information kept Soviet repression in the world spotlight and gave visibility to dissatisfied national and religious groups. From late 1976 the regime reacted vigorously, often applying Article 190/1. Particular targets were dissidents monitoring Soviet violations of the Helsinki Accords; several political trials of these leaders were staged in 1977–1978. Another police offensive of 1979–1980 brought arrests of nine Helsinki monitors and the internal exile of Andrei Sakharov to Gorkii. KGB tactics included trumped-up criminal charges

---

[7] Robert Lewis et al., *Nationality and Population Change in Russia and the USSR* (New York, 1976), pp. 350*ff.*

[8] Quoted in A. Rothberg, *The Heirs of Stalin* (Ithaca, NY, 1972), p. 170.

[9] Quoted in Rothberg, *Heirs of Stalin,* p. 301.

[10] Quoted in Rothberg, p. 304.

[11] Quoted in Rothberg, pp. 332, 338.

[12] Robert Sharlet, "Growing Soviet Dissidence," *Current History* 79 (October 1980), pp. 96–100.

against dissidents, increased use of psychiatric terror, and the employment of official hooligans to beat up dissidents or burglarize their homes. There was a major increase in forced deportations of prominent opponents of the regime. Nonetheless, the strength of the Soviet counterculture and information about its activities in the West increased.

Economy and Society

After a decade of moderate growth and relative prosperity, the Brezhnev regime faced declining economic growth rates and increasing demands on limited Soviet resources. Weather conditions caused fluctuations in agricultural production, but the general trend was slower growth. Some Soviet economists affirmed that the Stalinist model was holding back economic development. Reformers urged drastic changes: eliminating much central planning of prices and introducing competitive bidding between the State Planning Commission (Gosplan) and individual plants. However, the party apparatus and the bureaucracy refused to dismantle the central planning empire, relax controls, or move toward market socialism. Conservative ideologists opposed any concessions to capitalism.

Premier Kosygin, supporting reform, backed many suggestions of Professor Evsei Liberman of Kharkov University, who advocated that state enterprises sell their goods and be expected to show a profit. Liberman also rejected Stalinist economics based on commands from above and absolute obedience from below and the stress on quantity regardless of cost or quality. He wished to free the individual enterprise from outside controls, except for overall production and delivery goals. Wage increases and bonuses for managers and workers would depend on profitability—that is, on the sale of products—not on fulfilling centrally decided production norms. Using supply and demand, suppliers and manufacturers would deal directly with one another rather than going through central economic ministries. In July 1964

Khrushchev authorized an experiment with aspects of Libermanism in two clothing combines. Profits and sales increased sufficiently to encourage the new leadership to try Liberman's theories on a modified basis in some 400 consumer enterprises. Greater ability to adjust to consumer demand and more emphasis on quality resulted.

This experiment was underway when Kosygin's proposals for general economic reform, heralded as "a new system of planning and incentives," were approved in September 1965. That April Kosygin had challenged the party's role in planning:

> We have to free ourselves completely . . . from everything that used to tie down the planning officials and obliged them to draft plans otherwise than in accordance with the interests of the economy. . . . We often find ourselves prisoners of laws we ourselves have made.[13]

The September 1965 reforms included Liberman's managerial economics and profit ideas, but Kosygin also restored the central economic ministries, often under their Stalinist bosses. Khrushchev's *sovnarkhozy*, defended chiefly by local party officials anxious to retain control of regional industry, were scrapped. The Moscow technocrats regained all of their pre-1957 powers: The new head of Gosplan, N. K. Baibakov, had been removed from that post by Khrushchev in 1957!

Opposition from conservative party elements and Stalinist managers first watered down the Kosygin reforms, then halted their implementation. By January 1967 some 2,500 enterprises had adopted the new incentive system; by 1970 the reforms supposedly applied to all firms, but plant managers' authority was reduced as the ministers determined daily operations more and more. Gross value of output, not profit, remained the key index. Conservatives realized that to free managers from central tutelage would reduce bureaucratic power over industry. To orthodox party

---

[13] Quoted in Michel Tatu, *Power in the Kremlin* (New York, 1968), p. 447.

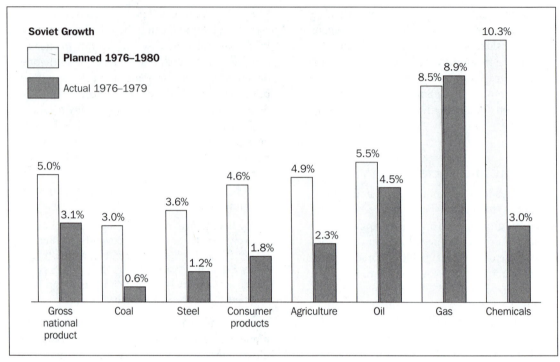

Figure 40.1
Soviet economic growth under Brezhnev: Planned versus actual

members, Libermanism was "goulash commu-nism"; to allow market forces to prevail over cen-tral planning would be "unscientific." Many managers, fearing responsibility, acted in the old Stalinist manner. Thus the 1965 reforms eventu-ally failed; rather than implementing Libermanism, they temporarily took up slack in the old system. A Soviet economist lamented: "I thought they [the leaders] understood from their experi-ence that repressive measures would never achieve results and that they were therefore ready to employ purely economic tools. Now I see there was nothing to it."[14]

As industrial growth rates under Brezhnev declined, Soviet planners were faced with a clear need to improve productivity and quality. (See

Figure 40.1.) The traditional Soviet economic policy of concentrating on heavy and defense-related industries and on quantity produced great imbalances and backward light industry and ser-vice sectors. Huge investments were required to maintain even lower levels of growth; bottlenecks were promoted by overexpansion of key indus-tries. The centralized Soviet system's economic inefficiencies included a waste of capital on ill-conceived, protracted construction projects, underutilized capacity, mismanagement of human resources, overcentralization, inertia, lack of initia-tive, and excessive bureaucracy.[15] Key goals of the Ninth (1971–1975) and Tenth (1976–1980) Five Year Plans were not fulfilled, even though scaled well below levels of previous plans and consump-

[14] Quoted in R. Conquest, "A New Russia? A New World?" *Foreign Affairs* 54 (April 1975), p. 487.

[15] George Feiwel, "Economic Performance and Reforms in the Soviet Union," in D. R. Kelley, ed., *Soviet Politics in the Brezhnev Era* (New York, 1980), pp. 70–101.

Table 40.2 Collective and state farms

	1940	1960	1976
Kolkhozy			
Total number	235,000	44,900	27,300
Workers per farm	110	445	542
Sown area per farm	500 hectares	2,746	3,597
Livestock	297 head	3,031	4,509
Tractors	4.4	14.4	39
Sovkhozy			
Total number	4,200	7,400	19,617
Workers per farm	381	783	559
Sown area per farm	2,750	9,081	5,680
Tractors	20	54	57

SOURCE: D. R. Kelley, ed., *Soviet Politics in the Brezhnev Era* (New York, 1980), p. 57.

tion was slated to grow about as fast as accumulation. Complicating the picture in the 1980s were high labor turnover, labor shortages, and rising consumer demand. At the 25th Party Congress of 1976, Brezhnev urged a rapid increase in productivity, a sharp cutback in manual labor, increased automation, and improved quantity and quality of consumer goods. However, such exhortations had little effect.

Although output rose during Brezhnev's early years, agriculture remained a weak link in the Soviet economy. Unfavorable weather and inefficient, oversized farms caused the USSR to suffer seven bad grain harvests in a row beginning in 1979. Soviet grain exports shrank; by the 1980s the USSR imported more grain than any other country. In *Letter to the Soviet Leaders* (1973), Solzhenitsyn urged scrapping the entire collective farming system. Soviet agriculture remained subservient to ideology and under tight central bureaucratic control. Despite higher investments, agricultural growth slowed: a roughly 26-percent increase during Brezhnev's first decade compared with a 41-percent increase under Khrushchev. Fluctuating grain yields—for example, a record 237.2 million metric tons in 1978 falling to 179 million in 1979—prompted Brezhnev to conclude long-term import agreements with the United States and Argentina. Although costs were high, in 1975

Soviet storage capacity was increased to 40 million metric tons. Brezhnev emphasized extension of irrigated lands and undertook a vast land-improvement program for the northwest. With agricultural production roughly 80–85 percent of U.S. output, the Soviet population received enough total calories and proteins, but lacked variety and quality.

Under Brezhnev the trend away from collective farms (*kolkhozy*) to state farms (*sovkhozy*) continued. (See Table 40.2.) Soviet farms became huge, impersonal rural factories whose farmers were controlled as strictly as by the estate manager under serfdom. Soviet farmers tilled about 70 percent more land area than did farmers in the United States, with more than seven times the manpower, but with only about one-third the tractors and trucks and 60 percent of the grain combines. The Brezhnev regime did establish a minimum wage for collective farmers and raised the income of all farmworkers. In 1980 the average collective farmer received 116 rubles per month, compared to 170 rubles for an urban worker; state farmers' income fell in between. Despite these improvements, in 1977 about 15 million private plots, averaging about one acre, produced 27 percent of all Soviet agricultural products, including 34 percent of livestock products and almost half of its vegetables and potatoes.[16] Private crop yields per acre and livestock output per animal exceeded substantially those on collective and state farms. These superior results reveal the stronger incentives to produce on private farms than on collective and state farms. More than 50 million people worked on private plots at least part-time. Whereas Khrushchev had taken steps to curtail and restrict private plots, Brezhnev promised to foster them. Small garden machines began to be manufactured for sale to private farmers.

Soviet foreign trade in the 1970s rose sharply, spurred by imports of Western technology and grain and exports of oil and natural gas. In a marked departure from traditional Soviet policies of autarky, the USSR was opened more to foreign technology, especially to increase its output of energy. Besides military equipment and gold, about 85 percent of all Soviet hard-currency exports were raw materials; more than half of these earnings came from petroleum. Soviet oil exports rose from 96 million tons in 1970 to about 125 million in 1975, mostly to Europe and Cuba. However, Soviet oil output then peaked at 12–13 million barrels per day. Output in older Soviet oil fields in the Caucasus fell rapidly, partly because of technological bottlenecks, while exploitation of newer Siberian fields required advanced and expensive foreign technology.

Soviet living standards, having risen markedly during the early Brezhnev years, leveled off during the 1970s and remained the lowest of the major industrial countries. (See Table 40.3.) The average citizen obtained an adequate but uninspiring diet featuring potatoes and cabbage, suffered chronic meat and milk shortages, and lived in shabby, overcrowded housing. Consumption in 1970 amounted to about 57 percent of total output (GNP), considerably less than in the United States and other industrial countries. Strong consumer

Table 40.3 Selected consumer goods per thousand

Item	1965	1970	1975	1977
Watches, clocks	885	1,193	1,319	1,408
TV sets	68	143	215	229
Refrigerators	29	89	178	210
Washing machines	59	141	189	200

SOURCE: D Kelley, ed., *Soviet Politics in the Brezhnev Era* (New York, 1980), p. 116

pressure spurred the Brezhnev regime, anxious to avoid strikes like those in neighboring Poland, to provide more and improved consumer goods and services. A more selective urban populace demanded quality products, especially automobiles, motorcycles, and carpets. But for such "high demand" goods no credit was available: The purchase price had to be paid in cash before delivery. Considerable resources were devoted to producing private cars, providing repair facilities, and building decent roads. Five Year Plans under Brezhnev channeled much more state investment into consumer products than ever before. Brezhnev's speech to the 26th Party Congress in 1981 stressed the political significance of improving consumption:

> The problem is to create a really modern sector producing consumer goods and services for the population, which meets their demands. . . . The store, the cafeteria, the laundry, the dry cleaners are places people visit every day. What can they buy? How are they treated? . . . The people will judge our work in large measure by how these questions are solved.[17]

Nonetheless, compared with earnings, the prices of Soviet consumer goods remained very high.

Under Brezhnev there was growing official concern over crime and corruption, symptoms of social malaise. A new gun-control law of February 1974 prescribed up to five years' imprisonment for unauthorized possession of firearms. As crimes of

---

[16] Karl-Eugene Wädekin, *The Private Sector in Soviet Agriculture* (Berkeley, 1973); Roy Laird, "The Political Economy of Soviet Agriculture Under Brezhnev," in Kelley, *Soviet Politics*, pp. 55ff.

[17] Quoted in Robert F. Byrnes, ed., *After Brezhnev: Sources of Soviet Conduct in the 1980s* (Bloomington, IN, 1983), p. 74.

violence increased, notably in southern areas, severe penalties were imposed for drug abuse, especially involving hashish and marijuana. Juvenile delinquency increased sharply. As the food situation outside of major cities deteriorated, parts of the USSR instituted rationing and even Muscovites searched for food and other consumer goods. As items of real commercial value disappeared from state stores into illegal or semilegal channels, the black and gray markets became crucial for most Russians. Old values and restraints broke down, as cheating and stealing from the state increased. As Russians lost faith that things would improve and regarded the promise of communism as a cynical joke, public morale plummeted. Many Russians told George Feifer, an American journalist: The whole country is sick and getting sicker.[18]

That seemed to be literally true. Whereas earlier the USSR was in the forefront of improving public health, raising life expectancy, and reducing infant mortality, after 1960 an astounding reversal occurred, marked by rampant alcoholism, burgeoning infant mortality, and declining life expectancy. Measured by its public health, noted Nick Eberstadt in 1980, the USSR was no longer a developed nation.[19] In no other European country, not even primitive Albania, were lives so short or the infant death rate so high. Western accounts emphasized the devastating effects of alcoholism, especially on Russian men, but also on women and even children. In the early 1970s the Soviet per capita consumption of hard liquor was more than twice the American or Swedish level. Despite sharp increases in state vodka prices, consumption rose, and almost as much moonshine (*samogon*) was consumed as legally purchased liquor. Alcohol purchases accounted, noted Feifer, for almost one-third of consumer spending in food stores. Christopher Davis and Murray Feshbach, leading

Western experts on Soviet society, attributed the Soviet health crisis to a number of factors, including poor-quality baby foods and nursing formulas, rising illegitimacy and abortion (averaging six to eight per woman during childbearing years), alcoholism, high accident rates, pollution of the air and soil, and a breakdown in the health-care system. The Brezhnev regime, busily building up its military forces, economized at the expense of public health: The Soviet Union devoted a declining percentage of total output to combating illness.[20] Another Western scholar suggested that the Soviet system itself might be wearing down from a combination of inefficiency, corruption, and rampant cynicism.[21]

Nor, despite official claims, did women's equality exist in the USSR. The Soviet leadership pursued the goal of sexual equality until it conflicted with economic or military priorities. Under Brezhnev males continued to dominate the higher ranks of all scientific disciplines and most other branches of the economy. However, Soviet women finally had achieved equal pay for equal work and equal entry into most professions.[22] In 1970 women represented 53.9 percent of the Soviet population and 51 percent of the workforce. However, women comprised only 22.6 percent of party members, and just 14 of some 300 full or candidate members of the Central Committee were women. The USSR had a higher percentage of women doctors, lawyers, and machine operators than any Western country, but women had only token representation in top economic, cultural, and political bodies. That situation partly reflected traditional Russian male predominance. Women were channeled mainly into low-skilled, low-income, physical-labor job categories. Lingering

---

[18] George Feifer, "Russian Disorders," *Harper's*, February 1981, pp. 41–55.
[19] Nick Eberstadt, "The Health Crisis in the USSR," *New York Review of Books*, February 19, 1981.

[20] The USSR spent about 9.8 percent of GNP on health care in 1955 but only 7.5 percent in 1977; in the United States, largely due to Medicare and Medicaid, the percentage rose from 8 to 11. Eberstadt, "The Health Crisis," p. 25.
[21] Robert Wesson, *The Aging of Communism* (New York, 1980).
[22] D. Atkinson et al., eds., *Women in Russia* (Stanford, 1977), pp. 219, 224, 355.

traditional concepts of women's role in the home and at work promoted their dual exploitation. The Brezhnev regime, while admitting problems, promoted legal equality of women but permitted economic, cultural, and political inequality to persist.

Soviet society under Brezhnev, despite reduced wage differentials, remained one of concealed privilege and inequality. The "new class"—an elite of party, police, state, and military leaders—had established itself as an hereditary aristocracy. This Communist aristocracy, without manners, taste, or real competence, passed position and wealth on to its offspring and seemed mainly concerned with its creature comforts. It possessed limousines, special luxury apartment blocks, country estates (dachas), and sanatoria closed to ordinary citizens. It utilized special shops with quantities of otherwise unobtainable goods at heavily subsidized prices. The elevated status of this privileged minority, as in tsarist Russia, separated it from a resentful mass of ordinary workers and peasants. Industrial workers still enjoyed high status in Soviet media, but their wages and pensions remained low. Collective farmers, their position improved by wage and pension increases under Brezhnev, remained at the bottom of the social ladder. "Developed socialism" in Brezhnev's USSR seemed a far cry from the Marxist ideal.

Foreign Affairs and Armed Forces

Abroad, a generally prudent Brezhnev regime, carrying a bigger military stick, avoided Khrushchev's dramatic initiatives, threats, and violent reversals. Until 1968 Soviet foreign policy seemed to lack self-confidence. Successful military intervention in Czechoslovakia, halting the erosion of Soviet control over eastern Europe, reversed this picture. Brezhnev thereafter became more decisive and self-assured. As the Sino-Soviet quarrel continued to rage, détente with the West produced important agreements with West Germany and the United States.

Détente and Defense Spending

The new leaders' initial approach abroad was conciliatory, with this message: We are not angry with anyone. They sought to mend their fences with China, but from 1965 on Sino-Soviet competition sharpened over influence in Asia; the gap widened between the bellicose Chinese stance and the moderate Soviet position in the Vietnam War. Exploiting this quarrel to enhance its autonomy, Romania established warm relations with China and increased its trade with the West. In 1966, as the so-called Cultural Revolution began in China, the Chinese boycotted the Soviet 23rd Party Congress, and Russians in China were abused and beaten up. Chinese students left the USSR, and Sino-Soviet trade shrank almost to zero. In January 1969 *Pravda* called Maoism "a great power adventurist policy based on a petty bourgeois nationalistic ideology alien to Marxism-Leninism." As friction mounted along the 4,000-mile Sino-Soviet frontier, the Soviet writer Evgeni Yevtushenko compared the Chinese unflatteringly with the Mongols of Chingis-khan. War between the Communist giants seemed a real possibility, despite the contrary assertions of Marxist-Leninist doctrine. In March 1969 began six months of intermittent but bloody frontier skirmishes over their disputed Ussuri River frontier. According to the dissident historian Roy Medvedev, Brezhnev, who was rabidly anti-Chinese, personally ordered a massive artillery assault and a deep penetration into Chinese territory that killed several thousand Chinese soldiers and poisoned Sino-Soviet relations for years. Rumors circulated that the Soviet military was considering a preemptive nuclear strike against China. In any case, the Chinese were intimidated and agreed not to patrol in areas claimed by the USSR. Meanwhile the USSR began a major buildup of ground forces along the Chinese border.

Faced with this rising menace in the East, Soviet leaders scrupulously avoided trouble in the West while increasing the USSR's military strength. The Soviets stepped up trade with western Europe, and during Charles de Gaulle's presidency sought to exploit Franco-American coolness in order to split NATO. The similarly independent roles of Romania and France suggested the weakening hold by the two blocs over their members, as contacts increased between eastern and western European countries. The Cuban missile crisis of 1962 had altered Soviet-American relations considerably. Both sides, noted Hans Morgenthau, an American political scientist, renounced active use of nuclear weapons but retained them as deterrents; both sides aimed at a balance of power and realized that neither could achieve true predominance.[23] Their rivalry in the Third World began to cool as they discovered that neutral countries would not commit themselves totally to either side. In their relations, the United States and the USSR deemphasized ideology and stressed pragmatic power considerations. During the late 1960s, heavy American involvement in Vietnam poisoned their relations; its subsequent decline fostered détente.

In the late 1960s and early 1970s, Soviet policy in the Third World produced both setbacks and successes. Several pro-Soviet regimes collapsed, notably those of Sukarno in Indonesia in 1965 and Nkrumah in Ghana in 1966, and were replaced by anti-Communist military governments. The Brezhnev regime shifted to practical economic assistance and military aid. Seeking to build up India as a bulwark against China, Moscow viewed the Indo-Pakistan War of 1965 with dismay. Premier Kosygin met with Pakistani and Indian heads of state in Tashkent early in 1966, and the resulting settlement enhanced the USSR's image as a peacemaker in Asia. India's dependence upon Soviet industrial, military, and diplomatic support increased, trade between the two nations expanded, and Soviet naval vessels in the Indian Ocean challenged the former Western monopoly. In the Middle East the USSR supplied major economic and military aid to Egypt and Syria to undermine the Western position and win political influence. Their defeat by Israel in the June 1967

war was a costly setback to Soviet policy, but it increased Arab distrust of the West and dependence on Moscow. After the war the Soviets rebuilt their clients' military forces, and thousands of Soviet advisers trained Egyptians to use more sophisticated equipment. Iraq, the Sudan, and Algeria also relied heavily on Soviet arms. Soviet influence in the Middle East reached unprecedented proportions, only to decline considerably during the early 1970s. President Anwar Sadat of Egypt in 1972 expelled all Soviet military advisers. Then in October 1973 Israel, with which the USSR had severed diplomatic ties, again defeated Egypt and Syria.

A crucial turning point in Brezhnev's foreign policy was the Soviet invasion of Czechoslovakia in August 1968. (See Problem 15 at the end of this chapter.) Earlier that year Czechoslovakia, under Premier Alexander Dubček, had moved rapidly toward democratic socialism, virtually ended domestic censorship, and increased ties with the West. Soviet intervention followed months of hesitation and an apparent agreement with the Czechoslovak Politburo at Čierna-nad-Tisou. Large Soviet forces and token contingents from several Warsaw Pact countries met only moral resistance, and Moscow disregarded Yugoslav and Romanian objections and Western denunciations. This move, successful from the Soviet viewpoint, revealed that the Brezhnev-Kosygin collective leadership could act decisively. Without hindrance from the United States, the USSR placed six Soviet divisions in Czechoslovakia, altering the strategic balance in central Europe. The Soviet press even echoed Bismarck's famous statement: "Whoever rules Bohemia holds the key to Europe." The subsequent so-called Brezhnev Doctrine warned that the USSR would tolerate neither internal nor external challenges to its hegemony in eastern Europe and that it would use force if necessary to prevent the overthrow of a fellow Communist regime. The Yugoslavs and Romanians wondered whether Brezhnev might apply his "doctrine" against them, but their clear determination to resist apparently dissuaded Moscow. Nonetheless, the Czech intervention reconsolidated the Soviet

---

[23] "Changes and Chances in American-Soviet Relations," *Foreign Affairs* 49, no. 3 (April 1971), pp. 429–41.

Bloc in eastern Europe and muted the Yugoslav and Romanian challenge of national communism.

After this major success, the USSR early in 1969 adopted a flexible foreign policy and tried to improve relations with the West. To accelerate Soviet economic growth, Brezhnev sought increased trade with the West and American technology. The replacement of Konrad Adenauer's hard-line rule in West Germany with that of Willy Brandt, a Social Democrat who favored reconciliation with the USSR, weakened NATO and helped Brezhnev heighten his influence in Europe. During 1970 landmark treaties were concluded among the USSR, Poland, and West Germany confirming their post–World War II boundaries and undercutting U.S. bridge-building with eastern European countries. Next the Soviets sought a general European security conference, again to weaken NATO and relax tensions on their western frontiers. But the Soviet hold over eastern Europe remained insecure because of persistent nationalism and the waning force of Marxist ideology. Riots in Poland in 1971 forced the conservative Gomulka to resign and brought the more flexible regime of Edward Gierek to power.

Major increases in military strength enhanced Soviet power and prestige under Brezhnev and created a new world balance of forces. Thus by 1979 the USSR spent an estimated $165 billion on defense, with armed forces totaling some 3.65 million men and women, nearly twice the personnel of the United States' forces. The Red Army, with about 160 divisions, had some 30 percent of its strength along the tense Sino-Soviet border. Possessing huge numbers of tanks and supporting aircraft, the Red Army proved its efficiency and power in the invasion of Czechoslovakia. Whereas during the Cuban missile crisis of 1962 the United States held at least a 3-to-1 advantage in strategic nuclear weapons, by 1969 the USSR had equaled the United States in intercontinental missiles and a decade later was well ahead in ICBMs and submarine-launched missiles.

The achievement of approximate nuclear parity and the growing expense of nuclear armament encouraged the two superpowers to reach signifi-

cant agreements to limit nuclear weapons, including the first Strategic Arms Limitation Treaty (SALT I). Until April 1971 the Soviet commitment to SALT remained tentative, but then Brezhnev apparently accepted the concept of strategic parity and championed détente. To Brezhnev this meant developing a working relationship with the United States, although Soviet ideology required him to regard the leading capitalist power as an adversary. Explained a Soviet publication of 1972:

> Peaceful coexistence is a principle of relations between states which does not extend to relations between the exploited and the exploiters, the oppressed peoples and the colonialists. . . . Marxist-Leninists see in peaceful coexistence a special form of the class struggle between socialism and capitalism in the world, a principle whose implementation ensures the most favorable conditions for the world revolutionary process.[24]

At their Moscow summit meeting of 1972, President Nixon and General Secretary Brezhnev agreed to limit construction of antiballistic missile defense systems and reached an interim accord on offensive missiles. Additional modest steps toward limitation were taken at meetings in Moscow and Vladivostok in 1974, which set a ceiling on the number of offensive missiles for both sides. These agreements slowed the arms race and inaugurated better relations between the two superpowers. At the European Security Conference, which included all European countries except Albania, plus the United States and Canada, the Helsinki Declaration of August 1975 was signed. The nearest thing to a peace conference ending World War II, it announced: "The participating states regard as inviolable all one another's frontiers . . . and therefore they will refrain now and in the future from assaulting those frontiers." The signatories, including the USSR, also pledged to respect human rights.[25]

---

[24] Shalva Sanakeev, *The World Socialist System* (Moscow, 1972), pp. 289–90.

[25] J. Nogee and R. Donaldson, eds., *Soviet Foreign Policy Since World War II* (Elmsford, NY, 1988), p. 263.

During a Soviet-American détente lasting until 1980, the Brezhnev regime moderated Soviet policies to permit large-scale Jewish emigration, more contacts with the outside world, and limited diplomatic cooperation to end the Vietnam War. As Robert Kaiser pointed out, during eight years of détente the Soviet Union became a more open society than it had been since the 1920s, and the West learned much more about its internal workings—political, economic, and military—than before.[26] Tens of millions of Soviet citizens listened regularly to Western radio broadcasts, which undercut the official Soviet version of the truth. The Soviet economy, no longer seeking self-sufficiency as under Stalin, became inextricably linked with the world capitalist system and dependent on Western technology and credits; the eastern European states were increasingly dependent on Western markets and credits. Soviet political controls over the eastern European bloc relaxed somewhat, but its members relied more on Soviet energy sources.

Improving Soviet-American relations failed to halt an ominous Soviet military buildup. After the mid-1960s the Soviet navy was greatly strengthened, becoming second only to the American. The Soviets established a naval presence in all oceans, especially the Mediterranean Sea, to support their Middle East policies. *Red Star,* the Soviet army newspaper, declared in 1970: "The age-old dreams of our people have become reality. The pennants of Soviet ships now flutter in the most remote corners of the seas and oceans." Russia's voice must be heard the world over, declared Foreign Minister Gromyko. Russia's merchant fleet became one of the world's largest. A new, more technically trained generation of Soviet army and navy officers took command of these growing forces from retiring World War II commanders. The armed forces' role in Soviet politics, however, remained stable. Military representation in the Politburo and Central Committee stayed small,

and the military did not wish to disrupt a regime that supplied its forces so generously.

The War in Afghanistan

Détente ended in 1980 after growing disillusionment with its fruits on both sides. In December 1979 the USSR, partly to prevent collapse of a Communist regime, abruptly invaded neighboring Afghanistan, a primitive country of warring Muslim tribesmen, where British and Russian imperial interests had clashed in the 19th century. During 1977, under apparent Soviet pressure, the Afghan Communists, divided between a Khalq faction led by Nur Mohammed Taraki and the Parcham group under Babrak Karmal, reunited. In April 1978, in a bloody coup, army officers and Communists seized power from the unpopular republic led by elderly President Daoud. Taraki promptly set up a one-man dictatorship—"the People's Democratic Republic of Afghanistan"—and aligned it closely with the USSR. His regime carried out large-scale purges and executions of opponents and removed army leaders and members of the Parcham faction. Babrak Karmal, the Parcham leader, took refuge in Moscow. Khalq leaders, headed by H. Amin, sought to implement socialism overnight in a backward tribal society, violating every Afghan cultural and religious norm. The new regime's blatant brutality and its identification with atheism and the USSR alienated much of the Afghan population.

In August 1978 Afghans from every province rose in revolt against the Taraki-Amin regime under Muslim leaders who proclaimed a jihad (holy war) against godless communism; parts of the Afghan army defected to the rebels. Originally delighted by the Communist takeover, Moscow was now appalled at the new regime's unwise and hasty policies. "The revolutionary transformations [were] . . . accompanied by gross errors and extremist exaggerations on the left, which failed to give due consideration to religious and tribal trends," declared a Soviet spokesman. Initially Moscow supported Taraki, but in September 1979, after a shootout in the palace, Amin removed

---

[26] Robert Kaiser, "U.S.-Soviet Relations: Goodbye to Détente," *Foreign Affairs* 59, no. 3 (1981), pp. 500–21.

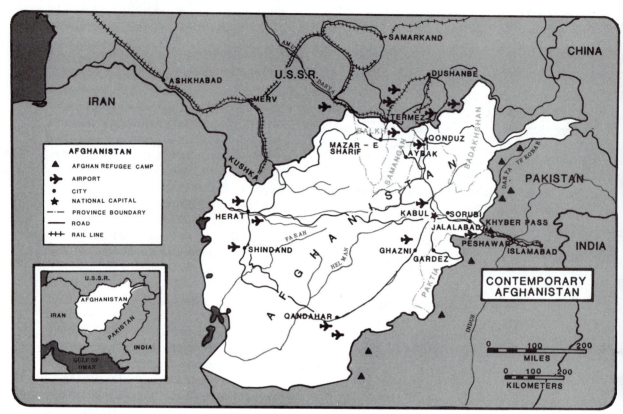

Map 40.2 Afghanistan at the time of the Soviet invasion

Taraki and ruled as dictator. As the popular revolt against him intensified, the Soviets escalated their role until by November there were some 4,500 Soviet "advisers" backing Amin in Afghanistan, and Soviet pilots were bombing rebel positions. (See Map 40.2.) Moscow was being sucked gradually into an Afghan civil war much as the United States had earlier been drawn into the Vietnam imbroglio.

Meanwhile, as he had done in Czechoslovakia in 1968, General I. G. Pavlovskii surveyed the situation in Kabul and concentrated Soviet troops and equipment. On December 24, 1979, regular Soviet units invaded Afghanistan; three days later a special Soviet assault force attacked the palace in Kabul and killed Amin and his family. As in Czechoslovakia, the Soviet incursion was massive

and militarily efficient, but again the political and propaganda aspects were handled with incredible clumsiness. The Afghan "request" for military "assistance" arrived in Moscow three days *after* the invasion began! Only hours after a Soviet minister had called on President Amin, Moscow announced that Amin had been executed for crimes "against the noble people of Afghanistan." Babrak Karmal, installed as the new Afghan leader, arrived from Moscow four days later in the baggage train of the Soviet army. Then Moscow proclaimed that its army had intervened, overthrown the government, and killed the president in order to forestall "foreign intervention," adding the absurd charge that Amin had plotted with the CIA and Muslim fanatics to destroy Afghan socialism! Yet that September Brezhnev had congratulated Amin upon his becoming president.

The Soviet invasion produced counteraction by the United States. President Carter declared that this Soviet action "has made a more drastic change in my own opinion of what the Soviets' ultimate goals are than anything they've done in the previous time I've been in office." Washington proclaimed the Persian Gulf vital to American security, imposed partial embargoes for a while on shipments of grain and technology to the USSR, and organized a partially successful Western boycott of the 1980 Moscow Olympics. The United Nations urged the "immediate and unconditional withdrawal of foreign troops from Afghanistan," but Moscow paid no attention.[27]

Was the Soviet incursion part of an aggressive design to dominate the Persian Gulf region or a defensive move under the Brezhnev Doctrine to prevent the fall of a client Communist regime to Muslim fundamentalism? Was this action unprecedented, as some Western observers believed, and thus a dangerous turning point in Soviet foreign policy, or merely the Asian counterpart of the Czech intervention? Even before the invasion, Afghanistan had been within the Soviet sphere of influence, affirmed Thomas Hammond, an American scholar.[28] Thus the Soviet move was really nothing new: Consistent with earlier actions by Moscow in the Third World, the invasion sought to secure Soviet frontiers by surrounding them with friendly and subservient clients and to prevent the fall of any Communist regime. Contributory causes included Soviet fears of Muslim fanaticism spreading into Soviet Central Asia and the Soviet desire to demonstrate effective support of its allies. The invasion of Afghanistan also continued traditional Russian imperialism in the area and aimed to create a more effective and obedient regime.

Babrak Karmal assumed the top posts in the new Soviet-installed government and named token non-Communists to his cabinet while protesting his patriotism and sincere support for Islam. He failed to win much public support because he was known to be an atheist, a Communist, and a Moscow puppet surrounded and controlled by Russian advisers who carried through progressive Sovietization of Afghanistan. Feuding Afghan tribal factions achieved unprecedented unity in a national liberation struggle and holy war against Russians whom they hated and despised. The rebels (*mujaheddin*) soon controlled most of the country despite the influx of some 115,000 Soviet troops. The strength of the unreliable Afghan army fell sharply. Soviet forces used massive firepower, indiscriminate bombing, and apparently chemical weapons in abortive efforts to root out the rebels. By 1984 some 3 million Afghans, or 20 percent of the total population, had fled their increasingly devastated and impoverished homeland; most went to neighboring Pakistan. The Soviet invasion and brutal conduct of the war undermined Soviet influence in Muslim lands of the Third World, hastened American rearmament, and severely drained Soviet resources.

Problems with Poland

During 1980 another and potentially even graver threat to the Soviet Bloc developed in Poland on the Soviet Union's western flank. Beginning in 1970 Edward Gierek, succeeding Gomulka as chief of the Polish Communist Party, had pushed a program of rapid industrialization, fueled by Western technology purchased on credit. After a boom period (1971–1975) and rising living standards, severe recession gripped Poland. Skyrocketing energy costs, delays in completing large industrial projects, and rising consumer demand produced alarming deficits in Poland's balance of payments with the West. In the summer of 1980 a series of worker strikes triggered formation of an independent trade union movement, Solidarity, which soon obtained the support of most Polish workers. Gierek was forced from office, but his replacement, Stanislaw Kania, failed to stem the workers' campaign for benefits and freedom. As the Polish

---

[27] Cited in *New York Times,* January 6, 1980.
[28] Thomas Hammond, *Red Flag over Afghanistan* (Boulder, CO, 1984).

economy neared collapse and farmers and students also began to organize, party control was threatened. Reports multiplied of a massive Soviet military buildup on Poland's frontiers, and veiled threats of intervention from Moscow were designed to restore the Polish Workers' Party's monopoly of power.

The Soviets confronted an acute dilemma: Military intervention might provoke Polish armed resistance and complete Poland's economic ruin, but inaction would imperil fragile Communist regimes in East Germany and Czechoslovakia, and possibly foment discontent within the Soviet Union. Solidarity demanded the virtual replacement of communism with democracy; Polish farmers followed suit by organizing Rural Solidarity. The Poles sought not merely free trade unions but elimination of censorship, establishment of independent courts, removal of the police from party control, and institution of free elections. Wisely shunning any demand to withdraw Poland from the Warsaw Pact, the Poles urged reducing its military forces. Clearly the USSR could not tolerate such a program any more than it could approve the "Prague Spring." (See Problem 15.) But instead of resorting to direct military intervention, which could cause a bloodbath, Moscow

encouraged the Polish army under a moderate, General Wojciech Jaruzelski, to take power and proclaim martial law (December 1981). Poland's military regime forced Solidarity underground and promised decentralizing economic reforms like those in Hungary. However, Jaruzelski failed to remedy a desperate economic situation.

The 26th Party Congress (February 23–March 3, 1981) in Moscow brought no real solutions to these difficult problems in Europe and Asia. Secretary Brezhnev, aged but still ascendant, sounded a conciliatory note by proposing a summit conference and renewed arms talks with President Ronald Reagan; otherwise there was complete reaffirmation of the status quo. Indeed, for the first time every full and alternate member of the Politburo and every member of the Secretariat was "reelected." The 5,002 delegates, including 12 cosmonauts, heard endless speeches praising the "titanic labors" and "colossal life experience" of Leonid Brezhnev. Premier Tikhonov appealed for greater efficiency and higher labor productivity; he promised more food and better consumer goods. The goals of the new Eleventh Five Year Plan (1981–1985) announced at the congress reflected continuing deceleration of Soviet economic growth.

Problem 15

Soviet Intervention in Czechoslovakia, 1968, and Its Repudiation, 1989

The armed invasion of Czechoslovakia on August 21, 1968, by the Red Army and smaller contingents from four Warsaw Pact allies shocked many in the Soviet Bloc as well as Communists and others in the West. Soviet intervention occurred only weeks after apparent agreement between Soviet and Czechoslovak leaders at Čierna-nad-Tisou just inside Czechoslovakia. Condemning

the action, only Romania refused to participate in the massive Warsaw Pact invasion. The military operation was smooth, unopposed, and revealed Soviet military efficiency, but Czechoslovak passive resistance surprised Soviet leaders and military personnel. Why did the Soviet Politburo decide suddenly, even if reluctantly, to invade an ally still ruled by the Communist party? Was it Czechoslovak domestic liberalization under Alexander Dubček or the danger that the movement would spread to the rest of the Soviet Bloc that proved decisive? And why did the Soviet Union and its allies 21 years later repudiate their intervention as mistaken and unjustified?

Defiant Czech youth waves national flag before a Soviet tank after the Red Army's unpopular occupation of Prague, Czechoslovakia, in August 1968.

Problem 15 continued

Soviet invasion followed almost a year of liberalization in Czechoslovakia (the so-called Prague Spring), hitherto one of the most conservative Stalinist members of the Soviet Bloc. Profound change followed the downfall in January 1968 of the unpopular Stalinist leadership headed by Antonín Novotný despite Soviet objections and halfhearted support. Although before World War II Czechoslovakia had been the most democratic and economically advanced eastern European country, since 1963 it had suffered a grievous economic decline. Early in 1968 much of the rigid, overcentralized Stalinist economic system was dismantled. Under Dubček, the first Slovak to govern Czechoslovakia, liberal Communists instituted far-reaching economic and political

reforms, wide freedom of the press, equality for the Slovaks, thorough party reform, and efforts to increase trade and improve relations with the West. Previous Soviet interference in Czechoslovak domestic affairs was denounced publicly by party members and intellectuals. This provoked alarm and fear in conservative Communist regimes in East Germany and Poland and among Soviet leaders that the Czech liberal fever might infect Ukraine and other Soviet republics. Initially Dubček apparently convinced Soviet leaders that he could control liberalization and restrict it to Czechoslovakia; he assured Moscow that his country would remain in the Warsaw Pact as a Soviet ally and that the Czechoslovak Communist Party (KSS or CCP) would retain its power monopoly.

The following excerpts depict the Soviet intervention from several contrasting viewpoints. Included are official Soviet explanations and justifications, Soviet dissident reactions, Czechoslovak protests and refutations of Soviet assertions, a Western view, and the 1989 Soviet repudiation.

Official Soviet Views

The following excerpts from the Soviet Communist Party newspaper, *Pravda*—one before the invasion and the other after—emphasize the deadly peril to socialism in Czechoslovakia and the Bloc posed by alleged Czech reactionaries aided by American and West German agents. *Pravda* asserted that Soviet forces were invited into Czechoslovakia by elements loyal to socialism and that the Soviet Union and other Warsaw Pact countries had the right and duty to act forcefully in the face of such blatant threats to the entire socialist world.

A month before the August invasion, an open letter "To the Czechoslovak Communist Party Central Committee" appeared in *Pravda*, July 15, 1968.

On behalf of the Central Committees of the Communist and Workers Parties of Bulgaria, Hungary, the G.D.R. [East Germany], Poland, and the Soviet

Problem 15 continued

Union we send you this letter, which is dictated by sincere friendship based on the principles of Marxism-Leninism and proletarian internationalism and by concern . . . for strengthening the positions of socialism and the . . . socialist commonwealth of the peoples.

The developments in your country have aroused profound anxiety among us. The reactionaries' offensive, supported by imperialism, against your party and the foundations of the Czechoslovak Socialist Republic's social system . . . threatens to push your country off the path of socialism and, consequently, imperils the interests of the entire socialist system. . . . We have not had and do not have any intention of interfering in affairs that are purely the internal affairs of your party and your state or of violating the principles of respect, autonomy and equality in relations among Communist Parties and socialist countries. . . .

. . . It is the common affair of our countries, which have united in the Warsaw Pact to safeguard their independence, peace and security in Europe and to place an insurmountable barrier in front of the schemes of imperialist forces, aggression and revanche. . . .

The forces of reaction, taking advantage of the weakening of party leadership in Czechoslovakia and demagogically abusing the slogan of "democratization," unleashed a campaign against the C.C.P. . . . with the clear intention of liquidating the party's guiding role, undermining the socialist system and pitting Czechoslovakia against the other socialist countries. The political organizations and clubs that have cropped up lately outside the framework of the National Front have in essence become headquarters for the forces of reaction. The social democrats persistently seek to create their own party . . . and are attempting to split the workers' movement in Czechoslovakia and to secure leadership of the country so as to restore the bourgeois system. Antisocialist and revisionist forces have taken over the press, radio and television and have turned them into platforms for attacking the Communist party, for disorienting the working class . . . , for carrying out unchecked antisocialist demagoguery and for subverting the friendly relations between the Č. S. R. and the

other socialist countries. . . . The reactionaries appeared publicly before the whole country and published their political platform, entitled "The 2,000 Words."

A month after the invasion, "Sovereignty and the International Duties of Socialist Countries" by Serge Kovalev was published in *Pravda,* September 26, 1968.

The question of the correlation and interdependence of the national interests of the socialist countries and their international duties has acquired particular topical and great importance in connection with the events in Czechoslovakia. The measures taken by the Soviet Union, jointly with other socialist countries, in defending the socialist gains of the Czechoslovak people, are of great importance for strengthening the socialist community. . . .

The peoples of the socialist countries and the Communist Parties certainly do have and should have freedom to determine the roads of advance for their respective countries. However, none of their decisions should do harm either to socialism in their own country or to the fundamental interests of other socialist countries. . . . This means that each Communist Party is responsible not only to its own people but also to all socialist countries and to the entire communist movement. . . .

. . . When a socialist country seeks to adopt a "non-affiliated" attitude, it . . . retains its national independence precisely thanks to the strength of the socialist community, and above all the Soviet Union as its central force, which also includes the might of its armed forces. The weakening of any of the links in the world socialist system directly affects all the socialist countries, which cannot look on indifferently when this happens. Thus, with talk about the right of nations to self-determination the antisocialist elements in Czechoslovakia actually covered up a demand for so-called neutrality and Czechoslovakia's withdrawal from the socialist community. . . . In discharging their internationalist duty to the fraternal peoples of Czechoslovakia and defending their own socialist gains, the USSR and the other socialist states had to act decisively, and they did act, against the anti-socialist forces in Czechoslovakia. . . .

. . . The troops of the allied socialist countries who are now in Czechoslovakia . . . are not interfering in the country's internal affairs; they are fighting for the principles of the self-determination of the peoples of Czechoslovakia.[29]

This Soviet rationale for armed intervention in other Bloc countries became known as the Brezhnev Doctrine.

Protests by Soviet Intellectuals

The invasion of Czechoslovakia soon produced a protest movement by many Soviet intellectuals and the development of a dissident movement in the USSR. Among some courageous objections was one by a leading Soviet poet, Evgenii Yevtushenko, who telegraphed Chairman Brezhnev:

> I cannot sleep. . . . I understand only one thing, that it is my moral duty to express my opinion to you. I am profoundly convinced that our action in Czechoslovakia is a tragic mistake. It is a cruel blow to Czechoslovak-Soviet friendship and to the world Communist movement. This action detracts from our prestige in the eyes of the world and in our own. For me this is also a personal tragedy because I have many friends in Czechoslovakia, and I do not know how I will be able to look them in the eye. . . . I tell myself that what has happened is a great gift to all the reactionary forces in the world, that we cannot foresee the overall consequences of this act.[30]

Roy Medvedev, a dissident historian, asked, "Was the Invasion a Defense of Socialism?"

> *Pravda* writes that the Soviet Communist Party has had an "understanding attitude" toward the decisions made by the CPC at the January 1968 plenum of its Central Committee. But *Pravda* says nothing about the mistakes and crimes of the Novotny group, which brought Czechoslovakia to

its present state of political crisis. *Pravda* asserts that the Soviet Communist Party leadership has no desire to impose its views on the CPC concerning forms and methods of social control or the road to socialism. But the facts testify to the opposite.

> During the past six months we have tried to impose on the CPC our false understanding of events in that country, and when our point of view was rejected, we resorted to military action. *Pravda* admits that the Czechoslovak leaders insisted that they were in full control of the situation in their country. But the Soviet Party leadership [concluded] that "the course of events was such that it could lead to a counterrevolutionary coup." This was a totally wrong conclusion, based . . . on hysterical appeals by the Novotnýites . . . and by their obvious allies in the Soviet embassy in Czechoslovakia. There was no danger of a counterrevolutionary coup either in the spring of 1968 or later. . . .

> . . . By violating Czechoslovak sovereignty, affronting the government of the CSSR and the leadership of the CPC, and offending the national sensibilities of the Czechs and Slovaks, we have weakened, not strengthened, the position of socialism in that country. Our action in Czechoslovakia was not the "defense of socialism" but a blow against socialism in Czechoslovakia and throughout the world.[31]

Aleksandr Ivanov, wrote of "Russia's Shame."

> So here we see the Stalinists of our huge country, frightened to death, trying to drown out with the clatter of tank treads the voice of those Communists who in tiny Czechoslovakia were a bit too hasty in trying to cleanse the *human face* of socialism of the trappings of pseudo socialism. . . . With the blow of the iron fist they have, for the moment, saved themselves and the Czech Stalinists—ridiculously small in numbers!—from the irreversible forward march of socialism.

> . . . August 1968 was a blow at the *practical reality* of socialism and at the Communist movement throughout the world. It was a blow against the ideas of socialism, against genuine Marxism, against the prestige of Communists in the eyes of all progressive humanity, because this blow was struck in the name of socialism and its ideas. . . .

---

[29] A. Rubinstein, *The Foreign Policy of the Soviet Union*, 3d ed. (New York, 1972), pp. 302–04.

[30] Stephen F. Cohen, ed., *An End to Silence: Uncensored Opinion in the Soviet Union*, pp. 279–80. Copyright © 1982 by W. W. Norton.

[31] Cohen, *An End to Silence*, pp. 281–84.

But it was our own "young and green" soldiers who carried out this reactionary deed. They did it without knowing or asking *who* they were going after, *who* they were crushing—whether it was a counterrevolution or a revolution. This blind and obedient willingness to follow any order, this unwillingness to consider the significance of one's own actions . . . —that is our national shame, the national disgrace of our times! . . . We are responsible for the enormous harm done to Czechoslovakia's development toward Communism, for all the consequences of our reactionary intervention.[32]

A Czech Reaction to the Invasion

In the first weeks after the Soviet invasion of August 21, the Czechoslovak people were mobilized in a movement of massive passive resistance by their press, radio, and television, freed from Stalinist controls earlier that year. The following extract is from "Commentary of the Day," *Reportér* no. 35 of August 26, 1968:

A country that does not need to be saved from anything or freed from anything, that is not asking for it and is actually rejecting it for weeks in advance as an absurdity—such a country cannot be "liberated." Such a country can only be occupied—unlawfully, brutally, recklessly. . . . These are unpleasant truths, and one cannot be surprised that the occupiers do not want to read them on the asphalt of the roads, on the walls of houses, . . . on millions of posters throughout the country. . . . But they cannot do away with these truths, least of all by driving the "natives" into the streets under their automatics and forcing them to tear down the posters. . . . Are they not acting "in the interests of socialism," have they not come as "class brethren" performing their "noble internationalist duty"? It is totally inconceivable to them that they should be compared with those who subjugated this country in an equally brutal manner three decades ago. . . . They did not come to liberate socialist Czechoslovakia on the 21st of August,

but to trample it down; they did not come to save the Czechs and Slovaks, but to enslave them. . . .

. . . Stealthily, not like a government of a decent country, but like medieval conspirators, behind the backs of all the legal organs of this country, they joined in a compact with a handful of discredited political corpses and stool pigeons who feared punishment for their participation in the crimes of the 1950's and while still pretending to conduct a dialog in their formal contacts, they forcibly invaded the country. Like gangsters, they abducted the Premier of the legal government of a sovereign country, the Chairman of the legal parliament of that country, the First Secretary of the leading political party, and they restricted the movement and action of the head of state, the President of the Republic, a bearer of the highest medals of their own country.[33]

They trampled upon all agreements that had bound them with that country and yet they had enough arrogance to claim that they were doing so precisely on the basis of those agreements. They brutally surrounded the parliament of that country with their tanks and machine guns. . . . Within three days, they flooded that small country with 26 military divisions and 500,000 soldiers, with thousands of tanks and even rocket weapons, which they aimed against our capital city. They drove the voices of this country, its press, radio, and television, underground, and they tried to replace them with their disgusting prattle disseminated out of [East] Berlin in an insulting distortion of our language. . . .

Encountering the calm of the people, a country that fails to offer a single proof in support of their nonsensical pretext for aggression, they started a futile barrage from all their weapons in the middle of the night—perhaps to be able to pretend to themselves that there is, after all, a need to fight. . . .

Can all this be called a rescue, can all this be called a liberation? How does it actually differ from 15 March 1939?[34] Is this not a replica of all that we already went through once? Of *Wehrmacht* and

---

[32] Cohen, pp. 293–95.

[33] President Ludvik Svoboda was one of very few foreigners to receive the highest Soviet military decoration, Hero of the Soviet Union.

[34] On that date the Nazi armies of Hitler occupied Prague and the remainder of Czechoslovakia.

Problem 15 continued

Gestapo, of blood and iron? Of injustice and arrogance, cruelty and recklessness? Is anything changed by the fact that all this is being perpetrated not by enemies but by "friends," not by recognized aggressors but by allies, not by those of whom we might have expected it but by those whom we would never have thought capable of it?[35]

A Western Evaluation

In a scholarly study, Galia Golan, lecturer in political science at the Hebrew University of Jerusalem, ends with an examination of factors leading to the Soviet invasion of August 1968. She emphasizes the dangers to the Kremlin posed by the "Czechoslovak road to socialism."

> While Czechoslovakia's reforms did not lead her to demand genuine independence from the Soviet Union, the growing pressures upon her did prompt more and more frequent references to sovereignty, equality, and a "Czechoslovak" road to socialism. The sources of these pressures, specifically Gomulka, Ulbricht, and the Kremlin, may well have believed that the reform movement would, eventually, lead Czechoslovakia out of the bloc. But subsequent actions—and revelations—suggested that what worried them most was this "Czechoslovak road to socialism," i.e., the threat it presented for socialism as the Soviets conceived it, both in Czechoslovakia and in the other countries of the Soviet bloc. . . . This issue was certainly used by both the East Germans and the Soviets in their accusations against Prague (*viz.* their efforts to link the reform movement with Bonn, revanchism, and the Sudeten Deutsche), but the Soviets never brought to bear all the means at their disposal to forestall such relations. Rather it would seem that something much more serious was deemed to warrant a full-scale invasion: . . . the threat to the continued rule of the party, the threat of pluralism, and the dangers of freedom of expression—all considered incompatible in Soviet eyes with the

continuation or building of socialism. Thus Soviet and subsequent conservative Czechoslovak attacks focused on the abolition of censorship, the criticism of the militia (read security organs), and the tentatives towards pluralism, specifically the clubs, of the 1968 revival. . . .

> The Soviets made every effort publicly to create the impression that their fear was that Czechoslovakia was falling into the hands of persons who wished to take her out of the socialist alliance, defy the Soviet Union and move towards the West. . . . Moscow's concerns focused on Czechoslovakia's traditional tendencies to democratic socialism, with all its implications for Eastern Europe and the Soviet Union. Like the Comintern and Cominform before them, Moscow, Warsaw, and Pankow were unwilling to accept or believe that this type of socialism could lead to and preserve communism. Specifically, the concept of the leading role of the party . . . had become so intricately connected with the concept of communist rule that Moscow could not conceive of a communist party's remaining in power if it were to abandon its leading role. . . . The implications of this danger were clear: pluralism in Prague . . . might well spread to other countries. . . . The fall of the communist regime in Prague would mean the loss of Czechoslovakia as a reliable ally or even friendly neighbor. . . . It was the democratic nature and content of the Czechoslovak experiment, rather than some fabricated "neutralism" or pro-western tendency, which precipitated the invasion.[36]

The Repudiation of 1989

In November 1989, encouraged by dramatic political change in neighboring Poland, Hungary, and East Germany, the hard-line Communist regime of Czechoslovakia led by Miloš Jakeš fell before a massive but peaceful popular revolution. On December 2 the newly formed Czechoslovak government issued the following statement:

> The Government of the Czechoslovak Socialist Republic considers the entry into Czechoslovakia of the armies of the five states of the Warsaw Treaty

---

[35] Czechoslovak "Black Book," in R. Remington, ed., *Winter in Prague* (Cambridge, MA, 1969), pp. 407–09.

[36] Galia Golan, *The Czechoslovak Reform Movement: Communism in Crisis, 1962–1968* (Cambridge, 1971), pp. 316, 327–28.

Problem 15 continued

in 1968 as an infringement to the norms of relations amongst sovereign states. The federal Government entrusts its chairman, Ladislav Adamec, to inform the Soviet Government of this position.

The federal Government proposes, at the same time, to the Government of the Soviet Union to open negotiations on an inter-government agreement which concerns the temporary stay of the Soviet troops on the territory of the Czechoslovak Socialist Republic. It entrusts the Minister of Foreign Affairs, Jaromir Johanes, to conduct the negotiations. It premises that the question of the departure of the Soviet troops must be settled in conformity with the advance of the European disarmament process.

The Government of the Czechoslovak Socialist Republic is prepared, together with the other countries involved, to create a group of historians who would consider, from all angles, the context of the events of August 1968.[37]

On December 4, 1989, in Moscow the USSR and the four Warsaw Pact allies that had joined in the 1968 intervention in Czechoslovakia jointly condemned that action. Furthermore, Soviet leaders agreed to discuss with the new Czechoslovak regime the withdrawal of Soviet troops that had been garrisoned in Czechoslovakia ever since August 1968. Here are the texts of the Soviet and Warsaw Pact repudiations of the intervention:

Soviet Statement
The Czechoslovak society is at the stage of a critical reassessment of the experience of its political and economic development.

This is a natural process. Many countries undergo it in one way or another.

Regrettably, the need for constant socialist self-renewal and realistic appraisal of the events has not always been taken for granted, particularly in situations when such events intertwined in a contradictory way and required bold answers to the challenges of the times.

In 1968, the Soviet leadership of that time supported the stand of one side in an internal dispute in Czechoslovakia regarding objective pressing tasks.

The justification for such an unbalanced, inadequate approach, an interference in the affairs of a friendly country, was then seen in an acute East-West confrontation.

We share the view of the Presidium of the Central Committee of the Communist Party of Czechoslovakia and the Czechoslovak Government that the bringing of armies of five socialist countries into Czechoslovak territory in 1968 was unfounded, and that that decision, in the light of all the presently known facts, was erroneous.

Warsaw Pact Statement
Leaders of Bulgaria, Hungary, the German Democratic Republic, Poland and the Soviet Union, who gathered for a meeting in Moscow on Dec. 4, stated that the bringing of troops of their countries into Czechoslovakia in 1968 was an interference in internal affairs of sovereign Czechoslovakia and should be condemned.

Disrupting the process of democratic renewal in Czechoslovakia, those illegal actions had long-term negative consequences.

History showed how important it is, even in the most complex international situation, to use political means for the solution of any problems, strictly to observe the principles of sovereignty, independence and noninterference in internal affairs in relations among states, which is in keeping with the provisions of the Warsaw Treaty.[38]

Conclusion

Explaining the Soviet invasion of Czechoslovakia in 1968, Soviet spokesmen emphasized that a powerful "reactionary movement" had sought to overturn socialism there, allied with West German militarists and revanchists. Moscow claimed the right to intervene anywhere in the "socialist world" to prevent the collapse of socialism and a consequent reversion to capitalism or feudalism. However, the Soviets failed to convince even their own intellectuals, to say nothing of foreign

---

[37]*New York Times*, December 3, 1989.

[38]*New York Times*, December 5, 1989.

Problem 15 continued

Communists, that such threats existed. Both groups deplored an invasion that tarnished Soviet prestige and undermined the world Communist movement. Faced with overwhelming Czechoslovak opposition to the invasion, the Soviets found few citizens who would welcome them into the country. By the intervention the Brezhnev regime regained its self-confidence and reconsolidated its hold over eastern Europe. However, the costs proved high: recementing the NATO alliance, alienating Eurocommunism, and exposing the USSR as a blatant violator of international law and national self-determination.

The eastern European revolutions of 1989 induced the Soviet regime to reassess drastically the 1968 invasion of Czechoslovakia. M. S. Gorbachev, the Soviet president, clearly encouraged the popular revolt in Prague, which was preceded by the appearance on Soviet television of Alexander Dubček, leader of the Prague Spring of 1968. Moscow hailed that movement as the harbinger of the Gorbachev reforms in the USSR. Soviet support for the removal of the Stalinist Czechoslovak regime confirmed Gorbachev's earlier repudiation of the interventionist Brezhnev Doctrine. ■

Suggested Additional Reading

THE BREZHNEV ERA

AMALRIK, A. *Will the Soviet Union Survive Until 1984?* (New York, 1970).

ANDERSON, R. D. *Public Politics in an Authoritarian State: Making Foreign Policy During the Brezhnev Years* (Ithaca, NY, and London, 1993).

BENNIGSEN, A. *The Islamic Threat to the Soviet State* (New York, 1983).

BERMAN, R. P. *Soviet Strategic Forces* (Washington, DC, 1982).

BIALER, S. *Stalin's Successors: Leadership, Stability and Change in the Soviet Union* (Cambridge, 1981).

———, ed. *The Domestic Context of Soviet Foreign Policy* (Boulder, CO, 1981).

BORNSTEIN, M., ed. *The Soviet Economy: Continuity and Change* (Boulder, CO, 1981).

BRADSHER, H. S. *Afghanistan and the Soviet Union* (Durham, NC, 1983).

BREZHNEV, L. *Peace, Détente and Soviet-American Relations* (New York, 1979).

COLTON, T. J. *Commissars, Commanders, and Civilian Authority: The Structure of Soviet Military Politics* (Cambridge, MA, 1979).

DORNBERG, J. *Brezhnev: The Masks of Power* (New York, 1974).

EDMONDS, R. *Soviet Foreign Policy: The Brezhnev Years* (Oxford, 1983).

ELLISON, H., ed. *The Sino-Soviet Conflict: A Global Perspective* (Seattle, 1982).

ENCAUSSE, H. C. D'. *Decline of an Empire: The Soviet Socialist Republics in Revolt* (New York, 1979).

FRANCISCO, R., et al., eds. *Agricultural Policies in the USSR and Eastern Europe* (Boulder, CO, 1980).

FREEDMAN, R. U. *Soviet Jewry in the Decisive Decade 1971–1980* (Durham, NC, 1984).

FRIEDGUT, T. *Political Participation in the USSR* (Princeton, 1979).

GALEOTTI, M. *Afghanistan: The Soviet Union's Last War* (London, 1995).

GELMAN, H. *The Brezhnev Politburo . . .* (Ithaca, NY, 1984).

HAMMOND, T. *Red Flag over Afghanistan* (Boulder, CO, 1984).

HOUGH, J. *Soviet Leadership in Transition* (Washington, DC, 1980).

———, and M. FAINSOD. *How the Soviet Union Is Governed* (Cambridge, MA, 1979).

HUNTER, H. *The Future of the Soviet Economy, 1978–1985* (Boulder, CO, 1978).

HUTCHINGS, R. L. *Soviet–East European Relations: Consolidation and Conflict, 1968–1980* (Madison, WI, 1983).

KAKAR, M. H. *Afghanistan: The Soviet Invasion and the Afghan Response, 1979–1982* (Berkeley, 1995).

KELLEY, D. R. *The Solzhenitsyn-Sakharov Dialogue* (New York, 1982).

KUSHNIRSKY, F. I. *Soviet Economic Planning, 1965–1980* (Boulder, CO, 1982).

LIGHT, M. *Troubled Friendships: Moscow's Third World Ventures* (Royal Institute of International Affairs, New York, 1994).

LITVINOV, P., ed. *The Demonstration on Pushkin Square* (Boston, 1969).

LÖWENHARDT, J. *The Soviet Politburo* (New York, 1982).

MARCHENKO, A. *My Testimony* (New York, 1969).

MEDVEDEV, R. *A Question of Madness* (New York, 1971).

PIPES, R. *U.S.-Soviet Relations in the Era of Détente* (Boulder, CO, 1981).

ROTHBERG, A. *The Heirs of Stalin* . . . (Ithaca, NY, 1972).

RUTLAND, P. *The Politics of Economic Stagnation in the Soviet Union* (New York, 1992).

RYAVEC, K., ed. *Soviet Society and the Communist Party* (Amherst, MA, 1978).

RYWKIN, M. *Moscow's Muslim Challenge* (New York, 1982).

SAKHAROV, A. *Sakharov Speaks* (New York, 1974).

SMITH, H. *The Russians* (New York, 1975, 1984).

SMOLANSKY, O. M., and B. M. SMOLANSKY. *The USSR and Iraq: The Soviet Quest for Influence* (Durham, NC, 1991).

ULAM, A. B. *Dangerous Relations: The Soviet Union in World Politics, 1970–1982* (Oxford, 1984).

WESSON, R. *The Aging of Communism* (New York, 1980).

YANOV, A. *Détente After Brezhnev: The Domestic Roots of Soviet Foreign Policy* (Berkeley, 1977).

CZECHOSLOVAKIA 1968

GOLAN, G. *The Czechoslovak Reform Movement: Communism in Crisis, 1962–1968* (Cambridge, 1971).

HOFFMANN, E. P., and F. J. FLERON, JR. *The Conduct of Soviet Foreign Policy,* 2d ed. (New York, 1980).

LITTELL, R., ed. *The Czech Black Book* (New York, 1969).

REMINGTON, R. A., ed. *Winter in Prague: Documents on Czechoslovak Communism in Crisis* (Cambridge, MA, 1969).

VALENTA, J. *Soviet Intervention on Czechoslovakia, 1968: Anatomy of a Decision,* 2d ed. (Baltimore and London, 1991).

ZARTMAN, I. W., ed. *Czechoslovakia: Intervention and Impact* (New York, 1970).

41

The Soviet Gerontocracy, 1982–1985

In a desperate holding action by the old men of the Politburo, for a decade beginning in 1975 the Soviet Union was ruled by the aged and the infirm. What a far cry from the revolutionary vigor and optimism of 1917, exemplified by Lenin and Trotskii! The Bolshevik Revolution of November 1917 had ushered in a Soviet regime led by dedicated, cosmopolitan revolutionaries with a vision of the socialist future and intellectually the equals of any leadership in the world. Only 60 years later Soviet rule had degenerated into a stagnant bureaucratic regime based on blatant privilege for an elite minority and endemic corruption. Deadly afraid of basic political, social, or economic reform, all long overdue, this conservative oligarchy proved unable or unwilling to tackle a formidable agenda of problems that Marx had never envisioned for a developed socialist state: a stagnating economy, dissatisfied and restive national minorities, and the embers of resurgent religion amid the ashes of Leninist ideology. The average age of Politburo leaders by 1982 was almost 70. With the general secretary often unable to mount unaided the steps of Lenin's Mausoleum, the Soviet Union at Brezhnev's death was

drifting. The Stalinist economic system, consolidated under Brezhnev, once an attractive model for underdeveloped countries, was being repudiated even by some members of the Soviet Bloc as they sought to cast off the confining shackles of centralized planning and overemphasis on heavy industry. One of the elderly rulers, Iurii Andropov, inaugurated significant reforms but died before much progress could be made in implementing them.

Domestic Politics

Brezhnev: 1982, the Last Gasps

Evidence mounted during 1982 that Leonid Brezhnev, the consensus politician, was no longer in real command. The struggle for succession apparently began back in 1975, when Brezhnev suffered a stroke that removed him from political activity for several months. During that time Mikhail Suslov and Andrei Kirilenko shared leadership of the party. In 1978 Brezhnev's health weakened again, and from then on he relied

Carter and Brezhnev at 1979 meeting to sign SALT II.

increasingly upon Konstantin Chernenko, promoting this faithful follower by 1979 to party
secretary and full member of the Politburo. Chernenko became Brezhnev's clear choice to be his
successor. Economic failures and scandals involving Brezhnev's cronies and family damaged Chernenko's prospects, however, as Brezhnev's power
eroded. First breaking late in 1981, corruption
scandals compromised General Semen Tsvigun,
Brezhnev's main ally in the KGB. In January 1982
the KGB chief, Iurii Andropov, who had directed
the investigations, informed Suslov, the powerful
"kingmaker" and chief ideologist, of the general's
involvement. After a showdown between them,
Tsvigun apparently committed suicide, and Suslov
died of a stroke a few days later. Early in March
foreign correspondents in Moscow reported that
Brezhnev's daughter, Galina, had been involved in
a diamond smuggling ring through her intimate
friend, Boris Buriata, nicknamed "the Gypsy."

Apparently Andropov had leaked this information
in an effort to discredit Brezhnev and undermine
Chernenko.[1]

The death of Suslov in January 1982 paved the
way for the other political changes of that year,
destroying the stability and balance of the ruling
oligarchy and removing the guardian of proper
behavior in the Politburo. Indirect attacks on
Brezhnev by the Andropov group were directed
against his protection of corrupt cronies. On his
return flight from Tashkent in March Brezhnev
suffered another stroke and was taken near death
to the Kremlin hospital, where he remained
speechless for several weeks. During this illness
Andropov consolidated control over Suslov's
vacant ideological fief, delivered the main speech

---

[1] Zhores Medvedev, *Andropov* (New York, 1983), pp. 93–96;
Harry Gelman, *The Brezhnev Politburo* . . . (Ithaca, NY, 1984),
pp. 183–86.

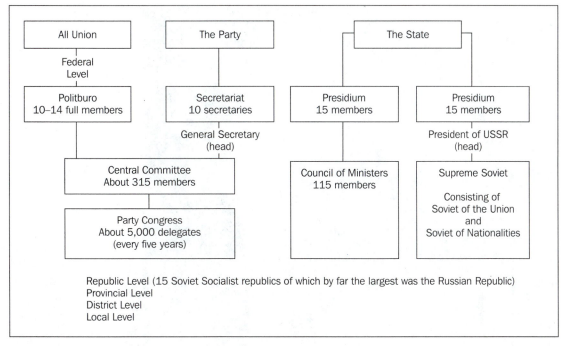

Figure 41.1
Top Soviet power centers, 1980s

on Lenin's birthday (April 22), and spent most of his time in the Central Committee. (See Figure 41.1 for a chart showing the hierarchy of power.) In May, at a crucial Politburo meeting, Andropov was chosen to succeed Suslov as chief ideologist over the opposition of Brezhnev and Chernenko. In this dress rehearsal for the Brezhnev succession, Andropov moved back into the Secretariat as its second ranking secretary while his candidate, Vitaly Fedorchuk, replaced him as KGB chief. That summer, with the ailing Brezhnev on vacation in the Crimea, Andropov took charge of the Secretariat and arranged the dismissal of two corrupt Brezhnev stalwarts, who were regional party secretaries. Returning to Moscow that fall, Brezhnev, in an address to military leaders, sought to demonstrate that he was still in charge. However, Andropov's supporters then leaked rumors that Brezhnev would resign at the end of the year for reasons of health. That might indeed have

occurred had Brezhnev not died of natural causes in November, after clinging to power to the end.

Andropov: The Sick Reformer

In Moscow, the first hint that a top Soviet leader had died came on the evening of November 10, 1982. Instead of a scheduled pop concert, a film on Lenin was televised. At 9 P.M., the appearance of a newscaster in formal dress suggested that someone had died, but who? Next morning, more than a day after his actual demise, came simultaneous announcements by Soviet radio and television:

> The Central Committee of the Communist Party of the Soviet Union, the Presidium of the Supreme Soviet of the USSR and the Council of Ministers of the USSR inform with deep sorrow the party and the entire Soviet people that L. I. Brezhnev, General Secretary of the CPSU and President of the Supreme Soviet,

Iurii V. Andropov, general secretary of the CPSU 1982–1984 (right), conferring with Andrei A. Gromyko, Soviet foreign minister 1975–1985.

died a sudden death at 8:30 A.M. on November 10th.

Like all Soviet leaders except Khrushchev, Brezhnev had died in office. His death was probably hastened by an appearance three days earlier at the frigid celebration in Red Square of the anniversary of the November Revolution. Brezhnev had held the key post of general secretary of the CPSU for 18 years, longer than anyone but Joseph Stalin; he had dealt with five American presidents and four British prime ministers.

Thus the transfer of power to a new leader loomed as an apparent turning point in Soviet history. The swift and smooth transition that then elevated Iurii Andropov to the post of general secretary concealed the lengthy power struggle described previously. The 300-odd members of the Central Committee who filed solemnly into the Council of Ministers building November 12 knew they were merely to ratify the decision made on November 10 by an enlarged Politburo (including candidate members, marshals, and key Central Committee members). That Andropov would be selected had been foreshadowed by his appointment as chairman of Brezhnev's funeral committee. Andropov spoke briefly extolling Brezhnev's services, then Chernenko rose to nominate Andropov, who had outmaneuvered him in the competition for succession. After the Central Committee's unanimous approval was registered, the official power transfer was over. Commented a Soviet engineer: "We used to complain some . . . and tell jokes about the old man. But now that Brezhnev is dead, I feel sad because he conveyed a sense of security and stability."[2] Whereas after Stalin's death 30 years earlier there had been fear and near panic, now the Moscow public remained calm, hopeful of reform.

Iurii V. Andropov's rise through the party ranks had been speeded by Stalin's purges. Born in the village of Nagutskoe in the north Caucasus in June 1914, the son of a railway worker, Andropov left school at 16 to work as a Volga boatman and a telegraph operator. At age 22 he began his political career as an organizer for the Komsomol, the Communist youth organization. Later he resumed his education at a technical college, but he lacked a university degree. Andropov rose rapidly in Komsomol ranks in the short-lived Karelo-Finnish Republic, where he won the valuable support of Otto Kuusinen, later a Politburo member. During World War II, as a political commissar, he organized guerrilla forces behind German lines during their occupation of that region. Afterward he became a party official in Petrozavodsk near Leningrad, and in 1951 he was transferred to Moscow where he joined the staff of the Central Committee Secretariat. From 1954 to 1957 Andropov served as ambassador to Hungary, playing a significant role in the Soviet suppression of the Hungarian Revolution of 1956 and elevation of János Kádár to head the Hungarian Communist Party. During his stay in Hungary, Andropov grew more sophisticated about eastern European problems. In 1957 he returned to Moscow to direct the foreign affairs department of the Central Committee dealing with Bloc countries. At the 22nd Party Congress (1961), Andropov became a Central Committee secretary, serving under Khrushchev and Brezhnev and traveling to various eastern European countries. Then, in 1967, he became head of the KGB and a candidate member of the Politburo. Serving longer than any other KGB chief, Andropov proved very adept at suppressing

the dissident movement while giving that dread agency a better public image. Andropov was the only head of the KGB to survive that job while increasing his own power and influence. Eliminating remnants of arbitrary terror of the Stalin era, he combated corruption in the party and state apparatuses; he also inaugurated more flexible,sophisticated methods of control and more carefully prepared political cases. He acquired a reputation as a strong, just guardian of the Soviet system.

Andropov's return to the Secretariat in May 1982 proved crucial in his becoming general secretary of the CPSU six months later. He obtained the backing of the powerful Soviet military establishment, represented in the Politburo by Marshal Dmitrii Ustinov, and the influential elder statesman Foreign Minister Andrei Gromyko. Andropov, at 68, was the oldest man to rule the party. His age and ill health—he suffered from diabetes and kidney disease—may have been the reason for his haste to implement changes and make a mark on the Soviet system. Contrary to some earlier predictions, Andropov swiftly consolidated his power. Within eight months he had become president of the Supreme Soviet and chairman of the Defense Council, posts that Brezhnev had acquired only after many years. Unlike previous Soviet successions, this time there was no prolonged power struggle as the new leader moved smoothly into a position of dominance.

However, Andropov found it harder to accumulate sufficient power to force political change than it was to acquire titular positions. Having achieved power without the support of the network of regional party secretaries who had backed Khrushchev and Brezhnev, he found it hard to move trusted supporters into key positions in the Politburo and Secretariat. Until the end of 1983 the only addition to full membership on the Politburo was the former Azerbaijan party secretary Geidar Aliyev, seemingly a consensus candidate. The coalition that had elevated Andropov to power proved reluctant to allow him to reshape and dominate the Politburo, and he was opposed there by a Brezhnevite "old guard" headed by his

---

[2] "Changing the Guard," *Time,* November 22, 1982, p. 14. See also Myron Rush, "Succeeding Brezhnev," *Problems of Communism* 32 (January–February 1983) and Medvedev, *Andropov.*

defeated rival, Chernenko, and including the elderly premier, Tikhonov. To be sure, Aliyev's designation as deputy premier made him the second most powerful figure in the state apparatus and put him in a position to inherit Tikhonov's position. Two other former subordinates of Andropov soon obtained key posts: Fedorchuk became interior minister, being replaced as KGB chief by his deputy, Viktor Chebrikov; and N. I. Ryzhkov was named a junior member of the Secretariat. Nonetheless, in his first year in office, wrote the American Sovietologist Harry Gelman late in 1983, Andropov failed to impart new dynamism or give new flexibility to Soviet policies. Instead the formidable weight of bureaucratic inertia impeded substantive changes. Only Andropov's political style was different: He needed fewer aides and advisers than the senile Brezhnev and made it clear that his speeches would be brief, frank, and infrequent. A key adviser was Iurii Arbatov, head of the Institute of the USA and Canada, a leading Soviet intellectual.

Between June and December 1983 Andropov, while losing a battle against kidney disease, managed to implement significant personnel and political changes. The Central Committee plenum in June confirmed the replacement of retiring A. Kirilenko with the former Leningrad party secretary Grigorii Romanov as a Central Committee secretary. The death of aged Arvid Pelshe enabled Andropov to replace him with Mikhail Solomentsev, who became a candidate member of the Politburo. Returning to Moscow from vacation in October, Andropov apparently realized he had only a few months to live and stepped up his campaign. Although too ill to attend the December plenum, Andropov nonetheless persuaded the Politburo to promote Solomentsev and Vitalii Vorotnikov to full Politburo membership and make Egor Ligachev, another KGB protégé, a Central Committee secretary.

He was greatly aided in these moves by a key ally in the Politburo, Mikhail S. Gorbachev, who was also in the Secretariat. Andropov rewarded Gorbachev, the youngest and best educated of the ruling oligarchy, with additional power over personnel changes in the Secretariat. Gorbachev, who shared Andropov's reformist sentiments and had become his choice as successor, was one of only two men who conferred regularly with the leader following his return to Moscow. They and Andropov's doctors perpetrated a deliberate deception by issuing reports of Andropov's imminent recovery and return to public view to enable him to retain full power until the end of his life. Acting through Gorbachev and Ligachev, Andropov, between November 1983 and January 1984, replaced almost one-fifth of all regional party secretaries, the greatest turnover in 20 years. Finally, claims Zhores Medvedev, Andropov enhanced and regularized the status of the second secretary of the Central Committee, who would chair Politburo meetings in the absence of the secretary general.[3] Chernenko, who held that post, favored this step, which received Politburo approval, but it would strengthen Gorbachev's position after Andropov's death. Also approved was Andropov's proposal to reduce administrative personnel in central and local organizations and the number of party and state officials in the Supreme Soviet while increasing the proportion of workers, farmers, and engineers. Having taken steps to undermine the power of the "old guard," Andropov died of kidney disease on February 9, 1984.

The Chernenko Succession: The "Old Guard" Hangs On

An emergency Politburo meeting convened the evening after Andropov's death failed to choose a successor. Indeed, not until Monday, February 13, was Chernenko selected. The delay suggests a power struggle between the Brezhnevite "old guard" favoring Chernenko, and the Andropov group, whose candidate was M. S. Gorbachev. Would an old, loyal party hack or a dynamic, sophisticated younger man be selected? If the Politburo were to remain deadlocked, the choice

---

[3] Medvedev, pp. 217ff.

under party rules would devolve upon the about 315-member Central Committee, which favored Chernenko. Thus Gorbachev's supporters in the Politburo, affirms Medvedev, agreed to support Chernenko's nomination as new party leader and keep the decision in the Politburo. In exchange, the Politburo would approve all of Andropov's recent suggestions on political reform. Gorbachev received the newly formalized post of second secretary, becoming the heir apparent behind the elderly Chernenko. This arrangement was apparently confirmed by the emergency Central Committee meeting of February 13 at which Premier Tikhonov nominated Chernenko as general secretary. Chernenko's previous appointment as chairman of Andropov's funeral commission suggested this outcome.

Andropov's funeral was smooth, efficiently organized, with a sense of continuity and propriety, and a total absence of grief. Recent party chiefs had been absent due to illness almost as much as they had been present and seemingly had become more a symbolic than an active force. About Andropov one Muscovite commented: "It is a pity. He was just, but he didn't have enough time." Those leaders closest to Andropov during his brief rule—Defense Minister Ustinov and Mikhail Gorbachev—lingered to pay their respects to his bereaved widow, Tatiana. E. M. Chazov, Andropov's chief physician, confirmed that the leader's kidneys had ceased functioning in February 1983, and that he had been on a dialysis machine after that.[4]

At age 72, Konstantin Ustinovich Chernenko succeeded Andropov as the oldest man ever chosen to lead the Soviet Union. Short and white-haired with slightly hunched shoulders, he delivered a lengthy, rambling, and stumbling acceptance speech, frequently mentioning Andropov and pledging to follow his reform initiatives. Significantly, there was no reference to his longtime mentor, Leonid Brezhnev. The old guard

Konstantin U. Chernenko, general secretary of the CPSU 1984–1985.

in party and state greeted Chernenko's accession jubilantly, believing that it would allow them to prolong their tenure of power. Chernenko's triumph represented a remarkable political comeback for this peasant's son from Siberia with little formal education. However one might assess his intelligence and ability—and there were numerous scornful comments from Russians and foreigners—this man from the people deserved respect for loyalty, toughness, and persistence. An ideologue who emphasized old-fashioned party slogans and virtues, his style was derived from many years of working in *agitprop* (agitation and propaganda) in Siberia and Moldavia and for the Central Committee. In the introduction to a collection of his speeches and articles, Chernenko wrote:

> I was born into a large and poor peasant family in the Krasnoiarsk region of Siberia in 1911. I left my mother when I was a young boy. At 12 I went to work for a wealthy master to earn my living. New Soviet life was just coming into its own and I felt its fresh winds when I joined the Young Communist League [Komsomol]. That was back in 1926. We studied and held down our jobs at the same time. We were underfed and poorly clothed, but the dreams

---

[4] John Burns, "Reporter's Notebook," *New York Times,* February 13, 1984.

of a radiant future for all fascinated us and made us happy.[5]

Chernenko stood forth proudly as a self-made Soviet man who, by dint of hard work, loyalty, and dedication to Leninist ideals, had climbed steadfastly to the top of the Soviet pyramid.[6] During a 50-year party career, Chernenko had never initiated projects nor enunciated original ideas. As an ideologist, carped Medvedev, he was even duller than his predecessor, Suslov. A pure product of the party apparatus, Chernenko remained an obscure provincial official until meeting Brezhnev in Moldavia in 1948. He followed his mentor upward through the party ranks, becoming a full member of the Central Committee in 1971. In 1976 Chernenko replaced Kirilenko as Brezhnev's closest colleague and heir apparent, being promoted with almost indecent haste as a party secretary in 1976 and full member of the Politburo in 1978. His philosophy was profoundly conservative: All problems could be solved with Leninist ideology, propaganda, and party discipline. Chernenko's short-lived regime, representing a holding action by the gerontocrats, was a throwback to Brezhnev's final years. Visibly feeble when he succeeded Andropov, Chernenko, like his two predecessors, was frequently out of public view, laid low by emphysema. As the torpor of the last Brezhnev years resumed, Andropov's 15 months in power stood out by contrast as an interlude of dynamism, initiative, and forward movement.

By early 1985 signs multiplied that the Chernenko era would be brief. Behind the scenes in the Kremlin, the dynamic Mikhail S. Gorbachev positioned himself for the succession. In December 1984 Marshal Dmitri Ustinov, defense minister and a powerful force in the Politburo, died and received a massive funeral. Chernenko appeared at the marshal's bier, pale and unsteady, but was absent from the burial ceremony conducted in bitter cold. Instead Gorbachev led the way in escorting the burial urn, followed by his rival, Grigori Romanov. The replacement of Ustinov by his deputy, Marshal Sergei Sokolov, suggested the aged leaders' reluctance to yield authority to the younger generation. During January 1985, as Chernenko failed to reappear, Soviet spokesmen admitted that he was gravely ill; rumors circulated that he would soon resign as general secretary. In late February he made two brief appearances on Soviet television, looking very feeble. However, contrary to initial fears, Chernenko, instead of undoing Andropov's reforms, continued them more gradually. One Moscow intellectual noted: "We have come to peace with Chernenko. He has contributed nothing new, the pace has slowed, the results are humble, but at least he has not turned back the clock."[7]

Economy and Society

"The Soviet Union simply does not have the resources to invest in all the necessary sectors. The leadership is going to have to make tough decisions on allocations of capital, raw materials, and labor," stated Robert Legvold of the Council on Foreign Relations. "The probable loser in the short term will be the Soviet consumer, accustomed since the 1950s to a steady, if unspectacular, rise in living standards. With Brezhnev's legacy of declining economic growth rates, Soviet citizens clearly would have to settle for minimal improvements during the 1980s," declared the American Sovietologist Walter Laqueur. Such statements reflected economic policies under Brezhnev's successors.

At Brezhnev's death, wrote Marshall Goldman, the USSR faced a severe economic crisis. The country had failed to adapt the rigid, highly centralized Stalinist planning model, which emphasized production of iron and steel, to meet radically new economic needs. Whereas

---

[5] Konstantin Chernenko, "Introduction," *Selected Speeches* (Philadelphia, 1984).

[6] Serge Schmemann, "A Bolshevik of Old Mold Rises to the Top," *New York Times,* February 14, 1984.

[7] "Chernenko's Status Shrouded in Rumor," *New York Times,* January 31, 1985.

Khrushchev had predicted confidently in 1958 that the USSR by 1980 would surpass levels of production of the United States and enjoy abundance, Soviet GNP (gross national product) during the early 1980s hovered between 55 and 60 percent of the American figure. The Stalinist system had developed a momentum of its own, continuing to churn out steel when food and consumer goods were required. As Khrushchev himself once stated:

> The production of steel is like a well-traveled road with deep ruts; here even blind horses will not turn off because the wheels will break. Similarly, some officials have put on steel blinkers; they do everything as they were taught in their day.[8]

With fulfillment of the central plan becoming an end in itself, with managers and planners rewarded for gross output and value of production, many resources were wasted by being diverted to needless increases in the capital intensity of industry producing large, expensive, and useless commodities. The Stalinist economic system neither rewarded intelligent decisions nor punished stupid ones. The obsolete could not readily be discarded, nor could innovation and technological change be readily fostered. Well-suited only to heavy industry and most difficult to restructure, the Stalinist model built up powerful political and economic vested interest groups resistant to basic changes. Reforms, when instituted, tended to get out of control, making the leadership loath to overhaul an outmoded system as long as it showed even minimal growth. Avoided far too long, economic change became more difficult with each passing year.

Yet by 1982 something clearly needed to be done. In 1981 Soviet steel production, previously a source of great pride for outpacing that of the United States, fell below the 1978 level; coal and oil output apparently had peaked, having become increasingly difficult and expensive to extract from remote regions. With almost a quarter of its own crop rotting in the fields or failing to be transported to markets, the USSR had become the world's largest importer of grain. The Soviet worker, with few incentives to produce or conserve and with few desirable consumer goods to buy, was suffering from falling morale and discipline. Beginning in 1980, strikes, demonstrations, and riots broke out in various cities; food rationing had to be reintroduced in major centers for the first time since the 1940s. Meanwhile Soviet leaders remained committed to a steadily rising military budget and an empire costing more than $20 billion per year in subsidies. How little the economy was serving consumer needs was revealed by a huge and growing volume of savings (from 91 billion rubles in 1975 to 156.6 billion in 1980), as consumers awaited desirable goods. This situation had stimulated development of a vast black market, estimated at almost 25 percent of GNP, but even that failed to close the gap between supply and demand.[9] Any sudden decontrol could trigger panic, huge inflationary pressure, and unemployment. Economic distortions had become too massive to be rectified quickly. A bold leader undertaking basic reform, predicted Goldman, must deal with prolonged inflation, severe unemployment, shortages of desirable capital, surpluses of outmoded capital, profiteering, and severe balance-of-payments deficits—evils from which only capitalist countries were supposed to suffer. Could the Soviet political system survive such severe strains? No aged or infirm interim leader would take such risks.

How then did Brezhnev's successors deal with these grave economic problems? Andropov began with harsh criticisms of the existing system's shortcomings, rather than with Brezhnev's ritualistic praise of past economic achievements; he bluntly distributed responsibility for current inadequate performance equally among government, workers, and farmers. His aim was not to introduce drastic reform of the economic system, which

---

[8] Marshall I. Goldman, *USSR in Crisis: The Failure of an Economic System* (New York, 1983), p. 36.

[9] Gregory Grossman, "The Second Economy of the USSR," *Problems of Communism* 26 (September–October 1977), p. 25.

he feared, but to improve management and worker efficiency, reduce waste, and ensure that everything produced or harvested would be made available. His priorities included raising productivity through harder work and better discipline, use of new planning methods, and accelerating introduction of new technology. Thus Andropov sought to make the old Stalinist system function more efficiently. In December 1982 he reorganized the Ministry of Railways and suggested improving coordination of all forms of transport. Lacking a new solution for agriculture, he echoed Brezhnev's expensive Food Program of May 1982 and campaigned for a reduction in food wastage and better storage facilities for farmers. Tougher policies were instituted to promote better work discipline. The police cracked down on loafing and absenteeism; they even corralled slackers in Moscow bathhouses! However, the regime's efforts to stifle the "second economy" by prohibiting unregistered freelance work proved premature and counterproductive and were soon abandoned.

Amid Western speculation that Andropov would institute economic reforms like those in Hungary (decentralization and more scope for market forces, for example), Soviet economic measures of early 1983, noted Medvedev, resembled those of General Wojciech Jaruzelski's martial law regime in Poland. The government raised food prices by rapidly expanding "commercial" trade by cooperatives, diverting more food into that system where prices and quality were far higher than in state shops. At a well-publicized meeting with workers and engineers at a Moscow machine tool plant that January, Andropov stressed better work discipline, stricter observance of the plan, and reduction of absenteeism and deliberately slow work if workers were to obtain more and better goods.[10]

Andropov also accelerated the anticorruption drive, which he had used earlier to undermine and discredit Brezhnev. Reports of high-level corruption and peculation appeared in the Soviet press.

Penalties against embezzlement and bribery were increased by a decree in January 1983. So readers would know the source of this campaign, Soviet newspapers published an unusual report entitled "In the Politburo of the CPSU," revealing that the Politburo had discussed numerous letters from workers and farmers complaining of shoddy work, false statistics, poor use of materials, and embezzlement of funds:

> The Politburo drew the attention of the Procurator General of the USSR and Ministry of Internal Affairs to the fact that it is necessary to take proper measures to improve socialist legality in towns and villages taking into consideration the fact that these problems are very frequently the cause of complaints in letters which are sent to the central Party organs.[11]

As Andropov intensified the anticorruption drive, millions of letters from citizens complaining about local abuses flooded into top agencies, which party leaders could not afford to ignore. Corruption at all levels had grown so widespread that the public believed that shortages of food and consumer goods resulted from officials' diverting better-quality goods into their closed shops and distribution centers.

British journalist Jonathan Steele and TV writer Eric Abraham claim Andropov supported the approach of M. S. Gorbachev, the Politburo's expert on agriculture, in encouraging decentralization and local initiative to stimulate the economy; both men favored fostering greater production on private peasant plots to supplement Brezhnev's Food Program.[12] An industrial reform program of July 1983 reduced the number of centrally imposed economic indicators and gave local managers more autonomy. Reintroducing some aspects of Premier Kosygin's 1965 reforms, it fell far short of the Hungarian economic reforms; there was no attempt to move away from the system of centrally administered prices. Andropov was merely willing to tolerate some experiments

---

[10] Medvedev, pp. 127–34.

[11] *Pravda*, December 11, 1982, quoted in Medvedev, p. 142.
[12] Jonathan Steele and Eric Abraham, *Andropov in Power*, Garden City, NY, 1984, pp. 162–65.

and limited decentralization to foster lower-level initiative, coupling these with greater social and industrial discipline. His economic reforms may have been limited by opposition within the Politburo, Gosplan, and the party bureaucracy. In his message to the December 1983 Central Committee plenum, Andropov warned: "The most important thing now is not to lose the tempo and the general positive mood for action." That became his legacy.[13]

Under Chernenko there was little apparent progress in remedying grave economic shortcomings. Observed one skeptical intellectual:

> The wheels are still turning from momentum. But they are beginning to slow down. And rot is setting in. But it will take a long time for anything conclusive to happen. It won't happen in my lifetime.

At least economic problems were being discussed more candidly in the Soviet press, noted Robert Kaiser, an American journalist.[14] Dr. Abel Aganbegyan of the Siberian department of the Academy of Sciences noted that too few people were entering the workforce. Raw materials and energy sources were disappearing from European Russia, where most industry still centered. Siberia and the Soviet Far East accounted for 88 percent of raw material and energy resources, which were becoming increasingly difficult and expensive to extract. Aganbegyan advocated radical reforms to prevent central industrial ministries from interfering with individual enterprises. He complained that Andropov's experimental reforms had been too tentative and limited.

A significant debate over economic policy proceeded under Chernenko between the Brezhnev "old guard" and reformers led by Gorbachev. While noting Andropov's "clear creative mind" and "keen sense for the new," Chernenko pleaded for caution and proven methods. Younger Politburo members (Gorbachev, Vorotnikov) and Central Committee secretaries (Ligachev, Ryzhkov) promoted by Andropov, taking positions contrary to Chernenko in their election speeches, credited Andropov personally for successes in 1983 in raising output and urged continuing his policies and accelerating the tempo. Gorbachev became the chief advocate of innovation, presenting himself as Andropov's standard bearer and Chernenko's main challenger. Thus in Stavropol in February 1984, Gorbachev interpreted the party's task as to "consolidate and develop the positive trends, and bolster and augment *everything new and progressive that has become part of our social life recently.*" He advocated "the acceleration of the development of the national economy and the improvement of its efficiency, . . . a profound reorientation of social production toward increasing the people's well-being." In sharp contrast with Chernenko, Gorbachev called for training "cadres capable of thinking and acting in a modern way." Their divergent attitudes and proposals revealed major contradictions at the top level between "conservatives" and modernists, suggesting an ongoing power struggle between Brezhnev's "old guard" and Andropov's "Young Turks."[15]

Despite the absence of basic reforms, the Soviet economy showed signs of an upturn. In the wake of an encouraging trend during 1983, there was a 4.2-percent increase in industrial output and a 3.8-percent improvement in labor productivity in 1984. However, agriculture failed to advance, and there was a disquieting decrease in oil production.[16]

Foreign Policy

At Brezhnev's death the Soviet Union faced major and intractable problems abroad in a number of areas. A virtually bankrupt and resentful Poland drained Soviet resources and typified increasing

---

[13] Ernest Kux, "Contradictions in Soviet Socialism," *Problems of Communism* 33 (November–December 1984), pp. 1–4.

[14] Robert Kaiser in *Boston Sunday Globe,* September 30, 1984.

[15] Kux, "Contradictions in Soviet Socialism."

[16] Serge Schmemann, "Chernenko's Status . . . ," *New York Times,* January 31, 1985.

Soviet difficulties in eastern Europe. East Germany, Romania, and even Hungary were only slightly less in debt to Western banks than unfortunate Poland. A second set of problems related to Sino-Soviet relations, which had remained generally bad under Brezhnev. The Chinese had been alienated not only by the border conflict of 1969–1970 but also by the later Soviet invasion of Afghanistan and predominance in neighboring Vietnam. In addition, Beijing was still worried by large Soviet military forces stationed along China's frontiers. Third, the USSR appeared deeply mired in Afghanistan, seemingly committed to a military and political victory regardless of the cost in money, men, and prestige. Meanwhile, Soviet-American relations had plumbed depths of tension and acrimony not equaled since the worst period of the Cold War. Apparently despairing of reaching positive agreements with a fiercely conservative Republican administration whose chief, Reagan, had denounced the USSR as an "evil empire," Soviet leaders realized that American hostility might well deny them the high technology and equipment they needed to modernize their economy while driving up military expenditures as they strove to keep pace with a wealthier United States in a new arms race.

Changes in Soviet foreign policy under Andropov were limited primarily to style, greater flexibility, and personal command. Such new trends followed immediately after Brezhnev's death. His funeral brought an unprecedented number of high-level foreign delegations to Moscow; Andropov talked at length in friendly fashion with the Chinese foreign minister and President Zia of Pakistan. His meeting with Vice President Bush of the United States revealed an intelligence and flexibility in spontaneous exchanges on a variety of issues. Andropov made it clear to some 100 foreign delegations that he would direct Soviet foreign policy firmly and reasonably; the period of diplomatic stagnation was over.

A distinct improvement in Soviet relations with China occurred under Andropov and continued under Chernenko. Brezhnev's speeches during 1982 revealed that Moscow had decided to improve Sino-Soviet relations. Andropov promptly initiated a conciliatory policy toward China: Articles critical of China ceased to appear in the Soviet Union, and the Chinese found it much easier to deal with Andropov than they had with Brezhnev. Nonetheless, normalization of Sino-Soviet relations proceeded slowly, hampered by continuing friction over Afghanistan and Vietnam. Under Chernenko progress continued, marked by the visit of an important Soviet official, Ivan Arkhipov, to Beijing and agreements to expand trade and cultural relations.

No significant change in Soviet relations with eastern Europe was evident under Andropov and Chernenko, both of whom considered preservation of Soviet preeminence there of the highest importance. In his November 1982 speech, Andropov declared that the USSR should make better use of the experience of friendly socialist countries, perhaps an allusion to the successful Hungarian economic reforms. Meanwhile, both he and Chernenko welcomed General Jaruzelski's political success in controlling ferment in Poland by martial law and continued to supply some economic aid. Despite the lifting of martial law by 1984, the Polish economy continued to decline. The Polish economic plight adversely affected neighboring Communist countries as well as the USSR.

As to dealings with the West, Andropov from the outset possessed the distinct advantage of knowing more about the United States than Reagan did about the Soviet Union and employing more competent advisers on American affairs (notably Professor Iurii Arbatov, a close friend) than Reagan did on Soviet affairs. By late November 1982 the Western press was alluding to Andropov's "peace offensive," which began in earnest with a speech in December. By mid-January 1983 the West was considering some 20 new Soviet proposals in military fields. This offensive was provoked by the imminent installation in western Europe of 572 Cruise and Pershing II missiles and some divergence about them between western European NATO countries and the

United States. When the Reagan administration failed to respond very positively to this Soviet initiative, negotiations stalled.

Late in 1983 a tragic incident caused Soviet-American relations to deteriorate sharply. On September 1 a Korean commercial airliner, KAL-007, on a regular flight from the United States to Japan, flew far off course into Soviet airspace over Kamchatka Peninsula and was shot down by a Soviet missile off Sakhalin Island, killing all 269 passengers and crew. At first Moscow denied any responsibility for the plane's destruction, claiming that while Soviet pilots were tracking it the plane suddenly disappeared from their radar screens. Five days later, faced with aroused world opinion, Moscow admitted that one of its pilots had indeed destroyed the plane, but claimed that it had been performing a secret surveillance mission for U.S. intelligence. (See Figure 41.2.) In a dramatic nationwide address President Reagan asserted that the destruction of KAL-007 was a deliberate, brutal, and unjustifiable murder.[17]

The Soviet government responded that the Korean airliner had been mistaken for an RC-135 American spy plane that had been flying a parallel course. Soviet defense forces had merely exercised the right to protect Soviet airspace from unwarranted intrusion into a sensitive military area. American leaders, affirmed the Soviet statement, had staged this provocation precisely when ways of preventing a nuclear war were being discussed with the United States. Belatedly Moscow declared:

> The Soviet government expresses regret over the death of innocent people and shares the sorrow of their bereaved relatives and friends. The entire responsibility for this tragedy rests wholly and fully with the leaders of the USA.[18]

The KAL-007 incident of September 1, 1983, brought a measured response from the Reagan administration, which left his right-wing supporters dissatisfied. An order of 1981 denying Aeroflot,

the Soviet airline, the right to land in the United States was reaffirmed. Reagan asked the U.S. Congress to pass a joint resolution denouncing the Soviet action. The United States suspended negotiations on several bilateral matters and demanded compensation to relatives of the victims; the Soviets refused. The affair effectively torpedoed nuclear arms negotiations on the basis proposed by Andropov and ended any plans for an Andropov-Reagan summit. The incident also raised disturbing questions about Soviet military confusion and bureaucratic rigidity. Secretary General Andropov apparently played no direct role in the Soviet decision to shoot down the plane.

In a thorough, balanced analysis of the KAL-007 affair, R. W. Johnson, a leading English scholar, discussed the four chief explanations for shooting down the plane: (1) the flight had strayed off course by accident, (2) the pilots had deliberately sought to shorten their route to save fuel, (3) the Soviets had attempted deliberately to lure the plane off course by electronic interference with its navigational equipment, and (4) the plane was involved in an American surveillance mission. Dismissing the first three as virtually impossible, Johnson concluded that the flight had been a risky attempt by the American military to obtain information about the newly discovered Krasnoiarsk radar installation in Siberia.[19] Interviewed July 19, 1984, Ernest Volkman, editor of *Defense Science*, stated:

> As a result of the KAL incident US intelligence received a bonanza the likes of which they have never received in their lives. . . . It managed to turn on just about every single Soviet electromagnetic transmission over a period of about four hours over about 7,000 square miles.[20]

Afghanistan remained a stumbling block in the path of improving Soviet relations with both China and the United States. Under Brezhnev the

---

[17] *New York Times*, September 6, 1983.
[18] *New York Times*, September 7, 1983, p. 16.

[19] R. W. Johnson, *Shootdown: Flight 007 and the American Connection* (New York, 1987), pp. 310ff.
[20] Johnson, *Shootdown*, p. 339.

1 An American RC-135 reconnaissance aircraft is spotted on radar at a Soviet air-defense station on Kamchatka Peninsula. It is a routine flight that provokes no Soviet reaction.

2 Another blip appears on the Soviet radar, and the Kamchatka command, suspecting it is a second spy plane, scrambles fighters to intercept the plane.

3 Flight 007 re-enters international airspace over the Sea of Okhotsk. The Kamchatka pilots observe it once again veering into Soviet airspace over Sakhalin. Low on fuel, they break off the chase and alert Sakhalin air defense of the incoming aircraft.

4 The American RC-135 lands at its base on Shemya Island.

5 Three Sakhalin Island interceptors, two Su-15s, and one MiG-23 catch up with the mystery plane. One Su-15 pilot makes visual contact with the plane from a distance of 1.2 miles.

6 Flight 007 has only seconds left inside Soviet airspace. The Su-15 pilot falls back behind the passenger plane and fires air-to-air missiles.

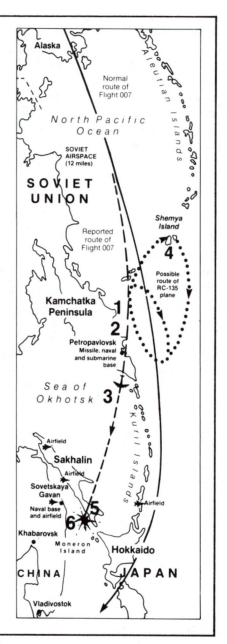

Figure 41.2
Confusion and mistakes doom KAL Flight 007

Soviet observers apparently mistook KAL Flight 007, an unarmed passenger plane, for an American RC-135 spy plane. The Soviets claimed they had tried to warn the KAL plane before they shot it down, but transcripts of the pursuit pilot's talk cast serious doubt on this claim. The incident imperiled Soviet-American relations.

(For more information, see *Newsweek*, "Death in the Sky" September 12, 1983)

Soviet media remained overwhelmingly silent about the war there except to make ritual accusations against both powers for "intervening" in Afghanistan's internal affairs. Under Andropov, who was inclined to greater frankness and realism, this attitude began to change. Finally, after almost five years of downplaying Russia's first war since World War II, the Soviet press discovered a war hero, a Byelorussian farm youth named Nikolai Chepik. In February 1984 Chepik reportedly sacrificed his own life to save his comrades while taking 30 of the enemy with him. Wrote *Literaturnaia Gazeta* in January 1985: "The last thing he could see was the peaks of the Hindu Kush, and above them the huge, bright sky, a sky stretching all the way to his motherland." The official creation of a Soviet war hero was part of increasing coverage of the Afghan conflict. Soon a song was composed about the exploits of Chepik, and many schools set up "Chepik corners" where the pupils could study his heroic deeds. Chepik was even awarded posthumously the coveted decoration Hero of the Soviet Union. Increasing parallels were drawn between the Soviet struggle in Afghanistan against the allegedly murderous and brutal rebels and the Nazi invasion of the USSR.[21] The Afghan war continued to drain the Soviet economy and to complicate Soviet foreign relations.

Suggested Additional Reading

ARBATOV, G. A. *The Soviet Viewpoint* (New York, 1983).

BERGSON, A., and H. LEVINE, eds. *The Soviet Economy* (Winchester, MA, 1983).

BINYON, M. *Life in Russia* (New York, 1984).

BONNER, E. *Alone Together,* trans. A. Cook (New York, 1986). (By Andrei Sakharov's wife about their internal exile.)

BRUCAN, S. *The Post-Brezhnev Era: An Insider's View* (New York, 1983).

BYRNES, R. F., ed. *After Brezhnev: Sources of Soviet Conduct in the 1980s* (Bloomington, IN, 1983).

CHERNENKO, K. U. *Selected Speeches and Writings* (Elmsford, NY, 1982).

DUNLOP, J. B. *The Faces of Contemporary Russian Nationalism* (Princeton, 1983).

GOLDBERG, B. Z. *The Jewish Problem in the Soviet Union* (New York, 1982).

GOLDMAN, M. I. *USSR in Crisis* (New York, 1983).

GROMYKO, A. A. *Peace Now, Peace for the Future* (New York, 1984).

HAZAN, B. *From Brezhnev to Gorbachev: Infighting in the Kremlin* (Boulder, CO, 1987).

HOLLOWAY, D. *The Soviet Union and the Arms Race* (New Haven, CT, 1983).

HUTCHINGS, R. *Soviet Economic Development* (New York, 1982).

———. *Structural Origins of Soviet Industrial Expansion* (New York, 1984).

JOHNSON, D. G., and K. McBROOKS. *Prospects for Soviet Agriculture in the 1980s* (Bloomington, IN, 1983).

KEEBLE, C., ed. *The Soviet State: The Domestic Roots of Soviet Foreign Policy* (Aldershot, England, 1985).

KELLEY, D. R. *Soviet Politics from Brezhnev to Gorbachev* (New York, 1987).

LAIRD, R., and E. HOFFMAN, eds. *Soviet Policy in a Changing World* (New York, 1986).

MCCAULEY, M., et al., eds. *The Soviet Union After Brezhnev* (New York, 1983).

MEDVEDEV, Z. A. *Andropov* (New York, 1983).

MILLAR, J. R., ed. *Politics, Work, and Daily Life in the USSR: A Survey of Former Soviet Citizens* (Cambridge, 1987).

PARKS, J. D. *Culture, Conflict and Coexistence* (Jefferson, NC, 1983).

RUBINSTEIN, A. Z. *Soviet Policy Toward Turkey, Iran and Afghanistan* (New York, 1982).

SHEVCHENKO, A. N. *Breaking with Moscow* (New York, 1985).

SHIPLER, D. K. *Russia: Broken Idols, Solemn Dreams* (New York, 1983).

TREML, V. G. *Alcohol in the USSR: A Statistical Study* (Durham, NC, 1982).

ZEMSTOV, I. *Andropov: Policy Dilemmas and the Struggle for Power* (Jerusalem, 1983).

[21] Seth Mydans, "An Afghan Footnote: Legend of a Soviet Farm Boy," *New York Times,* January 16, 1985, p. 2.

42

The Gorbachev Revolution, 1985–1991

The succession of Mikhail Sergeevich Gorbachev as Soviet leader in March 1985 marked a major turning point in Soviet history both at home and abroad. Taking power after a decade of gerontocracy, stagnation, and growing demoralization of Soviet society and intelligentsia, Gorbachev faced daunting problems, resembling those facing the reforming emperor, Alexander II, and the reforming first secretary, Nikita Khrushchev. Succeeding Nicholas I and his undiluted autocracy under which the Russian Empire lagged further behind western Europe economically, technologically, and politically, Alexander II had instituted Great Reforms, which brought much change but remained incomplete. (See Chapter 24.) The heir of Stalin's brutal dictatorship, Khrushchev had attempted to liberalize the Soviet system and provide a better life for its people. All three reform leaders sought to improve the position of Russia or the USSR in the world by ending some of their predecessors' many restrictions or "iron curtain" on contacts with western Europe. Aiming to preserve basic institutions and ideologies, all three sought to rule over a sprawling empire by making it function more

efficiently and humanely. The sad experience of his predecessors anticipated the ultimate fate of Gorbachev's reforms. Alexander II was assassinated by leftist extremists, and many of his reforms were halted; Khrushchev was removed by his Politburo colleagues and succeeded by Brezhnev's conservative regime; Gorbachev saw his country disintegrate.

The Leader and the Succession

At his accession to power Gorbachev seemingly possessed a sophistication and political skill greater than either Alexander II or Khrushchev. He was born March 2, 1931, of Russian peasant stock in a village in Stavropol province of the north Caucasus. Only 10 when Hitler invaded the Soviet Union, he was too young to fight in that conflict (though his father did), which left his native village devastated. Young Gorbachev worked summers on the local collective farm, driving a combine and assisting his father. Hard physical labor gave him both satisfaction and self-confidence. Interested in a wide variety of subjects, Gorbachev received a silver medal when he completed secondary school in 1950. At age 18, for excellence in political work in the Komsomol (Young Communist League) and physical labor on the *kolkhoz,* he was given the Order of the Red Banner of Labor.[1]

Those honors facilitated Gorbachev's acceptance by the law faculty of prestigious Moscow State University in 1951. There he met his future wife, Raisa Titorenko; they married in 1954 in a simple wedding. As a student he served as secretary of the law faculty's Komsomol organization and at age 21 joined the Communist Party. Graduated with honors in 1955, Gorbachev returned to Stavropol as a full-time Komsomol official. For his intelligence, dedication, and hard work, he was promoted rapidly, shifting to the party in 1962 and four years later becoming first secretary of the Stavropol party committee. In 1971 he was named to the Central Committee of the All-Union Communist Party, the youngest official to be so honored. He cultivated useful ties with several Politburo members and won their support. In September 1978 Gorbachev held crucial meetings with Brezhnev, Chernenko, and Andropov (his three predecessors as party chief) during their visits to Stavropol and the north Caucasus. Two months later he was called to Moscow as Central Committee secretary for agriculture, and in 1980, at 49, he became a full member of the Politburo.

Following Brezhnev's death in 1982, Gorbachev rose swiftly to the top of the Soviet power pyramid. With some younger Central Committee members, he backed Andropov's successful drive to succeed Brezhnev; he then served as his spokesman in the Politburo after the ill Andropov could no longer attend meetings. Checked temporarily when the old guard selected Chernenko as party leader in 1984, Gorbachev as de facto second party secretary controlled many power levers, including responsibility for ideology and personnel. His trip to Britain that summer and his

well-publicized meeting with British Prime Minister Thatcher enhanced his position as evident successor to the ill Chernenko.

On March 11, 1985, the Kremlin announced Chernenko's death after only 13 months as general secretary and Gorbachev's appointment as chairman of the funeral commission. Only hours later Moscow confirmed that the Central Committee had named Gorbachev first party secretary. *Pravda*'s front page featured Gorbachev and his reform program; Chernenko's obituary was relegated to page two. Gorbachev's accession confirmed a decision evidently reached earlier. During Chernenko's illness he had apparently presided over Politburo meetings. As the eighth paramount Soviet political leader, Gorbachev at 54 was the youngest since Stalin to assume control, younger than anyone else in the Politburo or Secretariat. Foreign Minister Andrei Gromyko, the older generation's most respected leader, had nominated him warmly as first secretary. Mourning was minimal at Chernenko's funeral as a self-confident Gorbachev talked with the many world leaders who attended. Gorbachev's acceptance speech revealed his eager impatience to begin work: "We are to achieve a decisive turn in transferring the national economy to the tracks of intensive development." Later, he noted: "The very system was dying away; its sluggish senile blood no longer contained any vital juices."[2]

Gorbachev's succession of a pathetic and aged leader facilitated his swift consolidation of power. The Soviet public greeted its youthful, energetic new leader with unconcealed enthusiasm, hopeful that their manifold problems would now finally be tackled. "After ten years of gerontocracy," commented a young Soviet writer, "it is like spring. Since Khrushchev we have had nothing done for the people, only repression and rhetoric. Now that generation has come to an end." Leaving foreign policy initially in the capable although inflexible hands of Gromyko, Gorbachev focused on domestic problems.

---

[1] On Gorbachev's difficult and challenging youth, see Mikhail Gorbachev, *Memoirs,* trans. Georges Peronansky and Tatjana Varsavsky (New York, 1996), pp. 19–35.

[2] Gorbachev, *Memoirs,* p. 168.

At Gorbachev's accession four of ten full Politburo members clearly opposed him: Grishin, Kunaev, Romanov, and Tikhonov. Apparently it had been the Secretariat and perhaps the Central Committee rather than the Politburo that had elevated Gorbachev to power. In any case, he transformed these top party bodies with unprecedented speed. Two party secretaries allied with him soon received full Politburo membership. Egor K. Ligachev assumed control over personnel and ideology; Nikolai I. Ryzhkov was to plan economic reforms. KGB chief Viktor Chebrikov, another Gorbachev ally, became a full Politburo member. In July 1985 Gorbachev abruptly removed his leading rival, Grigori V. Romanov, from the Politburo and Secretariat for "reasons of health" and nudged his own elderly sponsor, Gromyko, "upstairs" into the titular post of Soviet president. Replacing him as foreign minister was a Gorbachev man with minimal experience in foreign affairs, Edvard A. Shevardnadze, former first secretary of the Georgian party. In September Nikolai Ryzhkov succeeded Tikhonov as premier, confirming the passage of leadership to a new generation.

Early in 1986 Gorbachev consolidated his hold. In March conservative Moscow party chief Viktor Grishin was replaced on the Politburo and in Moscow by Boris N. Yeltsin, a radical reformer. During Gorbachev's first year as party chief, five new full members entered the Politburo. The Secretariat too was transformed, with seven of its nine secretaries selected in that time span.[3] The 27th Party Congress of March 1986 brought 125 new members, mostly Gorbachev partisans, into the 307-member Central Committee. And in the executive branch, 38 of the 100 ministers were removed and 8 more received new posts.

Most of the leaders Gorbachev selected were recently arrived in Moscow and not identified with the Brezhnev regime. At Brezhnev's death most of these men had relatively low status and less

seniority than Gorbachev, and they owed their subsequent promotions to him. A majority of those elevated into key power positions had worked with Gorbachev either in Stavropol or elsewhere in the Caucasus, had been Komsomol leaders, or were graduates of Moscow University in the 1950s. By August 1987 almost three-fourths of republic and regional first secretaries had been selected since Brezhnev's death while Gorbachev was either personnel chief or first party secretary, which gave him unprecedented control over the party apparatus. At the June 1987 Central Committee plenum, Gorbachev made three party secretaries who were his personal supporters full Politburo members: Viktor Nikonov, Nikolai Sliunkov, and Alexander Iakovlev.[4] (See Table 42.1.)

Glasnost and Political Reform

While consolidating control that first year, Gorbachev enjoyed a remarkable political honeymoon. Helpful to him were his youthfulness, vigor, openness, and skill at public relations revealed in a series of bold, frank speeches, radically different from previous stilted party pronouncements. Repeatedly Gorbachev waded into friendly crowds of ordinary Soviet citizens and workers to exchange banter as the populist Khrushchev had. Gorbachev, his highly educated and attractive wife, Raisa, and their children resembled the Kennedys and were featured at receptions, parades, and official gatherings in a drastic departure from Soviet traditions of secrecy. Gorbachev's restless activity, intellectual grasp, and directness contrasted completely with Chernenko's standpat and secretive regime. At first avoiding major controversial reforms that might alienate important groups, Gorbachev emphasized that the Soviet Union must emerge swiftly from political and economic stagnation or face inevitable decline. Enthralled with his style, the Soviet public and Western media overlooked the fact that Gorbachev had reached supreme power

---

[3] Jerry Hough, *Russia and the West: Gorbachev and the Politics of Reform* (New York, 1988), pp. 168–70.

[4] Hough, *Russia and the West,* pp. 170–72.

Table 42.1 Membership in Politburo of the Party Central Committee, 1989

Full Members	Year of Birth	Year Elected Full Member	Position and Year Assumed
M. S. Gorbachev	1931	1980	General Secretary, Central Committee (1985)
V. M. Chebrikov	1923	1985	Chairman KGB (1983)
E. G. Ligachev	1921	1985	Agriculture Secretary of Central Committee
N. I. Ryzhkov	1929	1985	Premier (1985)
E. A. Shevardnadze	1928	1985	Foreign Minister USSR (1985)
V. I. Vorotnikov	1926	1983	Chairman Russian Republic Council of Ministers (1983)
A. N. Iakovlev	1923	1987	A Central Committee Secretary
V. A. Medvedev	1929	1989	A Central Committee Secretary
N. N. Sliunkov	1929	1987	A Central Committee Secretary
L. N. Zaikov	1923	1986	A Central Committee Secretary
V. V. Shcherbitskii*	1918	1971	First Secretary, Ukraine (1972)
V. P. Nikonov	1929	1987	

*Removed during 1989.

after a 30-year political apprenticeship in the Komsomol and party apparatus.

Before undertaking major economic reform, or *perestroika* (restructuring), Gorbachev sought to build support for essential changes among the Soviet intelligentsia with far greater openness—*glasnost*—in the public media. This *glasnost* would be a spotlight exposing problems. Soviet and Western reporters received freedom comparable to that in other world capitals to cover stories, interview Soviet officials, and reveal facts formerly shrouded in secrecy. The Soviet press began publishing sensitive statistics and reports of crimes and disasters previously only whispered about furtively by individuals. Growing Western fascination with Gorbachev and his policies soon made him and his Soviet Union a leading news story. *Glasnost* also involved efforts by the Gorbachev regime to educate Soviet citizens from above in new traditions of freedom and tolerance. Inevitably this provoked unsuccessful efforts by conservatives to block or curtail *glasnost,* especially in sensitive areas of culture and history. Party control over the media remained firm, but *glasnost* gathered force rapidly as a formerly dull press now captivated Soviet readers with amazing revelations. In the Baltic republics the official press

became so outspoken that conservative Moscow newspapers accused it of being anti-Soviet.

Glasnost was severely tested and the Gorbachev regime embarrassed by technological and natural disasters. Late in April 1986 a near meltdown occurred at the Chernobyl nuclear energy station near Kiev, spewing radiation north and west into Byelorussia, Poland, and Scandinavia. Although Soviet authorities, including Gorbachev, were informed immediately and reacted swiftly, in an apparent repudiation of *glasnost* the outside world was not told that anything was wrong until three days later. Apparently Soviet authorities hoped to conceal the whole disaster as had been done in the past. Only 18 days later did Gorbachev speak publicly about Chernobyl, seeking to counter a public relations disaster. Chernobyl cast grave doubt on the future of nuclear power in the USSR and provided live ammunition to the growing environmental movement.[5] After this

---

[5] See Nigel Hawkes, ed., *Chernobyl: The End of the Nuclear Dream* (New York, 1986). In his *Memoirs,* Gorbachev affirmed that Chernobyl severely affected his regime's reforms "by throwing the country off its tracks." He added: "I absolutely reject the accusation that the Soviet leadership intentionally held back the truth about Chernobyl. We simply did not know the whole truth yet" (p. 189).

came a series of railroad accidents, coal-mine disasters, and ship and submarine mishaps that severely bruised Gorbachev's popularity. Then on December 7, 1988, while Gorbachev was visiting the United States, a massive earthquake in Soviet Armenia killed about 25,000 people and left more than half a million homeless. Costs of cleaning up and rebuilding the Chernobyl plant and devastated Armenia together kept on escalating. However, the unprecedented openness of Soviet authorities following the Armenian earthquake and massive American and worldwide aid to its victims confirmed the reality of *glasnost,* and enhanced Gorbachev's reputation and Soviet-Western relations.

As Gorbachev encouraged the press "to fill in the blank spots" in Soviet history, *glasnost* exposed the monstrous crimes of the Stalin era in an extension of Khrushchev's de-Stalinization. While attacking Stalin and Stalinism, the media generally defended Lenin's policies and ideology. Novelists, playwrights, and journalists pioneered in historical reevaluation as professional historians hung back cautiously. Reexamining Soviet history, declared Iurii Afanasiev, new liberal rector of the Moscow State Historical-Archival Institute, resembled "awakening from a prolonged mythological dream." As Soviet citizens learned more about their past, "to many in the USSR it has become obvious that there is no people and no country with a history as falsified as Soviet history." In 1989 Afanasiev elaborated on that theme:

> To give a legal foundation to the Soviet regime in the USSR is, it seems to me, a hopeless task. To give a legal foundation to a regime which was brought into being through bloodshed with the aid of mass murders and crimes against humanity, is only possible by resorting to falsification and lies—as has been done up till now. It must be admitted that the whole of Soviet history is not fit to serve as a legal basis for the Soviet regime. By admitting this, we

would be taking a step toward the creation of a democratic society.[6]

At a Central Committee plenum of January 1987, Gorbachev urged accelerating the application of *glasnost* to Soviet historical scholarship. After Stalin had been depicted very negatively in film and literature, Gorbachev's speech in November 1987 referred openly to Stalin's crimes. Abel Aganbegyan, Gorbachev's chief economic adviser, described "the misery and brutality of rural life" under forced collectivization. Lacking basic human rights, collective farmers had been paid less than subsistence wages.[7] The critique of forced collectivization under Gorbachev went far beyond anything revealed during Khrushchev's regime. Its beginning was described as a negative turning point in Soviet history, when Lenin's NEP was discarded in favor of Stalin's bureaucratic socialism.

Along with efforts to refurbish NEP as a truly Leninist model of reform came political rehabilitation of Stalin's opponents. In January 1988 Moscow's Central Lenin Museum displayed photographs of Bukharin, Zinoviev, Kamenev, and Trotskii—victims of Stalin's Great Purge. Bukharin's full civic rehabilitation in February 1988 contrasted his conciliatory, moderate rural program and political policies with Stalin's terror and "revolution from above." Khrushchev too was partially rehabilitated as Gorbachev described his beneficial reforms and praised his efforts to free the USSR from negative aspects of Stalinism, decentralize the economy, and democratize Soviet politics somewhat. However, Khrushchev was criticized for capricious behavior and unstable policies and for fostering his own personality cult.[8] Positive reassessment of Khrushchev's period coincided with a multifaceted critique of the Brezhnev era (1964–1982) as "the period of stag-

---

[6] Iurii Afanasiev at the Kennan Institute, Washington, DC, October 6, 1988; "Soviet Rule Questioned," *Radio Free Europe* 6, no. 30 (July 20, 1989).

[7] Abel Aganbegyan, *The Economic Challenge of Perestroika* (Bloomington, IN, 1988); Gorbachev, *Memoirs,* p. 113.

[8] M. S. Gorbachev, *Perestroika* (New York, 1987), p. 43.

nation." Gorbachev blamed Brezhnev for failing to institute timely political and economic changes and for the USSR's loss of momentum and declining economic growth after 1975. He stressed Brezhnev's vindictiveness.[9] Brezhnev became a convenient scapegoat for most ills of Soviet society, politics, and foreign policy.

Historical *glasnost* even invaded the formerly sacrosanct preserves of Leninism and Soviet foreign policy. Stalin, affirmed one article, for personal political reasons had grossly exaggerated the danger of a capitalist-sponsored and French-led invasion of the USSR in 1928–1929.[10] Stalin's policy of "social fascism," alleged another, had split the German working class and contributed to Hitler's seizure of power and eventually to World War II. One scholar denounced the Nazi-Soviet Pact of August 1939 as a cynical act.[11] In the Baltic republics that pact was denounced as the basis for their forced incorporation into the Soviet Union in 1940. Efforts to uncover the roots of Stalinism led to scattered criticisms of Leninism, chiefly in literature. Marxism-Leninism, suggested Vasili Seliunin, had played a destructive role by denigrating the principle of economic self-interest.[12] Unwittingly, Gorbachev had opened a Pandora's box of revelations that soon would undermine the entire Soviet system and its ideology.

Beginning in 1986, shocking revelations appeared in the Soviet press about a deteriorating Soviet social system. Statistics were published on infant mortality, incidence of disease, and numerous deaths from suicide and alcohol poisoning. Soviet commentators demanded open reporting of party affairs, even Politburo meetings; the 19th Party Conference in 1988 advocated more publicity in those areas. *Glasnost* did not imply an independent or free press, however, but rather instructions from above combined with frequent reminders by the leadership of limits and a contin-

ued need for controls. Inevitably *glasnost* provoked conservative efforts to curtail liberal probing of sensitive areas of culture, history, and foreign policy.

An offshoot of *glasnost* was the dramatic reappearance in the USSR, for the first time since the 1920s, of informal, voluntary organizations. Early "informals" were often devoted to the preservation of threatened historic monuments such as churches or to protection of the environment. *Pamiat* (Memory), a right-wing nationalist Russian organization with anti-Semitic overtones and an incipient political party, began as a preservationist group. By late 1985 informals had spread throughout the country, and in August 1987 their representatives meeting in Moscow's Hall of Columns called for creating a federation of informals and establishing a dialogue with the party. In 1988 the regime invited them to help defend *perestroika*. Their number doubled from an estimated 30,000 such organizations in 1988 to 60,000 in 1989. During 1989 many of these groups put forward political goals and planned to operate as political parties and establish foundations for genuine political democracy in the USSR. Popular fronts, first set up in the Baltic republics during 1988, by 1989 were successfully challenging the leadership of the party and electing deputies to the Congress of People's Deputies. From the Baltic republics this popular front movement spread to other minority republics. One freelance Soviet journalist, Liudmila Alekseevna, concluded in October 1988 that informals had made Gorbachev's program of democratization irreversible. By then some 70 percent of Soviet youth aged 14 to 17 belonged to informals concerned with popular music.[13]

By 1990 Gorbachev's USSR had progressed much further toward political reform than toward economic transformation. At an early stage Gorbachev realized that implementation of essential economic change depended on political reforms.

---

[9] Gorbachev speech of January 26, 1987; *Pravda*, March 1, 1987.

[10] *Komsomolskaia Pravda*, June 19, 1988.

[11] Dmitry Volkogonov, *Pravda*, June 20, 1988.

[12] V. Seliunin, *Novyi mir*, no. 5 (1988).

---

[13] L. Alekseevna, "Informal Associations in the USSR," Kennan Institute, October 24, 1988; Fred Starr, "Informal Groups and Political Culture," at the Kennan Institute, December 9, 1988.

Expressing impatience at the slow pace of reform to the Central Committee in February 1988, Gorbachev attacked opponents of change and urged accelerating the "process of democratization" by restructuring the Soviet political system. He singled out the soviets as the place to start. In February 1987 a limited experiment of competitive elections to some local soviets was launched. In June 1987 elections, about 5 percent of deputies were so chosen in scattered districts, but the results were heartening. Deputies to local soviets were to be limited to two five-year terms. Elected representatives began to achieve some power over the bureaucrats. In June 1988 Gorbachev told the 19th Party Conference that prescribed quotas in the soviets of women, collective farmers, and workers were no longer necessary:

> We should not be afraid of the disproportionate representation of various strata of the population. . . . All that needs to be done is to create a well-adjusted competitive mechanism ensuring that voters choose the best possible people out of this group. Then all the basic groups of the population and their interests will be reflected in the make-up of the soviets.[14]

At the 19th Conference significant political reforms were announced, including a new legislature—the Congress of People's Deputies—that was to be more freely elected and the new and powerful post of President of the Supreme Soviet for Gorbachev. (See Figure 42.1.) Gorbachev later called the conference "the real turning point when *perestroika* became irreversible."[15] (Party conferences were convened periodically, usually to deal with a specific issue, whereas Congresses after Stalin's death met every five years and were far longer.) Officeholders were to be limited to two five-year terms, and local elections were to be contested. Meanwhile debate escalated between radical reformers like Boris Yeltsin and conservatives led by Egor Ligachev. Even more extreme

was the neo-Stalinist letter of a Leningrad school-teacher, Nina Andreeva.[16] Following animated Politburo discussion, on April 5, 1988, *Pravda* issued a sharp rebuttal, approved by Gorbachev, defending the reforms. The 19th Conference engineered a more reformist Central Committee than that elected in March 1986 without awaiting the 28th Party Congress scheduled for 1991.[17] However, in the United States former dissident Andrei Sakharov criticized Gorbachev's attempt to implement "democratic reform through undemocratic means." Elections to the new 2,250-member Congress, he predicted, would be controlled by the state administrative apparatus. By holding power as both party general secretary and Soviet president, Gorbachev or a successor might abuse it.[18]

Nonetheless, the March 1989 elections came as a welcome surprise to supporters of democratization. "For all their unfairness, fraud, undemocratic framework and stage-managing," wrote a Gorbachev critic, "the present elections will go down in history as the most democratic elections the Soviet people have seen in the whole period of Communist rule." After balloting for 1,500 territorial deputies was completed, one Muscovite exclaimed, "It was as exciting as . . . when we celebrated the defeat of Nazi Germany."[19] As party conservatives withdrew, stunned by their almost universal repudiation, 90 percent of Muscovites voted for Boris N. Yeltsin, a leading spokesman for radical political change. In one Moscow district Arkadi Murashov—a young engineer advocating a multiparty political system—triumphed. In Leningrad the five highest party officials met defeat when more than half the voters crossed out their names! However, more or less free elections were held in only 200 to 300 districts out of thousands; in most others, hand-picked party candidates ran unopposed. Despite

---

[14] Gorbachev to the 19th Party Conference, June 1988, p. 15.
[15] Gorbachev, *Memoirs*, p. 237.

[16] In *Sovetskaia Rossiia*, March 13, 1988.
[17] Michel Tatu, "19th Party Conference," *Problems of Communism* 37 (May–August 1988), pp. 1–15.
[18] Sakharov at the Kennan Institute, November 14, 1988.
[19] Alexander Amerisov, *Soviet-American Review* 4, no. 2 (February 1989).

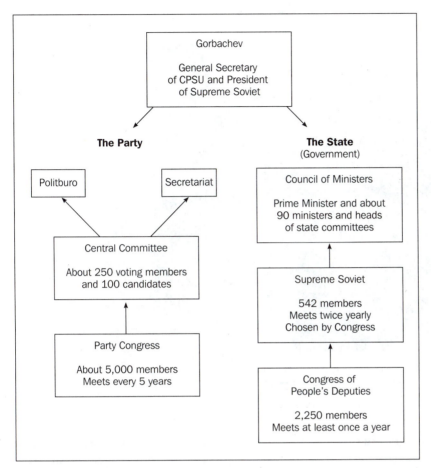

Figure 42.1
Soviet political structure, June 1990

their deficiencies, the March 1989 elections opened the way for a difficult evolution toward democracy.[20] Soon thereafter Gorbachev was elected president of the new Supreme Soviet, which at its initial sessions in spring and fall 1989 subjected him and other leaders to unprecedentedly frank questioning. Containing a growing liberal opposition, that body was no rubber stamp.

The ouster and subsequent resurrection of Boris Yeltsin throws an interesting light on politics

under Gorbachev. An ardent reformer, Yeltsin was named a Central Committee secretary in July 1985 and first secretary of the Moscow city committee in December, replacing Grishin. He issued emotional appeals for social justice and denounced privileges of the party elite (*nomenklatura*). But after a Central Committee plenum of October 1987 Yeltsin, denounced by conservatives and criticized by Gorbachev, was abruptly fired as Moscow party chief and removed from the Politburo soon thereafter. Receiving a modest post in the construction industry but soon named to the

---

[20] Amerisov, *Soviet-American Review* 4, no. 3 (March 1989).

Boris Yeltsin (1931–), maverick Soviet politician, meets the public in
Moscow. In 1991 Yeltsin was elected President of the Russian
Republic.

Council of Ministers, Yeltsin made a rapid comeback as spokesman for the Moscow intelligentsia
and electoral reform.[21] Overwhelmingly elected to
the Supreme Soviet over a conservative, Yeltsin
took a leading role among its liberal opposition.
During 1989 he emerged as Gorbachev's chief
left-wing critic, protesting that Gorbachev's
reforms were proceeding too slowly. On the right,
Ligachev claimed that the pace of reform was too
rapid. Gorbachev continued to hold the middle
ground in Soviet politics.

[21] Timothy Colton, "Moscow Politics and the Eltsin [Yeltsin]
Affair," *The Harriman Institute Forum* 1, no. 6 (June 1988).
Commented Gorbachev on Yeltsin's speech at the Central
Committee plenum: "His remarks sounded like an ultimatum and caused a sharp reaction. Speakers mentioned his
'wounded pride' and 'excessive ambition.'" Added Gorbachev: "I never lowered myself to his level of kitchen
squabbling." Gorbachev, *Memoirs,* pp. 243, 248.

The first lawyer to run the party since Lenin,
Gorbachev fostered major improvements in
human rights and advances toward a genuine rule
of law. Nearly all political prisoners were freed and
rehabilitated. Gorbachev's report to the 27th Congress in 1986 outlined desired legal changes, and
the 19th Party Conference of June 1988 reiterated
this theme. Henceforth laws were to be applied in
a democratic, evenhanded manner. Moves were
made to abolish or dramatically curtail capital
punishment, involuntary exile, and forced incar-
ceration in mental institutions. The Conference
recommended that "presumption of innocence"
be incorporated in a new Soviet law code. The
Central Committee decreed in November 1986
that defense counsel be admitted to preliminary
investigations in all criminal cases. Endorsing
many proposed legal reforms, the 19th Party

Conference gave this laudable campaign new momentum.[22]

The dramatic and sudden eastern European democratic revolutions of 1989–1990, encouraged by Gorbachev's evident unwillingness to repress them forcibly, accelerated Soviet political democratization. In the spring of 1989 Gorbachev told Hungarian party leaders that he sought "pluralism within a single party system" for the USSR. He told Soviet workers in February that a multiparty system in the Soviet Union was "rubbish." In November, reassuring worried Moscow conservatives, Gorbachev insisted that Marxism would be revived by the party and that the party would continue to lead Soviet society. He defended Article 6 of the Soviet Constitution, which prescribed a leading political role for the party, and headed off efforts by reformers to debate that issue in the Supreme Soviet.

However, in the face of an eastern European democratic tide and the fading popularity of the Soviet Communist Party, President Gorbachev had to reverse his position. In December 1989 the Lithuanian parliament voted overwhelmingly to abolish the party's power monopoly. In January 1990, confronted in Vilnius, Lithuania, by huge crowds chanting for democracy, Gorbachev declared that he saw "no tragedy" in a multiparty system for the USSR. At a dramatic party plenum in February, he advocated revoking Article 6, which was then implemented in a vote by the Congress of Peoples' Deputies. In republic elections from December 1989 to June 1990, the public repudiated many party-sponsored candidates. The opposition took over the governments of the USSR's three largest cities—Moscow, Leningrad, and Kiev. Power was shifting from a largely discredited Communist Party to the soviets. Gorbachev was losing control of the political system; his prestige was declining while that of Yeltsin and other radical reformers increased. In June 1990 a separate party organization dominated by conservatives was formed for the Russian Republic.

In early July 1990 the 28th—and last—Party Congress convened in Moscow in an effort to reorganize the CPSU and arrest its precipitous decline. "It was a battle between the reformist and orthodox-conservative currents in the Party," recalled Gorbachev. With some exaggeration, Gorbachev concluded: "The Party at this Congress condemned totalitarianism and swore allegiance to democracy, freedom and humanism." However, he admitted the congress widened the gulf between reformist and conservative forces in the CPSU.[23]

Nationalities and Nationalism

Under Gorbachev the Soviet nationalities emerged swiftly from apparent obedience to assert long-repressed aspirations to autonomy and even independence. This movement was spearheaded by the three Baltic republics, the most Westernized portion of the USSR. (See Map 42.1.) In some areas, notably the Caucasus and Central Asia, ethnic unrest led to widespread violence that threatened the entire fabric of Soviet federalism. Meanwhile Russian predominance declined further. According to the 1989 Soviet census, Russians comprised barely over 50 percent of the Soviet population. The USSR's 53 million Muslims, the second largest group, were increasing four times as fast as the overall Soviet population.

In July 1988 a large crowd gathered in a soccer stadium in Vilnius to celebrate a reborn Lithuanian national identity repressed since 1940, when Lithuania, Latvia, and Estonia were annexed forcibly to the Soviet Union. Participants bore pre-Soviet Lithuanian flags, demanded self-rule, and sang their long-banned national anthem. Algirdas Brazauskas, Lithuania's first party secretary, endorsed "economic sovereignty" for Lithuania. Moscow permitted this, and a popular front dominated Lithuania's March 1989 elections. Such leniency stemmed partly from Baltic leadership in implementing *perestroika*, which lagged

---

[22] William Butler, "Legal Reform in the Soviet Union," *The Harriman Institute Forum* 1, no. 9 (September 1988).

[23] Gorbachev, *Memoirs,* pp. 361, 372.

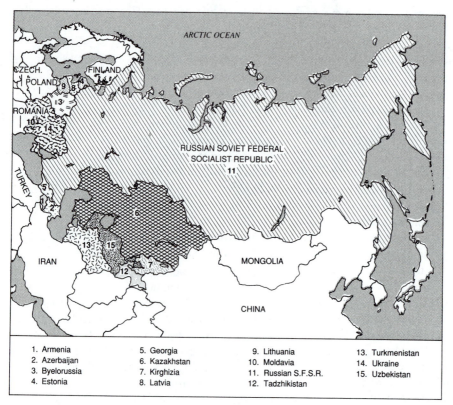

Map 42.1 Soviet Union Republics, June 1990

SOURCE: *Forbes*, February 19, 1990, p. 107. Map by Robert Mansfield.

elsewhere.[24] However, Lithuania's declaration of independence in March 1990 provoked Moscow to cut off industrial and fuel supplies to the republic. In July that conflict was settled temporarily when the Lithuanians agreed to postpone independence and Moscow lifted its sanctions. However, all three Baltic republics remained committed to eventual independence.

Beginning in 1988, Gorbachev faced an explosive and bloody ethnic and religious dispute between Armenians (Christians) and Azeris (Muslims) over the Armenian enclave of Nagorno-Karabakh inside the republic of Azerbaijan. (See Map 42.2.) In February 1988 hundreds of thou-

sands of Armenians went on strike, demonstrated, and demanded control over Nagorno-Karabakh. In ethnically mixed Sumgait, Azeris reacted by killing more than 30 Armenians. Moscow responded mildly at first, then used troops to suppress rioting in Sumgait. Armenians and Azeris emigrated en masse from areas where they comprised minorities. While rejecting Armenian demands to annex Nagorno-Karabakh, Moscow made some minor concessions. In November 1988 Gorbachev expressed deep concern over ethnic unrest:

> We live in a multi-ethnic state, the Soviet Union is our common home. When drawing up and implementing plans of revolutionary perestroika . . . , we cannot count on success if the work for the transformation of society does not take into account the interests of all the

---

[24] Robert Cullen, "Human Rights: A Millenial Year," *The Harriman Institute Forum* 1, no. 12 (December 1988).

Lithuanians demonstrate in their capital, Vilnius, for independence, January 1990. Signs read "Independence for Lithuania" and "Leave Lithuania."

nations inhabiting our vast country. . . . Our future is not in weakening ties among the republics but in strengthening them.[25]

Such soothing statements were combined with some repression, including arrests of some Armenian nationalist leaders. In January 1989 Moscow imposed "special situation status" in Nagorno-Karabakh, resembling actions taken by the government of India in handling ethnic conflict. For the first time Soviet leaders recognized that the USSR shared common ethnic problems with various foreign countries and could learn from them. Further decentralization, warned Gorbachev, might lead to disastrous results in the USSR as in Yugoslavia.[26]

As feuding continued, Moscow issued a decree in mid-January 1990 declaring a state of emer-

gency in Nagorno-Karabakh and surrounding areas. Later that month, as the Azerbaijan Popular Front sought to assume power from a weakening Azerbaijani party, Gorbachev ordered Soviet troops into Baku, the Azerbaijani capital, where a general strike had brought industry to a halt. Armed Azeri resistance was broken, but no solution emerged to the Armenian-Azeri quarrel. However, Latvia invited Armenian and Azeri leaders to Riga to work out a compromise, bypassing the federal government in Moscow—another dramatic demonstration of the growing power of popular front movements.

During 1989 ethnic violence erupted also in Central Asia between Uzbeks and Meshketians, a small population in the Caucasus deported to Uzbekistan by Stalin, inducing Soviet authorities to remove many of the latter to European Russia. Commented Soviet émigré Valeri Chalidze:

Separatism . . . is far from being the main problem of nationality relations in the USSR. The majority of people of non-Russian nationality has not even considered the possibility of

---

[25] Philip Taubman, "Gorbachev Says Ethnic Unrest Could Destroy Restructuring Effort," *New York Times,* November 28, 1988.
[26] Paul Goble at the Kennan Institute, January 23, 1989.

Map 42.2 The Southern Caucasus Region

After the Soviet assault in Baku, Nakhichevan proclaimed
independence. Nagorno-Karabakh, an Armenian-inhabited
region inside Azerbaijan, remains a focus of conflict between
Armenians and Azerbaijanis.

SOURCE: *New York Times,* January 21, 1990. Copyright © 1990 by The New York
Times Company. Reprinted by permission.

separation from the Soviet Union. I believe
these people do want free development of
their national culture and protection of their
national uniqueness from unification . . . and a
voice in solutions to their own problems.[27]

Chalidze cited past denial of political autonomy
and massive persecutions of most Soviet nationalities, falsifying their histories to claim that they
had joined the USSR voluntarily, massive corruption (especially in Central Asia), and ecological
problems as causes of friction. There was an
increasing tendency in virtually all Soviet republics
to assert their rights—political, cultural, and linguistic—against the Russian center.

During the first half of 1990 the disintegration
of the Soviet Union accelerated dangerously, and
the country was spinning out of control. Following

Lithuania's lead, other Baltic and Caucasian
republics asserted their sovereignty. Potentially
most serious was a decision by the legislature of
the Russian Republic (RSFSR) under its new president, Boris Yeltsin, that its laws would take precedence over those of the USSR. A nationalist tide
was rising throughout the Soviet empire, threatening its continued existence. In June President
Gorbachev promised that the Soviet Union would
be reformed to accord broad sovereignty to the
individual republics, but some of them continued
to press for full independence. As public order
began to break down, numerous Russian refugees
poured into Moscow seeking to escape ethnic
violence in the Caucasus and Central Asia.

Under Gorbachev, emigration from the USSR
of Germans, Jews, and Armenians was liberalized,
partly because of *glasnost* and partly to win foreign
approval and induce the United States to lift
trade restrictions. Relaxing restrictions on emigra-

---

[27] Valeri Chalidze, "Nationalities in the USSR," *Commission
on Security and Cooperation in Europe Digest*
(October–November 1988).

tion reflected a trend toward loosening central controls, recognizing more human rights, and promoting the rule of law. Starting in 1986, considerable numbers of Jews, especially "refuseniks," emigrated, and even more Soviet Germans departed. However, there was little emigration of Russians or other nationalities.

Russian nationalism was rekindled under Gorbachev as a backlash against Russophobic agitation outside the Russian Republic and as an outgrowth of an intraparty struggle between radical reformers and conservatives. Initially, Russian nationalism aimed to protect historic monuments and the environment. Nationalists successfully opposed a vast project designed to shift the course of Russian rivers to irrigate arid areas of Central Asia; it was abandoned in August 1986.[28] As Gorbachev's reform plans matured during 1987, neo-Stalinists and conservative Russian nationalists allied against *perestroika;* they objected especially to official encouragement of Western "mass culture," which appealed to Soviet youth. However, many Russian nationalists hailed Gorbachev's initiative to celebrate in June 1988 the millenium of the Christianization of Rus, including his well-publicized meeting with Patriarch Pimen. *Pamiat,* the leading Russian nationalist group, whose members wore black military shirts or army greatcoats, advocated "a great undivided Russia" free of Jews. By 1990 this Russian nationalism represented a significant, potentially dangerous force, but its fragmentation into several subgroups reduced its political strength.[29]

Perestroika's Impact on the Economy and Society

Political democratization and opening of the public media were designed to buttress Gorbachev's

radical overhaul of the Soviet economy, or *perestroika.* The chief problem—a monumental one— was to shift a huge economy from a state-owned and -managed system, highly centralized and bureaucratized, to a semimarket economy in which some degree of individual initiative and local decision making would prevail. Another formidable problem was to transform a totally unrealistic price structure into one in which prices and costs would reflect market forces. In short, Gorbachev aimed to move from state to market socialism by using capitalist techniques without restoring a capitalist system.

Under Gorbachev, economic reform in 1985–1986 featured traditional approaches such as tightening work discipline and shifting investment. A second stage, beginning early in 1987, aimed to overhaul the state economic sector and create a socialist market economy. Richard Ericson dubbed a third phase, beginning in 1988, "the privatization of Soviet socialism" in a desperate effort to overcome stagnation; its reforms included a law on individual labor activity and a law on cooperatives, granting long-term leases to private producers, especially in agriculture. The purpose was "to rescue *perestroika* for the Soviet consumer" by creating institutions promoting genuine competition and removing excessive central coordination and planning. But without steps to legalize essential middlemen, these changes remained ineffective. Legal, bureaucratic, and even public opposition and foot-dragging crippled the new private sector.[30]

Attempts at Agricultural Reform

Nowhere was reform more urgently required than in agriculture, which remained in the paralyzing grip of roughly 50,000 huge state farms (*sovkhozy*) and somewhat smaller but still large collectives (*kolkhozy*). On these grossly inefficient units that absorbed vast state subsidies, farmers still had few

---

[28] Nicolae Petro, "The Project of the Century," *Studies in Comparative Communism* (Fall 1987), pp. 235–52.
[29] John Dunlop, "The Contemporary Russian Nationalist Spectrum," *Radio Liberty Research Bulletin,* December 19, 1988.

[30] Richard Ericson, "The Privatization of Soviet Socialism," *The Harriman Institute Forum* 2, no. 9 (September 1989).

inducements to work hard or produce much. Meanwhile small individual garden plots, strictly limited in size by law, produced roughly one-third of Soviet vegetables, fruits, and other consumer staples. Gorbachev's initial response to this dilemma was to create Gosagroprom, an agricultural superagency, in November 1985, while continuing to provide huge state subsidies, especially for meat and milk production.

When this traditional approach failed to overcome the agricultural crisis, Gorbachev in October 1988 proposed leasing substantial amounts of land for up to 50 years to small groups of farmers with the state retaining overall land ownership. Teams of farmers were to purchase agricultural machinery, feed, seed grain, and fertilizers. After fulfilling annual delivery quotas to the state, they could dispose at will of any remaining surplus. Urging adoption of this leasing system throughout Soviet agriculture, Gorbachev by implication condemned Soviet forced collectivization: "What has happened is that people have been alienated from the soil. . . . Comrades, the most important thing today is to make people full-fledged masters of the land again."[31] At a Central Committee plenum early in 1989, Gorbachev urged a radical reversal of 60 years of centralized farming. The superagency Gosagroprom was to be dismantled and free markets introduced gradually. After a transition period, farmers should receive "complete freedom" to market their products. Previous efforts at agricultural reform, such as Premier Kosygin's program of 1965, had failed, noted Gorbachev, because they had not been radical enough: "The essence of economic change in the countryside should be to grant farmers broad opportunities for displaying independence, enterprise, and initiative." At that March 1989 plenum, Gorbachev spoke more frankly than any previous Soviet leader had about the shortcomings of collectivized agriculture. The most inefficient farms, he urged, should be allowed to go bankrupt, then broken up

and leased out to farmers or merged with more successful neighboring collectives. Egor Ligachev, leading the party conservatives, advocated supplying even larger state subsidies to bolster state farms. That policy, retorted Gorbachev, had proven its utter failure under Brezhnev.[32]

During a month-long tour of Soviet collectives in 1989, Mark Kramer, an American journalist, was told by a Soviet agronomist: "Our farms are disaster areas." Locally, the old failed system remained deeply entrenched. "Even if a collective farm earns money with honest labor," lamented a leading agrarian reformer, "in order to spend the rubles, to build a barn, you still need 1,000 signatures." Lack of incentives and a stifling bureaucracy meant that most collectives lost money. "There are still 200,000 orders, decrees, official instructions, and ministerial instructions. Our economy is tied by all these like a bound child."[33] Even if freed from controls imposed by a million bureaucrats, were there enough genuine Soviet farmers left to rescue the country from agricultural disaster?

Fiscal Crisis Hampers Industrial Production

Gorbachev inherited an economy in the midst of a grave financial crisis. For years the USSR had been running up huge, carefully concealed budget deficits, amounting in 1985 to almost 20 percent of GNP, roughly twice the U.S. figure. Defense expenditures in the 1980s had continued to increase roughly 3 percent annually to pay for strategic weapons, missiles, and submarines. Soviet state banks had automatically loaned vast sums to inefficient state enterprises. These deficit rubles paid workers but produced no goods for them to buy. Thus from 1970 to 1986 personal deposits in Soviet savings banks rose fivefold because of endemic shortages and low-quality

---

[31] Gorbachev's Proposal to Lease Farms . . . ," *Radio Free Europe* 6, no. 4 (November 1, 1988).

[32] Bill Keller, "Gorbachev Urges New Farm Policy," *New York Times*, March 16, 1989.

[33] Mark Kramer, "Can Gorbachev Feed Russia?" *New York Times Magazine*, April 9, 1989.

consumer goods. Meanwhile the ruble remained unconvertible inside the Soviet Union and worthless outside; currency black markets flourished. The USSR owed huge financial obligations to its citizens that it could not meet.[34]

Revamping Soviet finances and the economy proved far more difficult for Gorbachev to achieve than political reform. More radical economic reformers, for a time converting Gorbachev, urged abandoning centralized state planning and artificial prices set by the state for a system in which market forces would allocate most goods, services, and prices. They redefined socialism to embrace rules of the marketplace and private ownership of land. For a time Gorbachev envisioned speedy price reform by 1990–1991 to establish a realistic system; he backed away from such reform when faced with negative reactions from Soviet consumers and workers accustomed to state subsidies to keep prices low. Creating a market economy, realized Gorbachev, would be very difficult technically and dangerous politically.

Abel Aganbegyan, an advocate of such radical reformist views and a chief Gorbachev economic adviser, favored rapid and drastic price reform with sharp price increases. Confirming what Western economists had long affirmed, Aganbegyan admitted that in 1981–1985 there had been virtually no Soviet economic growth. Centrally dictated prices, he argued, should be retained "only for the most essential products in order to control their rate of growth and stave off inflation."[35] Soviet economic reformers, noted Ed Hewitt, created difficulties for themselves by allocating broad decision-making powers to individual enterprises before instituting price reforms. That allowed them to operate for several years "with distorted prices arbitrarily giving profits to new enterprises and losses to others." For the Soviet economy to become competitive and market oriented, argued

Hewitt, it would have to integrate more fully into the world economy.[36] Gorbachev attempted this by abolishing the Ministry of Foreign Trade's monopoly and encouraging joint ventures with Bloc countries and capitalist companies, reflecting a dramatic change in Soviet attitudes.

Early efforts by the Gorbachev regime to reform Soviet industry mostly failed. A party plenum in June 1987 approved the complex law on state enterprise (LSE), which aimed to discard Stalinist economic practices and make Soviet enterprises into autonomous, democratic, financially independent producers. Individual firms were to exercise initiative, be fully accountable financially, and receive no guaranteed state financial support. Such a change would require overhauling the banking and credit systems and implementing a price reform at the start of the 13th Five Year Plan in 1991. (Later those measures were deferred.) Indirect economic levers were to replace the former central command mechanism.[37] In January 1988 implementation of this radical industrial reform began, but soon it grew evident that the scheme was simply not working. "*Perestroika* has lost its first decisive battle," lamented a Soviet legal specialist. A major purpose of the LSE was to restrict the power of the ministerial bureaucracy by letting enterprises set their own annual and five-year plans partly through contracts freely negotiated with customers and suppliers. However, enterprise directors, used to receiving orders from above, ensured that state orders would still represent 80 to 90 percent of their output, rather than the intended maximum of 50 to 70 percent. Factory managers remained bound to the ministries, obeying their orders as before and regularly ignoring decisions reached by workers and their elected councils. This situation resulted partly from the vaguely phrased LSE. The centralized Stalinist

---

[34] Judy Shelton, *Gorbachev's Desperate Pursuit of Credit in Western Financial Markets* (New York, 1989).

[35] Abel Aganbegyan, *The Challenge: Economics of Perestroika*, ed. N. Browne (Bridgeport, CT, 1988).

[36] Ed Hewitt, *Reforming the Soviet Economy* . . . (Washington, 1988).

[37] Jerry Hough, *Opening Up the Soviet Economy* (Washington, 1988).

Pizza prepared by cooks from Trenton, New Jersey, being served to Muscovites at the start of a joint Soviet-American enterprise in 1988.

industrial system and its vast bureaucracy revealed an amazing capacity to survive.[38] (See Table 42.2.)

Despite Gorbachev's exhortations for drastic economic changes, during his first five years they failed to take root. (See Figure 42.2.) Growth rates in 1987 and 1988 were only about 1.5 percent, and agricultural output actually fell in 1988. Only about two-thirds of the state's priority projects scheduled to be commissioned were actually completed. The backlog of unfinished and abandoned construction grew steadily. Reduced state revenues—combined with rising expenditures for investment, defense, subsidies to unprofitable factories, and Armenian earthquake relief—swelled budget deficits and inflationary pressures. Modernization of industry and real price reforms were postponed, and the USSR lagged technologically even further behind the West and Japan,

especially in advanced microcircuits and main-frame computers.

Consumer Complaints Increase

Faced with rising consumer dissatisfaction and bureaucratic obstruction, Gorbachev revised his economic policies in the realization that he could not achieve his goals as quickly as he had hoped. The 1989 plan stressed consumption, cut state investment for the first time since 1945, promised a major reduction in defense outlays, and deferred retail price reforms. Priority went to retooling Soviet plants, proceeding with land leasing, and encouraging the private sector.[39] In 1985 *perestroika* had been launched with a barrage of new regulations, slogans, and resolutions, which often proved contradictory and remained mere verbiage.

---

[38] "Economic Reform Stalled in the USSR," *Radio Free Europe 6*, no. 8 (December 10, 1988).

[39] Report by CIA and Defense Intelligence Agency of April 1989, *The Soviet Economy in 1988: Gorbachev Changes Course* (Washington, 1989).

Table 42.2 Industrial production figures
(January–February production as a percentage of preceding January–February)

Product	Brezhnev 1982 1981	Andropov 1983 1982	Chernenko 1985 1984	Gorbachev 1986 1985
Electricity	103.4%	103.0%	103.3%	104%
Petroleum (inc. gas condensate)	99.8	102.0	96.3	101
Natural gas	106.4	108.0	109.1	107
Coal	99.3	100.5	98.4	106
Steel	95.6	104.0	92.2	111
Fertilizer	97.7	111.0	98.0	116
Metal-cutting tools	101.5	104.0	103.6	114
Robots	—	147.0	100.0	142
Computer technology	76.8	109.0	110.0	123
Tractors	99.6	102.0	104.0	105
Paper	93.3	108.0	93.7	113
Cement	88.3	113.0	93.7	111
Meat	93.6	106.0	106.3	113
Margarine	100.0	110.0	92.6	108
Watches	100.0	105.0	96.4	108
Radios	98.9	111.0	93.0	106
Television sets	99.9	108.0	100.0	106

SOURCE: Marshall Goldman, *Gorbachev's Challenge* (New York, 1987), p. 70.

In several key areas the leadership's efforts to decentralize the economy were emasculated by the bureaucracy or simply abandoned. In November 1989 the government set new production quotas for factories and limited some exports. Although Deputy Premier Leonid Abalkin called such measures "temporary," clearly *perestroika* had stalled as had the Kosygin reforms of 1965. Meeting with economists Gorbachev conceded, "We have a long way to go from formulating a concept to obtaining the goals we have set and changing the quality of our society."[40]

Problems plaguing a Soviet economy being reformed from above were exemplified by the soap crisis of late 1989–1990. At the slightest hint that soap, detergent, or washing powder might be sold, Russians lined up for hours outside stores. On the black market such items fetched several times the official state price. Nor was soap the only consumer product in short supply: 1,000 of 1,200 everyday items were hard to obtain, noted official figures. Dangerous public dissatisfaction induced the government in 1989 to spend a whopping $16 billion on emergency imports of consumer goods. While preparing even more radical reforms, Gorbachev's economic team admitted it had underestimated the difficulties of reform. Gorbachev told Soviet economists in October 1989: "We can neither return to the beginning nor can we stop half way."[41] The graphs in Figure 42.3 reveal the Soviet dilemma.

Gorbachev relied heavily on the "human factor" to spur the lagging economy. Many corrupt officials were fired, drastic measures were adopted in 1985 to curb alcohol consumption, and Soviet workers were exhorted to abandon casual attitudes toward work. In September 1988 Gorbachev

[40] Peter Gumbel, *Wall Street Journal,* November 21, 1989, pp. 1–2.

[41] Gumbel, *Wall Street Journal.*

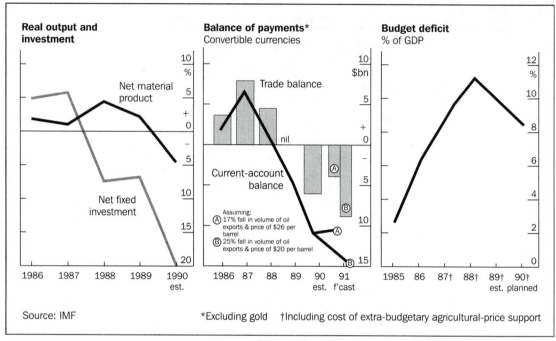

Figure 42.2
The Gorbachev Economic Balance Sheet, 1985–1990

SOURCE: *The Economist*, January 19, 1990, p. 40.

told representatives of the Soviet media: "We must free the social consciousness from such harmful complexes as the faith in 'a good tsar,' in an omnipotent center, in the idea that someone will impose order and organize *perestroika* from above." Seventy years of Soviet socialism, noted a journalist, had produced a psychology of social dependency: "Give me a free house, cheap meat, and get rid of my neighbor who is working on his own and lives better than I do." Many Soviet citizens responded to Gorbachev's pleas by forming "young peoples' residential complexes," competing to build their own apartment houses with money and materials provided by the state. Cooperatives proliferated—there were more than 32,000 by July 1988—to provide consumer services, formerly sadly lacking, such as repair facilities and private restaurants. However, they encountered the "red-eye" disease of envy by

those unwilling to see their fellow citizens prosper, and many cooperatives were burned down.[42] During 1988 Gorbachev retreated, criticizing cooperatives; he rescinded tough anti-alcohol measures after a surge in illegal production (*samogon*) caused losses of state revenue and sugar shortages.

Consumer dissatisfaction during Gorbachev's first five years reflected rising public expectations that the regime failed to satisfy. Per capita consumption remained virtually stagnant. Reduced farm output, inadequate storage facilities, and processing and distribution problems produced serious shortages of some foods. With supplies of meat, fruit, and vegetables sporadic in state stores, prices at collective farm markets rose considerably,

---

[42] "Gorbachev Calls for New 'New Soviet Man,'" *Radio Free Europe* 6, no. 6 (November 20, 1988).

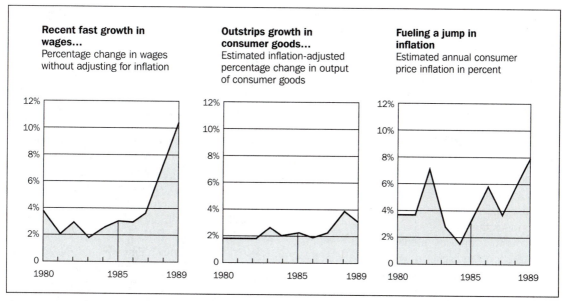

Recent fast growth in wages...
Percentage change in wages without adjusting for inflation

Outstrips growth in consumer goods...
Estimated inflation-adjusted percentage change in output of consumer goods

Fueling a jump in inflation
Estimated annual consumer price inflation in percent

Figure 42.3
The plight of Soviet consumers in the 1980s

SOURCE: PlanEcon Inc.

as did those of manufactured goods. Unsatisfied consumer demand for goods in 1988, noted Premier Ryzhkov, totaled over 90 billion rubles, or 20 percent of consumer purchases.[43] Soviet citizens continued to enjoy free health care and education while housing and necessities remained heavily subsidized, but overall living standards lagged far behind those of the West. "In terms of per capita consumption of goods," estimated Alexander Zaichenko, a Soviet economist, "the USSR . . . occupies between 50th and 60th place in the world." In 1985 almost two-thirds of the United States' GNP went for wages, compared to only 37 percent in the USSR, and the United States was outspending the USSR in education, health care, and social security. In 1985 a typical Soviet family of four with two wage earners spent 59 percent of its income on food, compared with only 15 percent for an American family. Soviet meat

consumption per capita was less than city dwellers had consumed in tsarist Russia. Zaichenko's figures provoked consternation among Soviet officials, who questioned those on tsarist meat consumption.[44]

Rapid urbanization added to consumer woes. Since 1917 Soviet cities had been transformed, noted an American geographer. Urban growth rates approximated 5 percent annually as the percentage of Soviet people living in cities rose from 18 percent in 1917 to 66 percent in 1985. Whereas in 1926 only Moscow and Leningrad exceeded 1 million people, in 1985 there were 21 such cities, and 292 with more than 100,000. Whereas advanced rural and urban planning prevailed in the Baltic states, cities in the Urals and Siberia could not provide nearly adequate services.[45] Under Gorbachev the media published

---

[43] CIA Report, *The Soviet Economy in 1988.*

[44] "USSR Living Standards Far Below Those of the West," *Radio Free Europe* 6, no. 17, 1989.
[45] George Demko at the Kennan Institute, October 3, 1988.

many revealing accounts of drug abuse, a serious and growing problem previously dismissed as nonexistent in the USSR. "Concealing an illness will not make it go away," wrote one newspaper. "We have come to realize that openness is needed in the struggle against drug addiction."[46]

National Security and Foreign Affairs

Introducing dramatic changes in Soviet foreign policy, Gorbachev elaborated a sharply altered view of military power and security. In superpower negotiations the Soviet Union agreed to drastic arms cuts and unprecedentedly intrusive measures of verification. Gorbachev downgraded the military's public role, encouraging civilian defense analysts to propose radical revisions of Soviet military policies. Replacing most of the high command he had inherited, he brought in the obedient General Dmitri Iazov as defense minister and appointed liberal-minded civilians to oversee important aspects of security policy. Most foreign observers viewed Gorbachev's "new political thinking" as constituting a revolution in Soviet security policy.[47]

Some of Gorbachev's statements before 1985 suggest that he had been a defender of Brezhnev's 1970s view that expanded military power, combined with arms control and diplomatic negotiations, would enhance Soviet security. However, beginning in 1983, Gorbachev opposed increased defense spending and expressed mounting concern over the USSR's industrial lag. Once in power he urged "civilized relations" with the West, unveiling in January 1986 a proposal for phased but sweeping arms reductions. As the 27th Congress that followed, he declared that growing

East-West interdependence required radical improvements in their relations.[48]

At Gorbachev's accession the Soviet Union remained a garrison state with enormous military forces built up over the previous 15 years at high economic and social cost. The USSR under Brezhnev had relied on military might to provide security at home and to serve as its primary instrument of foreign policy. Under Gorbachev this approach was revised substantially. Even in the early 1980s Soviet marshals had wondered whether a creaking economy could support the highly technological armed forces of the future. Policy changes under Gorbachev proved more far-reaching than at any other time in Soviet history. His "new thinking" rejected the Brezhnev military buildup as economically prohibitive and politically disastrous. Meanwhile there was growing public criticism of the Soviet military as bloated, expensive, and even morally corrupt. By 1988 some military men questioned the need for a huge standing army.

When two Soviet officers chained themselves to a lamppost outside the Defense Ministry in April 1989, they drew attention to the miseries of Red Army life. To their amazement, the next day they were sitting in Defense Minister Dmitri Iazov's office complaining about poor living conditions, scandalous health care, and insensitive political indoctrination. Although soon discharged from service, they revealed how *glasnost* had uncovered widespread discontent and caused unsettled times in the Soviet military, which were exacerbated by the unpopular war in Afghanistan.[49]

The Soviet economy had been grievously distorted and overstretched by Brezhnev's military buildup. A weak technological base, warned Marshal Nikolai Ogarkov, could not produce new sophisticated weaponry. Advances in high tech-

---

[46] John Kramer, "Drug Abuse in the Soviet Union," *Problems of Communism* 37,(March–April 1988), pp. 28–40. In 1988, 52,000 persons reportedly were officially registered in the USSR as drug addicts.

[47] Raymond Garthoff, "New Thinking in Soviet Military Doctrine," *Washington Quarterly*, Summer 1988, pp. 131–58.

[48] Bruce Parrott, *The Soviet Union and Ballistic Missile Defense* (Boulder, CO, 1987), pp. 55–56; and "Soviet National Security Under Gorbachev," *Problems of Communism* 37 (November–December 1988), pp. 1–35.

[49] Bill Keller, "Restlessness in Soviet Ranks," *New York Times*, April 21, 1989.

nology elsewhere, he noted, threatened to make obsolete 20 years of Soviet military growth. Discerning Soviet military men realized that problems of high technology could be solved only if the Soviet economy were redirected away from defense.[50] Gorbachev's team viewed Brezhnev's foreign policy, dependent on military power, as a disaster. The invasion of Afghanistan had triggered enormous American rearmament while alienating Japan and China from the USSR. Rejecting Brezhnev's idea of deploying forces that could defeat any combination of foes, Gorbachev accepted the American "zero option" proposal for Intermediate Range Ballistic Missiles even though it required the Soviets to destroy about four warheads for every American one. Gorbachev's United Nations speech of December 1988, in which he offered to cut Soviet forces unilaterally by 10 percent, reflected this new approach. Discussion on creating a smaller professional Soviet army also proceeded in Moscow.[51]

Supporters of *perestroika* sharply criticized the swollen Soviet military in 1988–1990 as blocking substantive progress on basic economic reforms. Attacks on the military as an institution multiplied. An article by Andrei Sakharov, the dissident scientist, virtually accused the Soviet military of genocide in Afghanistan. Some Red Army officers favored eliminating conscription. An army that had expanded by a million men from 1970 to 1985 was proving too costly to maintain, especially since its traditional Russian core was shrinking. More than one-third of Soviet soldiers were now Muslims who spoke little Russian, creating severe ethnic tensions within the armed forces. A smaller, chiefly Slavic professional army would alleviate such problems.[52]

In a wide-ranging debate in 1989 on national security issues, "new thinkers" advocated a permanent shift away from military means of ensuring security; they proposed channeling most resources into economic development. "Technocrats" favored a short-term shift of resources to militarily relevant sectors of the civilian economy to develop advanced weaponry. "Old thinkers" continued to urge heavy military spending. The "new thinkers," including Gorbachev, generally prevailed and urged an evolution of Soviet foreign policy toward cooperation; they argued that overall economic strength was fundamental to national security. "If we become stronger, more solid economically . . . , the interest of the capitalist world in normal relations with us will grow."[53] This victorious view represented a fundamental shift away from the rigid, militaristic thinking of the Brezhnev era.

Soviet foreign policy under Gorbachev was transformed. A peaceful international environment, it was hoped, would enable the USSR to realize major domestic reforms without sacrificing its status as a superpower. Gorbachev faced painful decisions over Afghanistan, eastern Europe, and German reunification. Almost immediately he sought to improve Soviet-American relations and mend fences with China so he could trim military expenditures and concentrate on domestic reform. Similarly, Alexander II had sought to maintain Russia's role as a leading European power while achieving major domestic change. Repudiating Brezhnev's policies, Gorbachev blamed his regime for the USSR's declining growth and power. Seeking to demilitarize and stabilize East-West relations, Gorbachev integrated the Soviet Union increasingly into the world capitalist economic order.[54] Defending his

---

[50] Report for the Joint Economic Committee, *Allocation of Resources in the Soviet Union and China—1986* (Washington, 1989).
[51] Condoleeza Rice, "Gorbachev and the Military: A Revolution in Security Policy Too?" *The Harriman Institute Forum* 2, no. 4 (April 1989), pp. 1–8.
[52]*Radio Free Europe* 6 no. 13 (February 1, 1989).

[53] Matthew Evangelista, "Economic Reform and Military Technology in Soviet Security Policy," *The Harriman Institute Forum* 2, no. 1 (January 1989).
[54] George Breslauer, "Linking Gorbachev's Domestic and Foreign Policies," *Journal of International Affairs* 65 (Spring 1989), pp. 267–82.

innovative foreign policy before the 28th Party Congress, Gorbachev declared:

> I tried to show that only incorrigible "hawks" could see anathema in a policy that did away with hyper-militarization of the country, turned the world back from the nuclear precipice, and created the basis for our integration into the economic and political structures of the world.[55]

Gorbachev's bold policies prompted George F. Kennan, a veteran American diplomat and an architect of the American post–World War II policy of containing the USSR, to urge Washington to negotiate reductions of nuclear and conventional weapons with a liberalizing USSR as steps toward normal relations. Kennan told the Senate Foreign Relations Committee in April 1989:

> What we are witnessing today in Russia is the break-up of much, if not all of the system of power by which that country has been held together and governed since 1917 . . . [especially] in precisely those aspects of Soviet power that have been the most troublesome from the standpoint of Soviet-American relations, namely: the world-revolutionary ideology, rhetoric and political efforts of the early Soviet leadership, . . . [and] the morbid extremism of Stalinist political oppression . . . [whose] remnants are now being dismantled at a pace that renders it no longer a serious impediment to a normal Soviet-American relationship.

Kennan cited three factors that still troubled U.S.-Soviet relations—swollen Soviet armed forces, continued Soviet hegemony over eastern Europe, and the arms race—but he discerned a changing Soviet security policy, military cuts, and a weakening Soviet hold over the Bloc. Declared Kennan prophetically: "So tenuous is the Soviet hold over these [eastern European] countries today that I personally doubt that military intervention . . . would now be a realistic option of Soviet policy." Praising Gorbachev's initiatives on arms control, Kennan concluded that the USSR should no

longer be viewed in the United States as an enemy:

> That country should now be regarded essentially as another great power . . . whose aspirations are conditioned outstandingly by its own geographic situation, history and traditions. . . . It ought now to be our purpose to eliminate as soon as possible by amicable negotiations the elements of military tension that have recently dominated Soviet-American relations.[56]

The course of Soviet-American relations from 1985 to 1990 provided a basis for Kennan's optimism. Already in April 1985 Gorbachev in a *Pravda* interview repudiated the former Soviet policy of confrontation. Citing President Reagan's apparent pursuit of military superiority through the Strategic Defense Initiative (SDI), dubbed "Star Wars,"[57] as the chief obstacle to rapprochement with the United States, Gorbachev urged achieving a breakthrough through arms control agreements. In a *Time* magazine interview in August 1985 Gorbachev reiterated the crucial importance of a Soviet-American accord to limit nuclear weapons and ban weapons in outer space. At their Geneva summit meeting that November, after extensive private talks, Reagan and Gorbachev issued a positive joint statement. Soviet newspapers, which had previously depicted Reagan as a trigger-happy cowboy, now described him talking amicably with Gorbachev. Later Gorbachev told the press that their talks, the first between an American and a Soviet leader in more than six years, had been "unquestionably a significant event in international life."

After Geneva both sides moderated their hostile rhetoric. However, Reagan's continued insistence on SDI and his refusal to join with Moscow

---

[55] Gorbachev, *Memoirs,* pp. 365–66.

[56] George F. Kennan to the Senate Foreign Relations Committee, April 4, 1989, quoted in the *New York Times,* April 5, 1989.

[57] See R. W. Johnson, *Shootdown: Flight 007 and the American Connection* (New York, 1986), pp. 109–10. Johnson describes how Reagan's national security adviser, William Clark, converted the president to the "Star Wars" scheme, keeping this a secret for a month from the secretaries of state and defense.

Raisa and Mikhail Gorbachev arrive at Reykjavik, Iceland, in October 1986 for summit talks with U.S. President Reagan.

in a nuclear test ban moratorium slowed progress. Then Gorbachev proposed another summit, and he met with Reagan in Reykjavik, Iceland, in October 1986. They had almost reached agreement to ban all nuclear weapons within a definite time span only to stumble over the issue of testing Reagan's SDI. With Reagan becoming absorbed in the Iran-Contra scandal, Soviet leaders doubted that meaningful agreements could be reached with his administration.

But during 1987 Soviet-American relations moved forward as Reagan moderated his former anti-Soviet stance. In December in Washington he and Gorbachev achieved a major breakthrough by signing a treaty to eliminate medium- and short-range missiles. Scoring a great triumph with the American media and public, Gorbachev announced that the two sides had "emerged from protracted confrontation." The final two Gorbachev-Reagan meetings in 1988 produced no major new agreements but deepened their personal relationship. At the largely ceremonial

Moscow summit of May 1988 Reagan, who earlier had dubbed the Soviet Union an "evil empire," chatted happily with Soviet citizens and lectured Soviet intellectuals on democracy. Gorbachev's brief meeting with Reagan and President-elect George Bush in New York that December reinforced their rapport and fostered its continuation under the Bush administration.[58] Conferring in Malta in November 1989 against the backdrop of the eastern European democratic revolution, Gorbachev confirmed his resolve not to intervene against it and to continue efforts at arms reduction and European integration. Bush and Gorbachev reached substantial agreement on the difficult issue of German reunification, which proceeded more rapidly than either of them anticipated.

Fundamental changes in Soviet relations with eastern Europe after 1985 supported Kennan's predictions and fostered improved Soviet-U.S. ties. Late in 1988, as Hungary and Poland liberalized their political and economic policies, Iurii Afanasiev, a liberal Soviet reformer, declared eastern Europe should be free to choose its own path even if that meant abandoning socialism. On a June 1989 visit to France, President Gorbachev expressly repudiated the Brezhnev Doctrine, used earlier to justify the intervention in Czechoslovakia, as outmoded. Instead Soviet officials espoused the "Frank Sinatra Doctrine," or "do it your own way." Praising varying eastern European responses to popular demands for greater freedom, Gorbachev intimated that they were merely implementing *glasnost* and *perestroika* in their own manner.

This major shift in Soviet policy toward the Bloc reflected further development of Khrushchev's theme enunciated 30 years earlier of "separate roads to socialism" and of a "socialist commonwealth." However, neither Khrushchev nor Brezhnev would allow Communist regimes to fall, as interventions in Hungary, Czechoslovakia, and Afghanistan confirmed. By contrast, under

[58] Gordon Livermore, ed., *Soviet Foreign Policy Today: Reports and Commentaries from the Soviet Union,* 3d ed. (Columbus, OH, 1989), pp. 42–73.

Soviet President Mikhail Gorbachev smiles as U.S. President George Bush tries on a headphone during their joint press conference at Malta summit meeting, December 1989.

Gorbachev ideology was largely repudiated in the conduct of foreign policy, permitting eastern Europe to go its own way and enabling the Soviets to withdraw from Afghanistan. By downplaying ideology, Gorbachev enhanced the USSR's image abroad. Meanwhile eastern Europe had lost much of its strategic importance for the USSR because under Communist rule it was draining Soviet resources. Gorbachev, the realist, became willing to cooperate with the West to stabilize eastern Europe on a new basis, although surely he did not anticipate how fast events would move there. During 1988–1989 Communist power was undermined first in Poland and Hungary, then popular movements overturned conservative Communist regimes that lacked popular support in East Germany, Czechoslovakia, Bulgaria, and Romania. This dramatic movement toward political democracy and market economies left only tiny Albania, where the USSR had little influence and no troops, under a Stalinist regime in June 1990. The collapse of the East German Communist regime accelerated the process of German unification and left the Soviet occupation army in East Germany isolated until it was withdrawn beginning in 1991.

Another remarkable shift in Soviet foreign policy was the Soviet military withdrawal from Afghanistan early in 1989. The Communist-led Afghan regime of Najibullah remained to face divided Afghan rebels, but was buttressed with generous Soviet military aid. Soviet withdrawal produced many compensations to the USSR. It helped improve Soviet-American relations, so crucial for Gorbachev. It undermined arguments of American "hawks" that the Afghan intervention had proved the aggressiveness of "Russian imperialism towards the Persian Gulf." Soviet retirement seemed to vindicate those who viewed the Soviet invasion as a product of miscalculation and circumstances.[59] It also allowed relaxation of Soviet tensions with China and a reduction of

---

[59] Mark Urban, *War in Afghanistan* (New York, 1988); Joseph Collins, *The Soviet Invasion of Afghanistan* (Lexington, MA, 1986).

Soviet forces on China's frontiers and improved the Soviet image in the Muslim world, especially in Iran. Although the war had grown highly unpopular inside the Soviet Union, returning Soviet troops were welcomed home by brass bands and assurances they had accomplished their "international mission."

The Gorbachev regime blamed the Afghan intervention on a small hawkish group in the Politburo surrounding the moribund Brezhnev. Very ill at the time of intervention, Brezhnev reportedly had signed the decision slipped to him hastily by Defense Minister Dmitri Ustinov. The Soviets, affirmed Joseph Collins, had "habitually attempted to pursue their interests in Afghanistan by using the lowest level of resources possible . . . , but each rung in this ladder of escalation brought the Soviets into deeper involvement with the Afghan problem."[60] In October 1989 the Kremlin issued a formal apology to the world for the invasion of Afghanistan:

> When more than 100 U.N. members for a number of years were condemning our action, what other evidence did we need to realize that we had set ourselves against all of humanity, violated norms of behavior, ignored universal human values? I am referring of course to our military engagement in Afghanistan. It should teach us a lesson that in this case gross violations of our own laws, intraparty and civil norms and ethics were allowed.[61]

A close parallel was evident between American policies in Vietnam and Soviet intervention in Afghanistan, ending in similar discomfiture for both superpowers. Both cases confirmed the strength of resistance by nationalist guerrillas even against a superpower.

After the Afghan withdrawal, Gorbachev charted a new and promising course in northeast Asia with arms control initiatives and overtures to China, Japan, and South Korea. Moscow sought to

alleviate tensions there to permit the USSR to reduce its military forces and outlays, end confrontation with China, and encourage Japanese investment in the Soviet economy. From 1981 to 1988, as Soviet leaders strove to end conflict with China, Sino-Soviet trade increased tenfold. Among the troop reductions announced in Gorbachev's U.N. speech of December 1988 were 200,000 to be cut from Soviet forces in Asia.

Finally, Gorbachev transformed Soviet policy toward the United Nations, reflecting multifaceted efforts to restore the USSR to the civilized world. His article in *Pravda* of September 17, 1988, contained a remarkable agenda: an enhanced role for the secretary general in preventive diplomacy, greater use of U.N. peacekeeping forces in regional conflicts, mandatory acceptance of decisions of the International Court of Justice, a global strategy for environmental protection, and negotiations to make national laws conform to international human rights standards. Previous Soviet leaders had opposed efforts of any secretary general to strengthen U.N. influence and refused to consider third-party arbitration of bilateral disputes. Some Western observers dismissed the new Soviet rhetoric about the United Nations as propaganda and an attempt to make the United States, which under Reagan often failed to pay its dues, look bad. Was Gorbachev, needing many years of external stability to implement *perestroika*, seeking to use the United Nations to help extricate the USSR from overextension abroad? Apparently Gorbachev aimed through the United Nations to make the USSR a major player in world diplomacy, having abandoned class warfare in favor of a new philosophy of international relations to achieve global interdependence and cooperation.[62]

Until his fall, President Gorbachev continued to play a major international role. After seeking unsuccessfully to arrange a peaceful solution of the Persian Gulf crisis, Gorbachev sacrificed the

---

[60] Collins, *The Soviet Invasion*, pp. 124–25.
[61] Eduard Shevardnadze's speech as quoted in the *New York Times*, October 25, 1989.

[62] Richard Gardner at the Harriman Institute (March 23, 1989), "The Soviet Union and the United Nations," *The Harriman Institute Forum* 1, no. 12.

special Soviet position in Iraq and Syria and backed the efforts of the United Nations to force Iraqi strongman Saddam Hussein out of Kuwait. However, the overwhelming American military victory there confirmed the United States as undisputed number one world power. During 1991 the end of the Cold War was confirmed, as the Warsaw Pact dissolved and most Soviet troops withdrew from eastern Europe. At a July summit in Moscow with President Bush, Gorbachev concluded further far-reaching agreements on reducing nuclear armaments.

During his six and one-half years in office, Mikhail S. Gorbachev became a hero in the West for relaxing authoritarian controls in the Soviet Union, permitting eastern Europe to free itself from the Soviet grip, and ending the Cold War. However, Gorbachev became unpopular at home as store shelves emptied and the USSR's economic and political troubles mounted. The Gorbachev regime, noted economist Anders Äslund, took inherited economic stagnation and turned it into drastic and precipitous economic decline. In seeking to reorganize and save the Soviet Union, Gorbachev undermined and finally destroyed it.[63]

Suggested Additional Reading

ÄSLUND, A. *Gorbachev's Struggle for Economic Reform . . . 1985–88* (Ithaca, NY, 1989).

BALZER, H., ed. *Five Years That Shook the World: Gorbachev's Unfinished Revolution* (Boulder, CO, 1991).

BENN, D. W. *From Glasnost to Freedom of Speech: Russian Openness and International Relations* (New York, 1992).

BESCHLOSS, M. R., and S. TALBOTT. *At the Highest Levels: The Inside Story of the End of the Cold War* (Boston, 1993).

BOETTKE, P. J. *Why Perestroika Failed: The Politics and Economics of Socialist Transformation* (New York, 1993).

BOLDIN, V. *Ten Years That Shook the World: The Gorbachev Era as Witnessed by His Chief of Staff,* trans. Evelyn Rossiter (New York, 1994).

BONNER, A. *Among the Afghans* (Durham, NC, 1987).

BROWN, A., ed. *New Thinking in Soviet Politics* (New York, 1992).

BRZEZINSKI, Z. *The Grand Failure: The Birth and Death of Communism in the Twentieth Century* (New York, 1989).

BUTLER, W. *Soviet Law,* 2d ed. (London, 1988).

CERF, C., and M. ALBEE, eds. *Small Fires: Letters from the Soviet People to Ogonyok Magazine, 1987–1990* (New York, 1990).

COLLINS, J. *The Soviet Invasion of Afghanistan* (Cambridge, 1986).

CROUCH, M. *Revolution and Evolution: Gorbachev and Soviet Politics* (New York, 1989).

CROZIER, B. *The Gorbachev Phenomenon: Peace and the Secret War* (London, 1990).

DANIELS, R. V. *The End of the Communist Revolution* (New York and London, 1993).

DAVIES, R. W. *Soviet History in the Gorbachev Revolution* (Birmingham, England, 1987, and Bloomington, IN, 1989).

DESAI, P. *Perestroika in Perspective: The Design and Dilemma of Soviet Reform* (Princeton, 1989).

DODER, D., and L. BRANSON. *Gorbachev: Heretic in the Kremlin* (New York, 1991).

DUNSTAN, J., ed. *Soviet Education Under Perestroika* (New York, 1992).

DZIAK, J. *Chekisty: A History of the KGB* (New York, 1988).

FARMER, K. C. *The Soviet Administrative Elite* (New York, 1992).

FREEDMAN, R., ed. *Soviet Jewry in the 1980s* (Durham, NC, 1989).

FRIEDBERG, M., and H. ISHAM, eds. *Soviet Society Under Gorbachev . . .* (Armonk, NY, 1987).

GLEASON, G. *Federalism and Nationalism: The Struggle for Republican Rights in the USSR* (Boulder, CO, 1990).

GOLDMAN, M. *Gorbachev's Challenge: Economic Reform in the Age of High Technology* (New York, 1987).

———. *What Went Wrong with Perestroika?* (New York, 1991).

GORBACHEV, M., *Memoirs,* trans. Georges Peronansky and Tatjana Varsavsky (New York, 1996).

———. *Perestroika: New Thinking for Our Country and the World* (New York, 1987, 1988).

———. *Selected Speeches and Articles,* 2d ed. (Moscow, 1987).

---

[63] Anders Äslund, *Gorbachev's Struggle for Economic Reform . . . 1985–88* (Ithaca, NY, 1989).

GURTOV, M., ed. *The Transformation of Socialism: Perestroika and Reform in the Soviet Union and China* (Boulder, CO, 1990).

HARLO, V., ed. *Gorbachev and Europe* (New York, 1990).

HAZAN, B. *Gorbachev and His Enemies . . .* (Boulder, CO, 1990).

HIDEN, J., and P. SALMON. *The Baltic Nations and Europe . . . in the 20th Century* (White Plains, NY, 1991).

HILL, K. *The Soviet Union on the Brink: . . . Christianity and Glasnost* (Portland, OR, 1991).

HILL, R. J. *Communist Politics Under the Knife: Surgery or Autopsy?* (London and New York, 1990).

HOSKING, G. *The Awakening of the Soviet Union* (Cambridge, MA, 1990).

HOUGH, J. *Russia and the West: Gorbachev and the Politics of Reform* (New York, 1988).

ITO, T., ed. *Facing Up to the Past: Soviet Historiography and Perestroika* (Sapporo, Japan, 1989).

JACOBSEN, C. G., ed. *Soviet Foreign Policy: New Dynamics, New Themes* (New York, 1989).

JONES, T. A. *Perestroika: Gorbachev's Social Revolution* (Westview, CT, 1990).

JOYCE, W., et al., eds. *Gorbachev and Gorbachevism* (New York, 1989).

KAGARLITSKY, B. *Farewell Perestroika: A Soviet Chronicle* (London, 1990).

KAISER, R. G. *Why Gorbachev Happened: His Triumphs and His Failures* (New York, 1991). (Excellent summary of Gorbachev's years in power.)

KNIGHT, A. *The KGB: Police and Politics in the Soviet Union* (Boston, 1988).

LAPIDUS, G. *State and Society in the Soviet Union* (Boulder, CO, 1989).

———, and V. ZASLAVSKY, eds. *From Union to Commonwealth: Nationalism and Separatism in the Soviet Republics* (New York, 1992).

LAQUEUR, W. *Black Hundred: The Rise of the Extreme Right in Russia* (New York, 1994).

LEWIN, M. *The Gorbachev Phenomenon* (Berkeley, 1988).

LIGACHEV, Y. *Inside Gorbachev's Kremlin: The Memoirs of Yegor Ligachev* (Boulder, CO, 1996).

LÖWENHARDT, J., J. OZINGA, and E. VAN REE. *The Rise and Fall of the Soviet Politburo* (New York, 1992).

MARPLES, D. *Chernobyl and Nuclear Power in the USSR* (New York, 1987).

MEDVEDEV, R. *The Truth About Chernobyl* (New York, 1991).

MEDVEDEV, Z. *Soviet Agriculture* (New York, 1987).

MELVILLE, A., and G. LAPIDUS. *The Glasnost Papers: Voices on Reform from Moscow* (Boulder, CO, 1990).

MIKHEYEV, D. *The Rise and Fall of Gorbachev* (Indianapolis, 1992).

MILLER, J. *Mikhail Gorbachev and the End of Soviet Power* (New York, 1993).

MOSKOFF, W. *Hard Times: Impoverishment and Protest in the Perestroika Years* (Armonk, NY, 1993).

OLIVIER, R. *Islam and Resistance in Afghanistan* (Cambridge, 1986).

PLESSIX, F. DU. *Soviet Women* (New York, 1990).

PRYCE-JONES, D. *The War That Never Was: The Fall of the Soviet Empire, 1985–1991* (London, 1995).

RALEIGH, D. *Soviet Historians and Perestroika: The First Phase* (Armonk, NY, 1990).

RAMET, S., ed. *Religious Policy in the Soviet Union* (New York, 1993).

SAIVETZ, C. R. *The Soviet Union and the Gulf in the 1980s* (Boulder, CO, 1989).

SAKWA, R. *Gorbachev and His Reforms, 1985–1990* (New York and London, 1991).

SENN, A. E. *Gorbachev's Failure in Lithuania* (New York, 1995).

SHANSAB, N. *Soviet Expansion in the Third World* (Silver Spring, MD, 1986).

SHCHERBAK, I. *Chernobyl: A Documentary Story,* trans. Ian Press (New York, 1989).

SMITH, G. *Soviet Politics: Continuity and Contradiction* (New York, 1987).

TARASULO, I., ed. *Gorbachev and Glasnost: Viewpoints from the Soviet Press* (Wilmington, DE, 1989).

———, ed. *Perils of Perestroika: Viewpoints from the Soviet Press, 1989–1991* (Wilmington, DE, 1992).

URBAN, M. *War in Afghanistan* (New York, 1988).

WILLERTON, J. P. *Patronage and Politics in the USSR* (New York, 1992).

WOODBY, S. *Gorbachev and the Decline of Ideology in Soviet Foreign Policy* (Boulder, CO, 1989).

YANOV, A. *The Russian Challenge and the Year 2000,* trans. J. Rosenthal (New York, 1987).

ZACEK, J. S. *The Gorbachev Generation: Issues in Soviet Foreign Policy* (New York, 1988).

ZASLAVSKYA, T. *The Second Socialist Revolution . . . ,* trans. S. Davies and J. Warren (Bloomington, IN, 1991).

43

Soviet Culture after Stalin, 1953–1991

The death of Stalin ushered in the first of a series of "thaws" in Soviet culture culminating in the Gorbachev revolution. A largely spontaneous outburst of activity in the arts, coupled with Khrushchev's efforts to rid the Soviet Union of the worst aspects of Stalinism, produced a remarkable cultural revival. Soviet cultural policies under Khrushchev and Brezhnev fluctuated between "thaws" and "freezes," but there was no full-scale return to the Stalin-Zhdanov approach. But until the Gorbachev era, socialist realism persisted as the guiding principle in literature and the arts, and the regime intervened decisively to prevent overt expression of dissident viewpoints— as the careers of Alexander Solzhenitsyn, Boris Pasternak, Andrei Amalrik, and Zhores Medvedev revealed.

The Thaw, 1953–1956

An article of May 1953 deploring the lack of human emotion in Soviet films reflected an initial cautious reaction against Zhdanovism. It decried

depersonalized "human machines," standard in Soviet films, as untrue to life. A heroine agreeing to marry the hero only if he overfulfilled his production norm was a travesty on human feelings, it claimed. Socialist quotas were important for socialist realism, but individual lives amounted to more than that. Such a view could not have been expressed openly in Stalin's final years. In the new, freer air bold ideas found their way into print. The new collective leadership recognized the utter sterility of Soviet culture under Zhdanovism and permitted freer discussion of alternative approaches.

An article that November by composer Aram Khachaturian, "On Creative Boldness and Imagination," directly attacked bureaucratic interference, which had almost destroyed Soviet musical culture: "We must once and for all reject the worthless interference in musical composition as practiced by the musical establishments. Problems of composition cannot be solved bureaucratically." Without repudiating socialist realism, Khachaturian insisted on artistic integrity. "Let the individual artist be trusted more fully, and not be constantly supervised and suspected."[1]

Others joined the burgeoning criticism. The respected poet Alexander Tvardovskii, editor of the prestigious journal *New World,* denounced Soviet literature as "arid, contrived and unreal." Ilia Ehrenburg, a well-known author and former apologist for Stalin, concluded sadly that Russian classics were more popular with the public than contemporary authors because the older works dealt with human emotions and feelings. Could anyone "imagine ordering Tolstoy to write *Anna Karenina*?"[2]

Not everyone shared these liberal views. Stalinist hard-liners had their spokespersons too, and there was some sharp infighting. But party leaders allowed the artistic intelligentsia freer rein. The mood of the times was captured in Ehrenburg's short novel *The Thaw* (1954), which aptly describes these years. Stalinist Russia had been frozen solid, rigid, and somber. The post-Stalin era was an intellectual spring heralded by melting of ice that had prevented growth. Ehrenburg's novel marked a new path for Soviet culture to follow. Writers of "the thaw" stressed recognition of the gulf between the real and the ideal and emphasized truth in all its complexity, rejected tyranny and fear, and expressed concern for human dignity and the individual; they admitted shortcomings in Soviet life. Ehrenburg believed that these fundamental artistic aims could best be achieved within socialist realism. Great enthusiasm about these issues led to an outburst of literary activity from 1954 to 1956. Poetry annuals and literary almanacs appeared without formal approval by the Writers' Union, and new poetic and prose talents emerged.

Despite high optimism among younger Soviet writers and artists in these years, conservative and Stalinist writers fought hard to defend Zhdanovist principles and retain control of literary institutions. At the Second Congress of Soviet Writers in December 1954, A. Surkov, the Stalinist secretary of the Writers' Union, sharply denounced the new mood and trends and demanded a return to Zhdanovist ideological purity. But others at the congress insisted on even greater freedom, rehabilitation of disgraced writers, recognition of émigré writers, and publication of banned works. Liberals in the Writers' Union looked to Ehrenburg and young writers; conservatives relied on old-line Stalinists who controlled the union. Because party leaders did not intervene, the two factions fought to a stalemate.

At the 20th Party Congress (February 1956) the pendulum swung toward the liberals. Surkov's hard-line diatribe was answered boldly by Mikhail Sholokhov, who denounced literary bureaucrats and hacks who claimed to speak for all Soviet literature. "A writer can learn nothing from Surkov," he concluded. "Why do we need such leaders?" That Sholokhov said this openly at the 20th Party Congress indicates a climate tolerating intellectual debate. Khrushchev's secret speech had compromised many Stalinist writers, temporarily weakening their influence in the Writers' Union. Thus some works sharply critical of aspects of contemporary Soviet life were published. In 1956 *New World* issued Vladimir Dudintsev's novel *Not by Bread Alone,* which exemplified liberal cultural trends. It castigated the exploitation and victimization of talent by arrogant Soviet bureaucrats, outraging literary bureaucrats like Surkov.

Dr. Zhivago and the Refreeze

In this optimistic atmosphere of 1956, Boris Pasternak (1890–1960) submitted his now famous novel *Dr. Zhivago* to *New World.* Pasternak enjoyed the reputation of an outstanding poetic talent even before the Revolution, but had remained largely silent under Stalin, publishing occasional poems, essays, and translations. His extraordinary translations of Shakespeare set a standard for all Soviet translations. Pasternak remained an aloof loner and internal exile, quietly completing his novel in 1955. Revealing his political naiveté, he fully expected *New World* to publish *Dr. Zhivago.*

---

[1] Aram Khachaturian, *Sovietskaia Muzyka,* November 1953.
[2] Quoted in E. J. Brown, *Russian Literature Since the Revolution* (New York, 1969), p. 241.

Like Zamiatin and Pilniak 30 years before, he gave a manuscript copy to an Italian publisher, Feltrinelli, for preparation of an Italian edition after the work appeared in the USSR. To Pasternak's dismay, *New World*'s editors politely refused to publish the novel, but Feltrinelli, despite Surkov's protests, published an Italian translation in November 1957. Soon *Dr. Zhivago* appeared in English, and an original Russian version was published in the West. It was hailed abroad as a masterpiece, and Pasternak was awarded the Nobel Prize for literature in October 1958, but he was pressured by party authorities to reject it. Viciously denounced in the Soviet press, he was expelled from the Writers' Union and constantly hounded by the authorities, literally to death in 1960, another victim of the Soviet literary inquisition.

The intensely personal *Dr. Zhivago* traces the story of Iurii Zhivago from prerevolutionary times through the Soviet period. Zhivago's life is a shambles; he never uses his medical training. His life's work is a slender volume of poetry included at the end of the novel—Zhivago's legacy to humankind. Pasternak was proclaiming that though he had produced nothing practical, his poetry, like Zhivago's, could stimulate people to think and act creatively. Zhivago's poems, among Pasternak's most profound creations, contain the novel's essence, affirming the constant renewal of life as suggested by Zhivago's name, meaning "living" (*zhivoi*). Pasternak served as a living bridge from the prerevolutionary Russian literary tradition that stressed human spiritual qualities to contemporary Soviet life. In *Dr. Zhivago* Pasternak's essentially religious conception of the future is based on unwavering faith in resurrection and salvation for Zhivago and Russia itself.

Believing the Soviet public unprepared for such a message, party authorities prevented the novel's publication in the USSR. However, "Lara's Theme" from the 1965 film's score became a hit in Moscow, although the film was banned there.

Even before the Pasternak "affair," the pendulum had begun swinging back as the screws tightened again on Soviet culture. Soviet armed intervention in Hungary in October 1956 struck at burgeoning de-Stalinization. The more relaxed atmosphere of the thaw ended as Khrushchev moved decisively to halt a headlong race toward liberalization. He warned students at Moscow University to be careful or they would face the full force of his regime. Two hundred students were expelled and the rest intimidated. Stalinism remained fresh in people's minds.

Culture under Khrushchev

Khrushchev's de-Stalinization campaign had loosened the Soviet grip on the Communist Bloc. Hard-pressed by party conservatives, he adopted a more conventional cultural militancy. The abrupt change in official policy caught many off guard. Late in 1956 the Soviet poet Evgenii Yevtushenko published a provocative poem proclaiming: "Certainly there have been changes; but behind the speeches/Some murky game is being played./ We talk and talk about things we didn't mention yesterday;/ We say nothing about the things we did ourselves." This devastating criticism of party leaders and Khrushchev revealed that the more Stalin's actions were discredited, the more present leaders were implicated in his crimes. Such an attack could not go unchallenged. Yevtushenko was summarily dismissed from the Komsomol (Young Communist League) and stripped of many privileges.

When intellectuals proved slow to respond to Khrushchev's insistence on greater ideological conformity, he personally demanded compliance with his directives. He told Moscow writers at a garden party at his dacha that they were expendable; unless they cooperated, he would use force. Hungary's difficulties in the 1956 revolt could have been avoided, he declared, if intellectuals who had stirred up rebellion had been shot. Khrushchev assured the stunned writers: "My hand will not tremble" [if force is required]. The initial post-Stalin thaw had fallen victim to Khrushchev's political requirements and ambition.

Consolidating his personal power by March 1958, Khrushchev cautiously resumed de-Stalinization and built bridges to the West. Some foreign travel was permitted, and cultural exchanges were negotiated with Western countries, including the United States. The literary thaw resumed. Promising and talented young writers published works that focused more on individual concerns in a complex industrial society rather than on "building socialism." Writers picked up threads of the earlier thaw and wove them into a new, more sophisticated literature. Despite opposition from party conservatives, fearful of liberal works and cultural rapprochement with the West, the liberals regained their ascendancy. Debate, disagreement, innovation, and experimentation were tolerated within limits. At the Third Congress of Soviet Writers in 1959, Khrushchev expressed satisfaction with the cultural atmosphere. He would be liberal, in Soviet terms, if writers supported the party.

Numerous works appearing in the next years testified to the imaginative power of young, unknown Soviet writers such as Aksionov, Nagibin, Kazakov, Tendryakov, and Voinovich. Discarding the literary didacticism and moralizing of much socialist realist literature, their stories and novels revealed a renewed concern for style, psychology, and human emotions. Attracting much popular attention, their works were avidly read and discussed. Taboo subjects were now openly debated. In 1961 Yevtushenko published his famous *Babi Yar,* an extraordinarily powerful poem about the 33,000 Soviet Jews slaughtered by the Nazis in 1941 in Babi Yar ravine near Kiev. Memorializing the innocent Jews, the poem castigated anti-Semitism, whether in fascist or Communist guise. Russian anti-Semitism still "rises in the fumes of alcohol and in drunken conversations." The poem was attacked violently by conservatives as slandering the heroic Russian people who had sacrificed so much to destroy Nazism. Liberals lauded Yevtushenko's courage in confronting squarely a problem deeply rooted in the Russian psyche.

The liberal tendency gained ground elsewhere, too. Early in 1962 the respected art critic Mikhail Alpatov published a defense of modern, abstract art. Others followed, suggesting that "the 20th

Monument at Babi Yar.

century is becoming an age of triumphant abstractions." Why was the USSR so backward in appreciating modern art? Moscow's venerable Tretiakov Gallery began cautiously opening its vaults to exhibit some innovative early-20th-century Russian artworks, such as those of Kandinskii and Malevich. The poet Bella Akhmadulina proclaimed optimistically in 1962: "I think the time has become happy for us, that it now runs in our favor. Not only can my comrades work, but they are given every encouragement in their endeavor."[3]

During 1962 the liberals pushed their advantage. In October Yevtushenko's poem "The Heirs of Stalin" appeared in *Pravda.* It was a remarkable commentary on the times: "He [Stalin] has worked out a scheme./ He merely curled up for a nap./ And I appeal to our government with a

---

[3] *Literaturnaia Gazeta,* October 2, 1962, p. 4.

plea:/ to double,/ and treble/ the guard at his slab,/ so that Stalin will not rise again/ and, with Stalin —the past."[4] Yevtushenko bluntly confronted the possibility of the revival of Stalinism:

No, Stalin has not given up.
He thinks he can outsmart death.
We carried him from the mausoleum.
But how carry Stalin's heirs away from Stalin?
Some of his retired heirs tend roses thinking
    in secret
Their enforced leisure will not last. . .

No wonder Stalin's heirs seem to suffer
these days from heart trouble.
They, the former henchmen, hate this era
Of emptied prison camps
And auditoriums full of people listening to poets.[5]

Acknowledging that he had personally authorized publication of Yevtushenko's poem, Khrushchev hinted at a new round of de-Stalinization.

Further confirmation of this came when Khrushchev authorized the unexpurgated publication of Alexander Solzhenitsyn's *One Day in the Life of Ivan Denisovich* in *New World*'s November 1962 issue. Solzhenitsyn's first published work was a powerful portrayal of everyday life in a Stalinist prison camp. Based on his own experiences in the camps, it was understated, dispassionate, and nonpolemical, bringing to life in searing detail one ordinary day in Ivan Denisovich's prison life. It recorded the agony of an inmate reduced to animal level for survival but whose dignity and humanity remain intact. Ivan Denisovich symbolized the indomitable courage of the Russian people in their continuing struggle for freedom and human dignity. *One Day* became an instant sensation, touching millions of Soviet citizens who had experienced years of days like Ivan Denisovich's. Public sentiment about the brutal inhumanity of Stalin's terror was stirred again in apparent preparation for renewed de-Stalinization.

Just as this new campaign began, Khrushchev was immersed in the turbulent political waters of the Cuban missile crisis (October 1962) and an open Sino-Soviet dispute (see Chapter 39). These crises abroad combined with growing economic problems at home again threatened Khrushchev's control of party and state. Sharp consumer price increases that autumn caused outbreaks of violence among workers. All this persuaded Khrushchev to renounce further de-Stalinization.

"Stalin's heirs" prepared a counterattack on the cultural front in November 1962. To a retrospective art exhibition, "Thirty Years of Soviet Art," at the huge Manezh Gallery near the Kremlin were added about 75 modernistic canvases and sculptures, apparently as an elaborate "provocation" by cultural conservatives. On December 1 Khrushchev and several Presidium members visited the gallery unannounced. He spent most of his time in three small rooms viewing modernistic works of contemporary Soviet artists. His reaction was what conservatives had anticipated—violent and vulgar. Khrushchev's vicious verbal attack startled liberals, then enjoying a heyday. Pausing before an abstract painting, he remarked:

I would say this is just a mess. . . . Polyanskii [Presidium member] told me a couple of days ago that when his daughter got married she was given a picture of what was supposed to be a lemon. It consisted of some messy yellow lines that looked . . . as though some child had done his business on the canvas when his mother was away and then spread it around with his hands.

Further on, he lashed out against jazz music: "When I hear jazz, it's as if I had gas on the stomach. I used to think it was static when I heard it on the radio." Proceeding through the exhibition, he declared:

As long as I am chairman of the Council of Ministers, we are going to support a genuine art. We aren't going to give a kopeck for pictures painted by jackasses.

Speaking to one artist but referring to all modernist painters, Khrushchev fulminated:

---

[4] Evgenii Yevtushenko, *The Collected Poems, 1952–1990,* ed. A. Todd, trans, G. Reavey (New York, 1991).

[5] Quoted in Priscilla Johnson, *Khrushchev and the Arts,* trans. G. Reavey (Cambridge, MA, 1965), pp. 93–95.

You've either got to get out [of the USSR] or paint differently. As you are, there's no future for you on our soil. . . . Gentlemen, we are declaring war on you.[6]

Hours later began a war for "ideological purity." Press editorials demanded that all unions of writers, artists, composers, and cinema workers be amalgamated in order to prevent nonconformity. The message was clear: centralize and control. Some Stalinist bureaucrats ceased "tending roses" and returned to prominent posts. At a meeting between party authorities and cultural leaders to discuss the current situation, Leonid Ilyichev, the Central Committee's chief ideologist, deplored recent demands by intellectuals to end all Soviet censorship and attacked the inexorable advance of Western "bourgeois" influences on Soviet culture. Following his hard-line speech ensued remarkably candid informal exchanges between party officials and writers and artists. Ehrenburg boldly defended the new freedom, insisting that modern art was not a cover for political reaction. Yevtushenko defended abstract painters, arguing they needed time to straighten out problems in their art. Khrushchev reportedly broke in shouting: "The grave straightens out the hunchback." Unintimidated, Yevtushenko retorted: "Nikita Sergeevich [Khrushchev], we have come a long way since the time when only the grave straightened out hunchbacks."[7] The assembled writers and artists broke into applause with Khrushchev joining in. The intellectuals' unity and sense of common purpose at this meeting provided conservatives with ammunition in the battle against modernism.

The affair of Shostakovich's 13th Symphony further revealed the tense situation. Its first movement was a musical version of Yevtushenko's poem *Babi Yar.* The new symphony was to premiere the evening after the great gathering of party officials and intellectuals. Allegedly, Ilyichev demanded its withdrawal, but Shostakovich

refused. At the premiere many musicians and the choir hesitated, fearing reprisals. After a second performance, further performances were canceled. As Moscow's frigid winter descended, a new ideological freeze chilled the intellectual community.

It culminated in March 1963 at a gathering of more than 600 intellectuals. Ilyichev again attacked writers in general and Ehrenburg in particular. Ehrenburg had argued in his memoirs, *People, Years, Life* (1960–1961), that he and others had known full well what was occurring in the USSR in the 1930s but had to remain silent with "clenched teeth." Ilyichev accused Ehrenburg of enjoying special privileges under Stalin and of having frequently praised him hypocritically whereas he (Ilyichev) and his colleagues had flattered Stalin allegedly out of sincere conviction. Ehrenburg considered that Ilyichev's false remarks made a reply unnecessary.

Khrushchev then delivered a devastating speech partially reaffirming Stalin's straightforward, uncomplicated tastes in art and literature and partially rehabilitating Stalin himself. Khrushchev sought to exonerate Stalin's entourage, and himself, of complicity in his crimes. He then realized the dangers of further de-Stalinization, which might raise questions such as "What were you doing during Stalin's criminal rampages?" Ilyichev affirmed he had not known what was happening. Ehrenburg argued that he knew of Stalin's crimes but had remained silent, thus admitting complicity or cowardice. It was clearly better to leave Stalin's ghost alone. De-Stalinization ended as Stalin's conservative heirs used abstract art to dissuade the party from further liberalization. Khrushchev had to yield to mounting pressure within the party, and his personal cultural tastes seemed closer to the conservatives than to the liberals. Anyway, the lid slammed down again. Throughout 1963, at meetings organized by the party, leading cultural figures acknowledged their "errors" and pledged to abide by the party's wise guidance in all matters. Shostakovich, Yevtushenko, Voznesenskii, and many others submitted. Open ferment ended or

---

[6] Johnson, *Khrushchev and the Arts,* pp. 101–105.
[7] Johnson, p. 121.

was submerged. A light frost prevailed with only occasional sunshine.

Culture under Brezhnev

Khrushchev's fall in October 1964 did not herald a new thaw. Brezhnev and Kosygin maintained the status quo: comprehensive cultural controls and inflexible conformity. Writing for "the desk drawer" or painting for "the closet" continued, becoming more widespread after fleeting moments of relative freedom. Literary works in increasing numbers circulated surreptitiously in manuscript copies; artists showed their latest abstract works privately. An organized Soviet counterculture emerged.

New developments in liberal literary circles included *samizdat* and *tamizdat*. *Samizdat,* a play on *Gosizdat*—State Publishing House—meant "self-publication" by authors, not the state. Because individuals lacked access to printing presses, most *samizdat* materials were produced on typewriters or mimeograph machines. Smudged carbon copies circulated from hand to hand; new copies were made when needed. *Tamizdat* referred to materials published abroad—"over there"—that were then smuggled back into the Soviet Union. By these means a considerable body of clandestine literature accumulated in the USSR not subject to official control or censorship.

The Trial of Siniavskii and Daniel

Writing for the desk drawer was often frustrating and unrewarding, so authors sought other means of uncensored expression. Publishing abroad had always been dangerous, as the fate of Zamiatin and Pasternak had shown. Their works had been published abroad out of confusion and misunderstanding, not from conscious intent to evade Soviet censorship. That did not save those authors from vilification and abuse, but neither one was put on trial. Andrei Siniavskii, a distinguished literary critic, and Iuli Daniel, a young writer, consciously evaded party literary controls by smuggling manuscripts out of the USSR for publication abroad under the pseudonyms Abram Tertz (Siniavskii) and Nikolai Arzhak (Daniel), beginning in 1956 when the first thaw ended. For nine years they escaped detection and published stories, short novels, and essays highly critical of Soviet life. These were the first examples of *samizdat* and *tamizdat*.

Siniavskii's publications abroad included a long essay, "On Socialist Realism" (1960), denouncing that doctrine as old-fashioned and inappropriate for the modern USSR. Soviet literature was "a monstrous salad" whose content was distorted by a rigidly imposed form, in which bureaucrats regularly interfered. Siniavskii urged abandoning socialist realism and returning to Mayakovskii's literary experimentation of the 1920s. Also published abroad was *The Trial Begins* (1960), a fictional exposé of Soviet justice as fraudulent, cynical, and arbitrary. Other works poked fun at Soviet foibles or satirized Soviet life. All criticized Soviet institutions, but none was directly anti-Soviet.

Daniel's works were, from a Western perspective, rather harmless literary exercises, less sophisticated than Siniavskii's. Of his four stories published abroad, "This Is Moscow Speaking" and "Hands" are the most interesting. The former is a macabre tale about a Public Murder Day supposedly decreed by the Politburo: On August 10, 1961, all citizens over 16 could kill almost anyone they wished between 6 A.M. and midnight. When people failed to use this license to kill, the party condemned it as sabotage, thus implying that mass terror could be reintroduced in the USSR without much public response. The story "Hands" deals with the psychological impact of terror. A former Cheka officer suffers from chronically shaking hands after being ordered as a young secret policeman to shoot priests accused of counterrevolutionary activities. His friends played a joke on him by loading his pistol with blank cartridges. When the priests implored the young officer not to shoot, advancing with outstretched hands, the officer had shot repeatedly as the priests "miraculously" continued to advance. That experience

ITAR-TASS/SOVFOTO

Andrei Siniavskii (right) and Iuli Daniel at their Moscow trial in
February 1966 for allegedly slandering the Soviet system in writings
published abroad.

so unnerved the officer that his hands shook
constantly.

The KGB (security police) mounted an intensive campaign to identify Tertz and Arzhak. (Computers analyzed their writing styles.) Finally,
Siniavskii and Daniel were arrested in September
1965, accused under the infamous Article 70 of the
criminal code of disseminating "slanderous" and
"defamatory" inventions about the Soviet system.
After the defendants were convicted in the press, a
public trial was held in February 1966. Siniavskii
received seven years of hard labor (the maximum
sentence) and Daniel five years.

The Siniavskii-Daniel trial was unique in Soviet
justice. Never before had writers been tried for
their writings. Many writers—including Zamiatin,
Zoshchenko, and Pasternak—had been publicly
denounced and accused of various "crimes," and
many more had disappeared during the purges,
but none had been tried in open court. A brilliant
young Leningrad poet and eventual Nobel laureate, Josef Brodskii, had been tried and convicted in
1964, not for his writings but as a "parasite" lack-

ing gainful employment. (He was a poet but not a
member of the Writers' Union.) Unlike defendants
in other Soviet public trials, Siniavskii and Daniel
defended themselves valiantly.

The harsh sentences shocked Soviet intellectuals. With remarkable unity, liberal intellectuals in
the arts and sciences wrote to party authorities to
protest the treatment of Siniavskii and Daniel. The
only major Soviet writer to support the regime
fully over this issue was Mikhail Sholokhov, Nobel
Prize laureate, who declared that the sentences
were much too mild! Party leaders were unmoved
by the storm of protest over the sentences. The
trial had aimed to intimidate dissenters. Siniavskii
and Daniel were scapegoats for a new "get tough"
policy. The trial warned Soviet intellectuals that all
works by Soviet citizens were subject to censorship. Succumbing to public pressure would have
undermined that aim.

Still, the Siniavskii-Daniel trial backfired,
becoming a milestone in a continuing struggle
between party leaders and the intellectual elite.

From the 1920s onward the literary intelligentsia had been preoccupied with a search for truth based on the conviction that it could be found only in artistic or intellectual freedom. Writers had sought to liberate the creative process from arbitrary party interference. They sought to foster the artistic and moral values of traditional Russian literature: deep concern for the individual, psychological truth, intellectual honesty, and a multifaceted realism. Siniavskii's and Daniel's advocacy of these values led them into direct conflict with the authorities. After their trial, the Soviet intelligentsia realized that the artistic rights they sought could be achieved only with basic political freedoms.

This new consciousness triggered by the Siniavskii-Daniel affair created an unprecedented movement of dissent. Questions were asked about topics previously taboo even in liberal periods of Soviet history. The lack of basic rights, such as freedom from fear and freedom of speech, press, and assembly—all supposedly guaranteed by the Stalin Constitution—was widely discussed by Soviet intellectuals. The realization grew that Soviet citizens' fundamental rights were violated daily. The Constitution did not authorize censorship. How, then, could the party dictate what writers could or could not write or proscribe peaceful protest? These questions deeply disturbed many intellectuals.

Protesting the harsh sentences in the Siniavskii-Daniel trial, four young intellectuals, led by Alexander Ginzburg, collected extensive materials on the trial, including a verbatim transcript. Their aim was to induce the authorities to reopen the case and review the sentences. In January 1967 copies of these materials were sent to the KGB and Supreme Soviet deputies. The official response was to arrest the four young compilers, but a copy of the "white paper" had reached the West and was published. In January 1968 the four were tried and convicted under the notorious Article 70. The sentences of two, Iurii Galanskov and Ginzburg, were harsher than those of Siniavskii and Daniel. The Galanskov-Ginzburg trial

evoked unprecedented public protests and triggered a broader civil-rights movement.

Andrei Sakharov, the leading Soviet nuclear physicist and "father of the Soviet H-bomb," organized the Human Rights Movement in 1970. It was designed to protest official policies that violated fundamental individual rights guaranteed by the Soviet Constitution. These freedoms were specified in the UN Declaration on Human Rights, which had been signed by the USSR. Prominent Soviet intellectuals joined in the clamor of protest. The regime responded with further unpublicized arrests and repression. The dissenters sought to inform the public of illegal official actions in *The Chronicle of Current Events,* a remarkable *samizdat* account of arrests, harassments, and exiles. The Brezhnev regime found it increasingly difficult to hide behind a veil of secrecy. The Human Rights Movement aimed not to overthrow the regime or alter the basic Soviet legal structure but merely to have existing laws enforced fairly and uniformly. Its patriotic members sought to have Soviet constitutional provisions observed in practice.

Alexander Solzhenitsyn

Intimately associated with the movement of dissent in the late 1960s and early 1970s was Alexander Solzhenitsyn. His renown grew steadily after publication of his novel *One Day in the Life of Ivan Denisovich* in 1962, though only a few more of his stories were published. Born in 1918, he studied mathematics and physics, became a teacher, and fought valiantly as an artillery officer in World War II. Near the war's end he was arrested and sentenced to the labor camps for referring to Stalin in a personal letter seized by the security police as "the man with the moustache." After eight years in labor camps and three more in exile in Central Asia, Solzhenitsyn in 1956 was considered fully rehabilitated, all charges against him were dismissed as groundless, and his civil rights were restored. *One Day* earned him recognition as a powerful writer and moral authority. Nevertheless, his few published works enraged party conservatives, and under Brezhnev the authorities decided

Alexander Solzhenitsyn.

UPI/Corbis-Bettmann

despises. Rusanov's antithesis is another cancer patient, Kostoglotov, a veteran of the labor camps and exile. He has suffered and survived, but no longer values life nor fears death. With literally nothing to lose, he has much strength to combat cancer. Rusanov, by contrast, has everything to lose—position, wealth, and family—and fear of death makes him desperate. He cannot accept his condition or combat it rationally.

Another Solzhenitsyn novel, *The First Circle,* an extension on a different level of *One Day,* was published in the West in 1968, but not in Brezhnev's USSR. It depicts a prison housing scholars, scientists, and engineers, all convicted of state crimes. Required to work on state scientific projects, they do not feel the physical anguish of Ivan Denisovich; although well-fed and well-housed, they experience a mental anguish more degrading and destructive than physical suffering. Again Solzhenitsyn deals with a central theme that reappears constantly in his works: the indomitable human spirit triumphant over adversity.

Another of Solzhenitsyn's major works is the broad historical panorama *August 1914,* published in the West in 1971, the first of a series of historical works dealing with Russia's travails in World War I and the Revolutions of 1917. Solzhenitsyn contrasts the Russian people's heroic struggle with the tsarist government's criminal incompetence. A historical parallel between Russia in World War I and the Soviet Union in World War II is evident.

Publication in the West of Solzhenitsyn's works led to a mounting campaign of persecution and public vilification against him. His international reputation and the Brezhnev regime's sensitivity to world opinion provided him a security that other dissenters, except for Sakharov, lacked. Like Kostoglotov in *The Cancer Ward,* Solzhenitsyn had suffered all that the Stalin regime could subject him to, and life held no terrors short of physical annihilation; he could not be intimidated or silenced. He spoke out courageously against censorship, repression, and injustice. "No one can bar the road to truth," he proclaimed in a famous letter circulated at the Fourth Congress of Soviet Writers in 1967, "and to advance its cause I am

that no more of his works should be published. Despite this decision, Alexander Tvardovskii, editor of *New World,* accepted a major Solzhenitsyn novel, *The Cancer Ward,* for publication there in 1968. The type was already set when the party abruptly ordered Tvardovskii to halt publication. The Galanskov-Ginzburg trial and accompanying protests caused the regime to block publication of a novel dealing with repression, abuse of power, and moral decay. Meanwhile a manuscript copy reached the West and was promptly published over Solzhenitsyn's objections. Nonetheless, the Soviet press orchestrated vicious attacks on the author.

The Cancer Ward deals with the terrifying experiences of Rusanov, a high Soviet official. After discovering he has cancer, Rusanov is unable to use his connections to enter an elite clinic and is confined in an ordinary cancer ward, packed with inconsequential, unsympathetic people whom he prepared to accept even death." Solzhenitsyn demanded an end to all censorship, insisting on absolute freedom for writers and artists:

> Literature cannot develop in between the categories of "permitted" and "not permitted," "about this you may write" and "about this you may not." Literature that is not the breath of contemporary society, that does not transmit the pains and fears of that society, that does not warn in time against threatening moral and social dangers—such literature does not deserve the name of literature; it is only a facade. Such literature loses the confidence of its own people, and its published works are used as wastepaper instead of being read.[8]

In 1970 Solzhenitsyn was awarded the Nobel Prize for literature. The anti-Pasternak scenario of 1958–1959 was reenacted as party hacks attacked Solzhenitsyn as a "leper" and had him expelled from the Writers' Union. This public assault failed to intimidate Solzhenitsyn as it had Pasternak. He proudly accepted the Nobel award but declined to go to Stockholm to receive it for fear of being denied reentry to the USSR. His eloquent Nobel lecture was smuggled to the West and published there in 1972. It was a dignified plea for freedom everywhere and reaffirmed strongly the moral responsibility of the writer and artist "to conquer falsehood." Harassment of Solzhenitsyn intensified in 1973. Fearing for his life, he managed to transmit some key manuscripts to friends in the West to prevent his enemies from silencing him even by death. He instructed his friends to publish them if anything happened to him.

In September 1973 the KGB pressured a Solzhenitsyn typist into revealing the whereabouts of a major underground manuscript she had typed. Solzhenitsyn promptly signaled his Western friends to publish the manuscript, previously smuggled abroad. The first volume of the monumental *The Gulag Archipelago, 1918–1956* was published in Paris in December 1973 and in numerous translations, including English, in 1974.

Volumes two and three were issued in 1975. *The Gulag*, a powerfully moving history of the Soviet prison camp system, is dedicated "To all those who did not survive." Solzhenitsyn traces the prison camp system back to Lenin, although it developed into a monstrous structure only under Stalin. This remarkable account of man's inhumanity to man was based on Solzhenitsyn's personal experiences in the camps and those of hundreds of former prisoners (*zeks*) who shared their stories with him. Publication of *The Gulag Archipelago* in the West provoked an unprecedented campaign of slander and abuse of Solzhenitsyn in the USSR and an equally tremendous international outpouring of support for him. The Brezhnev regime hesitated momentarily in the face of world opinion, but in February 1974 had Solzhenitsyn arrested and charged with treason. The next day he was taken to the Moscow airport and put on a plane for West Germany and involuntary exile. Soon his family joined him and they settled in the United States, where he continued to write and denounce tyranny until his return to Russia in 1994.

In exile Solzhenitsyn identified himself with Russian Orthodoxy and criticized injustice and corruption not only in the Soviet Union but also in the West. He denounced détente, arguing that it helped perpetuate the Soviet dictatorship. Solzhenitsyn grew increasingly strident in his criticisms of the Soviet Union. Like Alexander Herzen, a 19th-century Russian exile in Europe, Solzhenitsyn continued from a Vermont farm his struggle against tyranny in his native land.

Other Soviet Writers

Under Brezhnev significant changes occurred in Soviet culture. While the state continued to determine what would be published officially, writers and artists achieved greater latitude than under Stalin or even under Khrushchev. During the 1970s some literary and artistic experimentation in form was permitted, producing some excellent results. The best Soviet writers created a literature with credible characters in real situations. They

---

[8] Quoted in *Problems of Communism* 17, no. 5, p. 38.

wrote about personal conflicts and aspirations, not building communism. Renouncing the reformist political writing of the mid-1950s, they stressed concern with self and everyday problems and shifted away from the novel to the novella and short story. In this genre authors focused on isolated incidents, chance occurrences, and private moods and feelings.

The best writers under Brezhnev walked a tightrope between free literary expression and state-defined aesthetics. Iurii Nagibin's stories portray human love and passion on an intimate level. After visiting the United States, he described his impressions with great insight. Iurii Kazakov's characters have received little from Soviet society and are embittered, frustrated rejects. The characters of talented, youthful Vasili Aksionov often reflect dehumanizing aspects of the Soviet regime and closely resemble the drifters and dreamers of American fiction of the 1950s and 1960s. In the 1970s he examined the macabre, pursuing new directions that ultimately proved officially unacceptable.

The derevenshchiki ("village writers") favored contemporary rural settings, often in Siberia, for tightly woven, realistic portrayals of the peasantry and daily life. Valentin Rasputin explored the pathos of peasant life objectively and clearly. His novella Live and Remember portrays the tribulations of a peasant deserter from World War II who depends on his wife's wisdom to outwit the authorities. In this simple story of struggle for survival, Rasputin passes no judgments. His gripping tale of rural life, "Money for Maria," describes the problems of a peasant woman managing the village general store. An official audit reveals a large cash shortage for which she is blamed. Respected in the village, she receives much support, but even the entire village cannot cover the shortage. In despair her husband seeks help from a relative in a distant city. Rasputin never reveals whether Maria is exonerated or if the authorities punish her, but the strength and dignity of the peasant community triumphs. Rasputin's timeless story simply ignores the

tenets of socialist realism. In the 1980s Rasputin spearheaded the drive to save Lake Baikal from pollution.

Vasili Shukshin's death at age 45 represented a serious loss for Soviet fiction, film, and theater, for he was innovative in all three fields. In his compelling human-interest stories, Shukshin epitomized the derevenshchiki movement. His novella The Red Guelder Rose treats the formerly taboo subject of the criminal in Soviet society. After serving his sentence, a convict reforms and resolves to labor honestly in a village as an agricultural worker. His ideal world includes wife, family, and socially useful labor, but he cannot discard his criminal past. Eventually the criminals from whom he had sought to escape murder him.

Literary innovation and artistic spontaneity also flourished among non-Russians. The popular stories of Fazil Iskander, a Georgian from Abkhazia, possess a remarkable conversational quality. "Something About Myself" (published in English in 1978) begins:

> Let's just talk . . . about things we don't have to talk about, pleasant things. Let's talk about some of the amusing sides of human nature, as embodied in people we know. There is nothing more enjoyable than discussing certain old habits of our acquaintances. Because, you see, talking about them makes us aware of our own healthy normality.[9]

Iskander's "talk" is very incisive and symbolic. In "The Thirteenth Labour of Hercules," a parable about the efficacy of humor in facing reality, Iskander argues:

> It seems to me that ancient Rome perished because its emperors in all their marble magnificence failed to realize how ridiculous they were. If they had got themselves some jesters in time (you must hear the truth, if only from a fool), they might have lasted a little longer. But they just went on hoping that the geese would

---

[9] Fazil Iskander, "Something About Myself," in The Thirteenth Labour of Hercules, trans. R. Dalgish (Moscow, 1978), p. 7.

Michael Curran

Kolkhozniki—collective farm workers. The values of the rural heartland are reflected in works of the *derevenshchiki* writers. These peasant faces reveal those values.

save Rome, and then the barbarians came and destroyed Rome, the emperors and its geese.[10]

Was this intended for an aging Politburo under a moribund Brezhnev? Whatever Iskander's intent, his tales won him a deserved reputation as a gifted storyteller and subtle critic of the Soviet system. His two major works, *Sandro of Chegem* (1983) and *The Gospel According to Chegem* (1984), published in English translation but not in the USSR until recently, capture the spirit of the patriarchal village succumbing to inexorable modernization and Sovietization:

> In my childhood I caught fleeting glimpses of the patriarchal village of Abkhazia and fell in love with it forever. Have I perhaps idealized the vanishing life? Perhaps. A man cannot help ennobling what he loves. We may not recognize it, but in idealizing a vanishing way of life we are presenting a bill to the future. We are saying, "Here is what we are losing; what are you going to give us in exchange?" Let the

future think on that if it is capable of thinking at all.[11]

Iskander portrays the modern history of Abkhazia in the Caucasus in stories featuring Uncle Sandro and many other unforgettable characters from Chegem village. Sandro is a fearless, independent spirit, irreverent toward the Soviet regime.

Iskander's digressions as narrator proved unacceptable to Soviet censors. For example:

> With characteristic frankness, Lenin confessed to Gorky . . . that he was humorless. . . . Lenin partially compensated for his deficiency in humor through his magnificent work as an organizer. After Lenin, unfortunately, the Bolsheviks, although they did not possess his genius, decided to follow his lead with respect to humor. . . . They appointed their most unsmiling man [Stalin] to be the country's leader, in the mistaken belief that the most unsmiling man was the most earnest one. This is what revealed the tragedy in the lack of a

---

[10] F. Iskander, *The Thirteenth Labour of Hercules,* p. 51.

[11] F. Iskander, from Foreword to *Sandro of Chegem,* trans. S. Brownsberger (New York, 1983), p. viii.

sense of humor. Yes, he did smile into his moustache with satisfaction, but only later, after 1937 [the Great Purge].[12]

Iurii Trifonov (1925–1981) balanced artistic integrity and political acceptability in his short career. His father, an Old Bolshevik, perished in the purges, but Trifonov adapted to party demands: An early novel of his received a Stalin Prize. In middle age, disdaining party approval, he established his reputation with a series of novellas that probed the past and its influence on the present. The past, he suggested, must be confronted in order to free the future from Stalin's savage legacy. *The House on the Embankment* depicts perceptively the impact of the Stalin era: the problems of growing up, seeking meaning in life, and finding a place in Soviet society from World War II to the mid-1970s. Flashbacks allow Trifonov to explore shifting Soviet values. The successes and failures of Glebov, the main character, are chronicled with nostalgia and resignation, symbolizing the ambiguities of Soviet life: "He dreamed of all the things that later came to him—but which brought him no joy because achieving them used up so much of his strength." Was that perhaps the fate of Soviet people struggling for small joys only to discover that their struggle merely entailed more travail? Here is no view of a radiant future, nor the party's triumph over adversity, but only the tribulations of an ordinary, unheroic person. One can pity Glebov and his periodic waverings, but the Soviet authorities failed to find Trifonov's work uplifting.

Trifonov's somber novellas became immensely popular with Soviet readers, who mourned his untimely death in 1981. Trifonov's passing stilled a voice that had spoken appreciatively of ordinary people and everyday experiences, unlike socialist realism's often grandiose portraits, which seemed more and more divorced from Soviet reality. Trifonov's career revealed that genuine talent could flourish to some degree within narrow Soviet confines. Few others negotiated as successfully the delicate boundary between artistic integrity and party dictates.

From a similar background, Vasili Aksionov became an even more famous writer. More politically engaged, he clashed frequently with the authorities until he was forced to emigrate in 1980. Aksionov first won acclaim for his novella *Halfway to the Moon* (1961), recounting experiences of the first generation of Soviet youth to be deeply influenced by the West. His stories, plays, novels, and cinema scripts gained him a reputation as a prolific and outspoken writer.

What triggered Aksionov's expulsion from the USSR (he still resides outside Russia) was his leadership in creating the literary anthology *Metropol*, which relentlessly demanded artistic freedom. Defying censorship, it was published in an edition of only 10 copies! Increasingly frustrated with literary censorship, Aksionov had his explosive novel *The Burn* published in Italy (1980) and the United States (1984) without authorization. Depicting Moscow intellectuals' alienation during the post-Stalin thaw, it became an instant success. Deeply influenced by the contemporary West and derived from Aksionov's experiences as a visting lecturer at UCLA in 1975, it is an intense and generally negative portrait of contemporary Soviet society. In a style reminiscent of Thomas Pynchon, *The Burn* chronicles the adventures of five men with the same name. The novel has a memorable cast of characters, but the plot is weak and poorly developed.

More interesting is Aksionov's *The Island of Crimea*, a fantasy:

> What if Crimea really were an island? What if, as a result, the White Army had been able to defend Crimea from the Reds in 1920? What if Crimea had developed as a Russian, yet Western, democracy alongside the totalitarian mainland?[13]

---

[12] F. Iskander, *The Gospel According to Chegem*, trans. S. Brownsberger (New York, 1984), pp. 264–65.

[13] V. Aksionov, from Preface to *The Island of Crimea*, trans. M. Heim (New York, 1983), p. ix.

Aksionov imagines a Crimea resembling contemporary Taiwan or Hong Kong replete with superhighways, neon lights, designer boutiques, and sun-worshipping bathers on beaches all within sight of the totalitarian mainland. Andrei Luchnikov, the main character and son of a White leader, successfully defends Crimea against the Red Army. Handsome, rich, and powerful, Luchnikov owns a newspaper that leads an unlikely and curious campaign to reunify capitalist Crimea with the Communist mainland. After his emigration, Aksionov's reputation continued to grow both abroad and in the USSR.

Other Cultural Fields

Although leaders in music and art under Brezhnev pushed the regime to the limits of the acceptable, little was produced that openly challenged party authority. The cinema remained largely a wasteland, despite a few exceptional works such as Andrei Tarkovskii's excellent and innovative film *Andrei Rublev,* about the great 14th-century Russian iconographer. Because of its religious theme, it could not be shown widely in the USSR, but it received an award at the Cannes Film Festival. The heroism of the Soviet people in World War II still strongly influenced filmmakers, who found in it a virtually inexhaustible supply of themes.

In music, Dmitrii Shostakovich remained the leading Soviet composer of the Brezhnev era. He continued to produce innovative, rather bitter masterpieces right up to his death in 1975. Both his 13th (*Babi Yar*) and 14th symphonies, whose leitmotifs were death, were works of protest. In this period Soviet classical music underwent a slow but inexorable modernistic evolution and increasingly used Western composition techniques. New composers such as Boris Tishchenko and Rodion Shchedrin imitated Western experimentalism. To the unconcealed disgust of second-rate conservatives such as Tikhon Khrennikov, longtime head of the Composers' Union, they moved ever further from socialist realism's hallowed but deadening tenets. However, under Brezhnev none dared challenge ideological orthodoxy directly. During the 1970s the role of regional composers from various national republics grew significantly more important.

Culture under Gorbachev, 1985–1991

At first the new regime moved cautiously in the cultural realm, until Gorbachev realized that his program of *perestroika* required endorsement and support from the entire country, especially the cultural elite. *Glasnost* greatly widened freedom for all the arts; artists' responses were enthusiastic but wary. Decades of cultural conditioning and conformity could not be discarded overnight. Prior experience taught that "thaws" were followed inevitably by "frosts" or even hard "freezes." However, it soon grew evident that Gorbachev was serious about reform, and bold individuals decided to test *glasnost*'s limits. The dissidents had already created bases for a Soviet counterculture. Their ideal—an open, freer cultural atmosphere without state-defined norms—fast became reality. The counterculture surfaced rapidly, as many radical works, formerly considered unacceptable, now appeared, raising questions about censorship. Works that challenged traditional limits became catalysts of free expression. Artists and journalists led this remarkable transformation of Soviet culture.

Cultural organization grew more important as controls shifted from state organs, such as the Ministry of Culture, and as unions won greater influence over culture. But not all unions were dominated by emerging "liberals." The powerful Writers' Union remained under conservative control but grew more tolerant of diverse literary approaches. Innovative leaders prevailed in other unions. Journal editors, historians, and scientists supported *glasnost* ardently.

An outspoken cultural leader was a Ukrainian writer, Vitali Korotich, named editor of the influential journal *Ogonek* (*The Little Flame*) in 1986 and elected to the new Congress of Peoples' Deputies in 1989. He transformed a stodgy, uninteresting journal into a progressive vehicle of opinion, focusing on issues of *glasnost.* Stimulating the new national passion of recapturing the past honestly, Korotich published articles critical of Stalin and Stalinism, openly confronting formerly taboo social problems such as prostitution, drug abuse, and the Afghan war. His willingness to test *glasnost*'s limits made *Ogonek* extremely popular. But Korotich realized that *glasnost* offered no guarantees: "It's like flying. There's a feeling of exhilaration, but you always have the thought in the back of your mind that the plane might crash."[14]

Gorbachev's political reforms and the freedom to criticize, publish, and exhibit sparked a creative renaissance in the USSR. Gorbachev recognized that for his revolution to succeed it had to enlist the country's most creative minds and free them from party-imposed conformity. The USSR had to be opened to outside influences and reintegrated into global culture. Nonetheless, opposition to *glasnost* and *perestroika* persisted, and Gorbachev's critics denounced his policies. At a "conservative" rally in Moscow in February 1988, a Leningrad schoolteacher, Nina Andreeva, warned a wildly cheering crowd that Russia was faced by a "counterrevolution" that threatened to pose grave problems, such as strikes, ethnic violence, and moral degradation. These problems, she argued, stemmed from Gorbachev's efforts to "Westernize" the country and introduce "capitalist exploitation in all our cities."[15]

Literature: New and "Lost" Works

Established authors continued under Gorbachev to publish respectable if unimaginative works with broad appeal. A younger generation of talented, innovative writers emerged, but as of the early 1990s had not really found its true literary voice. *Glasnost* produced a major movement to recapture the portion of Soviet literary tradition long repressed by rigid cultural policies. Works that had languished in desk drawers or circulated in

tattered manuscripts were now published at a furious rate, straining press capacity. Among long-suppressed classics finally issued in the USSR were Zamiatin's *We,* Pasternak's *Dr. Zhivago,* Akhmatova's *Requiem,* and Solzhenitsyn's *Cancer Ward.* Even Solzhenitsyn's *Gulag Archipelago* was published in 1990. Other long-banned writers were rehabilitated, included Bulgakov, Pilniak, Mandelshtam, and Siniavskii. Soviet readers were introduced to long-forbidden émigré authors and Western writers formerly considered decadent. Works by Nobel laureates Josef Brodskii and Vladimir Nabokov were published, as was James Joyce's *Ulysses.* Recent émigré works such as Aksionov's *The Burn* and Voinovich's *The Life and Extraordinary Adventures of Private Ivan Chonkin* were also issued.

These "lost" works, analyzed in literary journals, were then reintegrated into the USSR's literary legacy. Restrictions on literature brought into the USSR were virtually eliminated. Taboo subjects almost disappeared, as indicated by publication of Anatoli Rybakov's *Children of the Arbat.* Written in the 1960s but set in 1933, this novel boldly records the sinister beginnings of the Great Purges and contains a chilling portrait of Stalin, depicting his callous disregard for human suffering and insatiable lust for power.

An avalanche of works about the Stalin era burst forth, calling attention to the extent of Stalinist repression, which struck the peasantry through collectivization, national minorities through deportation, religious believers through persecution, and the intelligentsia by intimidation. Many of these books had been written decades earlier but had never been published in the USSR. One example is Vasili Grossman's *Life and Fate,* a massive novel about World War II, in scale comparable to Tolstoy's *War and Peace;* it was published in the West in 1985 and in the USSR in 1988. It portrays with devastating honesty the trauma of war in the Soviet Union, especially in the Battle of Stalingrad, which unleashed Russian venality, prejudice, and suspicion. Grossman holds a mirror to Soviet society, which had glossed over negative aspects of the Soviet Union's wartime role. He

---

[14] *Remaking the Revolution: The Soviet Union 70 Years Later* (Los Angeles, 1988), p. 31.

[15] *New York Times,* February 24, 1988, p. 6.

draws disturbing parallels between Nazi Germany and Stalin's Russia and holds Lenin responsible for Stalinism and other evils in Soviet society. Completing the novel in 1960, he submitted it to the journal *Znamia* (*The Banner*), which rejected it as "anti-Soviet." The KGB then confiscated the manuscript and harassed Grossman, who died in poverty and isolation in 1964.

Similarly, Vladimir Dudintsev, best known for *Not by Bread Alone* (1956), in 1988 published *White Robes*, a stunning fictional account of the struggle by honest scientists against Trofim Lysenko's perversion of Soviet science under Stalin (see Chapter 36). Daniel Granin's curiously titled *Aurochs or Bison* (*Zubr*) depicts the moral dilemma of a Soviet scientist who flees the USSR because of political control of science to pursue his scientific work in Nazi Germany. Such works, questioning the validity of the entire Soviet experience, could not have been published in the USSR prior to Gorbachev.

Also published officially in the USSR was Fazil Iskander's cycle *Sandro of Chegem* and *The Gospel According to Chegem,* which some critics believe may become a 20th-century Russian classic.[16] Anna Akhmatova's poem "Requiem," also published under Gorbachev, is an impassioned solemn chant for her son arrested during the Great Purges:

> Silent flows the Don
> Yellow moon looks quietly on
> Cap askew, looks in the room,
> Sees a shadow in the gloom,
> Sees the woman, sick, at home,
> Sees the woman, all alone,
> Husband buried, then to see
> Son arrested . . . Pray for me.[17]

Georgii Vladimov's novella *Faithful Ruslan,* published in the USSR in 1989 (1979 in the West), is a frightening parable about a loyal and determined trained guard dog at a Siberian forced labor camp. When the camp is closed, Ruslan cannot understand his new role. When the former prison camp becomes a cellulose factory with free workers, Ruslan and other guard dogs cannot differentiate them from prisoners and harass the workers as they had once harassed the prisoners. Behavior cannot be changed easily after long conditioning, argues Vladimov. Human beings, like dogs, cannot escape their past.

Such literary archives, once opened, helped Soviet citizens come to grips with their brutal totalitarian past. Under Gorbachev, literary attention focused on that past rather than on new, experimental literary works. Noted the critic Georgii Baklanov in 1988:

> Three years ago we would never have dreamed of achieving what we have now achieved in the cultural sphere. Nevertheless, we are still lacking a lot . . . because our society is putting all its energy into convalescing.

However, such "convalescing" is essential if former Soviet citizens are to understand massive current changes and place them in accurate context. Another critic, Tatiana Ivanova, wrote in *Ogonek:*

> Our time does not pass in vain. Who can measure the impact of the publication of Grossman's novel [*Life and Fate*] on many thousands of shocked minds? Is it possible for us not to notice the impact of reading *Children of the Arbat,* or *White Robes*? . . . The effect is enormous. . . . We will become different.[18]

A fascinating episode from the Gorbachev era was the national debate over a play not yet produced. The playwright, Mikhail Shatrov, published *On and On and On!* in the journal *Znamia* (*Banner*) in 1988 and overnight became a celebrity. Himself a victim of Stalinism, having lost his parents and close relatives in the purge, and trained as a mining engineer, Shatrov began writing plays in the early 1950s. Some of the early ones were about Lenin; all were controversial. *The Peace of Brest-Litovsk* (written in 1962, published in 1987)

---

[16] Deming Brown, "Literature and Perestroika," *Michigan Quarterly Review* 27, no. 4 (Fall 1989), p. 769.

[17] In *Selected Poems,* ed. Walter Arndt (Ann Arbor, MI, 1976), p. 147.

[18] Tatiana Ivanova, "Who Risks What?" *Ogonek,* no. 24 (June 11–18, 1988), p. 12.

unleashed heated protests. *Pravda* denounced him for "distorting" Soviet history. That was minor compared to the controversy over publication of *On and On and On!,* which raised disturbing questions about the Bolshevik Revolution. His characters ask whether Lenin, had he known the Revolution's outcome, would have led the Bolsheviks in a forceful seizure of power in November 1917. Stalin is portrayed as confronting dilemmas and resolving them violently because of his sadistic, paranoid personality. Shatrov wonders whether Lenin could have intervened successfully to prevent Stalin's rise to power. Exploring alternatives, Shatrov suggests that Stalin's rule was not preordained.

Shatrov's irreverent treatment of the great icons of the Bolshevik Revolution and his questioning of its legitimacy ignited vehement protests. Three historians accused him in *Pravda* of "falsifying" history by portraying Lenin as weak and vacillating. In light of Marxist economic determinism, his critics argued, how could Shatrov suggest that the Bolshevik Revolution was an "accident"? Nina Andreeva castigated Shatrov for spurning socialist realism. Why, she wondered, this obsession with criticizing Stalin? Numerous letters about the play streamed into *Znamia,* mostly praising the play and its publication. A policeman and party member from Irkutsk wrote:

> I want you and Shatrov to know that honest people who value truth and justice are grateful to you for your work which strengthens our belief in the irreversibility of the revolutionary reconstruction of our country.

An unsigned letter from Kiev expressed a very different view:

> Where is your responsibility to the party, your civic honor and simple human dignity when you allow your magazine to publish the vulgarity, anti-Sovietism and political muck produced by Shatrov? . . . Whose mouthpiece have you become?[19]

---

[19] "Perestroika and Soviet Culture," *Michigan Quarterly Review* 38, no. 4 (Fall 1989), p. 589. *Znamia* reported that the letters ran 5 to 1 in support of the play.

This debate reflected a continuing dispute in Soviet society over *glasnost* and *perestroika.* Shatrov sought above all to help audiences recapture the past and recognize complex truths. Gorbachev's reforms included an effort to "restructure" the past, and Shatrov sought to assist him in *On and On and On!*

Art

Soviet artists too were deeply affected by Gorbachev's reforms. Many artworks hitherto proscribed emerged from closets and cellars into public view. The rigid confines of socialist realism were shattered, and the distinction between "official" and "unofficial" art faded. Soviet artists participated more fully in world art. In July 1989 Sotheby's, a major international art auction house, organized a Moscow auction of 120 contemporary Soviet works. More than 11,000 people attended the preauction exhibition and more than 2,000 the auction itself; receipts, far exceeding expectations, totaled $3.4 million. For many previously unknown artists, such commercial success enabled them to pursue creative work full-time.

Earlier Soviet artist-émigrés staged successful exhibitions in the USSR. Mikhail Chemiakin, a Leningrad artist who had won international acclaim in Paris and New York, held a major retrospective exhibition in Moscow in 1989. While evading the criteria of socialist realism, Chemiakin's art is neither radical nor anti-Soviet. His subject matter comes from traditional Russian culture and history.

Another Soviet artist who won critical applause in the West is Ilia Kabakov. His multipaneled works combine images with text. Dubbed "albums" or "portfolios," his works portray lives of ordinary characters moving through life, as he comments on physical and intellectual activity.

Abstract art was long derided in the USSR as decadent, antisocialist, and devoid of social content, but even before *glasnost* Soviet artists experimented with "unofficial" forms of expression. Under Gorbachev, competing styles and forms were openly accepted. Among well-known Soviet artists who rejected socialist realism in order to continue the earlier abstract tradition of Malevich and others were Boris Sveshnikov and Anatoli Zverev. Soviet abstract painters, winning wider acceptance at home and abroad, sought to enter the mainstream of world art. The enthusiastic response to the first public auction of contemporary Soviet art indicated how far these pioneers had come in only a few years.

Film

The Cinema Workers' and Theater Workers' unions underwent dramatic leadership changes under Gorbachev. The distinguished director Elem Klimov became head of the Cinema Workers, and the liberal Alexander Kamshalov took over Goskino, which supervised the Soviet film industry. Together they opened the film archives and released scores of films repressed over the previous 30 years. Among them, Klimov's own *Agony,* shown in the West as *Rasputin,* portrays the decadence and depravity of the Russian imperial court in the twilight of tsarism. Alexander Askoldov's film *Commissar* (1968), released for showing in 1988, deals with issues such as anti-Semitism, abortion, and child abandonment. It reveals moral dilemmas confronting a young Red Army "commissar" in the Civil War who becomes pregnant, considers abortion, has the child in a poor Jewish home, leaves the child with the family, and then returns to the front.

Glasnost's most celebrated film was *Repentance* (1983, released for viewing in 1987) by the Georgian director Tengiz Abuladze. Surrealistic and filled with symbolism that strikes at the heart of totalitarian dictatorship, the film denounces Stalinism and reaffirms human dignity expressed under the greatest adversity. The film was a sensation, viewed by millions who were deeply affected by its humanistic message. The film's final line of dialogue became the key question for many: "What good is a road that does not lead to a church?" In 1988 Abuladze received for *Repentance* the Lenin Prize, the highest state award for creative work; in 1989 the film was recognized at the

Cannes Film Festival. Formerly taboo subjects for film, such as alcoholism, family conflicts, and environmental problems, became acceptable. The film *Little Vera* caused a sensation in 1988 because it dealt with sex and drugs and, for the first time in Soviet cinema, featured on-screen nudity.

The Stalinist past provided abundant subject matter for films and documentaries that raised nagging questions about the purges, the betrayals by family and friends, and the issue of responsibility for the past. In documentaries people spoke out about their sufferings in the prison camps, the terror, and people's heroism in combating it. This examination is part of the vital task of accepting the past.

The most confrontive and controversial film to appear was Stanislav Govorukhin's documentary *This Is No Way to Live.* An unrelenting chronicle of more than 70 years of Communist brutality, corruption, criminal activity, and stupidity, the film paints everything a uniform "black," just as former socialist realist films painted everything "rosy." It is, however, yet another vehicle designed to help recapture a lost past, not as a novel or as history, but as a documentary virtually all Soviet citizens could relate to based on their personal experiences. It was, therefore, a powerful tool to wrench Soviet citizens out of their apathetic acceptance of authoritarian misrule. Many cannot understand the decision to allow such a devastating indictment of Communist rule to be shown publicly, but Gorbachev reportedly reviewed the film personally and approved its release. Gradually the former Soviet people were regaining their historical memory, and this film was an important part of that process.

Music

The cult hero of *glasnost* was the deceased young balladeer Vladimir Vysotskii, recognized as a symbol of the triumph over repression that had strangled Soviet culture for decades. Officially Vysotskii was an actor in Iurii Liubimov's famous Taganka Theater in Moscow who also appeared in films. But he was best known as a poet-bard whose

ITAR-TASS/SOVFOTO

Vladimir Vysotskii (1938–1980), popular Russian poet and balladeer,
at a concert in Yaroslavl in February 1979.

bitter, satirical protest songs won him a huge following among youth and members of the intelligentsia. His songs circulated widely in *magnitizdat*, poor-quality homemade recordings made at his many concerts and private songfests. Living in the fast lane, Vysotskii died in 1980 as a widely recognized underground hero. Under *glasnost* he emerged "above ground" to be acknowledged as a "seer" and "legend." His works have sold hundreds of thousands of copies, TV documentaries have recorded his life, and he has achieved huge success in the popular press.

A highly dramatic event associated with musical *glasnost* was the triumphant return to Moscow in February 1990 of the distinguished cellist and conductor Mstislav Rostropovich, who with his wife, the acclaimed soprano Galina Vishnevskaia, was exiled from the USSR in 1974. They had been accused of "acts harmful to the Soviet

Union" for offering shelter and support to Solzhenitsyn prior to his own expulsion. Rostropovich's return to the USSR, restoration of his citizenship (revoked in 1978), and the return of his Moscow apartment heralded a new era in Soviet music. The press glorified Rostropovich for his contributions to music and his heroic defense of justice and freedom. Asked about his view of President Gorbachev, Rostropovich commented that Stalin had tried in the 1940s to frighten Prokofiev and Shostakovich into writing more "socialist" music. "I know Gorbachev does not give [music] lessons to my friend, Alfred Schnitke."[20] The distinguished Russian-born pianist Vladimir Horowitz also returned to the

---

[20] Quoted in the *New York Times,* February 14, 1990, p. B1. Schnitke is considered a leading Soviet contemporary composer.

Russian-born pianist Vladimir Horowitz returned triumphantly to
the USSR for a concert tour in 1986 after 51 years in exile.

Soviet Union for a concert tour in 1986. *Glasnost*
thus relaxed controls and provided greater access
to the international musical world.

Conclusion

A great artistic revival under Gorbachev contributed mightily to a cultural catharsis in the
USSR. Recapturing the past, artists and historians
liberated the populace from the deception of Stalinism and the stagnation of the Brezhnev era. The
strongest support for Gorbachev's restructuring
program came from Soviet artists and writers
seeking to energize the nation and generate positive attitudes toward the future.

Alexander Kabakov, a young journalist, published in *Iskusstvo Kino* (*Film Art*) in 1989 a projected script for a science fiction film, *The
Non-Returnee.* In this antiutopian film script,
Kabakov portrays a future USSR totally disintegrated and locked in civil war. The country is ruled
by roving bands of terrorists, national minorities
have all left the Soviet Union, and the economy
has sunk to a bare subsistence level. His purpose,
stated Kabakov, was to deliver "a stern and sober

warning of what could happen if we do not manage to cope with destructive anti-*perestroika*
processes present in our society. *Perestroika* may be
the last chance."[21] Were Kabakov's views
prophetic? Soviet culture has often marched
ahead of Soviet politics.

Suggested Additional Reading

Most works of literature and literary dissent mentioned in this chapter have been translated into
English. Consult your library for the most recent
editions and anthologies.

KHRUSHCHEV ERA

BETHEA, D. *Joseph Brodsky and the Creation of Exile*
(Princeton, 1994).

FIELD, A., ed. *Pages from Tarusa: New Voices in Russian
Writing* (London, 1964).

GERSTENMAIER, C. *The Voices of the Silent* (New York,
1972).

---

[21] Quoted in *Report on the USSR, Radio Free Europe* . . . 1, no.
33 (August 18, 1989), p. 9.

GIBIAN, G. *Interval of Freedom: Soviet Literature During the Thaw, 1954–1957* (Minneapolis, 1960).

GOLDBERG, A. L., and P. GOLDBERG. *The Thaw Generation: Coming of Age in the Post-Stalin Era* (Pittsburgh, 1993).

JOHNSON, P. *Khrushchev and the Arts: The Politics of Soviet Culture, 1962–1964* (Cambridge, MA, 1965).

KARLINSKY, S. *Marina Tsvetaeva . . .* (New York, 1986).

LIVINGSTONE, A. *Pasternak: Dr. Zhivago* (New York, 1989).

LOWE, D. *Russian Writing Since 1953: A Critical Survey* (New York, 1987).

OKUDZHAVA, B. *A Taste of Liberty,* trans. Leo Gruliow (Ann Arbor, MI, 1986).

PROKOFIEV, S. *Prokofiev by Prokofiev: A Composer's Memoir,* ed. D. H. Appel, trans. G. Daniels (Garden City, NY, 1979).

REAVEY, GEORGE, ed. and trans. *The New Russian Poets, 1953–1966: An Anthology* (New York, 1966).

ROBIN, R. *Socialist Realism: The Impossible Aesthetic,* trans. C. Porter (Stanford, 1992).

ROTHBERG, A. *The Heirs of Stalin: Dissidence and the Soviet Regime, 1953–1970* (Ithaca, NY, 1972).

SCATTON, L. H. *Mikhail Zoshchenko: Evolution of a Writer* (New York, 1993).

SCHWARZ, B. *Music and Musical Life in Soviet Russia, 1917–1981,* enlarged ed. (Bloomington, IN, 1983).

SJEKLOCHA, P., and I. MEAD. *Unofficial Art in the Soviet Union* (Berkeley, 1967).

BREZHNEV ERA

AKSYONOV, V. *The Burn* (New York, 1984).

———. *The Island of Crimea* (New York, 1984).

———, et al., eds. *Metropol* (New York, 1983).

AMERT, S. *In a Shattered Mirror: The Late Poetry of Anna Akhmatova* (Stanford, 1992).

BENYON, M. *Life in Russia* (New York, 1983).

BROWN, D. *The Last Years of Soviet Russian Literature: Prose Fiction, 1975–1991* (Cambridge, 1993).

BRUMBERG, A., ed. *In Quest of Justice: Protest and Dissent in the Soviet Union Today* (New York, 1970).

DODGE, M., and A. HILTON, eds. *New Art from the Soviet Union* (Washington, 1977).

DUNLOP, J. B., R. HOUGH, and A. KLIMOFF, eds. *Aleksandr Solzhenitsyn: Critical Essays and Documentary Materials* (Belmont, MA, 1973).

GILLESPIE, D. *Iurii Trifonov: Unity Through Time* (New York, 1993).

HAYWARD, M., ed. *On Trial: The Soviet State Versus "Abram Tertz" and "Nikolai Arzhak"* (New York, 1966).

HOSKING, G. *Beyond Socialist Realism: Soviet Fiction Since Ivan Denisovich* (New York, 1980).

KERBLAY, B. *Modern Soviet Society* (New York, 1983).

KIRK, I. *Profiles in Russian Resistance* (New York, 1975).

KOLESNIKOFF, N. *Yury Trifonov: A Critical Study* (Ann Arbor, MI, 1991).

MEDVEDEV, Z. *The Medvedev Papers: The Plight of Soviet Science Today* (New York, 1971).

MONONOVA, T., ed. *Women and Russia: Feminist Writings from the Soviet Union* (Boston, 1984).

NEPOMNYASHCHY, C. T. *Abram Tertz and the Poetics of Crime* (New Haven, CT, 1995).

OKUDZHAVA, B. *A Taste of Liberty,* trans. Leo Gruliow (Ann Arbor, MI, 1986).

PARTHE, K. *Russian Village Prose: The Radiant Past* (Princeton, 1992).

POLLAK, N., ed. *Mandelshtam: The Reader* (Baltimore, 1995).

POLUKHINA, V. *Joseph Brodsky . . .* (Cambridge, 1989).

REDDAWAY, P., ed. and trans. *Uncensored Russia: Protest and Dissent in the Soviet Union . . .* (New York, 1972).

ROTHBERG, A. *Aleksandr Solzhenitsyn: The Major Novels, 1953–1970* (Ithaca, NY, 1972).

SCAMMELL, M. *Solzhenitsyn: A Biography* (New York, 1984).

SHALAMOV, V. *Kolyma Tales,* trans. J. Glad (New York, 1980).

SHIPLER, D. *Russia: Broken Idols, Solemn Dreams,* 2d ed. (New York, 1989).

SOLZHENITSYN, A., et al. *From Under the Rubble: Essays* (New York, 1975).

TOKES, R., ed. *Dissent in the USSR: Politics, Ideology and People* (Baltimore, 1975).

TRIFONOV, I. *Another Life and House on the Embankment* (New York, 1984).

———. *The Old Man* (New York, 1984).

VISHEVSKY, A. *Soviet Literary Culture in the 1970s. The Politics of Irony* (Gainesville, IL, 1993)

VISHNEVSKY, P. *Soviet Literary Culture in the 1970s: The Politics of Irony* (Gainesville, FL, 1993).

VOLKOV, S., ed. *Testimony: The Memoirs of Dmitri Shostakovich* (New York, 1979).

WALL, J. *Invented Truth: Soviet Reality and the Literary Imagination of Iurii Trifonov* (Durham, NC, 1991).

GORBACHEV ERA

AITMATOV, C. *The Day Lasts More Than a Hundred Years* (Bloomington, IN, 1983).

ANDERSON, R., and P. DEBRECZENY, eds. *Russian Narrative and Visual Art: Varieties of Seeing* (Gainesville, FL, 1993).

BARTLETT, R. *Wagner and Russia* (Cambridge, 1995).

BERRY, E., and A. MILLER-POGACAR, eds. *Re-entering the Sign: Articulating New Russian Culture* (Ann Arbor, MI, 1995).

BROWN, D. *The Last Years of Soviet Russian Literature: Prose Fiction, 1975–1991* (New York, 1993).

CHANCES, E. *Andrei Bitov: The Ecology of Inspiration* (New York, 1993).

GARRARD, J., and C. GARRARD. *Inside the Soviet Writers' Union* (New York, 1990).

GROSSMAN, V. *Life and Fate* (New York, 1985).

ISKANDER, F. *Rabbits and Boa Constrictors* (Ann Arbor, MI, 1989).

KETCHIAN, S. *The Poetry of Anna Akhmatova: A Conquest of Time and Space* (Munich, 1986).

LAHUSEN, T., and G. KUPERMAN, eds. *Late Soviet Culture: From Perestroika to Novostroika* (Durham, NC, 1993).

LAWTON, A. *Kinoglasnost: Soviet Cinema in Our Time* (New York, 1993).

MUCKLE, J. *Portrait of a Soviet School Under Glasnost* (New York, 1990).

ORLOV, Y. *Memoirs of a Russia Life,* trans. T. Whitney (New York, 1990).

"Perestroika and Soviet Culture," *Michigan Quarterly Review,* 1989. (An extremely valuable collection of essays and translations providing a comprehensive account of Soviet culture under Gorbachev.)

PETRA, S., ed. *Rocking the State: Rock Music and Politics in Eastern Europe and Russia* (Boulder, CO, 1994).

POLOWY, T. *The Novellas of Valentin Rasputin . . . ,* vol. 1 (New York, 1989).

RASPUTIN, V. *Siberia on Fire,* trans. G. Mikkelson and M. Winchell (Dekalb, IL, 1989).

REEDER, R., ed., and J. HEMSCHEMEYER, trans. *The Complete Poems of Anna Akhmatova* (Boston, 1992).

Remaking the Revolution: The Soviet Union 70 Years Later (Los Angeles, 1987). (Selections from the *Los Angeles Times'* coverage of the Soviet Union.)

ROSS, D., ed. *Between Spring and Summer: Soviet Conceptual Art in the Era of Late Communism* (Cambridge, MA, 1990).

RYAN-HAYES, K. L. *Contemporary Russian Satire: A Genre Study* (New York, 1995).

RYBAKOV, A. *Children of the Arbat* (Boston, 1988).

———. *Heavy Sand* (New York, 1983).

SEGEL, H. *Twentieth Century Russian Drama: From Gorkey to the Present* (Baltimore, 1993).

SHNEIDMAN, N. *Soviet Literature in the 1980s . . .* (Toronto, 1989).

SMITH, G. S., ed. and trans. *Contemporary Russian Poetry: A Bilingual Anthology* (Bloomington, IN, 1993.)

SOLOMON, A. *The Irony Tower: Soviet Artists in a Time of Glasnost* (New York, 1990).

TAUBMAN, W., and J. TAUBMAN. *Moscow Spring* (New York, 1989).

TUPITSYN, M. *Margins of Soviet Art* (Milan, 1989).

VLADIMOV, G. *Faithful Ruslan* (New York, 1979).

JOURNALS

Literaturnaia Gazeta, Moscow. (Now available in English as *The Literary Gazette.*)

Moskovskie Novosti. (English language edition is *Moscow News.*)

Ogonek (*The Little Flame*). (Available only in Russian, ed. Vitali Korotich.)

44

The Collapse of the Soviet Union, 1990–1992

The abortive coup of August 19–21, 1991, led by conservatives appointed to office by President Gorbachev, undermined fatally the already shattered structure of the USSR and destroyed Gorbachev's power. During the last months of 1991 the Soviet empire simply disintegrated into its constituent republics and was finally given a decent burial on December 25. The Soviet Union was succeeded by a loose confederation similar to the European Community and known as the Commonwealth of Independent States, led by Russia, the most powerful by far of the sovereign republics. Meanwhile, the economic situation in the former union grew more and more catastrophic, and ethnic tensions worsened. President Yeltsin of Russia stood forth as the most decisive leader of an extremely difficult transition era. This sudden collapse of a vast multinational empire and superpower was virtually unprecedented in world history. These cataclysmic events proved profoundly traumatic for the peoples of the former Soviet Union and for an anxious world.

Gorbachev Declines, Yeltsin Rises, 1990–1991

By 1990 the Soviet Union—politically, economically, and in national terms—was an empire in crisis and turmoil. Gorbachev had sought unsuccessfully to lead a perilous transition from Brezhnev's authoritarian, centralized system toward pluralism and market socialism. He had moved far beyond Khrushchev in encouraging a pitiless examination of previous Soviet policies and history, inducing many to question sharply the legitimacy of the Soviet regime. Fostering a degree of political debate and change unparalleled since Lenin, Gorbachev threw the party and state into contention, then disintegration.

In the spring and summer of 1990, amid unredeemed promises of drastic economic change, political reform and national disintegration accelerated. Within the Supreme Soviet Boris Yeltsin, favoring radical reform, helped organize a left-wing opposition to Gorbachev, supported on most issues by Andrei Sakharov. Within the party the Democratic Platform group, established in January 1990, advocated ending the party's leading role, electing its officials democratically, and creating a multiparty political system. That group, with Yeltsin as a leader, urged Gorbachev to break with party conservatives led by Egor Ligachev. Ligachev, in turn, accused Gorbachev of straying from Marxism-Leninism and adopting Western social democracy. The conservatives urged restoring Soviet unity under firm, centralized party control. At the Central Committee plenum of February 1990, Yeltsin's 10-point reform program, based on the Democratic Platform group and urging a decentralized, federal party, was rejected.[1] In March the Third Congress of People's Deputies, confirming the end of the Communist Party's political monopoly under Article 6, elected Gorbachev Soviet president. This uncontested "election" triggered public protests that he should have faced a nationwide vote, which he would probably have won. A variety of parties contested spring elections to parliaments in the Christian republics; in the Baltic republics, Georgia, and Armenia the Communists met defeat. Over Gorbachev's opposition, his leftist critic Boris Yeltsin was elected chairman of the Russian parliament. As the republics and regions gained in strength, the central Soviet government steadily lost authority and credibility. That summer Gorbachev and Yeltsin agreed briefly to enact radical economic change embodied in a so-called "500-Day Plan" designed by academician Stanislav Shatalin to introduce a genuine market economy and accelerate privatization of industry and land. However, supported by conservative state and party leaders, Gorbachev soon backed way from its proposals to transfer most economic power to the individual republics.

In the second half of 1990, disturbing extreme conservative trends gathered force in the Soviet Union, foreshadowing the August 1991 coup. In June was formed a "Centrist Bloc" of hard-line elements from the Communist Party, security services, and military demanding a return to cen-

tralized authoritarian rule. Its chief spokesman was the violent Colonel Viktor Alksnis, whose conservative Soiuz faction in the USSR Congress of People's Deputies claimed support from more than one-fourth of its 2,050 deputies. In December the so-called Committee of National Salvation from this bloc pressured Gorbachev to impose a national state of presidential emergency, suspend all political parties, and remove elected officials in the more democratically oriented republics. By the end of 1990 five of these republics—the three Baltic states, Georgia, and Armenia—had declared their independence. Early in 1991 Colonel Alksnis demanded publicly that President Gorbachev be removed from office and that the KGB and Interior Ministry then impose strong centralized rule over the country, by force if necessary. These demands foreshadowed the program of the leaders of the August Coup of 1991.

In the fall of 1990, worried by these trends, Gorbachev veered sharply to the right. He removed a number of top reformers from their positions; others, including Shatalin and Shevardnadze, abandoned him. After Gorbachev replaced Vadim Bakatin, the first Soviet interior minister respectful of the rule of law, with Boris Pugo, a belligerent hard-liner, Foreign Minister Shevardnadze in a dramatic speech on December 20 declared that democrats and reformers were departing and announced his resignation:

> A dictatorship is coming. . . . No one knows what kind of dictatorship it will be and who will come or what the regime will be like. . . . I am resigning. . . . Let this be my contribution, if you like, my protest against the onset of dictatorship.[2]

Believing that hard-line, conservative groups were determined to hold the USSR together by force, Shevardnadze saw Gorbachev yielding to them. The Fourth Congress of People's Deputies, at Gorbachev's urging, elected Genadii Ianaev, a colorless apparatchik, to the new post of vice pres-

[1] Jack F. Matlock, Jr., *Autopsy on an Empire: The American Ambassador's Account of the Collapse of the Soviet Union* (New York, 1995), pp. 305–16.

[2] Quoted in Matlock, *Autopsy,* p. 429.

ident of the USSR. After Gorbachev spurned the 500-Day Plan, the Soviet economy underwent a precipitous decline, and all of his promarket economic advisers resigned. The new Soviet premier, Valentin Pavlov, replacing the ill Ryzhkov, introduced an ill-conceived currency reform and invented Western economic conspiracies against the USSR. By early 1991 disgruntled reformers viewed President Gorbachev as an obstacle to necessary fundamental political and economic change.

In January 1991 Gorbachev sought to block Lithuanian independence with an ultimatum and a threat to use force. KGB troops attacked a television complex in Vilnius, killing some civilians. Awakened by his staff, President Gorbachev denied responsibility, but his explanations and those of Interior Minister Pugo were unconvincing. Yeltsin flew to Vilnius and challenged Gorbachev's right to control the Soviet armed forces against the wishes of republic governments. Clearly Gorbachev's authority was shrinking rapidly. Leaving the president's team, economist Nikolai Petrakov attacked Gorbachev openly in a letter:

> A regime in its death throes has made a last-ditch stand: economic reform has been blocked, censorship of the media reinstated, brazen demagogy revived, and an open war on the republics declared. . . . The events in Lithuania [are] criminal.[3]

However, in the spring of 1991 Gorbachev, again shifting course, encouraged decentralization and genuine federalism. Under strong foreign pressure, the independence of the three Baltic republics—Latvia, Lithuania, and Estonia—was approved. In March a nationwide referendum sponsored by Gorbachev favored the preservation of the Soviet Union, but the vote in Ukraine was very close, and six republics refused to participate. Although Gorbachev interpreted this referendum as a victory, it actually revealed dwindling support

Table 44.1
Recent Russian elections, president and legislature

Candidate	Presidential Election, June 12, 1991	
	Votes	% of Total
Boris N. Yeltsin	45,552,041	57.30
Nikolai Ryzhkov	13,395,335	16.85
Vladimir Zhirinovskii	6,211,007	7.81
Iman-Geldy Tuleyev	5,417,464	6.81
Vadim Bakatin	2,719,757	3.42
Albert Makashov	11,136	0.7

for any real union.[4] Nonetheless, on April 23 Gorbachev met with Yeltsin and leaders of eight other republics at a dacha at Novo-Ogarevo near Moscow. They agreed upon terms of a new union treaty that would create a loose federation in place of the old Soviet Union. In June, after a free and vigorous election campaign, Yeltsin was elected president of the Russian Republic on the first ballot, giving him, unlike Gorbachev, an undeniable popular mandate. (See Table 44.1.) On July 20, giving notice of his authoritarian governing style, President Yeltsin ordered the Communist Party excluded from factories and the armed forces. Hard-liners assailed his decree as an illegal move toward dictatorship.

The August Coup

At dawn on August 19, 1991, the eight members of the so-called Committee for the State of Emergency[5] attempted to seize power throughout the Soviet Union and establish a conservative, authoritarian regime.

The roots of the August Coup went back to 1989, when the KGB set up tight surveillance over Yeltsin and leaders of Democratic Russia by tapping their telephone conversations. Reading and

---

[3] Quoted in Matlock, p. 467.

[4] Matlock, p. 494.

[5] The Russian initials for the Committee—GKChP—noted one Muscovite, when pronounced sounded like a cat choking on a hairball!

Members of the Committee for the State of Emergency at a press conference in Moscow, August 19, 1991. Left to right: Alexander Tiriakov, Vasili Starodubtsev, Boris Pugo, Gennadii Ianaev (chairman), and Oleg Baklanov.

commenting on these secret surveillance reports, President Gorbachev bore full responsibility for illegal activities that would later be employed against him. By August 4, 1991, the KGB had prepared all the documents for the coup, including the draft of a state of emergency in the USSR. On August 7 some of the coup leaders began meeting at a KGB "safe house" in Moscow. Leaving on vacation August 5, Gorbachev dismissed warnings from Russian colleagues and the Bush administration of an impending coup.[6]

After ordering President Gorbachev detained at his summer home in the Crimea, the Emergency Committee announced that he had been removed from power temporarily because of illness and had been replaced by Vice President Gennadii Ianaev. The conspirators moved swiftly to control the Russian public media but inexplicably failed to seize or silence Russian President Yeltsin, who

promptly and unequivocally denounced the putsch as illegal and unconstitutional.

The Emergency Committee, composed of hardline leaders of the Communist Party, the KGB, and the military, warned in its proclamation to the Soviet people: "A mortal danger has come to loom large over our great Motherland." President Gorbachev's reform policies, it claimed, had "entered a blind alley." Pledged the Committee: "We intend to restore law and order straight away, end bloodshed, declare a war without mercy on the criminal world, and eradicate shameful phenomena discrediting our society." The proclamation called on all loyal Soviet citizens to rally around the Committee and support its efforts "to pull the country out of its crisis." At a hastily called news conference, Acting President of the USSR Ianaev declared quizzically:

> Mikhail Gorbachev is now on vacation. He is undergoing treatment in the south of our country. He is very tired after these many years and will need some time to get better, and it is

---

[6] John B. Dunlop, *The Rise of Russia and the Fall of the Soviet Empire* (Princeton, 1993), pp. 192–93.

our hope that as soon as he feels better, he will take up again his office.[7]

"The great irony of this coup," noted S. Tarasenko, adviser to former Foreign Minister Shevardnadze, "is the fact that those people who demoted Gorbachev are his friends." Gorbachev had appointed all of the "gang of eight" to their posts; now they sought to end his rule and reforms.

What had caused this sudden conservative backlash? The trigger was the scheduled signing on August 20 in Moscow of a new union treaty, dismantling the old Soviet order and transferring many of its hitherto awesome powers to the individual republics. That treaty posed a direct and immediate threat to the power of the institutions represented in the Emergency Committee: the Communist Party, state police agencies, economic technocrats, and some senior military leaders.

Underlying the coup were Gorbachev's efforts to balance off two irreconcilable and uncontrollable forces: a generation of new popular leaders such as Yeltsin and a group of hard-liners and custodians of stability whom Gorbachev had appointed to power. During the previous two years Gorbachev's gyrations between seeking democratic reform and tolerating hard-line crackdowns had grown more and more desperate. Each measure designed to satisfy one side had alienated the other, until he resembled a captain in a storm rushing from port to starboard to keep his ship afloat. The conservative "gang of eight" had thus acted to cancel Gorbachev's political reforms, which threatened the Soviet Empire's cohesiveness and status as a superpower, as well as their own high positions.

In his account of the coup, Gorbachev designated it an inevitable and decisive clash "between the forces of reaction and democracy." Not only was the draft Union Treaty ready for signature, but Gorbachev had called into session the Council of the Federation for August 21 to discuss accelerating economic and financial reforms. "The plotters

saw that time was fast running out for them, and so they chose that moment to put their plans into action."

On August 18—the day before the coup—President Gorbachev spoke by telephone with presidents of key republics and with Vice President Ianaev. Just before 5 P.M., told that a group accompanied by a KGB security leader was demanding to see him, Gorbachev discovered that all his telephone lines had just been severed. He promptly resolved to resist any pressure or blackmail, and his family concurred. The delegation of the Emergency Committee demanded that Gorbachev sign a decree transferring power to Vice President Ianaev and the Committee. Refusing pointblank, Gorbachev warned: "You and the people who sent you are irresponsible. You will destroy yourselves, but that is your business and to hell with you. But you will also destroy the country and everything we have already done."[8] Gorbachev was receiving foreign radio reports describing growing public resistance to the coup and support from top world leaders for him and President Yeltsin. Gorbachev's courage and confidence in the Soviet people helped frustrate the coup attempt.

Meanwhile Yeltsin coordinated public opposition. Army vehicles sent into downtown Moscow to enforce the Emergency Committee's decrees were encircled by indignant crowds; soldiers mobilized to disperse them refused to obey orders to fire on the people. Before the parliament of the Russian Republic—the so-called Russian White House—Yeltsin climbed up on an armored truck and appealed for a general strike the next day to protest the coup. By nightfall on August 19 some Russian Republic troops and armored combat vehicles were guarding Yeltsin's headquarters. By then Anatolii Sobchak, mayor of Leningrad (soon to be renamed St. Petersburg), Moscow's deputy mayor, and other republic leaders were openly supporting Yeltsin's defiance of the Committee.

[7]*New York Times*, August 20, 1991, p. 9.

[8] Mikhail Gorbachev, *The August Coup* (New York, 1991), pp. 15–22.

President Yeltsin and followers in front of the Russian parliament building, defying the attempted August coup.

On August 20, its second day in power, the Emergency Committee ordered a curfew imposed on Moscow and sent new armored forces into the city. This move provoked clashes with angry civilians, three of whom were killed. Large crowds gathered before the Russian parliament building to protect the defiant Yeltsin. An even larger crowd filled Palace Square in Leningrad to hear Mayor Sobchak denounce the coup and the Committee, whose junta showed increasing signs of disunity and confusion. President Bush, calling Yeltsin on an open telephone line, pledged his support and expressed the view that the poorly prepared coup could be reversed.

On August 21—the third day—the coup collapsed ignominiously, and President Gorbachev returned to Moscow. A key turning point came at dawn, when army tanks under the Emergency Committee's control failed to assault the Russian parliament building guarded by only a handful of defenders. The coup fizzled as Russians rallied behind President Yeltsin and the plotters proved irresolute and divided. Long columns of tanks and

personnel carriers, some decorated with Russian flags, moved out of Moscow to cheers from jubilant Muscovites. A major casualty was communism as a political force. Even the coup leaders failed to wave the drooping flag of Marxism-Leninism. Some Muscovites gloated: "We knew the Communists couldn't do anything right!" Early that day the coup leaders fled the Kremlin; some reached the Crimea, where Gorbachev was quarantined aboard a presidential airplane. "When the plotters turned up at the dacha, I gave orders that they should be arrested," wrote Gorbachev.[9] After President Gorbachev was restored to power, the leaders of the Emergency Committee were arrested or committed suicide.

Why had a coup engineered by the USSR's most formidable military and security agencies failed so ignominiously? The August Coup amazed observers on the scene and abroad by its indecisiveness and incompetence. It was indeed strange that President Yeltsin and other leading

---

[9] Gorbachev, *The August Coup,* p. 36.

democrats had not been arrested, that satellite connections had not been cut, and that foreign correspondents continued reporting freely from Moscow. It was puzzling that KGB chief Vladimir Kriuchkov, a Committee leader who had helped suppress the Hungarian Revolution of 1956, could not even organize a successful coup in Russia. It was a rather stupid attempt, noted American political scientist Jerry Hough, by lackluster leaders who failed to plan ahead or present even a minimally attractive program to the Soviet people.[10] Promising law and order, they failed to establish it and could not even take effective control of the government.

During the 60 hours the junta exercised some control, it sought to halt the process of reform instituted by Gorbachev. Its failure owed something to the public forces unleashed during the previous six years by *glasnost* and *perestroika.* Counting on Russia's authoritarian tradition, public disillusionment with *perestroika,* and a yearning for the "good old days" of order and relative plenty under Brezhnev, the coup leaders miscalculated how the Soviet public would react. Thanks to the efforts of Gorbachev and Yeltsin, no longer was Russia a nation of docile slaves. The methods, timing, and even the language used by the August junta resembled those of Brezhnev and company in ousting Khrushchev in 1964. But unlike the Brezhnev coalition, the Emergency Committee failed to obtain support from commanders of the armed forces, or even from rank-and-file troops. Two new factors in August 1991 were the popular resistance centering in Moscow and Leningrad, and alternative centers of power—Yeltsin's national Russian government, Sobchak's city government in Leningrad, and other republic governments, all of which had greater legitimacy than did the junta. Crucial in the coup's collapse was the split within Soviet military forces; most key commanders either refused to participate or remained on the fence. Such divisions, noted Hough, were mostly generational. The military of

the future—younger leaders such as General Evgenii Shaposhnikov—defeated the army of the past headed by World War II officers such as Marshal Dmitrii Iazov and Sergei Akhromeev (a suicide after the coup failed). Believing that Gorbachev was a traitor for yielding wartime gains, they aimed to suppress democracy and restore a stable Soviet Union.[11]

The Demise of the Soviet Union, 1991–1992

In the immediate aftermath of the failed August Coup, democratic and reform elements in the Soviet Union and world opinion rejoiced. The chief hero of that hour of triumph was Russian President Boris Yeltsin, who had stood stalwartly on a tank before his Moscow headquarters as the symbol of democratic defiance of reaction. While Yeltsin's popularity and power soared, Soviet President Gorbachev returned shaken and shrunken. Initially Yeltsin insulted Gorbachev publicly and, without consulting his own legislature, outlawed the Communist Party in Russia and closed down Communist newspapers. He even threatened to seize Russian-speaking areas of Ukraine and Kazakhstan should they insist on secession. These dictatorial measures alienated some intellectuals and other supporters. Wisely, Yeltsin soon backed away from such arbitrary measures. During the months following the coup Yeltsin took over most of the powers of the former Soviet central government.

President Gorbachev, his authority crumbling, continued to press stubbornly for formation of a federal union, arguing that the republics' outright secession and full independence would lead to catastrophe and even civil war. In September the USSR Congress of People's Deputies granted theoretical power to the republics while vesting considerable authority in a new Soviet State Council chaired by Gorbachev and composed of leaders of the republics. However, that body soon

---

[10] Jerry Hough, "Assessing the Coup," *Current History,* vol. 90 (October 1991).

[11] Hough, "Assessing the Coup."

proved largely impotent because the republics simply ignored its decisions.

The August Coup accelerated the USSR's disintegration into its national components. By discrediting the central agencies—the party, state bureaucracy, and KGB—and by splitting the army, which had previously held the USSR together, the coup transferred most de facto authority to the republics. It remained uncertain whether the vast Russian Republic, containing more than 100 distinct nationalities, would remain united. The mortal blow to the Soviet Union—and to Gorbachev's hopes of preserving the center—was Ukraine's overwhelming vote in the referendum of December 1, 1991, in favor of full independence. Elected as Ukraine's president was Leonid M. Kravchuk, long-time Soviet apparatchik, who underwent a sudden conversion to Ukrainian nationalism only after the August Coup collapsed.

The failed coup dealt a devastating blow to the Communist Party, especially in Russia, where President Yeltsin proclaimed it dissolved and ordered its property seized. Communist elites in some other republics sought to preserve their power by swift proclamations of independence. The KGB, emasculated as an organization, lost its awesome power over the police. With the collapsing Soviet government no longer able to finance them, most of the swollen central ministries were abolished or greatly reduced in personnel. As most army recruits refused to serve outside of their own republics, the new defense chief, General Evgenii Shaposhnikov, advocated a sharply reduced, professional military force. Even before its independence referendum, Ukraine considered constructing its own armed forces. A crucial issue was control of some 27,000 nuclear warheads located in late 1991 in four Soviet republics.

After the coup a question that perplexed Soviet and foreign leaders was whether in the future there would be a single Soviet foreign policy. At first President Gorbachev and foreign supporters such as President Bush insisted that the center would continue to conduct the international business of the Soviet Union. Immediately after the coup Foreign Minister Alexander Bessmertnykh,

implicated in it, was removed by President Gorbachev and replaced by Boris Pankin, the ambassador to Czechoslovakia. When it became evident that Pankin had little international prestige, he was replaced in November by former Soviet Foreign Minister Eduard Shevardnadze, the architect of Gorbachev's "new thinking" in foreign affairs. However, only a month later President Yeltsin abruptly abolished the Soviet foreign ministry and claimed the USSR's permanent seat on the United Nations Security Council for Russia.

The failed coup accelerated the sharp diminution of Soviet power and international influence evident since the collapse in 1989 of eastern European Communist regimes. The Warsaw Treaty organization dissolved and most Soviet troops withdrew from eastern Europe, spurred by generous financial aid from Germany. With the end of the formidable Soviet Bloc in eastern Europe, warmer relations were established between a fading Soviet Union and western European countries, especially Germany. The removal of Soviet power and influence from eastern Europe marked a startling reshuffling of power. The collapse of the coup undermined most remaining Communist regimes worldwide. Cuba's Fidel Castro, still defiantly Communist but isolated and vulnerable, saw Soviet aid to his battered economy disappear. North Korea's aging hard-line dictator, Kim Il-sung, shocked by Gorbachev's overtures to prosperous South Korea, moved toward accommodation with the south. Communist Vietnam, deprived of Soviet aid, turned toward the United States.

After central Soviet ministries were transferred to the control of Yeltsin's Russian government, the formal dissolution of the Soviet Union approached. In the days before his resignation President Gorbachev warned of the dangers ahead if the union were ended, foreseeing ethnic strife, economic chaos, and the disintegration of Russia. Sending a message to the December 21 meeting of republic leaders in Alma-Ata, Kazakhstan, Gorbachev argued for common citizenship and a centralized command to control nuclear weapons. He urged that the USSR Supreme Soviet be convened to dissolve the Soviet Union formally, adding:

> We should begin a new era in the history of the country with dignity and in conformity with standards of legitimacy. . . . We have both the prerequisites and the experience needed to act in the framework of democratic rules.

Earlier Yeltsin had agreed that the Soviet Union should end officially at midnight on December 31, 1991, but then he pressed for an earlier transfer of power. On December 25 Gorbachev delivered his resignation speech on television, then instructed that the nuclear weapons codes be transmitted to General Shaposhnikov representing President Yeltsin.[12] On Christmas Day the Soviet flag, which had flown over the Kremlin for 74 years, was lowered ceremoniously for the last time. The Soviet Union was no more.

The Commonwealth of Independent States

On December 8, 1991, the presidents of the republics of Russia, Ukraine, and Belarus (formerly Byelorussia), meeting in the latter's capital, Minsk, declared that the Soviet Union no longer existed and announced formation of a Commonwealth of Independent States (*Sodruzhestvo Nezavisimykh Gosudarstv*). The leaders of the three Slavic republics, linked historically for centuries, urged establishment of "coordinating bodies" for foreign affairs, defense, and the economy, with their seat in Minsk (in order to meet Ukrainian fears that Russia might dominate any new state). A common "economic space" was to be formed with the ruble as its common currency, and the Commonwealth was to remain open to all former Soviet republics and outside countries "sharing the aims and principles of this agreement." They pledged to fulfill Soviet international obligations and to ensure unified control over Soviet nuclear weapons. The three presidents agreed to carry out "coordinated

radical economic reforms" and create market economies. Soviet President Gorbachev denounced this agreement as "illegal and dangerous," but he was powerless to prevent it.

Two weeks later, at the Alma-Ata meeting, the Commonwealth of Independent States (CIS) was reformed to include central Asian republics, and by the end of December all former Soviet republics had joined it except the three Baltic republics and Georgia, then torn by a violent power struggle between President Zviad Gamsakhurdia and a rebel opposition movement that accused him of dictatorship. On December 25, 1991, President Gorbachev resigned as Soviet chief of state, the Soviet seat at the United Nations was assumed by Russia, and foreign governments recognized the former Soviet republics as independent countries.

Meeting in Minsk on December 30, 1991, the republic leaders agreed to establish governing councils of presidents and prime ministers of their respective states as the chief coordinating bodies of the new CIS. However, they failed to draw up either a political charter for the CIS or a cohesive plan for economic reform, or to establish unified armed forces. Individual republics could form their own armies, declared Yeltsin, although he hoped they would opt for a unified command. Marshal Evgenii Shaposhnikov of Russia would continue indefinitely as interim commander of the CIS's armed forces and its nuclear weapons.

In mid-1992 the former Soviet Empire appeared to be suspended in a vacuum containing the vague and disputatious CIS. Russia was emerging as successor to the old USSR in some ways, as Russian President Yeltsin had supplanted former Soviet President Gorbachev. Russia loomed so much larger territorially, politically, and economically than other republics that it naturally assumed a role of leadership. Thus in January 1992, when Russia introduced its "price liberalization," the other republics partially and hesitantly followed suit. Under the Russian reform consumer prices were to be set by manufacturers, regional authorities, and retailers, not by centralized state

---

[12] Matlock, pp. 645–47.

economic agencies as before. The Russian government maintained price ceilings on basic foods and fuels, allowing them to rise moderately. Most other price controls were lifted, many small businesses were privatized, and the budget deficit was reduced, but privatization of farm property lagged. Increasing numbers of industrial workers were laid off, military plants closed, and exports, imports, and industrial output plummeted, leaving most Russians near or below the poverty level. Other republics continued to follow suit reluctantly.

To alleviate the former Soviet Union's mounting financial crisis, the Group of Seven advanced industrial nations (United States, Germany, Japan, Canada, France, Great Britain, and Italy) on April 1, 1992, announced a $24 billion aid package (mostly credits) for Russia over a three-year period, including $6 billion to stabilize the ruble. Two weeks later an official of the International Monetary Fund (IMF) predicted that other CIS countries would require an additional $20 billion to ensure continued progress toward market economies. "The magnitude of the problem facing the 15 republics is unprecedented," stated an IMF spokesperson. "They go far beyond what is generally understood by the concept of economic transformation. These peoples are creating new nations from scratch and in a very brief period."[13] Soon thereafter Russia and other CIS members were invited to join the IMF. This invitation constituted a major step toward their eventual economic integration with the West, a process begun five years earlier by Gorbachev. Declared President Bush: "The stakes are as high for us now as any that we have faced in this century. . . . Future generations of Americans will thank us for having had the foresight and conviction to stand up for democracy and work for peace."[14]

Meanwhile the former Soviet Army, with some 3.5 million men the largest armed force in the world, survived in a dead empire, "orphaned, bankrupt, humiliated, demoralized, often for sale."[15] Morale among officers and men plummeted and desertions and draft-dodging were rife, but preserving this army seemed preferable to massive military unemployment. Russian submarines, aircraft, and weapons were being sold to foreign countries to raise cash. Housing was lacking for hundreds of thousands of former Soviet troops withdrawn from Germany and eastern Europe. President Yeltsin of Russia advocated unified Commonwealth armed forces, but President Kravchuk of Ukraine demanded that the 700,000 former Soviet soldiers on its territory swear loyalty to Ukraine. Thousands of long-range nuclear weapons remained in Russia, Ukraine, Kazakhstan, and Belarus.

Controversy between Russia and Ukraine, the two most populous republics, over control of the Black Sea Fleet and possession of Crimea threatened to fragment the infant CIS. On behalf of the Commonwealth's Unified Command, President Yeltsin insisted that the Black Sea Fleet, the smallest of four former Soviet naval fleets, constituted an integral part of the CIS's strategic forces. Some Russian nationalists demanded the retrocession to Russia of Crimea, whose chief city, Sevastopol, was Black Sea Fleet headquarters. Crimea faced a referendum on independence from Ukraine, to which Khrushchev had arbitrarily transferred it from Russia in 1954. After contending over Crimea and the fleet, the presidents of Russia and Ukraine in April 1992 agreed to work out a plan to divide the fleet. "If we are wise enough and calm enough," stated President Kravchuk, "we can solve the [fleet] question in the interest of our states and our people."[16]

After the USSR dissolved, rising national feelings and ethnic tensions threatened also to tear apart the Russian Federation, which contained at least 39 different nationalities. However, President

---

[13] Steven Greenhouse, "$44 Billion Needed," *New York Times,* April 16, 1992.
[14] Andrew Rosenthal, "Betting on Boris," *New York Times,* April 5, 1992, sec. 4, p. 1.

[15] Serge Schmemann, "The Red Army Fights a Rearguard Action Against History," *New York Times,* March 29, 1992.
[16] Celestine Bohlen, "Black Sea Fleet Dispute Cools," *New York Times,* April 10, 1992.

Yeltsin scored a major success on March 31, when 18 of 20 main subdivisions of the Federation signed a federal treaty creating a new post-Soviet Russian state. While binding them together in a single Russian Federation (or Russia), the treaty accorded local units considerable political and

economic autonomy. Although largely Muslim and oil-rich Chechen-Ingushetia (bordering on Georgia) and Tatarstan refused to sign it, the federal treaty nonetheless outlined a way of preserving the Russian Federation intact.

Problem 16

Why Did the Soviet Union Collapse?

How could the apparently powerful and formidable Soviet empire, which had dominated half of Europe since World War II while holding its people in impotent obedience, suddenly disintegrate and collapse in 1991? There has been considerable debate both in the former Soviet empire and in the West since then as to the causes of this sudden death that few anticipated. Did the USSR fall of its own weight from accumulated political, social, and economic imbalances and errors, or was General Secretary Gorbachev responsible by his policies of *glasnost* and *perestroika?* Was this last great world empire bankrupted by excessive military spending under Brezhnev? Were Brezhnev's heavy outlays designed to keep himself in power, or were they a response to major American rearmament by President Reagan? Again is posed the issue: Has Russia's, and the USSR's, fate been determined chiefly by internal or external factors? Should the West—notably the United States—rejoice and take credit for the demise of Soviet communism, its enemy in the Cold War? Was the allegedly false ideology of Marxism-Leninism, based on lies and deception, to blame for the collapse once the Soviet people, partly as a result of foreign radio broadcasts, discovered the truth? Did the West and the United States foster the collapse or seek to prevent it?

Sigmund Krancberg: A Soviet Postmortem

The American scholar, Sigmund Krancberg argues that the "grand failure" of the Soviet system was rooted in the failure of Marxist-Leninist ideology to provide a viable basis for the Soviet regime and its actions.

> The degeneration of the Bolshevik dictatorship into "a power that is not limited by any laws, not bound by any rules, and is based directly on force" compromised and impoverished the Communist ideas and plans for social development as an ordered and continuous process of social growth. In the long run, with the lack of legal safeguards against the abuse of power, the sordid reality of Soviet social and political life contributed to the fragility and collapse of the Soviet system—a system that originated "in a utopia that led to its practical failure." Bolshevism—in a massive attempt to substitute ideology for reality—lost in the course of its history the political, moral, and intellectual standing in the countless inhuman excesses of War Communism and forced collectivization, in the extensive purges and Moscow trials, in the Hitler-Stalin pact, and in the autocratic, cruel, and oppressive treatment of the Soviet people after the Second World War. And all these atrocities were committed in the name of a Marxist-Leninist ideology that considered violence as the midwife of history. . . .
>
> . . . The growing recognition of the terrible inefficiencies of the Soviet system, with its social decay and the faltering command economy, was reflected in Gorbachev's catchword of *"perestroika"*. . . . Despite its novelty and great significance, *perestroika* failed to alleviate the deepening economic

crisis exacerbated by the tradition of rigid planning, poor growth in productivity, and lagging technological performance.[17]

George Urban: American Democracy Aided Communism's Collapse

A former director of Radio Free Europe, George Urban, while agreeing that mistakes and inadequacies of the Soviet system itself were the primary factor in its demise, affirms that the West, and especially the United States, contributed to that result. Urban stresses particularly the impact of broadcasts by Radio Free Europe and Radio Liberty.

> In what sense can it be said that we in the West made a contribution to the fall of the Soviet system? We did so, as I see it, in at least three different ways. First, American rearmament under President Reagan, and especially the SDI (Strategic Defense Initiative) project, conjured up for an already declining Soviet economy the prospect of so heavy an extra burden that the Soviet leadership was propelled to surrender Moscow's outposts in the colonial empire as well as its glacis in Central and Eastern Europe. . . . President Reagan had caused the USSR to spend itself into near-bankruptcy; and when bankruptcy began to loom, the USSR sent itself into liquidation.
>
> The second way in which we hastened the demise of the Soviet system has been by example: the mere existence of relatively rich and relatively free capitalist countries, side by side with the Soviet Union and its satellites, carried its own message. The spirit of rebellion grew from nothing more dramatic than geographic proximity. . . . What could be bought in Germany, spoken in France, and printed in Holland could not be bought, spoken or printed in the USSR or Poland. With *glasnost*, the abolition of jamming, growing economic links, cultural cross-fertilization and international

travel, it proved no longer possible to isolate the Soviet system from the rest of the real world. Something had to give—and it did. We can now see why Stalin and the Stalinists were, from their point of view, right to segregate their empire from the rest of humanity. . . .
>
> The third contribution to the fall of the Soviet system has been a deliberate policy of identification with the nations under Communist tutelage. Back in the early 1950s, farsighted Americans recognized the need to equip Western—especially U.S.—foreign policy with a psychological arm to enable us to talk to the peoples of the extended Soviet empire. Radio Free Europe and Radio Liberty . . . turned out to be . . . one of the most successful political investments the U.S. has ever made, for much of World War III was fought and won in terms of ideas and culture.[18]

John P. Maynard: Soviet Communism Collapsed on Its Own

Maynard, a pseudonym for a staff member of the United States Congress, asserts that the West deserves no credit for the USSR's collapse—that, in fact, the United States helped the Soviet Communist Party retain power right to the end by providing economic and technical assistance. Instead the Soviet system collapsed because of the basic flaws of socialism.

> It is hard to see how anyone can seriously claim "We won," when we, the West, were primarily responsible for keeping the Soviet Union alive for over seventy years. We did not win. They lost—notwithstanding our efforts to keep them alive!
>
> . . . Franklin Roosevelt came to the aid of the Soviet tyrants many times beginning in 1933 when he extended diplomatic recognition to the Stalinist regime and continuing into World War II . . . in a multitude of ways which we are only now coming to hear about. Most disgraceful was Yalta, when against Churchill's objections, Roosevelt agreed to hand over the entire eastern half of Europe to brutal Marxist depredation under Stalin.

---

[17] Sigmund Krancberg, *A Soviet Postmortem: Philosophical Roots of the "Grand Failure"* (Lanham, MD, 1994), pp. 140–43.

[18] William Barbour and Carol Wekesser, eds., *The Breakup of the Soviet Union: Opposing Viewpoints* (San Diego, 1994), pp. 19–20.

Problem 16 continued

Notwithstanding the Cold War and the U.S. containment policy, every U.S. President since Roosevelt has in some way provided economic and technical assistance which has in effect served to keep communism alive. Most recently, when the "evil empire" began to break up, official U.S. policy was to preserve the Soviet empire intact—denying freedom and self-determination to the various peoples that had been forcibly incorporated into it. George Bush did his best to keep Gorbachev in power. . . .

. . . U.S. financial and technical assistance was undoubtedly used to build up the Soviet military machine. . . . The Soviet economy was aided consciously or unconsciously, by U.S. Presidents and Western industrialists and merchants like Armand Hammer. . . . Ford Motors even constructed and financed the factory that built the large military trucks used by the Soviets in their invasion of Afghanistan. Now our leaders have the gall, the audacity, to say "We won." . . . Socialism collapsed in the USSR under its own weight *despite* the help it constantly received from the West. . . . The collapse of the Soviet Union is a living example of the effects of socialism. . . . The inefficiency, bureaucratic incompetence, inherent nepotism, and the deadening absence of human freedom which kills the soul, were the causes of its collapse.[19]

Michael Mandelbaum: Gorbachev's Reforms Doomed the USSR

A professor of political science at Johns Hopkins University in Baltimore, Mandelbaum argues that it was the well-intentioned but poorly conceived political reforms of a humane Soviet leader, Mikhail Gorbachev, that ultimately destroyed the Soviet system that he had attempted to reform and make freer. However, he praises Gorbachev's humanity and refusal to use violent means to preserve the Soviet empire.

[19] John P. Maynard, "What's Sad about the Soviet Collapse," *Conservative Review*, April 1992.

How did it happen that a mighty imperial state, troubled but stable only a few years before, had come to the brink of collapse in 1991? Who and what was responsible? The chief architect of the Soviet collapse was Mikhail Gorbachev himself. During the August 1991 coup, as a prisoner of the junta in his Crimean villa, he was the object of a struggle between the partisans of the old order and the champions of liberal values. But it was Gorbachev who had in the period between his coming to power in 1985 and the fateful days of August 1991, created the conditions that had touched off this struggle.

The Soviet leader had created them unintentionally. His aim had been to strengthen the political and economic system that he inherited, to strip away their Stalinist accretions and make the Soviet Union a modern dynamic state. Instead he had fatally weakened it. Intending to reform Soviet communism he had, rather, destroyed it. The three major policies that he had launched to fashion a more efficient and humane form of socialism—glasnost, democratization, and perestroika—had in the end subverted, discredited, and all but done away with the network of political and economic institutions that his Communist Party had constructed in Russia and surrounding countries since 1917. . . .

Glasnost enabled the people of the Soviet Union to lay claim to the public sphere after seven decades of exile from it. Through democratization they had the opportunity for the first time, to act collectively in that sphere. . . . The experiment in democracy that he launched did not demonstrate, as Gorbachev had hoped, that he enjoyed popular support. . . . Elections discredited the official dictum that the Communist Party had earned public gratitude and support for the "noble farsighted" leadership it had provided since 1917. . . . Democratization also created the opportunity for the beginning of an alternative to the communist political elite to emerge. In Russia its main orientation was anticommunism and Boris Yeltsin became its leading figure. . . .

Glasnost and democratization were for Gorbachev, means to an end. That end was the improvement of Soviet economic performance. Economic reform was the central feature of his program . . . to lift the country out of the economic stagnation into which it had lapsed at the end of

---

Problem 16 continued

the Brezhnev era. . . . Gorbachev's most enduring
and destructive legacy . . . [was] a severe fiscal
imbalance. The center's obligations expanded as it
poured more and more money into investment and
tried to buy public support with generous wage
increases. At the same time its income plummeted,
as republican governments and enterprises . . .
refused to send revenues to Moscow.[20]

John L. H. Keep:
An Element of Chance
Was Involved

John Keep, a leading British scholar, attributes
the collapse of the USSR largely to social change
over a period of decades and declining economic
growth rates. However, he does not view the fall
of the Soviet system as inevitable until 1989 and
notes elements of chance as well.

In the USSR the accession to power of Mikhail
Sergeevich Gorbachev in March 1985 unleashed a
chain reaction. Within less than seven years it led
to the extinction of the world's number two superpower. Historians are naturally tempted to see such
an astonishing development as foreordained, and to
try to explain it by the working out of long-term
processes. Yet clearly an element of chance was
involved as well. . . .

Perhaps the end of Soviet Communism, like its
beginnings, can best be explained by weighing up
probabilities at successive historical moments. In
the earlier case the road led to an increasingly
violent catastrophe as various alternative courses of
development were successively ruled out. . . .
During the Brezhnev era a new generation of Soviet
citizens came to the fore who could not be satisfied
by the simple certainties of the official ideology.
Better educated than their parents or grandparents,
and accustomed to a modest level of prosperity, the
members of this urban elite sought greater individual autonomy and material well-being. These
yearnings evoked a response among writers and

other intellectuals whose views became widely
known, despite the censorship. In this way an
informal "second culture" took shape that was
potentially as subversive of collectivist values as
the "second economy" was of the state-socialist
order. By the mid-1980s there were many pointers
to impending crisis: falling growth rates, major
ecological disasters, and the army's inability to
defeat the Afghan *mujaheddin*—to mention only
three of the most obvious.

All this made systemic change likely, but not
inevitable. Other options were still open. The most
plausible scenario was that by embarking on a
program of reform the Party would restore its
shaken credibility and maintain its rule, perhaps in
slightly amended form. This required both a peaceful international environment and an unusual
degree of skill on the part of the reformist leaders.
They needed to know just where they were heading
and to take the people into their confidence. In the
event Gorbachev did permit a fair measure of freedom of expression (*glasnost*), but failed to answer
clearly the question what *perestroika* (restructuring)
really involved or how it was to be achieved. . . . He
was basically a pragmatist, but could not shake off
a residual Marxist-Leninist dogmatism. . . . He
tried to be both Luther and the Pope.

. . . In the face of emerging conservative and
radical lobbies he had to take a "centrist" line,
advancing or retreating as the constellation of
power changed. But each successive tactical shift
reduced his area of manoeuvre and added to the
ranks of the disaffected. They seized on the new
opportunities to make their views known. The
greater the amount of liberty conceded, the more
difficult it became to check its unwelcome consequences without resorting to coercive methods that
had supposedly been abandoned. From 1989
onwards the regime began to lose control.

• • •

Contrary to all earlier expectations, it was
Ukraine . . . that would deal the final knife-thrust to
the tottering USSR. From mid-1990 onwards there
was a fatal weakness at the heart of the empire
symbolized by the Yeltsin-Gorbachev dyarchy. The
conservative *coup* of August 1991 made it infinitely
more difficult to keep the Union together. It was
less the cause of the empire's disintegration than a
symptom of the cancer that was eating it away. This
had its origin in the inability of Communism . . . to

---

[20] Michael Mandelbaum, "Coup de Grace: The End of the Soviet
Union," *Foreign Affairs*, Autumn/Winter 1991–1992.

Problem 16 continued

contain centrifugal pressures that had been build-ing up for decades.[21]

Conclusion

Controversy persists whether the chief causes of the sudden collapse of the Soviet Union in 1991

---

[21] John L. H. Keep, *Last of the Empires: A History of the Soviet Union 1945–1991* (Oxford and New York, 1995), pp. 331–32, 383. Reprinted by permission of Oxford University Press.

derived from fundamental flaws in a system rely-ing upon a decayed and false ideology, an unfree political setup, and an outdated command econ-omy that could no longer satisfy people's needs, or from pressure applied by the West, notably the United States of President Reagan. The allure of freedom prevalent in the West appears to have contributed to the demise of a system that had long concealed its basic shortcomings from its citizens and from the outside world. The USSR's huge natural resources may have helped prolong its survival until 1991. Was the result inevitable or speeded by a well-meaning Presi-dent Gorbachev? ■

Suggested Additional Reading

ALLISON, G., and G. YAVLINSKY. *Window of Opportu-nity: The Grand Bargain for Democracy in the Soviet Union* (New York, 1991).

ANDERSON, J. *Religion, State and Politics in the Soviet Union and Successor States* (Cambridge, 1994).

ARNOLD, A. *The Fateful Pebble: Afghanistan's Role in the Fall of the Soviet Empire* (Novato, CA, 1993).

"The August Coup," *New Left Review,* no. 189 (September–October 1991).

BARBOUR, W., and C. WEKNESSER, eds. *The Breakup of the Soviet Union: Opposing Viewpoints* (San Diego, 1994).

BERMEO, N., ed. *Liberalization and Democratization: Change in the Soviet Union and Eastern Europe* (Balti-more and London, 1992).

BUTTINO, M., ed. *In a Collapsing Empire: Ethnic Conflicts and Nationalism in the Soviet Union* (Milan, 1993).

DUNLOP, J. B. *The Rise of Russia and the Fall of the Soviet Empire* (Princeton, 1993).

D'ENCAUSSE, H. C. *The End of the Soviet Empire: The Triumph of the Nations,* trans. Franklin Philip (New York, 1993).

FESHBACH, M. *Ecological Disaster: Cleaning Up the Hidden Legacy of the Soviet Regime* (New York, 1995).

GILL, G. *The Collapse of a Single Party System: The Disin-tegration of the Communist Party of the Soviet Union* (Cambridge, 1994).

GORBACHEV, M. *The August Coup: The Truth and the Lessons* (New York, 1991).

GRAHAM, L. R. *The Ghost of the Executed Engineer: Technology and the Fall of the Soviet Union* (Cambridge, MA, 1996).

GWERTZMAN, B., and M. KAUFMAN, eds. *The Collapse of Communism: By the Correspondents of the New York Times,* rev. ed. (New York, 1991).

HEWETT, E. A., and C. G. GADDY. *Open for Business: Russia's Return to the Global Economy* (Washington, 1992).

HOLMES, L. *The End of Communist Power: Anti-Corruption Campaigns and Legitimation Crisis* (New York and Oxford, 1993).

KRANCBERG, S. *A Soviet Postmortem: Philosophical Roots of the "Grand Failure"* (Lanham, MD, 1994).

KRASNOV, V. *Russia Beyond Communism: A Chronicle of National Rebirth* (Boulder, CO, 1991).

LAPIDUS, G., et al., eds. *From Union to Commonwealth: Nationalism and Separatism in the Soviet Republics* (Cambridge, 1992).

LAUBE, E., ed. *Chronicle of the Soviet Coup, 1990–1992: A Reader in Soviet Politics* (Dubuque, IA, 1992).

LIEVEN, A. *The Baltic Revolution: Estonia, Latvia, Lithua-nia and the Path to Independence* (New Haven, CT, 1993).

LOORY, S. H., and A. IMSE. *Seven Days That Shook the World: The Collapse of Soviet Communism* (Atlanta, 1991).

MATLOCK, J. F., JR. *Autopsy on an Empire. The American Ambassador's Account of the Collapse of the Soviet Union* (New York, 1995).

MILLAR, J., and S. WOLCHIK, eds. *The Social Legacy of Communism* (Cambridge, 1994).

MORRISON, J. *Boris Yeltsin: From Bolshevik to Democrat* (New York, 1991).

"Moscow, August 1991: The Coup de Grace," *Problems of Communism*, 39 (November–December 1991), pp. 1–62. (Articles on the August Coup.)

One Nation Becomes Many: The ACCESS Guide to the Former Soviet Union (Washington, 1992).

PEI, M. *From Reform to Revolution: The Demise of Communism in China and the Soviet Union* (Cambridge, MA, 1994).

REZEN, M., ed. *Nationalism and the Breakup of an Empire: Russia and Its Periphery.* (Westport, CT, 1992).

ROEDER, P. G. *Red Sunset: The Failure of Soviet Politics* (Princeton, 1993).

SMART, C. *The Imagery of Soviet Foreign Policy and the Collapse of the Russian Empire* (Westport, CT, 1995).

SOLCHANYK, R. *Ukraine: From Chernobyl to Sovereignty* (New York, 1992).

SOLOVIEV, V. *Boris Yeltsin: A Political Biography* (New York, 1992).

STOKES, G. *The Walls Come Tumbling Down: The Collapse of Communism in Eastern Europe* (New York and Oxford, 1993).

WALLER, M. *The End of the Communist Power Monopoly* (New York and Manchester, 1994).

WHITE, S., et al., eds. *Development in Soviet and Post-Soviet Politics,* 2d ed. (Durham, NC, 1992).

YELTSIN, B. N. *Against the Grain: An Autobiography,* trans. Michael Glenny (New York, 1990).

45

The Legacy of Soviet Communism and Troubled Transitions in the 1990s

At the end of 1991 most citizens of the former USSR appeared to agree that the Soviet legacy was overwhelmingly negative. The Soviet system, established in November 1917, had proven a colossal failure in virtually every aspect, inducing some to repudiate the November Revolution and its leader, V. I. Lenin, as historical aberrations.

Nowhere was Soviet communism's failure more evident than in economics and finance. The centralized economic system outlined by Lenin but created largely by Stalin during the First Five Year Plan, churned out vast amounts of steel, coal, and oil, which made the USSR a leading military power from World War II until 1990, but it was an economy of shortages that provided little for most Soviet consumers. After 1975 most Soviet citizens saw their living standards and buying power fall further and further behind not just the United States and Japan but virtually every European and many Asian countries. The massive heavy industries established in the 1930s became increasingly obsolete under Brezhnev and his successors and caused unprecedented environmental pollution. In agriculture the collective and state farm system,

created forcibly under Stalin, had killed or exiled millions of the best Soviet farmers as alleged exploiters (kulaks), enslaving the rest under a 20th-century version of serfdom. Condemning millions to starvation by famine, Stalin disrupted Russian and Ukrainian agriculture, which before 1914 had exported millions of tons of grain. Agriculture became the perpetually backward and inefficient stepchild of Soviet communism, compelling Khrushchev and his successors to import massive amounts of grain from the capitalist West.

During the last years of tsarism Russian workers had enjoyed improving working conditions, rising real wages, and increasing rights to organize and strike. Under the so-called proletarian Soviet dictatorship of Lenin and Stalin they soon lost all these gains and any right to choose their jobs or determine their pay. Low real wages and a cradle-to-grave system of state-provided benefits undermined the Soviet worker's desire to work hard and well. This was summed up in the post-Stalinist quip, "We pretend to work, and they pretend to pay us." The worker's plight was exacerbated by burgeoning corruption, massive stealing from the state, and rampant cynicism. Workers and farmers alike were deprived of any real incentive to strive for quality, and Soviet products were spurned in world markets.

In the 1890s, under Count Witte, Russian state finances were placed on the gold standard and the ruble became fully convertible. Russia prior to World War I enjoyed exemplary credit, which made possible large-scale foreign borrowing to finance advancing industrialization. Under the Soviet regime this progress was totally negated and reversed. By 1991 the USSR had a massive external debt that it could not service and a huge budget deficit. Its currency, the ruble (or better: rubble!), had become virtually worthless inside and outside the country; hyperinflation loomed. The expiring Soviet Union, despite possessing huge quantities of salable raw materials, depended on foreign charity to avert bankruptcy.

Politically, imperial Russia in 1914 was moving, if uncertainly, toward constitutional monarchy, public debate, and the rule of law. It was an empire in which individual minority groups, except for Jews and Poles, enjoyed broader political and cultural rights than in previous centuries. Russia appeared to be following the positive political course taken earlier by western Europe; its links with Europe were growing ever stronger. Then the Soviet regime of Lenin and Stalin imposed a brutal despotism on the peoples of the empire, reintegrating most of them forcibly into a new Soviet empire. The fake federalism embodied in the Stalin Constitution of 1936 left them under Russian rule without real autonomy or decision-making power. Between 1936 and 1953 millions of Russians, but especially non-Russians, were exiled and executed. Entire peoples were uprooted from ancestral homelands and exiled forcibly to Siberia and Central Asia, notably Crimean Tatars, Volga Germans, Chechens, and Baltic peoples. Stalin's minions murdered at least 25 million people of various nationalities, partly to assuage a paranoid dictator.

Soviet foreign policy, after positive beginnings under foreign commissars Chicherin and Litvinov, ended disastrously. Stalin, after helping Hitler achieve power, concluded the Nazi-Soviet Pact in order to dominate eastern Europe; it triggered World War II. Afterward the Stalin regime provoked a lengthy and incredibly costly Cold War with the West. It subjugated eastern Europe, wiping out those who resisted, especially in Poland, imposing by force Soviet-style regimes on its helpless peoples. Thrice the Soviet army intervened with massive force—in East Germany, Hungary, and Czechoslovakia—to suppress popular revolts and perpetuate regimes that lacked local roots. The Cold War saddled the Soviet and Western peoples with huge burdens in order to maintain bloated military forces and huge arsenals of weapons of mass destruction. Soviet foreign policy was based on monstrous lies mouthed by thousands of obedient diplomats or secret police operatives masquerading as diplomats.

Late imperial Russia had seen an unprecedented flowering of creativity in literature, music, and art and had made great contributions to world culture. Russia was becoming increasingly integrated into European civilization. Lenin's Soviet regime severed these promising links, as hundreds of Russian writers, composers, and artists chose exile to escape its tyranny. Many others were later murdered in Stalin's purges. Those who remained in the Soviet Union were subjected to a stifling and pervasive system of state controls euphemistically called "socialist realism," which glorified mediocrity and persecuted originality and creativity. The result, prior to Gorbachev's *glasnost,* was the devastation of the brilliant and creative Russian cultural tradition.

The entire perverted Soviet system rested on the ideology of Marxism-Leninism, based in the USSR on an interlocking network of lies and deceptions. The Soviet people in 1917 had been promised abundance, peace, and freedom under socialism but instead received hardships, shortages, enslavement, and war. In place of a true socialist system based on the equality promised by Marx and Lenin emerged a new class of parasitic apparatchiks and partocrats with special stores and clinics, luxurious dachas, and a myriad of special privileges. That new class exploited the labor of the Soviet masses for its own selfish benefit. Marxist ideology, thoroughly perverted and robbed of all meaning under Stalin, became a mask to conceal massive inequality and injustice. Efforts to liberalize and humanize this corrupt Soviet system under Khrushchev and Gorbachev led instead to its deserved and mostly unlamented destruction in 1991. As had been said of the Roman Empire, the amazing thing was not that it collapsed, but that it persisted so long.

A Devastated Land

Among the staggering problems confronting the countries of the former USSR, none is more daunting than their devastated environment. Like other industrialized nations, the Soviet Union ignored environmental consequences as it exploited abundant natural resources to create a massive industrial base. For more than 70 years the USSR assaulted the environment relentlessly and undermined the population's health. The drive to fulfill centrally determined economic plans preempted every other concern. The legacy of that relentless drive has been unprecedented environmental destruction.

However, from the start there were those in Soviet Russia who were aware of the dangers of wantonly disregarding nature. Some Soviet environmentalists were well ahead of European and American colleagues in recognizing the dangers industrial development posed for the environment. They realized that natural resources needed to be expended rationally and husbanded with an eye to their preservation and replenishment.[1]

In the Soviet Union a struggle erupted between "modernizers" advocating rapid technical progress to achieve a modern "heaven on earth" and "preservationists" who believed desecrating

nature was an excessive price for "progress." Some Soviet scientists opposed economic bureaucrats advocating human "mastery of nature" and its systematic exploitation by the state. This reflected a struggle between the Communist Party, seeking to monopolize all decision making, and some scientists, especially conservationists, who believed that rational economic progress could be achieved with careful guidance. The latter wished to block development that threatened nature. However, the Bolsheviks proved unwilling to accept any restraints on their decision making, especially in the economic sphere, where socialist construction became the focus of the Soviet regime.

The battle to protect the environment and the people's health was lost during the Stalin era when the party's primacy in scientific and economic decision making went unchallenged; it remained so virtually to the end of Soviet rule. Economic decisions were never subject to debate; one either accepted them or remained silent. Politburo or Central Committee decisions were implemented through the economic ministries without regard for scientific or public opinion. Despite scientists' growing concerns about environmental problems, little could be done about them until the Gorbachev era.

Seeking to demonstrate the socialist system's superiority, from the 1960s on impressive pollution control policies were adopted and Soviet environmental legislation was touted as the world's most stringent. Declared the Soviet Minister of Public Health B. V. Petrovskii in 1968:

> Problems related to air and water pollution are being discussed in a host of capitalist countries. But the capitalist system by its very essence, is incapable of taking radical measures to ensure efficient conservation of nature. In the Soviet Union, however, questions of protecting the environment from pollution by industrial wastes occupy the center of the Party's and government's attention. It is forbidden to put industrial projects into operation if the construction of purification installations has not been completed. The Soviet Union has

---

[1] For early Soviet debates on conservation and ecology, see Douglas R. Weiner, *Models of Nature: Ecology, Conservation and Cultural Revolution in Soviet Russia* (Bloomington, IN, 1988), pp. 19–84.

been the first country in the world to set maximum permissible concentrations of harmful substances in the air of populated areas.[2]

The 1977 Soviet Constitution boasted:

> All necessary steps will be taken to protect and make scientific, rational use of the land and its mineral and water resources, and the plant and animal kingdoms, to preserve the purity of air and water, to ensure reproduction of natural wealth, and to improve the human environment.

Article 42 guaranteed Soviet citizens the right to a healthy environment, and Article 67 obligated them "to protect nature and conserve its riches." At best pious hopes, mostly for international consumption, environmental concern and enforcement were minimal until the end of Soviet rule.

Soviet environmental legislation was so strict that local enforcement was virtually impossible, and the legislation was mostly ignored with impunity. Ultimate responsibility for its enforcement belonged to the Supreme Soviet and the Council of Ministers. The State Planning Committee (Gosplan) was responsible for planning development of the Soviet economy. Environmental aspects of the economic plans were handled by an elaborate structure of ministries and state committees responsible for both conservation and production. Whenever these two conflicted, production prevailed. Noted one American scholar:

> Instead of serving as a referee between polluters and conservationists, government officials usually supported the polluters. . . . The most important criterion for any government official (or factory manager) who seeks promotion or recognition is how much his production has increased in his region (factory), *not* to what extent his rivers have been cleaned up this year. . . . Few government officials (or factory managers) are likely to be particularly

sympathetic to those who threaten the attainment of new production records.[3]

Thus enterprises easily ignored environmental legislation because monitoring agencies were also those responsible for meeting production goals. The economic plan always took precedence over environmental considerations, with tragic results.

Seeking to remedy this sorry state of affairs, Soviet authorities in the late 1970s entrusted power to monitor the environment to the State Committee for Hydrometeorology and Environmental Control (*Gidromet*). However, it lacked essential powers of enforcement, remained the creature of the economic ministries, and was largely ignored by polluters. After the Chernobyl disaster of 1986 a new agency—the USSR State Committee for Environmental Protection (*Goskompriroda*)—was to supervise the environment, theoretically with broad powers over the ministries, but from the beginning it was underfunded and understaffed and lacked real enforcement authority over the economic ministries. Its chairman was called "a general without an army."

Under Gorbachev a "green movement" flourished briefly and became an outspoken critic of Soviet power. However, with the end of the Soviet Union this movement declined, yielding to pressing problems of economic survival. Environmental concerns, while receiving lip service, have been largely ignored by a Yeltsin government striving to develop a genuine market economy. State funds are lacking even for the most urgent environmental problems. The legacy of Soviet environmental neglect and mismanagement must be ended soon if previous grievous damage to the former Soviet land and people is to be overcome. A full assessment of this damage has yet to be made. Recognizing the problem's dimensions and establishing priorities are urgent for a solution to the area's enormous environmental problems.

---

[2] *Current Digest of the Soviet Press,* July 17, 1968, p. 16.

[3] Marshall I. Goldman, *The Spoils of Progress: Environmental Pollution in the Soviet Union* (Cambridge, MA, 1972), pp. 69–70.

How great was the environmental damage caused by irresponsible Soviet economic policies? Two leading American experts suggest:

> When historians finally conduct an autopsy on the Soviet Union and Soviet Communism, they may reach the verdict of death by ecocide [ecological suicide]. . . . No other great industrial civilization so systematically and so long poisoned its land, air, water and people.[4]

Public health has been so undermined by the polluted environment that in Russia alone among industrialized nations, life expectancy has declined sharply—from 66 in the 1960s to 58 in 1993—and is still declining.[5]

Once boasting majestic stands of forest, pristine lakes and rivers, Russia has become a vast arena of pollution and sickness. While transforming Russia into an urban-industrial giant, Soviet authorities ruthlessly polluted and destroyed rivers and lakes, killed a giant sea, destroyed vast tracts of the world's richest supply of forest, and sacrificed the lives of countless citizens. Five Year Plans created gigantic industrial complexes. Huge industrial centers like Magnitogorsk, Norilsk, and Cheliabinsk churned out millions of tons of iron, steel, and chemicals, relentlessly burning natural resources without regard for pollution of air and water and creating acid rain. With Russia possessing seemingly inexhaustible natural resources, few in the USSR cared about the tremendous waste—that rivers turned purple with oil-well runoff and the sky turned orange in the glow of burning natural gas. Such destruction occurred despite theoretically stringent environmental standards. This wanton disregard of nature is hard to measure and understates the true dimensions of the tragedy. The examples that follow merely suggest the unprecedented damage caused by decades of environmental neglect.

[4] Murray Feshbach and Alfred Friendly, Jr., *Ecocide in the USSR: Health and Nature Under Siege* (New York, 1992), p. 1.
[5] See *New York Times*, March 28, 1994, p. A5.

Destruction of the Aral Sea

Once larger than most of the Great Lakes, the Aral Sea east of the Caspian Sea on the Kazakh-Uzbek border has lost two-thirds of its volume and 44 percent of its area. In 1960 it measured 26,000 square miles, but by 1990 11,000 square miles of seabed had become desert. Within a generation it will likely disappear completely.

The destruction of the Aral Sea resulted from decisions made in Moscow, more than 1,000 miles away. Its two primary feeder rivers, the Amu Daria (1,578 miles long) and Syr Daria (1,370 miles long), dumped only one-eighth as much water into the sea in 1990 as in 1960. Cotton consumed these rivers' clear waters as a sacrifice on production's altar. Moscow's central economic planning agencies decided to create a cotton monoculture in Central Asia. Cotton harvests increased 70 percent between 1965 and 1983 following the diversion from the Amu and Syr rivers of huge quantities of water to irrigate almost 18 million acres of cotton.

The water passed into poorly constructed and maintained irrigation ditches, wasting as much as 90 percent of the diverted water before reaching the cotton fields. These waters also carried an increasing chemical runoff from overuse of chemical fertilizers on the cotton crop: phosphates, ammonia, nitrates, and chlorinated hydrocarbons. Virtually all the groundwater in a region of more than 35 million people was poisoned. The Aral Sea's rapid evaporation had unforseen effects on the climate: Temperatures rose in summer and fell in winter to unprecedented extremes. Huge dust storms occurred with increasing frequency as the exposed seabed turned into a great salt desert.

> Yearly in the 1980s the storms carried between 90 and 140 million tons of salt and sand from the 11,000-plus square miles of exposed seabed to Byelorussian farmlands 1,200 miles to the northwest, and half as far southeast to the snowfields of Afghanistan where the Amu Daria rises.[6]

[6] Feshbach and Friendly, *Ecocide*, p. 75.

This ecological disaster affected not only the region's soil and water but its people as well. Whole industries were destroyed:

> Once there were 10,000 fishermen working out of Muynak [a center of the fishing industry formerly on the coast and now 65 miles inland], taking pike, perch, and bream as fat as piglets from the Aral. The town produced three percent of the Soviet annual catch. There were 24 native species of fish in the Aral. Today there are none, and the commercial fishing industry is dead.[7]

During the 1980s infant and maternal mortality rates in the region doubled and tripled, respectively. Throat cancers and respiratory and eye diseases have soared from large clouds of gritty salts that clog the air around the Aral Sea. Concluded Feshbach and Friendly: "The sea turning to desert was a symbol of a sixty-year pattern of ecocide by deliberate design."[8]

What of the future? Even heroic measures can never restore the Aral Sea to its condition in 1960. At best the situation might be stabilized so the sea will not disappear completely. But resources to initiate such a stabilization seem unavailable and whatever remains of the Aral Sea will be largely useless, five times saltier than the oceans, a "dead sea."

Air Pollution

Despite stringent air quality norms, air pollution remains a major environmental problem. According to data presented to Soviet prosecutors late in 1990, the life expectancy of Moscow residents—ten years below what it had been in 1970—ranked the metropolis 70th among the world's largest cities. Congenitally deformed children were being born in Moscow one-and-a-half times as often as in the USSR as a whole. With infant mortality two to three times higher in Moscow than in other republic capitals in 1989, "more inhabitants . . .

died than were born."[9] The worst air pollution, however, was in Norilsk, Siberia, above the Arctic Circle, where in 1990 270,000 residents breathed in almost 2.4 million tons of industrial atmospheric pollutants. Sao Paulo, Brazil's largest city, is considered "severely polluted" from 250,000 tons of industrial air pollutants annually, but Norilsk per capita is *222 times* as polluted as Sao Paulo.[10] More than 100 cities in the former USSR have air pollution levels five times or more higher than Soviet standards permitted, exposing millions of people to dangerous respiratory diseases and cancer.

The Chernobyl Accident

The single greatest ecological disaster occurred on April 26, 1986, when Unit Number 4 of the V. I. Lenin Chernobyl Nuclear Power Station was rocked by two explosions, releasing more toxic radioactive material into the atmosphere than the combined bombings of Hiroshima and Nagasaki in World War II.

> A new study suggests that the explosion threw out 100 million curies of dangerous radionuclides, such as cesium 137—twice as much as previous estimates. The World Health Organization reckons that 4.9 million people in Ukraine, Belarus, and Russia were affected. But the consequences, though obviously tragic in some aspects, remain unclear.[11]

The fallout from that accident persists amid growing concern that hasty efforts to seal off reactor 4 were woefully inadequate. Some 180 tons of uranium fuel lie buried inside the sealed-off reactor, and 10 tons of radioactive dust covers everything inside the steel and concrete sarcophagus that encapsulates the damaged reactor, which suffered total meltdown of the core—something originally denied by Soviet authorities. Because the steel and concrete shell is structurally un-

---

[7] William Ellis, "A Soviet Sea Lies Dying," *National Geographic* 177, no. 2 (February 1990), p. 84.
[8] Feshbach and Friendly, p. 75.

[9] Feshbach and Friendly, p. 9.
[10] Feshbach and Friendly, p. 10.
[11] Mike Edwards, "Lethal Legacy: Pollution in the Former USSR," *National Geographic* 186, no. 2 (August 1994), p. 104.

sound, any shifting of debris buried inside could topple the entire structure and high winds could cause it to collapse, releasing a new, lethal cloud of radioactive dust across an already contaminated landscape. It is agreed that the remaining operative reactors on site are unsafe. Because of continuing safety problems at the site, international efforts have been made to have all remaining reactors at Chernobyl shut down. Energy-starved Ukraine has refused—the Chernobyl reactors supply 17 percent of its energy—until alternative sources of energy are on line. In summer 1994 the government ordered reactor 2 restarted.

The full dimensions of the reactor core meltdown are only now emerging. The Chernobyl Union, a citizens group, estimates that at least 5,000 people have died as a direct result of the accident, and the number is increasing each year. More than 30,000 people have been disabled. The spread of cancers and other radiation-related illnesses grows daily; genetic disorders are clearly rising. More than 30,000 square miles of rich farmland have been contaminated, costing billions of dollars. Chernobyl's damage consumes some 15 percent of Ukraine's annual budget, and would cost even more if the government could cope with the growing health problems. Ukraine cannot provide adequate medical diagnosis and treatment, reclamation programs, or adequate measures to prevent future accidents. The future of nuclear power in the CIS states is being publicly debated on local, national, and international levels.

Lake Baikal

For more than 35 years a battle has raged to protect Lake Baikal, the "Pearl of Siberia," from pollution. Battle lines formed between the state bureaucracy and industry, on the one hand, and scientists and public opinion, on the other. That struggle's final outcome remains uncertain, but the efforts to save Lake Baikal have helped define the environmental movement in the former Soviet Union.

Situated in southeastern Siberia, Lake Baikal is the largest body of fresh water on earth—12,200 square miles, up to 5,346 feet deep, a total of 5,520 cubic miles of water. The lake's surface area is about that of Lake Superior, but Baikal holds almost as much fresh water as *all* the Great Lakes combined. Lake Baikal is a natural reservoir for 336 feeder rivers and is drained by a single river, the Angara, flowing northward to the Arctic Ocean. If the water in all the feeder rivers were diverted and the Angara River were allowed to drain the lake, it would take some 400 years to drain it completely.[12] Baikal's waters are so translucent and clear that divers can see clearly to a depth of 150 feet. Baikal comprises a unique ecological system with more than 1,200 forms of unique aquatic life.

Until a century ago, when construction of the Trans-Siberian Railroad intruded, this pristine environment was largely untouched. Even after the railroad appeared, very little development occurred along the lake's extensive perimeter— a few small towns and fishing villages. Serious human challenge to Siberia's "radiant orb" began only in 1957, when Moscow economic planners decided that the lake's pure waters and surrounding stands of timber should be exploited for a very specific purpose, which was revealed only later. In 1979 Ze'ev Wolfson, a knowledgeable Soviet scientist and official, using the pseudonym Boris Komarov, published abroad a devastating account of environmental mismanagement in the USSR. Wrote Komarov:

> At the time [1957], the Ministry of Defense needed new durable cord for heavy bomber tires. Such things are referred to tersely as "strategic interests of the country" and are not subject to discussion even within the Council of Ministers. The immunity of the Baikal projects from any criticism is explained by these "strategic interests." They had sealed Baikal's fate by 1959.[13]

---

[12] Peter Matthiessen, "The Blue Pearl of Siberia," *New York Review of Books* 38, no. 4 (February 14, 1991), p. 37.
[13] Boris Komarov (Ze'ev Wolfson), *The Destruction of Nature in the Soviet Union* (White Plains, NY, 1980), p. 16.

The plan was to build a cellulose-cord processing enterprise at Baikalsk, on the lake's southern shores, and a smaller cardboard manufacturing plant on the major feeder river, the Selenga. The decision to build these plants was based on the need for high-quality, heavy-duty tire cord for long-range strategic bombers, a matter of "national security." Baikal had virtually unlimited supplies of two essential ingredients: pure water and timber. But inasmuch as paper and cellulose manufacturing produce notoriously high levels of toxic wastes, unprecedented opposition developed swiftly to siting the plants in the Baikal region. Outspoken opposition from the scientific community and the public induced the Soviet authorities to compromise by agreeing to install "state-of-the-art" water treatment facilities in order to minimize the dangers to the lake and its environs.

Unfortunately, the plants opened in 1966 before water treatment facilities were available, and loggers began clearing out the vast taiga along the lake's shores. Forest regenerates slowly in the harsh climate, and promised planned reforestation was never initiated. The lakeshore therefore eroded rapidly, and landslides dumped vast quantities of silt into the lake and feeder rivers. Harvested timber was floated down the feeder rivers, and much of it became waterlogged and sank before reaching processing plants. As the timber decayed, bacteria depleted the water's oxygen, destroying fish and aquatic life and the purity of the water in both rivers and lake. Under pressure from scientists and the public, Soviet authorities sought in the 1970s and 1980s to reverse the damage. Logging was banned in a wide belt around the lake, reforestation began, rotting logs were removed from rivers, and log-rafting was banned (logs had to be transported aboard ships).

The worst problem, however, was effluent from more than 100 factories operating on the lake's shores without proper purification facilities. Their untreated wastes were dumped directly into the lake, contaminating it with mercury, lead, zinc, tungsten, and molybdenum. The Baikalsk cellulose factory used enormous amounts of fresh, pure water, discharging it untreated back into the lake. The factory finally had to install expensive water-purifying equipment to treat badly polluted *intake* water. More than 23 square miles of the lake's floor became a "dead zone," where no life survives. The Intourist hotel at Listvianka, a fishing village on the lakeshore north of the Baikalsk plant, can no longer serve drinking water directly from the lake.[14] Agricultural enterprises send chemical fertilizers directly into the feeder rivers. The largest feeder, the Selenga, carries effluents from the industrial center Ulan Ude, 60 miles upriver. Partially treated and raw sewage and effluent from more than 50 factories pour down the Selenga into the lake.

In a classic case of Soviet mismanagement, it soon became clear that the primary purpose of the Baikalsk and Selenga plants had disappeared. As the plants began operating in 1966, it was discovered that nylon cord was more suitable for bomber tires than super cellulose cord, and far cheaper to produce. Many of the superfluous Baikal plants nonetheless still operate. After almost 30 years in service, defying stringent Soviet and Russian emission standards, the Baikalsk plant alone has dumped almost 2 billion cubic meters of untreated industrial wastes directly into Lake Baikal. Closing the plants has been discussed, but that would cost about 30,000 workers their jobs.

Lake Baikal became the first real battlefield between an incipient "green movement" and Soviet planners. The pollution of Lake Baikal first aroused public interest in state policy formulation and led to questioning the Moscow industrial ministries' arrogant power. Public outcry against the needless destruction of a treasured natural resource finally forced Soviet officials to consider environmental protection as an important component of industry. Not wholly successful, the campaign to save the "Pearl of Siberia" launched a Soviet environmental movement that continues today.

---

[14] Matthiessen, "The Blue Pearl," p. 40.

Conclusion

Few resources are currently available to begin restoring environmental balance in Russia and the CIS states, but public awareness is growing that something must be done to protect the environment and population. One outspoken environmentalist, the Siberian author Valentin Rasputin, is pessimistic:

> I remain gloomy and sad about the environmental prospects. . . . Almost all our country's rivers and lakes, especially in Europe, are polluted to a very high degree . . . and even in Siberia there are regions where the water problem is truly serious. There are many groups trying to save the Aral Sea, the Volga Basin, but it is doubtful they will succeed. It will cost billions of rubles, and nobody has the slightest idea where the money will come from. To be sure ecological consciousness is growing, but many still argue against environmental protection.[15]

Improving environmental quality and public health must remain a top Russian priority into the next century and beyond. Continued environmental deterioration would further complicate and perhaps even scuttle the reform process. Russia and the CIS states cannot undertake unaided the many tasks of environmental reclamation. A cooperative international program is required, but Russia must take the lead and make the necessary sacrifices to begin the lengthy process of environmental restoration.

Troubled Transitions, 1992–1998

Beginning in 1992, the former Soviet Union underwent an extremely traumatic triple transition: from an autocratic Communist-ruled state toward a decentralized democracy in Russia; from a centralized command economy featuring heavy industry and state-owned land to a consumer-oriented, privatized economy; and from a multinational empire ruled from Moscow to 15 uneasily

---

[15] Quoted in Matthiessen, p. 47.

coexisting and theoretically independent countries. In mid-1998 it remained uncertain whether this transition could be achieved successfully in Russia and the "near abroad," although considerable economic and political progress had been scored, especially in Russia. The danger remained that this vast area, spanning one-sixth of the globe, could follow the disastrous path taken by former Communist Yugoslavia. Here we will examine key developments there in the realms of politics, economics, and foreign relations during this difficult period.

Politics

A power struggle intensified during 1992–1993 between President Yeltsin and the Russian parliament as his support there declined. Following its session of December 1992 to March 1993, at an emergency meeting in March the parliament sought to curtail the president's powers. The two sides argued over a referendum on Yeltsin's reform policies. Despite parliament's efforts to prevent it, the April 1993 referendum endorsed the president's reform policies by a narrow margin. Yeltsin then called for a constitutional convention in order to replace the outdated Brezhnev Constitution, but the parliament blocked this temporarily. In summer 1993 the Russian Federation seemed on the verge of disintegration as its provinces and even cities began declaring themselves independent republics.

In September 1993 the parliament, led by Ruslan Khasbulatov and Vice President A. V. Rutskoi, sought to enact antireform measures and reduce President Yeltsin, who had been issuing numerous authoritarian decrees, to a figurehead. On September 21 Yeltsin responded by ordering parliament dissolved and announcing that new parliamentary elections would be held in December. Parliament then declared Yeltsin "deposed" and "installed" Rutskoi as president of Russia. Yeltsin retaliated by sealing off the "White House" where the parliament convened. Many of those inside it, ironically, were those who with Yeltsin had defied the August 1991 plotters, while the

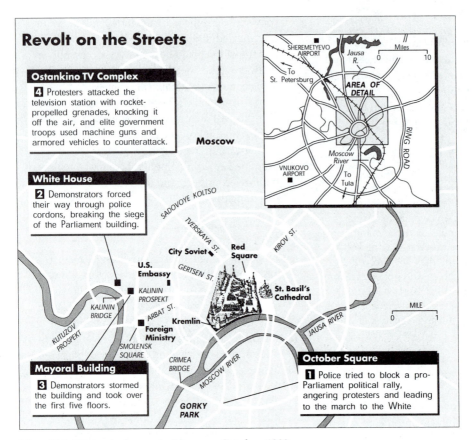

Revolt on the Streets

Ostankino TV Complex

4 Protesters attacked the television station with rocket-propelled grenades, knocking it off the air, and elite government troops used machine guns and armored vehicles to counterattack.

White House

2 Demonstrators forced their way through police cordons, breaking the siege of the Parliament building.

Mayoral Building

3 Demonstrators stormed the building and took over the first five floors.

October Square

1 Police tried to block a pro-Parliament political rally, angering protesters and leading to the march to the White

Map 45.1 Attempted coup in Moscow, October 1993

siege was directed by Yeltsin, the chief opponent of the August Coup. At the beginning of October, in an effort to resolve the impasse, negotiations were conducted in Moscow's Danilov Monastery under the auspices of Patriarch Aleksii of the Orthodox Church and Mayor Iurii Luzhkov. When these negotiations failed, Khasbulatov and Rutskoi attempted a military coup on October 4, sending armed detachments to seize the mayor's office and the Ostankino television tower. (See Map 45.1.) Confirming that parliament was controlled by extreme paramilitary groups and hard-line Communists, this resort to force proved a fatal blunder. Yeltsin's government, with army backing, quickly mobilized far greater force, bombarded the "White

House," and forced its surrender. The parliamentary leaders were marched off to prison.

Two days after the White House siege ended, President Yeltsin in a television speech proclaimed himself the savior of Russia. On November 10, 1993, with the publication of Yeltsin's draft constitution, a new constitutional structure was established in Russia. A 450-member State Duma was to be elected for two-year terms; the 178 members of the new Federation Council would likewise serve two-year terms. The election of December 12 approved the new constitution by a bare majority, as 45 percent of the electorate abstained and only 31 percent voted yes. Fascists and Communists won a majority of seats in the Duma; almost

Vladimir Zhirinovskii, leader of the Liberal Democratic Party of Russia, enthusiastically gestures during a press conference at the Parliament building in Moscow, June 22, 1995.

25 percent of the party-list votes and about 14 percent of the seats went to the new, misnamed Liberal Democratic Party led by extremist Vladimir Zhirinovskii, who had stressed Russia's national "humiliations." (See Table 45.1.) In part this was a protest vote against rising crime, threatened political chaos, and squabbling reformers. This election nonetheless marked the emergence of political parties and of television as major forces in the new Russian politics. An intriguing new party with much potential influence called itself the New Women of Russia.

Beginning in December 1993, the Yeltsin Constitution created a new, seemingly more stable political framework for Russia with most players abiding by its rules. Noticeable, however, was a rising disillusionment with democracy for failing to produce prosperity and restore Russia's power. By 1994 Russia had a fairly normal parliament, constantly sniping at the government, but a dubious presidency as Yeltsin failed to build a strong political party or movement. Despite a weak and ineffective central government, President Yeltsin dominated a rather featureless political landscape. Almost 10 years after emerging on the national scene, Yeltsin remained a unique, enigmatic, and unpredictable figure. As rumors and reports proliferated about his alleged abuse of alcohol, and between bouts of illness and periodic seclusion, he remained from 1990 the chief agent of Russian political change. From 1989 he had generally, albeit rather inconsistently, supported economic and political reform. Under the 1993 Constitution he obtained strong executive powers backed by a rapidly expanding presidential apparatus. However, as his physical health declined, his popularity sank to single-digit levels, making it highly uncertain whether he could achieve reelection in 1996.

Table 45.1 Russian Duma election, December 12, 1993

	Party Lists			
Parties and Blocs	% of Vote	Seats	Single-Member Constituency	Total Seats*
Liberal Democratic Party	22.79	59	5	64
Russia's Choice	15.38	40	18	58
Communist Party of the Russian Federation	12.35	32	16	48
Agrarian Party	7.90	21	12	33
Women of Russia	8.10	21	2	23
Yavlinsky-Boldyrev-Lukin (Yabloko)	7.83	20	2	22
Party of Russian Unity and Accord	6.76	18	1	19
Democratic Party of Russia	5.50	14	1	15
Democratic Russia Movement			5	5
Russian Movement for Democratic Reforms	13.39	—	4	4
Others			153†	153
Total	**100.00**	**225**	**219‡**	**444‡**

In mid-January 1994, according to Western estimates, the parliamentary factions in the State Duma were as follows: Russia's Choice (76 seats); New Regional Policy (centrist faction comprising independents—65); Liberal Democratic Party (63); Agrarian Party (55); Communist Party of the Russian Federation (45); Party of Russian Unity and Accord (30); Yavlinsky-Boldyrev-Lukin (Yabloko—25); Women of Russia (23); Democratic Party of Russia (15).

†Including 130 members without party affiliations.

‡Totals exclude one deputy from Chechnia and one from the Naberezhnye Chelny district of Tatarstan, where the election was boycotted, and four deputies from the remaining constituencies of Tatarstan (where fewer than 25% of registered voters took part, thereby invalidating the poll). However, in March 1994, in fresh elections in Tatarstan, the five deputies were successfully elected to the State Duma, bringing its total membership to 449.

SOURCE: *The Europa World Yearbook 1994, vol. 2, p. 2497.*

In mid-1995 Premier Viktor Chernomyrdin stood as the second most influential Russian political figure until eclipsed by the Communist leader, Gennadii Zyuganov, then by General Alexander Lebed. Chernomyrdin, a former Soviet gas magnate and cautious moderate, showed considerable success in handling Russia's perilous political and economic transition, gaining a personal triumph in June 1995 by negotiating a truce in Russia's ill-advised war in Chechnia (discussed later in this chapter). He stressed stability, a home for Russians wanting "progress without shocks or revolutions, who are tired of disorder and lies, who are proud of Russian statehood."[16] On the other hand, extreme nationalist Vladimir V. Zhirinovskii, whose influence peaked with the December 1993 parliamentary elections, lost much of his popularity subsequently.

In the elections to the Russian Duma of December 17, 1995, the revived Communist Party led by Zyuganov defeated Chernomyrdin's government party, Our Home Is Russia, more than 2 to 1—roughly 22 to 10 percent. In second place emerged the ultranationalist and misnamed Liberal Democratic Party of Zhirinovskii. (See Table 45.2.) Seeking to explain this result, Premier Chernomyrdin commented:

> The Communist Party has already been operating for 97 years in Russia and got 20 percent of the vote. Our Home Is Russia has only been working four or five months, and we immediately got almost 10 percent.[17]

---

[16] Steven Erlanger, "Russia's Premier: Too Popular for His Own Good?" *New York Times,* June 26, 1995, p. 4.

[17] Alessandra Stanley, "Communists Lead the Ruling Party," *New York Times,* December 19, 1995, pp. 1, 8.

Viktor Chernomyrdin, Premier of Russia.

Wojtek Laski/Gamma

Sergei Karpuk/AP/Wide World Photos

Gennadii Zyuganov, leader of the Communist Party, addresses an emergency session of the Duma in Moscow, January 11, 1995.

The only other political party to win the required 5 percent for admission to the Duma was Grigorii Yavlinskii's liberal Yabloko Party. The extremists' victory provoked speculation that they might form a coalition in the new Duma. However, under the 1993 Constitution the Duma's powers are very limited. Igor M. Kliamkin, director of a Moscow public opinion institute, commented:

> Even together, the Communists and the nationalists cannot really decide anything about the fate of the former Soviet Union from Parliament, but they can foster an imperialistic mood here and further isolate Russia from its neighbors and the West.[18]

The four successful parties filled only half the Duma seats; the remaining 225 seats went to candidates running as individuals. Some observers compared the Russia of 1995 politically with Germany's Weimar Republic before Hitler overthrew it. Others pointed out a resemblance to Charles de Gaulle's successful though authoritarian Fifth Republic in France.

President Yeltsin rebounded physically to conduct a vigorous campaign for reelection. In June and July 1996 Russia underwent two dramatic and crucial elections for president that tested its progress toward democracy. In the first round of voting on June 16, with ten competing candidates, including former President Gorbachev, President Yeltsin scored a narrow victory by 35 to 32 percent over his chief rival, Communist Party chief Gennadii Zyuganov. Coming in a surprisingly strong third with 15 percent was retired General Alexander Lebed. Yeltsin promptly recruited him as his new security chief. Yeltsin then arranged for the runoff vote to be held on a weekday, July 3. In that runoff Yeltsin scored a decisive victory, gaining almost 54 percent of the vote against about 40 percent for Zyuganov. (See Table 45.3.) This result was hailed with relief both in Russia and abroad as a great victory for democracy and reform. The victorious Yeltsin promptly reappointed the moderate, Viktor Chernomyrdin, as prime minister, and pledged to continue on the path of reform.

---

[18] Stanley, "Communists Lead," p. 8.

Table 45.2 Russian Duma election, December 17, 1995

Party	Percentage of Party-List Votes	Party-List Seats	Single-Candidate Seats	Total Seats	Seats Won in 1993
Communist Party	22.30%	99	58	157	45
Liberal Democratic Party	11.18	50	1	51	63
Our Home Is Russia	10.13	45	10	55	—
Yabloko	6.89	31	14	45	25
Parties needed a minimum of 5 percent of the vote to win party-list seats.					
Women of Russia	4.61	0	3	3	23
Working Russia	4.53	0	1	1	0
Congress of Russian Communities	4.31	0	5	5	—
Party of Svyatoslav Fyodorov	3.98	0	1	1	—
Democratic Choice of Russia	3.86	0	9	9	76
Agrarian Party	3.78	0	20	20	55
Power to the People	1.61	0	9	9	—
Other parties	Unavailable	0	17	17	—
Independents	—	0	77	77	—

SOURCE: *The New York Times*, December 30, 1995. Copyright © 1995 by The New York Times Company. Reprinted by permission.

After undergoing quintuple bypass heart surgery in November 1996, President Yeltsin, despite pneumonia, made an excellent recovery. By early spring 1997 Yeltsin returned to regular work in the Kremlin, and in April he appointed a new team of reformers led by Anatolii Chubais, a top economist, and Boris Nemtsov, the youthful former governor of Nizhnii-Novgorod, as First Deputy Premier in charge of free market reform. The most popular political figures in Russia were General Alexander Lebed, a powerful former paratroop general, blunt and outspoken and generally credited with ending the disastrous war in Chechnia, and Iurii Luzhkov, mayor of Moscow, noted for his face-lift of the Russian capital and for attracting foreign investment and business. Meanwhile the popularity of both Vladimir Zhirinovskii, and extreme nationalist, and Gennadii Zyuganov, the chief Communist leader, fell sharply. Russia appeared to be continuing along a shaky and uncertain path toward political democracy.

Important Russian regional elections in the summer of 1997 for governor of Nizhnyi-Novgorod and mayor of Samara, noted an American scholar, provided hints about the next presidential elections scheduled for the year 2000. Whereas Russian electoral politics from 1990 to 1996 had been polarized between "Reformers" and "Communists" (Yeltsin and Zyuganov), after the 1996 presidential elections five categories of potential candidates emerged pointing toward the year 2000: the liberal, youthful reformer, Boris Nemtsov; the nonideological boss, Iurii Luzhkov, mayor of Moscow; the moderate, Viktor Chernomyrdin; the anticommunist and antiregime protest candidate, General Alexander Lebed; and the traditional communist, Gennadii Zyuganov. In Nizhnyi-Novgorod a boss like Luzhkov won while in Samara a protest candidate triumphed; both Reformers and Communists lost. If Russia were to remain politically fairly calm until 2000, McFaul predicted, Luzhkov would win the presidency; otherwise a Lebed victory was more likely. The provincial elections had suggested that traditional communists could not win major Russian elections; they also revealed the relative weakness of

Table 45.3 Russian presidential election, June 16 and July 3, 1996

Candidate	First ballot	Second ballot
Boris N. Yeltsin	26,665,495	40,200,000*
Gennadii A. Zyuganov	24,211,686	30,110,000*
Alexander I. Lebed	10,974,736	—
Grigorii A. Yavlinskii	5,550,752	—
Vladimir V. Zhirinovskii	4,311,479	—
Svyatoslav N. Fedorov	699,158	—
Mikhail S. Gorbachev	386,069	—
Martin L. Shakkum	277,068	—
Yurii P. Vlasov	151,282	—
Vladimir A. Bryntsalov	123,065	
Total	**74,515,019†**	**73,900,000†**

*Provisional.

† Including votes cast against all candidates and (in the first ballot) 308 votes cast for A. G. Tuleyev, who withdrew from the election after early voting had begun.

SOURCE: *The Europa World Yearbook*, 1996, vol. 2, p. 2688.

General Alexander Lebed.

the present "party of power" led by President Yeltsin.[19]

While democracy seemed to be taking root, the political uncertainty continued in 1998. President Yeltsin's health remained questionable as he disappeared in December 1997–January 1998, suffering from what was described as a "severe cold." He returned to work in the Kremlin in late January looking healthy and vigorous. In late March he introduced new uncertainty by sacking his entire cabinet, including Prime Minister Viktor Chernomyrdin who had loyally served for five years. Yeltsin announced that Chernomyrdin was being relieved of his responsibilities so he could properly prepare to run for the presidency in 2000. Just what the decision to select an entirely new administration means is not entirely clear.

Economics

Would basic economic reform undermine the Russian Federation's unity? Dismantling the inefficient state sector required active cooperation of regional and local officials, most of whom were members of the former Soviet *nomenklatura*. Would they implement Moscow-ordered reforms or cater to the interests of their own regions? When most prices were freed during 1992, inflation surged. In 1993 consumer and industrial wholesale prices rose by 940 and 1000 percent, respectively. Severe inflation seriously reduced agricultural and industrial output in all CIS countries.[20]

Between 1992 and 1995 privatization proved the most successful aspect of Russian economic reform. (See Figure 45.1.) By October 1, 1992, 150 million privatization vouchers were distributed to the Russian population with a face value of 10,000 rubles each for investment in enterprises or to pay for goods and services. The private sector of the Russian economy expanded rapidly and enormously. During 1992–1993 most small shops and restaurants were privatized; then came the turn of

[19] Michael McFaul, "Russian Regional Elections: Presidential Primaries?" *Analysis of Current Events* Vol. 9, No. 9 (September 1997), pp. 1–4.

[20] John Löwenhardt, *The Reincarnation of Russsia* (Durham, NC, 1995), p. 120.

Laski Diffusion/Gamma-Liaison

Boris Nemtsov, Russia's First Deputy Premier, former governor of Nizhnii-Novgorod.

medium- and large-scale enterprises, some 70 percent of which were private by the end of 1994. As the production of larger state firms fell sharply, at the end of 1993 the net material product (the actual production by the economy without counting illegal output) reached only 68 percent of the 1991 level. Entire new branches of business were developed, notably computers, advertising, and insurance. The whole economy was shifting rapidly away from manufacturing to services, from capital goods to consumer products. The private sector was driving Russia inexorably away from the former Soviet command economy and was shaping a future capitalist Russia. By 1995 well over half of all Russian economic activity was in private hands, although few of the inefficient state

enterprises had actually closed down. As economist Anders Äslund concluded, "Russia could (and did) reform, and it has become a market economy."[21]

Benefiting from privatization and forming a class of nouveaux riches were primarily former members of the *nomenklatura*. The effects on the bulk of the Russian population were very negative; at least one-third fell below the official subsistence level in 1993. Pensioners and single-parent families suffered the most. In 1993 alone the Russian population declined by 300,000; life expectancy fell as alcoholism and suicides continued to rise. Heavy industry defended itself vigorously and continued to extract large state subsidies. Resigning in January 1994 after failing to prevent this, Finance Minister Gaidar stated: "Russia never experienced shock therapy. Yes, there were deep reforms in the direction of privatization and price liberalization, but financial policy always remained soft and weak."[22] However, by 1995 Premier Chernomyrdin's team had reined in inflation also.

Organized crime profited greatly from privatization, proliferating throughout Russia and the CIS following the Soviet collapse. By 1994 the territory of the Russian Federation was divided among some 5,000 criminal gangs, and many police and public officials were corrupt. Organized crime controlled major sections of private industry, trade, and banking, accounting for almost one-third of Russia's gross national product.[23] Penetrating every aspect of Russian life, this mafia was usurping political power, taking control of state firms, and engaging in forgery, assault, contract killing, drug running, and arms smuggling. Declared President Yeltsin in 1993: "Corruption is devouring the state from top to bottom."[24] In order to complete a successful transition to market capitalism, Russia would have to bring this crime

---

[21] Anders Äslund, *How Russia Became a Market Economy* (Washington, 1995), p. 316.

[22] Löwenhardt, *Reincarnation of Russia,* p. 55.

[23] Löwenhardt, p. 170.

[24] Claire Stirling, "Russia's Mafia," *The New Republic,* April 11, 1994, pp. 19–22.

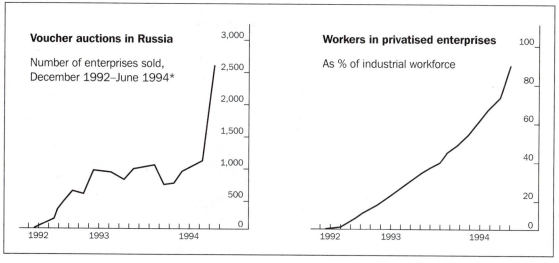

Figure 45.1
Going private

*Sales ended June 1994.

SOURCE: *The Economist,* April 8, 1995, p. 6. © 1995 The Economist Newspaper Group, Inc. Reprinted with permission. Further reproduction prohibited.

wave under control. In mid-1998 that had still not been done. However, Russia in 1998 faced the prospect of its first year of economic growth since the Soviet Union collapsed (see Figure 45.2).

Foreign Relations

After the demise of the Soviet empire, Russia sought to adjust to a new and unfavorable geopolitical situation as the other former Soviet republics became the "near abroad." As of 1992 Russia's new frontiers in Europe resembled those of 1613 after the Time of Troubles. For the first time in centuries Russia lacked borders with Turkey, Iran, or Afghanistan and was without direct contact with the Middle East. The country was deprived of most of its Caspian and Baltic coastlines. Russia's former chief naval base, Sevastopol, now lay in an independent Ukraine. As Muslim separatist movements threatened to fragment the Russian Federation, Russia's relationships with its former colonies and dependencies remained uncertain. Initial hopes that the CIS

would become a substitute for the USSR were soon dashed.

Sporadic tension and violence marred Russia's relations with its neighbors in the "near abroad." (See Map 45.2.) In June 1992 a conflict erupted in Moldova involving Russia, Ukraine, and Romania, centering around the newly proclaimed Dniester Moldavian Republic, consisting mostly of Russians. In July President Yeltsin signed an accord with the Moldovan president to introduce a Russian peacekeeping force there. Another disputed issue related to the withdrawal of Russian troops from Estonia and Latvia, which Moscow linked with protecting the rights of their Russian minorities. Potentially the most serious of these crises arose over relations between Russia and Ukraine. The issue of the large Russian minority there became fused with disputes over Crimea and the Black Sea Fleet. The Russian parliament claimed Crimea for Russia, pointing out that roughly 70 percent of its population was Russian. Ukraine and Russia also quarreled over the 400-ship Black Sea Fleet, rotting in its harbors. In August 1992

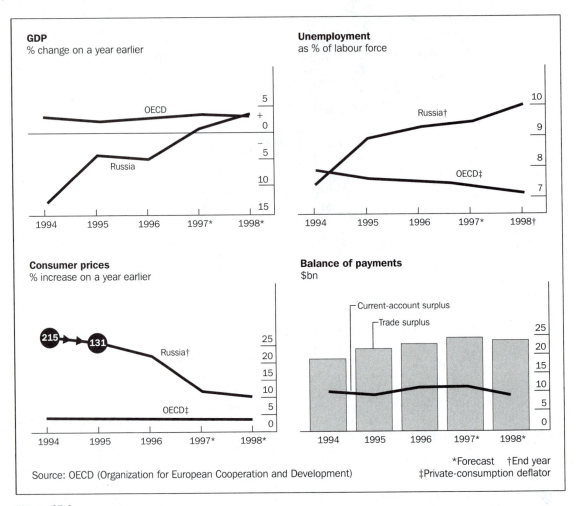

Figure 45.2
Russian economic trends, 1994–1998

SOURCE: *Economist*, December 13, 1997, p. 98.

Presidents Yeltsin and Kravchuk agreed to a joint command for three years, but then in June 1993 agreed to accelerate the splitting of that fleet. Disputes over Crimea and the port of Sevastopol dragged on into 1994, threatening to degenerate into military conflict. It required 14 months of threats and negotiations before a trilateral agreement among Russia, Ukraine, and the United States provided for dismantling and scrapping Ukraine's 1,600 nuclear warheads in Russia

in return for security guarantees and some compensation.

These tensions with Ukraine and the status of approximately 25 million Russians living in the "near abroad" soon spurred changes in Russia's foreign policy. Initially, President Yeltsin and Foreign Minister Andrei Kozyrev had pursued a strongly pro-American and pro-Western set of policies and had sought Russia's reintegration into Europe. Late in 1992, however, they began moving

Map 45.2 Ethnic trouble spots in the Russian Federation

	Income per Person $, Nov. 1994	Population '000 Jan. 1995	% of Russians 1989
Ethnic trouble spots			
6 Chechnia	na	1,006	22.0
Chuvashia	36.3	1,361	26.7
Dagestan	49.1	2,009	9.2
5 Ingushetia	na	228	23.0
3 Kabardino-Balkaria	35.7	787	32.0
2 Karachevo-Cherkassia	35.7	435	42.4
4 North Ossetia	40.5	664	29.9
Tuva	57.4	308	32.0
Resource-rich republics			
Karelia	116.2	789	73.6
Komi	98.7	1,203	57.7
Yakutia (Sakha)	142.6	1,035	50.3
Volga republics			
Bashkortostan	51.8	4,077	39.3
Kalmykia	36.4	320	37.7
Mari-El	41.7	767	47.5
Mordovia	37.0	959	60.8
Tatarstan	48.7	3,754	43.3
Udmurtia	47.9	1,641	58.9
Others			
1 Adygeya	36.2	450	68.0
Altai	70.6	200	60.4
Buryatia	45.2	1,052	70.0
Khakassia	56.9	583	79.5
All Russia	89.9	148,200	81.5

away from this pro-Western stance toward the positions adopted by their nationalistic critics. Russian politicians and military leaders increasingly defined Russia's sphere of influence as consisting of all former Soviet republics and much of eastern Europe. During President Yeltsin's visit to Brussels late in 1993, his spokesman declared, "Russia considers itself to be a great power and the successor to the Soviet Union and all its might."[25] During the sharpening conflict in Bosnia-Hercegovina, Russia provided consistent and strong support to Serbia and the Serbs, while opposing the aspirations of its former eastern European clients—Poland, Hungary, and the Czech Republic—to forge closer relations with the West.

Illustrating the dangers threatening Russia in its difficult transition was its war against Chechnia in the Caucasus region. In an earlier era the Muslim leader Shamil had long defied the large army of Emperor Nicholas I. The region was important to Russia because it controlled access to the oil of Azerbaijan. After the Soviet collapse Chechnia became a major center of drug running, arms smuggling, and holdups. In October 1991 General Dzhokar Dudaev forcibly seized power in Grozny, its capital. Stating his intention to break away from Russia, he won the Chechen presidency in disputed elections. For the next three years he remained head of a semi-independent state, running Chechnia's internal affairs as he wished.

On December 9, 1994, President Yeltsin issued a decree on restoring order and Russian control of Chechnia; on December 11 began a Russian military invasion. Yeltsin later justified this attack by the need to hold the Russian Federation together and to crush organized crime there. Actually the Russian Federation, shaky in 1992, appeared quite solid by late 1994, and Chechen organized crime was declining. The invasion was poorly planned and incompetently carried out by badly trained troops of low morale. Despite the boast by Russian Defense Minister Pavel Grachev that Russian

troops could take Grozny in a few hours, initial Russian assaults were repelled. Even after Grozny was finally subdued, Russia faced the difficult task of overcoming Chechen guerrillas in the mountains. The invasion cost Yeltsin the support of many democratic leaders and revealed his shaky control over the Russian military. In May 1996 Yeltsin, in a pre-election move, worked out a ceasefire in Chechnia with the successor of Dudaev in Moscow. That ceasefire was short-lived and the bloody conflict continued into summer 1996. Following Yeltsin's July election victory, his new security chief, General Lebed, worked out an agreement with the Chechens that ended the armed conflict but did not resolve the issue of Chechnia's political status as autonomous or independent. President Yeltsin and the Chechen president signed a peace treaty in Moscow in May 1997.

Russia's use of force in Chechnia, suggests former American ambassador Jack Matlock, may dissuade its leaders from resorting to military action elsewhere. Russia had avoided using military force against its neighbors in recent controversies with Kazakhstan and had handled carefully and peacefully the touchy Crimean issue with Ukraine. Matlock therefore doubted Russia would seek to reabsorb territories of the former USSR: "Russia cannot afford an empire again and the regions will not go along with it."[26] The weak central government had allowed the de facto development of federalism since 1992. Thus Tatarstan and Sakha (formerly Iakutia), avoiding talk of secession or full sovereignty, had driven hard bargains with the Moscow center. The war in Chechnia revealed a clear need to reform the disintegrating Russian army and police.

Post-Soviet Culture

When the USSR collapsed in 1991, Marxism in Russia was thoroughly discredited. As Russia

---

[25] Löwenhardt, p. 32.

[26] Kennan Institute (Washington), *Meeting Report* 12, no. 15, May 1, 1995.

strives to emerge from the rubble of Communist rule, Russian culture, plagued by chaos and confusion, struggles to reshape itself and to find a new identity. Replacing a controlled Soviet culture will be one more decentralized, diffuse, and dissonant.

Literature

This rupture with the Soviet past is especially evident in literature. The writer/poet in Russia was viewed as society's moral conscience. Literature enjoyed a quasi-religious status, reflecting the popular "soul," as the bearer of truth and justice. During the Soviet era writers were expected to exemplify the regime's moral authority, becoming "engineers of the human soul." Poetry and prose had been among the Soviet regime's most powerful weapons in seeking to legitimize the Communist system and conquer the souls of the people. Osip Mandelshtam, a literary victim of Stalin's Great Purge, declared: "Poetry is respected only in this country—here, people are killed for it. There is no country in which *more* people are killed for it." Clearly, today that is no longer true.

The return of Alexander Solzhenitsyn, the Nobel laureate, to Russia in May 1994 after 20 years of forced exile, mostly in seclusion in Vermont, indicated how dramatically the cultural climate has changed. Abroad Solzhenitsyn was lionized as a great Russian writer like Leo Tolstoy. With his highly publicized return and slow railroad journey from Vladivostok to Moscow, he sought to act as the great Russian writer revitalizing his country by his presence and moral authority. But his homecoming served instead as a graphic example of how greatly the cultural terrain had shifted since the fall of communism.

The idea of a great writer as the nation's conscience had become an anachronism. Educated young Russians may be curious about Solzhenitsyn, but few have read his books; they disdain his moral posturing and divorce from post-Communist Russian reality. Gregori Amelin, a young Moscow critic, stated that Solzhenitsyn, "with a Hollywood beard, and a conscience shined

to an incredible lustre, fails to realize that his appearance in Russia is shamelessly outdated. Who needs him anyway? No one." In October 1994 Solzhenitsyn excoriated the Russian parliament for its failures and false claims to represent the Russian people. Bemused by his philosophical chastisement, many parliament members considered him entirely out of touch with Russian realities and paid him no heed.

Russian writers no longer epitomize the truth. No longer struggling with the "cursed questions" of society, they are no longer indispensable to the nation's welfare, nor are they now "heroes on the barricades" as before. As writer Alexander Kushner explained to David Remnick, an American journalist:

> The writer in Russia was for so long like an uncrowned prince. Even an unpublished poet had a place of respect. Now this is gone. Why? In those days, literature was the one real door open to people of a certain kind. Now there are lots of doors to walk through. You can go into business, play on the Israeli soccer team, play for a New York hockey team, make your fortune in Greece, or even go into politics, if you should choose. At the same time, literature in the eyes of the people has lost its exceptional importance. Literature will always have a place, as it does in America. Marginal, but important. Small, but beautiful. Of course, if a monster, a fascist, like Vladimir Zhirinovskii, is ever elected President of Russia, literature will have to assume its old role. But for now, no.[27]

Cultural Institutions

The old Soviet cultural institutions have crumbled, and nothing new has appeared to replace them. The Soviet Writers' Union, overseeing and controlling literature for the party, disintegrated after the failed August Coup of 1991. Remaining is the dark, foreboding hulk of the Central House of Writers, formerly an elite Soviet cultural center

---

[27] Quoted in David Remnick, "Exit the Saints," *The New Yorker,* July 18, 1994, p. 52.

where Writers' Union members basked in privilege and comfort. The demise of cultural institutions such as the Artists' Union and Composers' Union has left a void in which writers, artists, and composers are drifting. Instead of fretting about the size of editions of their published works, they worry now about survival and the commercial value of the creative process in a highly competitive market. Gone are generous state subsidies and commissions. Like everything else in post-Communist Russia, culture too must find a market. Today bookstores and kiosks bulge with translated Western detective stories, romance novels, and soft-core pornography. Readers demand entertainment, not moralizing or propaganda. The guideline is what sells. Lacking government subsidies, publishers realize that the market will determine their fate, that they must produce commercially successful books.

Literary institutes, cultural think tanks where numerous intellectuals churned out scholarly works about Russian and Soviet literature, have fallen victim to the drought in state subsidies. Literary scholars now find themselves irrelevant, unread, alienated, and preoccupied with mere survival. They have lost their patron and their audience.

Few readers want yet another book about Dostoevskii or Gorkii. Everywhere people read trash novels, books on the occult, or works of long-suppressed authors. Escalating prices have limited public access to the book market. Well-established writers now must write for the market rather than from the heart. Some Russian writers have found a better audience abroad than at home. Andrei Bitov, Vladimir Kushner, Tatiana Tolstaia, Vladimir Sorokhin, and other younger writers are little known in Russia or abroad. Nevertheless, they carry on Russian literary traditions by seeking an audience that will respond positively to their works. They are not cultural heroes like their predecessors under communism.

Music shops contain the latest Western rock music and marginal Russian rock imitators. Radio stations broadcast a steady stream of Russian "top 40" music, drowning out classical. Television features "feel good" pop culture, deplored in the West as vacuous and banal. Cheap, often pirated, cassette tapes of Western and Russian rock music fill music shops and shabby kiosks. Private art galleries have proliferated, filled with various artistic works, many created for the tourist trade or the supposed market.

The painful transition to a market economy has been agonizing for all cultural workers now struggling to survive amid market conditions they do not understand. State funding for the arts, libraries, and educational institutions has been drastically reduced or eliminated. State subsidies are no longer available, and the public cannot afford to support cultural activities. The high cost for Russians of theater and concert tickets denies many Russians access to cultural events. Ticket sales alone cannot sustain theaters and theater companies, concert halls and musicians. Theaters are half empty as the quality of productions deteriorates. Scenery and costumes are shabby and threadbare, as are theaters and concert halls. Even the best productions seem seedy. The best performers and companies, committed to past traditions of excellence, seek opportunities abroad or are driven from their chosen professions. Theater companies and music groups compete for scarce foreign tours in order to meet expenses at home.

Russian cinema features American action films of Arnold Schwarzenegger and Sylvester Stallone and blockbusters like *Jurassic Park* and *Titanic*. Snickers candy bars and Marlboro cigarettes are hawked on many street corners and at corner kiosks. Commercial advertising everywhere has replaced Soviet propaganda slogans. Western designer boutiques, promoting current Western fashions, have replaced many of Moscow's and St. Petersburg's drab shops, but most of their fashionable merchandise is out of reach of most Russians, generating anger and hostility toward the West like that of the Cold War era. These changes have left many Russians confused and resentful of what they perceive as a callous alien cultural invasion.

Maintenance of Russia's cultural heritage is haphazard and inconsistent. Should the Soviet cultural heritage be preserved or destroyed?

Despite the natural tendency to discard a discredited past, much produced under communism is worth preserving. Many Soviet monuments remain but without a consensus on what should be destroyed or retained. Meanwhile, monuments of the Communist past deteriorate physically.

Inadequate funding has postponed efforts to preserve most cultural monuments. Without proper scientific supervision, historical monuments and valuable archives are threatened. Currently only minor state resources can be invested in cultural projects. Realizing the dangers facing the Russian cultural heritage, people at the grass roots seek to raise funds at home and abroad to assure survival of the best of Russian and Soviet culture.

Religion

Religion has reemerged to fill a part of the void created by communism's precipitous collapse. The Russian Orthodox Church, existing precariously under Soviet rule, has sought to reestablish itself as a major social force, but not without competition from other religious organizations that view Russia as fertile prosletyzing territory. Major Protestant churches, evangelical and New Age groups, Hare Krishnas and Jehovah's Witnesses compete actively for souls in today's Russia. The Orthodox Church lacks adequate resources to restore its presence among the people. Thousands of churches need restoration or rebuilding; a new generation of priests must be recruited and trained. The Orthodox Church is poorly prepared to manipulate the modern media, utilized so effectively by well-trained, well-funded foreign religious groups. The Church also must refurbish an image tarnished by accusations of collaboration with the Communists and of spying on people for the KGB. It must also compete with the Orthodox Church Abroad, established largely by Russian émigrés, claiming to speak with greater moral authority after its unrelenting, decades-long struggle against communism. Communists carefully controlled the number and assured the political reliability of recruits in Soviet theological schools.

The existing Orthodox clergy, insufficient in number, is compromised by complicity with the former regime, tainting its moral authority. All this complicates the Church's ability to compete in the open religious marketplace.

Despite these obstacles, the Orthodox Church is reasserting a central role in society. Churches are reopening, renovation is progressing, often with volunteer labor, Church publications are widely disseminated, and the clergy speaks out on social and economic issues. People are responding as they search for new ethical moorings following Marxism-Leninism's collapse. By far the largest number of believers identify with the Russian Orthodox Church. Currently about 40 percent of Russians consider themselves believers, of whom a majority identify with Orthodoxy. Even nonbelievers feel a historical and cultural affinity for Orthodoxy. With a potentially receptive audience, the Church is thus well situated to exert significant social influence. However, its public influence is being undermined by internal authoritarian and ultranationalist tendencies. The Orthodox hierarchy is divided between conservatives refusing to recognize the legitimacy of other religions and a more ecumenical group that welcomes the cooperation of other denominations in spreading Christian ideas. Patriarch Aleksii II, elected in 1990, while not rejecting Russian religious nationalism, has shown some limited interest in closer ties with other Christian denominations.

The Russian Orthodox Church, like other Russian institutions, is attempting to define its role in the new Russia and in the religiously diverse world beyond Russia's borders. It seeks to minister to the more than 25 million ethnic Russians living outside Russia's borders. How can the Moscow Church assert its authority over these souls and prevent Orthodox hierarchies in other former Soviet republics from declaring independence? Traditionally, national Orthodox churches have been autocephalous, and independent Orthodox churches in Ukraine, Belarus, and Georgia would reduce the status of the Russian church. A large Russian Orthodox diaspora and competition within Russia have stimulated nationalism and intolerance within the Church. Anti-Semitism, long a blot in the Orthodox Church, has revived. The Church faces the daunting task of emancipating itself from its past history, notably its association and compromises with Communist and tsarist regimes. To reassert its moral authority, it must stand above politics, speaking directly to the people's spiritual needs.

The Future

As Russia seeks to develop a viable democracy and a market economy, Russian culture struggles to reestablish an equilibrium recognizing its historical continuity while responding to the demands of a rapidly changing Russian scene. Russian culture seeks to reemerge on the stage of world culture and express a diverse Russian creativity. Having given much to the world in many fields, Russian creativity hopefully is destined to contribute importantly in the future as Russia itself moves to a new plateau of development.

Suggested Additional Reading

A DEVASTATED LAND

FESHBACH, M., and A. FRIENDLY, JR. *Ecocide in the USSR. Health and Nature Under Siege* (New York, 1992).

GOLDMAN, M. I. *The Spoils of Progress: Environmental Pollution in the Soviet Union* (Cambridge, MA, 1972).

KOMAROV, B. *The Destruction of Nature in the Soviet Union* (White Plains, NY, 1980).

MEDVEDEV, Z. *The Legacy of Chernobyl* (New York and London, 1992).

MOORE, J. L., ed. *Legacies of the Collapse of Marxism* (Fairfax, VA, 1994).

PETERSON, D. J. *Troubled Lands: The Legacy of Soviet Environmental Destruction* (Boulder, CO, 1993).

PRYDE, P. *Environmental Management in the Soviet Union* (New York, 1991).

STEWART, J. M. *The Soviet Environment: Problems, Policies and Politics* (New York, 1992).

WEINER, D. R. *Models of Nature: Ecology, Conservation and Cultural Revolution in Soviet Russia* (Bloomington, IN, 1988).

TROUBLED TRANSITIONS

ÄSLUND, A. *How Russia Became a Market Economy* (Washington, 1995).

BATALDEN, S., ed. *Seeking God: The Recovery of Religious Identity in Orthodox Russia, Ukraine and Georgia* (DeKalb, IL, 1993).

BLUM, D. W., ed. *Russia's Future: Consolidation or Disintegration?* (Boulder, CO, 1994).

BREMMER, I., and R. TARAS, eds. *New States, New Politics: Building the Post-Soviet Nations*, 2d ed. (Cambridge, 1996).

BROWN, J. F. *Hopes and Shadows: Eastern Europe After Communism* (Durham, NC, 1994).

BUZGALIN, A. V. *Bloody October in Moscow* (New York, 1994).

COLTON, T., and R. LEGVOLD, eds. *After the Soviet Union: From Empire to Nations* (New York, 1992).

DAWISHA, K., and B. PARROTT. *Russia and the New States of Eurasia: The Politics of Upheaval* (Cambridge, 1994).

DENBER, R., ed. *The Soviet Nationality Reader: The Disintegration in Context* (Boulder, CO, 1992).

DILLER, D. C. *Russia and the Independent States* (Washington, 1993).

DUNLOP, J. B. *The Rise of Russia and the Fall of the Soviet Empire* (Princeton, 1993, 1995).

FUNK, N., and M. MUELLER, eds. *Gender Politics and Post-Communism from Eastern Europe and the Former Soviet Union* (New York, 1993).

GINSBURGS, G., et al., eds. *Russia and America: From Rivalry to Reconciliation* (Armonk, NY, 1993).

GOLDENBERG, S. *Pride of Small Nations: The Causasus and Post-Soviet Disorder* (Atlantic Highlands, NJ, 1994).

GOLDMAN, M. *Lost Opportunity: Why Economic Reforms in Russia Have Not Worked* (New York, 1994).

HANDELMAN, S. *Comrade Criminal: The New Russian Mafia* (New Haven, CT, 1995).

HOLDEN, G. *Russia After the Cold War: History and the Nation in Post-Soviet Security Politics* (New York, 1994).

JOHNSON, T., and S. MILLER. *Russian Security After the Cold War: Seven Views From Moscow* (Washington, 1994).

JUVILER, P., et al., eds. *Human Rights for the 21st Century, Foundations for Responsible Hope: A US–Post-Soviet Dialogue* (Armonk, NY, 1993).

KARTSEV, V. P. *Zhirinovsky* (New York, 1995).

KHASBULATOV, R. I. *The Struggle in Russia: Power and Change in the Democratic Revolution* (New York, 1993).

KHAZANOV, A. *After the USSR: Ethnicity, Nationalism, and Politics in the Commonwealth of Independent States* (Madison, WI, 1995).

KNIGHT, A. *Spies Without Cloaks: The KGB's Successors* (Princeton, 1996).

LAPIDUS, G., ed. *The New Russia: Troubled Transformation* (Boulder, CO, 1995).

LÖWENHARDT, J. *The Reincarnation of Russia: Struggling with the Legacy of Communism, 1990–1994* (Durham, NC, 1995).

MALIK, H., ed. *Central Asia: Its Strategic Importance and Future Prospects* (New York, 1994).

MARSH, R., ed. *Women in Russia and Ukraine* (New York, 1996).

MCFAUL, M. *Post-Communist Politics: Democratic Prospects in Russia and Eastern Europe* (Washington, 1993).

———. *The Troubled Birth of Russian Democracy* (Stanford, 1993).

———. *Understanding Russia's Parliamentary Elections: Implications for U.S. Foreign Policy* (Stanford, 1994).

MICHKA, V. *Inside the New Russia* (Broken Arrow, OK, 1994).

MOTYL, A. *Dilemmas of Independence: Ukraine After Totalitarianism* (New York, 1993).

NIMMO, W. F. *Japan and Russia: A Reevaluation in the Post-Soviet Era* (Westport, CT, 1994).

ODOM, W., and R. DUJARRIC. *Commonwealth or Empire? Russia, Central Asia, and the Transcaucasus* (Indianapolis, 1995).

PATTERSON, P., ed. *Socialist Past: The Rise of the Private Sector in Command Economics* (Boulder, CO, 1993).

POPOV, N. P. *The Russian People Speak: Democracy at the Crossroads* (Syracuse, NY, 1994).

POSADSKAYA, A., et al., eds. *Women in Russia: A New Era in Russian Feminism* (London and New York, 1994).

RA'ANAN, U., and K. MARTIN, eds. *Russia: A Return to Imperialism?* (New York, 1996).

RA'ANAN, U., et al., eds. *Russian Pluralism—Now Irreversible?* (New York, 1993).

RAMET, S. P., ed. *Rocking the State: Rock Music and Politics in Eastern Europe and Russia* (Boulder, CO, 1994).

SAIKAL, A., and W. MALEY, eds. *Russia in Search of Its Future* (Cambridge, 1995).

SAIVETZ, C., and A. JONES, eds. *In Search of Pluralism: Soviet and Post-Soviet Politics* (Boulder, CO, 1994).

SESTANOVICH, S., ed. *Rethinking Russia's National Interests* (Washington, 1994).

SHLAPENTOKH, V., et al., eds. *The New Russian Diaspora: Russian Minorities in the Former Soviet Republics* (Armonk, NY, 1994).

SMITH, A. *Russia and the World Economy: Problems of Integration* (New York, 1993).

SMITH, G. B. *Reforming the Russian Legal System* (Cambridge, 1996).

TURPIN, J. *Reinventing the Soviet Self: Media and Social Change in the Former Soviet Union* (Westport, CT, 1995).

VACHNADZE, G. N. *Russia's Hotbeds of Tension* (Commack, NY, 1994).

WHITE, S. *Russia Goes Dry: Alcohol, State and Society* (Cambridge, 1995).

———, et al., eds. *The Politics of Transition: Shaping a Post-Soviet Future* (Cambridge, 1993).

WILSON, A. *Ukrainian Nationalism in the 1990s: A Minority Faith* (Cambridge, 1996).

YAKOVLEV, A. *The Fate of Marxism in Russia*, trans. Catherine Fitzpatrick (New Haven, CT, 1993).

A

Russian and Soviet Leaders, 1328–1998

1. Muscovite grand princes

Ivan I, "Kalita"	1328–1340	Vasili II	1425–1462
Simeon	1340–1353	Ivan III, "the Great"	1462–1505
Ivan II	1353–1359	Vasili III	1505–1533
Dmitri Ivanovich "Donskoi"	1359–1389	Ivan IV, "the Terrible"	1533–1547
Vasili I	1389–1425		

2. Russian emperors (tsars)

Ivan IV, "the Terrible"	1547–1584*	Anna Ivanovna	1730–1740
Fedor I	1584–1598	Ivan VI	1740–1741
Boris Godunov	1598–1605	Elizabeth I	1741–1762
Dmitri I	1605–1606	Peter III	1762
Vasili IV	1606–1610	Catherine II, "the Great"	1762–1796
Mikhail I Romanov	1613–1645	Paul I	1796–1801
Alexis I	1645–1676	Alexander I	1801–1825
Fedor II	1676–1682	Nicholas I	1825–1855
Ivan V	1682–1696	Alexander II	1855–1881
Peter I, "the Great"	1682–1725	Alexander III	1881–1894
Catherine I	1725–1727	Nicholas II	1894–1917
Peter II	1727–1730		

* Crowned tsar in 1547

3. **Soviet leaders** (all except Lenin were general or first secretaries of the Communist party of the Soviet Union)

V. I. Lenin	1917–1924	L. I. Brezhnev	1964–1982
J. V. Stalin	1924–1953	Iu. V. Andropov	1982–1984
G. M. Malenkov	1953	K. V. Chernenko	1984–1985
N. S. Khrushchev	1953–1964	M. S. Gorbachev	1985–1991

4. **Chairmen of the Council of People's Commissars** (prime ministers after 1946)

V. I. Lenin	1917–1924	N. A. Bulganin	1955–1958
A. I. Rykov	1924–1930	N. S. Khrushchev	1958–1964
V. M. Molotov	1930–1941	A. N. Kosygin	1964–1980
J. V. Stalin	1941–1953	N. A. Tikhonov	1980–1985
G. M. Malenkov	1953–1955	N. I. Ryzhkov	1985–1990

5. **Full members of the Politburo** (Presidium, 1952–1966) of the Soviet Communist Party

V. I. Lenin	1919–1924	N. A. Bulganin	1948–1958
L. D. Trotskii	1919–1926	A. N. Kosygin	1949–1950,
J. V. Stalin	1919–1953		1960–1980
L. B. Kamenev	1919–1925	V. M. Andrianov	1952–1953
N. N. Krestinskii	1919–1921	A. B. Aristov	1952–1953,
G. E. Zinoviev	1921–1926		1957–1961
A. I. Rykov	1922–1930	S. D. Ignatiev	1952–1953
M. P. Tomskii	1922–1930	D. S. Korochenko	1952–1953
N. I. Bukharin	1924–1929	O. V. Kuusinen	1952–1953,
V. M. Molotov	1926–1957		1957–1964
K. E. Voroshilov	1926–1960	V. V. Kuznetsov	1952–1953
M. I. Kalinin	1926–1946	V. A. Malyshev	1952–1953
Ia. E. Rudzutak	1926–1932	L. G. Melnikov	1952–1953
V. V. Kuibyshev	1927–1935	N. A. Mikhailov	1952–1953
L. M.		M. G. Pervukhin	1952–1957
Kaganovich	1930–1957	P. K. Ponomarenko	1952–1953
S. M. Kirov	1930–1934	M. Z. Saburov	1952–1957
S. V. Kosior	1930–1938	N. M. Shvernik	1952–1953,
G. K.			1957–1966
Ordzhonikidze	1930–1937	D. I. Chesnokov	1952–1953
A. A. Andreyev	1932–1952	M. F. Shkiriatov	1952–1953
V. Ia. Chubar	1935–1938	A. I. Kirichenko	1955–1960
A. I. Mikoyan	1935–1966	M. A. Suslov	1955–1982
A. A. Zhdanov	1939–1948	L. I. Brezhnev	1957–1982
N. S. Khrushchev	1939–1964	G. K. Zhukov	June–Oct. 1957
L. P. Beria	1946–1953	E. A. Furtseva	1957–1961
G. M. Malenkov	1946–1957	N. I. Beliaev	1957–1960
N. A. Voznesenskii	1947–1949	N. G. Ignatov	1957–1961

Full members of the Politburo (Presidium, 1952–1966) of the Soviet
Communist Party (continued)

F. R. Kozlov	1957–1964	A. A. Grechko	1973–1976
N. A.		G. V. Romanov	1976–1985
Mukhitdinov	1957–1961	K. V. Chernenko	1977–1985
N. V. Podgorny	1960–1977	N. A. Tikhonov	1979–1985
D. S. Polianskii	1960–1976	M. S. Gorbachev	1980–1991
G. I. Voronov	1961–1973	G. A. Aliyev	1982–1987
A. P. Kirilenko	1962–1981	M. S.	
A. N. Shelepin	1964–1975	Solomentsev	1983–1988
P. E. Shelest	1964–1973	V. I. Vorotnikov	1983–1987
K. T. Mazurov	1965–1978	V. M. Chebrikov	1985–1991
A. Ia. Pelshe	1966–1983	E. G. Ligachev	1985–1991
V. V. Grishin	1971–1985	E. A.	
F. D. Kulakov	1971–1978	Shevarnadze	1985–1991
D. A. Kunaev	1971–1989	N. I. Ryzhkov	1985–1991
V. V.		L. N. Zaikov	1987–1991
Shcherbitskii	1971–1989	V. P. Nikonov	1987–1991
Iu. V. Andropov	1973–1984	N. I. Sliunkov	1987–1991
A. A. Gromyko	1973–1988	A. N. Iakovlev	1987–1991
D. F. Ustinov	1973–1984		

6. **President of the Russian Federation**

Boris N. Yeltsin	1991–

B

Areas and Populations
of Former Soviet Union Republics

Republic	Area (in thousands of square kilometers)	Population (in thousands)	Date	Capital	Population (in thousands)
Armenian SSR	29.8	3,580	1/91	Erivan	1,215
Azerbaijani SSR	86.6	7,145	1/90	Baku	1,757
Belorussian SSR	207.6	10,259	1/90	Minsk	1,612
Estonian SSR	45.1	1,573	1/89	Tallinn	503
Georgian SSR	69.7	5,449	1/89	Tbilisi	1,264
Kazakh SSR	2,717.3	16,690	1/90	Alma-Ata	1,132
Kirghiz SSR	198.5	4,372	1/89	Frunze	626
Latvian SSR	63.7	2,681	1/89	Riga	915
Lithuanian SSR	65.2	3,690	1/89	Vilnius	582
Moldavian SSR	33.7	4,341	1/89	Kishinev	720
Russian SFSR	17,075.4	147,386	1/89	Moscow	8,967
Tadzhik SSR	143.1	5,112	1/89	Dushanbe	604
Turkmen SSR	488.1	3,621	1/90	Ashkhabad	339
Ukrainian SSR	603.7	51,704	1/89	Kiev	2,602
Üzbek SSR	447.4	20,322	1/90	Tashkent	2,079
USSR	22,402.2*	287,925			

*Approximately equivalent to 8.65 million square miles
SOURCE: *Europa World Yearbook* II, (London, 1991), pp. 2679–80.

C

Populations of Principal Cities of the Russian Federation

City	Population (est. 1/1/92)	City	Population (est. 1/1/92)
Moscow	8,746,700	Astrakhan	512,200
St. Petersburg*	4,436,700	Tomsk	504,700
Novosibirsk	1,441,900	Tyumen	496,200
Nizhnii-Novgorod*	1,440,600	Viyatka*	492,500
Ekaterinburg*	1,370,700	Ivanovo	480,400
Samara*	1,239,200	Murmansk	468,300
Omsk	1,168,600	Bryansk	460,500
Chelyabinsk	1,143,000	Lipetsk	463,600
Kazan	1,104,000	Tver*	455,600
Perm	1,098,600	Magnitogorsk	441,200
Ufa	1,097,200	Cheboksary	438,900
Rostov-na-Donu	1,027,100	Nizhnii Tagil	437,400
Volgograd	1,006,100	Kursk	435,200
Krasnoyarsk	925,000	Archangel	413,600
Saratov	909,300	Kaliningrad	410,700
Voronezh	902,200	Groznyi	387,500
Tolyatti	665,700	Chita	376,500
Simbirsk*	656,400	Ulan-Ude	366,000
Izhevsk*	650,700	Kurgan	365,100
Vladivostok	647,800	Vladimir	356,100
Irkutsk	637,000	Smolensk	351,600
Yaroslavl	636,900	Kaluga	346,800
Krasnodar	634,500	Orel	346,600
Khabarovsk	614,600	Sochi	344,200
Barnaul	606,200	Makhachkala	339,300
Novokuznetsk	600,200	Stavropol	331,800
Orenburg	556,500	Vladikavkaz*	324,700
Penza	552,300	Saransk	322,000
Tula	541,400	Komsomolsk-na-Amure	318,600
Ryazan	528,500	Cherepovets	317,100
Kemerovo	520,600	Belgorod	314,200
Naberezhnye Chelny*	515,400	Tambov	310,600

* Some towns that were renamed during the Soviet period have reverted to their former names: St. Petersburg (Leningrad); Nizhnii-Novgorod (Gorkii); Ekaterinburg (Sverdlovsk); Samara (Kuibyshev); Simbirsk (Ulyanovsk); Izhevsk (Ustinov); Naberezhnye Chelny (Brezhnev); Viyatka (Kirov); Tver (Kalinin); Vladikavkaz (Ordzhonikidze).

SOURCES: UN, *Demographic Yearbook. Europa World Yearbook* II, (London, 1996), p. 2681.

Glossary of Foreign Words

apparatchik derogatory term for professional party worker

artel primitive producers' cooperative

ataman chieftain

barshchina labor service by peasants, corvée

Blitzkrieg lightning war (Ger.)

bog god

bogatyr ancient hero

boyar or boiar Kievan or Muscovite titled nobleman

bunt spontaneous uprising

bylina (pl. byliny) saga of old Rus

cheliad slave

chernozem fertile black soil

chernyi bor special tax

chin service rank

diak state secretary

dolia Petrine taxation unit

Dreikaiserbund League of Three Emperors (Ger.)

Duma, duma (pl. dumy) parliament, assembly

dusha (pl. dushi) literally "soul," male serf

dvorianin (pl. dvoriane) courtier, service nobleman or gentry

dvorianstvo service nobility, gentry

dvorovye literally "courtyard people," domestic serfs

fabrika factory, industrial concern

fiskal(y) informer on financial matters

gensek (generalnyi sekretar) general secretary of CPSU

gimnazium classical secondary school

glasnost openness, publicity

golova "head," mayor

gorod town, city

gorodischche ancient fortified settlement

gorodskaia duma (pl. gorodskie dumy) city council

gost(y) member of privileged merchant elite

grivna coin of early Rus

groznyi awesome, dread, terrible

guberniia (pl. gubernii) province

hetman elected Cossack leader

hromada society

iarlyk(i) patent of authority

izba (pl. izby) Muscovite administrative department; also peasant hut

kabala temporary bondage, indenture

kagan ruler, khan

kazna treasury

kholop(y) slave

kino-glaz "camera eye"

kino-kulak "film fist"

kino-pravda "film truth"

kolkhoz(y) collective farm

kolkhoznik(i) collective farmer

kolokol bell

kombedy "committees of the poor" 1918–1921

konets (pl. kontsy) "end," ward or borough of old Rus and Novgorod

kopek 1/100th of a ruble

702

kormlenie Muscovite "feeding" system to support local officials

kulak(i) better-off peasant

kupechestvo merchantry (**kupets**, merchant)

kuriltai Mongol general assembly

kustar handicrafts

liberum veto free veto of Polish nobility

liudi "people," middle-class freemen of Kievan Rus

meshchanstvo petty bourgeoisie (**meshchanin**, pl. **meshchane**, petty bourgeois)

mestnichestvo Muscovite system of "place" based on noble birth

mir peasant commune; also means world and peace

mirovye posredniki peace mediators

molodshie liudi literally "younger men," lower-class townsmen of Rus

mujaheddin Afghan Muslim rebels

muzh(i) upper-class freeman of Rus and Novgorod

Nakaz Instruction of Catherine II to Legislative Commission

namestnik(i) governor

Narkomindel People's Commissariat of Foreign Affairs

narod the people

narodnichestvo populism (**Narodnik**, Populist)

nemetskaia sloboda "German Suburb," foreign settlement near Moscow

nomenklatura ruling party elite

oberfiskal financial supervisor and investigator

obrok peasant rent and tax on side earnings

obshchina peasant commune

okolnichii Muscovite court rank just below boyar

oprichnik(i) member of Ivan IV's Oprichnina

partiinost party spirit and loyalty

podzol poor, ashy soils

pomestie service fief

pop priest

posad(y) commercial district, section

posadnik(i) governor, mayor

posadnitsa female mayor

poshlost banality

Posolskii prikaz Ambassadorial Board

pravlenie executive board

prikaz(y) Muscovite bureau or board

Prodameta metallurgical cartel

provintsiia (pl. **provintsii**) province

Rada, rada assembly, central council of Poland or Ukraine

raznochinets (pl. **raznochintsy**) "man (men) of various ranks," from various social groups

Realschule(n) practical secondary school stressing science and mathematics (Ger.)

Rodoslovets Book of Genealogy of Muscovite nobility

Russkaia Pravda Russian Truth or Justice, law code of Kievan Rus

samizdat "self-publication," underground literature

samogon moonshine liquor

seim Polish or Lithuanian assembly

shliakhetstvo nobility (derived from Polish **szlachta**)

sloboda (pl. **slobody**) settlement, district

smerd(y) literally "stinker," peasant of Kievan Rus

sobor, sobranie gathering

sokha wooden forked plow; also tax unit

soslovie semicaste, highly stratified social group

sotnia (pl. **sotni**) "hundred"; Cossack cavalry unit; street of Novgorod

soviet council; **Soviet Gospod**, Council of Notables (Novgorod)

sovkhoz(y) state farm

sovnarkhoz(y) regional economic council

starozhilets (pl. **starzhiltsy**) "old resident," longtime peasant resident

starshina elder; the Cossack elite

sto hundred; Novgorod trade guild

strelets (pl. **streltsy**) Muscovite musketeer, palace guard

Strigolnik(i) literally "shorn head," Novgorod religious sect

sudebnik law code

szlachta Polish gentry

tamizdat work published abroad

tysiatskii chiliarch, leader of 1,000 men (Kievan Rus)

udel(y) appanage, hereditary feudal territory

uezd district

Ulozhenie Law Code of 1649 (formally **Sobornoe Ulozhenie**)

ulus segment of Mongol Empire

veche (or **vieche**) town assembly of early Rus and Novgorod

vladyka lord, ruler

voevoda (pl. **voevody**) military commander or governor

volost(i) rural district, township

volostel(i) district official

"Vor" "The Brigand" (Second Pretender)

Vostochnik(i) "Easterner," advocate of Russian imperialism in Asia

votchina (pl. **votchiny**) hereditary landed estate

vyvoz exportation; removal of peasants

Wachtparade watch parade (Ger.)

yarlyk (or **iarlyk**) patent of authority issued by Golden Horde

zakup(y) semifree laborer

zemshchina Russian outside Oprichnina (1565–1572)

zemskii sobor Assembly of the Land (1566–1682)

zemstvo (pl. **zemstva**) local self-government system, elected district councils

Zhdanovshchina period of Andrei Zhdanov's preeminence (1946–1948)

Zhenotdel Women's Section (established 1920)

zhitye liudi well-off people

Bibliography

Abbreviations of Scholarly Journals

AEMA = Archivum Eurasiae Medii Aevi
AHR = American Historical Review
ASEER = American Slavic and East European Review
BS = British Studies
Byz. St. = Byzantine Studies
Cahiers = Cahiers du monde russe et soviétique
Cal. SS = California Slavic Studies
CanAmSlSt = Canadian-American Slavic Studies
CH = Church History
CQR = Church Quarterly Review
CSP = Canadian Slavonic Papers
CSS = Canadian Slavic Studies
DOP = Dumbarton Oaks Papers
EEHE = East European History Essays
EEQ = East European Quarterly
EHR = English Historical Review
FOG = Forschungen zur Osteuropäischen Geschichte
HJAS = Harvard Journal of Asiatic Studies
HOEQ = History of Education Quarterly
HSS = Harvard Slavic Studies
HUS = Harvard Ukrainian Studies
Ind. SS = Indiana Slavic Studies
Int. Hist. Rev. = International History Review
JAOS = Journal of the American Oriental Society
JAS = Journal of Asian Studies
JBS = Journal of Baltic Studies

JCEA = Journal of Central European Affairs
JEBH = Journal of Economics and Business History
JEH = Journal of Economic History
JfGO = Jahrbücher für Geschichte Osteuropas
JHI = Journal of the History of Ideas
JMH = Journal of Modern History
JUH = Journal of Urban History
MERSH = Modern Encyclopedia of Russian and Soviet History
NCMH = New Canadian Modern History
OSP = Oxford Slavonic Papers
PCRE = Proceedings of the Consortium on Revolutionary Europe
PHR = Pacific Historical Review
PP = Past and Present
RoP = Review of Politics
Rus. Hist. = Russian History
Rus. Rev. = Russian Review
SBB = Studies in Bibliography and Booklore
SEEJ = Slavic and East European Journal
SEER = Slavonic and East European Review
SEESt. = Slavic and East European Studies
SOVS = Soviet Studies
SR = Slavic Review
SS = Slavic Studies
SSH = Soviet Studies in History
TRHS = Transactions of the Royal Historical Society
UQ = Ukrainian Quarterly

The following brief bibliography contains only major reference works relating to Russian and Soviet history, some key general histories in English, and some collections of essays not relating to a specific period. For works on specific periods and topics, see the suggestions for additional reading at the end of each chapter of the text.

Reference Works

AKINER, S. *Islamic Peoples of the Soviet Union* (London and Boston, 1983).

ALLEN, R. *Russia Looks at America: The View to 1917* (Washington, 1988).

ALLWORTH, E., ed. *Soviet Asia—Bibliographies: The Iranian, Mongolian and Turkic Nationalities* (New York, 1973).

American Bibliography of Russian and East European Studies (Bloomington, IN, 1957–) (Books and articles, annually since 1957.)

BENNIGSEN, A., AND S. E. WIMBUSH. *Muslims of the Soviet Empire: A Guide* (Bloomington, IN, 1986).

BEZER, C., ed. *Russian and Soviet Studies: A Handbook* (Columbus, OH, 1973).

BOYM, S. *Common Places: Mythologies of Everyday Life in Russia* (Cambridge, MA, 1994).

BRISTOL, E. *A History of Russian Poetry* (New York, 1991).

CARPENTER, K. E., comp. *Russian Revolutionary Literature Collection* (New Haven, CT, 1976).

CARTER, S. K. *Russian Nationalism, Yesterday, Today, Tomorrow* (New York, 1990).

CLARKE, R. A., AND D. J. MATKO. *Soviet Economic Facts 1917–1981* (London, 1983).

COHEN, A. *Russian Imperialism: Development and Crisis* (Westport, CT, 1996).

CROWTHER, P. *A Bibliography of Works in English on Early Russian History to 1800* (New York, 1969).

CRUMMEY, R., ed. *Reform in Russia and the U.S.S.R.: Past and Prospects* (Champaign, IL, 1990).

DAVIES, R. W., et al., ed. *The Economic Transformation of the Soviet Union, 1913–1948* (New York, 1994).

DMYTRYSHYN, B., ed. *Imperial Russia: A Source Book, 1700–1917,* 3d ed. (Fort Worth, TX, 1990).

———, ed. *Medieval Russia: A Source Book, 850–1700,* 3d ed. (Fort Worth, TX, 1991).

DMYTRYSHYN, B., AND F. COX. *The Soviet Union and the Middle East: A Documentary Record of Afghanistan, Iran and Turkey, 1917–1985* (Princeton, 1985).

EGAN, D., AND M. A. EGAN. *Russian Autocrats from Ivan the Great to the Fall of the Romanov Dynasty: An Annotated Bibliography of English Language Sources to 1985* (Metuchen, NJ, 1987).

EKLOV, B., ed. *School and Society in Tsarist and Soviet Russia* (New York, 1993).

FITZPATRICK, S., AND L. VIOLA, eds. *A Researcher's Guide to Sources on Soviet Social History in the 1930s* (Armonk, NY, 1990).

FORSYTH, J. *A History of the Peoples of Siberia: Russia's North Asian Colony* (Cambridge, 1992).

FULLER, W. C. *Strategy and Power in Russia, 1600–1914* (New York, 1992).

GERON, L. AND A. PRAVDA, eds. *Who's Who in Russia and the New States* (London and New York, 1993).

GRAHAM, L. *Science in Russia and the Soviet Union: A Short History* (New York, 1993).

———, ed. *Science and the Soviet Social Order* (Cambridge, MA, 1990).

Great Soviet Encyclopedia: A Translation of the Third Edition, 10 vols. (New York, 1973).

GREEN, B. B. *The Dynamics of Russian Politics: A Short History* (Westport, CT, 1994).

HAMMOND, T., ed. *Soviet Foreign Relations and World Communism: A Selected Annotated Bibliography of 7,000 Books in 30 Languages* (Princeton, 1965).

HELLER, A., AND F. FEHER. *From Yalta to Glasnost* (Cambridge, MA, 1991).

HORAK, S. M. *Junior Slavica: A Selected Annotated Bibliography of Books in English on Russia and Eastern Europe* (Rochester, NY, 1968).

HORECKY, P., ed. *Basic Russian Publications: A Selected and Annotated Bibliography on Russia and the Soviet Union* (Chicago, 1962).

———. *Russia and the Soviet Union: A Bibliographic Guide to Western Language Publications* (Chicago, 1965).

HOSKING, G. *Empire and Nation in Russian History* (Waco, TX, 1993).

HUBBS, J. *Mother Russia: The Feminine Myth in Russian Culture* (Bloomington, IN, 1989).

HUSKEY, E., ed. *Executive Power and Soviet Politics: The Rise and Decline of the Soviet State* (Armonk, NY, 1992).

KAHAN, A. *Russian Economic History: The 19th Century* (Chicago, 1989).

KASACK, W., ed. *Dictionary of Russian Literature since 1917* (New York, 1988).

KATSENELINBOIGEN, A. *The Soviet Union: Empire, Nation, and System* (New Brunswick, NJ, 1990).

KATZ, Z., ET AL., eds. *Handbook of Major Soviet Nationalities* (New York, 1975).

KAVASS, I. *Demise of the Soviet Union: A Bibliographic Survey of English Writing on the Soviet Legal System, 1990–1991* (Buffalo, NY, 1992).

KERNIG, C., ed. *Marxism, Communism and Western Society: A Comparative Encyclopedia,* 8 vols. (New York, 1972).

KOLLMAN, N. S., ed. *Major Problems in Early Modern Russian History* (New York, 1992).

KON, I. S. *The Sexual Revolution in Russia: From the Age of the Tsars to Today,* trans. J. Riordan (New York, 1995).

KOZLOV, V. *The Peoples of the Soviet Union,* trans. P. Tiffen (London, 1988).

LAQUEUR, W. *Soviet Reality: Culture and Politics from Stalin to Gorbachev* (New Brunswick, NJ, 1990).

LEVIN, N. *The Jews in the Soviet Union Since 1917: Paradox of Survival,* 2 vols. (New York and London, 1988).

LIEVEN, D. *Russia's Rulers Under the Old Regime* (New Haven, CT, 1989).

LITTLE, D. R. *Governing the Soviet Union* (New York, 1989).

MAGOCSI, P. R. *Ukraine: A Historical Atlas* (Toronto, 1985).

MAICHEL, K. *Guide to Russian Reference Books* (Stanford, 1962).

———. *Guide to Russian Reference Books II: History, Auxiliary Sciences, Ethnography and Geography* (Stanford, 1964).

MARTIANOV, N. N. *Books Available in English by Russians and on Russia* (New York, 1960).

Modern Encyclopedia of Russian and Soviet History, 59 vols. (Gulf Breeze, FL, 1976–1996). Supplement, 1 vol., 1995, ed. J. L. Wieczynski. (Extremely useful.)

MOSSE, W. E. *Perestroika Under the Tsars* (New York, 1992).

NATION, R. C. *A History of Soviet Security Policy, 1917–1991* (Ithaca, NY, 1991).

NERHOOD, H., comp. *To Russia and Return: An Annotated Bibliography of Travelers' English Language Accounts of Russia from the Ninth Century to the Present* (Columbus, OH, 1968).

ORLOVSKY, D., ed. *Social and Economic History of Prerevolutionary Russia* (New York, 1992).

PALLOT, J., AND J. SHAW. *Landscape and Settlement in Romanov Russia* (New York, 1989).

PEARSON, R., ed. *Russia and Eastern Europe: A Bibliographic Guide* (Manchester, 1989).

PIERCE, R. *Soviet Central Asia: A Bibliography,* 3 vols. (Berkeley, 1966).

PINKUS, B. *The Jews of the Soviet Union . . .* (Cambridge, 1988).

POMPER, P. *Lenin, Trotsky, and Stalin: The Intelligentsia in Power* (New York, 1989).

PUSHKAREV, S. G. *A Source Book for Russian History from Early Times to 1917,* ed. A. Ferguson et al., 3 vols. (New Haven, CT, 1972).

RAEFF, M. *Political Ideas and Institutions in Imperial Russia* (New York, 1994).

RAGSDALE, H., ed. *Imperial Russian Foreign Policy* (New York, 1993).

RAMET, S. P., ed. *Religious Policy in the Soviet Union* (New York, 1993).

RYAN, M., comp. and trans. *Social Trends in Contemporary Russia: A Statistical Sourcebook* (New York, 1993).

SAUNDERS, D. *Russia in the Age of Reaction and Reform* (New York, 1992).

SCHULTHEISS, T., ed. *Russian Studies, 1941–1958: A Cumulation of the Annual Bibliographies from the Russian Review* (Ann Arbor, MI, 1972).

SHAPIRO, D. *A Selected Bibliography of Works in English on Russian History, 1801–1917* (New York and London, 1962).

SHTEPPA, K. F. *Russian Historians and the Soviet State* (New Brunswick, NJ, 1962).

SHUKMAN, H., ed. *The Blackwell Encyclopedia of the Russian Revolution* (Oxford, 1988).

SMITH, G. S., ed. and trans. *Contemporary Russian Poetry. A Bilingual Anthology* (Bloomington, IN, 1993).

STEEVES, P. D., ed. *The Modern Encyclopedia of Religions in Russia and the Soviet Union* (Gulf Breeze, FL, 1988–).

STEPHAN, J. J. *The Russian Far East* (Stanford, 1994).

SZEFTEL, M. "Russia Before 1917," in *Bibliographical Introduction to Legal History and Ethnology*, ed. J. Glissen (Brussels, 1966).

VOLKOV, S. *St. Petersburg: A Cultural History*, trans. A. W. Bouis (New York, 1995).

WAGNER, W. *Marriage, Property and Law in Imperial Russia* (Oxford, 1994).

WOZNIUK, V. *Understanding Soviet Foreign Policy: Readings and Documents* (New York, 1990).

ZILE, Z. L., ed. *Ideas and Forces in Soviet Legal History: A Reader in the Soviet State and Law* (New York, 1992).

General Histories

BLACK, C. E. *Understanding Soviet Politics: The Perspective of Russian History* (Boulder, CO, 1986).

BRUMFIELD, W. *A History of Russian Architecture* (Cambridge, 1993).

DANIELS, R. *Russia: The Roots of Confrontation* (Cambridge, MA, 1985). (General treatment of Russian and Soviet history.)

DMYTRYSHYN, B. *USSR: A Concise History*, 4th ed. (New York, 1984).

DVORNIK, F. *The Slavs in European History and Civilization* (New Brunswick, NJ, 1975).

DZIEWANOWSKI, M. K. *A History of Soviet Russia*, 4th ed. (Englewood Cliffs, NJ, 1993).

ELLIS, J. *The Russian Orthodox Church: A Contemporary History* (Bloomington, IN, 1986).

FLORINSKY, M. T. *Russia: A History and an Interpretation*, 2 vols. (New York, 1953).

FULLER, W. C., JR. *Strategy and Power in Russia, 1600–1914* (New York, 1992).

GADDIS, J. L. *Russia, the Soviet Union, and the United States: An Interpretive History*, 2d ed. (New York, 1990).

GRAHAM, L. *Science, Philosophy, and Human Behavior in the Soviet Union* (New York, 1987).

HELLER, M., AND A. M. NEKRICH. *Utopia in Power: The History of the Soviet Union from 1917 to the Present* (New York, 1986).

HEYMAN, N. M. *Russian History* (New York, 1993).

HOSKING, G. *The First Socialist Society: A History of the Soviet Union from Within*, 2d ed. (Cambridge, MA, 1993).

KEEP, J. *The Last of the Empires: A History of the Soviet Union, 1945–1991* (New York and Oxford, 1995).

KOCHAN, L. *The Making of Modern Russia* (New York, 1983).

KORT, M. G. *Soviet Colossus: The Rise and Fall of the USSR*, 4th ed. (New York, 1996).

LAUE, T. VON. *Why Lenin? Why Stalin? Why Gorbachev?: The Rise and Fall of the Soviet System*, 3d ed. (New York, 1993).

MARTIN, J. *Medieval Russia, 980–1584* (Cambridge, 1995).

McCAULEY, M. *The Soviet Union, 1917–1991*, 2d ed. (London and New York, 1993).

McCLELLAN, W. *Russia: A History of the Soviet Period and After*, 3d ed. (Englewood Cliffs, NJ, 1994).

McNEAL, R. H. *Tsar and Cossack: 1855–1914* (New York, 1987).

MEDISH, V. *The Soviet Union*, 4th ed. (Englewood Cliffs, NJ, 1991).

MILIUKOV, P., et al. *History of Russia*, trans. C. Markmann, 3 vols. (New York, 1968).

MOSER, C. A., ed. *The Cambridge History of Russian Literature* (Cambridge, 1992).

MOSS, W. G. *A History of Russia*, 2 vols. (New York, 1997).

NOGEE, J. L., AND R. DONALDSON. *Soviet Foreign Policy Since World War II*, 4th ed. (New York, 1992).

NOVE, A. *An Economic History of the USSR, 1917–1991*, 3d ed. (New York and London, 1992).

RAEFF, M. *Understanding Imperial Russia: State and Society in the Old Regime* (New York, 1984).

RAUCH, G. VON. *A History of Soviet Russia*, 6th ed. (New York, 1972).

RIASANOVSKY, N. V. *A History of Russia*, 5th ed. (New York, 1993).

RIHA, T. *Readings in Russian Civilization,* 2d ed., 3 vols. (Chicago, 1969).

ROGGER, H. *Russia in the Age of Modernization and Revolution, 1881–1917* (London and New York, 1983, 1988).

SPECTOR, I. *An Introduction to Russian History and Culture,* 5th ed. (Princeton, NJ, 1969).

SUMNER, B. H. *A Short History of Russia* (New York, 1949, 1962).

TREADGOLD, D. W. *Twentieth Century Russia,* 7th ed. (Boulder, CO, 1990).

ULAM, A. *A History of Soviet Russia* (New York, 1976).

WESTWOOD, J. N. *Endurance and Endeavour: Russian History 1812–1981,* 4th ed. (New York, 1992).

WREN, M. C. *The Course of Russian History,* 4th ed. (New York, 1979).

Collections of Essays

BARON, S. AND N. KOLLMAN, eds. *Religion and Culture in Early Modern Russia* (DeKalb, IL, 1997).

BIALER, S., AND M. MANDELBAUM, eds. *Gorbachev's Russia and American Foreign Policy* (Boulder, CO, 1988).

BLACK, C. E., ed. *The Transformation of Russian Society* (Cambridge, MA, 1960).

BOCIURKIW, B., AND J. STRONG, eds. *Religion and Atheism in the USSR and Eastern Europe* (Toronto, 1975).

CHOLDIN, M., AND M. FRIEDBERG, eds. *The Red Pencil: Artists, Scholars and Censors in the USSR* (Boston, 1989).

CRISP, O., AND L. EDMONDSON, eds. *Civil Rights in Imperial Russia* (Oxford, 1989).

CURTISS, J. S., ed. *Essays in Russian and Soviet History in Honor of G. T. Robinson* (Leiden, 1963).

FLERON, F., et al. *Soviet Foreign Policy: Classic and Contemporary Issues* (New York, 1991).

FRIEDBERG, M., AND H. ISHAM, eds. *Soviet Security Under Gorbachev* (Armonk, NY, 1987).

GERSCHENKRON, A. *Continuity in History and Other Essays* (Cambridge, MA, 1968).

GLEASON, A., et al. *Intelligentsia and Revolution: Russian Views of Bolshevism, 1917–1922* (New York, 1986).

GOODPASTER, A., et al., eds. *U.S. Policy toward the Soviet Union . . . 1987–2000* (Lanham, MA, 1988).

HAIMSON, L., ed. *The Mensheviks from the Revolution of 1917 to the Second World War* (Chicago, 1974).

HAJDA, L., AND M. BEISSINGER, eds. *The Nationalities Factor in Soviet Politics and Society* (Boulder, CO, 1990).

HAMBURG, G., ed. *Imperial Russian History I, 1700–1861* (New York, 1992).

————, ed. *Imperial Russian History II, 1861–1917* (New York, 1992).

HENDEL, S., AND R. BRAHAM, eds. *The U.S.S.R. After Fifty Years . . .* (New York, 1967).

HOFFMAN, E., AND R. LAIRD, eds. *The Soviet Polity in the Modern Era* (New York, 1984).

HUNCZAK, T., ed. *Russian Imperialism from Ivan the Great to the Revolution* (New Brunswick, NJ, 1974).

JUVILER, P., AND H. KIMURA, eds. *Gorbachev's Reforms: U.S. and Japanese Assessments* (New York, 1988).

KORBONSKI, A., AND F. FUKUYAMA, eds. *The Soviet Union and the Third World . . .* (Ithaca, NY, 1987).

LANE, D., ed. *Elites and Political Power in the USSR* (Brookfield, VT, 1988).

LAPIDUS, G., AND G. SWANSON, eds. *State and Welfare USA/USSR* (Berkeley, 1988).

LEDERER, I., ed. *Russian Foreign Policy* (New Haven, CT, 1962).

LEGTERS, L., ed. *Russia: Essays in History and Literature* (Leiden, 1972).

LERNER, L., AND D. TREADGOLD, eds. *Gorbachev and the Soviet Future* (Boulder, CO, 1988).

MCLEAN, H., et al., eds. *Russian Thought and Politics. HSS 4* (Cambridge, MA, 1957).

MILLAR, J., ed. *The Soviet Rural Community: A Symposium* (Urbana, IL, 1971).

MORTON, H., AND R. TÖKES, eds. *Soviet Politics and Society in the 1970's* (Riverside, NJ, 1974).

NOVE, A., ed. *The Stalin Phenomenon* (New York, 1993).

OBERLÄNDER, E., et al., eds. *Russia Enters the Twentieth Century* (New York, 1971).

OLIVA, L. J., ed. *Russia and the West from Peter to Khrushchev* (Boston, 1965).

PIPES, R. *The Russian Intelligentsia* (New York, 1961).

RABINOWITCH, A., et al., eds. *Revolution and Politics in Russia: Essays in Memory of B. I. Nicolaevsky* (Bloomington, IN, 1972).

RYWKIN, M., ed. *Russian Colonial Expansion to 1917* (London, 1988).

SHANIN, T., ed. *Peasants and Peasant Societies: Selected Readings* (New York, 1987).

SMITH, G., ed. *The Nationalities Question in the Soviet Union* (London, 1990).

STAVROU, T., ed. *Russia under the Last Tsar* (Minneapolis, 1968).

TIMBERLAKE, C., ed. *Essays on Russian Liberalism* (Columbia, MO, 1974).

TÖKES, R., ed. *Dissent in the USSR: Politics, Ideology, and People* (Baltimore, 1975).

VUCINICH, W. S., ed. *The Peasant in Nineteenth Century Russia* (Stanford, 1968).

———. *Russia and Asia: Essays on the Influence of Russia on the Asian Peoples* (Stanford, 1972).

WHELAN, J., AND M. DIXON, eds. *The Soviet Union in the Third World . . .* (Elmsford, NY, 1986).

Index

EARLY RUSSIAN PRINCES AND GRAND PRINCES

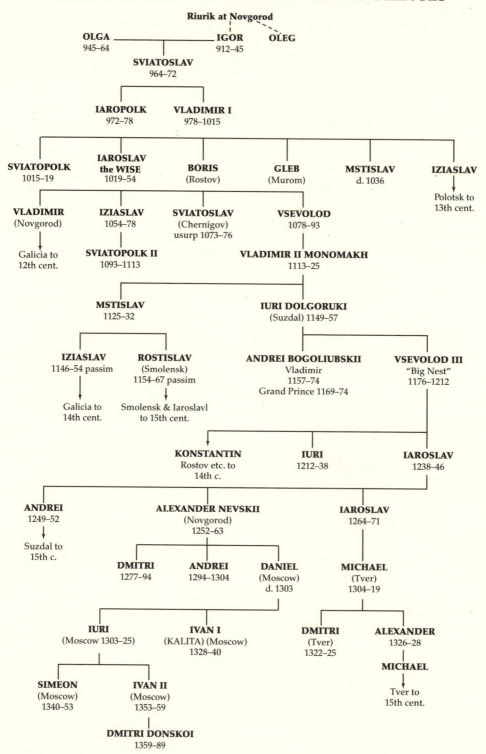

Riurik at Novgorod

OLGA
945–64

IGOR
912–45

OLEG

SVIATOSLAV
964–72

IAROPOLK
972–78

VLADIMIR I
978–1015

SVIATOPOLK
1015–19

IAROSLAV
the WISE
1019–54

BORIS
(Rostov)

GLEB
(Murom)

MSTISLAV
d. 1036

IZIASLAV

Polotsk to
13th cent.

VLADIMIR
(Novgorod)

Galicia to
12th cent.

IZIASLAV
1054–78

SVIATOPOLK II
1093–1113

SVIATOSLAV
(Chernigov)
usurp 1073–76

VSEVOLOD
1078–93

VLADIMIR II MONOMAKH
1113–25

MSTISLAV
1125–32

IURI DOLGORUKI
(Suzdal) 1149–57

IZIASLAV
1146–54 passim

Galicia to
14th cent.

ROSTISLAV
(Smolensk)
1154–67 passim

Smolensk & Iaroslavl
to 15th cent.

ANDREI BOGOLIUBSKII
Vladimir
1157–74
Grand Prince 1169–74

VSEVOLOD III
"Big Nest"
1176–1212

KONSTANTIN
Rostov etc. to
14th c.

IURI
1212–38

IAROSLAV
1238–46

ANDREI
1249–52

Suzdal to
15th c.

ALEXANDER NEVSKII
(Novgorod)
1252–63

IAROSLAV
1264–71

DMITRI
1277–94

ANDREI
1294–1304

DANIEL
(Moscow)
d. 1303

MICHAEL
(Tver)
1304–19

IURI
(Moscow 1303–25)

IVAN I
(KALITA) (Moscow)
1328–40

DMITRI
(Tver)
1322–25

ALEXANDER
1326–28

MICHAEL

Tver to
15th cent.

SIMEON
(Moscow)
1340–53

IVAN II
(Moscow)
1353–59

DMITRI DONSKOI
1359–89